CENTURY OF SERVICE:

THE HISTORY OF THE SOUTH ALBERTA LIGHT HORSE

1905 2005

A Century of Service

This important history of the South Alberta Light Horse was written to preserve the history of achievement, courage and sacrifice of the senior militia regiment in Alberta and to mark the centennial of the Province of Alberta. Free distribution to all public libraries and post secondary institutions in Alberta has been made possible through a grant from Canadian Heritage.

L'histoire de South Alberta Light Horse a été écrite pour conserver l'histoire des exploits, des sacrifices et du courage du régiment senior de la mélisse de l'Alberta et pour marquer le centenaire de l'Alberta. Des fonds ont été attribués aux bibliothèques publiques et aux institutions post secondaires en Alberta, grâce à une subvention du Patrimoine canadien.

Canadian Heritage   Patrimoine canadien

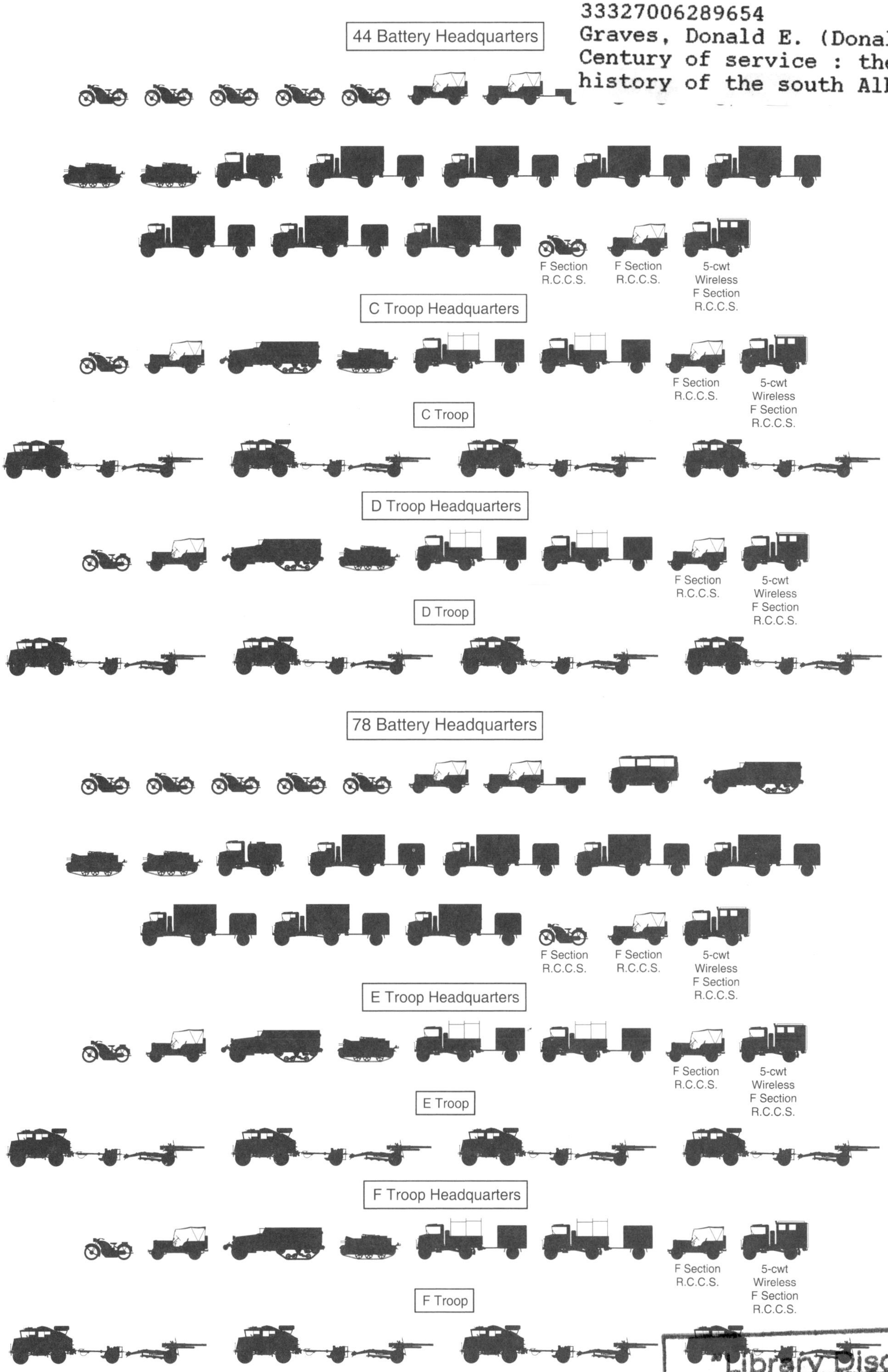

44 Battery Headquarters

F Section
R.C.C.S.

F Section
R.C.C.S.

5-cwt
Wireless
F Section
R.C.C.S.

C Troop Headquarters

F Section
R.C.C.S.

5-cwt
Wireless
F Section
R.C.C.S.

C Troop

D Troop Headquarters

F Section
R.C.C.S.

5-cwt
Wireless
F Section
R.C.C.S.

D Troop

78 Battery Headquarters

F Section
R.C.C.S.

F Section
R.C.C.S.

5-cwt
Wireless
F Section
R.C.C.S.

E Troop Headquarters

F Section
R.C.C.S.

5-cwt
Wireless
F Section
R.C.C.S.

E Troop

F Troop Headquarters

F Section
R.C.C.S.

5-cwt
Wireless
F Section
R.C.C.S.

F Troop

Front endpaper

13th Field Regiment, Autumn 1944

This diagram shows 13th Field Regiment after it reorganized with 25-pdr. guns in the late summer of 1944. The Regimental Headquarters contained the command element of the unit and its administrative units which supplied the administrative echelons of the three batteries. A Light Aid Detachment for vehicle repair was attached to Headquarters.

The three batteries were semi-independent units, each having a battery headquarters element, an administrative echelon with supply vehicles and two troops each of four 25-pdrs. In 13th Field, 22 Battery controlled Able and Baker Troops, 44 Battery controlled Charlie and Dog Troops and 78 Battery controlled Easy and Fox Troops. The guns in each troop were numbered from 1 to 4, thus Able 1, Baker 2, Charlie 3, etc. Also attached to 13th Field Regiment but not shown in this diagram was a signals section from the Royal Canadian Corps of Signals.

Drawing by Chris Johnson

CENTURY OF SERVICE

THE HISTORY OF THE
SOUTH ALBERTA LIGHT HORSE

DONALD E. GRAVES

Maps and drawings by
Christopher Johnson

Original artwork by
Ron Volstad

Additional research by
Lieutenant-Colonel R.B. McKenzie, MMM, CD,
Captain Colin Michaud, CD,
and Master Warrant Officer James Ogston, CD,
South Alberta Light Horse

Published for
THE SOUTH ALBERTA LIGHT HORSE
REGIMENT FOUNDATION

by

ROBIN BRASS STUDIO
Toronto

Published and distributed for
The South Alberta Light Horse Regiment Foundation
Suite 101, 11111 – 82nd Avenue, Edmonton, Alberta T6G 0T3, Canada
by
Robin Brass Studio Inc.
10 Blantyre Avenue, Toronto, Ontario M1N 2R4, Canada
www.rbstudiobooks.com

Printed and bound in Canada by Friesens, Altona, Manitoba

Library and Archives Canada Cataloguing in Publication

Graves, Donald E. (Donald Edward)

    Century of service : the history of the South Alberta Light Horse / Donald E. Graves ; maps and drawings by Christopher Johnson ; original artwork by Ron Volstad ; additional research by R.B. McKenzie, Colin Michaud, and James Ogston.

Includes bibliographical references and index.

ISBN 1-896941-43-5

    1. Canada. Canadian Armed Forces. South Alberta Light Horse – History. 2. Canada. Canadian Army. South Alberta Light Horse – History. 3. World War, 1914-1918 – Regimental histories – Canada. 4. World War, 1939-1945 – Regimental histories – Canada. I. Johnson, Christopher II. Volstad, Ron III. South Alberta Light Horse Regiment Foundation. IV. Title.

UA602.S678G72 2005   358'.18'0971   C2005-901191-2

FRONTISPIECE

LIGHT HORSEMEN AND PREDECESSORS, 1885-2005

Top row (left to right)
Unknown Rocky Mountain Ranger, 1885
Unknown corporal, 15th Light Horse, c. 1906
Trooper Ottreal, 19th Alberta Dragoons Service Squadron, 1915
Unknown sergeant, 3rd Canadian Mounted Rifles, 1915

Second row
Unknown sergeant, 31st Battalion, CEF, 1919
Lieutenant-Colonel E.S. Doughty, commanding 31st Battalion CEF, 1919
Unknown officer, 15th Canadian Light Horse, 1922
Unknown soldier, South Alberta Regiment, c. 1938

Third row
Captain F.A. Thorne, 13th Field Regiment, Normandy 1944
Corporal A.G. Tuft, South Alberta Regiment, 1945
Trooper Clifford Allen, South Alberta Regiment, 1945
Major Reid Ainscough, South Alberta Light Horse, 1962

Fourth row
Warrant Officer Ron Grover, South Alberta Light Horse, 1967
Corporal Brett Walton, South Alberta Light Horse, 1988
Master Warrant Officer John Szram, South Alberta Light Horse, 1995
Captain Troy Steele, South Alberta Light Horse, 2005

This book has been written to
commemorate the Joint Centennial in 2005 of
the Province of Alberta and the South Alberta Light Horse.

It is intended to be a monument to honour the dedication,
hard work and self-reliance of the men and women who,
in the last century, have served both Alberta
and its senior militia regiment.

The publication of
Century of Service: The History of the South Alberta Light Horse
has been made possible by the generosity of our major sponsors shown below
and numerous other individuals and corporations who are not listed
and to whom we will remain forever grateful.

EnCana Corporation

Honorary Colonel Stanley A. Milner, OC, AOE, CD, LL.D,
South Alberta Light Horse, Edmonton

Honorary Lieutenant-Colonel John D. Watson, FCA,
South Alberta Light Horse, Calgary

Honorary Colonel (Ret'd) Fred P. Mannix, CD,
Calgary Highlanders, Calgary

and

In Memory of
Sergeant Thomas E. Milner, DCM, BSc., P.Eng.
The South Alberta Regiment
(29th Canadian Armoured Reconnaissance Regiment)
by his family, in recognition of
his valour and service

CONTENTS

LIST OF MAPS

BUCKINGHAM PALACE

Honorary Colonel Stanley Milner, OC, CD
President,
South Alberta Light Horse Regiment Foundation

Please convey my warm thanks to the Officers, Warrant Officers and Senior Non-Commissioned Officers, Junior Non-Commissioned Officers, Soldiers and the Regimental Foundation Board Members of the South Alberta Light Horse Regiment Foundation for their message of loyal greetings sent on the occasion of their Centenary.

I was interested to read the history of the Regiment and send my best wishes to all those concerned during this most memorable anniversary year.

ELIZABETH R.

February 2005

FOREWORD

Honorary Colonel S.A. Milner, OC, AOE, CD, LL.D.
and Honorary Lieutenant-Colonel J.D. Watson, FCA,
South Alberta Light Horse

The year 2005 marks the Centennial of both the Province of Alberta and the South Alberta Light Horse. To celebrate this important occasion, we are delighted to present *Century of Service*, a history of Alberta as it unfolded through the eyes of those who were prepared to sacrifice their lives for their fellow Albertans and Canadians in the wars of the 20th century. The story below actually begins in the days before Alberta became a province, when the volunteers of the Rocky Mountain Rangers stood ready to protect their communities from the threat of a major uprising. Those were difficult and uncertain times as Alberta struggled towards provincial status and a magnificent destiny, but we Albertans have experienced periods of great uncertainty ever since and, indeed, these trials have shaped our character.

As *Century of Service* explains, the South Alberta Light Horse embodies the tradition and heritage of some of the most renowned cavalry, infantry, armoured and artillery units in Canadian history, all of them Alberta-based. Its ancestor regiments fought at Vimy Ridge and Ypres in the First World War. They took part in the first tank attack in history at the Battle of Courcelette in September 1916, and mounted the last Canadian cavalry charge at Iwuy two years later. In the Second World War, they acquired fifteen new battle honors as the South Alberta Regiment, an armoured unit that fought through France, Belgium and Holland to final victory in Germany in 1945.

Over the last half century, through a series of amalgamations, the South Alberta Light Horse has emerged as the proud descendant of many distinguished predecessor units: the famous 31st Battalion of the First World War, the South Alberta Regiment and 13th Field Regiment in the Second, and a half dozen others as this book details, all now manifesting themselves in the SALH. As with all Militia regiments across Canada, the Light Horse and its predecessors have fought two different types of battles – they waged war for Canada during times of international conflict and struggled to survive in the cost-cutting times of peace. And perhaps it is in this way more than any other that the Light Horse's history of struggle corresponds with the history of the province which provided most of the soldiers who served in its ranks.

Like the Regiment, and like the whole Canadian Militia, Alberta has had to struggle from time to time for very survival. The victory of the Rocky Mountain Rangers and Canadian Militia units in the Northwest Rebellion of 1885, for instance, was not followed, as everyone had expected, by a mass influx of settlers, but by a ten-year recession that almost destroyed our first railway. With the turn of the century came the first big provincial boom – fortune smiled upon us and we thought it would do so forever. We were wrong. Shortly before the First World War, a recession settled upon the Province which would last for more than thirty years, so that Edmonton streets developed and largely serviced in 1912 stood without houses, the forlorn evidence of economic disaster, until the early 1950s. Since that time, there have been two periods of awesome growth with a devastating recession between them.

But adversity builds a tough people and it was this same toughness that saw Alberta's 31st Battalion and other Canadian units become the shock troops of the triumphant Canadian Corps in the final phase of the First World War. In the Second, it caused Major-General Frank Worthington, the father of the Canadian armoured corps, to make the South Alberta Regiment the pathfinders for his 4th Canadian Armoured Division as it advanced through Northwest Europe. One can sense this same dedication to the job in the young people who join the South Alberta Light Horse today as citizen-soldiers.

Unfortunately, not enough Canadians realize how vitally important it is that our modern Militia units be sustained and properly equipped. One of the decisive strengths of the western democracies over the last two centuries is that they have not maintained enormous standing armies. Given its size and responsibilities, even the armed forces of the United States have never reached the relative proportions of the nations that posed a threat. This gives the democracies a double advantage. Not only does it prevent the phenomenon of the "military coup" and resultant "government by generals" so depressingly familiar in other parts of the world. It also enables these democracies to direct much more of its resources to the development of industry and the economic well-being of their people.

However, this system depends wholly on democratic governments meeting two responsibilities. First, they must maintain a small but highly efficient – and superbly-equipped – permanent military establishment, ready at any moment's notice to become the nucleus of a much larger fighting force. Second, they must be sure that within the civilian population there are well-trained citizen-soldiers, willing and able to be called to active duty whenever the need arises. This need might be provided by the menace of a hostile military power. Just as possibly, it could be provided by a natural disaster to our nation, such as the *tsunami* that struck the nations in East Asia just as this history neared completion. By the citizen-soldier we refer, of course, to the men and women of the Militia.

We need the Militia. It is as essential to the effective functioning of a democracy as a police force, fire department, medical or emergency services. But it depends upon there being a population of young people ready to devote much of their spare time to the service of their country. As this book so adequately illustrates, Canada has had such young people when it confronted great perils in the past. As the roster of our Regiment illustrates today, we still have such young people. But we need more of them, and we need to equip them far more adequately than we are at present. That is the implicit message of the pages that follow.

HONORARY COLONEL S.A. MILNER, OC, AOE, CD, LL.D.
Edmonton

HONORARY LIEUTENANT-COLONEL J. WATSON, FCA
Calgary

FOREWORD

Lieutenant-Colonel Thomas E. Putt, CD,
Commanding Officer, South Alberta Light Horse,
Jefferson Armoury, Edmonton

Among the finest of the many fine traditions of the Canadian army is the regimental system. For more than three centuries, while Commonwealth soldiers may have gone to war for such slogans as "King and Country" or "making the world safe for democracy," they have actually fought wars for "the Regiment," a much smaller but elusive ideal. Reduced to its simplest terms, what this ideal means is that, when Commonwealth soldiers enter battle they do not do it alone but as part of a small and distinct community forged by history and tradition, marked by certain uniform distinctions, and bound by pride and comradeship. It is a community in which the strengths of the individual are directed toward the common good, and the weaknesses buttressed by a common goal. Indeed, it is why many of us volunteer to serve our nation.

I have the privilege of commanding the South Alberta Light Horse and it is my particular privilege to command the Regiment during its Centennial Year of 2005. To mark this important milestone, the Light Horse, in conjunction with the South Alberta Light Horse Regiment Foundation, decided to organize a number of special heritage projects. There will be two special exhibits relating to the history of the Regiment opened at The Provincial Museum of Alberta in Edmonton and at the Esplanade Museum in Medicine Hat. The Light Horse will be staging a number of parades across the Province of Alberta including a ceremonial Trooping of our Guidon. In March 2005, a project that is particularly important to all the soldiers of the Light Horse will be completed and that is the complete restoration of "Old Reliable," the veteran command half-track of the wartime South Alberta Regiment, to running order in its original 1943 state. Last but not least, the Regiment and the Foundation decided to commission a comprehensive history of the South Alberta Light Horse.

Our choice as author was Donald E. Graves, the well-known Canadian military historian, a choice that was particularly apt as Mr. Graves wrote *South Albertas: A Canadian Regiment at War*, the story of one of our most distinguished predecessor units and a work regarded by many as one of the finest Canadian regimental histories ever published. The result is *Century of Service: The History of the South Alberta Light Horse*.

In the pages that follow, Donald Graves tells the story of the South Alberta Light Horse. It is an interesting tale full of interesting people that actually begins some decades before the Regiment's first official predecessor unit was authorized in 1905. In *Century of Service*, we march behind Alberta's oldest regiment as it experiences victory and defeat in times of war, and struggles to stay alive in times of peace. We suffer with it at the Somme, Passchendaele and the Kapelsche Veer, we savour its triumphs at Vimy Ridge and on JUNO beach on 6 June 1944, and we are there when its most famous predecessor becomes the only unit in the Canadian Armoured Corps to win the Victoria Cross during the Second World War and the only unit of the Canadian army to win that decoration during the 1944 Normandy campaign.

What *Century of Service* makes clear is that, while in the past, the predecessors of the Light Horse have fought in a variety of roles under a variety of titles, all these units shared common characteristics. These include an emphasis on good leadership at all levels, initiative, drive, adaptability and resourcefulness, a willingness to try new methods if old ones fail, and an eagerness to embrace the latest technology. The members of the Light Horse family have always exhibited a preference for practical results as opposed to outward show – the Light Horse have always been soldiers for the working day – and, while they take their work seriously, they never quite take themselves seriously and always manage to have a little fun on the way. As the Commanding Officer of the South Alberta Light Horse, I am happy to state that all these characteristics still flourish today in my Regiment.

Many of the qualities of the Light Horse and its predecessors are shared by the people of Alberta, from which the Regiment is recruited, and I am very glad that Mr. Graves has included much provincial historical background in the pages that follow. The South Alberta Light Horse is not only the senior militia regiment in Alberta, it is truly a pan-provincial unit. In the century it has existed, it has forged historical links with almost every community in Alberta and, if greater proof is needed for that statement, it will be found in the map on page 49 which depicts those communities that have ties with the Regiment.

In closing, I would like to say that I feel that *Century of Service* has captured the story and the spirit both of the Light Horse and of its home province very well and I have no doubt that readers will find the following pages as fascinating as I have. With such a splendid past behind it, the South Alberta Light Horse can move with confidence into its second century and will continue to serve – according to its motto, *Semper Alacer*, "Always Alert" – both the Dominion of Canada and the Province of Alberta.

LIEUTENANT-COLONEL THOMAS E. PUTT, CD
Commanding Officer
South Alberta Light Horse

AUTHOR'S INTRODUCTION
AND ACKNOWLEDGEMENTS

When Honorary Colonel Stanley Milner of the South Alberta Light Horse called me in late 2003 to ask if I would write the history of his regiment, I hesitated. I had already completed the story of one of the Light Horse's most distinguished predecessors, the South Alberta Regiment of the Second World War, and I had sworn that I would never undertake another similar project. It was not that my work on the SAR project was unenjoyable – far from it – but any historian who has written a regimental history knows that it is a task which, if it is to be done well, requires an incredible amount of sheer drudgery. I was intrigued, however, by Colonel Milner's proposal because my work on the history of the South Albertas had provided me with considerable background knowledge and I was fully aware that the South Alberta Light Horse possess a distinguished and lively military heritage. I therefore agreed to Colonel Milner's request but, in a weak moment (which I have had many, many occasions to regret in the last year or so), recklessly suggested to him that it might just be possible to have the book in print by the time of the Regiment's 100th Birthday on 3 July 2005. That I was able to successfully meet that objective was only made possible by the assistance afforded me by the following persons and institutions.

First and foremost, my thanks must go to the serving members and former members of the South Alberta Light Horse, and the veterans of the South Alberta Regiment, 19th Alberta Dragoons and 13th Field Regiment, RCA, who consented to be interviewed for this book. In particular I wish to pay tribute to two Alberta officers. Colonel George Lynch-Staunton, CD, served in three of the Light Horse's predecessor units, the 15th Canadian Light Horse, 13th Field Regiment and the 19th Alberta Dragoons while, in a similar vein, Lieutenant-Colonel Harry Quarton, CD, served with both the SAR and the 19th Dragoons before ending up as the commanding officer of the Loyal Edmonton Regiment. These gentlemen were therefore in a unique position to help me and they did so, unreservedly.

Second, I must acknowledge my gratitude to three serving members of the Light Horse. Lieutenant-Colonel R.B. McKenzie, MMM, CD, whose father not only served in the wartime Calgary Highlanders but also commanded the postwar SAR, was a treasure trove of regimental lore and legend. Captain Colin Michaud, CD, and Master Warrant Officer James Ogston, CD, whose unparalleled knowledge of Light Horse history was invaluable, made a significant contribution to the writing of a book that could not have been completed without their help.

As usual, the staff of the Directorate of History and Heritage, DND, many of them former colleagues, were extremely helpful and I am grateful to Major James McKillip, CD, Doctors Stephen Harris and Ken Reynolds, and Warrant Officer Carl Kletke for their aid. I would like to acknowledge my particular gratitude to Major Paul Lansey, CD, of the Heritage section who helped me untangle the Light Horse's convoluted lineage. Last, but not at all least, Major (Retd.) Robert Caldwell, CD, not only provided me with his helpful expertise on the early history of Western Canada but also, being a participant in some of the events discussed below, happily agreed to be interviewed for this book.

Two old colleagues, friends and soldiers came to my aid during the course of my work on this book. I shall be eternally grateful to Major (Retd.) Michael R. McNorgan, CD, the co-author of *The Royal Canadian Armoured Corps*, for putting at my disposal much of the background research done for that title, particularly information relating to early cavalry matters in Canada. As a former (but humble member) of the Royal Canadian Artillery I was looking forward, for the first time in my professional career, to writing some gunner history but I quickly realized that the technical aspects of this arm were far beyond my limited knowledge. I am therefore grateful to Lieutenant-Colonel (Retd.) Brian Reid, CD, a former Chief Instructor in Gunnery at the Combat Arms School at CFB Gagetown for assisting me, both on the technical aspects of artillery and for matters relating to the South African War. I would also like to acknowledge the assistance given to me by the staff of the Royal Canadian Artillery Museum at Shilo, Manitoba, who provided me with copies of very rare artillery manuals.

This is a book about Alberta as well as its soldiers so it will be no surprise that many in the province helped me along the way. In Calgary, Lieutenant (Retd.) Barry Agnew, CD, and Corporal Michael Dorosh, CD, of the Calgary Highlanders temporarily put aside regimental affiliations and hunted down rare archival sources while the late Joseph Harper made available his considerable expertise on the lineage of all Canadian military units of the last two centuries. Reg Hodgson of St. Albert, editor of *Army Motors*, provided advice on his subject of expertise and some interesting photographs while Lucia Gillespie of Banff National Park put me firmly on the trail of "Heinie," the elusive pony. In Edmonton, Colonel Milner and his staff of The South Alberta Light Horse Regiment Foundation – Charmaine Milner, Gerri Pappas and Susan Angus – were unflinchingly helpful and met many desperate requests for information. In particular, I must acknowledge my gratitude to Tom and Patricia Campbell for their rigorous editing of early drafts and, where I chose below to disregard their sound advice, the result must be on my head. Colonel Paul Wynnyk, CD, of Base Edmonton was another critical but positive editor and he and his staff are responsible for amassing many of the pictures of rare badges that grace the colour section of this book. Tony Schnurr of Edmonton also contributed to the badge section and James Design Studio of that city did much of the preparatory graphic work. Finally, Vern Klotz of the Northern Alberta Institute of Technology took the fine photos of "Old Reliable" and the restoration crew found in the colour section of this book.

There are others that I must not forget. Hugh Halliday of Ottawa placed at my disposal his comprehensive notes on Second World War awards and decorations. Professor Emeritus S.F. Wise of Ottawa, a former teacher, read through the First World War chapters and saved me from many embarrassing blunders. Major Tonie and Mrs. Valmai Holt of Woodnesborough, Kent, gave me permission to reproduce the Bairnsfather cartoons that grace the First World War chapters while Lieutenant (Retd.) Patrick Clay of Ottawa, formerly of 13th Field Regiment, permitted me to use his cartoon work from the Second World War. Dr. Reg Roy of Victoria gave me permission to use the photograph of Private Donald Fraser of the 31st Battalion and to quote from his excellent edited version of that soldier's compelling First World War Journal. I am also indebted to two young people who are just getting their feet wet in terms of historical research. Joseph W. Temple, an undergraduate in history at Carleton University in Ottawa, proved to be a very reliable research assistant while Miss Sylvia Grodzinski of Kingston, a Grade IX student, began the onerous task of compiling an accurate list of the commanding officers of the predecessor units of the SALH by extracting them from *Militia Lists* and General Orders. Such was the quality of the work of these two young people that I am confident that the future of my chosen profession will rest in capable hands.

There are also those who only suffered. David and Sandy Atack, personal friends in Wolf Grove, sat glassy-eyed many evenings, politely and silently enduring lengthy disquisitions on obscure matters relating to the history of Alberta and its militia, a subject I found fascinating, but they probably did not. In this respect I do not think it inappropriate to thank the friendly staff of the Bistro Cafe in Edmonton for permitting me, on a succession of enjoyable evenings in September 2004, to spread papers out on my table while fetching, at the crucial moment, potable reinforcement.

One request that I made before undertaking this project was that I bring back The Old Gang who had worked on the South Alberta project and other titles with me – Robin Brass on design, Christopher Johnson on maps and graphics and Ron Volstad on colour artwork – and, thankfully, this request was granted. These three gentlemen are leading experts in their particular fields but it is still a source of puzzlement to me as to why they ignore my sound advice on how they should do their work. Whether they take my advice or not (mostly they do not) the result, however, is always very good, as indeed will be seen in the pages below.

Finally, I would like to offer my heartfelt thanks to my wife, Dianne, who set aside her own writing in order to assist me, in many ways, meet the tight deadline for this book. Too often, in the last year she has put up with a husband whose body was present but whose mind was roaming along the trail of the Light Horse somewhere between Fort Macleod in 1885 and Wainwright Camp in 2004.

And so, with the help of all those above (and I pray I have not forgotten any), the job was done and it was done on time. Whether it was done well is not for me to judge but I will say that writing the history of the South Alberta Light Horse has been a fascinating task and I am now thankful that I overcame my initial reluctance and undertook to tell the colourful story of "Her Majesty's Cowboys" (my preferred title) and the province from which they come. In closing, therefore, it is entirely appropriate that I extend 100th Birthday Greetings to Alberta and its senior militia regiment, and wish them both many happy returns.

DONALD E. GRAVES
Wolf Grove, Upper Canada
February 2004–January 2005

A NOTE TO THE READER

During the approximately 120-year span covered by this book, military terminology and abbreviations suffered many changes. This is particularly true in the three decades since the unification of the Canadian Forces, as Ottawa appears to issue new abbreviations and acronyms on a weekly basis. In order to assist the reader not well versed in military jargon, I have included in Appendix I a glossary of the major terms, abbreviations and acronyms, etc.used in this book.

As during most of the period covered by this book, Canada and her soldiers used Imperial measure, it has been retained in the text.

Finally, the reader should note that the index is in two parts: the general index and an index of illustrations.

D.E.G.

CENTURY OF SERVICE:
THE HISTORY OF THE SOUTH ALBERTA LIGHT HORSE

Getting it right: After Action Review, ACTIVE EDGE, 2004
Following a training exercise, personnel gather to carry out a post-mortem. Left to right are: Corporal Gutowski (getting out of turret); Captain J.R. Watt (with map in turret); and Corporal Adby in driver's position. On the ground, from left to right, are: Major Lockhart (wearing crew helmet without camouflage); Lieutenant Yanda (with map); Lieutenant Peeling; Warrant Officer Bergt (back to camera) and on far right, Sergeant Rosendaal. On the vehicle behind is Corporal Stock.
COURTESY, BRETT WALTON

(Below) **Cougars' den**
Light Horse personnel draw their vehicles and equipment at the Militia Training and Support Centre at Wainwright Camp before commencing Exercise ACTIVE EDGE, August 2004.
COURTESY, BRETT WALTON

"Alpha This Is 4-1, Report When Set ... Out."

WAINWRIGHT, ALBERTA, AUGUST 2004

The South Alberta Light Horse, Alberta's senior militia regiment, is two days older than the province itself. The Regiment marks its birth date as 3 July 1905, the date of a general order which authorized the raising of the 15th Light Horse, its oldest predecessor unit, while Alberta came into being on 5 July 1905, the day legislation was passed in the House of Commons creating it and Saskatchewan from the former Northwest Territories. These are indisputable facts but it is very doubtful that the soldiers of Regimental Headquarters and B Squadron of the Light Horse, sitting in a Canadian Forces Highway Cruiser bus driving east along Alberta Highway 14 on the morning of Saturday, 21 August 2004, gave much thought to this important historical information.

For one thing, they were engrossed in watching a video film, "Mars Attacks" on the overhead screens and, for another, they were in a rather flat mood. "Mars Attacks," a black comedy based on series of bubble gum cards issued in the early 1960s, which features an invasion of earth by small and aggressive aliens who are only defeated after it is discovered that the loud playing of a record of Jeannette MacDonald and Nelson Eddy singing "I'll Be Seeing You" causes the invaders' brains to implode into green mush, was about par for Light Horse intellectual endeavour. Certainly, it coincided with the mood in the bus which was rather low, a combination of the cold, grey, threatening weather and the minimal expectations that all experienced soldiers learn to cultivate before going into the field because, as the saying goes, "expect the worst and you will never be disappointed." On the other hand, since life in the Canadian army never corresponds with that magical world depicted in the gaudy painting that adorned the side of their bus – with its impossibly handsome young men and women in impossibly well-fitting and nifty uniforms cheerfully doing all those interesting jobs that lure the unwary into recruiting offices – the soldiers on board were pretty sure that there were some poor devils who had it worse.

On that Saturday in August, the poor devils in question were personnel from the Light Horse A Squadron who were riding in two large panel vans north up Highway 41, the old "Buffalo Trail," through one of the most sparsely populated parts of Alberta. Not only had A Squadron left its armoury in Medicine Hat earlier than their comrades of RHQ and B Squadron, but they faced a longer drive, some 240 miles, and had neither soft seats to lull them asleep nor videos to entertain them. The most notable thing about A Squadron's journey, besides the 30-mile stretch of Highway 41 where the sign warns you to watch out for "snakes crossing" (without telling you that they are mostly rattlesnakes) was the obligatory stop at the large gas bar near Oyen – which is about a hundred miles from nowhere, in every direction – to refuel and, as the armoured corps likes to say, "ease springs."

The destination of both Light Horse elements was the Land Forces Western Training area at Wainwright, a sprawling, rolling area of some 240 square miles of semi-arid and rocky soil, covered with prairie grass and dotted with patches of scrub birch, located about two and a half hours east of Edmonton. They were headed for Wainwright, a place depressingly familiar to all Western Canadian soldiers, to participate in week-long exercise codenamed ACTIVE EDGE 04, a major training event staged by the three Western Canada militia (reserve) brigade groups – 38th Brigade from Saskatchewan, Manitoba and northern Ontario, 39th Brigade from British Columbia and 41st Brigade from Alberta. ACTIVE EDGE, which involved some 750 regular and militia personnel, was the largest such exercise to be held in eight years, years that were blighted by government financial cutbacks. Although the Light Horse were excited about the coming week, nobody was foolish enough to admit it, under the practical philosophy that if you think it is going to be bad, it will not be as bad as you think. The last Martian brain had imploded and the credits were rolling on the video screen by the time the bus dipped when Highway 14 descended into the valley of the Battle River a few miles west of Wainwright, a terrain feature that let the soldiers know they were nearing their destination.

At about 10.30 A.M. that Saturday, the bus turned right off the highway, drove past the small tank farm, crossed the railway overpass and proceeded through the main gate of the base. This year, unlike the previous occasions the Light Horse had been at Wainwright, there would be no opportunity to explore the

Unsung heroes: The Echelons
Armoured units require good supply services and these are provided by the soldiers of the Echelons, essential personnel whose work is too often forgotten. Here, the soft-skinned vehicles of the field squadron Echelon for ACTIVE EDGE concentrate, preparatory to carrying out their important work.
COURTESY, BRETT WALTON

bars and pizza joints of the adjoining town of the same name – not that they were anything to write home about, but there was always a chance that you might encounter the infamous Midget, a short and aggressive female who haunts these establishments and who, over a couple of decades, has become the stuff of legend among successive generations of Canadian soldiers. No chance of that this day because, having passed by the buffalo compound with it straggling collection of shaggy beasts, the Highway Cruiser pulled up at the large modern structure of the Militia Training Support Centre. Here the Light Horse, an armoured unit, would marry up with their vehicles which were stored and maintained by the staff of the MTSC.

Fortunately, as it turned out, the Light Horse had earlier been issued a box lunch, which they ate on the concrete floor of the Support Centre, before they commenced the lengthy process of signing for and equipping their AVGP (Armoured Vehicle, General Purpose) Cougars, the standard training platform of Canadian militia armoured units for nearly a quarter of a century, as well as their B Echelon or soft-skinned, non-fighting vehicles. The Service Centre staff, no fools they, required numerous signatures for every little item of kit as, if anything went missing, they were determined it would not come back on their heads. The result was that it all took time, a lot of time. When the Light Horse finally completed the process and finished equipping their vehicles for the field, it was time to do radio checks to make sure all communications equipment was functioning properly. Since, inevitably, some of it was not, non-functioning items (headsets are always a problem) had to be exchanged for new items, which of course meant more signatures … and so it went for several hours.

This done, everybody was good to go but, the army being the army and armies never changing, they promptly sat down to wait. The fact was the Light Horse were not the only unit taking part in ACTIVE EDGE and some British Columbia units, who had to fly in, did not reach Wainwright until early in the evening of 21 August. At long last, however, the combined squadron formed by the armoured units involved in the exercise began

to move out, troop by troop, to the field training area. Unfortunately, it had started to rain while the Light Horse were getting their vehicles and equipment and, as they emerged from the large MTSC building, the drizzle turned into a downpour which caused one trooper to think that, instead of going on exercise, they should perhaps think about building an ark. It wasn't long before water was sloshing around the bottom of the "boats" (the popular term for Cougars) and, no matter how careful you tried to be, you inevitably got wet, as did anything that dropped on the floor, including one troop leader's order book and check list for the exercise. Closing the hatches, even if it was permitted, would not have helped, because the hatch seals on the Cougar are notoriously inefficient. Slice it any way, the only thing to do was grimly endure, while at the same time contemplating your decision to join in the first place and the old saying, "if it ain't raining, you ain't training," was no comfort.

By dusk on that wet and miserable Saturday, everyone was in position in their first "hide," an armoured corps term for a temporary overnight position. This first night, as there were still units to arrive, was "non tactical," meaning that there was not much to do besides maintaining a radio watch (listening to the set for possible orders or information), and "routine maintenance," a neat little phrase that conceals a fair amount of work, particularly for the Cougar drivers who had to check their fluid levels, hubs and air filters, the last task involving removing the heavy engine cover at the front of the vehicle. At the appointed time, or approximately the appointed time, the squadron sergeant-major drove up to each vehicle and flipped over the correct number of brown bags containing IMPs (Individual Meal Packs), the standard field ration of the modern Canadian army. On the other hand, if the sergeant-major was late, the Light Horse crews were not fussed about it as, being experienced and used to the vagaries of the supply system, most had brought their own emergency rations with them, beef jerky being a favoured item – but then what else would the Queen's cowboys pack?

Individual Meal Packs are not issued by contents but only by the number required. In a rare display of thoughtfulness, however, the army lists the main contents on the outside of each insulated bag, thus permitting crews to switch according to taste, and there is a great variety of meals to barter. You might get ham steak, sausage and hash browns, beans and wieners, lasagna in tomato sauce, shepherd's pie, Hungarian goulash, pork chow mein, salisbury steak, and other main dishes, along with a variety of deserts ranging from fruit cocktail to strawberry and rhubarb compote. Not only that, but a benevolent government includes in each IMP bag an amazing variety of small but potentially useful items such as little packets of jam or jelly, tea, coffee (very strong), candy, chocolate bars, sugar, salt, pepper, artificial sweeteners, matches, mini-biscuits, juice, a toothpick, matches and, to clean up afterward, a moist towelette. Regardless of choice, each crew heated up their rations in the little pressure cooker that is part of a Cougar's kit and, then having erected the triangular tent that is also part of the vehicle's equipment, settled down for the night.

The rain fell through the night and into Sunday morning, 22 August, most of which was spent waiting for the final elements of the battle squadron to get themselves sorted out and into the field. Exercise ACTIVE EDGE had three distinct elements, each intended to train troops for the various situations that modern Canadian soldiers may possibly face on overseas deployments – what National Defence Headquarters likes to call "Three Block War." "Three Block War" involves different but overlapping activities: assistance to local authorities; security operations against what the Canadian Broadcasting Corporation terms "militants" but clear-thinking people call "terrorists"; and full scale warfighting. The composite battle squadron formed by the armoured units was slated to train for warfighting, which made the Light Horse happy, as learning how to negotiate with a local village headman (who, judging by his short hair, looked suspiciously like a hastily-impressed spare military person) or being taught how to conduct vehicle searches at roadside check points was not what they signed up to do – and that was to put as many main gun rounds down range as possible.

Before they were permitted to do that, however, the battle squadron had to pass through the various stages of "Gateway" training. This is an exercise intended to polish basic armoured skills such as road movement, advance-to-contact, fire and movement, establishing fire bases, and quick attacks. It began at about 1 P.M. on Sunday afternoon when the squadron, having finally got all its elements together, moved into the field in a serious way, and continued through Monday, 23 August, all under a continuous downpour. Gradually, beginning with the simple things, the squadron progressively worked up to larger and more sophisticated manoeuvres. There were the usual problems to be worked out but, by late Monday afternoon, everybody was in the swing of it and the two Cougar troops of the squadron, as well as its headquarters and supply echelons, began to function smoothly as they bumped around the muddy fields and along the rocky roads of Wainwright to the soundtrack of radio messages:

"4-1, this is 4-1 Bravo, Black Snake now… over."

"4-1 Roger, Charlie, push farther left… over."

"Charlie, roger… out."

"Alpha this is 4-1, report when set… out."

"4-1 Alpha, set… out."

The Light Horse were hard at it all through Monday, 23 August, and when they went into their "hides" that night, despite the rain, they were content because the following day promised to be an interesting one with a combined armour-infantry-engineer assault on a defended obstacle.

We're going to leave the South Alberta Light Horse for the time being, munching on turkey and vegetable stew, or green pepper beef, or Tarragon chicken strips, or whatever, while we tell the story of this distinguished regiment. It a lengthy tale and perhaps the best place to begin would be the year 1874 ……

The Old Originals – G Squadron, Canadian Mounted Rifles, 1903
The first Alberta militia units were raised in 1903 when three squadrons of mounted rifles were authorized at Calgary, Fort Macleod and Medicine Hat. G Squadron at Calgary soon outstripped the others and here the men of that unit pose proudly in 1903 during their summer camp held on the estate of James Walker east of Calgary. Walker himself can be seen at the left of the front rank. The swords are 1896 Pattern heavy cavalry swords. GLENBOW MUSEUM, PB-869-2

"The Queen's Cowboys"

In the early autumn of 1874, a long column of horsemen and wagons wound its way through a rolling country just east of the foothills of the Rocky Mountains, which formed a blue line on the horizon. It was a picturesque sight, this column, led by about 200 red-coated men of the Northwest Mounted Police, five divisions or squadrons in all, with the men of each division riding horses of a distinct colour: dark brown, light chestnut, grey and buckskin and black. Behind the horsemen trailed 73 wagons, 114 two-wheeled Red River carts, 142 draft oxen, 93 cattle, two 9-pdr. field guns and several implements of farm machinery. Recruited and organized to bring law and order into the Canadian West, these mounted policemen had left Fort Dufferin in Manitoba the previous July to make a gruelling 900-mile march across arid plains, a march that ended in the bountiful land that would later be known as Alberta. One of the riders in that column was a man who will feature largely in our story. His name was James Walker and he was to become not only one of Alberta's leading pioneers but also the first commanding officer of the regiment known today as the South Alberta Light Horse.

James Walker was born in 1848, the son of Scots parents who had emigrated from their homeland in the late 1830s to begin a new life as farmers near Carluke, Ontario. Walker's father was interested in breeding horses and his son acquired this interest as he worked on the family farm. Walker was educated in public schools and a business college but, from an early age, evinced an interest in military matters. He was commissioned as a lieutenant in an Ontario militia infantry battalion in 1867, commanded a company on active service during the Fenian Raids of 1870, and obtained First Class Certificates from both the Infantry School in Toronto and the Artillery School in Kingston. He had reached the rank of major by 1873 when he was asked by

> Our dailies team with daring deeds,
> And books are filled with fame,
> Brass bands will play and cannons roar
> In honour of the name,
> Of men who held commissions, and
> Were honest, brave and true,
> But still the question comes to me,
> WHAT DID THE PRIVATES DO?
>
> All honour to the brave, wild boys,
> Who rallied at the call –
> Without regard to name or rank
> We honour one & all.
> They're passing over, one by one
> And soon they'll all be gone
> To where the books will surely show
> Just what the boys have done.[1]

Lieutenant-Colonel George French, the first Commissioner of the North West Mounted Police, to help equip the newly-established force and, between them, French and Walker chose every horse purchased for the organization.

Commissioned a sub-inspector in the spring of 1874, Walker accompanied the NWMP on their march west that summer and proved invaluable during this gruelling ordeal. When a thunder storm caused the column's horses to stampede and run away, leaving their riders stranded on foot, it was Walker who rode more than a hundred miles to round up and return them. When the exhausted mounties were nearing the end of their trek, it was the 6-foot, 4-inch Walker who picked up 14-year-old Bugle Boy Fred Bagley and carried him the last few miles of the march. Promoted an inspector in 1875, Walker served with the NWMP for the next five years and also acted as an Indian Agent, earning a reputation among the aboriginal peoples for being fair but strict in all his dealings with them. As a young man, James Walker was therefore privileged to see the first horsemen of Alberta – the aboriginal plains peoples – before they were swept aside by a flood of white settlement.

"Something happens to a man when he gets on a horse": The first horsemen

The aboriginal peoples had been in the West for thousands of years but they had entered the area on foot and they were drawn to it by the buffalo. Roaming the plains of North America in numbers that might once have been as many as 60 million, the buffalo thrived on the grass on the continental interior and were a plentiful source of food for the native peoples who followed their annual migrations and hunted them by stratagems including buffalo "jumps." This method of hunting required a high degree of cooperation which, in turn, led to the evolution of a culture whose life was bound up with its prey. By the early

The first horsemen: Assiniboine camp, 1874
The aboriginal peoples residing on the western plains were quick to take to the horse and gun, innovations that reached them in the early 18th century. Their way of life depended on the buffalo that constituted their food supply, and as the buffalo declined, that way of life came to an end. NAC, C-81793

(Right) **"Something happens to a man when he gets on a horse": Cree Warrior, 1880s**
The culture of the plains people was based on the horse, gun and buffalo. It began to disintegrate in the mid-19th century when the buffalo began to disappear and these proud people were overwhelmed by the advancing tide of white settlement. NAC, C-33473

18th century the area that would later become Alberta was the territory of the Blackfoot Confederacy, with its constituent and allied peoples, in the south, and of the Cree and Assiniboine peoples in the north and northeast.

The aboriginal peoples living on the central plains were far removed from developments on the Atlantic shores of the continent. They may have heard about the arrival of Europeans and acquired a few useful or attractive trinkets from Indian traders who passed their way but they certainly became aware of the new arrivals when two European innovations – the horse and the gun – reached them. The first horses arrived in Alberta in the third decade of the 18th century and guns appeared almost at the same time, brought in by aboriginal traders who had obtained them from the British and French. The plains peoples took quickly to these two innovations and the horse, gun and buffalo became the foundations of a new culture. "Something happens to a man when he gets on a horse," wrote a scholar of the plains warriors, "in a country where he can ride at a run forever, it is quite easy to ascend to an impression of living in a myth."[2]

The western horse warriors lived that myth and were relatively immune to the pressures exerted on the other Indian nations by the increasing numbers of Europeans who began to penetrate the interior. The first white man known to have encountered the Blackfoot was Anthony Henday of the Hudson's Bay Company who, in 1754, undertook an exploratory mission to convince the peoples of the plains to trade at the company posts. In October of that year Henday met a large band of Blackfoot near the Red Deer River who told him politely but firmly that they were not interested in his proposals. As Henday recorded, the Blackfoot thought the European posts were "far off, and they could not live without buffaloes flesh, and that they never would leave their horses, and many other obstacles which I think very just, the chief of which was, they never wanted provisions."[3]

Matters began to change, however, in the late 18th and early 19th centuries as the fur trading companies built new posts at Edmonton House and Rocky Mountain House in the central part of what would later be Alberta. The horsemen started to trade with the whites and, like all the native peoples, they suffered from this association – between 1819 and 1870 perhaps half their numbers died from epidemics of diphtheria, measles and smallpox. During the same period, overhunting led to a progressive decline of the buffalo and this in turn led to armed conflict between the aboriginal peoples. The plains warriors also faced a challenge from a new western people, the Métis, the offspring of British and French fur traders and aboriginal women. Employed at first by the trading companies, the Métis gradually established settlements along the banks of the Red River at the eastern edge of the plains and later, along the banks of the North Saskatchewan River farther to the west. As farming could not support

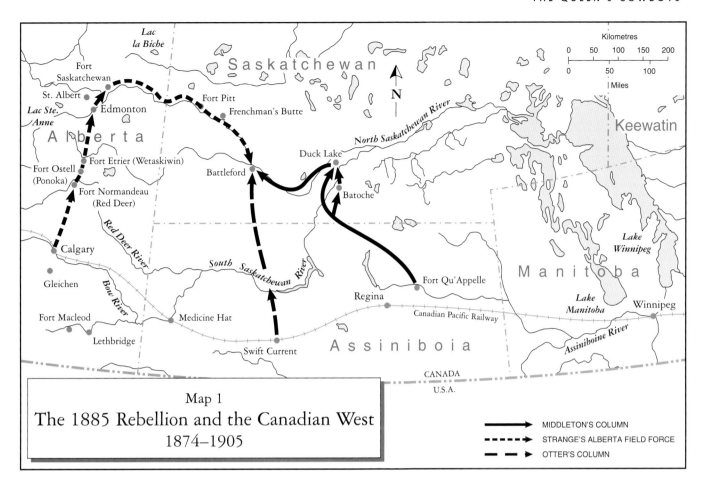

Kilometres
0 50 100 150 200

0 50 100
Miles

N

Map 1
The 1885 Rebellion and the Canadian West
1874–1905

MIDDLETON'S COLUMN
STRANGE'S ALBERTA FIELD FORCE
OTTER'S COLUMN

their numbers, the Métis turned to buffalo hunting which, in turn, caused them to clash with the aboriginal peoples.

Such was the situation by the 1860s when the Hudson's Bay Company, having outlasted all its rivals, became the sole proprietor of a huge area, encompassing the modern provinces of Manitoba, Saskatchewan and Alberta and much of British Columbia and the Northwest Territories. The company was concerned about the relentless advance of the America frontier to the south and, knowing it could not defend this vast territory, began to contemplate disposing of it. The most likely purchaser was the newly-formed Dominion of Canada, created by the Confederation on 1 July 1867 of the British colonies in Eastern North America. The first prime minister of the new nation, John A. Macdonald, was interested in the West as a future place of settlement for the expanding population in the East and as a market for the products of eastern industry. He also wished to include the Pacific coast colony of British Columbia in Confederation and that would require the construction of railway across the western

plains. On 1 November 1869, for the bargain price of £300,000, Canada acquired an area of 1,800,000 square miles, stretching from Hudson Bay to the Pacific.

Acquiring this territory proved easier than governing it. No one in the federal government had thought to consult the Métis

Mounted Police constable, 1870s

Formed in 1873 to maintain law and order in the Canadian west, an object they admirably accomplished, the Mounted Police were nearly overwhelmed during the Northwest Rebellion of 1885. The result was that military forces were stationed in the west – at first regulars and later militia.

SASKATCHEWAN ARCHIVES BOARD, S-879

25

The North West Mounted Police on parade, c. 1883
The NWMP were equipped with artillery and here an artillery section trains on a field gun while a troop suffers the indignities of infantry drill.
NAC, PA-118756

about the transfer of power and the Métis were concerned that their culture and landholding system would be threatened by eastern settlers. In late 1869 and early 1870, before the Canadian government took over firm control of the new territory, the Métis in the Red River area rose in rebellion under the leadership of the charismatic Louis Riel. This rebellion – actually not much more than an armed protest – was settled with minimal loss of life after British troops were rushed to the area. In May 1870, the southeastern corner of the new Canadian West was transformed into the Province of Manitoba and the remaining 1,789,000 acres became the Northwest Territories with a regional government established at Regina.

Cattle, cowboys and cayuses: The whites arrive in numbers, 1870-1885

Throughout the 1860s, as overhunting began to kill off the once almost countless herds of buffalo, hunger forced the Cree and Assiniboine to encroach on the territory of the Blackfoot Confederacy and this led to open warfare. The last battle of the horse warriors took place in 1870 with victory going to the Blackfoot. Year by year, however, the numbers of buffalo continued to decline and, worse yet, another outbreak of smallpox decimated the plains peoples. Almost as bad as the evil wrought by the white man's disease was that wrought by American whisky traders who came over the border to sell alcohol in return for whatever a once proud people had to barter. When drunkenness and violence led to the massacre of 30 innocent Indian men, women and children by American traders in the Cypress Hills area in the summer of 1873, the Canadian government moved to restore order in the West.

The government had a good plan. In 1872, Prime Minister Macdonald had sent the adjutant of the Canadian militia, Colonel P. Robertson-Ross, on an inspection tour of the Territories to advise on the best way to establish a military presence in the

area. It was Robertson-Ross's belief that a force of a thousand men should be raised, "supplied with horses and equipment as mounted riflemen," to provide for the security and "the preservation of good order" in the West.[4] Macdonald agreed that this force should be "Mounted Riflemen, trained partly as Cavalry, but also instructed in rifle exercise" and "in the use of artillery."[5] He did, not, however, think that it should "be expressly military but should be styled Police, and have the bearing of the Irish Constabulary." The result was the creation in 1873 of the North West Mounted Police.

In June of the following year, the NWMP, with 26-year-old James Walker among them, entered the West, and quickly established the rule of law for all, including whites, Métis and Indians, in the Territories. They built a series of posts across what would later be Alberta – Fort Macleod and Fort Calgary among others – but did not like the look of the old Hudson's Bay fur trading station at Fort Edmonton and instead constructed their post, Fort Saskatchewan, some 15 miles to the northeast. The police were fair in their dealings with the Indians and oversaw the signing of the two treaties, No. 6 in 1876 and No. 7 in 1877, by which the Crees, Assiniboines, and the Blackfoot Confederacy renounced the rights to their land in return for small reservations, education, instruction in farming and the federal government's not overly-generous welfare. When the Sioux nation under Sitting Bull, having wiped out Custer and most of the 7th United States Cavalry, fled north to British territory, the NWMP escorted them to a place of refuge and maintained a watchful eye on them until they returned to the United States in 1881. Not the least of the many contributions made by the NWMP to the settling of the West was that the force brought a singularly hardy and self-reliant group of young men to the area who, liking what they saw, remained after their terms of service had expired and proved to be very successful pioneers. Among them was James Walker who secured his release from the NWMP in 1880 to take over the management of the Cochrane Ranch west of Fort Calgary.

It quickly became clear to the new settlers that a country which had been ideal for buffalo would be just as suitable for cattle. Some of the early fur traders had brought cows with them but it appears that the first man to drive cattle into what would later be Alberta was the Reverend John McDougall who brought a small herd to his mission at Morleyville in 1873. Others followed McDougall's lead and it was discovered that cattle let loose on the prairie in the autumn could survive through the winter unassisted, as they could shelter in the many coulees, creeks and river beds while the Chinook – the warm westerly wind off the Rockies – resulted in frequent winter thaws that uncovered meadow grass. In 1881, the ranching industry was given a tremendous incentive when the federal government passed an Order-in-Council allowing one man or company to lease annual grazing rights in the West for cattle for one cent per acre. That same year James Walker drove the first big herd of 7,000 head in from Montana and ranching was given an additional boost when the government directed the NWMP not to raise their own cattle and horses but to procure them from civilian establishments. By 1884 there were 47 ranches in what was now officially known as the District of Alberta – including such large establishments as the Cochrane, 76, Bar U, Military Colonization, Quorn and Walrond Ranches, and the Cypress Cattle Company. With the cattle came the cowboys and with the cowboys their horses – the prairie cayuse or quarter horse – sturdy little animals not much to look at but good for 75 miles a day and which, like the cattle, were often let loose to graze on the open plains in winter where they prospered. In the 1880s, white society in the southern part of the District of Alberta was just as horse crazy as that of the plains warriors which had preceded it.

Mary Inderwick, the wife of an Alberta rancher, recorded that "if I did not ride," her husband's employees would have had "nothing to do with me."[6]

Outwardly, both the ranching and agricultural sectors of Alberta society resembled their American counterparts but differed in one major aspect – the NWMP maintained the rule of law. There was very little of the violence found in the American West, violence that has provided Hollywood with much dramatic material, some of it even true. The Mounted Police were respected by the lawful inhabitants and feared by the lawless but that is not to say, however, that there were not some colourful characters and colourful times in the early history of the District of Alberta, particularly around Fort Macleod, the hub of ranching activity. The centrepiece of this little town was the Macleod Hotel, run by Kamoose ("Squaw Thief") Taylor, sometime whisky trader and preacher, who delighted in posting eccentric signs in his establishment:

> All guests are requested to rise at 6 a.m. This is imperative as the sheets are needed for tablecloths.

> Towels changed weekly. Insect Powder for sale at the bar.

and perhaps his most famous:

> The Bar in the Annex will be open day and night. All Day drinks, 50 cents each; Night drinks, $1.00 each. No Mixed Drinks will be served except in case of death in the family.[7]

However, men like Kamoose Taylor (and many of his guests) – no matter how much they added to its character – did not represent the social elite of the District of Alberta. That was

Home on the Range
In the early 1880s, cattle ranching thrived in the southern part of the District of Alberta and when the Northwest Rebellion broke out in 1885, cowboys proved to be natural light cavalry. Here, cowpokes brand cattle on a ranch near Medicine Hat in the 1880s. GLENBOW MUSEUM, NA-631-2

formed by the officers and men of the NWMP and Alberta, in its early years, always had a distinctly British style, even if the weather differed considerably from the Mother Country. There were some very cosmopolitan men in the ranks of the Police – Inspector Samuel B. Steele, who served at Fort Macleod in the 1880s, remembered that among the sergeants at his post were three university graduates, three former NCOs of the Royal Irish Constabulary, an ex-sheriff from New Brunswick and a West Point cadet who had been "rusticated" for some offence.[8]

The NWMP dictated the tone of the surrounding communities and invitations to their social functions were eagerly sought after. At the larger police posts the biggest event was the annual ball. William Antrobus Griesbach, the young son of the commander of Fort Saskatchewan in the early 1880s, remembered that the toughest challenge was finding female partners for the men so, on the day of the event, almost every team and sleigh at the post was busy picking up young ladies in Edmonton and bringing them out to the fort where a barrack room, scrubbed top to bottom and provided with clean linen and blankets, was set aside for them. It was not regarded as ready, however, until it had passed a white glove inspection by Mrs. Inspector Griesbach and, throughout the event, there was always a reliable married constable standing post at the door. Dancing took place in the enlisted men's mess which was "profusely decorated with evergreens, coloured panels bearing suitable mottoes and the like" while streamers "forming stars and other artistic designs flowed from the ceiling" but this room, too, had to pass inspection by Mrs. Griesbach before festivities could commence. The dancing usually began at 7 PM and continued until dawn with a break for supper and it was formally conducted by a grand master of the ball who directed what appeared, to young Griesbach's untutored eyes, to be "a series of manoeuvres which bore a startling resemblance to the musical ride."[9]

The other big NWMP celebration was Christmas Dinner. As Inspector Steele at Fort Macleod recalled, this was serious business:

Our Christmas dinners … were always in the evenings, no daylight dinners for us. All, from the commissioner to the latest recruit, realized that Christmas comes but once a year, and that we must have a good time. Our civilian friends, to the number of 20, sat down with us, and our bill of fare consisted of turkeys, wild geese, antelope, other venison, buffalo tongues, boss rib, plum pudding, California fruit, raisins, nuts and milk punch, for which a permit had been obtained to enable us to pass the Christmas satisfactorily. The proceedings were enlivened by songs, speeches and toasts, the Queen, the Governor General, the army and navy and other loyal toasts being duly honoured. The President of the United States was toasted in honour of our guests, who with few exceptions were citizens of the great Republic, and was responded to by every American at the table.[10]

In the 1880s the West began to change as the Canadian Pacific Railway reached the prairies. This great venture was part of Prime Minister Macdonald's plan to tie British Columbia to Confederation and to settle the West. The coming of the railway was eagerly awaited in the District of Alberta as it would not only provide communication to the outside world but also a means of transporting the area's cattle and crops to market. At this time, the area around Edmonton had the largest population in the District, with some 700 people living in the little town and the surrounding communities of Fort Saskatchewan, Lac La Biche and Lac Ste. Anne. Fort Calgary could only muster 75 persons on a good day while about 500 whites lived in the ranching community around Fort Macleod. By June 1883 the CPR had reached the South Saskatchewan River at a point where a bridge was built and the settlement that grew up around the construction site adopted the Indian name for the locality which was *saamis* or "medicine hat." By August the tracks were through to little Calgary, which dropped "Fort" from its name and soon boasted some 750 people, and were moving on to the Rockies. In the spring of 1885 there were approximately 3,500 white and Métis settlers in the District of Alberta while the Indian population was perhaps three times that number. Everyone, with the possible exception of the aboriginal peoples, believed the future looked bright.

"I see by your outfit, that you are a cowboy":
Alberta rancher, 1880s
Frederick Charles Inderwick was typical of the many men who engaged in ranching in the early days. He had come to Canada as an aide-de-camp to Lord Lansdowne, the governor general, but in 1883 established the North Fork Ranche, 22 miles from Pincher Creek. In this studio shot Charlie Inderwick poses proudly in his cowboy outfit, complete with chaps, lariat and, of course, a prominently displayed six-gun. GLENBOW MUSEUM, NA-1365-1

The "Hat," 1885

In the summer of 1883, the Canadian Pacific Railway built a bridge across the South Saskatchewan River at a place that the aboriginal peoples called *saamis* or "medicine hat." The community that grew up around the bridge adopted the name and Medicine Hat has retained its distinctive moniker. Throughout its history, Medicine Hat has always supported its local military – from the Rocky Mountain Rangers of 1885 to the South Alberta Light Horse of 2005. SALH ARCHIVES

"First-class men": The Northwest Rebellion and the Alberta Field Force, 1885

Trouble, however, was brewing. The tensions that ultimately led to the outbreak of rebellion in the Northwest Territories in the spring of 1885 had been simmering for more than a decade but had accelerated with the construction of the CPR. The Métis, many of whom had moved farther west to settle along the North Saskatchewan River when English-speaking settlers began to flood into Manitoba after 1870, again felt their culture and landholding system threatened. For their part, the Assiniboine and Cree peoples, on government reservations, complained that the federal government had not lived up to its obligations to them and they were verging on starvation. Tensions came to a head in 1884 when the Métis invited Louis Riel, who had fled to the United States after his abortive rebellion in 1870, to return to Canada to plead their cause with Macdonald's Conservative government. Ottawa, however, dragged its heels and only awoke to the seriousness of the situation in the spring of 1885. By this time it was too late – on 18 March Riel seized the federal Indian agent at Batoche and announced the formation of a provisional Métis republic. When a small force of mounted policemen and settlers serving as special constables marched on Batoche to re-establish federal authority they were met at Duck Lake by a Métis force which decisively beat them, inflicting a loss of 23 men killed and wounded. The NWMP, which had a strength of only 550 officers and men to police an area nearly as large as Western Europe, were unable to contain the uprising and the federal government began to mobilize military forces.

These forces were led by Major-General Frederick Middleton, a British soldier who held the appointment of General Officer Commanding, Canadian Militia. A few days after the disaster at Duck Lake, Middleton arrived by rail in Winnipeg to organize an army composed of militia units, both from Manitoba and Eastern Canada, and units of the tiny Canadian regular force. Mounted troops were essential in the West but Middleton, an experienced campaigner who had seen active service in Australia and India, did not have much faith in either the regular cavalry "school corps" with a total strength of 84 all ranks, or the Governor-General's Body Guard, a militia cavalry regiment from Toronto, which formed part of his force. Instead he followed the advice of Prime Minister Macdonald who advised that he could "get men enough from the Prairies" who would "of course be much more serviceable than town-bred men who compose our cavalry."[11] When he moved against Batoche in late April 1885, Middleton left the regular cavalry and the Toronto boys to guard his lines of communication and put his trust in Boulton's Scouts, a volunteer unit mounted on quarter horses and armed with Winchesters and a knowledge of the ground. The wisdom of this decision was confirmed when, early in his march toward the seat of the rebellion, the Scouts prevented his column from being ambushed.

Farther west in the District of Alberta a minor panic ensued when news arrived of Duck Lake. There were only 6 NWMP officers at Calgary and there was great fear that the Blackfoot Confederacy, estimated to 5,000 warriors strong, would burn and loot the little town. Not least among the fearful was the mayor and town council who, one local businessman remarked, became "much the worse for liquor" during the crisis.[12] This eyewitness, who confessed himself "familiar with the doings of the Mayor, Council and a few more of Calgary's drunken beauties," accused them of spreading rumours and trying to fortify the NWMP barracks "by building bastions and a thousand more foolish and unnecessary requests, while we the sober and better class are trying to do our duty in a quiet orderly way." Inspector Sam Steele of the NWMP, who arrived in Calgary on the CPR at almost at the same time as the news from Duck Lake, recalled that "many ladies were at the train with their families, on their way east."[13] Fortunately for the District, cooler heads prevailed, among them Thomas Strange, proprietor of the Military Colonization Ranche near Gleichen.

Thomas Bland Strange was a 30-year veteran of the Royal Artillery who had seen service in the West Indies, Gibraltar and India. The last ten years of his career had been spent commanding one of the "school" batteries of artillery which were the first units of the Canadian regular army. Strange had retired, rather unwillingly, in 1881 and had obtained financial backing to operate a grazing lease on 70,000 acres in the Alberta District. He was on familiar terms with many of the Blackfoot leaders, including Crowfoot, the most powerful chief. Strange did not believe that the Blackfoot Confederacy, except for a few young and virtually uncontrollable warriors, would join the Métis, Assiniboine and Cree forces along the North Saskatchewan River. Appointed by Minister of Militia Adolph Caron to command the forces of the Alberta District, Strange immediately took steps to raise troops and prepare a force to march north to Edmonton which, being closer to the centre of the uprising, was believed to be in peril. He was hampered by shortages of every kind of military materiel including weapons, uniforms, saddlery, horses and equipment and, as he later remarked, in Alberta when it came to military matters in 1885, "there was nothing but brick-making without straw."[14]

Strange established his headquarters at Calgary and authorized Steele and George Hatton, his ranch foreman and a former militia officer from Ontario, to raise two small volunteer mounted units – to be known as Steele's Scouts and the Alberta Mounted Rifles – for the march north. Strange recorded that the mayor and town council of Calgary were most unhelpful as they "did their best to prevent the enrolment of men, telling them they would be forced to march with me, while the town, left unprotected, would be plundered and burnt by the Indians."[15] The citizenry were mollified somewhat when the capable James Walker, who had left the ranching business two years before to establish a sawmill and farm on the banks of the Bow River just east of Calgary, was put in command of a home guard unit to defend that town and the area south to Lethbridge and north to the Red Deer River. Strange, Hatton and Steele found no shortage of recruits among the drifting population of young men who worked in the ranch country – as a visitor to Calgary in the spring of 1885 remarked, the town seemed to be

the very paradise of cowboys, horsemen and scouts, for the place was full of the great, rough, good hearted fellows, fairly bristling with arms. Belts of cartridges round the waist and slashed across the chest held supplies for the Winchester rifle and Colt's revolver; great leather leggings called "Schaps," bowie-knives here and there about the person, huge jingling spurs, immense grey hats turned up at one side, "the cavalry swagger," and somewhat ferocious language were the prevailing characteristics. These men were magnificent riders, more at home in the saddle than on carpets; and they had the run of the town, the sight of a number of them, with their wild horses at full speed along the principal streets, was quite common.[16]

The long riders may have appeared exotic to easterners but Strange thought they were "excellent stuff," the majority being cowboys "out of a job; unfortunately the long Winter had obliged many of them to sell their horses and saddles, though most of them had stuck to their Winchesters and six-shooters."[17]

Steele and Hatton had no sooner commenced recruiting cowpokes when the local citizenry (who truly seemed to have been an awkward lot) implored Strange not to enlist such "rowdies" who "would never submit to discipline."[18] But Strange had lived too long among cowboys "not to know their good qualities as well as their little weaknesses." He recorded that, from "start to finish, they never gave me the slightest trouble, and were the best-behaved men of the Force, always to the front, yet never grumbling." Strange's high opinion of these men was echoed by Steele, who believed that, as a light cavalryman, the cowboy "has no superior in the world," and "takes to the order of military experience as if he were born to it."[19] For his part, Steele was only too glad to enlist "cow-punchers" and "broncho busters" who were "first-class men, ready for hard work, good-tempered and obedient."

It was not difficult to find good men in the District of Alberta but it was much harder to find weapons and equipment. After bombarding Ottawa with telegrams Strange finally received 150 Winchester rifles, ammunition, and a shipment of saddlery for the Alberta Mounted Rifles. Unfortunately the saddles were cheaply made, "flimsy affairs, put together with tin-tacks" which the Mounted Rifles' half-broken horses "bust up with lightness of heart."[20] As a result the first mounted parade of the Rifles was a sight worth seeing:

The men were good riders, but to sit a bucking broncho is one thing, and to hold on the saddle also when the girths give way is quite another. Consequently the prairie was in a few minutes strewn with men, rifles, revolvers, and relics of saddles, in which some horses were tangled up, while others careered around until they were lassoed by the men with reliable saddles. The broken ones were patched up, and after some severe marching and patrolling there was no more equine exuberance."[21]

Strange's command was augmented by the arrival of three militia infantry battalions – the 9th Voltigeurs and 65th Carabiniers Mont Royal from Quebec and the 90th Winnipeg Rifles – and, less than two weeks after his appointment as commander of the District, he was ready to move north with about 400 men. On 18 April 1885, the first element of the Alberta Field Force left Calgary for Edmonton to be followed, over the next few days, by the remainder of the force. Scouting ahead of the main body was Reverend John McDougall and four warriors of the Stony nation. This was the same Reverend McDougall who had brought the first cattle into Alberta in 1873 and who, in Sam Steele's opinion, "was one of the best scouts in the west, being as much at home in the canoe, on the trail, or running wild buffalo as he was in the pulpit."[22] A few days later Reverend George Mackay, another member of the church militant, joined Strange after riding 200 miles from Fort Macleod to offer "his services in any capacity." "Brave as a lion, an excellent horseman, a good shot and speaking Cree fluently," Reverend Mackay was, for Steele, "just the man for the cavalry" and the inspector was pleased when Strange assigned him to Steele as the chaplain for his Scouts.[23]

McDougall reached Edmonton on 25 April to find the inhabitants nervous but no sign of hostiles. Five days later, Strange arrived at the "scattered little town" on the banks of the North Saskatchewan dominated by the gray wooden stockade of the Hudson's Bay Company fort with its flag "displaying the wondrous letters 'H.B.C.,' which are a whole history of the 200 years of British pluck and energy."[24] The sight of that flag prompted a question from one of the Englishmen in the force as to the meaning of the initials displayed on it, a query that received a swift reply from a Canadian: "I guess that's 'Here Before Christ.'"

Strange halted at Edmonton for about five days to prepare for a move to Fort Pitt and Frog Lake, the western seat of the rebellion. He utilized the time to both train his raw volunteers and militia and construct boats to carry the supplies he would need as there was little to be had between Edmonton and his objective. William Griesbach, last met as the puzzled young observer of Mounted Police dancing, never forgot the day the general trotted into his father's post at Fort Saskatchewan:

Strange was a tall man with a ferocious black beard. He rode at the head of his column wearing artillery trousers (with a broad red stripe) tucked into long jack boots, a dark blue frock coat and a black felt hat with the brim pinned up on the left side; a sword hung from his sword-belt, worn outside the frock coat. I was tremendously impressed and decided, then and there, at the age of seven that the only thing worth-while was to be a general, particularly when my father saluted him smartly and, standing to attention, was full of "Yes, sir; certainly sir; quite sir."[25]

Finally, on 14 May 1885, Strange felt ready to continue. Leaving a portion of his force to garrison Edmonton and Fort Saskatchewan, he set out down the North Saskatchewan River, his troops moving by land and his supplies by boat. By Sunday, 24 May, his column had reached Frog Lake and since this was not only the Lord's Day but Queen Victoria's birthday, he felt constrained to point this out to his troops. Referring to the Sovereign, Strange told them that "we have not time to celebrate and can't have fireworks, but let us hope we soon will have fireworks with the enemy."[26] Having got that out the way, the general then turned to the matter of religion:

Boys, this is also Sunday but we have no time for service today; we must push on the march. I am reminded of an old soldier who on going into battle prayed "O God, I often forget thee. I will be very busy today. I am sure to forget thee, but do not forget me." Boys, we will sing together, "Praise God from whom all blessings flow."[27]

When the last note died away, the Alberta Field Force moved out.

It took eleven days from Edmonton to reach Fort Pitt which Strange found abandoned but three days later, on 28 May 1885, he encountered a strongly-entrenched Cree force under their chief, Big Bear, in a very good defensive position at Frenchman's Butte. Strange did not have enough infantry to mount a fron-

Officers of the Rocky Mountain Rangers, 1885
From left to right, Lieutenant Henry Boyle, Captain Edward G. Brown; unidentified officer, Captain Lord Richard Boyle; and Major John Stewart, commanding officer. NAC, C-2872

Rough and ready – the Rocky Mountain Rangers, 1885
A group of Rangers pose at Fort Macleod in 1885 shortly after their unit was raised. Note the variety of civilian clothing and that each man has a revolver somewhere on his person. All are armed with the Winchester Model 76 .45-75 rifle. MEDICINE HAT ARCHIVES, PC 404-14

"Armed to the teeth": The Rocky Mountain Rangers, 1885

While Strange was campaigning in the north, the security of the southern part of the District of Alberta, meanwhile, was in the hands of not only James Walker's homeguards at Calgary, Fort Macleod, High River and Medicine Hat but also a volunteer mounted unit, the Rocky Mountain Rangers. The Rangers were the brainchild of John O. Stewart, a 31-year-old former resident of Ottawa who came West in 1881 to found the Stewart Ranche Company near Pincher Creek to provide horses to the mounted police and beef to the Indian Department. Stewart was in Ottawa when the rebellion had broken out and he approached Caron, the minister of militia, with a proposal that he raise a mounted unit of 150 all ranks from ranch employees. These men would supply their own horses and saddles and wear "their own serviceable Western apparel," but would receive weapons and pay from the government.[29] Caron approved this proposal and Stewart returned to the West to commence recruiting in the Pincher Creek-Fort Macleod area. In just twenty days, he formed three troops of Rangers who included in their ranks many men who were already, or would later, be prominent in the history of Alberta.

Among the officers were Captain Lord Richard Boyle and Second Lieutenant the Honourable Henry Boyle, adventure-loving sons of the Earl of Shannon who delighted in wearing cowboy costume. These sprigs of the Anglo-Irish aristocracy had come to the West in 1881 to found the Alberta Ranche Company near Pincher Creek with a lease of 47,750 acres. Captain "Honest" John Herron, a veteran of the NWMP, had been Stewart's sergeant-major in an Ottawa militia cavalry unit. Stewart's adjutant was Duncan John D'Urban Campbell, his ranch partner and, like Stewart, a native of Ottawa and former Ontario militia cavalry officer. The troop surgeon was Doctor Leverett George De Vreber, late a surgeon with the NWMP, who had established a practice in Fort Macleod. The sergeant-major was John Henry Gresham Bray, a veteran of both the British army and the mounted police who was also a horse rancher. Among the enlisted Rangers was the renowned John "Kootenai" Brown, a former British cavalry officer and NWMP scout. There were also many early pioneers in the ranks including Albert M. Morden, one of the first settlers of Pincher Creek; Frederick Inderwick, a former aide-de-camp to the governor-general and owner of the North Fork Ranche near the same settlement; and Alfred Lynch-Staunton, owner of the Antelope Butte Ranch which runs cattle to this day. There was also some infamous men like John "Rattlesnake Jack" Robson who claimed to have served with the NWMP, a claim that unfortunately cannot be substantiated although his criminal record can.

High born or low, famous or infamous, by the last week of April 1885 the Rangers were raised and ready for service at Fort Macleod and Pincher Creek. They did receive some very basic training, with an emphasis on the basic. One ranger recalled that his troop officer gave the orders, "'Mount, Walk, Trot,' and then when we got in front of the little log saloon [possibly Kamoose Taylor's place] – Halt! Everyone dismount and have a drink.' That

tal assault, nor did he wish to as, despite his many eccentricities, Thomas ("Gunner Jingo") Strange was no fool and had no wish to "commit Custer."[28] He sent Steele and his scouts to find an open flank but, when Steele reported that there was no unguarded approach to the Crees' position, Strange decided not to needlessly waste lives but to withdraw to Fort Pitt.

He returned to Frenchman's Butte a few days later to find that the Cree had disappeared. Steele and his Scouts were sent on their trail and, although they came very close, they never caught up with the elusive Big Bear. A few days later Middleton, having taken Batoche and defeated the major Métis forces, arrived with the main field column and Strange's independent command ended. So, for that matter, did the rebellion – Riel had already surrendered and Middleton spent the first three weeks of June scouring the area around Fort Pitt for Big Bear who finally surrendered on 2 July 1885, bringing the entire business to a conclusion.

When Strange had moved east, the defence of Edmonton and the surrounding district was left in the hands of Lieutenant-Colonel Ouimet of the 65th Carabiniers Mont Royal. Ouimet constructed three fortified posts: Fort Etier (modern Wetaskiwin), Fort Normandeau (Red Deer) and Fort Ostell (Ponoka). He also armed a group of mounted Métis volunteers from St. Albert who had been serving under NWMP command at Fort Saskatchewan. About 60 strong, they were popularly known as the St. Albert Mounted Rifles and, after more eastern militia units arrived to garrison Edmonton, they rode to the mission at Lac La Biche under their commander, Captain Samuel Cunningham. For the remainder of the rebellion, the St. Albert Rifles patrolled the aboriginal reserves in the Lac La Biche area and they disbanded in Edmonton when the insurrection ended.

Cause for celebration: Medicine Hat, 1885

A group of Rangers, Indians, Métis, militia and citizens celebrate the opening of the Hat's first brewery in 1885. The bearded man seated in the front row holding the container from which the celebratory whisky bottle was removed (the bottle is in the hand of the seated man third from the left) is James "Kootenai" Brown (1839-1916). A former British cavalry officer, gold miner, pony express rider, whisky trader, U.S. cavalry scout and big game guide, "Kootenai" Brown served as the chief scout of the Rocky Mountain Rangers. He later dabbled in oil exploration but ended up as the first warden of what would later become Waterton Lakes National Park. MEDICINE HAT MUSEUM ARCHIVES PC 234-2

We see by his outfit: Rocky Mountain Ranger, 1885

Typical of the cowpokes who made up the Rangers is this unidentified man who poses proudly with his Winchester Model 1876 .45-75 rifle and bandolier. Note the small calibre pistol (for insurance) tucked into the waist band of his chaps and the "seegar." The Rangers were a hard riding outfit spoiling for a fight but never found one. GLENBOW MUSEUM, NA 670-5

was all the drill we got."[30] Another remembered hearing a Ranger call out, after failing to respond to several calls from his officer to fall in, "Hold on, Cap, till I cinch my horse!"[31] The Rangers may have lacked discipline but they certainly did not lack colour. When Number 1 and 2 Troops rode out of Fort Macleod for Medicine Hat on 2 May 1885, the local paper exulted that they were

> composed of a particularly fine body of men, and as they marched past armed to the teeth with Winchesters, and waist and cross-belts jammed full of cartridges, there was but one opinion expressed regarding them, and that was that they would make it extremely unhealthy for several times their number of rebel half-breeds or Indians, should occasion require.[32]

No less impressed was John D. Higginbotham, the town druggist, who penned for the eastern press a lively description of what he chose to call "The Cowboy Cavalry":

Headed by their youthful but intrepid commander, Capt. Stewart, the Rocky Mountain Rangers presented quite a formidable appearance as they left Macleod, amid the loud huzzas of the garrison. Their tanned faces almost hidden beneath the brims of huge Spanish sombreros, strapped on for "grim death". Around many of their necks were silk handkerchiefs, which besides being an embellishment, prevented the irritation by their coarse brown duck or "Montana" broadcloth coats. Over pants of the same material were drawn a pair of chaps (leather overalls). Cross belts pregnant with cartridges, a "sixshooter", sheath knife, a Winchester slung across the pommel of the saddle and a coiled lariat completed the belligerent outfit. Mounted on "bronchoes" good for 60 to 100 miles a day, they soon disappeared in the distance, a loud clanking of bits and jingling of their huge Mexican spurs now gave place to the rattling of the transportation wagons.[33]

Two days later, the Rangers rode into the Hat and were welcomed by the citizens who had been digging rifle pits for their own defence. Stewart then sent his men on continuous patrols along the Canadian-American border to the Rockies and along the railway and telegraph lines. In mid-May, when eastern militia units arrived to relieve the Rangers of the burden of defending the railway, they concentrated on border patrols. Although

33

"The Horsemen" – North West Mounted Police, 1894

A detachment from G Division of the NWMP parades in full dress uniform. The Mounted Police, a para-military force, provided security for the District of Alberta in its early days but the Norhwest Rebellion demonstrated that there was a need for more conventional military units.

they were spoiling for a fight, and certainly armed for one, the Rangers never found a scrap and their period of service ended in late June 1885 without incident. In fact, it appears that their worst enemy was the eastern press who apparently made some slighting remarks about their reputation. Stewart, himself a scion of the Ontario establishment, responded in a speech he delivered during the splendid banquet held at Fort Macleod in August 1885 to celebrate the Rangers' achievements. Noting the adverse comments, Stewart made the entirely truthful claim that, in the District of Alberta, "a body of Mounted men could be raised superior to ANY CAVALRY IN THE DOMINION" and challenged journalists in Eastern Canada "to take this statement up and deny it."[34]

Stewart also proposed to Caron that the Rangers be retained in service, as an auxiliary "mounted corps" composed of "ex-policemen and cowboys would prove very valuable allies to the police" in the District.[35] Not only did Caron turn Stewart down, he added insult to injury by refusing to reimburse the Ranger commander about $1,200 which Stewart had paid out of his own pocket to purchase necessary items for his men.

And so the hard riding Rocky Mountain Rangers galloped off into history without ever firing a shot in anger. Nonetheless, they form an important part of our story as, nearly half a century later, the Rangers were accorded a Battle Honour, "North West, 1885," which has come down to the South Alberta Light Horse, the modern regiment that maintains their traditions.*

---

* The modern day Rocky Mountain Rangers, a British Columbia militia unit, have no official connection with the Rangers of 1885. The SALH is the only Alberta militia regiment to possess a Battle Honour for the 1885 Rebellion.

"No red coats, lace and long boots": The regular cavalry comes west

It was clear that the Northwest Territories, an area of a quarter million square miles, needed a military presence to back up the NWMP in an emergency. On this subject, Major-General Frederick Middleton had some definite ideas and, in May 1885, well before hostilities in the Northwest had ended, he offered some advice to the government. Middleton was no admirer of the NWMP whom he considered to have been singularly ineffective during the rebellion. Instead, he proposed that a new force be raised of "distinctly mounted infantry, dressed properly for the duty required – no red coats, lace and long boots but Khaki coloured uniform with Winchesters and Sword bayonet."[36] This new entity would be similar to the volunteer scout units that had served during the Rebellion but, in Middleton's view, it had to be a military force of no less than 1,000 all ranks that would "supersede the Mounted Police altogether."

The general's proposed strength figure, which would in effect double the size of the tiny regular Canadian military establishment, found no favour in Ottawa. Now that the rebellion was over, Macdonald's government could see no threat that required an increase in defence spending – the Métis and aboriginal nations were no longer a concern and the United States was preoccupied with its own problems.

There was also the question of cost and, as we shall see, throughout the history of Canada its government has always demonstrated a singular tendency in peacetime never to spend a penny on defence it did not have to spend. Caron did go so far, however, as to authorize the creation of a "School of Mounted Infantry" at Winnipeg to consist of two companies with a strength of 100 enlisted men. This tiny regular unit was recruited in the autumn of 1885 and, when Middleton inspected it in November of that year, he was pleased with the selection of the school's four officers, three of whom were veterans of the recent rebellion. But he also cautioned that

> For Indian warfare this arm (mounted infantry) will prove of value, but care must be taken that the original object of the organization is not lost sight of and that they do not try to be cavalry either in dress or movements.
>
> It is, also, of course, most necessary that Mounted Infantry should be good shots and no expense or trouble should be spared in making them so.[37]

A year later, Middleton felt again constrained to warn that the mounted infantry school confine itself to its intended role, "that of Infantry moving on ponies or horses for rapidity of movement only, and never attempting to fight mounted" otherwise the new corps might end up being "bad and expensive Infantry and indifferent Cavalry."[38]

These terms "cavalry" and "mounted infantry," a matter of concern to Middleton, require some explanation. Almost from the time the first soldier rode into battle on a horse, the major cavalry tactic in western armies was the use of shock produced by a charge delivered by hundreds of horsemen, armed with edged weapons, either swords or lances. In shock tactics, the horse's weight and momentum was the real weapon because the charge was basically a moving wall of men and horses, riding knee to knee. The mounted arm did have other tasks – advance and rear guards, reconnaissance and the pursuit of a beaten enemy – but every true cavalryman's dream was to deliver a charge against opposing cavalry or infantry. In the mid-19th century, however, the introduction of rifled weapons with increased accuracy and range meant that the traditional shock tactic of a charge with swords or lances over "clear, open ground" that had "hitherto been a cavalryman's ideal," now became very costly because this was precisely the same ground where infantry rifle fire produced "its greatest effect."[39] The result was a major change in the tactical employment of mounted troops, particularly in North America, which first became notable during the American Civil War of 1861-1865 in which the traditional charge was rarely used and, even then, usually only against enemy cavalry. Increasingly, horse soldiers began to fight dismounted, using their steeds only as a means of getting to battle and not as the arbiter of its outcome – in effect they became mounted infantry. This process was accelerated late in the war when the Union cavalry received multi-shot magazine weapons that exponentially increased their firepower.

From this time on, two schools of thought emerged – the traditional cavalry school which continued to believe that a charge with edged weapons would be decisive in battle, and the progressive "mounted infantry" school which held that firepower was the dominant factor on the battlefield and the horse simply a means of locomotion. It would seem, however, that the attraction of becoming true cavalry and charging with out thrust swords was just too strong for the Mounted Infantry School in Winnipeg. In 1891, although it had recently been redesignated the Canadian Mounted Rifle Corps, the new commander of the Canadian Militia, Major-General Ivor Herbert, ordered the School to be reorganized as a troop of cavalry and a year later, when it became B Squadron of the Royal Canadian Dragoons, it primarily trained as conventional cavalry.

"Fine horses and fine horsemen": The military and Alberta, 1885-1899

The debate over mounted tactics did not attract much attention in the District of Alberta which, for sixteen years after the 1885 Rebellion, continued to exist without any armed force except the NWMP. In 1886, the citizens of Calgary, remembering the anxiety the city experienced during the recent troubles, petitioned Ottawa to authorize a militia unit but this request disappeared into some dusty pigeon-hole. In the decade following the Rebellion, the growth of the District of Alberta was steady if not spectacular. Many eastern militiamen, who had come out during the recent hostilities, returned to settle and they were joined by about 1,000 new settlers a year until the early 1890s when the influx of newcomers increased, fed by immigrants from Britain, the United States and Europe. By 1891 the District had over 17,000 white and 9,000 Indian inhabitants – four years later there were 30,000 whites. The discovery of gold in the Klondike in 1897-1898 provided a strong impetus to the growth of Edmonton which became the gateway to the north and, by the end of the decade that city and neighbouring Strathcona had a population of 4,176 souls while Calgary had 4,392.

In 1898, some twelve years after the citizens of Calgary had petitioned Ottawa to authorize a militia unit for their city, it appeared that something might finally be done about the matter. In that year Major-General T.H. Hutton assumed the post of commander of the Canadian militia. Hutton had an extensive background in the organization and deployment of mounted infantry in Africa and Australia and possessed firm views on the subject. He suggested temporarily moving the Dragoon squadron from Winnipeg to Kingston to train the eastern militia cavalry, leaving only a small cadre in the West that would have the job of training a new militia regiment "consisting of two battalions of Mounted Infantry" which Hutton proposed raising in Manitoba and the Northwest Territories.[40]

In the autumn of 1899 Hutton travelled to British Columbia on an inspection tour and took the opportunity to stop in Calgary and address a very well-attended public meeting held at the Albert Hotel on 7 October. On the platform with Hutton were Commissioner Herchmer of the NWMP, Major V.A.S. Williams who commanded B Squadron of the Royal Canadian Dragoons at Winnipeg, Richard B. Bennett, a Calgary lawyer who was making a name in local politics, and James Walker. By now one of the most prominent citizens of Calgary, Walker's

Major John Stewart (1854-1893), 1885
The son of a prosperous mill owner in Ottawa and a former militia cavalry officer in that city, Stewart came west in 1881 to manage the Stewart Ranche near Pincher Creek, which supplied horses and cattle to the government. When the 1885 Rebellion broke out, he raised the Rocky Mountain Rangers to patrol the southern part of the District of Alberta. Stewart died in 1893, at the young age of 39. GLENBOW MUSEUM NA-1724-1

"Gunner Jingo": Major-General Thomas Bland Strange (1831-1925)
A somewhat eccentric but thoroughly professional soldier, Strange had retired from the army and was ranching in the west in 1885 when the Northwest Rebellion broke out. He took command of the military forces in the District of Alberta and organized a column that marched north to succour Edmonton. A stern disciplinarian, Strange nonetheless praised the cowboys who filled the ranks of his mounted units as natural-born light horse soldiers. Strange had many detractors but he outlasted them all, dying in 1925 at the green old age of 94. AUTHOR'S COLLECTION

The young professional: William Antrobus Griesbach (1878-1944), 1901
The son of an NWMP officer, William Griesbach had a long connection with military matters in Alberta. His father commanded Fort Saskatchewan during the 1885 Rebellion and, as a boy, Griesbach witnessed Strange's Alberta Field Force arrive at that post. In 1900 he served in South Africa with the 2nd Battalion, Canadian Mounted Rifles, and appears here at the age of 22 in his uniform, which is khaki wool field service dress. Griesbach helped to raise the independent squadron of mounted rifles in Edmonton that later became the 19th Alberta Dragoons. During the First World War he accompanied the Dragoon squadron that went overseas in 1914 before taking over the 49th Battalion CEF (perpetuated today by the Loyal Edmonton Regiment). After the war, Griesbach served both as a Member of Parliament and Senator from Alberta but always maintained his military connections and was a major-general when he died in 1944. FROM W.A. GRIESBACH, *I REMEMBER*

Western war horse: Samuel B. Steele (1849-1919)

Seen here as a major-general in 1915, Sam Steele had a long connection with the military in Alberta. He rode west with the NWMP in 1874, raised Steele's Scouts in the 1885 Rebellion and commanded Strathcona's Horse during the South African War before commanding Military District 13 (Alberta) from 1907 to 1911. Steele's last appointment was general officer commanding, 2nd Canadian Division, in the First World War. In this photo, Steele is wearing a frock coat. GLENBOW MUSEUM, NA-4008-1

Father of the Light Horse: Lieutenant-Colonel James Walker (1847-1936), c. 1912

James Walker came west with the NWMP in 1874 and took his release to settle in the Alberta District. He drove the first large cattle herd into the district from the United States in the early 1880s to begin the ranching industry and later expanded his commercial activities into mining and forestry. Walker commanded the Calgary home guard during the 1885 Rebellion and in 1905 he was appointed the first commanding officer of the 15th Light Horse and was serving as its honorary colonel when he died in 1936. A pioneer of Alberta, Walker can not only be termed the father of the provincial militia, he was prominent in the creation of the province itself. In 1974, James Walker was proclaimed "Calgary's Citizen of the Century." FROM MACRAE, *HISTORY OF THE PROVINCE OF ALBERTA*

Lieutenant-Colonel Robert Belcher, c. 1900

Belcher, a civilian doctor in Edmonton and a former medical officer in the NWMP, fought in South Africa and later became the first commanding officer of the 19th Alberta Mounted Rifles, later the 19th Alberta Dragoons. In 1911 he was promoted colonel and given command of the 5th Cavalry Brigade, the formation to which all Alberta mounted units belonged, succeeding Colonel James Walker. Belcher commanded the 138th Battalion, CEF, during the First World War. In this photo, Belcher is wearing South African War uniform. GLENBOW MUSEUM, NA-299-4

"Goodbye, Dolly Gray": Alberta volunteers for South Africa
Albertans enthusiastically enlisted in the mounted units raised for the war in South Africa and proved to be some of the best light horsemen in the British Empire. Here, volunteers pose in front of the recruiting office at Pincher Creek in early 1900. GLENBOW MUSEUM, NB-9-21

presence on the platform was no accident as he always took a keen interest in any matter relating to the military in the West. Hutton came straight to the point – in his opinion, a military unit such as he proposed could only be raised in three areas of the British Empire: South Africa, Australia and Western Canada. The District of Alberta, Hutton continued, was great ranching country and "when you have a Briton with a horse you generally have a gun or a rifle, so that the description of the militia most likely is a mounted one, and the class of force which I propose here would be suited to the country, namely mounted rifles."[41] When Hutton had finished, James Walker, noting that in Alberta there was "nothing but fine horses and fine horsemen," warmly promised his full support as did Commissioner L.W. Herchmer of the NWMP, Mr. Bennett and all those on the platform. As the *Calgary Herald* enthused, the advantages of having a militia unit, "social, protective, patriotic and other wise, are palpable great."

In a second meeting held the following day at Medicine Hat, Hutton elaborated on his plans before another enthusiastic audience. He informed his listeners that he proposed to raise companies of mounted rifles in that town, Calgary and Fort Macleod and promised that the men who joined would receive fourteen paid days annual training a year, which brought much applause. A few weeks later, Major Williams of the Dragoons addressed similar meetings at Fort Macleod, Lethbridge and Pincher Creek and again the response was very positive. But the plans of General Officers Commanding go oft awry and Hutton's intention to raise mounted militia units in Western Canada was shortly overtaken by events in distant Africa.

"A particularly workmanlike class of men": The war in South Africa, 1899-1902

Ever since Britain had acquired the Dutch colony at the Cape of Good Hope in the early 19th century, there had been problems between the British authorities and the Dutch-speaking inhabitants, popularly called the "Boers" after the Dutch word for farmers. Tension led to many Boers leaving British territory and founding two small republics, the Orange Free State and the Transvaal Republic, in the mid-19th century but relations did not improve and a British attempt to make the perpetually obstinate Boers see the light of Imperial reason led to a war in 1870, a conflict which came to a negotiated end after the British army suffered some humiliating reverses. For some time there was peace but the discovery of gold in the two republics and British territorial aspirations ultimately led to increased tensions which, by 1899, brought Britain and the Boers to the brink of war. Outright hostilities began when Boer forces invaded British territory in October of that year.

In Ottawa, Prime Minister Wilfrid Laurier's Liberal government, faced with strong opposition from its Quebec wing against any involvement in Imperial adventures, tried to sit on the fence but pressure from English Canada, coupled with offers from Australia and New Zealand to provide troops, ultimately forced the Liberals' hand. On 14 October 1899, Laurier announced that Canada would send an infantry battalion totalling 1,000 men to fight in South Africa. This unit, designated the 2nd (Special Service) Battalion, Royal Canadian Regiment, was raised from every province in Canada and, in a miracle of improvisation, embarked and was on its way just sixteen days after the government's announcement. There was no attempt to recruit for the Special Service Battalion in the Northwest Territories, a seeming slight that caused the *Calgary Herald* to grumble about westerners "being so treated in this manner," yet "another instance of the way in which the people of the effete east ignore" the people of the West.[42]

Events in South Africa – particularly during the "Black Week" in early December 1899 when the Boers inflicted three successive major defeats on the British – resulted in the raising of a second Canadian contingent. The early operations of the war had brought some nasty surprises to the British army which discovered that its opponents were skilled horsemen, often armed with modern Mauser magazine rifles that utilized smokeless powder and were accurate at long range. The Boer "commandos" were highly mobile small forces that might concentrate for a major action but would disappear only to turn up again in an unexpected place – ironically, they were the mounted riflemen that Middleton had been so keen to see formed in the West. The British regular cavalry, slow, overloaded, and rigid in mentality, were frustrated by the fact that the Boers would usually not stay in one location long enough to receive a charge or, if they did, would cut it down with long range rifle fire from hastily-dug entrenchments. What was needed to counter the Boers were horsemen who could match them and, in December 1899, Canada's offer of a unit of four squadrons of mounted rifles organized in two battalions, was gratefully accepted by the British government who advised that "it is indispensable that the men should be trained and good shots."[43]

Recruiting began almost immediately and this time Albertans got their chance. The 1st Battalion of Canadian Mounted Rifles, based on the Royal Canadian Dragoons, was raised in Eastern Canada and Manitoba but the 2nd Battalion, formed around an NWMP cadre, was recruited in the Territories. The mounted po-

lice provided 134 enlisted men and 9 of the unit's 16 officers including the commanding officer, Superintendent L.W. Herchmer, and the second in command, Superintendent Samuel B. Steele (erstwhile commander of Steele's Scouts in 1885). One squadron commander was to be a serving police officer and the other was to be James Walker but his wife's illness prevented Walker from proceeding overseas. Police officers opened recruiting stations in Calgary, Edmonton, Lethbridge, Fort Macleod and Pincher Creek and the response was overwhelming. Men flocked to enlist, men Steele described as "expert horsemen and good shots," and in a matter of days the 2nd Battalion was complete.[44]

Among these eager would-be soldiers was 21-year-old William A. Griesbach of Edmonton who, fourteen years before, had gazed with awe at the impressive figure of Major-General Thomas Strange when he rode into Fort Saskatchewan. Griesbach, who knew he was under the minimum weight, managed to pass the medical examination by surreptitiously holding a heavy piece of coal behind his back while on the scales, which brought him a half pound over the required figure. In Fort Macleod, 25-year-old Jefferson Davis, a Métis cowboy signed up, while Pincher Creek contributed a number of men including Fred Morden, the son of former Rocky Mountain Ranger, Albert Morden, one of the first settlers in the area. In all, 190 men joined the 2nd Battalion from the District of Alberta and, in the first week of January 1900 they left by rail for the East – as his train pulled out, young Griesbach was somewhat distressed to see his overwrought mother following it down the tracks. After a short stop in Ottawa long enough to be kitted out, inspected by the governor-general and to partake of a number of banquets provided by patriotic civilians, the men of the 2nd Battalion left for Halifax and by early February were on their way to the war.

Shortly after the 2nd Battalion had left, recruiting began for a new mounted regiment, Strathcona's Horse, which had

Rough and ready in South Africa: "The Queen's Cowboys," 1900
William A. Griesbach (marked "9") poses with comrades from the 2nd Battalion, Canadian Mounted Rifles, somewhere in South Africa in 1900. Raised in western Canada from cowboys and mounties, the 2nd Battalion, CMR, were a rather rough and ready lot. After their return to Canada, there were some wild scenes when the boys, whose "idea of a good time was to raise hell and fire off their weapons indiscriminately," terrorized eastern communities on their way home. Most of these men are wearing either wool field service dress jackets or khaki wool shirts. PROVINCIAL ARCHIVES OF ALBERTA, B-5395

originated in an offer by Donald Smith, Lord Strathcona, then Canadian High Commissioner in London, to raise and equip at his own expense a mounted regiment for the British army. Lord Strathcona specifically requested that his regiment be drawn from Western Canada as he had a high opinion of the horsemen of the plains and Sam Steele shifted from the Canadian Mounted Rifles to take command, gaining promotion to lieutenant-colonel. In early February 1900, recruiting began in British Columbia, Manitoba and the Northwest Territories and, as Steele recalled, volunteers "were not wanting; one could have got thousands of the best men in Canada."[45] The response was enthusiastic and the new regiment was filled within four days, including 180 men from the District of Alberta who were soon off to Ottawa where they were armed, equipped, inspected and feted before boarding the train for Halifax, stopping briefly for a banquet in Montreal on the way. On 16 March Strathcona's Horse embarked for South Africa.

By the time the three Canadian mounted units arrived at the front, the nature of the war in South Africa had undergone a marked change. After the British had forced the surrender of the main enemy army at Paardeberg in February 1900 and occupied the capitals of the two Boer republics, senior commanders were confident that hostilities would end. But there were still more than 35,000 Boers in the field, most of them mounted riflemen, and they refused to play by the British rulebook, resorting instead to guerilla warfare, using small, semi-independent, commandos that struck at supply columns, rail lines and outposts and disappeared before any force could be organized to catch them. The British response was to form light, mobile columns composed of regular cavalry, mounted infantry and colonial mounted units from Australia, Canada, New Zealand and South Africa to track down and eliminate these marauders. The colonial units proved much better at this work than the regular British cavalry who were, to their great disgust, told to hand in their swords and lances in return for rifles. The three Canadian mounted units (which some British observers called the "The Queen's Cowboys," either because of their stetsons and Colt revolvers or because of their behaviour) were often deployed on this service, particularly as advance guards riding ahead of the columns to prevent ambush – work that one likened "to hunting for a gas leak with a candle."[46]

Despite the fact that they did not receive the best horses – which went to the overloaded and rather ineffective British regulars – the Canadians proved adept at this mobile warfare.

Canadian hero, Sgt A.H. Richardson, VC (1873-1932)

A former mountie, Richardson enlisted in Strathcona's Horse during the South African War. He won the Victoria Cross in action at Wolver Spruit on 5 July 1900 when he rescued a wounded comrade while under fire by throwing him on the back of his horse. In this portrait photo, Richardson is wearing his VC medal and ribbon on his khaki wool field service dress jacket. GLENBOW MUSEUM, NA-1159-1

A British general, who had Strathcona's Horse under his command for some time, said of them that he had "never served with a nobler, braver or more serviceable body of men."[47]. The reason for the Canadians' reputation, according to Lieutenant E.W.B. Morrison from Ottawa, was simple – they knew how to utilize ground:

I have seen every variety of mounted troops out here – regular cavalry, mounted infantry, regular and irregular, and none of them are in it with the "Canydians" for the sort of work to be done. Their outpost work is the best I have seen by long odds, for the simple reason that they know how to keep under cover. So far, all the British soldier has learned is to keep under cover when he is being fired at. When not being fired at, he chooses for preference a conspicuous portion of the sky line or a hill top, and the Boers know just exactly where he is and how many of him there are. The Canadians keep under cover all the time, taking up their position before daylight and the Boers never know where they will stumble on them or how many there will be.[48]

In this type of fighting, westerners coming from a country not unlike that of the African veldt, had a definite advantage.

Although the major battles were over by the time they got to the war, the Canadian mounted units fought in some notable smaller actions. On 22 June 1900 four Mounted Riflemen, all from Pincher Creek, were manning an outpost, termed a "Cossack post," near the train station at Honing Spruit when they were attacked by a superior force of Boers. Corporal Fred Morden and Private R.J. Kerr fought until they were killed while Lance Corporal Thomas R. Miles and his brother, Private Henry Miles, both wounded, kept fighting until they were relieved. A few weeks later Sergeant A.H. Richardson of Strathcona's Horse, a former NWMP constable, won the Victoria Cross for rescuing a wounded comrade under fire by throwing him over his saddle and galloping to safety.

The Canadians and Boers came to have a healthy mutual regard for each other – Griesbach noted that his comrades "never hated the Boers and never ceased to have profound respect for them as fighting men."[49] There was a personal element to this war as both Boers and Canadians were able to identify their opponents by name and sometimes, rightly or wrongly, would attempt to exact revenge. Such was the case in October 1901 when Corporal "Casey" Callaghan from Maple Creek and Private Jefferson Davis from Fort Macleod encountered a Boer leader named Villamon whom they believed responsible for the murder of two Canadians who had surrendered after a previous skirmish. Callaghan and Davis had taken up a concealed position, hoping to snare another Boer leader,

> when they sighted Villamon riding along all gallant and gay. They knew the country and they raced for a point to cut off the Boer's retreat and succeeded. He raced for another kloof and was soon floundering girth-deep in one of those treacherous Transvaal bogs. This was what the Canadian scouts had been playing for. They rode down to the edge of the bog, dismounted with much deliberation and proceeded to take pot-shots at Herr Villamon at 500 yards. Finding his horse hopelessly mired, he jumped off and ran on through the bog. They hit him the first shot but did not drop him. ...... They hit him three times in five shots. ...... The last shot caught him in the back of the head, scattering his thoughts upon the grass, and he died. They took his rifle, horse and bandolier and told some natives to bury him. The killing of Herr Villamon made a considerable impression on the surrounding commandoes.[50]

After nine months service, the Canadian Mounted Rifles returned to Halifax in January 1901 and were immediately disbanded. Each man received the thanks of a grateful nation and, perhaps more important, nearly a year's pay in Canadian money as well as his uniform, his Lee-Metford rifle and bayonet, his Colt .45 revolver and a train ticket home. It was generous gesture and one quite unlike the Canadian government but the authorities soon had reason to regret it. Private William Griesbach headed with ten of his comrades to Ottawa where they did just about "everything that young men do who have been away from civilization for some time and have lots of money to spend." Most of their accumulated pay went on fine hotel rooms, expensive dinners, fancy liquor, theatre tickets and flowers for pretty actresses – the rest the Riflemen just wasted. When he left the capital, Griesbach had fifteen cents in his pocket but, thanks to the generosity of patriotic civilians, he still had the same amount when he arrived home in Edmonton. Along the way, he heard many stories about men of the 2nd CMR, "involving the shooting up of some peaceful eastern towns and of bloody battles with the police." When he got to Rat Portage, Ontario, Griesbach, at the request of the police chief, convinced one of his comrades that he should stop sniping at the local constabulary whom the irate Mounted Rifleman believed had treated him "in a manner inconsistent with his dignity." In Griesbach's opinion, this devilry occurred not because his comrades were criminals but because "their idea of a good time was to raise hell and fire off their weapons indiscriminately" which is not surprising considering that many "were real cowpunchers, and others were merely the synthetic variety."[51]

The war in South Africa, however, continued. After their own period of service had concluded, some of the more adventurous spirits in the Canadian mounted units joined irregular scout forces created to counter Boer raiding. Among them was that deadly pair, Callaghan and Davis, and, in February 1901, they added to their already considerable reputations when they were ordered to carry dispatches from General Kitchener, the British commander in South Africa, to Major General Smith-Dorrien, commanding one of the mobile columns. Their route led through 40 miles of Boer-controlled territory and, on the way, they had a few problems which they overcame. A British officer who met the two shortly afterward recorded that

> They had a marvellous ride: one had to bury the despatches and dodge the Boers. Davis … was taken prisoner, but escaped by shooting several Boers with his revolver. At night Callahan dug up the despatches and got them in safe. It reads like Fenimore Cooper. I have no time to write details, but it was a wonderfully exciting ride.[52]

General Horace Smith-Dorrien remembered this incident somewhat differently. As he recalled, Jefferson Davis

> appeared before me and, saluting, handed me the dispatch with as much unconcern as though it had been an Aldershot field-day. I asked him how he had got through, and he told me, and when I asked how he had not been discovered, he said at one moment in the advance he noticed a Boer looking at him rather interestedly, and as dead men tell no tales he had pushed the muzzle of his carbine into his back and pulled the trigger; but excepting that incident, nothing unusual had happened.[53]

Even as Callahan and Davis were making a reputation on the veldt, new mounted units were being raised in Canada. At the request of the British government the Dominion agreed to recruit for the South African Constabulary, a police force not unlike the NWMP raised to maintain law and order in the newly-conquered Boer republics. Lieutenant-Colonel Sam Steele, just returned from commanding Strathcona's Horse and a man ever hellbent on seeing action, supervised the raising of this force. Recruiting began in October 1900 and offices were opened in the major towns in the District of Alberta. As usual, there were no problems finding recruits and in the space of a few weeks just over 1,200 men, about a quarter of them recent South African veterans, were enlisted. In all, six Canadian squadrons of the Constabulary were sent to South Africa in the spring of 1901, two of them (C and D Squadrons) from the District of Alberta. Theirs was a dangerous occupation and no less than 52 officers and men died on active service.

In November 1901 Britain requested Canada to provide a fourth mounted unit that would serve as part of the British army and that month recruiting began for the somewhat confusingly titled 2nd Regiment, Canadian Mounted Rifles, a six-squadron unit with an authorized strength of 901 all ranks. In the District of Alberta, men were enlisted at Calgary, Edmonton, Lethbridge, Fort Macleod and Pincher Creek but it is not certain how many Albertans joined this unit which concentrated at Halifax in early January 1902 and arrived in South Africa in late February. It participated in the last major operations of the war which witnessed massive drives by large British forces trying to pin the elusive Boers against the British defence lines. As usual, it did not work but the 2nd Regiment, CMR, participated in one of the most hard-fought small battles of the war, at Hart's River (now Boschbult) on 29 March 1902. As part of a force of about 1,800 mounted troops commanded by a British officer who deployed them very poorly, the 2nd Regiment fought off an attack by 2,500 Boers supported by artillery. A group of Mounted Riflemen, 21 in number, were cut off when the British troops on their flank unexpectedly retreated but continued to fight until 17 were killed or wounded and the last four taken prisoner when the Boers overran their position. This action cost the 2nd Regiment 61 casualties.

But the 2nd Regiment of Mounted Rifles was not the last Canadian unit to be sent to South Africa. In early 1902 Canada agreed to recruit 2,000 mounted men, to be formed into four regiments. Recruiting started in March and, as usual, the District of Alberta was prominent with men crowding into the offices set up in the larger towns. Business was so brisk that recruiting was closed after the third day and, even then, excess numbers were taken. All of the recruits, including 191 men from the District, were sent to Halifax where they were organized into four regiments, each about 500 strong, along regional lines with most of the Alberta men ending up in the 5th Regiment, Canadian Mounted Rifles, whose commanding officer, Lieutenant-Colonel A.C. Macdonell, noted that his ranks included

a particularly workmanlike class of men, of good physique, good shots and riders, and thoroughly accustomed to prairie and camp life. A good many (about one-third) had previous service in the British army, the Permanent Corps, or the North-west Mounted Police and other corps.

Among the cow-boys and ranchers who enlisted, thirty-two were professional packers from the Rocky Mountains, and sixty-four were professional "broncho busters," horse-breakers and ropers from western ranches.[54]

Macdonell's regiment embarked at Halifax in late May but were at sea for only a week when the war came to an end on 31 May 1902.

"Put through their goose steps": The first Alberta militia units, 1901-1905

When the shooting was over, Canada was proud of the record established by what one citizen called "our little army in the field."[55] A total of 8,300 Canadians had enlisted, including a battalion for home service, and 89 were killed and 252 wounded in action while 135 died from accident or sickness. Canada's participation in the conflict, which had witnessed the first dispatch of Canadian troops to fight overseas, had a number of consequences. First, a precedent had been set and, as far as English Canada was concerned, if the Mother Country called on Canada again, she would be ready to serve. Second, the war increased public interest in military matters – as one enthusiastic commentator put it:

Since the South African War, there has been manifested in Canada a growing disposition to recognize the importance of maintaining an efficient military spirit. The country realizes that its whole life has been stimulated, the standard of its manhood built up, the national character strengthened ...... True, the laurels have been moistened with the tears of Canadian mothers, but a price has to be paid for everything that is worth having. The mother of a coward does not often weep.[56]

This interest led to an increase in government expenditure on defence – the annual defence budget rose from $1.6 million in 1900 to $7 million in 1911 – and this in turn led to an expansion and reorganization of both the regular and militia components of the Canadian army. From 1901 onward, the strength of the permanent force was raised and administrative, engineer, intelligence, logistic and staff elements were added to it. The number of militia nearly doubled in the same period, from 35,000 to 66,000, and, more importantly, increased funds were allotted for training, meaning not only were more men in service, they were better prepared men. Much of this useful work was accomplished during the long tenure (1896-1911) of Frederick Borden as minister of militia in Laurier's Liberal government; Borden, who had lost a son in South Africa, was sensitive to military matters.

The reorganization of the militia actually commenced before the war had ended. In the spring of 1901, plans were set afoot to accomplish what Hutton had proposed nearly two years earlier, the establishment of a force of mounted militia in the West. Known officially as the Canadian Mounted Rifles, this new organization was to consist of a regular component, B Squadron of the Royal Canadian Dragoons, stationed in Winnipeg and eight, later raised to ten, independent militia squadrons across Canada. The regular squadron, which would serve as the training unit for this new organization, was redesignated A Squadron (Permanent) Canadian Mounted Rifles while the militia units were given letter designations as Independent Squadrons of Canadian Mounted Rifles. Three of these squadrons were to be located in the District of Alberta and, in April 1901, Lieutenant-Colonel T.D.B. Evans, the District Officer Commanding, Military District 10, which at this time included the Northwest Territories, held meetings at Fort Macleod, Medicine Hat and Pincher Creek to discuss matters relating to the new units. He found interest in Alberta very keen and some communities, no-

Getting started, c. 1903

There is no positive identification for this unit but it is possible that it is one of the three squadrons of Canadian Mounted Rifles authorized in 1903, most likely either H Squadron at Fort Macleod or I Squadron at Medicine Hat. The unit has not yet received its uniforms, saddlery and weapons, hence the incredible variety of weapons (although most appear to be Winchesters) and civilian tack. Nonetheless, the officer at the far left has procured a sword and though they may not look like soldiers, they have made a start. GLENBOW MUSEUM NA-1075-19

tably Medicine Hat, had already started preliminary recruiting. In June 1901, three independent squadrons of mounted rifles were authorized in Alberta: G Squadron at Calgary, H Squadron at Fort Macleod and I Squadron at Medicine Hat.

Authorizing units on paper was one thing, actually raising them was quite another. Throughout its brief history, the squadron at Fort Macleod suffered from leadership problems caused by political partisanship until it was disbanded in September 1904. At Calgary, G Squadron, under the command of Captain W.M. Inglis, and I Squadron at Medicine Hat, commanded by Captain E.F. Fewings, a real estate agent in that city, did better. In early 1902, a number of the newly-appointed Mounted Rifle officers attended the Royal School of Cavalry held at Winnipeg by the regular A Squadron and this course was repeated each winter. G Squadron at Calgary received its uniforms in February 1902 and began holding drill nights in March with the *Calgary Herald* reporting that the "men were put through their goose steps" by Sergeant-Major Bagley and "acquitted themselves very creditably."[57] By May the squadron was conducting mounted drill on the ranch of Captain J.H.S. Gordon near Calgary and it marched in the 1902 Dominion Day parade. It fired a Royal Salute to celebrate the coronation of King Edward VII in August of that year and was part of the civic parade, where the most popular float was that of the Calgary Brewery, which included "a gang of men employed bottling beer, bottles of which were thrown to the crowd."[58] It participated in the Calgary Exhibition in September and held its first major social event, a Thanksgiving Dinner, at Hull's Opera House the following October. Both G and I Squadrons held their first summer camps in June 1903. The Calgary squadron tented on the property of James Walker

on the banks of the Elbow River east of the city adjacent to a military rifle range, constructed on property that Walker had sold to the government. The Medicine Hat squadron went under canvas at Police Point near that town and, having received its uniforms, marched that summer in the Hat's Dominion Day parade.

With the population and resources of a large urban centre to draw on, it was not long before G Squadron outstripped the other two units. In January 1904, the squadron formally opened the drill hall it had built with private funds on 12th Avenue SW near the CPR Depot with Calgary's first Military Ball at which the "sound of revelry by night" and "bright lights shone o'er fair women and brave men."[59] Unfortunately the evening was cut short when officers and men were called away to assist the Calgary Fire Department fight a conflagration in the downtown business district. In the following summer, the squadron not only formed an active and popular band but also a 16-man "Musical Ride" which performed at the Dominion Exhibition held that year in Winnipeg.

By 1905, G Squadron of the Canadian Mounted Rifles had established Calgary as the leading military centre of the District of Alberta but rumours were floating around that there were going to be organizational changes and when the squadron went under canvas at Victoria Park in June 1905, it learned that the authorities had decided to create a new cavalry regiment with headquarters at Calgary. Its title would be the 15th Light Horse and its commanding officer would be James Walker, the prominent Calgarian who, for more than three decades, had been involved with military matters in the West.

And so it was, from these proud and colourful beginnings, that the South Alberta Light Horse was born.

Wetaskiwin's finest: 19th Alberta Mounted Rifles, c. 1910
A squadron of the 19th Alberta Mounted Rifles poses on the main street of Wetaskiwin about 1910. Note the young lad in the first rank. It was not uncommon to unofficially enlist underage boys in the militia – they were not paid but it kept them out of mischief. Despite their somewhat rough appearance, the Alberta mounted units were carrying out very advanced training prior to the First World War. The saddles appear to be Universal Pattern 1890 Steel Arch models, the bits the 1902 Universal Pattern Portsmouth, and the bridles are the so-called "1902 Pattern." The men are equipped with 50-round "Mounted Infantry" bandoliers and their rifles are carried in Mounted Rifle buckets. GLENBOW MUSEUM, NA 579-11

CHAPTER TWO

"Our Training Is for War"

"Blowing in her majesty": The birth of the Regiment and the province

With his extensive background, both in the military and in the west, the newly-promoted Lieutenant-Colonel James Walker was the ideal man to command the infant 15th Light Horse. Headquarters and A Squadron of the unit were to be located in Calgary while the remaining three squadrons would be located in smaller towns south of that city. This pattern of sub-unit distribution would prevail throughout much of the Light Horse's history as a cavalry regiment as, owing to the almost unceasing expansion of Calgary, there were fewer and fewer horses in the city and fewer and fewer places where mounted drill could be carried out. Although it was clear that the new regiment was intended to replace G Squadron of the Canadian Mounted Rifles, that squadron held a camp in June 1905 in the fair grounds at Victoria Park – the site of the Calgary Agricultural Fair, founded by James Walker in 1886, and the future home of the Calgary Stampede – and remained in existence until the following December when most of its officers and men enlisted in the 15th Light Horse.

The big news, however, during the summer of 1905 was that the District of Alberta was to be shortly combined with the western part of the District of Athabasca to form the province of Alberta with a population of 73,000 souls. Edmonton had been chosen as the provisional capital (only provisional, Calgarians were quick to remind everyone), a feat accomplished by some neat gerrymandering and the fact that the District representative was a Liberal who had close connections with the government in Ottawa. Edmonton was planning a mighty celebration to mark the coming of provincehood but many Calgarians thought the northern fur trading post was getting ideas above

> I've come to say goodbye, Dolly Gray,
> It's no use to ask me why, Dolly Gray,
> There's a murmur in the air,
> You can hear it everywhere,
> It's the time to do and dare, Dolly Gray.
> Can't you hear the sound of feet, Dolly Gray,
> Marching in the village street, Dolly Gray,
> It's the tramp of soldiers so true,
> In their uniforms of blue,
> I must say goodbye to you, Dolly Gray.
>
> Goodbye Dolly, I must leave you,
> Though it breaks my heart to go.
> Something tells me I am needed,
> At the front to fight the foe.
> See – the boys in blue are marching,
> And I can no longer stay,
> Hark! I hear the bugle calling,
> Goodbye Dolly Gray![1]

its station. Bob Edwards, publisher of the Calgary *Eye-Opener*, at that time the most enjoyable, honest and well-written newspaper in Canada, warned that

> They are getting very toney up in Edmonton with their fair and inauguration festivities in sight. Many of the smart young ladies have taken to wearing open-work shoes to display pretty hosiery, a charming idea. It is now in order for the men of Edmonton to start wearing open-work hats for the purpose of displaying the wheels revolving in their heads.[2]

On the other hand, Edwards was no more complimentary about his own hometown which he once harpooned as being

> Picturesquely situated so as to be within easy reach of the brewery, Calgary extends right and left, north and south, up and down, in and out, expanding as she goes, swelling in her pride, puffing in her might, blowing in her majesty and revolving in eccentric orbits round a couple of dozen large bars which close promptly at 11.30 right or wrong.[3]

On the great day, 1 September 1905, crowds estimated as high as 20,000 showed up in Edmonton to watch the celebrations as the governor-general, Earl Grey, (best remembered now for his football trophy) and Prime Minister Wilfrid Laurier ushered the new province into Confederation. There was a magnificent parade including the G Squadron band from Calgary, C Squadron of the Royal Northwest Mounted Police, 200 strong, and just about anything that could ride or walk including "a very excellent float advertising Ochsner's beer" from which bottles of cold

First summer camp, 1906

The 15th Light Horse pose during their first summer camp, held on the estate of Lieutenant-Colonel James Walker east of Calgary. All three squadrons appear to be present and although the unit is only a year old, it could already muster a respectable strength. GLENBOW MUSEUM, NA-33-35

beverage were "handed out to any thirsty individual who held up his hand in the crowd."[4]

Now that Edmonton was the capital (still the provisional capital according to Calgarians), it seemed only fitting that it too should have a military unit of its own. The human materiel was certainly available as it had been the custom in the first few years of the new century for young men interested in horses and marksmanship to hold riding and shooting competitions in the Edmonton area. William Griesbach, last seen in 1901 when he was spending a year's accumulated pay on young actresses and other such foolishness, was practising law in the capital and had become active in local politics. Griesbach remembered that, during the period immediately following the South African War, he "had forwarded, as either chairman or secretary of committees, a number of petitions urging the extension of the militia system to Edmonton and district, at the same time including a list of names of those willing to serve."[5] On 1 December 1905, Ottawa finally paid heed and the Department of Militia authorized the raising of three new squadrons of mounted rifles in the central part of Alberta: A Squadron in Edmonton, B Squadron in neighbouring Strathcona and C Squadron at Fort Saskatchewan. As part of this organizational initiative, I Squadron of the CMR at Medicine Hat was redesignated D Squadron. Major S.C. Paton commanded A Squadron and Major F.C. Jamieson, an Edmonton lawyer, took command of B Squadron. Griesbach was invited to take a commission as a lieutenant in A Squadron, an appointment that almost ran afoul of politics because, at this time, the Canadian militia was a highly politicized organization and party connections influenced the choice of officers. Despite the fact that he was well qualified, Griesbach was a Conservative

and, since the Liberals held power in Ottawa, many Edmonton Liberals were annoyed by his appointment and asked that, if his commission could not be withdrawn, at least "steps should be taken by the Government to see that" he was "not be allowed to become too prominent."[6] Since Griesbach would end his military career as a major-general, this is comment sufficient on the inanity of basing officer selection on political grounds.

By May 1906 the three new squadrons had received their uniforms, weapons and equipment and in June held their first annual camp at a location on the north bank of the North Saskatchewan River west of Edmonton. Part of this site was currently being leased by the Edmonton Golf Club which patriotically and "cheerfully" granted permission for the Canadian Mounted Rifles to manoeuvre on their land, only stipulating that the troops "avoid the putting greens."[7] Almost from the start, the three new squadrons were very active which is an indication of the amount of local interest. A and B Squadrons performed ceremonial drill in front of the crowds attending the Industrial Exhibition in Edmonton in July 1906 and they carried out their first field day on the Thanksgiving weekend. Farther south, the 15th Light Horse went to camp at the military range abutting the Walker estate where they were joined by the Alberta Rangers, a unit created by the redesignation in April of the Light Horse squadron at Fort Macleod.

The year 1907 was an important one in the history of the Alberta militia. In April Military District 13 was created with headquarters at Calgary meaning that no longer would Alberta units have to communicate with far-off Winnipeg but would have the advantage of having a regular headquarters staff close at hand. The first District Officer Commanding was Lieutenant-

GLENBOW MUSEUM, NA-3063-2

GLENBOW MUSEUM, NA-3624-1

The 15th Light Horse, 1905-1914

The new regiment quickly established itself and, in their stetsons and red serge jackets with yellow facings, as seen on this unidentified Light Horse corporal at upper right, became a common sight in Alberta. In 1906 it was inspected by Field-Marshal Lord Aylmer, the Chief of the Imperial General staff (right), an event important enough to be recorded by the *Calgary Herald*. From the left are Lieutenant-Colonel James Walker, Aylmer and Lieutenant-Colonel T.B. Evans, commanding Military District 13. Its band, seen above, became very popular in Alberta and made a European tour in 1907. Below, the men of a squadron pose for their portrait at Victoria Park in Calgary. The two officers wearing white hat bands in the first row and the two men in slouch hats in the last row are most likely from the 23rd Alberta Rangers.

SALH ARCHIVES

GLENBOW MUSEUM, NA-2883-46

Colonel Samuel B. Steele, stalwart veteran of the early days of the NWMP and the wartime commander of Strathcona's Horse. Steele remembered arriving in Calgary in June 1907 to be met by his old mounted police comrade, James Walker, "on whose powerful shoulders the winters of the north and the struggles with the forces of nature had no effect, whose hearty hand clasp and frank, kindly gaze said, 'You can depend on me.'"[8]

Sam Steele, who had ridden west with the NWMP in 1874, found it hard to believe the changes that had occurred since he had last seen Alberta:

> I was not long in visiting Edmonton on duty, and found a beautiful and bustling place, towering above the fine river, with stores and residences that would be a credit to a place a hundred years old. It was hardly credible that this was the place where we wintered in 1875, with only half a dozen poplar log homes in sight, and later, during the rebellion, only a village!
>
> It was the same all over western Canada, and we, who had been the pioneers of this glorious change, were permitted by Providence to see the fruits of our labours and our hardships.[9]

Steele immediately inspected Walker's regiment, which, with the Alberta Rangers, was under canvas on Walker's own property. The strength of the Light Horse was 28 officers, 225 enlisted men and 217 horses while the newly-formed Alberta Rangers had 8 officers, 54 other ranks and 58 horses. On Dominion Day, both units participated in the parade held to mark the national holiday in Calgary. In the north, meanwhile, the independent squadrons of the CMR came together, 240 officers and men and 211 horses, at a camp near St. Albert. Also in attendance were men from the new E Squadron, raised in St. Albert and Morinville. Lord Aylmer, the Inspector General of the Canadian militia, visited both camps in 1907 and was impressed, reporting that "the horses could not be better for this class of work" and that all the units contained young men "who have had military training either in the Imperial service" or the regular Canadian units and "there are many more waiting to do likewise in other parts of the 'great and last west'".[10]

Later that summer, the popular band of the 15th Light Horse was invited to play at the International Exhibition in Dublin. For a period of two weeks, dressed in scarlet tunics and stetsons, they performed two shows daily, with one of their most popular numbers being "The Indian Company," described in the official programme as a whimsical piece portraying life in the "far wild west."[11] The band rendered it, complete with the "music of various Indian dances, intermingled with war whoops and yells," ending it "on a peaceful note with the playing of the *Andante Religiose* prayer." Following their Dublin performances, the 15th Light Horse band played in Manchester and Liverpool before returning to Canada. Lieutenant-Colonel Walker accompanied them on this tour.

In 1908 the provincial militia experienced an increase in strength and a major reorganization. In February of that year the four independent squadrons of Canadian Mounted Rifles in Edmonton and surrounding district were consolidated into a new unit, the 19th Alberta Mounted Rifles, with command going to Lieutenant-Colonel Robert Belcher, a 59-year-old doctor in civil life. On 1 April the former Mounted Rifles' D Squadron at Medicine Hat was reorganized as the cadre of another new regiment, the 21st Alberta Hussars, with headquarters at The Hat and squadrons in that town and surrounding area, while the Alberta Rangers were raised to regimental status as the 23rd Alberta Rangers, with headquarters at Fort Macleod. To round out the increase in cavalry, a new independent squadron of light horse was raised at Red Deer which, for purposes of administration and training, was attached to the 15th Light Horse. Up to now, mounted units had dominated the provincial militia but 1908 also saw the authorization of the first artillery unit, the 25th Battery, Canadian Field Artillery, at Lethbridge and the first infantry unit, the 101st Regiment with headquarters at Edmonton. This latter unit would shortly take the title "Edmonton Fusiliers."

"Keen as mustard": The province and its militia, 1908-1913

The growth of the provincial militia only paralleled the growth of Alberta which was phenomenal in its first nine years as a province. A constant stream of immigrants, attracted by good and cheap land and determined to strike it rich at something, anything, flowed into Western Canada. When Ochsener's Brewery employees were handing out cold beer to thirsty crowds in September 1905, Alberta had 73,000 people; by 1910 it had 374,000 and by 1914 there were 474,000 people and an estimated 254,000 horses in the province. Horses were still important in

Dobbin takes a dive, 1909
An officer of a Canadian mounted rifles squadron from the Edmonton area demonstrates a popular tactic as he shelters behind his horse. Dobbin does not look particularly happy with this part of the training syllabus. PROVINCIAL ARCHIVES OF ALBERTA, A-3880

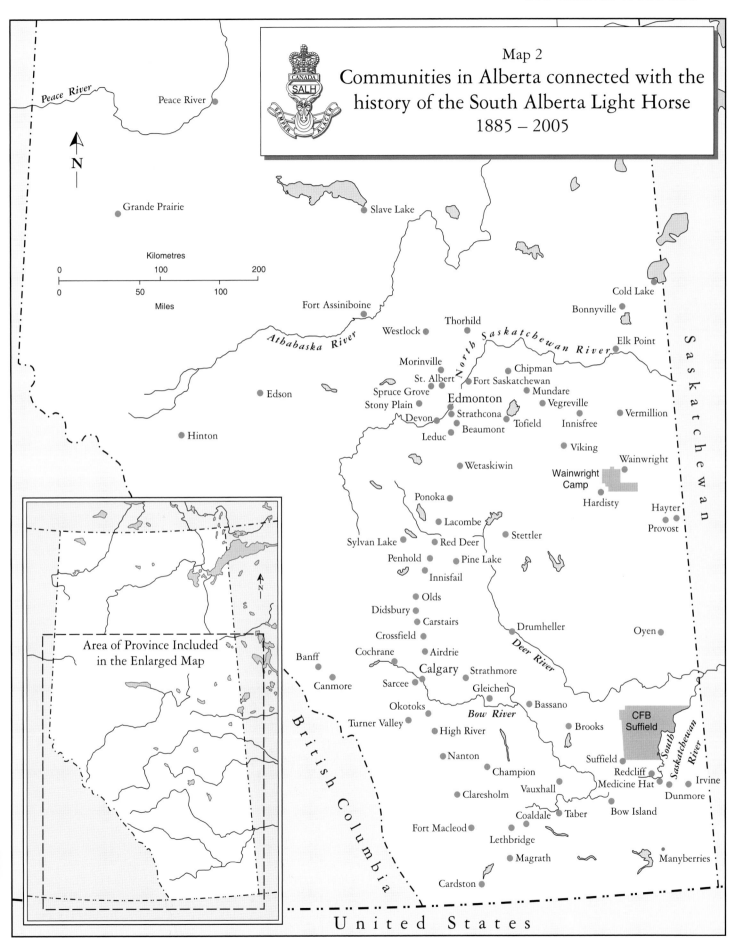

Map 2
Communities in Alberta connected with the history of the South Alberta Light Horse
1885 – 2005

Officers, 23rd Alberta Rangers, c. 1907

Officers of the 23rd Alberta Rangers at summer camp, probably Sarcee. Authorized originally as an independent squadron in 1906, the Rangers were raised to regimental status in 1908 and were the fourth mounted unit to be formed in Alberta. It appears that the Rangers favoured slouch hats turned up on the left, as opposed to stetsons, as they are most often seen in this headgear in pre-1914 photos. GLENBOW MUSEUM, NA-1876-1

Provisional School of Cavalry, 1908-1909

The permanent force, or regular army, acted as instructors for the militia. Training courses run at regular garrisons were called "Royal Schools" while those held at militia facilities were known as "Provisional Schools." Instructors and students of the Provisional School held at Calgary in the winter of 1908-1909 pose here for their course photo. The two men with white collars are probably from the 23rd Rangers while those with white hat bands may be 21st Hussars. The men in khaki are probably regular instructional staff. GLENBOW MUSEUM, NA-2380-3

Alberta although the days of the great ranches had passed, their grazing areas being gradually encroached on by small 160-acre freeholds which limited their access to water. The death knell of big ranching was rung by the winter of 1906-1907, the worst in living memory and a lengthy horror of low temperatures and blizzards that killed off nearly half the cattle in the province. Thereafter, although beef was still an important industry, the ranches were smaller and more efficiently run. When the first Calgary Stampede was held in September 1912, it was partly to mark the passing of this colourful period in Alberta's history but, even so, all the horses for that first stampede were supplied by the Turkey Track Ranch near Medicine Hat and the Turkey Track ran 22,000 cattle and 700 horses. It is noteworthy that Lieutenant-Colonel James Walker, along with other surviving veterans of the 1874 march west, dressed in the original uniforms of the NWMP, had an honoured part in the first Stampede parade.

In Edmonton, they discovered that being a capital meant a steady if not spectacular civil service payroll and that community grew from about 14,000 people in 1905 to 72,000 in 1914. In the same period, Calgary increased from 14,000 to 74,000 and Medicine Hat from 2,500 to 15,000. All three cities were able to boast fine new hotels – splendid establishments that were a far cry from Kamoose Taylor's eccentric hostelry at Fort Macleod in the good old days. There was the MacDonald in Edmonton, the Palliser in Calgary and the Cosmopolitan in Medicine Hat. In all these cities and in smaller towns across Alberta, construction was continuous and that led in turn to real estate booms, the first in 1906 but the biggest and most famous in the autumn of 1911 and spring of 1912, when the price of a lot in Calgary worth $150 in 1895 changed hands for $300,000, while in Edmonton a property that went for $5,000 in 1910 fetched $73,000 in 1912. In that latter year, 82 of the 200 registered businesses in Edmonton were real estate brokers but when the bubble finally collapsed in May 1912, the city council was stuck with 75,000 city lots on which no taxes were being paid.

Medicine Hat, smaller but more determined than its larger rivals, experienced much the same cycle of boom and bust. In 1910 the city council somehow became convinced that changing the Hat's unique name would encourage investors and announced that a plebiscite would be held on the matter. Many were opposed and the question was finally put to rest after the British author, Rudyard Kipling, who had visited the Hat three years before, was consulted and replied that a name change would go against "the old Cree and Blackfoot tradition of red mystery and romance that once filled the prairies" – and there

19th Alberta Mounted Rifles on parade, 1909
As the mounted unit in the capital, the 19th were often involved in ceremonial events. Here members of A or B Squadron provide an escort to the lieutenant-governor on the opening or closing of the legislative assembly. The men are wearing stetsons and blue serge patrol jackets, blue pants with a yellow stripe and black boots with black leather gaiters. They are equipped with the South African War, "Mounted Infantry" pattern 50-round bandolier although it cannot be seen whether they are armed with Ross or Short Magazine Lee-Enfield rifles. COURTESY, CITY OF EDMONTON ARCHIVES #EA10-2438

Mounted Rifles in the field
A squadron of the 19th Alberta Mounted Rifles pose for their photograph in 1908-1909. They are wearing straw hats or slouch hats turned up on the left side and with what appears to be a red hat band, khaki shirts and dark blue breeches with a side stripe which is probably red but the colour cannot be determined. They have their rifles slung on their backs. PROVINCIAL ARCHIVES OF ALBERTA, B-5454

Western cavalry – a small-town squadron, 19th Alberta Mounted Rifles, c. 1910
The militia cavalry squadrons stationed in smaller towns had advantages and disadvantages. They benefited from the availability of horses but suffered from having to draw their members from a smaller population. Nonetheless, their pride is evident in this photograph taken about 1910. These men appear to be armed with Ross rifles but note the variety of headgear and clothing. GLENBOW MUSEUM, NC-6-1203

Alberta Combined Military Services Rifle Team, 1910
The militia put great emphasis on marksmanship and there were frequent inter-unit, inter-provincial and national competitions. Here, the provincial military team for 1910 pose in Ottawa where the national match was held. Almost every militia unit in the province is represented on this team as well as civilian marksmen. Lieutenant-Colonel W.C.G. Armstrong, commanding the 103rd Regiment, "Calgary Rifles," is fourth from the left in the centre row. GLENBOW MUSEUM, NA 2370-3

the matter ended.[12] The Hat kept its heritage and, gradually, became a centre of pottery, brick-making, and greenhouses fuelled by its impressive reserves of natural gas and, of course, ranching.

During the first decade of Alberta's existence as a province, many new industries started or expanded including mining, lumbering and railway construction – there were no less than 3,600 miles of track laid in Alberta by 1912 – but the biggest industry was agriculture, either farming or ranching, which employed about two-thirds of the population. The federal government's generous immigration policy attracted people from Eastern Canada and around the globe including Britons, Americans, Europeans and Scandinavians as well as a host of other nationalities. It was not an easy land to homestead – some were successful but others were not and drifted into the cities, adding to a growing social problem. A distinct species by themselves were the many young, single Englishmen who seemed to know nothing and appeared incapable of learning anything. Many were well-educated and there is a story, which may be apocryphal but certainly is typical, that when a foreman working for the city of Calgary overheard four of his ditch-diggers conversing in an unknown language that turned out to be Latin, he became convinced they were anarchists plotting revolution and so informed the authorities.

Throughout this period the Alberta militia made progress. In the summer of 1908, all four cavalry regiments went into camp near their hometowns where they were visited by the inspector-general of the Canadian militia, Major-General Percy Lake, who observed that "the western cavalry corps are ahead of those in the east" which he attributed to the fact that there was "no doubt, that the western men are better riders and, on the whole, better horsed."[13] Any Albertan could have told Lake that simple truth and saved him the long journey from Ottawa. The following summer the 15th Light Horse, 21st Hussars and 23rd Rangers attended camp at Calgary while the 19th Mounted Rifles held a separate camp near Edmonton. In 1910, Military District 13 said goodbye to Sam Steele who was appointed to the command of Strathcona's Horse, as the regular A Squadron of the Royal Canadian Mounted Rifles had just been re-designated. It would shortly become Lord Strathcona's Horse (Royal Canadians) by which title it is known to this day. Steele's replacement was Colonel Ernest A. Cruikshank, a former Ontario militia officer.

That year also saw the creation of the Alberta's second infantry unit – the 103rd Regiment in Calgary – and the organization of the 5th Cavalry Brigade under command of the newly-promoted Colonel James Walker, which included all four of the provincial mounted regiments, and which sent 409 men and 458 horses to a joint camp held at Calgary that June. Walker's replacement as commanding officer of the 15th Light Horse was 48-year-old Lieutenant-Colonel George Macdonald, the medical health officer of Calgary. The Light Horse now had their Head-

Lieutenant-Colonel W. Frederick ("Fat Freddy") Carstairs
Freddy Carstairs, the first commanding officer of the Edmonton Fusiliers, was a well-known Edmonton character. He fought in the 1885 Rebellion as a constable in the NWMP and was later commissioned an officer in the Royal Nigerian Constabulary and helped stamp out the slave trade and cannibalism in West Africa. Freddy had to use a chair to mount his horse and the owner of Lewis's Lunch in Edmonton once said that he hated to see Freddy come through the door "because he would consume a bottle of ketchup and a loaf of bread while waiting for his main course." FROM HISTORY OF THE 101ST REGIMENT EDMONTON FUSILIERS ... 1908-1913

And the band still played on

Fusilier bandsmen pose in full dress uniform in 1912. Bands were an integral part of militia units, raising their profile in the community and acting as a recruiting incentive. The white Colonial Service helmet was standard full dress headgear for many infantry units, regular and militia, in the period before the First World War and a variant is still worn as part of the modern full dress of Princess Patricia's Canadian Light Infantry. PROVINCIAL ARCHIVES OF ALBERTA, B-5396

(Below) **Alberta Ranger, c. 1910**

Wearing the comfortable hot-weather uniform – stetson, shirt and trousers – a member of the 23rd Alberta Rangers poses during a summer camp at Pincher Creek in 1910. Note the use of the leather bucket to hold the butt of the soldier's rifle, an awkward arrangement that left the mounted man with only one hand free. It was replaced after 1911 by the rifle boot or holster which freed both hands. GLENBOW MUSEUM, NA 102-3

Rough and ready, junior version

Clearly a squadron mascot, this young Alberta Dragoon mounted on his pony strikes a fierce pose for the photographer. The Lee-Metford carbine he is holding, however, is not a toy. PROVINCIAL ARCHIVES OF ALBERTA, B-5428

quarters and D Squadron in Calgary, A Squadron in Crossfield, B Squadron in Elbow River and C Squadron at High River. The officer commanding A Squadron, Major Russell Boyle, had been wounded while serving with the artillery in South Africa, and was a big, intelligent, energetic local rancher liked by all who knew him.

In 1911, the 19th Alberta Mounted Rifles were redesignated the 19th Alberta Dragoons. Their commander, Lieutenant-

Colonel Robert Belcher, was promoted to colonel and given the command of the 5th Cavalry Brigade on the retirement of Colonel James Walker which occurred early that year. Walker, however, did not cut his military links as he became Honorary Colonel of the 23rd Alberta Rangers. Lieutenant-Colonel F.C. Jamieson, an Edmonton lawyer, now took over the Dragoons. In Lethbridge, meanwhile, the 25th Field Battery continued to make steady progress and, on the occasion of the state funeral

A place for everything and everything in its place
In 1906, the three squadrons of Canadian Mounted Rifles in the Edmonton area held their first camp on the grounds of the Edmonton Golf Course west of the city. Note that the horse lines are located close to the bell tents of the men. PROVINCIAL ARCHIVES OF ALBERTA, A-3878

(Below) **"Take aim!" The Light Horse at camp**
The 15th Light Horse practise skirmishing tactics at summer camp, probably about 1908. All the Alberta cavalry units were trained to function as mounted rifles – they rode to battle but fought dismounted – and their training was very advanced compared to the cavalry of other nations prior to 1914. The double yellow trouser stripe was standard on on light cavalry uniforms. SALH ARCHIVES

(Left) **Taking a break**
A troop of the 19th Dragoons takes a break during camp, probably at Victoria Park west of Edmonton. PROVINCIAL ARCHIVES OF ALBERTA, B-5421

(Below) **Ready for inspection**
Men of the 19th Dragoons prepare for an inspection of their saddlery and horse tack. PROVINCIAL ARCHIVES OF ALBERTA, B-5419

Equestrian training
Although the men of the country squadrons often owned their own animals, the city squadrons were usually provided with rented animals at camp. This made for some interesting times during the first days of training and most mounted units had "rough riders" standing by should one of the "rent-a-steeds" take off for greener pastures. These men are equipped with 1902 Universal Pattern steel arch saddles, 1902 Universal Pattern Portsmouth bits and the so-called "1902 Pattern" bridles. SALH ARCHIVES

(Right) **Pay Parade**
The high point of camp was the pay parade when men received the government's bounty which was literally paid, "cash on the barrel." In a time before there was paid vacations, militia camp was the only holiday many men got, and the fact that it was a paid holiday made it even better. SALH ARCHIVES

(Below) **And then it was time to go home**
Summer camp functioned as an enjoyable holiday for many men in a time when there were no legislated vacations. All too soon, it was over and this photo taken at Sarcee shows one of the final tasks – a detail from the 15th Light Horse taking down tents. The bell tent shown was standard issue in the Canadian army from about 1900 to the mid-1970s. SALH ARCHIVES

(Above) **Dobbin gets new shoes**
A farrier at Sarcee shoes a cavalry horse. Government funding allowed two new shoes for each horse that attended summer camp, and they usually went on Dobbin's forelegs. The farriers and veterinary officers attached to each mounted unit were important personnel with critical duties. GLENBOW MUSEUM, NA 5483-36

(Below) **The social side**
Militia units always provided an active social life for their members. Here, the officers of the three squadrons of the Canadian Mounted Rifles entertain their ladies to tea at camp on the North Saskatchewan River west of the city about 1907. PROVINCIAL ARCHIVES OF ALBERTA, A-3879

Officers, 23rd Alberta Rangers, summer camp, c. 1912
Wearing naval service pattern caps, the officers of the 23rd Alberta Rangers pose at summer camp, probably at Reservoir Park near Calgary, shortly before the First World War. Lieutenant-Colonel A.C. Kemmis, commanding officer, with a white cap cover, is seated on the left. Note that the officer standing second from the left is wearing medal ribbons, almost certainly from the South African War. These officers are wearing scarlet patrol jackets with white facings and Stohwasser gaiters, and are armed with 1896 heavy cavalry officer's swords. GLENBOW MUSEUM, NA 2380-20

Vice-regal inspection, 1912
The boys of the Edmonton Fusilier cadet corps await inspection by the Duke of Connaught, the governor-general, in 1912. Prior to the First World War, the cadets were an extremely popular organization, almost all schools required boys to belong to cadet corps, which were often attached to, and supervised by militia units. FROM *HISTORY OF THE 101ST REGIMENT EDMONTON FUSILIERS ... 1908-1913*

for Edward VII which took place on 20 May 1911, fired a 68-gun salute, the first major artillery salute fired in Alberta. To do so, the gunners had to make their own blank rounds using black powder, for a total cost of $44.30 to the taxpayer and, although they had confidence in their ordnance manufacturing abilities, they wisely had a doctor standing by throughout the process.

In the following month, the largest militia camp to date was held at Reservoir Park, on the edge of Calgary, and all the provincial units – horse, foot and artillery – attended. The cavalry camp, which included all the units of the 5th Brigade, turned out 913 all ranks and 730 horses and, on Coronation Day, 29 June 1911, the brigade participated in a massive parade through Calgary. The *Calgary Herald* complained that many enlisted men from the camp could be seen on the streets of the city in the evening, without "belts, and unwashed in many cases" but did admit that, no matter "what these men may look like when they are off duty, they are wonderfully smart looking on parade."[14] A big feature of the 1911 camp was the tactical scheme, or "mock battle" as the journalists termed it, and the writer from the *Herald*, who had the misfortune to be "taken prisoner" by the Edmonton Fusiliers, noted that their commanding officer's "blood was up and he was bent on capturing everybody and everything in sight who might be, by any chance, connected with the enemy."[15]

This aggressive Fusilier commander was Lieutenant-Colonel William Frederick Carstairs, a native Ontarian who had served in the militia of that province, the NWMP, and in the Royal Nigerian Constabulary. Concerning his experiences in the latter corps, it is recorded that Carstairs commanded the "Unwana column of the Arrow expedition which comprised 1,500 of the rank and file and 3,000 porters and carriers and was the means of stamping out forever the slave trade in West Central Africa and in destroying the Long Ju-Ju cult of human sacrifice and cannibal feasting."[16] Arriving in Alberta in 1907 as a musketry instructor for Military District 13, "Freddy," as he was universally known, married one of Sam Steele's nieces and settled in Edmonton where he sometimes ran a hotel but devoted most of

his time to the Edmonton Fusiliers, which he raised in 1908. An impressive figure, who weighed about 300 lbs. in his stocking feet, Freddy had to use a chair to mount his long-suffering horse but woe betide anyone who tried to interfere with Freddy or the "Hunger and Thirst," as the Fusiliers called themselves. On one memorable occasion, when an Edmonton streetcar driver insisted on driving through the ranks of the regiment as it was parading through the downtown business area, chaos resulted. Enraged, Freddy caught up to the miscreant driver's vehicle on horseback, drew his sword and used it to uncouple it from its power line, bringing it to an abrupt and unscheduled stop.

In June 1912, the 5th Cavalry Brigade again went under canvas at Reservoir Park. This time they were reviewed by Major-General W.D. Otter, Inspector-General of the Canadian Militia, who not only complained that the stetson "was a useless commodity and should be abolished" but also bluntly queried: "Have not the plaudits awarded for a church parade or ceremonial parade lulled us into a belief that we are fit for any military strain coincident with invasion?"[17] These comments can be better understood if they are placed in the context of the man who spoke them for not only was Otter an infantryman, he was also a Torontonian which may go some way to explaining his behaviour. Be that as it may, when Lieutenant-General Sir John French, the senior officer of the British cavalry, inspected the 5th Brigade at camp in June 1913, he was impressed. "The Western Cavalry are fine," he reported, adding that the "physique of the men is just right. They ride daringly and well. They are keen as mustard, and their horses, the broncos of the prairies, show blood and stamina."[18] Attending camp that year was a new regiment, the 35th Central Alberta Horse, formed from the Independent Squadron of Light Horse that had been in existence at Red Deer for the past five years. By this time, there was also a full slate of service and support units in Military District 13 including a cavalry field ambulance, ordnance corps and army service corps detachments, field engineer troops and a veterinary section.

Throughout the decade prior to 1914, the Alberta militia carried out many ceremonial duties and gave exhibitions. The two Edmonton units were sure to be included in any activity involving the provincial legislature and paraded in strength when the fine new Legislature Building was opened in October 1912. The band of the 15th Light Horse was recognized as one of the best in the province and, by 1912, both the Light Horse and the 19th Dragoons had trained "Musical Ride" teams which often performed at annual exhibitions and fairs across Alberta. At these events, cavalrymen also competed in jumping, tent pegging (picking up a tent peg embedded in the ground with the tip of a sword or lance while at a gallop) and bareback wrestling contests, against each other and usually against a team from the RNWMP. One of the most popular contests included at these festivities was the "Victoria Cross Ride" – possibly modelled after the feat accomplished by Sergeant Richardson of Strathcona's Horse in South Africa – in which a trooper rode to a "wounded" man, jumped off his horse and then returned to the start line with his comrade draped across the saddle. The tricky part was that, while performing this stunt, which was timed, the contestant was under constant fire from men firing blank cartridges filled with soft soap which could inflict stinging and painful wounds, particularly if the cartridges had been filled sometime previous and the soap had hardened.

"War is closer than you dream": Dark clouds on the horizon

Times were so busy in Alberta that few in the province took note of the dark clouds gathering on the horizon because the world was moving, slowly but surely, to war. The origins of the tensions that ultimately led to war in 1914 can be traced back to the Prussian victory over France in 1871 and the creation of

"On parade": 15th Light Horse, 1912

A troop of the 15th Light Horse poses for the camera in this photo taken at the Calgary Exhibition grounds. These men are wearing red serge jackets with yellow facings, are equipped with the "Mounted Infantry" 50-round bandolier and appear to have Ross rifles. Their horse equipment includes a 1902 Universal Pattern Portsmouth bit and either 1890 or 1902 Universal Pattern saddles. GLENBOW MUSEUM, NA-1909-5, NA-1909-10

the German *Reich* which incorporated all the many independent German states into a new national entity. France, determined to exact revenge for her defeat and take back Alsace-Lorraine, which she was forced to cede to Germany after her defeat, made a defensive alliance with Russia. Germany, in turn, concluded a defensive alliance with the Austro-Hungarian empire, an alliance later joined by Italy. By the end of the 19th century Germany's remarkable economic progress made her the most powerful state in Europe outside Britain, which attempted, as always, to stay out of entanglements on the continent. The German decision in the late 1890s to build a powerful, modern high seas fleet, however, was viewed by Britain as a threat and in 1904 she therefore concluded an *Entente Cordiale* (an alliance in all but name) with France, which was later extended to Russia. By 1907 Europe was split into two great rival alliances and any incident involving one member of those blocs threatened to start a chain reaction that would drag all their member nations over the precipice.

The most likely place for a war to start was in the Balkans. Once part of the Turkish Empire, by the early 20th century most of the Balkan peoples had won their freedom in a series of revolutions and wars. The small but fiercely nationalistic Balkan nations were split along ethnic, religious and linguistic lines but the most powerful and aggressive was Serbia, a Slavic country which enjoyed the protection of Russia because that empire regarded itself as the leader of the "pan-Slav movement," and dreamed of uniting all the Slav peoples under one banner. Inevitably, Russia came into conflict with the Austro-Hungarian Empire, an aging polyglot of different ethnic groups more or less held together by police and military repression, which itself had aspirations in the Balkans. Tensions were exacerbated in 1909 when Austria-Hungary annexed the two principalities of Bosnia-Herzegovina, incurring the undying enmity of Serbia which regarded these territories as part of "Greater Serbia." On a number of occasions in the early years of the 20th century, Europe came close to the brink of war over Balkan problems but each time hard-working diplomats managed to pull it back from the brink.

By the beginning of the second decade of the century, however, the desire for peace had been eroded by a belief among the leaders of the major nations that a war could solve both their external and internal problems. This belief was particularly strong in Germany which possessed the most professional army and the

Alberta Hero: Major R.A. Boyle, 15th Light Horse, 1912

Major Russell Boyle, a rancher from Crossfield, Alberta, fought in South Africa with the Royal Canadian Field Artillery and was wounded in action. He later joined the 15th Light Horse and held the rank of major when the war broke out in 1914 when he assumed command of the 10th Battalion CEF. Boyle was killed during the attack on Kitcheners' Wood, part of the battle of 2nd Ypres in April 1915. SALH ARCHIVES

second-largest navy in Europe, and a head of state, Kaiser Wilhelm II, who was a professional sabre-rattler and the instigator of several international crises. Although there had been wars between individual states, there had not been a general war in Europe since 1815 and everyone expected that should such a conflict break out, it would follow the pattern of recent hostilities – short in duration and clear in outcome.

Although far from the scene of these tensions, Canada and the other self-governing Dominions of the Empire were affected by them. As Britain changed her traditional foreign policy of "splendid isolation" and brought the greater part of the Royal Navy back to home waters, she called upon the Dominions to strengthen their own military and naval forces and to make greater contributions to Imperial defence. Wilfrid Laurier's Liberal government, cautious about British entanglements, tried to keep Canada's commitments as minimal as possible but Laurier was finally forced to increase defence spending and to create a Canadian navy. When Robert Borden's Conservatives came to power in the general election of 1911, attitudes changed and defence spending was increased – from $7,000,000 in 1911 to $11,000,000 in 1914. Much of this spending was prompted by Sam Hughes, Borden's minister of militia and one of the most infamous personalities in Canadian public life.

A native of Northumberland County in Ontario and a former railway promoter and newspaper editor as well as a veteran of South Africa, Sam Hughes was an athletic, energetic, jingoistic, egotistic and supremely self-confident man, highly critical of the faults of others and blind to his own. Prime Minister Borden, who knew Hughes well and suffered greatly from him, once noted that about half the time his explosive minister of militia exhibited correct judgement and produced excellent results while on other occasions he was "extremely excitable, impatient of control and almost impossible to work with" and sometimes "his conduct and speech were so eccentric as to justify the conclusion that his mind was unbalanced."[19]

Major William Griesbach of the 19th Dragoons thought that Hughes's many faults were balanced by his virtues, chief among which was the ability to get things done quickly, and also by his passionate interest in the militia. Griesbach remembered that after Hughes took office, the militia "realized that they were receiving support now that they had never received before and this had a beneficial effect in itself."[20] Griesbach, however, was a lifelong Tory; others had a different opinion of Hughes includ-

Fusiliers on parade, Victoria Park, Calgary, 1912
Wearing the field uniform of straw hat, shirt, pants, and boots, the Edmonton Fusiliers pose for their photo at Victoria Park outside Calgary in 1912. Front and centre is "Fat Freddy" Carstairs, their overweight commanding officer, on his long-suffering horse. Despite constant admonitions from his doctors to diet, Freddy kept eating and was pushing 80 when he died in 1940. FROM *HISTORY OF THE 101ST REGIMENT EDMONTON FUSILIERS ... 1908-1913*

ing a future officer of the Canadian Expeditionary Force who rendered the cutting verdict that Hughes's career "is a warning to democracy of the inevitable man that will arise when defence in time of peace is a matter of no serious concern; his fate is an admonition to all men lest they attempt things beyond their reach."[21]

It seems that everybody had a strong opinion, good or bad, about Sam Hughes and Sam Hughes had a strong opinion about the immediate future – Germany was going to start a war in Europe. In a 1912 speech he spelled out this belief to his audience: "Gentlemen, we are not more than half civilized today, and war is closer than you dream; the great peril is from Germany. Why? Because Germany must have colonies within a generation or she will begin to go down."[22] Although not an admirer of regular soldiers, particularly British regular soldiers, Hughes was determined that, should such a conflict begin, Canada would be in a position to send her promised contribution to Britain which was to be an infantry division and a mounted brigade equipped "to meet the requirements of active service in a civilized country in a temperate climate."[23]

The question pondered by professional soldiers during these years of increasing tension was what form this war would take as it was sure to be different from any previous conflict. For one thing, armies would be larger as most major nations had some form of conscription in place and, with the advent of railways and telegraphs, these large armies could be moved, supplied and commanded over long distances. There was also the consideration that the raising, training, arming, equipping, deploying

and supplying of such large armies would require not only a larger and more professional military staff, but a greater proportion of a nation's economic output and thus the nation that had the largest and most efficient industrial base was most likely to be victorious. But the real difference from past wars would come about as a result of the technical advances made in the last half century, which had resulted in a quantum leap in the lethality of weaponry. The infantry of major armies were now armed with breech-loading, magazine rifles with an accurate range of 1,000 yards and a rate of fire of up to 12 rounds per minute and they also possessed machineguns capable of firing 400-450 rounds per minute at nearly the same range. The artillery arms of the major states were equipped with so-called "quick firing" breech-loading guns with hydraulic recoil systems that permitted them to stay on the target after every round and were fully capable of firing 15 rounds of high explosive or shrapnel per minute.

Much of this new weaponry was used in the Russo-Japanese War of 1905 and European military observers tried to draw the appropriate lessons. They seemed to believe, however, what they wanted to believe although some of the more observant noted the increasing use of temporary trenches by soldiers trying to protect themselves against modern firepower – and also the tremendous casualties that resulted when infantry tried to attack these same trenches, particularly if defended by machineguns. Yet, despite all the warning signs that a future conflict would require a huge economic effort and result in high casualties, professional soldiers persisted in thinking that if war came, it would be short, mobile and won by the offensive spirit.

Elan, dash, ironmongery and the magazine rifle:
The cavalry world, 1900-1914

Military theorists also pondered what role cavalry would play on a battlefield dominated by firepower. In the British Empire, the experience of South Africa seemed to provide a clear verdict that fire would be the deciding factor as the proponents of the "mounted infantry" school been asserting for nearly three decades. During that conflict no less than 28 temporary battalions of mounted infantry were formed and it was noted that these units "tended to attract the pick of the younger infantry officers and the most intelligent and adventurous other ranks."[24] The matter was seemingly settled in 1903 when the lance was withdrawn as a weapon from the British army. A year later a new manual, *Cavalry Training*, was issued which emphasized fire as opposed to shock tactics and Field-Marshal Lord Roberts, a soldier with half a century of active service behind him, contributed a preface which summed up the matter:

It is hardly too much to say that the change which has taken place in cavalry is as great as that which occurred to the infantry when the cross-bow and pike were replaced by the rifle and bayonet. ......

But what does the development of rifle fire consequent on the introduction of the long range, low trajectory, magazine rifle mean? It means that instead of the firearm being an adjunct to the sword, the sword must henceforth be an adjunct to the rifle; and that cavalry soldiers must become expert rifle shots and be constantly trained to act dismounted.

Cavalry officers need have no fear that teaching their men to fight on foot as well as on horseback will in any way interfere with that *élan* which is so essential for cavalry soldiers to possess. It will, I am satisfied, only serve to increase their confidence in themselves and their branch of service. ......

I think the improvement in fire arms will give the victory to the side which can first dismount on ground less favourable to a charge than an open plain.[25]

In the same year the new manual was released – and also a Canadian version entitled *Cavalry Training, Canada* – an up-and-coming young British politician, Winston Churchill, who had participated in a traditional cavalry charge at Omdurman in 1898, was even more blunt and insisted that the cavalry "throw away 'ironmongery' altogether" because modern war was "fought with firearms, and if cavalry is to play a great *role* in the battlefield in the future, they will have to use modern weapons, and not the sharp sticks and long irons with which the wars of savagery and medieval chivalry were conducted."[26]

It was not long, however, before the traditionalists mounted a counterattack, led by Lieutenant-General Sir John French and Major-General Sir Douglas Haig, two officers who would become prominent in the very near future. After Roberts retired in 1904, they managed to influence a revision of the 1904 manual so that when the next edition appeared in 1907, shock action was given almost equal emphasis with firepower. It was the feeling of the traditionalists that the "true cavalry spirit" could not be quantified by calculations based on the cold statistics of range, accuracy and rounds per minute and that "dash, the most precious possession of the cavalry soldier, should never be tampered with, either in training or in war."[27] It was all a question of "cavalry spirit" and that was apparently a difficult thing for cavalrymen to define for lesser mortals. Sir John French noted that its attributes, notably "elan" and "dash" and "fixed determination always to take the offensive and secure the initiative" and it was his opinion that such "a spirit can never be created in

Wilson's "Wonders": Alix, Alberta
Sergeant R.W. Wilson, on the far right poses with the men of his troop at Alix in 1912. Note the young lad fourth from the right, possibly an underage boy soldier. This is most likely a troop of the Independent Squadron of Horse or the 35th Central Horse which had its headquarters at Red Deer.
GLENBOW MUSEUM, NA-2925-4

a body of troops whose first idea is to abandon their horse and lie down under cover in the face of a swiftly-charging mass of horsemen."[28]

By 1912, an attempt was made to balance the conflicting schools through the expedient of creating different types of horse soldiers: cavalry; mounted rifles; and mounted infantry. The manual, *Yeomanry and Mounted Rifle Training*, issued that year by the War Office in London, contained fairly precise definitions of their weapons, tactics and roles. Cavalry were the elite and, although they were armed with rifles, they were also trained with the sword and lance and always sought for a way to use shock action in battle. Mounted rifles were horse soldiers "trained to use the rifle as their principal offensive or defensive weapon" and although they might be trained for shock action, it was "for use on special emergencies only, and altogether secondary to fire action." At the bottom of the heap were the mounted infantry who used horses "only for the purposes of locomotion" and were an unwashed species "not to be regarded as horse-soldiers" but merely as infantry "possessing special mobility."[29]

With the benefit of hindsight provided by knowledge of what was about to come, one should not be unduly critical of the traditionalists. British mounted troops of whatever stripe were at least trained to shoot, which was not the case with the French and German cavalry, which continued to emphasize shock action. Even the United States cavalry – which should have known better as they had recent experience in the Civil War that most European armies lacked – stressed shock over firepower as the dominant factor on the future battlefield in the decade prior to 1914.

"Keep off the skyline": Cavalry training in Alberta, 1910-1914

The Alberta militia cavalry used British manuals and were familiar with *Yeomanry and Mounted Rifle Training*, which was adopted in Canada, but they did not pay much attention to the military social delineations contained in it. Major William Griesbach of the 19th Dragoons has left a record of how that regiment trained in the last years of peace and much of what he says probably applies to the other horsed units in the province. To Griesbach, the distinctions between cavalry and mounted rifles – not to mention mounted infantry – were completely artificial. He attributed it to the inherent conservatism of the British cavalry officer and to the fact that the British army recruited poorly-educated enlisted personnel who were difficult to teach. In Alberta, Griesbach noted, "we had in our ranks a very high-class body of men who were very keen and quick to understand and learn."[30] This being the case, Alberta cavalry officers believed a soldier

who was a good horseman and of a superior intellectual type could be taught to be both a Cavalryman and Mounted Infantryman at the same time, and I think we were right. We, therefore, trained our men to seek for the opportunity of a cavalry charge, such an opportunity presenting itself, the men slung their rifles, drew their swords and rode at top

Dragoon staff, 1913

The headquarters staff of the 19th Alberta Dragoons pose at summer camp in 1913. Standing left to right are Captain McDonald (quartermaster), Captain Hislop (adjutant), Lieutenant Edmiston (musketry officer), Captain Hislop (medical officer). Seated are Lieutenant-Colonel F.C. Jamieson (commanding officer) and Captain Carruthers (chaplain). Jamieson would take the 19th Dragoons overseas in 1914. COURTESY, PAUL WYNNYK

speed to strike the enemy when he was shocked by artillery fire or surprised by our action, and when he presented to us a favourable target. On the other hand, we endeavoured to train our men for mounted rifle action and practised, in particular rapid changes of position to enable us to escape shell-fire and to confuse the enemy as to where we were or what we were going to do next.[31]

As he later wrote, Griesbach took over the training of the 19th Dragoons "for the main reason that I could do the job" and drilled the regiment, particularly the officers, rigorously.[32] In good weather, they were out almost every weekend and, it should be noted, that they were not paid for this work. As Griesbach remembered:

We devoted Sunday afternoon to practice with sword and lance, scouting, reconnaissance work and the writing properly of field reports and messages. Meanwhile the officers took various courses. Each officer had to equip himself with a horse, uniform, arms and accoutrements, and each officer was required to spend a good deal of time and money on the work which he undertook. ……

I had many other interests and made a division of my time to permit me to give some six hours a day to my military job. I brought my squadron up to strength and continued the training in our own time. The squadron acquired a stable where the men kept their horses. I constantly sought to improve the calibre of the men enlisted so that ultimately nearly all my men who went to the War of 1914-18 won their commissions in the field.[33]

Griesbach was one of the few cavalry officers in Military District 13 who admired Colonel E.A. Cruikshank, the district commander. A lifelong militia officer from Ontario in his sixties, Cruikshank had been brought into the permanent force five years earlier and was a pedantic, stern and somewhat inflexible personality who, since his background was the infantry, had firmly fixed ideas about tactical matters. As nearly all the units in the district were cavalry, Griesbach remembered that there were inevitable clashes between Cruikshank and his cavalry commanders (many of whom were veterans of the South African war) "when it came to the question of the use of horses."[34]

Curiously enough, the rigid old colonel and the intelligent young squadron commander got along well as they shared an interest in military history which both were convinced was an effective tool for teaching tactics. Griesbach noted that, when planning a training scheme for the annual Alberta militia camp, Cruikshank "never drew up anything fictitious but took an incident of the American Civil War or the Franco-German War, 1870, which had to be worked out by the troops under his command."[35] Alberta officers like Griesbach often found themselves attempting to carry out one of Jeb Stuart's raids "with time and distance allotted to correspond" with Stuart's actual movements "behind the federal lines." Certainly, Griesbach's prescription for the tactical training of the 19th Dragoons – which was probably used by the other Alberta mounted units – has more than a whiff of the methods of the famous Confederate commander:

Thus, one of our frequent practices was to seek first a covered position for our horsemen and then a rapid advance over open ground, usually at a gallop towards a good firing position or a position from which we could deliver an infantry assault, always keeping the horse as close to the men as possible. The foothills in the Sarcee Camp, at Calgary, are very suitable for this form of training. When confronting an enemy position we aimed to gallop forward by troops, and then, on reaching dead ground in front of the enemy position, to attack frontally with the rifle or ride to a flank, always moving at high speed. By this method we were frequently able to appear on the flanks of the enemy.[36]

Reflecting on the matter in later years, Griesbach noted that, while prior to 1914, the training of the 19th Dragoons and the other provincial mounted units was intended "for open warfare in which troops moved freely over the terrain," it had to be remembered that at the time it was "generally the opinion of all soldiers" that the next major conflict would feature "open warfare.[37]

Not that the Alberta cavalry neglected the more recent military innovations, including aircraft. The British army used aircraft for the first time on a major military exercise in 1910 but it is remarkable that, within a few years, the Alberta cavalry were training against a possible threat from the air. At a time when many British cavalry officers were arguing for a return to the sword and shock action, and the French cavalry (who had never believed in this business about giving a mounted man an accurate rifle), were busy raising more lancer units, Alberta mounted units

practised concealment and evasive action against aeroplanes. We dismounted our squadrons, having first taken a wide extension. When dismounted, the men hugged their horses closely and allowed them to graze, putting their hats on the shiny seat of the saddle to eliminate sun flash. Someone then recollected that horses always graze up the wind to avoid the flies. Consequently, on dismounting, the men turned their horses' heads up-wind and endeavoured to convey the impression of a herd of horses grazing. The men were taught not to look up, since a man's face is noticed from the air. ......
We also taught the men to open fire with their rifles at an aeroplane. There were distinct possibilities in this since, with a hundred men so extended firing, there were likely to be ugly concentration of bullets in the air in the neighbourhood of the enemy airplane.[38]

In the winters, when it was not possible to train outdoors, Griesbach continued with his study of military history to the point where he believed that, in his subsequent career, "I was never confronted with a military situation for which my mind had not been prepared."[39] He used both his reading and practical experience gained in South Africa to prepare a series of lectures for the sergeants of the 19th Dragoons that he delivered over the winter of 1913-1914. These were later collected in a small manual, *Observations on Cavalry Duties. Some Hints for Western Canadian Cavalry Men*, which he had printed at his own expense the following spring.

Observations on Cavalry Duties is a succinct, well written little primer of basic cavalry knowledge, with an emphasis on patrol work, divided into chapters discussing advance, rear and flank guards, outpost duties, scouting, map reading, message writing and entraining horses. Griesbach offered practical pearls of wisdom gained, no doubt, through personal experience in South Africa. "Keep off the sky line," is an injunction he repeats several times. And then there was the humble subject of dust, which can provide useful information to the trained eye. Heavy low, clouds of dust usually indicate a column of marching infantry while thin, high dust clouds usually mean cavalry and thin, low dust clouds artillery. One of the few unwittingly hilarious passages in the manual is found in the author's strictures (again, no doubt, based on personal experience) about the adverse effect the mat-

Alberta's first gunners
In 1913 the 25th Battery, Canadian Field Artillery, of Lethbridge became the first artillery unit formed in Alberta. It was equipped with modern quick-firing 13-pdr. field guns, the standard light fieldpiece of the British Empire. The Lethbridge boys were proud of these weapons as they were the same as those used by the Royal Horse Artillery and Royal Canadian Horse Artillery. GLENBOW MUSEUM, NA-567-5

ing habits of the equine species can have on the equilibrium of a railway box car: "Stallions are very undesirable, but, if you must have them, stand them at the extreme end of the car; next to him stand a mare not in season, and tie head to head."[40] The point of Griesbach's work, however, is encapsulated in an early passage in which he stresses that, "if in doubt or without orders, there is an old rule which still holds good, 'Go to the gun fire,' in other words, 'Get into the game.' Our training is for war. The soldier is a fighting man. Get into the fight."[41]

These were serious words but William Griesbach was an intelligent man who could analyze and interpret what he read in the newspapers and what he read and what he heard, convinced him, like Sam Hughes, that trouble was brewing and that he and his comrades "were definitely preparing for the War which we knew was coming."[42]

"The sweetest music a soldier can hear": The last peacetime militia camp, 1914

In the summer of 1913, Canada experienced its most severe economic depression in two decades. Because of its agricultural base, this setback was not as bad in Alberta as in Eastern Canada but construction, both of buildings and railways, nearly halted and thousands in the province were thrown out of work and drifted into the already overcrowded cities where accommodation was scarce with the result that many ended up living in tents in vacant lots and on the outskirts. At this time in Alberta there was a severe gender imbalance, single men outnumbered single women nearly two to one and there was little for this horde of unemployed or underemployed bachelors to do – and not much money to do it with. Many passed their time in the numerous bars to be found in all Albertan cities and the sight of unconscious drunks on the street was common. This aroused the ire of the strong and outspoken provincial temperance movement formed by an alliance of church and women's groups and it began to agitate not just for moderation but outright prohibi-

tion. So influential was this movement that it even managed to gain the support of Bob Edwards of the *Eye Opener* which was surprising as Edwards, like many good writers (and some good historians) had a weakness for the dram.

There was positive news on the economic front, however, as the militia prepared for their 1914 summer camp at Reservoir Park in Calgary – oil had been discovered in the Turner Valley in May. The price of oil shares rose from $2.50 to $200 and, within three days, nearly a hundred new oil brokers had set up shop in Edmonton. The Calgary *Western Standard Illustrated Weekly* added a new section on the provincial oil industry, complete with beautifully-drawn plans showing how close the site of the strike was to the property of the many new companies offering shares at amazingly low prices. "The Alberta Oilfields," the *Standard* assured its readers, "May Soon Rival Those of California" and advised that investment in oil was just too good a chance to miss.

Thus, when the 5th Cavalry Brigade went to camp, it appeared to many Albertans that happy days were just around the corner. For the 19th Dragoons, the annual concentration began in the evening of Sunday, 14 June 1914, when A Squadron rode through the streets of Edmonton to the CPR station, hooves clattering and sabres clanking, to board the train for Calgary. The band and two companies of the 101st Regiment were there to send them off and it is likely that the Fusilier bandsmen played "Dolly Gray" which, in the previous decade, had become a popular "loath to depart" tune for military units leaving station. As was standard practice at this time, militia cavalry units attended camp before the infantry – the 101st Fusiliers would be going at the end of the week. At the station, A Squadron quickly loaded their 80 horses (among which, according to one eyewitness, were some "fiery untamed steeds") onto the box cars taking care, no doubt, to heed Griesbach's sage advice not to hitch stallions in close proximity to mares in season.[43] The unit's arms and equipment were placed in two baggage cars and, finally, the

The last camp – 5th Cavalry Brigade parades through Calgary, June 1914
The 5th Cavalry Brigade rides through Calgary on its way to the unveiling of the South African War Memorial at Central Park on 20 June 1914. The lead unit is possibly the 23rd Alberta Rangers. Note the officer on the right, the unit padre. The 1914 summer camp, which took place just a few weeks before the outbreak of war, was regarded as the best ever held in the province. SALH ARCHIVES

men took their seats in six green-painted Colonist Cars, probably cursing the hard wooden slat benches which were, with some truth, believed to brand an indelible pattern on one's posterior. To the cheers and hurrahs of the crowd, the train pulled out for nearby Strathcona where a brief stop was made to pick up B Squadron and then, as Trooper Lathern produced his fiddle to provide a little entertainment, the men settled down for the overnight journey south.

The Dragoons arrived at Calgary station at 8 A.M. the next morning. Monday, 15 June 1914, was a busy day for the railwaymen in that city as cavalry units from all over the province – the outlying squadrons of the 15th Horse, the 21st Hussars, 23rd Rangers and the 35th Central Horse – came in on chartered CPR, Grand Trunk Pacific and Canadian Northern Railway trains. Some men had a long ride from their homes just to get to the railway – Corporal W.H. Widden of the 21st Hussars rode 170 miles in three days to reach Red Deer and board the camp train of the 35th Horse – while others elected to ride the entire distance to Calgary, including a detachment of the Corps of Guides from Banff who spent two nights camping on the way. One train brought in nothing but horses for the city squadron of the 15th Light Horse. There was no shortage of experienced wranglers to get this collection of barely halter-broke mounts, rented in outlying small towns for the camp, safely through the streets of the city to the Light Horse armoury where they were awaited by nervous urban troopers. It says much for the efficiency and experience of the Alberta cavalry that all units offloaded

their horses, men, equipment and arms without confusion and delay before setting out on the three and a half mile march to the camp site at Reservoir Park near the Sarcee Reserve west of the city. They arrived to find lines of bell and marquee tents awaiting them, the product of hard preliminary work done by No. 14 Company, Canadian Army Service Corps and Nos. 4 and 6 Field Troops, Canadian Engineers. Just as the units entered their lines, the "official camp thunderstorm" broke but it was soon over and did nothing to repress the spirits of mostly young men who were happy and boisterous because, for many, militia camp was their only holiday.[44]

Camp discipline, however, was more strict in 1914 than in previous years. There was no drinking at Reservoir Park because Sam Hughes was a committed teetotaller and had expressly forbidden the presence or sale of alcohol at camps, which led militiamen to sing, to the tune of "John Peel,"

> D'ye ken Sam Hughes, he's the foe of booze;
> He's the real champeen of the dry canteen;
> For the camp is dead, and we're sent to bed,
> So we won't have a head in the morning.[45]

Nor was there any gambling – not even semi-innocent (although often profitable) games of "Crown and Anchor" – as this too was prohibited. There is no doubt that these regulations were rigorously enforced at Calgary as the commander of Military District 13, Colonel Cruikshank, was a humourless stickler who followed regulations to the letter. He had served more than 30 years in the Ontario militia before being brought into the permanent force and, such was his reputation as a martinet, that, when commanding a militia brigade in the Niagara area, miscreant units were often assigned to his formation as a form of punishment. Cruikshank also tried to forbid the traditional camp amusement of blanket tossing – in fact regimental commanders had been trying to get rid of this practice for the past six years – but even Cruikshank did not try to outlaw inter-unit arm wrestling contests, an always popular activity. As for drinking and gambling, maybe it didn't take place at Reservoir Park but the attractions of Calgary were close at hand and men were generally off duty after the evening meal, although they still had to be back in their lines by 10 P.M.

On Tuesday, following reveille at 5.30 A.M., everyone got down to work. The cavalry units carried out individual dismounted drill while the 25th Battery went off to the range to fire live rounds from their 13-pdr. guns. The Lethbridge boys had only recently received these modern weapons and were very proud of them, no doubt telling anyone willing (or unwilling) to listen that these were the same guns manned by the Royal Horse Artillery and the Royal Canadian Horse Artillery. The gunners had a good time at the range until time came to fold up shop for the day when a final ammunition check revealed that they could not account for one shrapnel round. This discovery promptly set off a frantic search of the ammunition limbers and gun area but the hunt was to no avail until some bright spark thought to check the guns themselves and the round was discovered in the breech of one of the 13-pdr. guns with its fuse set to "0" or the minimum range setting possible, which would have detonated it not far out of the muzzle. What made matters worse was that the weapon in which the missing shell was loaded was known to have a defective safety mechanism. Letting their collective breath out while at the same time saying a quiet prayer of thanks to Saint Barbara, the patron saint of gunners, the Lethbridge battery packed up and returned to its lines in the main camp.

Beginning on Wednesday, 17 June, each unit in turn spent a day at the rifle ranges. In 1914 the Canadian militia took marksmanship very seriously, not just because Sam Hughes was a fanatical shooter but also because a militiaman had to score a minimum of 42 out of 70 possible points on the ranges to get the few cents extra "efficiency pay" to add to his 50 cents a day camp pay, and an enlisted man had to get efficiency pay before he could gain promotion. Those cavalry units not firing on the range commenced mounted drill while the 25th Battery practised deploying for action, gun drill (with probably a little extra time spent on the correct procedure for clearing a gun after action) and displacing to new positions. Not all the cavalry were good riders, particularly the men from the city squadrons who, to make matters worse, were usually issued the half broken "rent-a-steeds." Every cavalry unit, however, had experienced roughriders on hand who were tasked with breaking unruly horses or rescuing hapless troopers "not familiar with either the

disposition or the wonderful possibilities of a western cayuse."[46] When a runaway took place – and it apparently happened quite often – these specialists would rope in an unridden horse or, if the rider was still gamely "in distress, hanging on the back of a rearing, plunging" cayuse, they would come alongside and shout "a few queer phrases of their own to try and instill him in a little self-confidence."[47]

This routine continued for the remainder of the week although Thursday morning was given over to the District Commander's inspection which, according to the newspapers, was passed with flying colours. The annual camp was big news in Alberta and its activities were covered in all the hometown papers although it is puzzling that the *Edmonton Journal* assured its readers that B Squadron of the 19th Dragoons was the best squadron at camp in 1914, while the *Medicine Hat News* stated with equal confidence that the honour belonged to C Squadron of the 21st Hussars. The media were frequent visitors and the reporter for the *Calgary Standard* was impressed when he arrived at Reservoir Park to find

everything in the best military order and the camp second to none in point of order, industry and cleanliness. No one was idling, even those "off duty" seemed busy, and the prairie near the Sarcee reserve was alive with scarlet and khaki-clad men, undergoing severe tests of their abilities in squadron drill, signalling, marksmanship, foot drill and wagon drill. For infantry drill, the men have been supplied with very picturesque and appropriate sun-hats, and though the drill is carried out in the face of a strong sample of Alberta sunshine, no heat prostrations are recorded.[48]

This same journalist was also intrigued to see the many mascots in the tent lines as each unit had brought its own well-groomed pony, dog or other pet beast. He was pleased, that is, until he encountered a monkey, the pride of one unidentified unit (one suspects the Central Horse, a new regiment eager to impress, or the Lethbridge battery because gunners are known to be a little strange), which promptly ate his notes when he stopped to pet it and then tried to bite the aspiring young Hemingway after he refused to render up his pencil for the simian's dessert. This was perhaps not the best example of military-media relations but, on the other hand, 1914 was a distant happy time before the invention of Public Affairs Officers.

On Thursday night, 18 June, most of the officers in camp attended, by invitation, the "Rose Ball" at the Palliser Hotel in downtown Calgary. This was a fundraising event staged by the Imperial Order of Daughters of the Empire because the good and loyal ladies needed to pay for the impressive new memorial, dedicated to the fallen of the South African War, which they had just erected in Central Park. The social elite of the city and – more important for young cavalry officers – all their beautiful unmarried daughters were on the invitation list. The absence of most of the officers probably resulted in a better run camp, as the NCOs took over and no doubt peace and reason reigned in the tent lines (plus a little discreet "Crown and Anchor" and perhaps the odd nip as the district staff were all known to be down at the Palliser). By every account the ball was a great success and enjoyed by all, including a number of junior officers who, it is reported, weaved their way back to their tents shortly before reveille, heads full of both champagne punch and troubling visions of bare, pale, soft shoulders wreathed in silk, organza or tulle. This should come as no surprise, however, because young officers often display a distressing tendency to drink to excess and stay up too late while, when it comes to young ladies, they generally live in perpetual hope.

The following day – and it turned out to be a very hot and dry one – it was back to mounted drill and range work. Quite possibly there were some pale-faced subalterns on morning parade and squadron commanders, taking note, would make an effort to assign such unfortunates extra duties involving the loud shouting of orders and considerable riding back and forth in the dust of the prairie under a mind-baking sun. They did this not only because it was an essential part of a junior officer's training but because all young gentlemen must learn that war really is hell. It might also be possible that some of these subalterns, suffering from mildly guilty consciences as well as thick heads, dodged hastily behind tents that evening when they spotted the matrons of the IODE, many of whom were protective mothers of attractive young ladies, making serene and majestic progress through camp to solicit funds from the enlisted men for their memorial. The District Commander had given the good Daughters permission to do so, while at the same time issuing an order that they "be welcomed with the utmost civility."[49]

During the weekend there was some relaxation of activity, at least training activity. Much of Saturday, 20 June 1914, was given over to a full dress parade – with stetsons instead of straw hats for the cavalry – by all 2,000 men in camp to downtown Calgary to attend the unveiling the South African War Memorial in Central Park. That afternoon, the 101st Fusiliers, 325 strong, arrived at the station from Edmonton and marched in – fat Freddy Carstairs leading the column – with their Colours flying and their band playing a stirring march. The 103rd Rifles, being a local unit, first attended the memorial parade before coming out, with 200 all ranks, to Reservoir Park. On Sunday morning, the Catholics were mustered and marched off to St. Mary's in Calgary for service while the Protestants (or members of any other faith for that matter as the army in 1914 had a rather simple concept of religion) were formed in a hollow square, in the centre of which was an altar created by one of the 25th Battery's 13-pdr. guns covered by a Union Jack. Services were then conducted by a number of local ministers who probably took full opportunity of having a captive congregation to increase the length of their sermons. Things got better in the afternoon, however, as it was largely given over to some rest and relaxation, involving arm wrestling contests, baseball games and displays of horsemanship complete with broncho-

busting, jumping and short distance races, all of which were watched with great interest by crowds of civilians who took post on nearby ridges.

Now that all the units in Alberta were present, as William Griesbach recalled fondly some thirty years later, morning reveille was truly impressive:

At five-thirty in the morning the morning gun was fired in the artillery lines, fifteen squadron trumpeters blew reveille, the artillery trumpets and the infantry bugles joined in. The air throbbed with the sweetest music that a soldier can hear. When the trumpets had finally ceased, brass bands of the infantry then marched through the camp and the pipers made their contribution of "Hi! Johnny Cope."

Then began the sounds inseparable from a Cavalry camp. Sergeants went through the lines inviting all concerned to "show a leg" and presently the morning roll-call was underway. The men broke off to "stables" and the horses greeted them with snickering and neighing. Then one heard fearful and ferocious threats of the men addressed to their horse; such as "Get off my foot or I'll brain you." It invariably ended with tickling the offending horses between the hind legs.[50]

The second week was somewhat busier than the first. On Monday, 22 June, the infantry spent the day on the ranges firing their Ross rifles while the cavalry units conducted brigade drill under the direction of Colonel Robert Belcher, commander of the 5th Cavalry Brigade. That evening Belcher held an Orders Group for all unit commanders during which he issued instructions for the forthcoming tactical scheme. The two infantry regiments were brigaded with the 21st Hussars and 35th Central Horse under Lieutenant-Colonel Frank Sissons of the Hussars as "Blue Force", while Belcher took command of 5th Cavalry Brigade as "Red Force" with the 15th Light, 19th Dragoons, 23rd Rangers and the Lethbridge battery. No details of this scheme have survived but it would seem from the division of the units that Cruikshank, whose regular staff served as umpires, wished to approximate a meeting engagement between a mounted brigade with attached horse artillery, and an infantry force with a light cavalry screen which would make entire sense as Military District 13 was largely regarded as a cavalry district and training emphasis was usually put on the mounted arm. It is also very probable that this scheme was based on an actual operation from the American Civil War.

On Tuesday, while the infantry finished their range qualification, the cavalry continued brigade drill but, at 8 A.M. sharp on Wednesday, 24 June 1914, the two forces left camp in different directions and marched into the country south of Calgary to carry out the scheme. It lasted two days with the troops going into bivouac on the Wednesday night before returning late on Thursday.

The following day, the infantry carried out company and battalion drill while the cavalry and gunners packed up and prepared to go home. The chartered trains, full of tired but happy men and tired but happy horses, began to pull out of the Calgary on Friday evening. Everyone who was there was in general agreement that the 1914 Alberta militia summer camp, attended by 2,459 men and 1673 horses, was the best ever held in the province.

"Volunteers, fall in line!" The world goes over the edge, 1914
The 19th Dragoons were one of the last cavalry units to get away and did not arrive in Edmonton until Saturday evening where they were met by a large and enthusiastic crowd of families and friends. The *Edmonton Bulletin* and *Edmonton Journal* did not publish on Sunday and when the morning editions appeared on Monday, 29 June 1914, the major news was not the summer camp but the assassination of Archduke Franz-Ferdinand, heir to the throne of the Austro-Hungarian Empire, by a Serbian extremist, which had taken place the previous day in Sarajevo, an obscure town somewhere in the ever-troublesome Balkans. Noting the doleful influence this event would have on a tottering European dynasty, the *Journal* prophesied with unwitting but fatally chilling accuracy that it was possible that "the course of history has been largely altered by this deed."[51]

In the next few weeks, however, the Alberta papers did not give much attention to what became an escalating crisis in Europe. After making sure of Germany's backing, Austria-Hungary issued a ten-point ultimatum to Serbia on 23 July. The Serbs agreed to all the points except one but when their answer was received in Vienna, Austria-Hungary declared war on Serbia. It now became a matter of plans and carefully orchestrated train timetables as the mobilization process, once started, could not be stopped. Russia mobilized in support of the Serbs and when Germany, who had already begun her own mobilization, requested that St. Petersburg halt the process, the Russians refused and Germany declared war on Russia on 1 August. In accordance with her defensive alliance with Russia, France mobilized that same day and two days later Germany declared war on France.

Through much of July 1914, however, Canada and Alberta appeared blissfully unaware of the coming storm – the big news in the provincial papers that month was the investigation into the tragic sinking of the liner, *Empress of Ireland* in May with the loss of 964 people, the more recent tragedy in a mine at Hillcrest in June that had claimed the lives of 189 men, troubles in Northern Ireland and the depredations of the Mexican revolutionary Pancho Villa against the border towns of Texas. Also of interest was the claim of a New York lawyer – on what grounds it is not entirely certain – that the invention of the tango had resulted in a 50% increase in the divorce rate and, finally, there was the curious situation at the recent Calgary Exhibition where no less than 260 of the 770 babies displayed by proud Albertan mothers had received prizes.[52]

During the long days of mid-summer, Britain acted as an honest broker to try and bring an end to the European crisis by negotiation – it had worked before but it was not to work this time. On 2 August 1914 Germany presented a note to Belgium requesting the free passage of her troops across that nation to attack France. Belgium refused and since Germany was a signatory, along with Britain, to an 1839 treaty preserving Belgian neutrality, this caused the British government to deliver an ultimatum to Germany that if she did not respect that obscure treaty, a state of war would exist between the two nations. This ultimatum was set to expire at 11 P.M. British time, Tuesday, 4 August 1914.

In 1914, when Britain was at war, Canada was at war and, in the first few days of August, Canadians suddenly took an active interest in European events. In Alberta, Monday, 3 August, was a public holiday and Albertans, by this time thoroughly excited, followed the course of the crisis in the hourly bulletins posted on the windows of newspaper offices. In Lethbridge, home of the 25th Battery, as the hours ticked away on Tuesday, 4 August, with no response from Germany to the ultimatum, crowds gathered by the bandstand in the park to hear the latest information read to them by the staff of the *Lethbridge Herald*. In Edmonton, the street in front of the *Journal* office at First Street and Jasper Avenue was, the editor of that paper bragged, as crowded as King and Yonge in Toronto, and lined ten deep with people. In Toronto itself where, ironically, the theme of the forthcoming Canadian National Exhibition was to be "1914: The Year of Peace" there were indeed crowds of that size on that busy downtown intersection. By late afternoon, Sam Hughes in Ottawa lost his patience and, convinced that Britain was going to "skunk it," ordered the Union Jack flying over the Militia Department to be hauled down.[53]

"Fighting Sam" did not have to worry. At 8.55 P.M., Ottawa received the telegram from London that, in the absence of a reply from German government, a state of war now existed between that nation and the British Empire. At almost the same time, word reached Alberta and the province went wild – in front of a bandshell in a small town in the southern part was heard "the mightiest cheer that ever rent the atmosphere that hovers over the tranquil city of Lethbridge."[54] In Calgary, the orchestra at the Palliser Hotel and the musicians at the picture shows interrupted the programmes to play the national anthem to thunderous applause. In Edmonton, an estimated 10,000 people watched an impromptu parade form in front of the United Service Club and then march through the streets to the CPR station blocking all traffic until the early hours of the next morning. Led by a veteran on a grey horse and accompanied by the Citizens' Band and the Edmonton Caledonian Pipers playing patriotic marches, this procession featured a truck draped with a large banner reading: "United Service Club. Loyal Call to Arms. Veterans, Ex-Service Men and Volunteers, Fall in Line!" – and they did by the hundreds.[55]

And so Alberta and Canada went to war but, as the *Medicine Hat News* cheerfully assured its readers, there was no need to worry unduly because Lloyds of London was giving even money that it would all be over by Christmas.

Brigade commander's inspection, Calgary, 1915
Shortly before the 31st Battalion left Calgary, it was inspected by Brigadier-
General H.D.B. Ketchen, commanding the 6th Brigade of the 2nd Canadian
Division. Here, Ketchen, wearing an "officer's warm" coat, stops to talk
to a staff sergeant but it is unlikely that the sergeant had any complaints.
Directly behind Ketchen is Lieutenant-Colonel A.H. Bell, who commanded
the 31st Battalion from 1914 to 1918. GLENBOW MUSEUM, NA-1165-1

"The Honour and Integrity of the Empire"

THE GREAT WAR TO SEPTEMBER 1915

We are Sam Hughes's army
Thirty thousand strong are we.
We cannot march, we cannot shoot,
What bloody use are we?
And when we get to Berlin
The Kaiser he will say,
"*Hoch, Hoch, Mein Gott*, what a bloody odd lot
To get six bob a day."[1]

"A call to arms like the fiery cross": The creation of the Canadian Expeditionary Force

Now at war, Canada was determined to make every effort to maintain "the honour and integrity of the Empire."[2] Without significant debate Parliament approved the creation of an overseas military contingent totalling 25,000 and the staff of the Department of Militia dusted off plans to send it to fight "in a civilized country in a temperate climate" – in short, France.[3] Sam Hughes, however, had other ideas. He ignored the draft mobilization plan in favour of what he later described as "a call to arms, like the fiery cross passing through the Highlands of Scotland or the mountains of Ireland in former days."[4] On 6 August 1914 Hughes sent a telegram to the 226 militia unit commanders across Canada authorizing them to recruit physically fit volunteers between the ages of 18 and 45, with preference given to single men and married men without families, for an overseas expeditionary force. The volunteers were to concentrate at Valcartier, Quebec, in a few weeks time.

Armouries across Alberta were immediately besieged by men wanting to enlist and unit strengths dramatically rose. The Edmonton Fusiliers had only been able to bring 325 officers and men to camp the previous June but, within a week of Hughes's message, they had more than a thousand on their rolls and a similar phenomenon occurred in the other provincial units. In those hectic August weeks recruiting also went on in Alberta for a new regiment – Princess Patricia's Canadian Light Infantry – which originated in an offer by a wealthy Quebec businessman, Hamilton Gault, to raise at his own expense a unit in Canada for the British army. Princess Patricia, daughter of the governor-general, lent her name and recruiting started on 12 August. Nearly 500 men, about half the strength of the PPCLI, were enlisted in Alberta – including the Edmonton Caledonian Pipe Band which joined as a group – and by 12 August they were on their way east.

Most of the provincial commanding officers hoped that when the dust settled from Hughes's "call to arms," their units would go overseas as distinct entities but, in the meantime, they signed up many willing men. The 15th Light Horse, 21st Hussars, 23rd Alberta Rangers and 35th Central Alberta Horse all expanded to between three to four times their prewar strength but the fifth provincial cavalry regiment, the 19th Alberta Dragoons, experienced a more balanced increase. In the mobilization plan, the Dragoons were slated to provide a squadron for the infantry division that would eventually be organized from the mass of the expeditionary force and this part of the plan was followed. The Dragoons' selection for this role over every other militia cavalry unit in Canada (including some of the socially-elite Montreal and Toronto units with good political connections) was a reflection of the high esteem in which they were held. Lieutenant-Colonel F.C. Jamieson, the Edmonton lawyer who commanded the Dragoons, received orders to mobilize the active service squadron on 7 August and, although he was somewhat concerned about the competition for recruits, he quickly set about the task. Almost the entire peacetime strength of the Dragoons enlisted *en masse* and Jamieson had no problem finding additional men although he only took those who had previous military training and were "able to ride and shoot."[5] Within a week, Jamieson had not only recruited his authorized strength of 6 officers and 165 other ranks but also a reserve troop of 85 all ranks.

It wasn't hard for the Dragoons to find good men, but they also had to find good horses. Jamieson received permission to purchase mounts locally and the unit began to look for horses costing not more than $175, "sound in wind and limb and free from all blemishes," 8 to 15 years in age, 15 to 16 hands in height and between 1,000 and 1,400 lbs. in weight, with the preferred colours being brown, black or chestnut but not bay or roan.[6] With a provincial horse population estimated to be 254,117 head in 1914, Jamieson's wranglers had no problem finding good stock. The unit also acquired another four-legged recruit, a friendly yellow husky named "Ogema" who began to attend the daily drill parades held that August outside the Dragoons' armoury on 106th Street, and was eventually mustered in, and issued a collar plate reading "Husky, Divisional Cavalry, Edmonton."[7]

By the third week in August, 28,553 officers and men had joined the First Contingent of the Canadian Expeditionary Force and, unit by unit, detachment by detachment, they began to move to Valcartier. The Edmonton Fusiliers, with a strength of 1,247 all ranks dressed in khaki, red tunics and civilian clothes, marched to the station on 24 August. As they tramped along the streets of the provincial capital, one Fusilier shouted "God Help the Kaiser if we get hold of him!" which brought thunderous applause from the crowds who lined the route.[8] At Red Deer, the send-off was not so well organized. The 35th Central Horse were out on a training march at 10 A.M. in the morning of 26 August when a telegram came informing them that their train for Valcartier would be arriving in an hour. They made a prompt about turn and went directly to the station while frantic details gathered up stores, and families and friends bundled up belongings and brought them to the station. As the crowds "cheered and cheered again" and the town band played patriotic airs, the 35th Horse left Red Deer at 11.15 A.M.[9] The 19th Dragoons, 205 officers and men, 240 horses and one yellow husky strong, left Edmonton that same day. Despite the frantic activity of the last few weeks the unit still found the time and the resources to participate in the Edmonton Exhibition, mounting a musical ride on 11 August and two days later joining the Fusiliers in staging a military tattoo. As the Dragoons boarded their train to leave Edmonton, Major William Griesbach recorded, they had a "good send-off" and the cheers of the crowd followed them down the line as they headed east for the war.[10] Similar scenes took place across Canada as the Canadian Pacific, Canadian Northern and Grand Trunk railways undertook the massive task of transporting thousands of men and their weapons, horses, vehicles and equipment to Valcartier Camp, 20 miles north of Quebec City.

"Onward Royal Canadians": Valcartier, August and September 1914

When the 19th Dragoons arrived at Valcartier, what they saw from the windows of their coaches was a miracle of improvisation impelled by the frantic energy of Sam Hughes. A few weeks earlier, when Hughes decided it would be the mobilization point for the Canadian Expeditionary Force, Valcartier had been noth-

Sam Hughes

Assuming a typical Napoleonic stance, Colonel Sam Hughes, the Minister of Militia, watches the First Contingent of the Canadian Expeditionary Force depart for Britain in October 1914. Always a controversial figure, Hughes displayed impressive but mindless energy, which often did more harm than good. His course was run by late 1916 when Prime Minister Borden fired him. NAC, PA-002468

ing but sandy farm fields and scrub pine. The first workmen arrived a few days after that and, in less than three weeks, a camp large enough to accommodate 30,000 men had been created with a railway siding, a 1,500-target rifle range, administrative and store buildings, water points and drains, electricity, telephone and telegraph, magazines, and seemingly endless rows of white bell tents erected by units of the regular force. With the military came the civilians and, by the time the troop trains arrived, there were huts and canteens located just outside the camp boundaries offering their military clientele a wide range of items including candy, soft drinks, pastries, clothing, books, postcards, badges, jewellery for sweethearts but not alcohol – at least not openly – as teetotaller Sam Hughes was determined that "his boys" would not be led into temptation.

Hughes, mounted, and wearing a colonel's uniform, was a constant and often disturbing presence at Valcartier. Riding through the camp accompanied by a large staff, he would harass, bully, compliment, abuse, promote and demote at will, leaving general chaos in his wake. He puzzled one infantry unit at its drill by ordering them to "form square," a tactical formation dropped from the manuals decades before, and he berated an unfortunate and low-voiced officer in his front of his men by shouting: "Pipe up, you little bastard, or get out of the service!"[11] On three separate days in September 1914 Hughes stopped all training activity to stage reviews for Prime Minister Robert Borden, the governor-general and other, lesser, functionaries including several of his personal political cronies. The troops did not know what to make of the unpredictable Hughes but he was good entertainment value and he certainly contributed to the festive mood at Valcartier, a mood that was a compound of militia summer camp, old time revival meeting and small town carnival.

As men poured in, more than 35,000 in all, Hughes organized them into provisional units. Militia commanding officers now learned that their units would not go overseas as distinct entities but as numbered battalions of the Canadian Expeditionary Force. It took Hughes several attempts to draft an order of battle, but by early September he had divided the contingent into a divisional headquarters and 16 infantry battalions. In this new organization, only the 19th Dragoons retained their prewar title, the remainder of the Alberta units went into four of the new CEF units. The 35th Central Alberta Horse, 116 strong, were com-

Fig. 8.

67. First movements on horseback.

1. The recruit should be impressed with the importance of not hanging on by the reins and should be told that if he does so he will injure his horse's mouth and make it difficult to ride.

FIG. 6. VIEWED FROM FRONT.

Bit-reins shown shaded.

FIG. 7. VIEWED FROM ABOVE.

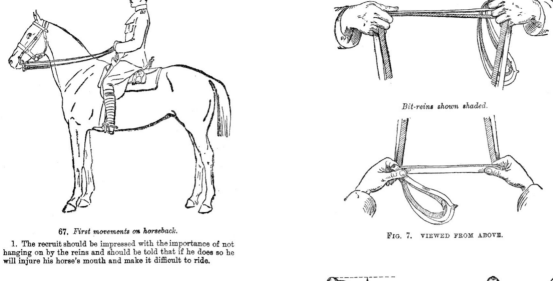

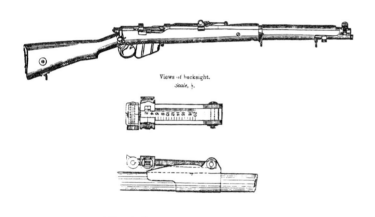

Views of backsight.
Scale, ½.

Saddlery, universal—
Bucket, rifle, Cavalry. (Mark I.) ... ... 1 Leather, reversible.
See § 12714.

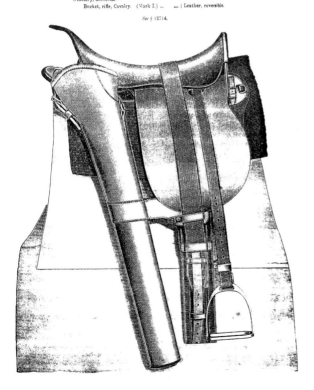

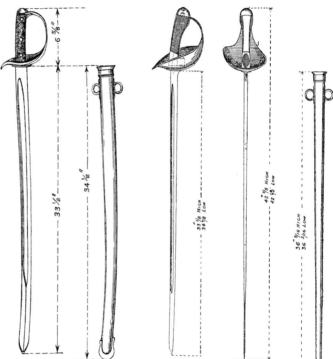

The cavalry world, 1914

Illustrations from period military publications depict important elements in the world of the mounted soldier in 1914. The picture at upper left is the correct position for sitting on a horse while that at upper right demonstrates the correct method of holding the reins. Cavalry weapons depicted are the .303 calibre Short Magazine Lee Enfield Rifle Mk III, and the 1890 (left) and 1908 Pattern Swords. The 1908 Pattern Sword, with its thin blade, was the last combat sword to see service in the Commonwealth armies and is still worn on parade today by Canadian armoured officers. Below is the 1912 Universal Pattern Saddle, with its rifle boot or holster, a long overdue improvement. SOURCES: *LIST OF CHANGES IN BRITISH WAR MATERIAL*, VOL 2 (SWORDS, RIFLE AND SADDLE) AND *CAVALRY TRAINING, 1912* (MOUNTED FIGURE AND REINS)

"It's a Long Way to Tipperary": Strathcona CPR station, 26 August 1914
The 19th Alberta Dragoons get a rousing send-off from the people of Edmonton as they depart for Valcartier Camp. The Dragoons were the only militia cavalry unit in the First Contingent to go overseas as an intact unit; all other militia mounted units were converted to infantry. The war is clearly a great adventure still and the civilian well-wishers fully expect these men to be back shortly – if not by Christmas, not long afterward. GLENBOW MUSEUM, NC-6-1210

bined with cavalry units from British Columbia, Manitoba and Saskatchewan to form the 5th Battalion, CEF, popularly known as the "Western Cavalry," while drafts from the 15th Light Horse, 21st Hussars and 23rd Rangers ended up in the 6th Battalion. The Edmonton Fusiliers, which had arrived at Valcartier with a strength of 1,247, were combined with a tiny detachment of 77 officers and men from Ottawa to form the 9th Battalion while the 103rd Regiment "Calgary Rifles," 846 strong, was combined with the smaller 106th "Winnipeg Light Infantry" to form the 10th Battalion (Canadians).

Hughes despised the Canadian permanent force and made no provision in the order of battle for regular units. He exiled the Royal Canadian Regiment to Bermuda to replace the British garrison, told the Royal Canadian Dragoons and Lord Strathcona's Horse they could only go overseas if their officers and men enlisted individually in the new CEF infantry units and informed the artillery, engineers and service corps their primary function would be to instruct the volunteers. He was forced to relent on these decisions, partly because of political pressure and partly because the regular units were needed to provide some efficiency for the CEF. The Dragoons and the Strathconas became part of the First Contingent and, as a result, the Alberta Dragoons lost their reserve troop which was distributed as reinforcements to these regular mounted units.

Very little practical training was done at Valcartier because there was a general shortage of uniforms, weapons and equipment and, above all, expertise – not to mention the constant interference of the minister of militia. The regulars did what they could and much of the training involved range work as Hughes was a fanatic about marksmanship – "I want, first of all,

men who can pink the enemy every time" he told the volunteers – and about the Ross rifle, which he had been instrumental in getting chosen as the standard longarm of the Canadian army despite the misgivings expressed about it by ordnance experts.[12] Gradually, as Canadian manufacturers geared up to meet the lucrative contracts Hughes distributed freely to firms with Conservative connections, the men began to look like soldiers even if they were still largely a civilian mob dressed in identical clothing. They quickly learned the first lesson of army life which is to "hurry up and wait," and wait they did, for equipment issues and just about everything else in the five weeks the First Contingent remained in Canada. To many, however, it was great fun and the civilian-soldiers retained their sense of humour – sing-songs around the campfire were popular and units composed their own songs including the 2nd Battalion (Eastern Ontario), which sang, to the tune of "Onward, Christian Soldiers":

> Onward Royal Canadians,
> Marching to the range,
> Marching for your breakfast, is this nothing strange?
> Onward Royal Canadians,
> Wash your dirty clothes;
> Where the soap is coming from,
> The orderly sergeant knows.[13]

The 19th Dragoon squadron was fortunate because it had a clearly defined role. Shortly after their arrival at Valcartier the Dragoons were issued swords, as they had wisely left their own in Edmonton and – both more impressive and more useful – Colt .45 automatics. They took a few days to get settled in and then Griesbach, responsible for squadron training, started serious work. His syllabus was often interrupted by Hughes's latest whim and the general confusion, not to mention an argument he had with the squadron veterinary officer whom he had replaced and the necessity to attend horse boards for the more than 8,000 animals in camp, nearly 300 of which were found unfit, including one aged nag which turned out to have been rejected 15 years before for service in South Africa. There was great excitement on 13 September 1914 when a stampede occurred at the Remount Depot which led to some lively scenes in the tent lines. From the diary that he kept during September 1914 it would appear that Griesbach managed to give the Dragoons 10½ days training that month, mostly mounted and dismounted drill, range work and sword drill although the squadron did have four successive field days with each of the four infantry brigades in the Contingent during which they practised scouting and screening, advance to contact, advance, flank and rear guards.

All too soon, it was time to sail. The Dragoons received embarkation orders on 24 September and spent the next five days packing stores and equipment, taking their mounts into Quebec City to be loaded on the horse transports and cleaning up their tent lines. Two days later, the squadron had a half holiday which they spent playing football, doing "bicycle sports" and having a "sing-song at night."[14] Over the next four days, the units at Valcartier began to move into Quebec City to board the transports and the Dragoons went on board the SS *Arcadian* at 9 P.M on 29 September.

When the camp broke up, the happiest man was Sam Hughes. The government had authorized a strength of only 25,000 for the First Contingent but by early September there were nearly 35,000 assembled at Valcartier and, although just under 5,000 were eventually released for one reason or another, Hughes was still 5,000 men over the authorized strength. Dreading the decision that would have to be made about which units would have to be left behind, Hughes put it off. When he confessed his problem to Borden, the prime minister told him that all 30,000 could go and the mercurial Hughes burst into tears. When he bid "his boys" farewell Hughes assured them that, in the unlikely event "of the war lasting until the spring he himself would take the field" at their head – a promise many must have heard with a sinking heart.[15]

As the transports carrying the First Contingent made their way down the St. Lawrence on 1 October 1914, Sam Hughes darted from ship to ship in a steam launch to distribute bundles of his farewell message, "Where Duty Leads," to his "boys." It informed them that the world regarded them as a "marvel" because they had "been perfected in rifle shooting" and were "as fine a body – Officers and men – as ever faced a foe." Now they were off on the great crusade to defend the "gigantic power of liberty" and although some would not return, Hughes assured them that the man "who goes down in the cause of freedom never dies – Immortality is his."[16] As the minister's boat receded into the distance, hundreds of copies of his prose littered the rippling surface of the St. Lawrence.

"Greatest conflict in all history": The opening weeks of war

Throughout August and September 1914, while men across Canada besieged recruiting offices and assembled at Valcartier, the armies marched in Europe. Of the major combatants at the outbreak of war, only Germany possessed an offensive war plan, which was based on the probability that she would face a war on two fronts. Since Russia would be slower to mobilize, the German General Staff calculated that a single, massive blow would defeat France before Russia would be able to cross Germany's eastern frontier. To avoid being delayed by the French fortresses on that nation's frontier, this plan called for a major offensive by three large armies, totalling nearly 800,000 men, to traverse Belgium and move west in a gigantic wheeling movement that would ultimately swing around Paris, take the French armies massed on the border in the rear, and squash them up against their own frontier. For its part, the French general staff played right into these calculations by advancing into Alsace and Lorraine, on the German left flank.

On 5 August, only a few hours after the British ultimatum had expired, German forces entered Belgium. The small Belgian army, six divisions strong, fought gamely but was more or less brushed aside, although the necessity of besieging the Belgian frontier fortresses imposed some delay on the Germans. At the same time, the French movement into Alsace and Lorraine came to an ignominious end when the French army discovered that offensive spirit withered in the face of machineguns and modern artillery. Suffering heavy casualties, the French withdrew behind their frontier but convinced, despite all evidence to the contrary, that the weight of the German attack was going to come in the centre, they massed at that point to launch another attack that was also repulsed with heavy losses. By 22 August, the powerful German right wing had crushed Belgian resistance and was advancing on the drab industrial town of Mons where, for the first time, they encountered the British Expeditionary Force (BEF), a cavalry and four infantry divisions, under Field-Marshal Sir John French.

The true nature of the enemy's movements were becoming clear to the French general staff and, desperately trying to redeploy to the northeast, they asked the British commander to make a stand to gain time. Sir John agreed and, on 23 August 1914, the British army fought its first battle in Europe since Waterloo. The commander of the Third German Army, the leading enemy force, completely unaware of the presence of British regulars in his front and encountering unexpected resistance by an unknown enemy made a series of hasty and un-coordinated attacks that were beaten off by British regulars who could deliver 12-15 aimed rounds of rifle fire per minute. The stand at Mons gained a respite for the two Allies and, by the time the BEF withdrew the next day, the French had begun to re-assemble to protect Paris. On 26 August, the British fought a second delaying action at Le Cateau which so impressed the enemy that they did not immediately pursue when the British again pulled back. The French realignment was now nearly complete and the German decision to wheel inward of Paris, not outward as planned, exposed their flank to fresh

French forces which promptly attacked it. They were beaten off but German senior commanders were starting to lose their nerve – the master plan had failed and, on 9 September, they ordered a withdrawal to positions along the Aisne River.

The Allies now went over to the offensive and launched a series of attacks along the Aisne which were beaten back by artillery and machineguns. The lethality of modern weaponry had been made apparent in the first four weeks of fighting and men began to dig hasty entrenchments, "scrapes" the British called them, to reduce their vulnerability – the beginning of trench warfare. September and October witnessed the so-called "race to the sea" as the opposing armies tried to find an open flank to break the deadlock and by the first week of October the BEF was in Flanders where it would more or less remain for the next four years

In Canada, the course of the war was followed in newspaper reports that were often incorrect but usually dramatic. A typical approach was that of the *Red Deer News* which, on 19 August 1914, devoted its entire front page to a couple of lengthy and breathless headlines:

GREATEST BATTLE IN WORLD HISTORY
PROCEEDING
The Greatest Conflict in All History is Now in Progress with Battle Lines Extending Two Hundred Miles Long. So Appalling is the Situation that Never in the History of the World Has There Been Such Immense Hosts Opposed to Each Other With Every Death-Dealing Device Modern Ingenuity Can Devise. Two Immense Armies of a Million Men Each Are Now Face to Face.[17]

Two weeks later, the *News* informed its readership that the Russian army might reach Berlin by the end of September, an outrageously inaccurate statement considering that German forces had just decisively defeated the large but poorly-led Russian armies in two decisive battles at Tannenberg and the Masurian Lakes, bringing to a halt a Russian offensive into eastern Germany.

The Central Powers of Germany and Austria-Hungary were less successful on other fronts. An Austro-Hungarian invasion of Serbia was stopped by the latter's determined resistance, resulting in a stalemate. But a conflict that had begun in the Balkans relentlessly spread until it was global in scope: Turkey joined the Central Powers while Japan joined the Allies, and Bulgaria, Italy and Rumania teetered on the edge. By the late autumn of 1914 there was fighting in Africa and central and southeast Asia as the Allies began to roll up Germany's overseas colonies.

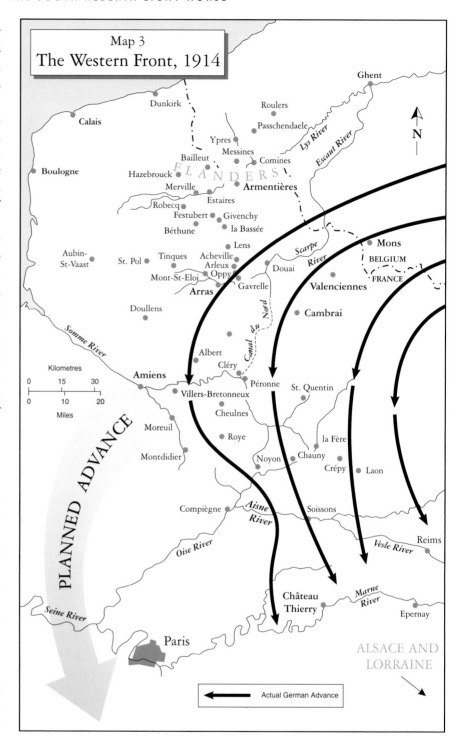

"If you have the guts": The First Contingent in England, October 1914 to January 1915

The First Canadian Contingent crossed the Atlantic without incident and this was just as well because on the 19th Dragoons' transport, the *Arcadian*, there was no accommodation for nearly 200 men who had to sleep in life boats and on hatch combings. The convoy, the largest escorted by the Royal Navy up to that time, arrived in Plymouth in the early morning of 14 October and, one by one, the grey-painted transports, many decorated with maple leaf foliage brought from Canada, made their way up Plymouth Sound to anchor in the historic naval base. As the

Swimming on Salisbury Plain, 1914
The men of the First Contingent on Salisbury Plain had to endure the wettest winter in six decades and their plight was so bad that the Canadian government officially protested the conditions. Subsequent Canadian units were more comfortably (and dryly) housed. It was all still an adventure, however, and the boys remained in good spirits as this picture demonstrates. *THE WAR PICTORIAL*, 1914

first Dominion troops to arrive from overseas, the Canadians attracted considerable attention and a British journalist who was present remembered that

> A big steamship was coming directly shorewards, like a vast phantom emerging from the mist …… And then suddenly, it seemed like to me like a cinema transformation, her contour seemed to be traced in khaki … then I caught the wavering sounds of a band playing somewhere on board and gave a start as the revelation came upon me for the first time that it was "The Maple Leaf For Ever" ……
>
> A naval petty officer paused at my side and exchanged looks, "The Canadians" he said in a voice tense with pent-up enthusiasm, "Thirty-one transports full of them!"[18]

The troops disembarked the next day and marched through streets lined with cheering locals to board the quaint little English trains that took them to Salisbury Plain, a rolling stretch of Wiltshire countryside dotted with farms and small villages.

Here the Contingent went under canvas in several large, adjoining camps. They enjoyed fine weather for a week and then it began to rain and it continued to rain on 89 of the next 129 days, including one awful stretch of 75 days, of which only 5 were dry. The tent lines quickly became a quagmire and almost everyone, with the exception of those fortunate few billeted in houses, remained wet or at least slightly damp for weeks on end. The horse lines were such a swamp that the cavalrymen rode their horses to be watered as they could not lead them on foot without losing their boots in the clinging, sucking mud surrounding the troughs.

At this point the First Contingent, soon be re-designated the Canadian Division, was still largely a collection of civilians. Discipline was lax, leave (authorized or unauthorized) was frequent and there were problems in the pubs of the surrounding villages where drunken soldiers (and officers) created disturbances. Five days after the arrival of the Contingent, the 19th Dragoons

were ordered to send mounted patrols to these villages to police them and they continued to do so until Major-General Edwin Alderson, the British officer appointed to command the division, authorized the establishment of regimental wet canteens in the camps. This did not please the teetotal Sam Hughes but it improved the behaviour of the division.

Nor was Hughes pleased with the criticisms Alderson and other British officers made about the Contingent's uniforms, weapons and equipment, hastily supplied by Canadian manufacturers. The Canadian pattern tunic was too tight and not only chafed the wearer but frequently split along its seams; the overcoats issued were neither wind nor waterproof while the load-carrying equipment, foisted on an unsuspecting militia department in the 1890s by Dr. William Oliver, a British army surgeon, was a nightmare tangle of straps, buckles, belts and attachments. It was modified at the outbreak of war to take into account some of the criticisms that had been levied against it for nearly a decade but even the improved version came under fire for having a "yoke not adjustable; canvas valise tears away from leather braces; pouches unsuitable; waist belt too narrow; entrenching tool heavy and difficult to carry, chafes thighs and bangs about, not bullet proof; colour of equipment too light."[19] The issue entrenching tool – one of Sam Hughes's bright ideas and patented in the name of his secretary Ena McAdam – had a folding blade with a hole in it that could supposedly be used as a shield for a rifleman lying prone who would stick his muzzle through the aperture. It was a piece of useless junk and everyone knew it but it was kept in service. Many had doubts about the Ross rifle, which had a distressing tendency to jam if fired rapidly but no one wanted to voice those doubts loudly because of Hughes's intense personal conviction that the Ross was the finest military longarm in the world. The worst thing, however, were the Canadian-made boots which "might do very well for a farmer making an excursion to his barns on a Sunday afternoon, or for his daughter going to church" but which soon "were reduced to a sodden mass, and the paper from which the heels

1914: How they thought it was going to be
An Alberta Dragoon takes cover behind his long-nosed chum while training on Salisbury Plain. Note the mud on the horse. The cavalry soon learned that these tactics did not work on the Western Front. *THE WAR PICTORIAL*, 1914

were made returned to its primitive pulp."[20] Men forced to wear these articles on Salisbury Plain in the wet winter of 1914-1915 bitterly called them "Sham Shoes."

Many former militia officers, used to relaxed peacetime ways when an officer could be popular with his subordinates, found it difficult to adjust to the stricter discipline of a wartime army. Others made the transition easily and one such was Lieutenant-Colonel Russell Boyle, formerly of the 15th Light Horse and now commanding the 10th Battalion (Canadians). Faced with an unruly faction in his unit that constantly questioned his authority and criticized his actions, Boyle resolved his problem by standing in front of his battalion, stripping off his tunic and issuing an invitation to all comers: "If you have the guts … we'll have it out right here."[21] One look at Boyle, 6 feet tall and a beefy rancher from Crossfield, as well as a decorated veteran of the South African War, was enough – no one stepped up and Boyle thereafter had no problems in the 10th Battalion.

In the 19th Dragoons, Lieutenant-Colonel Jamieson handled matters more traditionally – a defaulter charged with being "Absent Without Leave" for 28 days received 28 days Field Punishment No. 2. Normally reserved for major transgressions, this punishment entailed being "kept in irons" and "made to labour as if he were undergoing punishment with hard labour."[22] Jamieson was also strict with his officers. Learning that some of his subalterns had not been attending "Stables," the thrice-daily cavalry parade when men curried, combed and fed their "long-nosed chums," but had been leaving the NCOs to supervise this important task, he issued a regimental order which was read out to the squadron that in future all troop officers were to attend this important function, no matter what their other tasks were at the moment. Thereafter, when the squadron trumpeter sounded the traditional call ("Come to the stable, all ye who are able, and give your old horses, a little more hay, and give your old horses, a

Royal inspection, November 1914

The 19th Dragoons, the divisional cavalry squadron of the 1st Canadian Division, proudly ride past King George V on Salisbury Plain on 3 November 1914. For once, it is not raining. The Dragoons and, later, the Canadian Light Horse were the only Canadian mounted units to retain the stetson for overseas service. *THE WAR PICTORIAL, 1914*

little more hay") young lieutenants headed for the horse lines.[23]

The Dragoons continued training throughout the autumn and into the early winter. They commenced with troop mounted and dismounted drill and then progressed to squadron drill on foot and horse, interspersed with sword drill which most men probably did not take seriously. When Major William Griesbach, ordered to return to Canada to command a new battalion of the CEF, left them at the end of November, they were exercising with the Divisional Cyclist Company which had been attached to Jamieson's command, possibly under the incontestable logic that mounted troops were mounted troops, no matter what they rode. In early December, the squadron moved into billets at Newfoundland Farm and were finally able to get most of their horses under good shelter and, in the New Year, transferred to hutted accommodation at Bulford Barracks although they still had to shelter some of their mounts in marquee tents.

Throughout all this time the rain kept falling although, thankfully, it held off on 3 November 1914 when the squadron rode in review on Salisbury Plain past Their Majesties King George V and Queen Mary. By Christmas the squadron War Diarist had given up recording the weather although it probably rained that day and on New Year's Day, which was a full holiday for officers and men. The weather was definitely fair on 13 January 1915 when Lieutenant Kenneth Edmiston of 3 Troop married Miss Mary Allen of Ottawa in the parish church at nearby Netheravon. The lieutenant's troop accompanied the bridal couple to the church as a mounted escort while the entire squadron rode to Netheravon to attend the service. As the happy couple emerged, they walked under the traditional triumphal arch of swords formed by Edmiston's fellow Dragoons.

In January 1915, when the Canadian Division was confident that it would shortly be transferring to the continent, Alderson made the decision that Hughes should have made four months previously – since his division had to conform with the War Establishment of a British infantry division, which was three brigades each with four battalions, four of the 16 battalions in the division would have to be removed. Alderson's choices were the 9th, 11th, 12th and 17th Battalions. Thus, the Edmonton Fusiliers, which more or less formed the 9th Battalion, were left behind as a training and reinforcement unit. Outraged Fusiliers

blamed this decision on politics as their commanding officer, Lieutenant-Colonel Garnett Dunham, was a Liberal and Hughes always played favourites with Conservative officers. Be that as it may, the division carried out more intensive training in January than it had before. The 19th Dragoons concentrated on range work and were thankful that, unlike the infantry which had the cranky Ross, they were armed with Lee-Enfield cavalry carbines, a more reliable weapon. On three separate day-long exercises, the squadron acted as a "skeleton enemy force" against each of the three infantry brigades in the division and also did some practical schemes in advance and rear guard work.[24] It was all very interesting but the question on the mind of most of the Dragoons and soldiers suffering under the teeming rain on Salisbury Plain was – when were they going to France to win the war?

They need not have worried because the beast was patiently waiting for them. In October 1914 the opposing armies on the continent manoeuvred north and south from the Aisne. Except for a small enclave on the Channel, Belgium was now almost entirely occupied by German troops and it was against this enclave that the enemy launched his next major attack. The Belgians beat it off and the Germans switched south towards the Belgian market town of Ypres (pronounced "Eee-preh" but universally known to English-speaking soldiers as "Wipers"), only to run head on into the BEF which was advancing from that same town. On 24 October 1914 the Germans threw four newly-raised and poorly-trained corps of youthful reservists, mostly volunteers from universities and technical schools, against entrenched British regular infantry and the resulting slaughter is still known in Germany as the *Kindermord von Ypern* (the children's murder at Ypres). Five days later, the Germans tried again but were beaten off with heavy losses while a third and final attempt on 11 November was also rebuffed. The arrival of winter in December, which put an end to active operations, found the opposing armies entrenched in continuous positions – what one historian has called "a ribbon of death" but more popularly known as the Western Front – that ran nearly 500 miles from the English Channel to Switzerland.[25]

All the combatants had suffered terrible losses in the opening months of the war. France lost 900,000 men, including a large part of her prewar regular army. German losses were somewhat less, but still heavy being 130,000 at the 1st Battle of Ypres alone. Particu-

Love conquers all

Lieutenant Kenneth Edmiston, 24, of the 19th Alberta Dragoons married Miss Mary Allen from Ottawa at Netheravon church on 3 January 1915 in a service attended by the all ranks of the 19th Dragoons. As the happy couple emerge from the church, Edmiston's troop forms the traditional arch of swords. Edmiston, a graduate of the Royal Military College and a pre-war Dragoon, survived the war. Although the bride would probably not be interested, her arch is formed by 1890 Pattern swords. *THE WAR PICTORIAL*, 1915

larly hard hit was the small British regular army – between August and December 1914, the seven British regular infantry divisions that fought in Europe lost 3,627 officers and 86,237 men killed or wounded, about 90% of their strength. There were still regular units in overseas garrisons, territorial or reserve units in the home islands, and there were also the military forces of the Empire but their numbers were not enough to wage a conflict that consumed men seemingly without pause. For all intents and purposes, Britain would have to recruit, arm, equip and train an entirely new army, a process that would take nearly eighteen months.

"Maintain order with fixed bayonets": The 31st Battalion is raised

For their part, Canada and Alberta were ready and eager to provide more men. The First Contingent had no sooner left Canadian waters than an offer was made to Britain to raise a Second Contingent. Before it was officially accepted by the British government on 31 October, Hughes informed the military district commanders that this new force would be raised and over the next few weeks, its composition was debated until it was agreed that it would consist of fourteen infantry battalions, numbered 18 to 31, which would be recruited across Canada with Military District 13, Alberta, assigned the task of raising the 31st Battalion. Separate from this Second Contingent, the government also decided to create thirteen regiments of mounted rifles, a decision apparently prompted by the disappointment in Western Canada that mounted units had largely been excluded from the First Contingent. It was felt that, until mobile warfare returned to the Western Front, they might usefully serve in Palestine against the Turks. Military District 13 was therefore directed to organize the 3rd, 12th and 13th Mounted Rifle Regiments.

There was keen interest in Alberta in these new units, particularly the 31st Battalion which was popularly called the "Alberta Battalion" because it was raised across the province (although this title was never officially authorized). Recruiting offices were

Mugging for the camera: Dragoons, 1915

Having just survived the Second Battle of Ypres in April 1915, Corporal John A. Jackson (left) and Lieutenant John W. Tipton of the 19th Alberta Dragoons mug for a postcard they sent home in July 1915. Both men belonged to the prewar Dragoons and, here Tipton shows off a souvenir acquisition. Tipton and Jackson survived the war. Meanwhile, to the right, Troopers Ottreal (left) and Eisler pose just after the Dragoon squadron landed in France. Both men are armed with Model 1911 Colt .45 automatics in leather holsters and are wearing leather magazine carriers on their waist belts. COURTESY, COLIN MICHAUD

opened in Calgary, Claresholm, Edmonton, Lethbridge, Medicine Hat, Pincher Creek, Red Deer, Wetaskiwin and Youngstown with a quota set for each office ranging from 375 for the two larger cities down to 25 from Youngstown and area. Recruiting began on the morning of 16 November and many men waited through the night to sign up. The first man to officially enlist was Lance-Corporal F. Clement of the 103rd Regiment who did so at Calgary at 9.30 A.M. that day and he was followed by hundreds of other eager volunteers until recruiting was temporarily suspended when the limited supply of uniforms and equipment ran out. When it resumed nine days later, the crowds were even larger and more eager, so much so that the 101st Regiment in Edmonton had to call out a guard "to maintain order with fixed bayonets."[26] In just two active days of recruiting, the 31st Battalion was completed to a strength of 36 officers and 1,134 other ranks with 27 officers and 409 other ranks from Calgary, 5 officers and 348 other ranks from Edmonton, 100 and 101 other ranks from Medicine Hat and Lethbridge respectively and the balance from smaller towns. Recruiters had their pick and they chose the best, turning away hundreds. Although he might be forgiven for bias, it was the opinion of one of the unit's senior officers that no "finer body of men were ever brought together," a sentiment that was echoed by every senior officer who inspected the Alberta Battalion.[27]

The shipping list or muster roll of the 31st Battalion permits some analysis of the background of the men of the unit. Recruits to the Canadian Expeditionary Force were asked to provide their country of birth and the address of their next of kin, crucial questions bearing on their nationality. Approximately 80% of the recruits to the 31st Battalion stated that they were born in the British Isles. This is in excess of the 65% figure for the whole CEF in 1914, a figure some Canadian historians have assumed means that the vast majority of the men who joined the CEF in the early years of the war were actually British citizens. This assumption, however, does not take into account the heavy immigration into Canada from the British Isles in the preceding three decades and many of the recruits who stated they were born in the British Isles, probably came to Canada as small children. If the question had been asked (and, indeed, if Canadians had made the distinction between being a British citizen and a Canadian citizen in 1914), they would most likely have described themselves as Canadians because they had clearly established roots in the country. The proof of this statement can be found in the addresses of the next of kin contained in the shipping list – if men born in the British Isles, who gave North American addresses on their enlistment papers, are listed separately from those providing British addresses (the true "British born"), the latter category falls from 80% to 49.8% The ethnic composition of the 1,286 officers and men of the 31st Battalion was as follows:[28]

Born in the British Isles (next of kin in Britain):		640 (49.8%)
England:	407	
Scotland:	165	
Ireland:	37	
Wales:	25	
Channel Islands:	3	
Isle of Man:	3	
Total:	640	
Born in the British Isles (next of kin in North America):		381 (29.7%)
England:	199	
Scotland:	153	
Ireland:	21	
Wales:	6	
Channel Islands:	2	
Total:	381	
Born elsewhere in the British Empire (next of kin not in North America):		19 (1.5%)
Born elsewhere in the British Empire including Canada (next of kin in North America):		202 (15.7%)
Other Nationalities:		39 (3%)
Miscellaneous:		5 (.05%)
Total:		1,286 (100%)

Appointed to command the new battalion was Lieutenant-Colonel Arthur H. Bell, an officer of Lord Strathcona's Horse who had served in South Africa and had been on the staff of Military District 13. The second-in-command was Major W.H. Hewgill, a native of Moose Jaw, Saskatchewan. The unit was quartered in the Horse Show Buildings in the Exhibition grounds at Calgary and, in the first week of December, commenced training which mainly consisted of parade ground drill, route marching, skirmish tactics and range work with their "Maggie Ross" – the Ross service rifle. Other than that, there was not much real work done to prepare the men for the Western Front because no one in Canada in the winter of 1914-1915 knew how to properly train soldiers for modern warfare. The unit's activities were followed closely by hometown papers which assured their readers that local boys were being well fed and cared for in the army. The 31st Battalion was particularly popular in Calgary where it was feted at civic banquets by service clubs, provided with free passes to the moving picture shows and generally acclaimed by one and all. The people of Calgary contributed funds to buy it musical instruments so that by the first week in January 1915, the battalion had a band and, in April, the Anglican element in the unit marched behind it to Sunday service at the Church of the Redeemer. This annoyed Captain J.C. Macpherson, a Presbyterian who, not wanting to be outdone by the "adherents of any rival denomination,"

got together a few pipers and organized a pipe band of his own. Thereafter, for a few Sundays, the Presbyterians marched to Divine service to the martial music of the homeland of their faith, and continued in this prideful path until the unofficial band was suppressed by the Commanding Officer. Whether this drastic step was taken by reason of an inherent, if ill-judged, dislike of the pipes on the part of Col. Bell, or in order to spare the citizens of Calgary unnecessary suffering, or merely to prevent bloodshed and an internecine religious war, the records do not reveal.[29]

All in all, the nearly six months the 31st Battalion spent in Calgary were a pleasant time that was later fondly recalled.

Sharing the Exhibition Buildings at Calgary with the 31st was the 12th Regiment of Canadian Mounted Rifles. Raised principally from recruits of the 19th Dragoons and 23rd Rangers, it was under the command of Lieutenant-Colonel George MacDonald, formerly of the 15th Light Horse. The other Alberta Mounted Rifle units, the 3rd and 13th, which mobilized and trained at Medicine Hat and Pincher Creek respectively, also drew heavily on the five prewar militia cavalry units in the province, the 3rd being formed from the 15th Light Horse and 35th Alberta Horse while the 13th took men from the 15th Light as well as the 19th Dragoons, 21st Hussars and 23rd Rangers. The regiments of mounted rifles were very popular in Alberta but they were never to see action as units – in early 1916 they were converted to infantry and distributed as reinforcements for existing units on the Western Front.

Winter wear on the Western Front, 1915-1916
Lieutenant Walter Kingsley ("King") Jull shows off his goatskin vest, issued during the battalion's first winter in the trenches but disliked because it made the wearer smell like a goat. A former member of the 103rd Regiment, "Calgary Rifles," Jull joined the Alberta battalion in 1914 at age 23 and won the Military Cross in action. He continued in the postwar militia, rising to be CO of the Calgary Regiment (Tank) in 1939. GLENBOW MUSEUM, NA-3868-33

Lieutenant-Colonel Nelson Spencer
The former mayor of Medicine Hat, Spencer joined the 31st Battalion in 1916 when the unit he raised, the 175th Battalion, was broken up for reinforcements. He commanded the Alberta Battalion in the last two months of 1918 and won the DSO. Spencer served as a postwar member of the Alberta Legislative Assembly. GLENBOW MUSEUM, NA-3456-2

(Right) **Private Donald Fraser**
Fraser, a 32-year-old bank clerk from Calgary, joined the 31st Battalion in November 1914. He fought with the unit in 1915-1916 before transferring to the 6th Brigade Machinegun Company and was badly wounded at Passchendaele in November 1917. Fraser kept a diary of his wartime experiences which he expanded while recovering from his wounds. It survived and is one of the most compelling memoirs of the life of a private soldier on the Western Front. Here, he is shown in the goatskin vest issued during the winter of 1915-1916. COURTESY, PROFESSOR REGINALD ROY

Private Howard J. Exton on his way overseas, 1915

Exton, a 22-year-old bookkeeper from Calgary and a former member of the 103rd "Calgary Rifles," joined the 31st Battalion in November 1914 and survived the war, being awarded the Meritorious Service Medal. Exton served in the Provost Corps and the Pay Corps during the Second World War and ended his military career in 1956 as a captain and paymaster of the South Alberta Light Horse. GLENBOW MUSEUM, NA-3868-4

(Above) **For whom they waited**

Typical of the photos that graced the mantel of many an Alberta home in the war years is this picture of Sergeant Edward Guy Gibson taken at Bramshott in England. Gibson, a married 34-year-old rancher from the Red Deer area, enlisted in the 187th Battalion in May 1916 but when this unit was broken up, he was sent to the 31st Battalion and fought at the Somme, Vimy Ridge, Passchendaele and Amiens. Gibson was another of the lucky ones – he was wounded but made it back to Red Deer and his wife, Bella. GLENBOW MUSEUM, NA-3183-1

(Left) **Private Arthur N. McIlveen, 1914**

A former member of the 103rd Calgary Rifles, McIlveen was 22 when he enlisted in the 31st Battalion in November 1914 and, although wounded, survived the war and was awarded the Military Medal for gallantry in action. GLENBOW MUSEUM, NA-3868-4

81

In the last week of April 1915, the units of the Second Contingent began to move overseas and the 31st Battalion expected that it would shortly be leaving Calgary. The big news, however, was the rumour that the 1st Canadian Division had been in battle on the Western Front. Details were sketchy and often conflicting – the *Red Deer News* held that "Canadians Had Covered Themselves in Glory" while the *Calgary Herald* took a very different view – "Canadians Mowed Down Like Sheep."[30] These references were to the 2nd Battle of Ypres fought on 22-27 April 1915 – and both papers were right.

"We didn't know enough … to know that we were licked": Ypres, April 1915

When the 1st Canadian Division on Salisbury Plain was reviewed a second time by King George V on 4 February 1915, its officers and men were sure that they would shortly be going to France. Five days later, the division moved to Avonmouth and embarked in a motley fleet of small transports. It was a wretched crossing, racked by three days of storms and everyone was truly thankful when they disembarked on 12 February at the small fishing port of St. Nazaire on the Brittany peninsula – particularly the 10th Battalion which, spotting an unguarded cask of rum on the docks, managed to purloin it as a useful incentive to unit morale. At St. Nazaire, the Canadians made their first acquaintance with the "40 and 8s," the small French railway cars marked "40 *hommes*, 8 *chevaux (longs)*" in which they travelled to Hazebrouck on the Belgian border. Although still part of the Canadian Expeditionary Force (CEF), they now came under the command of the BEF which controlled British Empire troops on the Western Front and would share the fate of that entity for the next three and a half years. Unit by unit, including the Dragoon Squadron, the men of the division spent 48 hours in the frontline trenches with experienced British units to learn the tricks of the trade. In early March the division took over a quiet sector near Neuve Chapelle.

It was not quiet for long. Following their failure to take Ypres in November 1914, the German army had gone on the defensive in the west in order to shift troops to the Eastern Front where the Russians were again massing. The severe winter of 1914-1915 slowed operations although the French, anxious to recover the German-occupied part of their country, mounted a series of unsuccessful attacks in December 1914 and January 1915. For his part, Sir John French, the commander of the BEF, did not feel that his army, crippled by its losses in 1914 and short of heavy artillery and shells, was capable of a major attack. It was not until March 1915 that he agreed to make one to secure a limited objective – the Aubers Ridge near Neuve Chapelle, to the right of the Canadian sector. This operation was carried out on 10 March and Alderson's Canadian division was tasked with distracting the enemy forces opposite their sector by engaging in a concentrated display of artillery and rifle fire. The British attack was initially successful, the German frontline trenches were taken but a breakdown in communications, confusion and, above all, a shortage of artillery, limited success. For their part, the Canadians had a good time making noise although they made the disconcerting discovery that their Ross rifles were prone to jamming.

The Canadian Division remained another two uneventful weeks near Neuve Chapelle. It was during this period that the 19th Dragoons found that, because there was little need for mounted troops on the Western Front, they had become the divisional "maids of all work." The Dragoons served as orderlies, traffic police, guides, and labour details and also took over the responsibility of distributing remounts to the other units in the division. Occasionally they carried out reconnaissance patrols but the trench system severely restricted their effectiveness. At other times, they carried out mounted and dismounted drill and, on 14 April 1915, when the division was ordered to move to the Ypres Salient, acted as guides to ensure that the three infantry brigades reached their assigned areas.

This projection into the German lines around Ypres had resulted from the fighting of the previous autumn. The Salient, as everyone called it, was a low flat area, cut across by canals and dykes, and exposed on three sides to German observation and artillery fire. Between 14 and 17 April the 2nd and 3rd Infantry Brigades took up positions along the Gravenstafel Ridge northwest of Ypres while the 1st Brigade remained in reserve. On the Canadians' left flank were two French divisions scheduled to be relieved in the near future by British troops. Shortly after the Canadians arrived, however, German deserters brought disconcerting information that an enemy attack was planned on the Salient and it would include the use of poison gas.

This information was accurate. The Russians had recently launched a major operation against Austria-Hungary and

No complaints about the food: Dinner time for the 31st Battalion
Men of the Alberta Battalion eating at an outdoor mess. Note the cooks in the upper left corner. The caption to this photo suggests that it was taken in England but the uniforms, belts and the fact that there are men in civilian clothing among the happy munchers indicate that it was more likely taken at Calgary in the autumn of 1914 before the battalion was fully clothed. GLENBOW MUSEUM, NA-3456-5

Taking a break

Men of the 31st Battalion take a break while on a route march not far from their barracks in the Calgary exhibition grounds, which can be seen in the distance. Judging by the rather careless way these men are handling their weapons, this picture was taken not long after the battalion was raised in the autumn of 1914. They would learn quickly that even the slightest speck of dirt would cause the Ross rifle to jam – a distressing defect that often had fatal consequences in action. GLENBOW MUSEUM, NA-3868-5

Vienna's appeals for assistance forced the Germans to transfer major forces from the west to the east. To disguise this movement and to test out a frightening new weapon, the German high command decided to attack the Salient. The Germans had previously used tear gas against both the French and the Russians but this time they intended to deploy more than 5,000 cylinders of poisonous chlorine gas. The attack was set to begin at 5.45 A.M. on 22 April but gas is a weapon that is dependent on the weather and at dawn that day there was no wind. The attack was therefore postponed until the afternoon and German assault troops, nervous enough about this new weapon and closely packed in the forward trenches near the chlorine cylinders, spent more than ten tense hours waiting until a southerly breeze sprang up late in the afternoon. At 4 P.M, the German artillery brought down a furious bombardment on the French and Canadian forward positions and an hour later the cylinders were opened to discharge a deadly yellowish-green cloud that was carried on the breeze south towards Ypres.

The two French divisions on the left of the Canadians bore the brunt of this terrible weapon although some hit the left flank of the Canadian position. Captain F.A.C. Scrimger, the medical officer of the 14th Battalion (Royal Montreal Regiment), quickly concluded that the gas was chlorine and saved many lives by telling men to urinate in their handkerchiefs and hold them over their mouths and noses to neutralize the effect. The Canadians stood steady but, within minutes, the greater part of the two French divisions disintegrated into a mass of men, horses and wagons fleeing toward Ypres. Corporal Louis Younger of the 19th Dragoons was enjoying a meal with a comrade in an *estaminet* or cafe in Ypres that afternoon. Both men had heard the guns firing to the north but were not concerned until French troops who "were quite demoralized and had thrown away all their equipment," began streaming down the street "in great confusion, claiming that the war was finished as the Germans were using poison gas."[31] A British Cockney soldier went to the door of the cafe and began "denouncing these troops in a wonderful flow of adjectives as they streamed past" to no effect. At the same time, a Canadian artillery officer moving north from Ypres was amazed to encounter a mass of French ambulances, ammunition wagons and transport vehicles "galloping across country through hedges, ditches, and barbed wire" with artillery horses "being used for quick transportation, sometimes with two and three men on their backs."[32] Isolated groups of French soldiers did stand but, in the space of two hours, the Germans advancing slowly (very slowly as they were themselves afraid of their own gas), had pushed a bulge into the Allied lines about 4 miles wide and 2 miles deep.

The Canadian left flank was wide open and all was confusion but Alderson cobbled together a defence line, using almost anyone who could fire a rifle. The 19th Dragoons were ordered to send out small patrols along the front as accurate information about the position of friendly and enemy troops was scarce. Corporal Younger took a patrol to the village of Boesinghe, about 3 miles north of Ypres, and remembered passing "a troop of French cavalry, dressed in their blue uniforms and shining helmets – quite a target for the Germans."[33] Younger found a French artillery battery still in position and firing at Boesinghe and was able to confirm that French were holding on the west side of the Yser Canal and the Divisional Cyclist Company was dispatched to reinforce them.

Early in the evening the French asked for Alderson's support in a counterattack they were planning against the village of Pilckem north of Ypres. In response, Lieutenant-Colonel Russell Boyle's 10th Battalion (Canadians) and Lieutenant-Colonel R.G. Leckie's 16th Battalion (Canadian Scottish) were ordered "to clear" Kitcheners' Wood, a straggling copse about a mile and half southeast of the French objective. At 7 P.M, Boyle's battalion moved forward, the men singing "The Maple Leaf Forever," to the assembly area at Mouse Trap Farm, 500 yards south of their objective. There they waited for the 16th Battalion which did not arrive until 10 P.M and while they did so, Boyle told his battalion that "we have been aching for a fight and now we are going to get it."[34] Just before midnight, the two battalions, with a total strength of about 1,600 officers and men, formed in column of companies with each company deployed in two ranks and 30 yards between companies, moved forward with bayonets fixed to carry out Canada's first attack of the war.

Unfortunately, given the hasty preparations and the general confusion, there had been no time to make a proper reconnaissance of the area, although it was suspected that the fields south

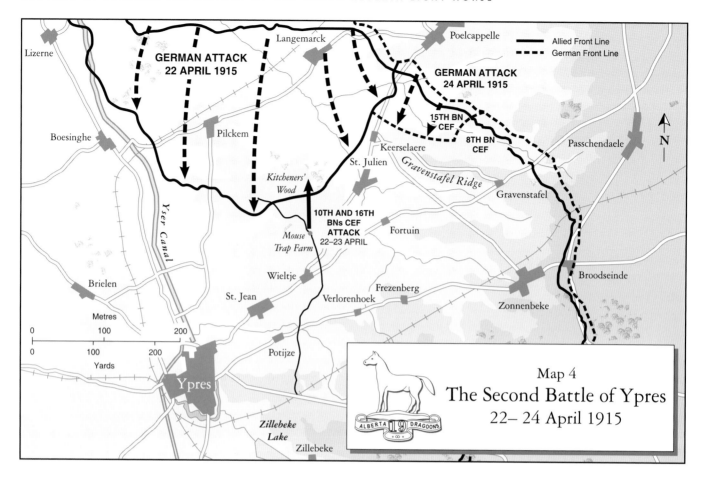

Map 4
The Second Battle of Ypres
22– 24 April 1915

of the Wood were enfiladed by machineguns. The two battalions advanced steadily, trying to keep their formations intact, and all went well for 300 yards until suddenly a flare arched into the night sky and the Maxims opened up – one private of the 10th remembered that the tree line in front "seemed to be lined with machine guns."[35] The lead companies withered away and casualties were heavy in the following companies but the Canadians charged the remaining 200 yards to the Wood only to discover that it was bordered by a hedge with a barbed wire fence, behind which was a shallow trench full of Germans. Cutting, hacking and thrusting their way through this obstacle the Canadians fell on the enemy and hand-to-hand fighting ensued until the Germans retreated into the darkness.

There was now a pause while officers tried to regroup as the two battalions had become jumbled in the fighting. When this was done, they advanced through the Wood which turned out to be full of sandbagged machinegun nests. Vicious and confused fighting followed as small groups of Canadians and Germans shot at each other's muzzle flashes in the underbrush. Boyle was mortally wounded by machinegun fire; his second-in-command was hit and the adjutant took over command of the 10th Battalion. By first light at about 4.30 A.M., the two units, reduced to a quarter of their strength, were holding a line on the north edge of the woods. Knowing he did not have the strength to beat off the German counterattack that was certain to take place, Leckie of the 16th ordered a withdrawal to the shallow trench

at the southern edge of the woods and here he was reinforced by the 2nd Battalion (Eastern Ontario) and the 3rd Battalion (Toronto) which had been led up to the Wood by guides from the 19th Dragoons. The 10th Battalion had gone into the battle for Kitcheners' Wood with 816 all ranks – it came out with 193 and the losses of the 16th Battalion were almost as grievous. For their part, the French did not attack Pilckem that night.*

Throughout the next day, 23 April 1915, as British units arrived to reinforce Alderson's shaky line, the 19th Dragoons guided them into position and also established straggler collection points to gather up the many men who had become detached from their units the previous day. There was heavy fighting around Kitcheners' Wood that day and to the west, with attack being met by counterattack, but at last light the line still held. At this point the German commander, Albrecht, resolved to use gas a second time and this time the target selected was Brigadier-General Arthur Currie's 1st Brigade holding the tip of the salient. If weather conditions were right, this attack was to take

---

* A request by the 10th and 16th Battalions, CEF, for a Battle Honour for Kitcheners' Wood was denied but permission was given for a special badge commemorating the action to be worn by the postwar units that perpetuate these two battalions. As Kitcheners' Wood was an oak plantation, it is in the form of an oakleaf and acorn, and is today worn on both shoulders by the soldiers of the Calgary Highlanders and Canadian Scottish, which perpetuate the 10th and 16th Battalions respectively.

place at 4.30 A.M. the following day and, throughout the preceding night, Currie's men were disturbed to see German flares going up in a near circle around their positions.

At dawn on Saturday, 24 April 1915, a gentle breeze was blowing toward the Canadian lines. Promptly at 4.30 A.M. a heavy artillery bombardment came down on the 1st Brigade just as the men of the 8th (90th Rifles) and 15th (48th Highlanders) Battalions saw a green-yellow wall of vapour about 15 feet high drifting toward them. Fortunately, the 8th Battalion had been expecting a gas attack and had taken the rudimentary precautions of having buckets of water in their trench lines in which men could wet cloths and towels to cover their noses and mouths. The soldiers of that unit still felt the effect of the noxious vapour, however, and found themselves coughing, spitting and wheezing but it did not prevent them from stopping the advancing Germans cold with rapid rifle fire. To the left the 15th Battalion had it worse as the gas concentration was heavier in their area and the unit was unable to prevent their forward trench from being overrun by Germans estimated to be ten times their strength. The 15th fell back to its reserve trenches and the Germans were able to penetrate the northern tip of the salient but were brought up short when reinforcements hastily set up a new defence line. Canadian attempts to stop the German advances were frequently frustrated by their Ross rifles which kept jamming – one man remembered "fellows crying in the trenches because they couldn't fire their damned rifles."[36] Many threw the wretched things away and picked up British Lee-Enfields wherever they could find them.

Throughout the day British troops arrived to shore up the threatened salient. The 19th Dragoons continued to operate straggler collection points and Jamieson recalled that, at one point, most of a British battalion that "had been rushed over from England to reinforce the line were drifting back in groups" was halted by the Dragoons.[37] His dragoons and the nearby Cyclist Company formed a line to stop them until they were reorganized and again sent forward. Heavy fighting continued on the following day, 25 April, as a see-saw battle waged back and forth but, for the infantry of the Canadian Division, this marked the end of their serious involvement in a battle which had now become a British affair. Over the next few days, Alderson's three infantry brigades were gradually withdrawn although the Canadian artillery remained in action at Ypres for nearly two more weeks because the battle was far from over. It was during this time that an officer of the 1st Brigade, Canadian Field Artillery, paused a few minutes one morning to scribble a short poem about poppies blooming among the soldiers' graves in the fields of Flanders. His name was John McCrae and every 11 November in Canada, and across the English-speaking world, his verse is recited or at least brought to mind.

The casualties resulting from the 2nd Battle of Ypres were nothing short of horrendous. The Canadian Division lost 6,036 men killed, wounded, captured and missing – approximately half its infantry strength. The formation's inexperience had been evident throughout the action but so had its courage. Allied se-

nior commanders praised the Canadians and even the Germans grudgingly admitted that they were tenacious opponents. Reflecting on the matter in later years, however, many Canadian participants concluded that they had not retreated from an impossible situation because they simply did not realize how bad it was – they "didn't know enough about it to know that we were licked."[38] But the survivors had also learned, as one historian has pointed out, "what they could never grasp on Salisbury Plain, at Valcartier, or at countless militia camps" – that wars "are ugly, merciless struggles, in which skill and ruthlessness alone determine the outcome."[39]

"Fighting sons from the Dominion": The 31st Battalion overseas, May-September 1915

It took some time for both the Canadian government and newspapers to obtain accurate information about the Ypres casualties. Speculation was rife – a week after the Canadian part in the battle had ended, the *Red Deer News* warned that "Casualties Feared Heavy" in recent fighting while other Alberta papers provided estimates ranging from 500 to 10,000 killed and wounded. The first reliable information arrived in early May and long lists of dead, wounded and missing began to fill page after page of newspapers across Canada. The *Medicine Hat News* printed the first instalment of the Ypres casualty list on 6 May 1915 and continued it in almost every issue until 17 June, although most Alberta papers chose only to print the names of men from the province or their local area. There was widespread grief in almost every community in the country but it was also noted that, in the immediate aftermath of the battle, men entered the recruiting stations in increased numbers.

At Calgary on 11 May 1915, Lieutenant-Colonel A.H. Bell received orders to prepare the 31st Alberta Battalion to move overseas. The unit was packed up ready to go and, the next day,

"Don't worry, we'll be home by next Christmas": The 31st Battalion leaves Calgary, 1915
D Company of the 31st Alberta Battalion, recruited in Medicine Hat, bids farewell to well-wishers as they prepare to leave on a Canadian Northern Railway train for Halifax in the spring of 1915. They were off on a great adventure although, by this time, news of the heavy casualties suffered at the 2nd Battle of Ypres in April made that adventure look distinctly less glamorous. GLENBOW MUSEUM, NA-3863-1

85

marched to the station behind the bands of the newly-formed 50th and 51st CEF Battalions, to board Canadian Northern Railway trains for the journey to Quebec City, their port of embarkation. Calgarians, forgetting that the 31st was recruited from across the province, had by now claimed the unit for its own and the *Western Standard* wished "Calgary's Mighty Thirty-First" good luck in the future.[40] The battalion arrived in Quebec on the morning of 17 May and immediately embarked on the old Cunard liner, SS *Carpathia*. It was not a comfortable crossing as there was insufficient food and accommodation and life boats for only half the passengers, but everyone on board cheered up when they arrived in Plymouth on 28 May. While their band played patriotic airs, the men of the Alberta battalion crowded the decks of the liner to get a glimpse of what was for many their first sight of England – and England gave them a splendid reception:

> The masts and yards of the picturesque training ships, reminiscent of the time of Nelson, which lay at anchor in the harbour were manned by the cadets of the Royal Navy, who cheered the "Carpathia" as she passed; cheering crowds lined the terraced slopes of the Hoe, and the whole of the city shore-line; every steamship in the sound and every dockyard and factory on shore kept their sirens blaring as the liner made its way to its berth. Surely few on board the incoming liner could have remained unmoved by the heartiness of the first welcome extended by the Mother Country to her fighting sons from the Dominion.[41]

The next day the battalion disembarked and travelled on the little British choo-choo trains to their training area.

The 31st Battalion and the other units of the Second Contingent were fortunate that they were not sent to suffer on soggy Salisbury Plain. The British War Office had heeded the complaints of the Canadian government and assigned the Second Contingent to a tented camp in a pastoral setting near Shornecliffe on the scenic chalk cliffs of Kent. On clear days the French coast was clearly visible and if the wind was favourable the rumble of artillery on the Western Front could be heard in the tent lines. This was the concentration area of the 2nd Canadian Division, as the contingent was now redesignated (with the original Canadian Division now becoming the 1st Division). The 31st Battalion, along with the 27th Battalion (Winnipeg), 28th Battalion (Northwest) and 29th Battalion (Vancouver), became part of the 6th Infantry Brigade, a formation from Western Canada under the command of Brigadier-General H.D.B. Ketchen, a regular force officer and a former Strathcona. The division commander was Major-General Steele, the same Sam Steele who had played such a notable role in the early history of Alberta but Steele would not be going into action in this new war as he was too old and infirm. When the division's time came to go to France, it would be led by Major-General Richard Turner, who had won the Victoria Cross in South Africa and commanded the 3rd Infantry Brigade at Ypres.

The 31st Battalion spent three months on the Kent Coast, undergoing the usual training syllabus for that period of the war, which was heavy on route marches, field exercises in skirmishing, and musketry instruction. The 2nd Division was more fortunate than the 1st Division because not only did it have a longer period to prepare, it also received marginally more useful training. The infantry got some instruction on the construction of trenches and the newly-developed military skill of "bombing," as grenade throwing was termed. Major W.R. Hewgill of the 31st Battalion recorded in his diary that the "boys are doing well with the live bombs and should be able to give the Germans what for."[42] Training was interspersed with the occasional inspection and review, leave was generously granted, the weather was mild and, all in all, the men of the 2nd Division spent a rather pleasant summer.

A scant 200 miles across the Channel, things were not pleasant at all. Following the 2nd Battle of Ypres, the 1st Division was withdrawn from the line to rebuild. Personnel from the four battalions left in England the previous winter were drafted into its ranks and those units in the division that had not suffered heavy casualties were combed out for infantry replacements. On 14 June the 19th Dragoons Squadron was nearly crippled when it lost 19 NCOs sent for commissions and a quarter of its troopers posted into the infantry. So many officers were struck off strength for one reason or another that, at one point, there was only a single lieutenant remaining in the squadron. Throughout the weeks following the battle the Dragoons continued to carry out mundane but necessary tasks – orderly service, traffic control and remount distribution. They also acquired a new job as they spent several weeks "cleaning up" the battlefield at Ypres, burying the dead and salvaging weapons and equipment. Occasionally they were able to engage in mounted drill but, by this time, almost every man in the squadron knew that cavalry had only a limited role on the Western Front.

Allied military leaders, however, still believed that trench warfare was only a temporary phase and that, if they could just discover the proper means to break through the German defences, they would be able to regain mobility and bring the war to a swift and successful conclusion. In the summer of 1915, however, victory seemed a long way off – in April an Allied amphibious landing on the Straits of the Bosphorus, intended to knock Turkey out of the war, had floundered at Gallipoli; in May a German offensive on the Eastern Front had thrown back the Russian army; in June a French attack in the Artois area and a second British attack at Neuve Chapelle had failed, largely because of a lack of artillery ammunition and heavy guns. The inability of British industry to provide the heavy ordnance and ammunition necessary for adequate support of the attacking infantry and to counteract the far superior Germany artillery (at one point British gunners on the Western Front were restricted to 3 rounds per day) led to the "Shell Scandal" and the formation of a coalition government in Britain. There was, however, some good news: Italy joined the Allies in June and,

Royal inspection, Shornecliffe Camp, 1915

The 31st Battalion is inspected by King George V in September 1915. By now the men have been issued the looser 1907 Pattern British 5-button service jacket and the 1908 Pattern British web equipment but still retain their Canadian headgear and, of course, the miserable Ross rifle. A Royal inspection usually meant that a unit would shortly be moving to the front and the 31st Battalion crossed to France a few weeks later. GLENBOW MUSEUM, NA-3620-16

by mid-1915, no less than 21 new divisions had been created in the British army.

In response to appeals from France to assist by staging offensive operations, Sir John French, the commander of the BEF, agreed to mount more limited attacks in the British sector near Neuve Chapelle. Their purpose was not so much to take ground but to wear down the enemy "by exhaustion and loss until his defences collapsed" – in short, attritional warfare.[43] The first of these attacks went in against the Aubers Ridge on 9 May 1915 but failed because the German positions had been considerably strengthened since the battle of Neuve Chapelle the previous March. French tried again on 15 May when, following an intense and lengthy bombardment, British troops managed to capture the German frontline trench before being checked. Reinforced with the 2nd and 3rd Canadian Infantry Brigades of the 1st Canadian Division, they tried again on 20-21 May but only made minor gains at the cost of heavy casualties. There was now a pause for three weeks and then came a second attack from the village of Givenchy, mounted by the 1st Canadian Brigade after very careful preparation and an increased artillery bombardment. It was marginally more successful but the assaulting troops were unable to hold the ground they had captured. When the French ended their operations in Artois, operations on the British sector also came to an end and there was a lull on the Western Front that lasted until September.

After the 2nd Battle of Ypres there had been many complaints about the Ross rifle – one Canadian battalion commander stated bluntly that, "after firing 15 to 30 rounds rapid fire, the rifles jam" and to "loosen the bolt it was necessary to use the boot heel or the handle of an entrenching tool."[44] Repeated complaints led to Alderson submitting the Ross to tests by ordnance experts who, after considerable experimentation, concluded that

the Canadian rifle would only work well with Canadian-manufactured .303 ammunition, not the commonly available British .303 round. This conclusion led Sir John French to order that the infantry of the 1st Canadian Infantry Division be supplied with British Lee-Enfield rifles for the attack at Givenchy – in fact about 3,000 soldiers in the division had already procured the British weapon on their own initiative. This decision infuriated Hughes, who was a blind adherent of the Ross, and he exerted enough pressure to retain it in Canadian frontline service although he directed that the rifle's chamber be bored out to accept British-manufactured .303 rounds. In early September the infantry of the 2nd Division at Shornecliffe paraded with their weapons to have this done by a mobile ordnance workshop. After the procedure had been completed, each infantryman "was allowed to fire two shots into a bank of earth, and if the bolt did not jam, the weapon was declared to work to perfection."[45]

This was one of the last tasks the division carried out in England as, on 14 September 1915, it received a warning order to prepare to cross to France. By now the men had received British tunics which were looser in cut and more durable than the Canadian pattern and they had also been issued British load-carrying gear in place of the despised Oliver equipment. On 18 September, along with the other infantry units of the division, the 31st arrived by train at Folkestone and marched down from the station to the harbour and boarded the transport *Duchess of Argyll*. They marched along a street that in later years would be named "The Road of Remembrance" since, sadly, for hundreds of thousands of men who passed along it to the vessels that took them to France, it was a one way trip. The Alberta battalion was 32 officers and 991 other ranks strong when it embarked for the Western Front and many of these men would never see Canada again.

CHAPTER FOUR

"A War in Which Blood Counts, Not Bone"

THE WESTERN FRONT, SEPTEMBER 1915 TO OCTOBER 1916

"Fritz has a very nasty disposition": The winter of 1915-1916 in the trenches

The 31st Alberta Battalion landed at Boulogne at 9.30 P.M. on 18 September 1915. A short but slow overnight train journey on the "40 and 8s" brought them to Bailleul near the Ypres Salient. Here they were inspected by Lieutenant-General Edwin Alderson, recently promoted to command the newly-formed Canadian Corps consisting of the veteran 1st Division and the green 2nd Division. The last leg of their journey was a 14-mile route march to billets just behind the line. It was hot day and Private Donald Fraser of A Company, a 33-year-old former bank clerk from Calgary, remembered that the weight of packs and equipment began to tell as, one by one, "unnecessary articles were flung to the side of the road, boots, shirts, underclothing, brushes, etc.," were "strewn along the roadside for several miles."[2] One of the first things to go was the useless McAdam shovel which soon decorated ditches behind the marching columns. As the 2nd Division passed through the billets of the 1st Division, the veterans of that formation "lined the last mile or so of the march" and, with the sensitivity so typical of infantrymen, "greeted their new comrades with the usual derisive and unprintable pleasantries."[3] The next few days were taken up with demonstrations including gas attack drill with the recently-issued "smoke helmet," which the regimental history notes, "was altogether neither easy to breathe through nor comfortable to wear."[4] On 25 September Alderson informed the 6th Brigade

When Very lights are shining,
Sure they're like the morning light
And when the guns begin to thunder
You can hear the angels shite.
Then the Maxims start to chatter
And the trench mortars send a few,
And when Very lights are shining,
'Tis time for a rum issue.[1]

that it would be taking over a section of the front line near Wytschaete Ridge ("White Sheet Ridge" to Canadians).

That same day the BEF launched a major attack at Loos in Artois, 60 miles to the south. The summer of 1915 had been fairly quiet on the Western Front but elsewhere there had been heavy fighting. In May Italy had entered the war on the side of Britain and France and an Italian offensive was making some gains but the Central Powers had pushed the Russians back into their own territory and Serbia was now completely overrun. An Allied landing at Salonika, intended to succour that Balkan nation, was floundering as was the amphibious attack at Gallipoli, where stubborn Turkish resistance had confined Australian, British, French and New Zealand troops to a narrow and vulnerable beachhead. As if all this was not bad enough, German U-boats were becoming active in the waters around the British Isles.

In September 1915 the French armies carried out a massive attack in the Champagne district but it failed at the cost of heavy casualties. In support of this operation, Field-Marshal Sir John French, the commander of the BEF, somewhat reluctantly agreed to a limited attack at Loos. He was concerned about his lack of heavy artillery and artillery ammunition, both of which were in short supply as British industry was just coming into full wartime production. French did, however, have plentiful quantities of poison gas and, on 25 September 1915, Britain carried out its first major chemical attack of the war using 5,000 cylinders of chlorine. The results were mixed as much of the vapour drifted back to friendly lines but the initial attack made some gains, at a heavy cost, before it was stymied by a well-sited second defence line. Three weeks of heavy fighting followed that resulted in 50,000 British casualties, spawning a controversy that resulted in French's replacement by General Sir Douglas Haig, a fellow cavalryman. Having studied recent Allied operations, Haig was convinced that only careful preparation, heavy artillery bombardment and a massive and violent infantry assault could break the deadlock on the Western Front. He therefore resolved that,

---

(Facing) **All Quiet on the Western Front**

For the moment at least. These soldiers are resting in a communication trench, complete with elaborate "funk-holes" with overhead protection. Three men catch some sleep while a fourth writes a letter, probably telling the folks at home that he is fine and doing well. Note the rifles stacked in the bay in the left foreground, an indication that this is not a forward trench as, if it was, the men would have them closer to hand. Note also that the soldier sleeping in the foreground has his gas mask carrier open – just in case. CANADIAN ARMY PHOTOGRAPH, O-2533

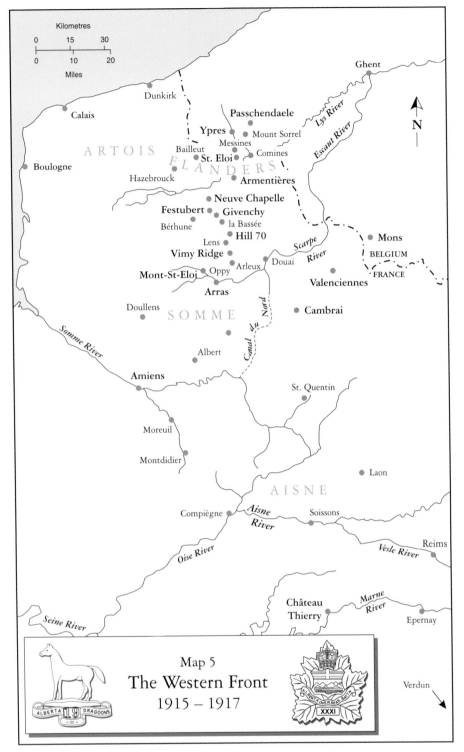

Kilometres
0   15   30

0   10   20
Miles

Map 5
The Western Front
1915 – 1917

tributed to the sense of nightmare unreality."[5] Private Donald Fraser found the stench in the trenches "almost unbearable" because frequent shelling had brought "refuse or dead bodies to the surface."[6]

By the time the Alberta Battalion arrived on the Western Front, warfare had become a matter of established routine. The trenches were constructed in three distinct but parallel lines: firing, support and reserve. The firing or front-line trench closest to the enemy was dug in a "zig-zag" or "dog's tooth" form, both to protect troops from enfilading fire down its length and to limit the effect of shelling. It was basically a series of short sections or firing bays, each divided from the next by traverses that intersected it from the front or rear. Firing trenches were normally about seven feet wide at the top and two to three feet wide at the bottom, the side facing the enemy was the parapet while the rear side was the parados and both were reinforced with timber, corrugated iron and, most commonly, sandbags. The parapet was constructed with a firing step which the defenders could man in case of attack but, most often, daytime observation of the "No Man's land" between the opposing lines was accomplished by the use of periscopes. In a well-established firing trench, saps or tunnels were dug to listening posts forward of it, which were manned at night. As a rule, there were not many "dugouts," or small, reinforced caves in the firing trench, these were normally located in the support and reserve trenches to the rear but frontline troops often burrowed small one-man "funk holes" in the parapet to provide protection from shelling. The firing trench was always protected by a belt of barbed wire, as thick as those defending the trench could make it, strung on iron or wood posts and work on this wire belt was unending.

The second trench system was the support line, generally about 200 yards back from the firing trench, where immediate reserves were stationed to reinforce the firing line if necessary or from which counterattacks could be mounted to recover any portion of it lost to the enemy. When a battalion entered the trenches, the general rule of thumb was that one of its four companies would man the firing trench while two companies took post in the support trenches and the last in the reserve line. There was a constant rotation of companies during the battalion's frontline tour and, under normal circumstances, a company would not spend more than 48 hours in the firing trench before being rotated back through the support trenches to the reserve line. Support

before he mounted a major offensive, he would have the weight of numbers and materiel on his side.

In the last days of September 1915, while the BEF banged its head against Loos, the 31st Battalion began its first tour in the front line. As the men filed through the muddy, wet communication trenches that led to the forward area, one remembered that the "enshrouding gloom, the persistent rain, the silence in which the slowly moving column advanced, the muddy, crater-pitted desolation of the surrounding terrain, the ignorance of the men of their own position and that of the enemy, all con-

trenches, subject to less intense enemy action, were often more elaborate and here would be found more dug outs, including a battalion's headquarters and its Regimental Aid Post, or medical station. Support trenches were connected to the firing line by communication trenches, again constructed in a crooked fashion to prevent enfilade fire, and similar communication trenches linked the support line to the reserve line about 400 yards to its rear. All trenches – firing, support, reserve and communication – were identified by a code number, used for the benefit of the staff in the rear. Frontline soldiers generally gave them names and since most had originally been built by British soldiers,

some of the most dangerous positions bore rather homely titles – "Leicester Square;" "Clapham Junction," Tram Car Cottage," "White Horse Cellars," "Lulu Lane," "Regent Street" and "Pall Mall," to name but a few.

Although there were infinite variations, the general system was that a division would keep one of its three brigades in the firing and support trenches and one in the reserve trenches, while the remaining third enjoyed life in divisional reserve at a rest camp or billets behind the lines. Approximately every 5-7 days there would be a rotation of brigades because it was impossible to keep men longer than this in the front lines without risking

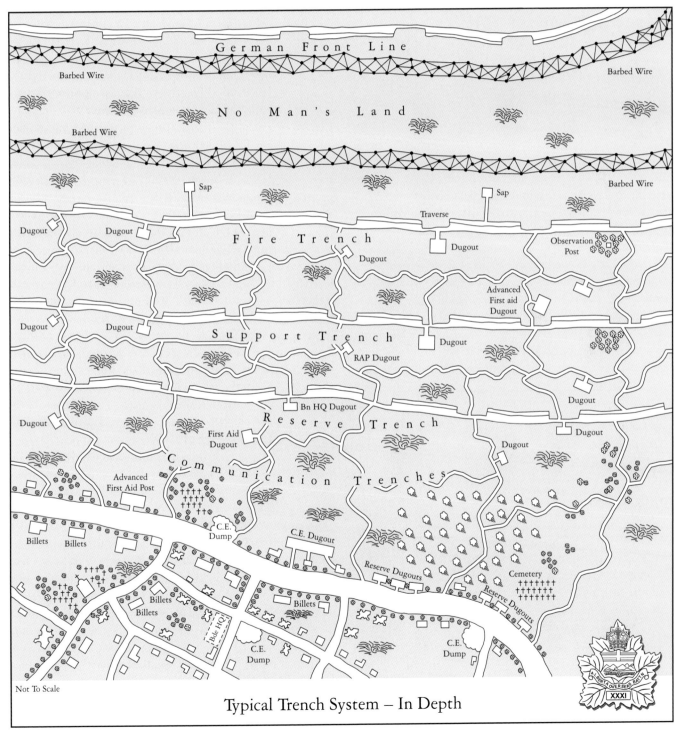

Typical Trench System – In Depth

Not To Scale

a loss of efficiency. Between 25 September 1915 and 31 March 1916, the 31st Battalion served thirteen tours in the trenches, totalling 75 days in the frontline and support trenches. They spent 65 days in brigade reserve, and 41 days in the divisional or corps reserve rest camps which were generally, but not always, located outside German artillery range.

A typical day in the trenches began at dawn with a "stand to" for between 30 minutes and an hour when a battalion fully manned its lines, weapons ready, as this was often the time chosen by the opposing side to attack. The "stand down", or signal to relax, was often followed by the "morning hate" or "frightfulness" during which both sides engaged in rapid rifle and automatic weapons fire, sometimes accompanied by light artillery or trench mortar bombardment just to let the opposing team know they were in good fettle. This was normally followed by a tacit truce while the opponents cooked their breakfast and then daily chores commenced (unless there was heavy shelling which made everyone quite literally go to ground) such as digging, repairing and reinforcing trenches with wooden props or sandbags and replacing the wooden duckboards laid along their bottoms. A very necessary task was the spreading of chloride of lime or creosote on refuse, latrines or corpses as a sanitary measure. While this was going on, assigned sentries kept watch on the enemy's line by periscopes while those men not detailed for fatigues generally tried to get some sleep – in dug-outs if they were lucky, "funk holes" if they were not. Everyone kept their head down as the Germans had perfected the art of sniping to a very high degree and German snipers were assigned to a specific sector for long periods so that they were very familiar with every foot of the Allied trenches opposite.

After the dusk "stand to" and the arrival of darkness, the trenches came to life. The cover of night provided opportunity to carry out major repairs on the parapet facing the enemy or repair the barbed wire belt in "No Man's Land" that protected it. Night was when rations and bulky stores were brought up as the infantryman on the Western Front was also a beast of burden, particularly in the early years of the war, and it was also when major movement, such as the relief of units, was made. While this was going on, listening posts forward of the firing trench were manned and sentries, almost always in pairs, kept watch on the enemy line. Both sides were very alert and it was not unusual for rifle and machinegun fire to be periodically let off and for

Typical Firing Line and Communication Trench Layout

Communication Trench
3′ to 5′ Wide

Traverse
8′ Wide

Firing Line Trench

Firing Bay

Sandbags

Parados

Parapet

6′ to 8′

4′ to 6′

Fire Step

2½

artillery (and also machineguns) to fire on the known or suspected location of communication trenches or road junctions in the rear areas. The firing of Very lights or flares, was common and what with the flares, smallarms and artillery fire, no one got much sleep during a night on the Western Front.

Danger was ever present. Even on a quiet day there would be some shelling, either by artillery or trench mortars, and there were frequent exchanges of rifle and machinegun fire. By the time the 31st arrived on the Western Front, all armies on the Western Front were plentifully supplied with automatic weapons. The British army had commenced the war with two machineguns per battalion – by the autumn of 1915 there were 16, and by 1918 there would be 32 such weapons with each battalion. The most feared weapon, however, was HE (High Explosive) and shrapnel shells fired by either conventional artillery or the recently-introduced trench mortars. As it was a matter of survival, soldiers learned quickly to judge where a shell might fall from the noise it made. "A noise like a train overhead," one recalled, "meant a destination miles to the rear; a sharp shriek or a deep growl meant imminent danger; and between the two there lay a wide variety of pitches, which one soon learned to interpret properly" or one died – but then sometimes one died anyway.[7] In the front line the most detested enemy weapon was the trench mortar as the Germans, a technically ingenious people, had developed an impressive variety of these deadly contrivances, ranging from the small *Granatenwerfer* or grenade launcher to the dreaded 250 mm *Minenwerfer*, capable of throwing a 200 lb. projectile with an explosive charge of 100 lbs. a distance of 500 yards that, when it struck, created a room-sized crater. The British answer was the 3-inch Stokes mortar, not as large nor as lethal as the German weapons but lighter and easier to move. When it came to audibility, German mortar bombs were in a category of their own – a "dull pop" from the enemy lines signalled that one was on the way, either large or small, and it was soon visible, resembling a large and deadly sausage wobbling high through the air over "No Man's Land" making its peculiar "swish, swish" and "wa-wa" sounds.[8] All eyes followed its course but mortar bombs were very tricky as it was difficult to judge from their trajectory just where they were going to land – miscalculations were frequent, and often final. Even an average day on the Western Front was a continual test of a man's psychological stamina and, as Private Donald Fraser of the 31st Battalion commented, his

comrades were fighting "a war in which blood counts, not bone; nerve is the test and not strength."[9]

Curiously enough, poison gas was not as feared as artillery or mortar shelling. The casualty statistics for the British Empire forces during the war would seem to confirm this belief – only 9% of all Imperial casualties from 1915 to 1918 were caused by gas and, of these, only 3.18% died. Since the prevailing winds in northwest Europe were from the west, the Germans may have had cause to regret introducing this weapon. The difficulties of controlling the direction of gas clouds released from cylinders led to increasing use of gas shells fired by conventional artillery. These were usually fired in conjunction with conventional artillery rounds to mask their deployment, but the introduction of improved gas masks and strict anti-gas discipline largely countered their effect despite the introduction of the more deadly phosgene, which could immobilize and kill a man in 41 seconds, in place of chlorine gas which took, on average, 4 minutes to achieve the same effect. Later came mustard gas which did not have to be inhaled to take effect but caused painful irritation to the exposed skin of a victim, who was often unaware that he had been afflicted. As one Canadian veteran of the Western Front noted, however, gas was quickly dispersed by sun and wind and was only truly effective on still nights. He greatly preferred hearing the soft "plop" of a gas shell to the detonation of conventional artillery rounds and his conclusion was that gas was only "a new way to do rather poorly a work that was already accomplished most effectively by high explosives."[10] During the winter of 1915-1916 the 31st Battalion suffered at least two gas attacks but their War Diary does not record any significant effects that resulted. Very generally speaking, gas was most effective if the weather conditions were right – no wind and humid – and if the target was in low-lying ground. The evidence is inconclusive but the most effective use of gas may not have been on the infantry in the frontline trenches but against the rear areas, since it was devastating against horse transport and effective against artillery positions because it was extremely difficult for gunners

Shrapnel shell bursts

Artillery was always the most feared weapon and men on the Western Front often had to endure days of heavy bombardment. Here, sappers working near Vimy Ridge duck as two bursts come close. NAC, PA-001131

(Left) **Nighttime working party on the Western Front**
The darkness hours were when most of the work was done. Here a working party carries duckboards forward as the flash of the camera lights up strands of barbed wire and makes them resemble flares. This picture was not taken within range of the enemy because such a flash would bring down prompt and heavy German fire. Note that the soldier carrying the duckboard has a cigarette in his mouth – one had to be careful where one smoked as German snipers were alert and deadly. The expression, "Never three on a match," had its origin on the Western Front as it was known that a sniper spotted the flare of the match when the first smoke was lit, took aim as the second smoke was lit, and fired when the third was lit. BY KIND PERMISSION OF THE TRUSTEES OF THE IMPERIAL WAR MUSEUM, Q 6420

"Funk holes"
Man-size holes such as these were often cut into the sides of communication and rearward trenches for protection from shellbursts and the rain. Given the depth of the trench, it is probably a communication trench. NAC, PA-000723

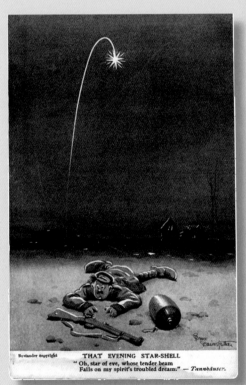

"That Evening Star-Shell"
Another contribution by Bruce Bairnsfather shows a private carrying the rum ration forward in its earthenware SRD (Supply and Replenishment Depot) jug caught out by a flare. COPYRIGHT TONIE AND VALMAI HOLT, REPRODUCED WITH PERMISSION FROM *THE BEST OF FRAGMENTS FROM FRANCE*

wearing masks to make the physical exertion necessary to fire their weapons.

The six months that the Alberta Battalion served in the trenches near Kemmel during this first winter in France were for the most part quiet. But "quiet on the Western Front" was a very relative term as even a quiet day might still result in the loss of about 300 men killed or wounded in the British sector – losses staff officers termed "normal wastage." Occasionally, incidents occurred that interrupted the daily routine, usually making it more dangerous. On 13 October, in support of a nearby attack, the 31st Battalion mounted a demonstration (a "Chinese attack" in soldiers' parlance) to distract the enemy. This demonstration included a heavy artillery bombardment and the loud shouting of mock orders and blowing of whistles. The bombardment was truly impressive causing "clouds of smoke and spouting columns of earth shot skyward from the red flashes of the bursting projectiles, while sudden whitish puffs of smoke, slowly spreading and diffusing against the sky, marked the explosions of shrapnel in front of and over the trenches."[11] The demonstration concluded with the entire battalion manning the firing trench and letting off 15 rounds rapid with their Ross rifles but no less than 138 weapons jammed, nearly 20% of those in use. Private Fraser remembered his frustrated comrades having to kick open their bolts to eject rounds and commented that the whole affair was a "poor advertisement" for the Ross.[12] The "Maggie Ross" had by now become a bitter joke in the Canadian Corps and Fraser was unsparing about its faults:

The effect of artillery bombardment
These battered German trenches show the effect of heavy, prolonged artillery bombardment. On the Western Front, it was discovered that the first line of enemy trenches could be taken with artillery support – the problem came when an attacking force tried to take the subsequent trench lines as communications were just too primitive for commanders to control the battle at a distance. NAC, PA-000811

Its chief defects were it was too long and showed above the trenches. It was continually catching in the overhead trench signalling wire. It did not balance on the shoulder well and often tilted to the side, the muzzle catching in the mud. With so much open metal surface and mechanism it was difficult to keep clean and from rusting. But the principal objection was that it jammed. The least thing would jam it – a speck of dust, a shower of rain, even a burst of rapid fire.[13]

The Albertans, like their comrades of the Canadian Corps, came to know the enemy well. The Germans were often hated, sometimes feared, but always respected – as one veteran remarked: "We rather admired the technical efficiency of the Germans, even if we suffered from it, and we were most proud of ourselves when we surpassed it."[14] The German artillery – and they had more of it than the Allies in the first two years of the war – inflicted heavy losses as did the ubiquitous Maxim machineguns with their mechanical chatter. Occasionally there would be a local frontline truce to gather up casualties but these occasions became increasingly rare as the war progressed. More common was an arrangement to "live and let live" unless senior officers were expected to visit the frontline.

Among the armies fighting on the Western Front, the Canadians acquired a distinct reputation as souvenir-hunters and were extremely acquisitive collectors of German spiked helmets, badges, medals, "*Gott Mit Uns*" belt buckles, buttons, daggers, revolvers, watches, field glasses and mess tins, which were particularly desirable as the German version was deeper than the British issue and had a useful handle. The French civilian population, noting this national trait, believed that the French soldier fought for his country; the British soldier fought for drink; and the Canadian soldier fought for souvenirs.

There was the occasional incident of humour. On the Somme one morning, a German unit placed a rocking horse on its parapet, presenting an attractive target that was promptly knocked off by rifle fire. It reappeared a few minutes later, bandaged in two places. More common were incidents such as that recorded by Major William Hewgill in October 1915: "Fritz has a very nasty disposition and this morning at 'Stand To' gave us a lot of bombs etc. Will fix him tomorrow." When the next day came and the Germans "started funny work," the 6th Brigade responded by bringing down 30 rounds of 18-pdr. HE rounds and 3 rounds from every mortar in range onto the enemy's trenches – "Silence," Hewgill noted later that day, "now reigns supreme."[15]

The Germans were nasty enough but the weather was almost as bad. Flanders is a low, flat, well-watered area and the winter of 1915 was unusually wet – Hewgill recorded 40 days between October and January on which it rained and only constant work could prevent the trenches from dissolving. "As fast as the men rebuilt the crumbling and water-logged parapet, the battalion historian recorded, "it slipped back again into the trenches."[16] Dugouts and shelters filled with water and became nearly un-liveable while sump holes overflowed and the latrines "drained their sewerage into communication trenches." Of that winter, Private Fraser remembered that he and his comrades had to "shovel, shovel and keep on shovelling but it is of no avail" as "the mud sticks to the shovel and after vigor-ous attempts to dislodge it, it only comes off to fall in the trench again."[17] The unit history records that, "Bunyan's Slough of Despond was a happy and comparatively salubrious spot by comparison with the stinking, shell-tortured and bloody ooze of Flanders on that Christmas Day of 1915," a Christmas Day the 31st spent in reserve under a torrential fall of rain.[18] The down-pours continued into January 1916 until the landscape around Kemmel and White Sheet Ridge was

Gas mask
The use of poison gas was yet another of the many horrors of the First World War. Both sides made increasing use of it and introduced more deadly types as the war progressed. The answer was the gas mask, which protected the soldier but severely limited his vision and breathing and, ultimately, his effectiveness. This is a late war pattern mask. NAC, PA-000928

butter (tinned), jam or marmalade (all too often a heartily-despised mix-ture of plum and apple), tinned bully beef or (rarely) fresh beef, tinned stew (a greasy, thin concoction supposedly containing meat and universally called "McConochie" after its most prominent British manufacturer); bacon (rarely); cheese (tinned); rice (very scarce and, in any case, hard to prepare); dried veg-etables (officially termed "desiccated vegetables" but known as "desecrated vegetables" to soldiers) and, occasion-ally perhaps, bottled onions or pickles. The rations were brought up to the re-serve trenches during the night and it was usually some luckless corporal's job to go back and collect them in a sand-bag (which resulted in an interesting combination of food types) and then attempt to divide them fairly among the men of his platoon – a task that was patently hopeless and certain to invoke howls of complaint. If it was possible to light a fire in the lines, small cook-ers or braziers were utilized to heat the food; if not it was consumed cold. Din-nertime ended with the traditional re-mark, "Well, if that's dinner, roll along supper!" – but supper normally con-sisted of the cold remains of dinner.[21] There never seemed to be enough to eat – particularly for men forced to do hard physical labour under conditions of extreme stress – and rations were ex-tremely variable from day to day, depending on their availability and enemy shelling of the communication trenches.

a sea of mud, plentifully pitted with the deep pools of water-filled craters. Through this deso-late morass men floundered back and forth from the mud-clogged trenches to the muddy rearward areas, drenched for the most part, to the skin, and shivering with the raw, damp cold. Trenches and communication trenches were frequently knee deep in mud and water, and in some places waist deep. The water-logged parapets were continually collapsing into the trenches until, in some parts, the shallow depression in the mud that alone remained was a trench only in name. The bringing up from the rear of rations, ammunition and supplies became a task of ever-increasing difficulty and dan-ger.[19]

Everyone in the battalion was overjoyed when the temperature dropped at the end of January because Albertans could handle cold and the frost also solidified the ground, reducing their la-bour. "More snow this morning and cold," enthused Hewgill on 23 February 1916, "Real western Canada weather."[20]

Throughout all this misery, mud and murder, the men of the 31st Battalion tried to keep their spirits up. In the line what kept them going were three things: food, rum and tobacco. The high point of the day was the midday meal which would usually include tea and bread or hardtack and might include

Rum and tobacco were also distributed and, at least, had the benefit of reducing hunger. The rum came up in large jugs marked "SRD" which was interpreted as meaning everything from "Service Rum Demerara" through "Service Rum Diluted" to the entirely possible (in the eyes of the privates) "Sergeants' Ration, Double." Actually "SRD" meant none of these things – it stood for "Supply and Replenishment Depot." Rum was the soldier's friend – Fraser believed it aided the circulation which tended to get sluggish on "cold nights for want of movement" and eulogized that "Time and again it has come to the rescue and many owe their freedom from colds, rheumatism, and kin-dred troubles to the timely inward application of this liquor."[22] Almost as good was tobacco and, although there were very few non-smokers or atheists in the trenches, even those men who did not smoke took their cigarette ration to use for barter. Fraser recalled that, for many of his comrades, the craving for ciga-rettes was irresistible and

Goulash cannon

A mobile cooking stove belonging to the 2nd Canadian Division is seen behind the front line. Hot food was a luxury in the trenches and most infantrymen had to do their own cooking over braziers. Things got better when they were out of the line as equipment like this could be utilized to provide a decent meal. Note that one cook is cleaning his rifle while the other tends to the culinary duties. NAC, PA-0001931

Food for the inner soldier

A unit meat ration, including sides of beef and crates of corned beef, at a railhead supply point in July 1916. Among the many horrors experienced by soldiers on the Western Front was the quality and quantity of their rations and most relied on tobacco and ration rum to get them through a tour in the front lines. A particularly despised item was the ubiquitous plum-apple jam (actually a mixture of turnips, plums, apples and rhubarb) which only too often appeared instead of the much preferred strawberry. Nobody knew where the strawberry jam went, but it was rarely seen in the trenches. NAC, PA-000255

> In the firing line it is almost their whole existence. It appears to sooth the jaded nerves and make them tractable. Without fags I am sure many a soldier would soon go to pieces. One of the most noticeable things after a soldier is wounded is that he will call for a fag.[23]

On 1 April 1916, when the 31st Battalion went into corps reserve in billets near Bailleul, it had completed just over six months service on the Western Front. Casualties during this period had been constant but not severe – 35 killed and 150 wounded – although the sight of burial parties had become common. As the unit's historian remarked:

> Custom stales, and after a while, all such things lose their significance. Burials become a daily occurrence – a mere matter of routine. In the same way sights which at first caused physical nausea by their sheer ghastliness are seen and passed over without a second thought. In the fierce furnace of war the finer sensibilities are tempered and toughened, and the whole personality must, of necessity, become inured to things that would once have greatly moved it.[24]

(Left) The soldier's friend
"When they smoke a cigarette, they have the steadiness of nerve to do their duty" was how a tobacco company described the beneficial effect its product had on fighting men. The ad also stresses the stoic courage of a British naval officer who calmly puffed away on the bridge of his warship while his vessel was sinking after being torpedoed by a U-boat. Tobacco and rum kept many men going in the trenches and nobody worried too much about the long-term health effects as "long-term" on the Western Front meant staying alive for another day. AUTHOR'S COLLECTION

Unfortunately, the battalion would be conducting a great many more funerals in the immediate future.

"Some mother's son gone to glory;" The St. Eloi craters, April 1916.

In December 1915, the Allied leaders held a conference to plan strategy for the coming year. The past twelve months had seen their military operations in all theatres stymied or defeated by the Central Powers. The amphibious landing at Gallipoli, intended to knock Turkey out of the war, had gone nowhere and would shortly be abandoned while an expedition up the Euphrates River had been blocked at by the Turks at Kut. On both the Italian and Russian Fronts, German and Austro-Hungarian troops had emerged victorious. Recognizing that the enemy possessed the advantage of being able to switch forces rapidly from one front to another, Allied leaders decided to stage simultaneous offensives on all fronts to pin German and Austro-Hungarian forces in place. On the Western Front the major operation would be a joint British-French effort in the Somme, south of the Ypres Salient, and preparations began for this attack which would be the largest of the war to date. Until it was launched – and the projected date was 1 July 1916 – it was decided that only minor "wearing out" operations were to take place in the west.

In February 1916, the Germans forestalled Allied plans by launching an attack of their own against the city of Verdun, an objective they knew the French would be compelled to defend. The German purpose was not to achieve a breakthrough but to inflict losses on the French army – a strategy of attrition. This enemy operation began on 21 February 1916 and initially it went well, so well that the German commanders lost sight of their original purpose and converted it into a major offensive, one of the great strategic errors of the First World War. The fighting at Verdun, which saw heavy losses on both sides in some of the grimmest fighting of the conflict, continued for more than four months but, although the French came close to breaking, they managed to hold off the Germans.

The French asked for assistance from the British Expeditionary Force to divert enemy forces and Haig launched a number of small "wearing out" operations in the BEF sector of the front. One took place at St. Eloi, a small village in the Salient about 3 miles northeast of the positions the 31st Battalion had manned throughout the winter. The objective was "the mound," a clay bank held by the Germans about 20 feet above the flat, surrounding countryside, which permitted them to observe British troop movements. In the massive siege operation that was the Western Front, tunnelling and mining had by now become highly developed. Beginning in August 1915, British engineers dug a series of tunnels, 60 feet deep, under the "mound" and on 27 March 1916 blew six mines that more or less removed it from existence and created six large craters, numbered 1 to 6 from west to east. The British 3rd Division then moved forward to occupy these craters but confusion, poor staff work and the fact that it was hard for the infantry to get their bearings in what was now a lunar landscape, resulted in only Craters 1 to 3, 6 and a large shell crater numbered 7, being occupied. Craters 4 and 5, in the middle of the British line, were not occupied, the Germans promptly moved into them and heavy fighting followed for a week over Crater 5, which was finally taken. At this point, the British formation was relieved by the 2nd Canadian Division and Ketchen's 6th Brigade was ordered to take over the crater area with the 27th (Winnipeg) and 31st Battalions in the forward line.

The relief was carried out on the night of 3 April under heavy German shelling. As the battalion – everyone for the first time wearing steel helmets – filed through the communication

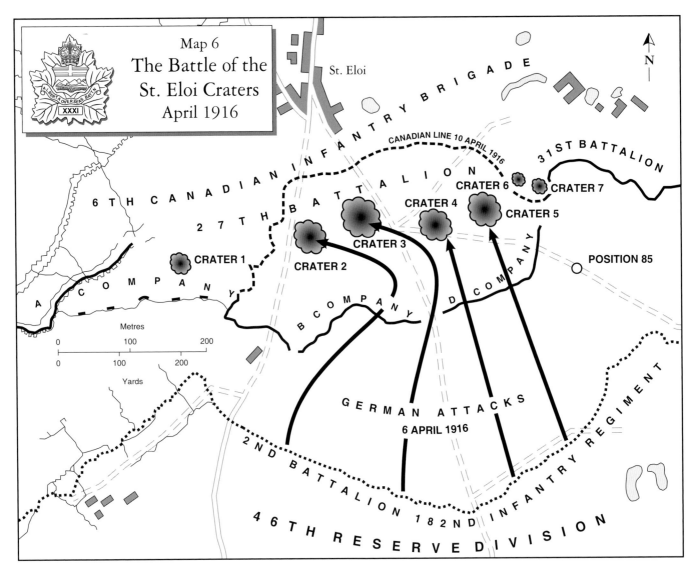

Map 6
The Battle of the
St. Eloi Craters
April 1916

St. Eloi

6TH CANADIAN INFANTRY BRIGADE

CANADIAN LINE 10 APRIL 1916

31ST BATTALION

27TH BATTALION

CRATER 6
CRATER 7

CRATER 4
CRATER 5

CRATER 3

CRATER 1

CRATER 2

A COMPANY

B COMPANY

D COMPANY

POSITION 85

Metres
0   100   200
0   100   200
Yards

GERMAN ATTACKS
6 APRIL 1916

2ND BATTALION 182ND INFANTRY REGIMENT

46TH RESERVE DIVISION

N

trenches, they encountered a young British soldier who "showed signs of visible distress." "Cheer up! Don't be downhearted!" they consoled him, only to receive the reply, "You'll be downhearted when you see what's up there."[25] This wasn't very reassuring but the Albertans kept trudging forward. When they got into their assigned positions, which were hard to distinguish as most of the trenches had been obliterated by shelling, three companies occupied the firing line which everyone believed to end with its right flank on Crater 5. As there were no trench maps, however, no time to reconnoitre and no intelligence about enemy positions (which were much farther forward than anyone realized), nobody was sure of their exact location. The 27th and 31st Battalion took what they thought was the correct position with the Winnipeg unit to the right but, at no time during the coming week were the two units in solid contact and there was a gap of 80 yards between their positions. The most pressing problem was to ascertain the position of the six mine craters as there were at least seventeen craters on the 6th Brigade front, "all much larger than any that the 31st Battalion had previously seen."[26] It was a confusing situation but once they got into what they thought was the approximate correct position, both battalions

began to consolidate by repairing the shattered trenches, digging new ones and installing pumps to drain all the trenches, which were knee deep in water. Throughout this nightmare relief, enemy shelling was unceasing.

"When day broke," Private Fraser of A Company remembered, "the sights that met our gaze were so horrible and ghastly that they beggar description." Grim evidence of recent heavy fighting was all around:

Heads, arms and legs were protruding from the mud at every yard and dear Lord knows how many bodies the earth swallowed. Thirty corpses were at least showing in the crater and beneath its clayey waters other victims must be lying killed and drowned. A young, tall, slim English lieutenant lay stretched in death with a pleasant, peaceful look on his boyish face. Some mother's son gone to glory. ...... Another English lieutenant was lying at the edge of the crater, huddled up, with his legs uppermost. One of the most saddening cases was a stretcher bearer near half a dozen dead Tommies, a little to the right of the trench – leading to crater 7. He was sitting with a bandage between his hands in the very act of bandag-

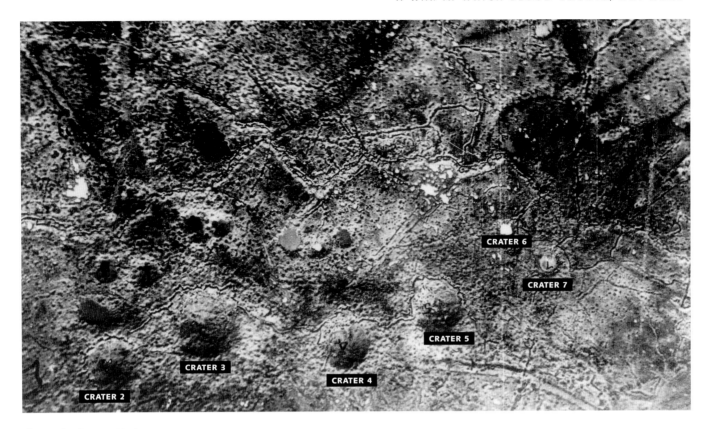

The St. Eloi Craters, 1916
This aerial photograph, taken on 16 April 1916, shows how a strong line of German trenches defend Craters 2, 3, 4 and 5 while comparatively weak Canadian trenches are in front of Craters 6 and 7. Fought in a water-logged lunar landscape, the Battle of the Craters was the Alberta Battalion's first major action and it was a costly business. NAC, C-043985

ing his leg, when his life gave out, and his head fell back. ......
Eight bodies of British soldiers were collected in the crater for burial, when a shell came over and burst amongst them, plastering Webber and Doull with gangrened flesh. At daybreak one of the bombers was shocked to find himself standing between a dead German and English officer, whilst close by was a German private and English Tommy. What trench mats there were seemed to rest on dead bodies.[27]

The shelling which had been heavy all night now began to pick up in tempo and there was soon a steady stream of casualties being evacuated with great difficulty through the ruined communication trenches. The German bombardment continued throughout the day of 4 April, through the night and on into 6 April – it fact it was unceasing for the five days the 31st Battalion spent in the frontline trenches. Captain Harold ("Iodine Joe") McGill had set up his Regimental Aid Post in a dugout in a clay bank to the rear, and for McGill and his orderlies, those five days were an unending procession of shattered men whom they treated with morphine and iodine (used for antisepsis on the Western Front), dressed with splints and bandages and evacuated to hospitals in the rear. McGill's diary records their work:

5th April 1916
12.00 hrs: Wounded have been coming in all morning and are being evacuated to BEDFORD HOUSE [an advanced dressing station to the rear]. Stretcher cases must be left in trenches until night. ......

6th April 1916
3.30 hrs: A most terrific concentrated enemy bombardment is taking place on our position in front of and about ST. ELOI, using trench torpedoes [mortar bombs] and shells of all kinds and sizes. Hundreds of shell are bursting per minute. We must expect heavy casualties. Bombardment continues all day from both sides. ......

We dress and send out wounded all morning and afternoon, practically all were walking cases. Stretcher Bearer Avery comes in with shell wound in back. Avery dressed wounded continuously for forty eight hours under shell fire, and carried on for some time after being hit.

Cases of shattered nerves are coming in. The worst of these I send to the Field Ambulance, but the majority I allow to lie down in an adjoining dugout. There are only half a dozen cases. Some men that have been buried by shells I also kept at R.A.P. dugout.[28]

"Notwithstanding that stretchers, ammunition, every requisite disappeared under an avalanche of shells," Fraser remembered, "our men never flinched … despite the fact that they were melting away, and the position intolerable and untenable." These were times, he concluded, quoting Thomas Paine, "that tried men's souls."[29]

At 3.30 A.M. on Thursday, 6 April, the bombardment increased in severity and when it lifted, two German battalions attacked directly against Crater 3, which was the remnant of the "mound." They caught the 27th and 29th (Vancouver) Battalions off guard as they were attempting a relief and occupied Crater 3 but the 31st Battalion to the east, positioned around what they thought were Craters 4 and 5 but which were actually 6 and 7, were in better case. "Rifle fire was brought to bear on them and many were killed and wounded, whilst the remainder fled or took refuge in shell holes."[30] The enemy, however, took Craters 2, 3, 4 and 5 and regained almost all the ground lost since the explosion of the mines ten days earlier. Over the next two days all three battalions launched small counterattacks to regain these positions but they were beaten off with heavy losses. On the night of 7 April, Major-General Richard Turner, commanding the 2nd Division, relieved the 6th Brigade with the 4th Brigade – even so, D Company of the 31st Battalion was so isolated and under such heavy artillery fire that it was another 24 hours before it could be extricated. On 9 April, the battalion re-assembled at a rest camp to the rear, having suffered 182 killed and wounded in the five terrible days at the craters.

It was not until 16 April that aerial reconnaissance confirmed that the 2nd Division had never properly occupied Craters 4 and 5. The fallout from this botched operation was considerable – the commander of the Canadian Corps, Lieutenant-General Edwin Alderson, wanted to remove both Major-General Turner of the 2nd Division and Brigadier H.D.B. Ketchen of the 6th Brigade for what he saw as their failure at St. Eloi. As both men were Canadians, however, politics entered the equation and, instead, Haig left Turner and Ketchen in place and removed Alderson, replacing him with Lieutenant-General Sir Julian Byng.*

By this time the Canadian Corps was growing in strength as the 3rd Division had arrived in France and a 4th Division was in the process of being formed. The expansion of the corps caused

"If You Knows of a Better 'Ole, Go To It!"
Captain Bruce Bairnsfather of the British army became the most celebrated cartoonist of the war and his work was reproduced throughout the English-speaking world. This is the most famous of Bairnsfather's cartoons and the one that made his reputation. COPYRIGHT TONIE AND VALMAI HOLT, REPRODUCED WITH PERMISSION FROM *THE BEST OF FRAGMENTS FROM FRANCE*

a major change for the 19th Dragoons squadron serving with the 1st Division. The squadron, with reduced numbers, had been used in a variety of administrative and logistical fatigues throughout the previous summer and had spent most of the winter of 1915-1916 manning a series of observation posts in the Salient near Ploegsteert Wood ("Plugstreet" to Canadians). In the early summer of 1916 there were three Canadian divisions overseas, each with its own cavalry squadron, and a decision was made to combine these squadrons into a new regiment with the somewhat awkward title, the Canadian Corps Cavalry Regiment, afterward wisely changed to the Canadian Light Horse. The newly-formed unit consisted of three squadrons, each with four troops and six Hotchkiss machineguns, with a total strength of 36 officers and 600 other ranks. The 19th Dragoons became A Squadron of the new unit while B Squadron was formed from the 1st Hussars of London, Ontario, and C Squadron from the 16th Light Horse of Regina. Members of the CLH usually wore their brass regimental flash on their shoulders but each squadron retained its original collar and cap badges and all ranks wore the stetson when not in the front lines. By this time, Lieutenant-Colonel F.C. Jamieson had returned to Alberta to command the large, new military camp constructed at Sarcee and Lieutenant-Colonel Ibbotson Leonard, formerly of the 1st Hussars, assumed command of the CLH.

There was not much call for cavalry on the Western Front but Haig was convinced that the mounted arm would regain its usefulness once the deadlock of trench warfare – which he regarded as only temporary – ended. For this reason he retained a great number of cavalry formations in the BEF and insisted that they keep up their mounted training, although they were occasionally used as infantry in the frontlines if reserves were lacking. From the time of its creation in 1916, therefore, the CLH continued to train for its mounted role as a corps reconnaissance unit but their efforts in this respect were continually frustrated by constant demands that their personnel serve as labour troops, medical auxiliaries and traffic police. Bitterly, the men of the

---

* Alderson is remembered today in Alberta by Mount Alderson in the Waterton Lakes area which is named after him.

CLH began to call themselves "Canada's Labour Hunters" or, somewhat more kindly, "Canada's Last Hope," "Colonel Leonard's Huskies" or "Coming Like Hell."[31]

"We managed to bag the most": Mount Sorrel, June 1916

The 31st Battalion remained in reserve in the St. Eloi area while it tried to rebuild its strength from reinforcement drafts. This was the first time the battalion had to undertake this process which, over the next two and a half years, would be unending. In mid-April it served another tour in the crater area but in brigade support and much of its time was spent on labour details necessary to repair trenches that were constantly being destroyed by almost incessant German artillery bombardment. Tours in the support lines alternated with tours at the front, the battalion did two more short tours which were not marked by heavy fighting. On 7 June the unit was ordered with the remainder of the 6th Brigade to relieve the 7th Brigade of the 3rd Division near the village of Hooge at the eastern tip of the Salient. This area, which contained some of the few remaining high points in the Ypres area including Mount Sorrel and a long, low elevation called Observatory Ridge, had long been coveted by the Germans. On the night of 1/2 June 1916, following the heaviest bombardment Canadian troops had yet experienced during the war, the enemy attacked the shaken 3rd Division troops holding the area, and pushed forward 600 yards – a considerable advance for the Western Front – and then , unaccountably, stopped. Canadian attempts to regain this vital ground on 3 June drove the enemy back a short distance at the cost of heavy losses but the Germans still held most of their gains. Another major operation, supported by considerable artillery, was planned for 12 June and, to give the roughly-handled 3rd Division time to prepare, Ketchen's 6th Brigade was brought in to reinforce it.

The brigade took up its positions during the night of 5/6 June under an intense German bombardment which caused heavy casualties in the 31st and unnerved a number of new men who had only joined the unit on the previous day. The 31st occupied a position in the line south of the remains of a copse called Zouave Wood. To its left was the 28th Battalion (Northwest) with two companies somewhat advanced around the little village of Hooge. The two units soon discovered that this was not a happy place as they were under observation from enemy positions on high ground on three sides and the Germans took full advantage of this asset. Beginning at 7 a.m. on 6 June a heavy and accurate bombardment commenced – at one point during the morning a hundred shells fell in the immediate vicinity of the battalion headquarters. Private Fraser recorded that the enemy artillery fire was

> of unprecedented accuracy. The shells were bursting in or near the trench and the gunfire would run from end to end. It played along the line as if worked by a hose. Gunfire so precise and methodical in execution strikes terror, even into the bravest hearts. Stuck in a trench, with shells creeping gradu-

> ally nearer and nearer to you from the right, and through a good piece of fortune you escape, only to go through the same ordeal as the fire sweeps back from the left, is unnerving to the last degree. All the time you hear the noise from the guns and brace yourself for the burst, which you expect every moment on top of you. …… This systematic shellfire, which aims at complete destruction of a helpless foe, has swelled our hospitals and asylums to the brim.[32]

The battalion endured more than eight hours of this hell and it was too much for many of the green men who "lost their heads and either scattered wildly or got jumbled up in the trench."[33] As if all this was not bad enough, it rained throughout the day.

At about 3 P.M., the Germans exploded four mines under the two forward companies of the 28th Battalion at Hooge. Two hundred yards of trench disappeared, one company was completely wiped out and the other lost most of its men. The Germans then attacked and captured most of the village although their advance was stopped by the remaining two companies in the support line. At the same time the 26th (Württemberg) Division attacked directly west against the positions of the 31st Battalion. The Germans came on in small groups of about 100 men, about 30 yards apart, and in short rushes. They "came over," Private Fraser remembered, "with full accoutrements evidently expecting a walk over."[34] If that was true, the Württembergers were in for a shock as the Albertans, only too glad that the German bombardment had lifted, manned their firing trench and cut them down with highly accurate fire. The battalion machinegunners "got in some useful work" but, as Fraser remembered, most of the killing was done by rifle fire. "Hunter got a bead on a Hun and dropped him. Macdougall accounted for an officer who was waving his men forward. A Hun going to his assistance got a renewal of the dose and dropped to the ground." The attack was completely repelled as was a second attack that took place a few hours later when the Germans, "several hundred of them," advanced again but "we managed to bag the most" although "some got about 30 yards of our parapet." In the late afternoon, the Germans gave up and the heavy shelling began again and continued for the next two days until the 31st Battalion was relieved on the night of 8 June. Five days later, after the heaviest artillery bombardment the Canadian Corps had yet mounted, the 1st and 3rd Divisions regained most of the lost ground and the situation was stabilized.

The Battle of Mount Sorrel cost the Alberta Battalion 50 killed, 196 wounded and 2 missing. At the rest camp in the rear, the unit absorbed another 200 new men from the 9th Reserve Battalion, the western Canadian reserve unit in England, and set out to rebuild itself again. The unit history records that by June 1916, only half the men who had sailed from England the previous September were still in the ranks and it was Fraser's opinion that, from this time on, the original battalion began to disappear although, for a short period at least, men from the Calgary days still constituted the greater part of the officers and NCOs. Their obstinate resistance at St. Eloi and Hooge had earned the 6th Brigade the nickname of the "Iron Brigade" or the "Iron Sixth" while, for their tenacity in the same battles, the 31st was dubbed "Bell's Bulldogs" after their commanding officer. It was at this time that a soldier of the 28th Battalion penned a poem about the brigade which celebrated each of the four units in the formation and which, the 31st Battalion historian assures us, was set to music and "not infrequently" sung on the march.[35] Of the Alberta Battalion, the poet said:

> A breath from Calgary's City, flung where the fight is worst,
> Still more of Canada's manhood is the gallant thirty-first.
> From prairie land and city, they've answered to the call
> And bravely shouldered rifle lest their Empire's honour fall.[36]

Be that as it may, after a final short tour in the trenches near Mount Sorrel, the 31st went with the remainder of the brigade to a rest camp on 29 June. On Dominion Day, 1 July 1916, the four battalions held a sports meeting in which the 27th and 28th Battalions walked off with most of the prizes but all through that day, the men could hear the sound of heavy artillery fire from the south as the long-awaited Somme offensive had now begun.

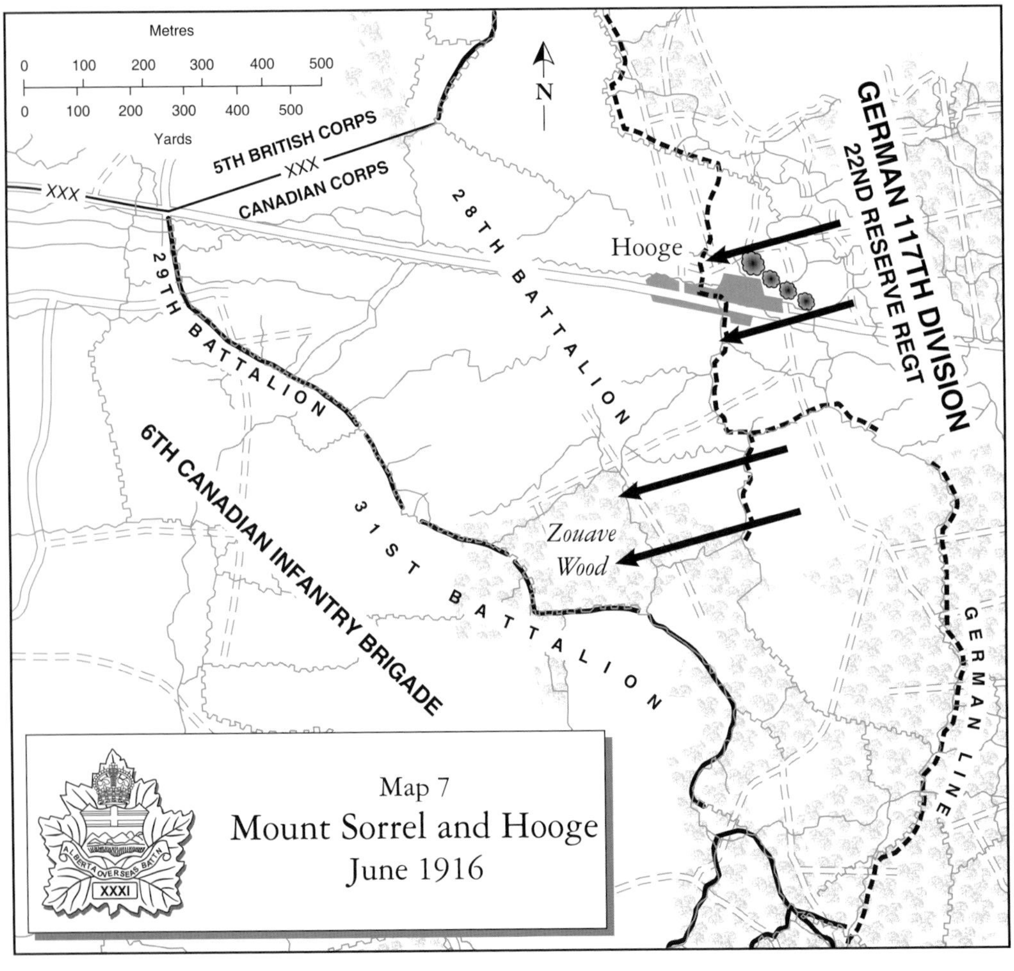

"I couldn't stop urinating": The Somme, July–September 1916

Haig's preparations were complete at the end of June 1916. The BEF, with contingents from the Dominions, now numbered over one million men organized in four armies and 58 divisions. In Haig's initial planning, the Somme operation had no overriding geographical objective, the area had been chosen because it was on the junction point of the British and French sectors of the Western Front and Haig's purpose was to relieve pressure on the French at Verdun, prevent German troops from being shifted to the Eastern Front where the Russians had launched another major offensive, and inflict casualties on the enemy. The continued fighting at Verdun reduced the French contribution to the attack and the Somme became a largely British and Dominion operation. More than half the British divisions allotted to the Somme attack were from the so-called "New Armies" raised in the previous eighteen months from civilians in the industrial midlands, many of whom had joined "Pals Battalions" made up of friends from the same school, factory, business or social club, who had enlisted under the promise that they would be allowed to serve and fight together. The "New Armies" were enthusiastic, inexperienced and poorly trained but, by this time in the war, Haig had plenty of artillery and ammunition – his staff assembled more than 1,500 guns for the assault and planned a week-long preliminary bombardment that would be followed, on 1 July 1916, by a massive attack by 13 divisions on a 16-mile front. Haig and his staff were confident that the weight of the bombardment would devastate the German frontline defenders and his infantry would simply walk into the enemy positions. For seven days the men in the assault divisions cheerfully listened as the unceasing artillery bombardment crashed into the German lines opposite. Much of the shelling was devoted to destroying the barbed wire belts in front of the German frontline trenches and artillery planners had used thousands of rounds of shrapnel for this purpose but, unfortunately, this was a major miscalculation and the wire was largely left unscathed. As the time crept down to the zero hour for the assault, 7.30 A.M. on 1 July, however, almost everyone was confident that this time it would be easy.

As the minutes ticked away, scaling ladders, previously brought into the firing line, were laid ready

Map 7
Mount Sorrel and Hooge
June 1916

to be thrown up when the whistles blew. Due to German counter bombardment, an attempt was made to thin out the assaulting troops but, as the last rounds came down one recalled,

The tension affected the men in different ways. I couldn't stop urinating ...... The ground shook and trembled, and the concussion made our ears ring. It was impossible to hear ourselves speak to a man lying alongside. It is strange how men creep together for protection. Soon, instead of four paces interval between the men, we came down to lying alongside each other, and no motioning could make them move apart.[37]

Promptly on time officers blew their whistles and climbed the ladders, enthusiastically followed by their men.

It was slaughter. The Germans emerged from the deep shelters that had protected them and manned the *Stottertanten* ("stuttering aunts") or *Nähmaschinen* ("sewing machines") – the 7.92 mm Maxim MG O8 machineguns firing 450 rounds per minute – which cut down the advancing troops, many of whom advanced shoulder to shoulder, by the hundreds, and then the thousands. Those few that got close to the enemy frontline discovered to their horror that the shrapnel had not cut the wire and they were pinned down, unable to move forward or back. Wave after wave of infantry went over that morning and whole battalions were decimated – 32 of the assaulting battalions lost more than 500 men each and one division suffered 6,380 casualties in six hours. In some places the attack was called off but,

On parade, Sergeant Samuel Lewis, A Squadron, Canadian Light Horse
Sergeant Samuel Lewis poses for the camera in late 1916 or early 1917. He is wearing a stetson with a 19th Dragoon badge, Dragoon collar badges and CLH brass shoulder titles and the CLH ribbon on his shoulder strap. He is mounted on a Universal Pattern Steel Arch Saddle, most likely the 1902 Pattern and is armed with a Model 1908 sword strapped to the saddle on the near (or left) side of his horse. His horse is harnessed with a 1902 Universal Pattern Portsmouth bit with the so-called "1902 Pattern" bridle and has been closely cropped except for its legs. COURTESY, COLIN MICHAUD

Canadian Light Horse Band, 1916
In the spring of 1916 the three divisional cavalry squadrons of the Canadian Corps were reorganized as the Canadian Light Horse. Shortly afterward, the regimental band posed for their picture wearing CLH brass shoulder titles and the CLH ribbon on the shoulder straps of their British pattern 5-button jackets. The three squadrons of the new unit continued to wear their original collar badges and thus the badge of the 19th Alberta Dragoons, now A Squadron of the CLH, can be seen adorning some collars in this photo as well as the badges of the 1st Hussars and 16th Light Horse which formed the other two squadrons. COURTESY, COLIN MICHAUD

Behind the lines, summer, 1916
Men of the Canadian Light Horse relax at a sports meeting in the summer of 1916. By this time in the war, senior commanders were beginning to realize that longer rest periods were necessary for soldiers if they wished them to retain combat efficiency. NAC, PA-448

35,493 wounded – and it can be truly said that 1 July 1916 marked the day that empire ended because such was the psychological shock of the first day of the Somme that it is still deeply etched within the British national consciousness.

Despite elaborate planning and the deployment of all available personnel, the medical services were simply overwhelmed by casualties that were three, four, five, a dozen times greater than anticipated. One small mercy was the close proximity of excellent road, rail and marine connections which permitted many wounded to be evacuated to England. In that country, where the artillery firing in the week-long bombardment could be heard in communities along the Channel coast, there was confidence, based on the first and inaccurate newspaper reports, that the attack had met with great success and losses were light. This mood was dispelled when overcrowded medical trains began to arrive day and night in cities and towns the length of England. The lightly wounded ("walking wounded" was the term in use) were sent to hospitals in the industrial midlands. A woman in Rochdale remembered seeing a procession of bandaged and bleeding men slowly climbing the steep hill that led from the station to the local hospital, helping each other, even pushing each other in hastily-procured bath chairs while medical personnel and civilians did what they could to assist. The seriously wounded, unable to survive prolonged journeys, were sent to hospitals along the southeast coast. A nurse stationed at a hospital in Hampstead where the ambulances had to be unloaded in the street was horrified to see

at this time in the war, the only effective means of communication was by runner and runners did not last long on 1 July 1916. Unable to get accurate information, many senior commanders continued to send troops forward to reinforce what they thought was a hard fight – they were actually sending these men to their deaths. One of the most tragic incidents on that most tragic of days was the fate of the Newfoundland Regiment, part of the British 29th Division. Assigned to attack near the ruined village of Beaumont Hamel, the Newfoundlanders were forced to bunch up to cross a few narrow gaps in the German wire and were massacred, losing 310 killed and 374 wounded in less than an hour. The Somme attack, however, continued until dark as unit after unit, division after division, moved forward. When night fell, the attackers had gained a toehold in the German line of about a mile deep and three miles wide. For this the British Empire paid a terrible cost – 19,240 men killed and

His Majesty's Land Ship: Mk I British tank, Courcelette, September 1916
The 31st Alberta Battalion participated in the first use of tanks in warfare at the battle of Courcelette on 15 September 1916. Three Mk I tanks supported the 6th Brigade that day but only one made it to the German lines, where it caused widespread panic among the enemy. Manned by a crew of eight, the Mk I was armed with two 57 mm guns in side sponsons as well as four machineguns and was capable of a top speed of about 3-4 miles per hour. The screen on top of the vehicle is to deflect grenades and the two wheels at the back of the tank were used for steering although this method was later dropped in favour of steering by the tracks. BY KIND PERMISSION OF THE TRUSTEES OF THE IMPERIAL WAR MUSEUM, Q 5572

fascinated schoolboys gathered around the vehicles and keeping up a loud and continuous stream of commentary: "Coo! He's got no hands ...... Blimey! Look, he's bleeding." She screamed at them to leave because it "was very upsetting for our boys, being stared at like freaks."[38] A few days later, the telegrams with the fateful phrase, "regret to inform you," went out and in almost every community across Britain there were houses with closed curtains and doors adorned with black crepe.

But the Somme offensive continued. Haig had to take pressure off the French at Verdun and prevent the enemy from shifting forces to Italy and the East where the Italian and Russian armies were making gains. The Allies were buoyed by the entry of Rumania into the war on their side and it was clear that the Germans were also suffering heavy losses. Gradually, the Somme offensive took on a life of its own as Haig decided that, instead of being a holding operation, it might just achieve decisive results. The attacks therefore continued through the summer in a battle of attrition which Haig calculated would reduce German strength to a point where he could deliver a final blow sometime in September. In August the four divisions of the ANZAC (Australian and New Zealand Army Corps) entered the fray – big rangy men who had established a magnificent reputation during the ill-fated landing at Gallipoli. They were committed to an attack on the village of Pozières on a commanding ridge and they took it in five weeks of heavy fighting, losing 23,000 killed and wounded in the process.

In the first days of September the ANZACs were relieved by the Canadian Corps, for it was now Canada's turn to enter the killing ground.

"A big surprise for the old Hun this time": Courcelette, 15 September 1916

The redeployment of the Corps from the Salient to the Somme was part of Haig's plan to mount a major "knock-out" blow against the enemy. He envisaged a two-army assault on a 10-mile front, intended to penetrate the German third line of defence as, despite heavy losses, the BEF had gradually ground its way through the first two enemy lines in the Somme. If a breakthrough was achieved, Haig planned to launch his cavalry into the open ground beyond, forcing a major German withdrawal and possibly breaking the deadlock on the Western Front. To accomplish this, he planned to employ a new artillery tactic – rather than a lengthy and heavy preliminary bombardment, his gunners would bring down a concentrated bombardment shortly before the attack went in and, as the infantry advanced, would fire a moving barrage immediately ahead of them to keep

Brewed up

British Mk I tank, bogged, brewed and abandoned by its crew at the Somme in 1916. The first use of tanks in this offensive terrified the German infantry but they recovered after they found armoured vehicles could be stopped by direct fire from field guns and that the tank crew's limited visibility was a drawback in action. The Germans then turned all available weapons on any tank that appeared and this made the tanks unpopular with their supporting infantry as they attracted fire. NAC, PA-001012

the Germans in their dugouts. Finally, Haig planned to employ a secret weapon that had been in development for more than a year – 45 recently-manufactured tanks which would accompany the assault waves to take out any Maxim guns that survived the bombardment and barrage. The Canadian Corps was given the job of securing a formidable series of defences in front of the ruined village of Courcelette, a mile northeast of Pozières, with the main assault to be delivered by the 4th and 6th Brigades of the 2nd Division, including the 31st Battalion. Zero hour was set for 6.20 A.M., 15 September.

After a two-day train journey from the Salient the 31st Battalion reached the Somme on 6 September 1916. As they marched to a billet just behind the line, they could hear the rumble of artillery and could see no less than 19 tethered observation balloons hovering in the sky. Moving forward they passed an Australian infantry unit marching out, their appearance "bore out that they had undergone terrific hardships, their faces being wan, eyes weak and watery, shoulders drooping and marching irregular."[39] For its part, the 31st was in good fettle. It was now nearly three months since the battalion had seen heavy fighting and it had recovered from its ordeals at St. Eloi and Hooge. In August the 2nd Division had at long last exchanged its despised Ross rifles for Lee-Enfields and another novelty was the recent issue of unit identification patches worn on the upper arm. These were in various combinations of shapes and colours which, at a glance, permitted a trained observer to identify a man's division, brigade and battalion. As the fourth battalion in the third brigade of the 2nd Division, the men of the 31st now wore a dark blue square surmounted by a smaller square of the same colour. For its part, the Canadian Light Horse adopted a badge consisting of a three-colour ribbon worn on the left shoulder strap, the colours being taken from the colours of the three divisions from which its squadrons had been taken: red for the 1st Division, dark blue for the 2nd and blue-grey for the 3rd

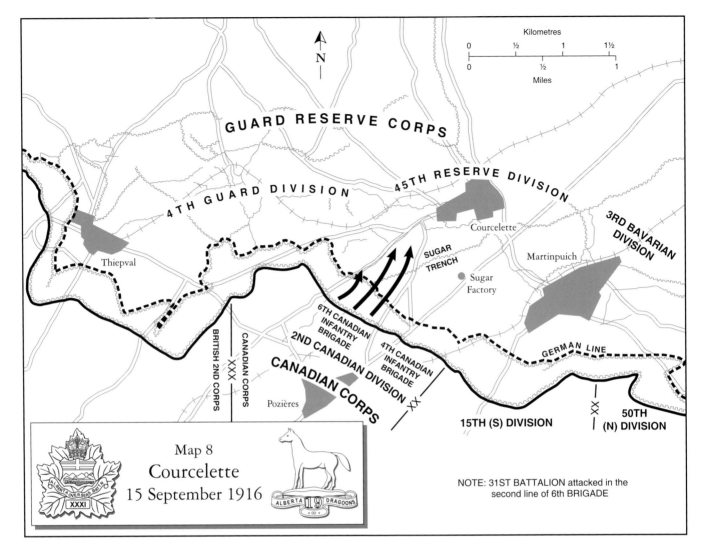

Map 8
Courcelette
15 September 1916

NOTE: 31ST BATTALION attacked in the
second line of 6th BRIGADE

Division. This ribbon was woven in the form – dark blue, red, blue-grey – and worn with the dark blue strip next to the point of the shoulder.

On the night of 11 September the 2nd and 3rd Canadian Divisions relieved the 1st Division which had been holding the line and began making preparations for the assault. On the following day both divisions were fascinated witnesses of an aerial dogfight above their trenches:

> We had a great view of an aeroplane fight this morning which ended in a victory for our man. The fight took place right over our lines (support) and they went at it hard and at very close quarters too. The machines were almost touching at times. At last our man got in a good shot and hit the Hun gas tank, no doubt, as he took fire and came tumbling down in a sheet of flames. The boys gave our man a great cheer as he flew away.[40]

That night Major William Hewgill and the senior officers of the two assault brigades were taken to see a demonstration of the new secret weapon. Hewgill was enthusiastic:

> We have a big surprise for the old Hun this time – We have a machine which is built something like a submarine. It was invented by a Naval man and they are called H.M.L.S. (His Majesty's Land Ship) and are given names such as *Cupid Chartreuse – Gordon Gin* and *Cream de menthe*. ...... These machines are built on the Caterpillar style and shaped as I said before like a submarines – They are armour plated and are fitted with a periscope (2) two six pound guns and several machine guns and Automatic rifles. The crew gets inside and closes the door and then look out – They can go over trenches – shell holes – ditches – climb a wall and in fact can go almost anywhere. They weigh about 30 tons and up to the present have been an absolute secret. We have six attached to our B[riga]de. and there will be sixty (60) of them taking part in the Big Push which starts on 15th. ...... Rifle fire or shrapnel fire has no effect on them and nothing but a direct hit from a high explosive shell will stop them.[41]

Actually, the number of tanks available was far fewer and only three were allotted to the 6th Brigade but everybody was convinced that they would bring the war to a swift and successful end.

The plan was that the 27th and 28th Battalions would advance in four company lines each, followed by the 29th and 31st which would do the necessary "mopping up" and carry extra ammunition, grenades and sandbags to consolidate the captured enemy position. The distance to be covered between the lines varied from a quarter of a mile to a mile and since men of the battalion were loaded down with extra ammunition and equipment, Private Fraser of A Company decided that "speedy manoeuvre was practically impossible."[42] At 9.30 in the evening of 14 September, the four companies of the 31st moved into the communication trenches. Fraser recalled that his comrades' "attitude was possibly a little more serious and quieter than usual" but that the jokers in his company started making funny cracks and it was "impossible to quell them, and when all is said and done, they are the best men to have in the ranks in modern warfare" as "a jovial temperament seems to be an antidote to morbid thought, fear or cowardice." The men huddled in the communication trenches during a very restless night and were glad to be ordered into the firing line at 3.30 A.M. ready for the attack. The communication trenches were so crowded that it "was impossible to move forward or backward," Fraser recalled, and, among his comrades, "wrath as usual began to rise and imprecations were showered upon those in charge" all the way up, it is certain, beyond Haig to King George V. Fed up, A Company left the trenches and dodged from shell hole to shell hole to reach their forming up position but, running into another traffic jam, became jumbled with the men of the 29th Battalion.

Friday, 15 September 1916 dawned clear and calm. Promptly on time the gunners brought down a heavy bombardment on the closest German positions and then the infantry moved forward in lines. Hewgill, who was at the battalion headquarters, recorded that the attack "was successful from the beginning" while Lieutenant-Colonel D.E. McIntyre of the 28th Battalion, also in the rear, wrote in his diary that "the objectives were all reached and captured by 7 A.M."[43] It is uncertain which battle these two officers were describing as, according to Private Fraser who took part in it, the attack on Courcelette was not at all an easy victory and his detailed account is worth quoting at length.

When the attack began, Fraser climbed out of the trench with his comrades and ran forward, hunched over and dodging shell holes, until, as he remembered,

I raised my head for the first time and looked at the Hun trench, and to my astonishment, saw Heiny after Heiny ranging along the line, up on the firing step, blazing wildly into us, to all appearances unmolested. Seriousness and grim determination took possession of me as I stared hard and menacing at those death-dealing rifles. Strange to say they all seemed to be pointing at me, an illusion but nevertheless that is how it appeared. My eyes were for a moment glued a little ahead to the right on Sgt Hunter, who was leading with Lt. Newlands beside him. He appeared a picture, heroic in the extreme; his rush had dwindled to practically a walk, and he

strode forward with body erect, right in the forefront, a target for innumerable shots. As I was levelling up on the left, it seemed a thousand miracles that he was not laid low. ......

Immediately above, the atmosphere was cracking with a myriad of machine-gun bullets, startling and disconcerting in the extreme. Bullets from the enemy rifles were whistling and swishing around my ears in hundreds, so that to this day I cannot understand how anyone could have crossed that inferno alive. As I pressed forward with eyes strained, to the extent of being half closed, I expected and almost felt being shot in the stomach. All around our men were falling, their rifles loosening from their grips. The wounded, writhing in their agonies, struggled and toppled into shell holes for safety from rifle and machinegun fire, though in my path the latter must have been negligible, for a slow or even quick traverse would have brought us down before we reached many yards into No Man's Land. Rifle fire, however, was taking its toll, and on my front and flanks, soldier after soldier was tumbling to disablement and death, and I expected my turn every moment.

At this point Fraser took shelter in a shell hole and looked back to see "waves of men coming on, right away back to the parapet [of the Canadian firing trench], but they were collapsing right and left and not a single one got as far forward as the remnants of our own Company."

Pinned down, Fraser and the other men of A Company brought the Germans under aimed rifle fire until Lieutenant F.P.D. Newland

rose up a little from me and gallantly endeavoured to signal us forward by a sweep of his hand, but the time was inopportune and no one moved. He himself was hardly up, when he was wounded and fell back in the shell hole. In the adjoining shell hole, almost touching ours, Lt. Foster got up almost simultaneously with Newland and promptly collapsed back again, having been hit in the upper arm or shoulder. Freudemacher jumped in beside him to render first aid. It seemed that Foster was painfully hit, for I could see for a minute or two, an arm waving backward and forward above the shell hole, as if he were in pain.

It seemed to Fraser that the assault had failed and that "our only hope lay in waiting until darkness set in and then trying to win our way back."

It was at this critical point, with the assault battalions pinned down in front of the German lines, that a huge, gray object came in view that slowly "crawled along like gigantic toad, feeling its way across the shell-stricken field." It was big, beautiful Creme de Menthe, the only one of the three Mk I tanks assigned to the 6th Brigade to make it as far as "No Man's Land." As the tank rumbled forward, Fraser remembered, men rose from the ground "as if from the dead, and running from the flanks to behind it, followed it in the rear to be in on the kill. The sight of this behemoth rumbling toward them was too much for the Germans and most threw down their weapons, jumped out of their trenches and headed in the general direction of Berlin. The men of the 6th Brigade promptly ran forward into the German firing trench only to find no enemy capable of resistance.

The objective secured, everyone now got down to the serious work of collecting souvenirs, chasing "up and down the trench looking for Iron Crosses." Fraser cut the buttons off the coat of a dead German but found it a tough job as they had been fastened with wire. He got a dagger with a fancy tassel, a revolver which he gave to his sergeant (always a good idea to keep NCOs happy), a purse with money, a cheap watch, two helmets, a couple of caps and some postcards, all of which he deposited in his loot bag, an empty sandbag brought along for just such a purpose. The Albertans, who had long been told that the enemy was on the verge of collapse, were amazed to find the German trench system well constructed, scrupulously clean and plentifully supplied with cigars, rations and white rum which everyone "greatly appreciated" but thought "it did not compare with our S.R.D." This enjoyable pause for refreshment completed, A Company and the rest of the battalion began to consolidate and begin the construction of communication trenches back to the Canadian line, work that was done under the orders of the NCOs as no officers appeared to be about. German shelling and sniping increased in tempo throughout the day and the battalion was glad at 5.15 P.M. to be ordered back to its position of the morning.

On the return trip, Fraser and his comrades came across "a fellow, minus equipment, lying on his back yelling and kicking up a deuce of a row." Thinking the man was badly wounded, Fraser went closer only to find "Mackintosh of No. 4 Platoon, helplessly full of Fritz's rum, as happy as a lark, and trying to sing for all he was worth." They left Mackintosh to his revels and arrived back in the Canadian lines only to find out why there were so few officers around – of the 22 officers of the battalion who had gone forward that morning, 13 had become casualties including all four company commanders. The 31st had also lost about half its enlisted men. The attack, however, had been so successful that the 5th Brigade was brought in to consolidate the gains and managed to capture Courcelette. That night Private Fraser went back with three other volunteers to bring in the body of Major George Splane, the dead commander of A Company, and they encountered detachments from the other three companies on similar missions. By this time, the Germans were bringing down heavy artillery fire so, once they had recovered Splane's body, Fraser's group hurried as quickly as possible back to their own lines.

The 31st Battalion had not only successfully accomplished its support mission, but three "battle patrols" it sent out with the 27th and 28th Battalions penetrated farther into Courcelette than any other troops that day. Many prisoners were taken by the Iron Brigade – the 31st might have brought in more but, as Hewgill cryptically noted, "after the way the Boche acted I don't think the boys can be blamed."[44] The 28th Battalion, however, collected very few Germans and when a brigade officer accosted a soldier from that unit to ask what the Winnipeggers were doing with their prisoners, he received the blunt reply: "We're not taking any, they blew mines under us twice."[45] Many of those prisoners that did make it back alive to the Canadian rear area were horror stricken by the tanks and one complained that the use of these infernal new machines was not war but "savage butchery."[46]

"Go forward and tangle with the enemy": Thiepval Ridge, 26-29 September 1916

The Alberta Battalion was relieved on 16 September and spent the next week in a series of bivouacs in the rear while it tried to absorb a draft of 275 reinforcements. During this time, the 1st and 3rd Divisions attempted to push north and east of Courcelette but paid heavy losses for only small gains. It was becoming clear to Lieutenant-General Sir Julian Byng that another major assault would have to be mounted from Courcelette with the objective of taking a German trench running along Thiepval Ridge, commanding ground about a 1000 yards northeast of the village. The Iron Brigade got the job and this time Ketchen put the 29th and 31st Battalions in the lead with the 27th and 28th in support. The attack was to begin at 12.30 on 26 September following heavy preliminary bombardment but when the brigade moved into position in the forward trenches on 25 September, it suffered many casualties from heavy German shelling. Lieutenant-Colonel Arthur Bell and Major William Hewgill then went forward to make a personal reconnaissance of the ground over which the battalion would have to advance and became concerned that the heavy shelling indicated that the enemy was forewarned.

But orders were orders and the attack had to go ahead. In the crowded forward trenches, the men crouched because the shelling was relentless all through the night of 25/26 September. As always, the hours of waiting were the worst part:

> Men stand in silence, or converse in low voices, often breaking off absent mindedly in the middle of a sentence; feet move restlessly, and hands pluck irritably at the collars of shirt or tunic; officers, at the cost of an effort known only to themselves, preserve an outward nonchalance which is betrayed by the too frequent glances at the dials of their wrist watches. To all the minutes pass on leaden feet until at last the waiting is over and the tension snaps into swift and desperate, but welcome, action.[47]

The enemy shelling increased on the morning of 26 September but, at 12.30 P.M., the whistles blew and the men went forward as their own artillery brought down a furious bombardment on the German forward positions. Unfortunately, their range was incorrect and most of the rounds landed harmlessly some 50 yards to the rear of the target while the Germans responded with a terrific counter-bombardment which fell squarely on the waiting assault troops.

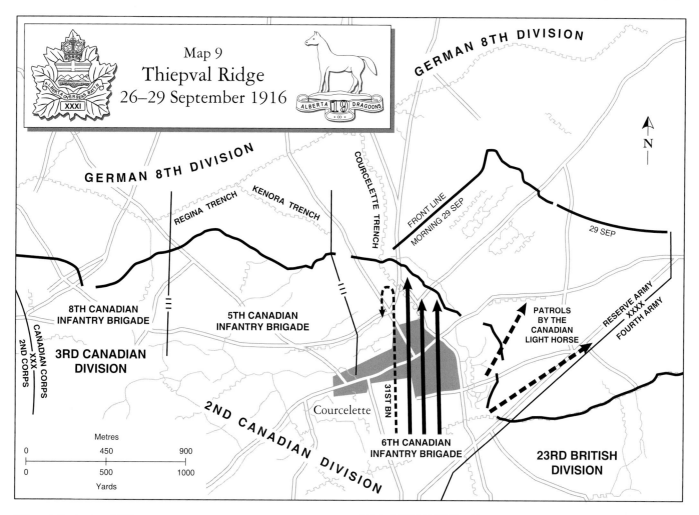

Map 9
Thiepval Ridge
26–29 September 1916

GERMAN 8TH DIVISION

GERMAN 8TH DIVISION

REGINA TRENCH

KENORA TRENCH

COURCELLETTE TRENCH

FRONT LINE MORNING 29 SEP

29 SEP

8TH CANADIAN
INFANTRY BRIGADE

5TH CANADIAN
INFANTRY BRIGADE

PATROLS
BY THE
CANADIAN
LIGHT HORSE

CANADIAN CORPS
XXX
2ND CORPS

RESERVE ARMY
XXXX
FOURTH ARMY

3RD CANADIAN
DIVISION

2ND CANADIAN DIVISION

Courcelette

31ST BN

6TH CANADIAN
INFANTRY BRIGADE

23RD BRITISH
DIVISION

Metres
0   450   900

0   500   1000
Yards

Thiepval, September 1916

Aerial photo of the junction of Regina and Kenora (lower) trenches northeast of Courcelette. Note the numerous shell craters made by heavy artillery bombardment which has almost obliterated the previous system of trenches. The 31st Battalion attacked Thiepval Ridge just east of this point on 26 September 1916 and suffered 392 casualties, almost half the unit's strength, including 16 of the 22 officers who participated in the assault. By the time this action, the last major battle of the 1916 Somme campaign had ended, there were only four officers in the battalion left from of its early days in Calgary – and two of them were non-combatants. After two months of furious and costly fighting, Haig's 1916 offensive had ended in stalemate, at the cost of between 480,000 and 680,000 casualties. NAC, C-14151

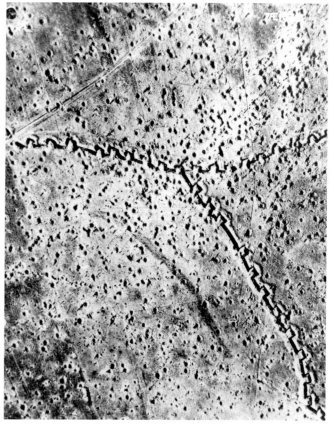

Nonetheless, over they went, only to encounter "a murderous fire from rifle and machine gun."[48] It was clear that the Germans were far from demoralized and the leading companies were forced to take cover until their officers got them going again. There had not been time to properly train or integrate the many raw reinforcements in the unit and, as Fraser noted, these men soon became "unnerved by the roar of artillery and noise of bursting shells and the thought of facing death was too much of a strain on them and they failed to grasp the situation and understand that they had to go forward and tangle with the enemy."[49] Leading by example, the officers and NCOs got those veterans who were still on their feet close enough to the German firing trench to engage in a mutual grenade exchange. "Attempt after attempt was made to … come to grips with the enemy," the regimental historian wrote, but "time after time the ranks of the attacking troops withered under the hail of rifle and machine gun bullets from the enemy positions."[50] Every officer in the two leading companies, B and D, was killed or wounded and Lieutenant H. Kennedy came over from A Company to take command of the assault elements. Kennedy then made two attempts to close with the defenders but each time his men were forced to take cover from the furious small arms fire and here they stayed until dark. Things got serious in the late afternoon when A Company, which was holding the battalion's positions to the rear, received a German counterattack which they managed to beat off.

As dusk fell, Bell received orders from Ketchen to make another attack at 11 P.M. Gathering up the remnants of the four companies he found that his strength was half of what it had been that morning. A short bombardment was brought down on the German position but, again, the gunners had the range wrong and it fell harmlessly to the rear. The battalion then moved forward only to be pounded by a German bombardment and the enemy gunners had the range to the exact foot. Casualties were again heavy but some of the survivors managed to reach and occupy a small section of the German trench and this position was gradually expanded. When morning came on 27 September it became clear that the enemy had withdrawn and fresh units were brought up to reinforce the 31st and consolidate the position – by this time A Company was less than platoon strength.

September 26 and 27 1916 were a very busy time for Captain Harold McGill who established his Regimental Aid Post in a deep German dugout in Courcelette:

[26 September]
12.35 hrs: Zero hour. Bombardment for attack begins. Enemy barrage comes back almost immediately. Very intense bombardment.

14.00 hrs: Wounded begin to arrive and a constant stream keeps up all afternoon. Some very severe cases. Sgt. E. Barnes, stretcher bearer, had leg blown off at knee. …… Have sent to Field Ambulance collecting post for help to clear the wounded.

18.00 hrs: 31st. Battalion attack repulsed. Constant stream of wounded. 3 stretcher cases are lying at door of dug-out.

Terrific Enemy shelling around R.A.P. One of the cases at the door walks out. Orderly Willis brings another in. The third case has disappeared. We can find no trace of him and do not know whether he has crawled away or has been blown to pieces.

19.00 hrs: We have cleared a large number of wounded but still have 8 stretcher cases in R.A.P.

22.00 hrs: Enemy shelling very heavy. We now have 9 stretcher cases in dug-out.

Orderly Willis takes out party and brings in Sgt. Tripp, 27th Battalion, from shell hole in village. Our door partly smashed in, by heavy shell, direct hit.

[27 September]
6.00 hrs: Bright morning. Walking casualties have been passing through all night. …… We send out a number, by parties of slightly wounded men, as carriers. We also utilize some stragglers. 4 Field Ambulance squads, work, clearing from R.A.P. to collecting post.

Lieut. Mee and Lieut. Scott are passed through on stretchers. The latter was shot through pelvis yesterday. Peritonitis beginning.

15.00 hrs: We have all our stretcher cases cleared. Battalion has reached objective. ……

20.00 hrs: Night quiet. A few walking cases coming through. Since yesterday morning we have passed through 3 Officers and 68 O.R. of 31st Battalion.[51]

During the night of 29 September the Albertans were relieved and moved back to a rest camp in the rear where Major William Hewgill recorded the aftermath of Thiepval:

Of 22 officers going in only six returned, the balance being either killed, wounded or missing. The casualties among the men were 370. We are bivouacked for a few days in the Tara Valley and we reorganize the B[attalio]n. Our total trench [fighting] strength including reinforcements is now 360. It is a cold and miserable day.[52]

While the 31st was suffering on Thiepval Ridge, the 19th Dragoons – as A Squadron of the Canadian Light Horse – were seeing action not far away. The CLH sent out a number of mounted patrols to the west of Courcelette during the fighting of 26-29 September both to ascertain enemy positions and to keep contact with 23rd British Division on the right of the Canadian Corps. These came under German machinegun fire and were turned back. The Light Horse's main contribution to the attack on the Thiepval Ridge, however, was the provision of two 120-man stretcher parties to the 2nd and 3rd Infantry Brigades when they attacked about a thousand yards west of the 31st Battalion on 26 September. Sergeant-Major George Stirrett was in charge of a bearer detachment attached to the 8th Battalion and 26 September 1916 was a day Stirrett never forgot:

I was going from shellhole to shellhole which at the Somme almost interlocked. In a shellhole ahead, I spotted a boy from Saskatchewan, lying wounded. He looked like my younger brother Jack, who was with the artillery. I touched the boy and he opened his eyes. I asked him what I could do for him.

"Sergeant major" he said "Will you answer a question honestly for me?" I said I would. "Sergeant major" he said "Do you believe in God?" My answer was yes. "Sergeant major" he said "Will you pray to God for me? I'm going to be with him in a few minutes." You could not fool with this request. Then he told me to go and help others. But I was to come back later and empty his pockets and answer the letters which I would find there. He wanted to be alone.

What happened to me then, I don't know. But all fear was gone. I walked and went any place I wished to that day and night without fear. I came back in about an hour and emptied his pockets. We worked that day, that night, and the next day as stretcher bearers under continuous fire. ……

In my diary for this date, I have written "Whoever it was that said War is Hell was correct."[53]

The fighting on the Somme continued until early November 1916 and ultimately all four divisions of the Canadian Corps became involved in it. When Haig finally called a halt to operations, he had gained a strip of ground 20 miles wide and 6 miles deep but the farthest penetration was still 3 miles short of Bapaume, his primary objective the previous July. Haig had relieved the German pressure on Verdun, prevented Germany from transferring forces to the Eastern Front and had certainly inflicted heavy losses on the enemy – between 450,000 and 680,000 according to different sources – including, as one enemy general remarked, what was left of the "old first-class, peace-trained German infantry."[54] Against this, the British Empire had suffered losses of 419,654 men (24,029 of them Canadian) while the French had lost 204,253. The Somme was a turning point and the men of the BEF were never the same after it – acute observers noted that, from this time on, soldiers tended to sing much less than they had in previous times.

As for the 31st Battalion, Canadian Expeditionary Force, their losses in their four major battles of 1916 – St. Eloi, Mount Sorrel, Courcelette and Thiepval Ridge – had cost the unit 202 officers and men killed, 753 wounded and 147 missing, a total of 1,092, a figure that does not count those lost in so-called "quiet" periods or from sickness. When the battalion marched out of the Somme on 4 October 1916, only a hundred men remained of those who had marched with it into that killing ground a month before. Major William Hewgill noted in his diary that there were just four officers remaining who had been with the battalion at Calgary in the spring of 1915: the commanding officer, Hewgill himself, the medical officer and the padre.

But the human spirit is an amazing thing and the survivors gradually began to recover – on 8 October while the Alberta Battalion was enjoying a rest camp in Warloy, Hewgill crowed to his diary: "*A great event happened today. I had a bath in Soft Water. Somme Bath.*"[55]

Still not downhearted but very tired
Canadian infantrymen come out of the line in November 1916. During three months at the Somme, the Canadian Corps experienced its hardest fighting yet in the war, suffering heavy casualties in the process. Unfortunately, things would get worse the following year. NAC, PA-000914

Regimental mascot, 187th Battalion, Canadian Expeditionary Force
Richard Robinson, the son of Lieutenant-Colonel C.W. Robinson, commanding the 187th Battalion CEF, and clearly the unit mascot, poses proudly in his miniature officer's uniform in front of the Regimental Colours at Sarcee Camp in 1916. Dick Robinson acquired a liking for soldiering and joined the Calgary Regiment in 1931 before transferring to the South Alberta Regiment in 1940, where he served as the unit's technical adjutant from Normandy to the Baltic. GLENBOW MUSEUM, NA-3232-67

Home Fires

CANADA AND ALBERTA
DURING THE WAR

God save our splendid men,
Send them safe home again,
God save our men.
Send them victorious,
Patient and chivalrous
They are so dear to us,
God save our men.[1]

Victory Bonds and "temporary" income tax: How Canada financed the war

While the men of the Canadian Expeditionary Force suffered the gruelling ordeal of the Western Front, their families at home faced their own problems and it is now time to look at civilian life during the "Great War," as people were already calling it.

Canada, which had existed for less than a half century when the war began in August 1914, was experiencing her first major trial as a nation. The country had been in a state of recession when the conflict began and there was great fear in the business sector that it would go bankrupt; while the crowds cheered and sang patriotic songs, the Montreal stock market closed to prevent a selling panic. These fears proved to be groundless as, by a number of innovative measures, the government was able to finance its military expenditure, and the war ultimately provided a stimulus to the national economy.

The first of the financing measures was the implementation of what modern economists would term "user fees" on such items as telegrams, railway tickets and insurance policies. This did not bring in enough revenue so in 1916 the government turned to direct taxation, first a war tax on industries profiting from the conflict and then, in 1917, Ottawa introduced income tax as a "temporary measure" which, although it was fairly low – 3% on a family income of more than $3,000 annually or on an individual earning more than $1,500 per year – was to end when the war was over. Place not your trust in the promises of government, one is tempted to say, as this "temporary" tax is still very much with us. The main method of financing the war effort, however, was by borrowing, at first on American markets – to a total of $220 million by 1916. To offset this, Ottawa somewhat nervously floated a Victory Loan to Canadians in November 1915. The government wanted to raise $50 million and offered good terms, (5% of tax free interest annually) on "Victory Bonds." To Ottawa's amazement, this venture brought in $179 million and, thus encouraged, it mounted five more Victory Loans during the course of the war, collecting an additional $1.5 billion as

Canadians scrambled to pick up a sure thing. The result was that, by the end of the conflict, much of the nation's war debt was owed to Canadian, not foreign, investors.

Many sectors of the economy prospered during the war. Beginning in late 1914 small orders from British firms began to flow to Canada for artillery shells and war materiel. The response of the federal government, in the form of Sam Hughes who interfered in the procurement process, was somewhat erratic and when Britain threatened to suspend orders as a result, Ottawa created the Imperial Munitions Board under Toronto millionaire Joseph Flavelle in December 1915. An organizational genius who quickly became one of the most powerful men in the country, Flavelle put military manufacturing on a rational basis and, by 1917, the Board controlled 600 factories employing 250,000 workers which produced two million dollars worth of products every day. The steel, automobile, textile, lumbering and pulp and paper industries all enjoyed increased wartime orders, and both profits and wage packets increased.

Alberta, like much of Western Canada, did not get a large share in the wartime jackpot experienced by eastern manufacturers, and this was a source of much complaint. The province did, however, enjoy increased demand for coal, lumber, beef and horses but the big money maker during the war was wheat, which went from 91 cents per bushel in 1914 to $1.33 in 1916, and $2.40 in 1918. Wheat acreage in the province doubled between 1914 and 1917 and in the summer of 1915, perfect weather conditions resulted in the "Big Crop of 15" which yielded record results of between 26 and 31 bushels an acre compared to 5.7 bushels in 1914. This was the high point, however, and thereafter a combination of drought, stemrust and the refusal of many farmers to leave land fallow, resulted in a decrease to 9.7 bushels per acre in 1919, although this was offset by the fact that the bushel price nearly doubled in the same period.

The bounty enjoyed by the agricultural sector was felt throughout the provincial economy as newly-wealthy farmers spent their money freely. Car ownership in Alberta increased fivefold during

3rd Canadian Mounted Rifles, Sarcee, 1915
Major Frank Fane, commanding C Company of the 3rd Canadian Mounted Rifles, receives a Union Jack at Sarcee, probably in 1915. Fane was a squadron commander in the prewar 19th Alberta Dragoons and joined one of three mounted rifle regiments raised in the province during the war, along with many other members of the prewar militia cavalry.

CITY OF EDMONTON ARCHIVES EA458-70

the war, compared to the national average of fourfold, and many of the new vehicles were the simple and rugged Model T Fords. The farmers' major problem was labour because so many men were in uniform. In response, the federal government encouraged women and schoolboys to assist with the harvest and, in 1917, many aliens who had been interned at the beginning of the war, were released to work in agriculture. Such was the shortage of labour that farmhands nearly doubled their income, from $50 a month in 1914 to $100 a month in 1918. Almost everyone in the province had more money to spend although inflation ate up much of the increase, the purchasing power of the dollar was halved during the war and wages did not entirely keep up with inflation.

"Talked to death by the preachers and newspapers": Wartime recruiting, 1914-1916

Most of the money raised by Ottawa was needed to finance the large army that Canada mobilized during the war. In the first twelve or so months of the conflict, as the CEF experienced a radical increase in strength, it seemed that almost every young man in Canada either donned, or was contemplating donning, khaki. This expansion was the brainchild of the energetic but erratic Sam Hughes. Ignoring sound advice from his own staff, Hughes kept increasing the size of the CEF by authorizing more and more new units. There had been no problem recruiting the 14 infantry battalions of the Second Contingent and the 13 regiments of mounted rifles in 1914 and, thus encouraged, in 1915 Hughes went on what can only be termed a "recruiting bender" raising infantry battalions literally a dozen at a time. By the end of that year, no less than 158 battalions, fully or partly up to strength, were in service. Prime Minister Robert Borden appears to have contracted the same mania – he increased the total authorized strength of the CEF to 150,000 in June 1915 and to 250,000 in October. Borden and Hughes's confidence that these numbers could be met seemed to be born out by the statistics, as men kept enlisting throughout 1915, particularly in Ontario and the west, which had 61% of Canada's population but which provided 73.3% of the recruits in the first two years of the war. This being the case, Canada was in a position to offer a third overseas division to Britain and then a fourth, all of which were eagerly accepted by London. In vain, Major-General Willoughby Gwatkin, the chief of the general staff, pointed out that experience on the Western Front indicated that an infantry division

with 12 battalions needed replacements equal to 60% of its total strength each year – about 12,000-20,000 men – and, thus, to keep four divisions with 48 battalions overseas would require 80,000 new men each year the war lasted. Gwatkin, having crunched the numbers carefully, concluded that Canada would have difficulty maintaining three divisions in the field, let alone four or more, and advised that a more rational system should be put in place whereby recruits would not be formed into new battalions but sent to existing units.

Borden and Hughes ignored him. Hughes kept raising more battalions in 1915 and 1916 even though the limited military facilities in Canada were overstrained – there was not enough accommodation to house the new units during the winter, there were no proper training facilities and arms, uniforms and equipment were in short supply. When his staff pointed this out, Hughes came up with a brilliant idea – each electoral district that raised a battalion or more of infantry would have the men of that unit billeted in private homes at government expense at the rate of 60 cents per man per day. Hughes was quite aware that this would limit company and battalion training but he directed that each new recruit be given "a drill book free of charge" and, "from the most efficient of the recruits," would be chosen the officers and NCOs of a newly-raised unit.[2] This radical concept, which not only flew in the face of military discipline and efficiency, but all reason, was disastrous and fortunately lasted only a few months.

Borden was no better. On New Year's Day 1916, without consulting his cabinet, he announced that the strength of the CEF would be raised to 500,000 men. At first, the beleaguered staff of the Department of Militia assumed that this was to be the total strength but they were subsequently horrified to learn that Borden actually intended to maintain an army in the field numbering half a million men. In desperation, they pointed out that such a strength would require 300,000 new recruits every year and that the total strength of the CEF in early 1916 had not yet reached the 250,000 mark set just four months before. Again, the prime minister and his minister of militia paid no attention but went on their merry way – in the first six months of 1916, Hughes authorized no fewer than 34 new infantry battalions.

The manpower supply, however, was beginning to dwindle.

The bedrock of all armies – NCOs of the 3rd Canadian Mounted Rifles, 1915

It is an immutable truth that warrant officers and sergeants run armies and it is their constant complaint that they could do a much better job of doing so if only the officers would stop interfering. The faces of these sergeants of the 3rd Canadian Mounted Rifles photographed in Calgary in 1915 reflect their firm belief in the importance of their place in the universe. GLENBOW MUSEUM, NC-6-1301

Recruiting officers had already noticed that, by the end of the first year of the war in August 1915, the best men had joined and what they were now getting were either very young or older men without any previous military experience. Although the regulation that required a married man to have his wife's permission to enlist had been abolished and although the agricultural community had been mollified when farmers' sons were granted harvest leave – to the prejudice of their training – it was still found necessary to reduce the physical standards. Two battalions were permitted to recruit "bantams," men under the newly-lowered height of 5 feet, 2 inches. In last months of 1915, the quality of the men coming in noticeably declined but medical officers, trying to meet their commanding officers' quotas, passed men as fit who would never prove an asset to the army and only clog its medical facilities. New units, desperate to fill their ranks, began to reach out to hitherto untouched sources of manpower – there were Scandinavian battalions, aboriginal battalions and even a series of "American Legion" battalions raised from the citizens of that country living in Canada, which were dissolved after protests from Washington. The men kept coming in, particularly in the west where 23 infantry battalions actively recruiting in the last three months of 1915 raised 21,897 men – but they began to tail off in the spring of 1916. The 34 battalions authorized by Hughes in January 1916 took six months to raise 22,539 men and they were certainly not the King's best bargains. Intensive recruiting drives were mounted across Canada including a project personally backed by Borden in his native Nova Scotia where an entire Highland brigade of four battalions was raised in January and February 1916. This was one drive that succeeded but most did not. The high point was March 1916 when no less than 33,960 men joined the ranks but thereafter the numbers dropped away. In May 1916, the strength of the CEF reached 250,000, half the figure Borden wanted to send overseas, and seven months later it would be just under 300,000 men. Still, this was an impressive figure for a nation whose population of men of military age (18-45) was estimated to be two million at the outbreak of the war.

By the summer of 1916 the writing was on the wall for Hughes's madcap policy of unrestrained expansion and the government began to draft legislation for the compulsory registra-tion of males of military age, the preliminary step to imposing conscription. The hard working staff of the Department of Militia were finally able to get control of the recruiting and reinforcement process – very few battalions were recruited for overseas service after mid-1916 and most of those raised in the previous eighteen months were broken up as reinforcements. At the end of the year, a territorial system was put in place by which all recruits joined the depot battalion of a territorial regiment or regiments created in each province where they were trained before being sent to a reserve unit of that territorial regiment in Britain, which would eventually send them as reinforcements to an active battalion in one of the four infantry divisions – precisely the system that Gwatkin had been trying to implement since the beginning of the war. When the high casualty rates suffered on the Somme and in Flanders in 1916 became common knowledge, men became reluctant to enlist in the infantry and after that year, most volunteers chose the artillery, engineers or medical services where the chances of survival were better.

It was infantrymen who were needed in France, however, and the problem was how to get them, particularly if the government seriously wanted to maintain a combat force of half a million. As one unit commander pointed out in early 1917, Canadian men

And the band still played on: Recruiting in Medicine Hat

Throughout the war, recruiting never ceased in Alberta. Here, the band of an unidentified CEF unit plays in a downtown intersection in the Hat. By 1916, however, there were fewer volunteers signing up to serve for King and Country and the government began to consider conscription. GLENBOW MUSEUM, NA 3007-4

(Left) Military couple, 1915
The newly-wed Sergeant and Mrs. Frederick Harvey at Medicine Hat in 1915. Harvey joined the 13th Canadian Mounted Rifles at Fort Macleod in February 1915 and trained with the unit at Medicine Hat. She almost certainly told him to be careful but he wasn't – commissioned as a lieutenant in Lord Strathcona's Horse in 1916, Fred Harvey won the Victoria Cross the following year and ended his military career as a brigadier. GLENBOW MUSEUM, NA 3471-57

(Below) Innisfail's finest, 1916
The Innisfail platoon of the 187th Battalion CEF raised in 1916. The custom of raising companies and platoons from small localities promoted group cohesion but it could cause havoc in those communities if heavy casualties were suffered. The size of some of these men reflects the lowering of height standards throughout the war – on the other hand, short men possessed an advantage in the trenches. GLENBOW MUSEUM, NA-1709-03

Officers of the 12th Canadian Mounted Rifles, 1915
In late 1914 and early 1915, three regiments of mounted rifles were raised in Alberta and many prewar militia cavalrymen joined them. Sadly, they were broken up and used as infantry replacements. GLENBOW MUSEUM, NA-3348-6

Band of the 187th Battalion CEF, 1916

One of the first things most new CEF battalions did was to form a band to increase morale and promote recruiting. Civilian bands often enlisted *en masse,* the fastest method of getting martial musicians. In action, the bandsmen served as stretcher bearers. SALH Archives.

You're in the Army, Mr. Jones

Private Wilbur Jones of the 113th Battalion CEF ("Lethbridge Highlanders") poses proudly with his blanket roll and Ross rifle at Sarcee Camp in 1916. The training done by Canadian units prior to shipping overseas was very fundamental and bore little resemblance to what they would encounter on the Western Front. GLENBOW MUSEUM, NA-2144-2

(Left) Horse lines, Sarcee camp 1915

The horse lines of the 13th Canadian Mounted Rifles at Sarcee. The long-nosed chums are tucking into their fodder. Note the white-painted rocks on the ridge which spell out "20th Battery." Most of the units that were stationed at Sarcee left these memorials behind and some remain there today. GLENBOW MUSEUM, NA-5483-16

Officers of the 13th Canadian Mounted Rifles, 1915

All five Alberta militia cavalry units contributed men to the three regiments of mounted rifles raised in the province in late 1914 and early 1915. Unfortunately, cavalry were not needed on the Western Front and these units were used as infantry reinforcements. GLENBOW MUSEUM, NA-2370-5

Military art, c. 1916
The lines of the machinegun section of the 113th Battalion, Lethbridge Highlanders, at Sarcee in 1916. Despite the exhortation "Berlin or Bust," the 113th never made it to the German capital, being broken up for reinforcements. These decorations are long gone but bell tents were still being used in the militia as late as the 1970s. GLENBOW MUSEUM, NA-3419-7

had been "talked to death by the preachers and newspapers and magazines, and one half of the people of the country will recruit the other half."[3] According to this officer, the conclusion was inescapable – if the government wanted to send 500,000 men overseas, they would have to be conscripted, as those "are gone who are willing to go as volunteers."

"The Empire's need is greater": Alberta and the military during the war

By any method of of measurement Alberta's contribution to the national war effort was impressive. Between 1914 and 1918, the province's rate of enlistment was two and a half times the national average – of the 139,279 males of military age (18 to 45) estimated to live in Alberta at the outbreak of war, there were 18,000 in uniform by the end of 1915 and 33,671 by the end of 1916. When hostilities ended in November 1918, 48,885 Albertans had enlisted, of whom 36,165 served overseas. In 1915 Edmonton led the nation in rate of enlistment, no less than 13,000 men had volunteered from a municipal population estimated to be between 50,000 and 70,000 while the little town of Gleichen sent no fewer than 250 men into the army, of whom 50 did not return. In terms of units, 20 infantry battalions were raised solely in Alberta and another 9 were recruited partly in the province which also contributed three regiments of mounted rifles, two squadrons of cavalry, 4 batteries of artillery, a forestry battalion and medical, service, engineer and supply units.* The prewar militia made an outstanding contribution as, after the near hysteria connected with the raising of the First Contingent in August 1914, they functioned as recruiting organizations throughout the war. The militia also provided most of the commanding officers or deputy commanding officers for 20 of the 23 infantry battalions and mounted rifle regiments raised in the province. In this respect the 101st Regiment contributed twelve officers while six came from the 103rd Regiment, four each from the 15th Light

Horse and 19th Dragoons, three from the 23rd Rangers, two from the 35th Horse and one officer from the 21st Hussars.

One prominent member of the provincial militia determined to get into the war was Honorary Colonel James Walker of the 23rd Alberta Rangers, who was 66 when the conflict began. His offer to serve overseas in any capacity was refused because of his age and Walker reluctantly accepted an appointment as a recruiting officer for one of the infantry battalions being raised in Alberta. In 1916, when Walker learned that there was a need for trained forestry units in Europe to provide lumber for the Western Front, he became determined to get overseas and, finding a loophole in the regulations which permitted overage captains to go on active service, he got himself demoted to that rank and went to Europe as a supernumerary officer in an infantry unit. Once there, he switched to the Canadian Forestry Corps, was promoted major and commanded a six-company forestry battalion that operated sawmills in Britain and France. Walker did not to return to Calgary until September 1919 by which time he was 70 years old. As General Sir Arthur Currie remarked, the indomitable Walker was "a man who breaks out every fifty years and goes to war."[4]

Recruiting in Alberta was unceasing. After the Second Contingent – which included the 31st Battalion, recruited across the province, and the 49th Battalion from Edmonton and 50th from Calgary – and the three regiments of Canadian Mounted Rifles had departed, Hughes's ambitions resulted in wave after wave of new Alberta units being authorized. The 63rd and 66th Battalions began recruiting in April 1915; the 82nd Battalion in July 1915; the 89th, 113th, 137th, 138th and 151st Battalions in December 1915 with the final wave – the 175th, 187th, 191st, 192nd, 194th and 202nd Battalions – coming in July 1916. Many who joined these units were given the impression (and, in some cases, more than an impression) that they would serve and fight overseas in the unit in which they enlisted. Even when it became clear in late 1915 that the necessity for replacing losses more or less doomed most of the battalions raised after the spring of 1915 to being broken up as reinforcements, this military con game – for that is what it was – continued and only stopped with the reformation of the recruiting system in late 1916. Thereafter, all recruits ended up in the depot battalion of the Alberta Regiment at Sarcee Camp and from there they went to the 9th Reserve Battalion in England for ultimate transmission to the Alberta battalions in the Canadian Corps. There were four such units: the 10th (Canadians) Battalion, recruited partly in Alberta and Manitoba, which served in the 1st Division; the 31st (Alberta) Battalion in the 2nd Division; the 49th (Edmonton) Battalion in the 3rd and the 50th (Calgary) Battalion in the 4th Division, giving the province representation in each major formation of the Corps.

Throughout 1915 and 1916, recruiting activities were relentless and efforts to bring in men were assisted by service clubs, patriotic organizations and church groups which held rallies and meetings, and many of these events ended with the singing of the new wartime verse for "God Save the King!" quoted at the beginning of this chapter. Military recruiting parties roamed the

---

* A complete list of the military units raised solely or partly in Alberta during the First World War will be found in Appendix H.

streets of every city and town in the province and sometimes the rural areas. Every possible device was employed to get men to sign on the line – the 211th Battalion possessed a car which drove through the streets of Calgary carrying a large sign urging men to "Eat Your Christmas Dinner in England" by getting "A Free Ride to Duty – Jump On."[5] Most municipalities and many large companies forced young and single male employees to either enlist, in which case their jobs would be kept for them, or face dismissal. And then there were the newspapers which daily printed patriotic exhortations:

> Wives. If your Husbands Can Go. *Send Them.* The Dominion Government and the Patriotic Fund Will Look After You.

> Parents: If you have boys who can go. *Send Them*, if they want to go *Let Them*. In nearly all cases the Empire's need is greater than yours. Mothers who depend solely on sons will be looked after.

> Girls: Follow the example of Old Country Girls and use all your influence for your Country's Cause. Urge the boys to go.[6]

or

YOUNG MEN!

The time has come for every unmarried and physically fit young man to enter the service of his country. Your comrades in the trenches in France expect you. Duty offers no alternative. Leave your work for wounded soldiers and the physically unfit. The old battalions are moving out. Fill the vacant places.

JOIN THE 194th BATTALION, EDMONTON HIGHLANDERS[7]

Occasionally, the newspapers even attempted a little heavy-handed humour:

> Good old Bill, he left this place,
> With smokin' gun and smilin' face.
> But Bill won't mind if some good chap,
> Will follow up and fill the gap.[8]

No matter from which direction it came, the pressure on civilian men, particularly young, single men, to join was intense and they quickly learned to avoid public gatherings as they were often presented with the white feather symbol of cowardice by young women doing their own bit for King and Empire. To avoid such embarrassment, wounded veterans, those rejected for medical reasons and those engaged in essential war work, were issued official lapel buttons as a means of identification.

The Calgary "Riot," February 1916

As the figures for Alberta demonstrate, the results were impressive but there were tremendous problems in housing and training the new units. In April 1915, work began on a large camp on land leased from the Sarcee nation which adjoined Reservoir Park, the site of prewar militia camps. It was intended to provide accommodations and training facilities for up to 15,000 troops but it was not completed by the following winter, forcing the three infantry units then in the Calgary area, the 56th, 82nd and 89th Battalions, to house their men either in the exhibition buildings at Victoria Park or in converted warehouse buildings in downtown Calgary, or to simply billet them in their own homes. This was not conducive either to good training or discipline and the situation was made worse by the fact that it was a cold winter with temperatures in late January 1916 ranging as low as -36 degrees Fahrenheit, which more or less brought all outdoor training to a complete stop. The result was that approximately 3,000 poorly-disciplined soldiers, really just civilians in khaki, became bored and restless. This was a prescription for trouble and it came on 10 February 1916.

There was widespread anti-German sentiment in Alberta

Edmonton's senior officers
Edmonton had one of the highest enlistment rates in Canada. In this group portrait, from mid-1916, are shown the commanding officers of the units that recruited in the provincial capital: 19th Dragoons, 3rd Canadian Mounted Rifles and the 49th, 101st, 51st, 63rd, 66th, 138th, 151st, 194th, 202nd, 218th and 233th CEF Battalions. Most of these men were members of the pre-war militia, including Belcher, Fane, Griesbach and Jamieson, all of the 19th Dragoons. William A. Griesbach, who as a young boy witnessed the Northwest Rebellion, had reached the rank of brigadier-general by 1916. GLENBOW MUSEUM, ND-3-19

during the war and Calgary had the largest German population in the province, estimated to be 2,600. In the first week of February, rumours began to circulate among the soldiers that the White Lunch restaurant, which had two locations on 8th and 19th Avenues, had fired employees who were soldiers invalided out of the army and replaced them with aliens. On 10 February the manager of the White Lunch telephoned Brigadier-General Ernest Cruikshank, commander of Military District 13, to express his concern about these rumours, which were common knowledge in Calgary. Cruikshank, however, did nothing and that evening a mob of unruly soldiers, numbering several hundred, gathered outside the front of the White Lunch on 8th Avenue. Brushing aside fifteen Calgary police officers who appeared on the scene, they totally wrecked the establishment and, a short time later, another military mob ransacked the White Lunch on 19th Avenue. Cruikshank now appeared and ordered the men to return to camp, which most did, and he then posted unarmed pickets in front of the two restaurants.

Understandably, this incident evoked a storm of criticism from Calgarians but Cruikshank, who by now had a clear warning that all was not well in his district, tried to mollify municipal politicians with assurances that there would be no repetition of the incidents. He did go so far as to post pickets in front of a number of other Calgary businesses which had informed him that they had received threats from soldiers but, incredibly, he did not confine the men of the three battalions in the city to their quarters. On the evening of 11 February, a mob estimated to be 1,500 strong, mostly soldiers but with some civilians, many of whom had, as the Irish say, "drink taken," ransacked a German-owned hotel in the Riverside District. Despite the pleas of the three battalion commanders – all of whom who appeared on the scene – for their men to return to their barracks and billets, the mob continued into downtown Calgary with the intention of repeating the process at two German-owned restaurants. It was fortunately forestalled by a strong force of about 700 loyal troops who simply formed a cordon around these two establishments and, after a while, the rioters got bored and dispersed.

At this point, Cruikshank took the steps he should have taken after the first incident. He confined the battalions to their barracks, instituted frequent roll-calls to make sure the men were actually present, and formed roving patrols that arrested any soldier found on the streets of Calgary without a pass. Later,

HELP THE HORSE TO SAVE THE SOLDIER

"GOOD-BYE, OLD MAN"

PLEASE JOIN THE AMERICAN **RED STAR** ANIMAL RELIEF National Headquarters. Albany, N.Y.

Dobbin bites the dust

A poster from the American Red Star Animal Relief solicits funds to provide medical and other services for military animals. In a time when horse-drawn transport was prevalent, the long-nosed chums were everywhere on the Western Front and suffered heavy casualties, particularly from artillery. BY KIND PERMISSION OF THE TRUSTEES OF THE IMPERIAL WAR MUSEUM, Q 80217

he ordered the three battalion commanders to take their units out in the country on long winter route marches to keep them occupied. Following these riotous scenes, the German community in Calgary was understandably terrified but the reaction of the civic authorities was not at all sympathetic – it was the property loss that concerned them, not the fact that Germans were the targets – and shortly afterwards they dismissed or laid off all civic employees of alien nationality. The Calgary riot of February 1916 attracted considerable adverse attention in the media across Canada and the government was forced to take some action. Cruikshank was transferred out of the district but the Department of Militia refused to compensate the property owners for the losses they suffered. Gradually, the whole thing died down but this was not the last incident of this type to occur in Alberta as, in March 1917, men from the 211th Battalion wrecked the Greek Cafe in Medicine Hat.

The Calgary riot would have never occurred if firm leadership had been exercised and it was perhaps an indication that, by 1916, the best officers were already serving overseas. In defence of the senior officers involved, it has to be said that both the accommodation problem and the weather had contributed to the incident but, nonetheless, they should have taken earlier and more effective steps to prevent trouble, particularly because they were forewarned after the first incident occurred. As for the soldiers involved, they were very fortunate that they were not serving with the Canadian Corps in France where misbehaviour brought swift and drastic punishment. When a drunken Canadian soldier destroyed the furniture of a French seamstress, a subsequent court martial awarded him 56 days of Field Punishment No. 1, a sentence regarded as too lenient by the commander of the British First Army when he reviewed the proceedings. Some might disagree with that commander because Field Punishment No. 1, which differed from Field Punishment No. 2 described in Chapter 3, meant that, in addition to being kept in irons and made to do forced labour, a convicted soldier was also to,

(b) Be attached by straps, irons or ropes for not more than 2 hours in 1 day to a fixed object. Must not be attached for more than 3 out of 4 consecutive days or for more than 21 days in all.[9]

"Till the Boys Come Home": They also served who waited

For those soldiers from Alberta who left wives and families in the province, the government paid these dependents a $20 month separation allowance provided that a soldier also assigned at least 20% of his pay over to them. The welfare of most military dependents, however, was not looked after by the government but by a private organization, the Canadian Patriotic Fund, which was created in 1914 and based on predecessors established in the War of 1812 and South African War. Administered by local committees, whose members were often drawn from prominent families, the clergy and patriotic associations, the Fund was supported by private donations solicited from Canadians of all income levels. Its appeal was straightforward:

> "When the Boys Come Home They Will Ask"
> What Did *YOU* pay to care for *MY* family while I was fighting for *YOU* and *YOUR* family?
> What Will Your Answer Be?
> Subscribe to the Patriotic Fund[10]

Financially, the Fund was very successful and was able to supplement the government allowance to dependents with a monthly stipend that varied from $20 to $30 depending on the province. But the Fund also intruded into the lives of its clients – a wife could be cut off for evidence of infidelity or admonished for extravagance if she went to the cinema or tried to acquire a telephone. The attitudes of the Fund committees varied, as did its membership, but many soldiers deeply resented having to rely on what they regarded as charity to support their families, even though they really had no other choice.

In the meantime, the families and loved ones of soldiers waited through the long years of separation. Entertainment was at a premium during the war years, with moving picture and variety shows popular in the larger centres.

"Leave"

Bairnsfather portrays a British soldier happy to be home on leave. In this respect British soldiers were more fortunate than the men of the CEF, who were rarely given leave to Canada, and most men did not see their loved ones for years. COPYRIGHT TONIE AND VALMAI HOLT, REPRODUCED WITH PERMISSION FROM *THE BEST OF FRAGMENTS FROM FRANCE*

Sheep skins and healthy skins

It wasn't long before advertisers figured out that the war was profitable. On the Western Front, the "strong and manly physique" needed protection from a lot more than the "germs and microbes of disease." The sheep and goat skin vests issued to the men of the BEF during the first two winters of the war were intensely disliked because they stank. AUTHOR'S COLLECTION

This was a time, however, when people were more resourceful in terms of providing their own fun and when a piano (either manual or mechanical) graced many middle class homes and at least one family member usually knew how to play it. There was also the newfangled gramophone which had steadily declined in price in the years immediately prior to the war – a bottom line model could now be purchased for between $5 and $10. And if a family possessed neither a piano nor a gramophone, they were not embarrassed to sing. The result was a boom in music aimed squarely at the home front with songs like "Keep Your Head Down, Fritzie Boy," "A Handful of Maple Leaves," "You Bet Your Life We All Will Go," "Over There," "K-K-K-Katy, Goodbye," "What the Deuce Do We Care for Kaiser Bill?", "Will Daddy Come Home Tonight?", and so on. Particularly popular, as many women joined knitting and sewing circles to produce "comforts" for the troops overseas, was Al Jolson's 1917 recording of this tongue-twister:

> Sister Susie's sewing shirts for soldiers
> Such skill at sewing shirts
> Our shy young sister Susie shows!
> Some soldiers sent epistles,
> Say they'd sooner sleep in thistles
> Than the saucy, soft, short shirts for soldiers
> Sister Susie sews.

Perhaps the most popular homefront song of all, because it spoke directly to those who waited, was Ivor Novello's 1914 composition, "Keep The Home Fires Burning":

> They were summoned from the hillside,
> They were called in from the glen,
> And the country found them ready
> At the stirring call for men.
> Let no tear add to their hardships
> As the soldiers pass along,
> And although your heart is breaking
> Make it sing this cheery song:

Keep the Home Fires Burning,
While your hearts are yearning,
Though your lads are far away
They dream of home.
There's a silver lining
Through the dark clouds shining,
Turn the dark cloud inside out
'Til the boys come home.

Of course, no one told the folks who belted out this tear-jerker that the soldiers in France had their own version:

Oh, they've called them up from Westchurch
And they've called them up from Wen,
And they'll call up all the women,
When they've f____d up all the men.[11]

But then the horrors of war are best kept from civilians.

In Alberta, one casualty of the war was the saloon, not that it would have been frequented by many military dependents. In 1915, women's, church and temperance groups – believing in the essential goodness of human nature (if only it could be removed from temptation) – convinced the provincial government to enact prohibition, and the province went dry. Unfortunately, human nature takes neither kindly nor easily to reformist zeal and this measure did not stop the consumption of alcohol. The wealthy were able to procure it by mail from outside the province and the less wealthy frequented illegal "blind pigs" which sprang up to replace the now-closed and easily-policed bars and saloons. Drinking continued but it now went underground, creating a crime problem.

Mail was the only means of contact between families and a soldier whose formal portrait photograph, in which he was usually wearing the tight 7-button Canadian 1903 Pattern Service Jacket, graced many wartime mantels in Alberta. Mail call was one of the most eagerly waited events on the Western Front and, throughout the war, the Canadian postal service proved very efficient – a far cry from its present day successor – so that those separated by the war were able to maintain fairly frequent contact by post. Not that enlisted men could tell their loved ones much about the war as all their letters had to be censored by an officer which,

for many, was one of the most disliked aspects of service life. Soldiers were warned not to discuss military movements, battles, morale and weapons or to criticize their superiors but, on the other hand, most men were wise enough anyway not to not tell the truth as it would only cause undue worry for their families. Soldiers could send censor-free letters using a "green envelope" which bore a declaration that the soldier had to sign stating that the contents did not contain any military information. Green envelopes were subject to random checks by the military postal authorities and punishment for contravening this regulation was severe. They were issued at the rate of one per man per week, usually on Sunday, and were so popular that, as one veteran of the CEF noted, "they soon came to have a money value and to be the commodities of a substantial traffic."[12] For those soldiers who did not wish to write, either because they had no penchant for it or resented censorship, there was always the Field Service Post Card which contained the barest of details.

The coming of the postman was eagerly awaited on the homefront but not so the arrival of a telegram boy, that innocent harbinger of death. As the war progressed and the casualty lists in the newspapers grew increasingly lengthy, most papers gradually reduced the space accorded to them. Typical was the approach of the *Medicine Hat News* which devoted at least fifteen daily issues to reproducing the complete casualty list for the battle of 2nd Ypres in May and June 1915 but which, by June 1916, printed only one and a half pages of casualties, mostly men of the 31st Battalion, resulting from the battle of the St. Eloi Craters. By early 1917, the *News* had reduced its casualty coverage to a weekly list containing only the names of local men. The appearance of these sombre notices were accompanied by telegrams to homes in Alberta which, if they came (and understandably the telegram boys hated delivering them), would be from the Officer in Charge of Records at Militia Headquarters in Ottawa. A fatal casualty notification would contain only the most sparse of details as, for example: "Deeply regret to inform you that 234789 Private John Smith, 31st Battalion, officially reported killed in action (or died of wounds) on 1 July 1916." A few days or weeks later a letter would usually arrive from the man's officer or unit padre informing the family that he had died bravely doing his duty, that his death was instantaneous and he had suffered no pain, and that he was

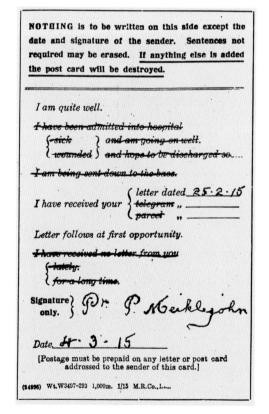

Field Service Post Card, 1915
Soldiers were permitted to send these postcards home weekly to keep their families informed about their condition. Note that if the soldier indicated that he had been wounded, he only has two choices -- he was either "going on well" or hoped to be discharged – and nothing in between. AUTHOR'S COLLECTION

popular with his officers and comrades and would be sorely missed – whether these things were true or not is entirely beside the point. If a man was wounded, the dreaded missive might contain more information but it was sometimes incorrect. A particularly bad case was the telegram sent to the family of Private John A. Macdonald, wounded at Willerval in 1917, which informed them that "Your son John wounded in arm, head severed" which must have caused consternation until the correction, "Your son John wounded in arm, head severe," arrived.[13] The statistics are not entirely reliable but approximately 6,140 fatal casualty notifications were sent for men from Alberta killed during the war, and 20,000 sent informing recipients of the wounding of men who had enlisted in Alberta.

"To win, at any cost, the coming election": Politics, problems and progress, 1916-1918

In the summer of 1916, as the monthly intake of volunteer recruits slowed to a trickle in comparison to previous years, Prime Minister Borden created the National Service Board to ascertain the manpower reserves of Canada. The Board distributed information cards to all men of military age asking them to complete and return them. This survey was, in effect, a form of registration and although the exercise was voluntary, approximately 80% of the men who received the cards, responded. The result revealed that there were 286,976 men in Canada available for military service – the problem was how to get them to voluntarily enlist.

Before he could deal with this problem, Borden had first to deal with the his troublesome minister of militia. Hughes had created a Canadian military establishment in England that had grown into a huge and bloated bureaucratic empire with several competing organizations and commands, many of which were run by Hughes's cronies. In the autumn of 1916, tired of Hughes's prevarications about cleaning up this mess, Borden appointed Sir

Canadian Colours on Wolfe's Memorial, Westminster Abbey, London
Only four infantry battalions raised in Alberta – the 10th, 31st, 49th and 50th Battalions – served in combat as units on the Western Front. All other Alberta infantry units were broken up as reinforcements and many temporarily laid up their Colours on Wolfe's Memorial in Westminster Abbey. Most of these standards were brought back to Canada after the war. GLENBOW MUSEUM, PA-3476-13

George Perley, one of Hughes's long-time political enemies, as Minister of Overseas Military Forces with powers rivalling that of Hughes himself. Having done that, he waited for the inevitable explosion. It was not long in coming but Borden, aware by this time that, because of the Ross rifle and a number of other disasters, Hughes was intensely disliked by the CEF, had come to the end of his tether as far as Sam was concerned. An abusive letter from Hughes led to Borden firing him in November 1916, despite the political fall-out that resulted. When Perley arrived in England he discovered that, while there were 2,526 officers and 105,640 enlisted men serving with the Canadian Corps in France, there were no less than 7,420 officers and 128,980, mostly half-trained, men stationed in England. Perley cleaned up this mess in fairly short order and instituted a rational reinforcement system.

Borden now turned to his major problem, procuring manpower. In the spring of 1917 he decided that, far from maintaining an army of half a million men in France, it would be necessary to implement conscription just to keep the four-division Canadian Corps at the front. As his parliamentary term was nearing its end, he invited Wilfrid Laurier, head of the opposition Liberal party, to join him in a coalition government that would implement conscription, even offering to vacate the prime-ministership if necessary, but Laurier, sensing a possible election victory, refused. Thereupon, Borden introduced the Military Service Bill, a conscription act, into parliament in June 1917 and it was passed after a bitter debate in which 25 Liberals deserted the opposition benches while 9 Tory members – all from Quebec which was dead set against the measure – went the opposite way. This debate fractured party allegiances and, after gathering support on both sides throughout the summer, Borden decided to go further and form a Union or coalition government.

The crucial election, 1917
In December 1917, Canadians went to the polls to vote on the issue of conscription. Prime Minister Robert Borden's Union government won and, not surprisingly, most of the soldiers on the Western Front voted in favour of the measure. Here, men of the CEF await their turn to vote at a military polling booth. NAC, PA-002238

On 6 October he dissolved Parliament and called an election, presenting the voters with a potential cabinet composed of both Liberal and Tory members. "Our first duty," he informed Unionist supporters, "is to win at any cost, the coming election in order that we may continue to do our part in winning the war and that Canada be not disgraced."[14] Toward that end, Borden possessed the advantage of recently-passed legislation drafted by his wily solicitor-general, Arthur Meighen, which permitted members of the CEF to vote and also – in a time before women had the franchise – their mothers, wives and sisters. At the same time, all Canadians from enemy countries, who had been naturalized since 1902, lost their franchise. In short, since most soldiers and their families were in favour of conscription while many recent immigrants were not, Meighen had stacked the deck in favour of the Union government. The resulting election campaign, fought on the issue of conscription, was one of the most bitter in Canadian history and, although it was very close, ended in a Union victory. Among the civilian population, the Union margin over the Liberals was only 97,065 of the 1,650,958 votes cast. The soldiers of the CEF, to nobody's surprise, voted overwhelmingly in favour of conscription, 215,849 as against 18,522 for the Liberals.

Canada now had conscription but making it work was quite another matter. The legislation imposing it provided a three-level appeal system and the result was inevitable – of the 40,000 men ordered to register in October 1917, 93% sought exemption by means of appeal. Matters were more serious in Quebec where local appeal tribunals granted blanket exemptions to French-speaking appellants but applied the law very rigorously to English-speaking appellants. This was not surprising because, almost from the outbreak of war, Sam Hughes had totally mismanaged the recruiting process in Quebec, turning what was at first enthusiasm on the part of the French-speaking population into disappointment which quickly moved to disillusion and then to distrust of the federal government. In August 1914 a brigade of four battalions of French-speaking troops could have been recruited in Quebec but, as a result of some very stupid decisions – including putting a Protestant clergyman who could not speak French in charge of recruiting in the province – although nine infantry battalions were raised in the province, only one active service unit, the 22nd (French Canadian) Battalion, reached the

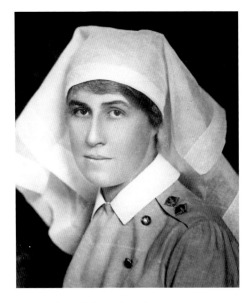

Nursing Sister Roberta McAdams
One of the first provinces in Canada to do so, Alberta granted women the right to vote in April 1916. In the June 1917 provincial election, Albertans elected two women to the Legislative Assembly, Louise McKinney and Roberta McAdams – the first women to be elected to any British or Canadian parliament or assembly. Nursing Sister Roberta McAdams, serving on the Western Front, was one of two armed forces representatives to the assembly. During the First World War, the first "total war," Canadian women made tremendous strides toward achieving social and political equality. PROVINCIAL ARCHIVES OF ALBERTA A.13, 185

Western Front and problems were encountered keeping it up to strength. The situation was not helped by the tendency of French-Canadian males to marry and have families at a younger age than their English-speaking counterparts, which made them less likely to contemplate joining the service. By 1918 French Canada was largely opposed to the war and certainly opposed to conscription. The crisis came in March 1918 when a mob burned the local Military Service office in Quebec City and looted businesses. Ottawa sent in troops to restore order and, on 1 April, they fired into a crowd of angry rioters, killing four of them. Farmers were even more resistant to the provisions of the law and waged a highly successful campaign to have their sons and employees avoid conscription, although they too had to give way eventually. The result was that, by one means or another, most of the men called up managed to avoid service or delay it. The government had stated that conscription would bring 100,000 new men into the CEF – by November 1918, when the war ended, 99,000 were in uniform but only 24,000 had joined combat units in France.

In other aspects, Borden's Union government, which did not suffer from party politics, proved to be both moderately efficient and progressive. The longstanding problem of there being too many railways in the country was solved when the government forced the Grand Trunk Pacific and the Canadian Northern Railway to amalgamate into a new entity, the Canadian National Railway. Following Alberta's early lead, prohibition was enforced nation wide and the mail-order liquor trade banned. The only way now to legally procure alcohol was by a doctor's prescription for "medical" use and, of course, doctors issued thousands of prescriptions. In 1918, the Union government enacted universal suffrage, giving women the right to vote in federal elections.

In this they were only following the lead of Alberta which had granted the vote to women in provincial elections in 1916 and which elected the first two women to any parliament in the British Empire – Louise McKinney and Roberta McAdams – in the provincial election of 1917. It was notable that Roberta McAdams was a nursing sister then serving in France, one of 2,428 Canadian nurses in the Canadian Medical Corps, while another 313 were serving with Allied medical services. Nursing was a traditional and respected role for women but Canadian women made other advances during the war. In Alberta many replaced men in the agricultural sector and across the nation, about 30,000 women worked in non-traditional factory jobs and another 1,325 were employed by the federal civil service. The Royal Flying Corps, which maintained a large establishment in Canada, had 1,200 women employees including 750 serving as mechanics. In Britain the Canadian Army Service Corps employed women drivers while personnel from the British Women's Legion and Women's Army Auxiliary Corps served with the Canadian Forestry Corps in England. The need to mobilize all sectors of the economy, including all available sources of personnel, possibly did more to advance the status of women than the previous three decades of political agitation. Their service was not without cost – 43 nursing sisters were killed by enemy action during the war including two women who died from an air attack on No. 1 Canadian General Hospital in Boulogne in May 1918 and fourteen who were killed the following month when the hospital ship *Llandovery Castle* was sunk by a U-boat. By 1918 women had proved to be such an asset that the Canadian government was actively contemplating the creation of a uniformed service, the Canadian Women's Army Auxiliary Corps based on the British model, but the war ended before actual steps were taken.

The majority of women, however, both in Canada and Alberta, remained in their homes, perhaps occasionally engaging in war work but also trying to keep their families together in very difficult circumstances. On the home front, the last year of conflict was the worst year. The nation was shocked by the civilian casualties – 1,600 killed and 9,000 injured – which resulted from the explosion of an ammunition ship in Halifax harbour in December 1917. That winter also brought fuel shortages that caused the frequent closings of schools and public buildings and restricted transportation and travel. Food shortages led to the imposition of an "honour rationing" system for such items as flour, eggs and milk. Many people had to make do with wartime bread, containing 20% non flour additives. As if this were not bad enough, the federal government inflicted Daylight Savings Time on Canadians in 1918 but the bureaucrats who came up with this supposedly brilliant labour-saving device, aimed primarily at the agricultural community, had no idea of farm life and did not realize that, just because the farmers got up an hour earlier, it did not mean that there had been enough sunlight to

How to Make Mask for Prevention of Influenza

Instructions as to the making and use of masks have been sent out by the provincial board of health. These are to be used when taking care of influenza patients, and beginning on Thursday morning on all trains and street cars in the province. Here is the method of making the mask, published in The Bulletin some days ago and here repeated by request.

To Make a Mask—Take a piece of ordinary cheesecloth, 8x16 inches. Next fold this to make it 8x4 inches. Tie cord about 10 inches long at each corner. Apply over mouth and nose as shown in the picture.

To be worn in the sick room when taking care of the patient and on street cars and railway trains.

Keep the nose and mouth covered while coughing or sneezing.
A mask should not be worn more than two hours.

Epidemic, 1918

A government notice on the manufacture and wearing of face masks, published in the *Edmonton Bulletin* in October 1918, the same month that the first cases appeared in that city. About one in six Albertans contracted the disease and about one in ten who did so, died from it – the death tally in the province was 3,259 men, women and children. Globally, more people died from the 1918 pandemic than were killed in battle during the war. PROVINCIAL ARCHIVES OF ALBERTA, A.13, 187

dry out the fields so that they could be worked. As spring approached in 1918 and news of a major German offensive in France reached Canada, civilian morale was at its lowest – and the worst was yet to come.

In June 1918 a new and virulent form of influenza began to appear in Europe. It acquired the inaccurate name of the "Spanish flu" and soon reached pandemic proportions. A particularly cruel disease because it had a severe impact on children and young adults – those who most needed nursing and those best able to provide it – approximately one quarter of its victims were under the age of 25. In the early autumn of 1918, as the newspaper headlines were reporting glowing victories on the Western Front, the "Spanish flu" pandemic reached North America. The first cases were reported in Calgary on 4 October and its assault was so overpowering that within two weeks all schools, churches and theatres were closed and all public meetings banned. This was followed by the shutting down of all but essential services and a provincial regulation requiring those who served the public to wear face masks, with fines for violations of this regulation. The disease was extremely contagious and no known form of prevention could stop its wildfire spread. It appeared in Edmonton on 19 October, seven days later there were 695 cases and by the end of the month more than 2,000 were afflicted. Medical science was helpless, there was no known form of treatment and the progress of the disease was swift. The first symptoms were a violent headache and general weakness, within a day this was followed by a high fever that rendered the victim delirious and, if the attack was mortal, the victim was usually dead within two days of the first symptom. Overall, approximately one in six people in Alberta contracted the disease and one in ten of those who did so, died from it – a total of 3,259 fatalities in the province. The mortality rates were staggering, the pandemic claimed 50,000 lives in Canada, 550,000 in the United States, 619,000 total in Britain, France and Germany, while in Asia, which was particularly hard hit, 16 million people died in India alone. The final statistics will never be known but the best estimates are that between 20 and 25 million people died from the global pandemic of 1918-1919, more than were killed by wartime action.

With some truth it can be said that, on the home front as on the Western Front, the First World War was an ordeal for all Canadians who lived through it.

CHAPTER SIX

"Hanging on the Old Barbed Wire"

1917 – THE YEAR OF TRIUMPH AND TRAGEDY

"Wading through the mud to work": The winter of 1916-1917

Following their trials on the Somme in September 1916, the 31st Alberta Battalion faced another winter on the Western Front. On 16 October the unit left the rest camp at Warloy to begin a frontline tour in the Lens sector. The two weeks of grace granted the battalion after the Somme had been put to good use resting, reorganizing and incorporating reinforcements. When they arrived in their new sector the Albertans were agreeably surprised to find it quiet, so quiet "that school children frequently approached within a mile of the line and sold chocolate and cigarettes to the troops."[2] Private Donald Fraser was delighted as, for the first time since he had arrived in France, he was billeted in a house with all its doors and windows intact and no holes in the walls or roof, and, better still, it was not crowded because Fraser had to sleep with only six comrades on the floor of an empty room – indeed elegant and spacious accommodation. The battalion spent most of its second winter in France around Lens and the weather was just as miserable as it had been during the first – Captain Harold McGill recorded that it rained on forty days between the end of October and the beginning of February. During this time the battalion followed the routine of five or six days in the trenches, interspersed with periods in reserve and the occasional spell in a rest camp. Much time in the line was spent repairing trenches caved in by the rain

If you want to find the politicians, I know where they are,
If you want to find the politicians, I know where they are,
They're drinking brandy at the House of Commons bar.
I've seen 'em!
Drinking brandy at the House of Commons bar.
I've seen 'em!
Drinking brandy at the House of Commons bar.

If you want to find the old battalion, I know where they are,
If you want to find the old battalion, I know where they are,
They're hanging on the old barbed wire.
I've seen 'em!
Hanging on the old barbed wire.
I've seen 'em!
Hanging on the old barbed wire.[1]

and exchanging the occasional round with the Germans. On 14 November a noteworthy event occurred when a flock of geese flew over the lines and both sides opened fire – Major William Hewgill watched as the Albertans hit one that fell behind their lines but failed to note whether the bird ended up in the pot that night.

Throughout the winter the Canadian Corps carried out an active programme of nighttime raids on the German positions, both to secure intelligence and to demoralize the enemy. One of the first and most successful of what could be very dangerous operations resulting in heavy casualties, was carried out on 24 November by the 26th Battalion on the immediate left of the Albertans' sector. The 31st supported this raid by providing a trench mortar bombardment but unfortunately this stirred up the German artillery which brought down a heavy bombardment on their wet forward trenches, collapsing many into the mud. Three days later, the 31st made its first raid when a small party of fourteen men crossed No-Man's Land and entered the enemy frontline trench opposite. A firefight and grenade battle ensued, which was won by the raiders, but when they examined the enemy dead they could find no means of identifying their unit. The officer in command therefore decided to bring two of the corpses back to the Canadian lines but the carrying parties were defeated by mud and had to abandon their burdens.

By late December the frontline trenches were in terrible shape. Hewgill noted that "water was coming in torrents and trenches were tumbling in all along the line."[3] Repair work was unending but, almost as soon as the trenches were rebuilt, they again collapsed. Fortunately, on Christmas Day the battalion was in a rest camp and consumed a splendid repast of turkey with sausage dressing, cabbage, roast potatoes, plum pudding and candy, the whole washed down with the "greatest treat of all, real English

(Facing) **"Are we downhearted? – Hell no!"**
Happy Canadian infantrymen wave and mug for the camera as they leave the Vimy Ridge area in May 1917. The Canadian Corps' successful attack on the supposedly impregnable ridge was one of its greatest victories, and it is fitting that Canada's National War Memorial for the First World War today stands atop that feature. NAC, PA-001267

Working party on break, March 1917

The winter of 1916-1917 was particularly wet and conditions in the trenches were thoroughly miserable. Here a working party, probably sappers from the Canadian Engineers, some wearing rubber hip waders, takes a break at a coffee stall behind the trenches. Note the sleeveless leather jerkins which were working dress in the British and Canadian armies in two world wars. NAC, PA-000926

beer."[4] Near the Corps headquarters at Divion, A Squadron of the Canadian Light Horse also enjoyed their Christmas celebration which took place on 24 December, particularly as the unit had put in several hard months on labour details in the trenches. The NCOs waited at the tables and Trooper George Hambley "enjoyed it as I have seldom enjoyed a meal."[5] The squadron consumed not only fine food but also stout, ale, beer, whisky, white wine and champagne, which led to "songs, speeches and recitations, all kinds of stunts as the wines got the boys started." When A Squadron went back into the line the next morning, they didn't "feel much like wading through the mud to work." It being Christmas Day, however, the officers "had a *parlé* with Fritz" and "all the guns were silent until one of our men got a bullet thru the shoulder and then our batteries began playing Hell with old Fritzie's line all day." Good will toward men never lasted long on the Western Front.

On New Year's Eve the 31st Battalion was back in the line when they inflicted a new form of "frightfulness" on the enemy. For some days they had been constructing a drain linking their frontline trenches with the German lines opposite and just before midnight they opened it, manned their pumps and "turned loose tons of water which found its way to the Boche lines" as Alberta's New Year's Eve present.[6] Promptly at the stroke of midnight all Canadian artillery within range brought down three rounds on the enemy frontline to wish the Germans a "Happy New Year." That was the high point of January, however, and the month passed slowly by under pouring rain, occasionally mixed with wet snow. In the last week of the month, photographers took pictures of those men remaining in the 6th Brigade who had landed with it in September 1915 – in the 31st Battalion, of a total strength of 1,027 all ranks at that time, only 227 of these veterans were still in the ranks. Given the wretched weather, everyone in the battalion was happy when it was pulled out of the

Lens front in early February 1917 and sent to the St. Eloi area. It was still wet but the craters, which had once been so problematic, now provided protection from surprise attack. The unit's tour in this area was nevertheless of short duration as, on 9 March 1917, they commenced intensive training for a major new offensive.

This operation resulted from high level Allied councils of the previous November. Things had not gone well for the Allied cause in 1916 – the strategy of simultaneous offensives on all fronts had failed completely, Rumania was knocked out of the war while Russian assaults on the Eastern Front had been blunted and that empire was tottering on the verge of revolution. There was stalemate on the Italian and Salonika fronts and, on the Western Front, the Somme had been a disaster and Verdun a bloodbath. Allied leaders decided that in 1917 their main effort would be made on the latter front and that France would launch it in the Aisne area under a new commander, General Robert Nivelle, who had earned a ferocious reputation at Verdun where his subordinates gave him the telling nickname of "*consommateur des hommes*" or "eater of men." Nivelle was convinced that, if enough artillery could be massed, he could deliver a knockout blow against the Germans.

Preparations for this offensive were considerably advanced by February, when the two German senior commanders, Generals Paul von Hindenburg and Erich Ludendorff, upset Allied calculations. Since the Kaiser was a mere figurehead by this time, these two officers assumed almost dictatorial powers for the remainder of the war, directing not only the German military effort but also that nation's diplomatic and economic activities. In late 1916 Germany began to feel the effects of the British naval blockade and put out a peace feeler to the Allied powers, but this initiative came to nothing after Berlin made it clear that it wished to retain much of the Belgian territory it had occupied at the outbreak of the war. In early 1917 Hindenburg and Ludendorff decided to remain on the defensive in the west and attack in the east. Toward this end, in February they ordered a partial withdrawal on the Western Front to a newly-constructed defensive position (dubbed the "Hindenburg Line" by the Allies) which shortened their front by 25 miles and made fourteen divisions available for deployment against Russia. Taken by surprise, the Allies were unable to take advantage of this withdrawal. That same month Germany commenced unrestricted submarine warfare in the waters around the British Isles and Allied shipping losses began to rise dramatically, partly because the Royal Navy refused to institute the convoy system. Hindenburg and Ludendorff were fully aware that this measure might ultimately bring the United States into the war on the Allied side, but gambled that the Allies would come to the negotiating table long before American military power could make itself felt.

The major U-boat bases and the airfields from which German bombers were attacking British cities were on the Channel coast of Belgium. For this reason, many British military and naval leaders supported the recently-promoted Field-Marshal Sir Douglas Haig's wish to stage an offensive in Flanders in 1917 as, if it was successful and Haig was confident it would be, it would blunt German sea and air

Dobbin does his bit for King and Country
Horses of the 20th Battery, Canadian Field Artillery, bring 18-pdr. shells forward to the battery position at Vimy Ridge March 1917. The 20th Battery was from Lethbridge, Alberta. NAC, PA-001231

attacks against Britain. But Haig was distrusted by Lloyd George, the British prime minister, who ordered him to undertake an offensive in the Arras sector to draw German reserves away from Nivelle's push in the adjoining Aisne area. BEF staff began to plan for a major attack involving three armies and, as part of the British First Army, Lieutenant-General Sir Julian Byng's Canadian Corps was assigned the task of taking Vimy Ridge.

"Clock-like precision": Preparations for the attack on Vimy Ridge

Vimy Ridge, from which it was said "more of the war could be seen than any other place in France," was a 9-mile long ribbon of high ground running north and south in front of the Douai Plain near Lens.[7] It had been held by the Germans since 1914 and it was an ideal defensive position as its long and gentle western slopes provided an excellent field of fire for infantry weapons while its steeper and wooded eastern slopes provided concealed positions for artillery. The ridge formed the lynch pin between the older German line and the new Hindenburg Line – it was a crucial position and the Germans were determined to retain it.

Byng's plan called for a simultaneous setpiece assault by his four infantry divisions in line, the first time all four Canadian formations would go into battle together. The main objective was to clear the ridge and the positions behind it and the assault troops, including 21 battalions of infantry in the first wave, would mark their progress by a number of phase lines – Black, Red, Blue and finally Brown – with the final line being on the eastern slope of the ridge. An impressive amount of artillery was concentrated for the attack – nearly a thousand guns of all calibres and averaging about one for every 20 yards of front – and the gunners planned a lengthy artillery programme that would start three weeks before the date of the assault, 9 April 1917, and would include bombardment, lifting barrages and counter-battery programmes. One aspect of the preparations for the attack

was that, for the first time, the attacking infantry would not be used as manual labourers. The job of providing all the logistical, transport and communications support was delegated to the engineer and auxiliary labour units and they were delighted with the chalky soil around the ridge, which had been quarried for centuries. Hardworking sappers extended the many existing tunnels and caves to create large underground shelters complete with electric lights, running water and even small railway systems.

The use of specialized construction troops was not the only innovation. Throughout the winter the senior officers of the Canadian Corps had been studying the tactics employed in previous battles and this resulted in changes to infantry organization and training. Emphasis was now put on the platoon, rather than the company, as the main fighting element and the platoon was reorganized into four teams: a rifle section; a Lewis light machinegun section with one, and later two, weapons; a rifle grenade section; and a "bombing" or grenade section. These mutually supporting teams were trained to manoeuvre to take out enemy positions and, at the same time, stress was placed on every officer and man knowing exactly what he had to do, when he had to do it and where he had do it. An accurate terrain model of the Ridge was constructed for purposes of study, large scale trench maps of their objectives were issued to each platoon and, most important of all, a practice area the same size as the objective was taped off where each infantry brigade spent several days rehearsing their part in the forthcoming operation. The turn of 6th Brigade came on 15 March 1917:

The area was laid out to represent as accurately as possible the terrain … to be attacked by the Brigade, the lifting of the barrage being signalled by means of flags. Contact work between infantry and aeroplanes was practised, and everything possible was done to make the rehearsal as near to the real thing as possible. The practice attack was carried out with a clock-like precision which augured well for the future, and which imbued all concerned with an added feeling of confidence. Further rehearsals on subsequent days brought the operation to as near mechanical perfection as was possible, and made of the Brigade as fine an aggregation of shock troops as had been seen on the Western Front.[8]

Nine days later, the 31st Battalion was ordered into the line near Neuville St. Vaast at the foot of Vimy Ridge. Shelling was bad on both sides. The Canadian artillery had begun their preliminary bombardment on 20 March and when the enemy artillery replied, their positions were carefully noted by the gunners who were plotting an impressive counter-bombardment programme. A staff officer with the 6th Brigade recalled that for weeks on end, the glass in the window of his office hut never stopped rattling from the incessant concussion of exploding shells. As usual, the weather was miserable – cold, wet and windy – but the men in the trenches were intrigued by the numerous air battles in the skies over the Ridge as German aircraft, many painted in bright colours, fought their Allied counterparts. Private Fraser, an interested observer of these dogfights, thought Allied airmen got the worst of the business because of inexperience or inferior aircraft. Fortunately for the Iron Brigade, its companies not in line could take shelter in the Zivy Cave, a huge underground shelter accommodating 5,000 soldiers – Signal-

ler Charles Craig of the 28th Battalion noted that it "was some 90 feet under the ground and from floor to ceiling about 40 feet high."[9] Soldier rumour was that 1,500 French gas casualties were buried somewhere in the cave, which may or may not have been true but Craig did remember that "the smell was pretty bad sometimes."[10]

As zero hour, 5.30 A.M. on 9 April 1917, approached, the Canadian artillery intensified their fire. By the end of March they had expended 285,000 rounds and now more and more guns joined in as they brought down furious bombardments and practice barrages across the entire German front. "Hour by hour and day by day," wrote the historian of the 31st, "the artillery pounded the enemy positions with high-explosive shells, blowing in dugouts, levelling trenches and ploughing up the ground."[11] During the night of 8 April, the 6th Brigade moved into its jumping-off position east of Neuville St. Vaast behind the 4th and 5th Brigades which would make the initial 2nd Division attack. Although the troops were fresh, it was a wearying march through the mud as the men were weighed down with haversacks, weapons, extra ammunition, iron rations, two canteens plus "bombs, flares, shovels, phones, flags" and "a host of other things."[12] Then came the long wait through a night punctuated by star shells "of every hue, flashes of guns, bursts of shell and shrapnel" that "filled the earth and air with such intermingled fires that no distinction was perceptible till some

The Canadian Corps becomes more professional, 1917
Before the attack on Vimy Ridge in April 1917, an intense effort was made to ensure that the assault troops knew their job. Part of this effort included walking over a scale terrain model such as this one, constructed by the engineers. It was another sign of the increasing professionalism of the Canadian Corps. NAC, PA-003666

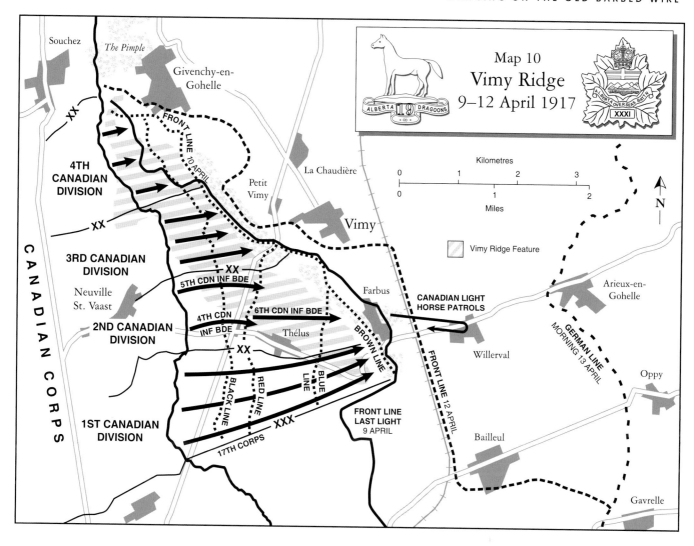

Map 10
Vimy Ridge
9–12 April 1917

particular explosion happened to reflect the wall of a ruin or give background to a tree."[13] As the time approached, the gunners began to lessen their fire, both to confuse the enemy and to gain time for last minute preparations. All guns ceased firing four seconds before zero hour. There was an unearthly quiet for the space of a breath and then, precisely at 5.30 A.M., 982 artillery pieces, from 15-inch howitzers down to 2-inch mortars, opened up with everything they had as the infantry went forward under a downpour of rain, snow and sleet.

"General, everything is jake!": Vimy Ridge, 9-12 April 1917

After weeks of preparation and the heavy and prolonged artillery bombardment, the assault on Vimy Ridge was almost anticlimactic – at least for the 1st and 2nd Divisions on the right flank. The 4th Division encountered determined resistance from an enemy position dubbed the "Pimple" which stymied its advance and also hampered the progress of the 3rd Division on its right. In the 2nd Division's sector, however, the 4th and 5th Infantry Brigades, moving close behind their lifting barrage, met very little opposition and their biggest problem was getting across muddy ground churned up by the bombardment. The two brigades reached the Black Line at 6.20 A.M. and the Red

Line an hour later. Here they halted for the 6th Brigade to come up and take over the advance. The Iron Brigade and the 31st Battalion were in position and ready to go at 9.10 A.M. when the gunners brought down another lifting barrage to cover their advance. They met only scattered resistance until they reached the Blue Line at the ruined village of Thelus, which was stubbornly defended by the Germans. Utilizing the new platoon tactics, however, the battalion managed to clear Thelus although snipers remained a problem throughout the day. In a dugout near the village the amazed Albertans found an elaborate German officers' mess with a well-stocked bar, a fine dinner laid out on the table and five mess attendants waiting to serve it. The waiters went into the bag and the dinner into the captors, while the contents of the bar were added to battalion stocks. At this point the 31st halted to consolidate and the 27th Battalion took over the advance to the final phase line, the Brown Line, which was reached early in the afternoon. The Iron Brigade then consolidated its positions just short of the village of Farbus. In the late afternoon a German counterattack was broken up by the artillery and, by night, with the exception of snipers, the occasional artillery round and isolated pockets of resistance, the brigade front was quiet.

The Canadian soldiers who participated in that memorable day never forgot it. To Private Donald Fraser the attack on Vimy Ridge was "the easiest and most successful that I ever was in. The going was arduous and tough, but the opposition was negligible, although after consolidation one was lucky to escape death from shell fire."[14] Trooper Hambley of the Canadian Light Horse who had been sent to assist the crews of the Canadian Machine Gun Corps lay down a barrage of automatic weapons fire ahead of the advancing troops, watched the infantry move up the western slope of the ridge "all headed in one direction walking leisurely enough with their rifles slung on their shoulders and their long, hungry looking bayonets protruding above their heads."[15] A few minutes later, "over came enormous strings of Fritzies with gestures of putting up their hands" and the Canadians "crowded to meet them and one young fellow I saw had his helmet snatched from his head before he ever got near our trenches – for a souvenir." To Signaller Charles Craig of the 28th Battalion the day was "all a haze as I don't remember anything very distinctly but have just a few very vivid pictures of it" but Craig did remember collecting souvenirs.[16] Souvenirs were also on the mind of Private Fraser who was disappointed when he returned to forage in

an interesting pile of German equipment and uniforms stripped from prisoners by their captors that he had seen earlier, only to find it had entirely disappeared. Throughout the late morning and afternoon, the German artillery brought down sporadic fire, sometimes using the occasional gas shell and, during one of these bombardments, Fraser had a very close call:

> I was on the point of climbing out of the trench when a shell with a dull pop burst on the parapet almost in my face. My breathing stopped at once. With mouth open I could neither breath in or out. Breathing was paralysed. It a peculiar sensation. In a flash I knew it was a gas shell and it completely fouled the air. In a fraction of a second, in fact my quickness astonished me, I had my respirator on and was breathing freely.[17]

For the Canadian Light Horse, however, 9 April 1917 was not a particularly good day. Two of the unit's squadrons had been dismounted to serve as carrying parties for the machinegunners and as stretcher bearers. Lieutenant-Colonel Ibbotson Leonard retained C Squadron with a strength of 211 all ranks on horse-

"Leaning into the barrage," Vimy Ridge, 1917
Behind the smoke and explosions of both Canadian and German artillery shells, Canadian infantry advance at Vimy Ridge. Given the terrain, these are probably men of the 1st Canadian Division on the right flank. All arms admitted that the success in this battle was due to the impressive work of the Canadian artillery. NAC, PA-001087

back as he had been warned that the Light Horse might be required to provide scouting parties on the far side of the Ridge. Around midday a request came through from the 1st Division, for mounted patrols to be sent in the direction of Willerval, a village a half a mile beyond the Brown Line. Leonard ordered Captain W. King to take two troops and a Hotchkiss machinegun section to a small wood near the adjoining village of Farbus where he was to leave one troop and try, if possible, with the other to secure a lodgement in the village. It is an indication of just how difficult it was for cavalry to operate on the Western Front when one reads in Leonard's report that, before dispatching this force, he first had to have a route cleared and taped for them through the shell holes, barbed wire and mud so that the horses could get past these obstacles. This was done and King took the two troops to Farbus Wood, set up his two Hotchkiss machineguns and, at 4.20 P.M., dispatched two small patrols into Willerval to ascertain whether it was occupied by the enemy.

It most certainly was and both patrols ran into trouble. That led by Lieutenant Murray came under fire as soon it crossed a railway embankment just beyond the Canadian line and lost three horses. Murray continued into the centre of Willerval

where he spotted a group of Germans at a crossroads in the centre. He ordered his troop to draw swords and charge and the Germans, probably amazed at the sight of horsemen galloping down at them, immediately surrendered but at almost the same time the troop came under machinegun fire. Murray ordered his men to retire but several men and horses were killed or wounded by automatic weapons fire. Murray himself was wounded and his horse killed, but when his troop sergeant rode over to help him, Murray told him to return to the Canadian lines with the by-now-obvious information that Willerval was held by the enemy in strength. This patrol lost 6 of its 13 men, including Murray.

The other Light Horse patrol, led by Sergeant T. Smith, fared no better. Just past the railway line it encountered "a large party of the enemy … lying in the open in extended formation." Smith reported what happened next:

> We approached within a 100 yards when we came under a cross fire from the village and the trench. I gave the signal to retire, and I had 4 men and four horses killed, and while trying to assist a man who was being dragged, I lost my other two horses. Corp[ora]l McMurray who was shot through the hand, and myself, managed to crawl from shell hole to shell hole and made our way back when I reported the result of my reconnaissance. My patrol consisted of 6, four of whom were killed.[18]

The survivors were back in the Canadian lines by early evening and the Light Horse's day was done.

It required three further days of fighting before the 4th Division was able to eradicate the "Pimple" and take their objective, the highest point of the ridge. The victory was now complete at the cost of 10,062 casualties which, although not light, were a remarkably small price to pay in the context of the Western Front, for a magnificent achievement. All arms had contributed to the triumph but, in the end, everyone admitted that the artillery had played the major role – in the words of the senior gunner of the Canadian Corps, Major-General E.W.B. Morrison, the artillery preparation and support in this battle "was as near

The Iron Brigade at Vimy Ridge, April 1917
Picking their way through the ruins of the German wire belt, men of the 29th Battalion CEF, the Alberta battalion's sister unit in 6th Brigade, move forward at Vimy Ridge. The preliminary bombardment was so ferocious that in the 2nd Division area only scattered resistance was met when the infantry advanced. NAC, PA-001086

The immortal Vickers
A section of Vickers machineguns is deployed by men of the Canadian Machine Gun Corps in a defensive position at Vimy Ridge. Introduced to the British army in 1912, this .303 calibre weapon which could fire 450 rounds per minute was the British equivalent to the German Maxim 08 and just as deadly. The standard British and Canadian medium machinegun in three wars, the immortal Vickers was finally declared obsolete in 1968. NAC, PA-001017

Off they go – Canadian Light Horse at Vimy Ridge, 1917
In the immediate aftermath of the attack on Vimy Ridge the Canadian Light Horse sent a number of mounted patrols to villages east of the last Canadian phase line. These troopers are wearing steel helmets, and are equipped with 90-round leather bandoliers and have their weapons in rifle boots. Dangling from their saddles can be seen a canvas water bucket and feed bag for Dobbin. NAC, PA-001111

perfection on a gigantic scale as the science of the arm has ever been brought."[19] Morrison also contributed an anecdote about the reaction of the corps commander to the victory.

> You know General Byng delights in Canadian slang. He repeats it over and chuckles to himself when it is expressive. He likes my expression "go to it." At the height of the battle when I got the report we had taken the Ridge, I went to him and said: "General, everything is jake! We are shelling the retiring Boches." He sprung his jolly smile and gave the historic order: "Morrison, go to it!"[20]

It was a great moment for the Canadian Corps but there were more battles to be fought before this miserable war ended.

"Jumping from shell-hole to shell-hole": The attack on Fresnoy, 3-7 May 1917

The assault on Vimy Ridge was the northern component of the British operations at Arras and the Canadian success was nearly paralleled by British troops who, in three days of heavy fighting, pushed the Germans back an average of 2 miles along an 18-mile front. On the Aisne, however, the French met with disaster. Confident of success, Nivelle had massed nearly 4,000 guns to support his two-army attack which began on 16 April but the assaulting formations encountered a new German defensive doctrine based on an elastic defence in depth. Frontline positions were only lightly held, for the main battle line was 2,500 yards behind and consisted of two fighting trenches and a network of concrete machinegun emplacements and deep dugouts that sheltered reserve forces for use in counterattacks. All trenches were protected by formidable belts of wire laid out so that machinegun fire could enfilade any possible approach. Nivelle's massive artillery bombardment fell on the enemy outpost line which his troops took without difficulty only to find themselves up against masses of machineguns behind uncut wire in the German main line. All attempts to penetrate these defences were unavailing and Nivelle gained only local success at the cost of 187,000 casualties. He lost his job as a result but the Aisne

disaster was too much for the despairing men of an army that, since 1914, had invariably suffered the highest losses of any of the combatants on the Western Front. French soldiers began to mutiny in mid-April and by June more than half the divisions in the army of the republic were refusing to carry out offensive operations, although they did agree to defend their positions. This massive act of protest was gradually brought under control but, for the remainder of 1917, it was clear that the BEF would have to shoulder the main burden on the Western Front.

To divert German attention from the critical French situation, Haig ordered a continuation of the Arras offensive, and what had originated as a subsidiary operation now became the main Allied effort. Haig's objectives were modest – a series of assaults by nine divisions on a 9-mile front – and he saw this renewed attack as being a battle of attrition rather than deep penetration. Unfortunately, when the attacks began on 23 April they encountered the new German defensive positions and the tactics that had worked earlier in the month at Vimy Ridge and other places no longer proved effective. Gains in terms of ground were minimal and casualties heavy as the BEF became involved in a number of "soldiers' battles" in which heavy bombardment of the enemy forward lines proved ineffective while, all too often, the infantry were pinned down by machineguns and pillboxes protected by uncut wire belts. The only major success of these operations was gained by the 1st Canadian Division, which stormed the fortified village of Arleux on 28 April. Now came a brief pause while Haig assessed the situation. He had to decide whether to continue operations in the Arras sector or commence a new operation in Flanders, an option he personally favoured. He decided to renew the attack and the Canadian Corps was given the task of seizing the hamlet of Fresnoy, a German strongpoint located a few miles southeast of Vimy Ridge.

The Corps plan for this operation was straightforward. Under a combined bombardment and barrage brought down by every available gun, the 1st Infantry Brigade would make a direct attack on Fresnoy while the 6th Infantry Brigade, in the form of the 27th and 31st Battalions, would advance to provide left flank protection. During the night of 1/2 May 1917 the assault battalions moved up in readiness to begin the attack at 3.45 A.M. on 3 May, but the Germans were alert and had plentiful artillery on call which inflicted heavy

"Hanging on the old barbed wire."
German wire belts protecting their forward trenches in 1918. Wire belts presented a formidable obstacle for the infantry and they were almost always covered by machineguns which, in the later years of the war, were emplaced in concrete pill boxes. It was discovered through trial and error that wire belts could be cut by High Explosive but they were still the cause of heavy casualties. NAC, PA-030372

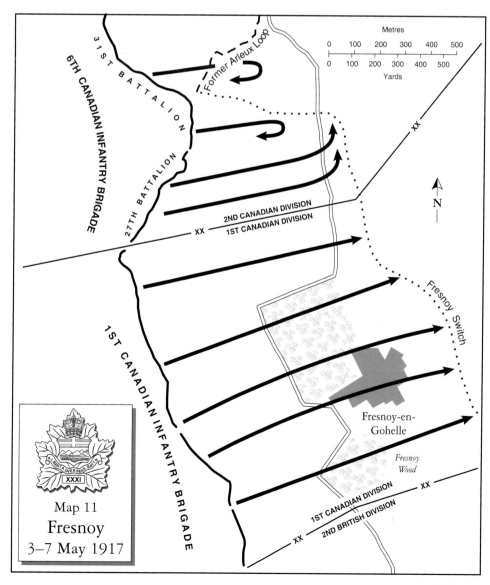

Map 11
Fresnoy
3–7 May 1917

casualties. Under cover of a lifting barrage the infantry went forward on time and the 1st Brigade, although meeting determined resistance, was able to secure Fresnoy and its final objective, a line 250 yards east of the village, by 6 A.M.

The 6th Brigade, however, ran into serious trouble. The 31st Battalion came upon an unexpected and uncut belt of concertina wire and the lead companies fell behind the barrage as the men desperately tried to find a way through. By the time they did so, the barrage had ended and the battalion found itself pinned down by automatic weapons fire from the German main line, while being severely shelled by enemy artillery. So many shells were falling that "it was difficult to distinguish between the shell-bursts from the supporting artillery and those from the enemy batteries" and C Company, caught moving through the wire, was particularly hard hit.[21] But the Albertans, by now much reduced in numbers, found gaps and pressed on to what they thought was the main enemy line, only to find more uncut concertina wire. It was now nearly dawn and the battalion lost cohesion as small groups found or made gaps in the wire and launched a series of separate attacks on the enemy trench behind.

Unfortunately, daylight revealed that the battalion was not in front of the main German line but pinned down before a hitherto unsuspected forward position and were only half way to their objective. Suffering from unrelenting shell and machinegun fire they were forced to ground in shell craters. Major William Piper, the senior surviving officer in the assault companies, attempted to consolidate the remnants of the battalion in a sunken road to the immediate rear but many men, under heavy and unrelenting machinegun fire, were unable to withdraw to this position. Nor was it possible to evacuate the wounded, many of whom kept up the fight by continuing to throw grenades. After he had regrouped what was left of the battalion, Piper sent two officers forward to make a reconnaissance of the German position and they reported that it might be possible to secure the closest enemy trench by a determined grenade attack. This was carried out by a small bombing party which entered the enemy position and methodically worked its way down it, clearing sections so that Piper could order a general advance, which was joined by many men who had been sheltering in shell craters. The German position was taken, but by this time it was clear that the Albertans were not going to attain their objective and, worse still, they were isolated and not in touch with the 27th Battalion on their flank.

At brigade headquarters, Ketchen was out of contact with

"They've evidently seen me"
Evidently they had – another example of Bairnsfather humour, and sometimes humour was all they had to keep them going. COPYRIGHT TONIE AND VALMAI HOLT, REPRODUCED WITH PERMISSION FROM *THE BEST OF FRAGMENTS FROM FRANCE*

the situation because of communications failure. In the early morning the numbers of enemy prisoners coming back appeared to be a positive sign and Donald Fraser, who had grudgingly accepted a promotion to lance-corporal and re-assignment to the brigade machine gun company, had watched as

about sixteen Huns came running towards our [machine] gun with their hands up. ...... As they approached closer and saw our guns spitting fire, up went their hands still higher. They were taken captives by a couple of our men and it was amusing to watch their cunning. They were delighted with themselves, smiling and wanting to shake hands. ...... Only a few moments before they were trying their hardest to kill us and now you would think they were our long lost brothers. The leader came towards me with his hand extended, crying in broken English, "You ween, you ween (win)." All you could do was smile, it was so funny.[22]

As the day wore on, however, it became increasingly clear to both Ketchen and Bell that the attack was an unmitigated disaster.

Meanwhile, the remnants of the 31st Battalion consolidated their hardwon position and made ready for the inevitable counterattack. It came in the afternoon and, according to one witness, it was carried out by troops "fresh from Belgium three days ago, with hot coffee in their bottles and sandwiches, new clothes and new equipment." The enemy advanced "jumping from shell hole to shell hole in bunches of about a hundred" but the Lewis "gunners and riflemen opened up on them and many of the enemy were killed and wounded."[23] Although they could not know it, the Albertans were having their first experience with a new German tactical doctrine developed on the Eastern Front – *Stosstruppen* or "storm trooper" tactics – which emphasized short rushes by small groups covered by fire from other small groups which leapfrogged through each other using fire and movement to seize their objectives. As no one had informed the battalion that these tactics were a remarkable innovation that had worked well against French and Russian troops, the Albertans forced the enemy, in this instance a Prussian Guard unit, to ground with small arms fire and, once that was accomplished, launched volleys of grenades at them. The Germans, despite "pressing forward with the utmost vigour and resolution in spite of casualties," were themselves pinned down, and by this time, communication having been established with the supporting artillery, an intensive bombardment was brought down on them which more or less ended the matter.[24]

All aboard for the rear
One of the most common forms of transport behind the trenches was hastily-converted London buses. Note that the windows have been boarded up, probably as a protection against artillery fire. On the other hand, unless they were coming out of the line, one trench was as bad as the next and these men did not need to see where they were going.

Still under heavy artillery fire, the battalion remained in place through the night, working feverishly to improve their positions and to locate and evacuate their wounded. It was a difficult and dangerous task as enemy snipers were active and German machinegunners, firing on fixed lines, periodically sprayed the Albertans' position with rapid fire. At 6 A.M. on 4 May the unit was relieved by the 29th Battalion and the survivors withdrew to the support lines, which proved almost as bad as the forward positions because, for three days, German artillery bombardment was unceasing, methodical and relentless. Lance-Corporal Fraser described it:

Starting on the north, a shell would explode in or near the trench; the next one would drop about ten yards further down, the third would alight a similar distance away. A series of explosions at very short intervals occurred for a distance of about three hundred yards. Then the fire would be reversed and shells would burst on the way back. Up and down the trench, with perfect regularity, shells were bursting with the result that the battalion men were shifting and bunching up and down the trench trying to keep ahead of the bursts, while a limited number, as soon as the shell burst, would race past the place of explosion to get to the other side. We were completely at the mercy of the shelling. …… The suspense was unnerving as the bursts neared you on the left, but when the shell passed over you and exploded on the right, the tension was released and you breathed again freely. Up and down the trench the enemy kept this type of shelling for a long time, making the situation almost unbearable.[25]

Just to make things more disagreeable, enemy aircraft made frequent bombing and strafing attacks on the Canadian trenches.

The 6th Brigade endured this torment for three days before it was relieved at 1 A.M. on 8 May and marched back to a bivouac at Thelus. Its travails were not over, however, as the Germans brought down a heavy gas shell bombardment while the relief was taking place and, as the 31st historian noted, many men in the battalion "suffered a good deal from the poison fumes."[26] Fraser remembered trying to sleep that night while lying on the ground wearing his respirator, nearly sickened by the "abominable smell" of gas until a lucky downpour of rain dispersed it.[27]

Fresnoy was disastrous for the Alberta Battalion. It had gone into the attack on 3 May with a strength of 23 officers and 568 other ranks; it lost 12 officers and 229 men killed, wounded and missing in that action, a casualty rate of 48% – C Company alone lost 95 men, probably about 80% of its strength. With good reason, Fraser remembered that the men of the 31st were "somewhat bitter" about the whole business and what made it worse was that it was all for nothing.[28] On the day after the 6th

Brigade was relieved, the Germans counterattacked, destroyed the British battalion holding Fresnoy, and recaptured the ground purchased at such a high cost in Canadian lives.

"Stretcher bearers, on the double!" Military medicine on the Western Front

Fresnoy was a failure but one of the tragic ironies of the First World War was that, whether an operation succeeded or failed, the casualties were inevitably heavy and the only difference was in degree, not kind. For example, the assault on Vimy Ridge, one of the outstanding military feats of the war, still resulted in 7,114 wounded Canadians who had to be tended by the medical services. The sheer number of casualties posed unprecedented problems for all combatants during the First World War and it is time to discuss the medical aspects of the conflict.

By 1917, the Canadian Army Medical Corps (as part of the Royal Army Medical Corps) had evolved a complex but efficient system for treating the wounded based on a number of successive stages. For a wounded man, immediate first aid and stabilization of his wound was undertaken at a Regimental Aid Post manned by a battalion's Medical Officer and his staff. He was then evacuated to a Relay Point where he was taken over by the Field Ambulance attached to each infantry brigade and brought back to the Advanced Dressing Station where he received further treatment. From here he went to the Casualty Clearing Station where treatment was more extensive and from there to general, base or specialized hospitals on the continent or in Britain. At each stage, medical treatment became progressively more elaborate but the first and most important link was provided by the battalion Medical Officer.

In the case of the 31st Battalion, from 1915 to 1917 this was Captain Harold W. McGill. A 38-year-old graduate of the University of Manitoba medical school, McGill had been on the staff of the Calgary General Hospital before joining the unit when it was raised in late 1914. As Medical Officer, McGill was responsible for the general health of his unit out of the line and for the initial treatment of its casualties in the line. In the rear area he supervised sanitation and cleanliness, advised and checked on rations and cooking, but his main duty was the daily sick parade at which he examined and treated all soldiers who attended, deciding whether to send them to a hospital or retain and treat them in the unit. In this respect, as the historian of the Canadian Medical Corps notes, the Medical Officer "must be tender to the weak, and harden his heart against the malingerer or him who would shirk."[29] In effect McGill was a general practitioner whose practice was the 31st Battalion, and through experience and personal knowledge of his patients, he became very adept at differentiating between the truly sick and those who merely wished to get sent to hospital for a rest, or at least put on light duties for a day or two. In his work, McGill was assisted by a small staff of six men from the medical corps.

Medical science had made tremendous advances in the previous three decades and the First World War was one of the first wars in history in which more soldiers died from enemy action than from sickness. Medical personnel managed to prevent widespread epidemics of disease, which is remarkable given the conditions under which the soldiers served on the Western Front. Typhus and dysentery were held in check, although precautions against meningitis were less successful. "Trench foot," a variant of frostbite resulting from prolonged immersion in water, was rampant in the early years of the war but was brought under control when tours in wet frontline trenches were reduced and it was made a disciplinary offence – meaning that a unit with a high incidence rate of trench foot was punished with stoppage of leave. Even the depredations of the "humble and friendly louse," a soldier's constant companion and a carrier of typhus, were lessened when it was discovered that lice and their eggs could be destroyed by subjecting infested garments to intense heat for short periods.[30]

The Medical Officer was of paramount importance when his battalion went into the line, particularly during an attack. It was an important boost to morale (and men who served on the Western Front needed all possible help in that respect) if soldiers knew they would receive immediate and proper medical treatment if wounded in action. This treatment was carried out at the Regimental Aid Post and its siting and function was one the primary concerns of the Medical Officer. RAPs were usually placed in large, deep and strongly-built dugouts in the support or reserve trenches (the cellars of ruined buildings was a favoured location) where they had some protection from artillery fire. In periods of active fighting, the Medical Officer would usually stay at the RAP and the casualties would be brought to him by the 16 stretcher bearers under his command, a number doubled or quadrupled if heavy fighting or other conditions warranted it.

During battle, lightly wounded men would make their own way to the RAP but the shout, "stretcher bearers, on the double!" would bring a pair of bearers to the location of the seriously wounded. They would evaluate his wound or wounds and render first aid, using the dressing every soldier carried in the skirt of his tunic, often coating a wound with iodine which was in general use as an antiseptic, and then carry him back to the RAP. Only in an extreme emergency, usually concerned with wounds causing major fractures or where the wounded had to be tended before being moved, would McGill leave the RAP to go to the man's location.

As the wounded came into the RAP, either by stretcher or on foot, McGill would carry out a more elaborate evaluation, stem bleeding with compresses or clamps, pack extensive wounds with sterile material, coat the wounds with iodine and dress or bandage them. He did not try to suture or close wounds, unless it was absolutely necessary to preserve life, as given the frequency of gas gangrene, this was usually left to the surgeons in the rear. He would inject the man with morphine and anti-tetanus serum (tetanus was another scourge of the Western Front). Again, only if necessary, he might carry out emergency surgery,

greatest source of comfort was morphine, administered in doses of a half grain per injection because it was found, through considerable experience, that morphine "given early and accompanied by quiet and warmth" was the most effective method of saving lives.[31] In this respect, the medical personnel were aided by the fact that in the immediate aftermath of being wounded, shock often meant the inflicted man suffered little or no pain. But, as the historian of the Canadian Army Medical Corps notes, "the pain was not long delayed" and it "became atrocious and had best not be spoken of even in a history of military medicine."[32] Morphine not only eased pain, it kept the wounded quiet and it was therefore used freely.

Wounded evacuated from the RAP entered the successive stages of the medical chain. From the RAP, they went to the Relay Point where they were turned over to the brigade field ambulance and taken to the Advanced Dressing Station where further triaging, dressing and some emergency surgery was carried out, and a more complete history recorded. From here the afflicted went by motor ambulance or light railway to the Casualty Clearing Station, which was located out of enemy artillery range. The CCS was actually a mobile hospital and one was provided for every division in the BEF. Medical treatment at the CCS was more elaborate and the majority of surgery was done at this stage by relays of surgeons working around the clock in large operating theatres that could accommodate four procedures at a time.

In a time before the introduction of antibiotics, one of the greatest problems surgeons faced was treating extensive tissue loss caused by artillery projectiles and the often concomitant gas gangrene. The soil of Flanders, fertilized for centuries with animal manure and, in more recent times beginning in 1914, by corpses, latrines and waste, was a fertile breeding ground for the amoebic bacteria that caused gangrene. As the war progressed, saline solutions were introduced to clean the wound but the most effective treatment for gas gangrene was the removal of all infected, or possibly-infected, tissue – and all too often, amputation was the only sure way to save lives.

The Casualty Clearing Station, which was often equipped with a blood bank and X-ray machines as an aid to diagnosis and treatment, was the most significant stage in the medical chain. Frontline medical personnel in the RAP and field ambulance worked under the guiding principle: "Get the wounded man to the casualty clearing station as soon as possible. Do all you can for him at the regimental aid post or the advanced dressing station, and do it as thoroughly and as quickly as you can, so that there will be no need to disturb the patient again, on his journey down."[33] The wounded might be retained in the CCS for a few days but only the most serious cases were kept there for longer periods, the remainder being transferred by ambulance train or

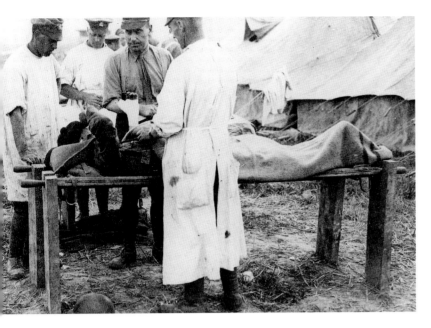

"Iodine Joe": Captain Harold W. McGill, Medical Officer, 31st Battalion

Dr. Harold McGill, a former Calgary doctor, served as the medical officer of the 31st Battalion from 1914 to 1917, an unusually long time in such a position. He was known to the enlisted men as "Iodine Joe" because of his predilection for iodine above all other forms of antiseptic. McGill is seen here in uniform observing surgeons treat a wounded man at Amiens in 1918 and it is clear they are out of range of enemy artillery, otherwise they would be in a dug-out. GLENBOW MUSEUM, NA-4938-17

usually amputation for wounds involving shattered limbs, but no surgery was carried out at the RAP that required a general anaesthetic. Fractures were secured with splints, many specially devised during the war, to keep the afflicted limb rigid. While he undertook these procedures, McGill also "triaged" his patients (although the term was not in common use during the First World War) meaning that he made a rapid diagnosis, rendered essential first aid and sorted out the casualties into categories. Lightly wounded men (the "walking wounded") were treated swiftly and dispatched to the rear, often serving as emergency stretcher bearers if they were able. The stretcher cases were then divided into three classes: men expected to die; men who could be sent to the rear after the Medical Officer had stabilized them; and men who required more attention before being evacuated (usually cases involving extensive haemorrhage). McGill made the "moribund" or those expected to die as comfortable as possible with morphine and placed them aside, then treated the two other classes in order of medical priority. He dispatched those who could be evacuated, and kept those who needed further attention until he felt they could be safely taken back to the rear.

Medical personnel took care to complete a brief record of treatment that would follow a wounded man through the evacuation system – marks, either "M" for morphine or "T" for tetanus, were made with iodine or indelible pencil on the forehead or wrists to record any injections and a wound card with details of injury, date and time was attached to the afflicted man's tunic button. A great effort was also made to keep the wounded warm with extra blankets and fortified with hot, sweet tea. But the

Stretcher bearers

The first treatment a casualty received was given by the regimental stretcher bearers, seen here bandaging a wounded man in August 1916. The bearers would next take him to the Regimental Aid Post, where a unit Medical Officer would render more elaborate treatment. NAC, PA-000794

Regimental Aid Post

The RAP, the station of a battalion Medical Officer, was usually a secure dug-out behind the firing trenches. Here, two stretcher bearers in 1916 leave a wounded man until he can be taken in for treatment. They will now make a trip for another man. NAC, PA-000518

(Below) **Too close for comfort: Shellburst near Medical Relay Point, the Somme, September 1916**
After initial treatment at the Regimental Aid Post, wounded men were brought back to a Relay Point where they were transferred to horse-drawn or motorized ambulances for evacuation to the next link, the Advanced Dressing Station. These relay points were still within artillery range as this photograph demonstrates. Note the wheeled stretcher on the right, these contrivances were only useful outside the trenches. NAC, PA-000625

Relay Point, Somme, and hospital train
At the Relay Point (above left), the wounded soldier was shifted to the vehicles of a Field Ambulance unit that would take him to an Advanced Dressing Station, where he would receive further treatment in preparation for evacuation to a Casualty Clearing Station. The last stage in the medical evacuation chain was the hospital train (above right) that took wounded men from the Casualty Clearing Station to a base or specialized hospital for extended treatment and convalescence. Here a Canadian Army Medical Corps train is seen in 1917 at the siding for No. 1 Canadian General Hospital near Abbeville. LEFT: NAC, PA-000680. RIGHT: COURTESY, COLIN MICHAUD

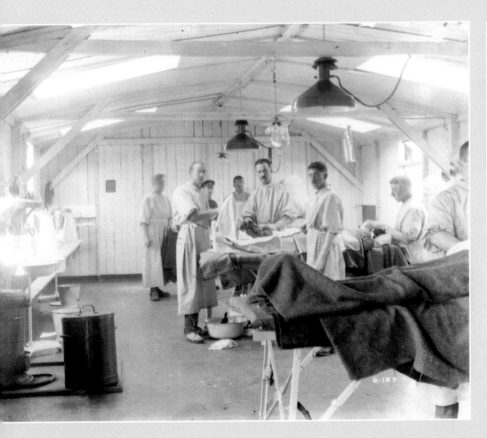

The Casualty Clearing Station
The main operating theatre at Canadian No. 3 Casualty Clearing Station photographed in July 1916, where as many as four simultaneous surgical procedures could be carried out. The CCS was actually a forward hospital and the major component in the medical evacuation system. The wounded soldier stayed at the CCS for some time until he was stable enough to be transferred to a general or base hospital. NAC PA-000104

"Bluebird"
Nursing Sister Blanche Lavallée, sketched by artist R.G. Mathews in 1916. More than 2,500 Canadian women served in the Canadian Army Medical Corps during the First World War and several were killed in action. Nicknamed "bluebirds" because of their distinct light blue uniforms, they exhibited grace under pressures that, during major offensives when the wounded came in by the thousands, were almost unbearable. COURTESY DEPARTMENT OF NATIONAL DEFENCE, PMR-C-86-419

barge to either general hospitals on the Channel coast or in Britain, or to special hospitals that afforded advanced treatment for, as examples, orthopaedics or plastic surgery.

Two types of casualties were particularly difficult to treat. The first were men wounded by gas. Medical personnel observed that the gas itself rarely killed its victim because treatment was available – oxygen for inhaled gases and standard medical procedures for men with burns caused by mustard gas. Rather, he died from complications involving bronchitis or pneumonia which usually occurred within a week of his being wounded. Otherwise, gas casualties usually survived but, nonetheless, many gassed men required a long recovery period that was often complicated by symptoms involving debility, irregular heart beat and vomiting that did not appear to be physical in origin. It became obvious to the medical staffs that, although they were physically healthy, many men who had been severely gassed suffered from considerable emotional trauma as the "apparently cured would relapse just before discharge from hospital" and, "in spite of all treatment these symptoms were frequently most persistent."[34]

The second problem casualty, and a related one, was the soldier suffering from psychological trauma. Such casualties had been known in earlier wars – although they were treated somewhat harshly – but the First World War differed from previous conflicts in the duration and intensity of combat and the lethality of the weapons in use, particularly high explosive shells fired by long-range artillery. In the early period of the war, men exhibiting psychological trauma were diagnosed as either suffering "shellshock," "hysteria" or "neurasthenia." There were important distinctions between them as the first was a wound caused by enemy action, while the others were conditions caused by fear. Nor surprisingly, as it affected both their subsequent pensions and the attitudes of their comrades, men preferred to be diagnosed as "shellshocked" and unit Medical Officers, who did not have the training to differentiate between the three, nor the time to deal with them, often simply wrote "Shell Shock (W)" on the man's medical label and sent him down the line. Also not surprisingly, malingerers and shirkers took advantage of this procedure and, by the midwar period, it was realized that the increasing numbers of men evacuated with shell shock

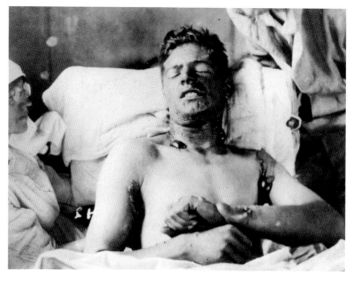

Mustard gas casualty, 1917

Mustard gas, a blistering agent, caused skin irritation that resulted in painful wounds. The use of gas became more frequent and lethal as the war went on as new and more deadly agents were introduced and gas bombardment was often mixed with High Explosive bombardment so that the gas shells would not be easily distinguished. NAC. C-080027

– many of whom made a swift recovery once they were away from the line – were overburdening medical resources. In June 1917 a general order was issued forbidding the use of the term "shell shock" on any medical report or document and directing that all cases of apparent psychological trauma would henceforth be labelled "NYD(N)" or "Not Yet Diagnosed (Nervous)" and sent to a special hospital, where they were kept under observation for a month to weed out the truly afflicted from the others. After the introduction of this measure, there was a dramatic decline in the number of such cases because being labelled "NYD(N)" was regarded as a stigma by frontline soldiers.

The whole question of psychological trauma was one that vexed military commanders and medical personnel. The origin of the problem was not fear – everybody was afraid – it was the inability of certain men to control that fear to the extent that they put their comrades in danger. All men in the frontline were afraid but most were more afraid of letting their fear show than of anything the enemy could do to them. Frontline soldiers distinguished between a man being "windy" or generally afraid and a man who was in a "funk," or so afraid that he could "not do his bit" or perform his duties and would thus endanger his comrades. The matter, however, was more complex because courage (perhaps most usefully defined as the ability to control fear under extreme stress) is a limited resource and the realities of trench warfare, particularly heavy artillery bombardment for days and weeks on end, steadily chipped away at a man's personal store until he snapped. It was extremely difficult for a battalion Medical Officer to distinguish psychological trauma resulting from an oversensitive or congenitally nervous disposition and that caused by horrific stress. In this respect the newly-invented science of psychology was not much assistance because, as Sir Andrew Macphail, the acerbic historian of the Canadian Army Medical Corps, acidly wrote, a battalion Medical Officer "had no knowledge of the jargon in which the problem was being discussed … could not distinguish hypo-emotive from hyper-emotive, or commotio cerebri from emotio cerebri," nor could he differentiate between "respective reflexes, dynamogenic, and dysocinetic explanations."[35] What he could do was weed out the shirkers "after consultation with the sergeant-major," label the rest "NYD(N)" and send them to the special hospital.

But the problem was never solved and it did not go away.

Private Fraser witnessed a man from his platoon, an otherwise reliable soldier, suddenly start talking gibberish about possessing supernatural powers – he was sent to the special hospital after McGill observed his behaviour for a period. At the battle of Courcelette of 15 September 1916, Fraser encountered a major (not from the 31st as all the majors in that battalion who took an active part in that action were killed) being led by the hand, crying and sobbing, to the rear. Frontline soldiers were not always sympathetic to men who broke down – possibly because they themselves were often finding it hard to control their own emotions. At Vimy Ridge Fraser remembered a "poor fellow, a big chap, … crying like a baby with shellshock. His nerves and control were absolutely gone and he was yelled at by everyone to shut up the moment he whimpered."[36] Captain Harold McGill noted that every time the battalion was warned it would be going back into the line, the number of men coming on sick parade with minor or imaginary ailments would double or even triple. This phenomenon was widespread through the BEF and on the eve of major attacks the number of NYD(N) cases sent back increased, as many units took the opportunity to get rid of men who would constitute a liability in action and Medical Officers willingly assisted in the process. Understandably, there was also an increase in NYD(N) or pseudo-NYD(N) cases during periods of heavy action. At the battle of Passchendaele in November 1917, when McGill was serving with a field ambulance, he encountered so many such cases – not all of them genuine – that he was forced to place one man under arrest. Desperate and terrified men might resort to desperate measures – there were 729 cases of self-inflicted wounds in the Canadian Corps during the war and they were severely punished with sentences ranging from imprisonment with hard labour to execution by firing squad. These draconian measures were so effective that a soldier who "tore his hand upon a wire entanglement would nurse his wound in secret" lest it be thought that he had inflicted it himself.[37]

"Ideal rest periods": The summer of 1917

After the hell of Fresnoy, the 31st Battalion was in urgent need of rest and reorganization, "and the same thing applied," wrote its historian, "in greater or less degree to every battalion in the Canadian Corps."[38] On 10 May 1917 the unit marched to a rest camp at Aux Rietz where it was to remain, except for a brief and an uneventful frontline tour late that month, until the end of June 1917. Throughout this period, the seemingly never-ending process of incorporating new men into the unit went on and the battalion counted itself very lucky to receive a draft of 250 reinforcements from the Edmonton 202nd "Sportsman" Battalion who were a "fine body of men, few being less than 5 ft. 8 ins in

Back into the line again
A company of the 8th Battalion CEF ("Little Black Devils"), perpetuated today by the Royal Winnipeg Rifles, on the march in October 1917. Judging by the solemn expressions on their faces and their state of cleanliness, these men are heading into the trenches, not coming out of them. Note the stretcher carried by a bearer and the Lewis light machinegun. NAC, PA-001994

height, and many of them being specialists in Lewis-gun work, bombing, signalling or sniping."[39] In May and June the battalion underwent a number of inspections by the brigade commander, the divisional commander and Major-General Sam Steele, who was returning to Canada because of illness but took this last opportunity to visit the fighting men of Alberta. All the senior officers complimented the battalion on its appearance but the enlisted men disliked these formal affairs, which they regarded as a waste of time. As Donald Fraser complained:

We were continually being pulled out of our billets to go through all sorts of parade drill as if this was the chief mission of our lives and war of secondary importance. Officers, [the] R.S.M. and C.S.M.'s, were jumping about and the Orderly Room giving out confusing instructions; one day it was pack dress, another day it was skeleton order, ultimately it became drill order. We were subjected to no end of button polishing and inspections, twice daily, until we were heartily sick of the whole affair …… There is no mistaking the fact that the business end of military life does not appeal very strongly to the barrack-room class of officer; on the parade ground he is in his element and as far as he is concerned it is there that all battles are won. Right turn and left turn are a delight to him, forming fours and "on the left form platoon" send him into ecstasy.[40]

The best of the best – No. 11 Platoon, 31st Battalion, 1917
Lieutenant Maynard E. Patterson (light coloured cap, middle of first seated row) and No. 11 Platoon, 31st Alberta Battalion, which won the competition for the best platoon in the Canadian Corps in the summer of 1917. The battalion itself won the Corps competition for marksmanship. Triumphs such as these were not only a boost to morale, they also indicated that the Alberta Battalion was one of the best units in the CEF. NAC, PA-003413

At Aux Rietz time not spent at drill, undergoing inspection or training was devoted to musical concerts and battalion and brigade sports events. The 31st walked off with the most of the prizes at the brigade athletics meet, their transport section won the top two prizes in the Divisional Horse Show and their scouts and snipers won two brigade contests in shooting and observation. The most important prize, however, came at the 6th Brigade Musketry Competition on 26 June when the 31st Battalion beat the other three battalions of the brigade on the ranges.

This interest in musketry or marksmanship resulted from an increased emphasis on the subject by the new commander of the Canadian Corps, Lieutenant-General Arthur Currie, who replaced Byng in early June 1917. Currie was an ardent collector and disseminator of information on tactical developments that would improve his Corps' training for battle and its performance in battle. He stressed the proper use of the rifle and bayonet, and created a musketry school to train instructors for all the infantry battalions. Effort was also placed on cross-training all members of a platoon to fire all weapons in the platoon so that, if necessary, they could take them over in action. Finally, renewed emphasis was placed on platoon tactics and junior officers were given a series of problems which they had to solve using their men while under observation from their superiors. At the same time as the training tempo was increased at unit level, Currie and the senior officers of the corps were studying recent operations to find innovations and improved methods that would help them in the next major action. The main thrust was to expand and improve what had worked at Vimy Ridge – the incorporation of all sources of intelligence about enemy defences, improved artillery co-ordination and infantry small unit organization and tactics, intensive preparatory training, massive logistical support, better communications (field radio

was just coming into use), aerial observation, and the use of phase lines – and discard what had not.

The Canadian Light Horse, smarting from their reverse at Willerval, meanwhile, enjoyed a quiet summer in reserve near the Corps Headquarters at Divion. Throughout that summer the training emphasis of the Light Horse was on marksmanship and mounted tactics. The unit spent most of June and July working at the troop level but in early August, the entire regiment went on a 6-day scheme in the field. This renewed interest in cavalry training stemmed from Haig's belief that the major offensive he launched in Flanders that summer might just lead to the long-awaited breakthrough and he wanted the mounted units of the BEF to be prepared in case they were needed. Other than that, the Light Horse carried out their normal duties of providing orderlies, traffic control, movement guides and remount service for the Corps.

By this time, the third summer of the war, the men of the Canadian Corps had come to regard themselves as being a cut above the rest of the Imperial military herd, a belief solidified by their spectacular triumph at Vimy Ridge. It was clear that a new national consciousness was taking shape in the Corps – its members were still proud to belong to the British Empire and its army but they were also aware that, as had been proved on a number of occasions, they could fight better than their British counterparts and they thought of themselves "as being more efficient than other corps."[41] Although they wore British uniforms, the Canadians took great care to transfer the maple leaf buttons from uniforms issued to them in Canada to their British-made clothing to serve as a mark of national distinction. This wish to differentiate themselves was boosted by the fact that most Canadian unit cap badges featured a maple leaf, while the system of identifying division/brigade/battalion by coloured shoulder patches was unique to the Canadian Corps. Many Canadians, however, longed for an easily-recognized national distinction such as possessed by the Australians and New Zealanders with their slouch hats but, in this respect, only the Canadian Light Horse stood out as they wore the stetson when not in the trenches.

There was always friendly rivalry between the Canadians and the Australians who, with some reason, also regarded themselves as elite troops, but there were differences between the fighting men of the two Dominions. On the whole, the Canadians tended to be more disciplined than the Australians, whose favourite pastime in the rear areas was forming posses to hunt down British military police and who might, if it was a fine day and they were in a good mood, salute their own officers but would rarely salute British officers, no matter what rank. By this time in the war, however, most British officers had learned through hard experience that they could not treat Dominion soldiers the same harsh way they treated their own men – and if they had not, they often got a rude awakening. Both Dominion contingents admired the British Highland regiments but did not have a very high opinion of the average British soldier. Britain, which had raised the upper age limit for conscripts to 50 in early 1917, was by this time scraping the very bottom of its manpower barrel and British soldiers were not only physically smaller but did not seem to be very aggressive. As one Canadian remarked, his comrades knew that the Tommies "would do their best" but "it would only be a second-best, lacking the energy and enthusiasm that comes from intelligent leadership."[42]

On Dominion Day, 1 July 1917, the units of the 6th Brigade held a church parade in memory of those who had fallen in the recent fighting. The 31st Battalion was under orders to return to the front and when the men marched to their billets in the afternoon, they received an issue of beer to mark the national holiday which made "a fitting climax to one of the most ideal rest periods in the Battalion's history."[43] A few days later the unit went into the line in the Lens area and over the next six and a half weeks did five tours in this sector, tours marked by heavy German shelling that included bombardments with the recently-introduced mustard gas, which fortunately did not cause heavy casualties. On 26 July, in response, the Royal Engineers put in a gas attack by projector and shell against the German positions and the German artillery fire died away for some time thereafter. On 14 August, the battalion was relieved to stand ready for the major Corps attack planned against Hill 70 west of Lens.

Haig ordered this operation in the hope of diverting German units from Flanders, where he had opened a major offensive at the end of July. Although many Allied leaders, including Britain's Prime Minister Lloyd George, neither liked nor trusted the commander of the BEF after his grim record on the Somme in 1916, the wider situation forced them to approve his Flanders offensive. In the spring and early summer of 1917, the Allied Powers' cup had become increasingly bitter. In March the Russian people overthrew the Czar and although the new Russian leaders prom-

ised to continue the war, that nation was verging on anarchy. In April the United States, angered by the German decision to wage unrestricted submarine warfare, entered the war on the Allied side but it would be a year or more before it could mobilize and train its armies. The Salonika Front remained in stalemate and, although the Italians had launched an offensive along the Isonzo River in May, it had sputtered out in June and the Central Powers were actively preparing a major counter thrust. On the Western Front the French armies were in a state of disarray and would not be able to undertake large operations for some time. The only bright spot in this depressing picture was the Middle East, where British forces were making impressive gains against the Turks. With all this in view, and fearing that Germany might deal a mortal blow to the shaken French, reluctant approval was given for Haig to undertake a major offensive in Flanders with the immediate purpose of clearing the Channel coast of enemy U-boat bases and airfields, and diverting German attention from the French situation.

This offensive, which began on 31 July 1917, was fought on almost the same ground that Canadians had defended in the spring of 1915, and from the outset, it ran into trouble. The Germans had instituted their new doctrine of elastic defence and, because the area was so low lying and flooded, had constructed numerous concrete pillboxes that proved invulnerable to all but a direct hit by a large calibre artillery piece. British staff work and planning proved faulty and preparation was inadequate, assault tactics were often incorrect and there was very little co-ordination between the infantry and artillery. But the worst problem was the ground which, soggy at the best of times, had been converted by nearly three years of shelling into a sea of mud and was made still worse by the fact that during the summer of 1917, Europe experienced the worst rainfall in three decades. As a result, the Flanders offensive degenerated into a grinding battle of attrition, where gains were measured in square feet of quagmire.

While his men pushed slowly forward, Haig wanted to keep the pressure on the Germans in other sectors. As a subsidiary operation he ordered Currie to take Lens in an attempt to get Ludendorff to shift forces from Flanders, but Currie insisted that first he had to take Hill 70, an area of high ground which dominated that city as if it could be secured, the Germans would have to counterattack to regain it or abandon Lens. Currie, certain that the Germans would counterattack, planned to break up any such attempts with massed artillery. It would not be an easy task as the German defensive positions on Hill 70 were very strong and included concrete machine-gun emplacements, thick belts of wire and deep dugouts and trenches. Currie's plan called for the 1st and 2nd Divisions to advance directly against the objective on a series of phase lines, while the 4th Division made a feint to distract the enemy. Much depended on the Corps artillery, which was considerably reinforced by British artillery units, and, for the first time, aircraft were used in a tactical role. While the assault troops rehearsed on a carefully laid out duplicate of the ground over which they were to attack – so detailed that the men even knew the names of the village streets they were to move along – the artillery and aircraft carried out preliminary attacks on the German rear areas to "soften" them up by destroying artillery and disrupting communications.

The assault on Hill 70, which began on 15 August 1917, went in behind three distinct lifting or moving barrages, timed to prevent German reinforcements from being brought forward. The 6th Brigade did not participate as it was in divisional reserve but provided carrying parties to get ammunition, rations and supplies up to the frontline. The whole operation went almost like clockwork as the infantry used the new platoon tactics to eliminate enemy strongpoints and the artillery, directed by improved communications systems, brought down fire on any target that held up the advance. By midday, almost all the objectives were taken and when the Germans began to counterattack during the afternoon, the gunners were ready for them and broke up attack after attack with heavy bombardments. One artillery forward observation officer recorded that "it was delightful to see the Germans coming out from their frontline in knots of 5 or 6 to form up for a counterattack and give them half a dozen rounds of gunfire."[44] In all, eighteen separate enemy attacks were beaten off by the Canadian infantry and artillery, whose ammunition expenditure was astronomical. The Germans tried for three days to recover the lost ground and did make some gains but only at the cost of heavy casualties. Currie's plan had worked perfectly. Throughout this period the 31st Battalion continued its supporting role and suffered only moderate casualties from enemy shelling before being relieved on 22 August.

For the next three weeks, the unit enjoyed a second lengthy rest period complete with the usual inspections, including one by Field-Marshal Sir Douglas Haig, and more training. It was at this time the 31st Battalion began to distinguish itself in athletic and military competitions. In September, the battalion won the Brigade Elimination for the Canadian Corps Rifle competition – its marksmen winning the battalion, company, platoon and "falling plates" competitions – and cleaned up at another brigade sports day. But the event that interested everyone was the competition for the best infantry platoon in the Canadian Corps. On 11 September, the battalion's No. 11 Platoon, under the command of Lieutenant Maynard E. Patterson from Medicine Hat, won the 2nd Division Elimination Competition and qualified to compete in the final event held on 21 September which matched twelve platoons drawn from the twelve brigades in the Corps. The first test in this competition was marksmanship, both with the Lee-Enfield and the Lewis gun, and No. 11 Platoon emerged the clear winner, scoring 624 points, 172 points more than the runner-up platoon from the 50th Battalion. It is interesting to note that, of the twelve battalions that competed in this event, the 31st Battalion was first, the 50th second and the 49th fifth, securely placing three Alberta infantry units among the top marksmen of the 48 infantry battalions in the Canadian Corps. The low scorer was the 116th Battalion from near

Toronto, which was disqualified when its witless Lewis gunner mistakenly fired at the rifle targets.

No. 11 Platoon was on a roll. Having established themselves as the best shots in the Corps, Patterson's men went on to win the Corps Platoon Competition which featured tests of turn out, tactics, employment of rapid fire from rifles and Lewis guns, the use of cover, and the use of fire to cover movement, all tests being done while in motion. The result was that the 31st Alberta Battalion clearly demonstrated that it was the best infantry unit in the Canadian Corps – at least as far as performance out of combat was concerned. It just couldn't get any better for "Bell's Bulldogs" that September, and that was good because three weeks later they marched out of very crowded billets near Hondeghem behind Lens and took the road north for the Salient to take part in a battle that, in later years, has come to epitomize all the many horrors of the First World War. It was part of Haig's offensive in Flanders and, although officially termed the 3rd Battle of Ypres, most Canadian soldiers knew it simply as Passchendaele.

"A wilderness of devastation and desolation": Preparations for Passchendaele

Lieutenant-General Arthur Currie was not pleased when he received an order from Haig on 3 October 1917 for the Canadian Corps to carry out a major attack in Flanders. After nearly two months of heavy fighting that had drawn in 51 of the 61 divisions in the BEF, Haig had advanced approximately 3 miles at the cost of nearly a quarter of a million casualties. Objectives that were supposed to have been captured on 1 July, the first day of the operation, were still not taken on 7 October, when Haig's two senior generals told him bluntly that the entire operation should be shut down. Haig persisted, however, in making one more attack on 10 October and it cost him 7,000 casualties although it secured a toehold on Passchendaele Ridge, the last remaining area of high ground in the Salient in German hands. Haig wanted the Canadian Corps to take this objective but Currie could see no profit in the business. "Every Canadian," Currie later wrote, "hated to go to Passchendaele" and he protested his orders to Haig, carrying that protest "to the extreme limit … which I believe would have resulted in my being sent home had I been other than the Canadian Corps Commander."[45] Currie pointed out "what the casualties were bound to be" but Haig, citing the overall grave Allied situation, ordered him "to go and make the attack." The Canadian Corps commander insisted, however, on being given enough time to make all possible preparations and Haig, somewhat irritated, reluctantly granted this request.

The main problem was the ground over which the Corps would have to attack. The area around Ypres was a low-lying plain composed of well-watered soft alluvial soil that three years of almost incessant shelling had pulverized and turned into a cratered landscape that choked the normal drainage system, forming marshes and small lakes. If that was not bad enough, the unusually heavy rainfall of the last three or so months, had transformed the entire area into a gigantic mud flat littered with the wreckage of three months of heavy fighting. A gunner of the 2nd Canadian Division has left a memorable description of what was, without a doubt, about the worst possible ground over which to conduct a military operation:

Presently dawn came in a dull sky, so that we were able to see the road ahead of us and the country around us. By the side of the road at intervals lay corpses of our own men and the Germans, dead animals, Red Cross ambulances overturned and abandoned, trucks left wrecked and derelict, munition wagons shattered and upset. …… On either side of the road stretched to the horizon a vast expanse of mud, pitted everywhere with shell-holes touching and over-lapping so that the surface resembled that of a honeycomb; and in most of the shell-holes lay pools of water and by some of them lay lifeless forms, once British soldiers. Here and there in the distance one could see a derelict tank, entirely useless in that sea of mud and water; and at intervals we caught sight of low cement structures which were quite clearly the "pill-boxes" which had sheltered German machine gunners and had in consequence proved such formidable obstacles to the soldiers who had preceded us in that front. There were relics of skeletons of trees, mere trunks with the remains of a branch or two, black and gaunt against the sky; there were a few traces of grass; there were small lakes in all the hollows, fed by the light but continuous rain. A wilderness of desolation and devastation it was, a whole countryside mangled and murdered as if by some frightful monster.[46]

The road referred to was the single road leading from Gravenstafel Ridge to the village of Passchendaele. Keeping traffic moving on that road without delay was the job of the Provost Marshal and throughout the operation, the Canadian Light Horse provided troopers for that purpose. As one staff officer remembered, they did their job well as the traffic was "very heavy but well regulated" with Light Horse pickets at intervals of 200 yards and, "as soon as a block starts" a CLH trooper would straighten it out.[47] German gunners had the range for every foot of that road and kept it under constant fire, their aim corrected by forward observers on the Passchendaele Ridge and the observation balloons tethered above their lines. The Light Horse lost a dozen men killed and wounded on traffic duty during operations at Passchendaele.

Passchendaele

The Germans were bad enough, but at Passchendaele in the autumn of 1917 the waterlogged, swampy terrain became a worse enemy. Passchendaele was a nightmare to the men who fought there and many wounded soldiers and animals drowned in ground like this before they could be rescued. NAC, PA-0002165

Stretcher party, Passchendaele 1917

One of the worst things about a battle that epitomized all the horrors of the Western Front was the plight of the wounded. With the flooded terrain, it sometimes took stretcher parties six to seven hours to get the casualties back for medical treatment. It was found that one wounded man needed up to eight bearers as they had to take frequent rests to cover the terrible ground. NAC, PA-002107

Heavy traffic, 1917

A congested road near the Somme. Moving in one direction are infantry, staff cars loaded with officers, and horsed transport while coming in the opposite direction are horse transport and an ambulance. This scene took place beyond the range of German artillery as it would have made short work of such an attractive target. The Canadian Light Horse performed traffic duty on busy routes like this, a very necessary task. BY KIND PERMISSION OF THE TRUSTEES OF THE IMPERIAL WAR MUSEUM, Q 5794

To attack over ground such as this, Currie received additional engineer units. The sappers commenced work on 17 October and worked round the clock for nine days to complete the preparations in time for the first attack, scheduled for 26 October 1917. They constructed stable gun platforms (many of the artillery pieces had sunk in mud up to their axles), attempted to drain the worst areas of flooding, repaired and strengthened the single road and constructed new plank roads and paths of duck boards to the forward lines. Miraculously the rain, which had been almost constant for months, held off for nearly a week.

It was recognized that one of the greatest problems would be the evacuation of the wounded. Medical personnel were informed that in previous operations in the area, it had taken six men six hours to carry one stretcher case from the frontline back to the evacuation points. They were also warned that "under the prevailing conditions, the evacuation of the wounded will be a matter of extreme difficulty" as, "owing to the almost complete absence of shelter of any kind, it will be impossible to keep cases under cover; and in consequence the wounded will suffer hardship if the weather is bad."[48] Casualties could only be evacuated in daylight because "stretcher parties lose themselves" at night as there were "no land marks."[49] Additional medical units borrowed from British and Australian formations were deployed and every effort possible was made to ensure that the wounded would be treated and evacuated as quickly as possible – in anticipation the number of stretcher bearers was increased to four times the normal complement.

The objective of the Canadian Corps was Passchendaele Ridge which ran north to south and was about 150 feet above the plain at its highest point. Located only a few miles east of the battleground where Canadians had fought their first major battle in France in April 1915, it was a very difficult proposition as there was only one very swampy road leading to it and the Canadian front was split by a flooded bog created by the Ravebeck stream. The German defences on the ridge were not based on continuous lines of trenches, which were vulnerable to artillery, but consisted of dozens of concrete machinegun positions, dubbed "pill boxes" by the Allies, linked with well-fortified craters and defended farm houses. The cellars and lower levels of the ruined houses and buildings in the little village of Passchendaele on the highest point of the ridge had also been turned into miniature fortresses. These positions were not intended to stem an attack but only delay it long enough for fresh troops, located in deep shelters to the rear, to counterattack and regain any lost ground. Defensive positions in depth such as these, combined with the awful terrain and plentiful enemy artillery, had stymied Haig throughout most of the summer and autumn, limiting his gains and inflicting heavy casualties.

Currie's plan called for three separate attacks on a very narrow front of only 2,000 yards to secure a series of phase lines that would ultimately end with gaining the entire ridge. A commander who always "took the most care of the lives of his troops" and held "an almost fanatical hatred of unnecessary casualties," Currie believed in using shells and not troops.[50] He therefore requested and got massive artillery support. A total of 420 guns would carry out a complex artillery programme that would include a preliminary bombardment programme to prevent the Germans reinforcing and supplying their forward positions; an intensive bombardment put down shortly before the attack by all heavy guns on all known German positions; a series of lifting barrages to take the infantry forward while further bombardment would come down on the forward German defences; and a heavy counter-bombardment that would neutralize enemy artillery firing at the Canadian assault waves, or break up German counterattacks. Both sides made considerable use of gas at Passchendaele, particularly mustard gas, and low-lying areas were saturated with it. Both sides also made use of airpower for observation, tactical air support and long range bombing of rear areas. In this respect the Germans had a marked superiority in numbers and, as the coming weeks would show, no part of the Salient, front or rear, was safe by day or night. All the lessons learned at Vimy Ridge and Hill 70 were incorporated in the preparations and the assault troops studied a scale model of the area over which they would operate before rehearsing the forthcoming attack over ground marked by the engineers to approximate the enemy positions.

This preliminary work paid dividends when the 3rd and 4th Divisions launched the first attack at 5.40 A.M. on 26 October under a heavy downpour. It met with varying success and some gains were lost to counterattacks, but after two days of intense fighting, the Canadians had secured firm ground from which to launch the next assault. This was carried out by the same two divisions on 30 October and, although losses were heavy, the attacking units took all their objectives in a day of heavy fighting. At a cost of 3,700 casualties, a jumping off point had been secured for the third attack, which was to take places in two distinct phases: the first to secure the village of Passchendaele and the second to clear the remainder of the ridge. In the ensuing pause, the hardworking engineers constructed new gun platforms so that artillery cover could be provided for the later operations and extended the communications trails and paths. This work was made difficult by heavy rainfall which made already terrible conditions worse, if that was possible. Each day, men, horses and mules who had fallen into the treacherous water-filled shell craters, had to be dragged out, although many of the animals were simply shot to put them out of their misery. The Salient "was never silent" because, day and night, the artillery of both sides "flashed and thundered, further pulverizing the tortured earth and flinging up great geysers of mud and water."[51] The soldiers lived, moved and slept in "muck and mire; the air was rank with dampness, the reek of mud, the stench of corruption and the acrid fumes of high explosive; rations tasted of mud and clothing was caked with it." While this was going on, Currie replaced the 3rd and 4th Divisions with the 1st and 2nd Divisions who would undertake the remaining phases. The 6th Brigade was assigned to the first attack and Ketchen planned to use three of his battalions – the 27th, 28th and 31st – in the initial assault scheduled for dawn on 6 November 1917.

"With bomb, bullet and bayonet": The Alberta Battalion at Passchendaele

The 31st Battalion arrived in the Passchendaele sector on 27 October. Over the next few days, officers and men studied the terrain model and rehearsed their attack by slipping and floundering over the taped replica of the ground under continuing heavy rain. On the night of 4 November, the battalion moved along to its jumping off area for its attack along a single duckboard trail that threaded its way in and around the water-logged landscape of shell craters and mud, mud and more mud. One man recalled that the long, thin column "would pass somewhere and the water would move a little and you would see men's heads bobbing up and down, drowned in sloughs – whether or not they were wounded or killed first, we didn't know, of course, and they had been there some time."[52]

Just past midnight the brigade reached its assembly area under heavy enemy shelling that inflicted some casualties. On the 6th Brigade front, the 27th Battalion was on the right, the 31st in the centre and the 28th on the left. Then, all that remained was to wait for thirty long hours in the crowded and wet frontline trenches in the rain and bitter cold and the men of the brigade were not happy when they received an order to remove their greatcoats so that they would be able to move more freely through the mud. The garments were left in the reserve lines, where German aircraft mistook the coats placed in neat lines for men assembled for an assault and called down artillery fire on them. On the other hand, it was better to lose coats than men.

At 6 A.M., on 6 November, an intense and heavy four-minute bombardment was brought down on the enemy positions. Then the whistles blew and A Company, the lead element of the 31st Battalion, went over the top and moved toward Passchendaele village, their immediate objective, behind a lifting barrage. Almost immediately they encountered a slough which forced them to divide into two elements, but the hardworking gunners had put down so much high explosive that the right element reached the southwestern corner of the village without significant casualties, and began the job of clearing it house by house, position by position. The left hand element ran into trouble when they were caught by German artillery fire while still on open, marshy ground but continued to move forward until Maxims came alive on the flanks and hit them with enfilade fire. While some fell dead or wounded, others stumbled into shell holes and were helped out by their comrades. Despite heavy casualties, the left element kept moving forward through the slime toward their first objective, a German machinegun position protected by a rubble heap. Both elements of the company now went to work using the tactical drill they had learned – while riflemen and Lewis gunners kept the Germans' heads down with covering fire, the rifle grenade sections moved in closer to launch their projectiles and restrict the enemy's vision so that the bombers could get in even closer to lob their grenades. When the time was right, the riflemen rushed the position with the bayonet, while being covered by the Lewis gunners.

There was much desperate fighting in the village and the unit historian states unequivocally that the Germans "fought gallantly, and offered a strenuous resistance."[53] Many of the enemy had been wounded by the opening bombardment and wore bandages but they did not surrender and many of the strongpoints had to be taken with the bayonet after a quick volley of rifle and hand grenades. Company Sergeant-Major Ferrie of A Company and many men were wounded by machinegun fire from a concealed position, and Lieutenant C.M. Scadden of that company went to their assistance only to be hit himself. Another officer, Lieutenant J.A. Cameron, who was also wounded, located the German position and charged single-handed into it with a rifle and bayonet (by this time most officers were using this weapon in preference to revolvers), "bayonetted a man in the act of throwing a bomb" and then "bayonetted several more of the enemy, forced twelve to surrender, and captured the machine gun."[54] A few minutes later Cameron was hit again and had to be evacuated along with Scadden, who was put on a stretcher carried by two German prisoners and sent to the rear. Sergeant-Major Ferrie ignored his wound and assumed command of A Company which continued to move forward until it reached its objective in the northwest corner of the village. There, after it had established contact with the 27th and 28th Battalions on the flanks, it began to consolidate its position

using seven captured machineguns to bolster its defences.

B and D Companies now passed through A Company on their way to the battalion's second objective, the enemy main line of resistance in a row of houses lining a street in the northwest corner of Passchendaele. Pinned down by a machinegun in the village church, D Company laid down covering fire, while small bombing parties worked around behind the building and killed its defenders with grenades. The two companies experienced a difficult time and lost many men taking a series of German positions, concrete dugouts and pillboxes, and several fortified shellholes. The tactical drill, however, of putting down covering fire with rifle and Lewis gunfire and then, progressively, occupying the defenders with rifle and hand grenades until an assault could be made, proved successful and the two companies were able to consolidate on their objectives.

It was now C Company's turn to go forward and take the third objective, the high ground of the ridge. But the German artillery was now in action and as the company moved forward in a series of rushes, it suffered heavily from shell fire and every officer except the company commander was killed or wounded. C Company kept going until it encountered two German pillboxes on its left flank which forced it to go to ground. The company commander, Major G.D. Powis, arranged for B and D Companies in the rear to lay down covering fire on these two

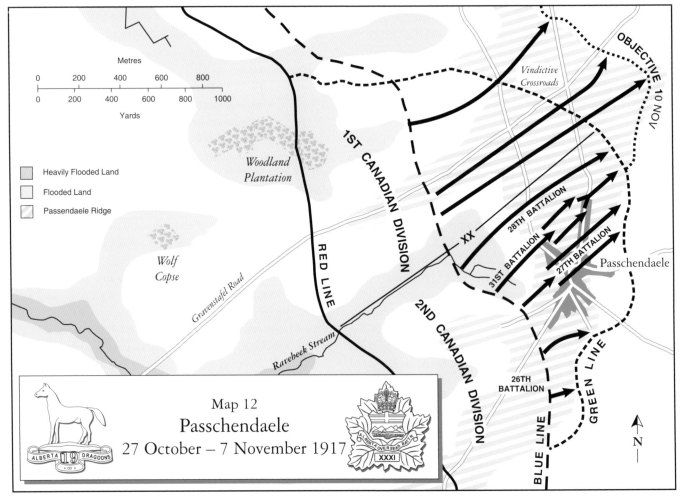

Map 12

Passchendaele

27 October – 7 November 1917

positions while he attempted to work around to their rear with a small party. Powis was almost immediately killed but Lieutenant H. Kennedy, one of two surviving officers in B and D Companies, sent the other surviving officer to take over C Company while he took on the two pillboxes with the help of his sergeant-major.

While everyone in range poured rounds on the firing slits, Kennedy and the sergeant-major crawled to within grenade range, lobbed several grenades and, when these had gone off, rushed the position and captured 3 officers, 34 enlisted men and the two machineguns. Thus encouraged, C Company moved onto its objective and spent much of the afternoon, as the battle was now about six hours old, searching out snipers and dealing with machinegun nests. The intrepid Lieutenant Kennedy and the battalion signals officer, Captain W. Jewitt, who arrived to take over C Company, jointly took the final remaining enemy position, crawling slowly and laboriously within striking range while being covered by every available weapon in range, until they could finally rush it. They captured six officers and six soldiers, four of the officers turning out to be the battalion commanders and adjutants of a Bavarian unit and a Prussian Guards unit who had been ordered to put in a counterattack on the village and had come forward to reconnoitre the ground. This ended German resistance in Passchendaele, and the Albertans consolidated their position.

Throughout the day a steady stream of walking wounded and stretcher cases made their way to the rear, often under German artillery fire as the restricted routes from the frontlines were known to the enemy who targeted them. The plight of the seriously wounded was particularly bad as it took hours for stretcher cases to reach the aid posts. A soldier of the 28th Battalion assigned to bearer duty remembered picking up two wounded men who had been lying exposed for two days but the mud "was up to our knees and we had to rest every 50 yds. with the stretchers."[55] They managed to get the men back but it took them four hours to move just 200 yards. Some wounded never made it to the aid posts, including Lieutenant Scadden who had fought so valiantly. The two German prisoners carrying him along the duckboard route became frightened by shellfire and abandoned him to scamper to safety. He was found the next morning by two battalion cooks who volunteered to search for him, but later died from a combination of exposure and wounds.

Poor bloody infantry, 1917
A Canadian infantry company trudges back from the front line in the autumn of 1917, a year that began with a triumph at Vimy Ridge and ended with a tragedy at Passchendaele. After more than three years of fighting, the stalemate on the Western Front continued. There was no end in sight to the killing and the dying and these men are very aware of that fact. CANADIAN ARMY PHOTO O-997

After a day of heavy fighting, the Iron Brigade had taken and held all its objectives and the other attacking formations were just as successful. "Through mud which made every movement slow and arduous," the battalion historian recorded, "through a barrage of shell which blew men to bits or deluged them under cascades of mud and water; through machine-gun fire and rifle fire and the attacks of hostile aircraft the Canadians had pressed on undaunted and, with bomb, bullet and bayonet, had driven the enemy before them all along the front."[56] The 1st and 2nd Divisions were now in a position to launch the second and final phase of the attack four days later which pushed the Germans completely off Passchendaele Ridge. The Canadian Corps had accomplished the job it had been given by Haig but the cost was heavy – 15,654 killed and wounded in the four major attacks. The 31st Battalion's share of this terrible bill was 53 officers and men killed, 206 wounded and 13 missing, the latter "probably drowned in shellholes."[57] The battalion was relieved on 7 November and trudged its weary way back to a bivouac in the rear under a steady downpour of rain. "For the men of Alberta," the unit historian wrote, "the Battle of Mud and Blood had ended."[58] Actually, it was not quite over – that night German aircraft bombed its tent lines killing two officers and wounding five men.

On 10 November 1917, the unit entrained for Caestre near Lens. It arrived in the late afternoon and marched to its previous billets at Hondeghem which, the War Diarist noted somewhat morbidly, were "not so crowded this time as our strength is considerably depleted."[59]

One year and one day later the war would end.

Poor bloody infantry, 1918

By the last year of the war the platoon had become the main infantry fighting element. Organized around the Lewis .303 calibre light machine-gun, it was capable of both fire and manoeuvre. This is a platoon of the 29th Battalion, Australian Imperial Force, but Canadian infantry platoons would have looked much the same. Note that among the sixteen men in this platoon there are no fewer than three Lewis guns. BY KIND PERMISSION OF THE TRUSTEES OF THE IMPERIAL WAR MUSEUM, E (AUS) 2790

CHAPTER SEVEN

A Thousand Yards, A Thousand Deaths

THE END OF THE WAR, DECEMBER 1917 TO JUNE 1919

I want to go home, I want to go home
The bullets they whistle, the cannons they roar,
And I don't want to go to the Somme any more.
Take me over the sea,
Where the Alleyman can't get at me.
Oh my! I don't want to die
I want to go home, sweet home.[1]

"Don't let the slacker throw you in the ditch": The winter of 1917-1918

As though to compensate for the horrors of the rainy previous autumn, the winter of 1917-1918 – the third winter Canadian soldiers spent on the Western Front – was relatively mild and dry. The Canadian Corps passed much of it holding a quiet sector of the line in the Lens-Vimy area and casualties were light, just the normal daily "wastage" incidental to trench warfare. In December political signs appeared in the rear areas as all ranks participated in the Canadian general election. It will come as no surprise that most of the signs supported conscription:

"If You Want Conscription, Vote For the Union Government"

Keep up Canada's Reputation. Don't Let the Slacker Throw You in the Ditch. If He Won't Come Voluntarily, Make Him! And The Way To Do This Is To Vote For The Government![2]

It is also no surprise that 90% of the men in the Corps voted in favour of the Union government and conscription. Christmas came and went and everyone noticed that there were more parcels from Canada than in previous years – the 31st Battalion was out of the line on the day and consumed a seven-course meal that included 1,200 lbs. of turkey.

During the first three months of 1918 the weather was exceptionally good and in February many Canadian units, including the 31st Battalion, turned to growing vegetables to supplement their rations although, as the unit War Diarist noted, agriculture on the Western Front had its problems. Volunteers for this work were warned that the plough might hit and explode a buried shell from previous battles while the unit transport horses so stubbornly resisted being rebadged as plough horses that they had to be ridden to get them to perform their new agrarian duties. In early April, Lieutenant-Colonel A.H. Bell said goodbye to his Albertans to take up an appointment as commander of

the 6th Brigade. His tenure in command had been an unusually long one – three and a half years – and this was fortunate for a battalion which had become so identified with their commanding officer that they were known throughout the CEF as "Bell's Bulldogs." His replacement was Lieutenant-Colonel E.S. Doughty, a former CPR employee and land agent from Medicine Hat.

By the first months of 1918, it seemed to many soldiers on the Western Front that the war had become a permanent institution, a feeling the historian of the 31st Battalion has aptly described:

The period before the war had become, to him, vague and unreal, like the memory of some other existence; the days of peace, which he realized must return sooner or later, he found difficulty in visualizing. For three years, each longer by far in its living than a peace-time year, the war had been his life, and imagination boggled at the thought of any other kind of existence. For three years he had lived in mud, or among dust and flies (depending on the season), with rats for bed-fellows and lice as lodgers; for half his time he had lived the life of a troglodyte and for the other half the existence of an overworked labourer; he was never really clear of danger and was often literally face-to-face with sudden death. The whole fabric of his being was so far removed from that of normal peace time that the latter seemed a fantastic unreality and the war alone seemed stable and real. ......

The whole mental attitude of the fighting man towards life and death is entirely different from that of the civilian, and perhaps few who took no part in the war can realize the depth and the width of the gulf that separates the two.[3]

During that winter, it not only appeared that the war was going to continue for a long time yet but also that, for the Allied powers, it was not going very well. On the Western Front the French army was still weak after the mutinies of the previous

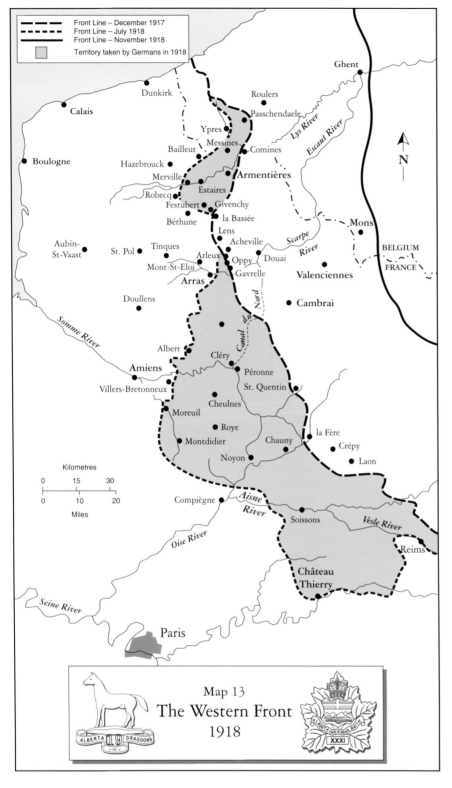

Map 13
The Western Front
1918

continue military operations during the previous summer had been defeated by German and Austro-Hungarian troops who launched a major offensive that led to the collapse of the Russian army which simply voted with its feet and went home. In November 1917 Lenin's Bolsheviks seized power in St. Petersburg and negotiated a separate peace with Germany and Austria-Hungary, thus permitting the Central Powers to shift forces from the Eastern Front to the west.

There had been some positive developments in 1917. The British had taken Palestine and were moving on Damascus and the implementation of the convoy system had brought the U-boats under control. And then there were the Americans – by the first weeks of 1918 there were 130,000 Yanks in France and more were on the way, their arrival delayed only by a general shortage of shipping.

Anxious to make up his heavy losses in 1917, Field-Marshal Haig had definite plans for the United States Army. He wanted to incorporate an American battalion in each brigade of the BEF but these hopes were dashed when Washington wisely issued instructions to General John Pershing, the American Expeditionary Force commander, that his troops were only to go into battle as a national force under American command. Haig was therefore forced to look elsewhere and, as Britain's manpower barrel was nearly empty, he was forced to reduce the number of infantry battalions in each of his British divisions from twelve to nine, and to break up some divisions to bring others up to strength. An attempt to have the Canadian Corps follow suit was rebuffed by Currie who managed not only to preserve the twelve-battalion division structure, but also to get the 5th Canadian Division in England disbanded and its infantry distributed to the other four divisions, with its artillery added to the corps artillery. Currie also beefed up the heavy machinegun units under his command. The result was that the Canadian Corps became one of the most powerful formations in the BEF – not only were its units up to strength, but each infantry battalion had 100 men overstrength as firstline reinforcements and it possessed at least 20% more artillery and automatic weapons than an equivalent British corps. Eventually, by the coming summer, enough American troops would arrive in Europe to tilt the scales squarely in favour of the Allies – but could they hold out until that time?

For their part, Hindenburg and Ludendorff were making calculations based on the same facts but in reverse – could they gain a decisive victory on the Western Front and force Britain

summer and the BEF was still recovering from Passchendaele. In Italy the Central Powers had mounted an offensive on the Italian Front in October 1917 that caused the near collapse of the Italian army and brought their forces to within 20 miles of Venice, forcing Britain and France to transfer troops from the Western Front to bolster their shaky ally. But the area of greatest concern was the Eastern Front where matters had gone from bad to worse. An attempt by the new Russian government to

and France into a negotiated peace before the Americans shifted the balance? The shortage of food and raw materials caused by the British naval blockade was causing civilian unrest in Austria-Hungary and Germany and would eventually limit the Central Powers' ability to wage offensive war. The demise of Russia had released German forces for transfer to the Western Front – 192 German divisions now faced 156 Allied divisions so, if an attack was to be launched, it had to be done before the arrival of the Americans in force. The two German leaders decided to carry out this offensive in March and actively prepared for it throughout the winter – the German divisions on the Western Front were reorganized into two types: three quarters were designated *Stellungsdivisionen* (literally "position divisons" although "defensive divisions" might be more appropriate in the context), largely consisting of older men that were only capable of defence while the remainder were classified as *Angriffsdivisionen* or assault divisions and supposedly received the best men and equipment. The assault formations were trained in a new German offensive doctrine that had been developed over the last two years. This emphasized the use of short bombardments of impressive weight and intensity, with prime targets being the opponent's artillery and lines of communication followed by an attack carried out by elite, heavily-armed *Stosstruppen* or "storm troopers" who operated in small groups to infiltrate through the defenders' lines, seeking weak points and leaving strongpoints to be dealt with by troops coming behind. By March 1918, German preparations for the coming attack were almost complete.

"Oh, oh, oh – it's a lovely war": Leisure, leave and love on the Western Front

Almost everyone in the British Expeditionary Force, from Field-Marshal Haig down to the lowest private, expected a German attack in the spring of 1918 and speculation as to its time and place were topics of daily conversation. In the meantime, since there was not much the average soldier could do about the approaching storm, he got on with his daily life in the line and tried to make the most of his off-duty activities. It might be well at this point in our story, while waiting for Ludendorff to finish his preparations, to take a look at those activities.

Reading was popular in the Canadian Corps, usually light fiction, as were card games such as poker, Black Jack and cribbage or games of chance such as craps and "Crown and Anchor." The latter, strictly forbidden in the Corps on pain of the most drastic penalties, was a vastly simplified form of roulette played with special die. It had been inherited from the British army and passed along with the traditional dealer's spiels: "All done, my lucky lads? Any more for any more? Three hooks, one lucky die. Who says one more on the old sergeant-major? All done? All finished? Nobody want any more?"[4] Out of the line, if they had the time and the weather was good, men played sports, baseball being a particular favourite. Occasionally, they could get away for a few hours to one of the coffee bars, canteens, reading rooms and cinemas operated by the Salvation Army or YMCA. The YMCA charged for its services and products, applying the profits toward purchasing athletic equipment and organizing musical shows and other entertainment for the Corps, but the Salvation Army was more respected as it only asked for a small donation, if possible.

These establishments, however, were under military supervision and many men preferred to visit one of the *estaminets* in nearby French towns and villages to get a plate of "Bombardier Fritz" (*pommes de terre frites* or French fries) and perhaps a glass of beer or wine. Not that the alcohol was any great delight – a member of the 31st described the beer as coloured water with a "medicinal flavour and a ghost of a froth that could only be produced by a three foot drop" while the wine "red or white, was weak, flat and sour" and "a perfect delight to the temperance advocate."[5] On occasion, according to their historian, the men of the Alberta Battalion would "drink to excess, and amusements of an even more dubious nature were not unknown."[6] If they were in the mood, they might also sing – but rarely patriotic civilian concoctions or popular tunes with the possible exception of such cynical favourites as J.P. Long and M. Scott's 1917 song, "Oh, It's a Lovely War":

Up to your waist in water, up to your eyes in sludge,
Using the kind of language that makes the sergeant blush
Who wouldn't join the army, that's what we all enquire,
Pity the poor civilians sitting around the fire.

Oh, oh, oh, its a lovely war
What do we want with eggs and ham,
When we've got plum and apple jam?
Form fours, right turn!
How do we spend the money we earn,
Oh, oh, oh, its a lovely war.

or R.P. Weston and Bert Lee's 1915 composition, "Good By-ee":

Goodbye-ee, goodbye-ee,
Wipe the tear, baby dear, from your eye-ee,
Tho' it's hard to part I know,
I'll be tickled to death to go.
Don't cry-ee, don't sigh-ee,
There's a silver lining in the sky-ee
Bonsoir, old thing, cheerio, chin, chin,
Nah-poo, toodle-oo, Goodbye-ee.

More commonly, the battalion historian assures us, the men preferred songs that "were anything but patriotic," and had "no bearing whatsoever upon the war" including many that were "lewd and unprintable."[7] In the army, some things never change.

As soldiers have always done, the men of the BEF and CEF created their own vocabulary which arose from shared experience and which enhanced membership in an exclusive, but beleaguered, community. Every frontline soldier dreamed of either leave to "Blighty" which was England and a "Blighty one" or sometimes just "a Blighty" was a wound that got him out of the trenches and into a hospital in Britain. The word derived from the Hindustani *belati* for "home," an expression taken over, as were so many First War expressions, from the prewar British regular army. Other examples were "bundook" for rifle from the Swahili *bunduki* or "friend" and "dekko" or look from the Hindustani *dekhna* or "to see, to look." The infantry, always caustic about other corps and services, looked down on "Ally Sloper's Cavalry" (the Army Service Corps, popularly believed to rob frontline men of the best rations); "Five-mile snipers" (the artillery) and "Rob All My

A Small Potato

What's that hat doin' floatin' round there, sergeant?"
" I think that's Private Murphy sittin' down, sir "

Over there: The "Sammies" arrive on the Western Front
Bruce Bairnsfather turns his attention to the American army, which wore campaign hats not unlike the Alberta cavalry's stetsons. COPYRIGHT TONIE AND VALMAI HOLT, REPRODUCED WITH PERMISSION FROM *THE BEST OF FRAGMENTS FROM FRANCE*

Comrades" (Royal Army Medical Corps, as frontline infantry were convinced that the medical orderlies picked the pockets of the wounded). The enemy were "Fritz," "Fritzie", "Heinie," "the Hun" or the "Boche" but when civilians began to use these terms, most combat soldiers switched to "Alleyman" after the French *Allemand* for German. Australians were "Diggers," British were "Tommies," "Limies" or "Woodbines" (after the detested British ration cigarette), and Americans were "Sammies" or "Yanks" or, in Cockney rhyming slang, "septic tanks."

Perhaps in an effort to minimize the horror that resulted and thus the fear they caused, various German artillery projectiles were termed "Flying pigs," "Jam Jars," "Rum Jars," "Toffee Apples," or "Wooly Bears." The terms "Black Maria," "Coal-box" or "Jack Johnsons" originated from the smoke that attended the explosion of some types of heavy projectiles – the first two are obvious while the black boxer, Jack Johnson, was the reigning world heavyweight champion in 1914. Particularly feared was the high velocity German 77 mm field gun, whose shell was known as a "whizz-bang" after the sound its projectile made when it was fired at you. The French language was tortured and mangled on an hourly basis and thus "van blank," "van rouge" and "tray beans" need no translation, while "van blank anglays" was whisky and "zig a zag" was drunk although "jig a jig" meant something quite other. By the latter years of the war, however, one word of French origin was used above all others – from the French *il n'y en a pas* meaning "there is none" or "there is nothing," a response heard all too often, English-speaking soldiers came up with "napoo." To be "napoo'd" was to be killed and everyone was eager to see the day when this wretched war would be "napoo finee."

Until that time, and nobody could see it in the early months of 1918, Canadian soldiers eagerly looked forward to leave. En-

listed men could expect a week to ten days leave a year and officers considerably more. London was the most common leave destination until 1917 when Paris became popular and in both cities, service organizations provided cheap accommodations and tickets to popular shows. Some men spent their leave touring cultural sites such as the British Museum or the Louvre but others sought less intellectual and more traditional forms of entertainment. Trooper George Hambley of the Canadian Light Horse, a devout Presbyterian, was utterly shocked by the "brute intellect" of his comrades and their "miry talk" about their main interests, which seemed to be drink and women, and he was horrified to find that in Divion, near Canadian Corps headquarters, there were "licensed houses of debauchery."[8] Hambley was also appalled by the behaviour of British and French women, which was certainly different from the girls he had known back home in Swan Lake, Manitoba. In his diary, he complained that, in France, even "old married women are after our lads – and how can the poor lads help it I don't know! when the temptation is so great – and access so horribly easy."[9] The result, he noted, was that "there will be many young Canadians in Divion before we leave as a new crop seems constantly to be on the way and no repugnance is now experienced in regard to them."[10]

Children were one product of this frantic socializing, another and much less desirable one was venereal disease. The Canadian Expeditionary Force vied with the Australian Imperial Force for having the highest Venereal Disease (VD) rate in the BEF. This resulted partly from the fact that the men of both nations were serving far from their homelands and sought comfort where it might be found (and they were not too discriminating), partly by relaxed wartime morality and partly because Australian and Canadian soldiers were paid four to five times as much as their British counterparts – having more tin in their pockets, they got into more trouble. The problem was compounded by the fact that, unlike the more worldly French who took the necessary steps to control infection, British authorities refused to implement the necessary public health programmes until late in the war. Despite the fact that the Canadian army treated its infected soldiers very harshly, isolating them in special hospitals akin to leper colonies, the problem was just barely kept under control. Naturally, the attitude of the average soldier differed from that of the authorities – as Trooper Hambley recorded in 1918:

the talk turned in spite of me (as usual) to venereal diseases – the cause for which and means of getting it are probably the most popular talk of each of them and the average man – at least here – can think and talk of nothing that pleases him better than to hear and talk of his associations with girls in Paris and all that it means – exactly and solely what they go there for and nothing else and the resultant disease has come to be looked upon by most (the average man) as I look upon a bad cold.[11]

It was a great puzzlement to Hambley why his fellow soldiers did not devote their leisure time, as he did, to spiritual and intellectual improvement instead of relentlessly looking for cheap alcohol and friendly women. For his part, Hambley liked to read and discuss religious and philosophical tracts and spent the last eighteen months of his military service studying Pelmanism, a system for memory improvement. Understandably, Hambley's views were not popular with his comrades, who must have cursed if duty forced them to much spend time alone in the company of a man whose conversation was a series of morally-uplifting epistles – George Hambley didn't even like baseball.

"With our backs to the wall": The German offensives, 1918

The long-anticipated storm broke early in the morning of 21 March 1918 when Ludendorff launched Operation MICHAEL against the British Fifth Army. After an incredibly heavy but short bombardment by more than 10,000 artillery pieces and trench mortars, 43 assault divisions overwhelmed the defenders and, within a week, drove a salient nearly 20 miles deep into the BEF's front that threatened the vital communications centre of Amiens. At the end of March, however, the Germans began to run out of steam as the assault troops became exhausted and their horse-drawn supply system failed to keep up with the advance. Allied resistance stiffened but, by the time Ludendorff called a halt to the operation on 4 April, he had inflicted 178,000 casualties on the BEF, including the loss of 70,000 prisoners, and 77,000 casualties on the adjoining French armies. German losses had not been light, however, and included many of the elite *Stosstruppen*.

There was now a brief lull while the Germans regrouped and re-supplied and then on 10 April, they attacked in the area of Armentières in Flanders. Again, they broke through the British defences and the situation became so desperate that, the following day, Haig issued a special order to the BEF informing his officers and men that there was "no other course open … but to fight it out. Every position must be held to the last man: there must be no retirement. With our backs to the wall and believing in the justice of our cause each one of us must fight on to the end."[12] Nonetheless, in late April Haig was forced to abandon the Ypres Salient, that grim piece of real estate that the BEF had doggedly retained for more than three years. This time, however, the German offensive was shorter in duration as Ludendorff's supply situation was critical and there were cases of indiscipline when some units, including the vaunted *Stosstruppen*, stopped fighting in order to loot captured supply depots.

For the Allies, one positive outcome of this dark period was that *Maréchal* Ferdinand Foch was appointed supreme commander on the Western Front with the power to co-ordinate strategy. The advantages of this measure, which should have been adopted years before, were evident when Ludendorff mounted two further but limited attacks in the Armentières area in late April. Although they gained some ground, they came up against British and Australian reinforcements made available when Foch began to shorten the amount of line held by the BEF, thus making reserves available, and the Germans ground to a halt within a matter of days. Throughout May there was another pause as both sides prepared for a renewal of operations. Allied losses in nearly five weeks of ceaseless fighting had been heavy but they had withstood the worst the Germans could offer and the Americans were now arriving in numbers – there were 430,000 US soldiers in France by 1 May 1918 and, although still green, they counterbalanced the 332,000 Allied losses suffered in the recent fighting. Ludendorff could not expect to make up the 348,000 men he had lost in March and April 1918 and although he still possessed the numerical advantage, it was a dwindling asset. Despite the misgivings of some of his senior generals who recognized their losses were irreplaceable, Ludendorff decided to mount further attacks.

This time he hit the French along the Aisne. On 27 May Ludendorff commenced Operation BLÜCHER with a 4,000-gun bombardment followed by a furious infantry assault that, in a few hours, destroyed the better part of eight British and French divisions. That day the German armies advanced 12 miles – the largest single day's gain ever made on the Western Front – and two days later were just 60 miles from Paris. But this was the high water mark and Foch blunted the enemy advance with a series of counterattacks, including one at Chateau-Thierry undertaken by two American divisions, an ominous portent for the Germans. Nonetheless, Ludendorff refused to give up and continued to attack in late June and July but, although his troops took ground, the threat was blunted by Allied counterattacks supported by large numbers of tanks.

By early August Ludendorff's gamble had failed and his only hope was to go on the defensive and make the Allies pay such a heavy price that they would enter into peace negotiations. The best place for his armies to do this would be in prepared defensive positions such as the Hindenburg Line but Ludendorff was reluctant to give up his recent gains and so, instead of withdrawing, the Germans remained in place. The indomitable Haig, sensing the tide was beginning to turn, received Foch's permission to stage a major offensive to drive the Germans away from Amiens and its vital railway network. To carry out this attack Haig chose his best troops – Lieutenant-General John Monash's Australian and New Zealand Corps and Lieutenant-General Arthur Currie's Canadian Corps.

"Willing, eager and capable": The Canadian Corps in the summer of 1918

The Canadians were in fine fettle as the greater part of the Corps had not been involved in the heavy fighting that took place between March and the end of June. The 1st Motor Machine Gun

Brigade and the Canadian Cavalry Brigade had participated in a number of rearguard actions and the corps artillery had occasionally supported British formations, but most of the Corps had continued to hold the line near Vimy Ridge. As British divisions were redeployed to face the German onslaught, it gradually took over a larger and larger sector and therefore displayed an extremely aggressive attitude toward the enemy opposite in order to prevent them, in turn, becoming aggressive. In May and June, a number of highly successful trench raids were mounted including two by the 31st Battalion on 21 May and 24 June. During the latter raid, which involved 500 men from both the 27th and 31st Battalions, the Alberta raiders penetrated the German strongpoint of the village of Neuville Vitasse and, before withdrawing, planted in the most conspicuous spot a pole bearing the Red Ensign and a message addressed to the local German commander informing him that the "Morale of your Company is damned rotten" and the "Next time we raid you we will go through to your Battalion Headquarters."[13] A few days later, the enemy withdrew from Neuville Vitasse and the raiders earned sincere congratulations from General Sir Julian Byng of the Third Army, under whose command the Corps was operating at the time. On 26 June, along with the rest of the 2nd Division, the Alberta Battalion was pulled out of the line for an intensive training period that was to last until the end of July.

This instruction was actually the final polish on a programme the Corps had been carrying out during the spring and summer of 1918 for all formations and units. In July, however, the emphasis was on mobile warfare and each infantry battalion received lectures and demonstrations on movement in the open, and practised tank-infantry cooperation and field manoeuvres. "Everything that was possible was done," wrote the 31st Battalion historian, "to perfect officers and men in the tactics of the new type of warfare which was confidently anticipated."[14] A pleasant break in their work came on Dominion Day, 1 July 1918, when all units not in the trenches were given a holiday and a Corps sports event, attended by 50,000 men, was held at Tinques with Prime Minister Robert Borden and the Duke of Connaught, the governor-general, as guests of honour.

For its part, the Canadian Light Horse resumed mounted training during the early summer of 1918. According to Trooper George Hambley of A Squadron, that was a good thing as the Light Horsemen had by this time become "fed up" with being used as auxiliary traffic police, labourers and carrying parties. They wanted an opportunity to distinguish themselves in a mounted role as the Royal Canadian Dragoons and Lord Strathcona's Horse had done at Cambrai the previous November and Moreuil Wood in March, actions that had garnered two VCs. Hambley and many of his comrades were convinced that there was something wrong with a unit "such as ours whose sole ambition seems to be to prepare" and nothing else – his fellow Light Horsemen were "willing, eager and capable" and asked only for a chance to make the "Woodbines sit up and take notice."[15] They were therefore hopeful that, if mobile warfare resumed, the cav-

Taking the salute, 1918
On a visit to the front in July 1918, Prime Minister Robert Borden of Canada acknowledges the March Past of a Canadian infantry battalion while General Sir Arthur Currie, commanding the Canadian Corps, returns an officer's salute. Borden led the only government in Canadian history that truly supported the nation's army and Currie led the finest fighting force Canada has ever produced. NAC. PA-002746

alry would at last come into its own again, overlooking the fact that Cambrai and Moreuil Wood had resulted in heavy losses for the mounted units involved.

At the end of July 1918, when the Canadian Corps began to move to its assembly area for the planned Amiens attack, it was up to strength, as well trained as it could be, and its morale had never "been better, nor its spirits higher."[16] The movement of the Corps' four infantry divisions and attendant artillery and corps troops was a masterpiece of staff work and deception that was carried out in the utmost secrecy. The units moved by road, bus and rail, mainly during the night using different and devious routes. Once they reached the assembly area, no fires were permitted at night and only limited movement in the day. Fortunately the weather did not favour German aerial observation and, although German intelligence officers learned of the presence of Canadian units in the Amiens area, they did not realize that the entire Corps was assembling for a major offensive.

The forthcoming operation differed from previous major attacks in that it depended on the element of surprise. Massed armour, 604 tanks in all, would replace lengthy preliminary bombardment and there would be copious artillery, 2,070 guns, available to support the infantry once they attacked. The plan incorporated all the hard-learned lessons of 1915 to 1917: communications would depend on wireless or radio; use would be made of tactical air support; advancing troops would be supplied with ammunition by specially designed armoured vehicles and, above all, the infantry would make use of "fire and movement" to advance, leaving strongpoints in their rear to be mopped up by the tanks. Working in the favour of the Allies was the fact that the defenders along the 14-mile front consisted of fourteen mainly weak divisions, which had not constructed strong defensive positions. There were none of the thick wire belts or pillboxes that had rendered the defence so formidable the previous year and the enemy positions consisted mainly of discontinuous trenches, fortified shell holes and strongpoints located in natural obstacles such as woods. Another factor was the ground, which was rolling countryside that not been churned up by artillery fire and over which troops could move swiftly. The overall plan called for the Canadian Corps to attack in the centre, the Australian Corps and a British corps on the left and the French on the right. Currie planned to make the initial assault using the 1st, 2nd and 3rd Divisions and the objectives were phase lines codenamed Green, Red and Blue. In the 2nd Division, the 4th and 5th Brigades would be responsible for securing the first two, after which Bell's 6th Brigade would move through them to secure the third. The attack was set to commence at 4.20 A.M. on 8 August 1918.

"Black day of the German army": Amiens offensive, August 1918

The efforts to maintain surprise were assisted by a heavy ground mist that blanketed the front at dawn on the day. At zero hour, a short but intense bombardment was brought down on all the German forward positions, which had been carefully located both by intelligence and by aircraft in the preceding two weeks. Then the infantry and tanks went forward and met with success everywhere as the defenders, demoralized by the bombardment and terrified by the large numbers of noisy armoured vehicles that suddenly appeared out of the mist and smoke, were incapable of putting up much resistance. Meanwhile, terrific dogfights

took place overhead as Allied fighters tried to prevent German fighters from interfering with the tactical aircraft attacking the enemy positions. Many Canadian soldiers took time out to watch these aerial battles with field glasses found in captured enemy positions, as 8 August 1918 was a red letter day for the souvenir hunters. Late in the morning the infantry heard an unfamiliar sound approaching from the rear, a drumming noise that grew louder and louder until men finally realized it was the sound of thousands of hooves. At long last, the cavalry – two full divisions including the Canadian Cavalry Brigade – were being sent in to exploit the breakthrough. It actually worked, although the light Whippet tanks attached to the mounted troops probably did more damage, and by early afternoon the Canadians had advanced beyond the Red Line.

Now came the turn of the 6th Brigade which, throughout the morning, had been moving forward, and from the front,

through the thinning mist, came the staccato rattle of rifle and machine-gun fire, where the lines of khaki-clad infantry were steadily pushing into German territory. Here and there the red flash of bursting shells glowed for an instant through the fog, and winked out in brown columns of up-flung earth and dust. All along the divisional front clouds of cavalry were already on the move, and already in the rear guns were being

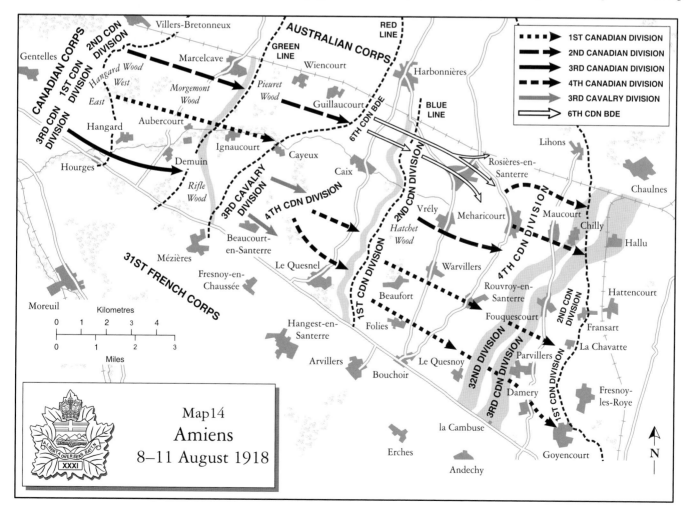

Map 14
Amiens
8–11 August 1918

hauled forward into new positions. Over the uneven ground tanks lurched and rolled, firing as they advanced, while in the air British pilots swooped and turned, bombing and machine-gunning the retiring Germans.[17]

The brigade was committed to an attack to secure the Blue Line in the early afternoon and made progress against uneven German resistance. They obtained their objective by 7.15 P.M. and captured numerous prisoners including a shaggy Russian pony, barely 12 hands high, "and of a sociable and friendly disposition."[18] He was such a likeable little fellow that the Albertans decided to keep him and "Heinie," as he was named, was duly entered on the rolls as the official mascot of the 31st Battalion.

By the end of that memorable day, the Canadian Corps had advanced an average of 6 miles, capturing more than 5,000 prisoners and nearly 200 artillery pieces. The Amiens offensive was the single most successful operation carried out by Canadian soldiers in the history of their nation and it spelled the end for Germany. As report after report came into Ludendorff's headquarters of positions overrun, troops surrendering in large numbers and Allied advances measured in terms of miles not yards, the German commander despaired. As he later noted, 8 August 1918 was "the black day of the German army in the history of the war," and he informed the Kaiser that Germany should immediately begin peace negotiations with the Allied powers.[19] For the time being, however, the war would have to continue and, during the night of 8/9 August, Ludendorff reinforced the dispirited troops in the Amiens sector with seven divisions, in an attempt to hold back the Allied onslaught.

The presence of fresh German troops became apparent on 9 August when the Allied advance, hampered by staff confusion and the fact that the progress of the previous day had placed the forward troops beyond the range of artillery support, began to slow down. The Iron Brigade's objective that day was a German defence line running through the village of Rosières-en-Santerre but to reach it, the brigade would have to move across a long, gradual open slope. The task of the 31st Battalion was to take the village of Rosières itself but when Lieutenant G.A. Cunliffe of D Company surveyed through his field glasses the ground over which his men would have to advance, he got a really bad feeling. Cunliffe asked a nearby soldier how far he thought it was to the village and when the reply came that it was about 1,000 yards,

The end for a German rearguard, Canal du Nord, October 1918
During the last months of the war, German rearguards, built around automatic weapons, offered stubborn resistance. They usually fought to the end and, even if they tried to surrender, were often shot out of hand because of the casualties they inflicted. This dead German was well armed – his Maxim 08/15 machinegun (a lightened version of the standard automatic weapon) lies at the edge of his hole along with a Mauser 98 rifle and a "potato masher" grenade. Another grenade and a fighting spade are in the hole beside the body. NAC, PA-0003202

the young officer's comment was: "One thousand deaths."

The brigade was supposed to have tank support but, due to some mix up, the tanks were not up when, late in the morning, following a rather feeble bombardment from the few guns in range, it attacked. Cunliffe was one of the first fatal casualties and his prediction turned out to be entirely true – the Alberta Battalion was immediately caught in murderous crossfire from automatic weapons and then subjected to an artillery bombardment. The advance came to a halt as the men went to ground but, urged on by their officers and NCOs, they again went forward, in short rushes by sections, one covering the other, and then switching roles. Every yard was paid for in blood. The tanks finally arrived but, with no mist or smoke to cover them, they suffered from German artillery fire and anti-tank rifles and only one made it to the village although they did manage to dampen German machinegun fire long enough to permit the battalion to get a toehold in Rosières.

No sooner were the Albertans among the houses than the enemy infantry launched a counterattack but this was beaten off by the battalion Lewis gunners, assisted by tactical aircraft that strafed the oncoming Germans and sent them to ground. It took the battalion several hours to clear the village in vicious fighting in which few prisoners were taken, and while doing so, they were attacked in turn by German aircraft which bombed and strafed them from an altitude of 100 feet. None of the Albertans who had survived the murderous crossing of that open slope wanted to return to it, however, and they hung on grimly and cleaned up Rosières house by house, street by street, until at 2.30 P.M. it was completely in Canadian hands. This was no sooner reported to brigade headquarters than the Germans mounted a second counterattack with about a thousand infantry but this time, however, it was the enemy's turn to cross open fields and the Lewis gunners broke up the attack without difficulty. As dusk fell, the 6th Brigade had achieved all its objectives – but at a heavy cost.

The advance resumed on 11 August but German resistance was stiffening and the gains were small. Although fighting continued in the Amiens sector for another week, it was apparent that there would have to be a pause while preparations were made for a new operation. Overall, the results had been impressive. The Canadian Corps and its allied formations had driven forward 14 miles and captured more than 9,000 prisoners and huge quantities of weapons and war materiel. Balanced against this was the loss of 11,822 Canadians killed and wounded including 2,400 men in the 2nd Division alone. The Alberta Battalion's share of this "butcher's bill" was 3 officers killed and 12 wounded, 26 other ranks killed and 204 wounded, and 8 missing, for a total of 253, almost all suffered on 9 August. The unit historian, searching for some positive aspect in these statistics, noted that in the Amiens action, "the ratio of killed to wounded in the Canadian casualty lists was about 1 to 6, as compared with an average of around 1 to 4 in trench warfare."[20] This was optimism indeed but, as the next three months would demonstrate, although mobile warfare had returned to the Western Front, it did not mean a lessening of the casualty rates – 20% of all Canadian fatal casualties in the First World War occurred during the last one hundred days of the conflict.

"The gas hung low, and caused considerable trouble": Arras to Cambrai, August to October 1918

Following Amiens, Ludendorff continued to reject the advice of his senior staff to withdraw to the prepared defences of the Hindenburg Line. Instead he decided to hold in place all along the Western Front, lest a withdrawal further demoralize a German army already shaken by the disaster at Amiens. This decision played straight into the hands of his Allied counterpart, *Maréchal* Foch, who, determined to maintain momentum and prevent the Germans from concentrating their reserves, planned a series of attacks at widely spaced sectors of the Western Front. In the last ten days of August, American, British and French forces staged offensives in the Argonne, Flanders, Somme and Arras sectors. The Canadian Corps took part in an operation in the Arras sector with the ultimate objective of the city of Cambrai, a vital communications centre. To get there, however, the Corps would have to penetrate no less than four German defence lines – the Fresne-Rouvroy Line, the Drocourt-Quéant Line, the Canal du Nord and the Hindenburg Line itself – beyond which lay open country. Between late August and early October 1918, the Corps made a series of frontal attacks against some of the strongest German positions on the Western Front.

The first of these operations, which began on 26 August, saw the 2nd and 3rd Divisions breach the Fresne-Rouvroy Line in

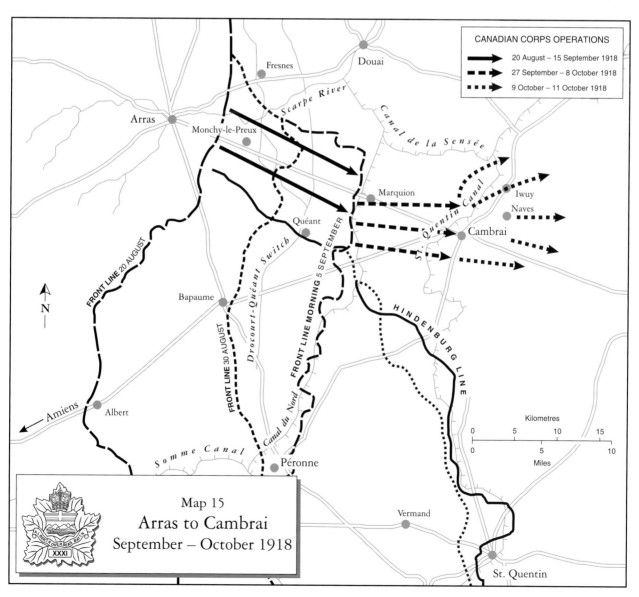

Map 15
Arras to Cambrai
September – October 1918

four days of heavy fighting. The 31st Battalion – now under the command of Lieutenant-Colonel Nelson Spencer, a 42-year-old real estate agent from Medicine Hat and former mayor of that city – was in support throughout this operation, nor was it involved when the 4th Canadian Division penetrated the Drocourt-Quéant Line on 3 September. It moved back to the front, however, for a five-day tour on 7 September while preparations were advanced for the next operation – the securing of a bridgehead over the Canal du Nord in front of Cambrai. The Albertans had just got into their positions about 1 A.M. on 7 September when the German artillery laid down the most intense gas shell bombardment the battalion had yet suffered, and it lasted until 6 P.M. on the following day. So heavy was the concentration of phosgene and mustard gas that most of the battalion had to wear their respirators for four hours while B

Company, which was particularly hard hit, had to wear theirs for six hours. Matters were made worse by the rain that fell during the night as "owing to the dampness … the gas hung low and caused considerable trouble, the men being compelled to wear their gas masks all the time."[21] An hour later a change of wind direction dispersed much of the gas and many men removed their respirators only to be caught when a reversal of the wind blew "light concentrations of the deadly vapour across the Battalion positions" causing numerous casualties. At this point the Germans brought down an intense mixed gas and high explosive bombardment lasting for two hours.

The casualties that resulted from this episode were the heaviest losses the battalion "had ever experienced in a single day from hostile artillery action."[22] No fewer than 107 men had to be sent back with gas poisoning and for this reason the 31st was placed

Advancing at long last, 1918

A Canadian Light Horse squadron moves forward in the last days of the war while German prisoners assist lightly wounded Canadians to the rear. The Light Horse spent three and a half frustrating years working as labour troops and stretcher parties before resuming mounted operations in the autumn of 1918. (Right) When the war entered a mobile phase after August 1918, cavalry came back into its own for reconnaissance work. Like their human counterparts, however, the four-legged troopers needed frequent breaks while on the march and they can be seen here grazing while their riders debate how much longer the war will last. CANADIAN ARMY PHOTOGRAPHS O.3230, O.3236

in brigade reserve the next day. B Company suffered so many casualties that it was broken up and its healthy men distributed to the other three companies until it could be rebuilt with reinforcements. The 31st Battalion was still in reserve when the 1st and 4th Divisions took the Drocourt-Quéant Line on 26 September.

The Germans, determined to retain Cambrai, poured reinforcements into the area. There were four German divisions facing the Canadian Corps when it attacked the Drocourt-Quéant Line, but ten enemy divisions and thirteen independent machinegun corps facing the Canadians when they attacked the Canal du Nord on 1 October. They made only limited gains. Realizing that his troops were becoming exhausted, Currie called off the operation and prepared a new assault timed for 8 October. Although the Canadian commander could not realize it, the recent fighting had also exhausted the German army which, in the last half of September, had to defend against no less than four major Allied operations. Having no reserves left, Ludendorff reluctantly decided to give up Cambrai and the German troops in that city were just beginning to withdraw when the Corps attacked during the night of 8 October. Within a few hours, Cambrai was in Canadian hands.

"Let's go boys": The last charge, 10 October 1918

Currie wanted to keep pressure on the Germans to prevent them from preparing new defensive positions behind the next water obstacle – the Canal de L'Escaut, which runs northeast of Cambrai. Beyond that barrier lay open country and if the Corps could cross it, they could keep pushing the enemy back relentlessly to the next objective, the city of Valenciennes 25 miles northeast. To maintain momentum, Currie chose Brigadier-General Raymond Brutinel's Independent Force, a mobile battlegroup centred around the 1st and 2nd Motor Machine Gun Brigades equipped with motorized gun carriers and trucks. Brutinel's command had performed outstanding service the previous spring when it was one of the few Canadian units involved in holding back the German onslaught. This had not gone unnoticed and the Independent Force had been steadily augmented throughout the summer and early autumn. By September 1918 Brutinel controlled not only the two motor machinegun brigades but the Canadian Corps Cyclist Battalion, a battery of field artillery and two cavalry regiments – one British, the other the Canadian Light Horse.

After their long wait, it appeared to the men of the Light Horse that they would finally get a chance to prove themselves. While the rest of the Canadian Corps had been involved in heavy fighting in August and September, the Light Horse had actually enjoyed a fairly quiet time. Their main activities had been to provide traffic guides and prisoner escort during the operations at Amiens and when not so employed, they had continued to train intensively for mounted action, heartened by the mass employment of cavalry at Amiens. In late August the regiment lost its Hotchkiss machinegun sections to the Independent Force and the remainder of the Light Horse came formally under Brutinel's

Blitzkrieg, 1918 version
Near Amiens in August 1918 an Autocar of the Independent Force advances, followed by cyclist infantry while on the side of the road, troopers of the Canadian Light Horse rest their mounts. In 1918, Brigadier-General Raymond Brutinel's Independent Force, highly mobile and commanded by radio, was one of the most advanced combat formations in the world. NAC, PA-003015

command in early September. There had been no opportunity during the operations against Cambrai for either the Light Horse or the Independent Force to be employed but that changed when the city fell on 8 October, as there were no prepared enemy defensive positions east of it. Brutinel was therefore ordered to secure crossings over the Canal L'Escaut and "to exploit success" along the roads from that city to Valenciennes.[23]

On 9 October 1918, the 5th Brigade seized a crossing over the canal at Escaudoeuvres outside Cambrai and the Independent Force went forward to seize the high ground near the village of Iwuy (pronounced "Ee-way"), about 4 miles east of from Cambrai. Brutinel sent B Squadron of the Light Horse ahead of his main column, but they came under heavy machinegun fire from German positions in the village of Naves about 800 yards from the main road between Cambrai and Iwuy, and lost 12 men and 47 horses. This made it clear that the enemy was in strength and that infantry would be needed to continue the advance. During the night of 9 October, the 5th Brigade moved forward to Naves while the 6th Brigade, working both sides of the Canal de L'Escaut, reached the village of Thun l'Evêque, a few hundred yards west of Iwuy.

Early the next morning, the Independent Force and the supporting infantry began the task of clearing Naves and taking a bridge over the little Erclin River (actually a creek), in preparation for seizing Iwuy and the high ground around it. While infantry of the 5th Brigade took Naves, Brutinel sent a mixed group of armoured cars and cyclists to the Erclin, but they were unable to cross as the only bridge had been destroyed and, worse still, they were pinned down by machinegun fire coming from a sunken road, running along a ridge behind Iwuy which completely dominated the area. When the Canadians gathered bridging materials to get a rough structure across the Erclin,

New tanks arrive as mobility returns to the war

Infantry move past a British Medium Whippet A tank in 1918. Designed for pursuit and mobile operations, the Whippet was twice as fast as the standard British tank and could reach a top speed of 8 mph. The Whippet, manned by a crew of three and armed with four machineguns, was used in great numbers in the last months of the war. BY KIND PERMISSION OF THE TRUSTEES OF THE IMPERIAL WAR MUSEUM, Q 9821

A new type of warfare, a new type of force

Formed in 1918, Brigadier-General Raymond Brutinel's Independent Force was a highly mobile formation of motorized machinegun carriers, cyclists and traditional cavalry. It proved effective at fighting rearguard actions during the German offensives of that year and also during the fluid phase of the war which began in August 1918. Here, a column of machinegun carriers takes a rest east of Arras in September 1918 but note that the men keep their gas masks close at hand, indicating they are not far from the front. The arrow symbol on the front of the vehicles is the insignia of the Canadian Machine Gun Corps. NAC, PA-003399

The iron steed arrives on the battlefield, 1918

A crew member paints a unit marking on a Canadian-built Autocar of Brutinel's Independent Force. Mounting two Vickers .303 machineguns, the Autocar was not used as an armoured fighting vehicle – that is, its crew did not engage the enemy while on the move – but as quick transport for its automatic weapons. Note the soldier doll on the front of the vehicle, clearly a lucky charm. Soldiers tend to be superstitious which is not surprising because any positive belief is a help. NAC, PA-002003

(Below) Combined arms training, 1918

Men of the 5th Battalion CEF, a unit originally raised from cavalry units in western Canada, train with a Mk IV tank in the summer of 1918. The fact that this is a training exercise is clear as the men are not wearing helmets or gas masks. At Amiens in August 1918, Australian and Canadian soldiers would mount the first successful tank–infantry attack in history.

NAC, PA-003025

(Below) The old and the new, 1918

A column of machinegun-carrying trucks of the Independent Force pauses just east of Arras in September 1918. Note the white identification panels tied across the hoods of each vehicle, the chains on the tires and the water pail, probably needed as the engines of the time frequently overheated. Also note that the men have their gas mask carriers to hand, indicating that they are not far from the front. Behind can be seen a squadron of the Canadian Light Horse, the mounted component of the Independent Force. NAC, PA-003398

the Germans responded with a very heavy and effective artillery bombardment. About midday, however, Brutinel laid down a machinegun barrage on the ridge that permitted a brave platoon of cyclists (without their cycles) to seize a position on the sunken road but this small force had no success clearing the remainder of the ridge and were immediately pinned in place by heavy fire. The Germans defending this area were from the 6th Prussian Infantry Division, a well-trained assault division, and they were determined not to abandon the best defensive position immediately east from Cambrai without a stiff fight.

As the infantry of 5th and 6th Brigades were still coming up, Brutinel decided to take a chance and ordered Lieutenant-Colonel Ibbotson Leonard of the Canadian Light Horse to advance and seize a hill behind Iwuy that dominated the enemy position on the sunken road. To do that, the Light Horse would have to cross about 1,400 yards of open, grassy ridge swept by German machinegun fire and, with the Canadian artillery still out of range, they would be unsupported if they attacked on foot. Leonard reasoned that a mounted advance might be able to get over that fireswept ridge with minimal casualties to reach the objective. When he learned that the 5th Brigade intended to attack the sunken road at 2 p.m., which might distract the enemy defending it, Leonard decided to mount what would be Canada's last cavalry charge.*

To do so he had two troops of A Squadron of the Light Horse and three troops of C Squadron with their Hotchkiss machinegun sections, a total of 5 officers and about 75 men. Leonard ordered Lieutenant Matheson, commanding C Squadron, the 1st Hussars squadron, to cross the Erclin and move directly up the ridge while the two A Squadron troops came in from the west. Meanwhile, B Squadron, which had suffered heavily the day before, would remain in reserve. At about 2.25 p.m., just after the 5th Brigade attacked the ridge, Matheson's three troops went forward with Lieutenant Robert Hocken's No. 1 Troop leading, followed in order by No. 2 and No. 4 Troops. Hocken's men encountered great difficulties getting over the gulley formed by the Erclin, which was about 12 feet deep and 15 feet wide, but eventually most of the troop got across and began to climb the ridge. It immediately became clear that the Germans were in no way distracted by the infantry attack going in on their left and, before the men of 1 Troop could get up speed, they brought them under heavy artillery and machinegun fire that killed Hocken and 15 of his troop's 16 horses,

and wounded 9 men. That anyone from Hocken's troop survived at all was due to the actions of Trooper Stewart Thornton, who charged the sunken road alone and took out a machinegun crew with rifle fire, and Lance Corporal Robert Hill, who provided covering fire from the troop's Hotchkiss gun. The following C Squadron troops fared nearly as badly – as soon as they got across the river they were hit by German shellfire which wounded 9 men and killed 10 horses. Unable to advance because of the heavy machinegun fire, the remnants of all three troops took cover in the Erclin River bed and kept up a steady fire with rifles and Hotchkiss guns on the ridge.

It was now the turn of A Squadron, the 19th Dragoons squadron of the Light Horse. Lieutenant Robert Fyfe's No. 1 Troop led off, followed by Lieutenant Alan Sharpe's No. 4 Troop. Trooper George Hambley was in Sharpe's troop and for the rest of his life he would remember the events of the next few minutes. Hambley watched as a mounted orderly came up and handed Sharpe a message which Sharpe read before riding over to his waiting men: "Well boys, we have to take those guns out of there. See over there is the farm house – and along that ridge there is a sunken road and the guns are in there. We'll come in from the left. … O.K. Get mounted" and "Let's go."[24]

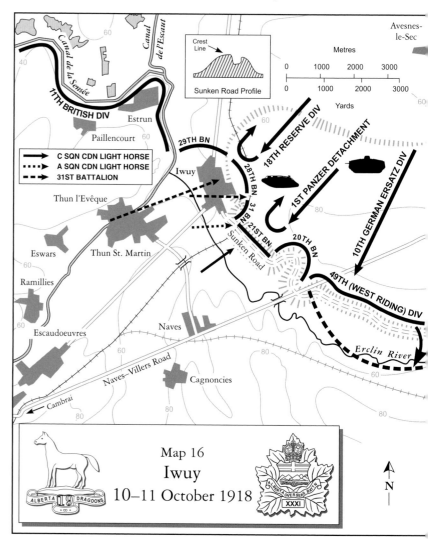

Map 16
Iwuy
10–11 October 1918

---

* It is a common misconception that the last Canadian cavalry charge was mounted by the Fort Garry Horse of the Canadian Cavalry Brigade near Le Cateau on 9 October 1918. As will be seen, the last charge was mounted by the Canadian Light Horse at Iwuy on 10 October 1918.

Following behind Fyfe's No. 1 Troop, Sharpe and his fifteen men

rode across a field and up over the railroad track and then down to cross that wide slope up to the sunken road. But before we could even get under way we came to quite a wide deep ditch [the Erclin River] with a very small trickle of water in it. We looked along the ditch and there were the men of 'C' Squadron. They hadn't gone on at all. One of them shouted "There's too many guns up there." Sharpe looked at them and said "Let's go boys."[25]

Riding behind Sharpe on his horse "Bill," the troop climbed down into the river bed but had a "hard scramble" getting up the other side. Troopers Dan Reavie and Joe Scanlon became caught up in some telephone wire and dropped out to disentangle themselves while the remaining men of the troop started up the grassy ridge. Before they could get even get their horses to a canter, they were hit and, as Hambley recalled,

Bullets began to plow up the dust and sizzle through the air. Every horse was doing his best. Everyone urging them on to the farm our objective. A bullet hit old Nix near the right temple – he went down like a stone. I came down on my head – Nix turned over right on top of me – quivered all over and never moved again. My helmet had rolled away somewhere. I attempted to get out from under my horse but had a hard struggle to free my feet – at last I raised his legs and got out. I lost no time in getting around behind the horse's body, out of the hail of bullets.[26]

From this vantage point, Hambley witnessed the fate of Sharpe's troop. He saw Sharpe's horse "Bill" hit and the troop commander tumble to the ground and then Trooper Quenton's horse "Croppy" was "shot full of holes and the blood spurted out from many of them" but "the noble horse kept on until Quenton got to the sunken road and started shooting all the Germans." "Zulu," the coal black horse of Troop Sergeant McRoberts and a favourite in the troop, was hit by several bullets and went down, throwing his rider. As Hambley watched, McRoberts, himself wounded in the leg, "crawled over and put his arms around Zulu's neck and the horse put his head on Mac's legs. Mac talked to the horse for he really cared for that big, black fellow and then he took out his [Colt .45] automatic and shot him through the head."[27]

Dressing the wounded, September 1918
During the last three months of the war, the Canadian Light Horse saw considerable action. Judging by the nature and position of his wound, this trooper has been hit by a shrapnel fragment from an air burst. Standing at left wearing glasses is George Hambley of A Squadron, the 19th Dragoons squadron, who left a detailed diary of his experiences. Dobbin pays no attention but grazes happily – his job was get his rider into battle, and nothing else. NAC, PA-002003

At this point, an amazing thing happened. Trooper Joe Scanlon, who had got fouled up in telephone cable at the Erclin, came thundering up, having "cut off his saddle, pulled out his sword, mounted the old mare bareback and dashed up the field" past Hambley. Scanlon made it to the top of the ridge but not many others were as successful. Hambley watched as "horse after horse went down and men rolled off – before the group had reached the road I saw Larry Bell roll off and his horse galloped away."[28] When it was over, there was a small knot of men from A Squadron fighting in the sunken road while the bodies of three of their comrades and all but one of the troop's 16 horses littered the grassy ridge in front. At this point, Hambley decided that

it would be madness for me to start up the field on foot as it was half a mile and the machine guns were still biting the dust all over the field. They were evidently firing at all the men laying in the field – some of the infantry men digging in and some dead. When I could get out in comparative safety I crawled to the first man whom I thought was one of us. It was Marlow – dead! I could do nothing for him as I got across into a large, shallow sand pit with the intention of getting up the road to the objective. A machine gun was still sniping at us. A number of infantrymen and three of our men with wounded horses were in the sand pit. Another man lay out in front, we thought him dead but I saw him move so went out and found it to be Stanley of 'C' Squadron shot very badly through the bowels. The other two fellows got a stretcher – one helped me carry Stanley into the pit where we put a couple of dressings over the bullet holes, put him on the stretcher, cut the blankets off the nearest dead horse and putting them on the wounded man we started out. Fellow came with an order to go back.[29]

But A Squadron's troubles were not over. As they sheltered from the machinegun fire, the Germans brought down an artillery bombardment of mixed HE, smoke and gas shells which forced them to don their respirators for more than an hour and which more or less finished off the "long-nosed chums" lying on the slope.

Leonard was about to commit B Squadron when he received orders from Brutinel not to send any more men up the ridge. The Independent Force would have to wait for the infantry to take the sunken road and the best they could do was to hang on to their positions in the face of heavy German fire. The charge had cost the Canadian Light Horse 4 men and 66 horses killed, and 19 men wounded. If anyone still needed conclusive proof

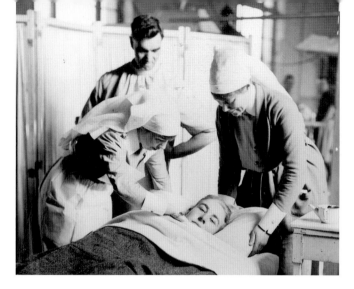

Life can sometimes be good

While a doctor looks on, a wounded soldier is tended by "bluebirds" – nurses of the Canadian Army Medical Corps – at a Casualty Clearing Station in November 1918. This is a staged publicity shot as conditions in a CCS were not usually this cheerful nor as comfortable. It was probably taken because the patient is Private Lawrence, who was hit at 10.45 A.M. on 11 November 1918 and thus was the last Canadian soldier wounded in the First World War. Lawrence was 17 years old and he does not look at all unhappy about being out of the fight. NAC, PA-003535

that, in warfare, the time of the horse had passed, it could be found in the dead animals scattered on a grassy ridge near the little French town of Iwuy.

During the night of 10/11 October the engineers managed to complete a bridge over the Erclin and elements of the motor machinegun brigades and the cyclist battalion moved up and reinforced the positions on the sunken road. The Germans, however, put up a determined resistance and Brutinel was unable to completely secure the position. It was now obvious that a full scale infantry assault would have to be made on Iwuy and the high ground behind it. The 5th and 6th Brigades were therefore brought forward and this attack went in under heavy artillery bombardment at 9 A.M. on 11 October.

The Iron Brigade's objective was Iwuy and the heights immediately behind. The 28th and 29th Battalions were to take the village and once that was secure, the 31st Battalion was to move through and secure the high ground. As the Alberta Battalion moved to its assembly area behind the two assault units, it was spotted by German artillery observers in the sunken road who brought a heavy and accurate artillery bombardment down on it and

> For a time hell was loose among the men of Alberta. The shells, as they fell, detonated off the trees that covered the Battalion's assembly area, and the wounds caused by the flying shell [and wood] splinters were terrible. Enemy machine-gunners, realizing that the Regiment was being cut up, poured belt after belt of machine-gun bullets into the area; and the deafening crash of bursting shells, the rending of riven timber and the continual stammer of the machine guns combined in an inferno of din sufficient to strike terror into the heart of the bravest.[30]

Casualties were heavy – 13 killed and 118 wounded – but the battalion moved back to cover, regrouped and, when it received word that Iwuy was clear, advanced through the village to attack the ridge. Unfortunately Iwuy was not clear and the 31st spent much of the day flushing out German machinegunners and snipers from the built-up area and surrounding woods.

The Germans, however, were determined to regain Iwuy. The Albertans were so preoccupied in the village that they probably did not even notice that late in the morning of 11 October the Germans mounted a counterattack – at least neither their War Diary nor their history makes any mention of it. It was obvious, however, to the troops on the sunken road, which by this time from Iwuy to a point at a bend about 1,500 yards east, was in the possession of 4th Brigade . The enemy attack, preceded by a heavy artillery bombardment, came in at 11 A.M. when five enemy infantry battalions moved towards Iwuy and the sunken road. Following behind the infantry was the rarest of all sights – German tanks. Captain George Stirrett of the Canadian Light Horse, who was up at the sunken road, remembered one of his men exclaiming: "My God, look at them houses moving!"[31] Lumbering towards them on the ridge were a clutch of thirteen captured British and German A7V tanks, each of the latter being 10 feet high and weighing 32 tons. Most of these vehicles broke down before they reached the Canadian lines and only one made it within range to use its two 57 mm guns and six machineguns. It was immediately put out of action by a Canadian officer using a captured 13 mm Mauser anti-tank rifle. The accompanying infantry fared no better, as the Canadians brought down a heavy bombardment from all guns within range and scythed down any survivors who tried to advance with machinegun and rifle fire. The position was held and that night, the Canadian units in the Iwuy area were relieved by British troops.

"Retreating war": The final days, October and November 1918

Following the battle for Iwuy, both the Light Horse and the 31st Battalion were withdrawn to rest and reorganize. The Alberta Battalion had suffered heavy losses on 10-11 October and, since there were no trained replacements available, it had to reorganize its companies on a three instead of four-platoon basis. For its part, the Light Horse had suffered more heavily in horses than in soldiers – it was given remounts and reinforced by a squadron of Royal North West Mounted Police, which became its D Squadron. Hambley remembered the burial of the four men lost at Iwuy:

> It was solemnly impressive. The four bodies side by side filled the large grave. …… Capt Martin of the 51st Div[isio]n read the ceremony, our men formed the firing party and our regimental trumpeter Chamberlain blew the "Last Post" and we showed that we appreciated these men …… There is something about Last Post that suggest the atmosphere of death, – as though the day being done, men call upon the Dusky Angel to take charge of the parade for the night.[32]

After a pause to resupply, on 14 October the Allied armies began to advance again all along the Western Front. Three days later, the 6th Brigade moved forward with the 2nd Division as the right flank of a general Canadian Corps movement toward Valenciennes. It was a memorable time, the battalion historian recorded, as

Although the weather was changeable, the mornings frequently dawned with brilliant sunshine that glistened from frost on trees, hedges and grass because the land, no longer a stark, barren shell-torn wilderness of mud and wreckage, lay in little pastures or cultivated patches from which grain had been harvested. Trees, many of them still in leaf, bore all the coloured beauties of an autumn well advanced. Retreating war, in its quickly-moving strides, left its scars mostly along the highways, railways and canals and at bridges, usually demolished. The war was now undergoing a rapid change from the drab stolidity of trench fighting to the more lively, intriguing and adventurous tactics of open warfare with its far-flung patrols, quick skirmishes and sudden assaults.[33]

The Canadian Light Horse provided small contact patrols for the infantry with orders "to draw fire from the enemy to show their positions" and, although they suffered significant casualties, it was Captain George Stirrett's opinion that, if the infantry had undertaken this work, the losses would have been in the hundreds. German resistance was variable, sometimes the enemy fought hard, at other times they seemed to give way easily and prisoners came in by the hundreds. Most of the enemy rearguards consisted of small forces built around the inevitable Maxims and the German machinegunners usually fought to the last – and with such effectiveness that they were rarely taken prisoner. As one Canadian soldier explained it, the Maxim gunners "who kept firing until the bayonets were upon them," and then tried to surrender, were given no mercy because, "if they had quit firing at least a minute or two before," they would have caused fewer losses.[34] Trooper George Hambley witnessed Canadian infantrymen, who had been pinned down by a Maxim in the second storey of a village house, enter the building from the rear and bayonet the German crew before throwing their bodies out of a window onto the street below.

Occasionally, while riding ahead of the Canadian Corps, the Light Horse did have some fun. Stirrett remembered taking a patrol into a Belgian village and, as they rode down the cobble-stoned streets,

All windows for 300 yards to the village square were drawn and covered. As we reached the village square at the Catholic church, we looked to see the road full of women, older men, and children, filling the road with anything they could wave. We dismounted and the old priest took me by the ears and kissed me. This started things. The priest kissed the three men with me. Then they all seemed to go crazy at once. They even kissed our horses. Then the priest called for prayer and

the entire village went to their knees at once, including my men and myself.[35]

Allied soldiers were beginning to realize that they were pursuing a beaten enemy and, although the German rearguards were obstinate, by 31 October the Canadian Corps was facing Valenciennes. The city fell four days later and the Canadians now pushed on to Mons. It was becoming clear to the men of the Allied armies that the war was coming to an end.

It had already been lost in the hearts and minds of the German soldiers and their leaders. After Amiens, Ludendorff and Hindenburg had informed the German government that it must begin peace negotiations, but nothing was done until the end of September when the two generals for the first time told German political leaders the true state of affairs on the Western Front. Bulgaria and Turkey had already sought peace and, on 4 October, both Germany and Austria-Hungary sent notes to President Woodrow Wilson of the United States asking for terms for a peace settlement. Wilson responded with very hard terms and although the German government was prepared to accept them, Ludendorff was not and he managed to delay further negotiations until he was forced to resign on 26 October. Thereafter, things moved fast and the newspaper headlines could barely keep up – within a matter of ten days, Austro-Hungary, Bulgaria and Turkey signed armistices with the Allied powers; the sailors of the German High Seas Fleet mutinied; the Kaiser abdicated and fled to neutral Holland; and the German government declared a republic. On 8 November a German delegation came to *Maréchal* Foch's railway car at Compiègne to discuss an armistice and did, indeed, receive very harsh terms. The German armies in Belgium and France would be permitted to return unmolested to their own territory but would have to leave behind or turn over an enormous amount of war supplies and weapons. These included 5,000 guns and 30,000 machineguns, 2,000 aircraft, 5,000 trucks and considerable other war materiel, which more or less removed any hope that Germany would have of resuming the war on land. At sea, the entire German High Seas Fleet was to sail to internment in Britain until its ultimate fate could be decided by an international conference that would negotiate the final peace treaty. In effect, the armistice amounted to an unconditional surrender – the German delegates had no choice but to sign, and sign they did. The armistice was to come into effect at 11 A.M. on Monday, 11 November 1918.

Early on the morning of that day the 31st Battalion marched from a bivouac near the Belgian village of Malplaquet, the scene of a famous 18th century battle, toward the village of Boissoit, about 6 miles to the east. Accompanied by a field artillery battery and some British cavalry, the unit was under orders to attack the German rearguard known to be holding Boissoit. Although all ranks knew of the impending armistice there had been no definite word before the battalion had left and the attack was just about to start at 10 A.M. when a messenger arrived from 6th Brigade Headquarters with orders cancelling it because the armistice would take place in one hour. During that last hour, the Albertans held their fire but the Germans brought down a light artillery barrage that wounded an officer and six men, the battalion's last wartime casualties. In front of B Company's position, German Maxim gunners on the outskirts of Boissoit fired lengthy burst after burst – shooting off unused ammunition so they would not have to pack it – but this tended to make everyone nervous and prompted retaliation from the Canadian artillery which fired a few rounds of HE in an attempt to get the enemy to mind their manners. Then, as hundreds of soldiers studied their wrist watches, the minutes ticked down to 11 A.M.

Some men have no luck. At 10.58 A.M., 256265 Private George Price of the 28th (Northwest) Battalion, Canadian Expeditionary Force, was hit and killed, possibly becoming the last fatal casualty on the Western Front. About 1,500 yards to the east of where this incident took place, the men of B Company of the 31st watched the enemy machinegun position in front of them. Precisely at 11 A.M., a German officer emerged from cover, fired a white Very light and then, as cheers and church bells rang out from every direction, he

> gave an order and from the ground arose the figures of his men. They dismantled their guns, pouring the water from the jackets. They packed their equipment with deliberate calm as men might lay down their tools when another day's work is done, and, lining up, walked off in the direction of the village of Boissoit.[36]

After 1,568 days of fighting and the deaths of between 8 and 9 million soldiers, the guns were finally silent.

Warrant officers and sergeants, A Squadron, Canadian Light Horse, 1918
By the relaxed looks on the faces of these men, this photograph was probably taken after the war had ended. Regimental Sergeant-Major John M. Heselton from Lloydminster is seated second from right while Signals Sergeant Harold E. Hecht, a former member of the 15th Light Horse, is seated to his right. These men are wearing brass CLH shoulder titles and CLH ribbons on their shoulder straps and most have 19th Dragoon collar badges. COURTESY, COLIN MICHAUD

"Good Bye-ee, Good Bye-ee": The long way home, November 1918 to June 1919

The shooting had stopped but the war was not yet over for the Canadian Light Horse and the 31st Battalion. Under the terms of the Armistice, Allied forces were to occupy bridgeheads over the Rhine and the 1st and 2nd Divisions of the Canadian Corps formed the lead element of the BEF on its movement to the German border. For its part, the 31st Battalion received the honour of acting as the vanguard of its division for much of this march and was "hailed in every town, village and hamlet" in Belgium.[37] Each municipality tried to outdo its neighbour in the warmth of its reception and an account of the battalion's arrival in Gosselies on 21 November is typical of the many happy scenes that took place during these memorable days:

> As the head of the column approached the village it was met by the Burgomaster and the village fathers, accompanied by a band consisting of half a dozen men playing with hearty good will but little harmony on flutes, fifes and a solitary but strident trumpet. This band played the men triumphantly into the village where the inhabitants swarmed, cheering through the street as the column made its way toward the town hall. Here the officers of the battalion were given an official welcome while the men fell out and proceeded to their billets.
>
> Within the village hall, two long tables had been set up and loaded with wines, but of food, significantly, there was little, and, after their long march, everyone was hungry. Many long speeches followed, and many toasts all duly and deeply honoured by the hungry but appreciative gentlemen from Canada.[38]

Food was in short supply because the Canadians had outstripped their supply services which had difficulty keeping up because German demolitions had disrupted much of the rail and road network. They found themselves feeding not only hungry civilians but also thousands of Allied prisoners of war who, released without any assistance by the Germans, were making their own way home. The Alberta Battalion was forced back on its own resources and Lieutenant-Colonel Nelson Spencer purchased a large cow for the stiff price of 2,000 francs to feed his hungry men. The beast "was not so young as it had been, and it must have led a hard life" but "it made good and nourishing soup despite the somewhat drastic after effects of eating the green meat."[39]

On 1 December the 31st Battalion reached Beho, a mile from the German border, whose inhabitants they found "pro-German and hostile" but they liked the surrounding countryside which, with its rugged hills and pine forests, was not unlike the foothill country in their native province.[40] That night, A Company slipped over the border to form an outpost line – just in case – and the Alberta Battalion thus became the first Canadian unit to enter Germany. The unit remained at Beho for two days, waiting for the logistical services to catch up and cleaning their weapons, uniforms and equipment for the formal entry into Germany. During this time they received a stern lecture from the com-

Taking the salute, the Rhine, 1918

General Arthur Currie, commanding the Canadian Corps, salutes as the Canadian Light Horse, passes in review on the Bonn Bridge over the Rhine in December 1918. The troops in this photograph are often wrongly identified as being another cavalry unit. NAC, PA-003798

mander of 6th Brigade, now Brigadier-General A.H. Ross, who had replaced Bell in October, and who emphatically warned them against fraternizing with German civilians. On 4 December, the 2nd Division crossed the frontier in column at 9 A.M.. The 31st Battalion was led by "Heinie" the pony who now returned to the land of his former masters, not that it made much difference to him. Nine days later, the little fellow again led the battalion when the 2nd Division, in a column that stretched for miles, crossed the Rhine bridge at Bonn, in battle order with bayonets fixed, flags flying and bands playing as Lieutenant-General Sir Arthur Currie and the Prince of Wales took the salute from a rostrum. As it was meant to, this display of martial pomp "created a lasting impression on the German population."[41]

The Canadians only remained in Germany for about a month. Their duties were not arduous and, despite all official prohibitions, there was considerable fraternization with German civilians, particularly female civilians. Trooper Hambley who, during the march through Belgium, had added the ladies of that nation to his list of European women with loose morals, now included German females. The behaviour of his comrades in the Canadian Light Horse perpetually perplexed and annoyed Hambley although it is interesting that he saw nothing wrong with joining them in the Bonn black market where they cheerfully sold army cigarettes, boots, blankets and bully beef for German marks with which to fund their active social lives.

George Hambley, however, was about to face his moment of truth. He was billeted with a German widow who had a very attractive daughter named Gerda. A former German army nurse, Gerda possessed many attributes in Hambley's eyes: she was highly intelligent, spoke good English, did not use cosmetics and – oh yes – had "Saxon blue eyes" and a "body bubbling

with youth and vivacious agility." Hambley found that his *kleine Schmetterling* or "little butterfly," as he christened Gerda, began to exert "quite a pull" on his heartstrings, particularly after she took to sewing in his room in the early evenings because, as she said, the light was better there. Things were moving to a dangerous pass and the crisis came one morning when Gerda's mother left to visit her sister for the day and Hambley encountered Gerda, dressed in a very pretty frock and with her silky blonde hair trailing in a fetching way over her shoulders, in the close confines of a downstairs hallway. Despite the Manitoban's best intentions, contact was made and a kiss exchanged – it was the supreme test for, as Hambley recorded in his diary, his "little butterfly" was "the right kind of a kiddie to make kissing a pleasure and not a sacrament as it should be." For a moment it looked like Trooper Hambley was about to go the way of all flesh but, managing to pull himself together at the last moment, he sternly informed the tearful Gerda that it could not be and quickly left the house not to return until after dark. Fortunately for Hambley, the Canadian Light Horse rode out for Belgium the next morning.[42]

They were followed by the 31st Battalion and the other units of the Canadian occupation force which in January 1919 moved to the area around Namur in preparation for demobilization and the journey home. The Canadians spent a couple of months in Belgium playing sports, attending the Khaki University – vocational courses run by the YMCA – and generally enjoying themselves. To add to all their other triumphs, it was during this time that the Alberta Battalion team won the Canadian Corps football championship. It was also during this period that most of the animals in the Corps were sold to the French and Belgian governments. "Heinie" was retained of course, but the Canadian Light Horse were no longer a cavalry unit. In connection with this matter, it might be worthwhile noting that the "long-nosed chums" had played an important role in the war and had paid the price – 284,886 horses serving in the British Expeditionary Force, including the CEF, were killed in action, succumbed to disease, or had been wounded during the conflict.

In late March and early April 1919, unit by unit, the Canadians departed for rather ill-named "Canadian Concentration Camps" or transit camps in England to wait for transport home. The Light Horse ended up at Ripon in Yorkshire, where they amused themselves by drinking and gambling or, in George Hambley's case, serious reading. On 10 April, when the Light Horse received word that they would be embarking for Canada in a few days, they held a dance to celebrate the event. Much against his will, Hambley was dragged along by his comrades but, predictably, did not enjoy the occasion. For one thing, his religion did not permit him to dance; for another the band started playing that "new jazz stuff" with its noisy mixture of banging "frying pans and ringing bells." But what really annoyed him were that most of the English girls at the dance were obviously "rather fast" and he became so annoyed that he "finally sat down beside one and told her off just on general principles giving her a piece of my mind – of course it made her peeved but that suited me immensely."[43]

Four days later, behind their band playing "Goodbye-ee, Goodbye-ee," the Light Horse marched out of Ripon to board the train for Liverpool where the S.S. *Belgic* waited to take them to Canada. On their way out to the open sea their convoy packed with men of the CEF home passed an Australian troop ship bound for "down under" and, while the bands of the two nations played "The Maple Leaf Forever" and "Auld Lang Syne," the best fighting men in the world cheered each other and waved good bye. The Light Horse arrived in Halifax on 24 April 1919 and were demobilized in Toronto a few days later. After three years of resisting temptation, George Hambley returned to Swan Lake, Manitoba with his virtue intact and went on to enjoy a long and productive life as a minister.

Sergeants, 31st Battalion, 1919
A shot of four sergeants of the Alberta Battalion taken outside their mess in Belgium in early 1919. They are wearing the British 1907 Pattern 5-button universal service jacket with fall down collar and the waist belt of the 1908 Pattern web equipment. These men have seen war and it shows – compare them with the faces of the men on page 117. GLENBOW MUSEUM, NA-3868-30

The 31st Alberta Battalion left Namur for Le Havre on 7 April 1919 to board a steamer for Southampton. This movement went without a hitch until an officious member of His Majesty's Customs Service spotted "Heinie" patiently waiting in line for his turn to mount the gangplank and declared that it was illegal to bring an animal into Britain unless it first spent six months in quarantine. This declaration tailed off when it was met by level stares from hundreds of hard-eyed Canadian infantryman each armed with a Rifle, Short Magazine Lee-Enfield, Mark III and its attendant Pattern 1907 Bayonet with a 17-inch blade. If the hapless official looked for support from authority in the form of officers or NCOs, he most likely found them studiously gazing the other way. Discretion being the better part of valour, it is not surprising that the impasse was broken and "Heinie," now Alberta bound, clumped his way on board. The battalion spent a month in a transit camp at Witley in Surrey before embarking on the SS *Cedric* for Canada on 19 May. They arrived in Halifax eight days later and then it was onto a waiting CPR train to commence the long train journey home. Amazingly enough, there were still 150 men in the unit who had served with it in Calgary in 1914.

In the early morning of 1 June 1919, there were "whoops and yells" when the 31st Battalion crossed the Saskatchewan-Alberta border. By this time the coaches were decorated with chalked slogans advising the girls of Canada that the boys within had "not yet been took" and inviting them "to take their pick." Groans came from the Calgary and Edmonton men when it was announced that there would be a stop in Medicine Hat so that D Company, which contained the Hat boys, could be properly feted. The Hat, however, did the battalion proud with a parade, minimal speeches from politicians and a splendid picnic in Riverside Park. Then it was back on the coaches for the last leg to Calgary. As they passed through the little towns on the way – Redcliff, Tilley, Bassano, Gleichen, Strathmore and all the rest – the train slowed while the local folk, waving little Union Jacks and Red Ensigns, stood by the tracks to cheer the boys home. When not responding in kind, officers and men cleaned their uniforms, arms and badges to be ready for their final parade.[44]

Sweet home, Alberta
After service in the Imperial Russian and Imperial German armies, Heinie was captured by the 31st Alberta Battalion at Amiens in August 1918. He was such a likeable little guy that he became the battalion mascot and was brought back to Alberta, where he was placed in the Whyte Zoo in Banff National Park. Heinie, however, did not like being penned and the superintendent, recognizing this, employed him as a pack animal. Heinie the happy pony was still alive as late as 1928. SALH ARCHIVES

Escort to the Colours
The 31st Battalion received its Colours in a ceremony in front of Namur Cathedral in April 1919. The sergeant standing between the two junior officers carrying the Colours is one of the old originals, indicated by the four chevrons on his sleeve, one for each year of service from 1914 to 1918. By this time, such men were becoming rare. SALH ARCHIVES

Home again, 1919
Led by Lieutenant-Colonel E.S. Doughty, the 31st Alberta Battalion marches in triumph with bayonets fixed through the streets of Calgary in June 1919. Doughty succeeded Lieutenant-Colonel A.H. Bell as commander of the 31st when Bell was promoted in April 1918. GLENBOW MUSEUM, NB-16-610

They got into Calgary at 5.45 P.M. The 31st Battalion was the first of the three Alberta infantry units to return from the war – the 49th and 50th Battalions were a few days behind them – and they received a splendid reception. Crowds lined the street around the station, the "tear wet faces of mothers, wives and sweethearts" were visible and the cheers were endless. It took some time to get things organized – "Heinie", who had made the journey in a baggage car, had to be cleaned up and the 120 Edmonton boys dispatched on a special train to their hometown – and then the remainder of the battalion formed under the command of Lieutenant-Colonel E.S. Doughty and marched out of the station for the Calgary Rifles armoury on

Eighth Avenue. Preceded by the Great War Veterans' Association Band, the Army and Navy Veterans' Pipe Band and a veterans' guard of honour, behind which plodded a glossy "Heinie", the Alberta Battalion marched through Calgary in battle order with steel helmets and skeleton web – and bayonets fixed. The streets were lined with troopers from Lord Strathcona's Horse to keep back what was estimated to be one of the largest crowds ever assembled in the city. Down Centre Street they went, under a triumphal arch bearing the slogan "Welcome to Bell's Doughty Boys" (a play on the names of the current and previous commanding officers), and then onto Eighth Avenue and finally to the armouries. Here they were quickly demobilized, each man turning in his arms and equipment to the storesmen ("respirator, one, check … respirator carrier, web, one, check … cartridge carriers, web, one set, check … haversack, web, one, check …" and so on until it all lay in a big heap on the counter) and completed their final paperwork. And then they left the army and went home.

As for "Heinie", the little guy was sent "to spend the remainder of his days in restful peace" at Banff National Park, grazing and gamboling among splendid surroundings.[45] At first he was placed in the custody of the Whyte Zoo but did not seem particularly happy so the superintendent of Banff National Park took him over as a working animal, and as late as 1928 "Heinie" was still alive.[46]

Many Canadian soldiers were not as fortunate as "Heinie." It has been said that Canada entered the First World War as a colony of Britain and emerged from it as an independent nation. If so, the price of nationhood came very high – some 66,500 Canadian servicemen and nurses were killed during the war or died of wounds in the four years that followed the end of hostilities in 1918, and 172,950 were wounded in action. The greater part of the fatal casualties during the war – 53,216 – were suffered by the Canadian Expeditionary Force on the Western Front and the statistics for the two units, whose stories concern us, the 31st Battalion CEF and the Canadian Light Horse, are as sobering. Of the 4,487 officers and men who served in the Alberta Battalion between 1914 and 1918, 941 were killed in action or died from accidents or sickness, and 2,312 were wounded while the Canadian Light Horse suffered 85 fatal casualties and 64 wounded.

In the memory of the men of the Alberta Battalion and Canadian Light Horse who fell in the First World War – and those other Canadians who have died for their country in uniform – every Remembrance Day the Ceremonial Troop of the South Alberta Light Horse mounts a Guard of Honour at the war memorial in the small town of Chipman, 25 miles east of Edmonton. Chipman was chosen as the Light Horse's major parade on this important date not because it played any great part in the regiment's history, but because it represents the many small communities across Alberta that sent forth the best of their youth to serve from 1914 to 1918.

Lest We Forget.

¾Lt. K.A.C. Clarke   2Lt. G.L. Macdougall   ¾Lt. R.M. Wynn   ¾Lt. L.M.K. Reed   ¾Lt. J.D. Menzies   Lt. E. Atkins

Col. Jas. Walker
Hon. Colonel

Lieut. R.D. Bryan   Major J.H. Beatty
2nd in Command
   Lt. Col. W.S. Quint
Med. Officer
   Lieut. J. Burton

Capt. S.L. Bosomworth   Major P.P. Littlewood, V.D.
O.C. "A" Squadron
   Lieut. Col. J.F. Scott
Commanding
   Major J.C. Valentine
O.C. "B" Squadron
   Capt. V.T. Bermejo

¾Lt. D.S. Clapperton   Capt. W.R. Coates
O.C. "C" Squadron
   Hon. Lt. Col. A.M. Berryman
Hon. Lt. Colonel
   Major L.C. Lane
Quartermaster
   Lieut. U.A. Jones, M.
Signalling Officer

Lieut. E.W. Lasher
Mach. Gun Officer
   Capt. A. Landale
Adjutant
   ¾Lt. S.O. Robinson   Major W.F. Macdougall
Vet. Officer
   Hon. Capt. J.M. Roe
Chaplain
   Lieut. F.J. Butler
Paymaster

OFFICERS
15th CANADIAN LIGHT HORSE

CHAPTER EIGHT

"We Stand on Guard for Thee (At Our Own Expense)"

THE LONG YEARS, 1919-1939

Return to peacetime soldiering: Alberta and its militia in the 1920s

The Great War was over. To the cheers of crowds in cities and towns across the country, the Canadian Corps, that magnificent, professional fighting force, was disbanded and its members returned to civilian life. Among them was Lieutenant-General Sir Arthur Currie, the best general Canada ever produced, who was so shabbily treated by the government on his return home that he shortly left the service to become the chancellor of McGill University. With the cry, "Never Again!," the veterans of the CEF resumed lives interrupted by four years of war but they were proud of their accomplishments and many were anxious that their wartime units continue to exist in the postwar order of bat-

> Yes, we have no pyjamas
> We have no pyjamas tonight.
> We've plenty of ear rings
> And solitary dear things
> We've necklaces too; and say –
> We have rolled-down silk stockings
> With expensive red clockings,
> But yes, we have no pyjamas,
> We have no pyjamas tonight.[1]

tle. This wish did not please senior militia officers who were just as anxious to maintain the existence of their prewar units.

To resolve this problem, the government appointed a committee under Major-General William D. Otter to examine and advise on the future military organization of the Dominion. The Otter Committee, convinced without any good reason that conscription would continue in peacetime, proposed that the postwar military structure should consist of 11 infantry divisions and 4 cavalry divisions, a huge and unwieldy organization, but one in which militia units would be linked with CEF units so that the latter would be perpetuated and their Battle Honours preserved. The committee also expanded the regular force by making the Princess Patricia's Canadian Light Infantry (PPCLI) and the Royal 22e Régiment permanent units and by creating the Canadian Machine Gun Corps with a single regular brigade (battalion) and twelve militia brigades. In 1920, all regular and militia units disbanded "for the purposes of reorganization" and then re-established themselves as part of a new postwar military establishment.

In Military District 13, or Alberta, the Otter Committee's work resulted in a major reorganization of the provincial militia which began in 1920 and went through several permutations until it reached a settled form about 1924. In that year, the Alberta militia consisted of the 5th Mounted Brigade with headquarters at Edmonton, comprising the 15th Canadian Light Horse (former 15th Light Horse) at Calgary, the 19th Alberta Dragoons at Edmonton, the 1st Regiment, Alberta Mounted Rifles (former 21st Alberta Hussars) at Medicine Hat and the 2nd Regiment, Alberta Mounted Rifles (former 23rd Alberta Rangers) at Pincher Creek. There were three brigades (regiments in modern parlance) of field artillery: the 18th Brigade at Lethbridge with batteries there and Fort Macleod; the 19th Brigade at Calgary with batteries in that city and Gleichen; and the 20th Brigade at Red Deer with a battery in that town and two more in Edmonton. Of particular interest to our story is the creation of 22 Battery, CFA, at Gleichen

---

(Facing) **Keepers of the Flame: Officers of the 15th Canadian Light Horse** During the interwar period, the militia struggled to stay alive in the face of public indifference and government parsimony. It was well that they did so because, by 1935 when the officers of the 15th Canadian Light Horse posed for a group portrait, another war was threatening. Among them is the seemingly-indestructible Colonel James Walker, who had founded the unit in 1905 but who would die in 1936; Lieutenant-Colonel J. Fred Scott, the commanding officer of the 15th Light Horse in 1935, who would command the Calgary Highlanders from 1939 to 1943; and Honorary Lieutenant-Colonel A.M. Berryman, a prominent Calgary businessman. Major J.H. Beatty, the second in command, was the only militia officer ever to win the Guides Challenge Cup, which he did in 1934. Among the younger officers in this picture, Second Lieutenants K.A.C. Clarke and G.L. Macdougall would see action with the South Alberta Regiment and would rise to the rank of major as squadron commanders, while Lieutenant E.W. Lasher served with the Calgary Highlanders and was wounded at the battle for the Walcheren Causeway, 31 October 1944. Second Lieutenant Sherwin Robinson also served with the Highlanders, commanded a company during the war with the rank of major and was wounded in Germany in 1945. The Light Horse's struggle for existence in the interwar period was paralleled by most militia units across Canada in the 1920s and 1930s but from their ranks would come the combat leaders of the Canadian army during the Second World War. SALH ARCHIVES

as it is a direct predecessor unit of the modern South Alberta Light Horse.*

The number of infantry units in the province increased to six battalions, grouped in two brigades. The 24th Brigade with headquarters at Calgary included the Calgary Highlanders and Calgary Regiment in that city, both derived from the prewar 103rd Regiment "Calgary Rifles," and the new South Alberta Regiment at Medicine Hat. Edmonton's 29th Brigade consisted of the Edmonton Fusiliers and Edmonton Regiment, both derived from the prewar 101st Regiment "Edmonton Fusiliers," and the new North Alberta Regiment at Killam. As part of the Canadian Machine Gun Corps, the 13th Machine Gun Brigade was created with headquarters at Calgary and a company in that city and companies at Edmonton and Medicine Hat. There was also a full slate of service and support organizations (which are only too often forgotten), including engineers, signals, transport, medical, veterinary and postal units. To preserve their memory, each of the combat units was linked with one or more CEF units and, thus, the 31st Battalion CEF, which had been recruited across Alberta, was perpetuated by the North and South Alberta Regiments, the two provincial infantry units based outside the larger centres of Calgary and Edmonton.**

An important postwar development was that, for the first time, regular troops were stationed in Military District 13. Headquarters and B Squadron of Lord Strathcona's Horse were transferred to Calgary in 1919 and, along with the District staff, shoved the Calgary militia out of the recently-built Mewata Armoury. The militia, however, rejoiced in the presence of nearby Sarcee Camp which, vastly expanded by a massive wartime building programme, offered excellent training facilities. With

regular officers and NCOs as instructors, good training facilities, modern weaponry from wartime stocks and a cadre of veterans, it appeared that the provincial militia faced a bright future.

Unfortunately, this was not to be. The election of Prime Minister Mackenzie King's Liberal government in 1921 led to defence expenditures being drastically slashed, a step that accorded with a global revulsion against war and matters military. By 1924, which saw the lowest defence budget of the interwar period, Canada was spending only one-fifth as much as the United States on defence and one-fifteenth as much as Britain. As most of the limited funds available went to the regular units, the militia had to make do with the scraps, with the result that its training suffered. Only one full-scale summer camp, attended by cavalry, infantry and artillery, was held in Alberta between 1919 and 1936, in1927, while the 5th Mounted Brigade was able to hold only one cavalry camp for all units in the province in 1924. In other years, funding permitted only "local headquarters training" or weekly parades in armouries or drill halls, "camp schools" or instructional courses run in the summer for selected officers and NCOs, and the occasional summer "brigade camp," mainly for mounted units. Headquarters training was useful but it did not give the units a chance to go into the field and practise what they were learning. The one bright point in this otherwise dismal picture was that the stationing of regulars in the province, and the close relationship between them and the militia, ensured that the quality and level of instruction was very high. This was particularly true of the mounted units which benefited from the presence of the Strathconas in Alberta.

It was a sad situation but in the 1920s most Canadians really did not care. There was a feeling that the "war to end all wars" having been fought, it was time to have fun and make money and this was certainly true in Alberta which, in almost every aspect, blossomed throughout the decade. Progress came in the form of paved roads, more railways, a provincial power grid and the beginnings of a modern air service, which began to open up the northern hinterland. Coal mines operated at peak capacity, the province's reserves of natural gas were developed,

---

* Following the First World War, an attempt was made to commemorate all the wartime CEF batteries by assigning their numbers to postwar militia batteries. For this reason, the new 22 Battery, CFA, at Gleichen was given the same number as a field battery of the Canadian Expeditionary Force which was raised in Ontario.

** A full list of the CEF units raised wholly or partly in Alberta during the First World War and their perpetuations will be found in Appendix H.

Officers of the 15th Canadian Light Horse, Sarcee, 1922
Lieutenant-Colonel A.G. Wolley-Dod, commanding officer, is seated in the centre; to the left in the same row is Major W.E. Tidball, who would take over the command of the Light Horse in 1926. Standing on the right is Lieutenant-Colonel H.C.A. Hervey, who would assume command in 1923. This was one of the first militia summer camps held after the First World War and the officers are wearing a variety of uniforms, some with rank on their shoulders and some on their cuffs, as was the older style. SALH ARCHIVES

and the neon lights and new buildings in the towns and cities. The population rose by nearly 20% between 1921 and 1931, from 593,000 to 732,000, with Calgary (83,751 souls) becoming the largest city, followed by Edmonton with 79,187, Lethbridge with 13,000 and Medicine Hat with 10,000.

It was agriculture, however, that underpinned the provincial economy and how the farmer fared in any given year was generally a measure of how Alberta fared. For the first three years after the war ended, the farmers fared very well indeed with good crops and high prices for wheat and livestock. In 1921, however, a minor agricultural recession led to unrest in the province and a decision by the United Farmers of Alberta, an agricultural interest group, to enter candidates in the June 1921

and the oil industry, which had fallen off after its brief period of excitement in 1914, picked up again in 1924 when renewed exploratory drilling in the Turner Valley, south of Calgary, resulted in further oil discoveries. These discoveries sparked off the inevitable speculation boom which ensnared the unwary including a British politician named Winston Churchill, who invested $5000 in an oil company that shortly went bankrupt. It was a prosperous time for Alberta, prosperity that was measured by the number of cars on the road, which doubled over the decade,

provincial election. To the amazement of many, including the UFA themselves, they won a sweeping majority and governed the province for the next fourteen years. The farmers' concerns were lessened by a bumper crop in 1923 and the creation of the Alberta Wheat Pool, a marketing co-operative, which helped stabilize grain prices. The crops of 1925, 1927 and 1928 were excellent and farmers, confident that the future would continue to be rosy, placed more and more wheat under cultivation and purchased expensive new machinery, mortgaging their property to do so. With the exception of the Palliser Triangle area in the southeast corner of the province where overfarming and drought had forced many off their lands, Alberta agriculture boomed throughout the first postwar decade.

In the 1920s, many Albertans only became aware

Inspection of the Alberta Mounted Rifles, Medicine Hat, 1921
The 1st Regiment of Alberta Mounted Rifles, formed from the 21st Alberta Hussars, undergoes an annual inspection by officers of Lord Strathcona's Horse at Medicine Hat in 1921. The regiment has a total of only 34 all ranks on parade, which was typical of the mounted rifle units in the 1920s. GLENBOW MUSEUM, NA-2637-4

of the militia when it participated in public events such as the opening and closing of the provincial legislature which usually involved the 19th Dragoons and Edmonton Fusiliers; Armistice Day, Coronation Day, Dominion Day and other civic parades; the funerals of prominent soldiers and community leaders; and an occasional appearance in the Calgary Stampede. On such occasions the militia tried to look their best but, although Ottawa permitted the wearing of ceremonial full dress uniforms, it had to be "at no expense to the public," meaning that honorary colonels or their friends usually dug into their own pockets to pay for expensive items of kit. Given the penny-pinching spirit of the times, there was always great excitement when a unit acquired a new item of ceremonial uniform – as its historian noted, after the sergeants of the South Alberta Regiment received scarlet sashes in the late 1920s, it "caused the parade to assume an added appearance of brilliancy, while the Armouries are scarcely large enough to accommodate the extra expansion carried on chests of aforesaid Sergeants."[2]

A major public event occurred in May 1925 when the Edmonton units – cavalry, artillery and infantry – with detachments from the Strathconas, RCNVR and RCMP, staged a Naval and Military Tournament in that city. The Strathcona B Squadron rode up from Calgary, taking five days to complete the journey, and arrived "covered in dust" to be greeted by the Edmonton garrison. The main event was a Friday evening show at the Edmonton arena which included a "combined arms demonstration" featuring cavalry, infantry, machinegunners, and artillery and a recreation of an aboriginal attack on a fur-trading fort, with members of the University of Alberta Canadian Officers Training Contingent playing the part of the warriors. The Strathconas performed a musical ride in scarlets and their vaulting team jumped over burning hurdles, "the flames of which surrounded both horse and rider."[3] On Saturday the Edmonton Regiment and Edmonton Fusiliers, assisted by 49th Battalion Pipe Band, carried out a ceremonial Changing of the Guard at the Edmonton Gardens while the 19th Dragoons demonstrated tent pegging – lifting tent pegs embedded in the ground with the point of the sword while at the gallop. The Military Tournament

was a popular but unusual event. More typical were occasions such as that which took place in Medicine Hat on 1 July 1927 when the South Alberta Regiment marched in the Diamond Jubilee Parade of Confederation, with the battalion band, "in their new Scarlet and Blue Uniforms" taking their place in the Parade."[4] The band made "a splendid showing and assisted further in the Programme during the Day and played for the Public Street Dance and Fireworks Display in the Evening."

Fancy dress was fun but it was no substitute for proper training, which suffered throughout the 1920s. The 15th Canadian Light Horse and the other Calgary units were fortunate that Sarcee Camp provided facilities, but limited funds restricted

Gunners at rest, Gleichen, Alberta, 1923
Formed at Gleichen, 22 Battery, Canadian Field Artillery, perpetuated a CEF unit raised in Ontario and is a direct predecessor of the modern South Alberta Light Horse. Here, three gunners from 22 Battery rest from drill on the prairie near Gleichen. Sergeant Frank Bates is on the left but the other men are unidentified. The weapon is an 18-pdr. (76 mm) gun, the standard British and Canadian fieldpiece from 1910 to 1939, which had a maximum range of 7,000 yards – not that the Alberta gunners got much live firing in the interwar period because government parsimony restricted ammunition expenditure. GLENBOW MUSEUM, NA-5613-34

the numbers who could attend (unless they went unpaid, as many did). Between 1921 and 1926, the 15th attended brigade or school camps at Sarcee with continually decreasing numbers – in 1921 they had 100 officers and men at camp; by 1924 they were allowed only 24 officers and men. The South Alberta Regiment, organized in 1921, was only permitted local headquarters training for the first seven years of its existence (although it was allowed a "school camp" at Sarcee with 15 officers and 50 men in 1927) and did not carry out its first battalion-level training at Sarcee until 1928. But even that had its drawbacks as the unit expended so much of its funds during that summer, it was forced to restrict local training in the autumn to three days for men who had been at Sarcee and twelve for those who had not.

The annual reports of the Department of National Defence from 1921 to 1926 bemoan the lack of funding for the militia which, on average, received between four and nine days paid training per year, with the artillery units getting the greatest number of days. Such was the parsimony of the government, however, that much of the gunners' range work was carried out using sub-calibre rounds, not the actual projectiles for their 18-pdr. guns and 4.5 inch howitzers. The artillery received instruction either at Sarcee from C Battery of the RCHA which annually came from its station at Winnipeg for this purpose, or went to Camp Hughes (later renamed Shilo Camp) in Manitoba. Often, funds did not permit the entire strength of a battery to attend these camps but only "firing parties" of selected officers and men. For most of the 1920s, artillery and infantry were funded for local headquarters training while the cavalry

Regiment at Killam which never mustered more than a weak platoon and appears to have become moribund about 1931. The 1st Alberta Mounted Rifles handed in their weapons and equipment in 1927 and were dormant until 1929, when they were revived while 93 Howitzer Battery at Fort Macleod existed in name only between 1927 and 1930. Ironically, the single largest unit in the province during the 1920s and much of the 1930s was the Canadian Officers Training Corps contingent at the University of Alberta in Edmonton.

Matters improved somewhat after 1926 when J.L. Ralston, a wartime battalion commander, became minister of defence. Ralston was able to get the defence budget gradually increased

South Alberta platoon, summer camp, 1920s
The uniforms, weapons and equipment are First World War vintage, as are the NCOs, but the South Alberta Regiment, created in the early 1920s, struggled on gamely throughout the interwar period. SALH ARCHIVES

utilized paid training days for "school camps," a sensible decision because most mounted units did not possess horses but only hired them for the camps. Sometimes this had dire results. In 1922 Lieutenant J. Fred Scott of the 15th Light Horse was riding a half-broken horse which, terrified by the noise of a band on inspection day, fell over on him, putting Scott out of action for several months with a crushed pelvis. This does not mean, however, that the mounted units did not train in the winter or that gunners and infantry did not train when funds ran out. They simply paraded without being paid and, in most units, the officers' pay and much of the enlisted men's pay was turned back to their unit to help keep it going.

Strengths were very low, an average of between 100-120 all ranks for cavalry regiments and infantry battalions, and 35-40 for artillery batteries, while brigade headquarters usually consisted of two men – the brigade commander and an orderly. The result was that some units began to fade away. The two regiments of Alberta Mounted Rifles, based in smaller rural communities, appear to have had trouble staying alive as did the North Alberta

and this led to the 1927 summer camp at Sarcee, the largest held in the 1920s, where the Edmonton and Calgary infantry units and the SAR received three or four days "school camp" training and the Alberta mounted units got a week. This was a particularly good camp for instruction as a rather large regular contingent of two Strathcona squadrons and two companies of the PPCLI was present, and even the fact that the camp was hit by the worst rain storm in years did not dampen the spirits of those in attendance. The following year, however, funding restrictions permitted only the Edmonton infantry units and the SAR to attend Sarcee and there were no summer camps in 1929. By that year, the commanding officer of the 2nd Alberta Mounted Rifles, which had experienced trouble throughout the decade maintaining its strength, admitted that his unit had more or less become moribund because of a lack of funds.[5] Overall, unit strengths continued to be weak – in 1929, excluding the university COTC contingent, there were 184 officers and 1,005 other ranks in the provincial militia.

Unfortunately, things were about to get worse.

"I can't hardly sleep for worrying": The Depression

In October 1929 the stock market crashed, creating the worst recession in modern history. The "Great Depression" hit western Canada particularly hard as its economy was based on the export of foodstuffs, raw materials and semi-processed goods to other countries, primarily the United States. A drastic decline in agricultural prices and the erection of high tariff barriers by most western nations combined to nearly ruin the province. The Alberta government was forced to bail out the provincial Wheat Pool, which could not sell stocks of wheat for which it had already paid farmers, while the farmers found they could not repay the loans taken out to grow crops they could no longer sell. Across Canada, all three levels of government struggled to cope with mass unemployment and the cost of providing relief or welfare. Mackenzie King's Liberal government was helpless in the face of the crisis and was replaced in the election of 1930 by Richard B. Bennett's Conservatives but Bennett had no better luck dealing with the disaster. At the lowest point, in 1931-1932, about 25% of all Canadians were unemployed and one in five were on some form of relief. An estimated 70,000 single men simply took "to the rails" and rode back and forth across the nation looking, mostly in vain, for employment.

The appalling figures do not reveal the true misery of the depression, misery that resounds in a letter written by an Alberta farm wife to Prime Minister Bennett in 1935. Confessing she felt "silly to write", the distraught woman informed Bennett:

> We are just one of many on relief and trying to keep our places without being starved out. Have a good half section, not bad buildings and trying to get a start without any money and 5 children all small. Have been trying to send 3 to school and live on $10.00 a month relief for everything, medicine meat flour butter scribblers. Haven't had any milk for 3 months but will have 2 cows fresh in March some time. Am nursing a 10 months old baby and doing all the work cooking washing mending on bread and potatoes some days. ......

> I am sure we can make a go of this place as its good land and doesn't blow if we would just manage until fall. Just had 70 acres in last year and the dry spell just caught it right along with the grasshoppers although we poisoned most of them there were hardly any left by fall. I can't hardly sleep for worrying about it. ......

> My husband doesn't know I am writing this letter but I just dont know what to do for money the children come to me about everything its the women + children who suffer in these terrible times, men don't notice things. ......

> Please help me by lending me some money and I will send you my engagement ring and wedding ring as security.[6]

To his credit, Bennett sent the woman $5 from his own pocket.

To fund relief, other government expenditures were slashed and, as always when it came to cuts, the defence budget was a prime target. By 1932 defence spending was 44% lower than it had been a decade earlier and for the next five years much of the militia's portion went to relief camps administered by the army which housed and fed single men while employing them on work projects. Between 1932 and 1936 the Department of National Defence assisted 170,000 men this way and although the camps were criticized for being an attempt to militarize Canada's youth, absolutely no attempt was made to turn these men into soldiers – the simple fact was that the army was the only organization in the country capable of moving, housing and feeding large numbers of people. The relief camps, however, took an undue portion of the already small defence budget and, in 1931, a general staff report warned that, if a greater proportion of that budget was not spent on matters of "direct defence," as opposed to the relief camps, "year by year the defensive capabilities of the present Militia Organization must diminish" as,

15th Canadian Light Horse, Sarcee, 1920s
With only 45 all ranks, this probably represents the total strength that the Light Horse were permitted to bring to camp (and be paid) that year. There is a variety of uniforms and many troopers appear to be wearing civilian white shirts. One item of uniform that is missing is the stetson as it was not commonly worn after 1919. SALH ARCHIVES

Officers of the 15th Canadian Light Horse, Sarcee, 1925

More uniformly attired than they were four years before (see photograph on page 179) the officers of the 15th Canadian Light Horse sit for a portrait at Sarcee Camp in the summer of 1925. Standing second from left is Captain J. Fred Scott, who would take over the Light Horse in 1935 and the Calgary Highlanders in 1939. Standing second from the right is Captain J.H. Beatty, who would win the Guides Challenge Cup in 1934. In the seated row are, second from the left, Major W.E. Tidball, who would assume command of the unit in 1926; Lieutenant-Colonel H.C.A. Hervey, commanding officer; and Major R.E.A. Lloyd, who would take command in 1930. GLENBOW MUSEUM, NA 2364-1

squadrons south to Red Deer. The 2nd Regiment of Alberta Mounted Rifles was re-titled the South Alberta Horse and stationed in the area south of Calgary while the 1st Regiment of Alberta Mounted Rifles, retitled the Alberta Mounted Rifles, was moved into the area north of Edmonton. For the future South Alberta Light Horse, a positive result of this change was that the Battle Honour, "North West Canada, 1885," earned by the Rocky Mountain Rangers during the Northwest Rebellion, was awarded to the newly-formed South Alberta Horse when that Honour received Royal approval in 1932.

Funding restrictions forced the staff of Military District 13 to alternate summer camps for infantry and cavalry units. In the summer of 1930, most of the mounted units were permitted only officer training at Sarcee, with the exception of the newly-revived 1st Alberta Mounted Rifles which managed to parade 100 all ranks and a Ford truck for "transport work" (rented for $8.00 a day from regimental, not government, pockets).[8] That same year the infantry

apart "from the obvious deficiencies in organization, the fighting power of existing units is steadily deteriorating, through increasing obsolescence in the arms, ammunition and equipment now available."[7] Despite such warnings, training funds were cut even further between 1930 and 1935.

One major change which took place at the outset of the Depression was a regrouping of the provincial mounted units in 1930-1931 to give them more rational recruiting areas to keep the rural units alive. The 15th Canadian Light Horse squadrons were concentrated in Calgary and the area north to Red Deer while the 19th Dragoons were concentrated in Edmonton with

were permitted a summer camp at Sarcee which involved all the provincial infantry – even the ailing North Alberta Regiment, which sent a platoon-size detachment. At this concentration for the first time since 1914, all the infantry units joined in a composite unit and, under the direction of PPCLI instructors, trained in battalion manoeuvres. The South Alberta Regiment managed to bring 14 officers and 101 other ranks to Sarcee that summer but it held no camps in the following two years. There were no summer camps for either the infantry or cavalry in 1931 and only unit camps or "school camps" for officers and NCOs at Sarcee in the summers of 1932 and 1933. In 1932 the 19th

Dragoons managed to hold a 10-day unit camp at Yekau Lake on the Stony Indian Reserve near Winterburn, about 14 miles from Edmonton, and, although they were only allowed funding for 65 all ranks and 50 horses, they were able to increase this to 76 all ranks for a 12-day period by voluntary contributions from those who did receive pay.

In July 1934 the 5th Mounted Brigade (at least the 15th Light Horse and 19th Dragoons) was allowed a 10-day brigade camp. The Light Horse were permitted an authorized camp strength of 85 all ranks but managed to bring 99 all ranks and an RMC cadet, 62 riding and 2 draft horses to Sarcee. It did this by paying the surplus officers and men with deductions "from all ranks pay and one day's pay from all officers, and reduction in horse pay from $1.25 allowed to 90 cents at day" while the advance party "contributed an additional half day each without pay."[9] The Light Horse B Squadron, 26 all ranks, marched to Sarcee from Innisfail, covering the distance of 95 miles in two days, and arrived at camp at 9 A.M. on the third day "with men and horses in good condition." They returned the same way thus "putting in three extra days in addition to the ten day period of authorized training." It was spirit like this that permitted militia units to survive the long years between 1919 and 1939.

The 1934 Mounted Brigade camp was marked by much socializing between regiments, many of whom had not been together for several years. Prime Minister Bennett, Honorary Colonel of the Calgary Highlanders, dined with them at Sarcee and there were a number of brigade and regimental dinners as well as a meeting of the Cavalry Association, the lobby group that represented the concerns of Canadian mounted units to the government. During these social events, Lieutenant-Colonel J.Fred Scott of the Light Horse grew increasingly weary of the insistence of Lieutenant-Colonel Norman Dingle, commanding the Calgary Highlanders, that his personal piper accompany him whenever Dingle made visits to other regiments, an insistence that was not only prejudicial to peace and tranquillity, but also caused undue excitement in the horse lines. Scott decided to retaliate and when he and Honorary Lieutenant-Colonel A.M. Berryman of the 15th paid a call on Dingle, they rode over to the Highlanders' lines with a "tiger skin under one saddle and a bearskin under the other, a Strathcona trumpeter leading the parade, four officers in blues carrying lances with pennants and, as outriders, two R.M.C. cadets in red blazers and white flannels." It was, as the historian of the 15th remarked, "truly a wonderful sight."[10] The 1934 camp was a highly successful event and, for the 15th Light Horse, marred only by the fact that the 19th Dragoons won the 5th Mounted Brigade Trophy "by a narrow margin."

This trophy was only one of a number of competitions in which militia units competed – there were district, brigade, regimental and inter-regimental tests for marksmanship, turn out, signalling, marching, drill, horsemanship and team jumping events. The 5th Mounted Brigade Trophy, instituted in 1927, was awarded in a hotly-contested competition that was run nine times until the outbreak of war in 1939 with the 19th Dragoons

Lieutenant-Colonel Maynard Patterson, South Alberta Regiment
Patterson commanded No. 11 Platoon of the 31st Battalion when it won the Canadian Corps platoon competition in 1917. He kept the trophy he received and used it as a trophy for the best platoon in the South Alberta Regiment, which he commanded from 1926 to 1936. Patterson is remembered today by Patterson Armoury in Medicine Hat, the home of the South Alberta Light Horse. SALH ARCHIVES

tying with the Alberta Mounted Rifles at three wins each, the 15th Light Horse receiving it twice and the South Alberta Horse once. In 1932 the 15th Light Horse won the newly-instituted Stockwell Challenge Cup, presented by the Cavalry Association to the militia mounted unit demonstrating the highest standard of skill in the reconnaissance role. Not to be outdone, their northern rivals, the 19th Dragoons, carried off the same trophy in 1938. The South Alberta Regiment had a very unique and precious trophy. Lieutenant Maynard E. Patterson, who had commanded 11 Platoon of the 31st Battalion when it won the competition for the best platoon in the Canadian Corps in 1917, presented the trophy shield he received to the SAR in 1921 as an annual prize for the best platoon in that unit. In 1926 Patterson was appointed to command the South Albertas and had the cheerful task of presenting the shield every year.

For the mounted units, however, the most coveted prize was the Guides Challenge Cup, which had been instituted in 1912 as an annual competition between members of the permanent force, the militia and the mounted police. The Challenge Cup was a test of horsemanship on a 15-mile course, which included six to ten jumps and a number of check points, each approximately two miles apart, which the contestants had to pass at a certain time. Competitors were judged by the time they took to complete the course, how they took the jumps, uniformity of pace and the state of their horses on arrival – they could be disqualified if their mounts exhibited spur marks. The Guides Challenge was not only difficult, it was also dangerous. Lieutenant-Colonel J. Fred Scott, who competed three times at Sarcee, recalled that he had seen three horses killed and two riders very seriously injured during Cup competitions.

The Guides Challenge was held eight times before it came to Alberta in 1928, with the winners usually coming from the Strathconas or the RCHA. The Cup was then run three times at Sarcee which gave the Alberta mounted units a chance to compete. In July 1928 Major J.H. Beatty of the 15th Light Horse came in second, the first time a militia officer had placed so high. At the next Alberta running in August 1930, Major Scott of the 15th placed second, behind an officer of the Strathconas, while the third place runner that year was Lieutenant Harry W. Foster of the Strathconas. Foster had been in the lead when, riding near the Elbow River, he saw two small children caught in some rapids and stopped to rescue them before carrying on to the end of the course. In August 1934, when the Cup was again staged at Sarcee, eleven riders entered, including three from the 15th Light Horse, among them Major J. Fred Scott, the second-in-command. Only four riders finished and the winner was Major J.H. Beatty of the 15th who beat officers from the Strathconas and RCHA, with Scott coming in fourth. This was the only occasion during the sixteen times the Guides Cup was run between 1912 and 1938 that a militia officer was triumphant, and it was a very proud moment for the 15th Light Horse.

"If it was worth carrying on": Surviving the grim years

Unfortunately, high spots like these were few and far between in the interwar period, particularly in the worst years of the depression. More typical was the experience of a squadron commander in a small Alberta town, recorded by Richard Cunniffe. From other information, we know that Cunniffe is describing C Squadron of the 2nd Regiment of Alberta Mounted Rifles at Nanton in 1930 or 1931 but his tale of woe would apply equally to any militia unit in any small Alberta community during the depression.

Early in June posters appeared in town asking for volunteers to attend a 12 day military camp at Sarcee early in July. Men wishing to enlist made their way to a small frame building (a former store) which was the headquarters and store room combined. There they were medically examined and sworn in as members of the local Militia unit. They were then issued with their uniforms, all wartime or pre-1914 manufacture, and certain articles of kit. In those happy days there was no mention of socks, boots, gloves or raincoat. The pay was $1.10 per day for the period of the camp and for the time travelling to and from the camp. A man providing his own horse was paid another dollar a day, and the horse was shod on the forefeet at government expense.

As few of the men had been in uniform before this, the veterans of last year's camp were kept busy showing them how to dress properly, how to roll puttees, how to pack the kit into kit bags, and how to handle the saddlery. Then, of course, there was the matter of polishing the articles of leather after a year of storage, and the polishing of buttons, badges and spurs. Times being what they were in the 1930s, some of the cavalrymen did not have sturdy boots, nor did they have ready cash to purchase cleaning material. This meant a cash advance from the unit's skimpy funds, and it was not unusual to see Militia soldiers wearing puttees with low shoes, brown or black.

Came the day for the Squadron to entrain for Calgary, and by this time the majority looked fairly respectable in

their uniform. On arrival at the big City the horses were off-loaded at the CPR platform on 9th Avenue at 6th Street SW, saddled up and then ridden along the dusty Avenue to the Strathcona stables on 14th Street, where they were watered. Then the long ride westward over the city streets, all gravelled or freshly tarred, and along the prairie trails to Sarcee Camp, seven miles away. The first few hours in camp were busy ones, as the NCO's instructed the soldiers how to wrap saddlery against the weather; to tie horses to a picket line; the art of filling a hay net; how to straighten a lop-sided bell tent. Then came an issue of mattress covers (palliasses) to be filled with straw, and two blankets and a rubber ground sheet made up the soldier's bedroll. Beds, mattresses, pillows and sheets were for the comfort of civilians, not for Canada's Militia soldiers. The move to camp was always made on a Saturday or a Sunday, and the weather was always hot, and that first ride from Mewata Armoury to Sarcee was always an ordeal – so, by evening most militiamen were glad to lie down on that rough, straw-filled bundle.

A few days of instruction on mounted drill from the instructional cadre of Lord Strathcona's Horse (RC) and the Squadron was reasonably ready to take part in squadron drill, later to be followed by regimental drill and manoeuvres. Be-

Colour party, 1st Alberta Mounted Rifles, 1920s
Although they tried bravely, the two regiments of Alberta Mounted Rifles fell behind the 15th Canadian Light Horse and 19th Alberta Dragoons when it came to maintaining their strength. By the late 1920s, both regiments were nearly "dormant." Here, a colour party of the 1st Alberta Mounted Rifles parades in Medicine Hat in the 1920s. Note that these men are all wearing the leather waist belt of the prewar Oliver equipment with its distinctive snake-clasp buckle but have added shoulder chains to their tunics. Also note that almost all of them are wearing First World War medals. One sergeant has a slightly different cap badge and it appears to be that of the 12th Manitoba Dragoons. SALH ARCHIVES

The South Alberta Regiment at Sarcee Camp, 1930
This was a big camp for the South Alberta Regiment, one of only two that they were permitted during their first decade of existence, and to mark the event, the entire regiment – all 100 or so officers and men including the band – assembled for a group photograph. Note the furled flags held by the signals section seated on the ground at the lower right. Judging by his summer khaki drill uniform, the NCO standing on the right is an instructor from the PPCLI. SALH ARCHIVES

cause of the good calibre of instruction from the Permanent Force Staff and the willingness to learn on the part of the militia soldier, the Militia units in camp were transformed within a very few days from (in some cases) an orderly mob into a fairly smoothly operating organization.

At camp other items of kit were issued to the soldier and these included a khaki shirt, khaki drill breeches, and to some units a straw hat. The latter was worn to distinguish friend from foe during the two day, and overnight, battle on the Sarcee Indian Reserve. Each unit provided its own cooks and it was soon proved that good cooks and good weather made a good camp. The ten or twelve days in camp went quickly because the soldiers were kept very busy. The daily training periods; the normal camp fatigues; caring for the horses; instruction on the rifle range; the overnight battles; a Church parade; a sports afternoon; a day at the Calgary Stampede, sometime riding in the military section, turning in kit to the QM stores; packing up for the return to the home station. ......

When the Squadron arrived back at its home station the men turned in their uniforms and saddlery, and were paid for the time spent at camp, less any monies previously advanced to them. In many Militia units this was the only cash payment the militia soldier received. In theory he received pay for every parade he attended during the year, but in practice that pay usually went into a regimental fund so that the unit could meet its expenses. After being paid, most of the erstwhile soldiers just disappeared from the locality because many of them were part of that floating population of the "hungry thirties" which was always on the move looking for employment. The following summer, when the squadron again prepared for camp, a new batch of men would likely answer the call for recruits and the Officer Commanding would be very thankful if a few of last year's seasoned veterans would show up.[11]

(Above) **Tactical scheme, 1930s**
Although it had become clear to most cavalry officers that the time of the horse in war was drawing to an end, they continued to train in mounted tactics throughout the interwar period – if for no other reason than the government was not going to spend the money to mechanize them. Here, the 15th Canadian Light Horse engages in a tactical scheme at summer camp, but restricted funding made these exercises much smaller than they had been prior to 1914. SALH ARCHIVES

Having got his squadron through summer camp, the squadron commander would then contemplate

the Winter training period. After his experiences last Winter (and the Winter before, and the Winter before that) he likely wondered if it was worth carrying on. He had one small building, most of which was taken up as storage for rifles, clothing and saddlery. The other portion had a very small training area, and a smaller office. He had Lee-Enfield rifles and a wartime Lewis machine gun, but no local rifle range where they could be used with safety. There was no heat in the building except a small gas radiant in the store room. A certain amount of basic drill and training was carried out in the lecture room, and there was instruction on map using, military law and similar subjects requiring little equipment. The attendance at the Winter parades varied according to weather conditions and the local employment situation. On a stormy evening the Squadron parade might consist of two officers, three N.C.O.'s and perhaps two troopers. Some of the men lived in the country and a few depended on the saddle horse for transportation. A good turnout sometimes brought the attendance up to about a dozen all ranks.

In the face of government apathy and public indifference, it required not only ingenuity but private funding to keep a militia unit alive. The officers in most units turned back their pay to their units and many of the enlisted men did the same. A captain in the service corps recalled that, during the 1930s, he used to provide streetcar fare out of his own pocket to get his man to parades, and went so far as to buy "a set of corsets for my Sergeant-Major's wife so she could go to a regimental dance" because "I had a good Sergeant-Major."[12] The Edmonton Fusiliers were particularly stringent about paying their personnel – in 1931 they were allotted eight paid training days for each enlisted man but, before a man could receive pay for those days, he had to attend 25 unpaid evening parades. The following year, however, on learning that there was no money to pay for an escort to the lieutenant-governor to open the provincial legislature, the Fusiliers to a man "volunteered to provide one without expense to the public."[13] The Calgary Regiment staged an annual masquerade ball, which was not only popular with the unit's junior ranks and civilians, but helped to fund the unit's training activities. Throughout the early 1930s, the annual reports of the Department of National Defence, while stressing that militia training funds had been cut back, often added the cheerful – and fatal – comment that a "large number of units, however, carried out additional training for which no pay was drawn."[14] Given the situation, it is small wonder that a common saying in the Alberta militia during the interwar period was: "We Stand on Guard for Thee (At Our Own Expense)."[15]

And yet, notwithstanding the problems, these were the same militiamen praised by the officers and NCOs of Lord Strathcona's Horse who were pleasantly surprised at

(Above) **Inspecting officers, Sarcee, 1930s**
One positive development during the interwar period was the stationing of regular troops in Military District 13. Lord Strathcona's Horse trained the mounted militia units and Princess Patricia's Canadian Light Infantry trained the infantry units. Here, inspecting staff officers (recognizable by the scarlet gorget patches on their lapels), accompanied by training officers from the Strathconas (wearing light khaki drill summer uniforms) watch the militia cavalry go through their paces. SALH ARCHIVES

(Below) **Brigade March Past, Sarcee, 1930s**
The 5th Mounted Brigade marches past at camp, probably Sarcee in 1934 or 1935. Such was the result of government cutbacks that the four-regiment brigade can only muster about as many men as a single regiment would have brought to camp before 1914. SALH ARCHIVES

Horsemen at play – tent-pegging

Tent-pegging, picking up an embedded wooded peg with the tip of the sword at a gallop, was a cavalry tradition and a useful training method in horsemanship and swordsmanship. The unit on display here is the Princess Louise Dragoon Guards from Ottawa but the Alberta cavalry also carried out public demonstrations of this sport. COURTESY RCAC ASSOCIATION

what can be done with these units, consisting as they do of a very large proportion of green men and certainly all green horses. After the first few days they are carrying out regimental drill and doing tactical exercises in a manner that reflects credit on all concerned. And this with only an occasional guiding touch from the Permanent Force instructors to the units. Certainly their keenness and indifference to the hardships and discomforts that a few days rain can produce in Sarcee is a standard that even regular troops might envy.[16]

In their turn, the Alberta mounted units were just as complimentary about the Strathcona instructors who "were all we could wish for, they knew their work and their method of imparting what they had to teach was of a high order."[17]

"The proper Cavalry spirit was shown": The social side of the militia

With conditions so bad and pay so small or non-existent, the question is why anyone would have joined the militia in the 1920s and 1930s? Perhaps the best answer is that there are always Canadians who, despite all the frustrations involved, believe firmly in service to their country even if the government of that country seemed inclined to ignore its own military forces. Another answer is that the militia provided a well-organized local club and, during the depression, a ready-made support network for its members. The social aspect of the militia cannot be over-emphasized and, although all units took their training seriously, they always took care to have a little fun on the way.

This was true from the first days of a unit's organization. Consider the South Alberta Regiment. The SAR held its first training parade on 4 January 1922 and its first regimental "smoker" just nine days later. The unit staged its first annual dance in December 1923, with all proceeds going to the regimental hockey team because sports were as important to the SAR as they were to other militia units. The South Albertas paraded three evenings (and were lucky if they were paid for one of these evenings) a week during the fall and winter training seasons, one evening being devoted entirely to sports. It took some time for the SAR to work up to more elaborate social events but, on 11 November 1929, the officers held their first "Armistice Military Ball" at the Independent Order of Foresters Hall on 3rd Street in the Hat. More than 150 couples attended and the "Khaki Uniforms, Mess Blues and Dress Suits and Gorgeous dresses of the Ladies made one of the most spectacular, enjoyable and successful dances ever staged in Medicine Hat."[18] In the 1930s, parade nights at the SAR were usually followed by a beer in the one of the messes and a few rounds on the horseshoe pitch, which the unit laid out beside its little armoury on Connaught Avenue.

The first six commanding officers

Taken at Sarcee Camp, probably about 1934, this interesting photograph shows the first six commanding officers of the 15th Light Horse. From left to right: Colonel James Walker (1905-1910); Colonel George Macdonald (1910-1920); Colonel E.G. May (1930-1935); Colonel A.G. Wolley-Dod (1920-1923); Colonel H.C.A. Hervey (1923-1926); and Colonel W.E. Tidball (1926-1930). James Walker is still wearing an old-style uniform with rank on the cuffs, but by this time he had been associated with the military in Alberta for more than half a century. GLENBOW MUSEUM, NA-92-3

Calgary Highlanders mess dinner, Sarcee Camp, 1935
The Highlanders were always a rather sociable lot and contributed to the off-duty entertainment at summer camp during the interwar period. In this group shot of the guests at their 1935 mess dinner are some of the leading military and business personalities of Calgary. GLENBOW MUSEUM, NA-3316-68

The social side of the militia was also important because it attracted recruits. An officer of the Calgary Regiment summed up the problems facing his unit in the 1920s and 1930s:

Before the Great War there was the glamour of full dress kit and the absence, in many centres, of other attractions, but the problem of creating and retaining interest in the Militia is now much greater. Those to whom the Militia had the greatest appeal had just finished a period of active service and the younger generation, steeped in years of war news, and the dash and excitement of an actual campaign, were ready to turn away from anything that smacked of the military. Then too, a much larger part of the civilian population with whom the wish was reality, were convinced that some miracle had happened with the Armistice [of November 1918] and that the Great War had purged the world of any thoughts of aggression and there was no further need for a defence force in Canada. Add to that the radio, the moving picture show and the dance hall as a counter attraction and you get some conception of the difficulty facing the Militia officer not only to get recruits but to retain them once they had enlisted.[19]

In terms of social functions, as in so much else, regiments in larger centres enjoyed advantages not shared by those in smaller communities. Every unit had its annual officers' mess dinner usually held on a day important in its history. The 15th Canadian Light Horse staged their annual event at the Garrison Officers' Mess at Mewata Armoury in Calgary and the dinner held on 12 December 1935 was a most memorable one. It had a "menu card in the shape of a horse-shoe done in red and gold with the regimental crest embossed in blue and a regulation Nose-Bag, in miniature for almond cases was one of the high lights of the dinner and greatly appreciated by all present."[20] Through the kindness of Honorary Lieutenant-Colonel A.M. Berryman, the vice-president of a Calgary metal manufacturing company,

"Hungarian Partridge was provided by those gentlemen" and "forty-five birds were thoroughly enjoyed." That elaborate menu card tells us that those present, including the commander of the 5th Mounted Brigade and the District Commander, sat down to dine on little gherkins, stuffed olives, ripe olives, wee onions, bouillon, filet of sole, the partridge augmented with wild grape jelly, Brussel sprouts, asparagus tips, creamed potatoes and mushroom patties plus Roquefort cheese, all washed down with coffee and, it appears, not a little wine. Following the formalities and the toasts to His Majesty King George V and the Light Horse's allied regiment, the 15th/19th King's Hussars, the commanding officer, Lieutenant-Colonel J.Fred Scott

called upon our Mr. Win [Wynn] Lasher for a song and he gave us the "Bold King's Hussar." This song was sent to us by our allied regiment. This was followed by another song and also recitation by Mr. A.H. Stewart, and thus the evening was spent in song and story.

The proper Cavalry spirit was shown all through the evening and it was particularly noticed that one certain Cavalry Officer of the Permanent Force of Welch descent (Major Powell) [Major F.C. Powell, MC, DCM, of Lord Strathcona's Horse] was actually bursting forth into song. This was an unheard of thing as the above mentioned gentleman has never been known to let himself go to that extent and by that one instance alone, all present knew that the dinner was a success.[21]

The 19th Dragoons, both officers and enlisted men, conducted a very active social life in the Connaught Armoury in Edmonton. In the officers' mess, the presence of Major Harcus ("Jock") Strachan, VC, MC – a very lively fellow it seems – resulted in some exciting times. Strachan introduced Mess Polo to the Dragoons which, although very popular, had to be banned by the Mess Committee who, while agreeing that it was "a rip-

Cavalry escort to the Prince of Wales, 1919

When the Prince of Wales visited Calgary in 1919, the military provided a ceremonial escort. As most of the militia units were dormant or reorganizing, the war having only ended months before, the escort was provided by the Strathconas who are seen here. The officer in the lead, however, is wearing the badges of the 15th Light Horse. GLENBOW MUSEUM, NB-16-13

Opening of the Legislative Assembly, 1929

As the cavalry unit in the provincial capital the 19th Dragoons usually provided ceremonial troops for official occasions. Here they are seen on a very cold day, waiting for the politicians to get on with it. The dragoons have turned up the collars of their coats for protection from the wind and Dobbin's opinion of the business can be seen on the ground under the escort commander. GLENBOW MUSEUM ND-3-5045(F)

"The Imperials": The 15th/19th Hussars, 1936

The 15th Light Horse and 19th Dragoons had separate alliances with the 15/19th Hussars, a British regiment with a long, distinguished record. In 1936 the Hussars sent their Canadian brothers a photograph of their mounted troop which took part in the Silver Jubilee celebrations of King George V. It must have made the Alberta cavalry feel really good. SALH ARCHIVES

(Below) Military Tournament parade, Edmonton, 1925

One of the largest public events held during the interwar period was the Royal Naval and Military Tournament staged by regular and militia units in Edmonton in May 1925. Here, a squadron of Lord Strathcona's Horse, who had ridden their horses to Edmonton from Calgary, pass the reviewing stand followed by the 19th Dragoons (in the left foreground).

GLENBOW MUSEUM, NC-6-11672A

(Right) Regimental Sergeant-Major Lawrence Blain, 19th Alberta Dragoons, 1939

RSM Blain, one of the men responsible for the creation and training of the Dragoon Royal Escort, poses beside the Connaught Armoury dressed in the escort uniform. He is perfectly turned out but that is only to be expected from the RSM and even Dobbin seems impressed by the splendour of his rider. The tunic and helmet are from the 6th Inniskilling Dragoon Guards and the RSM is armed with Pattern 1908 sword and equipped with a Pattern 1902 bridle. COURTESY, COLIN MICHAUD

(Left) The gunners were there too

78 Battery, Canadian Field Artillery, takes part in the Diamond Jubilee of Confederation on 1 July 1927 by parading through Red Deer. The original caption to this photo states that their guns are "horse and tractor drawn" and, sure enough, a magnifying glass reveals that at the end of the column is a civilian tractor pulling an 18-pounder. COURTESY, HARRY QUARTON

Church parade, Sarcee Camp, 1930s

The army was always concerned about the spiritual well-being of its men and church parades were compulsory, both for Catholics and Protestants (which included every other faith). This was all very well but ministers, having a captive congregation, did tend to drone on… and on. This was not peculiar to the Canadian army – Lieutenant-Colonel George S. Patton of the U.S. Cavalry restricted his regimental chaplain's sermons to a maximum of ten minutes and did so by sitting directly in front of the pulpit every Sunday and prominently displaying a very large pocket watch. It wasn't subtle but it kept sermons short and to the point. SALH ARCHIVES

RSM and NCOs of the 19th Alberta Dragoons, late 1930s

Regimental Sergeant-Major Harry Hind and the NCOs of the Dragoons pose for their portrait in the late 1930s. By now, many of the First War veterans had left the ranks of the militia and only four of the fourteen men in this photo are wearing medals or ribbons from that conflict. COURTESY, HARRY QUARTON

snorting game," regretfully concluded that, because of the breakage of chairs, and "owing to the present financial condition of the Mess we find that the up-keep in mounts is much too costly and while we hated to do it, the committee found it necessary to rule that the game be placed on the "retired list" together with "The Mountaineers" etc. etc."[22] Strachan was also very adept at the art of climbing tent poles and, at summer camps, liked to challenge regular officers from the district staff to compete in this difficult sport. One colonel, who responded to Strachan's invitation, "succeeded in passing the half way mark but got in difficulties when he reached the wire entanglements on which the lights were hung, the pole bent to such an angle and the tent shook to such an extent that the genial Colonel was forced to abandon his climb."[23]

The Dragoons' officers' mess produced an annual newsletter, "Sword Thrusts," which recorded some of the brighter witticisms brought forth after parade nights, including such examples as the following:

LIEUT. MARSDEN (first night in camp 1923): "I say, what is that bugler fellow blowing for?"
SENTRY: "That is for last post, Sir."
LIEUT. MARSDEN: "Good gracious is there one as late as this? You might just run along and see whether there are any letters for me?"[24]

Passing on as quickly as possible from Dragoon wit, it should be noted that all units held less formal events including ladies' dinners, dances and group outings. On 17 March 1934, we learn that the Light Horse chartered a bus to go from Calgary to Innisfail to attend the B Squadron dance and "Major J.G.F. Scott and Major J.H. Beatty, Lieut. and Mrs. Lasher, Lieut. and Mrs. Burton and approximately forty other ranks comprised the party. The cost of the transportation was borne by the Regiment with the exception of a charge of $1.00 in the case of each lady taken by any of the party."[25] A year later, we read that Headquarters and C Squadron of the Light Horse "attended the theatre to see the picture 'Lest We Forget.' They paraded at the corner of Ninth Avenue and Second Street West and marched to the Palace Theatre. There were 31 other ranks present who attended at the expense of the regiment."[26] The 15th Light Horse also had an active polo team which competed against rival military and civilian teams.

The South Alberta Regiment, which eased into the social side of things a bit more slowly, soon caught up and were soon staging some impressive events such at the 1936 Armistice Ball:

Soft pastel shades of pink and green formed the decorative motif of the smartly-arranged Military Ball which was held last evening at the Third Street Armouries. Always one of the chief events of the social season, last night's celebration of the Peace of eighteen years ago fully equalled all established precedent. Colored lights and streamers added their gay attractions to the dancehall, while the lounge boasted more practical appeal of chesterfield and easy chairs, quantities of spray 'mums and ferns continuing the color scheme. Snappy music by the Granada Serenaders, under the direction of Ronnie Sadler, kept the dancers on their toes until the wee small hours of the morning. A delicious midnight supper was served in the lower hall, nearly a score of tables being laid. The soft light from pink and green tapers gleamed on silver and cut glass, snowy napery and gracefully arranged flowers, as well as on the pink and green streamers and other decorations.[27]

"An interesting experiment was carried out": Things begin to improve, 1935-1938

In the depression, any form of entertainment that provided a few hours of escape from the grim realities of daily life was much appreciated. The national economy reached its lowest point in 1933 and then began a sluggish but uneven recovery although agriculture, hampered by low prices, high tariffs and a lack of cash, continued to limp along at a fraction of its pre-1929 state. The perilous condition of the western farmers affected the small towns that depended on them for their livelihood but things were no better in the larger centres where only soup kitchens and relief rolls kept many alive. Ironically, despite the depressed state of agriculture, the number of farmers in Alberta actually rose during the 1930s as many fled the cities to the rural areas. But even as the economy began slowly to recover, it seemed in western Canada that nature had decided to intervene against man. The winter of 1935-1936, one of the coldest on record, was followed by the hottest summer in thirty years which caused a drought so severe that crops withered in the field and the soil itself was blown away by unusually strong winds, laying waste the entire southern part of the province and leaving livestock in a desperate state. In the late summer the remaining crops were devoured by a plague of grasshoppers, followed by infestations of rust and sawflies. But there was no rain and when the true disaster year of 1937 arrived, a combination of wind, grasshoppers and drought blunted any attempts to grow crops and six million acres of once prosperous farmland in the Palliser Triangle became a near desert. When the rains finally came that autumn, the fields miraculously turned green – with an abundant crop of weeds.

Conditions such as these led people around the world to turn to political parties and leaders that appeared to offer a solution – workable or not – for their problems. France voted Socialist, the United States brought in Franklin D. Roosevelt's Democrats who promised a "New Deal" to the common citizen. Closer to home, Bennett's Conservative government was defeated in 1935 by King's Liberals and almost every provincial government in Canada changed during the 1930s. Neighbouring Saskatchewan supported the Co-operative Commonwealth Federation, a socialist party, Quebec adopted the *Union Nationale* and even Ontario went so far left as to vote in the Liberals. For their part Albertans turned to William C. Aberhart, a man who promised salvation in the form of a radical new economic theory.

In the early 1930s, Aberhart, a school teacher and a radio evangelist with a huge following in Alberta, became convinced that "social credit," an obscure economic doctrine developed by Major H.C. Douglas, an English engineer, was the solution to the depression. He tried to interest the UFA government in his theories and the government made a study of social credit but concluded it was unworkable. Rebuffed, in late 1934 Aberhart entered the political field and used his weekly radio broadcasts to spread a new gospel of political and economic change based on social credit. Aberhart was always short on details of just how it would work but loud in his conviction that it would work and that it would bring an end to the horrors of the depression. His most effective tactic, however, was his promise that, if elected, every adult in Alberta would receive $25 a month from the government in "social credit script." This was all desperate people needed to know and they seized on it – as one hardscrabble Alberta farmer put it:

You can strip down the appeal of Social Credit to the $25 a month. All of us farmers were in desperate straits. Here was William Aberhart promising $25 a month, and he was a minister of the gospel. I asked him about that $25 after one of his meetings, and he told me I must have faith.[28]

Voter turnout for the August 1935 provincial election was phenomenal and when it was over, the UFA had disappeared and Social Credit held 57 seats against 5 for the Liberals and 2 for the Conservatives. Aberhart's attempts, however, to introduce his new economic theories by legislation were declared *ultra vires* by the Supreme Court of Canada and, after a few rather shaky years, the Social Credit government settled down to become a very competent administration, guided by the capable hands of Ernest C. Manning, Aberhart's chief subordinate.

In Ottawa that same year, the new Liberal administration of Mackenzie King was faced not only with domestic problems but also by an increasingly dangerous international situation. For more than fifteen years, Canadians had felt that, because they "wished and hoped for peace, they seemed to believe that peace would endure. They showed no realization of the probable consequences if war did come and found their country unprepared."[29] These comfortable beliefs were shaken during the 1930s. In 1931 a militant Japan invaded Manchuria, initiating a conflict that, six years later, broadened into a full-scale war with China. In 1933, Adolf Hitler seized power in Germany and began a vigorous campaign of re-armament and an aggressive for-

South Alberta Armoury, Medicine Hat
Although constructed originally as a firehall, this structure served as the armoury for the South Alberta Regiment throughout the 1930s. SALH ARCHIVES

eign policy to regain German territory stripped from that nation by the 1919 Treaty of Versailles that had ended the First World War. In 1935 Italy, under the control of Benito Mussolini's Fascist dictatorship, invaded Ethiopia and used modern aircraft and poison gas against a backward nation and its peoples. The future was becoming darker and, shortly after the Liberals were elected, the Chief of the General Staff, Major-General A.G.L. McNaughton, warned the government that Canada's military forces were in a pitiful state:

> As regards reserves of equipment and ammunition, the matter is shortly disposed of. Except as regards rifles, and rifle ammunition, partial stocks of which were inherited from the Great War – there are none. ......
>
> (i) There is not a single modern anti-aircraft gun of any sort in Canada.
>
> (ii) The stocks of field gun ammunition on hand represent 90 minutes' fire at normal rates for the field guns inherited from the Great War and which are now obsolescent. ......
>
> (iv) About the only article of which stocks are held is harness, and this is practically useless. The composition of a modern land force will include very little horsed transport.[30]

Even Mackenzie King, a cautious politician determined to remain free from foreign entanglements, realized that something had to be done and, beginning in 1936, Canada slowly began to re-arm.

As part of a belated programme of increased defence spending, the army went through a major reorganization. This change was carried out under the precepts of Defence Scheme No. 3 drafted in 1932 which called, in the event of a future war, for the creation of a modern expeditionary force of seven divisions for service overseas. Using this as a blueprint, McNaughton undertook to reduce the unwieldy fifteen divisions of the army into a more manageable and balanced force. Surplus units, including 23 cavalry regiments, 51 infantry battalions and 12 machine-gun battalions, were given new roles, amalgamated or disbanded. The changes fell most heavily on mounted, infantry and machinegun units while the artillery and engineers were increased in strength. Some of the mounted units were designated as armoured car regiments and six infantry regiments were converted to tank battalions.

These changes rippled through Military District 13. The North Alberta Regiment, which had never truly caught hold, was disbanded. The 15th Canadian Light Horse was amalgamated with the South Alberta Horse in February 1936 to form the 15th Alberta Light Horse while the 19th Alberta Dragoons were joined with the Alberta Mounted Rifles and converted to an armoured car regiment. The Calgary Regiment was retitled a tank battalion, becoming the Calgary Regiment (Tank), and the Edmonton Fusiliers, with the disappearance of the 13th Machine Gun Brigade, were converted to the Edmonton Fusiliers (Machine Gun). Finally, a new field battery was added to each of the three Alberta field artillery brigades.

Many militiamen in Alberta, particularly cavalrymen, did not welcome these changes but did applaud the increased attention paid by the government to its armed forces and the increased spending. The army budgets for 1935 to 1937 were nearly twice what they had been just three years earlier. In 1936, for the first time in almost a decade, there was a full summer camp at Sarcee. The 19th Dragoons, proud but somewhat unsure of their new status, arrived at camp with no horses but a collection of 72 privately-owned motor vehicles with which they attempted to carry out training. The instructors from the Strathconas, themselves still riding horses, commented that

> Apropos mechanization, an interesting experiment was carried out this year with … the Alberta Dragoons … a Cavalry Motor Regiment. Of course the Department (of Militia) had not sufficient funds to equip them with a standardized vehicle, so we found our friends, the 19th, with a heterogeneous mass of gas buggies of all descriptions and vintages. However, the equipment was interesting, if only to prove that energetically used motor cars cover a deal more territory than the horsed variety, even over Alberta roads.[31]

The 15th Alberta Light Horse, however, weren't about to let the Dragoons forget they were no longer true cavalry and, since the camp of 1936 was a highly social one,

> On the last night several of the junior and senior officers of the Regiment borrowed a decrepit Ford car, and after enticing Col. Oliver, O.C. of the 19th A.D. from the guests he was entertaining in his tent, the car was placed in the centre of his tent. This was in honour of the mechanization of the 19th A.D.

Col. Oliver accepted the tribute in the spirit in which it was offered and later drove the car around the Camp with the Officers of this Regiment [15th Light Horse] supplying the motive power.[32]

The army was changing and one event that marked the passing of an era was the death of Alberta's foremost horse soldier, 86-year-old Colonel James Walker, in March 1936. The founding father of the Alberta militia and the first commanding officer of the 15th Light Horse, Walker's long and productive life encompassed much of the history of the province up to that point and it was only right that he was buried with full military honours, including detachments from every regular and militia unit in Calgary. The Calgary Highlanders Pipe Band played during the march to the cemetery, the buglers of Lord Strathcona's Horse sounded the "Last Post" at the grave site and the 15th Light Horse provided the firing party. At the time of his death, James Walker was the last surviving officer of the NWMP force that had marched west in 1874.*

During the late 1930s the strength of the Alberta militia increased – in 1930 it was 1,384 all ranks; by 1939 it had grown to 3,004 all ranks. In 1936, for the first time in nearly fifteen years, a military unit outnumbered the COTC at the University of Alberta. This was the 19th Dragoons who paraded 257 all ranks that year and thereafter until the outbreak of war, vied with the 15th Light Horse for the greatest number of men in uniform. Training also improved. Major camps were held at Sarcee in 1937 and 1938 and, for the first time in years, all units in the province received instruction. An innovation at these camps was the presence of 113 (Fighter) Squadron, RCAF (Militia), the new auxiliary squadron at Calgary, which flew antique Armstrong Whitworth Atlas biplanes, dropped "bombs" consisting of paper bags full of flour, carried out aerial observation and communicated with ground troops by throwing overboard messages in canisters with streamers attached. This appears to have been about the most advanced aspect of the training in the late 1930s and much of it still had a distinctly First War flavour. At camp in 1938 a squadron of the Strathconas gave a demonstration of a cavalry charge by attacking a trench defended by the South Alberta Regiment and the umpires ruled that Strathconas "won" – memories of Iwuy in 1918 seem to have dimmed. On the other hand, Lieuten-

ant-Colonel Scott of the 15th Alberta Light Horse was angered when a regular officer lecturing at the Alberta Military Institute in Calgary told his largely cavalry audience that: "You horse lovers should be first to see what the machine gun and barbed wire will mean to the cavalry charge."[33]

It was all good fun, if somewhat unreal, but during these same years Germany re-occupied the Rhineland and annexed Austria, while a vicious civil war in Spain gave Germany, Italy and the Soviet Union the opportunity to try out new weapons and tactics. Although many Canadians still steadfastly refused to believe it, another war was coming and some nations were actively preparing for it.

Preparing for war in Canada and abroad, 1919-1939

Germany was foremost among these nations. Prohibited by the Treaty of Versailles from possessing a large army, a general staff, tanks and modern aircraft, the German army devoted the 1920s to a diligent study of the operations of the First World War in an effort to be ready for a future conflict. Occupying a central position in Europe with potential enemies on all sides, the German solution was to emphasize manoeuvre and mobility with the aim of quickly destroying enemy forces in the field. The Germans, who had suffered from the use of tanks on the Western Front in 1916-1918, were aware of the strengths and weaknesses of that weapon system and were not convinced by the arguments of popular interwar armour theorists, such as J.F.C. Fuller and B.H. Liddell-Hart, that future armies would consist of vast numbers of tanks that would simply overrun their opponents. Instead a group of intelligent German officers critically examined the tank as a weapon system – among them a *Leutnant* Ernst Volckheim who had led the armoured counterattack at Iwuy in October 1918 – and decided that it was basically a highly

---

* James Walker's accomplishments and his contributions to Calgary and Alberta extended far beyond his military activities. He was instrumental in starting commercial ranching, lumbering and mining in the province. He was the first justice of the peace for Calgary, one of the first school trustees, a founding father of the Calgary Exhibition, which evolved into the Calgary Stampede, and very active in school Cadet Corps and the Boy Scout movement. Walker was also involved in agricultural research and was one of the founders of the Alberta Historical Society. In 1974, Calgary's centennial, James Walker was chosen as the city's "Citizen of the Century" and his home on the banks of the Bow River is now a provincial historical site.

The Connaught Armoury, Edmonton
Constructed in 1911 and one of the oldest armouries in Alberta, this structure was named after the Duke of Connaught, the governor-general. The Connaught Armoury was the home of the 19th Dragoons from 1911 until 1965.

Tankette, or toy tank

In 1933, Canada acquired its first modern armoured vehicles when a number of Carden-Loyd Mark VIA machinegun carriers were purchased for the regular infantry regiments. These little machines were four feet high, weighed 1.5 tons, had a maximum ⅓ inch of armour and their 4-cylinder gasoline engines could propel them at a top speed of 28 mph. They were better than nothing – but not by much. COURTESY, ROYAL CANADIAN HUSSARS MUSEUM

mobile gun platform that could be employed in a number of different roles. They concluded that the key to success in modern war would be a formation which, based on the tenets of "combined arms" tactics – with armour, artillery and infantry acting in concert – would not only be able to break through enemy defences but be able to pursue and destroy a beaten enemy. The Germans therefore created what they called the panzer or armoured division, a balanced mobile formation in which all arms and services were motorized and which was commanded by an extensive radio network. The theoretical aspects of this new entity were firmly in place in 1933 when Hitler came to power and began a programme of rearmament. The first panzer division was created in 1935 and valuable lessons were about its deployment were learned during the re-occupation of the Rhineland in 1936 and the annexation of Austria in 1938.

With the possible exception of the Soviet Union, no other major army made such a rigorous study of the First World War nor came up with quite the same advanced doctrine. Britain, which had been the pioneer in the development of the tank, gave up her lead in the 1920s and when she began to re-arm in the late 1930s, fell under the sway of a very dangerous belief that there should be different tanks for different purposes. Slow, heavily-armoured but lightly armed tanks would support the infantry, lightly-armoured but more heavily armed cruiser tanks would engage enemy armour and pursue a beaten enemy, while small light tanks, with thin armour and machineguns, would be used for reconnaissance work. Light tanks were issued to the cavalry, cruiser vehicles were grouped in tank-heavy armoured brigades, and infantry tanks were distributed in small "penny packets" among the infantry divisions.

Armour doctrine in France and the United States, although

not identical, was similar but thinking was different in the Soviet Union, which actually provided a secret test centre at Kazan for German armour development in the 1920s. The brilliant Marshal Michael Tukhachevsky, chief of staff of the Red Army, conceived an operational doctrine he called "deep battle" which called for the creation of powerful mechanized corps, with more than a thousand tanks each, to punch a narrow hole through enemy defences and then use mobility to strike deep into the enemy's rear. Unlike the German armour theorists, Tukhachevsky never satisfactorily solved the problem of how to command such formations and, in any case, he was purged by Stalin in 1938, along with more than half the senior commanders in the Red Army – a drastic step that came close to irreparably damaging Russian military capability.

In Canada these developments were only dimly perceived by those officers who seriously studied military journals. Even the most diehard Canadian cavalryman knew that the time of the horse was drawing to a close and that mechanization was the future but because it was expensive, it was not on the Canadian agenda in the interwar period. The cavalry units were content to carry on with mounted training, although many militia units did begin to employ motorized transport (the cost borne out of their own pockets) for logistical purposes on lengthy schemes. Attempts were made to mechanize the regular artillery batteries of the RCHA, small machinegun carriers (tankettes) were purchased for the regular machinegun battalion and later given to the three regular infantry battalions, and two prototype armoured cars constructed by Ford and General Motors were tested in the mid-1930s.

The 1936 reorganization brought about a quickening in the pace of change. The Canadian Armoured Fighting Vehicle School was created at Camp Borden in Ontario in 1938 under the energetic Major Frank F. Worthington, who had served in the Royal Tank Corps during the First World War, to train the personnel of the six new tank battalions. Equipped with a varied and rather cranky collection of obsolete vehicles, this school was able to provide the fundamentals of basic instruction in driving and maintenance. Since there were no vehicles for the newly-designated tank battalions – although they received the black berets of the tank corps – some units resorted to constructing their own prototypes to get some experience in their deployment.* The Calgary Regiment, for example made four "mock

---

* The black beret was adopted by the Royal Tank Corps in 1917 as a useful item of headgear to wear in the crowded and dirty interiors of early armoured vehicles. The original black beret was based on a pattern popular in girls' boarding schools in England before the war.

tanks" by fitting a canvas superstructure on Ford Model A cars. These developments, of course, were at the lower level – in terms of doctrine, the Canadian army followed the British lead although two young officers, Major E.L.M. Burns of the engineers and Captain G.G. Simonds of the artillery, engaged in a debate in the pages of the *Canadian Defence Quarterly* over the proper organization and utilization of armour. Burns's opinion was that armour should not be spread among all divisions but massed in a balanced formation while Simonds took the opposite view and one that followed the current British doctrine. Ironically, both officers would become corps commanders in 1944 and neither would prove particularly adept at deploying armour in mass.

The situation in Europe, meanwhile, became steadily more threatening. In the autumn of 1938, in an attempt to stave off the inevitable, Britain and France committed a cowardly act of appeasement by agreeing to what Hitler called his "final territorial demand" in Europe and signed away the freedom of the small state of Czechoslovakia, which was occupied by Germany. Most of the officers and men of the Canadian armed forces now became convinced that a war was only a matter of time. There was keen interest among the Alberta militia units when some of the first fruits of Britain's re-armament programme – the Bren .303 light machinegun, which would replace the Lewis, the Boys anti-tank rifle and a tracked infantry carrier – were displayed on a cross-country tour that came to the province in late 1938 and

early 1939, but all the militia got was a look because these items were not available. The artillery, including the three field brigades in Alberta, were intrigued to learn that the Royal Artillery had developed a new fieldpiece, a 25-pdr. gun/howitzer, to replace their aging First War vintage 18-pdrs., most of which were no longer safe to fire. But they also knew that they would have to wait before they would receive this sophisticated new weapon. At Camp Borden, the national armour inventory in early 1939 consisted of a museum collection of 37 obsolescent vehicles comprising light tanks, tankettes, armoured cars and an artillery gun tractor – and no spare parts for any of them. In fact, the only truly effective weapon that the Canadian army possessed in numbers was the Short Magazine Lee Enfield .303 rifle and bayonet.

"You look like a bullfrog trying to hump a bass drum, Sir!" The last days of peace, 1939

And so the spring of 1939 arrived. Despite the worsening situation in Europe where Hitler, not satisfied with Czechoslovakia, was trumpeting claims against Poland, there was optimism and excitement in Alberta – optimism because it appeared that the depression was finally at an end and excitement about the forthcoming tour of Canada by King George VI and Queen Elizabeth, the first visit by a reigning monarch in the nation's history. Unemployment was still high but, outside the hard-hit Palliser Triangle area in the southeast corner, agriculture was making a comeback. There were also encouraging developments in the Turner Valley where, in June 1936, Royalties No. 1 had paid off with a gusher at a depth of 6,838 feet. Nearly two hundred oil wells were drilled in the Valley over the next three years and Alberta, which up to 1935 had only produced 9,300,000 barrels of oil, was producing 10,000,000 barrels annually by 1939. Despite all the hardships of the previous decade the provincial population had actually increased by 64,000 people to just under 800,000 souls and Edmonton, with 93,817 citizens, had now outstripped Calgary, which had reached 88,904.

The excitement over the Royal Tour was shared by the 19th Dragoons, but they were also concerned as they would be providing an Escort to the Sovereign, an exacting ceremonial duty. Honorary Colonel F.C. Jamieson, Lieutenant-Colonel M.H. Wright, commanding officer, and Regimental Sergeant Major Lawrence Blain were determined that the Dragoons would do it right and months before the event, they set to work. Funding was obtained from Ottawa for a mounted escort of 36 all ranks under the command of Captain Robert A. Bradburn, and its members were carefully chosen from among the best riders in the regiment. A large marquee tent was erected on the grounds of the Connaught Armoury where the escort personnel ate and slept during a 12-day training period. Horses, also carefully selected, were obtained and housed in stalls built in the Strathcona Curling Rink located beside the Armoury, which was rented for the occasion. Finally, with great difficulty and much cost, borne out of regimental funds and donations, full dress dragoon uniforms and helmets were procured from Britain.

Getting ready, late 1930s

By 1938, it was clear to many militiamen that another war was coming and they did their best to prepare for it. Unfortunately, the Canadian army had almost no modern weapons but did seem to have a sufficient supply of gas masks, gas capes and gas goggles as modelled by this soldier of the South Alberta Regiment. His most effective piece of equipment is the Short Magazine Lee Enfield rifle he is holding. COURTESY, R.B. MCKENZIE

Escort to the Sovereign, 1939
Captain Robert A. Bradburn, at right, leads the 19th Alberta Dragoon escort troop during the royal visit to Edmonton in June 1939. The Dragoons drilled hard for months before this event and the results are clear in this photograph. Their biggest problem was finding proper uniforms but they were fortunate enough to purchase a stock of surplus uniforms of the 6th Inniskilling Dragoons of the British army, which had been amalgamated with another regiment some years before. The scarlet tunics had buff facings and collars (not quite correct for the 19th Dragoons), the crossbelts and cartouche were black leather and the sword slings and belts white leather. The badge of the 6th Inniskillings was hastily removed from the brass helmets and replaced with that of the 19th Dragoons but the buttons were Inniskilling. The Dragoon Escort Troop proved so popular that it rode in the Edmonton Exhibition and Calgary Stampede parades the following summer.
CITY OF EDMONTON ARCHIVES, EA 160-1329

The actual training of the escort was carried out by the legendary RSM W.C. "Cock" Roberts, MC, of Lord Strathcona's Horse. Roberts, a graduate of the Royal Horse Artillery equitation school in England, was the Strathcona Regimental Riding Instructor during the interwar period and every officer and man who joined that unit in the 1920s and 1930s – and not a few militiamen – passed through his hands before they were deemed suitable to appear on a horse, in uniform, in public. Roberts particularly delighted in the firm but gentle instruction of newly-minted second lieutenants fresh from the Royal Military College in Kingston. "You're just another dumb farm recruit who'll ride his horse like a jackass until he's properly trained by me, sir!" and "Bend that back! Not that way! You look like a bullfrog trying to hump a bass drum, Sir!" were among the more tactful encouragements he shouted at sweating young gentlemen.[34] When he had his pupils to a certain standard, Roberts liked to issue non-existent and impossible orders such as "Cross stirrups and fold arms" just to see what reaction would result. A demanding taskmaster but a superb instructor, Roberts had no problem in turning the handpicked Dragoon escort group into a fine ceremonial unit.

While the Dragoons were labouring under "Cock" Roberts's attentions in late May 1939, the King and Queen made triumphal progress across Canada. After landing at Quebec on 17 May, where they were welcomed by the governor general, Lord Tweedsmuir, and Prime Minister Mackenzie King they commenced an almost month-long visit. The tour served the purposes of both Britain, which wanted to strengthen ties with the Empire in the face of an impending war, and King who wanted to demonstrate to voters that not only the Conservative party had close ties with Britain. From Quebec, their Majesties boarded the Royal Train which took them, in turn, to Montreal, Ottawa,

Toronto and then out west. By 24 May they were in Winnipeg where thousands cheered and waved little Union Jacks and Red Ensigns as the King urged Canadians to "Hold fast to all that is just and of good report in the heritage which your fathers have left you."[35]

The royal couple visited Medicine Hat and Calgary, where the Strathconas in scarlet provided an escort, before continuing on to Vancouver and Victoria. They then swung back east by way of Jasper and daily bulletins in the *Edmonton Journal* recorded their progress toward the provincial capital. On 2 June 1939, a day on which it was estimated the population of Edmonton doubled, the King and Queen disembarked at the CNR station and drove down the newly-rechristened Kingsway Avenue through a sea of Union Jacks and an estimated 60,000 cheering spectators. At 101st Street, Captain Bradburn's Dragoons took over from the RCMP motorcyclists and escorted the royal couple to the Legislative Building where they were greeted by seven Alberta VC winners and listened to "God Save the King" sung in Cree by an aboriginal school group. Before they left the city, the King and Queen asked to see Bradburn and, complimenting him on the appearance of his troop, enquired whether it was the same regiment that had provided the mounted escort in Calgary a few days earlier. Biting his tongue, Bradburn tactfully explained the crucial difference between the 19th Alberta Dragoons and Lord Strathcona's Horse (Royal Canadians) and their Majesties responded that it was both "wonderful" and "marvellous" that soldiers who had been in training for only a few weeks could carry out ceremonial duties in such a fine manner.[36] That night it got better for the Dragoons and the remainder of the Edmonton garrison (and also the Calgary Highlanders who had been brought north for crowd control) when they sat down to a splendid banquet in the Masonic Temple.

The Royal Tour ended on 16 June 1939 when the King and Queen sailed from Halifax and were escorted out to sea by most of the tiny RCN and many of the operational aircraft of the even smaller RCAF. It had been a great success and had drawn Canada and Britain closer together and, at the same time, had cemented the Empire's bonds of friendship with the United States (for the royal couple had also visited that nation). This strengthening of friendships and alliances would be needed because in the early summer Adolf Hitler began to agitate for the abolition of the Polish corridor, the narrow strip of land between central Germany and East Prussia, which permitted Poland access to the Baltic. This time, however, he was resisted by Britain and France who signed treaties guaranteeing Polish territorial integrity. Doubting the resolve of the western Allies – not surprising considering that they had backed down on previous occasions – Hitler continued to bluster and the summer of 1939, a hot, dry one in Alberta, became like the summer of 1914, a succession of crises measured in the size of newspaper headlines.

Those headlines became very large on 22 August 1939 when Germany signed a non-aggression pact with the Soviet Union which gave her a free hand against Poland. That same day Britain warned Canada that hostilities were likely as German troops were moving toward the Polish border. In accordance with established procedure, at 11:15 P.M. on 25 August, the Chief of the General Staff in Ottawa sent a telegram to all military units in Canada ordering them to "Adopt Precautionary Stage against Germany."[37] That night, lights burned in armouries, camps and drill halls from Nova Scotia to British Columbia as units prepared to mount guards on vital points such as bridges and power plants and began preparations for mobilization. On 1 September 1939, Germany invaded Poland and, two days later, when Hitler ignored an ultimatum issued by Britain and France to withdraw his forces, those nations declared war against Germany. On 9 September, after an emergency debate, the Canadian House of Commons passed a motion declaring war on Germany, which was signed into law by Lord Tweedsmuir, the governor-general, on 10 September 1939.

The orders to mobilize, however, had already been issued. Lieutenant-Colonel J. Fred Scott of the 15th Alberta Light Horse had agreed to the request of Brigadier G.R. Pearkes commanding Military District 13, that, in the event of mobilization, he would take over the Calgary Highlanders as their commanding officer was not medically fit for active service. Years later, Scott remembered how it began:

> I received a terse order from Military Headquarters by phone – "Col. Scott?" – "Yes" – Mobilize!" When the order had sunk in, I slowly put down the file in my hands, and my pencil. Six years later, when I returned to my [law] office, the file was still in the same position, but the file by that time had built up very high indeed, as had many other piles of files.[38]

For the second time in a generation, Canadian soldiers – ignored, underfunded and undervalued – prepared to go to war.

The South Alberta Regiment Band greets Their Majesties, 1939
Although King George VI and Queen Elizabeth only stopped for a short period in Medicine Hat on 26 May 1939, it was a great moment in the city's history. The South Alberta Regiment could not match the efforts of the Calgary and Edmonton units but tried its best. Here, the SAR Band, dressed to perfection (or as close as they could get) marches to the CPR Station to participate in the official greeting. The drummer on the left of the first rank is Corporal Kenneth E. Perrin, who would be commissioned in the wartime South Alberta Regiment and killed in action at the Hochwald in 1945. COURTESY, MICHAEL CRAWFORD

CHAPTER NINE

"Keen-eyed Prairie Men"

THE YEARS OF WAITING, 1939-1944

> The S.A.R. won't ask for quarter
> In either work or play;
> Don't you ever cross our muskets
> Or we'll put you in the clay.
> We won't be beneath the table
> When the going's tough.
> The S.A.R. won't ask for quarter
> They never have enough.[1]

"Best type of men offering their services": The first months of war

Canada was again at war but there were differences from 1914. To avoid the chaos created by Sam Hughes in the opening days of the First World War, the general staff ensured that the mobilization plan, carefully worked out over the last two years, was followed to the letter. This plan, based on a 1937 revision of Defence Scheme No. 3, called for the creation of an overseas expeditionary force of two infantry divisions with ancillary troops that would be drawn from the existing regular and militia establishment. The choice of which militia units mobilized as part of this "Canadian Active Service Force" (CASF) was based on a wish to provide balanced representation from across Canada, with one infantry brigade from Western Canada included in each of the two divisions. The Edmonton Regiment was mobilized as part of the 1st Division and the Calgary Highlanders as part of the 2nd Division. In addition, although it took somewhat longer, 92 Field Battery (Howitzer) from Calgary eventually became part of the artillery component of the 1st Division and 20 Field Battery from Lethbridge, 23 Field Battery (Howitzer) and 91 Field Battery from Calgary and, eventually, 93 Field Battery (Howitzer) from Fort Macleod became part of the 2nd Division. So smoothly did the mobilization proceed that, at the same time as Lord Tweedsmuir was signing the Canadian declaration of war on Sunday, 10 September 1939, 400 officers and men in Edmonton, newly enlisted in the CASF, were attending their first church parade at the Protestant Cathedral.

(Facing) **In the blue Canadian Rockies, 1944**
In June 1944, the 31st Alberta Reconnaissance Regiment made what was the longest road movement by a Canadian military unit up to that time when they travelled 1,121 miles from New Westminster, B.C., to Wainwright Camp in Alberta. The unit started and ended with 118 vehicles, a perfect record. Here, an Otter Light Reconnaissance Car leads a column of similar vehicles wending its way through the Rockies. Note the markings on the nose of the vehicle. SALH ARCHIVES

There was natural disappointment among the other Alberta units – the 15th Alberta Light Horse, 19th Dragoons, South Alberta Regiment, Calgary Regiment (Tank), Edmonton Fusiliers (MG) and seven batteries of artillery – when they learned that they would not be mobilized but they pitched in and sent strong drafts of officers and enlisted men to the chosen units. The 15th Light Horse could take some pride in the fact that they at least provided a commanding officer for the Calgary Highlanders. Lieutenant-Colonel J. Fred Scott, the Light Horse commanding officer, was a cavalryman to the bone but he was also a veteran of the 50th Battalion CEF and he proved to be a good leader for the Highlanders during their first four years on active service.

Recruiting offices in Canada and Alberta were deluged with men anxious to enlist but, as a report from Military District 13 in mid-September 1939 indicates, they were not nearly as naive as their 1914 counterparts:

> Recruiting at all stations MD 13 exceeding expectation. Best type of men offering their services in numbers that tax capacity of medical boards. Units will have no difficulty in recruiting to strength well within the time limit. Complete absence of jingoism or war excitement. Men volunteering doing so with full realization of their responsibility.[2]

In less than ten days, the Edmonton Regiment enlisted more than 500 men and the Calgary Highlanders were nearly up to strength. By the end of September, 58,337 men and women (all nursing sisters) had volunteered for active service including no less than 4,205 CEF veterans. The problem, as usual, was not finding men, it was clothing, arming and equipping them as peacetime parsimony had reduced equipment stocks and many items – particularly boots – were in very short supply.

While this frantic activity was going on in Canada, Germany invaded Poland from the west and the Soviet Union invaded it from the east. There was little that Britain or France could do to assist and Poland was divided between the two dictatorships. The Western Allies, expecting a repeat of the First World War, now built up their forces along the French and Belgian frontiers and the war entered a static phase, dubbed the "Phoney War" or "Sitzkrieg" by the media, that was to last for nearly eight months.

This lull was not unwelcome to King's Liberal government which hoped to achieve maximum benefit from the war at the lowest cost. Anxious to avoid the heavy casualties of the Western Front and the resulting conscription crisis that had almost torn Canada apart in 1917-1918, King emphasized air, naval and economic commitments – the Canadian navy would escort Atlantic convoys, and the nation would train British and Commonwealth air crew and provide industrial products and raw materials,

Marching to the station: Medicine Hat, 11 June 1940
After a not unpleasant week in Medicine Hat where they drilled by day and went home at night, A Company of the SAR, recruited by the prewar regiment of the same name, marches down to the station to board the train for Edmonton. At this point, the boys do not have uniforms but can at least march in step. Private Robert Crawford, the young man on the far right wearing a white shirt and dark pants, was later commissioned in the SAR, captured in the Hochwald and spent three miserable months in a German prison camp. COURTESY, MICHAEL CRAWFORD

including foodstuffs. King knew that public opinion demanded that Canadian troops be sent overseas but he hoped to limit the extent of their commitment and he was determined that they would all be volunteers. Discussions with the British War Office, which was in the process of forming a new British Expeditionary Force for service in France, about the possible inclusion of Canadian troops brought the heartening response from General Sir Edmund Ironside, Chief of the Imperial General Staff, that "the reputation Canadians earned in the last war has not been forgotten, and that, except for regular and one or two territorial divisions, there are no troops the C[ommander]. in C[hief]. would rather have with him."[3] This being the case, plans were made to complete and send the 1st Division to Britain in December while retaining the 2nd Division in Canada over the following winter. Since, at this point in the war, financial considerations were paramount and costs were already running higher than expected, in early October the government suspended recruiting for the Canadian Active Service Force.

This decision frustrated the thousands of young men who wanted to join the army and many enlisted in the militia, seeing this as the best and quickest avenue into the Active Service Force when the doors opened again. Unit strengths mushroomed. Trooper George Lynch-Staunton, a 16-year-old member of the 15th Light Horse squadron in Pincher Creek, recalled that the strength of the Light Horse quadrupled over the winter of 1939-1940. He also remembered that Lieutenant-Colonel Harcus Strachan VC, MC, who had taken over the 15th Light Horse after Scott had given up command, was determined to raise

that unit's strength to War Establishment, or total authorized strength, with a view to having it mobilized in the near future and made the rounds of the province looking for men willing to enlist for active service. Strachan arrived at Pincher Creek on parade night, gave his spiel and then asked for volunteers to step forward. The entire squadron promptly took one pace toward him but Trooper Lynch-Staunton, three years under the minimum age to enlist for overseas service, was arrested in midflight by a shout from the squadron commander, Captain Frank Lynch-Staunton, who just happened to be his uncle: "Step back, George, I was at your father's wedding."[4] It would take young George Lynch-Staunton another two years of trying before he was able to get into the active army. In March 1940 the period of waiting for those who were of age ended when recruiting resumed for the active service force and, within a matter of weeks, the ranks of the 2nd Division were full.

"All right, you lot, come on in!": The South Alberta Regiment and 13th Field Regiment, 1940-1942

On 9 April 1940 the "Phoney War" came to an abrupt end when Germany attacked and overran Denmark and Norway in quick campaigns using air, ground and naval forces. With his northern flank secure, Hitler now unleashed the *Wehrmacht* against the Low Countries and France on 10 May and it quickly became clear the Western Allies faced a catastrophe as German forces, spearheaded by the swift-moving panzer divisions and supported by tactical aircraft, destroyed the Belgian and Dutch armies in a matter of days, and drove a steel wedge through the Allied lines. In less than three weeks, the BEF and the northern group of French forces were cut off and surrounded on the beaches of Dunkirk and German troops were advancing steadily on Paris. The Royal Navy proved equal, however, to the task of extricating the BEF from its predicament and returning it to Britain minus almost all its equipment and heavy weapons. French resolve, never strong because of that nation's heavy losses in the First World War, crumbled and French leaders were forced to suffer the humiliation of discussing surrender terms with the Germans in the same railway car that had been used for the negotiations that led to the Armistice of 1918.

Canada's response to this crisis was magnificent. Gone now were all thoughts of a limited war based on financial considerations – every modern warship in the Royal Canadian Navy and every operational squadron in the Royal Canadian Air Force was sent to Britain, and plans were made to accelerate the dispatch of the 2nd Division overseas. To make good the disastrous equipment losses of the British army, almost every modern rifle and machinegun in Canada – among them 75,000 Ross rifles – was transferred, as well as useful and precious stocks of other war materiel, including 6 million rounds of small arms ammunition. As it was now clear that it was going to be a long and dangerous war, the government undertook the mobilization of a 3rd and 4th Division of the Active Service Force as well as eight infantry battalions for home security purposes. These new forces were authorized on 27 May 1940, the same day as Operation DYNAMO, the evacuation of Dunkirk, commenced and the response was overwhelming – in four days, 6,909 volunteers came forward and, in the following three months, no fewer than 78,000 more men joined the ranks of the CASF.

The choice of militia units to be mobilized for the new divisions was again based on achieving balanced representation from across the country. In Alberta, 22 Field Battery from Gleichen and 78 Battery from Red Deer were mobilized as part of the 3rd Division while 95 Field Battery from Calgary, 96 Field Battery from Edmonton and 112 Field Battery from Lethbridge eventually ended up as part of the artillery component of the 4th Division. It was also decided that the 4th Division would include an infantry regiment from the province and it appears that the plan was for it to be titled "The Alberta Regiment" as it would be drawn from the five militia units in the province that had not yet been mobilized. This proposal was dropped, however, in favour of titling the new entity the South Alberta Regiment after the prewar militia unit in Medicine Hat. In actual fact, since it was to be an infantry battalion, this was the only title that could be chosen as the 15th Light Horse and 19th Dragoons were mounted units, the Edmonton Fusiliers a machinegun battalion and the Calgary Regiment nominally a tank battalion. It must be stressed, however, that, although the South Alberta Regiment (CASF) took the title of the prewar regiment, from the outset it was always a "Composite Alberta Regiment" with representation from across the entire province and more accurately should have been called "The Alberta Regiment."[5]

Each major militia unit in the province raised one company for the new regiment and who would contribute what was decided when the five commanding officers cut cards at a meeting held in Calgary on 2 June 1940. The result was that the Calgary Regiment (Tank) was given the task of raising HQ Company, the prewar South Albertas A Company, the 19th Dragoons B Company, the Edmonton Fusiliers C Company and the 15th Light Horse D Company. The five militia units also contributed five current or former commanding officers (Lieutenant-Colonels E.A. Pitman of the mounted brigade, Lieutenant-Colonel Harcus Strachan, VC, MC, of the 15th Light Horse, Lieutenant-Colonel M.H. Wright, MM, of the 19th Dragoons and Lieutenant-Colonels H.S. Davies and A. McLean of the Edmonton Fusiliers) who took a drop in rank to serve as second-in-command or company commanders. Finally, the five prewar militia regiments contributed no less than fourteen junior officers, many of whom would reach high rank during the war. From the outset, the South Alberta Regiment was to benefit from this infusion of experienced leadership.

There was no problem obtaining men when recruiting opened in Calgary, Edmonton and Medi-

Making do: Artillery training in 1940
There was a shortage of the standard Commonwealth fieldpiece, the 25 pdr. gun/howitzer, in the early years of the war and Canadian gunners had to train on the First War vintage 18-pdr. which was upgraded with a new carriage. By late 1941, with British and Canadian war industry coming into full tide, modern equipment began to reach units. Note the "Jungle Jim" hats worn by these gunners. NAC. PA-197865

203

cine Hat on 5 June 1940 and the five units competed against each other to turn out the best company for the new regiment. Competition to get in was so tough that 18-year-old John Galipeau, somewhat short, waited every day for a week outside the Prince of Wales Armoury in Edmonton and watched the sergeants select only the largest and most impressive physical specimens from the lengthy queue in front of the doors. Finally, late on Friday afternoon, just as Galipeau and the other hangers-on were about to give up, an NCO emerged and shouted: "All right, you lot, come on in, all of you!"[6] And so John Galipeau joined the South Alberta Regiment along with over eight hundred other young men, toughened by their Depression period youth, inured to physical labour in all weathers and very happy to have a job with regular pay and three squares a day. In less than three weeks the SAR recruited over its War Establishment or authorized strength and had concentrated at Edmonton to begin basic training.

But the South Albertas did not get all the good men in the province. At Red Deer where 78 Field Battery was in the process of mobilization, Gunner H.G. Cunningham remembered that Lieutenant Richard Scholten of the SAR, with two truckloads of recruits that he had picked up in Lacombe, made the fatal error of stopping by the Red Deer armoury and leaving them unattended for a few minutes. Cunningham's battery commander decided that the Lacombe boys were a likely looking lot and asked Cunningham to have a word with them so he strolled over and extolled the virtues of the artillery, emphasizing that, unlike the infantry, a man didn't have to march and promotion was swift and certain. Impressed, the Lacombe boys abandoned their vehicles and, to Scholten's consternation, promptly signed up with the Royal Canadian Artillery. As he had proved himself useful, the battery commander awarded Cunningham with an immediate promotion to lance-bombardier.

Over the summer of 1940, 22 and 78 Batteries remained in Alberta doing basic training before shifting to Shilo Camp in Manitoba in early October. Here they joined 44 Battery from Prince Albert, Saskatchewan, to form 13th Field Regiment, RCA. The men of this unit, as its historian noted, "were mostly from farms and rural areas and were imbued with qualities of independence, initiative, clear thinking and hard fighting."[7] Captain T.C. Greenlees, an RMC graduate from Ontario who was to join 13th Field later in the war, recalled that he found the attitude in this outfit from Western Canada always "more relaxed," and that "less time was spent on spit and polish than in an eastern unit."[8]

**"I'm a gun, it's plain to see":
Deficiencies**

During the early war years, deficiencies in equipment meant that, in training, some unfortunate gunners had to stand in for the missing item, as Sergeant J. Daimer of 12th Field Regiment indicates in this cartoon. By 1942, the Canadian artillery were well equipped with Canadian-made weapons and vehicles. FROM INTO ACTION WITH THE 12TH FIELD

In November 13th Field moved to winter quarters in a vacant department store, the Robinson Building in downtown Winnipeg and Bombardier James Moffat recalled some of their adventures and misadventures that winter:

The Robinson Building was the first time I ever saw a rat. I went into the kitchen one night while I was on fire picket to make a sandwich and turned on the light and there were about four rats. It was an old department store, a creaky thing. The latrines were downstairs and it was about a 30-foot trough divided up into sections. There was a great big water tank and very few minutes this thing would unload and a flood would go down the trough. One day some of the boys were in there while the RSM was taking a crap and they were up the line and they rolled up some toilet paper and set a match and let it go down under him.[9]

In February 1941 the regiment entrained for Debert Camp near Truro, Nova Scotia, where the units of the 3rd Division were being concentrated prior to being moved overseas. Here, for the first time, they got in some solid artillery training, using First War vintage 18-pdr. guns on more modern carriages. There was still a shortage of equipment and during training exercises, it was not unusual for some luckless gunner to be posted with a placard around his neck reading "No. 3 Gun," "Troop Command Post," or something similar. As the weather improved, the batteries got a chance in June and July to undertake prolonged range work at Tracadie, just over the border in New Brunswick. Such occasions were always welcomed as Debert Camp was a large camp with limited recreational facilities and it was nice to get away from its red mud and eat wild blueberries. All advanced training came to an end, however, in August 1941 when 13th Field was given embarkation leave in expectation of being transferred to Britain. As the units of 3rd Division had been moving steadily overseas throughout the summer, the regiment had been expecting this development but they would actually be on notice for embarkation for more than three months, during which they could not carry out any range work, only dry firing.

Finally, on 1 November 1941, the regiment embarked on His Majesty's Transport *Louis Pasteur* at Halifax and set sail. It was a journey that few of the men wanted to repeat as their small convoy took a northerly course to avoid U-boat concentrations and encountered severe storms in the North Atlantic. Bombardier Moffat recalled that the

Pasteur "started rocking before we got out of the harbour and rocked all the way across the Atlantic."[10] Gunner Drummond Cotterill remembered watching the warships escorting the convoy in rough seas, "coming to the crest of a wave and hanging there with the bow and stern exposed, just hanging there."[11] Bombardier R.J. Porter from Kinistino, Saskatchewan, was more blunt: "I'll never forget it. I was on that thing, the *Louis Pasteur* and, by jeez, I wish that sucker had gone down and stayed. I was seasick, seasick all the way over and it was not good. I don't go on the water to this day even if it is frozen."[12] On 11 November the *Pasteur* docked at Gourock in Scotland and a very thankful and wobbly-kneed collection of gunners disembarked to board the little British choo-choo trains for their regiment's first station at Farnborough in Hampshire. They were greeted on their early morning arrival with a breakfast of wartime ration sausages "which tasted like sawdust" and we can leave them here, stolidly munching, while we resume the story of the South Alberta Regiment.[13]

While 13th Field Regiment was enjoying the dubious pleasures of Shilo and Debert Camps, the South Albertas were undergoing their introduction to army life. In mid-June 1940, the regiment concentrated in Edmonton to live in huts built behind the Prince of Wales Armoury on the newly re-christened Kingsway Avenue. They now met the two men charged with turning them into soldiers – Lieutenant-Colonel James H. Carvosso. MC and bar, and RSM Christopher Seal, both former members of the PPCLI. Carvosso, a five-times wounded veteran of the First World War who had been commissioned from the ranks, was the perfect choice to mould an infantry battalion while Seal, a bull-voiced, eagle-eyed professional warrant officer and the very model of an RSM, was his perfect counterpart. Carvosso concentrated on the officers and Seal on the men. The old veteran had no time for the military pretensions of peacetime militia officers, particularly young officers, and treated them harshly whereas Seal managed to terrify everyone below him in rank while, at the same time convincing everyone above him to give him a wide berth. For three months the South Albertas went through a period of what the old army called "square bashing" – elementary drill, interspersed with lectures on weapons and regulations – with the occasional break of a horror-filled lecture from the Medical Officer on the perils of venereal disease. The men had a tough time on duty but evening passes were usually available and downtown Edmonton beckoned so, all in all, life in the army for the new recruits was not all that bad. In fact their biggest problem was their uniforms, fatigue suits manufactured by the Great Western Garment factory in Edmonton of a light brindle brown denim which, after one wash, turned to the colour of mustard.

One should never get too comfortable in the army as things do have a way of changing fast – for better or worse. In August 1940 the SAR was transferred to Dundurn Camp near Saskatoon. "The last place God ever made," as one South Alberta called it, Dundurn was an arid, semi-desert area that was to be-

come Carvosso's testing ground to weed out the halt, the lame and the weak and his chosen method was long route marches under full packs.[14] Over the course of five weeks the SAR made seventeen of these marches up to a distance of 20 miles and those unable to keep up, were dropped from the unit. The only good thing about Dundurn was that the regiment was able to get some practical field and range work at the company level

"Defaulters": Dundurn Camp, 1940
Defaulters are soldiers guilty of minor infractions and they are usually paraded every morning before officers or warrant officers, depending on the gravity of their offence. Defaulters are a sergeant-major's delight as they constitute a useful labour force for such necessary but disliked tasks as digging latrines and other holes, cookhouse help, painting things white (including stones), heavy lifting and a myriad of wretched tasks whose scope is only limited by his imagination. Knowing this, these miscreants do not look particularly happy about their situation although some are gamely giving the "thumbs up" sign. COURTESY, MIKE CRAWFORD

Wahkesiah Camp, 1940
After the desert conditions of Dundurn, the South Albertas were happy to transfer to Wahkesiah Camp near Nanaimo, B.C. – happy that is until it started to rain and their tent-lines flooded. They spent the wet winter of 1940-1941 in tents and, just as permanent barrack accommodation was completed, they were transferred to Ontario. On the other hand, if you can't take a joke, you shouldn't join up. SAR ARCHIVES

On Guard For Thee, Niagara, August 1941
The SAR spent nearly eight months guarding hydo-electric installations in the Niagara area of Ontario in 1941. Here, Private Fred Plahn, an unidentified soldier and Private R.C. Sims (right) prepare to go on guard.

SAR ARCHIVES

but, otherwise, there were few amusements to be had – in fact the most notable event was a massive outbreak of dysentery that laid low half the regiment and suspended route marching for a few days. In late September the South Albertas were overjoyed to be transferred to Wahkesiah Camp near Nanaimo on Vancouver Island, overjoyed, that is, until it started to rain a few days after their arrival and continued to rain for most of the eight months they spent on the west coast.

Major-General W.A. Griesbach, who first appeared in our story as a boy in 1885, was now the Inspector-General of Western Canada and he arrived at Nanaimo Camp in late April 1941 to examine the SAR. Griesbach was complimentary, reporting that the battalion "consists of a very fine body of men, rather on the large size" and that "some 15 N.C.O.s. have been promoted to commissioned rank and I would say that there are still a considerable number of N.C.Os. fit for such promotion."[15] By this time the SAR had a new commanding officer, Lieutenant-Colonel William Bristowe, a genial ex-British army officer dubbed "Buffalo Bill" by one and all. Bristowe proudly informed Griesbach that the enlisted men's canteens were making a profit of $500 per month, mostly from the dry canteen because "the consumption of beer is falling off ... due to the drinking of milk, chocolate milkshakes and soft drinks." Griesbach duly reported this to Ottawa but, being no fool, noted that beer was being sold in the SAR wet canteen at the rather high price (in 1941) of 20 cents

per bottle and suspected that the South Albertas' "abstinence from beer is largely, if not wholly, due to the price."[16]

By May 1941 when the SAR was transferred to Niagara-on-the-Lake in Ontario, its men were not only fed up with the climate but properly uniformed, armed and equipped, as the unit had begun to receive the first fruits of Canada's wartime production. The South Albertas spent the next eight months in Ontario, supposedly training when not guarding power installations and the Welland Canal connecting Lakes Erie and Ontario but such training as was done was only at the company level. Otherwise, Niagara was a rather pleasant time – if one overlooked the semi-tropical humidity of an Ontario summer – which was enhanced by the nearby fleshpots of Toronto and Buffalo. By the late autumn of 1941, however, the SAR, along with every other unit of the 4th Division, was getting anxious to get overseas, particularly as the 3rd Division had already shipped out to Britain. Their transfer was delayed, however, when most of the artillery and support units in the 4th Division were stripped from it to form the 5th Armoured Division, a new formation raised by Canada at Britain's request and it was only in December 1941, after eighteen months of service, that the 4th Division was able to concentrate all its units at Debert Camp, Nova Scotia. At Debert the South Albertas froze for two months trying to train in winter warfare until February 1942 when they learned the news that the 4th Division was to be converted to armour.

What followed was a very, very hectic period as the SAR, along with the remainder of the division, retrained for service in a new branch of the army. Men not up to the higher standards of the armoured corps were posted out while trained armoured corps men were posted in, and for five months, the South Albertas worked hard to learn new trades. There were never enough vehicles for instruction so courses were run in eight-hour shifts around the clock. Those unfortunates who could not get a vehicle had to make do with lengths of 2" x 2" nailed in an "H" configuration at the ends of which each member of a crew assumed the position he would have in a tank and off they would go to practice "troop tactics without tanks," all to the accompaniment of "a chorus of grumbling and muttering, drivers' imitations of engines running, gears crashing, and a goodly amount of laughter."[17] As there was not much to do in nearby Truro, a dry town

"Wish Me Luck As You Wave Me Goodbye": Halifax, 22 August 1942
One of a series of photos taken by Ivy Galipeau, wife of Trooper John Galipeau, from the women's washroom of a CNR car. It shows a Canadian corvette steaming toward the vessels of the convoy which would take the South Albertas overseas. It was strictly forbidden to take photographs of wartime Halifax harbour but fortunately Ivy Galipeau violated security to record the event for posterity.

COURTESY, JOHN GALIPEAU

in which the dance hall was located beside the Stanfield Underwear Factory, most men preferred to stay in camp and perhaps their biggest form of entertainment was the regular pep talks they received from the divisional commander, Major-General Frank F. Worthington, a straight-from-the-hip plain talking man who, when he informed the SAR in July 1942 that they would shortly be going overseas, added that "many of you will never see this land again."[18] Maybe so but when the South Albertas boarded His Majesty's Transport *Strathmore* at Halifax on 21 August 1942 they were glad, after more than two years in the army, to be getting closer to the action.

The army expands, 1940-1942

While the SAR had been training in Canada, the war had been running its deadly course. In the early summer of 1940, after the fall of France, the *Wehrmacht* massed on the Channel coast for the invasion of Britain while overhead the *Luftwaffe* duelled for air superiority with the RAF. Hitler was hoping that Britain would make peace but, in this, he was to be disappointed and since it was impossible for Germany, in the face of the overwhelming superiority of the Royal Navy, to launch an amphibious invasion of Britain, he drew back in the early autumn. Meanwhile Hitler's understudy, Mussolini, had his own dreams of conquest and late in 1940 invaded both Greece and Egypt. The Greeks sent the Italian army reeling back while, in December, British forces in Egypt launched a counter offensive that came close to overrunning most of Italian North Africa and resulted in so many prisoners that they could only be counted by the acre. Mussolini's debacles forced Hitler to intervene and, in the spring of 1941, German forces overran Yugoslavia and Greece while at the same time an aggressive young German general named Erwin Rommel landed in the North Africa with two German divisions and took the offensive, forcing British forces back to the Libyan-Egyptian border by June 1941. That same month, however, Hitler invaded the Soviet Union, making the fatal error of fighting a war on two fronts.

For Britain, the crisis came in the spring and early summer of 1941. In March that nation was technically bankrupt and was only saved by the American provision of Lend-Lease – basically ships, aircraft and weapons on credit – and by Hitler's decision to attack the Soviet Union. The question now was whether Brit-

"Worthy": Major-General Frank F. Worthington
The father of the Canadian Armoured Corps, Worthington, known to his men as "Fighting Frank" or "Fearless Frank," commanded 4th Armoured Division from 1942 to 1944. As the divisional armoured reconnaissance regiment, the South Albertas were under his direct orders and the crusty old soldier took a shine to his "keen-eyed prairie men," and carefully picked a commanding officer for the unit. Unfortunately, Worthington did not lead the 4th Division in combat as he was deemed too old. SAR ARCHIVES

ain could hold out until, inevitably, the United States entered the war on her side. Besides finances, Britain's most pressing problem was that German aircraft and U-boats, taking advantage of French bases on the Atlantic littoral, were threatening to cut her maritime life line. In this respect, her worries were reduced in the late summer of 1941 when President Franklin D. Roosevelt committed the United States Navy to escorting convoys in North American waters, technically an act of war. This assistance, combined with the fact that the Soviets, despite the loss of a vast amount of territory and men, finally managed to halt the German onslaught at the gates of Moscow in December, caused a momentary relaxation of tension. On 7 December 1941, however, Japan attacked in the Pacific and although this brought the United States into the war as an active ally, limited military resources were stretched even further. The spring and early summer of 1942 were the darkest hours for the Allies as the Japanese conquered Hong Kong, Singapore, the Dutch East Indies and the Philippines, and began to threaten Australia while the Germans, resurgent on the Russian Front, returned to the offensive and drove deep into Russia.

Throughout these anxious years, Canada played a major role. The two Canadian divisions in Britain, the only fully-equipped formations in that country after Dunkirk, guarded the Channel coast throughout 1940 and 1941. The RCAF, profiting from the establishment of the British Commonwealth Air Training Plan which trained aircrew in Canada, had steadily increased its strength, and sent squadron after squadron overseas while Canadian airmen also served with RAF units. Perhaps Canada's greatest contribution was made by the Royal Canadian Navy which, starting with less than a dozen warships in 1939, underwent an expansion unparalleled by other wartime navies as ships – mostly small and primitive – were built and commissioned almost by the dozen and sent out in the North Atlantic with a few trained officers petty officers and largely green crews. By 1942 there were nearly 200 Canadian warships in service and they were responsible for North Atlantic convoys from North American waters to the mid-ocean, a demanding, dreary and very dangerous job that would continue to the last day of the war.

The army, however, continued to wait. Between 1939 and 1943, it underwent a continuous expansion and the forces in

Britain steadily increased until First Canadian Army consisted of two corps with three infantry and two armoured divisions, and two independent armoured brigades. At home, the militia continued in existence as a recruiting and training organization for the Active Service Force.* A third and rather awkward element of the wartime army was created in 1940 by the passage of the National Resources Mobilization Act (NRMA) which permitted the conscription of men for military service in Canada and the powers granted under this act were used by the government to fill out the establishment of two new regular formations, the 6th and 7th Divisions, for the defence, respectively, of the west and east coasts. The units in these divisions were comprised of a mixture of active service soldiers and what officialdom termed men "enlisted under the National Resources Mobilization Act" but whom everyone else called "Zombies." In April 1942, when recruiting for the active force began to slow down, the Liberal government held a national plebiscite to ask Canadians whether they would release it from "any past commitments restricting the methods of raising men for military service?"[19] Outside Quebec, the answer was a resounding "Yes!" as 64% of voters voted in favour of what they thought would eventually mean conscription for overseas service but, for the time being, the Liberals continued to follow the somewhat tricky course of "conscription if necessary, but not necessarily conscription."[20] It was a phrase that would come back to haunt them.

There was also a fourth, and often overlooked, element in the wartime army. In 1941, along with the other two services, the army created a women's organization, the Canadian Women's Army Corps, in order to release men for combat duty – women were "to serve so that men may fight." Initially, CWAC personnel were only offered a limited choice of work in the clerical, mess and stores trades but as they proved themselves, the number of jobs taken over by women constantly increased until, by the late war period, they were performing almost every task in the army except those directly related to combat. It was discov-

* The terminology can be confusing. Prior to 1941, the Canadian military establishment consisted of the Permanent Active Militia (the regular or permanent force) and the Non-Permanent Active Militia (the reserve force equivalent to the Territorial army in Britain or the Army Reserve or National Guard in the United States). In that year, the titles were changed and the Canadian army consisted of the Canadian Active Service Force (units of volunteers mobilized for overseas service including all regular personnel and the Canadian Women's Army Corps) and the Reserve Army (the old militia). Men conscripted under the National Resources Mobilization Act existed in a limbo, being neither members of the active service force nor the reserves, one of the reasons that led them to being called "Zombies."

ered that women soldiers would work harder than male soldiers (although they received only 80% of the pay), were more reliable, required less supervision and presented fewer disciplinary problems.

Initially, of course, there were problems to be solved and adjustments to be made – as there always are when men and women serve together. Old line officers and NCOs, used to working up a good appetite for lunch in the mess by tearing wide and deep strips off defaulters on morning parade, were horrified when uniformed females standing at attention in front of them burst into tears on being admonished – a tactic that proved entirely unsuccessful with women officers and NCOs who proved to be just as merciless as their male counterparts (although possibly not as loud). And then there was the matter of drink. In 1942 three CWAC sergeants walked into a mess in Halifax and ordered a beer and the puzzled steward, having no instructions on the matter of dispensing alcohol to women in uniform, served them. When news of this reached Ottawa, it caused an uproar and the army promptly closed all enlisted messes in the Halifax area until a decision could be made as to whether women should enjoy the same privileges as men. Finally, with great reluctance and many reservations and regulations, it was decided that women soldiers might drink beer in army messes. As always, when young women and young men are placed in close proximity, conflagration sometimes ensued but, on the whole, male soldiers treated their female comrades with respect and – it being a patriarchal society in Canada in the 1940s – not a little protectiveness. Despite initial problems, the Canadian Women's Army Corps, which grew to a strength of 21,000 officers and women by 1945, all active service volunteers, proved such a successful idea that even the most hidebound and conservative male officers began to ask themselves why it had taken so long for such an organization to be formed.

Trooper, 31st Alberta Reconnaissance Regiment

The 31st Alberta Recce was mobilized in 1942 from drafts from the 15th Light Horse and 19th Alberta Dragoons. The men of the 31st Recce wore the cap badge of the 15th Light Horse as seen in this photo of an unidentified trooper. The unit spent two and a half years training in Canada before going overseas, but was broken up on its arrival in Britain. SALH ARCHIVES

"I'm volunteering for nothing": The 31st Alberta Reconnaissance Regiment, 1942-1944

During the first two years of the Second World War, the Alberta militia units carried on much as they had done in peacetime but with greater strengths and increased training budgets. Unfortunately, funding meant nothing when uniforms and weapons were scarce and active service units had first call on what little was available. Trooper George Lynch-Staunton of the 15th Light Horse recalled that, when that regiment went to summer camp at Sarcee in 1940 and 1941, along with the 19th Dragoons, the two units had a combined strength of nearly 400 men but, since uniforms were in short supply, they were issued the same awful brown denim overalls that had been inflicted on the South Alberta Regiment. At the 1940 and 1941 camps, the horses were left at home and the 15th Light Horse and 19th Dragoons trained as infantry. At this time, militia units were basically recruiting organizations for their linked active service units and many young men, under the minimum age of 19 for overseas service, joined the militia until they were old enough to go to the regular army. Many Alberta commanders still hoped that their regiments would be mobilized but, with the exception of the Edmonton Fusiliers, which formed an active service battalion in late 1940 and the Calgary Regiment (Tank) which went active service in February 1941, this was not to be.

A snapshot of the state of some of the provincial militia regiments in the early part of the war can be found in the papers of eagle-eyed Major-General W.A. Griesbach, who inspected them in the spring of 1941. Concerning the 15th Light Horse and 19th Dragoons, Griesbach noted that both units' training had suffered because they were not sure whether they would be employed as cavalry, infantry or armour. He found the active service battalion of the Edmonton Fusiliers a good unit but noted that it only possessed two obsolete Lewis machineguns, no Bren guns and a 2-inch mortar but no bombs for it. The 2nd or militia Battalion of the Fusiliers possessed 227 First War Enfield P-17 rifles but no ammunition for them, and 24 Ross Mk III rifles and three Lewis machineguns which were unserviceable. Griesbach found Lieutenant-Colonel Harcus Strachan, VC, MC, who had served briefly with the SAR but now commanded the active service battalion of the Fusiliers, to be "a gallant soldier and a man of distinguished appearance and excellent manners" but who possessed a "disinclination to concern himself with the multitude of small details which in the aggregate make for success in the command of a battalion."[21] He was harder, however, on the officers of the 15th Light Horse and the 19th Dragoons – the commanding officer of the former was characterized as "not the type of officer to command this regiment, either in peace or in war" while the commander of the 19th got off a bit easier, although Griesbach noted that he only "slightly" influenced his regiment.[22] However, Griesbach had nothing good to say about the officer commanding the Dragoon B Squadron in Edmonton whom he regarded as being "quite unfitted to command."

Matters in the militia changed in early 1942 when the entry of Japan into the war brought fear of an attack on the Pacific coast. New divisions were formed for home defence and more attention was paid to the militia, now re-designated the Reserve Army, with a view to making it an effective second line of defence in case of an invasion. All provincial militia units – cavalry, infantry, artillery, engineers, ordnance, medical, service corps and signals corps – now became part of the 41st Reserve Brigade Group with

headquarters at Calgary. Training was intensified and by 1943, with Canada's wartime production in full swing, the reserve units were relatively well dressed, well armed and well equipped. As a matter of historical interest, it should be noted that, in 1942-1943, Lieutenant Ernest Manning of the 2nd Battalion, Edmonton Fusiliers, soon to be the premier of Alberta, actively trained with his unit and attended summer camp at Sarcee.

To their dismay, in the early spring of 1942 both the 15th Light Horse and 19th Dragoons were informed that they would be made dormant for the remainder of the war and the 14th (Reserve) Army Tank Regiment (Calgary Regiment) would take over the mounted/armour role in Alberta. The good news, however, was that personnel from all three units would form the cadre of a new Alberta unit – the 31st Alberta Reconnaissance Regiment.* It was a sad time for the Light Horse and the Dragoons as they vacated their armouries to make way for others and packed their trophies and silver for storage. On 3 May 1942, when the 19th Dragoons marched out of Connaught Armoury to Holy Trinity Church in Edmonton to lay up their Colour, it was a day of memories.** Among the officers on parade was Lieutenant-Colonel F.C. Jamieson who had taken the Dragoon squadron overseas in 1914 while the general salute was taken by Major-General W.A. Griesbach. As the Dragoons exited the church, the band of the Edmonton Regiment played "John Peel," the regimental march of the 19th, in their honour.

The 31st Alberta Reconnaissance Regiment was formed at Sarcee Camp at the end of May 1942 from drafts contributed by the 15th Light Horse, 19th Dragoons and Calgary Regiment. Lieutenant-Colonel C.F. Smith, who had gone overseas with the 17th Duke of York's Own Canadian Hussars in 1939 but had been returned to Canada because of illness, was appointed to command. Smith was an experienced reconnaissance man and a good choice to raise and train the 31st Recce. He was also wise enough to try and preserve links with the dormant Alberta mounted units and, thus, the men of the 31st Recce wore the cap badge of the 15th Light Horse and (until told to take them down), the sergeants wore the badge of the 19th Dragoons above their chevrons.

Smith, however, faced a nearly impossible task because he had two distinctly different types of soldiers – active service volunteers and NRMA conscripts – with completely differing

---

* It might well asked whether the choice of unit number resulted from a wish to link the new regiment to the 31st Battalion CEF. This would, however, be asking for too much sensitivity from Ottawa – the number was simply assigned because the 31st Alberta Recce Regiment happened to be the 30th unit (there was no unit numbered 13th) in seniority when the Canadian Armoured Corps was reorganized in early 1942. Still, it would have been a nice thought.

** Throughout their history up to this point, the 19th Dragoons had been using the Union Colour of the 19th Alberta Mounted Rifles as their Regimental Colour. This was a Colour, or flag, not a Guidon as, under the regulations in effect in 1910 when the 19th received it, only cavalry regiments received Guidons; mounted rifle regiments received Colours.

attitudes. On the one hand, he had keen officers and enlisted personnel who were anxious to get overseas; on the other he had a substantial number (as much as half his enlisted strength) who were very much determined not to go overseas unless ordered by the government and who were, at best, "reluctant soldiers." Regulations made the distinction between the two perfectly clear. Active servicemen wore the "Canada" flash and the "General Service" badge and could gain promotion to NCO rank while, until the later years of the war, Zombies, or NRMA personnel, were not promoted above the lowest rank of private or trooper. The atmosphere in the barracks can be imagined but before one thinks too harshly of the NRMA soldiers, many had good reasons for not going active service. As one young private explained to a regular officer:

I'll go wherever I am ordered by the government because I am a loyal Canadian, sir. But I'm volunteering for nothing. Last war my dad volunteered. He was gassed at Ypres. When he came home he couldn't work. His pension was nothing. My mum had to run the farm by herself. We grew up poor. My dad was only 34 when he died. I'm all my mum's got now to look after her in her old age. If you had gone through what I did growing up, you wouldn't volunteer either.[23]

As if this were not bad enough, throughout its short and rather unhappy history, the 31st Alberta Recce was regularly raided for reinforcement drafts for overseas units and, of course, the unit lost its best active service personnel on these drafts. It its first year of existence the unit drafted 350 officers and men to Britain with the result was that Smith had to make one of his three squadrons a permanent training organization to handle the constant intake of recruits.

In August 1943 the regiment moved to Nanaimo to serve as the reconnaissance unit of the 6th Division with headquarters at Victoria. Since this division was more or less static, it had no real use for reconnaissance and the 31st Recce ended up as the mobile reserve for the Pacific Command, ready to rush at a moment's notice to repel a Special Naval Landing Force of the Imperial Japanese Navy should it splash ashore anywhere on Vancouver Island. The unit moved from Nanaimo to Otter Point near Victoria in October 1942, to New Westminster in May 1943 and to Vernon the following August. Over its first year in existence, the 31st Recce gradually acquired its War Establishment of combat vehicles – carriers and Otter Light Reconnaissance Cars. The latter was a rather high and ungainly Canadian-manufactured machine armed with a single .303 Bren gun and both vehicles were so thinly armoured that, in the immortal phrase of one veteran, "a well-oiled German could pee through them at 1,000 yards."[24] Attempts to train, however, were constantly frustrated by gasoline rationing (vehicles were generally grounded for two or three days each week) and the constant turnover of active service personnel – just as men learned their trade, they were posted out of the unit.

Things did not improve much when Lieutenant-Colonel H.H. Riley, the former commanding officer of the Calgary Highlanders, took over in August 1943 although the unit gradually began to undertake more offensive training and acquire more modern weapons including flamethrower carriers and 6-pdr. anti-tank guns. From December 1943 to February 1944, 31st Recce underwent instruction in amphibious warfare at the navy's Combined Operations Training Centre at Courtenay, which probably raised the hopes of its active service component that it would soon go overseas for the forthcoming invasion of Europe. If so, such hopes were quickly dashed when, having completed its course, the 31st Recce returned to New Westminster in February 1944 where it was to remain in garrison for four months.

Spirits lifted again, however, in June 1944 when 31st Recce, with 465 all ranks and 118 vehicles, was ordered to Wainwright, Alberta, where a large training camp had been constructed in

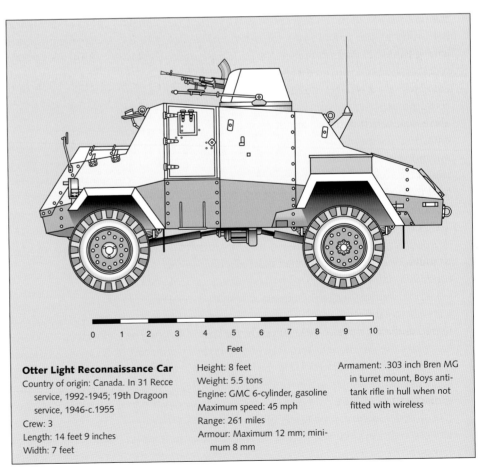

0 1 2 3 4 5 6 7 8 9 10

Feet

Otter Light Reconnaissance Car
Country of origin: Canada. In 31 Recce
 service, 1992-1945; 19th Dragoon
 service, 1946-c.1955
Crew: 3
Length: 14 feet 9 inches
Width: 7 feet

Height: 8 feet
Weight: 5.5 tons
Engine: GMC 6-cylinder, gasoline
Maximum speed: 45 mph
Range: 261 miles
Armour: Maximum 12 mm; mini-
 mum 8 mm

Armament: .303 inch Bren MG
 in turret mount, Boys anti-
 tank rifle in hull when not
 fitted with wireless

1941-1942. It made the journey of some 1,121 miles, quite possibly the longest road movement accomplished by a Canadian military unit up to that time, through the Rockies, travelling by way of Golden, Banff, Calgary and Edmonton and of the 118 vehicles that started, 118 finished. The unit arrived at Wainwright to settle into a new home "whose breath is dust and whose face a blazing sand dune pock-marked with tents – the mecca of the mosquito" – to commence an intensive three-month period of training.[25] And here we can safely leave it while we continue the overseas story of the South Alberta and 13th Field Regiments.

"A dagger pointed at the heart of Berlin": The South Albertas in Britain, 1942-1944

When His Majesty's Transport *Strathmore* docked at Glasgow on the morning of 31 August 1942, the men of the South Alberta Regiment learned for the first time the full details of the attack on Dieppe, which had taken place twelve days before. Too large to be a raid and too small to be an invasion, this operation had originated from persistent demands by the Soviet Union that a "second front" be launched in Western Europe to relieve German pressure on the Eastern Front. Operation JUBILEE was a disaster – just under 5,000 Canadian soldiers, drawn from the 2nd Canadian Division, attacked Dieppe in the early hours of 19 August 1942 but only 2,211 returned to England. The Calgary Regiment (Tank) had the unfortunate honour of being the first Alberta unit to enter combat in the Second World War; it landed 29 tanks to support the infantry on the main beach and every vehicle was lost, along with most of their crews.

Dieppe was a catastrophe but Dieppe was also a valuable if costly lesson. It provided a compelling demonstration that, before the Western Allies could mount a successful invasion of the European mainland, there would have to be a marked improvement in the doctrine, tactics and weapons used in amphibious landings. Over the next two years, while the problems inherent in this most difficult of military operations were analyzed and solutions found, the fortunes of war began to swing in favour of the Allies. The Soviet Union was able to blunt the German 1942 summer offensive at Stalingrad and after three months of desperate street fighting, the Red Army counterattacked and trapped an entire German army. In the Pacific, a Japanese thrust at New Guinea was stopped at Guadalcanal and Japanese naval airpower was eliminated at the climactic battle of Midway. The United States now began to prepare for the "island hopping" campaign that would ultimately bring it to the Japanese home islands. In October 1942 an energetic general named Montgomery led British forces to victory in

Egypt at El Alamein and drove Rommel's *Afrika Korps* back to Tunisia where it was trapped when Allied forces landed in North Africa in November. By the spring of 1943, the Japanese were on the defensive in the Pacific while, in Russia and North Africa, two German armies had been eliminated.

The South Alberta Regiment, along with the rest of First Canadian Army in Britain, only read about these events in the newspapers. By the fourth year of the war, Canadian soldiers overseas were beginning to get very restless. It was not that the boys disliked wartime Britain with its friendly people, mild weather, strong beer and large dance halls, it was because they had joined the army to fight and, in the spring of 1943, the prospect of combat still appeared to be distant. This long delay was an outcome of the Canadian government's insistence that its soldiers would only go into action as a complete national force under Canadian generals. For this reason, with the exception of Dieppe, First Canadian army took no part in the operations of

Calgary at Dieppe, 19 August 1942

In June 1940 the Calgary Regiment (Tank) contributed a company to the South Alberta Regiment and eight months later was itself mobilized for active service as part of 1st Army Tank Brigade. During the attack on Dieppe, the Calgary Regiment landed a squadron of Churchill tanks on the main beach, including the two vehicles, "Calgary" and "Bob," shown in this photo. There was never much chance that they would get off the beach but their crews remained with their vehicles to cover the withdrawal of the infantry. All the Churchills were lost and the crews killed, wounded or captured. Dieppe provided a valuable but costly lesson on how not to conduct an amphibious assault against a defended beachhead and the deaths of 807 Canadian soldiers were not in vain. COURTESY, KING'S OWN CALGARY REGIMENT MUSEUM

1940-1943, but remained in Britain engaged in seemingly endless training for the eventual return to the European mainland. Its commander, General A.G.L. McNaughton termed his command "a dagger pointed at the heart of Berlin" but that was putting the best possible face on a bad situation.[26]

The 4th Armoured Division, the parent formation of the South Alberta Regiment, being the last major formation to go overseas, was low on the priority list for almost everything. It arrived in Britain without its tanks in the late summer of 1942 and did not receive its full complement of vehicles until early 1943. The SAR, which spent that time at various stations in Hampshire, did what it could, along with the other units of the division, but unfortunately this only too often meant "troop tactics without tanks," walking about hanging on to wooden sticks while providing the necessary sound effects. The first vehicles started to arrive in the SAR lines in late 1942 at about the same time that the regiment learned it was going to be converted to an armoured reconnaissance regiment.

This change of role came about as part of a reorganization of the 4th Division which was in turn prompted by a British decision to change the War Establishment of Commonwealth armoured divisions. British planners, impressed by the swift German success in France in 1940, concluded that the enemy victory was due to the deployment of large numbers of tanks, supported by copious airpower. In actual fact the *Wehrmacht*'s success was based on the mobility of infantry, armour and artillery and a tactical doctrine that stressed the interdependence of the three arms in battle. To the Germans, tanks were only one part of the equation. To the British, tanks seemed to be the answer and, in 1940-1941, they created a huge armoured force of independent brigades and full divisions, the former to assist the infantry in the assault and the latter to carry out manoeuvre warfare. It proved impossible, however, to graft this new structure onto a very conservative army where each of the three arms persisted in a "shop mentality" and, too often, ended up fighting three separate battles instead of one. Experience in North Africa demonstrated that the British armoured organization was unwieldy – too "tank heavy" – and, in late 1942, it was re-modelled along what British planners thought was the German original. What British planners did not seem to comprehend was that the key to German success lay not in organization but in an effective tactical doctrine, and that aping German organization was not necessarily going to duplicate German success. Having no other choice, however, the Canadian army followed the British lead in these matters and, in late 1942 and early 1943, the two Canadian armoured divisions in Britain were restructured.

The introduction of the armoured reconnaissance regiment, modelled on the German *Aufklarungsbatalion*, was one outcome of this change. Unfortunately German reconnaissance doctrine differed from its British equivalent as the Germans were prepared, if necessary, to fight to obtain good and timely information and the *Aufklärungsbatallion* – a combination of medium and light armoured vehicles with mechanized infantry – was created for this purpose. British reconnaissance doctrine stressed more passive means of obtaining intelligence and the result was that nobody in the Commonwealth armies really knew what to do with this new unit.

South Alberta Sports Day, June 1943
A group of uniformed spectators observe the action using a radio truck as a bleacher. The South Albertas were enthusiastic athletes and competed successfully in football, hockey, marksmanship, and just about any other competitive activity but their greatest enthusiasm was reserved for boxing (and the attendant betting). The SAR boxing team, carefully picked and coached, was one of the best in the Commonwealth armies and its brightest star was Trooper Joe Main who won the Canadian army heavyweight championship in 1944 and 1945. CANADIAN ARMY PHOTO, 19601

For the South Albertas – now the 29th Canadian Armoured Reconnaissance Regiment (South Alberta Regiment)* – this change meant that they were now divisional troops – under the direct command of Major-General F.F. ("Fighting Frank") Worthington. Worthington informed them that they had been chosen for this role because, being "keen-eyed Prairie men," they could see farther than units from other parts of Canada.[27] While this may or may not be true, the crusty general definitely took a liking to the SAR – "Worthy," as people called him, was constantly in their lines and used them to test new equipment and weapons, including an experimental automatic rifle and a "baby" light tank. One of the prototypes that came the South Albertas' way in the spring of 1943 was an American M-3 half-track Armoured Command Vehicle, manufactured by the Diamond T Company, the first to be issued to a Commonwealth unit. The SAR tested it thoroughly and, based on their experience, made a number of suggested improvements which were incorporated into later models.

Worthington, whose experience with Lieutenant-Colonel

---

* When the Canadian Armoured Corps was created in 1940, all tank and recce units in the new organization were numbered according to their seniority and this number was used on all official correspondence. This measure was always unpopular with the regiments, who preferred their historic titles, and they waged an unrelenting struggle to, at first, retain their traditional titles, then to have their numbers put in brackets following their titles and, finally, to get rid of the numbers. During the war, the South Albertas always referred to themselves as such, and only used their number in official correspondence.

Bristowe had convinced him that Bristowe was too old for active service, also handpicked a new commanding officer for the South Albertas. His choice was Lieutenant-Colonel Gordon Dorward de Salaberry Wotherspoon (universally known to everyone except those under his immediate command as "Swatty" Wotherspoon), one of the rising stars of the Canadian Armoured Corps. A graduate of RMC, where he carved out an admirable academic record that has rarely been bettered, Wotherspoon was a prewar officer of the Governor-General's Body Guard and had been one of Worthington's protegées when that officer was creating and building the Canadian armoured force during the early years of the war. A brilliant leader and tactician, Wotherspoon was instructing at the Royal Armoured Corps Senior Officer's School when he received a summons from Worthington in May 1943 to take over the SAR. The always-unconventional Worthington greeted Wotherspoon's appearance in his office with the words: "you've got the SARs, they're my pride and joy …… You'd better do well with them."[28]

There was no fear of that. From the moment he entered their lines at Farnham near Aldershot (incidentally interrupting the C Squadron officers at their nightly crap game) Wotherspoon put his stamp on the South Albertas. Discipline was tightened and all officers were evaluated – those whom Wotherspoon deemed too old for combat were posted out of the unit to be replaced by junior officers whom he promoted after they had completed the requisite courses. Training became more intensive and more difficult as Wotherspoon, who discovered that nobody seemed to have any idea as to how an armoured reconnaissance regiment should operate, began to work out his own doctrine by writing bulletins on basic procedures for any foreseeable tactical situation. Wotherspoon, however, always emphasized that the "initiative of the junior leader must NOT be cramped or fettered in any way" as he was a firm believer that a commander should tell his subordinates what to do, not how to do it – with the corollary that they had better have a good idea of how to do it or he would be quickly on the scene.[29] This process went on for the remainder of 1943 and was hampered by the fact that the War Establishment of the armoured reconnaissance regiment was constantly being changed and because of the limited training facilities available in overcrowded wartime Britain. Nonetheless, when the 4th Armoured Division concentrated at

"Swatty": Lieutenant-Colonel Gordon Dorward de Salaberry Wotherspoon

A graduate of the Royal Military College and a rising star in the Canadian Armoured Corps, Worthington picked Wotherspoon to take command of the SAR in the spring of 1943 and he retained that appointment until the last weeks of the war. Not always liked but always respected by his officers and men, "Swatty" Wotherspoon was an outstanding leader and tactician. Here, he is seen in front of "Old Reliable," his half-track Armoured Command Vehicle at Maresfield in the spring of 1944. COURTESY, MICHAEL WOTHERSPOON

Brandon Camp in Norfolk in September 1943 to undertake two months of division level training (the first since it had been formed in June 1940 and the last – although no one knew it at the time – before it was committed to combat), the South Albertas did very well in their new role and Wotherspoon was pleased with their performance.

"Uncle Target! Uncle Target!": 13th Field and the SAR take on new roles, 1940-1943

We left 13th Field Regiment at Farnborough in November 1941 munching on sawdust-laden wartime sausages. Later that month they were fortunate enough to receive their full scale of 25-pdrs. and vehicles and for the next seven months the regiment, along with the remainder of 3rd Canadian Division, acted in the counter-invasion role along the Sussex coast. Beginning in the late summer of 1942, it began to train for offensive warfare and participated in all the major Canadian army schemes held in 1942-1943 including Exercises TIGER, HAROLD, SPARTAN and WELSH. In between times 13th Field carried out lengthy "shoots" at the ranges at Larkhill on Salisbury Plain and Sennybridge in Wales under the exacting and generally caustic supervision of Royal Artillery Instructors in Gunnery. Throughout this period of waiting, the gunners of 13th Field experienced the normal ups and downs of service life in wartime Britain: short rations, comfortable pubs; plentiful leave; hospitable people; crowded and lively London; quiet little country villages; frequent air raids and constant black-outs; not much snow and flowers blooming in February; and friendly young ladies – friendly that is until the better paid Americans started to arrive in great numbers. As Sergeant R.H. Porter of 13th Field commented: "We didn't like the Yanks because they were obnoxious bastards, just like the RAF."[30]

During their first two years in Britain, 13th Field had three commanding officers and two of them – Lieutenant-Colonels H.A. Sparling and W.S. Ziegler – were among the best gunners in the Canadian army and would reach high rank during the war. Sparling and Zeigler were able to quickly assimilate and train the regiment in the newly-developed Commonwealth artillery doctrine. Called either the "Parham system" after the officer primarily responsible for its creation, or the "Uncle Target system," after one of its significant contributions to artillery tactics, from 1943 onward it was to have a major effect in action.

(Left) **Marching, but not as to war: South Albertas at Dundurn, 1940**
B Company of the SAR, recruited in Edmonton by the 19th Alberta Dragoons, carries out yet another hot, dusty, wearying route march at Dundurn in the summer of 1940. The men are wearing sun helmets made out of compressed paper which they called "Jungle Jim" hats, a floppy fatigue sweater and, of course, the infamous mustard-coloured fatigue uniform. SAR ARCHIVES

(Left) **Lunch on the move – Brandon Camp, Norfolk**
In September and October 1943, the 4th Armoured Division concentrated at Brandon Camp in Norfolk to carry out the only divisional-level training it received before being committed to combat in August 1944. Here, five happy South Alberta munchers have a tailgate party in the field. COURTESY, MICHAEL CRAWFORD

(Right) **"Days in England" – 1939-1944**
The experiences detailed here by Sergeant J. Daimer of 12th Field Regiment were common to all the artillery units of 3rd Division, if not to every Canadian soldier in Britain from 1939 to 1944. It was a long wait. FROM *INTO ACTION WITH THE 12TH FIELD*

DAYS IN ENGLAND

YE OLDE COCK AND BULL

TEA IN THE MORNING WAS THE ORDER OF EVERY DAY!

QUIET EVENINGS WERE SPENT IN THE RESTFUL ATMOSPHERE OF THE ENGLISH PUB!!

COWFOLD!

"IT MUST BE AN AWFULLY INTERESTING LIFE ON A GOPHER RANCH!"

SUNNY WALES!

(Above) **Marching, marching, waiting, waiting: The Canadian army in Britain**
For four and a half years, the Canadian army in Britain marched, trained and waited for the invasion of the European mainland. It was not an unpleasant time but it was not what Canadian soldiers had enlisted to do. Note the sergeant in the lead, armed with a Thompson .45 calibre submachinegun. CANADIAN FORCES PHOTO UNIT, PMR 93-374

Changing tracks, Maresfield Camp, 1944
A heavy but necessary task in a tank unit was changing tracks. Here, a group of South Albertas pose for their photo while taking a break from this job at Maresfield Camp in February 1944. SAR ARCHIVES

(Below) Lecture in the field
During the long years of waiting, there were endless briefings, lectures, courses and drills. Here, Lieutenant Dave Mallet of C Squadron of the SAR delivers yet another talk to the men of his troop in Britain in 1943. NAC, PA-146663

(Left) Landing Craft, Tank
For their part in the forthcoming landing in Normandy, the field regiments of 3rd Division would use LCTs like this vessel seen on a training exercise in 1943. Four artillery regiments (12th, 13th, 14th Field and 19th Army Field) trained to fire their self-propelled 105 mm howitzers from these vessels, each troop of four guns being carried on one LCT. CANADIAN FORCES PHOTO UNIT, PMR 93-385

In matters of doctrine and training, the Royal Canadian Artillery followed the lead of the Royal Artillery. During the interwar period, in the interest of conserving ammunition and reducing costs, the RA had stressed pinpoint accuracy and a low rate of fire. While this emphasis was suitable in a peacetime environment, it did not work in wartime conditions as it required a lengthy targetting procedure and a long wait for infantry to obtain artillery support – sometimes as much as an hour. This shortcoming was notable in the French campaign of 1940 and a gunner veteran of that campaign, Brigadier H.J. Parham, began to look for a better and quicker method of engaging targets. Parham decided that, in mobile warfare, pinpoint accuracy would be hard to attain and, in any case, it was not really necessary – the same result could be obtained by simply drenching the area of the target with fire. It was his feeling that "the shock of a large number of rounds arriving simultaneously was far greater than that of a prolonged bombardment" and his solution was "to fire every gun that could bear as soon as it could be laid and loaded."[31]

The key to the Parham system was an efficient communications system based on radio. The gun positions would be fed target information from static OP (Observation Point) officers or mobile FOOs (Forward Observation Officers), located with the forward troops, or AOP (Air Observation Post) aircraft. Connected by radio with their regiments and batteries, these relatively junior officers would identify the target, give its approximate location (often based on a six-digit map reference) and could order a level of fire (that is, the number of guns to be used and rounds to be fired). This information was sent to the GPOs (Gun Position Officers) of each battery who would direct the guns under his command to fire on that target. A troop of four guns was generally the smallest fire unit used in the Parham system and a battery of two troops, or eight guns, was the most common. Parham developed a method which, if the situation warranted, could very quickly bring down heavy fire on the enemy. An observation officer, if authorized, could call for a "Mike," "Uncle," "Victor," or "Yoke" target. A "Mike Target" – the one most commonly used – would be engaged by the 24 guns in a field regiment; an "Uncle Target" by the 72 guns in the three field regiments of an infantry division; a "Victor Target" by all the guns in a corps,

Lieutenant Jack Summers, Maresfield Camp
Typical of the young westerners who served in the SAR, Jack Summers from North Battleford, Saskatchewan, enlisted as a boy soldier in the militia in the mid-1930s and, after going active service, was commissioned in the armoured corps. In early 1943 he joined the SAR and fought throughout the campaign in Northwest Europe, winning the Military Cross. Summers continued in the militia after the war and ended his military career in the 1970s as a brigadier-general commanding Prairie Command. He is seen here wearing the black denim coveralls which were standard armoured corps working dress during the war and after. SAR ARCHIVES

as many as 250 weapons; while a "Yoke Target" would receive the fire of every gun within range which, during the last years of the war, meant that it might be fired at by upwards of as many as 500 weapons.*

The Parham system began to be introduced in the Royal Artillery in late 1942 and in the Royal Canadian Artillery in 1943. As Canadian gunners mastered the new doctrine, their army, after more than three years of waiting and training, commenced sustained operations in July 1943 when the 1st Canadian Division participated in the invasion of Sicily. Following the successful conquest of this island, the Allies invaded the Italian mainland in September and commenced the long, hard job of fighting up the "Italian boot" in mountainous terrain that favoured the defender. Ultimately, the Canadian contribution in Italy increased to an entire corps, comprising the 1st Infantry Division and the 5th Armoured Division, while the 1st Armoured Brigade operated mainly with British troops. Understandably, the Canadian formations which remained behind in Britain – 2nd and 3rd Infantry Divisions, 4th Armoured Division and 2nd Armoured Brigade – began to get restless even though they knew they were being held back for the invasion of France.

By the summer of 1943 planning and preparations for this operation were in full swing. One of the main lessons learned from Dieppe was that, if infantry were to make a successful landing against fixed defences, they must have overwhelming fire support, including close fire support. This had been absent during Operation JUBILEE and the result was that infantry were pinned down on the beach and more or less slaughtered. Planners at Combined Operations Headquarters, the "fourth service" created to conduct amphibious landings for the Western Allies, studied this problem intensively and came up with a solution. It did not come about overnight but gradually evolved from experience gained during the major landings carried out in North Africa (Operation TORCH in November 1942), Sicily (Operation HUSKY, July 1943) and at Salerno and Anzio in Italy (Operation AVALANCHE, September 1943, and ANVIL, February 1944). This

---

* Although it was very rarely used, there was also provision for a "William" Target, a target to be fired at by every gun in an army. It is recorded that the first "William" Target fired by the Commonwealth artillery during the war was called for by Brigadier W.S. Ziegler, the Commander Royal Artillery, 1st Canadian Division, in Italy in 1943.

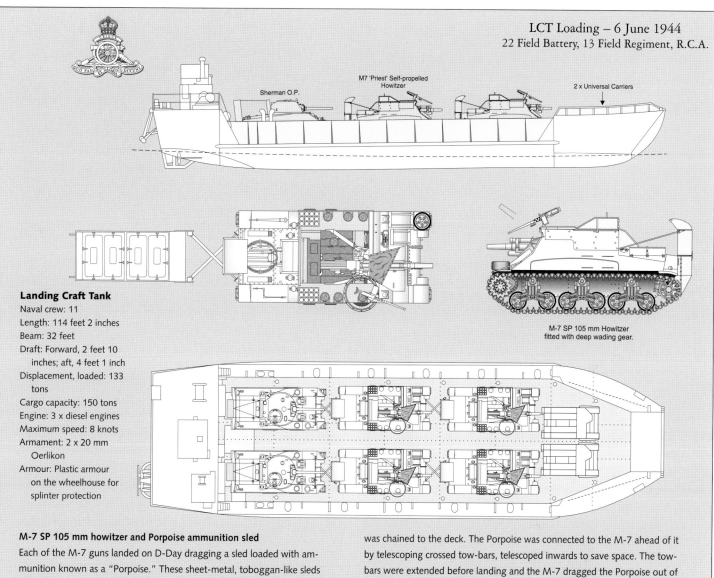

LCT Loading – 6 June 1944
22 Field Battery, 13 Field Regiment, R.C.A.

Sherman O.P.

M7 'Priest' Self-propelled Howitzer

2 x Universal Carriers

Landing Craft Tank
Naval crew: 11
Length: 114 feet 2 inches
Beam: 32 feet
Draft: Forward, 2 feet 10
  inches; aft, 4 feet 1 inch
Displacement, loaded: 133
  tons
Cargo capacity: 150 tons
Engine: 3 x diesel engines
Maximum speed: 8 knots
Armament: 2 x 20 mm
  Oerlikon
Armour: Plastic armour
  on the wheelhouse for
  splinter protection

M-7 SP 105 mm Howitzer
fitted with deep wading gear.

M-7 SP 105 mm howitzer and Porpoise ammunition sled

Each of the M-7 guns landed on D-Day dragging a sled loaded with am-munition known as a "Porpoise." These sheet-metal, toboggan-like sleds were designed to fit between the tracks and under the belly of a Sherman or Churchill tank. When loading an LCT, the Porpoise was dragged by chains hooked to its rear end into the craft and chained to the deck. A Sherman OP or M-7 reversed into the LCT and parked directly over the sled, where it too was chained to the deck. The Porpoise was connected to the M-7 ahead of it by telescoping crossed tow-bars, telescoped inwards to save space. The tow-bars were extended before landing and the M-7 dragged the Porpoise out of the LCT. It was never designed to be anything other than an expedient means to deliver extra ammunition in an assault landing, and M-7 crews soon learned that its thin steel bottom would wear through if dragged over rough terrain for any length of time.

experience was applied to planning for the main event – Opera-tion OVERLORD, the landing in France to be carried out in 1944 – and involved air, naval and ground forces. Aircraft, medium bombers and rocket-equipped tactical fighters, that would take out the enemy's coastal batteries, disrupt his communications and prevent reinforcements being moved forward to the assault area. Large warships would engage targets inland from the beach, while smaller warships would engage targets in the immediate landing area, their fire being directed by Forward Bombard-ment Officers (FBOs) who would land with the assault troops. The FBOs would also direct the fire of a great variety of gun and rocket-armed landing craft that would contribute inshore (less than 1,000 yards from the target) fire support squarely on the beach defences. The army's contribution was to be a "beach barrage" (actually a bombardment) using field guns firing from

LCTs (Landing Craft, Tank) that would keep the defenders' heads down during the final approach to the beach.

In July 1943 the 3rd Canadian Division was selected as one of the six Allied assault formations for Operation OVERLORD and for the next ten months it trained hard for this new role. In Sep-tember the division's three artillery regiments (12th, 13th and 14th Field Regiments) went to the Combined Operations centre at Inverary in western Scotland to learn amphibious techniques and to study ways and means of bringing down the "beach bar-rage." By trial and error it was discovered that a troop of four 25-pdrs. lashed to the deck of an LCT could fire an effective barrage using a director sight mounted on the vessel's bridge, which took the craft's axis as being the zero line. Fire could be brought down on either side of this line at varying ranges – it would not be highly accurate fire but, since the purpose of the beach barrage was to swamp the defenders with shells to keep them under cover, it did not have to be. As well as mastering this new technique, the gunners had to learn other new skills necessary for amphibious assaults – for example, swimming and waterproofing their vehicles – and also how to function while seasick. These skills were acquired at Inverary and the learning process was greatly encouraged when the crews of the landing craft provided the gunners with the navy's traditional daily tot of grog. In early October 1943, when the field regiments returned from Inverary, they went to the Bournemouth area on the Hampshire coast to undertake more advanced training with the naval and air task forces that would actually fight with them on the day.

A very distinguished visitor

One Distinguished Visitor Demonstration that no Canadian soldier minded was one for King George VI. On 25 April 1944 the Sovereign inspected the field regiments of 3rd Canadian Division and can be seen here, passing by the vehicles of Dog Troop, 14th Field Regiment, as the gunners, dressed in spotless uniforms, stand at attention on spotless vehicles. NAC, PA-145376

At the same time, the 3rd Division gunners began to receive new equipment. In order to reduce the number of vehicles to be carried on the landing craft and because there was a chance that, after landing, the gunners might become involved in close quarter fighting, it was decided that their 25-pdrs would be replaced by the American-built M7 self-propelled gun. This was a lightly-armoured 105 mm howitzer mounted on the running gear of the Grant tank which would later be christened the "Priest." In addition, for better protection, the artillery OP officers would use Sherman tanks instead of soft-skinned vehicles. This new equipment did not require a change of tactics since, once ashore, the regiment would continue to use the Parham system of artillery control, simply substituting their self-propelled guns for 25-pdrs. The first of the new guns and tanks began to arrive in 13th Field's lines in October and the regiment was very busy during the last two months of 1943 as the gunners learned to drive, maintain and fire from this new equipment. They set to it with a will and, as their regimental history records, it was not long before the self-propelled 105mm guns were

> roaring along the crowded streets of Bournemouth on their way, perhaps, to another of the many waterborne exercises, or to the New Forest area; their seven man crews perched on top beside the gun and among the shell cases or web equipment, all dressed in black coveralls and wearing the new assault type steel helmet."[32]

From late 1943 to the spring of 1944, the field regiments of 3rd Division carried out four full-scale exercises with Force J, the naval task force that would take them to France on the appointed day. The last of these training schemes was Exercise TROUSERS in early April which featured a full-scale landing at Slapton Sands on the southwest coast of England. Slapton was a place with features that closely resembled JUNO Beach, 3rd Division's future landing site in Normandy, complete with mock German defences based on intelligence from aerial photos. At this time, for security reasons, the officers and gunners of 13th Field did not know their actual landing site and codenames replaced actual names during training. Interspersed with the amphibious exercises, 13th Field carried out, along with the three other assault artillery regiments (12th and 14th Field, and 19th Canadian Army Field), two lengthy shoots at the British artillery range at Larkhill to sharpen their conventional skills.

In the spring of 1944 the regiment also experienced (or suffered) a number of DVDs (Distinguished Visitor Demonstrations) or inspections by senior officers. Among them was General Bernard L. Montgomery, recently appointed to command the Allied ground forces for the invasion. Surveying the men and equipment of the three field regiments of 3rd Division drawn up before him, Montgomery remarked: "I have never seen so many gunners together at one time before" but "to see so many is good as it is the gunners who win wars."[33] Monty probably said that to every artillery unit he visited that spring but it was the thought that counted and it was appreciated. For the gunners of 3rd Division, however, the DVD that really mattered was the inspection by King George VI – an unmistakable sign that action was approaching – which took place on 25 April 1944. "For days," the historian of the RCA wrote, the air around their camps was "heavy with green dust from relentless blancoing of web equipment, and redolent with the odour of Silvo."[34] Wearing their "knife-edge creased battledress and glistening boots," the gunners were subjected at "preliminary inspections to the scrutiny of officers at every level from troop commander up to the G.O.C. himself" before being viewed by the King, who was accompanied by Lieutenant-General H.D.G. Crerar, commanding First Canadian Army, and Vincent Massey, the Canadian High Commissioner to Britain. All went well on the day – at least the King had no complaints (but then he rarely did).

A few weeks later 13th Field Regiment moved to their final staging area at Park Gate Camp, just east of Southampton, to wait for the invasion. Up until this time, only the senior officers of the regiment knew all the details of the forthcoming landing but now junior officers and gunners were briefed, although with false code and grid references, "giving the suggestion that the landing was to take place farther north in the Calais area."[35] There were some disconcerting rumours floating around 3rd Division at this time

to the effect that it could expect to suffer 50-75% casualties on the beaches and that it was "given only a week to survive as a fighting division."[36] Men put information like this out of their minds but, just in case, took care to make out proper wills and write last letters to families or loved ones.

Meanwhile, about 50 miles to the east near Brighton in Sussex, the South Alberta Regiment was also preparing for their part in OVERLORD. For the SAR, the period since their two-month training period in Norfolk in September and October 1943 had been a very busy time. Late in the year their Ram II tanks had been replaced by Shermans and their carriers by Stuart V light tanks and they had to master these new vehicles and "shoot them in" which meant, for each squadron in turn, a trip

COMBINED OPERATIONS — PRACTICE. It took some time before the assault practice landings were able to go according to plan.

Combined operations – practice
Beginning in the summer of 1943, 13th Field Regiment began to train for its role in the forthcoming invasion of Europe. As the regimental cartoonist, Lieutenant Patrick Clay, emphasizes, it took time for the gunners to get acclimatized to the business. COURTESY, PATRICK CLAY. FROM *THE HISTORY OF 13 CANADIAN FIELD REGIMENT*

(Left) **Combined operations – theory**
As Lieutenant Clay indicates, relations between the army and navy were usually very friendly. FROM *THE HISTORY OF 13 CANADIAN FIELD REGIMENT*

COMBINED OPERATIONS — THEORY. The captain's cabin on board one of the landing craft where the "combined" part of the operations was most congenial.

north to Warcop Range in Norfolk. They had just finished this task in February 1944 and Wotherspoon and his three squadron commanders had just completed a training syllabus for the next three months when, in the space of two weeks, they were informed that the SAR would be reorganized on the War Establishment of an armoured regiment and would undertake a new role in battle, supporting the infantry of the 4th Division.

The man responsible for these changes was Montgomery. After he had taken over 21 Army Group – the Commonwealth forces gathered for the forthcoming invasion – in December 1943, Montgomery directed that all armoured reconnaissance regiments in First Canadian Army and Second British Army were to be reorganized as armoured regiments, although they were permitted to keep their distinctive titles. Second, he directed that henceforth, there would be no more talk of infantry and cruiser tanks but that in 21 Army Group, all armoured units would be trained to either support the infantry to break into the enemy's defences or to exploit a breakout, once those defences had been breached.

The result was yet another hectic period for the SAR as it reorganized for the third time in a little over a year. Once it was complete, the regiment consisted of a Regimental Headquarters to which were attached the Recce Troop of Stuart light tanks and the Anti-Aircraft Troop of Crusader III AA tanks. There were three fighting squadrons (A, B and C), each consisting of a Squadron Headquarters Troop of three Sherman tanks, and four fighting troops, each with four Shermans. Supply and transport vehicles were under the control of Headquarters Squadron (not to be confused with RHQ) which controlled the vehicles of A Echelon, which supplied the fighting troops with ammunition, gasoline and rations and B Echelon, which contained all the necessary but non-combat elements such as the cooks, paymaster, dentist, etc. With some minor variations, the SAR retained this structure, with which it possessed a total of 78 tanks, until the end of the war.

Having carried out this change, the South Albertas commenced training with the units of 10th Infantry Brigade commanded by Brigadier James Jefferson from Edmonton, who had

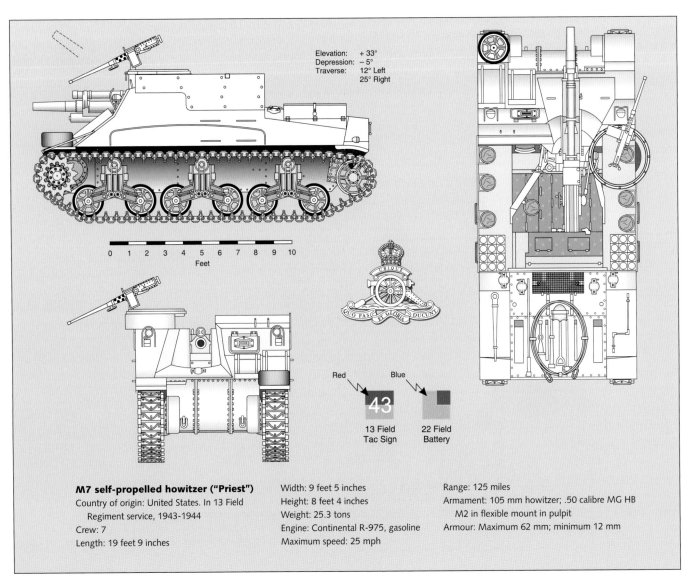

Elevation: + 33°
Depression: − 5°
Traverse: 12° Left
            25° Right

0 1 2 3 4 5 6 7 8 9 10
Feet

Red   Blue

43

13 Field   22 Field
Tac Sign   Battery

M7 self-propelled howitzer ("Priest")
Country of origin: United States. In 13 Field
    Regiment service, 1943-1944
Crew: 7
Length: 19 feet 9 inches

Width: 9 feet 5 inches
Height: 8 feet 4 inches
Weight: 25.3 tons
Engine: Continental R-975, gasoline
Maximum speed: 25 mph

Range: 125 miles
Armament: 105 mm howitzer; .50 calibre MG HB
    M2 in flexible mount in pulpit
Armour: Maximum 62 mm; minimum 12 mm

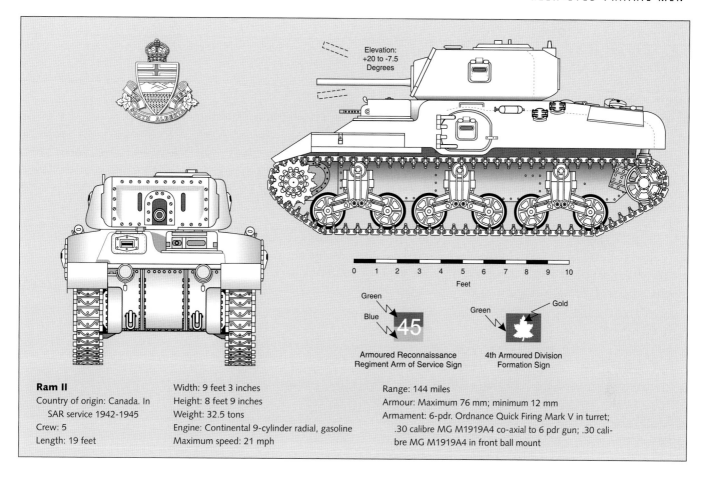

Ram II
Country of origin: Canada. In
   SAR service 1942-1945
Crew: 5
Length: 19 feet

Width: 9 feet 3 inches
Height: 8 feet 9 inches
Weight: 32.5 tons
Engine: Continental 9-cylinder radial, gasoline
Maximum speed: 21 mph

Range: 144 miles
Armour: Maximum 76 mm; minimum 12 mm
Armament: 6-pdr. Ordnance Quick Firing Mark V in turret;
   .30 calibre MG M1919A4 co-axial to 6 pdr gun; .30 calibre MG M1919A4 in front ball mount

won the DSO leading the Loyal Edmonton Regiment in the bitter fighting at Ortona in Italy in the previous December. In the early winter of 1944, when veterans from the Italian theatre were brought up to take over the senior appointments in 4th Armoured Division, Jefferson got 10th Infantry Brigade while Brigadier Leslie Booth, who had also won the DSO in that theatre, took over 4th Armoured Brigade. The biggest change, and one the SAR did not like as they were fond of their hard-bitten general, was that Worthington was replaced as divisional commander by Major-General George Kitching. Lieutenant-General Guy Simonds, the commander of 2 Canadian Corps, under which the division would fight in the forthcoming campaign, deemed Worthington too old for combat and the father of the Canadian armoured corps, who had built it up from scratch in the late 30s and early war years, was shuffled off to a training position in Canada.

Jefferson's 10th Infantry Brigade consisted of three Ontario infantry battalions: the Lincoln and Welland Regiment from the Niagara area; the Argyll and Sutherland Highlanders from Hamilton; and the Algonquin Regiment from the northern part of the province, supported by 15th Field Regiment and the New Brunswick Rangers which manned heavy mortars and medium machineguns. As the brigade historian commented, the coming of the SAR "was a great event because" the infantry of the brigade had always found the western tankers "most co-operative" and were "pleased to have armour with them, especially

S.A.R. armour."[37] In April 1944, just as the spring foliage of Sussex reached its best bloom, the South Albertas exercised with their flatfooted friends on the South Downs of Sussex. From the beginning, Wotherspoon insisted that each of his three squadrons train with one particular battalion so that the commanders would get to know each other and form effective teams. Thus, A Squadron was mated with the Lincoln and Welland Regiment, B with the Algonquin Regiment and C with the Argylls. In turn, each squadron and battalion completed up to ten days of joint training and, since almost all the senior SAR officers were former infantrymen, they did not find it difficult to undertake this new role. As Swatty Wotherspoon put it, to be "good tank support for the infantry, you had to be skilled in good infantry tactics, know what they should be doing and how they should do it."[38]

By early May 1944, Wotherspoon was satisfied that his regiment was as well prepared as he could make it. This was just as well as, on 20 May, the SAR was instructed to waterproof its vehicles, an onerous task that took it nearly two and a half weeks and which put an end to all active training because, once water-proofed, vehicles could not be moved any great distance. By now the South Albertas knew that the 4th Division would not be landing in the initial assault but would be part of the "follow up" forces and they therefore had a long time still to wait. They spent it route marching, doing small arms practice, map exercises and watching musical and variety shows that visited their camp. The officers' mess put a positive face on the matter by

221

"Break ranks and gather round": Monty addresses the troops, 1944

In the spring of 1944 Canadian units waiting to take part in the invasion of Europe suffered a number of DVDs (Distinguished Visitor Demonstrations) for senior officers such as Eisenhower and Montgomery. Perched on the hood of a jeep, Monty asks the gunners of the field regiments of 3rd Canadian Division to gather round so he can give them a pep talk. It was during this event that Monty assured his audience that "gunners win wars" – a fact they already knew. Note the dog, who is following orders by breaking rank. NAC, PA-132891

holding a weekly "farewell" dance every Saturday night to which they invited any gullible young female within 30 miles, who was willing to attend. In June, a popular form of entertainment was observing the German V-1 flying bombs pass over Maresfield day and night on their way to London and, one night, Captain Robert Allsopp, the adjutant, apprehended Captain A. Phillips Silcox, the padre, shooting at the things with a .38 revolver from a slit trench dug behind the officers' mess. Other than that, there was nothing else to do but wait, along with hundreds of thousands of other soldiers on both sides of the English Channel.

"Abide with me; fast falls the eventide": Final days, final hours

At Park Gate Camp near Southampton, meanwhile, 13th Field Regiment was "locked down" on 27 May 1944 with no one being permitted to enter or leave their lines. The men of the unit spent the final days before the invasion practising at loading their guns, OP tanks and other vehicles onto a mock up of an LCT that had been constructed at the camp. Because of the limited lift capac-

ity of Force J, the amphibious naval force, the unit would only be able to take its guns, OP tanks and the signals' carriers but not its administrative and supply vehicles which would land two days after the assault. Ammunition would be limited and, therefore, each of the guns was fitted with a "Porpoise," a metal sled packed with extra rounds of 105 mm ammunition which would be dragged behind each gun to its first firing position on shore. The "Porpoise" was one of those bright ideas conceived by staff officers that work better on paper than in reality and everyone was little nervous about the things – as Sergeant R.J. Porter of 44 Battery put it: "that SOB had enough explosive in it to blow us to pieces."[39] Having by this time in their service considerable experience with staff plans, the gunners wisely suspected that it might take longer for the supply echelons to come ashore, and this resulted in the vehicle crews stealing or scrounging "all sorts of material to fit our guns and vehicles up for the assault."[40] Vehicles were packed and repacked, waterproofing was checked and rechecked, gun detachments dry fired again and again, sig-

Recently scalped, Maresfield 1944

As the time for action approached, many South Albertas had their hair cut short in preparation for service in the field, as Sergeants Freeman and Jellis demonstrate. Freeman is wearing the black denim overall that served as a tank suit and fatigue uniform before the issue of the "zoot suit" in the autumn of 1944. COURTESY, WALLY JELLIS

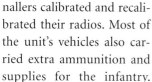

Landing Craft Tank in the Solent near Southampton, 4 June 1944
After the gunners boarded their landing craft, they still faced a five-day wait until they crossed the Channel to Normandy. In this photograph, the LCTs of 12th Field Regiment can be seen awaiting orders to form up for the cross-Channel voyage. FROM *INTO ACTION WITH THE 12TH FIELD*

nallers calibrated and recalibrated their radios. Most of the unit's vehicles also carried extra ammunition and supplies for the infantry. Other than that, the men waited and played volleyball and cards to pass the time, Sergeant Alex Brennand remembered that this time was "hard on the nerves as we knew the big push was coming but we didn't know when."[41]

On the morning of 29 May, the gunners of 13th Field figured it would not be much longer because the paymaster issued them French francs. That day passed like the others but the evening provided some unwelcome excitement when a German aircraft raided the Southampton area and dropped a single bomb on the crowded vehicle lines in Park Gate camp. It hit a B Troop gun and set off its contents including "mines, small arms, ammunition, grenades, mortar bombs and PIAT bombs."[42] Within seconds, the conflagration spread among the adjacent vehicles packed close around it but, as the regimental historian notes, the gunners of 13th Field reacted quickly:

> The drivers entered the vehicles even though some were burning and drove them to safety through a wall of fire and exploding ammunition. There is no question that their actions saved over half of the regimental equipment and many lives. Under the direction of Major Baird [officer commanding 22 Battery], the men also fought the blaze and explosions with a fire hose working from vehicle to vehicle using one vehicle for protection and bringing to bear the stream of water on the next vehicle ahead. The fires were eventually brought under control after three hours of explosions so violent at times that large portions of the armoured equipment were thrown some distance away. A motorcycle was found blown a distance of 800 yards. Besides the equipment, many houses in the district were wrecked, yet no one was killed or seriously injured.[43]

When it was over 22 Battery had lost four guns, two Shermans, a jeep and three motorcycles destroyed beyond repair.

Hurry up and wait – the final hours, June 1944
After nearly three and a half years in Britain, the gunners of 13th Field were anxious to get into action but they still had to wait for the final order to cross the Channel. They passed their time reading, talking, sleeping and playing cards. These men had been told that they can expect to take 50% casualties on the beaches but have put the thought out of their minds. FROM *INTO ACTION WITH THE 12TH FIELD*

Three of the guns were from B Troop and one, commanded by Sergeant James Moffat, from A Troop. Moffat remembered that his crew had "saved our rations and parcels from home and cigarettes and we lost all and that hurt the worst."[44] Moffat was given the surviving gun from B Troop which then received four new vehicles, and every officer and gunner in the battery pitched in to help the crews waterproof, provision and test the new vehicles, a job that normally took two weeks but which, with the extra help, was accomplished in two days.

On the morning after the bombing raid, advance parties left for nearby Bournemouth and Gosport and they were followed on 1 June 1944 by the assault element with their vehicles. The regiment was allotted six LCTs, each to carry the four guns of a troop, and two of the twelve OP tanks, with the remaining fighting echelon vehicles to come in a later lift. Loading, practised so many times before, went smoothly although it was always tricky getting the last gun on board as the driver had no room to manoeuvre and more or less had to skid into the correct position. The two tanks were loaded first, at the rear of the vehicle compartment, and two Porpoises were placed under them which were fastened by metal rods to the rear of the two guns which were loaded next. Two more Porpoises were then placed under these guns and fastened to the final two guns to come on board. Once each vessel was loaded, it steamed out into Southampton harbour to its allotted waiting position. The gunners passed the next few days in various ways, playing craps and poker, reading books (Gunner William McCrie remembered his chosen reading material was Martha Albrand's 1942 novel, *No Surrender,* about the Dutch Resistance), listening to the Armed Forces Network radio, or just napping. The crew of Sergeant Alex Brennand's gun managed to smuggle a rare bottle of whisky on board and that helped to pass the time. Although everybody was sure that this was the real thing, not another exercise, they didn't worry about it – Gunner McCrie expressed his comrades' philosophy: "we didn't have any idea but we weren't too inquisitive as we would go where we were sent and they knew best."[45]

The invasion had been scheduled to take place in the early morning of 5 June 1944 but bad weather prompted the Supreme Allied Commander, General Dwight D. Eisenhower, to delay it for 24 hours on Saturday, 4 June. By Sunday afternoon the weather had not greatly improved and everyone fully expected a further postponement. There was surprise, therefore, when the signals "Up Anchors," and "Take Station" were flashed to the vessels in Force J. As the six landing craft of the 13th Field group steamed slowly to their places in the formation, they were shepherded by Major George Baird in a fast motor launch which played "The Grenadiers," the artillery quick march, over its loudspeakers. When all vessels were in place, the regimental group moved slowly down the Solent behind Baird's launch and, as it passed a flotilla of Royal Navy destroyers, their crews manned the sides in honour of the men who would make the first assault on Hitler's *Festung Europa.* And then it was out into the open sea, guided by seemingly endless rows of twinkling, floating, luminous markers that provided a safe lane through the minefields protecting Southampton. At this point, to mark the occasion, Sergeant Brennand's comrades inserted a hastily-written message, "Liberators of Europe," into their now empty whisky bottle, corked it and threw it overboard.[46]

Once out of harbour, the ships' safes were opened and correct maps and air photos of the landing beaches, as well as final instructions, were distributed. The gunners of 13th Field were briefed on the forthcoming attack in minute detail and warned again that 50% casualties might be suffered on the first day but "that reinforcements were standing by ready to take their place on short notice."[47] This dire prediction had been heard so many times that it was beginning to lose its effect and, besides, as Sergeant Moffat of 22 Battery commented, "we were all volunteers, we weren't pushed into it."[48] Gunner Norman Hunter agreed – he recalled that his comrades "didn't know what to expect as we had never been shot at but we were in good spirits."[49]

Throughout the night Force J steamed steadily for Normandy on a very choppy sea which caused problems for some men. Gunner Drummond Cotterill of 44 Battery remembered that trip because it was the only time he ever became seasick during any of his wartime voyages. Lieutenant Patrick Clay was in charge of dispensing seasickness pills on his LCT but was himself so ill that he personally consumed most of the stock himself but did not find them very effective. Near midnight, the gunners, trying to sleep on their vehicles on the bobbing, pitching craft, looked up into a dark sky as hundreds of aircraft – bombers carrying out missions and transports carrying the 6th Airborne Division to its landing sites – passed overhead. After the throbbing of engines had died away, the quiet was almost deafening.

At about 5 A.M., the eastern sky began to lighten and the dawn of Monday, 6 June 1944, revealed a "dull, overcast day with everything in shades of gray," poor visibility and low cloud ceiling.[50] As the infantry began to climb down from their mother ships into the tiny assault landing craft, the six LCTs of 13th Field formed into two ranks of three craft and then, tossing and turning "in one of the roughest seas the men had ever experienced," moved slowly toward a shore that could just barely be seen by the naked eye.[51] In these final minutes, Honorary Captain H.L. Chappell, the regimental chaplain, held a brief prayer service on one of the LCTs which concluded with the singing of the old hymn:

> Abide with me; fast falls the eventide;
> The darkness deepens; Lord, with me abide;
> When other helpers fail, and comforts flee,
> Help of the helpless, O, abide with me.

Anxious eyes scanned the sky for the appearance of the tactical aircraft which were to lead off the bombardment but the air force was late that morning and the time passed, incredibly slowly, as the pitching LCTs moved inshore at a steady speed of 6 knots.

Suddenly, aircraft were overhead and on each LCT the command was shouted to "Take Post!" In response, the gunners mounted their vehicles, removed the canvas muzzle caps, sight and breech covers, checked mechanisms, and then set the ranges on their sights according to orders from the bridge of each landing craft where the troop leader was making the final calculations. This done, they loaded the first 105 mm round.

At 7.05 A.M., some 11,500 yards off Courseulles-sur-Mer on the coast of Normandy, came the order: "Open Fire!" In response, the No. 2 on each gun yanked the lanyard on the right side of the breech and 13th Field Regiment, Royal Canadian Artillery, entered the Second World War.

A Light Horse Colour Album

Guidon of The South Alberta Light Horse
Presented by HRH, Princess Alexandra, in May 1967, the Guidon bears the Battle Honours earned by the Rocky Mountain Rangers in the Northwest Rebellion, the 31st Battalion, CEF in the First World War, and the South Alberta Regiment (Canadian Active Service Force) in the Second World War. SALH ARCHIVES

Memorial Colour of the 29th Canadian Armoured Reconnaissance Regiment (South Alberta Regiment)
Prior to 1939, the South Alberta Regiment had not yet received its Colours and there was no time to procure them during the Second World War, nor before the regiment was amalgamated to form the South Alberta Light Horse. In 1995, the veterans of the wartime South Alberta Regiment procured a replica Colour and laid it up with great ceremony in the Alberta Legislature Building, where it can be seen today. SALH ARCHIVES

Colours of the 31st Battalion, Canadian Expeditionary Force
Received at Namur, Belgium, in early 1919, the King's and Regimental Colours of the 31st Battalion bear the Battle Honours earned by that unit during the First World War. Today, these Colours are laid up in the Pro-Cathedral Church of the Redeemer in Calgary. FROM H.C. SINGER, HISTORY OF THE 31ST BATTALION

Colours of the 101st Regiment, "Edmonton Fusiliers"
Presented to that unit in 1911, these Colours were used by the 19th Alberta Armoured Car Regiment, formed by an amalgamation of the 19th Alberta Dragoons and the Edmonton Fusiliers, after 1946. Today, they are laid up in Holy Trinity Church in Edmonton. FROM H.G. KENNEDY, HISTORY OF THE EDMONTON FUSILIERS

Ceremonial troop, 19th Alberta Dragoons, 1939
During the Royal Visit of 1939, the Dragoons formed a mounted troop in full dress uniform to provide an Escort to the Sovereign during the visit of King George VI and Queen Elizabeth to Edmonton. The troop trained intensively and the hard work paid off, as can be seen in this picture. COURTESY, HARRY QUARTON

We Will Remember Them
Every 11th November on Remembrance Day, the Light Horse Ceremonial Troop, dressed in the uniforms of the 15th Light Horse, mounts a Guard of Honour at the War Memorial in the little town of Chipman, east of Edmonton. Chipman was chosen as the venue for the Regiment's main activity on this important day because it represents the many small communities across Alberta who sent their sons forth to fight in the predecessor units of the South Alberta Light Horse: the 31st Alberta Battalion and the Canadian Light Horse of the Canadian Expeditionary Force; the 29th Canadian Armoured Reconnaissance Regiment (South Alberta Regiment) and 13th Field Regiment, RCA. The Regiment's Fallen are never forgotten. SALH ARCHIVES

Hat badge, Canadian troops,
South African War, 1899-1902

Hat badge, 15th Light Horse, used
with variations from 1905 to 1946

Hat badge, 15th Light Horse,
officer's pattern

Puggaree badge, 19th Alberta Mounted
Rifles, c. 1908-1911

Hat badge, 19th Alberta Dragoons, used
with variations from 1911 to 1946

Hat badge, 21st Alberta Hussars,
1908-1920

Hat badge, 23rd Alberta
Rangers, 1908-1920

Hat badge, 3rd Canadian Mounted
Rifles, 1914-1916

Canadian Light Horse, slip-on
and shoulder titles, 1916-1919

Hat badge, 13th Canadian
Mounted Rifles, 1914-1916

Hat badge, 12th Canadian
Mounted Rifles, 1914-1916

BADGES ARE NOT SHOWN TO SCALE

Hat badge, 9th Battalion, CEF,
1914-1919

Hat badge, 31st (Alberta) Battalion, CEF,
1914-1919

Formation/unit patches, 31st (Alberta)
Battalion, CEF, 1916-1919

Hat badge, 66th Overseas Battalion
(Edmonton Guards), CEF, 1915-1916

Hat badge, 113th Overseas
Battalion (Lethbridge
Highlanders), CEF, 1915-1916

Hat badge, 138th (Edmonton)
Overseas Battalion, CEF,
1915-1916

Hat badge, 175th (Medicine Hat)
Overseas Battalion, CEF, 1916-1917

Hat badge, 187th (Central Alberta)
Overseas Battalion, CEF, 1916-1917

Hat badge, 202nd (Sportsmen)
Overseas Battalion, CEF, 1916-1917

BADGES ARE NOT SHOWN TO SCALE

Hat badge, Alberta Mounted
Rifles, 1920-1936

Collar badges, 2nd Regiment,
Alberta Mounted Rifles,
1920-1931

Hat badge, South Alberta Horse,
1931-1936

Hat badge, Canadian Artillery and Royal
Canadian Artillery, 1919-1952

Hat badge, Edmonton Fusiliers,
1924-1926

Hat badge, Alberta
Regiment, 1920-1924

Collar badge, 1st Battalion,
Alberta Regiment, 1922-1924

Collar badge, 2nd Battalion,
Alberta Regiment, 1922-1924

Hat badge, South Alberta Regiment,
enlisted man, used with variations
from 1924 to 1954

Hat badge, South Alberta
Regiment, officer

Hat badge, Canadian Machine Gun
Corps, 1919-1936

Collar badge, 13th Brigade, Canadian Machine
Gun Corps, 1919-1936

Regimental flash, South Alberta Regiment,
29th CARR, 1940-1946

Beret badge, officer, South Alberta Regiment,
29th CARR, 1940-1946

Regimental flash, 31st Alberta
Reconnaissance Regiment, 1942-1945

Shoulder tab, 13th Field Regiment, RCA, 1940-1946

Regimental flash, 31st Alberta
Reconnaissance Regiment, 1942-1945,
variant

Shoulder tab, 41st Anti-Tank Regiment, RCA, 1946-1954

Regimental flash, Edmonton Fusiliers),
c. 1940-1946

Hat badge, 19th Armoured Car
Regiment (Edmonton Fusiliers),
1946-1949

Hat badge, Royal Canadian Artillery,
1952 to date

Hat badge, South Alberta
Light Horse, 1954-2005

BADGES ARE NOT SHOWN TO SCALE

UNIFORMS OF THE SOUTH ALBERTA LIGHT HORSE AND PREDECESSORS, 1885-2005

Displayed on this page and those following are paintings from the brush of Ron Volstad, an Edmonton artist who specializes in military subjects and whose work is internationally known. The seventeen figures (including twelve specially commissioned for this book) illustrated on these pages depict the uniforms, weapons and equipment of the South Alberta Light Horse and its predecessors over a 120-year period and colourfully show the transition from Winchesters, six-guns and chaps in 1885, through battle dress and battle bowlers in the 1940s, to CADPAT and Cougars in the 21st century.

Private
2nd Battalion, Canadian Mounted Rifles
South Africa, 1900

Dragoon
19th Alberta Dragoons
c. 1912

WESTERN CAVALRY

COURTESY OF THE DIRECTORATE OF HISTORY AND HERITAGE, DND

Rocky Mountain Ranger
Medicine Hat, 1885

Private
31st (Alberta) Battalion, CEF
Calgary, 1914

Squadron Sergeant-Major
Canadian Light Horse
France, 1918

VOLSTAD '05

PREDECESSORS OF THE SOUTH ALBERTA LIGHT HORSE (1)

Corporal
15th Light Horse
Calgary, 1908

Lieutenant
23rd Alberta Rangers
Fort Macleod, 1909

Fusilier
101st Regiment, "Edmonton Fusiliers"
Edmonton, 1913

VOLSTAD '05

PREDECESSORS OF THE SOUTH ALBERTA LIGHT HORSE (2)

Sergeant
31st Alberta Reconnaissance Regiment
New Westminster, 1943

Corporal
19th Alberta Dragoons
Royal Visit, Edmonton, 1939

Lieutenant, Forward Observation Officer
13th Field Regiment, Royal Canadian Artillery
Normandy, 1944

PREDECESSORS OF THE SOUTH ALBERTA LIGHT HORSE (3)

Sergeant
Khaki Drill
Niagara Camp, 1941

Lieutenant
Battle Dress
England, 1943

Trooper
Tank Suit
Rhineland, 1945

VOLSTAD 97

PREDECESSORS OF THE SOUTH ALBERTA LIGHT HORSE (4)
29TH CANADIAN ARMOURED RECONNAISSANCE REGIMENT
(SOUTH ALBERTA REGIMENT)

Lieutenant
Bush Dress
Sarcee Camp, 1962

Master-Corporal
Combat Dress
Serving with UNPROFOR, Medak Pocket,
Croatia, 1993

Trooper
CADPAT Uniform
Wainwright Camp, 2005

THE SOUTH ALBERTA LIGHT HORSE

The Rocky Mountain Rangers, 1885
A drawing by John Higginbotham showing the Rangers as they appeared at Fort McLeod in the spring of 1885. Buckskins, broncos, bandoliers and Winchesters are prominently displayed but why there is a goat on the roof of the building at right remains a mystery. CANADIAN PICTORIAL AND ILLUSTRATED WAR NEWS

(Right) **The Alberta cavalry in advertising**
Produced sometime shortly before the First World War, these little cards were part of a series depicting the uniforms of the British Empire that numbered more than one hundred. Such incentives to sell cigarettes and candy were popular throughout the 20th century and continue today. Unfortunately, the artist got almost all the details wrong except for the regimental titles – but the thought was nice. COURTESY, COLIN MICHAUD

OFFICER 23RD ALBERTA RANGERS
PINCHER CREEK ALTA

OFFICER 15TH LIGHT HORSE
CALGARY

19TH ALBERTA DRAGOONS
EDMONTON

Worthy and his Keen-Eyed Prairie Men
Major-General F.F. Worthington, Colonel-Commandant of the Royal Canadian Armoured Corps, poses with the officers of the South Alberta Light Horse during one of consecutive visits he made in 1962, 1963 and 1964 to Medicine Hat to present his trophy to the Regiment. Front row, left to right: Captain Doug Heine, Major Hank Sorenson, Lieutenant-Colonel N.R. Ray, commanding officer, General Worthington, Major R. Ainscough, Major G. McQueen, Major D. Moore. Second row, left to right: Lieutenant L. MacDonald, Lieutenant Herman Wahl, Captain Fairburn, Captain U. Carney, Captain Don Mulford. Top row, left to right: Lieutenant L. Eckroth, Lieutenant D. Merchant, Captain A. Taylor, Captain R. Thain and Captain S. Spavold. Worthy's visits were always scheduled around Grey Cup time in November as he liked to watch the game with the Light Horse and have a ride in "Old Reliable," Swatty Wotherspoon's wartime halftrack. SALH ARCHIVES

Keeping the peace, 1993

In the last decade of the 20th century, the soldiers from the SALH began to see service on overseas deployments with the regular Canadian army. Here, Light Horse personnel serving with NATO forces in Croatia in 1993 pose on a knocked-out Serbian T-34/85 tank. On the turret from left to right are Master-Corporal C. Howie, Trooper T.A. Louise and Corporal Chartier. On the ground is Corporal Henderson. SALH

(Below) **Cougars in the mist**

For nearly a quarter of a century the Cougar AVGP (Armoured Vehicle, General Purpose) has been the main training platform of militia armoured units and has served that purpose well. Below, Cougars of the combined battle squadron on Exercise ACTIVE EDGE arrive at the range early on an August morning in 2004. To the right, a Light Horse crew prepares for a battle run on Exercise ANTELOPE III in 1988 – from left to right are Master-Corporal D.M. Aasburg, Corporal G.M. Yanda and Trooper S.E. Kolke. COURTESY, BRETT WALTON AND CANADIAN FORCES

"Old Reliable" back on parade, 2005

After nearly 9,000 hours of hard work by a volunteer restoration team, "Old Reliable," the veteran trooper, was returned to pristine shape in its 1943 configuration in time for the Regiment's Centennial in 2005, marking its 62nd year of service with either the South Alberta Regiment or the South Alberta Light Horse. On the right are three members of the Light Horse restoration team: Sergeant Robert McCue (top), Corporal Adrian Winton (driver's seat) and Corporal Ian Christie (standing). Other members of the team were: Warrant Officer David Bergt, CD; Sergeant Jon Wilding; Master-Corporals Shawn Alexander, Christopher Elliott, Christine Fraser and Lindsey Manns; Corporals Kirk Routledge, CD, Sean MacIntyre, Falk Moehrle, Jocelyn Stickel, Francois Bergeron, Marshall Kartz; and Trooper David James. The upper photo shows the plaques mounted on the vehicle which list the names of the original crew and of the restoration team.

From Normandy in 1944 to Oldenburg in 1945, "Old Reliable" was present at every major battle fought by the South Alberta Regiment, but perhaps its most famous use was on Hill 117 north of St. Lambert when it provided communications for Lieutenant-Colonel Gordon ("Swatty") Wotherspoon to co-ordinate the battle to close the Falaise Gap in August 1944. This action resulted in the only Victoria Cross to be won by the Canadian Armoured Corps during the Second World War and the only VC to be won by the Canadian army in Normandy. PHOTOGRAPHS BY VERN KLOTZ

"Fire!" 7.05 A.M., Monday, 6 June 1944

Captain John MacIsaac, 14th Field Regiment, watches from the bridge of his LCT as the guns of Fox Troop, 81 Battery, RCA, open fire on JUNO Beach.

COURTESY, LIEUTENANT-COLONEL (RETD.) JOHN MacISAAC, 14TH FIELD REGIMENT

CHAPTER TEN

"Damned Fine Shooting"

NORMANDY, 6 JUNE–15 AUGUST 1944

"Everything that could shoot seemed to be firing": Day of Days, 6 June 1944

The first rounds fired were smoke shells. After observing their fall, the fire control officer for each of the four field regiments (19 Army Field Regiment had been assigned to 3rd Division for the landing) made the necessary corrections and transmitted them to the six LCTs carrying the guns of his unit, which then fired HE independently as the craft moved toward shore. On the bridge of each LCT, the naval captain held the line to the target while the artillery GPO (Gun Position Officer) called out the elevation to the crews of the four guns on his vessel. In response, the No. 2 gunner on each gun set the correct elevation on his sight, waited until the craft had levelled on its roll, and then fired. As the craft moved in toward the shore, the range dropped every 200 yards and the bombardment continued for about 30 minutes, the four field regiments sending an iron hail of more than 10,000 rounds of 105 mm HE onto the targets, the beach defences at Bernières-sur-Mer and Courseulles-sur-Mer.

The noise was deafening. As the gunners did not have ear plugs, they could barely hear after the first dozen rounds and, as if that was not bad enough, the battleships, cruisers and destroyers farther out to sea were firing over their heads. From time to time, men glanced around to see the impressive sight of dozens of specialized support craft – gun and rocket vessels – blasting away. "Everything that could shoot seemed to be firing at the beach" one remembered – while around them, the waves of tiny LCAs (Landing Craft, Assault), each carrying about 30 infantrymen, circled, waiting to land.[2] The rocket craft, firing salvos

We are the 44th of the 13th RCA,
Which is the finest regiment, in the 3rd Div, by the way
Its only modesty which makes us hesitate to say,
"Its the best in the Army too."

 Ask the infantry about us,
 Ask the Recce boys about us,
 Tanks would never move without us,
 And our guns to blast the way.

We came across the ocean blue to help to beat the Hun,
We landed up in Scotland in November 41,
Then for years we trained for war and how to serve the gun
And we lived on army stew.

 Ask the infantry about us ...

Then came June of 44, our chance had come at last,
We landed on the beaches and our hearts were beating fast,
We buckled down to business, for we knew the die was cast
For Hitler and his Nazi crew.

 Ask the infantry about us ....[1]

of 5-inch rockets, were most impressive but also dangerous. Several gunners witnessed an incident when a fighter aircraft "got caught in a cluster of rockets and disintegrated."[3] There was some return fire from the enemy – Gunner George Pugh of 22 Battery remembered that a shell splash erupted in front of his LCT, followed by a second splash astern and everyone on board braced, waiting for the third round to hit home, but it never came. At 2,000 yards off the beach, the guns on the LCTs ceased firing and the craft turned out to sea to wait their turn to disembark.

For the landing, 13th Field had been organized into an assault force consisting of the unit's 24 guns and the minimum number of personnel necessary to control and fire them. The plan was to land the guns in mid-morning after the infantry had secured a beachhead while the unit's A Echelon, necessary to supply the guns with ammunition and amounting to about 20% of its total strength, would come ashore later in the afternoon in a number of small detachments. For the actual assault, the regiment was supporting 7th Infantry Brigade by providing four FOO parties to land with the Regina Rifles of this formation in the first wave. As the LCTs headed back out to sea, they passed the LCAs carrying the infantry in to make the assault.

The FOO parties had a very dangerous job. Gunner George Lynch-Staunton from Pincher Creek, last met in 1939 as a member of 15th Light Horse, was in a 14th Field FOO party on that famous day and remembered it well:

It was still dark when we started getting ready on board HMCS *Prince Henry* at about 0430 hours, 6 June 1944. But we could

"Fire": D-Day, 6 June 1944

Some 11,500 yards off JUNO Beach, the 24 LCTs carrying 96 self-propelled guns of the four field regiments supporting 3rd Canadian Division opened fire. This is 12th Field Regiment firing on that famous Monday morning. FROM *INTO ACTION WITH THE 12TH FIELD*

The infantry go in – D-Day, 6 June 1944

As the gunners finished "drenching" their targets with heavy fire and turned back out to sea, the little LCAs (Landing Craft, Assault), each carrying about 30 infantrymen, moved in to land on JUNO Beach. They secured the beachhead but casualties were not light. FROM *INTO ACTION WITH THE 12TH FIELD*

Poor bloody infantry (1944 version): JUNO Beach, 6 June 1944

Infantry of 3rd Division move toward the beach in their LCAs. At this point all that was protecting them was heavy Allied naval gunfire and tactical aircraft. NATIONAL FILM BOARD

see aircraft coming over on bombing runs and could see and hear rockets being fired from the rocket craft. ......

As we got into the LCA which were lowered by ropes and tackle, one of the ropes jammed and we were lowered at a steep angle and one man fell out and we just heard a scream and that was that. We got onto the water and cast off from the ship and then there was a wait while we were being organized and I remember a man on a megaphone in a fast moving craft ordering people to line up to land. ......

We started to go in and then we were ordered to circle. It was rougher than hell and most of the men on board were sea sick. We made the run in, the front ramp went down and I ran out and I sank like a stone because of the weight of the No. 18 radio set on my back.

I came up and my feet hit bottom and then I started to move onto the beach. I remember the signaller in my FOO party, who was near me, saying "You're on fire, George, you are smoking." The radio set was smoking. I had not water proofed that set, someone else had done that and it was shorting out, so the signaller just cut the straps and I dumped the thing.

I also remember turning my back and facing the water and yelling to my FOO officer, Captain Jim Gartley, "grab my Sten!" Moments later, I was blown up and temporarily blinded but I could hear Gartley's voice saying "Over here!" I ran to the sound of his voice, as did the signaller, Bill Sharp, and we dived into a hole.

It was just a bit of a depression and we lay there for a minute or two until I came to, but I could only see out of one eye. My right eye ball had been grazed and I also was wounded in the head.

I then clearly remember my captain speaking on the only remaining radio set. He poked his head up to take a look and he fell back and died in my arms. The regimental history says a sniper got him but I remember seeing the backs of his hands full of little holes and that was shrapnel. I later found two holes in the back of my helmet. I think he was hit

(Left) Duplex Drive tanks foundering

High seas created difficulties for the DD amphibious tanks and many were swamped. The one in the foreground has foundered and been abandoned by its crew while a second tank keeps going with its crew on top of the turret in case a quick escape is necessary. NATIONAL FILM BOARD

(Below) The guns come ashore

A picture of Mike Green Beach just west of Courseulles-sur-Mer at about 9 A.M. shows an LCT of 12th Field Regiment landing guns and vehicles. Congestion on the beach delayed the arrival of 13th Field Regiment, which was scheduled to land west of this point. FROM *INTO ACTION WITH THE 12TH FIELD*

by shrapnel, or maybe shrapnel and a sniper.

Bill Sharp was also wounded, quite painfully, so I gave him a shot of morphine. ...... A sergeant from the Queen's Own Rifles crawled over and said "Get that f__king thing." He was talking about a machine gun nest which was firing down the beach at us. I turned on the remaining radio set but the dial did not move so I turned it around and the back was full of holes.

We were completely unserviceable. I lay there and then I saw the Fort Garry Horse coming ashore in their DD tanks and I was terrified that one would run over me as my legs were not working that well. I remember thinking that if I roll over I can get between the tracks but the driver must have seen me and they swerved off.[4]

Lynch-Staunton landed on NAN WHITE Beach at Bernières but things were no better on MIKE GREEN Beach, the 7th Brigade beach a thousand or so yards to the west near Courseulles. As the LCAs closed the beach, they discovered that the delay in landing occasioned by the choppy sea that retarded the assembly and deploy-

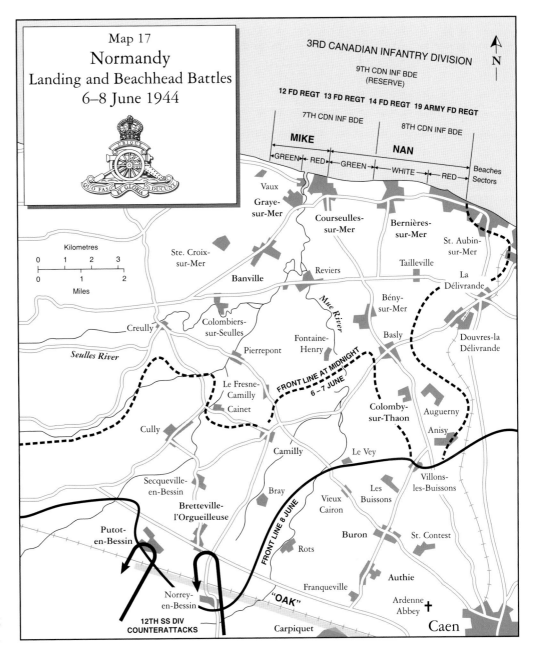

Map 17
Normandy
Landing and Beachhead Battles
6–8 June 1944

ment of the LCAs, meant that the rising tide had covered the beach obstacles – and the mines affixed to them. The Reginas lost half a company to these infernal devices and 13th Field lost one of its four FOO parties, commanded by Captain W.M. Dirks who was killed, and also the craft carrying Major G.F. Rainnie, the officer responsible for overseeing the disembarkation of the guns, killing that officer and three of his men. A third craft, carrying Major J.D. Young, the unit deployment officer, was destroyed by a direct hit from the beach defences that killed all on board. Force J was to suffer the heaviest loss in landing craft of any of the Allied naval assault forces on D-Day.

Nonetheless, the Reginas and their attached FOO parties splashed ashore, fortunately supported by the DD tanks of the First Hussars which cleared out a number of German defence posts, and moved into the village of Courseulles. As the infantry and FOO parties crossed the beach, German fire wounded Cap-

tain J. Else and killed his radio operator. Else kept going with his Able, or assistant, Gunner Jack Holtzman, into Courseulles but was hit a second time and had to be evacuated. Holtzman took over his duties and requested fire from 13th Field to deal with a stubborn German position that was delaying the advance. He was unable to get it as the regiment was not yet on shore, but managed to call up a Royal Marine artillery unit manning Centaurs (a Close Support version of the Cromwell tank armed with a 95 mm howitzer) and successfully directed its fire onto the target. This act earned him the Military Medal, one of the first of many decorations won by Canadian soldiers on 6 June 1944.

Meanwhile, the six LCTs containing the guns of 13th Field waited off shore under intermittent German mortar fire. The plan was for the unit to follow 12th Field onto the beaches near Courseulles but when that unit came ashore, it was forced to go into crash action on the beach. This upset the carefully-scheduled landing arrangements and 13th Field was not able to come ashore until late in the afternoon. As the LCTs neared the beaches, Sergeant R.J. Porter of 44 Battery was puzzled by "lumps that looked like blocks of wood" he could see bobbing up and down in the shallow waves. It was not until his vessel got closer that Porter realized to his horror that they were dead Canadian infantrymen, many "in full gear, with a rifle. They never fired a shot and they never got hit – the poor bastards were drowned."[5] The sight of dead bodies, German and Canadian, littering the landing area bothered Gunner William McCrie of 22 Battery but, as he later remarked, a soldier "had to build up an immunity when you see things like this as if you let that bother you, if you dwell on it, you are a goner. You build up an immunity that it is not happening to you."[6] The other thing that impressed McCrie was his first sight of the men who, for years, he had been waiting to fight and training to kill. As his vehicle passed a dejected group of German prisoners, McCrie's was amazed to realize that "those buggers look just like me." Gunner Hunter took it all in his stride, his first thought on coming ashore was "Good, I won't be seasick any more," and spirits in his troop were lifted, quite literally, when the troop leader passed around a bottle of scotch.[7]

As each gun came off the ramp onto dry land, it took its "Porpoise" with it and, trailing this metal sled full of ammunition behind, moved off to the first gun position. Unfortunately, the unknown but brilliant staff officer who conceived this novel method of transport had not thought the matter through completely. He had envisaged that these containers would be dragged across smooth sand but the sand only lasted a few hundred yards and after that the Porpoises scraped along rough, cobblestoned streets. By the time the regiment was in its first gun position near Banville, south of Courseulles, the metal on the bottom of many was worn paper thin. Once in position, the first thing the gunners did was to unload and discard the wretched things.

By last light on this, the longest of all days, 13th Field was in position and ready to fire. The men, many of whom had gone without sleep for days, were exhausted but were keyed up by sheer nervous energy. They were edgy, too edgy – when Lieutenant James Doohan entered the unit's lines after a patrol, he failed to respond quickly enough to a nervous sentry's challenge and was cut down with a burst of Bren gun fire which, fortunately, only wounded him.* Things got no better as the evening wore on because the *Luftwaffe*, absent during daylight hours, appeared to bomb and strafe the beaches and the dark sky was criss-crossed by tracer and lit up by the explosion of shells. All through the restless darkness hours, the gunners, huddling in hastily-dug slit trenches, could hear the sound of small arms fire around them in the dark. Nobody got much sleep that first night in Normandy.

---

* James Doohan from Vancouver, B.C., recovered from his wounds and later flew Auster AOP aircraft. After the war he became an actor and is best known for his role as "Scotty," the chief engineer of the starship *Enterprise* in "Star Trek."

Throughout the day and into the night, the medical personnel worked tirelessly to locate, treat and evacuate the wounded. Gunner Lynch-Staunton received first aid but was forced to lay on the beach through the night and when German aircraft started bombing, his first thought was "how can my helmet protect me" as "it could either protect my head or other parts and I remember trying to decide what to do with it."[8] Finally, Lynch-Staunton's turn came and he

was evacuated by a jeep ambulance on a stretcher and there was a stretcher above me. Something happened to that stretcher and it began to come down on me, it collapsed. I remember having to hold that stretcher up and the guy in it was really groaning and I could also remember red drips coming down.

We drove a short distance to a landing ship and up a ramp. ......

My stretcher was then placed in a compartment on metal pegs that projected from the side of the ship. One part of the compartment was screened off by a white sheet and that was an operating room. There was a large container full of sand outside it and, every so often, they would emerge from behind the screen and put an arm or a leg in it.[9]

What Lynch-Staunton was witnessing was but a small part of the price paid to get ashore in Europe. The total Canadian casualties on 6 June 1944 were 1,074 killed and wounded, of which 13th Field suffered 6 killed and 4 wounded. Although there had been stiff resistance, particularly at OMAHA Beach in the American sector, Operation OVERLORD had been a success and the Allies were now in France.

"Keep firing until your ammunition is gone": Battle for the beachhead, 7-10 June

None of the assault divisions, including 3rd Canadian Division, had managed to secure their D-Day objectives, which lay inland, although the Canadians came closer than any other Allied formation. The first order of business, therefore, on 7 June was to expand the D-Day gains and link up the separate beachheads to form a continuous front. For 3rd Canadian Division, this translated into securing a railway line codenamed OAK running between Caen and Bayeux.

At first light, just after 5 A.M., on 7 June the men of 13th Field "stood to" for a couple of hours before getting their breakfasts. At midday, the unit moved south, following behind 7th Brigade which reached OAK at noon and thus became the first Allied formation to take its D-Day objective – albeit a day late. To the east, 9th Brigade advanced in parallel and its forward elements took the villages of Authie and Buron. Up to this point, enemy resistance was weak and scattered – mostly isolated pockets of snipers and machinegunners – and both brigades had little problem dealing with it. In the early afternoon, however, the situation changed as 3rd Canadian Division now encountered

On guard: Normandy 1944
A gunner from a field regiment of 3rd Canadian Division stands guard while his comrades catch up on their sleep. By the time they landed, many men were exhausted but no one got much sleep that first night in Normandy because of German air attacks. NAC, PA-131440

Forward Observation party, 7 June 1944
A FOO party from 14th Field, operating beside their Sherman OP tank on the morning of 7 June, display visible signs of exhaustion. On the left is the Able or assistant to the FOO, in this case Lieutenant Garth Webb in the middle, while on the right is the radio operator who keeps Webb connected with his battery. NAC, PA-103417

a much more formidable foe – the 12th Waffen SS Panzer Division "*Hitlerjugend.*"

This formation, formed in the autumn of 1943 from hand-picked young volunteers from the Nazi youth organization, was trained and led by a cadre of veteran officers and NCOs taken from the elite 1st Waffen SS Panzer Division, "*Leibstandarte Adolf Hitler.*" With 20,000 men and more than 200 tanks or other armoured vehicles, the 12th SS Division was a major part of the German armour reserve, which now began to move to the Normandy area. Allied aircraft had hampered the division's march from its concentration area west of Paris and, it was only during the late morning of 7 June that its lead elements reached Caen and began to deploy in the face of the oncoming Canadi-

ans. One of the first of the division's units to arrive was the 25th SS Panzergrenadier Regiment under *Standartenführer* (Colonel) Kurt Meyer, a highly-decorated veteran of the Polish, French, Greek and Russian campaigns, who had orders to attack "the landed enemy and throw him back into the sea."[10]

Meyer had planned to wait until more of the 12th SS Division was in position but, sensing an opportunity as he watched 9th Brigade approach his positions on 7 June, he decided to make an immediate attack. At 2 P.M., just as the infantry of 9th Brigade were securing the village of Authie, they came under a heavy mortar bombardment that sent them to ground. A few minutes later, two strong battlegroups of German tanks and infantry attacked and forced the brigade to fall back from Authie and the neighbouring village of Buron to the north. The fighting was ferocious and both sides lost heavily but the Canadians were steadily driven back, and the Germans were only rebuffed when naval gunfire, including 16-inch shells from the battleship, HMS *Rodney*, was brought down on them. Having accomplished his immediate purpose which was to blunt the advance of the Canadians nearest Caen, Meyer now turned his attention to 7th Brigade to the west.

This formation was commanded by Brigadier Harry Foster who, as a young Strathcona officer twelve years before, had given up the lead in the Guides Challenge Cup to rescue drowning children from the Elbow River. Meyer's attack on 9th Brigade had tipped his hand, however, and knowing his turn was coming, Foster warned his units to expect an enemy attack. Shortly after midnight, the Germans began to probe the Regina Rifles' position at the village of Bretteville l'Orgueilleuse, less than a mile away from 13th Field's gun position near Bray. From about 1 A.M. on 8 June, the unit War Diary records that

> This regt was constantly called on to fire DF [Defensive Fire] and DF SOS [Emergency] tasks throughout the night while at the same time being constantly on the alert for small parties of enemy snipers. In actual fact throughout this morning until dawn, we kept the RRR [Regina Rifle Regiment] circled by a curtain of protective fire. Not a short round was dropped yet countless counter-attacks were beaten off and some tks killed. The morning light disclosed great numbers of enemy casualties and our own Bn [Battalion, meaning the Regina Rifles] fortress intact.[11]

Actually, this is not strictly accurate, the Germans did not mount any major attacks that night but only probed 7th Brigade with small fighting patrols to find weak points. Sergeant James Moffat of 22 Battery recalled that, because of the limited ammunition supply available, the gunners had been told that, once ashore, they would be limited to 25 rounds per gun per day. During the early morning of 8 June, Moffat remembered, this suddenly changed and the gunners were told to "Keep firing until your ammunition is gone."[12]

By 8 June, both tank battalions of 12th Waffen SS Division had

Dug in

A soldier of the Regina Rifles in a good defensive position during the first week in Normandy. The cotton bandolier around his shoulder contains stripper clips for his Short Magazine Lee Enfield .303 rifle and he is wearing, as did all the soldiers of 3rd Division, the so-called Mk III "invasion helmet." It was from positions like this that the Regina Johns were able to repulse the German attack on Bretteville during the night of 7 June.

NAC, PA-131423

arrived, as had four battalions of panzergrenadiers. Throughout the morning German infantry from the 26th SS Panzergrenadier Regiment attacked the Winnipeg Rifles' position at Putot and, by mid afternoon, three companies of that battalion had been destroyed and the hamlet was in German hands. Harry Foster wanted it back so, in the early evening, he sent in the Canadian Scottish, supported by a squadron of the First Hussars, behind a rolling or lifting barrage fired by 12th and 13th Field Regiments. After heavy fighting, the Scottish regained Putot.

The battle for Putot was still being waged at about 10 P.M. when Meyer launched an attack directly against the Regina Rifles' positions in the adjoining villages of Bretteville l'Orgueilleuse and Norrey-en-Bessin. To do so, he used a battlegroup consisting of a company of panzergrenadiers and two companies of Panthers, about 125 infantry and 30 tanks, supported by a battery of *Wespe* self-propelled 105 mm howitzers. Meyer, who led the attack on a motorcycle, was in overall command but the tanks were under the direct control of *Obersturmbannführer* [Lieutenant-Colonel] Max Wünsche of 12th SS Panzer Regiment, a highly-decorated veteran of the Eastern Front and one of Germany's leading tank aces. This being the case, it is curious why two such experienced officers would have not have used a stronger force, particularly in view of the fact that the recent fighting had demonstrated that, although inexperienced, the Canadians were tough opponents. The possible answer is that Meyer and Wünsche were somewhat over-confident and cer-

tainly there was no subtlety about their plan of attack. With the panzergrenadiers mounted on their decks, the Panthers drove along both sides of the road leading to Bretteville straight at the Regina Rifles' positions, all guns blazing.

Initially, the German attack met with success. The Panthers were able to knock out two of the 6-pdr. anti-tank guns at the outskirts of the village and enter Bretteville. Then the Reginas recovered and brought the German tanks under small arms fire that swept the panzergrenadiers off their back decks. A German infantry officer, *Untersturmführer* [Second Lieutenant] Reinhold Fuss, recalled that

> We were surprised by violent anti-tank fire. A great number of anti-tank guns seemed to be in positions along the edge of town. Canadian infantry were in position in the trenches to the left and right of the tree-lined road running from the northeast to Bretteville. They peppered the mounted grenadiers with wild rifle fire. I immediately ordered my *Zug* [platoon] to dismount on their own and to advance in infantry style.[13]

Few of the enemy infantry were able to get into Bretteville but the Panthers continued into the village. The tank crews were also surprised the weight of the fire brought to bear on them – *Sturmmann* [Lance-Corporal] Hans Kesper, a driver, remembered that their tanks "were taking heavy anti-tank fire" so his commander ordered: "Set the houses on fire so that we can see something!"[14]

Somewhat recklessly, the Panthers moved deeper into Bretteville. At one point, Lieutenant-Colonel F.M. Matheson, the Rifles' commanding officer, estimated that no less than 22 German tanks were circling about his command post. They did not stay there long as Matheson's men began to stalk them with PIATs and soon scored a hit on a Panther which

> halted for a moment, started again and after 30 yards was hit by a second PIAT. It stopped, turned around and headed out of town. A third PIAT finished it off so that it slewed around out of control, running over a necklace of 75 [anti-tank] grenades which blew off a track. The crew dismounted and attempted to make off but were killed by smallarms fire. During this incident a second Panther had remained further up the street. Seeing the fate of its companion, it commenced to fire both 75 and mg [machineguns] wildly down the street "like a child in a tantrum," doing no damage whatsoever except to set fire to the first Panther.[15]

By the time the German tank crews realized that their supporting infantry were pinned down at the edge of Bretteville and they were more or less sitting ducks, it was too late. Tank after tank was brewed up. *Obersturmführer* [First Lieutenant] Jürgen Chemnitz recorded that all three vehicles in his Panther troop took anti-tank hits at almost the same moment … The vehicle on the right burned as brightly as a torch, probably from a direct hit to the engine compartment. Its crew returned later, unscathed. My own vehicle took a hit which penetrated the turret. The loader was badly wounded, blinded, and had a number of broken bones. The electrical system failed. *Unterscharführer* [Sergeant] Rust's vehicle on the left only took a hit to the gear cover and remained ready for action. I reported to *Hauptsturmführer* [Captain] Berlin from this vehicle by radio and received orders to turn around. We pulled my loader from the interior and rested him on the rear [deck].[16]

The Reginas called for artillery support and got it very quickly as Lieutenant-Colonel F.T. Clifford, the commanding officer of 13th Field, was at Matheson's command post that night. FOO parties of the regiment began to call down fire on every target they could see and Bretteville was soon lit up by explosions. It was a dangerous place. Two of the three members of one 13th Field FOO party were killed and Gunner McCrie, who was acting as Clifford's radioman, remembered watching a Panther coming down the street "and it would fire left, boom, swivel to the right, boom!" until an anti-tank round

The Führer's finest
Panzergrenadiers of the 12th Waffen SS Division taken prisoner in Normandy in June 1944. Easily identified by their mottled camouflage smocks, the men of this formation were a determined, aggressive and tough enemy but the Canadians eventually overcame them. NAC, PA-129130

went through "one side of that tank and out the other."[17]

The Panthers began to retreat from Bretteville in all directions and, as they did so, they came under heavy artillery bombardment from all the field regiments in 3rd Division. *Sturmmann* [Lance Corporal] Leopold Lengheim, a Panther gunner, remembered looking through his sight to see "a virtual wall of fire coming at us from about 900 metres away" – then his tank was struck several times in succession by 105 mm HE rounds, one hit removing both the turret cupola and the crew commander's head.[18] Lengheim's driver turned around "at full throttle and drove into cover." German tanks, lost, wandered around the vicinity and a gun from Able Troop of 22 Battery engaged a Panther over open sights but was unable to see the results. For 13th Field there was no sleep again that night as those gunners not manning the 105s were deployed around the unit's gun position with PIATs and small arms, prepared to defend it.

After the surviving German tanks withdrew, the excitement had just died down in Bretteville when an incredulous Lieutenant-Colonel Matheson watched as a "daredevil German dispatch rider" raced through the village on a Canadian motorcycle.[19] Matheson knocked the impudent fellow off his saddle

Declawed Panther, Bretteville-l'Orgueilleuse, Normandy
During the night of 8 June, tanks and panzergrenadiers of the 12th Waffen SS Division mounted an attack against the Regina Rifles in and around Bretteville-l'Orgueilleuse. It was broken up by the determined resistance of the Rifles, who knocked out this Panther of I Battalion, 12th SS Panzer Regiment, at close range with a PIAT. NAC, PA-116529

Brewed-up, Bretteville, 8 June 1944
Another view of the Panther from I Battalion, 12th SS Panzer Regiment, which was brewed up by during the fight for Bretteville. During this vicious night battle, the field regiments of 3rd Division, directed by FOO parties in the village, brought down heavy fire on the enemy. NAC, PA-114983

Poor bloody infantry (dug in), Normandy, 1944

Flatfeet man their slit trenches in June 1944. As always, the infantry had the worst job and suffered the highest casualties, and the role of the armour and artillery was to get them where they had to go to do their job – alive. An infantryman's war was about 10 yards wide, but he was important as all wars ultimately come down to one frightened young man with a rifle against another frightened young man with a rifle. NAC,

PA-129043

with a burst of Sten fire, which was no small achievement, but a few minutes later, a German officer "drove directly up to the battalion command post" in a Volkswagen jeep, obviously having lost his way.[20] "He got out," Matheson remembered, "and looked around for a few seconds until an excited anti-tank soldier fired his rocket [PIAT] at him and scored a direct hit." Just before first light, Meyer pulled the survivors of his battlegroup back to its starting position. Both he and Wünsche had been wounded and their personnel losses had been heavy – 31 killed and 46 wounded – but surprisingly, despite all the wild fighting, only 6 Panthers were lost. Matheson's casualties were 11 men killed in action and perhaps twice that many wounded. When dawn came on 9 June Gunner McCrie remembered that there were two destroyed German staff cars and a Panther on the main street of the village but what pleased him most was that the gun of the German tank was "pointed right up at my building."[21]

Following the successful defence of Bretteville on 8/9 June 1944, there was a feeling in 3rd Division that they had taken the worst the Germans could throw at them – and survived. Sergeant Porter of 44 Battery puts it this way: "Them bastards had it over us, they had the experience but the Canadians were tougher than they figured we were."[22] The infantry of the division had done the hardest fighting and suffered the heaviest casualties but everyone – including the Germans – acknowledged the work of the artillery. The staff of 12th SS Panzer blamed the failure of their counterattacks "on the fact that reconnaissance and suppression of enemy artillery was impossible and its barrages could not be prevented."[23] The infantry were thankful that they had good artillery support in these early battles, their first experience of combat. A few days after the battle Sergeant Moffat remembered that his gun was "halted on the road and the

Reginas were going through us and this Regina sergeant jumped up and kissed my gun barrel."[24] To Moffat, "that was the breaking point" and, after that, he never doubted the ultimate Allied victory.

"You didn't dodge every shell": A slow June, a bloody July

For the next few days, there was continual fighting and much shelling from both sides in and around the forward positions of 7th and 9th Brigades. The gunners of 13th Field fired their first "Mike Targets" (regimental target using 24 guns), "Uncle Targets" (divisional target using 72 guns) and even a "Yoke Target" (a target using almost every gun in range) but the regiment also suffered from German shelling which killed 4 men and wounded several others. It became so intense that the unit was finally forced to pull back a mile to a new position near Camilly. By 11 June, however, things quieted down and it became clear that the campaign was entering a static phase while both sides paused to gather strength. The Germans had succeeded in cordoning off the beachhead but had failed to throw the Allies back into the sea while, for their part, the Allies had held their beachhead but were still short of their first objectives, including the city of Caen.

General Bernard Montgomery, the Allied ground commander, had a sequential plan calculated to bring victory in Normandy by D+90 (90 days after D-Day). While First U.S. Army cut the Cotentin Peninsula and captured the badly-needed port of Cherbourg, Second British Army was to take Caen and the relatively open terrain south of that city which was needed for airfields. Once this was done, Montgomery planned to launch the Americans in a series of offensives that would penetrate into Brittany and secure the deep water ports necessary to create the logistical lifeline to support the campaign on the continent. Before these plans could be put into operation, however, he had to build up his troop strength and supplies but, on 19 June, nature intervened on the side of the Germans when a fierce Channel gale destroyed one of the MULBERRIES, the artificial ports that had been constructed to ease the unloading of ships. For five days, not only was the logistical pipeline turned off, but the bad weather grounded Allied aircraft, thus permitting the Germans to build up their forces. By the last week of June, both sides were ready to renew the fighting.

The latter part of June was relatively quiet for 13th Field Regiment. Delays caused by storms and other problems prevented the arrival of the remainder of the unit from Britain and it was not until 24 June that the rear parties caught up and the regiment had all its personnel on the continent. There was relatively little German shelling during this time although by now, the gunners had "learned that you didn't dodge every shell you heard coming, only those that came close and you could tell by their sounds whether they were going to come close."[25] The most feared enemy weapon was the six-barrelled German *Nebelwerfer* mortar with its distinctive soul-freezing "whoo-ooh-whoo-ooh-whoo" wail that led it to be nicknamed the "Moaning Minnie" or "Sobbing Sister" by Allied troops. Despite overwhelming Allied air superiority, the *Luftwaffe* conducted almost nightly raids which, given the amount of anti-aircraft fire put up against them, ensured that nobody got much sleep. Gunner Pugh of 22 Battery remembered that when the Germans "came over at night, the fireworks were something to behold … tracer shells, white ones, green ones, red ones, some went out and sparkled off at the end and some went up in a big spiral."[26] German aircraft occasionally appeared during the day but as 13th Field War Diary entries indicate, if they did so, they had a short but exciting life:

1000 Hours [24 June 1944]
A ME 109 approaching from S.E. Hit by Spitfire Cannon Fire just before arriving over our position. Pilot baled out behind our lines. Plane circled around our position pilotless with Ack Ack fire pouring into it and crashed south of us. ……

1100 Hours [30 June 1944]
Messerchmidt over our position. Set onto by 12 Spits. Shot down and crashed south-east of us. Pilot had no time to bail out. ……

1315 Hours [3 July 1944]
Two ME 109 fighters engaged by Ack Ack fire S.W. of us. Came down to strafe. One passed over our field 30 ft high, strafing but causing no casualties. The other one was hit north of us by A/A fire and crashed 1/4 mile North East. ……

1500 Hours [15 July 1944]
15 ME 109s flew over our position and although they were not strafing our Ack Ack fired heavily as well as our AALMG [Anti-aircraft light machineguns] Nos. Five were shot down over our position – credit going to Gnr Teales L.F. whose Bren Fire was seen to have entered the plane before it lost its tail. It was a grand sight and no doubt the *Luftwaffe* will remember it as well as us.[27]

As the gunners grew used to combat, they became hardened to the awful sights of war, including the numerous enemy dead which littered Normandy. Sergeant Moffat of 22 Battery remembered that there was a dead German near his gun position and, as

> He was starting to swell up, we threw some dirt on him and when he swelled up some more, we threw some more dirt on him. Then the padre came along and gave us a little lecture about treating the dead properly but after he had left, we still didn't bury the German, we just kept throwing dirt on him when we thought he needed it. To us, it wasn't a person, it was a body in an enemy uniform.[28]

Many were surprised to find that the French civilians, far from greeting them as liberators, were somewhat circumspect in their attitude. As the War Diary of 78 Battery noted:

Easy Four firing, 28 June 1944
No. 4 gun of Easy Troop, 78 Battery, 13th Field Regiment, firing at targets around Carpiquet on 28 June 1944. This gun has just come into position as the crew have not yet unloaded their personal kit, which is strapped to its front. They have, however, piled the 105 mm rounds in stacks behind the weapon. NAC, PA-114577

> Contrary to what we expected they did not welcome us with outstretched arms but more or less with the diplomatic spirit of being "friends with whoever has the guns or the whip hand." The general feeling in the battery is that they would have treated the Germans the same way as they have us. In other words it seems immaterial to them who are here – the Germans or us.[29]

The biggest complaints were the lack of mail and the food. Limited shipping meant that mail was delayed reaching the bridgehead and also that the men had to exist on compo rations, rather than meals prepared by the regimental cooks. Mail only began to arrive on a regular basis in mid-July and compo rations remained the mainstay throughout the summer of 1944. For this reason, there was considerable excitement on 24 June when 22 Battery got its first fresh meat as a cow "had been killed by shrapnel at the 44th Bty" and 22 battery sent over a halftrack to bring back its share.[30] French livestock killed in action was considered a legitimate prize of war but Allied troops were under strict orders not to forage among the food supplies of the civilian population. Occasionally, however, tasty things did find their way into the pot. Gunner Geoffrey Hall of 44 Battery never forgot the day when

> this kind of slaphappy kid came in with 4-5 chickens flapping around in his truck. We killed and skinned them but we didn't know how old they were, so we decided to boil them. I wanted some new potatoes and remembered there was a French potato field down the road so went down there and they were lovely. So we had the chickens and the potatoes boiling on the fire when the BSM [Battery Sergeant-Major] arrived with orders for the next day including a general order

"Are we downhearted? Hell no!"
Tired but happy infantry toast their regiment, the Stormont, Dundas and Glengarry Highlanders, with glasses of calvados, the powerful apple liqueur produced in the Normandy region. The stuff was so plentiful that some gunners in 13th Field mixed it in jerricans with *creme de menthe* to produce an even more potent brew that not only raised morale but was a useful solvent for cleaning the grease from weapons. NAC, PA-169261

"Mail call": Normandy, June 1944
Mail was important to morale and there were many complaints in the first weeks of the campaign that it was slow in reaching frontline troops. The delay, due to shipping problems in the Channel, was finally resolved. Here, on 25 June 1944, Regimental Sergeant-Major Mike Harman (right) of 13th Field delivers mail to a happy Gunner Frank T. Butcher. NAC, PA-169266

about not looting French property. He took a long look and a long smell of our meal and finally someone said, "Why don't you stop for supper, sergeant-major." And he replied, "I think I will."[31]

There was no shortage of drink, however, as Normandy appeared to be full of stocks of calvados and wine. Gunner Pugh's crew in 22 Battery had a jerrican full of a volatile mixture of calvados and *crème de menthe*, which not only possessed morale value but was also useful for cleaning items of equipment.

Throughout this period, 13th Field was normally called on to fire only DF tasks requested by the infantry or HF (Harassing Fire) tasks which involved periodically bringing down a few rounds on known enemy positions or routes, crossroads being a favourite target. As ammunition was limited, the gunners knew something was about to happen on 24 June, the same day they got their first fresh meat, when 1,596 rounds were dumped at each battery position. At 3.30 A.M. the next day, the regiment fired a barrage and at 12 A.M. a second barrage, before engaging targets, as they were called for, at "slow rate."[32] Things were clearly beginning to heat up. On 26 June, 13th Field and thirty other artillery units commenced firing "the biggest barrage of the war," a total of one million rounds, before responding to 35 separate calls for fire, the gun crews firing for four hours without a "Stand Easy."[33] One of the British infantry divisions 13th Field supported that day acknowledged their gratitude with a message: "Damned fine shooting. Thanks a lot."

All this work was in support of Operation EPSOM, an attempt by Montgomery to outflank to the west the enemy defences north of Caen. The Germans managed to halt EPSOM after inflicting heavy casualties on the British troops involved and, frustrated, Montgomery decided to attack directly against Caen. The 3rd Canadian Division was given the task of taking Carpiquet airfield on the western outskirts of that city and the actual job went to 8th Infantry Brigade, which planned to make a setpiece

Catching up on the news
In a barn near Creully on 14 June 1944, Captains J. Draffin of 13th Field and W.B. Nixon of 12th Field Regiment take a break and compare the map in the *Maple Leaf*, the Canadian army newspaper, with the situation that they know first-hand. NAC, PA-167886

assault on 4 July. The brigade's attack would have massive artillery support, no less than 428 guns provided by one heavy, eight medium and twelve field regiments, as well as naval bombardment from battleships, monitors and heavy cruisers. The gunners of 13th Field were very active in the days immediately preceding Operation WINDSOR, as the attack on Carpiquet was codenamed, firing several "Victor Targets" (all guns in a corps in range), including one at "Scale 4" or 4 rounds per gun.

For 13th Field, Operation WINDSOR commenced at 5 A.M. on 4 July, when its three batteries began firing the timed, lifting barrage that went ahead of the infantry assault. Unfortunately, the defenders of Carpiquet, 12th SS Division, had been forewarned by lax Canadian radio discipline and increased reconnaissance activity that an attack was forthcoming and were prepared to meet it. As the infantry of 8th Brigade moved forward to attack the village of Carpiquet and the nearby airfield, the

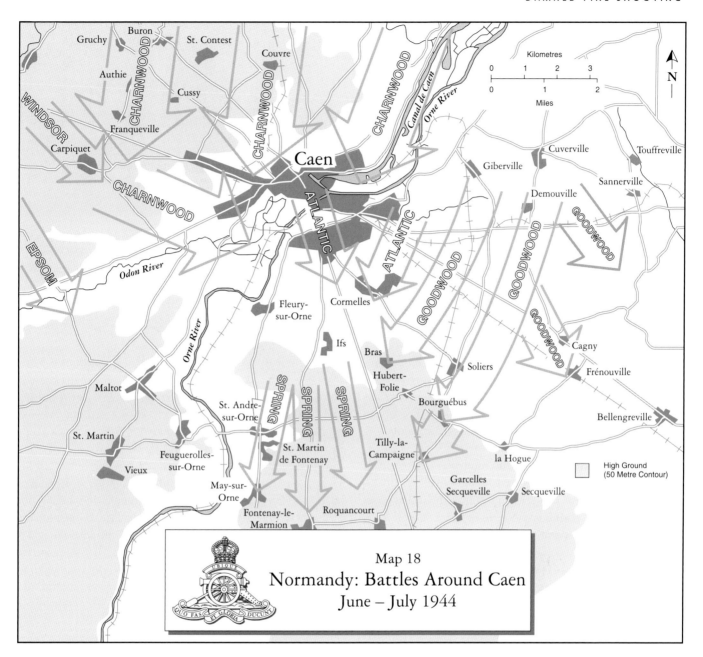

Map 18
Normandy: Battles Around Caen
June – July 1944

German gunners, who had excellent observation from nearby high ground, brought down a counter-bombardment which sent them to ground. By the time the attack got going again, the friendly barrage had moved far beyond the infantry and they had to attack across open ground against entrenched defenders. Casualties were heavy and they got worse in nearly three days of vicious see-saw fighting at Carpiquet. The three field regiments of 3rd Division supported the infantry with almost continuous fire, night and day.

Carpiquet, however, had not been completely captured when the next major attack, Operation CHARNWOOD, whose purpose was to take Caen and secure bridgeheads over the Odon River which bisected it, commenced on 8 July 1944. This initiated a period of intense and continuous action for 13th Field as Montgomery mounted a series of attacks, at first to take Caen and then to break out of it and move south. CHARNWOOD was preceded by a major air attack carried out by 428 aircraft from Bomber Command, which more or less flattened the northern part of the Caen, but did not do much damage to the enemy. Realizing that they could not hold that part of the city north of the Odon, the Germans withdrew to new defensive positions in the southern suburb of Vaucelles and on high ground south of Caen.

This brought about two new operations, GOODWOOD and ATLANTIC, intended to "pinch off" Caen. The first was mounted by three British armoured divisions east of the city, the second was undertaken by Lieutenant-General Guy Simonds's newly-activated 2 Canadian Corps. Operation GOODWOOD, the largest armoured operation carried out by the British army up to that time, achieved only very limited success. Preceded by another air attack by heavy bombers and unprecedented artillery support, it was brought up short by well-sited German anti-tank defences along the Bourguébus Ridge which ran east and west, south of Caen, and the three armoured divisions involved lost more than 200 tanks. The Canadian Operation ATLANTIC was successful, however, in clearing the Germans out of Caen but an attempt to take the strong German positions on Verrières Ridge, the western extension of Bourguébus Ridge, met with failure. By the time these operations ended on 20 July, Caen had fallen but the Germans were now in excellent defensive positions on high ground south of that city. The Second British Army, which at this time controlled the Canadian troops in Normandy, was a few miles closer to Berlin but it still faced an unbeaten opponent.

In the western sector of the beachhead, however, the Americans were starting to make progress. It had taken First U.S. Army nearly six weeks to take Cherbourg – only to find it rendered useless as a port by German demolitions – and to grind slowly through the bocage country, an area that favoured the enemy, to reach open terrain. The Americans were now in a position to launch Operation COBRA, the planned breakout from the bridgehead. It was scheduled for 25 July and, to keep the Germans occupied on the eastern side of the beachhead to prevent them switching their armoured reserves to face the Americans, Montgomery ordered Simonds to carry out Operation SPRING, an attack by 2nd and 3rd Canadian Divisions against the German positions on Verrières Ridge. It went in on 25 July and it was a costly disaster that, after Dieppe, incurred the worst single day's losses, 1,500 in total, suffered by the Canadian army during the war. One battalion, the Black Watch of 5th Brigade, lost 285 of 300 men it committed to this action, while the Calgary Highlanders of the same formation suffered 120 casualties. Operation SPRING has remained controversial since the day it was fought but, when it was over, the Germans still held most of Verrières and Bourguébus Ridges.

Advancing at last: Caen, July 1944
A self-propelled gun from one of the field regiments of 3rd Canadian Division enters the outskirts of Caen on 10 July. The city had been thoroughly flattened by Allied bombing and stank of death. NAC, PA-162693

"No greater hell than British artillery fire": 13th Field Regiment at work

During these weeks of heavy fighting, which lasted from 4 July to 25 July, 13th Field never stopped firing. Although the gunners knew the names of the various operations they were supporting and tried to follow the progress of the fighting, one day was much the same as the next on the gun positions and varied only in the intensity of their work. In July 1944, 13th Field carried out every kind of artillery fire: barrages (box and lifting or rolling), bombardments and concentrations, either independent or TOT (Time on Target, all shells landing at the same point at the same time); it undertook Defensive Fire, Harassing Fire, Counter-Battery Fire and many SOS or emergency tasks; and it fired on "Mike," "Uncle" and "Victor Targets." For three weeks, the guns were rarely silent and, if the gun crews were ordered to "Stand Easy," they still had the daily chores of ammunition re-supply and vehicle maintenance, which could occupy up to three hours a day.

Throughout these long, hot summer days, the three batteries were fed target information or taskings from static OP parties

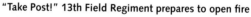

"Take Post!" 13th Field Regiment prepares to open fire
(Left) A troop from 13th Field prepares to open fire on 22 June. This was actually a quiet day for 13th Field, but 24 hours later it was hit by 150 rounds from a German 150 mm gun, losing three gunners. (Below) In the Canadian sector of the Normandy front, grain fields were more common than the bocage found in the American sector. This open terrain made it more difficult to camouflage gun positions but fortunately the sky was ruled by Allied aircraft throughout the campaign. NAC, PA-132921; NAC, PA-132922

sited with the infantry or mobile FOO parties. There was usually one OP for each of the six troops in 13th Field, connected to it by a land line, while the FOOs relied on radio communication. These observers, spread out across the entire front of the infantry brigade the regiment was supporting (usually, but not always, 7th Brigade), and also in the air in small AOP Auster aircraft, would call in targets to the batteries. In the area south of Caen, the observers found that church spires in the little villages that dotted the countryside were very useful – as an officer of 10th Infantry Brigade commented:

> It seemed oddly historic that the renowned Normandy spires should remain in pointed silhouette even after the terror and ravage of the modern hosts had passed in their victory and defeat. Their beauty might not have been the same, but many a harassed forward observation officer probably praised these houses of God for an accurate bearing.[34]

The observers would estimate the weight of fire required, which was never less than a troop of four guns, but if a single troop's guns were not deemed sufficient, the Parham system allowed an observer, a relatively junior officer, to increase the weight of fire up to an "Uncle Target," which would receive the fire of all three field regiments in 3rd Division, a total of 72 guns. As one gunner officer recalled, "Uncle Targets" were usually dramatic:

> There was always an air of emergency and trying to beat the clock about them. The opening call, an urgent, thrice repeated cry of "*Uncle Target! Uncle Target! Uncle Target!*" screamed into the microphone of a No. 19 set in that nasal tenor or soprano voice affected by all the best [radio] operators would galvanize the entire artillery net, waking up duty officers, demanding the straining of signallers and gun position officers for the next order and sending [gun] detachments to their posts in action.[35]

On one day in Normandy, 7 July 1944, 13th Field fired no less than fourteen "Uncle Targets" at "Scale 2" or 2 rounds per gun, meaning that each of these targets received 144 rounds of 105 mm HE. That wasn't all – on that same day the regiment engaged four "Victor Targets,"

fired by all guns in 2 Canadian Corps in range, possibly as many as 200 tubes, at Scale 4 and 5, meaning that these targets received between 800 and 1,000 rounds of 25-pdr., 105 mm, 4.5 or 5.5-inch rounds

No matter who called it in, target information and requests for fire would arrive either by radio or land line at the Battery Command Post which would relay it to the Troop Command Posts. Here the GPO would supervise his staff as they made the relevant calculations on the artillery plotting board and then issue firing orders via the Tannoy or loudspeaker system to the crews at each gun, normally in the sequence: type of target, type of ammunition required, type of fuze, number of propellant charges to be used, the angle of deflection, the angle of sight, method of ranging (by a single gun or all four guns in a troop), elevation and the scale of firing (number of rounds). The gun commander or No. 1, a sergeant, would transmit these orders

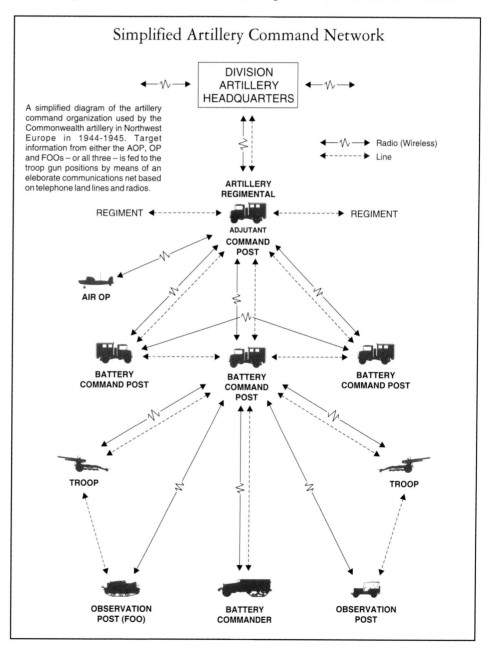

Simplified Artillery Command Network

A simplified diagram of the artillery command organization used by the Commonwealth artillery in Northwest Europe in 1944-1945. Target information from either the AOP, OP and FOOs – or all three – is fed to the troop gun positions by means of an eleborate communications net based on telephone land lines and radios.

DIVISION ARTILLERY HEADQUARTERS

Radio (Wireless)
Line

ARTILLERY REGIMENTAL

REGIMENT   ADJUTANT COMMAND POST   REGIMENT

AIR OP

BATTERY COMMAND POST   BATTERY COMMAND POST   BATTERY COMMAND POST

TROOP   TROOP

OBSERVATION POST (FOO)   BATTERY COMMANDER   OBSERVATION POST

Daily chores, Normandy 1944
Each gun required daily maintenance and, in action, that maintenance had to be fitted around firing tasks. Here, a gunner, working shirtless in the heat of a Normandy summer, performs maintenance on the hydraulic recoil chamber of his 105 mm howitzer. FROM *13 CANADIAN FIELD REGIMENT, RCA*

(Below) Getting ready for Carpiquet
The plan for the attack on Carpiquet Airport, which took place on 4 July 1944, called for an intense barrage and bombardment programme requiring a heavy expenditure of ammunition. A gunner of 13th Field prepares 105 mm rounds for firing. FROM *13 CANADIAN FIELD REGIMENT, RCA*

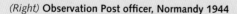

(Above) Troop Command Post
A Troop Command Post at Bretteville-l'Orgeuilleuse, June 1944. Targets from the OP and FOO parties were relayed to the Troop Command Posts which directed the fire of each of the six troops in 13th Field Regiment. The gunners learned quickly that they had to protect their positions. FROM *13 CANADIAN FIELD REGIMENT, RCA*

(Right) Observation Post officer, Normandy 1944
Captain H.L. Thorne of 13th Field poses for the camera in Normandy beside his Sherman OP tank. When the regiment switched to self-propelled guns, the OP officers changed from soft-skinned vehicles to Shermans, which provided an additional measure of protection. There were many complaints when the unit went back to towed guns in August 1944 and the Shermans were given up.
FROM *13 CANADIAN FIELD REGIMENT, RCA*

Smile for the camera: A gun crew, Normandy 1944
The unit is not identified but this photo, taken on 20 June 1944, shows a happy crew from one of the 3rd Division field regiments posed in front of their guns. The marking "B2" indicates the No. 2 gun of Baker Troop. Note the extra plate welded on the side of the vehicle for protection from smallarms fire, the camouflage net on the front and the rather unconvincing use of a tree branch for additional cover. With the exception of the man standing on the right, these gunners are wearing the Mk III "Invasion" helmet, with a wound dressing inserted under the camouflage net to break up the outline. The battle dress issued in Normandy was impregnated with an anti-gas chemical which made it stiff and hot to wear. NAC, PA-132886

Another day at the office (1): No. 2 prepares to fire
Seated under the ring for the .50 calibre machinegun on his self-propelled gun, the detachment No. 2 prepares to open fire. In his right hand, he holds the lanyard that fires the weapon while in his left hand is the lever that will open the breech and eject the empty shell casing after the gun fires. In front of him is the elbow sight used for anti-tank work. The gunner is Lance-Bombardier W.J. Pelrine and this is a gun of 14th Field Regiment. NAC, PA-114582

Another day in the office (2): No. 3 does his job
While the No. 1, or gun detachment commander, looks on, the No. 3 uses the panoramic telescope – fitted with an extension to raise it above the sides of the vehicle – to lay the 105 mm howitzer on the correct azimuth. Note the shells ready for use at the rear of the vehicle. This is actually a detachment from 14th Field and the No. 1 is Sergeant D. Mills while the No. 3 is Gunner H.W. Embree. NAC, PA-145374

Another day at the office (3): Ammunition numbers at work
Only Nos. 1, 2 and 3 actually fired the gun; the remaining gun numbers prepared the ammunition, located at the rear of the vehicle. Here, they are loading ready-use rounds onto a gun of 19th Army Field Regiment. 19 Army Field Regiment, although an army unit, was assigned to 3rd Division for the D-Day assault and fought with that formation through the Normandy campaign. Unlike the three field regiments of the division, it retained its self-propelled guns for the rest of the war. NAC, PA-190212

Air Observation Post, Normandy 1944
Assisting the ground-based OPs and FOOs were the Air OPs, light but unarmed Auster aircraft piloted by trained artillery officers which ranged the length of the front looking for targets behind the enemy lines. It was dangerous work, as not only did German flak try to bring them down, but *Luftwaffe* fighters made an occasional appearance. Here, an Auster AOP of the British AO Squadron 661, which worked with the 3rd Division in Normandy, prepares to take off. NAC, PA-162286

Operation ATLANTIC, 18 July 1944
On 18 July the field regiments of 3rd Division, including this gun from 12th Field Regiment, fired a barrage and then brought down heavy concentrations of fire to support Operation ATLANTIC, the Canadian attack on Verrières Ridge. The attack was a disaster that resulted in heavy casualties but there were no complaints from the infantry about the support they received from their gunner comrades. The expenditure of ammunition was prodigious as can be seen from the picture below of empty 105 mm shell casings and shell containers. BOTH FROM *INTO ACTION WITH THE 12TH FIELD*

to his detachment which consisted of the driver and six gunners who actually loaded and fired: the No. 2 on the right of the breech, who laid for elevation, operated the breech and fired the weapon; the No. 3 on the left of the breech who laid for deflection; Nos. 4 and 5 who were responsible for preparing and bringing forward the rounds; and the No. 6 (usually a bombardier and second-in-command of the gun), who supervised ammunition preparation.

As the crew compartment of the self-propelled 105 was crowded, only the first four gun numbers usually served on the vehicle, the others worked on the ground behind it where most of the ammunition was stored and prepared. The other major difference between the self-propelled gun and a standard artillery piece was that its 105 mm weapon only had a limited on-board traverse. If a new target bearing was ordered that varied considerably from the previous one, the driver would start up his engine and swing the vehicle onto a rough line so that the No. 3 could fine tune the bearing by means of the panoramic telescope fixed to the left of the breech. At the command, "Fire!," the No. 2 Gunner on the left of the breech would yank the lanyard sending – if the round was HE – a 33 lb. projectile at a

velocity of 1,020 feet per second out to a maximum range of more than 10,000 yards.

When a 105 mm HE round hit, a sequence of events took place. First, it would create a lethal blast area of about 35 yards in diameter. Second, it would disintegrate into hundreds of small, jagged metal shards, many of which buried themselves in the ground or went harmlessly up in the air but a great many of which also spread out to the front and forward quarters of the point of impact, creating an iron hail that would cut through anything but hardened armoured plate and concrete. Finally, the explosion would dig a crater up to 3 feet deep, throwing the earth up in the air in a miniature mushroom cloud of dirt and smoke, often containing rocks or stone fragments that were almost as lethal as the metal shards. The result of these events was that a single 105 mm round could kill human beings in a variety of ways: by simple blast (i.e. tearing them apart or even disintegrating them); by concussion created by the shock wave of the explosion which could rupture delicate lung tissue; by the deadly hail of metal, stone, rocks, wood splinters, and even hardened clods of earth that could kill, maim or create grievous wounds; and, finally, by burying them alive.

This was the effect of a single round of 105 mm HE but it must always be kept in mind that since the Commonwealth artillery rarely fired less than four rounds at a single target and usually many more, this effect has to be multiplied many times. One round could be effective, hundreds of rounds could be devastating and, even if they did not kill or wound the enemy, they might numb him with shock or drive him temporarily or permanently insane. The rule of thumb for Canadian gunners was that one round always got three men – one way or the other – and the effect of hundreds of rounds increased enemy casualties at an exponential rate. The Germans tried to return the fire with interest and, occasionally the gun positions came under counter-battery fire but, as Sergeant H.G. Cunningham of 22 Battery remarked, he and his comrades fired "10 rounds back for every round the Germans fired at us."[36] Cunningham recalled that the gun crews were so good and so fast that, when the gun fired, they could "load next round into the gun while it recoiled so you could fire it as soon as it went up," or returned to its firing position. Sergeant Moffat of 22 Battery was just as proud that his crew "could get off 8-10 rounds a minute and that I have no eye lashes today to prove it," those features having been permanently removed by muzzle flash.[37]

The expenditure of ammunition in July 1944 was prodigious – the War Diary of 22 Battery records that, when the battery left Britain, "no one ever thought that we would be using the amount of ammunition that we use now" but "then we had many ideas that changed considerably before we had been in action very long."[38] Re-supplying the guns was the job of the A Echelons whose trucks were in almost continuous motion between the ordnance dumps in the rear and the gun positions. Gunner Hall of 44 Battery, a truck driver in the Echelon, remembered how it worked:

At first the trucks would pick up the ammo right off the beaches where the dumps were and would drive them up to the guns. It was pretty steady firing at the start. They had mined the roads but the engineers checked them pretty thoroughly. As the frontline advanced, the dumps were moved farther forward.

We usually worked at night in convoys but did not use our headlights. There would be a guide in the front of each convoy and his vehicle would have a bit of a dim light. We also had our unit number on the tailgate with a dim light shining on it. The housing of the differential of the rear axle was also painted white. It usually wasn't too hard to keep up as you were following a convoy and we didn't move very fast.

When we got to the gun position, my helpers and I would unload the ammunition behind each gun as the gunners were usually too busy to help.[39]

The question remains, given the fact that the Germans continued to resist all attempts to break through their lines, whether all this artillery fire was producing results. Certainly, the enemy were impressed with the sheer weight of Allied artillery fire – the staff of Army Group B, the German higher formation in Normandy, noted, after Operations GOODWOOD and ATLANTIC, that "extraordinary vigour and the colossal superiority of the enemy in the fighting east of Caen on 18 and 19 July is indicated in the facts that he fired 103,000 artillery shells."[40] The 2nd Panzer Division submitted a "Lessons Learned" report on its first weeks of action in Normandy which emphasized that

The incredibly heavy artillery and mortar fire [of the enemy] is something new, both for the seasoned veterans of the Eastern front and the new arrivals from the reinforcement units. Whereas the veterans get used to it comparatively quickly, the inexperienced reinforcements require several

Into Caen: Sherman OP tank

Although often misidentified as a vehicle of an armoured regiment, this is a troop leader's tank of 19th Army Field Regiment, RCA. Just behind the bogie on the right fender can be see the edge of a "4" and the beginning of a white bar – "45" was the tactical sign of 19th Field and, being an army unit, its sign had a white bar under it. The "RC" designation indicates that this is the troop leader's tank of Charlie Troop. The indicator that this is an OP tank is the number of radio aerials. All four of the field regiments that landed with 3rd Division were equipped with Shermans as OP tanks and there was much grumbling when they were given up once 12th, 13th and 14th Field converted to towed artillery in early August 1944. NAC, PA-162667

"Enemy movement"

Such was the weight of fire that could be brought down in Normandy that this cartoon by Lieutenant Patrick Clay only slightly exaggerates. A call from a FOO for "Uncle Target Scale Five" would result in 360 rounds of HE landing in the vicinity of this hapless German. FROM *13 CANADIAN FIELD REGIMENT, RCA*

days to do so, after which they become acclimatized. The average rate of [Allied] fire on the divisional sector per day is 4,000 artillery rounds and 5,000 mortar rounds per day. This is multiplied many times before an enemy attack, however small. For instance, on one occasion when the British made an attack on a sector of only two [German] companies they expended 3,500 rounds in two hours. The Allies wage war regardless of expense.[41]

German artillery officers also stressed the quick response time of the Commonwealth gunners, the 326th Artillery Regiment complained that "counter battery fire was invariably brought down before our troops could fire more than 4-5 rounds."[42] But enemy artillery officers also noted that in major attacks, the Commonwealth artillery used unimaginative tactics as the main effort of the artillery "always informed" the defending troops "where the main infantry effort would be," one of the problems of using the setpiece infantry assault preceded by a bombardment or barrage.[43]

On a more subjective level, during their prisoner of war interrogations, two German prisoners expressed their personal feelings about the matter:

I fought in Poland, France, the Balkans, and Russia. I can honestly say that I have never in the whole of my experience as a soldier seen anything which remotely compared to the British artillery fire.[44] ……

I arrived at the Front firmly believing in the Fuehrer and a German victory. A few hours of British artillery fire and the sight of British tanks, together with the faultless organisation behind it all, was sufficient to make me realize how matters stand. Now I am confused, and don't know what to believe, but one thing I do know – there is no greater hell than British artillery fire.[45]

The only way for the Germans to survive the heavy bombardments brought down on them was to construct very strong and well-camouflaged positions with at least 3-4 feet of supported overhead cover to protect themselves against field artillery and much more for medium and heavy artillery. A member of the 12th SS Division recorded the efforts he and his comrades made to protect themselves from the Commonwealth artillery and the result of these efforts:

Heavy artillery fire woke us at a very early hour. Based on its intensity, we recognized that an attack was coming. We drew back into our slit trench which we had covered with farming implements, beams, girders and dirt. This would prove to be advantageous since we took at least four direct hits on our approximately 1.5 square meter [yard] trench. Since the shells were outfitted with highly sensitive impact detonators [fuzes], nothing much happened. There was only an immense

amount of dust every time. The whole terrain was covered by explosions, one could say, two per square meter.[46]

As soon as the Commonwealth gunners ceased firing, so as not to hit friendly troops, German soldiers like this man would emerge from similar well-constructed positions and begin to fight – as one Canadian infantry officer put it:

the intense concentrated pounding of a small area does not produce a great killing or even stunning effect. Defenders begin firing back almost immediately. … An additional advantage of the highly concentrated artillery fire is the dense smoke and dust raised.[47]

Another noted that one of the difficulties facing an infantry commander "is that while he realizes he has artillery resources to call on it is extremely difficult in the confusion to make use of [them]."[48]

As the Canadian experience in the operations carried out in July 1944 demonstrated, the proper use of artillery was one of a number of tactical problems that had to be overcome to penetrate well-sited and well-constructed German defences. First, the gap between the time the artillery stopped and the infantry reached its objective had to be reduced so as not to give the enemy time to recover from a bombardment. Second, some method had to be found of getting both the infantry and the armour on to the objective at the same time as, all too often, the infantry were sent to ground by enemy automatic weapons fire, leaving the supporting armour at the mercy of German anti-tank weapons with superior range and hitting power. The infantry could take out the anti-tank guns, and the armour could take out the German machineguns, but both arms had to do it at the same time and at the same place. In the final analysis, it was all about the infantry as only the infantry could *take and hold ground* – some method therefore had to be found to permit the infantry to cross fire-swept killing areas without suffering prohibitive casualties.

"The shelling makes a nervous wreck of him": The strain of battle

By 25 July, when Operation SPRING came to its bloody conclusion, 3rd Canadian Division had been in action without meaningful rest for 50 days and was beginning to show signs of strain. During the Second World War, American military psychiatrists estimated that the average soldier reached his peak effectiveness after his first 90 days of combat but after that point, his mental state and his morale would decline rapidly. These figures, however, were based on combat in North Africa, which was neither as intense nor as prolonged as combat in Normandy, particularly during the relentless fighting of July 1944. Soldiers in Normandy burned out at a much faster rate and, by late July 1944, 3rd Division was growing very tired, indeed.

Before D-Day the general belief in the division was that, given the heavy casualties expected during the landing, it would be withdrawn from combat after the beachhead had been secured. When this did not turn out to be accurate, the division continued in action but the arrival in France of every new Commonwealth formation gave rise to fresh rumours that it would soon be getting a rest. This was particularly true when 2nd Canadian Division landed in early July. When the expected relief did not occur and when the men of 3rd Division learned that British divisions which had been on the continent for less time were being sent back for a rest, they became dissatisfied. One gets a sense of their frustration in an entry dated 11 July 1944 in the War Diary of 78 Battery:

Second [Canadian] Division has been moving up through us all day and it is or was rumoured that they would be taking over from us and that we would be going back for a rest. However we learned later that they were relieving the 51st Highlander [sic] Division which is something we don't understand as we were in action two weeks before them. Rumour has it that the powers that be stated to some more powers that be that the Third Canadian Infantry Division didn't want a rest and so they relieved the 51st instead. Naturally all the boys are asking "who the Third Canadian Division was that was asked if they wanted to be relieved" because though our boys would go on fighting till they dropped, yet if they are in turn to be relieved, naturally they want to take it because they are sure in need of a rest and really deserve it.[49]

Shortly after this was written, 3rd Canadian Division suffered heavy losses during Operations ATLANTIC and SPRING. As always, the infantry bore the worst of the burden since about 75% of all combat casualties occurred in that arm and the number of "battle exhaustion" casualties – the 1944 term for post-trau-

matic stress syndrome – climbed dramatically. The War Diary of No. 1 Canadian Exhaustion Unit, a medical unit that specialized in the treatment of such casualties, records that it treated 175 cases during the three days that Operation ATLANTIC lasted – nearly 10% of all casualties suffered in that undertaking. These figures, however, were only for those men who were sent back from their units, almost certainly the worst cases. Most units tried to keep men suffering from "battle exhaustion" with them as it was known that, once such men were sent back through the medical stream diagnosed as "battle exhaustion" casualties, they rarely returned. The preferred method in combat units was to rotate men back to the unit's B Echelon, out of range of artillery fire, for a week or so where they could get some rest and hot meals.

Although gunners suffered fewer casualties than infantry, they too felt the strain of battle. For 13th Field Regiment, this was particularly true in July when the gun positions were under intermittent enemy artillery fire on a daily basis, often from the hated "Moaning Minnies." It was not long before some men began to exhibit symptoms of "battle exhaustion" and the commanding officer, Lieutenant-Colonel Clifford, and the battery commanders instituted a procedure that, as one veteran remembered, meant you got them "out of sight somewhere" for a while and "they'd be good again."[50] In this respect, the battery War Diaries of 13th Field are of interest because they contain some information on the fate of individual soldiers who suffered from the stress of combat:[51]

26 June
Gnr W Evacuated – Has been a pending case of shellshock for the last week and yesterday's shelling necessitated his evacuation. ……

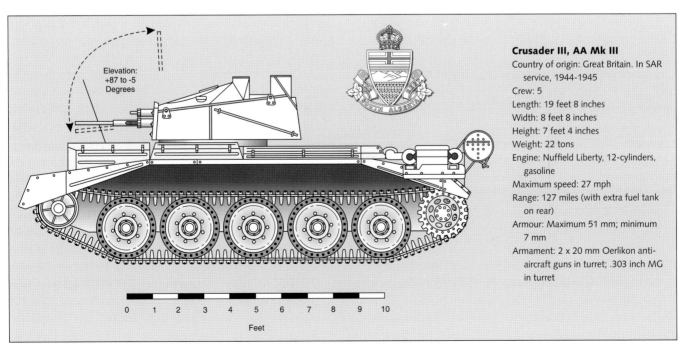

Crusader III, AA Mk III
Country of origin: Great Britain. In SAR service, 1944-1945
Crew: 5
Length: 19 feet 8 inches
Width: 8 feet 8 inches
Height: 7 feet 4 inches
Weight: 22 tons
Engine: Nuffield Liberty, 12-cylinders, gasoline
Maximum speed: 27 mph
Range: 127 miles (with extra fuel tank on rear)
Armour: Maximum 51 mm; minimum 7 mm
Armament: 2 x 20 mm Oerlikon anti-aircraft guns in turret; .303 inch MG in turret

Elevation: +87 to -5 Degrees

0 1 2 3 4 5 6 7 8 9 10

Feet

18 July

The shelling today affected Gnr X enough to warrant sending him back to "B" Echelon for a rest for a few days. He is one of the few we have who lets the shelling make a nervous wreck of him but with a few days rest he should be back on his feet again.

For some men, however, even a rest in B Echelon was not enough and they resorted to desperate measures:

26 July

Gnr Y. This man was returned to B Ech[elon] approx 15 Jul 44 for a rest as he was of a very nervous type and had been on O Pip work. Early in the morning of 23 Jul while on guard he was observed by Gnr _____ to put his rifle to his toe and pull the trigger. Whether it was accidental or otherwise is yet undecided. ……. His time for B Echelon was just about up and he was due to be returned to the front.

Gunner Y must have been desperate as, if found guilty by a court martial of a self-inflicted wound, he would receive a sentence of three to five years hard labour in a military prison. Some men, however, would rather undergo such punishment than return to combat.

As always, there were soldiers who tried to get out of doing their duty by pretending to be nervous cases. Such men were liabilities in action and they were generally got rid of as quickly as possible. Consider the case of Gunner Z who arrived at a battery on 29 July 1944,

with the typical "half mile" crime sheet. Brought from B Ech[elon] to F[ighting] Ech[elon] and immediately proved himself to be a shirker by refusing to dig in or help other people dig in – using the excuse that he was scared. It was quite apparent that he was trying to swing his way out and as we have no use for people like that – he was kicked out.

And, as always, there were men who tried to do more than duty called for and one such was Gunner J. Smith of 78 Battery who was ordered to the hospital on 24 July:

From a month before the invasion he suffered rheumatism badly but would not be attended to because he wanted to be in the invasion. Even after arrival over here he would not report sick, and probably never would have had he not been ordered to. …… but he stuck it out and most likely would have continued doing so.

Fortunately for the men of 3rd Canadian Infantry Division, in the last days of July 1944 it was relieved and pulled back for a rest. The turn of 13th Field came on 30 July after the unit had been in action for 53 days, during which time they had occupied thirteen gun positions, fired off hundreds of thousands of rounds and lost 26 officers and men killed and 55 wounded. The unit pulled out of its last gun position southwest of Caen at 11 P.M. that day and drove to its destination, a wheat field near Thaon, 6 miles to the north. After nearly eight weeks in action, it was so peaceful that it took some getting used to, as the War Diary of 78 Battery noted:

It is hard to realize there is a war back on here. When we pulled in around midnight – the sky was clear with a half-moon and it was warm and quiet. You couldn't hear a gun which was strange to us who for 53 days have heard the continuous firing of hundreds of them. All that told us that we were still fighting was the continual flash of guns on the horizon. Otherwise it is quiet and peaceful beyond the hopes and imaginations of all of us. But I don't have to add that it is welcomed. Everyone slept out on the flat ground while hardly anyone even bothered to dig a hole to jump into.[52]

"Ah sweet life," the diarist concluded, "but we suppose it won't last long."

"A goddamn sea of fire": Enter the South Albertas

While the men of 13th Field were enjoying a well-deserved rest, the South Alberta Regiment was moving up to the front. For the SAR, the six weeks that followed D-Day had been a frustrating time, all they could do was follow the course of the fighting by reading newspapers and listening to the BBC. The SAR – and the other units in 4th Armoured Division – were anxious to get across the Channel and into the fight, not the least of their reasons being that, since late April, training had been restricted because their vehicles were waterproofed. The divisional commander, Major-General George Kitching, realizing his men's frustration, visited all his units to assure them their time would come soon and that they would have the important task of leading the breakout battle. Until that time, they route marched, played cards, listened to the radio, and waited.

On Sunday, 17 July 1944, just as the officers were recovering from their seventeenth consecutive farewell party, the order came to move. Over the next two days, the unit's vehicles were loaded onto a convoy that set sail for France but storms in the Channel delayed their passage. As the vessels slipped by Dover in the darkness of the early hours of 22 July, a member of 10th Brigade recorded that they were treated to a magnificent fireworks display in the night sky:

Flying bombs were seen being launched from the French coast, growing from a tiny speck of light to the ultimate monstrous, flaming shape. One flew across our bows and the destroyer escort and our own ack ack guns shot the sky with tracers. The display on the Dover coast was magnificent. A wall of ruby spray went up at each successive bomb, and the heavy anti-aircraft guns sent flashes of brilliant silver winking across the sky. The drama of guns, men, and inhuman robots would reach its climax in a huge golden blaze as the pilotless plane exploded in its headlong flight.[53]

The SAR arrived off Normandy late in the afternoon of 24 July to begin disembarkation on a wide beach at Vaux, west of Courseulles. The following day 10th Brigade took over a portion of the front between the villages of Bourguébus and Bras on Bourguébus Ridge and, during the afternoon, the SAR moved to the little town of Cormelles near Caen ready to support the infantry. They were now within range of German artillery and, just as the men of 13th Field Regiment had done, they soon learned to dig slit trenches – deeply and quickly – and also to tell the crucial difference between the sound of "incoming" or enemy artillery fire and "outgoing" or friendly fire.

In the meantime, the balance of the campaign was tilting in favour of the Allies. On 25 July, First U.S. Army launched Operation COBRA which achieved a complete breakthrough of the German front. General George S. Patton's Third U.S. Army poured through the gap in the German lines and spilled out into Brittany. In order to keep the pressure on the German forces in the Commonwealth sector and prevent them from shifting troops to the American sector, Montgomery ordered the Second British Army and the newly-activated First Canadian Army to attack, harass and raid the enemy. In particular, the British general was keen that the Canadians mount another attack on the German strongpoint of Tilly-la-Campagne on Bourguébus Ridge, which had resisted two previous attacks. Orders came down to Kitching of 4th Armoured Division to attack Tilly, as a method of "easing" his division into battle.

Tilly was a tough objective. The defenders had reinforced the cellars of the houses in the hamlet and then dynamited the upper floors, creating bunkers protected by rubble. The only approaches were across flat, open fields swept by fire and the garrison consisted of nine companies of panzergrenadiers from the elite 1st Waffen SS Panzer Division, *Leibstandarte Adolf Hitler*, very determined soldiers who were backed up by tanks and self-propelled guns. The enemy strength was not known during the morning of 1 August when Kitching ordered the Lincoln and Welland Regiment, with support from the SAR, to attack Tilly that night. Problems caused by the fact that the Lincoln & Welland Regiment were going into action for the first time, meant that it was close to midnight before A Squadron was briefed on their role in the attack. The attack was an unmitigated disaster – the infantry were quickly pinned down by automatic weapons fire, communications broke down, and there was little the South Albertas could do to help except fire at enemy muzzle flashes. Lieutenant Gordie Irving of A-1 Troop remembered feeling helpless as he watched the flatfeet advance into "a goddamn sea of fire" in and around the village.[54] The Links were rebuffed with heavy casualties.

Four days later, at Jefferson's insistence, the Argylls, with Major Dave Currie's C Squadron in support, mounted a second night attack on the village. Again, problems were encountered

Enter 4th Armoured Division

A Sherman tank of 4th Armoured Division south of Caen in late July 1944. The units of this formation arrived in Normandy in the last week of July and went into action almost immediately. DND PHOTO, ZK-859

with the planning and Currie did not learn of the operation until late in the day, when he had difficulties locating the infantry in the dark and, finally dismounting, led his tanks forward on foot. The Argylls had no better luck than the Links and C Squadron lost four tanks to mines, but took no casualties. The problems encountered during the two abortive attacks on Tilly were an indication that the green 4th Division still had a lot to learn. Captain John Redden of C Squadron recalled that Dave Currie was very annoyed at the business but in Redden's opinion, despite the failure, the squadron "learned what not to do in the future."[55] The next day, 6 August, 10th Brigade was pulled back from Bourguébus Ridge to a rest area near Caen.

The Falaise Road (1): Operation TOTALIZE, 7-10 August 1944
During the five days that Jefferson's brigade had been banging its head on Tilly, major events had taken place in the American sector. Patton's advance into Brittany alarmed Hitler, who ordered the German commander-in-chief in Normandy, *Feldmarschall* Hans von Kluge, to counterattack with all available armoured divisions to cut off Patton's supply lines. In vain, von Kluge protested that, if he weakened his forces facing the Commonwealth armies, he would inevitably face a major attack in that area. Hitler was deaf to any form of logic and von Kluge obeyed orders

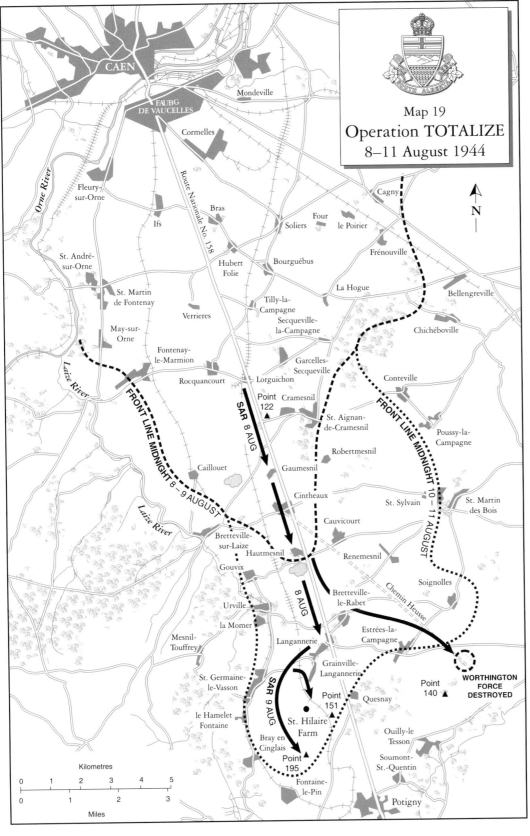

Map 19
Operation TOTALIZE
8–11 August 1944

German lines. Patton moved fast and by 11 August he was at Le Mans, at the rear of the German left flank and almost at the rear of the enemy forces facing the Commonwealth armies. The German armies in Normandy were now in danger of being encircled.

Before that could happen, First Canadian Army had to break through the enemy defence lines south of Caen. The terrain in this area consisted of gentle, rolling slopes and grain fields dotted with small villages, walled farmsteads, woods and orchards. Under orders from both Montgomery and General Harry Crerar, commanding First Canadian Army, to plan an operation that would penetrate these defence lines, Lieutenant-General Guy Simonds pondered how best to accomplish this task. Simonds had observed at first hand the failure of Operation GOODWOOD to overcome enemy positions on similar ground and he decided to attack at night to utilize the cover of darkness and to use all available artillery and airpower to break the defenders' will to fight. He also came up with a solution to the problem of getting the infantry and armour onto the objective at the same time – the armoured personnel carrier. Simonds later admitted that the concept of such a vehicle first came to him after he watched the SPGs from of one of 3rd Division's field regiments drive by him, and was struck by how useful they might prove as armoured

by sending four panzer divisions to attack in the Mortain area on 6 August. They were totally defeated after two days of heavy fighting and, with this threat removed, General Omar S. Bradley, commanding 12 Army Group, which controlled both First and Third U.S. Armies, ordered Patton to turn east behind the infantry carriers. As these units were about to exchange their self-propelled 105 mm howitzers for towed 25-pdr. guns, Canadian engineers created a crash programme to remove the howitzers from the vehicles and weld additional armour plate onto them, creating the first fully-tracked APC in history.

Simonds's plan of attack, codenamed TOTALIZE, was complex. The operation was to consist of two phases: Phase One would commence at 11 P.M. on 7 August with a heavy artillery bombardment and an attack by bombers on the German defences. Then the assault divisions (2nd Canadian and 51st Highland), with their leading infantry brigades in APCs and each supported by armour, would break through the German lines while their other brigades would follow on foot to mop up strongpoints left by the leading elements. Phase Two would begin at 1 P.M. on 8 August when, following a second bombardment by the U.S. Eighth Air Force, 4th Canadian and 1st Polish Armoured Divisions would advance on both sides of RN (*Route Nationale*) 158, which ran from Caen to Falaise, with the objective of seizing the high ground that overlooked the latter city.

The South Albertas' job in Phase Two would be to assist 10th Brigade take an area around the villages of Granville-Langannerie and Potigny. As the South Albertas prepared to move forward on the night of 7 August, the roar of aircraft was heard at 11 P.M. as RAF Bomber Command arrived to bomb the forward German positions. The bombers were still overhead when the artillery brought down a tremendous bombardment from hundreds of guns. Under its cover, and guided by searchlights, tracer shells and radio navigational beams, 3rd Canadian and 51st Highland Division moved to the attack behind a rolling barrage. A number of gunners from 13th Field participated in this attack, driving the converted SPs, now dubbed "Kangaroos." Although mines and enemy fire caused vehicle casualties, by first light on 8 August, most of the Phase One objectives were taken and there appeared to be nothing between First Canadian Army and the city of Falaise.

The commanders of the lead elements urged that the advance be continued but were told to wait until relieved by the two armoured divisions. Those divisions could not move, however, until the Phase Two air bombardment had been completed as, given the cumbersome nature of inter-Allied command, their attack could not be cancelled nor could its timing be changed. This delay was unfortunate because, although the initial attack had severely shaken the enemy, they had nearly six hours to rally and it was not long before Meyer, whose 12th Waffen SS Panzer Division was in reserve to the rear, was moving forward *ad hoc* tank and infantry battlegroups.

Promptly at 12.55 P.M. on 8 August, nearly 500 B-17s of the U.S. 8th Air Force swept in to hit the defended villages on either side of RN 158 and, unfortunately, some units in 3rd Canadian and 1st Polish Armoured Division, inflicting about 300 casualties including Major-General Rod Keller, the commander of 3rd Division, who was wounded. An hour late, the lead unit of

Operation TOTALIZE, 7 August 1944
Infantry of 2nd Canadian Division, identified by their flat Mk II steel helmets, wait on board improvised armoured personnel carriers created by removing the guns from the M-7 vehicles of the field regiments of 3rd Division. Many of the drivers from the field regiment remained with their vehicles and participated in the attack. Markings on the vehicle in the right foreground reveal that it is the former Dog One gun of 44 Battery, 13th Field Regiment. NAC, PA-129172

Waiting to go in, 7 August 1944
Infantry of the 2nd Division wait for the fun to begin. The "F4" on the side of the vehicle indicates that it is the former Fox Four gun of a 3rd Division field regiment. The driver, however, is wearing a black beret, which indicates that he is from the armoured corps. NAC, 129173

4th Armoured Brigade, the Canadian Grenadier Guards, crossed its start line and carefully advanced down the western side of the RN 158 but quickly encountered determined German resistance. This was not a good day for 4th Brigade which moved cautiously despite a personal tongue lashing given by Kitching to the formation's commander, Brigadier E.L. Booth. By 6 P.M. the brigade, more or less finished for the day, went into harbour to resupply. The Polish Armoured Division fared no better – its advance was disorganized because of traffic congestion and shortly after crossing their start line, its leading elements encountered a screen of German tanks and anti-tank guns positioned by Meyer, which brewed up 40 tanks in the space of two hours. At 4.30 P.M., the Poles informed Simonds that they were regrouping.

The South Albertas and the infantry of 10th Brigade had a better day. The regiment had completed a long and confusing night march, made worse by the fact that orders forbade the use of headlights, and by the clouds of dust stirred by hundreds of vehicles moving at the same time. When daylight came, the brigade was in its concentration area but all was confusion – Corporal John Galipeau remembered seeing all around him "trucks with infantry on board … trucks loaded with ammunition ahead of us and, in one case, we saw a kitchen truck come up but it went sailing off."[56]

Swatty and Jeff
Lieutenant-Colonel Gordon ("Swatty") Wotherspoon (left), commanding the SAR, and Brigadier James Jefferson, commanding 10th Infantry Brigade, discuss strategy in Normandy at the time of TOTALIZE. Jefferson always heeded the advice of his subordinate, as Wotherspoon was one of the best tacticians in the Canadian army, and the two got along well. Note that Swatty has removed his helmet – he hated wearing the thing but that did not prevent him charging any man under his command he caught without one in action.
NAC, PA-163410

During the morning the brigade column lurched forward again and, when the Phase Two bombing took place, was just north of Rocquancourt.

Jefferson's ultimate objective was Point 195 near the village of Potigny 7 miles to the south on the east side of RN 158. To get there, the brigade had to clear a series of villages on the east side of that highway and, with the Argylls and C Squadron leading, they commenced this task in mid-afternoon. There were stubborn pockets of resistance that had to be dealt with and, by 6 P.M., the lead elements of the brigade had only progressed as far as Hautmesnil, 4 miles short of Point 195. Jefferson had not taken his objective but 10th Brigade had made the farthest advance in Phase Two of TOTALIZE.

Simonds ordered Kitching to continue operations during the night to secure Point 195. To undertake this task, the commander of 4th Armoured Division dispatched a battle group consisting of the greater part of both the British Columbia Regiment (BCR) and the Algonquin Regiment under the command of Lieutenant-Colonel Don Worthington of the BCR. Worthington Force, as it was termed, moved off at 2 A.M. on 9 August but a tragic error in navigation found it, at first light, not on Point 195 to the west of the RN 158 but on Point 140 to the east of that highway and in the sector of the Polish Armoured Division. What was worse was that Worthington had inadvertently moved to within 2 miles of the headquarters of Meyer's 12th SS

Panzer Division, which had pulled back during the night to take up new defensive positions. Concluding, not unnaturally, that the Canadian battlegroup was where it was because it was supposed to be there, Meyer immediately brought down heavy artillery fire on Point 140 and threw every available tank and infantryman against it. By radio, Worthington requested support from 4th Division which could not provide it because, despite frantic efforts, the divisional staff could not pinpoint his location. The German attacks continued throughout the day and the Canadians were gradually whittled down with Worthington being killed and the commanding officer of the Algonquins badly wounded. At about 5 P.M., the remnants abandoned Point 140 and made their way independently to the Canadian lines, having lost 47 tanks and suffered 200 casualties.

Jefferson's 10th Brigade spent most of 9 August clearing out a series of small but connected villages south of Hautmesnil. Currie's C Squadron supported the Argylls as they captured a large quarry near that village and then Major Arnold Lavoie's A Squadron supported the Links as, in turn, they took the villages of Langannerie, Grainville-Langannerie and Vieille-Langannerie south of the quarry. German resistance was stiff but the defenders were gradually overcome. It was during this action that Trooper Robert Henning discovered that the flatfeet have a weird sense of humour. He saw an Argyll emerge from a house which Henning's tank had just demolished with AP fire, waving a German helmet with the owner's head still attached. Henning promptly threw up but, as he later recalled, he soon became inured to such sights. By 6 P.M. the brigade had finished their work and the South Albertas withdrew to Cintheaux, to harbour for the night.

Unfortunately, 4th Armoured Brigade, which had driven south from Hautmesnil on the west side of the RN 158 while 10th Brigade had been occupied on the east side, had no better luck than on the previous day. During the night of 9/10 August, Kurt Meyer had shifted all available forces to a new defence line running from Point 195 to Point 140. The central part of this line was Quesnay Wood, which straddled RN 158 about a mile and a half north of Potigny, and was an ideal defensive position. Here Meyer placed every available armoured vehicle, including a company of Tiger tanks, and a heavy screen of anti-tank guns. Advancing down the RN 158, 4th Brigade ran smack into this hornet's nest and the Governor-General's Foot Guards, the leading unit, lost 26 tanks and was forced to pull back.

By late afternoon it was clear to Simonds and Kitching that Point 195 was not occupied. Kitching ordered Lieutenant-Colonel Dave Stewart's Argylls to take that objective during the night and Stewart opted to take his battalion in by stealth on their feet, foregoing armour and artillery support. He personally scouted the route and then returned to his unit and led them, single file, through the dark, onto the objective. The Links made a similar night march to come in on the Argylls' right flank and, by first light on 10 August, the infantry were dug in on Point 195. Meanwhile, the remnant of the Algonquin Regiment moved forward to a position near St. Hilaire Farm abreast of Quesnay Wood.

This fine example of infantry fieldcraft took Kurt Meyer by surprise and he reacted vigorously. It was fortunate for the Argylls and Links that the main German defences were on a different spur of Point 195 or they might have run into them during the night. As it was, once the enemy discovered the new positions of the three battalions, they immediately brought down heavy artillery and mortar fire and put in a series of counterattacks, which were rebuffed. This was the first day that Wotherspoon of the SAR was able to properly employ his Recce Troop and three two-tank patrols went out early in the morning to ascertain the exact German positions. One patrol was shot up near the Quesnay Wood but, by 10 A.M., Wotherspoon had firm intelligence on the new German defensive line and sent his three squadrons forward to support their respective battalions. For its part, meanwhile, 4th Armoured Brigade – in the form of the Foot Guards and Grenadier Guards – tried again to advance against Quesnay Wood only to suffer heavy losses in tanks, despite the intervention of Typhoon tactical aircraft.

As 10 August wore on, it became clear to Simonds that Operation TOTALIZE was grinding to a halt. To the east 1st Polish Division had been stopped by a German defence line anchored on high ground north of the Laison River while, on either side of the RN 158, the strong enemy defence line in the Quesnay Wood and south of Point 195 had thwarted all 4th Armoured Division's attempts to advance. The corps commander decided to make one last attempt to break through and, late in the afternoon, 3rd Canadian Division was ordered to assault Quesnay Wood. It was nearly last light by the time the Queen's Own Rifles and North Shore Regiment advanced under the cover of a heavy artillery barrage, only to be pinned down by fierce German artillery, mortar and machinegun fire. To make matters worse, the Canadian artillery had to cease fire as, in the growing darkness, they were unable to distinguish enemy from friendly troops. The attack was a costly failure.

At 11 A.M. on 11 August, Simonds ordered 3rd Division to take over the positions of the two armoured divisions and allow them to regroup for a new attack. Operation TOTALIZE had succeeded in breaking through the German defence lines south of Caen and First Canadian Army had advanced about 7 miles but it had not taken its main objective, the high ground overlooking Falaise.

The Falaise Road (2): Operation TRACTABLE, 14-15 August 1944

The SAR was withdrawn to a rest area near Cauvricourt but nobody got much sleep because a nearby medium regiment fired its 5.5-inch guns directly over their heads for two days and two nights, covering them in dirt. Still, it was better than Point 195 and the men enjoyed hot meals provided by the B Echelon cooks and a visit to the "Chinese Hussars," as the army's Mobile Bath units were known, which furnished showers and clean underwear. Better still, the Salvation Army auxiliary services' truck finally caught up with the unit and the men were able to purchase soft drinks and candy and enjoy film shows.

In the meantime, 13th Field had enjoyed its four-day rest period and then, along with the two other field regiments of 3rd Division, commenced re-equipping with 25-pdr. gun/howitzers. The gunners were not entirely happy about the switch as the smaller 25-pdrs. looked like "pop-guns" compared to the 105 mm weapons they had been serving.[57] Even worse, they would now have to dig gun pits every time they changed positions, a chore that had not been necessary with the self-propelled equipment. But, as Sergeant Cunningham of 22 Battery noted, the regiment knew the 25-pdrs., having trained on them for years, "and they handled beautifully and you could get them into position quickly."[58] Despite all the grumbling, the bottom line, according to Sergeant Porter of 44 Battery was that, although his comrades "were not happy about the 25-pdr., we had to make the best of it and there it was."[59] Still muttering, the regiment left the rest area and went into position near Hautmesnil ready to take part in a new operation being planned by Simonds

Codenamed Operation TRACTABLE, it resulted from the quick eastward advance of Patton's Third U.S. Army which offered a chance to trap the German armies in Normandy somewhere between Falaise and Argentan. Montgomery therefore ordered Simonds to capture Falaise as quickly as possible and then "operate with strong armoured and mobile forces to secure Argentan."[60] Simonds's plan for this new operation was simple and direct – it would be a massive daylight tank thrust through the German defences north of Falaise that would avoid the strongpoint of Quesnay Wood. Following a short but intense artillery and air bombardment, the six armoured regiments of 2nd and 4th Armoured Brigades, formed in a massive phalanx, followed by an infantry brigade in the new Armoured Personnel Carriers, would smash through the German lines under cover of a heavy smoke screen. Jefferson's 10th Brigade and the 7th Brigade of 3rd Division would follow behind in trucks to mop up isolated pockets of resistance. Operation TRACTABLE was to set to commence at 1 P.M. on 14 August.

Simonds had been very dissatisfied with the performance of his armoured regiments in TOTALIZE. The day before TRACTABLE took place, he assembled every armoured unit commander in 2 Canadian Corps and gave them a lengthy and harsh dressing down, stating that this time there would be no excuses for a lack of success. These remarks were primarily aimed at Booth's 4th Armoured Brigade but Kitching was appalled by Simonds's lecture, particularly in view of the fact that TOTALIZE had been his division's first major operation. For his part, Swatty Wotherspoon regarded Simonds's words as a personal insult to both himself and his regiment and became furious with the corps commander. When Simonds "called me yellow," he recalled years later, "I never had great respect for the man after that, because neither my regiment nor I were yellow at all."[61]

On this same day, however, a far happier event took place. Major Bill Cromb, an Ortona veteran of the Loyal Eddies (the popular name of the Loyal Edmonton Regiment), was promoted and given command of the Lincoln & Welland Regiment. At the same time, Major Bob Bradburn of the SAR, whose military career had started 22 years before when, as a boy scout, he had accompanied the 19th Alberta Dragoons to summer camp, took over the Algonquin Regiment, which had lost its commander on Point 140. Bradburn was replaced in B Squadron by Major Thomas ("Darby") Nash, the commander of HQ Squadron and a prewar 19th Dragoon. These changes meant that the senior officers in 10th Brigade were men who knew each and had worked together for some time, an asset in battle. They also resulted in 10th Infantry Brigade taking on a distinctly Western Canadian tone, with the brigade commander and two of the four unit commanders being Albertans, while a third unit had been raised from across that province. The odd man out was Lieutenant-Colonel David Stewart of the Argylls, who was from Prince Edward Island, but Stewart would prove to be one of the most brilliant Canadian battalion commanders in Northwest Europe.

Early in the morning of 14 August, 10th Brigade – 79 armoured vehicles and more than 200 trucks – moved to a forming-up area marked out by the Provosts and engineers. Here they joined some 500 tanks and 1,500 soft-skinned vehicles of 3rd and 4th Divisions and 2nd Armoured Brigade. It was an amazing sight to see and one SAR officer commented that the numbers of tanks in view were "more reminiscent of a magazine advertisement for General Motors than warfare as we got to know it later."[62]

Promptly at 11.25 A.M., the artillery, including 13th Field Regiment, fired red smoke to mark targets for the medium and heavy bombers that appeared a few minutes later and then switched to a combination of HE and smoke to demoralize and confuse the enemy. At 11.40 A.M., the order came to "move now!" and the lead brigades rumbled straight ahead. Morale was high, an officer of the Lake Superior Regiment played the regimental march, "Light Afoot," on a trumpet while in the vehicles of 8 Field Squadron, RCE, the sappers, who had just received their rum ration, moved off "cheering and shouting and waving hilariously to our neighbouring vehicles."[63]

The massive formation simply overran the forward German positions. As a literary-minded officer of 10th Brigade wrote, the air and artillery bombardment had left

> nothing but churned mud. The enemy was shaken to the core, and when they saw this fantastic array of massed tanks and infantry, flame throwers and flails, beating down upon them, they must have recreated in their Teutonic minds a Wagnerian scene depicting the end, the wild bloody gloom of the last melée of all the gods of war.[64]

Be that as it may, progress was good until the leading elements reached the Laison River, about 3 miles north of the start line, which Simonds believed was fordable by tanks at all points. This belief turned out to be wrong and the advance stalled for several hours while hundreds of vehicles milled around the north bank of Laison waiting for the engineers to come up and bulldoze the banks to create crossing places. Chaos reigned at the Laison as units lost cohesion and then had difficulty sorting themselves out. The historian of the BCR recorded that even finding tanks of the same unit was difficult:

Lining up for the "Mad Dash": Operation TRACTABLE, 14 August 1944
Armoured and soft-skinned vehicles of 10th Brigade form up for the "Mad Dash" – Operation TRACTABLE – on the morning of 14 August 1944. In all, nearly 500 tanks and 1,500 other vehicles took part in this operation and the sight of so many Shermans gathered side by side caused one South Alberta officer to remark that it looked like "a magazine advertisement for General Motors." SAR ARCHIVES

"Hello Baker two. I am at RV now. Which is your vehicle?" …

"I am waving my arm from the turret." …

"Hello Baker two, are you the one waving his right arm or his left arm? Are you the one beside the tree or over at the fence?"[65]

By last light, however, 2nd Armoured Brigade had got over the Laison and was almost on its objective, the high ground overlooking Falaise. In contrast, 4th Armoured Brigade, whose commander had been killed, had stopped considerably short of its objective.

The South Albertas and 10th Brigade, coming behind, had an exciting day. When they received orders to move *en masse*, the Argyll, Lincoln & Welland and Algonquin infantry started "shouting, waving their caps in the air and giving forth Indian war whoops to express their high spirits."[66] With the SAR in the van, the brigade followed the visible tracks of the leading formations south to the village of Soignolles and were just approaching it when they were attacked by Allied fighter aircraft. The brigade fired off yellow smoke, the recognition signal for friendly troops, and all the vehicles spread orange and yellow panels along their tops to alert the airmen but it was to no avail – for 30 minutes, flight after flight of aircraft strafed the brigade formation, mercifully inflicting few casualties.

This was not the only mistake the air force made on 14 August 1944. As the waves of bombers flew over to attack targets in and around Quesnay Wood, they began to bomb short, dropping their deadly loads onto the rear areas of 3rd Canadian Division including the gun lines of 12th, 13th and 14th Field Regiments. Gunner William McCrie watched it happen:

The Pathfinders came over and dropped their bombs as they should, about two miles ahead. The first stream came over but the subsequent waves dropped a mile short of us but then the bombers

behind dropped shorter and shorter. We were getting out yellow parachute panels, the signal for friendly troops, we were firing off yellow smoke and we couldn't get them to stop. We could see the bomb bays open and the bombs coming right down on us. I jumped into a slit trench with a guy named Ford and Hector MacDougall. Then I thought that they might need me over at the battery CP [Command Post]. I jumped out and ran back to the CP. A bomb dropped on the slit trench and killed Ford and MacDougall.[67]

The attack lasted 90 minutes as wave after wave of four-engined Lancaster bombers, flying in stately procession, dropped their

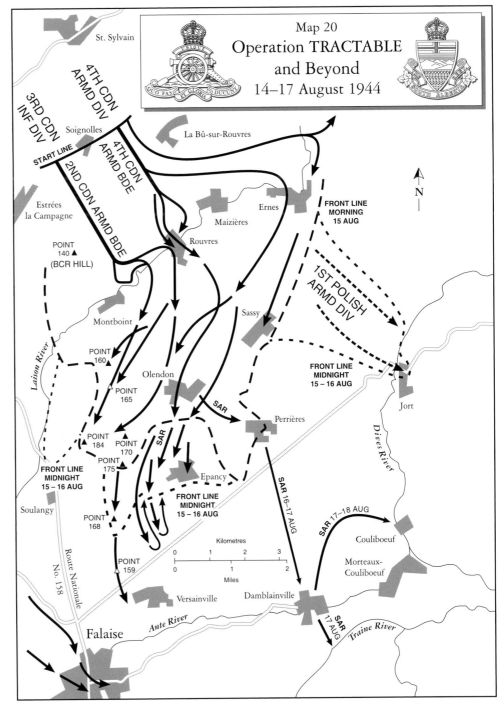

The terrible mistake

During the early afternoon of 14 August 1944, more than a hundred heavy bombers from RAF Bomber Command bombed their own troops by mistake, inflicting heavy casualties on the 3rd and 4th Canadian Divisions. This photograph, taken from the A Echelon of 12th Field Regiment, shows the towering pillar of smoke that resulted from this terrible error. Ironically, many of the aircraft were from the RCAF. FROM *INTO ACTION WITH THE 12TH FIELD*

What a soldier does not want to see overhead

During the Normandy campaign there were many (too many) occurrences of "friendly fire" when Allied aircraft attacked their own troops. One of the worst cases occurred during Operation TRACTABLE on 14 August when 126 heavy bombers (44 of them from 6 Group RCAF) such as this Lancaster attacked Canadian and Polish troops by accident, killing or wounding about 400 men. In vain, men on the ground shot off yellow smoke, the army's identifying signal for friendly troops, only to make things worse because the bombers were using yellow smoke as a target indicator. CANADIAN FORCE PHOTO UNIT, PC-44203

bombs on the smoke and explosions of the preceding wave. In desperation, ground troops spread yellow and orange recognition panels and fired off yellow smoke but it only seem to make matters worse. Sergeant James Moffat "counted 20 bombs coming out of one aircraft. You could look up and shake your fist and damn the airforce but nothing worked, not yellow smoke or anything."[68] Nothing worked because the pilots were under orders to ignore signals from the ground and, worse still, Bomber Command happened to be using the colour yellow as a target marker that day. Sergeant R.J. Porter was understandably bitter:

> There's something a man has to go through, to believe it, to see them big waves, them big suckers, you could see them coming from a long distance. We watched them and, by jeez, you see them doors opening up, you see the bombs dropping, and then you heard the whistle and then the explosions. They pretty well cleaned out the Poles next to us. They could see our recognition panels and they kept dropping. I really love airmen.[69]

When it was all over, Sergeant Cunningham of 22 Battery discovered a piece of bomb fuse near his gun stamped: "Stanley Tool Company. Made in Canada."[70]

A subsequent investigation of this incident by Bomber Command concluded that 144 aircraft had bombed short. Ironically, 44 of these aircraft were from 6 Bomber Group RCAF and the mistake had originated with two crews from 428 Squadron RCAF. The personnel responsible were demoted, transferred or retrained but this tragic error, only one of many made by Allied aircraft in Normandy, inflicted more than 400 casualties. The artillery units of 3rd Division suffered severely: 12th Field lost 13 killed and 53 wounded with 16 Battery losing every gun and vehicle; 13th Field lost 2 killed while 14th Field had no personnel casualties but lost all the vehicles in one of its batteries. A South Albertan, Trooper Gerry Scott, was also killed in this attack. As for the use of yellow smoke as the signal for friendly troops, Bomber Command at first denied that they had ever been informed of this important information but inquiries revealed that a formal letter on this very subject had been sent to the RAF well before D-Day but, unfortunately, had ended up in the "in basket" of a senior officer who had taken no further action on it.

As they moved south in the dust on 14 August, the men of 10th Brigade became aware that something was terribly wrong behind them as they could see billowing clouds of smoke in the rear areas. They pressed on, however, and reached the Laison only to get caught up in the massive traffic jam on the north bank. Jefferson now dismounted his infantry, who splashed across on foot to secure the village of Rouvres, before moving on to their next objective, the little village of Olendon, 3 miles to the south. Olendon was taken at 6 P.M. but, progress being good, Jefferson continued the advance during the darkness hours to Perrières which was in Canadian hands at about 2 A.M. on 15

August. The night of 14/15 August was a restless one with sniping, intermittent shelling and strange movement, and, again, nobody got much sleep.

It now only required a push onto the final objective, the high ground overlooking Falaise. Unfortunately for Simonds, this area was held by the remaining battlegroups of Meyer's 12th Waffen SS Panzer Division and that prescient soldier, suspecting an attack would come in this area, had surveyed a good defence line to hold it. When the fighting was renewed on 15 August, 3rd and 4th Divisions came up against this position and were able to make little progress. The SAR and the remainder of 10th Brigade did not play a major part in the fighting but 15 August was not a good day. For the second time, they were attacked by friendly aircraft as Typhoon fighter-bombers hit them with 20 mm cannon and rockets, inflicting several casualties. By last light on 15 August the Germans still held the high ground and Kitching was preparing to put in a night attack when Simonds ordered him to suspend it. Events to the south had brought about a change in plans and Operation TRACTABLE now drew to a close.

Disaster, 14 August 1944
Behind two rather badly-camouflaged SAR Shermans is the massive pillar of smoke from burning vehicles and ammunition caused by the mistaken bombing of Canadian troops on 14 August 1944. This was one of the worst of many incidents of mistaken attacks by Allied aircraft on their own troops in Normandy and, in First Canadian Army, dissatisfaction with the air force grew so loud that General Crerar was forced to issue a special order of the day pointing out that, without air superiority, the campaign could not be won. SAR ARCHIVES

Gunners firing down the Falaise road, 16 August 1944
Yet another busy day on the gun positions as First Canadian Army prepares to attempt to close the Falaise pocket and trap the German armies in Normandy. For the gunners, one day was much the same as the next, and differed only in the scale of the firing. NAC, PA-115569

CHAPTER ELEVEN

A Village Called St. Lambert

NORMANDY, 16–23 AUGUST 1944

Some folks come from the peaks and passes,
We're from the land of the waving grasses.
Now, while you fill up your glasses,
We'll continue bumping asses.

For we are the S-A-R!
For we are the S-A-R!

We're the boys from the bald-headed prairie,
We can ride anything that's hairy.
Ride them with, or without, a saddle,
Anything with hair on, we will straddle.

For we are the S-A-R!
For we are the S-A-R![1]

"A rather tough assignment": Background to a battle, 16-18 August 1944

By the end of their first week in action the South Alberta Regiment had lost 7 men killed in action and 46 wounded, and between 10 and 15 tanks. This casualty rate was bad enough but not nearly as bad as the other armoured units of 4th Division – during the same period the Grenadier Guards lost 36 killed in action and 68 tanks, the Foot Guards 34 fatal casualties and about 25 tanks, while the British Columbia Regiment suffered 51 fatal casualties and the loss of 47 tanks. The South Albertas' lower losses were not due to the fact that they seen less action – they had actually been in combat on more days than the other armoured units in the division – but resulted from a combination of good luck, good leadership and their tactical role.

Although all soldiers pray for it, and some get it, luck is no certain thing in war and – in August 1944 the South Alberta Regiment was lucky while other units were not. As for leadership, Swatty Wotherspoon had turned out to be an outstanding commander in action. He possessed an innate but rare ability to grasp the essentials of a situation, reduce them to simplicity, consider the various options, choose the best, and render his decision in clear and simple directions to his subordinates in a very

short time. Having issued his orders, Wotherspoon did not interfere with his subordinates when they carried them out because he was a firm believer in promoting initiative at all levels. Nonetheless, he was always aware of the situation – as one SAR officer noted, Swatty "had a knack of knowing what was going on out there."[2] Finally, and perhaps most important, the SAR's tactical role meant that they worked closely with the infantry battalions of 10th Brigade who protected them from enemy anti-tank guns while the SAR, in turn, protected the infantry from automatic weapons, a relationship that was mutually beneficial. By mid-August 1944, having survived their first two weeks in action without undue trauma (with the unfortunate exception of the Algonquin Regiment), the units of 10th Canadian Infantry Brigade were "shaking down" into a very effective combined arms team.

The brigade's efficiency was obvious during the three days that followed Operation TRACTABLE. It got a day of rest on 16 August but when Kitching ordered it south from its position near Olendon to secure a bridgehead over the Ante River near Damblainville, it was on the road during the night. This order resulted from the changing strategic situation. Patton's Third Army had reached Argentan, far in the German rear, and Kitching was ordered by Simonds to take Trun and attempt to close the gap between the American and Canadian forces, now only 15 miles wide. If this could be done, two German armies – Fifth Panzer Army and Seventh Army – would be caught in a trap. In response Major Dave Currie's C Squadron pulled out of Olendon with the Argylls on their decks at 11 P.M. on 16 August and drove through the night toward Damblainville. It was a fine march as, for the first time, the SAR entered an area untouched by war, a pleasant collage of farmyards, orchards and small villages.

By dawn on 17 August, C Squadron and the Argylls were on high ground overlooking Damblainville. The Argylls' scout platoon had already entered the village and found it free of the

---

(Facing) **Victoria Cross action: St. Lambert-sur-Dives, August 1944**
The main street of the village as it appeared about 1 P.M. on Saturday, 19 August 1944. Major David V. Currie, officer commanding C Squadron, South Alberta Regiment, holding his personal sidearm at the ready, watches as another group of German prisoners is led away. Immediately behind him are some SAR tank crewmen, identified by the bowl-shaped armoured corps helmets, and at their feet are blankets removed from the prisoners to be given to German medical personnel to attend to their own wounded. Farther down the street can be seen two SAR Shermans, one of which appears to be knocked out, while a third tank is positioned behind the prisoners. In the foreground is an officer holding his Browning 9 mm automatic at the ready. NAC, PA-116586

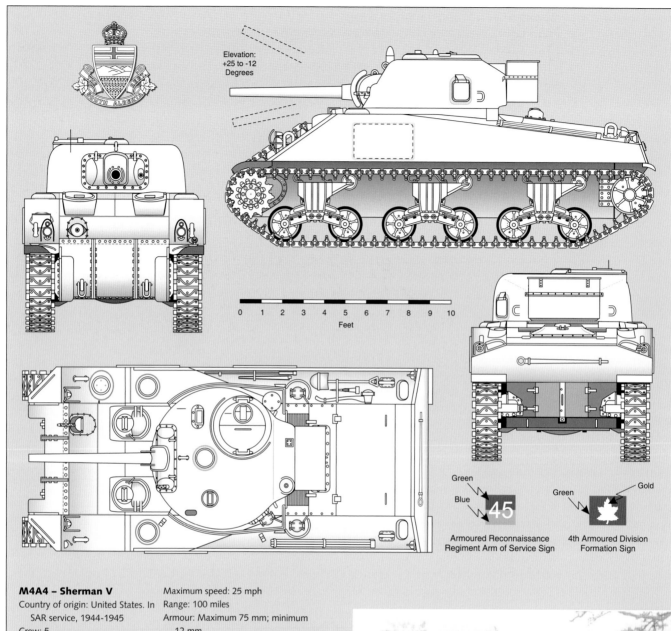

Elevation:
+25 to -12
Degrees

0 1 2 3 4 5 6 7 8 9 10
Feet

Green
Blue
45
Armoured Reconnaissance
Regiment Arm of Service Sign

Green   Gold
4th Armoured Division
Formation Sign

M4A4 – Sherman V

Country of origin: United States. In SAR service, 1944-1945

Crew: 5

Length: 19 feet 10 inches

Width: 8 feet 7 inches

Height: 9 feet

Weight: 35 tons (without extra armour protection)

Engine: Chrysler A57, 30-cylinder multibank, gasoline

Maximum speed: 25 mph

Range: 100 miles

Armour: Maximum 75 mm; minimum 12 mm

Armament: 75 mm gun M3 in turret; .30 calibre MG M1919A4 co-axial to 75 mm gun; .30 calibre MG M1919A4 in bow mount; .50 calibre MG HB M2 in flexible mount on turret top

Unsung heroes: Fitters' group, Normandy, 1944

Fitters were tank mechanics and they kept the South Albertas going – a necessary but unsung job. The SAR had good fitters and usually had a higher proportion of "runners" (operable vehicles) than any other armoured regiment in 4th Armoured Division. Showing evidence of the dust on the roads, this group posing around Trun includes, from the left, "Smitty," Sergeant George Muehllenner, "Fitzgerald," Captain Richard Robinson and "Sinclair." Robinson, the Technical Adjutant of the SAR, appeared earlier in this book as a child on page 114. These men are dirty and tired but excited as, at long last, the Germans are on the run. COURTESY, JACK PORTER

enemy except for snipers and the occasional vehicle. At 8.30 A.M., Currie's C Squadron and Lavoie's A Squadron moved into Damblainville to help the infantry clear it of snipers while B Squadron remained on the heights behind to render fire support. At noon, the Algonquins passed through the Argylls and secured a bridge over the tiny Traine River (actually a shallow stream) and then, with C Squadron in support, moved south toward the objective, the bridge over the Ante River (see Map 20). They were just nearing it when the entire area was blanketed with enemy mortar, artillery and small arms fire, sending the infantry to ground. Currie moved a troop forward to clean out the machineguns but almost immediately lost a Sherman to German SPGs (Self-Propelled Guns) and Tiger tanks sited in an ideal ambush position on wooded high ground south of the Ante. Currie ordered C Squadron to fire HE into the woods to keep the Germans' heads down while Wotherspoon who, by this time had reached the

heights north of Damblainville, called down artillery fire. At this point, the BCR and Lake Superior Regiment took over the advance but these two units could do nothing in the face of a well-sited and determined enemy. The result was a stalemate.

It was clear to Kitching that it would require a major operation to move through Damblainville to Trun. He therefore decided, with Simonds's approval, to sidestep his entire division 3 miles to the east to Morteaux-Couliboeuf, where a bridge over the Dives River had been taken that offered an alternate route into Trun. Led by the two Guards regiments, which had not been committed at Damblainville, this movement began at 4 P.M. and continued throughout the night of 17 August. It says much for the traffic control established by Lieutenant-Colonel John Proctor, the quartermaster of 4th Division, that this difficult night-time march went off without a hitch. By first light on 18 August the Grenadier Guards were on the outskirts of Trun but, as

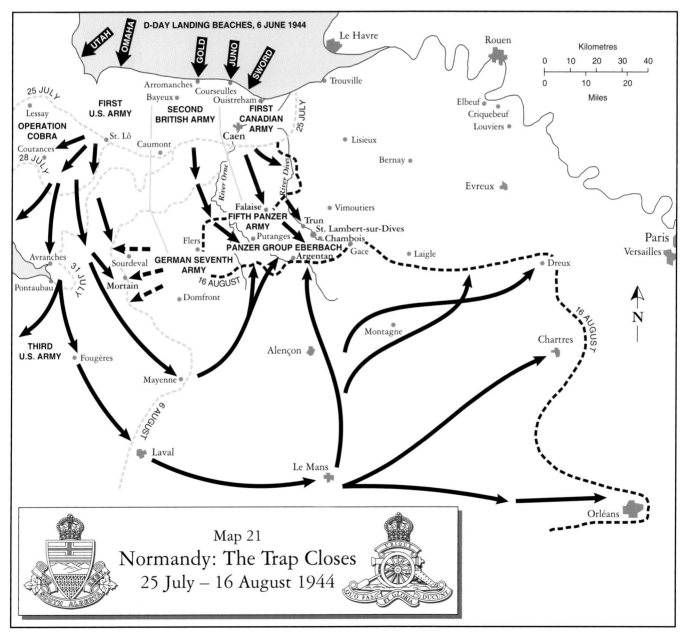

Map 21
Normandy: The Trap Closes
25 July – 16 August 1944

the infantry were not yet up, they did not enter the town. At mid-day the Links, supported by A Squadron, prepared to put in an attack but had to postpone it while they waited for Typhoon fighter aircraft to finish "beating up" the town, work that left much of it in flames.

Trun wasn't the only thing Allied aircraft beat up that day. By this time, with two German armies in full retreat, Allied fighters were ranging the entire area of the enemy pocket in the Falaise area, using cannon, rockets and bombs to attack the enemy columns moving east. Fighter pilots are an aggressive lot and excited fighter pilots faced with multiple targets but possessing only a sketchy knowledge of vehicle recognition are a dangerous lot. Over the next few days, the incidents of air attacks on friendly troops increased at an alarming rate. B Squadron was strafed by Spitfires on 17 August, while in position on the heights behind Damblainville but, fortunately, the only casualty was the canteen of SRD rum kept by one crew in

Trun, 18 August 1944
A crew from B Squadron takes a break in Trun on Friday, 18 August, 1944. Evidence of the damage caused by the Typhoon attack, which took place a few hours earlier, is all around. At about the time this picture was taken, Major Dave Currie was getting orders to take his squadron and a company of infantry to St. Lambert, a little village a few miles away. The South Albertas' most famous action was about to begin. COURTESY, GEORGE WHITE

its tank – a loss that resulted in howls of anger, fists shaken at the departing aircraft and curses shouted at the "Brylcreem Boys," the army's least nasty term of endearment for the air force.

A more serious incident occurred on the following day when two flights of Spitfires attacked Wotherspoon's tactical headquarters despite the fact that "Yellow recognition smoke was thrown and veh[icle]s with Allied recognition markings were in the open," and clearly visible.[3] Swatty, having been attacked by Allied aircraft on two previous occasions, had by this time

become exasperated by "friendly air" and ordered the two Crusader AA tanks which usually accompanied RHQ to fire at the Spitfires as they came around for a second pass. He was dissuaded by Padre Silcox who spread the large Union Jack he used for burials on the ground in the open while 20 mm cannon shells from the first flight hit all around him. The leader of the second flight fortunately realized what was happening and the Spitfires winged away, looking for other prey as the good padre, "shaking like a leaf," breathed a sigh of relief.[4] Wotherspoon promptly

The Valley of the Dives
This gentle, shallow little vale was the main route of the German troops trying to escape from the Falaise Pocket in August 1944. A tangle of sunken roads, woods, hedgerows, streams and gullies which offered concealment, the valley of the Dives was converted by three days of heavy fighting into a valley of death. PHOTOGRAPH BY DIANNE GRAVES

wrote up Silcox for the Military Cross but his deed was eventually acknowledged by the good padre being made a Member of the British Empire (MBE).

At Trun, meanwhile, the Typhoons had finished their work by mid-afternoon on 18 August and the town was largely in flames when the Links and A Squadron moved into it. Enemy vehicles, under the mistaken impression that Trun was still in German hands, kept rolling in and the infantry reported that the pickings were very good: "staff cars, reconnaissance cars, armoured half-tracks, horse-drawn carts, and a complete ambulance column."[5] Dave Currie, who had reached the heights behind Trun that morning, recalled that the men of C Squadron could, in the distance

see rising clouds of dust, and on closer examination, by field glasses, found that we were witnessing, what we later found out to be the remnants of the German Forces in France trying to escape the pocket. The columns were about three or four miles from our location and seemed to consist of every type and kind of vehicle, gun, tank and horse-drawn equipment that the German Army possessed. The column stretched as far as we could see. It was an awe-inspiring sight, and from the distance, it appeared to be a crushing force.[6]

The Germans were escaping and Montgomery, wanting this exodus stopped, ordered General Harry Crerar of First Canadian Army to close the gap between his forces and Third U.S. Army. When this order came down to Simonds at 11 A.M. on 18 August, he directed 1st Polish Armoured Division which, by this time was in the vicinity of Les Champeaux about 4 miles northeast of Trun, to advance to Chambois to link up with the Americans who were approaching that town from the south. Kitching's division, less the Algonquins and 4th Armoured Brigade were, meanwhile, directed to move southeast along the line of the Dives River toward Chambois. Brigadier Robert Moncel's 4th Armoured Brigade and the Algonquins were to move to the vicinity of Hordouseaux, 2 miles northeast of Trun, ready to continue the advance east to the Seine.

Jefferson apparently anticipated these movements because, in the afternoon of 18 August, he ordered Wotherspoon to send a squadron of armour and a company of infantry to secure the village of St. Lambert-sur-Dives, midway between Trun and Chambois. Swatty selected C Squadron for the job and Dave Currie remembered that, at about 3 P.M., he was called to RHQ to be told that he was going to get "a rather tough assignment" but an important one. Swatty ordered Currie to take St. Lambert and hold it until relieved and then cheerfully added that Dave would have "no immediate artillery support, but that later on, there should be some available."[7] As he left RHQ to round up his squadron, Currie later recalled thinking to himself that "up to now this has been a pretty good war, but this is it."

At 6 P.M., C Squadron, a total of 15 tanks, with a weak (only 55 all ranks) company of Argyll infantry on their decks, left

Trun, and moved down Highway D-13 to St. Lambert. It did not take long for the squadron to reach the village, which is only 2 miles from Trun. When they got to the outskirts, Currie could see no sign of the enemy and therefore decided to send a troop of tanks in first, with the infantry to follow. The first tank had just edged beside an outlying house when it was knocked out by AP fire, although the crew managed to escape.

Currie was listening on his radio to a report of this incident when two Spitfires attacked his squadron. Lieutenant Gerry Adams, one of Currie's troop leaders, remembered

we were bare-assing down that Trun–St. Lambert highway and I think my troop was the lead troop but I am not sure of that. We were really moving and I was standing in the turret watching this bloody airplane and the first thing I know, it attacks us. It flew over broadside and it swoops down on our tanks without any warning. I had my turret flaps open and I squatted down quickly in the turret when this thing fired at us but the shells ricocheted off one of the flaps and came down in the turret wounding me and my gunner. …… That held up the whole parade.[8]

Having wounded several men, the Spitfires came around for a second pass and, despite the fact that the frantic South Albertas threw out yellow smoke and spread the orange recognition markers attached to their tanks, this time the flyboys took out the medical half-track attached to the squadron. Satisfied at having done their bit for King and Country, the two intrepid

Medium gun firing, 1944

As soon as they came into range, the Canadian artillery added to the destruction in the Valley of the Dives. Here, a gun detachment from one of the six medium regiments in First Canadian Army fires a 5.5-inch gun. The 5.5, which could project a 100 lb. shell out to a maximum range of 16,200 yards, was controlled by army headquarters and allotted to lower formations as needed. NAC, PA-141715

Death from above: The Falaise Gap
Four photographs taken by 35 Wing RAF, the air reconnaissance unit of First Canadian Army, show the destruction in the Valley of the Dives on 18 and 19 August 1944 as Allied airmen shot up lengthy columns of German motorized and horse transport trying to escape the trap. FROM *35 WING*, COURTESY MICHAEL R. MCNORGAN

birdmen then winged away but it was all too much for Captain John Redden, who fired several long bursts at them from the .50 calibre machinegun mounted on his turret. He missed.

Currie, in radio contact with RHQ in Trun, requested jeep ambulances to come forward and pick up his wounded. Then, as it was growing dark, he made a personal foot patrol into St. Lambert to try and locate the enemy weapon which had knocked out his tank. He found it but realizing that he could not outflank the German position because of the Dives River, decided to dismount the crews of all but three of his tanks and, with the company of Links, make a nighttime assault on St. Lambert, using the three manned tanks for support. When he informed Wotherspoon of this plan, however, Swatty told him to sit tight until dawn as the remainder of the regiment was coming forward to join him near St. Lambert.

Darkness had now fallen and, as the South Albertas moved through ruined Trun, they witnessed a scene that

might have been the ravaging of some foreign village by the Danes a thousand years ago. The burning town threw the light of blood and pillage onto the square and the heavens. The shadows of cross streets, of walls and chimneys, were intensified in their blackness. Into this weird half light, from the darkness beyond came the ghostly figures of the enemy, silently, hopelessly, in their fives, their twenties, and their hundreds. To the right of the square, and looking onto it was the village inn its window reddened from without, and filled with flickering yellow candlelight from within. Behind a long table, his face fiery from the weeks of sun, and the glow of this conflagration, his hair white in vivid contrast, sat what might have been the chieftain. He was counting the spoils of the conquered and the table was covered with papers, with tens of thousands of francs, with wines and spirits, watches, binoculars and arms of all description.[9]

The barbarian chieftain was Lieutenant-Colonel Bill Cromb from Edmonton, commanding officer of the Lincoln and Welland Regiment, and Cromb and his men had clearly enjoyed a very good day on 18 August.

Wotherspoon left his half-track command vehicle in Trun as a radio relay and, just before midnight, moved down the D-13 to St. Lambert with RHQ Troop, Recce Troop, B Squadron and an attached troop of self-propelled 17-pdrs from 5th Anti-Tank Regiment. The combined force then harboured for the night in a large field on top of Hill 117, an elevation about 1,000 yards from the centre of the village.

"Jimmy, how do you get a job like this?" The first day, 19 August 1944

At first light, around 5 A.M., on 19 August, Wotherspoon ordered Currie to take St. Lambert. This time Currie sent the infantry in first, supported by a troop of tanks. At 6.30 A.M. the first Sherman had just got into the village on the D-13 Highway when

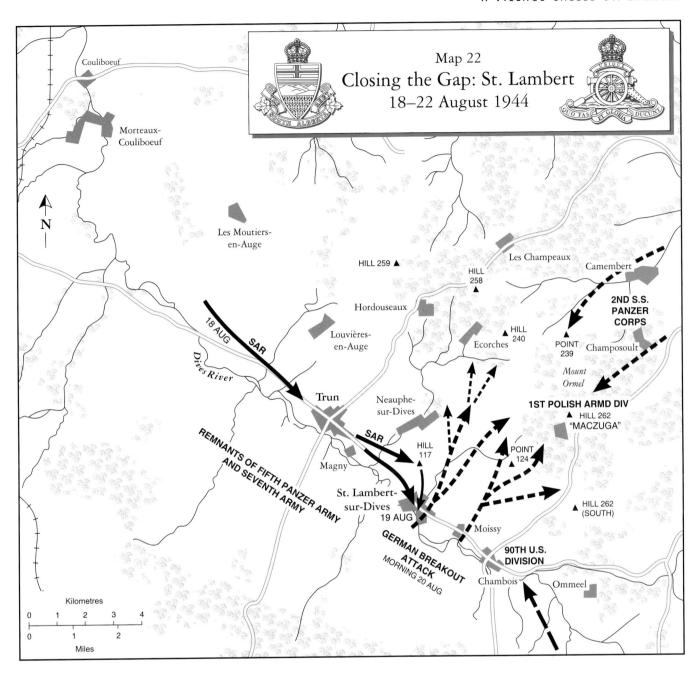

Map 22
Closing the Gap: St. Lambert
18–22 August 1944

it was brewed up by AP fire but the crew managed to bail out. This brought the advance to a halt but Currie, who had accompanied the infantry on foot, had spotted the opposition, two German tanks hidden behind buildings at the south end of St. Lambert. One of these armoured vehicles began to move up the D-13 toward the oncoming Canadians but it encountered Captain John Redden who, at the same time, was moving forward in "Clanky", Currie's command tank. As Redden came over and down the crest of Hill 117, he found that his crew had "a Mk IV Jerry tank at about 50 yards distance with his gun pointing away from us."[10] The gunner had HE in the breech of his 75 mm so Redden ordered him to fire that into the enemy vehicle's running gear and then "laced" the Mk IV with "about 6 AP rounds looking for the ammunition bin and the engine. He brewed up." This was the South Albertas' first confirmed tank kill in action

and the crew of "Clanky" got Wotherspoon's prize – a bottle of SRD rum.

The flatfeet now took over the lead and moved cautiously into St. Lambert, which is basically a long, thin built-up area on either side of the D-13. Another C Squadron tank was hit but the crew bailed out safely. The infantry worked slowly, section by section, down the main street of the village, one section covering another as it advanced, until they neared the little square by the *mairie* or town hall where a secondary road branched off and led to the two little bridges over the Dives River, which has a double course at this point. Here they spotted a German Panther tank whose crew commander was looking around from his open hatch. Approaching it from behind, Lieutenant Gil Armour of the Argylls jumped on the back deck and ended up exchanging punches with the German crew commander who refused to sur-

(Left) German tank killer – the 75 mm PAK 40 anti-tank gun

Although the German 88 mm dual-purpose weapon had a fearsome reputation, more Allied tanks were knocked out by its smaller brother, the PAK 40. Low-slung and easy to conceal, light and easy to manoeuvre, the PAK 40 was the standard divisional anti-tank gun in the last years of the war and the Germans deployed them by the hundreds. The PAK 40 was capable of penetrating 3.5 inches of armour at a thousand yards. PHOTOGRAPH BY DIANNE GRAVES

(Right) Knocked out: A Sherman in Normandy

This Sherman of the First Hussars, knocked out in the first days of the Normandy campaign, illustrates the problem Allied tankers faced in taking on German tanks and anti-tank guns with superior range and penetration power. This vehicle has been penetrated by at least six 75 mm rounds and the Germans probably kept firing at it because it did not brew up – a rarity for the Sherman, which was prone to igniting when hit. COURTESY, R.T. LESLIE, FIRST HUSSARS MUSEUM

(Below) War horse of the Panzerwaffe: The Mark IV

The standard German medium tank throughout the war, the Mark IV was constantly upgraded. This is the Model H armed with a 75 mm gun and two machineguns and capable of 22 mph on paved roads. DRAWING BY CHRISTOPHER JOHNSON

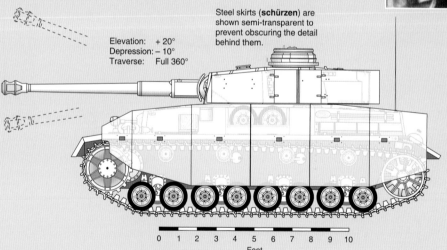

Elevation: + 20°
Depression: – 10°
Traverse: Full 360°

Steel skirts (**schürzen**) are shown semi-transparent to prevent obscuring the detail behind them.

0 1 2 3 4 5 6 7 8 9 10
Feet

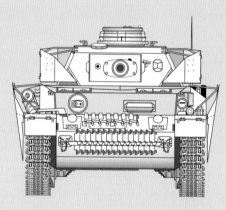

(Right) A deadly opponent: The Panther

The Panther was introduced in 1943 and quickly proved to be one of the best medium tanks of the war. Its high-velocity 75 mm gun, sloped armour and wide tracks gave it hitting power, protection and manoeuvrability. Most Panzer divisions had one battalion of these AFVs but this particular vehicle has been captured and put back into service by new owners. NAC, PA-169094

(Above) Simple but effective – the anti-tank mine
The mine was one of the most effective anti-tank defences. Easy and cheap to manufacture, German mine production in the last years of the war rose into the millions and even a dozen mines and the sign *"Achtung Minen!"* could bring an advance to a halt while the sappers used mine-clearing vehicles or dug the devices up as shown in this picture. NAC, PA-136278

(Above) The Firefly
One answer to superior German armoured vehicles was to upgun the standard Sherman with a 17-pdr. (76.2 mm) gun to create the Firefly, shown here. The problem was that, although the Firefly could take out German tanks at longer ranges than the standard Sherman, it was no better armoured and the Germans concentrated their fire on these vehicles, which were betrayed by their longer gun barrel. Note that extra armour plate has been welded in front of the drivers' compartments of this vehicle. DND PHOTO 4218

(Left) Combined arms fighting
As the campaign progressed, German armour became scarce on the First Canadian Army front and many armoured regiments found that their primary role was supporting the infantry as shown in this photo of a Sherbrooke Fusilier Sherman assisting infantry of the Fusiliers Mont Royal clear a street in the city of Falaise in August 1944. The South Alberta Regiment, attached to 10th Infantry Brigade for most of the campaign in Northwest Europe, became skilled at assisting their flatfooted comrades in a variety of terrains and settings. NAC, PA-132822

(Right) Tiger killer – the 17-pdr.
The British 17-pdr. (76.2 mm) was the most effective counter to the heavily-armoured German medium and heavy tanks. Introduced in 1943, it was used in a variety of roles, including direct fire against buildings as shown here, where it is taking out a German OP in a water tower. It was also mounted on the M-10 Motor Gun Carriage, which equipped the anti-tank units in armoured divisions, and on the Sherman Firefly. NAC, PA-137312

St. Lambert, 19 August 1944

An infantryman of the Argyll & Sutherland Highlanders moves cautiously past a brewed-up South Alberta Sherman at the edge of St. Lambert on 19 August 1944. Currie's C Squadron suffered casualties when they took the village that morning but German resistance was gradually overcome and by midday St. Lambert was in Canadian hands. NAC, PA-132192

render. Annoyed at the man's obstinacy, Armour killed him with his pistol and then lobbed a fragmentation grenade down the open hatch before quickly jumping off. There was no discernible sign of life in the Panther after the explosion but, just to make sure, the Argylls finished the thing off with a PIAT.

By mid-morning St. Lambert was in Canadian hands and Wotherspoon reported to Jefferson that the SAR were established in the village. Currie now deployed in defensive positions, placing Armour's platoon at the crossroads near the *mairie* with a troop of 3 tanks but withdrawing the remainder of his infantry and tanks to the north end of the village, which offered better fields of fire to the west. At this time, his strength was about 50 infantry and 12 Shermans. It should be noted that the population of the village had been evacuated to Trun some days earlier and this, in view of what was about to take place, proved to be a blessing.

While the South Albertas were securing St. Lambert, Simonds held an important O Group (Orders Group) for the divisional commanders of 2 Canadian Corps. Crerar had ordered Simonds to both seal off the Gap between the Canadian and American forces and be prepared to move east in pursuit of the beaten enemy. In response Simonds ordered 2nd Division to take over 3rd Division's positions along the line of the Dives between Damblainville and Trun so that the latter formation could be used to close off the enemy escape routes along the Dives between Trun and Chambois. Until this happened, the two armoured divisions were given the job of sealing the Gap and holding it shut. Major General Stanislaw Maczek's 1st Polish Armoured Division was to be responsible for the area of high ground east of Trun gen-

erally called Mount Ormel, and also for sending forces to take Chambois and to close the line of the Dives between that place and the hamlet of Moissy. Kitching's 4th Division got the job of sealing the Dives from Trun to a point outside Moissy, but since Simonds also wanted to be in a position to advance to the east, only the Lincoln and Welland Regiment and the SAR were made available for this task, the remainder of the division was placed in a forward position at Hordouseaux astride the Trun-Vimoutiers highway. No one seems to have questioned these orders, which effectively split 4th Division into two unequal components, the weaker one being given the most difficult task. At this time, however, the senior Allied commanders regarded the German armies in Normandy as a spent force and their eyes were fixed on the advance to the Seine River and, beyond that, Paris. The job of sealing the Gap was simply regarded as a "mopping up" operation against a beaten enemy.

Wotherspoon, whose regiment would suffer from these orders, knew nothing about them and, in any event, Swatty was having a great time up on Hill 117. After the morning mist had burned off, he found that his position provided excellent observation of movement in the Dives Valley. To the south, parts of the road from the Polish position at Mount Ormel to Chambois could be seen, as could Chambois itself, marked by its high stone Norman keep. To the west, he could locate the many little villages scattered through the valley by their church spires, and also some stretches of the roads and lanes between them, while to the south the wooded slopes of the Forêt de Gouffern could clearly be seen. Little enemy vehicle traffic was apparent that morning but it soon became clear that the Germans were moving on foot through the wooded areas surrounding Swatty's position. This being the case, he deployed for all-round defence. Lavoie's A Squadron and Recce Troop were posted on the western slopes of Hill 117 and along the line of the D-13 back to Trun, while RHQ Troop, AA Troop and four M-10s from 5th Anti-Tank Regiment were placed in defensive positions on the hill itself. Currie's C Squadron and the infantry in St. Lambert guarded the southern approaches to the hill while, for the moment, Nash's B Squadron was kept in reserve.

These were wise precautions because, as the day wore on, there was increasing German movement around Hill 117. In quick order, a Stuart was knocked out by a *Panzerfaust*, the crew of a bogged Crusader shot up as they tried to free their vehicle, and snipers became active. In response Wotherspoon established mounted patrols around the hill using Stuarts and Crusaders and the Crusaders routinely sprayed the tree line with bursts of 20 mm Oerlikon fire which had "devastating results" on enemy infantry.[11]

By midday, German vehicle traffic, marked by clouds of dust, was visible throughout the valley and Wotherspoon ordered all tanks within range to open fire. Once started, this firing went on throughout the afternoon as targets presented themselves. A Squadron, posted on higher ground facing the Dives, had the best positions and all four troops plus the troop of M-10s spent the day banging away at any target they could observe. The ranges were extreme for the 75 mm guns on the Shermans but, by trial and error, the tank crews evolved a rough-but-ready method of bringing down fire on the hapless enemy. Corporal Robert Rasmussen, a truck driver with A Echelon which, throughout the day continued to bring fuel, ammunition and food forward to Hill 117 from the dumps in the rear, was amazed when he observed through fieldglasses the effect of HE rounds fired by the tank of Sergeant Jim Gove on a column of German horse transport. Horses "went flying through the air," Rasmussen recalled and, turning to Gove, he shouted: "Jimmy, how do you get a job like this?"[12]

Things were moving along quite nicely in the early afternoon when Jefferson contacted Wotherspoon by radio to ask him if he had any contact with the Poles. From his position, Wotherspoon could see Polish troops moving down the road from Mount Ormel to Chambois and, after informing Jefferson of this fact, decided to move Nash's B Squadron into a position where they could support the Poles if necessary. Jefferson offered a company of Lincoln & Welland infantry to assist but, shortly after it arrived, the Poles reported that they could see American troops at Chambois. As it looked like the Gap would shortly be sealed, Jefferson ordered Wotherspoon to stand firm at St. Lambert and

await further orders. Swatty was glad to retain the Links on Hill 117 as he needed them to guard the growing number of prisoners being sent back from St. Lambert.

Down in the village, Currie and his men were starting to experience some trouble. Hundreds, if not thousands, of Germans had infiltrated into the surrounding woods and orchards, trying to find a way around the Canadian positions. Many were quite willing to surrender and did so – one Argyll private personally took 160 prisoners. Currie sent the Germans back in batches to the emergency Prisoner of War cage Wotherspoon had set up on Hill 117, and the South Albertas noted that the members of the *Wehrmacht* who surrendered that day were not exactly the pride of the Third Reich. Many were echelon, administrative or service personnel and they represented an amazing variety of nationalities, not a few being willing or unwilling volunteers acquired on the Eastern Front. There were other Germans, however, who wished to fight and, in the early afternoon, snipers inflicted a number of casualties, including Captain John Redden, who was wounded in his turret. Currie was also running low on fuel and ammunition and, since it was clearly dangerous to bring soft-skinned vehicles into St. Lambert, Wotherspoon arranged a shuttle service using the Crusaders of AA troop which trucked fuel and ammo down from Hill 117 into St. Lambert in

Main Street, St. Lambert, 19 August 1944 (1)
One of a series of photographs shot by Lieutenant Don Grant of 1st Canadian Army Film unit in the early afternoon of Saturday, 19 August 1944. This is a view of the main street of the village looking northwest to Hill 117. In the background, near Currie's headquarters at the north edge of the village, a column of German prisoners is marched into captivity. Note the abandoned and wrecked German transport and the knocked-out SAR Sherman just in front of the bus. NAC, PA-152373

Main Street, St. Lambert, 19 August 1944 (2)

These pictures were shot by First Canadian Army Film and Photographic Unit in the village. The top picture was taken by Lieutenant Don Grant, and the lower two are stills from an 8 mm film shot by Sergeant Jack Stollery. The upper two show Argyll infantry covering the approach of a German column up the main street from behind vehicles (one of them a German truck). The third shows the surrender of the column's commanding officer (with goggles on his hat), identified as a *Hauptmann* Rauch, to Company Sergeant-Major George Mitchell of the Argyll and Sutherland Highlanders of Canada. TOP, NAC, PA-115571. OTHERS, AUTHOR'S COLLECTION

small loads on their back decks. It was a dangerous job and, on a number of occasions, the Crusaders had to fight their way in and out of the village.

Just after noon, while Currie was trying to deal with these problems, two jeeps drove up containing the personnel of No. 1 Canadian Army Film and Photographic Unit under the command of Lieutenant Don Grant. Grant had heard that "something was up" in St. Lambert and had decided to see for himself. His detachment remained in the village for about ninety minutes, shooting both 8 mm film and a famous series of still photos and, when not performing their own duties, assisting the South Albertas and Argylls round up prisoners. As he drove out of St. Lambert back to Trun at about 3 P.M., Grant recalled that "there was a bit of a shoot up" at the southern end of the village.[13]

Unfortunately, it was worse than that. Germans began to pour into and around St. Lambert and firefights broke out throughout the entire extent of the village. "We were scrambling around a lot with the tanks," Corporal Robert Fairhurst later recalled, "trying to shake the Germans off and get better firing positions."[14] Enemy AP weapons began to join in and Currie lost another tank. The situation began to deteriorate until the tanks were forced to "delouse" each other by using their .30 calibre machineguns to "keep the enemy from climbing on top of them."[15] Just to make things more disagreeable, St. Lambert came under intermittent enemy shelling.

By this time, fortunately, friendly artillery was available as the 4th Division gunners, and some corps artillery units, had now moved within range. Assisted by a FOO from 15th Field Regiment, Wotherspoon began to call down fire on the many targets he could see moving in the valley, trying to arrange a fire plan using the 25-pdrs. of the field regiments to fire on certain roads and locations to "concentrate all the Jerries into an area."[16] Once that was done, Swatty and the FOO "would bring down the heavy corps artillery and as much additional artillery as we could find down on that one spot, and the pyrotechnics were wonderful to see." On the south side of the valley, the 90th U.S. Infantry Division was also bringing artillery onto the Germans while, overhead, Allied tactical aircraft roamed the length of the Dives Valley bombing, strafing and rocketing the wretched enemy.

Things continued to get worse in St. Lambert as the enemy continued to flood into the village, threatening to overwhelm C Squadron and the Argylls by sheer force of numbers. To break up the enemy momentum Currie asked Wotherspoon to bring down artillery fire as close as possible to his own positions. This request was granted and Dave warned his men to get under cover. Currie had been expecting a bombardment from the 25-pdr. guns of the field regiments, which were less dangerous to tanks but, as the first shells landed, he realized to his horror that Wotherspoon had called in the 4.5 and 5.5 guns of the medium regiments, which could destroy a tank. He complained about this to Swatty, only to get back the response: "is it killing more Germans or more of your people?"[17] Dave had to agree that it was killing more of the enemy but, understandably, neither he nor his men liked it much. It did, however, momentarily quieten things down in and around St. Lambert.

It was now late afternoon and the Poles were in Chambois. Just after 6 P.M., the Polish commander, Major H. Zgorelski, encountered Captain Laughlin E. Waters of the 359th Infantry Regiment, a unit of the 90th U.S. Infantry Division. Wotherspoon learned of this historic event at about 8 P.M. but, for his part, Swatty was still concerned about the situation in and around his positions on Hill 117 and St. Lambert. He contacted Jefferson to inform him that the SAR needed "relief in the form of infantry" and that, "unless relief comes," the enemy "will move back" into St. Lambert.[18] As Currie's need was greater than his, Wotherspoon sent the company of Links he had received in the afternoon to help hold the village during the night, plus a newly-arrived Argyll company which had orders to advance to Moissy. Wotherspoon's biggest headache was prisoners. He later estimated that he collected about 2,000 on 19 August and guarding them was stretching his limited resources. As fast as possible, they were sent back to the rear on the empty A Echelon vehicles after they had dumped their loads on Hill 117.

As the sun began to set, the South Albertas prepared for the night. Currie spread his infantry through St. Lambert, backing them up with his remaining tanks. On Hill 117, Wotherspoon "circled the wagons" into an all-round defensive perimeter while Lavoie's A Squadron and Recce Troop remained in positions along the D-13 to secure his communications back to Trun. Earlier in the afternoon, he had dispatched Nash's B Squadron to Point 124, east of his location, where they would be in a position to block any Germans that moved around St. Lambert or interdict any enemy movement up the Chambois-Mount Ormel road. This was a somewhat risky decision, as the squadron would be fairly isolated but, as Wotherspoon had been informed that Brigadier John Rockingham's 9th Brigade of 3rd Division would be arriving during the night to take over from the SAR, he planned to relieve Nash at first light. That done, the South Albertas and their attached troops settled down for the night, confident that, with the Gap nearly sealed and infantry on the way, this job would soon be over.

"No one got much sleep": A bad night and a worse morning, 19-20 August 1944

Unfortunately, the *Wehrmacht* had other ideas. What senior Allied commanders did not realize was that, on 19 August, some of the most combatworthy divisions in the German Seventh and Fifth Panzer Armies, were still west of the Dives River. The Allies were under the impression that the German retreat, which had officially begun on 16 August, was a continuous mass migration but, in fact, there had been three separate movements out of the Pocket. The first had been an unauthorized withdrawal by many divisional commanders of their rear echelon and service units. The second, which had commenced on 16 August, had been an authorized withdrawal of five panzer divisions and two infantry divisions, plus a mass of service, garrison and miscel-

laneous units. The panzer divisions had escaped without serious losses but the remainder had been caught by the Allied aerial onslaught and quickly transformed into a milling, terrified herd. These were the troops that the SAR had encountered during the day of 19 August.

Still remaining in the Pocket, however, as dusk came on 19 August were the remnants of six panzer divisions, seven infantry divisions, one parachute division and battlegroups from other formations. These troops had not tried to escape during the day but had stayed in camouflaged positions, content to let the rear echelon units bear the brunt of Allied artillery fire and air attack. Conditions were not good, however, and the senior German officer in the pocket, *Generalleutnant* Paul Hausser had decided, with the agreement of his senior subordinate, *Generalleutnant* Eugen Meindl, to undertake a breakout during the night of 19 August, which would be assisted by an attack into the Pocket by the 2nd SS Panzer Corps on the following day. The spearhead of the breakout would be paratroopers from Meindl's 2nd Parachute Corps who would attempt to find an escape route across the Dives to the area of Mount Ormel, where they would link up with friendly units attacking into the pocket. On the morning of 20 August, while five of the infantry divisions withdrew slowly and provided rearguards, the remaining formations, formed in several battlegroups built around divisional headquarters, would make a mass attack along the entire length of the Dives from Trun to Chambois. Their objective would not only be to break out but to secure the four crossing points over the Dives – at Trun, St. Lambert, Moissy and Chambois – because Hausser was determined to bring as many armoured vehicles as possible out of the trap.

When darkness fell, Meindl led the way. At around midnight, his 2,000 paratroops, formed in small but disciplined groups, began to infiltrate across the Dives north of St. Lambert. Scattered firing broke out as the South Albertas and their attached infantry opened up whenever they saw targets. By observing and analyzing the source of this fire, Meindl realized that the central points of his enemy's position were Hill 117 and St. Lambert. Wanting to avoid these areas he guided his men to the north and they crossed through A Squadron's positions near the Foulbec Stream, a wooded gulley that ran east and west north of 117. Although Lavoie's crews opened fire, they had no infantry with them and the paratroopers, moving cautiously and slowly and not returning fire, worked their way through A Squadron and continued on to the east. By first light, Meindl's spearhead was approaching the Polish positions at Mount Ormel.

In St. Lambert that night, Currie remembered that "there was considerable firing and no one got much sleep.[19] Earlier the previous evening, Major Gordon Winfield's C Company of the Argylls had advanced to Moissy in the dark, in an effort to carry out Simonds's orders of the morning. The company got into a night-time firefight with superior enemy forces, in which Winfield and the other company officers were wounded. It therefore retreated back to St. Lambert. Even with this reinforcement, Currie did not have enough infantry to hold the entire village so he placed some

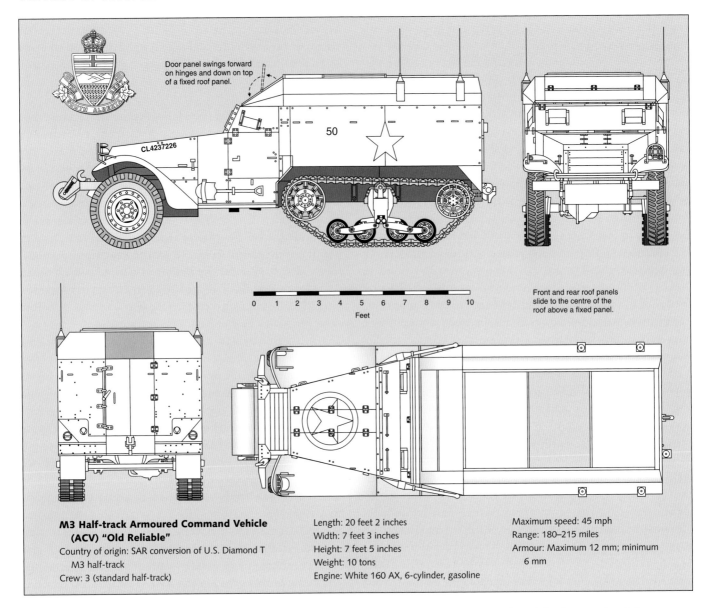

Door panel swings forward on hinges and down on top of a fixed roof panel.

CL4237226

50

Front and rear roof panels slide to the centre of the roof above a fixed panel.

0 1 2 3 4 5 6 7 8 9 10
Feet

M3 Half-track Armoured Command Vehicle (ACV) "Old Reliable"
Country of origin: SAR conversion of U.S. Diamond T
    M3 half-track
Crew: 3 (standard half-track)

Length: 20 feet 2 inches
Width: 7 feet 3 inches
Height: 7 feet 5 inches
Weight: 10 tons
Engine: White 160 AX, 6-cylinder, gasoline

Maximum speed: 45 mph
Range: 180–215 miles
Armour: Maximum 12 mm; minimum
    6 mm

in the crossroads by the *mairie*, supported by three SAR tanks, and the remainder in the northern part of the village and in the area of a low hill or hummock near the banks of the Dives. Currie was unable to prevent the Germans moving into the village across the two little bridges over the river and they began to pour through the southern end. It is important to note, however, that although the Germans regarded the St. Lambert bridges as crucial, there is not a single mention of these bridges in any of the 2 Canadian Corps, 4th Armoured Division, or 9th or 10th Brigades' orders, radio messages or War Diaries for the period, 18-21 August 1944.

The crew of Corporal Walter Fengler's tank, stationed at the intersection of the D-13 and the street leading to the bridge, quickly became aware of the enemy infiltration. Trooper Ed Davies of Fengler's crew recalled that, in the early hours of the morning, they heard movement around the tank. Fengler opened his hatch to have a look and closed it quickly, saying "hey, there are Jerries out there … what are we going to do?"[20] His crew responded that "the best thing we could do was do what we were supposed to do – start shooting." So they

swung the turret around and fired a couple of shots at vehicles moving behind us, swung around again and opened up with the machine guns and then we shot 75 mm AP rounds down the road, figuring there might be a tank among those vehicles which we could hear but not see. …… We set a truck on fire and it must have been full of mortar rounds, Moaning Minnies, and that stuff started going off and you should have heard it.

Fengler says, "pass me the Sten" and we gave it to him and he started firing out of the turret but it jammed. So he passed it to Young and got another one and was shooting out there. Young went to clear the goddamned thing and it fired and the bullet went right through my leg, between the knee and the ankle. I said to Young: "Jesus, you shot me" and he says, "I'm sorry."

Having got through the positions of A Squadron along the D-13 and C Squadron in St. Lambert, the flood of determined Germans lapped around the isolated position of Nash's B Squadron at Point 124. The crews of that squadron were anxiously awaiting the infantry of Rockingham's 9th Brigade but the infantry of the *Wehrmacht* reached them first and, in the early hours of 20 August, they became aware of movement all around their position – and there was also the noise of tank engines, which did not bode well at all.

Just after first light, Wotherspoon informed Jefferson that 9th Brigade had not arrived and that, during the night, there had been much "enemy filtration including some tanks which they [the SAR] are unable to stop as they are too thin on the ground."[21] At 7 A.M. Swatty elaborated on the situation, informing 10th Brigade that the Argyll company had been pushed back from their objective at Moissy but that they would probably return that morning. He again noted that no advance parties from 9th Brigade had yet arrived, something that was beginning to concern him. By this time, major enemy movement was visible to the west across the Dives and Wotherspoon requested that artillery fire be brought down on it. This request was refused, however, as there was to be no firing on targets west of the river because Second British Army, which had not been present on the Canadian situation maps for some time, was expected to move into that area during the day. This did not please Swatty who, at 7.45 A.M., again informed Jefferson that 9th Brigade had still not appeared and again requested that artillery fire be brought down on the enemy because the situation was beginning to worry him: "Must have all artillery support possible to hold firm today."[22]

Just as Swatty sent this message, the greater part of the German units involved in the break-out (armour and infantry) began to approach the Dives from the west. Their movement had been partially concealed by the morning mist and the woods, sunken lanes and orchards of the valley floor. They hit the South Albertas a few minutes after 8 A.M. and Currie's men in St. Lambert bore the brunt of the attack.

A Tiger rolled across the Dives bridges, blew the infantry stationed around the intersection of the D-13 and the road leading to the bridges out of their houses with AP fire, and brewed up two of the SAR tanks posted near the *mairie*. Waves of German infantry splashed across the shallow Dives (only chest deep at this point), surrounded the infantry holding the northwest corner of the village and came close to overrunning the SAR troop stationed to support them. The crew commanders hastily backed down a sunken lane to the northern end of the village only to find German infantry running along the banks, almost level with their turrets, firing at them. One troop leader was wounded but all the tanks got back to Currie's headquarters at the northern end of St. Lambert. The Germans, however, were not interested in taking the village, they just wanted to get through it and keep moving east. Nonetheless, the situation was serious – at one point Currie remembered "firing at snipers who were pinging bullets off the top of the tank and I had spotted them so I used a rifle I carried in the tank."[23] He was gradually forced back to the north end of St. Lambert and the Germans

were now in complete possession of the bridges. Currie met any enemy attempts to move up the D-13 with fire and called down heavy artillery concentrations on the area of the bridges – and that was about all he could do.

The enemy also came upon A Squadron, in position north of the village, but here they were less successful as Lavoie's crews had good fields of fire across open ground that the Germans had to cross once they left the tree-lined course of the Dives. The South Albertas cut them down with 75 mm HE rounds and .30 calibre Browning fire, but the enemy pressed on and managed to take out one tank with a *Panzerfaust* at close range. The Germans veered away from the squadron's positions and managed to get around them by using the wooded gulley of the Foulbec stream to move north of Hill 117. At 8.45 A.M. Swatty informed Jefferson that, unless he received support, he might be "pushed out" of his positions and followed this with a more serious message at 9.45 A.M.: "General attack is reported by 29 Recce and are asking for assistance."[24]

The Germans kept on coming and to keep them away from the crucial Hill 117, Wotherspoon reinforced Lavoie with his RHQ Troop and they "began to mow down the advancing Infantry."[25] Still, the enemy infantry kept advancing, so Wotherspoon ordered Lavoie to attack down the D-13 to the area of RHQ. Corporal John Galipeau participated in that attack and remembered crossing a field covered with stooks of grain which the Germans tried to use for cover to no avail, as the tanks "picked them off with the machineguns. It was just a slaughter."[26] In the middle of this mayhem Galipeau was amazed to see Corporal Herb Roulston, a crew commander, "out of the turret on top of his tank, sitting with his feet across the opening of the hatch, having a turkey shoot with a captured German rifle, sniping at the Germans running from stook to stook."[27] His troop leader ordered the brave but foolish Roulston to get back into his tank, only to receive the immortal reply: "Haven't you heard? There's a war on." Roulston then resumed his target practice.

Lavoie's attack ended the threat to Hill 117 but, by 10 A.M., there were thousands of Germans in and around the South Alberta positions. B Squadron had a particularly difficult time as their position was screened by woods that concealed the enemy infantry streaming by them. They nevertheless opened fire on every armoured and soft-skinned vehicle that came in view, nailing two Panthers and a column of trucks and half-tracks which they left burning. The enemy had hit the entire line of the Dives and although they had been rebuffed with serious losses at Trun and Chambois, they now had the bridges at St. Lambert and the ford at Moissy. The situation was steadily getting worse and, at 10.12 A.M., Jefferson signalled to all units in contact: "Enemy breaking through."[28]

This brought the Canadian and American artillery to life and they shelled the area of the German movement throughout the day. For the gunners the biggest problem was the location of friendly units in what was a very fluid situation and 13th Field recorded that the trace on their plotting boards "showing firing

"Tiffie" being armed, Normandy
Aircraft riggers load 20 mm cannon shells into a Typhoon fighter-bomber. Armed with four 20 mm cannon and eight 5-inch rockets, the Typhoon packed a devastating punch – unfortunately, only too often, Typhoon pilots hit their own troops instead of the enemy. DND PHOTO, PL 30936

restrictions, looked like a jig-saw puzzle and each day saw more amendments.[29] Nonetheless the gunners did their best – 15th Field Regiment, supporting the SAR, fired "three minutes intense" from its twenty-four 25-pdr. guns and then repeated this procedure several times to send 700 rounds "crashing onto a pinpoint target in a little over five minutes."[30]. There were so many calls for fire on so many targets that 13th Field recorded that it was a common sight, "to see the regiment engaging targets in one direction, with medium artillery nearby firing in the opposite direction."[31] German casualties were horrendous and *Generalmajor* Heinrich von Lüttwitz, commanding the remnant of the 2nd Panzer Division that was trying to get to St. Lambert, remembered the panic that broke out as vehicle convoys "ran into direct enemy fire of every description, turned back, and in some cases drove around in a circle until they were shot up and blocked the road."[32]

When word spread among the trapped German troops in the Pocket that the Dives could be crossed at St. Lambert and Moissy, they headed for these points. Late in the morning the energetic Meindl made contact with German forces outside the pocket and opened a clear escape route near the Polish positions at Mount Ormel. Maczek's Poles now came under attack from enemy forces both within and without the Pocket and were soon in serious trouble. The Polish commander lost contact with his units at Chambois and, as the day wore on, his situation started to become desperate as he began to run low on supplies. Both the Poles and the South Albertas were fighting hard but they did not have the strength to prevent the German breakout and needed assistance just to hold their positions.

"A team that could accomplish anything": The long afternoon of 20 August 1944

Unfortunately, they did not get it. Rockingham's 9th Brigade, which had been unable to move forward the night before because its own relief had not shown up, was lined up ready to go at 9.45 A.M. when it received Wotherspoon's appeal for assistance. It moved immediately but the situation was so confused that, instead of proceeding to St. Lambert, it turned off the D-13

and took up a position at Neauphe-sur-Dives, 1,200 yards to the north, too far away to support Wotherspoon. The remainder of the 4th Armoured Division, less those units at Trun and St. Lambert, had advanced that morning to the east and had reached Les Champeaux, where they were ordered to return to their starting point at Hordouseaux because of the situation along the Dives. They were now too far from St. Lambert to render any assistance whatsoever but they could observe the battle raging in the valley. Throughout the day and into the night of 20 August 1944, Major R.A. Paterson of the Argylls, watched the enemy's death throes:

> The air shook with the field, mediums and self-propelled guns and mortars firing into the struggling mass of chaotic, milling Germans. They fired all night and all day, and the destruction was enormous. The Typhoons circled and dove from dawn to dark, and were in a paradise of massed columns of all types of vehicles and men. …… When the sun set behind the purple western ridge of the pocket, the German planes in ones or twos would forlornly drone overhead, dropping clusters of flares to see what had become of an army.[33]

For the South Albertas, the situation quieted down somewhat during the early afternoon. By this time, the Germans had nearly cut the road between Trun and St. Lambert and, for the remainder of the day, A Squadron and Recce Troop were kept busy keeping it open. To the east, Darby Nash, whose B Squadron had come perilously close to being overrun during the morning, decided to withdraw to a new position about 1,000 yards north and closer to Neauphe-sur-Dives. Wotherspoon was not happy when he learned about this move as he would have preferred that Nash had stayed at Point 124 and "called the artillery down on top of his tanks" to deal with the enemy but, relying on his subordinate's judgement, he accepted it.[34]

In St. Lambert, meanwhile, Dave Currie was barely hanging on and could not prevent the enemy from streaming through the village. By this time Currie was down to five tanks and about 120 infantrymen and he positioned them to defend the five houses in the immediate vicinity of his headquarters at the north end of the village. The Germans moving through St. Lambert were very aware of the Canadian presence and later reported that, as they traversed the village, their tanks "concentrated the fire of their heavy guns on the enemy-held houses, which he had turned into fortresses."[35] The South Albertas and their attached infantry fought back so effectively that the Germans were convinced they were under constant attack from the north end of St. Lambert. Saturday, 20 August 1944, Currie recalled, was "hard on officers" and, by mid afternoon, he had lost all of his four troop leaders and most of his infantry officers.[36] He made frequent visits to his men's positions to keep them in the picture and to encourage them. Dave Currie's command style was low key, he would "come over, very calm, and say hello to us and ask how it was going," one South Albertan recalled.[37] Currie spent a lot of time with the infantry and was able to give them "the feeling of being a part of a team that could accomplish anything."[38] Sergeant John Gunderson remembered that the commander of C Squadron never showed any outward concern and

> just to go up and talk to him was enough to give us confidence. I still don't know how Major Currie did what he did – but without his example I do not believe we could have held out. He didn't give a damn how close the Jerries were, and he always had the same every-day expression, just as if we were on a scheme. He was wonderful.[39]

Although he did not reveal it, Currie was actually very worried and, in mid-afternoon, asked Wotherspoon for permission to withdraw his hard-pressed force from St. Lambert. Swatty, fully aware that a fighting soldier like Dave Currie would not have made such a request unless he regarded the situation as hopeless, reluctantly told him to stay put. Currie broke the news to his men. Trooper James Eastman remembered him coming up beside Eastman's tank and telling the crew "dig out everything you've got, all the shells – everything you've got, this is it."[40] Those crews he could not talk to personally, Dave informed by radio that "they were to sit pat because we weren't going anywhere."[41] As he later commented, the "usual answer" came back: "Okay, boss."

It was at this critical moment, about 3 P.M. on 20 August, that help arrived when two troops of towed 17-pdrs from 6th Anti-Tank Regiment pulled into the village. Their arrival was actually the result of a mistake – they had been at the end of the 9th Brigade column but, in the confusion of the morning, had failed to turn off with main body to Neauphe-sur-Dives and had continued straight on down the D-13 to St. Lambert. Once in the village, however, the gunners decided to join the party and immediately went into "crash action." There was no shortage of targets and, in the space of a few minutes, the 17-pdrs. had knocked out two armoured cars and two self-propelled guns. Shortly afterward a Tiger was spotted moving near the *mairie* and one gun en-

gaged it a range of 800 yards right down the D-13 "and scored a direct hit with an APC [Armoured Piercing, Capped] round."[42] The Tiger ground to a halt and the gun detachment then "fired a round of HE hitting the same hole enlarging it to about two feet in diameter. You could see right through the tank." After the initial wave of excitement had passed, Lieutenant J.R. Flowers, the anti-tank commander, left two gunners at each 17-pdr. and then, dismounting the .50 calibre machineguns from his Ram towers, deployed the remainder as infantry. The addition of eight heavy machineguns to the defence of the northern part of the village had an immediate effect and it was later estimated that they killed or wounded about 200 enemy infantry. For the time being, St. Lambert was secure.

By late afternoon, things began to quieten down and, at 5 P.M., Wotherspoon reported to 10th Brigade that the situation was "generally OK" and that he was engaging "targets of opportunity" with artillery fire.[43] Two hours later, he reported that things were "quiet" except for some shelling and "some mopping up to do."[44] Knowing his men were dead tired, Wotherspoon asked Jefferson "if relief could be sent, infantry particularly being needed."[45] That infantry, Rockingham's 9th Brigade, was close but, as evening fell, they were nowhere to be seen and the South Albertas and the troops under their command prepared to carry on during the coming night.

Knocked-out Panther, St. Lambert
Photographed in the southern part of the village, a calcined German corpse lies in front of a knocked-out German Panther. This is possibly the same tank that an Argyll platoon under Lieutenant Gil Armour took out during the morning of 19 August. BY KIND PERMISSION OF THE TRUSTEES, IMPERIAL WAR MUSEUM, B-9664

"I wonder where the hell we are?" The night of 20-21 August 1944

Throughout the day there had been ferocious fighting around the Polish positions at Mount Ormel and Maczek had pleaded for assistance from 2 Canadian Corps. The Polish commander recalled, however, that "my cries of alarm were received with a certain disbelief by the Canadian staff "who insisted that the troops at St. Lambert "sufficiently protected the Polish Division."[46] It was only when Simonds visited Maczek's headquarters late in the afternoon and got the true picture that things began to change – and they changed fast. Over Kitching's protests, Simonds directed him to order 4th Armoured Brigade to attack in the morning southeast from the Hordouseaux-Les Champeaux area to relieve the Poles.

Simonds then turned his attention to cutting off the German escape routes around St. Lambert. He placed Rockingham's 9th Brigade under Jefferson and directed that the Highland Light Infantry of 9th Brigade, supported by the First Hussars of 2nd Armoured Brigade, "seize the general area" around Point 124 which would interdict the tracks and lanes along which the Germans were moving.[47] Jefferson, concerned that there would be another major German movement out of the pocket that night, ordered Lieutenant-Colonel Douglas Harkness of 5th Anti-Tank Regiment to organize a screen of anti-tank units across the entire area and, for this reason, the two troops of 17-pdrs, which had fought so well in St. Lambert that afternoon, were pulled out of the village just before dark. They were supposed to be replaced by the North Nova Scotia Highlanders of 9th Brigade but that unit was incredibly slow in getting into position and did not even reach Hill 117 until about 10 P.M. The Highland Light Infantry and the Hussars were even more tardy, they did not marry up in Neauphe-sur-Dives until 10 P.M. and then waited while the two unit commanders made a recce of the area.

As this was going on, the Germans continued to move over the bridge at St. Lambert or across the ford at Moissy and make their way east. Wotherspoon continued to call in sighting reports and bring down artillery fire into the night. Jefferson passed this information on to 9th Brigade but, when he got no response, he asked for definite information as to the location of that formation's units. The HLI replied that they had been delayed by the need to make a recce but were "now in position" and that "everything was okay."[48] Actually, it was not okay – the commanding officer of the Hussars had decided that, contrary to his orders, he was not going to move forward through the wood in the dark to Point 124 but this decision was not reported to either Jefferson or Rockingham, who were under the mistaken impression that all was well.

In St. Lambert Dave Currie remembered the night of 20 August as passing "relatively quietly."[49] At 11 P.M., the lead company of the Nova Scotia Highlanders finally arrived in the village and for the first time in nearly two days, Currie felt secure enough to leave his command and report to Wotherspoon on Hill 117. Wotherspoon, who had himself just made a quick trip back to

Trun (having to "shoo off" some Germans on the way) to report to Jefferson, was glad to see him and they discussed the situation.[50] By this time there were Germans moving all around the SAR positions at Hill 117 and along the D-13. Lavoie's A Squadron, which had no infantry with it and which had to cover so much ground that the tanks were positioned about 100 yards apart, were fully aware of the enemy presence in the dark. As Sergeant Jim Gove recalled, the Germans came so close to the Shermans that some of the crews "would hear them feel the tank and whisper, 'Panzer! Panzer!' then skittle off into the darkness."[51]

The men of Nash's B Squadron were even more vulnerable. Throughout the day the squadron had waited for the arrival of the infantry but the flatfeet had not shown up and, as night fell, they began to get concerned about the enemy movement they could hear all around their isolated position. Having had no sleep for more than two days, Nash's men were tired but they remained alert which was just as well as, about 1 A.M. on 21 August, they came under attack. Sergeant James Nicholson recalled that, suddenly, there were enemy infantry "all around us."[52] Nash's men opened up a random fire with their .30 calibre machineguns and began to toss grenades from their turrets to keep the Germans away but one tank was immediately brewed up by what was later found to be phosphorus grenades. After a few minutes of hectic firing, shouts and explosions, Nash realized his squadron was being overrun and ordered his crews to make their way separately out of what was becoming a death trap, waiting until the last tank had passed before joining the tail end of the column. The tank of his rear link, Captain Wilfred Gallimore, unfortunately bogged in a creek bed and when the crew bailed out, two were cut down by small arms fire and Gallimore and his radio operator were taken prisoner.

The remaining seven tanks in the squadron made their way cautiously back to the area of Hill 117, although one took a wrong turning on the way. Nash became lost in the maze of farm lanes and roads south of Neauphe-sur-Dives and lost another tank to AP fire in the dark. Having no wish to blunder into the heavy defences of Hill 117, he asked Swatty by radio to provide a navigational aid. In response, Swatty ordered one of the Crusader crews to fire bursts of 20 mm tracer into the night sky and, using this beacon, his five surviving tanks, almost out of ammunition and fuel, made it back to Hill 117.

A seventh tank kept wandering about in the dark until it entered St. Lambert. After the fury of the daytime fighting, the night of 20 August was rather quiet in the village although Currie's men were fully aware of German vehicle traffic through the southern part. From time to time, they fired AP straight down the main street to let the enemy know they were still in the battle and, occasionally, an enemy vehicle made a wrong turn and came towards them, with the result that it was brewed up. The crews had just knocked out a German SPG in this manner when they heard engine noises approaching from the east along one of the farm lanes at the back of the village. Fortunately, they held their fire because when the vehicle stopped, they heard a voice speaking English saying: "I wonder where the hell we are?" It was the lost sheep from B Squadron, which was quickly put in the right direction to join the fold on Hill 117.

Word that B Squadron had been overrun reached the Hussars and the HLI when a dispatch rider who had been with Nash came through their area "in a highly excited state."[53] If the Hussars' commanding officer had been slightly nervous before, this information confirmed him in his decision not to move forward that night. The commander of the HLI proved no more aggressive and, despite both Jefferson and Rockingham constantly urging him by radio to get cracking, it took that battalion between six and seven hours to move a mile and a quarter to a position just east of Hill 117 – and there it remained until first light.

Dead Horse Gulch, Falaise Pocket, August 1944
A column of German horse-drawn transport destroyed by Allied artillery in a sunken road near St. Lambert. Much of the German army still used horse transport and thousands of poor beasts were killed or wounded during the fighting. BY KIND PERMISSION OF THE TRUSTEES, IMPERIAL WAR MUSEUM, B-9668

"The end was in sight":
The third day, 21 August 1944

When dawn came on Monday, 21 August 1944, it was clear that most of the Germans in the area had had enough and wished to surrender. Captain Gerry Stoner of the Hussars remembered seeing them coming out of the woods, with or without weapons, and thought to himself: "what the hell are we going to do with all these people?"[54] The Hussars and HLI began to round them up, a process which took two hours and then, at long last, the two moved forward to Point 124, the objective they had been ordered to occupy twelve hours before, arriving there about 10 A.M. without incident. Currie recalled that on this, the third day, there was a definite "change in the situation" and his men "could tell the end was in sight."[55] When he was relieved that morning by the North Nova Scotia Highlanders, Dave Currie – who had not slept for nearly four days – was so exhausted that "he actually fell asleep on his feet while talking to one of the relieving officers" but "one of the boys caught him before he could fall to the ground."[56]

Early in the morning 4th Armoured Brigade advanced to the Polish position on Mount Ormel which they reached about midday to the relief of the Poles, who were almost out of ammunition and food. The intrepid General Meindl, however, continued to hold the breach open near Mount Ormel but, as the day wore on, fewer and fewer troops came out of the pocket. The last organized detachment to escape was a battlegroup of the 10th SS Panzer Division which came by Meindl's command post at 11 A.M. and informed him that there was nobody behind them. At 4 P.M., having kept the escape route open for nearly a day, Meindl withdrew his paratroopers east to Vimoutiers.

The South Albertas spent much of this day rounding up and disarming prisoners, relieving them of such unnecessary burdens as Luger or Walther pistols, medals and decorations, pens, watches and wallets for, as one South Alberta put it, "where they were going, they didn't need money and they didn't need to know the time."[57] The crews collected amazing amounts of cash and, although most of it was nearly worthless German occupation script, Corporal John Galipeau's crew estimated they collected $50,000 that day. Some of the Germans spoke very good English and Trooper Ed Hyatt from Camrose was startled when he

> came across this German captain and he saw from my flash that I was from Alberta and he said, "what part?" I told him I was from the Camrose area and it turned out that he knew me as a boy when I was going to school and that he and my dad had both worked for the same farmer. I asked him why he went back to Germany and he said, "I had no choice, I was a captain in the German army and I was ordered back, … it would be my family or else." He told me exactly where my house was in the village.[58]

Modest hero: Major David Vivian Currie, VC
Wearing the ribbon of the Victoria Cross which he was awarded for his fight at St. Lambert-sur-Dives, 18-21 August 1944, Dave Currie poses for the camera. A somewhat shy man, Currie was admired for his courage and respected for his leadership by the men under his command. When this photograph was taken, shortly after his investiture at Buckingham Palace in December 1944, Currie had only been away from the front for a few days and the strain is evident on his face. SAR ARCHIVES

– making the SS understandably nervous because they naturally thought they were excavating their own graves. One member of the Waffen SS who was not captured in the Falaise Pocket, however, was *Brigadeführer* Kurt Meyer who, temporarily blinded by a head wound, was led out of the Pocket by his Cossack batman. As transport became available, the German prisoners were sent back in batches to a cage established by 3rd Division near Trun which infuriated Wotherspoon because that formation got the credit for the prisoners his regiment had collected over the past three days – as many as 5,000.

"Like trying to stop a buffalo stampede": The reckoning

There is no accurate figure for the number of Germans captured in the Falaise Pocket, the best estimate is perhaps 50,000. Unfortunately, more Germans got away than were captured – German records are understandably confused for this period but a recent study has concluded that 165,000 soldiers escaped from the trap during the period, 16-21 August, taking with them about 100 AFVs. Allied investigators later counted the wrecks of 187 tanks or self-propelled guns, 157 other armoured vehicles, 1,778 trucks, 669 cars and 252 artillery pieces in Dives valley, with the greatest concentration being in and around St. Lambert. About 10,000 Germans were killed in that formerly tranquil vale and it took weeks to clean up the mess. There were so many dead that bulldozers had to be used to bury them in mass graves and even hardened soldiers were impressed by the havoc. Sergeant R.J. Porter of 13th Field Regiment remembered driving through one of the valley roads,

when our vehicle stopped and right below us was a cardboard man, a German who had been run over so many times by tracked vehicles that he was about as thick as cardboard but we couldn't see him because of the dust and there he was although you would never believe it was a human being but it was at one time.[61]

It was not just humans who had suffered in the ferocious fighting. Much of the *Wehrmacht*'s transport was horse-drawn and thousands of horses had been killed and wounded. Many of the wounded animals had taken shelter in the bed of the Dives and their shrieks so affected the men of C Squadron that they spent hours putting the poor creatures out of their misery, a task that required hundreds of rounds. The worst of the destruction was in and around St. Lambert. Dave Currie noted that, when his men had first entered that place on 19 August, "it was a neat, small quiet French village" but when they left, it "was a fantastic mess," a terrible "clutter of equipment, dead horses, wounded, dying and dead Germans" – in fact, it was "a hellhole."[62]

This was all very impressive but the fact was that the Allied trap had failed and more Germans had escaped than had been killed or captured. In point of fact, the Falaise Gap was never properly sealed because the Polish Division did not carry out Simonds's orders to secure the D-13 from Chambois to Moissy

Many of the prisoners were wounded and these were sent back to the RAP on Hill 117 set up by Captain Wilfred Boothroyd, the Medical Officer of the SAR. Assisted by captured German medical personnel, Boothroyd spent three long days tending to the wounded of both armies. He was in constant danger of running out of supplies although they were augmented by stocks surrendered by the Germans. Mercifully, Boothroyd had plenty of morphine and remembered giving a bag of syrettes to a captured German medical sergeant who nearly burst into tears as "he could now go and administer to his worst patients."[59]

Among the prisoners were members of the Waffen SS, easily identified by their camouflage smocks, who "looked ugly and mean."[60] When the South Albertas observed that the *Wehrmacht* or army prisoners tended to stay away from the SS, they put Hitler's elite to work digging graves for the men who had died at the RAP on Hill 117 without telling them why they were digging

and the South Albertas did not have the manpower to hold the bridge at St. Lambert and secure the line of the Dives from that village to Moissy. All the Allied commanders must bear some responsibility for the failure but, since 2 Canadian Corps was tasked with the job of actually closing the Gap, Lieutenant-General Guy Simonds, the corps commander, has to be held primarily responsible for the failure and, to a lesser extent, Kitching and Maczek. Simonds seems to have regarded the task as a "mopping up" operation – his eyes were fixed on the next stage of the campaign, which is why he had ordered Kitching to deploy the greater part of 4th Armoured Division in a position where it could render very little assistance to the troops along the Dives. Brigadier John Rockingham's 9th Brigade must also come in for some share of the blame because its hesitant movements on 20 August resulted in there being no infantry on the ground during the flood tide of the German escape. Of all those responsible, however, it was Kitching who paid the bill – at 11 P.M. on 21 August, Simonds relieved him of command of 4th Division and replaced him with Major-General Harry Foster.

At the tactical level, the battle of the Falaise Gap was a much simpler business. It resolved itself into a single armoured regiment with three weak companies of infantry, two or sometimes three troops of anti-tank guns and a machinegun company – about 600-700 men with perhaps 70 armoured vehicles of all types – attempting to hold a 3-mile front against an estimated 60,000-70,000 Germans with as many as 100 AFVs. It was an impossible task and it was fortunate for the South Albertas that the enemy did not want to attack them, simply get around them. Reflecting on the matter years later, Lieutenant Jack Summers of B Squadron perhaps summed up the battle at St. Lambert best when he remarked that "it was like trying to stop a buffalo stampede, they went around us, they went over us and they went under us."[63]

One thing was certain about the battle for the Falaise Gap – the South Albertas had performed superbly during three days of heavy fighting. The action made the regiment's reputation in 21 Army Group and, as Corporal Robert Clipperton remarked,

We Remember

To mark the battle of St. Lambert for the ages, the South Alberta Regiment Veterans Association erected this monument and flagpole almost directly across the road from where Major Dave Currie was standing in the photograph that is the frontispiece to this chapter. In the postwar years, the SAR veterans have erected plaques and monuments from Normandy to the Hochwald to record the sacrifices made and the victories won by the unit in 1944-1945. SAR ARCHIVES

wherever he and his comrades went afterward, people "would look at our flashes and you would hear a comment: 'There's one of the SARs, they fought at St. Lambert.'"[64]

Every man in the regiment had done his best during those three awful days in August but one man in particular deserved to be singled out for his contribution to the battle – Major David Vivian Currie, officer commanding C Squadron. Swatty Wotherspoon put in an immediate recommendation for the DSO (Distinguished Service Order) for Dave but, on Foster's advice, later changed it to a recommendation for the Victoria Cross – the highest tribute for heroism that a Commonwealth soldier could win during the Second World War. It took nearly four months before the award was finally approved and the South Alberta Regiment became the only Canadian unit to win a Victoria Cross during the Normandy campaign and the only unit of the Canadian Armoured Corps to win a VC during the Second World War. Not that the tall, quiet man from Moose Jaw, Saskatchewan, ever let it go to his head – as he remarked the day after he received his medal from the hands of King George VI at Buckingham Palace:

I think it's the highest honour that can be paid on the field of battle but the honour belongs to the regiment: to the colonel for the very able direction and support he gave; to the other squadrons for the flank protection they gave during the job and particularly to my own boys and the boys of the Argylls who were with me on the spot. I also think that, if either of the other two fighting squadrons had been given the job, it would have been done just as well.[65]

He never varied that opinion to the day he died in 1986.

To return to Normandy in August 1944 – after being relieved Dave Currie finally got some sleep, his first in four days. When he woke up on the morning of 22 August, he recalled, the "birds were singing and all shell fire had ceased; it was so peaceful."[66] Almost immediately, orders arrived for the SAR to pull back to Trun to regroup in preparation for the advance to the Seine and beyond. After 77 days of fighting, the Normandy campaign was over – at a cost of 18,000 Canadians killed or wounded in action – but the war had not ended and more fighting lay ahead.

"Hulk Alley": The Huijbergsche Baan or the back road to Bergen

The Huijbergsche Baan provided a back way into Bergen-op-Zoom that bypassed the main German defences in front of the city. In the last week of October 1944, the South Albertas fought their way up it and, with good reason, it acquired the nickname "Hulk Alley." In this view can be seen a brewed-up C Squadron Sherman, a ruined Staghound from the 12th Manitoba Dragoons, what appears to be the remains of a carrier and, in the background, another knocked-out SAR Sherman. SAR ARCHIVES

CHAPTER TWELVE

"Vive la Mackenzie!"

THE LOW COUNTRIES, AUGUST–NOVEMBER 1944

"Thank you for liberating us": The great pursuit, August–September 1944

On 23 August 1944, the South Albertas and 13th Field Regiment, along with the rest of First Canadian Army, began to advance to the Seine River. As the long columns moved out, they encountered Provost Corps checkpoints which stopped and waved aside all non-regulation vehicles. Since fuel would be in short supply the farther the Allied armies advanced from Normandy, the more imperative it became that the number of vehicles be reduced, and since nearly every Canadian unit had picked up abandoned German transport, it was rigorously weeded out. Some of this mobile contraband was quite luxurious – four SAR sergeants from the Echelon had acquired a fine, large limousine in which they planned to motor in comfort to the Rhine while, in 13th Field,

> Each troop had two or three and sometimes more German army vehicles picked up on the way through the country. B[omba]d[ier]r Franklin of Able Troop, for example had a very useful motorcycle with side car. Bdr Morice of Baker Troop was driving a beautiful sports roadster. G[u]nn[e]r Slayter of the 78th Battery astonished everyone by successfully controlling a half-track personnel carrier, whose front wheels rarely stayed on the ground. BSM [Battery Sergeant-Major] Hillmann, L.M. drove an amphibious jeep. Others had 60 cwt [3-ton] trucks, light vehicles or enormous trailers where that extra kit bag or unwanted great coat found a home.[2]

It all had to go and, accepting no excuses, the red caps directed the drivers of these trophies to park them in the adjoining fields where they were destroyed. This measure particularly affected the field regiments of 3rd Division, as they had received British-built vehicles to replace the Canadian vehicles destroyed in the bombing of 14 August. To the gunners, German transport, no matter how cranky, was infinitely preferable to vehicles built in Britain – a belief emphasized in "The Fitters' Lament" quoted above.

> I'd rather be six feet under the sod,
> Than try to repair a Morris Quad.
> All the wheels shimmy and the water pump leaks,
> The whole darn body and the chassis creaks.
> The Quad is really something to scorn,
> In fact everything makes a noise but the horn.
> We pray every night that they'll take them away,
> But we're afraid the Morris is here to stay.[1]

As they moved northeast to the Seine, the Canadians experienced the joys of being liberators in areas of France untouched by war. In contrast to battered Normandy, wrote the historian of 13th Field,

> Gone were the wrecked houses and piles of brick, which indicated where houses had once stood. The country looked fresh, as if it had been sprinkled with a light rain. It was a picnic country with tree-lined highways and green fields. Gone, too, were the sight of sad-eyed war-weary civilians. These people stood on either side of the road and cheered and shouted, and passed out calvados, and bread and homemade butter and tomatoes and apples – in fact anything they could get their hands on quickly.[3]

At Bernay, the first big town on the way, the "local schoolmistress had her children lined along the main street singing in unison and in English, 'Thank you for liberating us.'"[4] Corporal John Galipeau of the SAR remembered that the civilians "crowded the sidewalks and spilled out into the road; our drivers had to just creep through the mobs" as the crews "were showered with flowers and fruit, bottles of cognac and cider, and there were girls all over the tanks and trucks."[5] Sergeant Alex Brennand of 13th Field recalled that the French would shout "Vive la MacKenzie!" in honour of the prime minister of Canada, a salutation that did not meet with much approval as King and his Liberal government were not popular with Canadian soldiers overseas. Frankly, it was all whacking great fun – Trooper John Lakes of the SAR Recce Troop, which often led the SAR column, remembered how the Recce boys

> would enter a village with the tank siren at full blast and proceed slowly to the village centre. We would be greeted by happy villagers, waving and offering flowers, and on occasion a pretty girl would find herself helped onto the tank. Very often there would be at least one elderly veteran of the First

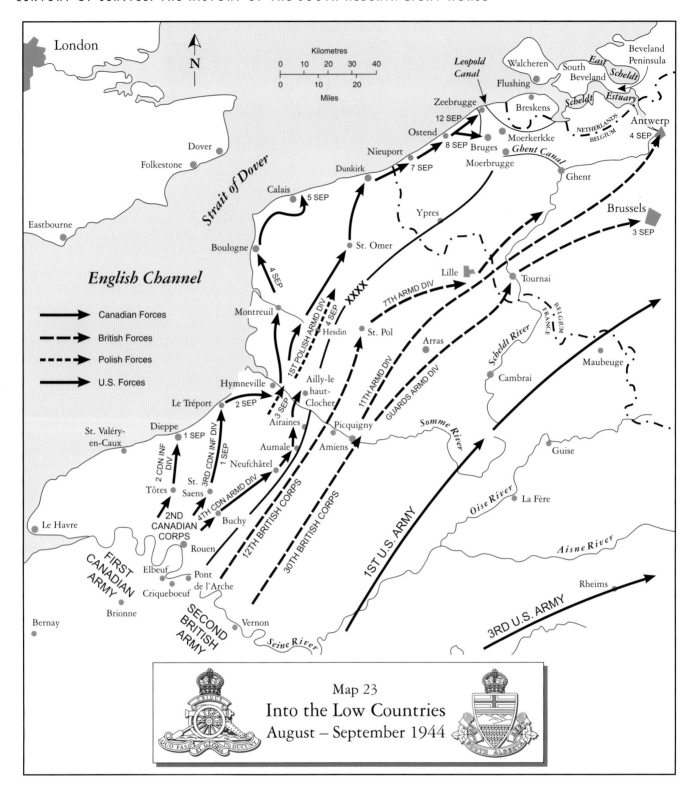

Map 23
Into the Low Countries
August – September 1944

World War wearing his old army tunic and cap, solemnly saluting with tears streaming down from his eyes as we drove past him.[6]

Staff Sergeant James Moffat of 22 Battery recalled one funny incident from this happy period. The battery had stopped for the night and "a couple of boys laid down on the side of the road to go to sleep and when they woke up," they found they had been covered with flowers by grateful civilians who thought they were dead.[7]

As the American and Commonwealth armies moved forward, they encountered little German resistance and there was general optimism that the war was winding down. Corporal Bob Clipperton of the SAR expressed these sentiments in a letter to his wife Andy on 23 August: "It's only a matter of time now & if I am not sent to Japan I should be home this year."[8] Paris fell to the Americans two days later and the general consensus was that the whole thing would be over by Christmas.

It certainly appeared that way to the Allied senior commanders as, on both fronts, the Germans were in full retreat. In the east the Soviet army had carried out a massive offensive that summer which brought it to the borders of the Third Reich. In the west, the Germans were pouring out of France and the immediate task was to keep them on the run and prevent them from establishing a firm defensive line. The problem was that, as the American, British and Canadian armies moved away from Normandy, the longer grew their supply lines, and logistical concerns began to dominate Allied planning. The newly-promoted Field-Marshal Montgomery, therefore, ordered First Canadian Army to take the ports of Dieppe, Dunkirk, Boulogne and Calais on the Channel coast to help ease these supply difficulties while Second British army advanced on its right flank into Belgium. To the south the three American armies of General Omar Bradley's 12 Army Group also pushed east.

On 25 August, the same day Paris fell, the lead elements of 10th Brigade reach La Haye Malherbe, just south of the Seine River. Simonds had ordered Major-General Harry Foster of 4th Armoured Division to seize a bridgehead "by coup-de-main" in the area of Criqueboeuf and the job fell to Bill Cromb's Links, supported by Lavoie's A Squadron.[9] The Links managed to get a company over the river by rowboat and, for the next three days, the brigade gradually expanded this bridgehead in the face of heavy fire from German rearguards positioned on the heights behind the river. The enemy resistance was strong enough for Simonds to decide to switch 4th Division to a bridge constructed at neighbouring Elbeuf and, on 30 August, the advance resumed, this time with 4th Armoured Brigade in the lead. It continued throughout the night and it was a long and tedious march. As drivers often fell asleep during the many halts, Wotherspoon, the SAR commanding officer, instituted a system to keep the columns moving – Corporal John Galipeau remembered how it worked:

On night runs we used no lights. The driver kept his position by watching the tail lights of the tank ahead. We were all of us dead tired, falling asleep in our seats. When we stopped, the co-driver would get out and lean on the tank ahead so that if the column started moving, he would wake up and go back and get his own tank going.[10]

Occasionally, tanks or vehicles got lost or started wandering around by themselves. On 2 September, Trooper John Neff's Sherman

Off they go!
Field Artillery Tractors (FATs) of a Canadian field regiment move through a ruined French town at the end of the Normandy campaign. In the fourth week of August, the Allied armies began to drive east into the Low Countries. NAC, PA-145557

was second to last in the convoy and the bridge in the town collapsed & our tank fell in the drink. Stan got a nasty cut on top of his head. A French Dr. was near by and took Stan to his house, I went along and drank brandy while he was fixing Stan up a bit. We helped search a bunch of Prisoners that were taken in the town. ...... I got many fine watches off the Germans and much loot. I gave a brand new lady's watch to some French Dame instead of selling it, must be slipping.

By 1 P.M. they had our tank out of the creek and we were on our way again, but we couldn't find the sqn. We were in good radio contact, but couldn't figure out just where we were on the map. Finally, we stopped and were admiring some nice fresh Ti-

Adjutants with "Old Reliable"
On the left is Captain Bob Allsop, adjutant of the SAR, and on the right Captain F.N. Hughes, the battle adjutant. This photograph was taken at Ailly-le-haut-Clocher in France, where the South Albertas enjoyed a few days rest before taking up the pursuit of the retreating Germans. This is a good picture of "Old Reliable," which, fully restored, is the pride and joy of the modern South Alberta Light Horse. SAR ARCHIVES

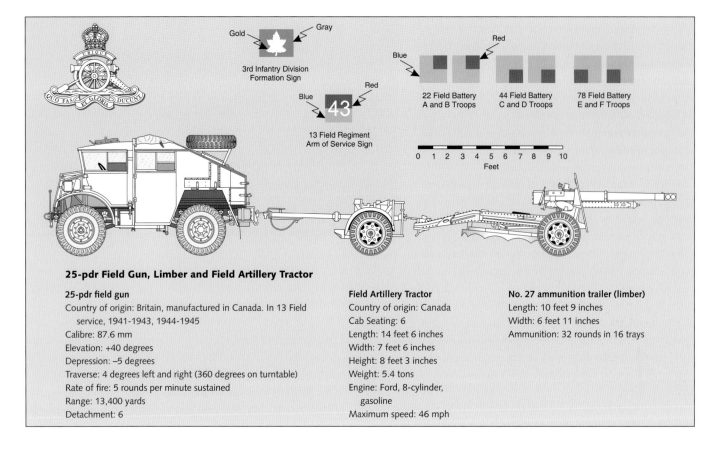

25-pdr Field Gun, Limber and Field Artillery Tractor

25-pdr field gun
Country of origin: Britain, manufactured in Canada. In 13 Field
    service, 1941-1943, 1944-1945
Calibre: 87.6 mm
Elevation: +40 degrees
Depression: –5 degrees
Traverse: 4 degrees left and right (360 degrees on turntable)
Rate of fire: 5 rounds per minute sustained
Range: 13,400 yards
Detachment: 6

Field Artillery Tractor
Country of origin: Canada
Cab Seating: 6
Length: 14 feet 6 inches
Width: 7 feet 6 inches
Height: 8 feet 3 inches
Weight: 5.4 tons
Engine: Ford, 8-cylinder,
    gasoline
Maximum speed: 46 mph

No. 27 ammunition trailer (limber)
Length: 10 feet 9 inches
Width: 6 feet 11 inches
Ammunition: 32 rounds in 16 trays

ger or Panther tracks. Just then a radio message gave this wood as the position of two Tiger tanks. The map reference was in clear so we could figure out just where we were. And we found ourselves in a small woods with two Tigers, a good mile ahead of the sqn. Now was our chance to win a VC or something, however, we remembered that discretion is the better part of valour so we high tailed it out of the woods to our own lines.[11]

By 3 September the SAR were at Ailly-le-haut-Clocher near Abbeville and not far from the Belgian border, where they were overjoyed to learn they would be granted a rest period. On that same day 13th Field was given a similar break at Hymneville on the banks of the Somme River. At Ailly, Wotherspoon decided to hold a party for the officers of 10th Brigade and, in short order, potables were secured from the surrounding area, a beef was purchased and cooked, and an interior wall in the chateau that served as headquarters was removed to create a large dining area. The party, held on 4 September 1944, was a great success although the meat tasted like old horse and the noise level became excruciating as the band and pianist were backed up by loud but off-key vocal accompaniment from all present. Not to be outdone, the sergeants staged their own party on the following day, providing (as is usual with sergeants' messes) better food and drink than that found among the officers. The two days of rest enjoyed by 13th Field were not as raucous as their history records that the unit padre "conducted short church services in each troop and the men caught up on their correspondence and washing" – but then gunners are generally a more restrained lot.[12]

During these early days of September 1944, the swiftly-advancing Allied armies came very close to breaking the back of the *Wehrmacht* in the west. Second British Army took Brussels on 3 September and Antwerp, the greatest port in Europe, the following day, trapping the German Fifteenth Army, which had been retreating along the Channel coast, on the south side of the Scheldt Estuary. Unfortunately, the British did not see fit to advance out of Antwerp and cut off the Beveland Peninsula on the north side of the Scheldt, an omission that not only permitted a large part of the Fifteenth Army to escape, it also left both sides of the Estuary in German hands, preventing the use of Antwerp as a supply port. The German retreat, however, continued and the *Wehrmacht* flooded into southern Holland in a panic-stricken migration. For the Dutch, 4 September 1944 was forever to be known as "Crazy Tuesday," as they watched long columns of enemy soldiers, sailors and airmen, mounted on a bewildering variety of transport, piled high with loot and lady friends, drive through their towns by day and night.

Sensing an opportunity, Montgomery had a plan in mind. He convinced General Dwight D. Eisenhower, the Supreme Allied Commander in Europe, to approve a daring but risky operation, codenamed MARKET GARDEN, using airborne troops to seize bridges on the major waterways in Holland that would create a corridor along which Second British Army could advance over the Rhine and into the Ruhr. Eisenhower approved MARKET GARDEN but also stressed to Montgomery the importance of clearing the Scheldt and opening Antwerp. Determined to get across the Rhine, Montgomery gave the job of clearing the

Scheldt to First Canadian Army – 21 Army Group's "maid of all work" – which was miles back and just beginning the task of clearing the Channel ports, even as Second British Army moved away from Antwerp and the Scheldt. This was a very dangerous deployment but in the heady days of early September 1944, it seemed a risk well worth taking.

Unfortunately, Montgomery's plans did not take into account the enemy, and the *Wehrmacht* was always a dangerous opponent to underestimate. The new German commander in the west, *Feldmarschall* Gerd von Rundstedt, was able to halt the panic-stricken German retreat through Holland. Collection points were created to round up stragglers who were formed into *ad hoc* battlegroups and placed in good defensive positions behind the many canals and waterways in that country. By dint of an extreme effort, 135,000 men were combed out of training establishments and the rear services, and sent west, the *Luftwaffe* alone contributing 30,000 men who were formed into the First Parachute Army. Rundstedt planned to halt the Allies along the Siegfried Line, the German counterpart to the French Maginot line but he needed six weeks to put its defences in order. To gain this time, Rundstedt ordered *General* Gustav von Zangen, commanding the Fifteenth Army, to hold a bridgehead in the Breskens area of the south shore of the Scheldt Estuary. Von Zangen immediately began preparing the defences of this "fortress" along the line of the Leopold Canal and, to prevent Allied interference, established a covering position along the Ghent Canal to the west. The German retreat was over and, on 8 September, 10th Brigade of 4th Canadian Armoured Division became some of the the first Allied soldiers to discover this fact.

"The wildest show and the bloodiest": Moerbrugge, 8-11 September 1944

Along with the other units of 4th Armoured Division, the South Albertas' rest period came to an end on 6 September when they resumed their advance. The unit covered 60 miles that day, the furthest single day's advance it ever made, and harboured that night close to St. Omer in the Pas de Calais region. In the late afternoon of 7 September 1944, 10th Brigade, with the South Albertas in the lead, crossed the border into Belgium. The men were impressed with the neatness and cleanliness of the Belgian towns compared to their French counterparts, and were intrigued by the countryside "which seemed to be arranged by a landscape gardener, everything so squared and trim, the copses just coming at the right junction of fields, and the poplars lining the cobblestone roads with geometric precision."[13] Corporal Galipeau of A Squadron recalled that, as he moved through the first Belgian village at dusk, he could see frightened civilians peering out from their doors or windows, unsure whether the military vehicle noise in the street was their liberation or the return of the *Wehrmacht*. On impulse, Galipeau shouted "Vive la Belgique!" from his turret and "immediately every door on the street was opened and the people came pouring out" to crowd around the tanks and attempt to kiss the embarrassed South Albertas.[14]

On the following day, 8 September, 10th Brigade received orders to secure a crossing over the Ghent Canal at the little town of Moerbrugge south of Bruges. Major Dave Currie's C Squadron, with the Argylls on their decks, was in the van and reached Oostcamp, just west of Moerbrugge, at about noon that day but experienced such a tumultuous reception that it took

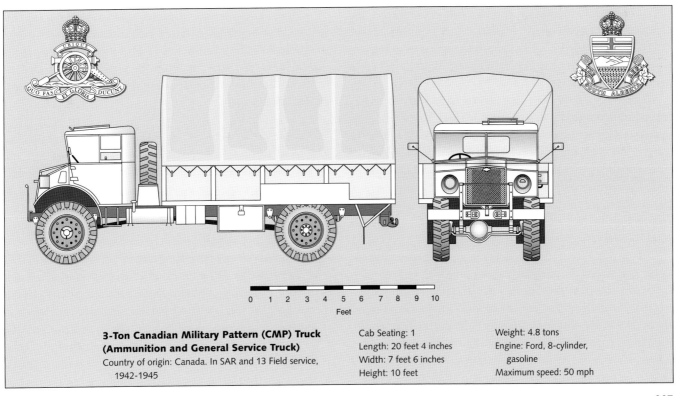

3-Ton Canadian Military Pattern (CMP) Truck (Ammunition and General Service Truck)
Country of origin: Canada. In SAR and 13 Field service, 1942-1945

Cab Seating: 1
Length: 20 feet 4 inches
Width: 7 feet 6 inches
Height: 10 feet

Weight: 4.8 tons
Engine: Ford, 8-cylinder, gasoline
Maximum speed: 50 mph

The Great Retreat: Holland, September 1944

As the *Wehrmacht* recoiled from Normandy, hope rose in Holland that the country would soon be free, hope inspired by scenes like this one, shot clandestinely by a Dutch civilian from an upstairs window. It shows a German 37 mm anti-aircraft gun being towed by a Dutch farmer's wagon and it appears that the Germans have not only conscripted wagon and horses, they have also conscripted the farmer himself. Unfortunately for the Dutch, the Germans were able to stabilize their front and they continued to occupy much of Holland throughout the following winter. SAR ARCHIVES

several hours for the column to thread its way through the town and approach the Ghent Canal. As the lead troop, C-2 under Lieutenant Jack Roberts, cautiously approached the bridge linking Oostcamp and Moerbrugge, the Germans blew it in front of them and Trooper David Marshall remembered "pieces of bridge falling all over and around us" and the enemy then opening up "with a barrage of anti-tank and small arms fire."[15] The Argylls began to clear the houses on the west bank of the canal while the remainder of C Squadron deployed along it. It was not long before the Highlanders made a wonderful discovery – a warehouse full of beer – and the war ground to a halt as the flatfeet and C Squadron took this opportunity to refuel. Trooper Marshall remembered that, when his Sherman moved away from the now empty building, it looked like "the Quarter Master's half track loaded with cases of extra 'rations.'"[16]

Harry Foster, convinced that he was faced with an enemy rearguard that would pull back after a "short, sharp fight," ordered the Argylls to establish a bridgehead on the far side of the canal.[17] The Highlanders looked around, "found a couple of old rowboats which were quite heavy and quite leaky" and, while B and C Squadrons laid down heavy covering fire from positions north and south of the selected crossing site, managed to get their companies across the 50 foot-wide waterway and secure much of Moerbrugge.[18]

The Argylls were fortunate that their crossing site happened to fall squarely on the boundary between the 64th and 245th Infantry Divisions, the two German formations tasked with holding the Ghent Canal, and each divisional commander assumed the other was responsible for the area. It did not take too long for the *Wehrmacht* to get itself sorted out, however, and when it did, a heavy mortar and artillery bombardment was brought down on the sappers who had come up to construct a Bailey bridge

over the canal while, at the same time, German infantry began to infiltrate into Moerbrugge to try and cut the Argylls off from the bridging site. Matters were made worse by the fact that supply shortages limited the amount of supporting fire that 15th Field Regiment could provide. Nonetheless, using the same leaky boats, all four rifle companies of the Argylls and three companies of Links were over the canal by nightfall on 8 September 1944. Fierce house-to-house fighting followed throughout the hours of darkness and, at first light on 9 September, the Germans brought the bridging site under 20 mm fire from three separate directions and then began to pound the west bank of the canal and Oostcamp with a heavy artillery bombardment.

That day was a long one for 10th Brigade. While the sappers worked hard to complete a bridge over the canal, B Squadron of the SAR provided direct fire support for the infantry from the west bank and Lieutenant Jack Summers managed to drive off several enemy SPGs which were firing directly at the infantry positions. The enemy artillery bombardment was intense – one South Alberta remembered it as the "worst shelling of the war bar none" – and it caused heavy casualties.[19] By late afternoon, however, FOOs from 15th Field had crossed into Moerbrugge and were able to direct artillery onto the German infantry, breaking up their attempts to form for attacks.

All that day the seven companies in Moerbrugge were hard-pressed. The best description of what the fighting was like in that little Belgian town on 9 September 1944 comes from the pen of Major R.L. Paterson of the Argylls, who commanded the left flank company on the far side of the canal. Paterson recorded that Moerbrugge

was ablaze that day with small arms fire, grenades and PIATs. The air was a frenzy of automatic fire and the shouts and groans of the wounded Germans. No one knows how many attacks they made, but they were many. Their stretcher bearers worked all day and were permitted into the company lines to clear the dead and wounded. It was the wildest show and bloodiest for a long time.

Toward evening the enemy teed up what was to be his last attempt at dislodging us. Counter attacks on both left and right flanks came in after a severe mortaring. One platoon on the right was overrun by sheer weight of numbers and the platoon commander killed. But the company on the left held, and those on the right forced the enemy back with great slaughter. They made three attempts to rush the defences, each time they formed extended line some three to 400 yards away in open fields. They came on in ragged lines, their grey greatcoats flapping at their ankles.

Each time the God-given Bren guns cut enormous swaths in their ranks. More ammunition had been secured for the artillery and with DF tasks called, and with the New Brunswick Vickers and the South Alberta Brownings sealing off the flanks, the enemy was held.[20]

The sappers worked desperately through the night and, by first light on 10 September, the bridge was nearly finished. On the other side, the tired infantry in Moerbrugge could hear the South Albertas gunning the engines of their tanks as they waited for the last planks to be put in place – "Jesus, what a glorious moment," one later recalled.[21] At 7 A.M. on 10 September, B Squadron rumbled across the Ghent Canal and, within a matter of minutes, the fighting died away in Moerbrugge. Major Paterson thought the relief was "a miniature Lucknow but instead of the faint skirl of pipe, it was the distant muttering of a Sherman that tormented the overwrought imaginations during this two-day siege."[22]*

With the bridgehead now secure, plans were made to expand it. Nash's B Squadron was to assist the Argylls' to advance north of Moerbrugge while Lavoie's A Squadron, supported by the Links, moved on Lekkerhoek, a hamlet about 3 miles to the west. Attempts to carry out these plans quickly revealed that, although the Germans had withdrawn from the immediate area of Moerbrugge, they had formed an anti-tank gun screen around it. B Squadron lost four tanks, one after another, that morning and Trooper John Neff of that squadron recorded some details of the fight in his diary:

> Once over the canal we started to fan out. We were with sqdn. HQ once more. We crossed over and took a position to the right at the edge of the town and at once started to burn houses & hay stacks. 1 tp was about 1/2 mile down the road ahead of us. Kroesing had his tank knocked out. Strathdee was hurt in the back and Devreker & Barnett were burnt about the face. Big Tony carried Strathdee & with his pistol shot two Germans and helped to take about a half Doz. more prisoners. ……. It was a bad day.[23]

Major Arnold Lavoie's A Squadron also suffered heavily when it attempted to advance on Lekkerhoek in the afternoon. Because of tank casualties, the squadron was organized in only three troops and, in a matter of minutes, it lost two troop leaders sniped in their turrets and eight tanks. The surviving A Squadron troop leader, Lieutenant Gordon Irving, gathered up

South Alberta tank casualty, Moerbrugge
The SAR lost heavily in men and tanks during the vicious fighting around Moerbrugge in September 1944. The extra tank treads welded to its hull did not protect this Sherman, which was hit during the fighting and now serves as a backdrop for happy Belgian civilians. *FROM DE SLAG OM MOERBRUGGE*

the four remaining Shermans and put down HE and Browning fire on every building, haystack, wood and ditch in range for 30 minutes before moving forward again, and was able to secure Lekkerhoek by late afternoon. One of the notable incidents of that day was the experience of Sergeant Alex Mackenzie who had two tanks shot out from under him in succession. When he went back after his second escape, Mackenzie fully expected to get a break but, instead, Regimental Sergeant-Major Jock Mackenzie, who happened to be his brother, told him to take over a third vehicle whose crew commander had been killed and go back to the fight. The sergeant survived but it is said that for some time afterward relations between the two brothers were very strained.

On 11 September, Dave Currie's C Squadron took over the lead and moved with the Links out of Lekkerhoek in the direction of Oodelem, the next town. Within a matter of minutes, the squadron lost four tanks to anti-tank guns and three crew commanders sniped in their turrets, while the infantry were forced to ground by automatic weapons fire. There was some confusion until the squadron could get itself sorted out and then the advance resumed, led by Sergeant Ted Palfrenier from Medicine Hat, commanding one of the first Sherman Firefly tanks to be issued to the SAR. Palfrenier's brand new vehicle had not gone more than 100 yards when it suffered a direct hit from an anti-tank gun and the crew bailed out, losing two men cut down by machinegun fire. Palfrenier escaped injury and took shelter behind a solidly-built stone farmhouse, only to be killed by an AP round that went through the building and into a half-track ambulance behind it. All C Squadron's attempts to move forward were completely frustrated by determined German resistance and both tank and infantry losses were heavy. The battle appeared to be a stalemate but the Germans withdrew late in the afternoon. Jefferson's 10th Brigade, however, was in no condition to pursue them..

---

* A reference to the siege of Lucknow during the Indian Mutiny where a British garrison, hard pressed for many weeks, was rescued by a relieving force preceded by a Highland unit and its pipers.

The battle for the Moerbrugge bridgehead cost the South Albertas lost 11 killed and 27 wounded. The SAR also completely wrote off 7 tanks while dozens more were out of action in the repair shops. Moerbrugge was a hard-fought action that made it quite clear that the great breakout run and the days of easy, joyous liberation had ended. It was now obvious to the Allied soldiers that the war would not be over by Christmas.

The day after the battle for Moerbrugge ended, 4th Armoured Division was ordered north to clear out the area west of the Ghent-Terneuzen Canal, which bisects northwestern Belgium. The division commenced the job that day and the South Albertas, moving ahead of 10th Brigade "had a grand day" as it "was back to its old role and worked as a Recce Reg[imen]t."[24] Splitting up into smaller elements, the three fighting squadrons, AA and Recce Troops spent the day investigating the many small bridges in the area between the Ghent and Leopold Canals before returning to harbour at Donk.

On 13 September, the lead elements of the division came up against the Leopold Canal, the boundary of the German stronghold that *General* von Zangen had created in the Breskens area. The enemy did not appear to be present in great strength and Foster decided to try to seize a bridgehead from which the armoured units of the division would "fan out in both directions to clear the North bank of the canal Leopold."[25] The job went to Bob Bradburn's Algonquins who attacked at 11 P.M., crossing the canal at a site near the town of Moerkerkke in 60 assault boats and other craft, under cover of a bombardment fired by

all the guns and mortars in the division as well as the SAR. By first light, all four Algonquin rifle companies were established on the German side but the Germans, sensitive to any attempt to obtain a lodgement in the Breskens pocket, reacted violently and brought down heavy artillery fire on the engineers who were attempting to build a bridge, and launched a wave of counterattacks against the Algonquins' positions.

By noon that day, Foster realized that his attempt to secure a lodgement had failed and, as the Algonquins were running out of ammunition, he ordered them to be withdrawn under the cover of a bombardment fired by every available barrel within range, the South Albertas alone contributing 1,600 rounds of 75 mm HE. The Algonquins suffered heavy casualties, losing 153 officers and men killed, wounded or missing and it was obvious both to General Crerar of First Canadian Army and Lieutenant-General Guy Simonds of 2 Canadian Corps that the elimination of the Breskens Pocket would require 2nd and 3rd Infantry Divisions, which were still pre-occupied clearing the Channel Ports.

Simonds ordered Foster to secure the Leopold Canal and to maintain contact with the enemy. During the ten days that followed the abortive attack at Moerkerkke, while the greater part of 4th Division held the line of the Leopold, the SAR helped to clear the Germans out of the area between the Leopold and Ghent-Terneuzen Canals, driving steadily north. They encountered more trouble from enemy demolitions and roadblocks than from the enemy but there were occasional rearguard actions. This was very good experience, one officer later remembered,

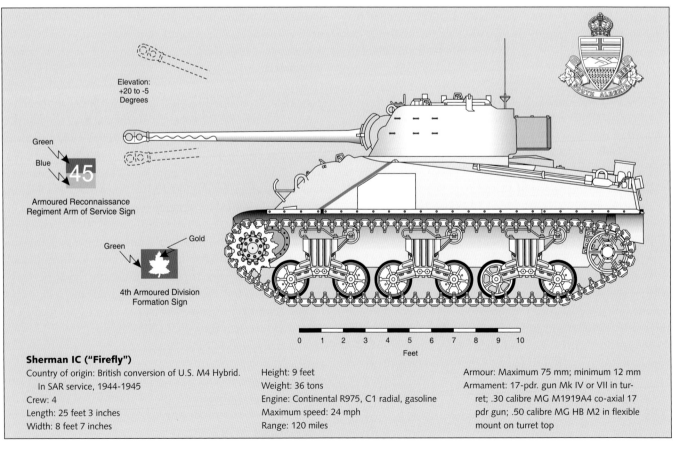

Elevation:
+20 to -5
Degrees

Green
Blue
45

Armoured Reconnaissance
Regiment Arm of Service Sign

Green — Gold

4th Armoured Division
Formation Sign

0 1 2 3 4 5 6 7 8 9 10
Feet

Sherman IC ("Firefly")

Country of origin: British conversion of U.S. M4 Hybrid. In SAR service, 1944-1945	Height: 9 feet	Armour: Maximum 75 mm; minimum 12 mm
Crew: 4	Weight: 36 tons	Armament: 17-pdr. gun Mk IV or VII in turret; .30 calibre MG M1919A4 co-axial 17
Length: 25 feet 3 inches	Engine: Continental R975, C1 radial, gasoline	pdr gun; .50 calibre MG HB M2 in flexible
Width: 8 feet 7 inches	Maximum speed: 24 mph	mount on turret top
	Range: 120 miles	

because it taught crew commanders how to think like Swatty Wotherspoon in terms of "what, who, where, when, how – and you had better think in those terms if he visited you or you had to report to him."[26] On Sunday, 17 September, everyone looked up to a sky filled with hundreds of aircraft as the men of three Allied airborne divisions flew overhead to commence Operation MARKET GARDEN, Montgomery's attempt to seize a bridge over the Rhine. The following day, Sergeant Albert Halkyard led a patrol from Recce Troop and he and his men became the first Canadian soldiers to cross into Dutch territory. Not only that, they engaged a 315 mm German railway gun and put it out of action before returning safely to their harbour that night.

By 25 September, the South Albertas were near Sluiskill in Holland when they received orders to take over a 40-mile stretch of the south coast of the Scheldt from Antwerp to the Ghent-Terneuzen Canal. Regimental Headquarters was established at Hulst and daily patrols were sent out along the coast roads but there was very little enemy activity. For the next two weeks the South Albertas had a rather quiet period and, for the first time since Normandy, the regiment was concentrated in one place. This, unfortunately, gave RSM Jock Mackenzie the opportunity to assert himself and matters of dress, deportment and drill were tightened up. Relations with the local Dutch civilians were uniformly good and on 9 October the South Albertas were sad to leave Hulst, which the press had dubbed "Albertania" to move to new positions around Brasschaet in Belgium. From this place, they would provide, along with the rest of 4th Division, flank protection for the 2nd Division which was about to commence the task of clearing the Beveland Peninsula. For the next ten days, the SAR carried out active patrolling to acquire information but, aside for the occasional enemy shelling, this also proved to be a fairly quiet time.

"A pretty sorrowful sight": 13th Field Regiment, September-October 1944

While the South Albertas were roaming through Belgium and southern Holland, 13th Field was taking part in the sieges of Boulogne and Calais. Following its two days of rest at Hymneville, the regiment moved north on 5 September to a gun position near Samer, southeast of Boulogne, to support 3rd Division's operations against that port. At this time, Lieutenant-Colonel F.D. Lace replaced Lieutenant-Colonel Clifford, who transferred to the staff of First Canadian Army. The German garrison of Boulogne consisted of about 10,000 men with 90 artillery pieces positioned in concrete fortifications on a ring of hills that surrounded the port. The morale of the defenders was known to be low and Major-General D.C Spry, who had replaced Keller as the commander of 3rd Division, decided that a single and sudden heavy blow – preceded by an attack of heavy bombers and supported by more than 300 artillery pieces – might just induce them to surrender. It took more than a week to complete the preparations for this operation, codenamed WELLHIT, and in the meantime, 13th Field supported the infantry of 8th Brigade

as it tightened the noose around the city but, given the supply situation and the need to deceive the enemy about the amount of artillery support available, firing was restricted.

On 8 September the regiment moved to a new gun position closer to Boulogne which was in range of the German artillery inside the fortress. The enemy kept a crossroads on the road leading to this position under continual harassing fire but it didn't do much good because, as Staff Sergeant James Moffat recalled, they "fired every two minutes so we would wait, and after they had fired, two or three vehicles would go by and then we would stop and wait."[27] It made no sense to Moffat and it was his opinion that Canadian gunners "could never do that, we would have slipped to a minute and a half" but nobody complained too loudly. While the preparations for WELLHIT went ahead, Allied aircraft were active, including Typhoons which made several rocket attacks on the German defences after they were targeted with red smoke from the artillery. The regiment also fired shells containing propaganda leaflets, summoning the garrison to surrender, and they liked to link such a bombardment with a Typhoon attack so as "to entice the Germans out into the open by the sight of some reading material and then to let go with a rocket" which rather defeated the intention of the psychological warfare experts but nobody worried too much about it.[28]

Operation WELLHIT commenced on 17 September 1944. It was preceded by an air bombardment from 792 aircraft from Bomber Command which dumped more than 3,000 tons of explosives on the German positions. There then followed an opening bombardment consisting of concentrations on all known German positions, followed by "stonks" or intense concentrations on particularly strong fortifications. Next, the infantry went in, accompanied by FOOs, but enemy opposition proved more determined than expected and it took the 3rd Division

Baker Troop, 22 Field Battery, September 1944
Baker One gun detachment takes a break during a lull in the fighting for Boulogne in September 1944. One of the reasons the gunners disliked switching from self-propelled 105 mm howitzers to towed 25-pdrs. was that they now had to dig a gun pit by hand every time they arrived at a new position. FROM *13 CANADIAN FIELD REGIMENT*

infantry five days to grind through the outer defences of Boulogne. Captain Don Baugh, serving as a 13th Field FOO, distinguished himself during the fighting, first by eliminating the crews of a battery of 88 mm anti-aircraft guns and then by trying to use these weapons against their former owners. Baugh's FOO party was under constant German shell fire for nearly three days but never stopped calling in the targets, an act that brought him the award of the Military Cross and his two gunner assistants, the Military Medal. After five days of heavy fighting and 634 Canadian casualties, the German garrison of Boulogne surrendered on 22 September but, as Sergeant Cunningham of 22 Battery lamented, "they drank up all the liquor before they came out," which infuriated the men of 3rd Division.[29]

The field regiments of the division now moved north to carry out Operation UNDERGO, Spry's plan for the attack on Calais. UNDERGO was a repeat of WELLHIT and, again, was preceded by heavy air bombardment as 633 heavy bombers dumped 3,000 tons of bombs on 20 September while all guns within range brought down suppressing fire on the German anti-aircraft positions. A medium bomber attack followed on 24 September but this time, for some unknown reason, the gunners were not ordered to suppress the flak batteries and the result was disastrous. Staff Sergeant Moffat remembered watching the medium bombers coming in at sunset, low, slow and level, "and they were perfectly silhouetted and they were nearly all shot down." Moffat had "never seen anything like it in my life. We had every German AA site spotted but there were no fire orders and we couldn't do anything. It was a pretty sorrowful sight."[30] As the horrified gunners looked on, the mediums kept flying in from the sea, and they "could see them being hit and the crews jumping out although they were too low – but they kept coming."[31] It was a disaster that cost the RAF 14 aircraft but there was no mistake on 26 September, the day after the infantry of 3rd Division began their assault with heavy artillery support. This time the gunners brought down fire on the flak batteries as 342 Lancasters landed 1,700 tons of explosive on Calais.

After this, there were very few German guns still in action and, as the infantry closed in on the city, the gunners of 13th Field had less work which suited them just fine. Their gun positions near Peuplingue were good ones, the 22 Battery CP being "very happily situated in a farm house which possessed all the comforts of home including four pretty daughters."[32] There was a 24-hour truce on 29 September to permit the civilian population of Calais to be evacuated and then every gun in range fired 65 rounds each on all known positions, followed by red target smoke for the Typhoons which roared in to make rocket attacks. The tactical aircraft were under stricter control than they had been in Normandy but, as usual, the fighter-bomber pilots did not lack aggression – Sergeant James Moffat of 22 Battery remembered

We were going through a village out in no-man's land and along came a Tiffie and he kept buzzing us a bit. We were on the other side of Calais when this damned Typhoon spotted us. We had a yellow smoke and a yellow flag out but it didn't do any good as he just came in and rocketed us, fortunately missing. Those goddamned Tiffies were wonderful but not when they were aiming at you.[33]

The massive Typhoon "beat up" on 29 September was the last straw for the defenders of Calais and they surrendered that day, as did the German coastal batteries in the surrounding area, bringing to an end what had been an intermittent four-year bombardment of Dover and area at the southeast tip of Britain.

The regiment spent a day tidying up and then held a party on 1 October to celebrate the fall of the Channel ports. The liquor stocks in Calais were found to be better than in Boulogne and the OP and FOO parties took the opportunity "to display souvenirs which they had obtained in the last few weeks," and sales to the gun detachments "were tremendous."[34] Everyone was just getting into the spirit of the thing when the regiment was suddenly ordered to move. "Somehow this was accomplished," their historian noted, and 13th Field left the Channel ports in a northerly direction.[35]

The regiment got a few days rest at Watou in Belgium until 5 October when they were ordered to move north to Maldegem to commence operations to clear the Scheldt Estuary. This move was carried out under the greatest secrecy and the men of 3rd Division were ordered to remove their regimental flashes and blue-grey divisional patch from their battle dress. As the columns rumbled through Belgium, Gunner Joe Shem-

Canada ends a German reign of terror
From 1940 onward, large German coastal guns like this 14-inch weapon in a heavily-fortified position near Boulogne, shelled the Dover area of England. This reign of terror ended in September 1944 when First Canadian Army took the Channel ports. The steel mesh curtain around the gun is for splinter protection. NAC. PA-131243

The Scheldt, 1944: Fighting below sea level
Extensive German flooding turned the low-lying Scheldt area into an interior sea. Here a Canadian convoy composed of amphibious vehicles moves along a road whose location can be ascertained only by the trees bordering its length. It took First Canadian Army 85 days to clear the approaches to Antwerp and it was a wearying and thankless task. NAC, PA-132422

rock, driving a battery command post half-track, acquired a new friend when Shemrock and his companion, the battery GPO, were adopted by a little white terrier, resembling a Jack Russell, whom they christened (with all that flashing wit for which gunners are famous) "Dog." Their new companion was an extremely intelligent little fellow who thrived on bully beef and hard tack and who knew instinctively, whenever Joe stopped, whether the halt would be for a long time or not. If the vehicle was stopping for a long period, "Dog" would jump out and disappear, foraging for rats and other food but if the stop was just a halt, "Dog" would not bother dismounting. If the little guy had disappeared and Joe had to move, he would give a loud whistle and "Dog" would appear in the distance and return to take up his position on the map console between the two front seats of the vehicle. Gunner "Dog" turned out to be an ideal travelling companion and his keen sense of smell and hearing were an asset at night when unfriendly strangers might be wandering about.[36]

The move to Maldegem was, for 13th Field, the beginning of nearly a month of continuous fighting to support the infantry of 3rd Division as it reduced the Breskens Pocket. This German position on the south side of Scheldt Estuary, roughly 18 miles long and 10 miles wide, was bounded by the Leopold Canal and there were only three usable approaches, all of which were heavily fortified by the Germans who had also flooded large areas of the Pocket. The garrison consisted of the 64th Infantry Division, a veteran formation which would prove to be obstinate opponents, their obstinacy reinforced by an order promulgated by Heinrich Himmler that any German soldier who surrendered in the Scheldt "fortresses" would be regarded as a deserter whose "ignominious behaviour" would "entail the most severe consequences for his family," including their possible execution.[37] Considerable artillery support was available for the reduction of the Breskens Pocket, a total of 327 barrels, which included not

only the artillery of 3rd Infantry and 4th Armoured Divisions but a Canadian and a British AGRA (Army Group, Royal Artillery), independent artillery formations of medium and heavy guns. The terrain, however, favoured the defenders as it was almost impossible for armoured vehicles to move on the Breskens except along dyke-top roads which were mined and covered by anti-tank defences. Basically, the Pocket was a heavily-defended swamp and the ever present mud reduced the fragmentation effect of HE rounds.

On 6 October, 3rd Division began the miserable job of clearing the Breskens, a task that would occupy it for four weeks. In a series of assaults in which the infantry moved in amphibious vehicles, the division's three infantry brigades, bit by bit, pushed the desperately resisting enemy back to the shores of the Scheldt. Day and night, 13th Field and the other gunner units fired in support of their flat-footed comrades and one day succeeded another in grim, grey procession. In the four weeks of the Scheldt battle, 13th Field fired 82,700 rounds at the Germans. The terrain limited the choice of gun positions and the individual troops were often placed in farmyards which were on higher ground. The gunners were amused to watch how the farm families, who lived in their cellars while the fighting was going on, persevered in collecting and replacing the pottery roof tiles dislodged by the concussion from the guns, only to have to repeat the process the next day. The presence of civilians sometimes made for funny incidents – during the first two weeks of the operation, the Command Post of 22 Battery was located about 150 yards from a local pub where

The boys drop in on their time off for an odd beer, or a shot of cognac, also to write letters or play cards. The lady who runs the "Pub" speaks only Flemish, and the only English she knows is: "Son-of-a-beech," which she has picked up from the boys. She has no idea what it means but says it every time the guns go off. It sounds very funny as she is rather the prim type of woman.[38]

By this time, 13th Field Regiment was functioning like clockwork. Everyone in the unit knew their job inside and out including the FOO and OP parties, the line crews who maintained communications, the command post staffs and the gun detachments manning the 25-pdrs. The line crews had a very dangerous job as they had to make constant repairs, often under German machinegun and mortar fire, to the telephone lines that connected the gun positions to the OPs. Despite heavy casualties, their dedication to this task never faltered. On 17 September a line crew of 78 Battery attempting to lay line in the forward areas disappeared. A search party from the battery went out with the advancing infantry and found the party's weapons "and some kit with a spool of wire opposite a German dugout" because this crew had unfortunately laid their line right into the enemy's positions.[39] Three men of the four-man party were taken prisoner and one killed.

The FOO parties were also dedicated men because they knew the infantry depended on them. It proved very difficult in the Breskens area to relieve the FOO parties on a regular basis because movement was difficult in the flooded terrain and they often stayed with the infantry for days on end. As the commanding officer of 13th Field later commented:

> Of all the gunners that fought, they were the heroes of the artillery. …… As far as I know, the guns were never out of action from D-Day until we got to Nijmegen in late November when the war settled down. They were supporting somebody all the time. While the guns were in action, somebody has to be directing them. So those FOOs were out there.
>
> They walked forward with the company or platoon commanders in the attacks; they were with them on the defence, usually exposed. When the company received relief, the FOO would be switched over to another company commander and still go on sweating it out. Some of them would begin counting – the ones that missed them and the ones that didn't miss. When the casualty figures get so high, you begin to say the odds are getting pretty small.[40]

Two captains of 13th Field won the Military Cross for their activities as FOOs during the clearing of the Breskens and their enlisted assistants were no less dedicated. During the attack on the town of Oostburg on 29 October, Lance-Bombardier Oliver Shaw, finding that communications with his officer had broken down, took a spare radio from the party's carrier and "proceeded on foot over a road swept by heavy enemy shell, mortar and smallarms fire," to reach his officer and restore contact. This act brought Shaw the Military Medal.[41]

The sappers were here: Pontoon bridge, Holland, October 1944
A Canadian artillery FAT (Field Artillery Tractor), or Quad, limber and 25-pdr. combination drives across a pontoon bridge over the Beveland Canal erected by the Royal Canadian Engineers. Although they were unsung, in the final analysis the campaign in Northwest Europe could not have been fought, let alone won, without the contribution of the sappers. NAC, PA-156498

After nearly four weeks, the Germans were pushed back to their last remaining position near Zeebrugge on the North Sea coast. Many had managed to escape to Walcheren Island on the other side of the Scheldt, which was being besieged by 2nd Division but, on 3 November, 13th Field fired its last rounds shortly before the Germans surrendered in the Breskens. At the cost of 2,077 casualties, 3rd Division had cleared the Pocket in a campaign unparalleled for misery and difficulty. As a result, there was great rejoicing in the division when its men learned that they were to get a 5-day rest in Ghent as a reward for their travails.

"Hulk Alley": 10th Brigade's drive to the Maas, 22 October–30 October 1944

While 3rd Division was occupied with the Breskens Pocket, 2nd Division had been clearing out the Beveland Peninsula on the north side of the Scheldt Estuary. The division, which had come to call itself "The Water Rats," commenced this task on 2 October and, if anything, encountered terrain that was worse than the Breskens. It took three weeks to seal the peninsula, fighting in an area reclaimed from the sea, much of it flooded by the Germans, and where vehicles could only move on the dyke tops which were mined, cratered with demolitions and under constant enemy fire. By the end of October the division had got as far as the causeway, 1,200 yards long and 120 feet wide, that linked the Peninsula with Walcheren Island, the last German strongpoint. The job of taking the causeway fell to 5th Infantry Brigade and each of its three battalions in turn attempted to cross this defile. The Calgary Highlanders were the second unit to go in and suffered very heavy casualties but its D Company under Major Bruce McKenzie from Medicine Hat, a prewar member of the

SAR, managed to seize a tiny bridgehead on the northern side. Attempts to expand it, however, were to no avail and during the heavy fighting that ensured, Captain Wynn Lasher, a former officer of the 15th Light Horse, commanding the Highlanders' A Company was wounded for the third time. After three days and 135 casualties, 5th Brigade was only too glad to turn over the area to the British 52nd Division which relieved it.

The long delay in clearing the approaches to Antwerp, which lasted throughout October, did not seem to worry Field-Marshal Montgomery. His eyes were firmly fixed on the Rhine but, although MARKET GARDEN had created a salient leading to that river, it had failed to take the Rhine bridge at Arnhem, the infamous "bridge too far." The situation did concern Eisenhower who wanted Antwerp opened to relieve the Allies' logistical problems, which were becoming critical. After a number of heated exchanges between Montgomery and other Allied senior leaders, Eisenhower finally issued the field-marshal a direct order to make Antwerp his first priority but even then, the British commander dawdled for six days before ordering Second British Army to support First Canadian Army in its unrelenting struggle to clear the Scheldt. The result was Operation SUITCASE, an attempt by four divisions, including 4th Canadian Armoured Division, under the command of British 1 Corps, to push the Germans north to the Maas River and cut off enemy communications with the Beveland Peninsula.

Operation SUITCASE began on 20 October and at first made good progress as the German troops in the area were second rate. The South Alberta Regiment did not play a major role in the opening stages of SUITCASE – that was born by 4th Armoured Brigade and the infantry of 10th Brigade which, by 22 October, were 7 miles southeast of Bergen-op-Zoom, their first major objective. The German commander in the area, *General Gustav von Zangen* of Fifteenth Army, had decided, contrary to orders from Berlin, to withdraw north of the Maas River, but realized that he needed to slow up the Canadian advance to buy time. He therefore moved his elite reserves, including the oversized 6th German Parachute Regiment and a combat group that contained elements of the Herman Goering Division, into strong blocking positions in the Wouwsche Plantage forest area south of Bergen. Their presence became apparent on 23 October when they decisively beat off an attempt by the Argylls and the Governor General's Footguards to move through the area.

That day the South Albertas concentrated at the town of Huijbergen to provide left flank protection for the advance on Bergen. On the following morning, Currie's C Squadron seized an intersection north of Huijbergen from which two roads branched off – a paved road leading north to the village of Wouwsche Plantage and a dirt road (actually a cleared route for a railway that had not yet been built) called the Huijbergsche Baan, which led northwest to Bergen-op-Zoom. Suspecting that this latter route might provide an opening through the German defences in the Wouwsche Woods to the east, Wotherspoon suggested to Jefferson that an advance straight up it might be very advantageous and Jefferson took it to Foster. Although he admitted it was workable, Harry Foster did not buy the idea and, instead, directed Jefferson to concentrate his main effort in the Wouwsche Plantage area, with a view to securing it and eventually cutting the main highway which ran due east from Bergen to the town of Wouw. Jefferson ordered Bradburn's Algonquins, with Nash's SAR B Squadron in support, to secure the village of Wouwsche Plantage while Lavoie's A Squadron and Currie's C Squadron would respectively provide right and left flank protection.

On 25 October Bradburn and Nash attempted to carry out these orders but encountered stiff German resistance in the Wouwsche Woods which slowed progress. Lavoie's A Squadron, meanwhile, moving to their right in more open ground, came up against enemy anti-tank defences that stymied their advance. By last light, Jefferson realized that a setpiece attack would have to be put in to secure both the village of Wouwsche Plantage and the nearby hamlet of Centrum. On the left, however, Dave Currie's C Squadron, made better progress up the Huijbergsche Baan and, as the day wore on, it became clear that Wotherspoon's guess

Not good tank country
The polder and dyke lands of Holland were the worst possible terrain over which to operate armoured vehicles. Note how this column of tanks of the Fort Garry Horse is restricted to a single muddy road bordering the dyke. The Germans planned their defences around these routes, forcing the Canadians to fight for every square inch. The poles in the background are a German defensive measure against glider landings. NAC, PA-138429

The medical system in operation during the Second World War was similar to that of the First War – a series of successive stages where the wounded soldier was given progressively more advanced treatment.

The wounded man was first attended by the stretcher bearers attached to each rifle company in an infantry battalion or those serving with the medical half-tracks in each armoured regiment. The stretcher bearers would administer immediate first aid and then transport the wounded to the Regimental Aid Post. Here, the unit Medical Officer (MO) would treat them or send them directly to the ADS (Advanced Dressing Station) located at the field ambulance unit attached to each brigade. At the ADS medical personnel would then triage the casualties into three groups. Group I casualties were those requiring immediate resuscitation and these might be treated at the ADS but were more normally taken by ambulance to a FDS (Field Dressing Station). Group II casualties were those requiring immediate surgical attention and they were transported by ambulance to an FDS to which was attached a Field Surgical Unit. From the FDS and ADS, depending on their condition, the wounded were ultimately removed to a Casualty Clearing Station and then to a military hospital. Group III casualties, which included all other casualties were evacuated directly from the RAP or ADS to the CCS and, ultimately, to hospital. Field Surgical Units were sometimes co-located at the FDS but usually at the CCS. After being treated, the wounded were usually kept at the CCS until fit enough to be evacuated by train or motor ambulance to a General Hospital in the rear. If their condition required advanced surgery and they were fit enough to travel, they were evacuated by air ambulance to Britain.

Lieutenant Jessie Morrison, an army nurse from Alberta, served with No. 10 Canadian General Hospital in Normandy and recalled that:

The convoys of wounded came to us usually after dark and streamed in all night. Medical officers examined the patients as they arrived and assigned them to whatever service was necessary. If they needed immediate surgery they were sent to an "E" block adjacent to the Operating Room.

Others who had less urgent needs were sent elsewhere. Those in shock and poor condition were sent to the Resuscitation tent, and there received blood transfusions, plasma or whatever else was required. Everyone worked through the night and day until every patient was cared for, and hundreds passed through our hands in a single night. In the Operating Room, the surgeons, anaesthetists, nurses and orderlies worked in teams. The patients' medical records were pinned to their uniforms, and notes made by anyone who had seen the man or given him any treatment were recorded on his medical sheet. ......

So it worked in a cycle – admit all one night, usually several hundreds though not always, then operate all that night and as far into the next day as required, allow the patients to "rest" two days, then evacuate to England and be ready for another convoy that night or next day.

To the medical personnel, intense periods of fighting would mean an unending procession of broken and dying men for days at a time, and sights that were truly heart rending. Major John Hills-

(Above) **Stretcher bearers**
The first step in the medical chain was the stretcher bearers who would take the wounded man back to the RAP. Here, four bearers evacuate a casualty wounded on the bank of the Rhine in April 1945. NAC, PA-140888

(Below) **Regimental Aid Post, Germany 1945**
The procession of wounded never stopped. A prisoner of war helps unload a casualty from a jeep ambulance somewhere in Germany in the last months of the war. Among the men in the background are two tank crewmen, easily recognized by their "zoot suits" or tankers' suits, which indicates that is probably an RAP for an armoured unit. Canadian Forces Photo Unit, PMR 93-376

man, a surgeon with a Canadian Field Surgical Unit in Northwest Europe, has provided a graphic account in his book, *Eleven Men and a Scalpel*, of what it was like to operate in the midst of the hell of battle:

During those days we became veterans. We saw the tragic sights from which we were never to be free for ten long months. Men with heads shattered, dirty brains oozing out. Youngsters with holes in their chests fighting for air. Soldiers with their guts churned into a bloody mess by high explosives. Legs that were dead and stinking – but still wore muddy boots. Operating floors that had to be scrubbed with Lysol to get rid of the stench of dead flesh. Boys who came to you with a smile and died on the operating table. Boys who lived long enough for you to learn their name and then were carried away in trucks piled high with the dead. We learned to work with heavy guns blasting the thin walls of our tent. We learned to keep our tent ropes slack so that anti-aircraft fragments would rain down harmlessly and bounce off the canvas. We became the possessors of bitter knowledge no man has ever been able to describe. Only by going through it do you possess it.

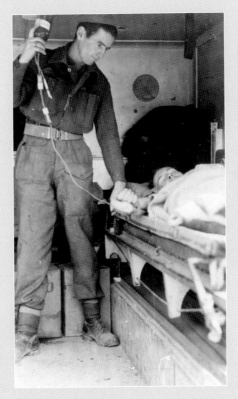

Inside an ambulance
A medical corpsman administers a blood transfusion to a wounded man in an ambulance. Medical advances during the Second World War, particularly the introduction of penicillin and sulphamides, saved many lives. CANADIAN FORCES PHOTO UNIT, PMR 93-369

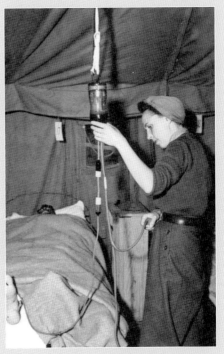

The Casualty Clearing Station
A Canadian nurse administers a blood transfusion to a wounded man at a CCS. Nurses generally did not work forward of the CCS in the medical chain, but even then, they occasionally came under fire. Wounded men often stayed at the CCS, which was really a forward hospital, for some time before being evacuated to a general hospital. NAC, PA 128234

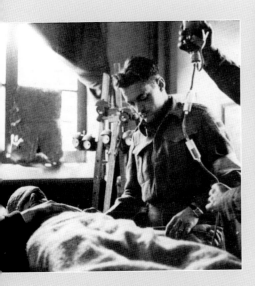

Advanced Dressing Station, Normandy
Captain Earl Bourbonnais, RCAMC, of 23rd Field Ambulance, 3rd Division, administers plasma to a casualty in an ADS set up in a house in June 1944. NAC, PA-131428

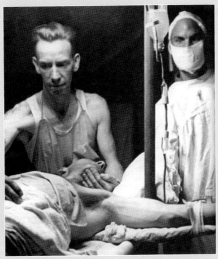

Field Surgical Unit
An orderly (left) and a surgeon prepare to carry out an operation on a wounded man. The Field Surgical Unit, often co-located with a CCS, saved many lives by performing surgery near the front. DND PHOTO

Air evacuation
As in the First World War, the close proximity of medical facilities in Britain was utilized to the fullest and the introduction of air ambulances saved many lives. Here a wounded man is loaded on a C-47 medical transport in Normandy. Note the nurse, who was probably a permanent member of the crew of this transport. NAC, PA-137357

Quotations from John Hillsman, *Eleven Men and a Scalpel*, and Ken Tingley, ed., *For King and Country: Alberta in the Second World War*.

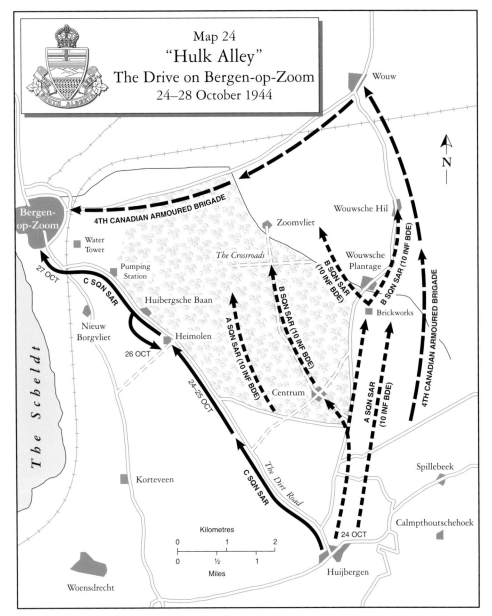

Map 24
"Hulk Alley"
The Drive on Bergen-op-Zoom
24–28 October 1944

men would have to go back up the dirt road again and, this time, a forewarned enemy would be ready for them. Major-General Harry Foster, who that day had been ordered by Montgomery to capture Bergen by 27 October, still believed that the best approach was north to the Bergen-Wouw Road and then east to the city. That night he directed Jefferson to make a major attack on the enemy strong points at Wouwsche Plantage village and Centrum and to clear the adjoining woods, while Moncel's 4th Armoured Brigade provided right flank protection to the east of the Wouwsche Woods. In response, Jefferson directed Stewart's Argylls and Bradburn's Algonquins, with A and B Squadrons of the SAR in support, to attack through the woods immediately east of the dirt road. Jefferson did, however, reinforce Wotherspoon with flail and flame-throwing Crocodile tanks from the 79th British Armoured Division and also gave him a rifle company from the Lincoln & Welland Regiment.

As it happened, 26 October 1944, was a terrible day for the 10th Brigade. With the help of B Squadron and British flame-throwing tanks, Bradburn's Algonquins were able to secure Wouwsche village, but an attempt to exploit north of it to the hamlet of Zoomvliet ran into trouble. Throughout most of the day, Lieutenant Leaman Caseley's B Squadron troop was cut off with a company

that this dirt road might be the easiest way into Bergen, was absolutely correct. Currie put three troops up that road behind each other and, by late afternoon, the lead troop, commanded by Lieutenant Danny McLeod of Medicine Hat, was within 2 miles from the city when it ran into determined resistance. When McLeod reported his position and asked for assistance, there was consternation at Regimental Headquarters as he was much closer to Bergen than anyone had realized. As the light was failing and there was no infantry available, McLeod was ordered to pull back down the dirt road to Currie's headquarters about 2 miles north of Huijbergen. By this time, however, McLeod's troop was nearly out of ammunition and was forced to resort to firing smoke shells into the wood to keep off the German infantry who managed to knock out one of his tanks with a *Panzerfaust*.

Swatty Wotherspoon was frustrated because he realized that, if infantry support had been available that day, he could have reached Bergen, bypassing the main enemy defences. Now his

of Algonquin infantry at a crossroads, and was only extricated, without its tanks, when 15th Field Regiment brought down a massive bombardment that kept the Germans' heads down long enough for a rescue convoy of Algonquin carriers to get them away. The heavy fighting cost Nash seven tanks and that night Trooper John Neff of B Squadron recorded in his diary, his impressions of a very hectic day:

Thurs. Oct. 26
First thing in the morning our tp. [troop] put in an attack on a brick yard [at Wouwsche], going in with two Churchill flame throwers. On the edge we routed out one poor little Jerry, nearly scared to death. The rest of the troops in the place were Foot-pads [Governor General's Foot Guards] and Lake Sups. [Lake Superior Regiment]. They should give one of them the V.C. for the way he braved our fire in order to get us to lay off. 4 tp. got itself cut off & started to cry for help. Al Holmes in 3 tp. lost his tank on a mine trying to get

Bogged down: Holland 1944
During the Scheldt campaign in the autumn of 1944 the Germans opened the dykes and flooded vast areas, forcing First Canadian Army to fight an amphibious operation. As the roads usually ran along the dykes, vehicle traffic was often subjected to heavy shelling. If it tried to move off the road, the result was often what is shown in this picture, taken near the Beveland Canal on 28 October 1944. This gun detachment has bogged its Quad and are preparing to tow it back onto dry land. NAC, PA-131257

through to them. Then in our tp. the new boss [i.e. troop leader] & Kroesing moved up to recover Holmes tank. All Hell broke loose and we rushed in to help "Crow" [Kroesing]. The bosses [sic] tank was already in flames and a bunch of green infantry did a run out on us. When the smoke cleared the new boss, Lt. Guyot, another new man, a gunner, Both Killed & J.D. White, Porter & Kenyon all wounded. This Mr. Guyot had come to us at Brasschat [sic] to gain battle experience, replacing Mr. Howard. Too bad he didn't last longer as he was a fine chap. The situation remained sticky all day & night.[42]

To B Squadron's left, Lavoie's A Squadron and the Argylls had no better luck in the woods, which turned out to be lousy with German mines and booby traps. Bergen-op-Zoom had long been the location of a *Wehrmacht* mine and demolition school and the instruction staff, experts in their field, had been called in to assist in the defence. Forced to constantly halt while sappers and pioneers cleared these devices, the Argylls and A Squadron made very slow and costly progress and, by last light, having lost four tanks either in the woods or on the neighbouring dirt road, pulled back to a position near the hamlet of Heimollen.

As for C Squadron, it was just as Wotherspoon had feared, the Germans were alert when the squadron, reinforced with Crocodile tanks, tried to move up the dirt road. In the lead for the second day, Lieutenant Danny McLeod was forced to call in the Crocodiles to take out an enemy position which the previous day had not been occupied. The defenders, mainly paratroopers, got one Crocodile with a *Panzerfaust* and a second with a controlled demolition charge so powerful that it upended the 35-ton vehicle and blew its turret 50 feet away. Forced to fire HE into the woods bordering the dirt road, the three troops of C Squadron, moving one behind the other, made slow progress that day because, as one troop passed, having dampened the Germans' enthusiasm, the paratroopers would re-occupy their positions and fire on the next troop. Although Currie was supposed to have a company of Links with him, it was delayed in arriving and did not reach the squadron until late afternoon, by which time McLeod's troop had almost reached the same position, 2 miles from Bergen, where they had been the previous day. As there was danger that the troop would again be cut

off, Currie ordered it to pull back down the road to the crossroads and Heimollen. By this time, the Huijbergsche Baan was littered with burning and destroyed Shermans, Crocodiles, carriers, scout cars and armoured cars, which earned it the name of "Hulk Alley." When the light faded, Harry Foster was no closer to taking Bergen than he had been in the morning and the 4th Division's advance had nearly ground to a halt.

The Germans, however, had accomplished their purpose, which was to delay the Canadian advance on Bergen long enough for them to retire behind a new defensive position north of the Zoom River which ran through the city. After the firing died down on 26 October, they used the cover of darkness to fall back and this became apparent the next morning when Foster, aware that the BBC had already "liberated" Bergen in a radio broadcast, ordered Jefferson to make a maximum effort, using the dirt road as the axis of advance. The brigade commander placed Cromb's Links under Wotherspoon's command and Swatty commenced his movement at 8 A.M. on 27 October. Only slight enemy resistance was encountered and Dutch civilians provided the information that the Germans had withdrawn the previous night. By early afternoon, McLeod's troop, in the lead on the dirt road for the third day running, had reached a pumping station less than a mile from the centre of the city. It was beginning to look like the way into Bergen was clear but as Wotherspoon did not want to get involved in house-to-house fighting, he decided to make a final recce and ordered McLeod to take his troop by the most direct route into the city while Sergeant Albert Halkyard of Recce Troop took his two Stuarts by a more roundabout way.

Guided by a Dutch resistance fighter who perched on the fender of his Sherman, McLeod set off in the early afternoon and, as he entered the outskirts of Bergen, it became clear that the Germans had pulled out. The population of the city, many of whom had been living in their basements for weeks during the recent fighting, went absolutely mad with joy and crowded around the troop's three Shermans. At 4.15 P.M., the troop pulled into the centre of the *Grote Markt*, the main square of Bergen-op-Zoom, to be greeted by a large crowd of overjoyed locals. At the same time, unnoticed by the frantically cheering crowd, Halkyard's two Stuarts entered the square from another direction. McLeod reported to Wotherspoon and Cromb, wait-

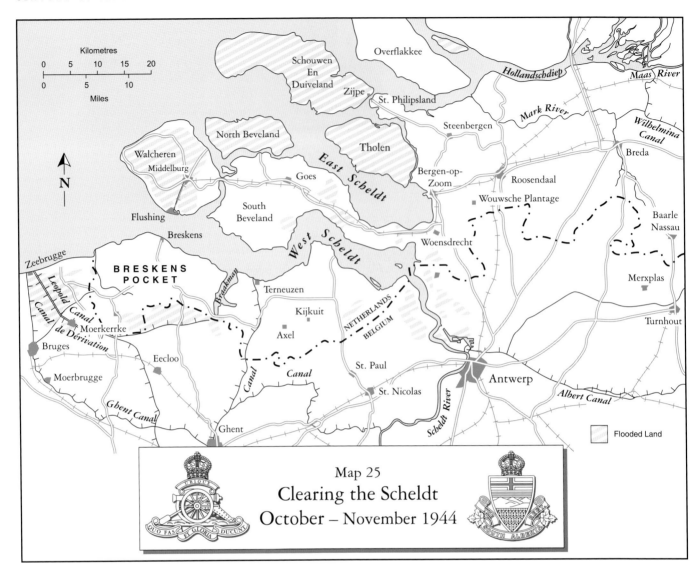

Map 25
Clearing the Scheldt
October – November 1944

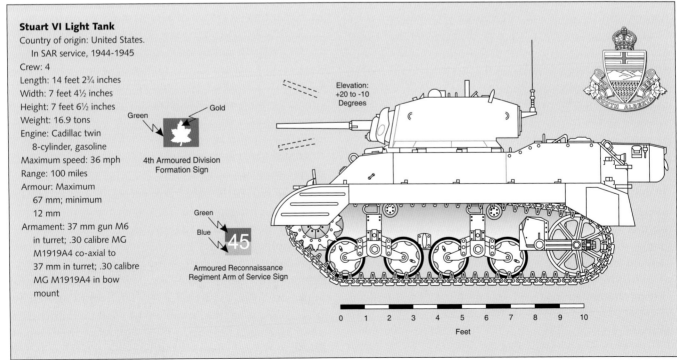

Stuart VI Light Tank

Country of origin: United States.
  In SAR service, 1944-1945

Crew: 4

Length: 14 feet 2¾ inches

Width: 7 feet 4½ inches

Height: 7 feet 6½ inches

Weight: 16.9 tons

Engine: Cadillac twin
  8-cylinder, gasoline

Maximum speed: 36 mph

Range: 100 miles

Armour: Maximum
  67 mm; minimum
  12 mm

Armament: 37 mm gun M6
  in turret; .30 calibre MG
  M1919A4 co-axial to
  37 mm in turret; .30 calibre
  MG M1919A4 in bow
  mount

Green → Gold
4th Armoured Division
Formation Sign

Elevation:
+20 to -10
Degrees

Green
Blue
45
Armoured Reconnaissance
Regiment Arm of Service Sign

Liberation Day, 1944
Argyll & Sutherland Highlanders perched on an almost invisible South Alberta tank experience the joys of being liberators in a small Dutch town in the autumn of 1944. Although the troops were pleased to be treated as heroes, the crowds and the generosity of the civilians often delayed or sidetracked operations. SAR ARCHIVES

ing at Swatty's tactical headquarters, that the city was clear south of the Zoom and was told to ascertain how strong the enemy defences were along that waterway. That being done, Swatty then turned to Cromb and, according to an eyewitness, said, "Hell, Bill, let's take the damned place," and the two colonels gave orders to their units to move into the city.[43]

As McLeod prepared to leave the *Grote Markt*, an unfortunate incident took place. A young Dutch boy, who had crawled on the front of his Sherman, jarred the .30 calibre Browning bow gun which accidentally triggered a burst into the crowd killing two teenage girls. The South Albertas were nearly made distraught by this tragedy but the head of the Bergen Red Cross took care of the matter as McLeod's three tanks pulled out of the square and headed for the Zoom. As they got near the main bridge on the Steenbergestraat, McLeod could see that its northern end was blocked by a huge concrete barrier. Moving slowly on either side of the broad boulevard that led to the bridge, the three Shermans were cautiously approaching this obstacle when the first German anti-tank gun opened fire and a round creased the turret of one of the tanks but otherwise did no damage. It

being clear the Zoom was defended, McLeod carried out the standard SAR drill for surprise contact with the enemy – "poof off smoke, pull all triggers and screw off in the ensuing confusion" – and withdrew to a sheltered position at a nearby intersection to await further orders.

For the next three days, there was heavy fighting along the Zoom which, at this point in its course, was actually a deep canal that formed an effective anti-tank ditch. While the sappers worked on demolishing the 3-foot thick concrete barrier across the Steenbergestraat bridge, 10th Brigade tried to get over the Zoom. The South Albertas, one squadron in rotation while the other two rested, provided direct fire support for the Argylls and Links who tried to secure a lodging on the north bank of the Zoom and some very vicious house-to-house fighting took place. Both sides exchanged artillery rounds across the city and the Germans fired every hour with Teutonic punctuality, an anti-tank round into the tower of the St. Gertruidnis Church on the *Grote Markt*, ringing its bell. It was a strange battle, infantry and tank crews would be exchanging fire with the enemy across the Zoom and, thirty minutes later, having been relieved, would be drinking beer at a nearby bar. Lieutenant Don Stewart of C Squadron, whose troop was occupying a large house along the river as a billet, decided to cook a hot meal for his men. He was forced to change his mind after the Germans, noting smoke issuing from the chimney of the house, put a 75 mm AP round through the front door which carried on down the hall into the kitchen, took out the stove on which Stewart's meal was being prepared, and continued on out through the back door into the garden where it demolished the outhouse.

There were also less comic incidents. During the afternoon of 29 October, a Canadian 5.5 shell landed short on the street where Dave Currie had his headquarters killing a dozen South Albertas and Argylls, and wounding many more.[44] After some stiff fighting, however, the Argylls and Links managed to secure toeholds on the north bank of the Zoom but, on the morning of 30 October, they discovered that the Germans were gone. By this time, 4th Armoured Brigade had cut the main highway running east from Bergen and von Zangen pulled back to his next defensive position, just south of the Maas River.

Not an inconsiderable obstacle – the Zoom in Bergen-op-Zoom
Intelligence officers reported that the Zoom River was not an obstacle for tanks. Guess again – the Zoom was not only a major obstacle, it formed an ideal defensive position and, after 10th Brigade entered the city, the Germans simply withdrew behind it and resisted every attempt to cross it. This picture of the blown Zandstraat Bridge was taken after the fighting had ended, a fact indicated by the Dutch children who have discovered that, courtesy of the *Wehrmacht,* they now have a new slide. SAR ARCHIVES

Gun detachment, Holland, autumn 1944

For the 85 days that the Scheldt Campaign lasted, the gunners backed the infantry and armour as they undertook the thankless job of clearing the estuary. Here a 25-pdr. detachment feeds the ever-hungry breech on their weapon. The No. 3, or gun layer, is to the left of the breech while the No. 2 is on the right. To the right rear of the piece is the No. 1, the detachment commander. Since he is looking at his watch, this weapon is probably engaged in a timed shoot. The other gun numbers are occupied in preparing the ammunition for loading. NAC, PA-115569

"They banished my gloom": Rest and relaxation, November 1944

Not that anyone cared much about the enemy after they disappeared from view because, on the advice of his senior medical officer who was concerned about the exhaustion of the men, Foster granted his division a 48-hour rest period in Bergen. Wotherspoon and Cromb, whose troops had been first into the city, had established their headquarters in the venerable Hotel de Draak on the *Grote Markt* and held on to it in the face of determined efforts by the divisional staff to take it over – attempts that only stopped after Wotherspoon somewhat slyly advised the staff officers that, with German artillery rounds coming down near the hotel, he needed it to conduct the battle. It was at the de Draak during a party on Halloween night 1944 that the musical Bill Cromb of the Links, who possessed a magnificent tenor voice, first performed his famous composition, "The Bergen-op-Zoom Song" to the tune of "The Blue Danube":

> In Bergen-op-Zoom, op Zoom, op Zoom
> I got me a room, a room, a room.
> I went to my doom, my doom, my doom,
> In Bergen op Zoom, op Zoom, op Zoom.
> The babes they were fair, were fair, were fair,
> Their forms were so rare, so rare, so rare.
> I was glad I was there, I was there
> Up in Bergen, Bergen-op-Zoom
> Oh I didn't say much, lest I get in Dutch,
> Up in Bergen, with a virgin.
> Oh they banished my gloom, in my nice hotel room,
> Up in Bergen, Bergen, Bergen-op-Zoom.[45]

The rooms, corridors and basement of the de Draak were soon full of happy, sleeping South Albertas and their flatfooted friends while, in the back patio, a C Squadron crew dug up the paving stones to create a barbecue pit over which they roasted a side of beef, acquired through nefarious means, on a spit.

Bergen was great. Everybody got a decent meal, provided by the army but cooked by the women of the city, a shower, and new uniforms and boots from the quartermaster. The Salvation Army auxiliary services took over a local cinema to show movies which both the soldiers and civilians enjoyed, although there was some excitement one evening when a Deanna Durbin musical was interrupted after a member of Recce Troop inadvertently put a 37 mm AP round through the building. The South Albertas carried out their vehicle maintenance on the streets of the town, watched by crowds of fascinated small boys to whom the crews fed candy in hopes of meeting their older sisters. There were girls around and some were friendly, but you had to be careful as two troopers from AA Troop discovered after they picked up a pair of young blondes on the *Grote Markt*, only to have the Dutch Resistance suddenly whisk them away with sincere apologies. When next the two men saw these girls, they were being paraded in tears along the streets by a crowd of abusive Dutch men and women, their hair shaven to the skulls as a mark of shame, and placards hanging around their necks which read, "I SLEPT WITH THE GERMANS." Perhaps the best thing about Bergen was the booze. The mayor thoughtfully provided Swatty and Cromb with a basket of wines and fine spirits as a thank-you gift for the city's liberation, nobody bought a drink if a civilian could buy it and, at the invitation of the populace and to their immense satisfaction, the men of 10th Brigade completely drained a distillery owned by a local collaborator in a matter of hours.

Sadly, all good things must end and, on 2 November, the SAR and 10th Brigade left Bergen and moved north to Steenbergen to pursue the enemy. Three days later, they had reached the Maas River and Operation SUITCASE was brought to a successful conclusion.

Meanwhile, 13 Field Regiment, having fired its last rounds in the Scheldt operation, headed for Ghent for its promised rest period. It arrived in that city of 200,000 just after dark on the evening of 4 November but, unfortunately, the advance party missed the guides who were supposed to conduct the unit to its billets and it drove aimlessly through the streets for some time. A rumour spread among the gunners that they were going to go right through Ghent and would not get their break. As the regimental column was at that moment traversing what appeared to be a very interesting red light district, an enterprising gun detachment

faked an accident by jack-knifing its vehicle and gun, which blocked the street and stalled a long section of the column.

Main Square at Bergen, 29 October 1944
Vehicles from RHQ, Recce Troop and AA Troop of the SAR are seen parked in the main square of Bergen-op-Zoom, conveniently close to the Hotel de Draak (fifth building from the left facing the square). It was during a banquet held at the De Draak on Halloween night 1944 that Lieutenant-Colonel Bill Cromb from Edmonton, commanding the Lincoln & Welland Regiment, first sang his famous composition, the "Bergen-op-Zoom Song." SAR ARCHIVES

Many of the men quickly piled out and disappeared into taverns and upstairs rooms. Vehicles farther back that could not move out of the jam began to hunt for similarly saturnalian locations of their own.[46]

When the regiment finally found its guides, the remainder of the night

consisted of enraged officers and NCOs racing around in jeeps, threatening soldiers out of taverns and out of the arms of women. Accompanied with images of penal servitude, the gist of their orders were: "Get into those vehicles, get them to the now-known compound, get introduced to your billets, and then you can come back and go crazy."[47]

And many did go crazy. Gunner William McCrie remembered that he and his comrades bought several bottles of 3-star brandy but not much after that except that he was later told by his friends that "I was dancing on the tables with the girls doing Hawaiian dances."[48] Gunner Drummond Cotterill had his picture taken in a photographer's studio but, when he sent it home to his mother in Edmonton, the first thing she said was, "my boy is drunk."[49] Sergeant Alex Brennand remembered that men of the 3rd Division "were given the key to the city and the Mayor declared that so long as a Canadian soldier was in a pub or cafe it was to stay open. Some nights they never closed."[50] After two days, officers began to warn their men that civilians were complaining that Canadian soldiers behaved worse than the Germans, who had always conducted themselves well in Ghent. This had the effect of restraining some of the wilder spirits but there will always be men who cannot be restrained, such as the miscreant gunner who walked into "a crowded drinking-hole one evening," removed his boots, "plunked them on the bar, … pointed to a bottle in exchange, clutched it by the neck and walked out the door in his sock feet."[51] Next day, he appeared at the quartermaster's stores wearing a pair of tattered slippers and asked for new

RELAY STATION. Day and night the men remained at their radio sets relaying messages.

Relations with liberated civilians were always good
Maybe not as good as Lieutenant Patrick Clay of 13th Field hints in this cartoon but still cordial. FROM 13 CANADIAN FIELD REGIMENT, RCA

boots to replace the ones that had rotted off him in the mud of the Scheldt. The quartermaster heard the story out to the end before telling the wet-footed gunner that he had been in the bar the previous night and witnessed the exchange.

On 9 November 1944, 13th Field Regiment pulled out of Ghent and headed for Nijmegen to take up positions for the winter along the south bank of the Maas River. After 85 days of fighting in appalling conditions in some of the worst terrain in Europe, First Canadian Army had opened Antwerp at the cost of 13,000 casualties, half of them Canadian. With their vital logistical lifeline secure, Allied leaders now began to plan the final offensives that would take them into the heart of Hitler's Third Reich. For the time being, after nearly five months of combat, the men of First Canadian Army could look forward to a quiet period guarding the lower length of the Maas River.

CHAPTER THIRTEEN

"Scrap Hitler with Scrap"

CANADA AND ALBERTA DURING THE SECOND WORLD WAR

Astounding statistics: The Canadian war effort, 1939-1945

As the South Albertas and 13th Field Regiment took up their winter positions along the Maas River, their families at home were preparing for their sixth wartime Christmas. By late 1944 Canada was a much different nation from the rather naive country that had gone, reluctantly but confidently, to war in September 1939. More than five years of conflict had changed the Dominion which, by any measurable standard, had made an outstanding contribution to the Allied cause. Perhaps the best way to comprehend the extent of that contribution is to look at the statistics as they are no less than astounding.

Starting with the three armed services – of a population estimated to be 11,295,000 souls in 1939, 1,029,510 Canadian men and 45,423 women served in uniform during the conflict. With the exception of the 99,407 men compulsorily enlisted under the National Resources Mobilization Act, they were all volunteers, and included 41% of all Canadian males aged between 18 and 45. The three armed services experienced an incredible expansion. The army went to war in 1939 with a strength of 55,679 all ranks in both the regular and militia establishments and reached a peak strength of 595,804 all ranks in March 1945 – an increase of nearly 11 to 1. The Royal Canadian Navy, which possessed 2,891 all ranks, regular and reserve, and 13 vessels in

I'm a Zombie, I'm a Zombie,
I'm a Zombie, yes I am,
I'd much rather be a Zombie,
Than an active service man.

Now come listen, all you Zombies,
You drink our wine, you drink our beer,
But you won't turn active service,
You're a handcuffed volunteer.[1]

1939, expanded 32 to 1 in terms of personnel and 33 to 1 in terms of ships in commission until, by 1945, its 92,441 men and women were manning 434 vessels and it had become the fourth largest navy in the world.* The Royal Canadian Air Force, which had a 1939 strength of 4,154 all ranks, with 20 regular and auxiliary squadrons deploying a total of 53 aircraft – most of which were obsolescent – grew by early 1945 to 222,501 all ranks organized in 70 operational squadrons flying some of the most modern combat aircraft in the world. Furthermore, RCAF personnel formed about 20% of the total personnel strength of the British Royal Air Force.

Canada made other contributions to the Allied war effort. Outside the British Isles, it was the only Commonwealth country with an industrial base large enough to engage in the mass production of weapons and nearly a million Canadian men and women were employed in industries directly related to the war effort. During the six years of war, Canada produced 815,000 combat and transport vehicles (including more than 4,000 tanks and self-propelled guns), about 12,000 combat aircraft, and 487 escort warships, 254 smaller warships, 410 merchant ships and 3,302 landing craft. As part of a joint venture with Britain, Canada oversaw the British Commonwealth Air Training Plan which trained 131,553 aircrew (including 72,835 Canadians) at 80 training stations established across the country. The RCAF was also heavily involved in Ferry Command, the organization created to transfer aircraft to the war fronts, and assisted in flying 9,300 military aircraft and 2,000 passengers to destinations in Europe and Asia. The RCN escorted 43,000 merchant ships across the Atlantic between 1939 and 1945 and it was Canadian warships that safely shepherded the largest wartime convoy, HXS

(Facing) "**Keep 'em flying!**" **Getting the job done**
A woman fitter works on the Cheetah engine of an Anson aircraft at No. 2 Air Observation School in Edmonton in February 1943. During the Second World War, Canadian women proved themselves just as capable, if not more, than men in a variety of occupations that had previously been closed to them. PROVINCIAL ARCHIVES OF ALBERTA, BL 529/3

---

* In terms of surface ships in commission, the RCN was actually the third largest navy in the world after the American and British navies. The German *Kriegsmarine* was third largest in terms of warships in commission in 1945 but by 1944 most of its strength consisted of submarines. It is a little known fact that by the war's end the Canadian navy was larger than the Soviet navy, the Imperial Japanese Navy and every other Allied navy including the French and Italian fleets. Canada being Canada, however, the inevitable postwar cutbacks left the RCN with fewer ships in commission in 1946 than it had in 1939 and one of them was a former German U-boat.

Meet the navy

Canada's contribution to the Allied war effort was nothing short of astounding and perhaps the most amazing aspect was the Royal Canadian Navy. When war broke out in 1939, the infant RCN had 13 vessels in commission but when it ended in 1945, it had 434 and was the third largest navy, in terms of surface vessels, in the world. This view of the naval base at Halifax in August 1944 shows more warships in the dockyard than there were in the navy in 1939. Intrigued by what was, to them at least, an exotic service, 7,593 Albertans joined the RCN during the war. NAC, PA-115367

300, which departed New York in July 1944 and arrived safely in Liverpool with 167 merchant vessels carrying more than a million tons of war materiel, vehicles, supplies and oil.

The cost of the war to Canada, both in lives and dollars, was high. A total of 96,456 servicemen and women were killed in action, died of war-related causes, or were wounded. Of the 42,361 who died on active service, 2,024 served in the RCN, 22,917 in the army and 17,101 in the RCAF. Between 1939 and 1950, the nation spent 21.7 billion dollars directly on defence matters (the postwar expenditures being for demobilization costs). On the other hand, nine successive Victory Loan drives resulted in Canadian citizens and corporations providing 18 billion dollars for the war effort. As had happened in 1914-1918, Canada largely paid its own way in the Second World War.

The price, however, was partly offset by the benefits the war brought Canada. The nation that entered the war in 1939, still recovering from the Depression, with an economy based largely on agriculture and the provision of raw materials evolved, by 1945, into a modern industrial state with a broad manufacturing base which included textile and machinery production, automotive and aircraft production, and shipbuilding that left it in a very competitive position in the postwar world. Generally speaking, unlike the First World War, the entire nation enjoyed

benefits from the six war years. Average annual income, despite the imposition of wage controls by the government, nearly doubled between 1939 and 1945 while the cost of living – restrained by strict price controls – only rose 20% during the same period. Canadians were subjected to rationing but it was not nearly as severe as that imposed in Britain. Alcohol consumption was reduced and there were shortages of sugar, vegetables, fruits and milk, but a federal government study undertaken in 1944 revealed that Canadians were eating better that year then they had in 1939, and certainly better than they had in the worst years of the Depression. The biggest shortages and the subject of the greatest complaints concerned the scarcity of nylon, tires and gasoline, all of which were strictly regulated by government agencies.

In fact, almost every aspect of life was regulated. Under the overall imposition of the War Measures Act and a plethora of lesser legislation, the federal government controlled almost every activity in the nation. Government agencies were created to supervise wage and price controls, rationing, labour disputes, agriculture, housing, manufacturing, the provision and direction of labour to high priority industries and travel. Bureaucratic intrusion into the lives of Canadians was sometimes mildly annoying and sometimes more serious. Daylight Savings

Nature's bounty
As in the First World War, agriculture was an important part of Alberta's war effort although labour shortages hampered many farmers. Here, a happy farmer contemplates his harvest in September 1943. PROVINCIAL ARCHIVES OF ALBERTA, BL 639/6

Time, unpopular during the First World War and dropped after that conflict, was re-introduced and this time it became permanent. The alcohol content of beer, the so-called "Canadian standard" of 5.5% alcohol by volume, was reduced to 5% and has remained so ever since. In a more serious vein there was strict media censorship and the RCMP was vigilant in combatting espionage and keeping an eye on enemy aliens including German, Italian and Japanese nationals. There was not a little paranoia in wartime Canada. In 1942, an opposition Conservative Member of Parliament was nearly charged with high treason for daring to question the Liberal government's official report on the fiasco at Hong Kong in December 1941 where two battalions of half-trained and poorly-equipped Canadian troops were overrun by the Japanese, until it was pointed out by the courts that he was perfectly within his rights to do so. Perhaps the worst example of wartime paranoia was the harsh treatment accorded to Japanese-Canadians living on the Pacific coast. Fearing that they might provide intelligence and aid to Japan, they were deported *en masse* to labour camps on the prairies and their homes and property sold for a fraction of its value. It took more than forty years for these largely innocent people to receive compensation for their losses.

Alberta during the Second World War

As Canada went, so Alberta went, and the province prospered during the war. The demand for agricultural products, both crops and livestock, was high although farmers complained about the imposition of price controls. The agricultural sector also experienced a shortage of labour caused by the absence of men in uniform and competition from wartime industries which paid higher wages, but this was ameliorated by the use of new sources of labour, including women, interned foreign nationals, prisoners of war and the Japanese-Canadian community. Alberta's textile, mining and forestry industries experienced a boom in production and sales. By 1945, the Great Western Garment company in Edmonton had become the largest producer of uniforms in the British Commonwealth, and was turning out 25,000 articles of military clothing each week. The province's crucially-important oil industry was also operating at full capacity, particularly the wells in the Turner Valley, and for the first time, serious consideration was given to tapping the resources of the Athabasca oil sands at Fort McMurray. Defence spending increased Alberta's prosperity. No fewer than twenty establishments of the British Commonwealth Air Training Plan were located in the province, many in smaller communities such as Bowden, Claresholm, DeWinton, Pearce, Penhold, and

Women played an important role
During the Second World War, Canadian women played a crucial role in the armed forces, industry and agriculture. As the number of male family members engaged in farm work in Alberta dropped by 13.3% and the number of male farm hands by 40% during the conflict, women stepped in to fill the gap. PROVINCIAL ARCHIVES OF ALBERTA, BL. 639/51

So that men may serve – Canadian Women's Army Corps, 1943
All three services created women's organizations to release men for combat duty. There was some trepidation on the part of conservative senior officers but servicewomen soon proved indispensable and took over a variety of non-conventional tasks and trades. The Canadian Women's Army Corps had a major training centre at Vermilion, Alberta, and a detachment from that centre shows the flag during a baseball game at Renfrew Park, Edmonton, in August 1943. PROVINCIAL ARCHIVES OF ALBERTA, BL 635/5

Vulcan, which experienced an economic bonanza that created thousands of short and long term jobs directly or indirectly connected with these installations. Currie Barracks in Calgary underwent a massive expansion to become one of the largest military bases in the country. In this regard, special mention must be made of the CWAC basic training centre located at Vermilion which, by 1943, was turning out 300 woman soldiers a month.

Wartime industries lured many rural residents to the larger centres. The rural population declined from 61% to 55% while the populations of Calgary, Lethbridge and Medicine Hat dramatically increased during the war years, creating a desperate shortage of accommodation which was never eased despite rent controls and the release of building materials for "wartime housing" units. Of all the cities in the province, Edmonton was perhaps most affected by the war. In 1940 Canada and the United States agreed to set up a Permanent Joint Board of Defence as a means of cooperating in the defence of North America. When the Japanese attack on Pearl Harbor in December 1941 created fears that the Pacific coast and Alaska were threatened, the two nations undertook three major projects to improve the defences of the area: the construction of a highway from Edmonton to Fairbanks, Alaska; the construction of the North West Staging Route, a series of airfields to permit aircraft to fly into the area; and the construction of an oil pipeline from Norman Wells, Northwest Territories, to Whitehorse in the Yukon. These projects brought thousands of American servicemen and civilian workers into Edmonton and northern Alberta – an estimated 33,000 by 1943 – and employed many thousands of Canadians. Generally, the citizens of the two nations got along very well, the American Military Police established joint patrols with the Edmonton Police Force and Canadians admired the Americans' energy and generosity but were amused that, for "foreign service," the Yanks received both medals and a 35% pay bonus.

Construction on the Alaska Highway, the "Road to Tokyo," 1,523 miles of road from Edmonton to Fairbanks, commenced in the early summer of 1942 and was completed by the following November, thanks to the efforts of 27,000 military and civilian workers using 7,000 pieces of rolling equipment. Overnight, Blatchford Field at Edmonton became one of the busiest airports in the world, handling 860 aircraft on one hectic day in 1943.

When heavy traffic outstripped even its vastly-expanded facilities, the United States constructed another airport, the largest in the world at that time, at Namao, 10 miles north of Edmonton. Aircraft repair and assembly became a major industry in the city, employing 2,200 civilians, of whom 30% were women. Attracted by the opportunities, people flocked into Edmonton and – although accurate statistics are lacking – the population rose from an estimated 89,000 in 1939 to an estimated 138,000 by 1943. Accommodation was at a premium and, despite rent controls and government supervision, unscrupulous landlords made small fortunes by charging high rents for what were basically converted chicken coops and garages. The city managed to construct 350 wartime housing units but this was but a small portion of what was needed and the housing shortage remained critical throughout the war.

There was a darker side to this prosperity. With fathers overseas and mothers in factories or in other non-traditional employment, children were less strictly supervised and this led to behavioral and social problems. In the larger cities there was an increase in juvenile crime and a high rate of absenteeism in the school system. Police departments, undermanned because of competition for personnel both from the armed forces and highly-paid civilian jobs, were hard pressed throughout the war years although it was noted that there was a significant drop in serious crimes because so many men in the 18-30 age group, traditionally the group most prone to criminal activity, were absent in uniform. The divorce rate soared which can only be expected when couples, who had often married after knowing each other only a short time, were separated for years. As a case in point, the men of the Loyal Edmonton Regiment who went overseas with the 1st Division in December 1939 were only given leave to Canada in late 1944, five years after they had left the country, and not many made it back before the war ended.

There were ups and downs to wartime prosperity but, unlike the First World War, which gave rise to the influenza epidemic, the Second World War only directly touched Alberta once in the late winter and early spring of 1945 when the province came under Japanese attack. The weapon system used was the rather curious one of incendiary balloons, fitted with explosive charges that would explode on landing, in an attempt to set massive fires

Heavy traffic – Edmonton Municipal Airport, 1942

During the war, as the air gateway to Alaska, the Edmonton Municipal Airport became one of the busiest in the world, handling a record 860 flights on one day in 1943. In this view, taken in 1942, can be seen Anson trainer aircraft, B-25 bombers, C-47 transports and Aircobra fighters, the latter on their way to the Soviet Union as part of the Allied lend-lease programme. PROVINCIAL ARCHIVES OF ALBERTA, A-5300

(Right) Edmonton, gateway to the North: The beginning of the Alaska Highway

On a cold day in March 1943 four American soldiers pose at what purports to be the beginning of the Alaska Highway at the south end of the 109th Street Bridge in Edmonton. In the background can be seen the bridge over the North Saskatchewan River and the Provincial Legislature Building. Actually, this was not the beginning of the highway, which was a few hundred yards away, but the photographer took a separate shot of the sign and then pasted it in here. PROVINCIAL ARCHIVES OF ALBERTA, BL 456/1

in the western forests of North America. Some 9,300 of these balloons were sent winging across the Pacific from February to April 1945 and, of these, about 20 either landed in Alberta or were spotted flying over the province. Although they did create some excitement, it was not well known at the time because wartime censorship meant that very few people, other than those in the armed forces and police, were even aware of the existence of Japan's secret weapon.

Two RCAF Mosquito fighter-bomber aircraft, stationed at the Lethbridge airfield for purposes of interception, scrambled in April 1945 when one balloon was spotted flying over the town and managed to shoot it down. Even more amazing was the incident involving a farmer near Foremost who, hearing his cattle bawling, investigated and found some of his livestock tangled up in the webbing of what he assumed to be a government weather balloon. He freed the animals and removed what he thought was the recording device and threw it in the toolbox in his truck. A

"Hi-ho, hi-ho, it's off to work we roll": Building the Alaska Highway

Heavy machinery moves through Alberta on its way to the Alaska Highway in November 1942. This massive project, which employed an estimated 27,000 workers for six months, resulted in a land link between Edmonton and Fairbanks, Alaska. PROVINCIAL ARCHIVES OF ALBERTA, BL 484/2

DON'T LET THIS HAPPEN !

It is time for action . . . Right now, enemy bombers lurk closer to Edmonton than ever before. Don't wait for your home . . . your business to be blasted to destruction . . . do your part to hold and drive back these threatening monsters by lending more and more money to supply our fighting men with more ships . . . more guns and more planes.

Buy **WAR SAVINGS CERTIFICATES** *Regularly !*

Space donated by **THE BREWING INDUSTRY OF ALBERTA**

Alberta under attack

It never quite got this bad and the greatest threat to the province during the war was Japanese incendiary balloons, which caused no injuries. Beer was one casualty, however, as the "Canadian Standard" of 5.5% alcohol by volume was reduced to 5% as a temporary austerity measure. Like such other "temporary wartime measures" as income tax and Daylight Savings Time, the reduction in the strength of Canadian beer became permanent. PROVINCIAL MUSEUM OF ALBERTA

level the detachment office" and "might also damage the telephone," and dispatched a bomb disposal squad to remove it.[2] The balloon attack did very little real damage as many of the items malfunctioned and – an indication of faulty Japanese intelligence – the forests were too wet in the late winter and early spring to be vulnerable. Nonetheless, balloons came down all over Western North America and were still being discovered more than a quarter of a century after the war ended.

"Socks for Soldiers": Life in wartime Alberta

If wartime life in Alberta can be summarized in one word, it was "organized" – both on the job and at home. Voluntary service organizations such as the IODE, Red Cross, Knights of Columbus, Salvation Army, Women's Institutes and many smaller organizations created drives to provide "Bundles for Britain," "Milk for Britain," "Socks for Britain," "Jam for Britain," "Seeds for Britain," the "Emergency War Fund, "the Russian Fund," the "China Fund," the "Overseas Cigarettes" and "Home Comforts" funds for the troops, the "Navy League" Fund," the Canadian War Services Fund and numerous "Buy an Aircraft" funds. There was an organization for everyone and it seems everyone on the home front was in an organization and working to collect money and other things including scrap metal ("Scrap Hitler with Scrap") and fats and bones ("Every Kitchen is an Arsenal"). Knitting circles abounded including one in Edmonton that produced 500 pairs of "Socks for Soldiers" each month.

All this activity paled, however, beside the effort put into the nine wartime Victory Loan campaigns which raised funds for the war effort. Everybody who was anybody in government, the armed forces or the entertainment industry participated in these campaigns, including a rather shy Major Dave Currie, VC, who duly made the rounds of factories and service clubs in the spring of 1945, doing his bit for the 8th Victory Loan. For those who could not afford to purchase war bonds, there were War Savings Certificates and War Savings Stamps in smaller denominations.

Life at home was not quite as grim as it had been in the First World War. The 1940s were the "Golden Age" of radio – and there was a radio in most Albertan homes by this time – bringing a wide variety of programmes including news, music (Benny Goodman, the Andrews Sisters, Guy Lombardo, Harry James and Glen Miller to name but a few), drama ("The Shadow" and "The Green Lantern") and comedy ("Jack Benny" and "Amos and Andy"). The BBC, which operated the Allied Expeditionary Forces Programming overseas, carried "Home News from Canada" nightly at 10.00 P.M. and programmes daily to appeal to Canadian military audiences: "Calling all Canadians;" "The Canada Show," "The RCAF Streamliners," "The Canada

few weeks later he entered the RCMP detachment at Foremost and, depositing the offending object on the desk of a mounted police corporal, gave him precise and profane instructions as to exactly what the Canadian government and the Royal Canadian Mounted Police could do with an apparatus that so disturbed a man's livestock. The police corporal, who did not know of the existence of the Japanese onslaught, phoned his superior at Lethbridge to request instructions and described the curious item sitting in front of him. The superior (who was knowledgeable about the balloons) calmly told the corporal that "he was holding a demolition charge which, if it exploded, probably would

Swing Show," and the "Canada Sing Show" as well as "Johnny Canuck's Review." The BBC also conducted interviews with Canadian soldiers overseas which were re-broadcast in Canada by the CBC and those listening on Monday evening, 4 December 1944, would have heard Major David Currie, just decorated with the Victoria Cross, explain to them what it meant for him and his regiment. Then as now, the most popular item was "Hockey Night In Canada" by which silver-tongued Foster Hewitt brought the National Hockey League into homes across the country and Canadians followed the progress of the Montreal Canadiens and their gifted young forward, Maurice ("Rocket") Richard, as he cut through Leaf defence lines like a knife through butter. It took Toronto nearly two years to do it but, by the spring of 1945 just as the war was ending, the Leafs finally figured out a way to slow down the "flying Frenchman" and won the Stanley Cup that year. On Monday, 6 June 1944, many Canadians listened as Prime Minister Mackenzie King addressed them and stressed that "the hearts of all in Canada today be filled with a silent prayer for the success of our own Allied forces and for the early liberation of the people of Europe."[3]

Outside the home, with money in their pockets for the first time in years, Albertans looked for ways to spend it. Restaurants, bowling alleys, dance and pool halls and soda fountains were full, as were bars and beer joints (sales of alcohol were rationed but there was no attempt at prohibition during the Second World War), and such was the demand that many municipalities permitted such establishments to open on Sunday. It was difficult to find a hotel room, even more difficult to get a cab and there was a shortage of people willing to work in the traditionally underpaid service industry – waiters and waitresses were at a premium and society matrons in Calgary complained that it was nearly impossible to obtain domestic servants. Dances were the most popular of all social activities and an examination of the War Diary of the South Alberta Regiment between 1940 and 1946 reveals that, unless the unit was in combat or had just moved into a new station, they held on average a dance every two weeks during those six years. The SAR staged its first dance a few days after it was concentrated for basic training in Edmonton in June 1940 and its last on the platform of the CPR station in Winnipeg while on its way back to Alberta in January 1946. In this, the SAR was no different than any other unit in the army, nor did it differ from the airforce or navy, and in any week during the war there was always a serviceman's dance being held somewhere in the province.

The other popular form of entertainment was the picture shows – two full-length features, cartoons and a newsreel, all for 15 cents or less. Unfortunately, apart from some of the classic British wartime productions such as "In Which We Serve," "Mrs. Miniver," "One of Our Planes is Missing" and "The Way Ahead," (the latter featuring a dapper British infantry lieutenant named David Niven and a slovenly but incredibly-talented private named Peter Ustinov) most of the film fare came from Hollywood which cranked out movies that reflected American tastes and beliefs on an assembly line basis. Hollywood did go so far as to get James Cagney into the RCAF in "Captains of the Clouds," which featured a clip of Air Vice Marshal William ("Billy") Bishop giving a pep talk to new recruits, and to parachute lantern-jawed Randolph Scott onto the bridge of a Canadian warship in "Corvette K-229" which actually included some footage shot in wartime Halifax, but that was about as far as it was prepared to go to cater to Canadian audiences. Other than that, fully convinced that Canada was populated by red-coated mounties, moose and check-shirted lumberjacks who spoke only French, Hollywood acted accordingly.

The Canadian press tried to make up for this attitude by finding or inventing a national connection with the leading ladies of the big screen. The 1940s were the classic age of the pin-up and Canadian newspapers delighted in publishing revealing photographs of actresses complete with rather trite commentary such as: "The name is Alexis Smith … she was born in Penticton, BC … she now is a Warner Brothers star … but hey, who's interested in facts when there's a figure like that handy?"[4] Alexis Smith, Yvonne de Carlo (also born in British Columbia) and Anne Rutherford (born in Toronto), were Canadian by birth, which was fine, but the media also attempted to claim any starlet who happened to have spent more than a week in Canada for one reason or another.

"I never cried one tear where anyone could see me": Keeping in touch

As in the First World War, mail was the means by which those Albertans who waited could keep in contact with their family members overseas and, throughout the war, the Canadian Post Office rendered yeoman service. In this as in everything else connected with the war effort, the statistics were nothing short of amazing – by the end of the war, 4,500,000 pieces of mail were being sent overseas from Canada each month. Christmas was always the busiest time as Canadians tried to ensure that their servicemen and women were not forgotten. During the Christmas season of 1943, the Post Office handled 8 million letters, 10 million pounds of parcel post, 2 million pounds of tobacco products and 308,400 pounds of newspapers. Many of the holiday presents were routinely marked, "Do not open until the 25th," a caution that was just as routinely ignored by recipients. Service personnel were subject to censorship and regulations forbade soldiers to make any criticism of the war effort or their superiors, or to discuss military operations, which more or less left the weather, food and the last letter from home as the only safe topics of conversation. Couples invented elaborate codes to discuss intimate matters, and acronyms such as SWALK (Sealed With a Loving Kiss) and BOLTOP (Better on Lips Than On Paper) were among the more innocent ways of expressing affection before the prying eyes of the censor. The "Green Envelope," as the "Active Service Army Privilege Envelope" was known, re-appeared and every soldier overseas was issued a limited number of these items which permitted him to enclose a maximum of three let-

THE LIGHTER SIDE: MILITARY CARTOONISTS AT WAR

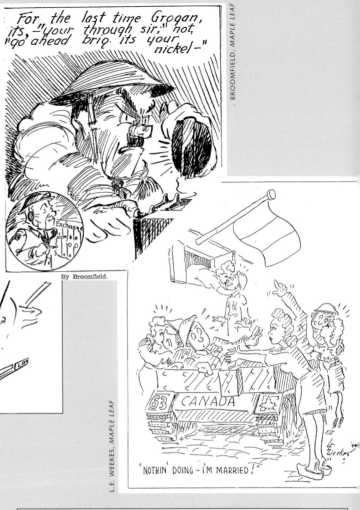

For the last time Grogan, its "your through sir," not "go ahead brig. its your nickel—"

By Broomfield.

DAMNED PEASHOOTERS!

REORGANIZATION. The men did not welcome the change-over from the 105 mm (S.P.) to the 25 pdr towed gun.

PATRICK CLAY, 13TH FIELD REGIMENT

"NOTHIN' DOING — I'M MARRIED!"

FAMOUS LAST-WORDS

"THIS IS DEFINITELY THE LAST JOB, AND THEN THE DIV GOES OUT FOR A REST!"

"COULD BE OUR OWN MEDIUMS LANDING SHORT!" (CALAIS, SEPT 1944)

"YEAH, IT'LL BE OVER BY OCTOBER!" (FALAISE POCKET, AUG. 1944)

"SOMEBODY'S GOING TO GET HELL!" (14 AUG. 1944)

OPERATION 'RELAX'

FOR FOUR DAYS THE BOYS WERE LEFT TO THEIR OWN DE-'VICES'!

"HIC! HOW DID I GET HERE!"

A QUIET TIME WAS HAD BY ALL — EVEN THE CHAUDS!

JUST CHARACTERS!!

GHENT OPENED HER DOORS WIDE TO US!

WELCOME

The Second World War produced a crop of military cartoonists who helped, through their sense of humour, to make the unbearable almost bearable. In this selection, taken from the histories of 12th and 13th Field Regiments and *Maple Leaf,* the newspaper of First Canadian Army, cartoonists portray the lighter side of life in the wartime army.

Opposite, Lieutenant Patrick Clay expresses the feelings of the gunners of 13th Field when they had to give up their self-propelled 105 mm guns for 25-pdrs. while Sergeant J. Daimer of 12th Field Regiment comments on latrine rumours and leave in Ghent and L.E. Weekes of the *Maple Leaf* underlines proper radio procedure and the perils of being a liberator. Below, Clay records the gradual progress of command post fashions, Weekes comments on German demolitions and Les Callan portrays one of the advantages of night patrols and the sudden popularity of francophone Canadian soldiers in Normandy.

AW — NOW JEAN BAPTISTE YOU KNOW I'M YER PAL ASK HER CAN I COME AROUND TOMORROW THEN TELL HER I'M A SWELL GUY EH ?

YOU KNOW THAT LUGER YOU BEEN WANTIN' BATEESE ?

"LEETLE BATEESE" IN THE DRIVER'S SEAT

BOTH: LES CALLAN, *MAPLE LEAF*

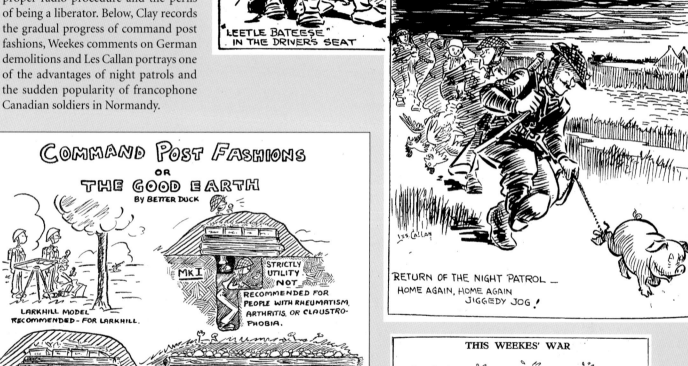

RETURN OF THE NIGHT PATROL — HOME AGAIN, HOME AGAIN JIGGEDY JOG !

COMMAND POST FASHIONS
OR
THE GOOD EARTH
BY BETTER DUCK

LARKHILL MODEL RECOMMENDED - FOR LARKHILL.

MK I
STRICTLY UTILITY. NOT RECOMMENDED FOR PEOPLE WITH RHEUMATISM, ARTHRITIS, OR CLAUSTROPHOBIA.

MK II
AS FOR MK I BUT DOUBLE CAPACITY. PRIVACY ENSURED.

MK III DELUXE MODEL - REQUISITIONED FROM WEHMACHT - TENDENCY TO DEVELOP INTO FLOPHOUSE - POKER DEN. MAYBE SHARED BY RATS (NOT WATER).

WHAM

MK IV ★ SAME, AMENDED.

MK IV - MODERN, UP-TO-DATE.. ALL THE COMFORTS OF HOME... WITH THAT ADDED TANG OF DANGER...

NIX IN DE WINKEL ALLES IN DE KELDER !
(WITH APOLOGIES FOR THE SPELLING)

PATRICK CLAY, 13TH FIELD REGIMENT

THIS WEEKES' WAR

BELGIUM

" HEY - YOU KNOW THAT CANAL BRIDGE ? - WELL ITS GONE !"

L.E. WEEKES, MAPLE LEAF

323

ters which were not censored, although random checks were routinely made. Gunner John Raycroft of 13th Field Regiment, a non-smoker, traded his cigarette ration for "Green Envelopes" and sent all his letters home in them.

Many couples were in the position of Corporal Myrtle ("Andy") Clipperton, CWAC, and her husband, Corporal Robert Clipperton from Hayter, Alberta, who fought with the SAR. The two met when both were serving at A-27 Recce School at Dundurn, Saskatchewan and when Bob was posted overseas in the summer of 1943, Andy wrote him every few days for the next two and a half years. Their correspondence, which has survived, provides an interesting insight into the trials and tribulations of a young couple separated by war.[5]

Andy to Bob, 17 July 1943 (First overseas letter)
The kids [her CWAC comrades] are so darn swell to me. They never mention you going away or anything, & I can't talk about you at all. I got your note but couldn't read it till night though, but don't worry, I never cried one tear where anyone could see me. I saw you go through a couple of times in the orderly room but thought it best for us both if I didn't speak to you. Short and Irene are here in the recreation room writing letters …… They've changed all the records on the Wurlitzer again & I'm glad. Some of them reminded me too much of you. ……

Andy to Bob, 25 July 43
You can't guess who I went to town [Saskatoon] with yesterday – Kay – we did some shopping & saw the show, "Ships in the Atlantic," with Humphrey Bogart. It was blood thirsty but

Happy Albertans
Whether it was weak or not, these happy fellows in an Edmonton bar appear to be enjoying their beer. After the long, grim years of the depression, the war brought prosperity to the province and, for the first time in many years, Albertans had money to spend on entertainment and luxuries. PROVINCIAL ARCHIVES OF ALBERTA, PA 610/1

sad & exciting. We came home at 11 p.m. in a Staff car with Cpl. Cave. I wanted to knit you a sweater so bad & it would have given me something to work at but we walked & walked even over to the west side & couldn't get any yarn. They just don't sell yarn any more. ……

Bob to Andy [August 43]
I am proud to say that I am the only guy of our draft who has heard from home. I think you had better stay where you are & not try to come over here as I don't think the war is going to last much longer. …… It sure picks up your spirits when you hear the planes going over for a couple of hours steady cause you know they have it coming. ……

Andy to Bob, 2 November 1943
Every one who bought a Victory Bond has a half holiday in town tomorrow & a free ride thrown in. …… We had a Lieut. Col. of the CWAC here yesterday and she gave us a talk. She said that we girls joined the army to release a man for overseas service, and so very few girls were sent over. She said they may send more over later & the ones to be picked would be the ones with the longest service & with clean crime sheets. ……

Bob to Andy, 13 January 1944
I went up to see the Imeson boys last weekend & we had a real old Hayter re-union. ……. I haven't heard from anyone at home. I never knew a thing about Mother having an operation. Good thing you keep writing or I wouldn't know I belonged to Canada. ……

Andy to Bob, [January 1944]
There has been a lot of romance sliding around here lately, in rather queer forms. Well, let's see now. Remember about the night when I told you about C. crying her heart out. Well I guess I can tell you about that now. It seems all the girls tell me their troubles. Well just as I expected, C. was pregnant. She was lucky the guy married her but the other girl in the same shape went to Saskatoon on a weekend & what she had done …… the poor kid was sick for a couple of weeks, I don't know how she stood it. I was the only girl who knew what was wrong with her. ……

Bob to Andy, 26 February 1944
Jerry came over about 10 o'clock and there was a dog fight right over camp. They shot him down and we could see the tracers. …… They put the searchlight on it as it came down & it was just a red glow going to beat hell & we could see the pilot bail out & his parachute open. …… I am glad that you are not here as last night, the glow over London lit up our camp and we are 40 miles away. Under no circumstances should you come over here unless you can't help it. ……

Andy to Bob, 22 April 1944
I was a blood donor again today. I have a button now. I tried to buy a Victory bond but no one had time to sell me one this afternoon. I wasn't going to buy one but then I thought Gee the money from my bond may buy the shell that saves your life & same with the blood donation. ......

Bob to Andy, 6 June 1944
I can tell you now that it's a great day & I am thinking of you always. Don't wonder & worry, just pray that we will be together in the near future ...... Just keep writing as often as you have. You've really kept my morale up with your regular letters & regardless of how often you hear from me, keep them coming. ......

Andy to Bob, 13 August 1944
This morning Enid & Maudie & I sat in the Area Canteen & played the Wurlitzer. Have you heard "I'll Be Seeing You"? It's one of my favourites. I was lucky enough to get 4 chocolate bars last night & 3 today. Three are your favourites "Crispy Krunch." They are for the next parcel. ......

Bob to Andy, 23 August 1944
I was in my first town with the whole population there & not a bombed building & were those people happy! They threw flowers on the tanks & brought wine out to us as we went through. ...... Another thing you will have to get someone to kill your chickens cause I will never pull another trigger ... as long as I live after the war. ......

Andy to Bob, 8 September 1944
Our new Col. is pretty swell. Today a boy on leave wired in "Having a wonderful time. Request 48 hours extension." They brought it in to the C.O. & he sent out a note for Anne to wire him back, "Congratulations on your wonderful time. We are all envious of you & wish we were with you. Extension granted." ...... Another time, a Cpl. on marriage leave wired back "It's lovely here. Please grant 4 days extension." The Col. wired back, "It's lovely anywhere. Extension not granted." ......

Bob to Andy, 13 September 1944
I've seen most of the boys from Hayter this week & they are all o.k. We have a saying here, "it isn't the shell with your name on it that worries you – it's the one marked TO WHOM IT MAY CONCERN. ......

Andy to Bob, 11 November 1944
It's a nice quiet Saturday afternoon – well not exactly? There are three radios on at this end of the Cwackery all blaring out a different tune & umpteen dozen girls running & squealing in all different outfits. I should talk – I'm wearing my issue sweater with my pyjama bottoms. I was going to throw the raggy looking box I keep my curlers in away tonight but then I noted that you had written your name all over it when we were on furlough, & I can't bring myself to throw it away. ......

Bob to Andy, 12 November 1944
Keep happy & remember that somewhere in Holland this man of yours is doing his best to get the war over & back to you. Also don't forget the prayers as it must be them that is keeping me the way I am. ......

Andy to Bob, 22 December 1944
It's getting awfully close to Christmas. All the kids have gone on leave & there are only ten girls left in our hut. Guess what I got? A sterling silver brooch with an SAR badge on it. I wear it on my tie. The way the war news is going I sure have been doing plenty of worrying about you. I hope your Christmas won't be too awful. ......

Bob to Andy, 21 February 1945
This is supposed to be my anniversary letter but though I am a bit behind (I don't mean the front line either). I sent you some flowers & hope you get them & like them. Every time I want to write a letter I have to be on the move or something. ...... There may be a let up in my letters but I will try to get a couple away a week to you & don't go worrying about me if you don't hear from me, so be calm & write as often as you can. ......

Andy to Bob, 25 February 1945
I wonder where little Edwards is? Remember the time we rode home from the wiener roast & he drove slow & stopped the truck a few times so we would have longer together? I was wishing the engine would fall out but those things never happen except in dreams or stories. Staff Q. asked me to go out today & Sgt. S. asked me three times yesterday – he doesn't give up easy. ......

Bob to Andy, 5 May 1945
At 8 a.m. this morning the Jerries called it quits and don't think we weren't happy. There was more ammunition fired off to celebrate than any battle we have ever been in! ......

Andy to Bob, 9 May 1945
Can't tell you how happy I am about V-E Day. Mostly because it means you are out of danger. I have worried terribly about you, especially in the last month or two & I've lost 15 lbs. We had a holiday yesterday & a celebration Monday night, church service Monday noon and last night a dance. I had a great time & it was because my heart has been lighter in the last two days than it has for months. It's really so exciting. I realize that it may be quite some time before you get home but I'm being optimistic & I'm not banking on you going to

the Pacific. ...... I've felt all along that it was part of a bargain I had with God that if I "waited" for you the way you'd like me to, then he would keep you safe for me. ......

There was one communication that everyone dreaded receiving – a telegram with the fatal opening phrase, "The Minister of National Defence sincerely regrets to inform you that ...". When they did come, family and friends gathered round to provide comfort and support. Corporal Clipperton recorded what happened when one of her woman comrades was informed that her husband had been killed in action:

It's funny, she & I never did chum together at all but when Nester was killed & the C.O. called her into his office to tell her, she asked for me right away & she wouldn't let me leave her at all. ...... Cpl. Lloyd drove her and I, in the Col's staff car, to Yorkton, where his folks live & she had to tell them. ..... I never had to do anything like that before & the kids felt sorry for me as it was harder on me than it would have been on some of the others because I felt that there but by the Grace of God go I. That day when I came out of the O.C.'s office, I tried to tell Staff Hill & I started to cry & couldn't speak – the place was full of guys too. Most of them figured it was you who had been lost. Hell of a war.[6]

"Every form of persuasion that could be thought of": The conscription crisis, 1944

Andy Clipperton was right – it certainly was a hell of a war and and it was costing thousands of lives, many of them Canadian. These losses eventually led to a crisis for the Liberal government which, although it had been released by 1942 plebiscite from its promise not to impose conscription for overseas service, had never attempted to impose it. Instead, trying to dodge the issue lest there be another repetition of the riots of 1918 which had nearly torn the country apart because Quebec in the 1940s was just as dead set against overseas conscription as English Canada was for it, Prime Minister Mackenzie King had steered a tricky course under the credo of "conscription if necessary but not necessarily conscription." He was successful for almost two years although his policy created two distinctly different types of Canadian soldiers: the general or active service volunteer who would fight overseas and the soldier drafted for home defence under the National Resources Mobilization Act of 1940 – the infamous "Zombie," who was not required to serve outside Canada.

The origin of this crisis, which was played out in late 1944, was a shortage of trained infantry replacements. It had arisen because Lieutenant-General Kenneth Stuart, who held the appointment of chief of the general staff during the army's expansion in 1941-1943, had taken British figures, based on that nation's experience in North Africa, as a basis for planning for replacements for casualties. The intensity of the fighting in Italy,

particularly at the vicious battle for Ortona in December 1943, revealed that the British figures were too low, with the result that 1 Canadian Corps in Italy began to run short of infantrymen. Rather than admit the error and take the necessary steps to correct it, Stuart, who by this time was chief of staff at Canadian Military Headquarters in London, compounded it by attempting to cover it up. Although his staff were concerned, in view of the forthcoming invasion of Normandy, Stuart forebade any communication going from London to Ottawa on the subject of manpower problems, ensuring that neither the government nor National Defence Headquarters were aware of the matter. Instead, he tried to remuster troops to the infantry from other arms, with mixed success and, although he finally admitted to Ottawa that there was a potential shortfall in infantry, he was confident that there would be enough men to replace expected casualties in the first four months of fighting after D-Day. Heavy fighting and heavy losses in Normandy during the summer exacerbated the matter, escalating it into a crisis, but Stuart kept sending optimistic reports to Ottawa based on fudged figures, while at the same time hoping for an early end to the war before the shortfall became known in high places. The situation kept getting worse. By 31 August 1944, First Canadian Army was short of 4,318 riflemen and at this point Stuart gave up trying to conceal matters and warned Ottawa that the army had a very real problem. Unfortunately, the Minister of Defence, J.L. Ralston, lulled by the previous eight months of optimistic lies, did not realize how serious was that problem.

The government and the Canadian public learned of the matter in mid-September 1944 when Major Conn Smythe, a prominent sports figure who had returned to Canada to convalesce from wounds suffered in Normandy, issued a statement to the press. Smythe not only stressed that there was a shortage of infantry in Europe, but that such replacements as were reaching frontline units were "green, inexperienced and poorly trained," and that "large number of casualties result from this greenness, both to the rookies and the older soldiers who have the added task of trying to look after the newcomers as well as themselves."[7] In Smythe's opinion, the only solution was to send the large numbers of trained NRMA personnel, the Zombies, to fight overseas, and he urged that Canadians "insist that no more money be spent on well-trained soldiers in this country except to send them to the battlefronts" and that voters, who had voted overwhelmingly in the 1942 plebiscite in favour of overseas conscription "should insist on the government carrying out the will of the people." This truly set the cat among the pigeons and caused an uproar across Canada and consternation in Ottawa, where the Liberal government was caught in a dilemma very much of its own making.

Ralston immediately departed on a trip to Europe to interview senior Canadian officers. What he learned troubled him and, concluding that if drastic steps were not taken, the pool of trained infantry replacements would be exhausted by the end of 1944, he urged the cabinet to send NRMA personnel to Europe

Joint patrol – Edmonton police and American MPs, 1943
By 1943, there were thousands of American servicemen in Edmonton and, although they were usually well behaved, the U.S. Army provided MPs to assist the municipal police. Generally, the Edmonton Police dealt with Canadians and the MPs with Americans, although both forces had the power of detention over the nationals of the other country. PROVINCIAL ARCHIVES OF ALBERTA, BL 625/1

cophone) had for years resisted volunteering and were not likely to change their mind at this late date. Brigadier F.M. Harvey, commanding Military District 13, who had won the VC as a cavalry officer during the First World War, informed the new minister that his NRMA personnel frankly did not believe that the government needed them overseas, otherwise it would order them to serve there. Major-General George Pearkes, another holder of the VC who commanded on the Pacific coast, was more blunt and told McNaughton that "the reason the men do not go active is because they do not want to go Overseas."[9]

Senior staff pointed out that, the previous April, a determined "gloves off" campaign to get the NRMA personnel in 13th Infantry Brigade, one of the better home defence formations as it had seen service during the invasion of the Aleutians, had been a dismal failure, getting only 769 volunteers from a total enlisted strength of 2,432. The brigade commander reported that his officers had

used every form of persuasion that could be thought of – interviews, discussions, sermons, films, speeches. We have appealed to their pride, to their manhood, to their patriotism and even to their self-interest. Be we have NOT used threats or intimidation nor subjected these men to extra fatigues or menial duties. On the contrary they have been employed throughout in properly organized training – no more arduous than that carried on by divisions of the army overseas, for the past 3 or 4 years. As I have personally told them the only discrimination has been that represented by the General Service badge on the arm of the volunteer, and all that badge implies.[10]

This same officer also underlined the essential difference between the active service and NRMA personnel and the tensions between the two:

It is not too much to say that the volunteer soldier in many cases literally despises the NRMA soldier. And it is an interesting psychological fact that when an NRMA man enlists [in the active service force] he frequently changes his own attitude to his former comrades with startling and even amusing suddenness and completeness.

The volunteer feels himself a man quite apart from the NRMA man. He regards himself as a free man who had the courage to make a decision. He seldom takes the trouble to analyze the manifold reasons put forward by those who won't enlist. He lumps them all together as no more than feeble excuses masking cowardice, selfishness and bad citizenship. In many cases no doubt he is right. In others he is wrong, but the fact remains that the antipathy between the two classes of soldiers starts right in the barrack room.[11]

This was to the point, and it is clear that the bad relations between the two types of Canadian soldiers, present through-

– in other words, the conscripts would go overseas. This did not please Mackenzie King who feared that such a move would "lead to spurts of civil war" and, still worse in King's mind, grave consequences for the Liberal party as it might cause the creation of a Union government as had happened in 1917 – and that, King determined "will not take place under me."[8] When several senior members of the cabinet indicated support for Ralston on the issue, King worried that there was a conspiracy to oust him and he initiated an intricate series of political manoeuvres culminating in Ralston's resignation on 1 November 1944. He was succeeded by General Andrew McNaughton, the former overseas commander. McNaughton, who believed that a determined campaign to get the NRMA soldiers to volunteer for active service would solve the problem, was far more acceptable to King in the important defence portfolio.

It is not certain where McNaughton, who had been away from military circles for more than a year, got the idea that the Zombies would volunteer in large numbers for active service and, in any case, military staff and senior commanders across the country soon disabused him of the notion. He was told that, although 54,434 men conscripted since 1940 under the National Resources Mobilization Act had gone active, the remainder, who in late 1944 amounted to 68,676 (of whom only 37% were fran-

Making do – 18-pdr gun detachment, Sarcee Camp, 1943
During the early years of the war, a shortage of weapons meant that Canadian gunners had to train on First War vintage 18-pdr. guns mounted on more modern carriages. As wartime production got into gear, these were replaced in the active units by the standard 25-pdr. but the militia artillery was forced to use the older weapons. Here, a gun detachment from an Alberta militia artillery unit trains at Sarcee Camp in August 1943. PROVINCIAL ARCHIVES OF ALBERTA, BL 618/15

out the war, began to worsen after the army entered sustained combat operations in 1943. In July 1944, a large-scale brawl, involving 150 infantrymen who resorted to rifles and bayonets, broke out at Currie Barracks in Calgary when active servicemen taunted their NRMA counterparts by singing the "Zombie Song" quoted at the beginning of this chapter. Officers and military police were able to separate the two groups before deaths or serious injuries resulted but, from that time on, NRMA recruits received their basic infantry training at Sarcee Camp, leaving Currie Barracks for active service personnel. The women soldiers of the CWAC, all active service volunteers, particularly despised NRMA personnel and, after a number of incidents that came perilously close to direct disobedience, the army removed Zombie NCOs from appointments where they had authority over CWAC personnel. Even federal civil servants disliked the NRMA soldiers and there was trouble in the greatly expanded Army Headquarters in Ottawa when NRMA NCOs were placed in supervisory positions over civilian staff.

The task facing McNaughton would have daunted a lesser man but he was determined to find the needed shortfall in infantry replacements – which he now knew to be 15,000 riflemen – from NRMA volunteers. A determined three-week national recruiting campaign conducted in the latter part of November 1944, however, resulted in only 3,626 Zombies going active service. This was bad enough but even worse was the fact that senior area and district commanders who, for four years had attempted to carry out a disastrous personnel policy which they knew would not work, began to contemplate resignation. The first to go was Brigadier R.A. MacFarlane of Military District 10 in Manitoba and McNaughton feared that others would follow. As he informed the prime minister, if the army's senior officers, "one after the other, began to resign, the whole military machine would run down, begin to disintegrate and there would be no controlling the situation."[12] Confessing that the failure of voluntary methods was like a "body blow," McNaughton regretfully informed King that overseas conscription was now a necessity.

The time had come for Mackenzie King to make the decision that he had been avoiding for more than four years. Although the wily prime minister, always somewhat nervous about the military, suspected that they also might be cooking up a plot against him, he was secretly relieved as he could blame the army for the failure of voluntary methods. He was now forced to impose a policy that was distasteful but which had to be done to preserve Liberal control of the government because William Lyon Mackenzie King was, if anything, a political animal and he promptly made an about face. As one historian has put it, the "interests of the ruling party now seemed to demand conscription just as stridently as they had formerly demanded a continuance of the voluntary system to the last possible minute."[13] This being the case, King drafted an Order-in-Council dated 23 November 1944 authorizing the dispatch of 16,000 NRMA troops to Europe. Four days later, the Liberals survived what amounted to a vote of confidence in the House of Commons, with a sizeable part of the Quebec wing of the party voting against the government but, in the end, it was done – the Zombies were going overseas.

"Greeted by loud cheers": The end of the 31st Alberta Reconnaissance Regiment, 1944-1945

The crisis was not over yet. When the orders came down to send NRMA personnel to Europe, there were near mutinies in some units and widespread desertion which, unfortunately affected the 31st Alberta Reconnaissance Regiment. We left 31st Recce just after they made a long journey by road from British Columbia to the newly-constructed Wainwright Camp in June 1944, where they had three months of excellent training, sometimes interrupted by terrible weather. It is ironic that, by the time this period had ended, 31st Recce was probably better trained than many units that had been in Britain for years, but had suffered from the lack of proper facilities in that crowded little island. In

Militia at Sarcee Camp 1943

During the war years the Alberta militia continued to function as a training organization for the active service units and as a secondary line of defence in case of invasion. Unit strengths were generally good and equipment got better as the war went on. Here, an infantry battalion, probably the Edmonton Fusiliers, marches into Sarcee Camp in the summer of 1943. Note the Rockies in the distance. PROVINCIAL ARCHIVES OF ALBERTA, BL 618/3

October 1944 the 31st returned to Vernon, BC, where they began to undertake familiarization with new equipment – the Fox Mk I armoured car which would replace their wretched Otter light cars in November, and Lynx scout cars to replace their universal carriers. They also received twelve Wasp flame-thrower carriers and each of the three squadrons deployed a troop of these vehicles.

On November 23, Lieutenant-Colonel H.H. Riley held a regimental parade and announced the government's decision to send conscripts overseas. In the week that followed, the officers and NCOs of the unit, all active service personnel, were proud that not a single NRMA soldier of 31st Recce participated in a number of anti-conscription marches staged by the Zombies of other units in downtown New Westminster. On 28 November, Riley received the word that his regiment would be sent to Britain and, when he assembled his officers in their mess to inform them of this news, it "was greeted by loud cheers followed by a 31st Recce toast."[14] On 1 December Riley informed the enlisted men of the news and asked each troop leader to personally interview every NRMA man in his troop to see if he would volunteer for active service. Unfortunately, as the War Diary recorded, the results "were not as good as had been expected."[15] Throughout December and early January, while the unit continued to train intensively and prepare for embarkation, more Zombies volunteered for active service, but the greater part of the NRMA troopers steadfastly refused to do so although there was no desertion. On 16 January 1945, all ranks received two weeks embarkation leave and, on the last day of the month, the unit re-assembled at Debert Camp in Nova Scotia, ready for embarkation.

To his horror, Riley discovered that, for the voyage, his unit, 503 all ranks strong, was to be increased by 1,773 additional NRMA personnel because it was to serve as a transit unit. In other words, he and his officers were to act as babysitters for Zombies being sent to Europe. These unhappy newcomers, from units from across Canada, proved to be insolent, unreliable, undisciplined and slovenly soldiers. Riley and his active service officers, NCOs and soldiers had a difficult time restraining these men and many tried to hide or desert when the order came to board the train for Halifax and the waiting transports. It was with great relief that the 31st Alberta Recce finally set sail for Britain on 1 February but, on their arrival a week later, Riley learned the bad news that the unit was being broken up to act as reinforcements for the combat units of First Canadian Army. He and his officers put the best face on the matter, reminding their men that, during its two and a half years in existence, the 31st Recce had trained and dispatched overseas the equivalent of two regiments. On 15 February 1945, the 31st Alberta Recce Regiment officially ceased to exist – its active service personnel were sent to the Canadian Armoured Corps reinforcement centre while its NRMA personnel were sent to the infantry reinforcement centre. Eventually, both types of soldiers would find their way to combat units on the continent where they would be needed as, in the last months of the war, the Canadian army was to become involved in heavy fighting.

CHAPTER FOURTEEN

"Where the Rubber Met the Road"

HOLLAND AND GERMANY, NOVEMBER 1944 TO MARCH 1945

"We would think we were back in England": Winter on the Maas, November 1944 to January 1945

While Canadians at home experienced their sixth wartime Christmas, 13th Field Regiment and the SAR held the line of the lower Maas River in Holland. On 10 November 1944, the batteries of 13th Field took up new positions in the Nijmegen area. This small city had been the scene of heavy fighting during Operation MARKET GARDEN the previous September and the wreckage of that battle was still lying about. The unit went into gun positions on Dutch soil but established an OP over the border in Germany, less than a mile away, giving 13th Field good claim to being the first Canadian soldiers on enemy soil. The regiment would remain in the Nijmegen area for almost three months, occupying two different gun positions, although many others were surveyed. Firing was often limited and although the OPs had a clear observation into the area of Wyler in Germany, where at least 2,000 enemy troops were positioned, it was rare to see a German soldier in the daytime. The gun detachments lived in

When you hear the spatter of Schmeissers in the night,
Then you might wonder, if your cause is right.
No matter how afraid you are,
You'll find me in the nearest bar,
Cause I am LOB, cause I am LOB.

When you hear the Tigers grinding by our slit,
Makes you start to wonder, if it's time to quit.
Just think of me in Gay Paree,
With some French wench upon my knee.
For I am LOB, for I am LOB.

When you meet the Wehrmacht, over the next canal,
I'll drink a toast and wish you luck, old pal.
When you go into the attack,
Just think of me, I'm ten miles back,
Cause I am LOB, cause I am LOB.[1]

dugouts beside the 25-pdrs. and it was not long before these dugouts became quite habitable. A detachment in Able Troop of 22 Battery boasted

a two room underground home, which accommodated the six men of the detachment and contained a carpeted floor, a chesterfield, many chairs, wall drapes, framed pictures and a coal stove. Add to this a radio and the electric lights found in all dugouts and houses, and you have a picture of what existed under a foot or two of snow, or beneath the sagging roof of a pup tent. It was rumoured that a gun has been fired from inside one of these homes using a long rope, but this has not been confirmed.[2]

Not to be outdone, a gun detachment in Fox Troop of 78 Battery added a piano to their home, the acquisition of which resulted from the work of a group of "aggressive, quick thinking and slightly dishonest gunners."[3] As the War Diary of 78 Battery recorded, life was getting so comfortable that, if the men of the unit had not been confined to their gun positions "we would think we were back in England."[4]

For their part, the South Albertas took over a stretch of the Maas between Raamsdonk and Waspik. Two squadrons maintained the line while the third was in reserve and there were frequent shuffles to give everyone a rest. The South Albertas mounted night patrols on their side of the Maas and enforced a strict curfew for local Dutch civilians. Sergeant Jim Nicholson of B Squadron recalled the night he was on patrol and saw a suspicious light in a house near the Maas. A figure left the house, Nicholson recalled, and came

(Facing) "Blackie's boys": South Alberta tank crew, Hochwald 1945
On their way to join in the attack on Veen in March 1945, Corporal Lyle ("Blackie") Levers's Firefly hit a mine and was put out of action. Nobody was hurt and the boys took advantage of the break to shoot some photos, including this one showing, from left to right, Trooper Elmer Stewart, Trooper Cliff Allen (holding that night's dinner) and Corporal Levers. Just above their heads can be seen the barrel of the 17 pdr. gun which has been wrapped in chicken wire and camouflage strips in an attempt to disguise its length as the Germans always fired at the Firefly tanks first. These men have just been through a week of heavy fighting in the Hochwald and it shows. COURTESY, CLIFF ALLEN

Field artillery, winter 1944-1945

One of the advantages artillery had over aircraft in the Second World War was that it was not affected by weather or darkness. Gunners fired 24 hours a day if necessary, summer and winter, rain or shine. Here, a 25-pdr. detachment in Holland fires across the Maas in the winter of 1944-1945. Note that the weapon is mounted on its Hogg platform which permitted it to be quickly traversed 360 degrees. NAC, PA-146868

towards me on a bicycle. When he was 20 feet away I hollered "Halt!", firing my sten gun into the air. He stopped and I asked him who he was and what he was doing outside after the curfew. Shaking, he replied that he was a doctor and had just delivered a baby in that house. I demanded to see the baby and indeed there was a young mother and a brand new baby. I urged them to keep the window covered and returned to my post.[5]

On 16 November Swatty Wotherspoon held the first South Alberta regimental parade in months to decorate men who had earned medals in the fighting in Normandy and the Low Countries. He told the South Albertas that, since August, they had averaged "better than 100 Germans a day" and singled out the troop sergeants for particular praise as "the success of the regiment to this point have depended mostly on the sergeants."[6] A few days later the unit moved back from the Maas to Vught to take over a former Dutch SS Barracks. It was at Vught that the SAR learned that Major Dave Currie had been awarded the Victoria Cross which, although great news, was tinged with sadness because the policy was that VC winners were sent back to Canada and Dave now left the regiment. The SAR also learned some less positive news – 4th Armoured Division was to get its fourth commander in nine months as Harry Foster was switched with Major-General Chris Vokes, commanding 1st Infantry Division in Italy. The move was popular with neither general and certainly not popular with the 4th Division who had come to respect and like Foster.

At Vokes's insistence, the units of 10th Brigade mounted raids on the opposite side of the river but this activity was not liked, as only too often there were few results for the ensuing casualties. Lieutenant-Colonel Dave Stewart of the Argylls became so incensed at the needless losses his battalion was suffering in these raids that he refused to carry them out, an action which resulted

in Vokes removing this fine officer from command. At the same time, Lieutenant-Colonel Bill Cromb of the Links, who had been overseas five years, went home on a long overdue leave and that unit was taken over by Major Jim Swayze. Not long after, Swatty Wotherspoon was called away to undertake a series of assignments that resulted in his being absent from the regiment for almost two months. Major Bert Coffin from Medicine Hat, his second in command, took over the SAR. Thirteen Field Regiment also experienced a change of command when Lieutenant-Colonel C.R. Ostrander succeeded Lieutenant-Colonel Lace in November 1944.

It was a strange sort of war for the men of both 13th Field and the SAR that winter, as they might be in action at the Maas by day and then return in the evening to comfortable billets in Dutch homes. The gunners could visit Nijmegen, where the streetcars were running and the bars, restaurants and film theatres were open, and one of the most popular places in that city was an establishment set up by the Auxiliary Services which served hamburgers and Coca-Cola. Sergeant James Moffat recalled that his gun detachment "would often take a gun Quad and go there to get a hamburger."[7] He also remembered another time when there were "12 of us and not one of us were dressed alike" for, by this time in the war, frontline soldiers followed their own individual preferences when it came to fashions and personal weapons.

The South Alberta tank crews rejoiced in their "Zoot suits," specially-designed overalls not unlike airforce flying suits, which possessed numerous pockets and zippers. In both the SAR and

Troop command post, Nijmegen, winter 1945

During the winter of 1944-1945 when 13th Field Regiment was in fairly static positions, command posts became more elaborate and comfortable. This position has an observation post, as seen here, connected to a heated log dug-out. FROM 13 CANADIAN FIELD REGIMENT, RCA

13th Field, a popular garment that winter was a sapper's long leather jerkin or vest to which the men sewed the sleeves of their issue overcoats. Gunner John Raycroft of 44 Battery recalled that captured German jackboots, with the tops snipped off, proved to be good footwear while many men in his battery also sported rabbit fur-lined German camouflage jackets captured the previous autumn. Sometimes it went too far – Raycroft remembered watching a carrier drive by his position with three men in it wearing top hats and tail coats. As for weapons, by this time many South Alberta tank crew members boasted either a Walther or Luger pistol and almost every tank had a German Mauser rifle or a Schmeisser MP 40 submachinegun. The gunners were no different, the crew of Raycroft's carrier had picked up a Schmeisser and also an MP 44 assault rifle, a deadly and accurate weapon which they much preferred to their own arms. Wisely, officers and warrant officers did not attempt to curb this tendency towards individual-

Staying warm, 1944-1945
A South Alberta crew poses in the winter of 1944. Many soldiers (including three men in this crew) sewed overcoat sleeves to the issue leather jerkin to create a garment that was warm and practical but also short – a consideration for tank crews. Note that no two men are wearing their beret the same way and none are wearing it in the regulation manner, an invariable custom among the South Albertas unless they were on parade. SAR ARCHIVES

ism in dress although, occasionally, some general would come for an inspection which would result in crumpled battledress being hastily pulled out of the kitbags stored with B Echelon and a frantic hunt for missing items of uniform.

Relations with the Dutch civilians were excellent as the men were often billeted in private homes. The Canadians not only brought their rations and fuel, they also brought cigarettes for the adults and candy for the kids and, in return, the Dutch provided the warmth of a family environment which was a welcome break for men who had not seen their own families for years. Both units held occasional dances to which they invited the local beauties. When 13th Field staged its first dance in Nijmegen on 14 December, Gunner McCrie remembered that "they brought truck loads of girls in to dance" but "a lot of boys had saved their tot of rum and, I tell you, the girls got out of the trucks and they wanted to get back in, the gunners were so unruly."[8] There was another dance the following night which, as the 22 Battery War Diary noted, was "just the opposite to the one last night, the only trouble being that not as many girls were there as last night."[9] Dances were popular but, as Trooper Arnold Dryer of the SAR remembered, it was "not easy getting an orchestra that's four years behind on the music and a hall that's been hit a few times,

no lights and make something out of it" although his squadron "got a good lunch from our rations and checked coats, hats, pistols and rifles."[10] These functions eventually proved popular with the Dutch girls although many soldiers suspected that the food the Canadians had was a bigger attraction than they were themselves. Not that the officers were any better in this regard, the RHQ officers of 13th Field held a tea party at which everything "but tea was served, from black coffee to Scotch Whiskey" but which was illuminated with "Feminine pulchritude … supplied courtesy of the Dutch interpreter."[11]

On 16 December, the war interrupted this happy idyll when the Germans launched a major offensive against the American forces in the Ardennes, 80 miles to the south of First Canadian Army's positions along the Maas. The enemy objective was to take Antwerp and split the Allied forces on the Western Front. Hitler committed his last reserves to this offensive, which at first made spectacular gains but was eventually slowed down and then halted by the timely arrival of reinforcements and air superiority. One panzer division came within 70 miles of Antwerp before it ran out of fuel but the German bolt was shot by the last day of 1944, although fighting continued in the Ardennes well into January. The offensive, however, did prolong the war as the Allied leaders were forced to postpone their own planned offensives against Germany until the enemy threat had been eliminated.

It also thoroughly spoiled Christmas for the South Albertas. Captain Tom Barford, the regimental quartermaster, had gone out of his way to prepare a good Christmas dinner for the boys but the celebration was ruined when the unit received a warning order early on Christmas day to be ready to move at 30 minutes notice. This order was later cancelled but it made dinner a little late, resulting in some thoroughly disgruntled diners. In Nijmegen, 13th Field had it better and each battery was able to have its own Christmas dinner complete with turkey and oranges as a treat.

It was around Christmas 1944 that the V-2 missile made its first appearance in the skies over the Maas and they were soon visible night and day, winging overhead toward Antwerp or London. Gunner McCrie remembered being at the hamburger joint in Nijmegen when one of these impressive objects flew across the sky, with its lengthy trail of flame, causing someone to

Besides trying to stay alive, eating was the main preoccupation of wartime Canadian soldiers. In this respect they were much better served than their fathers had been on the Western Front in 1915-1918 as the army devoted much time and energy to ensuring that they received good quantities of food, no matter where they were serving.

Wartime Canadian soldiers received a number of different rations. The first was the **Field Service Ration,** which was the military term for a hot meal prepared by the cooks in the fighting units' B Echelons. In this respect, the gunners of 13th Field were perhaps more fortunate than their comrades in the SAR, as they did not move so often and there was more opportunity for their cooks to prepare and deliver such meals.

More common was the **Composite Ration** or Compo Ration, intended to feed one man for 14 days or a tank crew of five men for three days (with somebody going short on the third day). The Compo Ration came in a wooden crate which, apart from food, contained cigarettes, salt, matches and toilet paper. It held non-varying food and semi-food items such as tea, biscuits, margarine, cheese and chocolate and a number of varying main meals, depending on which one of the nine types (A to G, and X and Y) it was. For example the "C-Menu" Compo Ration had 14 cans of Irish Stew while the "E Menu" had cans of haricot oxtail soup. The main meal was prepared by placing unopened cans in boiling water for a minimum of 30 minutes before consumption. Tea, pre-mixed with milk and

sugar, was a part of all rations, and was prepared by adding three heaping teaspoonfuls in one pint of boiling water. Soldiers cooked their food on a variety of small, gas-fuelled stoves, not unlike Coleman stoves, issued to them, but many resorted to using a cut-down metal container with a mixture of sand and gasoline which heated meals more quickly. The Compo Ration was designed to provide 3,600 daily calories per soldier.

An alternate to the Compo Ration, and often issued when the situation was very fluid, was the **24-Hour Ration** containing enough food (4,000 calories) for one man for one day. It came in a waxed cardboard box, which weighed about a pound, and included biscuits, porridge, tea, dehydrated meat, chocolate bars, sweets, chewing gum, meat broth, salt, sugar, and toilet paper. Understandably, most soldiers preferred the variety of the Compo Ration.

Soldiers also carried an **Emergency Ration,** which was only to be eaten when no other food was available and only by the order of an officer. The Canadian version, which came in a small tin, contained six bars of very high-calorie chocolate.

Finally, whenever possible, all Canadian soldiers supplemented their rather bland diet with supplies purchased from civilians, with eggs, milk and fresh bread being the favourites. When the army moved into Germany in 1945, the men were pleased to find that the enemy's food supplies were much better than those in the occupied nations and it was not long before chickens, cattle and pigs found their way (clandestinely, as it was against orders) into the ration system.

(Above) **Ration point, Normandy, August 1944**
Behind the fighting units of First Canadian Army was an extensive logistical element which provided food, fuel and ammunition. At this ration point in Normandy operated by the Royal Canadian Army Service Corps, compo rations (in wooden boxes marked with a clover leaf) are transferred to the A Echelons of frontline units, which will take them to the forward troops. For every soldier who fired a weapon, between four and five soldiers worked to supply him. NAC, PA-132903

(Above) **Receiving and distributing rations**
Trooper Bill Kennedy (left) and Sergeant Pete Woolf of AA Troop of the SAR sort out rations in Belgium in 1944. These are 24-hour ration packs. COURTESY, W. VAILLANCOURT

(Left) **Special issue – beer**
The men of AA Troop enjoy a ration of beer during a break in the advance from France. Alcohol was issued to the troops on an irregular basis, depending on the decision of officers, and was much appreciated. COURTESY, M. AMYOTTE

(Above) **Some help with the cooking, Bergen, October 1944**
Troopers Sutley and Warner of the SAR take instruction in cooking from a Dutch girl in Bergen. By this time, of necessity, the South Albertas were accomplished chefs, but a little advice from a pretty blonde lady was always welcome. Judging by the litter of packages, this is a 24-hour ration. NAC, PA-176887

(Left) **Hungry Highlanders: Veen, February 1945**
A platoon of weary Argyll & Sutherland Highlanders line up for a hot meal from the battalion cooks at Veen in February 1945. In forward areas it was not always possible for the troops to get hot food, and when the cooks could provide it, it was very welcome. Note the use of jerricans to carry tea. CANADIAN ARMY PHOTO, 47465A

(Above) **Good to the last drop**
Lance-Corporal Jackson of the Argylls drains his mess tin of hot, sweet tea in the Rhineland in 1945. Although Canadians were more fond of coffee, their rations were British in origin and, since the British army drank tea, they did too.
CANADIAN ARMY PHOTO, C47468

(Right) **"It's pork chops tonight, boys":
Louisendorf, Germany, February 1945**
Civilian food supplies were scarce in Holland but when the Canadians crossed into Germany, they found plentiful livestock and it was not long before they began to round it up. This happy private of the Lorne Scots is contemplating how many days of eating his platoon will get from this four-legged bounty. CANADIAN ARMY PHOTO 46988

(Above) **Tank crew enjoys a meal**
A crew from the Fife and Forfar Yeomanry of the British army, which often supported the 10th Brigade with their flame-throwing Churchill tanks in 1944-1945, pauses for a meal. They have cooked their meal on an improvised field stove dug partially into the ground and are eating it from a mixture of standard aluminum mess tins and the metal plates and cutlery in the compo rations. Judging by the expressions on their faces, they are content with the result. Note the tank suits and the thickness of the armour in their Churchill, as seen by the open hatch. CANADIAN ARMY PHOTO, 46993

Horror in Antwerp
After the Scheldt estuary had been cleared, Antwerp became the largest supply port for the Western Allies and a target for German air attacks. This grim photo shows the horrific scene after a V-1 flying bomb hit a crowded city square during noon-hour, killing dozens and wounding hundreds of office workers. In the background can be seen Canadian army medical vehicles and personnel assisting the local authorities to treat the casualties. NAC, PA-136790

There is just no escaping politicians – the polls come to the guns
Soldiers overseas were allowed to vote in provincial elections and here Gunner E.W. Casson of 22 Battery prepares to make a difference in the Alberta election held in early 1945. FROM *13 CANADIAN FIELD REGIMENT, RCA*

remark: "There goes a bundle for Britain."[12] On New Year's Eve, 13th Field celebrated with a bombardment of all known German positions "from every sort of weapon" and "the air was lit with tracers, flares, etc. and loud with the noise of weapons and bursting projectiles."[13] Heads were a little thick the next morning when the *Luftwaffe*, which had rarely been seen in the last few months, returned to centre stage with a vengeance when it launched a massive low-level raid on airfields in Holland and Belgium in an attempt to reduce Allied air superiority. Hundreds of enemy fighters flew across the Maas and the anti-aircraft gunners had a busy day. The headquarters of 10th Brigade were near a former German airfield close to Breda and the brigade historian recorded that all personnel "were subjected to, enjoyed, and suffered nothing from, the great daylight fighter and jet raid by the enemy" as the "Airdrome being so close, the fun was first hand" and the "Bofors crews were dizzy from having so many targets."[14]

In early January 1945, the South Albertas moved up to Kaatsheuvel on the Maas and, beginning on 11 January, the regiment began to engage targets on the other side of the river. It was rather pleasant work, individual troops would drive up to the Maas in the morning, shoot throughout the day, and return to their billets in the afternoon – regular banker's hours.

Lieutenant Ivan Donkin of B Squadron specialized in this task and was greatly admired by the Algonquin Regiment whose historian recorded that "Mighty Donkin" would "zig-zag up to the dike, poke the gun snout over, and blast away until he had several satisfactory blazes going."[15] More and more, one target, the island of Kapelsche Veer on the south shore of the Maas between Ramsdonk and Capelle, began to predominate and when strange artillery and engineer units began to arrive in the SAR area in the last half of January, it was clear that the war was about to heat up again.

"We were all scared": The battle for the Kapelsche Veer, January 1945

The Kapelsche Veer is a low, flat, treeless island in the lower reaches of the Maas River. When the Germans withdrew north of that waterway in November 1944, Allied troops did not occupy the Veer as it was felt it could be dominated by fire but they came to regret that decision in late December when the Germans established a fortified outpost on the island. The Polish Armoured Division, within whose sector the Veer was located, mounted two assaults that month to eject the interlopers but both were rebuffed with heavy losses. In mid-January 1945 the Royal Marine Commandos made a third attack but were also thrown back with great loss. Frustrated, Lieutenant-General John Crocker, commanding British 1 Corps, in which both 4th Canadian Armoured and 1st Polish Armoured Divisions were serving, attempted to have the Veer "drenched with heavy bombers and set alight with the new Napalm bombs developed by the U.S." but requests to obtain these weapons proved unavailing.[16] Crocker was determined to remove this thorn from his side because he felt that, if he allowed the enemy to retain

an outpost on the southern, or Allied side, of the Maas, it might engender "in the troops of 1st British Corps a belief in the superiority of the German soldier" – in short, it was a matter of prestige. He therefore ordered Major-General Chris Vokes of 4th Canadian Armoured Division to mount a fourth attack on the Kapelsche Veer.

The Veer was a tough nut to crack. The German defences, which consisted of concrete-reinforced tunnels and machinegun positions, were centred around two strongpoints – codenamed GRAPES and RASPBERRY – at the little ferry harbour in the centre of the island ("veer" is the Dutch word for "harbour"). The only approaches to this position were along the tops of two dykes, about 25-30 feet wide feet wide and 30 feet high, which formed the centre of the island and provided excellent fields of fire for the defenders. To offset these enemy advantages, divisional staff called for a massive smoke screen to be laid by artillery and smoke generators that would cover an infantry advance from the west and east ends of the island. At the same time, a 60-man canoe party, using Peterborough canoes flown over from Canada, would paddle down the Maas under cover of the smoke, enter the ferry harbour and seize the centre of the German position. To deal with the German defence works, the assaulting infantry would be supported by flame-throwing Wasp carriers and would also be issued "lifebuoy" portable flamethrowers. Despite the fact that the garrison of the Veer – a reinforced company of the 17th German Parachute Regiment – was almost certainly on the alert, divisional staff were confident that a surprise attack under thick smoke cover would meet with success.

The plan for Operation ELEPHANT, as it was codenamed, was handed to Brigadier James Jefferson of 10th Brigade who was told to carry it out without change. Jefferson selected the

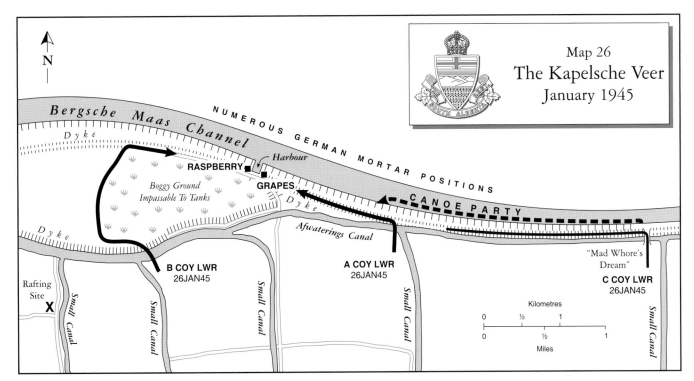

Death on the dyke: The Kapelsche Veer

The Kapelsche Veer, a small island on the south side of the Maas, was occupied by German paratroopers in late 1944. When attempts by the Poles and the Royal Marines failed to evict them, the job was given to 10th Brigade. Infantry from the Lincoln & Welland Regiment and the Argyll & Sutherland Highlanders, supported by SAR tanks, spent five miserable days trying to advance along dyke tops like this against very brave and determined opponents. PHOTOGRAPH BY DIANNE GRAVES

Lincoln & Welland Regiment to make the attack and he gave the unit a week to prepare. As there was much concern about the numerous German mortar units on the north bank of the Maas, Jefferson was allotted heavy artillery support – a total of 300 tubes ranging from medium artillery to 75 mm HE fired by a troop of South Albertas – but divisional staff cautioned 10th Brigade that "the extraordinarily good field works of the German garrison" were "practically impervious to neutralization or destruction," which was indeed a comforting thought.[17] The sappers of 9 Field Company, RCE, were more helpful and, in the week before the attack took place, managed to build a bridge from the mainland to the eastern tip of the island that was such a crazy, cobbled-together structure it was christened, (for reasons nobody really knows), the "Mad Whore's Dream."

Operation ELEPHANT commenced at 7.15 A.M. on Friday, 26 January 1945 and from the outset it went wrong. The smoke screen did not prove thick enough to prevent enemy observation and, in any case, the defenders were firing on fixed lines straight along the dyke tops. The canoe party, which had to go out in mid-channel because of ice on the Maas, came under fire from the north bank and was forced to land short of its objective after taking heavy casualties – 45 of the 60 men involved. The conventional infantry attacks fared no better. B Company of the Links crossed to the western tip of the island in Buffalo amphibious vehicles and, at first, made good progress on foot along the dykes toward RASPBERRY, the westernmost strongpoint, but were brought to a halt by German automatic weapons and mortar fire and forced to fall back. At the eastern end of the island, C Company of Links discovered that, because of ice, it could not get its flame-thrower carriers onto the dyke tops so it advanced with only the portable "lifebuoy" flamethrowers. Every man carrying one of these weapons was cut down by the Germans when he attempted to use

it. The Links' A Company, meanwhile, which had crossed in amphibious Buffaloes to a point on the Veer west of C Company, took heavy casualties when the thinning smoke screen permitted the Germans to hit several of these vehicles, sinking one. The company managed to land but could not get its surviving Wasp onto the dyke top. The company commander attempted to advance toward GRAPES, the easternmost strongpoint, but his men were stopped 30 yards from their objective by heavy machinegun fire which killed or wounded five of the six officers in the company. It lost cohesion and fell back to join C Company while the company commander, Captain Owen Lambert, was last seen advancing through the smoke alone against his objective, cursing and firing a sten gun from the hip. His body was found after the battle.

Two hours after it began, it was clear to Jefferson that the "surprise" assault was a total failure and that it would require a deliberate setpiece operation to take this useless piece of soggy real estate. He decided to push on the central strongpoints from opposite sides – the Links from the west and the Argylls from the east – and both battalions would have tank support from the South Albertas. At 3 P.M. on 26 January, Major Bert Coffin of the SAR, commanding in the absence of Wotherspoon, received orders to send officers to recce tank routes and, four hours later, while the engineers held their breath, two Stuarts from Recce Troop crossed over the "Mad Whore's Dream" and firmed up at the Argyll for-

Concealed German position, Kapelsche Veer

The Veer was covered with small, concrete positions such as this photographed after the war had ended. They were nearly invisible until the last moment when the occupants would open up with machineguns on infantry or *Panzerfausts* against armour. The whole wretched business on the Veer would have been finished sooner if higher authorities had seen fit to grant a request for napalm. SAR ARCHIVES

ward position about 1,000 yards east of GRAPES. As there was no bridge to the western side, 9 Field Squadron began to build a Class 40 raft in a small canal that joined the southern channel of the Maas. It took them all night, many sappers working up to their waists in water just above freezing point, and they had to down tools at one point to fight off an aggressive German patrol sent out from the Veer.

At 8.30 A.M., 27 January, Lieutenant Ken Little of A Squadron gently nosed his Sherman down the ramp onto the raft. Unfortunately the tide had gone out (the Maas is tidal at this point in its course) and the raft settled on the bottom of the canal, buckling under the weight of the tank. The sappers decided that not only would they have to build a new raft, they would also have to construct an approach ramp that would permit loading at any water level. They immediately set to work but came under heavy German 120 mm mortar fire from the north bank of the Maas which delayed work, as they were frequently forced to take cover.

On the island, meanwhile, the infantry were unable to make any progress along the narrow dyke tops in the face of German machinegun fire and when the flatfeet went to ground, they were mortared from the north bank of the Maas and suffered heavy casualties. In response, artillery FOOs on the Veer called down fire on the north bank, which was also bombarded by a troop of SAR tanks and attacked by fighter-bombers. It was to no avail as the German mortar detachments constantly moved their light weapons from one pre-registered position to another, shifting every few rounds to avoid being located. By mid-day, the Links and the Argylls had given up and simply dug in, as deeply as they could, into the mud of the dyke tops. They cheered up, however, late in the afternoon when Lieutenant Wilfred Kennedy of A Squadron of the SAR managed to bring two Shermans across the creaking, twisted "Dream." The arrival of these vehicles, an Argyll officer recalled, "a considerable achievement in itself, gave the riflemen new heart."[18] As darkness fell, Kennedy moved forward to cover a party from the Argyll pioneer platoon to clear mines on the dyke top so that the infantry and armour would be

able to advance in the morning. This operation was successful but, unfortunately, as Kennedy leaned down from his turret to congratulate Lieutenant Alan Earp, the Argyll pioneer officer, he was hit in the head and killed by a German sniper.

At almost the same time, the sappers finished their raft and began the onerous task of ferrying Little's three Shermans over to the west side of the island. Ken Little's tank went first and, propelled by four powerful outboard motors, the raft slowly made its way north along the canal to the south channel of the Maas. Unfortunately, the nighttime cold had caused the water to ice up and it soon became apparent that, even with all engines at full throttle, there was not enough power to cut through it. LVTs were therefore brought in to circle constantly around the raft and break the ice but a careless LVT driver rammed the thing, shifting one of the pontoons on which it floated and causing Little's Sherman to slide along the dark deck of the raft. Miraculously the raft held together and, after three hours, had progressed about 1,000 yards of the canal to reach the south channel of the Maas, where it encountered thicker ice. As it was impossible to go back, the engineers decided to go forward and found that, by turning their propellers alternately right and left, they gained a few feet every time. Slowly, very slowly, with LVTs breaking the ice and the sappers knocking it off the side of the craft with boat hooks, axes and oars as it formed on their vessel, they neared the island. Finally, nearly eight hours after it had set out, the raft was towed the last few hundred yards by an LVT to a point where Little's crew, who had "nearly fainted" several times during the voyage, were able to drive over 3 feet of packed ice onto dry land.[19] Cheerfully bidding farewell to Little's pale-faced tankers, the sappers turned their awkward vessel around to fetch his other two tanks.

They managed to get them over to the island and, with Shermans on both ends of the Veer, there were hopes that the thing could be wrapped up that day. Unfortunately the weather warmed up on 28 January and, instead of ice, the tankers now found they were faced with thick glutinous mud. In mid-morning, Little on the west side and Lieutenant Ernest Hill, who had replaced Kennedy on the west side, moved forward with their respective infantry units but, almost immediately, Little's second

Alberta on the Veer
Trooper Cliff Allen and Corporal Jake Wiebe (right) look out from their hatches while a nearby Bren section fires. The track links welded all over the Sherman did not help its mobility in the thick mud of the Kapelsche Veer. COURTESY, JAKE WIEBE

tank bogged, blocking the third behind it. He left them while he moved forward to give fire support to the Links and Hill did the same on the other end. Despite the fact that the Shermans laid down heavy fire from their main guns and machineguns, the infantry were soon forced to ground and, as the armour could not advance without close support, the attack bogged down on both flanks.

Hill and Little fell back while the infantry regrouped, and this being done, started back up the dykes in the early afternoon. For his part, Hill left his vehicle to work on foot, guiding his two Shermans and two Stuarts forward with the infantry. The Argylls had finally managed to get a Wasp up onto the dyke and it edged carefully past the tanks to move up with the infantry, but someone got confused and it drove past the flatfeet straight at GRAPES behind 30-foot bursts of flame. Before it got bogged in the mud and ran out of flame fuel, one awestruck observer reported that he had seen four German paratroopers on fire in a slit trench who, "after they had beaten out the flames, … continued to fight until they were killed."[20] This event, however, distracted the defenders long enough for Corporal Albert Broadbent, a warrior of the Cree people, to reach a slight bend in the dyke with his Sherman which permitted enfilade fire along the German positions on the north side of the dyke. Over the course of an hour Broadbent, observing carefully from the turret with fieldglasses, brought down accurate fire that killed or wounded 22 of the 25 men in the German platoon holding this position, a feat which brought him the award of the Distinguished Conduct Medal.* With this assistance, the Argylls managed to secure GRAPES late in the afternoon.

For his part, Little could see Hill's tanks coming toward him and he was able to shoot the Links into RASPBERRY at almost the same time. Unfortunately the paratroopers infiltrated along the dyke sides and popped up behind the Canadians causing such confusion that the Links fell back several hundred yards to regroup although Little remained in position, trying to support the Argylls. Running low on ammunition, he was forced to withdraw but as he opened his hatch to guide his driver back, he was killed by a German sniper. The Links, having meanwhile regrouped, surged forward again and secured RASPBERRY but they now had no tank support as Little's tank crew had bogged their vehicle after they brought his body back. In the few remaining hours of daylight that were left, the infantry threw demolition charges down the rabbit warren of tunnels and trenches around the ferry harbour before settling down for the night with the happy thought that this miserable job was almost at an end. Unfortunately, it wasn't as, at 10 P.M., the obstinate paratroopers, who had been hiding on the north side of the dykes, mounted a surprise counterattack which forced both battalions to give up their hardwon gains and withdraw down the dykes on their respective sides of the island.

When daylight came on 29 January, the fourth day of the battle, it revealed a nightmare landscape. The muddy dyke tops were covered, as Lieutenant Ken Wigg of the SAR remembered, with "the bodies of German and our own dead, wrecked vehicles, etc.," and resembled a First World War battlefield.[21] The Links and Argylls resumed the attack at 7 A.M. but the Links had no tank support as, by now, all three of the Shermans on the west side had bogged. On the opposite side, a Stuart had become so deeply mired that a call had to put into the sappers to bring a bulldozer onto the island and build a diversion or detour around it. Wigg was able to manoeuvre his two Shermans forward and support the Argylls as they recaptured GRAPES but all attempts by the Links to move forward to RASPBERRY without armour were doomed. By last light the German-held area had been compressed to a few hundred square yards around the latter strongpoint and there was hope that one more day would see an end to this wretched battle.

All three units tried to rotate their men, who were suffering from exposure and frostbite, on and off the island. Corporal Jake Wiebe of the SAR remembered that when his squadron sergeant-major asked for volunteers to replace a crew on the island, none of his comrades "were foolish enough to volunteer, and I certainly didn't volunteer" so the SSM had them draw straws and

Links and Winks
Four survivors of the Veer battle pose in their white camouflage suits on the day after it was all over. The Lincoln and Welland Regiment lost 50 men killed and 183 men wounded on the Kapelsche Veer, with 40 frostbitten, and took a long time to recover. NAC, PA-144706

---

* Broadbent's award of the DCM was based on evidence provided by *Stabsfeldwebel* Heinrich Fischer, the German paratroop platoon commander, who was captured. Despite the fact that Broadbent was his enemy, Fischer was so filled with "a soldier's admiration of a good job well done" that, at his interrogation, he singled out for praise the unknown (to him) tank commander who had nearly wiped out his platoon. It is believed that this is one of the few times in the history of the Commonwealth when the award of a decoration was based on information provided by an enemy.

Wiebe lost.[22] By now the South Albertas knew, as Corporal Bob Clipperton wrote his wife Andy, that they were up against "one of the toughest Parachute Divisions Jerry's got. The S.S. may act tough but these guy *are* tough & know it. They are quite happy to die rather than be taken prisoner."[23] Bad as conditions were in the unheated tanks on the Veer, it was worse for the infantry in the mud, some of whom spent 72 hours under intermittent but sometimes very heavy mortar fire. One infantry platoon commander on the Veer remembered that, "My men came to me and said they were cold and I gave them clothes, they said they were hungry and I tried to give them food, they told me they were scared and I told them we were all scared."[24]

During the night the indefatigable sappers managed to complete the detour around the bogged Stuart on the east side while, on the west, another Sherman was ferried onto the Veer. Unfortunately, when daylight came, all four tanks on the west flank bogged so that when the attack was resumed at first light on 30 January, the Links had no armour support and were quickly forced to ground, where they came under heavy mortar fire. On the east side, the attack was delayed when Wigg discovered that the barrels of his crews' .30 calibre Brownings were worn out from ceaseless firing and, as they had already gone through the spare barrels in their vehicles, there was a delay while replacements were rushed over from the mainland. This done, Wigg's Shermans and the Argylls made three attempts to cross the distance between the two strongpoints to secure RASPBERRY, but each time were beaten back by heavy automatic weapons fire and ceaseless mortaring from the north bank of the river that, despite all the efforts of the Canadian artillery (15th Field Regiment had by now fired 14,000 rounds of 25-pdr. HE in support of the operation) continued to harass the troops on the Veer. In mid-afternoon the Germans did hold their fire while Canadian stretcher bearers collected the wounded from the recent fighting and, once that was done, everyone opened up again. Wigg now received two more Shermans and his four tanks managed to shoot the Argylls into RASPBERRY in late afternoon by blanketing the entire area around the strongpoint with HE fire. In return, the Germans called down smoke from the north bank, obscuring their targets, and Wigg then turned his weapons on that area with little result. One of the problems was that the tanks could not depress their weapons low enough to hit the enemy who were very close to them and any attempt to open a hatch, resulted in "bullets zinging off them", and the loss of a crew commander[25]

All that remained now was to take the ground between RASPBERRY and the forward positions of the Links but it was so heavily swept by German fire that the infantry were quickly pinned down. At 6 P.M., Wigg decided to send one Sherman across this deadly area immediately ahead of the infantry while he provided fire support with his other three tanks. Corporal Mike Nichol edged his vehicle forward, covered by the fire of the other Shermans, but was forced to halt when he encountered a large crater in the dyke top. At that moment, a paratrooper popped up

and fired a *Panzerfaust* round which set the vehicle ablaze. The driver, Trooper Lloyd Laprade from Thorhild, Alberta, bailed out only to discover that the turret hatch had jammed and the turret crew were trapped. He freed them and then returned to the front of the tank to assist his co-driver, Trooper George Noble from Fallis, Alberta, who was wounded but both men were killed by small arms fire. There were no more attempts to go forward made that day.

At 8 A.M. on 31 January 1945, the fifth day of the Veer battle, Lieutenant Bob Crawford of the SAR, who now replaced Wigg on the east side, linked up with the troops on the west side. Few shots were fired as the greater part of the defenders had been evacuated during the night although a few dazed paratroopers staggered out of their holes with their hands up. The remainder of the day was spent recovering the dead, a grim task made easier by the fact that the corpses were frozen and easier to move – one Argyll remembered "stacking the fellows" like "they were pieces of wood …… you looked at them and you looked away."[26] Casualties were heavy. Jefferson's brigade had lost 133 killed and wounded which, if added to the 231 casualties suffered in the Polish and British attacks, came to 364 soldiers killed or wounded to take the Kapelsche Veer – a very high price to pay for prestige. An accurate count of German casualties was impossible because they had dumped many of their dead in the river.

The battle of the Kapelsche Veer was, in all respects, a thoroughly bad business. As the historian of 10th Brigade commented, the South Albertas and the engineers played a major part in achieving victory because "tanks were the decisive factor on the flat, sodden island where their use was undreamt of" and the engineers "performed miracles in even getting one across."[27] There was much bitterness in 10th Brigade over this costly, needless, and tragic action and much unrest in 4th Armoured Division over the way Vokes had handled the battle. Jefferson submitted a post-action report highly critical of the initial plans by the division staff, which he had been forced to execute, and, from that time on, had as little to do with Vokes as possible. Lieutenant-Colonel John Proctor from Edmonton, the quartermaster, who had loyally served three previous division commanders, went over Vokes's head to Simonds and requested a transfer because he just couldn't "serve him any more."[28] Proctor got both a transfer and a promotion. Vokes tried to have Major Jim Swayze, the temporary commanding officer of the Lincoln & Welland Regiment, removed from command but Simonds again stepped in and secured Swayze a transfer to a new appointment.

"Ankle deep in soup-like mud": The Rhineland (1), Operation VERITABLE, February 1945

The battle for the Kapelsche Veer was still being fought when First Canadian Army began preparing for a major new operation. The abortive German offensive in the Ardennes had delayed Montgomery's plans for a large scale attack to drive the Germans away from the west bank of the Rhine River from Nijmegen to Cologne but, in late January 1945, he issued or-

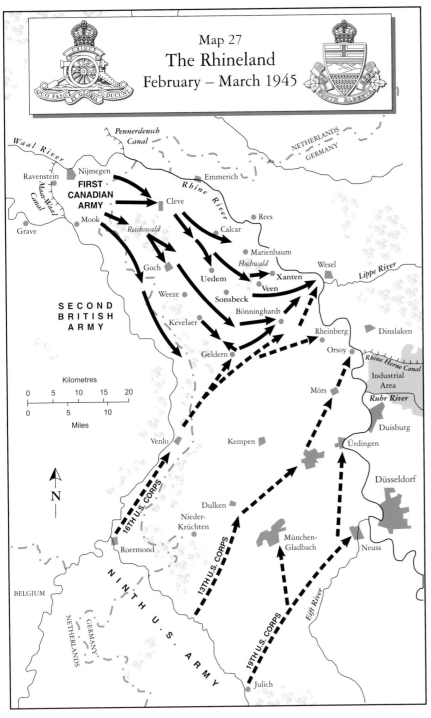

Map 27
The Rhineland
February – March 1945

the result was that VERITABLE became a grinding battle of attrition.

The plan for VERITABLE called for a three-phase attack. Phase One, to be carried out mainly by British troops of 30 Corps, which was under Canadian command, would commence on 8 February and involved a breakthrough of the Siegfried Line and the clearing of the Reichswald Forest. Phase Two, to be undertaken by 2 Canadian Corps, would clear the area to the immediate south and take the three towns of Goch, Calcar and Uedem to provide a springboard for Phase Three, a breakthrough of the German reserve line anchored along a ridge surmounted by the Hochwald-Balberger Forests. The terrain favoured the defenders, who had flooded all the low lying areas, restricting the approaches, and built concentric defensive lines utilizing the wooded areas of the Reichswald, Balbergerwald and Hochwald state forests. Every major town in the area had been turned, by the construction of numerous anti-tank ditches and defence positions, into an island of resistance. The German formations manning the forward line of defence where the initial Allied blow would fall, were not first-class troops but there were better quality units, both panzer and paratrooper, available in reserve.

To break through these defences, Operation VERITABLE relied on an incredibly heavy artillery programme. It would be fired in the first two phases by the artillery units in the two Canadian and five British divisions involved, supported by those of two corps and no less than five AGRAs as well as smaller additional units – a total of 1,034 guns ranging from 25-pdr. fieldpieces up to 240 mm heavy guns. Given this weight of artillery a call for fire on a "Victor Target" (a target engaged by all guns in a corps) might be answered by up to five hundred tubes. The planned ammunition expenditure was incredible, the 576 25-pdr. guns taking part would fire nearly 800 rounds per gun

ders for Operation VERITABLE. This was a massive offensive to be mounted by First Canadian Army southeast from Nijmegen while, at almost the same time, Ninth U.S. Army would mount a drive northeast from Aachen. Montgomery's objective was to compel the Germans to spread their forces along a broad front, so that they could be destroyed in detail on the west bank of the Rhine. Unfortunately, the Germans, anticipating these attacks, sabotaged the dams controlling the flow of water from the Roer River which created a huge lake in the area through which the Americans were to attack, delaying their offensive for two weeks while they waited for the water level to fall. This permitted the enemy to move troops north to face First Canadian Army and

in the initial bombardment alone. This was not all – included in the plan were a number of PEPPERPOT programmes, basically intense bombardments of selected targets by 466 non-conventional artillery weapons manned by anti-aircraft, anti-tank and infantry support units who were not otherwise engaged in supporting the assault troops. A PEPPERPOT was intended to "convince the enemy that it would be suicidal to move or come out above ground" and an enemy position selected as a target would be subjected to an intense 10-minute bombardment by Vickers heavy machineguns, 4.2-inch mortars, 75mm tank guns, 17-pdr. anti-tank guns and 40 mm Bofors guns.[29] Once a PEPPERPOT had finished, there would be a pause for ten minutes to let the Germans think that it was over, and then it would resume. Including the PEPPERPOT units, a total of 1,494 tubes were employed in support of VERITABLE – the largest number yet employed by the Commonwealth armies in a single operation during the war – making it truly "a gunner's battle."

Preparations began in the last week of January 1945 and security was very tight – the artillery regiments were not allowed to occupy their pre-surveyed positions until 48 hours before the attack began. The gunners of 13th Field Regiment became aware that something big was in the works when 40,000 rounds of 25-pdr ammunition was dumped near their gun positions outside Nijmegen. On 5 February, Major-General Dan Spry, commanding 3rd Canadian Division, visited the unit and spoke to the men, "impressing on all ranks that it was going to be a gunner's show and telling them what was expected of them."[30] The next few days were spent in sorting ammunition and getting ready for a move to Wyler in Germany, the regiment's next gun position. There was no firing at all on 7 February so that the men could get a rest and that night, the gunners were spectators when aircraft from Bomber Command and Second Tactical Air Force flew overhead at 10 P.M. to hit the fortified towns behind the first German lines.

All was in readiness in the grey, overcast and rainy morning of Thursday, 8 February 1944 and it was still dark when the gun detachments took post. Promptly at 5 A.M., the Commonwealth artillery opened up with "the greatest concentration of fire delivered in a single day by the British army up to that time."[31] The preliminary bombardment lasted for two and a half hours and the dark was pierced by a "strange, continuous light caused by muzzle flashes."[32] At 7.30 A.M. there was a pause for nearly two hours while the gunners got organized to fire the lifting barrage that preceded the first infantry attack and which shifted 300 yards every 12 minutes. That Thursday in 1945, the men of 13th Field fired continuously for eleven hours, sending about "500 RPGs up the spout during the day, leaving a tired but happy bunch of gunners."[33]

The assault troops, mainly British from 30 Corps, had no problems securing their first objectives. As they closed the main Siegfried Line defences, however, two factors hampered their progress: the Germans began to flood the area, reducing the number of usable roads; and the sheer number of vehicles moving along these roads soon resulted in a massive traffic jam. A combination of flooding and the heavy bombardment, which had turned the wet soil into the consistency of soup, prevented off-road movement and the commander of one assault division noted that, by the end of the first day, the vehicles of his formation "lay inert in the mud all over the battlefield" and that "it was raining and the weather forecast was bad."[34] Arguments broke out between divisional commanders over which formation had priority on the roads and relations between these officers were not "noteworthy for their cordiality."[35]

For the next two days, 30 Corps slowly but surely ground its way through the Reichswald Forest, hampered by atrocious weather which grounded air support, caused flooding and traffic jams and permitted the Germans to move up reinforcements from the south. By 10 February, after heavy fighting, the objectives for Phase One had been taken and 2 Canadian Corps now entered the battle to carry out Phase Two. It commenced on 16 February but 2nd Canadian Division encountered German armoured and paratroop divisions which, determined to defend their homeland, stubbornly contested every inch of ground and inflicted heavy casualties.

Throughout these operations, the three batteries of 13th Field Regiment were very busy. On 9 February, accompanied by Gunner "Dog," they became the first Canadian artillery unit to take up a gun position in Germany when they moved to Wyler, just over the border, which had been cleared by the infantry the day before. Wyler had been a common target for 13th Field during the previous three months and they were curious to see the results of their work:

> The houses are shattered hulks with bare walls and gaping rafters. The trees are little else but leafless, branchless skeletons, while the roads and paths are ankle deep in soup-like mud. Viewing the intricate system of trenches and dugouts that the Germans had here it is small wonder that we never observed any movement in daytime.[36]

Wyler had also been the scene of heavy fighting during Operation MARKET GARDEN and Gunner Pugh of 22 Battery remembered that there were airborne gliders lying about that "were full

German dead, Rhineland, 1945
Canadian gunners had a saying that one shell will "always get three men" and that appears to be the case with these Germans killed by blast from Canadian artillery in the Rhineland. Someone tried to render first aid to one of these unfortunates but, judging by the unravelled bandage, gave it up as hopeless. Note that the pockets of all three corpses have been rifled and their unwanted contents scattered on the ground about them. CANADIAN ARMY PHOTO, 46992

of things" but "you didn't get too close to them as the Americans had booby-trapped them and so had the Germans."[37]

Unfortunately the area was also lousy with mines which caused a number of casualties. Sergeant Alex Brennand was in a Quad that ran over a mine and blew up. Two of the six men in the gun detachment were wounded but Brennand was "thrown clear by the blast and covered with black soot."[38] He noted that a violin in the vehicle, which belonged to one of gunners, was totally destroyed by the blast, and there "wasn't a piece as big as a match stick left." The regiment remained in and around Wyler for eleven days and their activity was much hampered by the flooding which made movement almost impossible and mail was dropped by one of the little Auster aircraft of the Air OP, the only sure method of delivering it. After the first few days, things quietened down and firing became limited, mostly DF and HF tasks called for by 8th Infantry Brigade, which the unit was supporting.

Operation VERITABLE was a huge undertaking that occupied seven divisions and a number of independent brigades. At one point the ration strength of First Canadian Army was close to half a million men but for every soldier carrying a rifle in an infantry battalion or manning a gun in a field battery, there were five or more in the rear areas. Gunner Raycroft of 44 Battery, who spent much of his time during VERITABLE laying line to the forward positions, was surprised, when he went back to the rear to pick up his carrier which had been under repair, by the contrast between it and the frontline:

> We went through road junctions that were like Toronto's Bloor and Yonge without the lights. Military police in crisply-pressed uniforms, with white belts and gauntlets, were directing a constant string of traffic from all directions. Everywhere seemed to be crowded with soldiers, moving among big marquee-style tents and large enclosed trailers that were hospitals, dental offices, supply stores, sign-painting shops, Provost Corps (police) headquarters and so on. In the huge motor-transport repair area, men with uniforms hidden under overalls were swarming over vehicles.
>
> In contrast, when approaching a dug-in infantry position there were so few men visible that the atmosphere had a twinge of loneliness in it. ...... It was certainly never crowded up there.[39]

Despite the numbers and the weight of materiel, the Germans stubbornly resisted 2nd and 3rd Canadian Divisions and, by 21 February, Phase Two had ground to a halt without all its objectives being secured. The historian of 12th Field Regiment summed up the situation well when he commented that VERITABLE had stalled as

> Every thing had gone against us and the Germans were definitely fighting a last ditch stand with their backs against a wall. There were a great many Divisions fighting on a fairly narrow front and things, to say the least, were often a bit

mixed up. Intelligence was poor and so many Divisions were trying to do so much that one never knew when an attack was apt to be mounted through your particular front. Before the Operation was complete, eight British Divisions and three Canadian ones were involved and at that particular time the newspapers were full of queries as to the whereabouts of the British 2nd Army. Most of it was actually fighting under General Crerar and their front had been bled almost dry.[40]

Crerar decided that a pause was necessary before undertaking Phase Three which would be an entirely new operation codenamed Operation BLOCKBUSTER. The revised plan called for the 2nd Division to keep pushing through the Hochwald forest toward the Hochwald Gap, an area of clear ground between that wooded area and the neighbouring Balberger Forest. At the same time, 3rd Canadian Division, supported by 4th Armoured Brigade of 4th Division would secure Uedem and, when this had been accomplished, 10th Brigade would make a direct attack against the Hochwald Gap while 11th British Armoured Division secured the Balberger Forest. These orders brought the South Albertas into the Rhineland.

"Ceaseless Battering": The Rhineland (2): The Hochwald, 26 February–2 March 1945

Although they had been following the course of Operation VERITABLE, the SAR had been enjoying a quiet period at Kaatsheuvel following their travails on the Kapelsche Veer. For the regiment the biggest event was the army boxing championships which took place late in late January and early February. All winter, the SAR boxing team had been carefully coached by professional Dutch fighters paid by unit funds and they had no problem walking away with the brigade and division championships. Better still, for the second year running, Trooper Joe Main won the Canadian army heavyweight title.

Even better, the first allotments of leaves to Paris started coming in and several lucky groups of officers and men departed for the "city of lights." More common were 48-hour leaves to Brussels or Antwerp and two happy young troop leaders, Lieutenants Bill Luton and Fremont ("Tiger") Bowick, delighted to be doing so, travelled to the latter city. The sophistication of Europe often posed problems for the somewhat unworldly South Albertans. Troopers Marshall and Gregory found a mysterious device in the bathroom of their hotel room in Paris which puzzled them because it "shot water straight up but you wouldn't use it to do a job" so they cautiously left it alone.[41] Lieutenants Bowick and Luton encountered some difficulties with exotic European potables, difficulties that began, as Luton remembered, while walking to their hotel from the Antwerp train station:

> Tiger spotted a store selling booze and in the window a bottle of Kummel liqueur. "Best stuff you ever tasted, Bill," he said and promptly acquired it. We checked into the Atlanta Hotel, which had been commandeered as a Canadian officers'

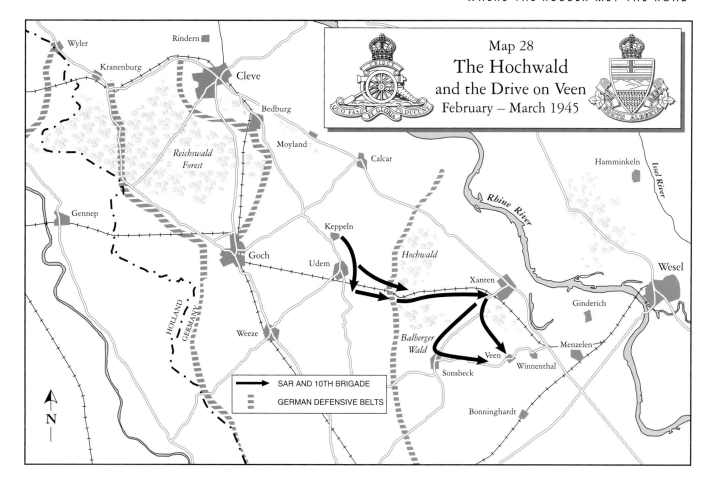

Map 28
The Hochwald
and the Drive on Veen
February – March 1945

SAR AND 10TH BRIGADE

GERMAN DEFENSIVE BELTS

leave centre. There had been no food on the train, and we were famished. So we sampled the Kummel: gin clear, very sweet and with the flavour of caraway seed – as Bowick had said, it was tasty. It went down so smoothly we proceeded to drink some more, well actually quite a bit more. It was now noon, our fatigue was gone, and we marched down to the "Palm Court" in fine fettle, promising ourselves a large lunch to make up for months of campaign rations and the previous 24 hours of no food whatsoever. To make things more gala, we ordered a bottle of champagne *each*. Bowick spoke French and encouraged by the mellow mood tried diligently, but unsuccessfully, to make a date with the waitress.

After the meal a little snooze seemed in order, and we started up the flight of stairs from the hotel lobby to our first floor room. During lunch those stairs had got a lot steeper, and as I climbed with exaggerated care, I had time to study the pattern in the avocado-green carpet that I still vividly remember. Strange thing about those stairs, as I was mounting they suddenly reared up and hit me smack in the forehead. ....

After he woke up in his hotel room, Luton remembered that neither he nor Bowick were feeling very good "but it was our only night in Brussels so we had to go out and do the town." In the course of the evening they acquired a couple of young British WAAF lovelies and, looking for a place to entertain them,

we pushed through a likely looking door in the blackout, and found ourselves in a plush lounge. So we sat down at a table and ordered a drink – and then wondered why everyone was staring at us. Another strange thing: the place was mostly filled with women, and women with very fancy clothes and made up to the nines. Realization began to filter through to our addled brains when one of our girls said, "I don't think we should be here." How right she was! Did you ever try bringing your own girl into a house of ill fame?

After that memory gets a bit hazy.[42]

Such misadventures could be funny but, unfortunately, there was a war on and, on 19 February, the SAR concentrated at the Dutch town of Best in preparation for a move into Germany. Three days later, just after midnight, the SAR moved out of Best and made a long and wearying overnight march to a position at the hamlet of Hau, near Cleve in Germany. As they crossed the border from Holland into the Third Reich, a sign reading "STOP SMILING. YOU ARE NOW ENTERING GERMANY" brought a sense of unease. Maybe so, but one thing the South Albertas noticed was that, in contrast to Holland where the population was existing on a near-starvation diet, there appeared to be no shortage of food in Germany and they quickly began to round up the livestock. RHQ Troop acquired three cows which provided them with fresh milk, the fitters kept a flock of hens to provide eggs and even RSM Mackenzie was observed driving a jeep with a large pig secured on the back seat. Major Bert Coffin, still in command in the continuing absence of Swatty Wotherspoon, drew the line, however, when he saw numerous beef carcasses being butchered while hoisted up on the barrels of the 17-pdr guns of the Firefly tanks, and strictly forbade this practice.

Coffin now learned the details of the regiment's role in the forthcoming attack, and he did not like what he heard. Conceived by Simonds and Vokes, it called for the SAR and the Algonquins (codenamed LION Force), less A Squadron, to put in a nighttime attack on the Hochwald Gap, a break in a high forested ridge. To get to that objective LION force would have to make a lengthy nighttime approach march and then cross a boggy, flooded valley (marked as "impassable for tanks" on the maps

Digging, digging, digging – yet another gun pit
Gunners of 13th Field dig yet another gun pit, this time in the wet, heavy soil of the Hochwald Forest area in February 1945. Each detachment had to dig a pit, about 15 feet in diameter, every time it changed position. It was one of the worst things about a gunner's job. FROM *13 CANADIAN FIELD REGIMENT, RCA*

provided), with woods on their left flank and a raised railway embankment on their right, both of which offered ideal enemy defensive positions. The attack was to go in at night and the assault troops would be guided by "artificial moonlight" provided by searchlights and 40 mm Bofors guns firing tracer to indicate the correct direction. Of course, these measures also indicated the same direction to the Germans but the worst part of this plan, however, was a proposed "right hook" by A Squadron and the Algonquin carrier platoon, which would advance independently to seize the southern end of the Gap while the main force seized the northern end. Both Coffin and Bob Bradburn of the Algonquins regarded this subsidiary operation as entirely too risky and suggested to Jefferson that it be dropped, but were told to carry it out.

For the South Albertas, Operation BLOCKBUSTER kicked off at 8 A.M. on 26 February 1945. While the other elements of the 4th Division carried out the preliminary attacks on Uedem, the

regiment moved out, with the Algonquins on its back decks, for the start line for the attack, scheduled for that night, which was near Kirseln, about 5 miles distant. It was a slow and hellish march through mud nearly 3 feet deep and there were constant delays when vehicles became bogged. By 7.45 P.M., after nearly twelve hours of slow and painful progress, the two units were still a mile away from Kirseln and the course of their progress was littered with mired tanks and vehicles. The operation was now eight hours behind schedule and the worst part of the march still lay ahead. Both Coffin and Bradburn realized that there was almost no hope, given the terrain, of beginning the attack before daylight on 27 February and therefore requested that it be delayed twelve hours so that it could be made under cover of darkness. Jefferson agreed and passed the request up to Vokes who took four hours before responding that LION Force was "to push on through" that day and cross the valley in front of the Gap by first light and "secure the objective by that time."[43] The right hook was also ordered to proceed.

By this time, the hardworking ARV crews had managed to unstick many of the bogged vehicles and, at 1.30 A.M. on 27 February, the march resumed. It took nearly four hours to move the last mile to the start line at Kirseln and, almost immediately, the eleven Stuart tanks of Recce Troop became bogged, as did all the wheeled vehicles, so Bradburn and Coffin transferred to the back deck of a Sherman and the procession continued. By 5.30 A.M., just before first light, LION Force – less Recce Troop and the company of Algonquins it had been carrying – reached the start line near Kirseln and were about a mile from the first objective. The two commanders decided to mount the attack using B Squadron and the three companies of Algonquins (one with only 30 all ranks) while C Squadron rendered fire support.

The attack on the Hochwald Gap commenced just as dawn was breaking on 27 February 1945. Assisted by the dim light, rain and mist, the assault force moved down off the Kirseln ridge into a shallow valley in front of the objective while the artillery brought down a heavy bombardment on the German positions. Surprisingly, there was little resistance but that really did not matter as the valley floor turned out to be a swamp. Only four tanks made it to the first German defence line, the first of three that had to be seized to take the Gap. The *Wehrmacht* now woke up and immediately brought down heavy artillery and anti-tank fire on the assault force from three different directions. In response, Bradburn and Coffin called down artillery fire on the ridge and the assault force kept going through the mud, the tanks slipping and sliding and the flatfeet trying to wade through the stuff, which was up to their knees. Despite increasingly heavy German fire, the second German defence line was secured by 8 A.M. but the assault force was now down to just two moving tanks of the fifteen or so that had started out, the remainder being bogged or trapped behind buildings by enemy anti-tank gun fire. The attached FOO was unable to help as his OP tank bogged shortly after the first calls for artillery support. Even worse, the infantry and tanks began to run low on ammunition and there were casualties to be evacuated. After a hurried consultation, Bradburn and Coffin decided to wait until dark before pushing on to the third and final German defence line at the top of the Gap. In the meantime all available tracked vehicles (wheeled vehicles simply could not move in the swampy valley) including the fitters' ARVs, infantry carriers and the medical half-tracks, were utilized to bring ammunition to the forward positions and evacuate casualties.

While the main part of LION Force was attacking the Gap itself, A Squadron, with Major Glen McDougall in command, and the attached Algonquin carrier platoon, attempted to carry out the "right hook." McDougall had difficulty getting around the town of Uedem, which was supposed to have been cleared the previous day by the 3rd Division, but turned out to be full of stubborn German paratroopers who lobbed *Panzerfausts* at his column. Uedem was also surrounded by a complicated maze of anti-tank ditches that claimed two Shermans before the column got clear of them. It took McDougall nearly three hours to circumvent the town and reach the railway from which his attack was supposed to start. This area had supposedly been cleared by 11th British Armoured Division the day before but, in fact, that formation had encountered such heavy resistance that they had not been able to accomplish this task. Unfortunately, this information was not given to 4th Armoured Division or to Mc-Dougall, and the result was disastrous.

The head of the column (which was now down to eight tanks, two having bogged and two having been left as rear link in Uedem, and four carriers) had just crossed a railway when they came under 88 mm fire from dug-in Tiger tanks and *Jagdpanther* self-propelled guns. The Germans quickly took out the lead tank of the column and German infantry in Uedem, thus encouraged, knocked out the last tank with a *Panzerfaust*. The tanks in the middle were trapped and the Germans then proceeded to destroy them one by one as their crews hastily bailed out. It was fortunate for the survivors that one of the Algonquin carriers was a Wasp flame thrower vehicle that, when hit, erupted and provided a smoke screen that covered a hasty retreat by the three remaining carriers and the South Alberta tank crews. Some of the

SAR crews made it out on the carriers and some escaped on foot but most were captured by the Germans.

During the last hours of 27 February Coffin and Bradburn revised their plan of attack. Throughout that awful afternoon on the ridge, the Argylls had begun to filter down into the valley and, with this reinforcement, Coffin and Bradburn decided to send C Squadron forward in the dark with the Highlanders to seize the objective while B Squadron firmed up with the remnants of the Algonquins at the second defence line. Unfortunately C Squadron had trouble getting through the mud on the valley floor so Lieutenant Leaman Caseley's B-4 Troop and Lieutenant Ed Reardon's B-2 Troop, a total of six tanks, went forward with the Highlanders. These plans were put into effect in the early hours of 28 February. There was surprisingly little resistance and, by first light, the Argylls had secured the Gap and had four rifle companies in line along the ridge. At this point the situation looked good as it was expected that 2nd Division, moving down from the north, would secure the Hochwald forest on the left side of the Gap, while the 11th British Armoured Division would take its objective, the Balberger Forest on the right side.

Unfortunately, neither of these formations were in close proximity on the morning of 28 February when the Germans, after

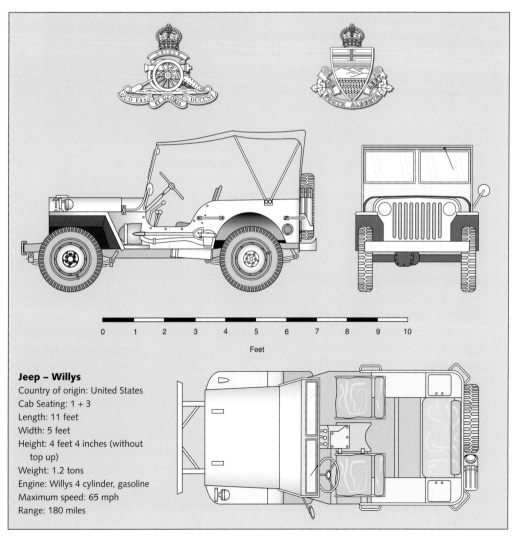

Jeep – Willys
Country of origin: United States
Cab Seating: 1 + 3
Length: 11 feet
Width: 5 feet
Height: 4 feet 4 inches (without top up)
Weight: 1.2 tons
Engine: Willys 4 cylinder, gasoline
Maximum speed: 65 mph
Range: 180 miles

And then it was their turn: German civilians, 1945
Appearing stunned by the magnitude of their defeat, disconsolate German civilians watch Canadian military traffic move along a secondary road in the Rhineland. For years the German population had been fed nothing but stories of victory, and the swift collapse of the Third Reich overwhelmed them.
CANADIAN ARMY PHOTO 47664

an extremely heavy artillery bombardment, put in a determined counterattack against both flanking forests. The attack on the Balberger Forest, which consisted only of infantry, was beaten off without trouble but the attack on the Hochwald forest, which included a mixed bag of about 15 armoured vehicles, including Tigers and *Jagdpanthers*, came close to overrunning the Argyll B Company which was in the most exposed position, and inflicted heavy casualties on it (the company would have only 17 unwounded men by nightfall). At one point a German tank commander shouted to the Canadians to "lay down their arms and surrender" but, in response, the commander of B Company killed him in his turret.[44] As the German armour surged around the Argylls, however, they exposed themselves to the six tanks of Caseley and Reardon which were in a fine ambush position about 200 yards down on the slope of the ridge. The crews immediately brought them under fire, destroying four Mk IV tanks or SPGs and bouncing so many 75 mm rounds off the Tigers that they hastily withdrew.

As the enemy assault died away, the ridge was again brought under heavy fire from the reverse slope and artillery bombardment from across the Rhine. In response, Coffin called in an air strike by Typhoons (bad weather had restricted the use of tactical aircraft on the previous two days). Although the aircraft mistakenly attacked a C Squadron troop that had taken up a forward position in the Balberger Forest, they managed to dampen German enthusiasm and, by last light, the ridge was still in Canadian hands – but just barely.

At this point, 4th Armoured Brigade entered the battle. During the early hours of 1 March, the Canadian Grenadier Guards made an abortive attack across the ridge only to lose ten tanks. When morning came, further infantry reinforcements arrived in the form of the Lincoln & Welland Regiment which put in an

"Cheers, Monty!"
When Montgomery visited the 13th Field at Wyler, Germany, in February 1945, he signed this photograph as a unit keepsake. Although the Americans detested him, British and Canadian soldiers respected Montgomery because they knew he would not commit them to battle without a careful plan and all available support.
FROM *13 CANADIAN FIELD REGIMENT, RCA*

attack against the Hochwald forest, supported by B Squadron, now down to 8 tanks. The Links encountered German armour on the reverse slope of the ridge and could make no progress but a hard fought little action ensued between B Squadron and the enemy tanks which resulted in four Mk IV tanks being brewed up with no casualties to the squadron. This was the last day of heavy fighting for 10th Brigade in the Gap as they were relieved on 2 March by 2nd Canadian Division and, thankfully, withdrew from that awful piece of ground. The brigade historian succinctly summed up the battle of the Hochwald Gap as an action that, for enemy bombardment and misery, was unparalleled during that formation's service in Northwest Europe. Once the initial attack had failed to cross the ridge line, "the game was up and the succeeding days of ceaseless battering were agonies of hopelessness."[45]

Throughout 10th Brigade's ordeal at the Hochwald, they had been supported by 13th Field from a gun position south of Calcar, a few miles north of it, which they had occupied on 23 February. This proved to be a very hot spot, as the regiment immediately came under heavy German counterbattery fire from medium guns on the east bank of the Rhine. On 24 February, a German shell hit and set on fire an ammunition truck being unloaded behind the position of 44 Battery. Bombardier John Stromquist although seriously wounded in the neck, called for a stretcher to evacuate the other wounded case and jumped into the truck and by throwing out cartridge cases and beating down the flames he was able to put out the fire. This action saved the explosion of many rounds of ammunition with the almost certain result of more casualties on the troop position. During the whole time the enemy continued to harass the gun position with shell fire. When the fire was put out B[omba]d[ie]r Stromquist collapsed and was then found to be seriously wounded.[46]

For his courageous act, Stromquist was awarded the Military Medal.

For the next week, 13th Field continued to support 2nd and 4th Divisions as they finally cleared the Germans out of the Hochwald and Balberger forests, preparatory to pushing them back into the Rhine. By this time, the men of 2 Canadian Corps were approaching exhaustion after nearly a month of ceaseless fighting. During the evening of 3 March 1945, Gunner John Raycroft of 44 Battery was tuning his radio when he picked up, by some freak of atmospherics, a North American radio station playing "Saturday Night is the Loneliest Night of the Week." As Raycroft, recalled, it was hard to keep turning his dial as

I imagined safe, happy people in clean clothes, and couples in the warmth and soft light actually touching one another. I looked at my little calendar. It was indeed Saturday night – still Saturday night, that is, in North America. But I broke away, tightened down onto a new frequency, and returned to the reality of the dark damp night and to the growl of distant killing.[47]

The "Mad Dash": Rhineland (3) – The battle for Veen, 4-10 March 1945

On the day after Raycroft's nostalgic moment, the German commander in the Rhineland, *Generaloberst* Alfred Schlemm, concluded that it was no longer possible to defend the west bank of the Rhine. The American Ninth Army, delayed by the flooding on the Roer River, was now pushing up from the south and his last good defensive position in the north, the Hochwald-Balberger Ridge, was in Canadian hands. He therefore decided to withdraw across the Rhine because, as he explained to his superiors in Berlin, if he did not, there would be no troops left to defend the east bank of the river against the inevitable Allied assault. That day, Schlemm began to pull his troops back from the Hochwald behind a covering position anchored on the fortified hamlets of Veen and Winnenthal, in which he deployed his best infantry, the First Parachute Army Assault Battalion, backed up by a heavy anti-tank gun screen.

For their part, the South Albertas got a single day of badly-needed rest after their ordeal on the Hochwald. On 4 March they were ordered by Vokes to "form a fast moving group" with Argyll infantry mounted in Kangaroo APCs and execute a "mad dash" to Veen, that "was to be pushed on ruthlessly," with any opposition "to be bypassed if possible."[48] They moved out in the early afternoon and, as they did so, they passed a film cameraman who

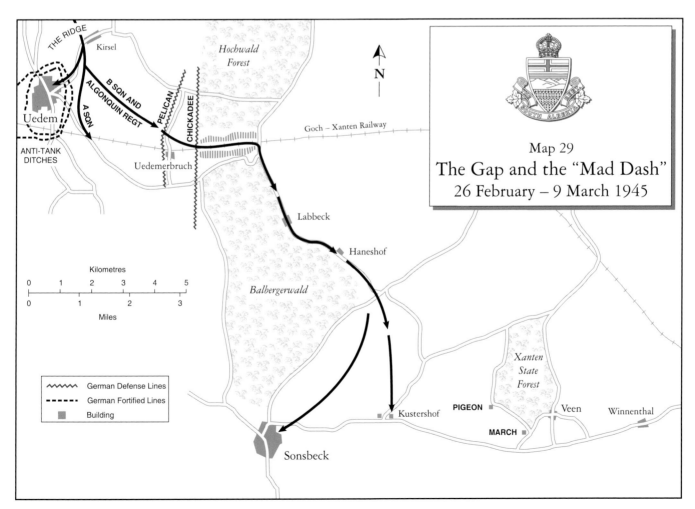

Rangers on the road

New Brunswick Rangers take a break near Louisendorf on 26 February 1945 just before the attack on the Hochwald. The New Brunswick Rangers (10th Independent Machine Gun Company) manned heavy Vickers machineguns and 4.2-inch mortars for the 10th Brigade. They were usually parcelled out among the three infantry battalions of that formation and as a result their contributions are often overlooked. Note the man with his name stencilled on the back of his jerkin, a popular practice. CANADIAN ARMY PHOTO 46987

Through the mud and the mud: The Hochwald, February 1945

A Sherman Firefly of the SAR attempts to navigate nearly three feet of mud on its way to attack the Hochwald Gap, a battle in which mud caused almost as many tank casualties as the Germans. By this time, the South Albertas resembled a well-armed Gypsy tribe. Note the variety of items stored on the vehicle, including a German rifle leaning against the turret, steel helmets and haversacks on the turret, a tent and ration box on the front glacis, a .30 calibre ammunition box on the right fender, what appears to be a Bren gun slung on the rear of the turret, and another ammo box and a shovel on the back deck. NAC, PA-113676

photographed the vehicles of Recce and AA Troops, which led the pack. This caused some interest and, as Corporal Bob Clipperton informed his wife Andy, "You should be able to get a glimpse of me in a future newsreel as they cranked a reel of us while we were shoving off."[49] That newsreel has survived in the archives of the British Pathe corporation (mistakenly titled "British troops liberating France") and it shows South Alberta Crusaders, Shermans and Stuarts moving in Germany in March 1945, most tanks having crumpled fenders, all burdened with an amazing variety of objects strapped all over them (including what appears to be a rocking chair), and hatches full of weary men in dirty tank suits wearing their berets in any but the regulation fashion. One of the Recce Stuarts has a big, fat army sock serving as a muzzle cap for its 37 mm gun which looks ridiculous until you realize that it was probably intentional as the co-driver could yank it off the muzzle without exposing himself (not the case if the regulation canvas muzzle cap was in place). All in all, the South Albertas setting out on the "Mad Dash" in March 1945 appear as rather piratical, but thoroughly professional, members of a combat armoured unit, which, of course, is exactly what they were.

Unfortunately, the "Mad Dash to Veen" proved to be an extremely difficult movement to make as the Germans had mined all the possible roads leading to that place and, in many areas, had used explosives to create craters – some as wide as 70 feet – on the approach routes. The "Mad Dash" turned out to be a slow, painstaking crawl down from the Hochwald Ridge that required nearly two days to complete and it was not until 6 March that the combined force was near the hamlet of Veen which, by this time, had been turned into a fortress by its paratrooper garrison.

The ground around Veen was flat and swampy and it proved almost impossible for vehicles, either tracked or wheeled, to move off the roads, which were covered by well-sited and well-concealed German anti-tank guns. Late in the afternoon of 6 March, an attempt to probe the objective came to grief when AP fire knocked out two Kangaroo APCs thus blocking the main road to the objective. For this reason, there was no tank support for the Argylls when they put in a two-company attack on Veen that night, an attack that was thrown back with heavy casualties, including the loss of 32 men taken prisoner. This called for some rethinking of matters as it was clear that Veen was going to be a difficult objective. It was decided to mount a two-battalion attack the next day, the SAR supporting the Algonquins and the

BCR supporting the Links, with the Sonsbeck-Veen road being the dividing line between the two forces. As friendly artillery, also hampered by the German mining and demolition of the approach routes, was still out of range, B and C Squadrons of the SAR were ordered to provide direct fire support while A Squadron went in with the infantry.

The attack started late in the morning of 7 March but it only got as far as two clusters of farm buildings, codenamed PIGEON and MARCH, before it was decisively stopped by a combination of mines, automatic and anti-tank gun fire. A Squadron, which was down to about ten tanks, lost five of them to mines or AP fire and, once in the area of the farm buildings, discovered that they were not only covered by concealed anti-tank guns but were mined and booby trapped. All attempts by either the Algonquins or the SARs to move out from the cover of these buildings met with a hail of fire – nor could they withdraw, as the approaches were also covered by enemy weapons. As a result, the remnants of A Squadron stayed with the Algonquins (whose rifle companies were by this time at about 25% of their authorized strength) for two days, totally stymied by the defenders. Attempts by the other squadrons to reinforce these forward positions were stopped by both mines and fire.

In his terse diary entries for 6 and 7 March 1945, Trooper John Neff of B Squadron provides a glimpse of his crew's experiences in and around Veen:

Tues. Mar 6
We advanced, bypassing Xanten going toward Veen. Here we saw 2 burned out Stag[hound]s. We halted by some farm buildings as the whole area was mined. We took on a ground mounted 88 and won for a change. Jerry moaning minnied us every 5 minutes at these cross roads where we pulled up.

Wed. Mar 7
Still pinned down at the cross roads. We keep pecking away at Jerry whom we can see about 400 yds to our left. We have burnt down all his houses, but he won't move out. He has our corner measured to the inch and mortars us every time we try to move about. We have the greatest concentration of Arty of the war backing this attack and what a noise.[50]

By last light on 8 March, the situation did not look very good and it was decided that a major attack, with artillery support, would be mounted on Veen the following day. That night, however, the defenders of Veen, having accomplished their purpose of delaying 4th Armoured Division's advance long enough for a complete evacuation of the east bank of the Rhine, quietly withdrew under cover of darkness and when 10th Brigade discovered this fact on 9 March, everyone rejoiced.

The Rhineland battles proved very costly for the South Alberta Regiment. The unit lost 61 tanks, almost its total AFV strength,

The Hochwald, February 1945
With their decks loaded with Algonquins, South Alberta tanks set off from Louisendorf for the nightmare approach march to the Hochwald. The attack was supposed to go in during darkness hours but the mud delayed the deployment of the two units and they were forced to carry it out in broad daylight. NAC, PA-113672

Tired but unbowed – Algonquins move up, March 1945

Led by a rather dashing lieutenant, a platoon of "Algoons" moves up to attack Veen. The Algonquin Regiment got off to a bad start in the European campaign, taking heavy casualties in Normandy and at Moerkerkke, but by 1945 they had recovered and were a very good outfit. Their commanding officer was Lieutenant-Colonel Bob Bradburn, formerly of the 19th Dragoons and the South Albertas, a tough, no-nonsense professional. CANADIAN ARMY PHOTO, 47462

and 83 casualties including 10 killed and 73 wounded or taken prisoner. B-3 Troop had gone into action on 27 February with 19 men and four tanks – it came out of it on 9 March with eight unwounded men and one tank. If the South Albertas and the other men of 4th Armoured Division were expecting praise for their efforts from Vokes, however, they were to be sorely disappointed. On 12 March Vokes assembled every officer in the division in a large field and proceeded to lecture them on their many faults, which had resulted in the recent operations not having achieved complete success, including a lack of drive, lack of physical stamina and outright cowardice. Justifiably angry, the officers bit their tongues but, as one South Alberta troop leader who was present that day commented, Vokes "should have been apologizing to us" for his ridiculous plan which sent inadequate forces across terrible ground against strong enemy defences, "instead of shouting the disgraceful comments he made."[51]

After the Kapelsche Veer, the Hochwald was perhaps the South Alberta's most terrible battle and it was with very good reason that, more than half a century later, the South Alberta Veterans Association erected a bronze plaque in the square of the little village of Uedemerbruch, the closest locality to the actual Hochwald Gap. It informs those who read it that, not far away, the SAR suffered its worst casualties in men and tanks in a single day of fighting.

"Where the rubber met the road": Waiting for the last act to begin, 12-23 March

When the SAR was pulled back to Tilburg in Holland for a rest period on 12 March, their vehicles were loaded with loot acquired in Germany. At Tilburg the tank lines soon began to resemble a gigantic flea market as they disposed of their ill-gotten gains – everything from bicycles to table linen – to the Dutch in exchange for hard cash or liquor. Padre Silcox, who always did his level best to tend to the spiritual wellbeing of his flock – a forlorn hope given the attitudes of the tough and profane young men who fought in the SAR – was somewhat distressed by this activity. At a church parade held on 18 March, he announced that he had thought about taking as the text of his sermon the scripture, "Let him that stole steal no more," but "decided to let it go for the time being."[52]

The South Albertas rejoiced when Swatty Wotherspoon returned to them at Tilburg after an absence of nearly two months occasioned by an appointment to run the divisional battle school and temporary command of both 4th and 10th Brigades. It was not that the South Albertas did not like Major Bert Coffin, who had led them through the difficult fighting on the Kapelsche Veer and the Hochwald, it was because they knew that Wotherspoon had no compunction about arguing with his superiors over bad orders. Wotherspoon was always a distant figure to his men but they wanted him around when they went into battle because they respected his abilities. As one SAR troop leader commented, the first question his crews would ask after he returned from an O Group for a forthcoming operation was whether Wotherspoon would be with the unit when it took place. If the troop leader replied that Swatty would be present, they were happy, but if he told his men that Wotherspoon would be absent, they

Rumbling by the flatfeet

A South Alberta Sherman passes infantry from the Lincoln & Welland Regiment near Sonsbeck on 7 March 1945. Although there was rivalry between the two arms in 10th Brigade, the Albertans looked after the infantry and the flatfeet looked after them. As the campaign progressed, 10th Brigade became one of the most experienced "combined arms" fighting teams in the Canadian army and the cutting edge of 4th Division. NAC, PA-115578

It was not all one way: German artillery fire

This photograph, taken on 7 March 1945, shows a heavy German smoke bombardment of 4th Division's forward units in the state forest between Xanten and Veen. The Germans had considerable artillery support during the Rhineland battles and they used it to good effect. CANADIAN ARMY PHOTO.

would get cranky, "bitch a lot" and threaten to disobey orders.[53] They would go into action, of course, but they were not happy about fighting without Swatty at the head of the regiment.

At Tilburg, the SAR got three days to rest and clean up, incorporate new reinforcements and vehicles and service its equipment. The heavy casualties suffered in the Hochwald meant that many new men joined the fighting squadrons, including some of the despised Zombies but Wotherspoon wisely concealed their identity and, in the end, they fought as well as the volunteers. The new men coming into the regiment were not always from Alberta or even from Western Canada but the old originals from 1940 still constituted the "senior management" of the SAR including most of the regimental staff and almost all the squadron and crew commanders. The result was, as Trooper David Marshall, himself from Ontario, commented, "a supportive family atmosphere" in the SAR as men "who had been with the regiment since mobilization were still there, which lent a degree of stability and a feeling of belonging that can only come with men who know each other well."[54]

There were many complaints from officers and NCOs about the quality of training of the new reinforcements and, wanting to work with the new arrivals, Wotherspoon moved the regiment from Tilburg to a suitable area near Loon op Zand on 17 March 1945, there to carry out five days of exercises. This was useful for the new men but did not particularly impress the veterans – Trooper Neff of B Squadron cynically recorded in his diary on 19 March that "the main reason for the move was to get the boys sober again" after their stay in Tilburg.[55] Lieutenant Bill Luton, who had been with the unit since December and regarded himself as a veteran, found the training "pleasantly routine" but noted that "combat with the enemy was where the rubber met the road" and that he "had learned more in two weeks of BLOCKBUSTER about *fighting* than in the previous two years of instruction."[56] The break, however, did not last long as on 22 March Wotherspoon attended an O Group at 10th Brigade to learn about the SAR's role in the forthcoming Rhine crossing

and, three days later, the SAR moved to a position on the bank of that river near Cleve.

Meanwhile, 13th Field Regiment was in position about 5 miles away near the small town of Wissel. Like the South Albertas, the gunners had enjoyed a period of rest and re-organization after the recent fighting but, unlike the SAR, they did not go back to friendly Holland but spent it near the destroyed city of Cleve on the banks of the Rhine. They moved there on 11 March and for the next ten days serviced their vehicles, recalibrated their guns and got ready for the next operation. Orders were issued that all vehicles were to be thoroughly cleaned, re-painted if necessary and their identification markings touched up if required. All non-regulation items carried in vehicles were to be thrown away and an inspection was held to make sure this latter order was obeyed. As Gunner Raycroft remembered, "pots and pans, sofa cushions, chairs, a small wood stove ... lengths of pipe ... and bed-rolls of immense proportions, usually because they contained "liberated" material" appeared in front of each vehicle in the regiment.[57] Raycroft's line crew hid their MP 40 Schmeisser sub-machinegun and MP 44 Assault rifle and also a large head of cheese, which they had found useful as an emergency ration while in the field. Gunner "Dog," stayed with Joe Shemrock as did a number of other pets who had decided to join the Canadian Active Service Force. That job done, the "Chinese Hussars" or mobile bath units arrived and 13th Field got a "hosing down" – the first one since the unit had left Nijmegen, forty days before. Of course, now that spring had arrived, 13th Field received its long overdue issue of winter clothing and then moved to gun positions surveyed near Wissel on the bank of the Rhine. They turned out be quite comfortable as Wissel had been abandoned and the gunners enjoyed good accommodation in unwrecked houses where such "novelties as china dishes, beautiful silverware, white sheets, pyjamas, dressing gowns, slippers, civilian radios and victrolas were plentiful and used freely."[58]

After that, it was just a matter of waiting for the last act to begin.

Firing over the Rhine

A 25-pdr. gun detachment fires across the Rhine to support the Allied assault in late March 1945. Note that the gun pit is fortified with empty shell crates packed with dirt, an indication that these gunners have been occupying it for some time. Also note that they are wearing rabbit-fur-lined German winter camouflage smocks, stocks of which had been captured the previous autumn and were a popular garment. NAC, PA-142108

CHAPTER FIFTEEN

"True Albertan Style"

"Over the Rhine, then, let us go": Operation PLUNDER, 23 March–1 April 1945

By late March 1945 Hitler's Third Reich was in its death throes. In the east the Soviet armies had lopped off East Prussia and were poised on the Oder River, gathering their strength for the final offensive that would take them to Berlin. On the Western Front, General Omar S. Bradley's 12 Army Group had secured a bridge over the Rhine River at Remagen and were preparing a massive drive to take the vital Ruhr industrial area. For his part, Montgomery had completed preparations for his 21 Army Group to undertake Operation PLUNDER, a massive assault crossing of the Rhine on a 20-mile front using Second British and Ninth U.S. Armies, which would be preceded by Operation VARSITY, an airborne landing. Crerar's First Canadian Army, although it would contribute some formations to the assault, was assigned the task of holding the west bank of the Rhine until bridgeheads had been secured, at which point it would cross and assume its by-now-traditional position on the left flank of 21 Army Group as it drove northeast to the Baltic. The Rhine crossing would be preceded by an air and artillery bombardment that dwarfed even that carried out for Operation VERITABLE. Comprising some 3,500 guns, the artillery plan called for using the Sherman 75 mm weapons of the armoured units of 4th Division to fire a diversionary bombardment on Emmerich, across the river from Cleve. By 23 March 1945, preparations for PLUNDER were complete and Montgomery issued a special order of the day to the troops under his command which contained the exhortation: "Over the Rhine, then, let us go. And good hunting to you all on the other side."[2]

The South Albertas learned about their part in the forthcoming operation on 22 March after Swatty Wotherspoon returned from an O Group at division headquarters. They were not very

> You wicked piece of vicious tin!
> Call you a gun? Don't make me grin.
> You're just a bloated piece of pipe.
> You couldn't hit a hunk of tripe.
> But when you're with me in the night,
> I'll tell you, pal, you're just alright!
>
> Each day I wipe you free of dirt.
> Your dratted corners tear my shirt.
> I cuss at you and call you names,
> You're much more trouble than my dames.
> But, boy, do I love to hear you yammer,
> When you're spitting lead in a business-like manner.
>
> You conceited piece of salvage junk.
> I think this prowess talk is bunk.
> Yet, if I want a wall of lead
> Thrown at some Jerry's head
> It is to you I raise my hat;
> You're a damned good pal … you silly gat![1]

happy about it because, as one troop leader remarked, if indirect firing "had been our cup of tea, we would have signed up for the artillery in the first place."[3] Nonetheless, grumbling, they moved to their positions just south of Cleve where the 75 mm gun Shermans were positioned in line and camouflaged, while the men from AA and Recce Troops, as well as the crews of the 17-pdr. Firefly tanks, were assigned the task of supplying ammunition to the firing vehicles.

H-Hour for Operation PLUNDER was 9 P.M. on 23 March 1945 but the pre-assault bombardment, fired by the artillery units of 2 Canadian Corps, began at 5 P.M. that day. So many guns were firing that, in the position of 13th Field Regiment near Wissel, Gunner John Raycroft recalled that, after the "horrendous first explosion, the noise blended into a solid roar."[4] The regiment's three batteries fired for an hour and five minutes and then rested for a couple of hours before commencing the fire plan intended to cover the landing of 51st Highland Division on the opposite bank. There was some German counter-battery fire and three gunners were wounded, although not seriously. Once they had started, 13th Field fired steadily for the next four days, meeting target requests from FOOs accompanying the assault troops and, when not engaged in that task, firing DF and pre-planned bombardments on known German positions.

For the men on the gun positions, these four days blended into one long one. The battery command posts would transmit firing orders to the individual gun detachments at each 25-pdr. by means of the Tannoy or loudspeaker system and these orders were acknowledged by the No. 1 on each gun holding his hand vertically above his head or, if not in sight of the battery command post, through the Tannoy itself. The No. 1 would then pass on the orders to his detachment: the No. 2 on the right of

Firing at night, Wissel, March 1945
Day and night for five days, the men of 13th Field Regiment fired on the east bank of the Rhine. FROM *13 CANADIAN FIELD REGIMENT, RCA*

Full recoil – firing across the Rhine, 1945
A 25-pdr. of 13th Field at full recoil during the bombardment of the east bank of the Rhine in March 1945. During five days of firing to support the Rhine crossing, Commonwealth gunners landed nearly four million rounds on enemy positions. FROM *13 CANADIAN FIELD REGIMENT, RCA*

the breech; the No. 3 or gunlayer on the small seat to the left of the breech who laid the gun by means of its various sighting devices; and the ammunition numbers, Nos. 4 to 6, who prepared the rounds. As the 25-pdr. carriage was mounted on a platform, not unlike a big cartwheel, it was relatively easy to traverse to a new bearing and this task was accomplished by the No. 1 using a handspike mounted on the trail. At Wissel in March 1945, targets, charges, fuzes and rates or scale of fire varied, but the projectiles were almost always the yellow-banded HE shells which the No. 4 would bring forward to the No. 2, who would ram them into the breech. When the order to "Fire" was given, No. 3 would pull the lever on the side of the breech and the gun would

fire with a short, sharp bark that pressed on the ear drums and the detachment would be surrounded by reeking cordite fumes. As the tube recoiled on its cradle, No. 2 pulled the lever to open the breech and eject the spent brass cartridge with a tinny clank. By this time, the No. 4 would have another round ready and the procedure would be repeated.

For three days the gunners of 13th Field fired across the Rhine amid noise, fumes and the unending work of feeding the ever-hungry breech, clearing away the empty cartridge cases, and bringing up fresh ammunition. It was a laborious job but one that required concentration, particularly on the part of the No. 3 or gunlayer who knew that even the slightest mistake on his part might result in a round falling on friendly troops bringing the dreaded "STOP!" order which froze all personnel, including the command post staff, who touched nothing until the Gun Position Officer found the source of the error and ascertained who was to blame. On and on it went, day after day, sometimes for hours at a stretch until the paint blistered from the barrels of the guns. Occasionally, the tired gun detachments snatched a bite to eat or took a quick nap beside their weapons so as to be ready in case there were orders for fresh firing, or an SOS (emergency) target. This unvarying and wearying routine was only broken by Gunner Germscheid, B Echelon cook and regimental wag, who somewhere "found a carriage and a couple of very fine horses" and, dressed "in tails and a top hat," drove back and forth along the main street of Wissel, "with all these shells going over" to entertain the boys.[5] When 13th Field finally stopped firing at 12 P.M. on 28 March 1945, Gunner George Lynch-Staunton who, having recovered from the wounds he had suffered on D-Day and joined 13th Field in March 1945, remembered, "the silence was deafening and we found that we were still yelling at each other for a long time after the guns were quiet."[6]

For their part, at 2.45 P.M. that same day, along with the other armoured units of 4th Division, the South Albertas began their diversionary bombardment of Emmerich. For the next 51 hours, with very few breaks, the SAR fired across the Rhine, at the slow rate of 5 rounds every two minutes, never seeing the target but simply obeying orders passed on to them by the artillery, and shifting their fire as required. The tank crews were spelled off by the men of Recce and AA Troops and everybody got a chance to load and fire the main guns of the Shermans. By the second day of this exercise, tempers were beginning to run hot and the guns themselves were exhibiting signs of stress – but it continued until 6 P.M. on 30 March when the "cease fire" order came after the SAR had dumped 38,325 rounds of 75 mm HE on the far bank of the Rhine.

"Crossing the mighty barrier": On the east bank of the Rhine, April 1945

Not surprisingly, the German defenders were overwhelmed by this massive bombardment and, by 31 March, 21 Army Group had a permanent foothold on the east bank of the Rhine. The sappers completed the first bridges over the river and 3rd and

4th Divisions prepared to cross. Just after breakfast that day, Swatty Wotherspoon held a squadron commanders' O Group to inform them that the regiment would be crossing the Rhine the next night. Once over the famous waterway, it would lead 10th Brigade which, in turn, would lead 4th Division north toward the Twente Canal and the SAR had orders to, if possible, capture an intact bridge over that obstacle. When the squadron commanders returned from the Regimental O Group, they held their own O Groups and Lieutenant Bill Luton of C Squadron recorded the details of the briefing of Major Stan Purdy, his squadron commander, in his notebook. There was the usual information about objectives, timings, routes, own and enemy forces which were thought to be three paratroop divisions, a panzergrenadier division and two Dutch SS brigades which caused Luton to wonder: "Why did we always seem to get the crack German divisions on our front?"[7] In view of the quality of the enemy, Purdy stressed that the troop leaders should "be very careful to conserve ammunition against the Paratroops" as "they would not be spooked by lavish, but ineffectual fire." At the end of the briefing, he emphasized that the troop leaders were also responsible for the behaviour of their men in Germany, and Luton's notebook entries for the O Group end with two lines in block capitals: "NO LOOTING" and "NO KILLING LIVESTOCK."[8]

As Luton remembered,

The meeting broke up hurriedly, since the junior officers had a lot to do in the next 12 to 18 hours. In my notebook, four more pages follow which cover my troop tasks for that period, including such items as "study map," "get morphine," "hold O-Group," and make an updated nominal roll. The men had lots to do as well: tank maintenance, refueling, stowing ammunition and procuring rations. The following morning Major Purdy was called back to RHQ for a second O Group with his opposite numbers in the Argylls, who would be going into battle with us. Upon his return my notebook acquired another page of jottings, dealing with troop tactics for the attack: C Squadron was to advance on a two-mile front, with 1 Troop and 3 Troop leapfrogging on the left, 2 Troop and 4 Troop doing the same on the right.

It was a busy time.[9]

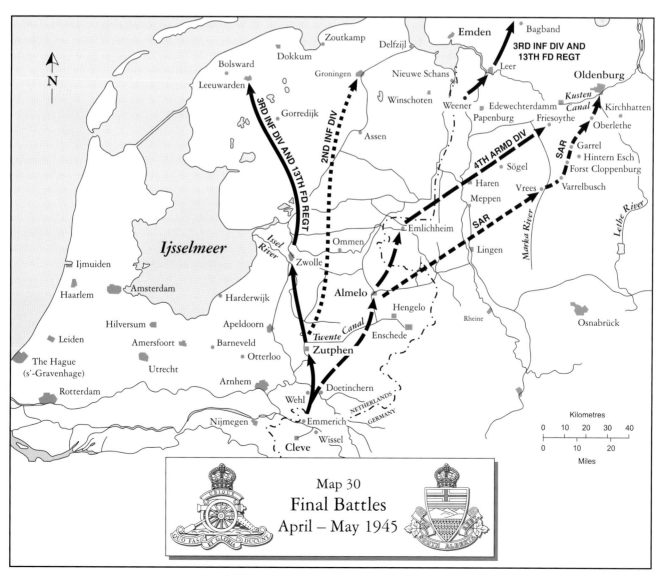

Map 30
Final Battles
April – May 1945

Not a Sherman but Sherwood Forest: SAR tank on the Rhine 1945
The crew of this tank has made a rather unsuccessful attempt to camouflage it in its position on the banks of the Rhine near the city of Cleve. For nearly three days the SAR bombarded the east bank of the Rhine, dropping 38,325 rounds of HE onto the German positions opposite. It was dreadful, boring, wearying work. SAR ARCHIVES

The rest of that day and the next was spent in preparing and, in the early hours of 1 April 1945, the South Albertas had the rather dubious honour of being the first armoured unit of the division to cross the Rhine on a lengthy pontoon bridge that the sappers had constructed over to Emmerich on the far bank. Moving along that pitching, rearing – and clearly temporary – structure, which required the drivers to keep their feet on their accelerators as though their vehicles were going uphill, was a unique experience that nobody wanted to repeat. Everyone got across safely, however, and, by first light, the regiment was in a harbour near Emmerich.

Wotherspoon now sent out patrols from Recce Troop to establish routes north to the Twente and waited for reports before putting the regiment on the road. Almost immediately the Recce boys informed him that the roads reserved for 4th Armoured Division were illegally occupied by a British division and the result was a clusterfuddle of massive proportions – happy April Fool's Day! The only Recce patrol to get clear of this mess was led by the intrepid Sergeant Albert Halkyard, who not only managed to winkle his way through it, but also to cross the border into Holland, thus becoming the first Canadian soldier to enter that country from Germany as well as the first to enter it from Holland. It took all day to straighten out the confusion and it was not until early evening that the South Albertas were on the road north to the Twente.

The going was better on 2 April and Recce Troop patrols spread out across the divisional front, looking for a bridge over the Twente. A two-tank Stuart patrol led by Sergeant Jimmy Simpson

spotted an unblown bridge but Simpson's tank was knocked out by an anti-tank gun before he could get close to it. He reported the news to Wotherspoon, who dispatched Lieutenant Bill Luton's C-1 Troop with an infantry company in an attempt to secure the precious crossing. Luton, thinking that "this could be a small version of the capture of the Remagen Bridge over the Rhine by American tanks," moved his troop forward as fast as possible.[10] As he brought the bridge under observation, Luton realized that taking it would not be an easy job – his troop would have to approach it in single file on the road which was probably mined, and there was high ground on the other side that would make an ideal position for an anti-tank gun. As Luton recalled,

> My appraisal was made quickly – more quickly than it takes to read – with a facility born of much practice. My plan, simple because so few alternatives existed, was to move C-11 [his tank] forward on the road, halt in a turret down position for further observation, move up to hull down, and if no fire was drawn, to move onto the near side of the bridge. From there, any approach by a demolition party could be prevented and a plan could be made for the next step. A quick order was sent out on the squadron net to the other tanks to cover our advance … and on the intercom to the driver to go ahead at full speed.

"Challenger" and its secret weapon
After the South Albertas crossed the Rhine, they found themselves engaging enemy infantry at frequent intervals. Sergeant Jim Nicholson decided that increased firepower would be useful and took the advantage of a rest period to manufacture a secret weapon – twin .30 calibre machineguns that could be fired from his crew commander's hatch – for "Challenger," his Sherman Firefly. SAR ARCHIVES

None of this was ever put to the test. My tank had only reached the end of the woods when a tremendous explosion shook the ground and a spectacular mass of debris shot far up into the air. The race had been lost.[11]

The bridge was blown and that night Wotherspoon concentrated the regiment at Lochem, ready to move in any direction. On the following day, the Links secured a bridgehead across the Twente at Delden, 20 miles east of Lochem, and the greater part of the division advanced in a northeasterly direction, continually moving farther away from the SAR. The regiment was given the task of holding the line of the Twente Canal which provided convenient flank protection for the division and they spent a rather quiet period exchanging the occasional round with the Germans on the other side of the waterway. The enemy across the canal were paratroopers and they had come up with a new trick of lobbing *Panzerfaust* rounds at high trajectory over the waterway, so the South Albertas replied with rounds from their PIATs, the Commonwealth equivalent.

Lieutenant Bill Luton was bothered by the fact that the South Albertas had no supporting infantry with them along the Twente. In contrast to most of the other armoured regiments in the Canadian army, Wotherspoon liked to leave his tanks in the forward infantry positions at night, rather than withdraw (as was the normal practice) to a secure harbour in the rear to refuel and re-ammunition. Actually it made sense as having friendly infantry around at night make the tanks a lot less vulnerable. There were no infantry, however, at the Twente and Luton was acutely conscious that

Distinguished gentlemen

If Canadians have one national characteristic, it is a fatal weakness for outlandish headgear. When they entered Germany, the boys discovered that most German homes contained top hats, used for formal occasions in Europe, and it was not long before they were sporting them. The sartorial splendour of the soldier in this photo is rather spoiled by the fact his comrade is holding a chicken. NAC, PA-137459

sion for a hurried visit so that the crossing was made with the active assistance of searchlights and ack-ack guns."[13] Over they went – including Gunner "Dog" perched in his half-track – although, while the regimental historian waxed eloquent about what a "great feeling" it was "to be across the river which had been an obstacle to victory for so long," Gunner Lynch-Staunton's reaction was more prosaic.[14] He took the opportunity to have a leak in the mighty Rhine from the tailgate of his truck as it drove over the long and swaying bridge.

For the next two weeks, 13th Field moved directly north as 3rd Division cleared the east bank of the Ijssel River. During this drive, which took place on Dutch territory, the regiment supported 8th Infantry Brigade (Chaudière Regiment, North Shore Regiment and Queen's Own Rifles) in a series of small actions as the flatfeet took town after town. In contrast to the unit's work during Operations VERITABLE, BLOCKBUSTER and PLUNDER, where it had contributed to massive artillery programmes, it now reverted to a smaller but more interesting operational level as its gunners

no slit trenches surrounded us complete with Bren guns and watchful men. The long winter nights on the Kapelsche Veer had been made less threatening by the comforting presence of white-clad men of the Links & Winks [Lincoln & Welland Regiment] and when cut off in the Hochwald Gap we had about us the stout Argylls from my home town of Hamilton. This was my first experience of a night position facing Jerry close at hand with no infantry and I did not like it at all. ...... Although I did not know this at the time, in the month ahead we were often to be without infantry. We had to learn to cope alone, and we did.[12]

Meanwhile, 13th Field drove over the Rhine during the evening of 1 April and, as "if the thrill of crossing the mighty barrier was not sufficient in itself, the German airforce took the occa-

getting away from being a small cog in the big wheel of Mike, Victor and Yoke concentrations, large barrages and fire plans, were now part of a more intimate battery show. Here the gun areas were selected, zero lines chosen, and administration carried out on a battery level. The fighting, too, became a battery and battalion affair, and information, received as to the progress made, was easier to obtain and more enthusiastically received.[15]

German resistance took the form of stubborn rearguards, often composed of very young soldiers who, though frightened, would fight very hard, making up with fanaticism what they lacked in combat experience. When 8th Brigade entered the town of Zutphen, there was some fierce house-to-house fighting and the opposing positions were so close that artillery fire could not be brought down on the Germans. Flamethrower vehicles were brought up to clear the enemy strongpoints and Gunner Raycroft, who was up at the front that day, laying wire with his crew to the OP stationed with the North Shore Regiment, remembered what happened next:

Shaw and I got into the house at the end of the block and had a perfect view down into the street, and also a perfect view of their target: the house across the intersection. The lead Wasp [flamethrowing carrier] nosed out into the open, slewed himself straight and came up the street, gathering speed, with the other two following behind. Their machine guns were blazing, and the enemy's fire was sending sparks off the carriers' steel. The first Wasp, and then the other two, let go their stream of flame.

When the fire went through the windows, I actually turned my head for fear of witnessing what I had heard often happens: men coming out in flames and screaming to death in agony. ......

But it didn't happen this time, and I had a treasonous feeling of relief. Those defenders must have dashed to the back of the house at the last second – or died instantly.[16]

During this push north, Dutch civilians were uniformly friendly and helpful, particularly the Orange Resistance organization, which provided accurate information on enemy positions and strengths. As the gun positions were some way back from the frontline and not often under enemy artillery fire, they were a popular attraction for the civilians and sometimes took on the atmosphere of a small village fair:

Nearly all the gun positions had a similar story to tell about the crowds of people who invaded their area to look in wonderment at the equipment, to ask for cigarettes and chocolate or just to be near activity. It was often the people's first day of liberation, and they made the best of it. Baker Troop was a typical example. Here the crowds around the guns and the command post were so great that BSM Hooper was forced to rope off restricted areas so that the troop could function properly. Even at that, some pretty "young thing" was sure to trip over the tannoy wire and break communications to one of the guns. Of course, the kitchen was a great attraction. To see what the men ate and, perhaps, obtain some of it! Many had never seen white bread for five years, nor tasted the weird and wonderful dishes which were just another monotonous meal to the soldiers. Two of the feature events for the spectators were the firing of the guns and the rides in the exchange crew carrier. The firing of a gun meant a chance for the braver ones to pull the firing lever and, also,

meant another cartridge case for a souvenir hunter to take home. The rides in the carrier were shared by all the teenage "kids" of the district. With flags flying and arms waving, the carrier would run regular trips along the road to the nearest town.[17]

Fortunately for 13th Field and the infantry they were supporting, the Germans were only fighting rearguard actions and 3rd Division drove them steadily north for more than a hundred miles. By this time, 1 Canadian Corps had arrived from Italy and, for the first time, all five divisions of the Canadian army overseas went into action together and some old acquaintances were renewed when the unit found itself in a position along side the gunners of 1st Canadian Division. By 18 April, the forward units of the division were at Bolsward near the north sea coast of Holland when 13th Field was informed that artillery support was no longer required as 3rd Division had completed its task of clearing the east bank of the Ijsselmeer. On 19 April, the regiment was pulled back to Gorredijk for a rest that was devoted to vehicle and gun maintenance.

"My knees were knocking something terrible": Armoured recce: The South Albertas' last battles, 11 April–4 May 1945

While 3rd Division rolled north through Holland the South Albertas remained along the line of the Twente Canal. On 11 April, when they were shifted to Meppen to get a couple of days of rest, 4th and 10th Brigades were near Friesoythe, about two thirds of the way to the 4th Armoured Division's final objective, the city of Oldenburg. The South Albertas had not seen any really hard fighting since crossing the Rhine on 1 April and, while

One more river to cross, April 1945
On 5 April, supported by 13th Field and the other field regiments of 3rd Division, the North Shore Regiment crossed the Ijssel River at Zutphen to begin their drive north. They suffered from sniper fire which inflicted the casualty seen here. Nearly 20,000 German civilians remained in their homes, which made fighting very difficult. NAC, PA-130059

they did not mind being away from the sharp end for a while, they were becoming annoyed about the nasty comments that they had become "lines of communication" troops.[18] The regiment was therefore happy when Wotherspoon returned from an O Group at division headquarters on the morning of 13 April with new orders: the SAR was to move north in the direction of Oldenburg, in an independent role with the job of maintaining contact between 4th Division and 2nd Division, its neighbour some distance to the east. As there were many small rivers to be crossed, Wotherspoon was given a troop of engineers and, for infantry support, three troops (platoons) of the British Special Air Service. Swatty translated these orders into a direction for the SAR to capture Oldenburg and he became determined to get that city before 2nd or 4th Divisions, notwithstanding the enemy or the terrain. In less than thirty minutes after his return to the regiment, C Squadron and Recce Troop were on the road toward the first obstacle, the Marka River.

Under fire, April 1945

A Canadian infantry section takes cover in a Dutch farm yard in April 1945. In the closing days of the war, German resistance varied but danger was ever present. NAC, PA-138284

For the next two weeks or so, the South Alberta Regiment carried out an independent odyssey as they moved northeast toward Oldenburg. The Stuart tank patrols of the Recce Troop, followed at a supporting distance by a troop of Shermans, went first. If the Recce boys encountered resistance, the Shermans came up to handle it and, if infantry were required, either the SAS or a company of Links that Swatty had managed to snaffle, would move in under the covering fire of the tanks and sort out the problem. Most of the resistance encountered were rearguards which attempted to use natural barriers to delay the advance but would withdraw if pushed hard enough. The biggest problem tended to be the boggy ground and the numerous small rivers (creeks in Canadian terms) that had to be crossed. To assist the engineers, Wotherspoon acquired a Valentine bridgelaying tank and formed a unit of South Alberta sappers, commanded by Captain Jack Summers of AA Troop and composed of echelon personnel under the command of Sergeant Wally Jellis (and known for that reason as "Wally's Commandos") to build bridges and clear mines. The "Commandos" developed a quick method of mine clearance – they used an armoured bulldozer to push abandoned German transport over suspected mines to detonate them. The destroyed vehicle was then moved to the side of the road and replaced by another wreck.

On 15 April, Halkyard's Recce Patrol with a B Squadron troop in support, came across an abandoned *Luftwaffe* airfield near the village of Varrelbusch. As Trooper David Marshall remembered,

When we first came up to it we thought it was just another farmer's field, as it appeared to be plowed, and it was, but this was a defensive measure to prevent our planes from using it. We pulled up to the open area of the airport through some trees and sat in the trees for a bit trying to see what was on the other side. We saw two enemy tanks and engaged them and, while doing so, we set the bush on fire allowing them to escape through the smoke.[19]

German tanks were not the only thing that bolted from the woods – a deer sprinted out of the trees in front of the amazed crews who, with visions of venison dancing in their heads, opened up with .30 calibre Brownings to bring it down but, as Marshall remarked, our "gunners should have been put on water and beans, all they managed to do was scare the poor thing."[20]

That wasn't all that was lurking around Varrelbusch. Sergeant Albert Halkyard was nosing out front when he came around the corner of a building and found himself staring straight down the muzzle of the 88 mm gun mounted on a Tiger II, the largest and most dangerous tank in the *Wehrmacht*. Halkyard screamed through his intercom at his driver to reverse just as the first 88 mm round narrowly missed his head but the driver, understandably flustered, stalled the tank which caused the entire crew to start screaming at him. The Tiger got off two more rounds before, thankfully, Halkyard got under cover, but when a Sherman Firefly of the supporting troop moved forward with its 17-pdr. gun to take it on, it was immediately knocked out for its troubles. Contact was then lost with the behemoth but word went around that a Tiger was on the loose and everyone was a little nervous.

That evening Lieutenant Danny McLeod's C-2 Troop was in the vicinity of the airfield when they encountered two German tanks and an SPG, which they managed to take out without too

It was the opinion of Father Raymond Hickey, padre of the North Shore Regiment, that his duties, like those of an infantryman, "depended on a strong pair of shoulders, a sturdy pair of legs, a stomach that could digest shoe leather, and two feet that wouldn't blister." Padres needed to be not only physically but spiritually strong as one of their many tasks was burying the dead. In battle, they often assisted the Medical Officer but, after the fighting was over (and sometimes during it), padres would search out and bury the men of their unit who had been killed in action, recording the details of the first field grave for the Graves Registration Units. When fighting was heavy and casualties numerous, this could be an oppressive duty. Padre J. Anderson of the Highland Light Infantry recalled the aftermath of the battle of Buron in June 1944:

> … at Buron we couldn't cope. I had to go back in a 60 Hundred-weight truck and took a man from each Company with me. We spent all day picking up. Not to bury them but to send them back to Beny-sur-Mer. The padres back there would bury them. We took one dog tag and left the other then wrapped the body in a blanket. We ran out of blankets.
>
> I went to our rear echelon. All gone. I continued back to rear division. When I asked for blankets, some clerk got my back up by telling me we were using too many. I was angry – out of my mind – I marched into the large Divisional marquee tent and gave them all Hell – then I started to cry.

Padre A. Phillips Silcox of the South Alberta Regiment has left a simple but eloquent account of this grim but necessary duty:

> We laid each on his blanket, wrapped him in its folds, and lowered him, under the Union Jack where possible, into the earth. …… We offered brief, simple prayers commending them to God's eternal love, sometimes accelerating those prayers to top speed and diving abruptly into any nearby grave ourselves for material protection.
>
> And when the fever of battle had passed for a spell, the quiet hours came round, then we sorted out little white sacks of personal stuff, valuables to be sent home, usables to his pals. Then we sat down to the toughest task of all and wrote letters to mothers and fathers, wives or sweethearts, to brothers in other regiments, to close friends, and casual acquaintances of whom we knew.

God alone can measure the tears we shed in silent solitude over those sincere letters to the folks at home.

Padre Silcox wrote many of these letters during the war. Each was different and each was personal because Silcox put a great deal of effort into this part of his duties. These are the words he wrote to the mother of Trooper F. Ross McKee, killed in action in September 1944.

> So far as the facts of the incident are concerned there is not much to add. …… Ross was driving the second of a patrol of tanks which was proceeding northward along a road which was in Belgium but the eastern edge of it was the border of Holland. The leading tank, commanded by their troop officer, used up its ammunition in the attack and the officer telephoned back to the second tank to assume the lead. As Ross's tank swung out to pass the leading tank it was actually astride the border line and as it came abreast of the other it was hit by an enemy shell fired from some distance to the east, and probably intended for the leading tank, which was saved by thus being shielded. Other members of the crew were wounded – I do not recall how badly but I think none seriously, but Ross was instantly killed.
>
> I was not able to come to the scene for an hour or two and by the time I had arrived the Chaplain of another regiment, H/Capt [Honorary Captain] Charles McLean from Nova Scotia, a Presbyterian, had already performed the sad duties, relative to his

The quiet man and his family
Padre Silcox poses with his family before going overseas. Despite having young children, he was one of the first in the SAR to volunteer for the Pacific when Germany surrendered. In 1945 Silcox was made an MBE for preventing, at the risk of his life, an attack on Regimental Headquarters by friendly aircraft in Normandy. After the war, having decided that his time with the South Albertas had spoiled him for ordinary parish duties, Silcox took a position as a chaplain with the Ontario Correctional Service and did much good work. COURTESY, SILCOX FAMILY

Father Raymond Hickey, North Shore Regiment, 3rd Division
Raymond Hickey, a Catholic priest from New Brunswick who served as the padre of the North Shore Regiment, left a moving memoir of his wartime duties, *The Scarlet Dawn*, published in 1947. Hickey died in Normandy in 1987, while attending a regimental reunion.
FROM *NORMANDY 1944: THE CANADIAN SUMMER*

(Left) **The padre makes his rounds**
Padre Silcox examines the burned-out interior of an SAR Sherman brewed up in Germany in April 1945. It was the padre's job to remove the incinerated remains of his flock from tanks such as this but he never complained about it. COURTESY, W. VAILLANCOURT

A padre at work
Padre R. Seaborne gives absolution to a dying soldier in Normandy. NAC, PA-136042

Canadian casualties ready for burial
Inverted rifles mark the resting place of four dead Canadian infantrymen who await the final administrations of the padres. Not only did the padres bury their own men, they also buried German dead. NAC, PA-141712

(Above) **Burial party**
Canadian soldiers carry a fatal casualty to his burial place on a stretcher draped with the Union Jack, Germany, 1945. NAC, PA-137038

burial. His officer assured me that he had not suffered an instant – and that in our eyes, who have seen too much of violence, is a merciful thing for which you will be thankful. He was temporarily buried not far south of Sans van Gent but on the Belgian side of the border. A little later our authorities will establish a large well-kept memorial park somewhere in Belgium to which all those who have laid down their lives will be gathered for their long rest – and at that time you will be advised of his grave's location.

However saddened you are by this loss you may have reason to be proud of your boy. I did not know him personally that I can remember, but it is no small tribute to a man's character that he is found in the very teeth of a battle in an armoured regiment. Weaklings have no place here. In these days you will be recalling the happy days of his babyhood and his school days – thinking of the hours that you laboured to care for him and teach him that he might become a good citizen. I know you did not then look for him to be a warrior – we are not that kind of people: we hope for more constructive careers for our children. But it is worth knowing that when this grimmer duty called him he was not found wanting.

We can see over here, probably better than you at home, how necessary this duty was and how worth-while have been our achievements so far, even though the task is not yet finished. For we have met thousands and thousands of common folk who are rejoicing in their new-found liberty. Even when their homes are smashed, their gardens destroyed in the combat – they are glad we came to chase out the Boche. Life is not easy for them yet but it is better and more hopeful – and they are happy. And this is our assurance that those who have been called to pay the full price of our victories have not done so in vain. It seems to be the kind of a world in which a few must die that many may live.

I pray that Christ may strengthen and console you as only He can and that He may hallow the memories of earlier years which you cherish. With the kindest wishes, I am

Yours very sincerely,
A. Phillips Silcox, H/Capt.
Protestant Chaplain

Although his official duties ended in 1945, Padre Silcox, like many other unit padres, corresponded and visited the families of men killed in action for years after the war.

Padre Silcox's letter courtesy of Helen Hanson. Quoted material from J.A. Snowie, *Bloody Buron* (Erin Mills, 1984); Raymond Hickey, *The Scarlet Dawn* (Campbelltown, 1949); and Walter Steven, *In This Sign* (Toronto, 1948).

Trooper F.R. McKee, South Alberta Regiment
Trooper Ferris Ross McKee, aged 27, was killed in action on 19 September 1944. Padre A.P. Silcox wrote the letter quoted here to his mother after his death. McKee was from Creelman, Saskatchewan, and today a bay on Montreal Lake in that province bears his name. COURTESY, HELEN HANSON

First field grave, Belgium, 1944
The first field grave of Trooper W.H. Andrew of the SAR, killed in action in Eekloo on 18 September 1944 and buried by Padre Silcox. Grateful civilians have covered the grave with flowers. COURTESY, JACK PORTER

The tanker's worst nightmare: King Tiger

The King Tiger was the ultimate in German tank design. Weighing 68 tons with armour almost 4 inches thick, it was armed with an 88 mm gun that could destroy any Allied tank with ease. The good news was that there were not too many of them. The SAR encountered one of these behemoths at Varrelbusch in Germany in April 1945 and took it out after a hard-fought little action. AUTHOR'S COLLECTION

much trouble. When McLeod reported this to RHQ, he was ordered to secure the airfield but, as he had heard about the Tiger, he decided to make a foot patrol through a small wood near his objective before exposing his four tanks. When he got to the edge of the trees, Danny spotted something in the fading light and, putting his fieldglasses to his eyes, found himself staring at the same Tiger Halkyard had encountered – he later recalled that it was so big that the "muzzle of this thing was sitting at the edge of my binoculars."[21] Returning to his troop, Danny talked the matter over with his troop sergeant, Tom Milner, and they decided to move slowly through the wood and engage the Tiger with the troop's two Firefly Shermans.

This was done and the two 17-pdr. tanks emerged from the treeline and opened fire. Trooper Carson Daley, Milner's gunner, recalled that he fired three rounds of AP but "they ricocheted into the air off the Tiger and my knees were knocking something terrible."[22] Danny now brought up his two 75 mm gun tanks and the troop opened up with everything it had. Someone managed to hit the muzzle brake of the Tiger's 88 mm gun, damaging it so the weapon was inoperable. At this point the German crew commander decided it was time to go and began to back away but, as he did so, he exposed his flank to C-1 troop and someone landed a round that set the engine compartment on fire. When it was over, Tom Milner recalled, the Tiger "lay all shattered and in pieces" and a nearby house and barn "had been blown to bits."[23] This little battle, one of the best single troop actions fought by the SAR during the war, was recognized by the award of the Military Cross to Lieutenant McLeod.

The SAR kept pushing toward Oldenburg. Just north of Varrelbusch, C Squadron was traversing a wooded area known as Forst Cloppenburg when Sergeant Tom Milner had a close call. As Sergeant Bob Fairhurst remembered it, Milner's tank was leading the troop

and we were just scouting around to see what we could see. All of a sudden this goddamned Jerry comes out of the bush with a bazooka [*Panzerfaust*] right in front of my tank to shoot Milner in the rear. He couldn't hear my tank. I stopped and he turned around and my boys put the Browning on him and he went down in a ditch. Then he stood up with his hands up but the Browning cooked off by itself and he got killed. I think he was a tankhunter because when we went up that road, there was a knocked out tank. But he wasn't smart enough.[24]

On 16 April the SAR were near the large town of Garrel. While C Squadron circled it and moved on to the next water barrier, B and C Squadrons entered Garrel to find only weak resistance – a few Germans who managed to take out one tank with a *Panzerfaust* before they skittered away. The town, however, turned out to be maze of obstructions, demolitions, obstacles, mines and the occasional sniper, and Wotherspoon thought it wiser to withdraw rather than stay overnight in what might become a deathtrap. A few days later, he decided that Garrel would be an excellent place to locate the Echelons and ordered the mayor to "organize the civilian population and get them to clear out all the mines in the area, to fill in cratered roads, to move the road blocks and to ensure the safety of our troops."[25] This official's reply that "it was not possible" brought a personal summons from Swatty, who told the German bluntly to do as he had been ordered and added that, if snipers or anyone else in Garrel harmed "a hair on the head" of a South Albertan, "five houses at the scene of the crime would be burned to the ground." This had an effect and, as the SAR War Diary notes, in a very short time "the civvies were working in the streets." At the end of the day, Garrel was free of nasty things.

By this time in the war many German soldiers were only too happy to give up and prisoners were plentiful. As for the enemy civilians, they were mostly passive, but the South Albertas were always on their guard. Trooper Peter Konvitsko who, because he could speak German, often served as an interpreter, remembered one incident that took place at Garrel. Konvitsko had just finished talking to a fresh batch of prisoners when he noticed that a small German boy was hanging around

and he was talking to the prisoners and I told him not to. He had his hand up his sleeve and I said "what have you got there" and he said nothing. So I grabbed his sweater and here he had one of these little 7.62 mm Mauser automatics and there was a round in the chamber so I got that away from him and sent him home to his mother.[26]

The South Albertas generally treated their prisoners well. They relieved the Germans of their weapons, binoculars, medals, watches, belt buckles and money so that they would have less to carry on their march to the rear, but freely handed out Canadian cigarettes, much preferred by the Germans to their own issue which had the consistency and taste of old army blankets. There was a certain rapport between the combat soldiers of the opposing armies, "between men who shoot at each other on the front line" because they had "an understanding of what the other fellow is going through."[27] Personnel from the rear echelons and services did not have this rapport and sometimes treated prisoners harshly. Sergeant John Galipeau remembered an incident in the last month of the war when a service corps officer who could not get his trucks up to the frontline, co-opted a half dozen prisoners that Galipeau's troop had just rounded up and

marched them to where he was taking the stuff off the trucks. Each loaded a ration pack or a jerry can of gasoline onto his shoulder and started back to the tanks. The officer decided he wasn't happy with them walking, so he ordered them to run. He ran them in, ran them back out to the trucks, put a second load on them and began running them back in again. We decided enough was enough. Two or three of us went out and told him to knock it off. ...... He wasn't too happy and made comments about how we were a bunch of German-lovers and so forth, but we told him we didn't care what he thought about it. He was not going to treat them like that in front of us. The guys were tired and beaten, and we were not going to see them abused needlessly. It just wasn't the Canadian way to kick a fellow when he was down.[28]

Swatty Wotherspoon now had Garrel but Oldenburg was his objective and he continued to press toward it, although the closer he came, the stiffer grew the German resistance. Unable to obtain artillery support from either 2nd or 4th Divisions, Woth-

erspoon ordered one squadron to act each day in the indirect fire role to provide HE on call from the leading elements. The Regiment got itself over the Aue River on 17 April, leaving only two more water barriers – the Lethe River and the Kusten Canal – before Oldenburg. By 21 April they were at the Lethe, even though that night German infantry infiltrated the regimental harbour and caused much trouble before they were ejected. Not much progress was made during the next two days because of resistance, estimated by the intelligence officers to consist of an enemy force in the strength of about two brigades composed of elements of the *Grossdeutschland* Panzer Division and the 61st Parachute Regiment. By this time, the SAS had disappeared and the single company of Lincoln & Welland infantry, which had accompanied the SAR north, was not strong enough to match the enemy's numbers.

Nonetheless, without risking his men unduly, Wotherspoon kept pushing forward during the day and then falling back to

FRIESLAND. The gun position, during a lull in fighting, sometimes took on the aspect of a Sunday picnic.

The last days
As Lieutenant Clay illustrates, although both the weather and the civilians were getting warmer, a war still had to be fought, despite all the interruptions. FROM 13 CANADIAN FIELD REGIMENT, RCA

secure harbours at night. It was during this time that Sergeant John Galipeau became exasperated with the green tank crew he had been issued just before the Rhine crossing, among them a gunner who didn't seem to know anything about his job and, even worse, couldn't shoot straight. Just outside Garrel, Galipeau's troop came under heavy mortar and artillery fire and he concluded that there was an enemy OP calling it in as "it was just too accurate."[29] Galipeau

spotted a church with a steeple, which was the kind of place they loved to put observers, and told the gunner to knock off the steeple. He fired a heavy explosive shell. I could see no sign of where the shell went. I put him on it again. Same story. After twenty minutes we had fired off everything we had, including the armoured piercing shells. There wasn't a shell left in the tank, and he hadn't hit a thing. Not one thing! I couldn't believe it. I asked myself again and again, "Where did these guys come from?"

Incredulous, Galipeau requested and received permission to pull back and re-ammunition. As he waited for the truck to come up from A-1 Echelon, Galipeau

> couldn't believe what happened next. So far as these guys were concerned, the war was over. They started to unload all their stuff from the tank, preparing to clean up and shave. I was boiling, and I really laid into them: "What are you guys doing? First of all we didn't hit that damned steeple because the gun sights were off, we've got to sight that damn seventeen-pounder. You're going to have ammunition to load, and all the guns have got to be cleaned. What are you doing messing around getting ready to shave when there's guys up there depending on us.
>
> They stood there with their mouths hanging open, but I must have got through to them, because they got busy cleaning the guns. By the time the truck came up with the ammunition, everything had been taken care of and as soon as we loaded we were on our way.[30]

During these last days, one never knew how the Germans would react, sometimes they would fight hard and sometimes they would just surrender. The haphazard nature of combat in these final days of the war is evident in the diary entries Trooper John Neff made in his diary during this period:

> Fri. Apr. 20
> Left A2 to rejoin the sqdn … oh goody. The sqn is at an Airport on the highway between Cloppenburg and Alhorn. We went out on Patrol and the whole tp got stuck in a peat bog. A recovery [vehicle] that came out to get us got stuck also. Then a Spitfire came over and bombed us.
>
> Sat. Apr. 21
> At the same place, went out on a Recce and shot up a German patrol. They came out to get their wounded waving a Red Cross flag as big as a house. An escaped French officer came up to our tank. I sure laughed when he started to kiss Lt. Orr on both cheeks.
>
> Sun. Apr 22
> Moved east to the Oldenburg-Quackenburg highway and put in an attack working with the Maisonneuves of 2nd Div. Lots of good shooting and many houses to burn. …… We advanced several miles, no one was hurt.
>
> Mon. Apr 23
> Still working our way up the highway. 3 tp lost a couple of tanks and hurried home. In the evening we went up and worked them over for a bit. Then back to our happy home.[31]

Neff's reference to B-3 Troop losing "a couple of tanks" on 23 April referred to an incident that had occurred that morning when that troop, led by Lieutenant Ivan Donkin, had set out with a company of the Régiment de Maisonneuve of 2nd Division to engage in some road clearing. Trooper David Marshall was commanding the troop's 17-pdr. Firefly and remembered the troop had just stopped at a farmhouse when they were hit by an enemy artillery and mortar bombardment. Looking around, the Canadians

> spotted a German demolition team working on the road about a half a mile away. We took some shots at them but they had already done their work. A few minutes later a tremendous explosion, probably caused by a 250 kilo aerial bomb, blew a deep crater in the road we were planning to use.
>
> With my tank fourth in line, the troop drove out of the farmyard turning north onto the road towards the crater. As this hole made the road impassable, we turned off through another farmyard into a large open field east of the road. The field must have been a half mile wide and a mile long surrounded by trees on three sides and the farms and roads on the other. While we were cruising in the park the infantry, "D" Company of the Maisies [Régiment de Maisonneuve] walked parallel to the road clearing the farmyards and buildings. We were spraying and shooting anything that looked as if it should be sprayed and shot at and got caught in heavy AP fire from the north and northeast as well as a concentrated artillery and mortar barrage.
>
> The troop was travelling abreast of each other, about 50 yards apart, with me on the left nearest the road. As the 17-pounder is the only gun that can do much damage to a German tank, and is not as good in the anti-personnel role as the 75 mm, its position in an advance will depend on what type of opposition is expected. If anti-tank guns are expected it will be forward, if not, the 75 mms will be in front. …… We were under a constant artillery barrage and we knew that they knew exactly where we were. However, we did not know if they had any anti-tank guns or if they planned to defend this particular spot. We soon found out. When German anti-tank gunners are given a choice of targets, they will destroy the 17-pounder first and then the tanks equipped with the 75 mm guns, which is exactly what happened.
>
> It was about 3.00 P.M. when we came under this AP fire. Each crew commander was trying to locate it when it got our range and we took an AP to the turret about a foot down from where I was standing. Except possibly in built-up areas where there may be danger from snipers, we always fought standing with our head out of the turret. As visibility is very

poor when you view the scene through the periscope, the only way of doing it properly is to stand up and look. The shell gouged out a hunk of the tank and showered me with fragments of it and blinded my right eye with blood.

I figured that was quite enough and ordered the crew out. The enemy gun was concentrating on my tank and it was hit again as we bailed out. The anti-tank gun turned its fire onto the other three tanks who right smartly headed for the shelter of the trees, as we still could not spot the gun(s).

A medic from the Maisonneuves put a dressing on Marshall's wound and told him "I wasn't going to die on his shift" or at least Marshall thought that was what he said as the words were spoken in French.[32] Marshall was evacuated to the rear and surgeons later removed more than twenty metal fragments from his face, which healed well.

By 24 April 1945 the SAR was at the Lethe River. Sergeant Tom Milner was approaching some farm buildings near the hamlet of Hintern Esch when his Sherman Firefly came under sniper fire. Milner's gunner, however, had spotted the German's muzzle flash and put about 200 rounds of .30 calibre into his immediate vicinity as well as a round of 17-pdr. AP for good effect, not only killing the sniper but destroying most of the building in which he was positioned. Having no friendly flatfeet with him, Milner did not want to get into close quarter action in a wooded area with enemy infantry but, spotting a slit trench filled with Germans, he decided to try and convince them to surrender without getting too near. He dismounted and filled an empty shell case with gasoline from the small supply kept for the cooking stove on the back of his tank. He then moved stealthily forward under cover until he was at an unoccupied end of the enemy trench, poured the gas into it and, withdrawing a safe distance, ignited it with a flare pistol. The spectacular result convinced the Germans that their war was over and twenty of them emerged with their hands up. This ingenious feat brought Milner the Distinguished Conduct Medal often known – because of the rarity with which it was awarded – as "the enlisted man's VC."

That same day, however, proved disastrous for Swatty Wotherspoon's ambition to take Oldenburg. The Lincoln & Welland company was removed by 4th Division and an appeal for infantry from the 2nd Division was refused as there were none to spare. Knowing that he could not get through the Germans ahead of him without infantry, Wotherspoon went to see Vokes to complain but returned empty-handed. All he could do now was to maintain contact with the enemy and, for the next ten days, the South Albertas moved forward during the day, shot up everything they could see and then returned to secure harbours at night. On the last day of April, as Russian artillery shells pounded the roof of his bunker in Berlin, Adolf Hitler committed suicide and it was clear to everyone that the war was coming to an end. This being the case, no one wanted to be the last fatal casualty and caution became the watchword of the day.

The regiment was at Oberlethe, 4 miles from Oldenburg, on 3 May when that city fell to 2nd Division, and it was Wotherspoon's opinion, which he expressed to his officers that night, that the South Albertas had "fought their last battle."[33] The next day, the Regiment's independent roving commission ended when it was brought back under the command of 10th Brigade and ordered to concentrate at Oldenburg airfield. For nearly three weeks, the SAR had waged a private little war during which they had fought as tankers, infantry, gunners and engineers, losing 40 tanks but very few men. They had done a job, the 10th Brigade historian noted, "unparalleled for initiative, and did it in true Albertan style – well."[34]

"Delaying action": The final days

As for 13th Field, their planned rest at Gorredijk came to an abrupt end on 19 April 1945 when they were ordered to support 8th Brigade in an operation to clear the approaches to Emden. This operation turned out to be "strictly a delaying action by the Germans as was the rest of the fighting until the end of the war."[35] Supported by all three field regiments in the division, 8th Brigade made steady progress towards Emden, experiencing more trouble with German demolitions than with German soldiers.

There was some stiff resistance at the town of Weener on 23 April and the three field regiments of 3rd Division brought down an intense 10-minute bombardment which was witnessed by Gunner Raycroft's line crew who were up with the North Shore FOO that day. Raycroft remembered that the whole area

Oldenburg: The South Albertas' objective, 1945
Senior German officers leave the Oldenburg provincial offices after discussing surrender terms with Canadian officers. Oldenburg was the South Albertas' objective for the last three weeks of the war but the conflict ended before they got there. DND PHOTO, 51586

"seemed to percolate and shake for those minutes, in one staccato of explosions." To Raycroft, it was "a savage, fascinating experience in power, efficiency and accuracy – and death – to be part of those fire orders, and then to hear the ordered rounds come over your head and explode on the target right in front of you."[36]

After this preliminary the North Shores took Weener without much trouble but found a lot of German wounded in the town, most being sailors from the *Kriegsmarine* who had been thrown into the fighting as infantry. Raycroft noted that the enemy wounded were tended by German nurses who moved "from one to the other with bandages and needles." This novel sight caused the North Shores to perk up their ears but their officers immediately declared the area of the German aid post out of bounds. Raycroft's carrier happened to be parked nearby, however, and he watched, fascinated, the nurses' "body movements in those sufficiently form-fitted uniforms." Unfortunately, the German girls entirely ignored him.[37]

With massive artillery support available on call, 8th Brigade advanced steadily north toward Emden. Nobody was pushing their luck, however, as it was obvious that the war was coming to an end and this being the case, there was a widespread hunt for souvenirs. As Gunner Raycroft remembers:

> The men were finding German equipment that had been left behind and were gathering up souvenirs, as they realized that the opportunities were just about over. And we were allowed to send parcels home.
>
> My first one went out on April 27, full of every object for which I had a duplicate, just in case it would never arrive. It contained German badges, medals, insignia, Nazi Party armbands, numerous swastika-stamped articles and air-dropped propaganda pamphlets of both sides.[38]

Sadly, it was during these final days that Gunner "Dog" met his fate. Joe Shemrock and his officer were in an advanced position when they came under heavy enemy mortar fire which caused them to up stakes and move quickly. "Dog" had gone off to forage but, when Joe whistled for him to mount up, he did not appear, probably very wisely having gone to ground until the mortar rounds stopped coming down. As Joe could not wait, he sadly turned his half-track around and moved back out of range, hoping that "Dog" would eventually catch up but there was no sign of him. A few days later Joe was talking to another half-track driver who recounted a strange incident. This driver had been coming through the same area where "Dog" had gone missing when the "darndest thing had happened" – a little white dog "kept trying to jump on the running board of his half-track, only to fall off as the vehicle moved." The driver told Shemrock that he "was about to stop and let the thing into the vehicle when the poor little bugger fell under the tracks and was squashed."[39]

On 3 May 1945, 13th Field Regiment went into a gun position near a town with the interesting name of Bagband, about

VE-Day! – 8 May 1945
Ecstatic Dutch civilians celebrate the official end of the war in Europe on VE-Day. Their country had been invaded nearly five years before and parts of it, the population starving, were still under German occupation at the war's end. From 6 June 1944 to 4 May 1945, 11,336 Canadian soldiers were killed and 33,003 wounded fighting in Northwest Europe.
NAC, PA-133153

15 miles east of Emden. The next day at 10.40 A.M., it fired its last rounds during the Second World War as, that evening, word came down that hostilities would cease at 8 A.M. the following morning. The South Albertas got the same information at the about same time at Oldenburg airfield where the unit had concentrated that day. In neither unit was there any great excitement, it had been obvious for weeks that the conflict was winding down and the official news of its end was almost anticlimactic. Gunner John Raycroft was sitting in his carrier on radio watch at 8.20 P.M. that night when he learned from the BBC that the German forces in northern Germany would formally surrender in the morning. His reaction was to start falling asleep as "the excitement all that day, and over the last couple of days, in anticipating the end was perhaps more exhausting than we realized."[40] Major R.A. Paterson, the 10th Brigade historian, perhaps summed up the mood of the troops best when he wrote that

> to us it didn't seem like the end of anything as yet. The skies were overcast, the rain dripped slowly from the thatched roof of the farmhouse, the lake looked grey and cold and a cutting wind shook steel-like raindrops from the new green leaves. ……. All was very quiet. …… One kept saying to oneself – "it's over, it's over," all the time half expecting to see a rainbow in the sky, to hear the shouts of the millions in Trafalgar

or Times Square, to experience some outward manifestation of joy, praise, thankfulness, or of great emotion flooding through the gates of restraint. But nothing happened. There were no bells in Germany, there were no happy people, and the conquerors were dumb in the greatness of their relief.[41]

"Lived for two days, conscious but courageous": The cost and the accounting

Over the next few days the padres of both units held voluntary church services which were very well attended as men took the time, not only to offer thanks for their own survival, but also to honour their fallen comrades. From the D-Day landing on 6 June 1944 to Germany in May 1945, during 333 days of fighting, 11,336 Canadian soldiers had been killed in Northwest Europe and many thousands more wounded. Of the two units whose story concerns us, 13th Field Regiment suffered 169 casualties from 6 June 1944 to 4 May 1945: 45 gunners killed, and 121 wounded in action, and 3 taken prisoner. In their nine months and three days in action, the South Alberta Regiment suffered 436 casualties: 82 killed in action, 339 wounded and 15 taken prisoner. In both units, an examination of the casualty statistics reveals interesting anomalies caused by the nature of combat in the armour and artillery arms. Nearly a third of 13th Field's total casualties, 61 in all, were suffered by the forward OP parties or the line crews who maintained their communications, an indication of the danger inherent in these duties. In the SAR, the figures demonstrate that being a troop leader was an extremely perilous occupation – of the 57 lieutenants who held troop commands in the unit between July 1944 and May 1945, no fewer than 40 became casualties, including 9 killed in action. This was a loss rate of 70% and an indication that, in the South Alberta Regiment, officers led from in front and paid the corresponding price.

Going home with a souvenir
This happy South Albertan, glad both to survive the war and to pick up a fine souvenir for the folks back home, poses proudly in front of a destroyed German fighter aircraft at Oldenburg airfield in May 1945. He won't be going home for another eight months but he will be going home. SAR ARCHIVES

The statistics are bad enough but statistics are numbers and numbers are neutral things. If one wants to truly comprehend the cost, there is no better place to start than the detailed records kept by Padre Silcox concerning the fatal casualties suffered by the SAR from Normandy to Germany. They make grim reading:

Troopers A and B
Their t[an]k. (Sherman) foundered in dry creek bed during night action in area infested with infantrymen … All five of crew crawled out and groped their way towards shelter but were fired on by enemy from trenches as they crossed a field. These two kd. [killed] outright. Other three taken prisoner … As I recall the scene – one of them was shot in the back, the other in abdomen, with single round in each case. ……

Corporal C
Stuart tank. Tank was hit by 88 round, crew bailed out. No one knows exactly what killed Corporal C. He was found half out of turret hatch several days later, by party returning to the scene. Lower half was burned. ……

Trooper D
In ambulance half-track. Stretcher bearer in co-driver's seat, driving through town when shelling started. Seeing, through [vision] slot, civilians in danger, Trooper D opened door 3 or 4 inches to see if they needed assistance. Just at that moment a shell burst against buildings overhead and a fragment came through that narrow opening, piercing his abdomen. D/W [died of wounds] an hour later. ……

Corporal E
Sherman tank squadron was employed in art[iller]y role, shooting up enemy positions …… At the moment a heavy fast stonk was ordered, Corporal E was loading one after another as fast as possible. One round stuck. He seized an empty [shell] case to hammer it home, struck the cap and exploded the shell. Eyes blasted out, right hand traum[atically] amputated, left thumb off and left middle finger smashed. Bad burns on face, neck and throat, etc. Lived for two days, conscious but courageous, but died in hospital.

Lieutenant F and Trooper G
Were in turret of Sherman …… I didn't see tank but it [the hit] must have been low, for both men were torn about the limbs. Lieutenant F was taken away by Jerry presumably toward their hospital, but was found later in one of their dug-outs dead. He had received inadequate first aid and I judge he died from loss of blood. One thigh was badly torn and not bandaged. The other leg was torn and fractured, wrapped with a thin gauze bandage only. Jerry invited us to come after Trooper G under flag of truce. He too had sustained severe thigh wounds which called for an amputation. He died following operation in our CCS [Casualty Clearing Station]. ……

Corporal H

Was one of six billeted in a house, arising at 7 a.m. when a sudden stonk fell, one shell coming through window and bursting in room. Corporal H struck on head by fragment, fractured skull, D/W about 24 hrs later. Others survived, tho' one lost one eye, injured other, and suffered a spray of splinters in his face. Another sustained a laceration of one leg which has healed well but later lost sight of one eye due to blast causing a bone to press on optic nerve. ......

Trooper I

88 shell penetrated front of tank in head-on shot, and pierced Trooper I through the abdomen (being driver). Others escaped, though two wounded. Trooper I k[ille]d. outright. Partly burned later. ......

Corporal J

Was sleeping with others of his troop on the ground in RHQ area when some shells, believed to be "friendly," fell some distance away. Evidently a fragment ricocheted off a tank and penetrated his chest. When general stand-to was ordered, he was found dead by sergeant who tried to waken him. ......[42]

"The Outcasts of Canada": The long wait to go home, May 1945–February 1946

The war in Europe was over but it would be some time before the men of First Canadian Army saw Canada again. In May 1945 there were 281,757 Canadian soldiers in Britain and on the continent and they faced a long wait for repatriation as the demands of the war in the Pacific had caused a worldwide shortage of shipping. The government had foreseen this problem, and not wishing to face a repetition of 1919 when Canadian troops had angrily rioted after been held in uncomfortable transit camps in Britain awaiting transport to North America, had devised a repatriation policy organized on a "first in, first out" basis. Men received points for every month of military service and additional points for every month of service overseas while married personnel, wounded personnel and personnel with dependants earned extra points. The higher the point score, regardless of rank, the earlier would come the trip back to Canada.

There was one way to get home quickly and that was to volunteer for the Canadian Pacific Force, a division-sized contingent being organized for the war against Japan. Men who joined this all-volunteer force were given priority in travel and 30 days clear leave in Canada before they had to return to duty. Many did volunteer, some because they genuinely wanted to continue fighting, others because they were betting that the war in the Far East would end before they would be called upon to serve again in combat. They won that bet as Japan surrendered on 17 August and the Second World War ended.

Men with low point scores – including many of the Zombies who had been ordered overseas the previous winter – were required to serve in the Canadian Army Occupation Force, a 25,000-man force organized for police duties in Germany. A great many men with high point scores, mainly young, single men who were not yet ready to settle down in civilian life, joined this force including Gunner George Lynch-Staunton of 13th Field Regiment.

As soon as the details of the repatriation policy were announced, there was much frantic calculation as everyone toted up their points. In the meantime, they were still in the army and still under military discipline – and there was much "tidying up" to do. The SAR left their bivouac at Oldenburg airfield on 9 May and moved into the local insane asylum, which was probably as good a place as any for them. Here RSM Mackenzie and the squadron sergeants-major, who were inclined to let matters slide a bit while the unit was in combat, now re-asserted themselves and the South Albertas began to look less like well-armed gypsies and more like soldiers. The big regimental event in the immediate postwar period was a picnic held in the nearby woods, where the men feasted on hot dogs and drank entirely too much, an excess that was made possible because, shortly before hostilities had ended, Captain Tom Barford, the regimental quartermaster, had captured the alcohol stocks of a German division. The unit also suffered through a number of parades for senior officers, including one for Vokes on 14 May, who was not only three hours late, it was clear to many when he did arrive, that he was intoxicated. In late May, along with the other units of First Canadian Army, the SAR moved into friendly Holland to await repatriation, ending up in the Raalte-Zwolle area where Wotherspoon snagged a local castle, to serve both as RHQ and the officers' mess.

The gunners of 13th Field had one last military duty to perform before they moved to Holland. Lieutenant-Colonel Ostrander was placed in charge of a force drawn from his own regiment and the infantry battalions of 8th Brigade, which was tasked with supervising the orderly withdrawal of German units from Holland back to their own country. This force policed a 40-mile stretch of highway in their vehicles, "kept the marching columns of soldiers closed up and made sure they did not take any stolen property with them."[43] "This last task was the biggest," noted the regimental historian, but when the Germans "passed through our lines they had in their possession little but their own personal equipment." The gunners removed a total of 240,000 guilders from their former enemy – about $50,000 in modern Canadian money – and turned it over to the Dutch government. This job completed, 13th Field moved to Lunteren in Holland and began to prepare for the big 3rd Division Victory Parade to be held in Utrecht, cleaning and repainting their guns and vehicles and marking them with the proper serial numbers and unit insignia. There was a brief panic when the regiment ran out of khaki paint but, by dint of prodigious efforts (and possibly a little discreet theft), 13th Field – both vehicles and gunners – looked shiny and clean on the day.

The Victory Parade at Utrecht was held on 6 June 1945, a year to the day since the 3rd Division had landed in Normandy. General Harry Crerar took the salute as the men of the division, including its three field regiments, marched or rolled past. It was a magnificent spectacle much enjoyed by the Dutch but, in the eyes of the historian of 13th Field, it "was not spectacular from the point of view of the men who knew the division or had served with it" because the appearance of the division wasn't right.[44] The vehicles and guns of 13th Field Regiment were "stunning" with "their new khaki paint, blackened tires and cleaned tarpaulins," but they looked artificial because

> that was not how they had been in action. There was something about the thin coat of dust or mud on the metal surfaces of the equipment that was a part of the memories. As the guns filed by there were other familiar sights missing too. The gun detachments were not sitting on the roofs of the FAT's now, waving and passing out cigarettes. Nor did the tops of the vehicles contain the innumerable necessaries such as bed rolls, camouflage nets, compo boxes, stoves, petrol tins and the innumerable luxuries such as beds, mattresses, chairs and radios all hidden beneath the massive tarpaulins. Nor did the jeeps look quite right without the many bed rolls in the back, the directors and gun markers strapped on the front, and a "reserved" sign protruding from one corner of the compartment.[45]

A few days later, 13th Field said goodbye to its guns, which were taken away to the ordnance parks, and the gun detachments, "who had cursed everything about them from the firing pin to the drag ropes were now a little wistful."[46]

At almost the same time, the South Albertas turned in their tanks. Many men were glad to see the armoured vehicles go because they would now have considerably less work, but others were saddened, including Sergeant John Galipeau who "felt a sense of loss" because

> their presence had been an essential part of our identity as an armoured regiment; their care and maintenance had structured our daily routine. I couldn't see any point in training without our tanks, and the rest of the troops seemed to feel the same.[47]

One vehicle not turned in was "Old Reliable," Swatty Wotherspoon's command half-track which had come to the SAR in the spring of 1943 and had made it from Normandy to Oldenburg without faltering. Under a programme which permitted each combat unit to send one vehicle to its home armoury to serve as a memorial, "Old Reliable" was put on board a ship and, after months in transit, arrived safely in Medicine Hat, where it was taken over by the reserve battalion of the SAR.

It was not long before men also started to leave for home or other duties. Lieutenant-Colonel Wotherspoon said goodbye to the SAR in early July to take over command of 4th Armoured Brigade. His replacement as the South Albertas' fourth and last wartime commanding officer was the newly-promoted Lieutenant-Colonel Thomas ("Darby") Nash from Edmonton, the

Germans returning to the Vaterland, May 1945
When the war ended, there were more than 100,000 German troops in Holland, and the Canadian army supervised their orderly withdrawal to their own soil. The gunners of 13th Field participated in this exercise and removed more than $50,000 of contraband money from the Germans which was turned over to the Dutch government. NAC, PA-137266

easygoing former commander of B Squadron. Padre Silcox, who had volunteered for service in the Pacific, also left at about this time and was missed for, as Corporal Bob Clipperton noted, in terms of padres Silcox was the "best one we ever had" and the "guys didn't seem to mind going to church & listening to him as he had a sense of humour."[48] The policy was that those men who did not have high point scores would return to Canada with units from their home provinces, so Albertans from other units were now posted into the SAR while non-Albertans were posted out. So many familiar faces were leaving and so many new faces arriving that Bob Clipperton felt that it was "hard to call it the South Alberta Regiment now."[49]

For the men overseas who just wanted to go home but had to wait their turn – and this was the great majority – the army instituted comprehensive educational, vocational, athletic, entertainment and leave programmes under the theory that if they were kept busy, they would stay out of trouble. Many took advantage of these programmes to upgrade their education or to learn new trades. Athletic equipment by the ton was distributed by the Auxiliary Services and there were inter-unit leagues for almost every sport. Generous leave was granted, about 25% of unit strength at any given time, and young Canadians who had grown up in the Depression were able to visit the cultural centres of Europe, and attend an endless variety of concerts, plays, musicals and films.

Of course, many men just wanted to have a little fun. In that respect, Holland offered plenty of opportunities as the skies were blue, the beer foamy and the women nearly all friendly – not to mention the fact that the country was bankrupt and the medium of exchange was the cigarette and if it was one thing Canadian soldiers had in plenty it was cigarettes. The result was that they were a very wealthy group of young men who could pay well for their entertainment, and the summer of 1945 was a slightly crazy time which would forever after be known to the Dutch as "the summer of the Canadians." Of course, the army being the army, it tried to control everything – even fun. In Zwolle, Trooper David Marshall of the SAR remembered,

> There were dances and shows and lots of pretty girls. The regiment had hired a dance hall, upstairs over the Harmony Cafe, and had dances three times per week which cost us 1 guilder, ladies free. A guilder was about 40 cents. The army kept up a barrage of orders concerning our conduct and putting off limits certain civilian "houses." You can be sure that anything that looked good was "off limits" or "out of bounds" or for "Officers Only."[50]

And so, one way or the other, the men tried to wile away the hours. "The time seems to go so slow & the weeks just drag," Corporal Bob Clipperton complained to his wife, Andy, serving in the CWAC at Borden Camp in Ontario,

> Guess it's because we can see the time when we will be going home, ahead of us. We have time to think now & before I had to spend most of my time figuring out how to stay alive. I've put a lot of things behind me & I hope I won't have to go through another war again.[51]

For the Clippertons, who had now been separated for two years, this was the cruellest time as the fighting was over and they just wanted to be together. By August 1945, most of the married men and men with dependants began to ship out for Canada but Bob Clipperton, who had only gone overseas in the summer of 1943, was still waiting. One can sense his frustration when he wrote Andy that

> They had a hell of a big riot last week [in a transit camp in Britain] and over 100 thousand pounds damage done. Things are pretty close around here & they have split us up into smaller groups & we have to turn all our weapons in tomorrow. I don't blame the guys though cause they could have us home in no time if they weren't trying to have the other nations believe we're so damn good & are such an orderly & obedient bunch of soldiers. I wish the people back home would do something about it cause a lot of the fellows figure now that the war is over they have forgotten about us over here & after all we do deserve a bit of consideration even though we are the outcasts of Canada.

The summer of 1945 passed very slowly for the Clippertons but, in September, rumours began to go round that married men with Bob's point total would be leaving at the end of the month. In anticipation, Andy obtained her discharge from the CWAC and the couple began to plan a romantic reunion at the Bessborough Hotel in Saskatoon, not far from Andy's hometown of Maymont, Saskatchewan. Their hopes rose to a high pitch when Bob was shipped to a transit camp in England in early October but, nearly two months later, he was still there. Totally frustrated, he wrote to Andy on 29 November,

> I guess you are wondering what the hell I am doing over in this country when I should be home but the Army doesn't look at it that way. I had two airmails from you yesterday & they [meant] more to me than any others you had written. For the last four nights I couldn't sleep worth a damn & last night I got so lonesome for you I got up at 4 A.M. & had a shower but it still didn't help any. All we do is sit around & we have roll call twice a day. Two shows a day, one in the morning & one in the afternoon. ...... We are senior [in terms of time in the transit camp] in this wing but there are still 18 other drafts senior to us in England.[52]

On that very same day, after having her hopes constantly raised and dashed, Andy wrote to Bob that

> I didn't think that this date would see me writing to you a letter but here I am with a prayer in my heart that you will never get it. It's all so disappointing but I can wait & as long as you *are* coming home then I'm happy & contented but Gee I'm lonesome for you. ...... I feel badly about writing so few letters but hope you will understand that I've been expecting you on every boat that docks & feel let down when no word comes.[53]

In the end, Corporal Bob Clipperton's ship came in, both figuratively and literally, on the last day of November, and on 9 December 1945, in Maymont, Andy got the telegram she had been awaiting so long: "Will arrive Saskatoon early Tuesday."[54]

Like all returning soldiers, Bob Clipperton got 30 days leave before he had to go through his discharge procedure. It was a wise regulation, particularly for married couples, because it permitted husbands and wives who had been separated for years to become re-acquainted with each other. Sergeant John Galipeau from Edmonton, who had only been married to his wife Ivy for 18 months before he had shipped overseas in 1942, recalled that, after "three years apart and all we'd been through, I was a different person and so was she."[55] "I didn't realize until some time later how much I'd changed," he remembered, and their first month back together was "very hard on Ivy." The Galipeaus and the Clippertons made the necessary adjustments and spent the remainder of their lives together but not all couples were so fortunate.

"Goodbye, the guns": Victory Parade, Utrecht, 6 June 1945
On 6 June 1945, a year to the day after they landed in Normandy, the field regiments of 3rd Canadian Division took part in a victory parade at Utrecht. The gunners spent days preparing for this event and their guns looked like they never had during eleven months of heavy fighting. A few days later, they turned into the ordnance park and 13th Field became gunners in name only. During the Second World War, the Commonwealth artillery performed superbly, living up to its motto, *"Ubique"* or *"Everywhere."* NAC, PA-192740

By the end of December 1945, 184,054 soldiers had left for Canada and the formations of the First Canadian Army were disbanded.* By now, most units consisted of only a couple of hundred low point men and cadres of young single officers and NCOs with high point totals, who had volunteered to remain behind to keep their units running. The remaining elements of 3rd Division were shipped back to Canada that month and 13th Field Regiment, by now a hollow shell, was disbanded in Ontario a month later. The South Albertas' turn came in December when they left Holland for a transit camp in England where they remained a few weeks before embarking on the *Queen Elizabeth* on 9 January 1946. Arriving at New York five days later, they commenced the long train trip west and reached Medicine Hat on 19 January to find Swatty Wotherspoon – who had made the trip out from his home in Toronto – there to greet them at a splendid reception arranged by the 2nd Battalion. When it was over, the Hat boys said goodbye to the Calgary and Edmonton contingents, who reboarded the train for the final leg of the journey, anxious to get to their own homes.

After each man had taken his 30 days homecoming leave, he made a brief trip to the headquarters of Military District 13 in Calgary to complete his discharge process. When Sergeant John Galipeau's turn came, he arrived at Calgary late at night and did

what he had done in similar circumstances in Europe, "wandered into the first barracks I could find, found an empty bunk by the light coming from the washroom door, took off my uniform and lay down on the mattress, pulling my greatcoat over me and went to sleep."[56] The next morning the men in the room treated Galipeau "like the plague" and the orderly officer informed him of his error – he had bunked in a privates' barrack room and was directed to the sergeants' mess. John was no more comfortable there as most of the NCOs present were young and none were wearing, as he was, battle and campaign ribbons on their uniforms. It was a miserable experience that made John Galipeau long for "the old gang" from the SAR but he did not have to put up with it for long. After a medical examination and more paperwork, he walked out the door, no longer Sergeant Galipeau but just plain Mr. Galipeau, and, like hundreds of thousands of other young men, went home to begin a new life as a civilian.

Among them was Technical Quartermaster Sergeant-Major Harry Quarton, who had enlisted in the SAR at the age of 17 in 1940 and had served with the regiment before transferring to the 4th Armoured Division Headquarters. With a job on the *Edmonton Journal* waiting for him and his final pay safely stowed in his wallet, Harry was in a good mood as he made his way out of district headquarters on 12 March 1946. He had just about reached the front door when he ran into Lieutenant-Colonel Thomas ("Darby") Nash, the South Albertas' last wartime commander. "Harry," said Darby, "we're standing up the 19th Dragoons again and you're going to join us – there's a meeting in Edmonton next week, you be there."[57]

---

* Special mention must be made of the wives and dependants of Canadian soldiers who married overseas. Between 1942 and 1948 the Canadian government transported 43,464 wives and 20,995 children from Europe to Canada, the vast majority from Britain.

Glory days

A Light Horse Sherman HVSS (call sign "Bobcat") rolls out on an exercise, probably at Suffield in the early 1960s. Major Gordon McQueen, second in command of the SALH, is in the turret at the left. This diesel-powered late wartime model of the Sherman served in the Canadian army from 1948 to 1972 and, being robust and easy to maintain, was an excellent training platform. SALH ARCHIVES

CHAPTER SIXTEEN

"This Is a Fine Regiment – You Can Make It the Finest!"

"A dagger pointed at the heart of Russia": The Alberta militia in the postwar decade

Lieutenant-Colonel John Proctor, OBE, was a happy man. The former quartermaster-general of 4th Canadian Armoured Division, who had returned to Edmonton at the end of the war to take up a position with the Department of Veterans Affairs, had been appointed to command the 19th Armoured Car Regiment, newly formed from an amalgamation of the 19th Dragoons and the Edmonton Fusiliers. As he gazed around the organizational meeting he had called at the Connaught Armoury in Edmonton in the third week of March 1946, Proctor saw staring back at him a group of young and experienced armoured officers and senior NCOs who would considerably ease his task of standing up a unit that had been dormant for almost four years and, better still, most of them were South Albertas. Rarely has a commanding officer been blessed with such an array of talent – Proctor had now-Major Darby Nash, the SAR's last wartime commander; Major Arnold Lavoie, the longest serving SAR squadron commander; Captain Bob Allsopp, the adjutant; Captain Newt Hughes, the battle adjutant; Captain Tom Barford, the quartermaster; and a dozen warrant officers and senior NCOs including Regimental Sergeant-Major Larry Blain and Mechanical Quartermaster-sergeant Sid Slater, Technical Quartermaster-sergeant Harry Quarton, Sergeant Wally Jellis of "Wally's Commandos" fame, Sergeant Bob Rasmussen, pride of the Echelons, and many, many others.

The postwar 19th Armoured Car Regiment (basically the wartime SAR with a different cap badge) may have been an exceptional case but to a lesser extent, their happy situation was mirrored in militia armouries across Canada. As the Canadian armed forces returned to peacetime establishment, the ranks of

Warm the night and dark the sky,
Shades of summer drifting by.
But cold am I, and stiff and numb,
Waiting for the lorry to come,
Yet, within my heart is light …
I am going home tonight.

First I see a Sarcee star,
Then a horn blows faint and far
Floating past a Sherman track,
Brings a thousand memories back.
As the headlight casts its glow,
Down past tents row on row,
How it makes my spirits bright,
I am going home tonight!

"Turn in boys" … and so to bed,
My haversack beneath my head.
'Til my weary eyes at last
Trade the present for the past.
Dreams of home! The militia's all right,
The troops are going home tonight![1]

the militia were full of experienced veterans and, in contrast to the years immediately following the First World War when the army had been drastically cut in the belief that there would be no more wars, a saner vision of the future prevailed in 1945. As Brooke Claxton, the Liberal Minister of National Defence put it, "Canada is not, and has never been, a warlike country" but the events of the past 25 years have provided a "lesson in preparedness" and it was essential, he felt, that the country have an army "which can be counted upon in times of danger."[2] In 1946 the government announced that the peacetime regular force (now called the Active Force) would number 25,000 all ranks – five times its 1939 strength – while the militia (now called the Reserve Force) would number 180,000, many times its prewar establishment (although these establishments were never fully recruited). The two components would be organized in two corps comprising six divisions, of which two would be armoured, and four independent armoured brigades. Changes were also made to the territorial organization of the army – the eleven traditional Military Districts were replaced by five geographical commands: Eastern, Quebec, Central, Prairie and Western. Alberta came under Western Command which was to have its headquarters at Edmonton, with British Columbia being a subordinate area within that command.

The new organization resulted in major changes to the Alberta militia. The infantry lost the Edmonton Fusiliers which were amalgamated with the 19th Dragoons to form the 19th Armoured Car Regiment (Edmonton Fusiliers) but the Loyal Edmonton Regiment, Calgary Highlanders and South Alberta Regiment continued to serve. The 15th Light Horse, which had been made dormant in 1942, was combined with some of the prewar militia artillery batteries (among them the 22 Battery at Gleichen) and redesignated the 68th Light Anti-Aircraft Regiment, with headquarters at Calgary. As the artillery at this time had responsibility for the anti-tank role, a new 41st Anti-Tank Regiment was formed, also with headquarters at Calgary, which took over some of the other former field batteries in the province. The King's Own Calgary Regiment (formerly the Calgary Tanks) and the 19th Armoured Car Regiment provided the armoured and recce components of the Alberta district respectively, becoming part of the newly-retitled Royal Canadian Armoured Corps.

All "black hats," as armoured personnel called themselves after their distinctive headgear, rejoiced when Major-General Frank F. Worthington was appointed Colonel-Commandant of the RCAC in 1948, following his retirement from active service. As Colonel-Commandant, Worthington was responsible for matters of tradition and morale and although he held an honorary, not a command, appointment, he still wielded great influence because "Worthy" truly was the "father" of Canadian armour. He had served in the Royal Tank Corps in the First World War, created the first Canadian armoured training school at Borden in the late 1930s, and trained and commanded the 1st Canadian Tank Brigade and the 4th Armoured Division in the Second World War. Almost as good was the news that the Corps would be receiving new equipment – in 1947 the government purchased 294 M4A2 HVSS Sherman tanks (often called "the Easy 8") from the United States at the bargain basement price of $62,000 a vehicle.

The HVSS was the latest model of the Sherman, which had been continuously upgraded since 1942, powered by a diesel engine and armed with a high velocity 76 mm gun. For the armoured car regiments, the government acquired Staghound armoured cars, Lynx scout cars and universal carriers.

The 19th Armoured Car Regiment was one of the first militia armoured regiments to receive their vehicles. This may have been intentional as the 19th had a definite role in the postwar world. In combination with the regular units of Western Command, it was tasked with protecting the Alaska Highway, the vital artery from Edmonton to Fairbanks, from a possible Soviet airborne invasion. The sad truth was that unfortunately for millions of people, particularly in war-ravaged Europe, who yearned for peace, the Allied victory over the Axis powers brought none, only a new and more dangerous international situation. Strains between the Western Allies and the Soviet Union in the latter years of the war broadened into outright hostility in the late 1940s after Moscow embarked on an aggressive foreign policy in Europe which resulted in the overthrow of the established governments of many smaller nations and their replacement with Communist puppet regimes. In quick succession, Bulgaria, Czechoslovakia, Estonia, Hungary, Latvia, Lithuania, Poland and Rumania came under Soviet domination and were shut off from the west by what Winston Churchill termed the "Iron Curtain." In 1948 Moscow blocked the land routes to West Berlin, which was surrounded by Russian-

Roll Past of 19th Dragoons, Edmonton, 1950
Looking somewhat incongruous, Dragoons in full dress conduct a Roll Past through downtown Edmonton in Lynx II scout cars and a jeep after retrieving their Colours from the church where they had been laid up. The Colours are those of the Edmonton Fusiliers, which were amalgamated with the 19th Alberta Dragoons in 1946. COURTESY, HARRY QUARTON

Dragoons take a break, 1949
In 1946 the 19th Dragoons amalgamated with the Edmonton Fusiliers to become the 19th Alberta Armoured Car Regiment (Edmonton Fusiliers). In this photo, from June 1949, a Staghound crew at summer camp is visited by Lieutenant-Colonel M.R. Dare of Western Command. From left to right: Sergeant J. Ellinger, Captain V.H. Kupchenko, Lieutenant-Colonel Dare, Captain F.M. Kohler and Trooper J.H. Collins. Lieutenant-Colonel Dare became the Director of Armour in 1958-1959. COURTESY, REG HODGSON

occupied East Germany, but was thwarted by an airlift mounted by Britain and the United States. This event ushered in the "Cold War," a time of unceasing hostility, just short of outright conflict, between the western world and the Communist bloc, which was to dominate the international scene for more than four decades.

The tension was made worse by the postwar process of decolonialization which resulted in a series of armed conflicts fought between European powers with overseas colonies and independence movements, often Communist led, in those colonies. Between 1945 and 1965, wars of independence were waged in Algeria, Cyprus, Indochina, Indonesia, Malaya, Palestine, Tunisia and many smaller nations. In 1949 Communist forces in China defeated non-Communist forces and that nation, with its large population and strategic location, became an active ally with the Soviet Union in what was a policy of world domination. The Cold War was made even more tense by the major powers' acquisition and deployment of nuclear weapons which meant that, should it turn hot, global self-immolation would be the result.

The immediate postwar decades were thus played out against a dangerous background of potential nuclear holocaust. Since it was known that the Soviet army included eight airborne divisions, there was a fear in the late 1940s and early 1950s that, in the event of war, the USSR might attempt to cut the Alaska Highway and seize the many airfields along its length. The plan was that Lord Strathcona's Horse would fight a delaying action down the Highway, buying time for the engineers to blow the bridges and create other obstacles. Since the river lines and bridge crossings were vital spots, the job of the 19th Armoured Car was to recce the Highway and assist the Strathconas in defending it. With experienced personnel under his command, Lieutenant-Colonel John Proctor had no problem getting his unit up and running – by 1948 the 19th Armoured Car had a strength of 200 all ranks, organized into four squadrons, with RHQ and A, B and C Squadrons at the Connaught Armoury and D Squadron in Wetaskiwin.

Dragoon Staghounds refuel
From 1946 until well into the late 1950s the Dragoons manned Staghound armoured cars, seen here refuelling prior to setting out on an exercise. As time wore on, these vehicles began to wear out and, gradually, the Dragoons began to train as an armoured unit, using the War Reserve of HVSS Shermans held at Wainwright Camp. SALH ARCHIVES

Dragoon lines at the Railhead
The 19th Dragoons took over the former American base at the Railhead in Edmonton which provided excellent storage and maintenance facilities. In this view, Otter light reconnaissance cars and Staghound armoured cars are seen in the garage. To the left is a Sherman turret trainer as the Dragoons always kept up with their tank skills. SALH ARCHIVES

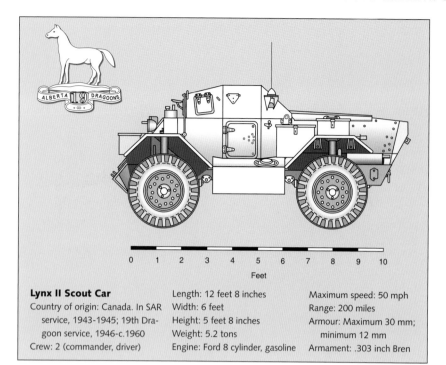

Lynx II Scout Car
Country of origin: Canada. In SAR service, 1943-1945; 19th Dragoon service, 1946-c.1960
Crew: 2 (commander, driver)

Length: 12 feet 8 inches
Width: 6 feet
Height: 5 feet 8 inches
Weight: 5.2 tons
Engine: Ford 8 cylinder, gasoline

Maximum speed: 50 mph
Range: 200 miles
Armour: Maximum 30 mm; minimum 12 mm
Armament: .303 inch Bren

The unit had 8 Staghounds and 5 Lynx scout cars, as well as a number of soft-skinned vehicles, and they rejoiced at taking over the garages and extensive workshops of the "Railhead," the wartime American base in Edmonton, which provided excellent maintenance facilities. As Harry Quarton recalled, the 19th was "the best outfitted unit in the country because we had all these workshops" including "a wireless wing, a gunnery wing, storage areas and even an auditorium."[3]

Like all militia units, the 19th also had the benefit of a decision on the part of Ottawa to post regular support staff to the reserves. Termed "A & T" (Administrative and Training) staff, they provided expertise and a model for parttime soldiers to

emulate. In this respect, the 19th were particularly lucky as their first MQMSM (Mechanical Quartermaster-sergeant-Major), the warrant officer charged with keeping their vehicles and equipment in running order, was Dick Muehllehner of Lord Strathcona's Horse, who had occupied a similar appointment with the wartime SAR. The Strathconas resumed the instructional role they had carried out prior to 1939 and formed close links with all militia armoured units in Western Canada. In the opinion of Captain George Lynch-Staunton, last met as a gunner in 13th Field Regiment and now an officer in the 19th, the "close bond" between the Strathconas and the Alberta militia was one of the reasons why the militia cavalry had been so efficient prior to the Second World War and why their successor armoured units were so efficient following it.[4]

In the late 1940s, Harry Quarton quipped, the 19th Dragoons were "a dagger pointed at the heart of Russia."[5] In preparation for the task of defending the Alaska Highway, Lieutenant-Colonel Proctor accompanied a group of regular force staff officers, headed by Brigadier-General George Kitching, the former commander of 4th Armoured Division in Normandy, who toured the Highway to study the problems of defending it. As Proctor recalled, he suggested one day to Kitching "that the man we really need to advise us" was Kurt Meyer because "he had thwarted every crossing we tried to make in Normandy."[6] Kitching quietly told him that the short, taciturn lieutenant in battle dress, who had been introduced to the group as a francophone officer, was actually former *Brigadeführer* Meyer, currently serving a life sentence in Dorchester Penitentiary in New Brunswick for the murder of Canadian prisoners by his division in 1944. With great dif-

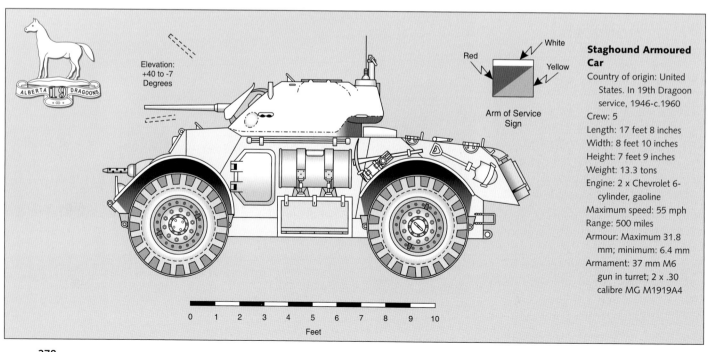

Elevation: +40 to -7 Degrees

Arm of Service Sign
Red White Yellow

Staghound Armoured Car
Country of origin: United States. In 19th Dragoon service, 1946-c.1960
Crew: 5
Length: 17 feet 8 inches
Width: 8 feet 10 inches
Height: 7 feet 9 inches
Weight: 13.3 tons
Engine: 2 x Chevrolet 6-cylinder, gaoline
Maximum speed: 55 mph
Range: 500 miles
Armour: Maximum 31.8 mm; minimum: 6.4 mm
Armament: 37 mm M6 gun in turret; 2 x .30 calibre MG M1919A4

ficulty, Kitching had managed to get Meyer – who gave his word of honour not to escape – out of Dorchester and he proved very helpful, rendering much sound advice that was incorporated into the defence plan for the Highway.

With experienced leadership – commissioned and non-commissioned – strong regular force support and a definite task, the 19th Armoured Car quickly became one of the best militia units in Western Canada. In the early 1950s, B Squadron moved to Westlock and C Squadron to Whitehorse in the Yukon but the regiment's strength remained strong in the postwar decade and rarely dropped below 200 all ranks. The 19th spent much time surveying the Alaska Highway and also carried out some interesting exercises with 418 RCAF, the reserve squadron in Edmonton, involving daytime camouflage and air defence. In the summer, the 19th concentrated at Wainwright, which was constantly being expanded during this period, to train with the KOCR and the Strathconas. In April 1950, it removed its Standard and the Colours of the Edmonton Fusiliers from Holy Trinity Church in Edmonton where they

The 19th Armoured Car Regiment carries out ceremonial duties, c. 1951
They used to do it with a mounted troop but the 19th Dragoons, now retitled the 19th Alberta Armoured Car Regiment, used vehicles to escort the Lieutenant-Governor to the opening of the provincial Legislative Assembly. The Dragoons would regain their traditional title in 1958. COURTESY REG HODGSON

had been laid up, and returned them to the Connaught Armoury. Also in 1950 Proctor turned over to Lieutenant-Colonel F.N. Hughes, who served for two years before being succeeded by Lieutenant-Colonel Arnold Lavoie, a former squadron commander in the wartime SAR.

The postwar decade was a good time for the 19th Armoured Car and happily remembered by men who served with the unit

19th Alberta Armoured Car Regiment vehicles, c. 1949
The unit lines up its vehicles in 1949, including Lynx II scout cars and Staghounds. Of interest is the vehicle fourth from the left, which is a rare type of Staghound mounting a British Crusader Mk III tank turret with a 6-pdr. (57 mm) gun. A smalll number of Staghounds were modified in this fashion during the war to give the vehicle more hitting power. COURTESY, REG HODGSON

Officers of the South Alberta Regiment, c. 1950

After the war had ended, the peacetime SAR reverted to being a militia infantry regiment with Headquarters at Medicine Hat. Here, the officers pose for a group photo, probably at Sarcee Camp around 1950. Note that every man is wearing medal ribbons. SALH Archives

during that period. There were the usual misadventures. In Exercise VERMILLION, held in June 1949, the regiment managed to start a prairie fire with mortar bombs, which brought a halt to all activities as all ranks fought the fire until it was put out. In the first five years after the war, the unit had a few wretched Otter Light Reconnaissance Cars, arguably the worst military vehicle ever produced in Canada. Captain George Lynch-Staunton recalled that he nearly lost his life one night in Wainwright when his driver "hit a slit trench and we went ass end up." Fortunately, the vehicle did not flip as Lynch-Staunton was in the turret "and would have been cut in half" but he was able to get clear before the turret slid off the hull.[7] Not that the Staghounds were much better, although they were certainly easier to drive as they had automatic transmissions. Sergeant Paul Fuog never forgot the time when, after returning from an exercise, he blocked the heavy traffic on the 109th Street bridge in Edmonton when the gear lever, which was not fully engaged, slipped just as he turned onto the structure and he hit a high curb. Fuog did little damage

to the vehicle but deeply slashed a tire which blew at the garage behind the back of the RSM just as he was berating Fuog for careless driving.

In the southern part of the province, meanwhile, the South Alberta Regiment continued as an infantry regiment with headquarters at Medicine Hat. In 1948, the SAR moved out of its little armoury at the corner of Division and Third Streets in the downtown part of the Hat and took over many of the facilities of the large wartime prison camp constructed on Dunmore Hill on the southern outskirts of the city. The main building, basically a large hanger with folding doors on its front, was the former camp auditorium and was named Patterson Armoury in honour of Brigadier-General Maynard E. Patterson, the prewar commander of the SAR, whose platoon of the 31st Battalion, CEF had won the Canadian Corps platoon championship in 1917. Headquarters and A and B Companies were at the Hat while C Company

Officers and NCOs of the 68th Light Anti-Aircraft Regiment, 1953

In the postwar reorganization of the Canadian militia, the 15th Alberta Light Horse and 22 Field Battery, RCA, were combined to form the 68th Light Anti-Aircraft Regiment with headquarters at Calgary. Here, the officers of that unit have their picture taken at Victoria, BC, where they concentrated for summer training in 1953. From left to right: Captain B. Bobey, Major I. McKenzie, Lieutenant E. Lomas, Lieutenant-Colonel P.W.H. Higgs, commanding officer, Lieutenant Harris and Sergeant C. Mellon. Back row left to right: Bombardier Anton, Lieutenant Valestuk, Captain E.G.M. McMullen and Lieutenant G. Bateson. Most of these gunners are wearing olive green, cotton summer field (bush) dress, introduced into the Canadian army in 1950. SALH ARCHIVES

was at Redcliff and D Company at Brooks. The SAR maintained good numbers in the immediate postwar period, fluctuating between 120 and 160 all ranks, and trained at Wainwright in conjunction with Princess Patricia's Canadian Light Infantry, the western regular infantry unit. In April 1951, the SAR carried out Operation WELLHIT, rendering support to regular troops who were trying to dynamite ice floes on the South Saskatchewan River that threatened to take out the bridges at the Hat. As these bridges were considerably downstream from the demolition site and, as it was difficult and dangerous to cross the frozen river on foot, the SAR signals platoon tried out a tactic found in its manuals and attempted to blow a land line from one bank to the other using a 2-inch mortar, without success. Finally, Lieutenant S.H. Wilkinson, the signals officer, enlisted the aid of an RCAF helicopter to carry it over.

During this same period, the new 68th Light Anti-Aircraft Regiment (15th Light Horse), RCA, was also actively training. Headquarters and 207 and 212 Batteries were at Mewata Armoury in Calgary, while 122 Battery (the former 22 Field Battery) was at Gleichen and there were troops at Bassano and Strathmore. Each battery was equipped with a self-propelled 40 mm Bofors and a towed gun, while RHQ

Operation WELLHIT, 1951

In times of emergency, the militia has always aided the civil power. In April 1951 when ice floes on the South Saskatchewan River threatened to take out the bridges at Medicine Hat, the South Alberta Regiment provided communications and logistical support for the regular troops who dynamited them. In this photo an SAR sergeant mans a No. 38 radio set. SALH ARCHIVES

had a four-barrelled 20 mm Polsten Oerlikon weapon. The 68th maintained good strength, averaging between 120 and 180 all ranks, but was somewhat hampered by the fact that its summer concentrations were at Esquimalt in British Columbia where the RCA held its western anti-aircraft training camp. Nonetheless,

Weapons of the 68th LAA Regiment, 1952

On a winter exercises in the Rockies, the 68th LAA mans its two main weapons: a towed Bofors 40 mm gun (top and bottom) and a 4-barrelled 20 mm. The unit also possessed a self-propelled version of the Bofors. This weapon, which had a maximum range of about 2,000 yards and could be brought into action in two minutes, was the standard medium AA gun of the Canadian army from 1940 until the 1980s. The 20 mm Polsten-Oerlikon gun, which could fire 450 rounds per minute out to a maximum range of about 1,200 yards, was the standard light AA gun in the 1940s and 1950s. SALH ARCHIVES

Weapons of the 41st Anti-Tank Regiment, 1951
The 41st Anti-Tank Regiment, with headquarters at Calgary, was equipped with towed and self-propelled 17-pdr. (76.2 mm) guns. These pictures, taken at a firepower demonstration held in 1951, show the towed and self-propelled versions lined up with HVSS Shermans of the King's Own Calgary Regiment; a 17-pdr. at full recoil while being fired; and an M-10 self-propelled 17-pdr. about to be fired. The M-10 utilized the chassis and running gear of the Sherman tank – note that the rear corner of the vehicle has been painted with luminous paint as a guide when driving at night. COURTESY, DIRECTORATE OF HISTORY AND HERITAGE, DND

the 68th sent strong detachments to camp, including a very impressive turn-out of 148 officers and men in 1949.

The headquarters of 41st Anti-Tank Regiment, which took its number from a reserve field regiment authorized in 1942, shared Mewata Armoury with the 68th LAA but its sub-units were very scattered. Only two of its four batteries were in Alberta – 78 Battery at Red Deer and 95 Battery at Calgary – while 62 Battery was at Courtenay, and 108 Battery at Kimberley in British Columbia. Each battery had one self-propelled M-10 17-pdr. and one towed gun, and the unit's overall strength fluctuated between 120 and 160 in the years immediately following its creation in 1946. It had an experienced commanding officer in Lieutenant-Colonel D.S. Harkness, GM, ED, who had commanded 5th Anti-Tank Regiment during the war and was the officer who organized the anti-gun screen in the Falaise Gap during the night of 20-21 August 1944. After a few years, Harkness retired from the militia to enter politics and ended up as a Liberal defence minister in 1960. By 1951, it seems that the intention was to turn the 41st into a field regiment and each battery, in turn, received a 25-pdr. gun/howitzer.

All these militia regiments carried out their activities against

a background of considerable international tension. In 1950, backed by Russia and China, the Communist puppet state of North Korea invaded South Korea. The United Nations responded by sending large military forces to fight what was euphemistically called a "police action" but was actually a vicious war that resulted in 1.6 million Communist casualties and half a million UN casualties. Canada contributed an infantry brigade with an attached armoured squadron, raised from volunteers, and in the four years that the Korean War lasted, 21,940 Canadian soldiers fought in Korea with 312 being killed and 1,245 wounded. It being clear that the postwar world was a very dangerous place, the Canadian government increased the size of its armed forces and defence budget. The regular army went from 20,000 all ranks in 1950 to 50,000 all ranks in 1952 and, for the first time in the history of the Dominion, outnumbered the reserve force. The regulars' main purpose was to provide a mobile brigade group in West Germany under the aegis of the North Atlantic Treaty Organization or NATO, formed in 1949 by the Western Allies to provide mutual defence against Communist aggression in Europe. This brigade group was a well-trained and – rare for Canada in peacetime – well-armed formation based on an armoured regiment equipped with Centurion main battle tanks purchased in 1952 from Britain. For the next four decades the NATO brigade was the major focus of the regular Canadian army.

Although these were troubled times for the world, Alberta fared very well in the postwar years. In 1945, there had been much concern that the province's population, which had only experienced a marginal increase to 803,000 souls in the last decade, would inevitably decline as Albertans were lured away to

Ontario or British Columbia by better economic opportunities. There were grounds for this concern. Agriculture, followed by lumbering and mining, was still the economic mainstay of the province and although farmers had done well during the war, most of the arable land in the province was under cultivation by 1945 and many young people had abandoned rural areas, attracted by the bright lights of the cities. The rural population was 20% less than in 1939 and the fear was that, without the stimulus of the wartime economy, there would be no jobs for them and they would be tempted to sail for distant shores.

This fear was dissipated by an event that took place in early 1947. On 13 February of that year Imperial Oil's Leduc Well No 1, located 17 miles southwest of Edmonton, struck oil at a depth of 5,000 feet and launched the province on an unprecedented economic boom. The Leduc oilfield, twice the size of the Turner Valley field, turned out to be an incredibly rich resource with an estimated 200 million barrels of recoverable oil. And this was only the beginning as, over the next 20 years, oil field after field was surveyed and tapped in Alberta. There seemed to be no end to this wonderful underground wealth – by 1971, it was estimated that the province's oil reserves were in the vicinity of 8 billion barrels and that figure did not include the incredibly rich Athabasca oil sands, 200 miles northeast of Edmonton, which possessed an estimated 300 billion barrels of recoverable oil although it was difficult and expensive to extract. Major development of the Athabasca sands began in 1964 and has continued to the present day. Oil was not the only underground bounty in Alberta, as huge reserves of natural gas were also discovered and the province, particularly the northern part, became crisscrossed with pipelines feeding oil and gas products to local refineries and the outside world.

The oil and gas boom – and its attendant effects on other commercial activities including construction and manufacturing – transformed Alberta. Attracted by the new-found bonanza, people flocked into the province and the population doubled between 1946 and 1971, from 803,000 to 1,600,000, an increase of almost 100% as compared to an increase of 72% for Canada as a whole. The major cities mushroomed, Edmonton experienced a 400% rate of growth to 449,000 people, Calgary went to 387,000 and Medicine Hat to 25,700. Not only were there more people, they were wealthier people – the average income in Alberta rose nearly eightfold between 1945 and 1971 – enjoying a high standard of living. The coffers of the provincial government overflowed from petroleum and gas revenues – in 1956 alone the province collected $250 million in tax revenue from this source and had a surplus in the same amount. By 1970, it had drawn $3 billion from the industry since its inception in 1947 and confidently expected that, in the next decade, it could count on $210 million annually from oil and gas revenues. In a remarkable turnaround, Alberta went from a province on the brink of decline in 1945 to becoming the economic powerhouse of Western Canada by 1970.

This bonanza was managed wisely by a provincial government that remained remarkably stable in the postwar decades.

William C. Aberhart's Social Credit Party had been re-elected in 1940 and when Aberhart died in 1943, he was succeeded by the very capable Ernest C. Manning, a former officer in the Edmonton Fusiliers. Manning won election after election and became the longest-serving provincial premier in Canadian history, completing 25 years until his retirement in 1968. He led a competent and responsible administration which, although friendly to business interests, particularly the American business interests which were underwriting the cost of the exploration and development of the oil and gas industry, efficiently supervised that industry in a manner that profited all parties. The largesse from the petroleum bonanza was invested back into the province's infrastructure and educational system until Alberta became the envy of Canada. As if all this was not bounty enough, in 1948 the Calgary Stampeders became the first Alberta football team to win the Grey Cup and Edmonton, not to be outdone by its southern rival, put an incredible Eskimos team, led by the magnificent Jackie Parker, onto the gridiron and took the Cup three years in a row from 1954 to 1956. The one dark shadow in this otherwise bright picture was that, from the 1930s to the 1960s, Alberta sent mainly Social Credit members to Ottawa and therefore did not have a loud voice in the halls of the federal government.

"Murdered by … an axe-man in Ottawa": The birth of the South Alberta Light Horse

In 1953, as Albertans were rejoicing in the first fruits of the oil and gas boom, the Korean War was coming to an end in a stalemate that preserved the *status quo ante bellum*. The regular army had experienced considerable difficulty in raising and training forces both for Korea and NATO and it was clear to the staff at Army Headquarters in Ottawa that the large six-division, two-

"Hello Baker, Hello Baker, report my signals"
Good radio communications are vital in modern warfare, particularly in an armoured regiment. Here a Light Horse corporal wearing parachute wings instructs a young trooper in the mysteries of the C-42 set. These soldiers are wearing the 1947 Pattern Canadian battle dress which featured an open collar and lapels and was worn with a tie. SALH ARCHIVES

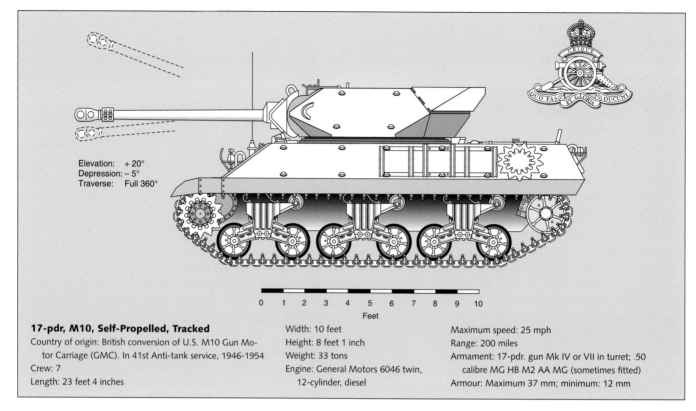

Elevation: + 20°
Depression: − 5°
Traverse: Full 360°

0 1 2 3 4 5 6 7 8 9 10
Feet

17-pdr, M10, Self-Propelled, Tracked
Country of origin: British conversion of U.S. M10 Gun Motor Carriage (GMC). In 41st Anti-tank service, 1946-1954
Crew: 7
Length: 23 feet 4 inches

Width: 10 feet
Height: 8 feet 1 inch
Weight: 33 tons
Engine: General Motors 6046 twin, 12-cylinder, diesel

Maximum speed: 25 mph
Range: 200 miles
Armament: 17-pdr. gun Mk IV or VII in turret; .50 calibre MG HB M2 AA MG (sometimes fitted)
Armour: Maximum 37 mm; minimum: 12 mm

corps structure created in 1946 would have to be streamlined. There was particular concern about the composition of the Reserve Force as the top-heavy structure had resulted in too many units competing for the available manpower with the result that many were sadly understrength. In May 1953 Lieutenant-General Guy Simonds, the Chief of the General Staff or professional head of the Canadian army, created a board of three senior officers, chaired by Major-General Howard Kennedy, to examine the training, organization and administration of the Reserves.

The Kennedy Board submitted its report in January 1954. It recommended returning to the traditional title of militia, replacing divisional and brigade headquarters with militia group headquarters and reducing the infantry and artillery components, but increasing the number of armoured units as the armoured corps would take over the anti-tank role. It is important to note that the Kennedy Board did not call for the disbandment of any of the seven infantry battalions that it suggested be struck from the order of battle. Instead, it proposed that they be redesignated, converted or amalgamated. The Board's report was discussed at a conference of Area Commanders held at Ottawa in March 1954, which generally accepted its recommendations – with one major exception. The Board had advised that the South Alberta Regiment in Medicine Hat be linked with the Loyal Edmonton Regiment but at the conference, a decision was made to disband the SAR, making it the only militia infantry unit in Canada to suffer this fate.

It is not clear why the SAR was singled out for this draconian punishment. Certainly, it was not because of its strength as it had 153 all ranks on its rolls and had sent the largest contingent to summer camp in 1953 of any militia unit in Alberta. In any

case, Brooke Claxton, the Minister of National Defence, was too politically astute to risk offending local sensibilities and when he outlined the future organization of the militia in the House of Commons on 21 June 1954, he stressed that "the procedure of disbandment would not be used where the amalgamation of units would accomplish the required reduction of units."[8] Army Headquarters got the message and when it issued a press release about the new militia organization, it stated that the SAR would "be replaced by elements of a new unit, 15th Alberta Light Horse (26 Armoured Regiment)" to be formed in southern Alberta by an amalgamation of the SAR, 68th Light Anti-Aircraft Regiment and 41st Anti-Tank Regiment.

The fact that the 15th Light Horse, dormant for twelve years, would soon be riding again was good news to the 68th in Calgary. Lieutenant-Colonel P.W.H. Higgs, commanding that regiment, confessed to Major-General Chris Vokes, commander of Western Area, that he was gratified that the 15th "has been reborn," as he had first been commissioned in the unit in 1939 and although his officers and men had "tried our best to be Gunners; it will be grand to be a Tanker again."[9] A few days after the official announcement, an elaborate party was held in the officers' mess at Sarcee, in the presence of Vokes, around three coffins containing the remains of the 15th Light Horse, the 41st and the 68th. The two artillery regiments, "murdered by remote control by an axe-man in Ottawa," were formally interred and then a trumpeter sounded "Reveille." On the last note, an officer wearing little more than a sporran jumped out of the coffin labelled "15th Light Horse" and "danced madly around the room" yelling "he was very happy to meet everyone again." And then, in the words of the *Calgary Herald* reporter who was present, "the mourners became what is known in polite international patois as 'bescwhippst' and in polite Canadian as a little happy."[10]

The Calgarians were rejoicing too soon. Medicine Hat was not going to let the SAR, the Hat's own militia regiment for three decades, die without a struggle and Mayor Harry Veiner of the Hat fired the first shot by sending a telegram to Claxton in mid-July 1954 protesting the proposed changes. This was followed up by protests from the Mayors of Redcliff and Brooks, who would lose the companies in their towns, and the veterans of the 31st Battalion, who disliked the fact that their Battle Honours would now be held by an armoured regiment. Supported by political riding associations, service clubs and Legion Branches, the local politicians waged a battle throughout July and August 1954. Major-General Chris Vokes quickly became aware of the strength of public feeling in southern Alberta – the Minister wasn't the only person receiving loud complaints and Vokes in Edmonton was a lot closer to the Hat than was Claxton in Ottawa. On 9 August Vokes sent a message to AHQ recommending that, because its strength compared favourably with other infantry units in Western Command and because Calgary was too far away, the SAR should be retained on the order of battle as an infantry regiment with headquarters in Medicine Hat.

This abrupt about-face was not what Headquarters staff wanted to hear and they complained that, if Vokes's suggestions were accepted, it would set a bad precedent that would "encourage other communities to adopt similar tactics" and, even worse, would "tend to create the impression that the Army had no firm plan for the reorganization of the Militia."[11] The result was that, on the same day he sent his message, Vokes received a phone call from Lieutenant-General Guy Simonds who, to put it plainly, leaned heavily on him. Vokes agreed to rescind and destroy all copies of the message he had sent that morning so that there would be no official record of any suggestion that the SAR be left alone. The two generals then discussed the situation. It was Simonds's opinion that, if the title "15th Light Horse" was not acceptable to the proponents of the SAR, the only choices "agreeable" to Army Headquarters would be either "South Alberta Horse (29th Armoured Regiment)" or "South Alberta Light Horse (29th Armoured Regiment)." Army Headquarters was prepared to go so far as to change the new unit's armoured corps number from "26" to "29" to placate the proponents of the SAR, but Simonds did not contemplate, nor did the two men discuss, retaining the title, "South Alberta Regiment."

Having more or less made their decision, Simonds and his staff tidied up the paperwork. On 13 August Simonds sent a memorandum to Claxton with information for "inclusion in any reply the Minister may wish to make" to the briefs he had received from the Hat area.[12] Simonds noted that, as two of the three regiments to be amalgamated in the new entity were from Calgary, it was "desirable from all aspects" that its headquarters be in that city. Regarding the title, Simonds stressed that, "as each of the units had just claims, the re-introduction of the 15th Alta Light Horse as a suitable title would be preferable" as it would "perpetuate the units now amalgamating and preserve their regimental traditions." "However," Simonds continued, sliding in something he had already discussed with Vokes, "if some other suitable designation is recommended which is acceptable to the units concerned it will receive favourable consideration." For his part, Vokes discussed the matter of a new title with the officers of the three regiments and it is clear that he gave them only two choices: "South Alberta Horse" or "South Alberta Light Horse." On 25 August, he reported back to Army Headquarters that the

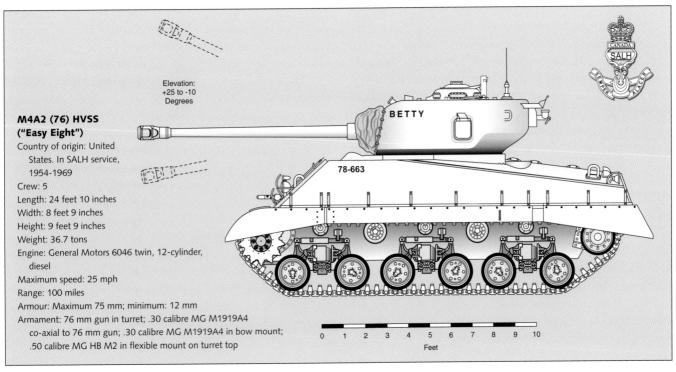

M4A2 (76) HVSS ("Easy Eight")

Country of origin: United States. In SALH service, 1954-1969

Crew: 5

Length: 24 feet 10 inches

Width: 8 feet 9 inches

Height: 9 feet 9 inches

Weight: 36.7 tons

Engine: General Motors 6046 twin, 12-cylinder, diesel

Maximum speed: 25 mph

Range: 100 miles

Armour: Maximum 75 mm; minimum: 12 mm

Armament: 76 mm gun in turret; .30 calibre MG M1919A4 co-axial to 76 mm gun; .30 calibre MG M1919A4 in bow mount; .50 calibre MG HB M2 in flexible mount on turret top

Elevation: +25 to -10 Degrees

BETTY

78-663

0 1 2 3 4 5 6 7 8 9 10
Feet

artillery regiments favoured "South Alberta Light Horse (29 Armoured Regiment)" but that the SAR wished "to retain its own title and will not compromise."[13]

The Hat, however, was not yet ready to give up the fight. At about the same time, Vokes sent a personal letter to Simonds enclosing a letter from Mayor Veiner which pointed out that Claxton's staff had apparently promised the mayors of Redcliff and Brooks that elements of the new regiment would be located in their towns, while Army Headquarters had just announced that these elements would be located in Calgary, Medicine Hat and Strathmore. It appears that Vokes, under intense pressure in Alberta, was again starting to waver, and Headquarters staff, anxious that he not weaken, propped him up with memoranda to the CGS and the Minister. On the matter of the proposed title, the staff noted that:

> The South Alberta Regiment is getting primary recognition in the accepted designation "South Alberta Light Horse (29th Armoured Regiment)". The two artillery regiments involved can only consider the term "Light Horse" as their contribution, by virtue of the fact that the 68th LAA Regt was converted from the 15th Alberta Light Horse.

It was quite clear where the staff's sympathies lay. It was their opinion that the 68th LAA and 41 Anti-Tank regiments

> have compromised and cooperated to a far greater degree in agreeing to the accepted title than the S Alta R (the latter having refused to consider any other title but its own), it would be wrong to put pressure on the two artillery units to accept the title S Alta R (29 Armd R).

This being the case, the staff continued, "there is no reason why the two artillery regiments should not be afforded some slight recognition in the accepted title," and Army Headquarters must "remain firm against any indication of high pressure being exerted by the community of Medicine Hat to retain the old infantry title for the new unit.[14] Such was the staff position and they were not going to budge because, as is so often the case in a bureaucracy, more time and energy is spent defending a bad decision than would be spent in correcting it. On 28 September 1954 Claxton signed the order bringing the South Alberta Light Horse into official existence and the matter was closed.

The failed struggle to preserve the South Alberta Regiment left a bitter taste in Medicine Hat. Although the 15th Light Horse, in the form of the 68th Light Anti-Aircraft Regiment, was the older of the two units to amalgamate and, indeed, by virtue of its date of raising, was the senior regiment of the Alberta militia, its title had been more or less dormant for twelve years. During that time the wartime South Alberta Regiment had carved out a magnificent record and it is difficult not to feel sympathy for the proponents of the SAR who had fought hard to retain the regiment. The question of the title, however, was only one part

of the controversy – even more galling to Medicine Hat was the move of the headquarters from that city to Calgary and, as we shall see, this would prove to be a mistake.

"Our problem of recruiting": The Light Horse and the 19th Dragoons, 1954-1959

The South Alberta Light Horse was created at the beginning of the 1954-1955 training cycle which delayed the process of converting gunners and infantrymen into armoured corps troopers. The new regiment, which had 351 all ranks in early 1955, was organized with its RHQ and C Squadron at Mewata Armoury in Calgary, B Squadron at Strathmore with outlying troops at Bassano and Gleichen, and A Squadron at Medicine Hat with outlying troops at Redcliff and Brooks. The SALH, which everyone immediately began to call the "Sally Horse" or "Light Horse," went to Sarcee in July 1955 where the Strathconas ran a one-week course in the three basic armoured trades: driving and maintenance; gunnery; and radio communications. Major Gordon McQueen recalled that, "at that time, we didn't have a hell of a lot to train on."[15] Corporal, later Sergeant-Major, A. Arelis, who had just joined the Light Horse from the engineers remembered the "armour part was rather vague and disjointed and nobody seemed to know what was going on."[16] It appears that the SALH received four Shermans that summer and armoured training intensified during the winter of 1955-1956 when the Light Horse held weekend exercises at Sarcee. As their Shermans had metal instead of rubber tracks and were thus not permitted on the highways, the KOCR lent its troop of four tanks so that, as Lieutenant-Colonel Higgs noted in his report to the RCAC Association for that year, "we managed to always have one troop of tanks running (out of a total of 8 allowing for repairs)."[17]

Unfortunately, it appears that the SALH soon began to experience problems. Higgs reported that he sent only 79 personnel to summer camp at Wainwright in July 1956 when, "with a strength of over 300, we should have sent at least 120."[18] He noted that, with a distance of 180 miles between A Squadron in Medicine Hat and C Squadron in Calgary, he had yet to hold a regimental parade but hoped "during the 1956-1957 training year that a March Past be held in the 'Hat' and the Honorary Lieutenant-Colonel takes the salute."[19] It was clear that, while the new regiment was taking root in Medicine Hat and Strathmore, it was having problems getting recruits in Calgary where it faced competition from the well-established KOCR. A Squadron in the Hat had 129 all ranks and B Squadron in Strathmore had 171, but RHQ and C Squadron in Calgary were parading only 51 officers and men in 1956.

Lieutenant-Colonel Higgs was interested in matters pertaining to regimental ceremonial and tradition. In this regard, there were many decisions to be taken as the SALH was formed by amalgamation and he appears to have tried to adopt traditions from all its predecessors. From the 15th Light Horse, he took the Regimental badge, which featured a pronghorn antelope, and also their motto, *Semper Alacer*. This has been variously trans-

Army display, Edmonton Exhibition, 1949
A fascinated group of civilians (mostly young boys) clamber over a 19th Dragoon Staghound at the Edmonton Exhbition. Militia regiments often used such events as both a recruiting tool and a public relations exercise. COURTESY REG HODGSON

Alberta Regiment. One of the most important decisions to be made was the choice of regimental colours, as this would dictate the appearance of the Regimental tie, ascot, lanyard and shoulder flash. Again, Higgs drew on the background of all the predecessors and opted for a combination of gold, red and blue that bears a marked resemblance to the regimental tie of the 15th/19th Hussars.

Matters of ceremonial and tradition are of great importance but they cannot take the place of weapons, equipment, training and recruits. In 1958 it appears that the Light Horse encountered some trouble as their strength dropped sharply that year. The reason for this decline is not certain and it is curious because in the summer of 1958 the SALH did some very effective training at Wainwright when it took over 12 Centurions provided by the Strathconas and carried out a 3-day exercise. The Light Horse conducted live firing, troop tactics,

lated as "Always Alert," "Always Brisk," "Always Lively" or "Always Swift," as, depending on context, it can mean any one of these things and, in any case, being alert, brisk, lively and swift are desirable qualities for Light Horsemen. From the South Alberta Regiment, Higgs adopted the Regimental march, "A Southerly Wind and a Cloudy Sky," which the SAR in turn had taken from the East Surrey Regiment of the British army. On the part of the SALH, he also reaffirmed that traditional alliances with the regiments of the British army held by its predecessors – that of the 15th Light Horse with the 15th/19th Hussars and that of the South Alberta Regiment with the East Surrey Regiment.* From the East Surrey he got permission for the senior Light Horse NCOs to wear a Surrey button as the top button on their blue patrols, a tradition that had originated with the prewar South

harbouring and leaguering in the field, night marches and camouflage discipline and seem to have come through with flying colours. About this time Lieutenant-Colonel Higgs obtained permission to form a regimental band which he thought would be of "great assistance to us in our problem of recruiting."[20] It appears, however, that when Higgs turned over command to Lieutenant-Colonel C.D. Williams in 1958, the SALH was having serious problems.

In contrast, up in Edmonton the 19th Alberta Dragoons were going from strength to strength. The Dragoons, who had regained their traditional title in 1954, had expanded to five squadrons: HQ, A and B Squadrons were in Edmonton at the Connaught and 109th Street Armouries, C Squadron (known as the "Northern Lights") was at Whitehorse in the Yukon and D Squadron was at Wetaskiwin. The Dragoons' numbers were good and fairly constant, averaging about 230 to 240 all ranks between 1954 and 1960, and they always sent a strong complement to the summer camps of 23 Militia Group at Wainwright. The unit's primary tasking was still the Alaska Highway – hence the creation of C Squadron at Whitehorse in 1958 – but as the decade drew to a close, the advent of long-range bombers and intercontinental ballistic missiles armed with nuclear warheads made the possibility of a Soviet airborne assault less likely and, frankly, unnecessary. More and more, the 19th trained as a conventional armoured regiment, using the Canadian army's battle reserve of HVSS Shermans which were stored at Wainwright and, by the time their Staghounds were taken out of service in 1959-

* The East Surrey Regiment became allied with the SAR in 1932 after Major Roupell, VC, was so impressed with the Alberta unit after he met it at Sarcee that he asked that an alliance be formed. It was an interesting connection since the 1st Battalion of the East Surrey Regiment was the former 31st Regiment of Foot and the SAR perpetuated the 31st Battalion, CEF. After recent amalgamations in the British army, the 15th/19th King's Royal Hussars are now the Light Dragoons while the East Surrey Regiment is now part of the Princess of Wales's Royal Regiment (Queen's and Royal Hampshires) and both are allied to the modern South Alberta Light Horse. It is somewhat ironic that the 15th Light Horse were allied with the 15th Hussars, and the 19th Alberta Dragoons with the 19th Hussars, before these two British regiments amalgamated in the 1930s to form the 15th/19th Hussars as now the South Alberta Light Horse, descended from the 15th Light Horse, is about to amalgamate with the 19th Alberta Dragoons.

We did it!
In 1956 the 19th Alberta Dragoons became the first Western Canadian armoured unit to win the prestigious Worthington Trophy, seen here being admired by, left to right, Captain Harry Meadows, Lieutenant Harry Quarton and Captain Steve Kruper, all wearing patrol dress, sometimes called "Blue Patrols." COURTESY, HARRY QUARTON

1960, the Dragoons were functioning primarily as a tank regiment. The 19th Dragoons were among the best militia armoured regiments in Western Canada and proof of that came in 1956 when they became the first western unit to win the Worthington Trophy (in a tie with the 8th New Brunswick Hussars). This trophy, created two years before by Major-General Frank F. Worthington, Colonel Commandant of the RCAC, was awarded to the militia armoured regiment achieving the best overall standard in the Corps. It was a proud moment for the Dragoons and they repeated this success in 1960 in another tie with the 8th Hussars.

As is often the case with efficient militia regiments, the 19th Dragoons were also a very social unit. A perusal of their professionally-produced newsletter, "The 19th," from 1954 to 1960 reveals an impressive social schedule of barbecues, officers and sergeants' mess dinners, VE-Day

balls, masquerade balls, "Klondike Nights" and an annual mess dinner held with the officers of the KOCR which alternated between the two regiments. In 1958 and 1960, the Dragoons staged two musical and variety shows, dubbed "Army Shows," at the Edmonton Jubilee Auditorium, with Dragoon personnel involved in all aspects of the production. For a brief period in the late 1950s the Dragoons formed a ceremonial mounted troop which took part in the annual opening and closing of the provincial legislature and provided escorts for distinguished visitors to Edmonton. It would seem that the only thing not improving with the Dragoons was their sense of humour as their newsletter, "The 19th," reveals that it was no better than when we last noticed it in the 1920s. The following examples will suffice:

> Trooper Perrin: "How about some old-fashioned loving?"
> Girl friend: "All right. I'll call grandmother for you."[21]

> Trooper Mottershead: "Would you like to see a model home?"
> Corporal Vanags: "Glad to. What time does she quit work?"[22]

Moving (as quickly as possible) back to the southern part of the province, by the beginning of 1959 the SALH was in difficult straits. Its strength had declined markedly in the previous twelve months and it appears that the RHQ and C Squadron in Calgary were almost dormant. The problem appears to have been the wide

The 19th Alberta Dragoons host a distinguished visitor
Lieutenant-Colonel David V. Currie, VC, visits the mess of the 19th Dragoons in the early 1950s and is greeted by some old South Alberta comrades. Kneeling in front is Lieutenant Harry Quarton and, seated from left to right, are Lieutenant-Colonel Ernest Hill, Lieutenant-Colonel Arnold Lavoie, Lieutenant-Colonel David Currie, Lieutenant-Colonel K.N. Clarke, Brigadier-General Bob Bradburn and RQMS Grant Flaws. Behind is SSM John Seccombe. With the exception of Clarke, every one of these men served with the wartime SAR and their presence in the postwar militia is an indication of the professional leadership it enjoyed. COURTESY, HARRY QUARTON

dispersion of the Regiment – its strength was concentrated in and around Medicine Hat and Strathmore but, facing competition in Calgary from the KOCR, it had never taken hold in the city. On 2 March 1959, the commander of 22 Militia Group passed sentence on the Light Horse. The squadrons at Calgary and Strathmore were to be taken over by the KOCR, its RHQ was to move to Medicine Hat but would remain dormant although A Squadron at the Hat was to continue as an "independent South Alberta Light Horse Squadron" until higher authority decided its fate – and few people had any doubt that it faced the chopping block. The future appeared bleak but, as is so often the case in the history of the Alberta cavalry, just when things looked their worst, the right man took over the reins.

"Orphan in the storm": Operation BOOMERANG, March 1959 to December 1960

In 1959 Major N.R. ("Rod") Ray was commanding A Squadron of the Light Horse and Ray was a man with a mission – he was determined to return the SALH to regimental status with headquarters in the Hat. A flamboyant, almost theatrical, personality blessed with seemingly boundless energy, Rod Ray was a veteran militiaman who had joined the Royal Canadian Corps of Signals during the war and had served as a signals officer with the BCR in Northwest Europe in 1944-1945. Employed by the Canadian Pacific Railway, he had joined the SAR when the CPR transferred him to the Hat in the late 1940s. As he later recalled, the situation of A Squadron, the surviving rump of the Light Horse, was perilous in March 1959 – it was "an orphan in the storm," an independent squadron without a parent and sure to be axed if there were any cuts in the militia.[23] That month Ray's squadron had about 35 all ranks and

> one Sherman, which was grounded and unable to be a runner or a gun tank … vehicles were in terrible shape … office equipment was at a premium – office space was non-existent … the Messes were run down … there was no canteen … authorities were considering disbanding the unit and leaving Medicine Hat without any Militia whatsoever.[24]

Obtaining a stay of execution from 22 Militia Group, Ray set out to restore the Light Horse to health and, much to everyone's surprise (particularly 22 Militia Group staff), he managed to accomplish this feat in the incredibly short period of nineteen months from March 1959 to December 1960.

Rod Ray was nobody's fool and he had a number of assets working in his favour. First and foremost was Medicine Hat's community spirit and the pride it had always taken in its local regiment. That pride had been injured by the 1954 amalgamation and the transfer of SALH headquarters to Calgary but the Hat's spirit was still strong and ready to be mobilized. Major Lorne MacDonald noted that recruiting was aided by the fact that the Hat's economy "was somewhat sluggish in the early 1960s and young people, particularly, were looking for paid work."[25] Ray proved to be a master of media and community

March Past, Patterson Armoury
The South Alberta Light Horse march past Major-General Chris Vokes at Patterson Armoury in the early 1960s when the Regiment was at its greatest strength. Leading the march is Lieutenant-Colonel N.R. Ray (saluting), followed by Major Gordon McQueen, the second in command. On the far left and behind Vokes is Brigadier-General Bill Howard, the commander of 22 Militia Group, with Headquarters at Calgary. All officers are wearing No. 1 patrol dress with belt, medals and sword. Patterson Armoury, basically a large wooden hangar, began life as a recreation hall and gymnasium for the prisoner of war camp at Medicine Hat. SALH ARCHIVES

relations – he quickly established good contacts with both the local paper and television station, and with civic officials. Even with their low numbers, the Light Horse squadron was certain to be included in any civic function and the press were sure to be invited to any militia function, no matter how modest. Toward this end, one of Ray's first acts in April 1959 was to form a band, using both civilian and military personnel, under the direction of Bill Wahl, the band instructor at the Medicine Hat High School. It quickly became an integral part of any public event requiring music staged in the Hat area.

Another asset Ray tapped was the nearby Suffield Experimental Station of the Defence Research Board of Canada, located about 30 miles northwest of Medicine Hat. Established in 1941 by the British and Canadian governments as a testing establishment for biological and chemical warfare, Suffield sprawled across some 1,000 square miles of arid, prairie grassland. Ray held initial talks with the Station director in 1958 and, a year later, received permission to use the 100 square miles of the "British Block" for training purposes. This gave the Light Horse their own private training area and range not more than a hour's drive from the Patterson Armoury, a tremendous advantage for instruction in corps (armoured) training. Not only that, but since many of his officers and men were employed at Suffield, Ray had close ties with the Station and even managed to obtain a loan of one of the government buses to transport his troops to and from Patterson Armoury on parade nights.

Ray also utilized the Young Soldier Training Plan, a federal government programme introduced in 1959, intended to provide recruits for both the militia and regular forces. Under the YSTP, young men between the ages of 16 and 19, who were attending school, trained with their local militia units through the winter and spring and then received six weeks at camp in the following summer. At the completion of their course, "Young Soldiers" could enlist directly in either the regular or militia forces but there was no compulsion for them to do so. It was a good programme for the lads and it was a great recruiting incentive for the Light Horse. In Medicine Hat, the YSTP entrants paraded at Patterson Armoury from 8 A.M. to 2 P.M. every Saturday and received a free hot lunch provided by the Light Horse – and they got paid for it. As the *Medicine Hat News* put it:

> To the boy who likes to shoot, to drive a vehicle or operate a wireless set, then the YSTP program is the answer. To top things off there's a friendly visit with paymaster Lt. Stan Spavold and $12 is tucked away for each four week period.[26]

The response on the part of local high school students was so great that, within a few months, there were usually large numbers of young men training at Patterson Armoury on any Saturday during the school year. Major Paul Mast recalled his early days in the YSTP:

> I joined in the spring of 1962. In those days in Medicine Hat, a boy either joined the militia or had a paper route. We got $3.25 a day and there was sometimes as many as 300 young soldiers on parade on a Saturday morning. We took National Survival training first and they issued us black overalls, puttees, boots and a field cap and white sash cord for a belt and we learned about 30 different types of knots. After that we got into our recruit course which was proper military training and had to start looking like soldiers. Then we did corps training either as Driver and Maintenance, track or wheel, Gunnery, or Signals. I was in Signals and worked with the No. 19 Set and if you could run one of those, you could run darn near anything that ever had a vacuum tube put into it. We'd be picked up at certain stops in the city by a 3-ton truck on Saturday morning. As far as I am concerned, the YSTP was time well spent.[27]

Ray did not overlook the young women of the Hat who, at this time, were only permitted to enlist in the CWAC. He shortly built up a sizeable CWAC in the SALH who trained and served as administrative staff, signallers (a function they performed superbly), wheeled vehicle drivers and storesmen. RSM Arelis recalled that the CWACS were "mostly young high school graduates and they were a very bright group of young people and it was just great to work with them."[28] To reassure parents, every member of the CWAC section was driven safely to her door on parade nights and CWAC personnel who attended summer camp "lived in separate billets … under CWAC Officer jurisdiction."[29] The Regiment seems to have had no problems attracting female recruits and, in 1962, Second Lieutenant Elizabeth Bajnok, commissioned after two years in the ranks, became the first woman officer to attend the annual SALH Vimy Dinner.

Gradually, but with increasing momentum, Ray built up his squadron's numbers and broadened its activities. The Light Horse went to camp at Sarcee in the summer of 1959 but, instead of armoured corps training, it engaged, as did all other militia regiments across Canada, in National Survival Training. Implemented by the government that year, NST was aimed at preparing the militia to assist the civil defence organizations in the event of a nuclear war. Units were formed into mobile columns equipped with soft-skinned vehicles that would enter the ruins of a major population centre and rescue, assist and evacuate the survivors – although not much mention was made of the danger of radiation. Derisively called "Snakes and Ladders" by the militia because it featured the frequent use of ropes, ladders and stretchers to rescue simulated casualties from the upper storeys of buildings, it was intensely disliked by the troops who preferred conventional military training. As Sergeant-Major Arelis put it, "it was demeaning to military personnel because it was a civilian job that civilians should have been trained to do."[30] The militia paid lip service to NST but managed one way or the other (and often clandestinely) to continue corps training during the four-year period, 1959-1963, when NST was their official role.

In this respect the SALH was fortunate because it received three new Shermans in the summer of 1959 and Ray ensured that all three, four trucks and four jeeps participated in the Calgary Stampede Parade that year. Sergeant-Major Arelis was enthusiastic about the tanks because "they were a great thing for recruiting as we would drive them in the open fields around the armoury and young people would come to watch."[31] These fields abounded in gophers and it was not uncommon for Light Horse crews to mount a .22 sub-calibre unit in the main guns of their Shermans and hunt them – "Driver, Halt! Gunner, target 3 o'clock! Traverse Right! On Target, Fire!"[32]

By late 1959, Ray's efforts were beginning to pay off as the squadron's strength increased fourfold to 134 all ranks in just six months. The following year saw a continuation of the progress despite the "Snakes and Ladders" training emphasis. Summer camp at Sarcee that year was also centred around National Survival activities and, along with the other units in 22 Militia Group, the Light Horse squadron formed mobile rescue columns and carried out civil defence activities. Fortunately, these exercises only occupied part of the camp time and the remainder was devoted to corps training. Ray stressed traditional armoured corps skills when he staged Exercise PEGASUS at Suffield that autumn and Light Horse tank crews managed to fire off 360 rounds on what was basically their own private gun range. The squadron increased its strength throughout the year and, by 1 December 1960, when 22 Militia Group accorded the SALH regimental status and re-

activated the RHQ at Medicine Hat, the newly-promoted Lieutenant-Colonel Ray had 14 officers and 199 other ranks under command. To celebrate the successful conclusion of Operation BOOMER-ANG, as he called it, Ray held an official parade, and a formal dinner and dance at Patterson Armoury to which he invited the Light Horse's many civilian boosters.

"Up to full War Establishment": Glory days, 1961-1964

For Lieutenant-Colonel Ray, getting back to regimental status was only the first step in a greater vision he held for the Light Horse and he now began to plan for the future. Having been pulled back from the edge, the SALH was on a roll by early 1961 and, having achieved momentum, Ray was determined to maintain it. Recruiting was unceasing and, although potential new entrants were warned that they would come under Military Law and any infractions would "result in immediate expulsion from the Regiment," they were assured that, in the event of war, there would be no "compulsion to serve in the active service force which would be mobilized."[33] Ray established a policy whereby on the regular Tuesday and Thursday parade nights, any civilian could flag down a military vehicle in the streets of the Hat and get a free lift to Patterson Armoury to discuss a golden future with the Light Horse. Not that the armoury itself, basically a Second World War aircraft hangar built as an auditorium for the wartime prisoner camp in Medicine Hat, was anything to brag about. The Regiment had to park its vehicles inside the building as they had no secure outside compound and on parade nights, the vehicles first to be taken outside and kept under surveillance so that the troops could take over the floor of the armoury. On cold winter

"The girls"
The Light Horse's four HVSS Shermans, "Agnes," "Betty," "Carol" and "Diana" at Patterson Armoury in the early 1960s. The Light Horse sometimes had as many as seven Shermans on strength but there was always a troop of four in running order. The problem was that the tanks were stored on the drill floor (note the trooper shovelling the mess) and had to be removed before parade nights. SALH ARCHIVES

As always, the high point of the militia training year was the summer camp or concentration, usually held at either Sarcee or Wainwright in the 1950s and 1960s. Here are a selection of camp scenes from those years.

1958 summer camp at Wainwright
Pictures from *Sabre and Spur,* the newsletter of the SALH show camp scenes in 1958.

Taking the crew tarining course were, L to R, Lt. D. F. Mulford (A), Major N. R. Ray (OC-A), Lt. E. M. Moore (A), Lt. T. Dent (RHQ), Lt. J. O'Brien (A). Seated is Sgt. F. C. Sturgess.

The busiest people in camp this year as in past years, were the orderly room staff. Pictured on the right are S/Sgt. J. Morris (A). S/Sgt. D. M. Lynes (RHQ), S/Sgt. R. F. Wiersma (RHQ) and WO2 R. J. Patterson (RHQ).

Centurion tanks, manned by Militia personnel of the Crew Training Course, prepare to move out on a scheme which included cross country driving, wireless, harbouring, leaguering and maintenance. Major R. N. Ray, O.C. "A" Squadron is on the foreground tank.

Some people found the train trip boring . . . . and some found it expensive! RSM W. N. Ross is pictured at the left—the quietest we've ever seen him. After taking the centre picture, we lifted the beret and found L/Cpl. D. M. Gilmour ("C") dozing beneath. It was replaced immediately so the snores would not disturb our other sleeping beauty. L/Cpl. R. M. Browne ("C") and B. P. White ("C") are shown on the right engaged in a "friendly game" with a couple of victims who shall remain anonymous, in case they forgot to mention their poker losses to the little woman.

(Left) **Light Horse officers, Sarcee, 1961**
Standing, from left to right, Lieutenant Harold Gunderson, Captain George Elliot (paymaster), Major Gordon McQueen (second-in-command), Lieutenant E.M. Moore, Captain Len Toole and Major Reid Ainscough. Lieutenant-Colonel N.R. Ray is seated. Ainscough commanded the Light Horse from 1964 to 1968 and Moore from 1972 to 1975. With the exception of Ray, who is wearing light khaki drill, these officers are wearing bush dress, a lightweight field uniform introduced into the Canadian army in 1951. Note the lanyards, ascots and armoured corps black web belts worn by most officers and the riding crops that replaced swagger sticks in the SALH. Colonel Ray has gone one better and sports a fly whisk instead of a riding crop, an old British cavalry tradition. SALH ARCHIVES

(Right) **Dragoons on the move, c. 1950**
A column of 19th Dragoon vehicles, including Lynx II scout cars, Staghounds, and even an Otter are seen on the road, probably on their way to Wainwright in the period, 1949-1951. At this time, it was the custom for Militia units to proceed to camp in their own vehicles, if it was not too distant. COURTESY, REG HODGSON

(Below) **Dragoons take a break**
It was traditional when moving to and from camp, to take a break for lunch on the road, as seen here where the command group of the 19th Dragoons poses by the Battle River in 1952. Lieutenant-Colonel Arnold Lavoie, a former squadron commander in the wartime SAR and commanding officer of the Dragoons, is kneeling in the centre of the front row. Some of these Dragoons are wearing the unpopular field summer cap, introduced in the early 1950s, which had a folding neck flap. Most soldiers preferred the beret. COURTESY, HARRY QUARTON

393

The "Northern Lights"
From the mid-1950s to the early 1960s, C Squadron of the 19th Dragoons, known as the "Northern Lights," was located at Whitehorse in the Yukon. Here the squadron gathers for summer camp in 1958 or 1959 and proudly informs everyone that theirs is the most northern militia summer camp in Canada. C Squadron later became part of the Yukon Regiment. COURTESY, REG HODGSON

days the diesel engines of the Shermans left a black fog of stinking fumes in the air as there was no venting system and it became necessary to remove them many hours before any human activities took place on the armoury floor. There was almost no administrative space so old wartime prisoner buildings located a considerable distance from the main structure were utilized for lecture rooms, and for the officers and sergeants' messes.

There was considerable international tension in 1960-1961. In May 1960 an American U-2 spy plane was shot down over the Soviet Union and a few months later Soviet premier, Nikita Khruschev, pounded his shoe on his desk during a meeting of the United Nations to emphasize the Soviets' anger. In April 1961 the United States mounted an abortive invasion of Cuba using refugees who had fled from that country when a Communist government under Fidel Castro had seized power two years before, and tensions in that area were at an all time high. That same month the Soviets put the first man into orbit around the world and there was considerable concern that the Communist bloc was going to take the "high ground of space" and dominate the free world. In Europe the Soviet Union was also eyeball to eyeball with NATO in Berlin, where the Communist East German government had become concerned about the continuing flight of its citizens to the west – a concern that resulted in the erection of the Berlin Wall in August 1961. In southeast Asia, Communist forces were close to toppling the American-supported government of South Vietnam and President John Kennedy of the USA authorized the dispatch of an increasing number of "military advisors" to assist the South Vietnamese army.

When 22 Militia Group concentrated at Sarcee in July 1961, the armed forces of both the Communist bloc and NATO were on alert and it was perhaps appropriate that the main training activity that summer was Exercise GONE FISSION, a simulated nuclear strike on an imaginary locality (constructed by the engineers) called "Greggsville" after Brigadier H.T.R. Gregg, commander of 22 Group. For four days, 800 militia personnel, including no less than 109 all ranks of the Light Horse (among them 16 members of the CWAC), formed in mobile columns, entered an area "devastated by nuclear attack" and engaged in rescue work. As Lieutenant Harold Gunderson, the SALH Public Relations Officer and a journalist with the *Medicine Hat News*, wrote

Smoke and flame poured out of burning buildings, high voltage wires sagged along the ground, fire-gutted cars were marked as radioactive. Above it all could be heard the cries of wounded victims who lay crumpled in bombed-out homes and collapsed basements. Slivers of glass and severed arteries protruded from gaping wounds … here lay a patient in a state of coma and a short distance away walked another victim in shock and suffering from radiation burns.[34]

Dramatic stuff indeed although nobody seemed to have worried about the very high level of radiation that would have resulted if this had been a real nuclear attack, and the militia personnel were not issued protective clothing. GONE FISSION was a major exercise and there was little time for corps training that summer although the Light Horse still won both the Murphy Trophy for the best armoured regiment in Western Command and the Rawlinson Trophy for the best signals work.

In the autumn of 1961 the Light Horse began to participate in the Special Militia Training Programme. Basically, this was a makework employment scheme created by the federal government to alleviate distress during the current economic recession in Canada. Under this programme, unemployed men received six weeks of military training with emphasis on National Survival Training, and were paid at the basic rate of a private in the regular army. Seeing the SMTP as another way to increase his numbers, Ray was anxious to become involved in this activity and from September 1961 to May 1962, Major Gordon McQueen, his second-in-command, assisted by both SALH and regular army personnel, ran four consecutive SMTP courses which graduated 477 men, 30 of whom joined the regular force and 70 of whom joined the Light Horse.

Exercise GONE FISSION and the SMTP were useful but they were not armoured training and Ray was very anxious that the Light Horse retain its core skills. To do so, he carried out a major exercise at Suffield which he dubbed Operation PEGASUS II, which involved not only the Light Horse but also 18th Field Regiment from Lethbridge and 19th Medium Regiment from Calgary. Operation PEGASUS II commenced on Saturday, 14 October 1961, when the two artillery regiments – a total of 200 gunners with four 105 mm howitzers and four 155 mm howitzers – moved to Medicine Hat. After an overnight stay in the Patterson Armoury and a hot breakfast provided by the militia RCASC company from Calgary, they joined the Light Horse, 300 personnel and 4 tanks strong, and moved at 8 A.M. to Suffield to begin a day of firing. The press, transported by the SALH, were present in number (as were a great many civilian spectators) and the journalist from the *Medicine Hat News* recorded that

Wind and dust, flame and smoke were the accompaniments to this tank and artillery field day; heavy trucks and tanks ground up the dry sandy Prairie soil and the strong wind kept the dust constantly on the move and fanned the flames when high explosive shells ignited the short, withered vegetation.[35]

Proper precautions against grass fires had been taken and the local fire services were on hand but, even so, the exercise had to be paused three times to let the firemen do their job.

The *News* journalist was most impressed with the work of the Light Horse who fired 400 rounds that day (but then the hometown boys always get the nod):

The SALH tanks were soon occupying a ridge overlooking falling ground and where four old cars had been towed out for use as targets. The command post and ammunition store was set up at one level of the ridge and some hundreds of yards farther back the transport and private cars were parked providing a grandstand view for personnel not required on the firing line.

The firing of the four Sherman tanks named Agnes, Betty, Carol and Diana, was very effective and a number of direct hits were scored. While the shells from the tanks were landing, puffs of smoke could be seen farther north in the target area where shells from the artillery were striking home.[36]

All in all, the *News* reporter concluded, "the roar of tank and truck engines" was a fitting accompaniment as "more than 500

Orphans in the storm, 1959
Major N.R. Ray (seated in front row with swagger stick across his knees), Officer Commanding A Squadron of the Light Horse, poses with the squadron, with a strength of 40 all ranks, at Patterson Armoury in March 1959. The Regiment had just been reduced to independent squadron status and the future did not look bright for the Light Horse. In the very short period of 19 months, however, Ray not only restored the unit to regimental status but transformed it into one of the largest militia regiments in Western Canada. COURTESY, A. ARELIS

soldiers carried out the biggest ever peacetime militia exercise in Alberta." This last statement – probably fed to the media by Ray himself as he liked to write his own press releases – was not quite correct but even if not true, made a good story.

Things were truly looking bright for the Light Horse – Sergeant-Major Arelis thought the SALH "had esprit de corps second to none."[37] The spirit of the Light Horse is perhaps best expressed in the motto conceived in the early 1960s by Major Henry Sorenson, officer commanding B Squadron, which, to this day, embellishes the north wall of Patterson Armoury: "THIS IS A FINE REGIMENT – YOU CAN MAKE IT THE FINEST!" Much of the credit was due to Lieutenant-Colonel Ray but, as his second-in-command, Major Gordon McQueen remembered,

Ray's background was in signals and not the combat arms. When we went to summer camp he usually turned the unit over to me. He was rambunctious but he was not a parade ground soldier. If we had a big parade or inspection coming up, I would have to go over his part and movement with him after I set it up with the RSM. Just before the event, he would call me into his office and go through it verbally with me and he would have it down cold. But then he would forget it and when the next big event came up, I would have to repeat the process.

We had a lot of young people who were in high school or had part time jobs would be around the armoury all the time and Ray would scrounge around and try and get some money for these people, he would write a letter and try to baffle group headquarters.

I used to have to try and restrain him sometimes when he was dealing with higher headquarters. He would get carried away and you would have to explain to him that it wouldn't work. On parade nights I would go in early and read the mail and when he came in, I would inform him of what paperwork needed to be looked at and he would say "tell me in ten words or less what has to be done." Sometimes he would write the wrong kind of letter to 22 Militia Group and I would read the carbon and tell him, "for God's sake, you can't do that" and he would say "can you do anything about it?" So I would phone a guy I knew up at Calgary and tell him that "you're going to get a letter from us on this but tear it up before you read it and throw it in the garbage" – and they would.[38]

Sergeant-Major Arelis admired his commanding officer because "he was a go-getter" and, "although people thought he was kind of pushy, I thought he was a person who could get things done."[39] True or not, it was a popular belief among the junior ranks of the Light Horse that Ray would phone the Minister of National Defence on a matter concerning his regiment – as the then Corporal Paul Mast put it: "This guy was the scourge of 22 Militia Group. He would pick up the phone and phone Ottawa and the Group commander would just cringe."[40]

Ray had big ambitions for the Light Horse which he outlined

The ladies lend a hand
In the 1960s, it was strictly against regulations for women soldiers of the CWAC to participate in weapons training but, nonetheless, the Light Horse would smuggle them onto the range. Here, two members of the Light Horse CWAC detachment assist Squadron Sergeant-Major A. Arelis load 76 mm ammunition for Sherman tanks. SALH ARCHIVES

in a memorandum to 22 Group that he sent in November 1961. Confessing that his regiment's phenomenal expansion was "as great a surprise to the present Commanding Officer … as it is all to all echelons of command," Ray expressed his firm belief that, by 1963, he might have as many as 900 all ranks on strength.[41] This being the case, his aim was

To build the SALH up to full War Establishment by the summer of 1963 as an Armoured Regiment together with all ancillary arms and services required to service an Armoured Regiment i.e. – RCAMC, RCASC, RCCS, RCEME, RCE, etc.

To train all SALH and attached personnel into a self-contained, self-administered and operational force capable of carrying out any or all roles assigned, without being interdependent of units based elsewhere or of civilian requirement.[42]

To accomplish this ambitious objective, however, Ray needed a few things from Group Headquarters – just a few small things – which he listed in detail. He asked for increased accommodation, including a doubling or tripling of the number of offices, small arms ranges, lecture rooms, medical facilities and quartermaster storage, and "sleeping accommodation" for "personnel in transit" that "would save hotel and motel expense." Ray also requested workshop accommodation for RCEME and RCE detachments and a "Food Servicing Section RCASC" to include "enclosed accommodation for training of cooks, cooking of rations, storing rations and a messing area." He very much wanted to have a paved parade ground, a secure vehicle compound and "a proper petrol point" for both armoured and soft-skinned vehicles. Concerning vehicles, he respectfully requested that a greater number of new soft-skinned vehicles be issued to the

SALH as its current transport was "old, and tired and in need of constant repair."[43]

Having got the minor items out of the way, Ray then got down to the main item on his agenda – he wanted more and better tanks. Noting he had already indented for six new Shermans in addition to the five running vehicles currently with the Light Horse, he expressed his concern that,

With ever increasing numbers of personnel completing all phases of NST [National Survival Training] an even greater number of tanks will be required to keep pace with the influx of personnel for this type of training. Here again, the difficulty of maintaining Sherman tanks in operational condition is becoming increasingly difficult due to shortage of remaining existing equipment.[44]

This being the case, he wished to know if 22 Group could kindly issue the SALH "Centurion type AFV's" and would they please supply "between 16 and 20 such AFV's" so that the Light Horse would be able "to fully train on a 'Squadron Basis.'" Lest Group Headquarters should feel this was a frivolous request, Ray noted that the Light Horse had its own 100-square mile training area at Suffield complete with tank ranges and had already carried out two "successful shoots in the area." With more modern tanks, he emphasized that the SALH could do more intensive and up-to-date training and, to sweeten the request for Centurions, Ray confessed himself willing to include infantry from 22 Militia Group (i.e. the Calgary Highlanders) in his next PEGASUS exercise at Suffield. Of course, such an increased training tempo raised the matter of instructional staff and, despite the fact that Group Headquarters had previously turned down such a request, he asked again if they could see fit to station "an adequate Senior Instructor and staffs" at Medicine Hat for this purpose.[45]

Ray had previously raised hackles at 22 Militia Group in Calgary, but this memorandum appears to have been the last straw for the staff. They began to take a closer look at the military phenomenon taking place in Medicine Hat and moved quickly to clip Ray's wings before he soared to even greater heights. The staff ordered him to suspend direct recruiting and began to behave with truculence toward any correspondence originating from the Hat. To make matters worse, a complaint, apparently originated by a disgruntled former member of the unit, led to a ministerial investigation into the unit's Young Soldier Training Plan. All youthful personnel "were required to produce a birth certificate with the result that some 56 troopers had to turn in kit" as they were found to be under the minimum 16 years of age.[46] By March 1962 Ray was complaining that

Each and every request for additional training aids to keep up the esprit-de-corps of the troops was turned down from above – including additional accommodation, additional tanks; additional vehicles; nothing done about the parade square or vehicle compound; no pamphlets; clothing in short supply; no shoulder cloth patches, no berets. The one bright spot was that some kind soul approved a flag-pole we hadn't asked for.[47]

Despite the active discouragement of 22 Militia Group, the Light Horse continued to increase in strength during the first half of 1962 – by means of the YSTP and SMTP, if not by direct recruiting. There were now three regular squadrons, HQ and A at Medicine Hat and C at Bow Island, while B Squadron at the Hat was composed of Young Soldiers. The records disagree on the exact number but what is certain is that in June 1962 the Light Horse reached a strength of between 450 and 500 all ranks – so many that Squadron Sergeant-Major Arelis remembered that it was impossible to hold a regimental parade in Patterson Armoury, even if the vehicles were removed, unless the hangar doors opened wide and "some people were put outside."[48] In July 1962, the Light Horse sent "the largest contingent thus far on record" to summer camp at Sarcee. By this time, however, National Survival Training was on its way out. It had proved so unpopular that there was a tacit conspiracy on the part of many militia headquarters and units across Canada to resume corps training. The SALH and the KOCR spent the last half of the 1962 camp working as armoured units, although the Light Horse were somewhat hampered by the fact that, due to budget restrictions, only two of their Shermans were running.

Throughout 1961 and 1962, Lieutenant-Colonel Ray expended much time and energy on ceremonial matters, a subject dear to his heart. By now all Light Horse officers had mess dress or blue patrols and, at the colonel's insistence, they had acquired riding crops to serve as swagger sticks. This was an old cavalry affectation but their commanding officer, always flamboyant, went one better and sported a fly whisk. Most Light Horse warrant officers and NCOs had blue patrols (with the top button being the regimental button of the East Surrey Regiment) and carried silver-headed canes in place of swagger sticks. There had been many complaints about the original version of the Regimental tie, so Ray worked hard in 1962 to procure a better quality replacement, through the good offices of a Medicine Hat haberdasher who had personal connections in the New York garment trade. For some reason, although never a popular measure with those who had to wear them, Ray chose red regimental blazers instead of the traditional dark blue or black. He also managed to procure a ceremonial mace or stave for the drum major of the SALH Band which, after winning numerous competitions, had by this time, evolved into one of the best military bands in Alberta. Most important of all, Ray initiated the onerous paperwork necessary to procure a Guidon, the cavalry/armoured equivalent of the infantry's Colours, as the Light Horse did not yet possess this most important of all military ceremonial devices.

Ray was also instrumental in getting "Old Reliable," the SAR's wartime half-track command vehicle, restored. In the decade following the war, the old veteran had rendered yeoman service to the SAR and then A Squadron of the Light Horse but, by 1961, it was immobile and rusting, behind Patterson Armoury. Over the years, a legend had evolved in Medicine Hat that "Old Reliable" had been smuggled back to Canada not shipped, as it indeed was, through proper army channels. Ray later recalled that he had often noticed this

wrecked and cannibalized vehicle sitting outside the Armouries but considered it was just junk so did not bother much about it …… However, after taking command, I listened to some Officers talking of "Do you remember when?" stories of WW II and they mentioned the Halftrack having been purchased by some SAR Officers in Holland and having it shipped back to Canada. Remembering the pile of junk, I looked it over the next day and lo and behold it WAS the self-same vehicle, after having the accumulated years of debris now practically covering it. It was horribly cannibalized, rusted and seeming useless. I had some very talented people in the unit vehicle party and we decided to see what could be done about it. It was loaded on a lowboy and hauled away to a workshop [at Suffield], taken apart, and with the help of the White Motor Company for some available parts for the motor, plus some track from salvage yards in the east, plus machining the parts we couldn't get, and scrounging some WW II paint – we managed to get some drawings and re-equipped the interior as it had been with the brackets to hold the wireless sets, etc. (also scrounged). It was then used operationally on our schemes with our Shermans on the firing range we had secured at DRES [Defence Research Estabalishment Suffield].

Worthy was delighted to see it as we drove him from the plane to the Armouries in it on his first inspection trip to the regiment – and he told me some of its history. And he had a ride in it, on each successive visit [he made to Medicine Hat].[49]

Ray was a firm believer in an active mess life. Major Gordon McQueen recalled that he kept the Light Horse officers and sergeants' messes, which were located in old

prisoner of war camp buildings, open almost seven days a week and since "a rye and water was 25 cents a shot, you couldn't afford not to drink."[50] A favourite officers' mess game during this period was to buy a bottle of champagne from the bar and sit in a chair directly across from the head of the pronghorn antelope that decorated a far wall – if you hit the head with the champagne cork, you got the bottle for free. The traditional officers' dinners and events were the Vimy Dinner, the Armistice Ball, the Grey Cup Party and the "At Home" on Boxing Day. The "warm up" parties for the formal mess dinners started a few hours before the main event and, not infrequently, continued on for another day or so after it ended. Major Lorne MacDonald particularly liked the Grey Cup Party where the traditional nourishment was "fried raw oysters and champagne."[51] The sergeants also had an active mess which, as Sergeant-Major Arelis was quick to note, was "nearly a mile from the officers' mess and that was a very good thing."[52] Some of the older corporals were permitted to drink in the sergeants' mess but for those members of the unit who were under the legal drinking age of 21 – meaning nearly all the junior NCOs and enlisted men, there was a soft drink club in the main building. Things were more relaxed in the field or at camp and, as Trooper Robert McKenzie recalled, underage personnel could get the occasional beer at Wainwright:

"Old Reliable" back in business

By the late 1950s, "Old Reliable," the wartime SAR's armoured command vehicle, had deteriorated to the point where it was no longer running. Deciding that a vehicle so important in the history of his unit had to be put back in shape, Lieutenant-Colonel N.R. Ray of the SALH managed, with the help of many volunteers and some government workshop space, to get "Old Reliable" back on the road. Here, it is being used as a range control vehicle, probably at Suffield in 1962 or 1963. In the hatch from left to right are Sergeant Bill Webb, Sergeant John Patterson and an unidentified man. On the ground, from the left, are WO 2 Turner, RCD, Captain Stan Spavold and Major Don Munroe of the REME. The warrant officer, who appears to be biting his nails, is probably a little nervous as he is the range control officer. SALH ARCHIVES

We were told unofficially that we could get served in the camp wet mess but we weren't sure if it was true so we sent a guy down to check it out but he never came back. They turned a blind eye to us drinking out in the field but we never abused it because we worked hard during the day and only played at night. I can remember coming back from the field over a ford in the Battle River and stopping the deuce and a half at mid point and everybody jumped in the water to cool off.[53]

Group Headquarters in Calgary, however, continued to worry about the size of the SALH. By mid-1962, the Light Horse was perilously close to outnumbering Lord Strathcona's Horse, the regular armoured regiment in Western Command, and, worse still, the Light Horse payroll for 1961, a total of $73,000 (approximately $475,000 in 2004), had eaten up a substantial portion of the group's personnel funds. What made it worse was that the Conservative government of Prime Minister John Diefenbaker, which had been in power for five years, was cutting back on defence expenditure and money was getting tight. Late in the summer of 1962, as Ray remarked, "the cold breath of austerity" began to blow from Calgary as Headquarters, citing an overexpenditure of budget, cut back the number of paid days allotted to the Light Horse, forcing the Regiment to delay the commencement of autumn training from September to October.[54] Cuts were also made to the Young Soldier Training Plan – the number of paid days was reduced and the lads no longer received a hot meal. These restrictions, combined with the end of the Special Militia Training Programme, cut into the strength of the Light Horse in the latter half of 1962 although it still carried 250 all ranks on its roll at the end of that year. Even so, the Light Horse managed to hold another live firing exercise at Suffield in the fall but, this time, the gunners were not present. Training that autumn was given impetus by the Cuban missile crisis in October when, for 13 days, the United States and the Soviet Union hovered on the brink of war following the Soviet deployment of missiles on that island. The forces of all NATO countries were on full alert and many Canadian schools conducted air raid drills to prepare their students for a possible nuclear attack.

Despite all the problems – both in the world and in the unit – 1962 was a banner year for the Light Horse. In September the Regiment learned that it had been awarded the Worthington Trophy. The 19th Dragoons had shared this trophy with other units in 1956 and 1960 but the SALH was the first militia armoured regiment in Western Canada to win it outright. Major-General Worthington paid a visit to Medicine Hat in late November 1962 to present his trophy in person and to attend the officers' Grey Cup party and a mess dinner. The Winnipeg Blue Bombers beat the Hamilton Tiger Cats that year but the Sally Horse were now on the top of their form and Worthy was back in the Patterson Armoury to eat fried oysters and watch Hamilton win in 1963 and British Columbia in 1964 when the Light Horse shared his trophy with other units. In the 42 years (1954 to 1996) that the Worthington Trophy was awarded in the armoured corps, the South Alberta Light Horse were the only western armoured regiment to either win it outright or share it, three years in succession. Worthy's visits were always popular events with the Light Horse and Sergeant-Major Arelis recalled that the crusty old general liked to be invited to the sergeants' mess, which he found most comfortable, so comfortable in fact that it was hard to get him to leave, even if the officers were waiting on him to start their own mess function. There is no doubt that Worthy took a shine to the Light Horse, the modern "keen-eyed Prairie men," just as he had taken a shine to their wartime predecessors, the South Albertas, when he had them under his command in 4th Armoured Division.

Although down from its peak in June 1962, Light Horse strength continued to be quite respectable in 1963 with 238 all ranks. That summer, for the first time in four years, corps training was emphasized over National Survival Training, which only gave official blessing to what had been unofficial practice for some time. The Regiment sent 85 officers and enlisted personnel to a very wet camp at Sarcee but, with only two Shermans running, it had to share tanks with the KOCR. All four vehicles were back on the road by the autumn, however, when the SALH carried out Exercise FLATFOOT, a two-day gun camp and range exercise at Suffield. Despite the fact that it was against regulations, the Light Horse smuggled their CWACs onto the ranges and let them fire both small arms and the main guns and .30 calibre machineguns on the Shermans as "some were very keen."[55] The Regiment maintained its strength throughout 1964, with 210 all ranks, and sent 79 to Sarcee in July who carried out corps training. One item worthy of note that occurred in 1964 was that an investigation revealed that, in a 47-month period, SALH transport drivers had driven 186,000 accident-free miles.

In November 1964, having spent three decades in uniform as a boy soldier, militiaman and wartime officer, Lieutenant-Colonel Rod Ray retired from the Canadian army. A remarkable man – part soldier, part showman, and all Sally Horse – he had saved his unit from extinction, raised it to its greatest peacetime strength, achieved perhaps its greatest peacetime triumphs and, above all, constructed a solid foundation for the Light Horse that has lasted to this day. In his farewell address, Ray summarized the achievements of his eight years in command of either A Squadron or the Regiment, and stressed that he had, "with God's help and yours, accomplished what I set out to do." He reminded his listeners that

Many of you people have grown up with this Regiment, not only in years but in wisdom gained from experience. Your esprit-de-corps is of the highest tradition and standards. I can now leave you, knowing the Regiment is in safe hands and can go only in one direction – and that of course is to even higher achievement.[56]

In bidding farewell to the Light Horse, Ray asked only that when the Regiment received its Guidon, he would have "a small place" in the parade. This request was willingly and enthusiastically granted.

CHAPTER SEVENTEEN

"Those Who Shall Follow the Guidon"

"They were just madder than hell": The demise of the 19th Alberta Dragoons

Lieutenant-Colonel Rod Ray's successor as commanding officer of the South Alberta Light Horse was Lieutenant-Colonel Reid W. Ainscough, a former gunner who had been wounded in Normandy and had joined the Light Horse as a major in 1961. Ainscough, a low-key personality (as are many gunners), had a more subdued command style than his predecessor but he was a very competent officer who was able to build on Ray's achievements. This was all to the good because, beginning in 1964, decisions were made in Ottawa that eventually came close to destroying the Canadian army, if not all three Canadian armed services.

These decisions were made by Paul Hellyer, Minister of Defence in the Liberal government of Prime Minister Lester B. Pearson from 1964 to 1968. Hellyer had served in the RCAF as a junior NCO during the Second World War and had been the Liberals' defence critic when the party was in opposition from 1957 to 1963. A self-made and successful businessman, Hellyer believed that private sector managerial concepts could be applied to the armed forces – as though they were a corporation in need of restructuring to produce a better bottom line on the quarterly financial report – and was determined to reduce waste, cost and duplication of effort. These were laudable objectives, to

> Troopers of the 19th ride in armoured cars,
> The eyes of the army occupied with Mars.
> We do our job quickly, silently,
> Way out in front of the infantry,
> For we are the 19th – the Armoured 19th.
>
> We used to ride on horses or march on weary feet,
> Before we were the 19th and mechanized complete.
> We blazed a trail through history,
> As cavalry and infantry,
> But we are now the 19th – the Armoured 19th.
>
> Cavalry they called them, very smart Dragoons,
> Fusiliers were proudly, numbered by platoons.
> Servied in the First War in the line,
> While Currie led – they crossed the Rhine,
> And we are now the 19th – the Armoured 19th.[1]

be sure, but Hellyer's chosen method was to at first integrate, and later unify, the three services into a single entity, the Canadian Forces. With an obstinacy bordering on fanaticism which brooked neither dissent nor informed opinion, Hellyer set out in 1964 to put this policy into effect and, over a period of four years, did away with the Royal Canadian Navy, Royal Canadian Air Force and Canadian army, replacing them with five functional commands (Mobile, Maritime, Air Defence, Air Transport, and Materiel and Training) in a single service possessing a common rank structure and, eventually, a common uniform.

For all intents and purposes, Mobile Command was the army – or what was left of it – but Hellyer was no admirer of the militia, which he regarded as a waste of money. In 1964 he decided to reduce the reserve component of the army, which numbered 75,000, to 30,000 all ranks with the intent of putting the funds saved toward the re-equipping of the regular force. To do so, he created a commission headed by a militia gunner, Brigadier E.R. Suttie, to select the units to be removed from the Order of Battle. The Suttie Commission commenced work in early 1964 and, like the Kennedy Board a decade before, travelled across Canada, holding hearings, investigating the status of militia units and inquiring into their problems. The militia held its collective breath while it waited for the Commission's final report which came in June 1964. It contained many positive recommendations, including higher pay and age restrictions paralleling those of the regular forces, but it also recommended the disbandment of many fine, old regiments, including four units of the armoured corps, which were placed on the Supplementary Order of Battle. None of the four armoured units condemned to the axe were in Alberta but Hellyer wanted further cuts and, in March 1965, National Defence Headquarters announced that three more ar-

---

(Facing) **The proudest moment, 25 May 1967**
Squadron Sergeant-Major Albert Arelis of the South Alberta Light Horse receives the Guidon from the hand of Princess Alexandra of Kent at Currie Barracks, Calgary. At the left are officers of the Calgary Highlanders, which received new Colours at the same time. Note the furled umbrella under the arm of the aide-de-camp to the Princess – it was needed as the weather was terrible that day. COURTESY, R.B. MACKENZIE

Playing with the big ones: Wainwright Camp, 1965
A Light Horse troop mans regular army Centurions at summer concentration in Wainwright in July 1965. It was not uncommon, if the circumstances were right and the vehicles were available, for the Light Horse to occasionally train on the Main Battle Tank of the regular armoured units. SALH ARCHIVES

moured units would either be amalgamated or "dormatized" by being sent to the Supplementary Order of Battle – among them the 19th Alberta Dragoons.

It is difficult to comprehend why this proud regiment was selected for "dormatization" as it was strong in numbers and had consistently been among the best militia units in Western Canada. Suspicion at the time was that politics – most of the Dragoon officers were Conservatives not Liberals – had come into play and the Dragoons were condemned because of Hellyer's personal spite. Be that as it may, it fell to the second-in-command, Major George Lynch-Staunton, and the quartermaster, Captain Harry Quarton, to supervise the closing down of the Dragoons as the commanding officer, Lieutenant-Colonel R.H. Summersgill, had recently been transferred by his employer to British Columbia. Quarton recalled that one of the first things he and Lynch-Staunton did, after receiving the official notice, was to lock all the offices and messes, to prevent the Dragoons' many trophies and memorials from being taken home for souvenirs. These were later catalogued and sent for safekeeping to the Provincial Museum of Alberta in Edmonton. Lynch-Staunton, who had expected shortly to assume command of the Dragoons, recalled that the two officers then decided that the next step, "other than to cry in our beer," was

> to counsel everybody in the unit as they were just madder than hell and they were terribly, terribly hurt. We had so many excellent people. So we counseled them. Some said "F__k it" and got out of the militia and some said "where do you think I should go?" I would advise them where I thought they should go: artillery, infantry, provost, service company or the intelligence company.

Before they disbanded, after more than half a century of service to their country, the Dragoons held a final regimental "smoker" for all ranks. Understandably, it was not the happiest

of occasions and many of those present were bitter and confused. A young trooper was heard to ask Technical Quartermaster Sergeant-Major Bob Rasmussen why the unit was being taken off the active order of battle? Rasmussen replied: "To make other regiments better."[2] He was right because the Dragoons' banishment to the Supplementary Order of Battle resulted in a diaspora of talent that was to benefit the provincial militia. Over the next decade, from the fourteen Dragoon officers who were on strength in 1965, were to come the future commanders of the Loyal Edmonton Regiment, 20th Field Regiment, RCA, the militia service, intelligence and provost companies in Edmonton, and a similar situation prevailed with former Dragoon warrant officers and NCOs. The 19th Alberta Dragoons may have gone into hibernation but their spirit and professionalism lived on and, as we shall see, their story is not yet ended.

"There's going to be rattle snakes in there": The last days of armour, 1965-1968

Although the Light Horse and the 19th Dragoons were friendly rivals, it is always sad when a regiment is removed from the Order of Battle, particularly a regiment with the distinguished history of the Dragoons. Feeling somewhat guilty at having survived, the SALH itself faced an uncertain future, made even more confusing by the many changes that took place as the newly-created Canadian Forces went through considerable teething pains. The increased pay was welcome but the new age restrictions meant that many veterans retired at this time, including some who had a decade or more of armour expertise. In a letter written in late 1964 to the King's Royal Hussars, the Light Horse's allied British regiment, Major D.F. Mulford, adjutant of the SALH, noted that the unit was "losing our older, and therefore better trained, personnel and we are finding it almost impossible to fill the gaps which are being created."[3] Higher formations also went through a number of permutations. Western Command and the militia group Headquarters were dissolved and eventually replaced,

In the field, Wainwright, 1966

Four scenes from summer concentration at Wainwright Camp in July 1966 show crews carrying out maintenance in the field. When the Light Horse trained at Wainwright, they used the War Reserve of HVSS Shermans, which were stored at that base, and not their own vehicles. The photo at top left shows one of the dirtiest maintenance tasks on the HVSS, changing the air filters. By this time, even the Shermans maintained by the regulars were beginning to show their age and spare parts were becoming scarce. Note the use of black denim overalls, standard armoured crew field dress in the 1960s. SALH ARCHIVES

after a series of permutations, by Alberta Militia District with headquarters in Edmonton. Perhaps the only positive thing to come out of the Suttie Commission was that, once and for all, it put a stake through the heart of the "Snakes and Ladders" survival training and the armoured units went happily back to corps training (which they had been doing anyway). It should come as no surprise, however, that the money saved by Hellyer's evisceration of the militia did not go toward re-equipping the regular forces but was soon eaten up by other government expenditure.

Mulford noted that the Light Horse's immediate task was "to provide a fully trained tank squadron by 1966" which would be a "formidable task," given the recent loss of key personnel.[4] The Light Horse went to work, however, with a will. Courses were held in Driving and Maintenance, Gunnery and Communications throughout the 1964-65 training year. Strength dropped somewhat during 1965, down to 203 and, like most of the surviving militia units in Canada, the Light Horse learned that higher pay

did not necessarily mean more money as Ottawa simply cut back the number of paid training days, a process that has continued almost to the present time. As always, however, much training was carried out on a voluntary basis without pay because the one asset that the militia has always possessed is raw enthusiasm. Budget cuts meant that the SALH was able to send only 44 officers and men to summer camp at Sarcee in July 1965 but did manage to get 49 officers and men qualified in needed armoured trades.

At this time, the direction on future armour policy coming out of Ottawa was very confusing. The regular armoured force wished to retain the Main Battle Tank for NATO service in Europe but Hellyer, who possessed a whim of iron, had become obsessed with "air transportability" and pushed for mobile, light armoured forces that could be airlifted around the globe to fight the "brush fire" wars that seemed to him to be the course of future armed conflict. The fact that light armoured vehicles were cheaper than conventional tanks only gave the concept added lustre in his eyes. "Light armour" became the buzz word and three armoured training regiments were created at bases across Canada, including Wainwright, to teach the new tactics to the militia. Captain Bob Caldwell of the Fort Garry Horse, attached to 1st Armoured Training Regiment at Wainwright, remembered that the regular instructors had a training package in the form of a lecture complete with a cloth table model which they "took on the road" to visit the various militia units and lecture on the future.[5]

This was all very well and good but the international situation was very tense in the late 1960s. In Southeast Asia the Vietnam war was in its most intense period as the Soviet Union and China backed the forces of North Vietnam against American forces in the southern part of that nation. In 1968, after Czechoslovakia exhibited signs of throwing off Communist rule, the Soviet bloc invaded that country and stamped out a putative attempt to establish democratic government. Senior Canadian officers knew that, if war did result, the major battles would be fought between NATO and the Soviet Union on the north German plain by conventional armoured forces equipped with MBTs, not light armour. As the Canadian army's major focus was its NATO brigade, regular armoured personnel were not happy with the "light armour" concept, while the remainder of the army, and the other two services, were unhappy and confused by the process of unification which, Hellyer insisted, must be carried to completion.

For the Canadian military, matters were made worse by two other factors. The first was changing social attitudes as a very young population (in 1967 more than half the population of Canada was under the age of 25), abhorring the violence in Vietnam that they watched nightly on their television sets, became anti-Vietnam war and, by extension, anti-military. The second factor was the election of Pierre Elliot Trudeau as Liberal Prime Minister of Canada in June 1968. Rare among Canadian political leaders, Trudeau had actually served in his country's armed forces, having briefly been a second lieutenant in a Montreal militia regiment during the latter years of the Second World War. As a student at that time, Trudeau, however, was exempt from conscription under the National Resources Mobilization Act and seems to have regarded joining the Active Service Force as being beneath his dignity. A privately-wealthy, 49-year-old bachelor from Montreal, Trudeau appeared to younger Canadians, the so-called "flower power generation," to be a leader who spoke to their values in contrast to his rather stodgy predecessors. An ambitious man, said by some to be brilliant, Trudeau embarked on a sweeping series of government, legislative, legal and political reforms that irrevocably changed Canada. Among his many initiatives was a review of the nation's defence policy which resulted in the NATO brigade being halved and defence expenditures being drastically reduced.

While these perambulations were taking place in Ottawa in the late 1960s, the Light Horse got on with the job. Blessed with its private training area at Suffield, the SALH held regular gun camps on its own range. Sergeant-Major Arelis remembered that

they would "drive down to Suffield, take all the tanks and just fire away at old car bodies. We'd set more prairie fires than you could count."[6] The Shermans, however, were by now more than two decades old and were beginning to show it. Although they were simple vehicles to maintain – "soldier and user-friendly" in then-Lieutenant Paul Mast's words – and the Light Horse was conscientious in carrying out maintenance, there were increasing mechanical problems.[7] Major Lorne MacDonald recalled that, by the mid 1960s,

> When we went to Suffield, we had to strap 45-gallon drums of water on the back decks because all the radiators and hose couplings leaked and that was the only way we could move them any distance without them overheating. My great fear was that one would stall on a bridge over the Trans-Canada Highway which was the route we took and would block traffic in both directions for hours.[8]

Major E.M. ("Mickey") Moore remembered that the vehicles were kept on the road because the Light Horse "had good mechanics, Fred Sturgess and Emil Chinook, and they did a lot to ensure we could keep tracks on those tanks and get them home. You're driving down the Trans-Canada highway and you lose a track and it's a bit embarrassing."[9]

The Light Horse were back at Suffield in October 1966, firing 350 rounds at new tank targets – broken-down HVSS Sherman hulls – which the Regiment had procured and "the destructive power of 'the 76' was a revelation to many of the younger members taking part in the shoot and a few of the old timers as well."[10] Captain Bob Caldwell of the regular Fort Garry Horse was at that gun camp and remembered it well. Caldwell, who had just completed a three-year posting in Germany as a troop leader and assistant adjutant of the Fort Garry Horse, had never served with the militia and, as he later recalled, "I knew regular Canadian soldiers, American, British, Belgian and German soldiers, but I had never met our own militia."[11] When he was formally introduced to the SALH, however, Caldwell was impressed:

> I thought they were very good. I met Colonel Ainscough and several of the majors. Instinctively, I knew they were a good unit and their strength was very good. What impressed me was their confidence and quiet competence and the fact that many of the officers were very well educated men on the staff of the Defence Research Establishment at Suffield. In fact they were much better educated than me and here I am lecturing men like this on "economy of effort" and "foresight" but that was the way it was in those days, these lectures had to be delivered by a regular officer.[12]

The Light Horse, in turn, liked Caldwell so they requested that he act as the RSO (Range Safety Officer) at the gun camp to be held that autumn at Suffield. As Caldwell relates, it was an interesting experience:

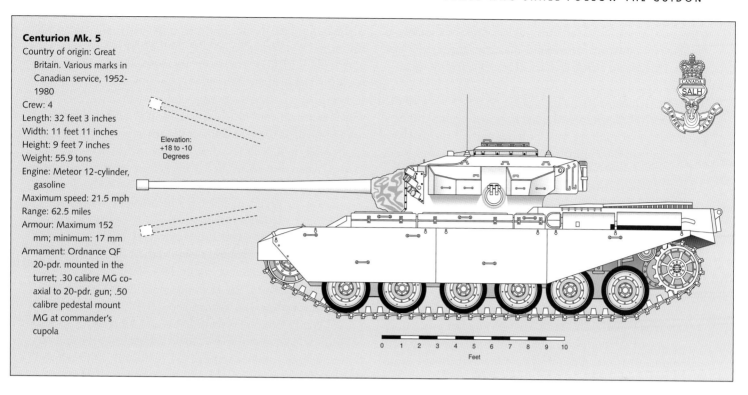

Centurion Mk. 5

Country of origin: Great
    Britain. Various marks in
    Canadian service, 1952-
    1980

Crew: 4

Length: 32 feet 3 inches

Width: 11 feet 11 inches

Height: 9 feet 7 inches

Weight: 55.9 tons

Engine: Meteor 12-cylinder,
    gasoline

Maximum speed: 21.5 mph

Range: 62.5 miles

Armour: Maximum 152
    mm; minimum: 17 mm

Armament: Ordnance QF
    20-pdr. mounted in the
    turret; .30 calibre MG co-
    axial to 20-pdr. gun; .50
    calibre pedestal mount
    MG at commander's
    cupola

Elevation:
+18 to -10
Degrees

0 1 2 3 4 5 6 7 8 9 10
Feet

They wanted a regular force guy to do the RSO job and I was good at tank gunnery, as it was my major passion. The problem was that I had never been in a Sherman turret, I had always been a Centurion man – in fact I learned how to drive a Centurion before I learned to drive a car. Anyway, they wanted to do this gun camp and I didn't even know enough to inspect the guns to see if they were safe or not but I had a sergeant on my staff who had been with the Strathconas in Korea and he knew Shermans so I told them "okay."

So we go out to the range at Suffield with the advance party and anyone who knows anything about Suffield knows that the place is full of rattlesnakes. I had never seen a rattlesnake in my life but I knew there were rattlesnakes in Suffield, everybody did. So we get there and they have a weatherbeaten old range shack where they store their targets and flags and stuff like that, which I have to check out. There was a very capable young sergeant in command of the advance party and I said to him, "You know, there's going to be rattlesnakes in there," meaning the shack, and he looked at me like I had just told him that the sun usually rises in the east and then replied, "we know, sir."

And so they went into action, his team of three or four soldiers, using pick handles. First they opened the door of the shack and let it slam, then they went around the outside walls banging on them with pick handles, and finally they went inside and started pounding on the floor with the pick handles. I didn't go with them, I hung back, in fact I just stood there and watched a bunch of snakes slither away from that shack – all you saw was a flash. After that, they stowed away their pick handles and got on with the job of setting up the range – you could tell it was part of their normal procedure but it sure impressed me.

I was very nervous because I did not know the equipment they were using but, on the other hand, I had great confidence in the SALH – from Ainscough all the way down to the young soldiers – as they had a quiet, calm way of going and did their work without bragging. In fact, I was much more nervous than they were.[13]

Despite all the enthusiasm, there was much uncertainty at this time in the armoured corps over the "light armour" concept. In his annual Christmas message to the Regiment in 1966, Lieutenant-Colonel Ainscough confessed that, although the future role of the militia and the Light Horse was still up in the air, he hoped to be able to clarify it in the coming months. He assured his personnel, however, many of whom were doubtful about the future, that, even after unification was completed, there would still be an armoured corps in the new Canadian Forces. Ainscough also mentioned a subject that was of great interest in the Light Horse – after two years of work the Regiment had finally procured its Guidon and Ainscough planned to hold an official presentation parade in the coming year.

"The most prized possession": The SALH receives its Guidon, 1967

From ancient times, soldiers have carried standards into battle – the Roman legions had their eagles, the Mongols their horsetail banners and the medieval knights their gonfalons and bannarets. These emblems served as a means of identifying friend from foe in battle, as a rallying point and guide for manoeuvre; and since the commanding officer or leader often took post near the standard, they were a convenient method of locating him. In the British and Commonwealth military tradition, regimental flags

– termed Colours in the infantry and Standards or Guidons in the cavalry – possess a status higher than any other ceremonial device. They are the visible emblem of a regiment's history as,

> On the Guidon and Regimental Colours are emblazoned the names of Battles in which units have distinguished themselves; they remind the men of those units of the past history and traditions of their Regiments. Guidons and Colours become more than rallying points, they are a symbol of a Regiment's past achievements and victories. As such symbols the Guidon or Colours are the most prized possession of a Regiment and are held in great veneration.[14]

The Guidon of an armoured or cavalry regiment is always treated with great respect and ceremony. It is carried on parade by a senior warrant officer who is escorted by a Guidon Party, or guard – soldiers salute when an unfurled Guidon passes and civilians should doff their hats as a mark of respect.

As early as 1747, the British army began to regulate the appearance of infantry Colours but it was not until 1768 that a Royal Warrant stipulated the appearance, dimensions and decoration of the Standards and Guidons of the cavalry. These regulations have not changed all that much in the intervening centuries and a light dragoon of the 18th century would instantly recognize the 21st century Guidon of a Canadian armoured regiment. The 1768 Royal Warrant, still largely followed today, stipulates that the Guidon be a swallow-tailed standard, made of red silk with a gold bullion fringe, possessing gently curved points in its fly, which are separated by a slit or indentation. It is 2 feet, 3 inches on its shaft and 3 feet, 5 inches at its greatest width in the fly.

Lieutenant-Colonel Rod Ray had initiated the lengthy process of obtaining a Guidon for the Light Horse in 1963 but it

Good to go

The Light Horse man a troop of Sherman HVSS tanks at Wainwright during summer camp in the early 1960s. The War Reserve of HVSS Shermans was held at Wainwright in the 1950s and 1960s and this was very convenient for the Western Canada militia armoured units as they could access these almost-new vehicles for training. Note the fuel truck at right – this troop is nearly fuelled up and good to go. SALH ARCHIVES

was not until 1966 that the finished product arrived in Medicine Hat. It was a very handsome item. In the first (upper left) and fourth (lower right) corners were the White Horse of Hanover, the Royal House in the 18th century, exactly as prescribed in the 1768 regulations. In the second (or upper right) corner was the gold Roman numeral "XXIX," the regimental number of the wartime South Alberta Regiment, surrounded by a wreath of maple leaves, while in the third (or lower left) corner were the initials, "SALH" again surrounded by a maple wreath. In the centre underneath the Queen's Crown and also surrounded by a maple wreath was the Regimental badge, with "SEMPER ALACER" on a scroll beneath. Around the badge were emblazoned the major Battle Honours of the Light Horse, earned by their predecessor units, commencing with "North West Canada 1885," awarded to the Rocky Mountain Rangers, continuing through "Vimy, 1917" and other First World War Honours gained by the 31st Battalion CEF, and ending with "St. Lambert-sur-Dives" and the other Second War Honours of the wartime South Albertas.

Before a Guidon or Colour can be carried by a regiment on parade, it must be officially presented – hopefully by Royalty or Royalty's appointed representative – and consecrated, or blessed, by a military chaplain. The presentation and consecration of new regimental Colours or Guidons is a solemn occasion and, since these devices often last decades before they are replaced, a rare but important event in the history of a regiment. This being the case, the South Alberta Light Horse wanted to mark the presentation of their first Guidon with all due pomp and circumstance.

It was fortunate that 1967, the Centennial of Confederation, was a special year in Canada and one in which all levels of government loosened their purse strings to fund a wide variety of celebrations and events. Visits by the Queen and other Royalty were planned and, when Lieutenant-Colonel Ainscough learned that HRH Princess Alexandra of Kent, the Queen's cousin and Colonel-in-Chief of the Calgary Highlanders, was scheduled to tour Western Canada in May and June of Centennial Year, he made an official request that she present the Guidon to the SALH during her tour. As there was no suitable area for the ceremony in Medicine Hat (having no parade ground at Patterson Armoury, the Light Horse was at this time still holding ceremo-

nial events on the grounds of the local high school) and because Princess Alexandra was going to present the Highlanders with new Colours, Ainscough arranged with Lieutenant-Colonel A.H. Brackenridge, commanding that unit, to hold a joint presentation at Currie Barracks in Calgary on Thursday, 25 May 1967. Ainscough also obtained funding for the Regiment to hold a series of ceremonial functions in Medicine Hat on the weekend following the presentation, including an inspection by Major-General Worthington, a March Past to mark the Freedom of the City which the city intended to bestow on the Light Horse, and the commemoration of a Tank Memorial at Riverside Park.

Once the plans were finalized, the Regiment sprang into action and the spring of 1967 was a hectic time for the Light Horsemen. A 100-man parade unit was formed and, with the help of instructors from the regular force, intensively drilled while the band, still one of the best in Alberta, practised continuously. There were also two-day drill parades on the five weekends preceding the ceremony which culminated in a full dress rehearsal held on the parade ground at Currie Barracks. Sergeant-Major Arelis would be receiving the Guidon on behalf of the Regiment and, as he remembered,

> I wasn't going to leave anything to chance so I had a special pole made to practise with that weighed about twice as much as the Guidon itself and the Guidon was fairly heavy with the embroidery, fringe and tassels. I practised for three months until my right arm had twice as many muscles as my left. It was a good thing I did that because the day of the presentation parade was cold and windy and I could have had some trouble controlling the Guidon.[15]

Corporal Robert McKenzie, who had only been in the SALH eighteen months in 1967, was promoted to lance-sergeant just before the parade because the unit still had a lot of "older guys from World War II who couldn't march and, even though I was 17 years old, they needed an NCO as left guide so they gave me that task and promoted me as well."[16] McKenzie thus became the youngest sergeant in 22 Militia Group.

By the great day – thanks to hard work on the part of all officers and men, and the contributions of a host of civilian volun-

teers, the Light Horsemen were ready. At 9.30 AM that Thursday morning in May, the combined guards of the Light Horse and Calgary Highlanders, 200 strong, marched, to the tune of "Highland Laddie" played by the bands of both regiments, onto the parade square at Currie Barracks which was lined by the men of the Queen's Own Rifles. The royal party, including Lieutenant-Governor Grant McEwen of Alberta and the Honorary Colonels and Lieutenant-Colonels of the two regiments, as well as Rod Ray by special invitation, took up their place on the rostrum and all was well except for the weather, which turned nasty with wind, rain and sleet. As then-Lieutenant Paul Mast recalled, "It was like we brassed off the weather gods."[17] Corporal Lindsay Fraser remembered it being so cold that his "hand was almost frozen solid" to the pistol grip of his FN C1 rifle.[18]

The weather didn't stop the ceremonies, which continued with an inspection of the guards by Princess Alexandra while the Light Horse Band played "Beaus and Belles", and then came the ceremonial "march off" of the old Highland Colours to "Auld Lang Syne" played again by the SALH Band. This was followed by the piling of the drums to form an altar upon which the new Guidon and Colours were laid. The Chaplain, Reverend Canon C.P. Bishop, then intoned the old and hallowed service of consecration and ended with the blessing: "Let thy gracious favour rest upon those who shall follow the Guidon and Colours now about to be committed to their trust."[19] The standards being consecrated, Princess Alexandra presented them to the waiting bearers, with Squadron Sergeant-Major Arelis receiving the Guidon. Next came the tricky parts: the March Past in slow time, the March Past in quick time, and the advance in review order – but it all went well and, after the royal party had departed, the two guards marched off to the tune of "Southerly Wind and Cloudy Sky" for the Light Horse Horse and "Black Bear" for the Highlanders. When it was over, every Light Horseman on parade or in the audience, particularly Sergeant-Major Arelis, breathed a great sigh of relief that nobody had tripped, fainted, wheeled the wrong way, missed the step or, the worst of sins, dropped a rifle – in fact, the execution of a complicated ceremonial event had been nothing short of splendid.

The events that took place in Medicine Hat on the following weekend were just as formal but possibly a little more relaxed as

Trooping the Guidon
On Saturday, 27 May 1967, the SALH trooped its Guidon in a public ceremony, one of a number of events held during the weekend that followed its presentation by Princess Alexandra. SSM Arelis is the Guidon bearer and is flanked on his left by Warrant Officer Ron Grover and on his right by Sergeant Fred Sturgess while behind comes RSM Paterson. The men of the Colour Party are wearing No. 1 Patrol Dress with medals, belt and sword while the troopers on parade are wearing battle dress and are armed with the FN C1 assault rifle, the standard Canadian army rifle from 1957 to 1988. SALH ARCHIVES

neither Royalty nor other regiments were present. In the Royal Canadian Armoured Corps, of course, Worthington enjoyed a status not much less than Royalty but Worthy was always fun to have around and, as usual, he did not disappoint the Light Horse, going out of his way to talk to the greenest recruit and stopping for a drink in the sergeants' mess. Many Light Horsemen, who remembered the tough old veteran from his many previous visits to the Hat, noted he appeared more frail than in former years and did not seem to possess his usual bouncing energy. What they did not know was that the father of Canadian Armour was already stricken with the mortal illness that would kill him within six months and, in fact, Worthy's May 1967 visit to the Light Horse was one of his last public appearances. Of course, that didn't stop him from attending the officers' mess dinner held on the Friday night, the inspection and review on the Saturday morning, the afternoon ceremony at City Hall granting the SALH the ancient right of Freedom of the City, nor the gala ball that evening and the memorial service on the Sunday.

On Saturday, 27 May, having received the Freedom of the City of Medicine Hat, the Light Horse immediately exercised their privilege of marching through it with Guidon flying, drums beating and bayonets fixed. Actually, they rolled past City Hall and the Regimental column was led by "Old Reliable," Swatty Wotherspoon's wartime half-track, and followed by the four Shermans, "Agnes," "Betty," "Carol" and "Diana." Worthy rode in the front passenger seat of "Old Reliable" while Sergeant-Major Arelis stood in the hatch proudly holding the Guidon aloft. It was a great day for the South Alberta Light Horse and it marked a high point in the history of the Regiment that would be recalled with fond memories during the difficult decade that lay ahead.

"We sucked it up and off we went": The longest decade, 1968-1978

Sadly, the Light Horse did not have their tanks for much longer. Ottawa had decided that all militia armoured regiments would be re-equipped as light armour and their Shermans were to be replaced with jeeps until suitable armoured recce vehicles were procured. As unit after unit turned in its tanks, there was plenty

of 76 mm ammunition around and Lieutenant Paul Mast remembered that, during the "last big shoot up" the Light Horse conducted at Suffield in the spring of 1968, "we must have cranked out 2,000 rounds."[20] The officers bet the sergeants a bottle of whisky over who could knock the turret off the target tank and the sergeants won. When the SALH went to summer camp in 1968, they did not take their Shermans and, as Mast recalled,

when we came back in September, the tanks were gone. What really upset me the most was the fact that we didn't give them a "Good bye, God bless you, kiss." We lost them and they had just put in new main packs [engines] and then they took them away. We didn't have a chance to give them a hug, if you will. We were an armoured regiment in the summer but when we returned in the fall, we were recce and it was like taking your shoes off and walking in your bare feet. But we sucked it up and off we went.[21]

The Light Horse received their first jeeps that winter, Model M38CDN (U.S. M38) vehicles – basically an upgraded version of the classic Second World War vehicle – and prepared to train for their new tactical role in the following summer.

That year, Lieutenant-Colonel Douglas Heine, in civilian life at scientist at Suffield, who had served both with the Light Horse and the 19th Dragoons, took over command. From the outset, Heine experienced difficulties and recalled that his four-year period of command was a troubled one:

We were struggling after we lost the tanks because all we had were the jeeps and our paid man days were cut way back. Things were difficult and we lost a lot of people. For me it was a very hard period as the equipment was very sparse and half the time it was unserviceable and trying to get things fixed was a major problem. The situation was anything but attractive and if you wanted to sum it up in one word, it was *frustrating.*[22]

Freedom of the City

As part of the celebrations attendant on receiving its Guidon, the SALH was granted the Freedom of the City of Medicine Hat, an ancient privilege that allowed it to parade through the streets with Guidon flying, bayonets fixed and drums beating. In the photo at right, Mayor Chuck Meagher congratulates Lieutenant-Colonel Reed Ainscough, commanding officer of the Light Horse, at City Hall. Eight years later, Meagher would take over the command of the SALH. (Above) The Light Horse immediately exercised their new freedom on 27 May 1967 by staging a Roll Past through the streets of Medicine Hat. Leading the parade is "Old Reliable" with WO Arelis proudly holding the Guidon aloft while behind is Lieutenant-Colonel Ainscough in a jeep, followed by "The Girls," the Regiment's four Shermans. Although he cannot be seen in this photo, sitting in the passenger seat of "Old Reliable" is Major-General Frank Worthington, Colonel-Commandant of the Royal Canadian Armoured Corps. BOTH, SALH ARCHIVES

With the prevailing anti-military attitudes, the removal of the Shermans which were a useful recruiting device, and the cutting back of both training days and payrolls, the strength of the Light Horse experienced a drastic decline. The SALH had paraded more than 200 in 1967 but by 1971 its strength had decreased to 78 all ranks. Lieutenant-Colonel E.M. Moore, CD, remembered that, when he succeeded Heine in 1972,

We were parading about 35 people at the time I took it over in December of that year but we managed to raise it to 75 by the next spring. We went to Sarcee that summer and we won every competition held, except one. Unfortunately, this was about the time that this master-corporal/corporal thing came out and I lost 20 men over pay issues when soldiers wearing the same rank were getting vastly different pay. I lost a lot of good people over pay issues and they were killing our numbers left, right and centre. Our budgets were watched very closely and the training days were drastically reduced.[23]

The problems caused by the new rank structure introduced during the unification process were not the only negative results of that lamentable process. Soldiers, sailors and airmen were

(Left) **In Memoriam**
Honorary Captain R.J. Thompson, padre of the Light Horse, reads the invocation at the commemoration of the tank memorial at Riverside Park in Medicine Hat on Sunday, 28 May 1967. Standing in the left rear is "Worthy" – Major-General Frank Worthington – a veteran of two wars and the father of the Royal Canadian Armoured Corps. Sadly, this was one of the old soldier's last public appearances as he would die six months later. SALH ARCHIVES

forced to wear the same green uniform, regimental badges were only permitted on headgear (the government even tried at one point to do away with regimental badges) and once a soldier removed his hat, there was no way of telling what service he belonged to, which was damaging to morale. By dint of extensive lobbying over a period of years, however, Mobile Command (the new name for the army) was able to get regimental badges on uniforms restored and the armoured corps was able to regain its

Founding Father, Colonel James Walker,
15th Light Horse

Lieutenant-Colonel P.W.H. Higgs, CD
1954-1957

Lieutenant-Colonel C.D. Williams, CD
1958-1960

Lieutenant-Colonel N.R. Ray, CD
1960-1964

Lieutenant-Colonel R.W. Ainscough, CD
1964-1968

Lieutenant-Colonel J.D. Heine, CD
1968-1972

Lieutenant-Colonel E.M. Moore, CD
1972-1975

Lieutenant-Colonel C.J. Meagher, CD
1975-1982

Lieutenant-Colonel B.F. McKinley, CD
1982-1984

Lieutenant-Colonel M. Moore, CD
1984-1988

Lieutenant-Colonel H.L. Fraser, CD
1988-1993

Lieutenant-Colonel R.B. McKenzie, MMM, CD
1993-1996

Lieutenant-Colonel B. Hodgson, CD
1996-2000

Lieutenant-Colonel N. Douglas, CD
2000-2003

Lieutenant-Colonel T.E. Putt, CD
2003 to date

distinctive black beret. Fortunately, during the grim years of the 1970s, the militia preserved many of the old traditions as they were permitted to keep their distinctive mess dress, patrol and full dress "until it wore out" and, of course, militiamen persisted in wearing these garments until they were positively threadbare. The Light Horse did not like the new green uniforms – particularly the garrison dress which featured a short, waist-length, zippered jacket – which they derisively termed "the bus driver's uniform" and, in the absence of anything better, preferred their black denim tanker's overalls.[24]

Equipment gradually arrived. By the early 70s the Light Horse had about 20 jeeps, either the M38CDN, M38CDN1 (often called the 52 or 54 pattern), M38A1CDN 2 (the 70 pattern) or the M38A1CDN3 (the 72 or 74 pattern) and some of the despised "67 pattern" vehicles that had a distressing habit of rolling easily, which were actually American-manufactured M151A2 jeeps. Depending on their strength, the Light Horse would form a number of troops, each consisting of about 5 vehicles. Communications were provided by C42 radios mounted in the backs of the vehicles and most of the jeeps had mounts for .30 calibre machineguns although an attempt to mount a .50 calibre weapon had to be abandoned because the vehicle was not strong enough to handle the recoil. One good thing about the jeeps was that they were easy to maintain and, as Sergeant Lindsay Fraser noted,

We were lucky to have guys like Emil Chinook, who was a heavy duty mechanic, self-appointed I think. We had Peter Eichelbaum, ex-RCEME warrant officer and for a while he

Last rounds, 1968

In the spring of 1968, the Light Horse held their last Sherman gun camp at Suffield and, as one soldier who was there remarked, "we must have cranked out at least 2,000 rounds." When the Regiment returned from summer camp that year, the Shermans were gone and, shortly afterward, they learned that their replacements would be jeeps as the SALH was about to become a recce regiment. SALH ARCHIVES

was able to get us spare parts. And then the army changed the rules and wouldn't give us spare parts so we had to send everything to Calgary to be repaired and once a vehicle went down, it was six months before it was operational again.[25]

Another asset the Light Horse exploited was the presence of the British Army Training Unit in Suffield (BATUS), created in 1971 to serve as a base and instructional organization for British combat units that rotated into Canada to carry out realistic training on the 1,000 square miles of that large base. The Brits occasionally let the Light Horse play with their Saladin armoured cars and Saracen personnel carriers and, from time to time, lent a hand. Corporal John Bray remembered that the Light Horse was having trouble

getting our C-42 sets repaired at base maintenance in Calgary. We cultivated some friendships with some of the British supply technicians and maintainers. They took about a half dozen of our C-42 sets that were down out there and repaired them. At that time the Canadian C-42 sets had tubes but the British models had solid state circuitry so they replaced our tubes with circuitry but neglected to tell us that. Then, we made a mistake of sending one of the radios up to Calgary and the regulars came back and said, "What the hell is going on here?" So they came down and took all the solid state radios away from us and probably gave them to the regulars.[26]

The Light Horse experienced many problems during this difficult decade – as did the Canadian militia in general – but there were also good times. Regardless of the difficulties, the Regiment carried on and many of the veterans of this time remember it as

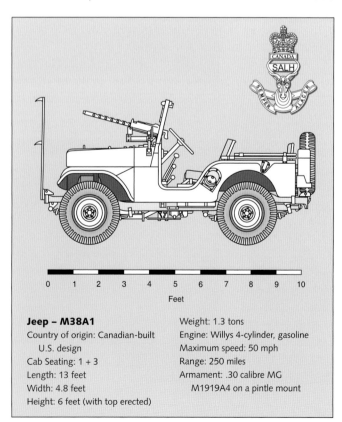

```
0   1   2   3   4   5   6   7   8   9   10
                  Feet
```

Jeep – M38A1

Country of origin: Canadian-built U.S. design	Weight: 1.3 tons
	Engine: Willys 4-cylinder, gasoline
Cab Seating: 1 + 3	Maximum speed: 50 mph
Length: 13 feet	Range: 250 miles
Width: 4.8 feet	Armament: .30 calibre MG
Height: 6 feet (with top erected)	M1919A4 on a pintle mount

being an interesting, as well as a strange, period. The SALH went through its annual cycle, beginning in September when training started, complete with autumn and spring exercises in the field, usually at Suffield, and public and social events, which culminated (if the funds were made available) in a summer camp, now known as Milcon (Militia Concentration). It was at the Milcons that the Light Horse got to use the proper armoured recce vehicles for their tactical role including the Lynx CRV (Command and Reconnaissance Vehicle), a tracked armoured vehicle based on the American M-113 armoured personnel carrier, which was a good piece of gear ideally suited to its purpose. The Strathconas loaned a CRV which was installed in Patterson Armoury as a training platform. Until about 1972 the fiction was kept up that militia armoured regiments would train as recce with jeeps most of the year but that, at Milcons, they would function as "armoured recce," using such vehicles as the regular force would make available to them. In 1972, all militia armoured regiments were re-designated recce units and, looking at the machinegun-mounted jeeps, many black hats cynically regarded their new function as being "recce by death" – that is to say, they drove along until the enemy knocked them out, at which point everyone knew where the enemy was positioned.

In 1975 the Light Horse went to CFB (Canadian Forces Base) Shilo in Manitoba for annual concentration and were able to get a close look at the *Bundeswehr* which used this base to carry out training similar to that of the British army at Suffield. Warrant Officer Robert McKenzie never forgot the time that two squadrons of German Leopard tanks roared at full speed past the Light Horse in their jeeps and "the ground shook."[27] Sergeant John Bray had good reason to remember that visit as he was out on a recce exercise with his troop "and the Germans were firing artillery and four 105 mm rounds landed about 300 yards away, and we took off quickly."[28] On the other hand, if you can't take a joke, you shouldn't join up.

The problems caused by prevailing social attitudes and funding restraints persisted. In 1973, the Regiment was forced to cancel its annual public "Trooping of the Guidon" ceremony, a popular event in Medicine Hat, because of funding cuts. The high point that year was the visit in April of Brigadier-General (Retd.) Gordon ("Swatty") Wotherspoon, DSO, the former commanding officer of the wartime SAR and Worthy's replacement as Colonel-Commandant of the RCAC, and Brigadier-General J.L. Summers,

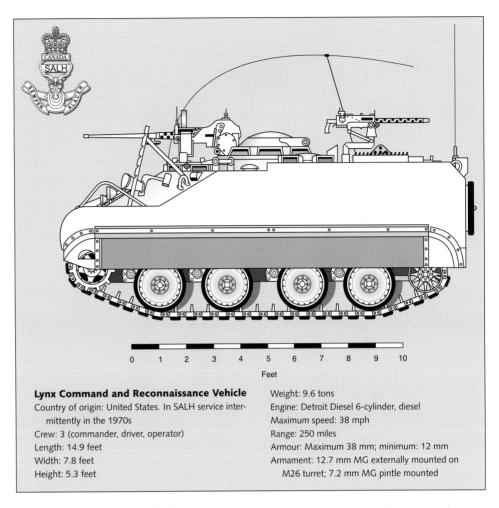

Lynx Command and Reconnaissance Vehicle
Country of origin: United States. In SALH service intermittently in the 1970s
Crew: 3 (commander, driver, operator)
Length: 14.9 feet
Width: 7.8 feet
Height: 5.3 feet

Weight: 9.6 tons
Engine: Detroit Diesel 6-cylinder, diesel
Maximum speed: 38 mph
Range: 250 miles
Armour: Maximum 38 mm; minimum: 12 mm
Armament: 12.7 mm MG externally mounted on M26 turret; 7.2 mm MG pintle mounted

MC, CD, a former troop leader in the South Albertas and the commander of Prairie District. Wotherspoon and Summers were there to attend the annual Vimy Dinner but, if these two veteran soldiers, who had watched hundreds of Canadian tanks go into action in Normandy, were disappointed to see the floor of Patterson Armoury covered with jeeps, they were tactful enough not say anything about it and, in any case, Jack Summers, a life-long militiaman, was only too aware of the problems facing the units in his command. Sadly, Swatty and Jack did not get to ride in "Old Reliable" because by this time the venerable half-track was not running and, the following year, the Light Horse bid farewell to this proud memento of their past when it was sent to CFB Calgary to serve as a static display vehicle.

In 1975, when Major Charles Meagher, the former mayor of Medicine Hat, took over as commanding officer, the Light Horse were in a perilous state. Budget cuts, social attitudes and the disinterest of the government had combined to reduce the unit's strength to the point where it was downgraded from "major" to "minor" status and Meagher therefore took command as a major. Then-Captain Paul Mast recalled that there were sometimes only 25 all ranks on parade and many of them were "not even signing in [to receive pay] and it was pretty grim" because of the "backlash from Vietnam."[29] It became particularly difficult to recruit young officers and the result was that, in a family tradition so to speak, the Light Horse began to "grow its own" just as

The 1970s: Recce by death

The 1970s were not a good time for the Canadian army, now renamed Mobile Command of the Canadian Forces, and it was a particularly bad time for the militia armoured regiments, which were all converted to recce units, with jeeps replacing their tanks. This led to the bitter joke that their new role was "recce by death," which is to say that their job was to locate the enemy by drawing fire which, given their equipment, could only have one result. Corporal Ray Gradwell and Trooper Jim Ogston, seen here in an M38CDN jeep at Suffield in the spring of 1975, do not seem particularly worried about it, nor about anything else for that matter. SALH ARCHIVES

the SAR had done during the war. A number of warrant officers were commissioned including two who would eventually command the Light Horse: Lieutenant-Colonels Lindsay Fraser and Robert McKenzie. But there were disconcerting rumours being put about that the SALH was about to be chopped from the Order of Battle and, frankly, matters did not look good.

The Light Horse's misfortunes during the 1970s were not shared by the province as Alberta prospered during that decade. This latest economic boom was brought about by events in the Middle East, where tensions between the Arab states and Israel had resulted in outright wars in 1956, 1967 and 1973, conflicts which saw Israel emerge as the clear victor. The result was that the largely Arab Organization of Petroleum Exporting Countries (OPEC) decided to increase the barrel price of oil in an attempt

to bring pressure against Israel and its western supporters and this created an international energy crisis. Alberta, blessed with some of the best oil reserves in the Western Hemisphere, benefited as a result and money and people flowed into the province – the Gross Domestic Product of the province tripled between 1971 and 1981 while the population increased by a third from 1.6 million to 2.4 million souls. Development of the Athabasca oil sands increased in tempo when the federal and provincial governments joined with the private sector in creating the massive Syncrude project to tap this wealth. The population trend away from the farms to the cities, which had continued through the immediate postwar decades, increased and, in 1971, a largely urban, affluent middle class ended Social Credit's lengthy rule by voting in the Conservative Party led by the charismatic but level-headed Peter Lougheed. Lougheed, however, proved to be as ardent a defender of Alberta as his Social Credit predecessors had been.

In 1976, Lougheed established the Alberta Heritage Trust Fund, which placed a portion of the oil and gas revenue bonanza from these non-renewable resources into long-term investments for the future development of the province. This provincial "rainy day" fund became the envy of other provincial governments, financially pressed during the 70s, which, in most of Canada, were stagnant years in economic terms. It also attracted the attention of the federal government which did not bode well for the future as, throughout the long tenure of the Liberal Party in Ottawa which – with a brief intermission of less than two years – lasted from 1964 to 1984, the province had almost no voice in the federal government because most Albertans did not like the Liberals and would not vote for them. This situation was not helped by the fact that Lougheed and Trudeau, two very different personalities, soon came to cordially detest each other, particularly when Ottawa began to make threatening noises about acquiring a great share of the province's oil and gas revenues. Ironically, as Ottawa and Edmonton began to square off over energy policy, it was a Liberal who came to the rescue of the South Alberta Light Horse.

Horace ("Bud") Olson, a rancher from near Medicine Hat, was first elected to the House of Commons as a Liberal MP in 1957, a highly un-

Dress and deportment are important: Junior NCO course, c. 1970

A Light Horse Junior NCOs conducted by RSM A. Arelis poses for their photo. During the early years of unification, stocks of the new CF green garrison uniforms for Mobile Command (the new name for the army) were in short supply so many units came up with an expedient. They took the pockets and shoulder straps off their battle dress shirts and sewed them onto the issue sweater (seen unaltered on the corporal standing to the left) to create a smart and serviceable order of garrison dress. COURTESY, A. ARELIS

Trooping the Guidon, 1970

In an annual popular event in Medicine Hat, the SALH "trooped" or paraded its Guidon in front of all ranks of the Regiment. This event was usually well attended by civilians but, unfortunately, budget cuts in the 1970s caused it to be cancelled. The decade from 1968 to 1978 was a difficult period for the Light Horse and Mobile Command (the new name for the army) and most militia units concentrated on one thing – surviving until better times. COURTESY, A. ARELIS

usual event as the election that year saw a resurgence of the Conservative Party in the west. Olson was re-elected in the next four federal elections and, by 1968, he was serving as Minister of Agriculture in Pierre Trudeau's first cabinet. Given the scarcity of Liberals west of Ontario, Olson was assigned responsibility for western affairs which made him a very powerful and influential figure in Ottawa. In 1970, Olson agreed to become the Honorary Colonel of the SALH and, although it appears that he did not maintain close links with the Regiment in the early 1970s, it was to Olson that Meagher turned in 1976 for help in saving the Light Horse from "the axe man in Ottawa." The response was not long in coming and the unit shortly received a "Winter Works" employment programme which enabled it to start a major recruiting drive that increased its strength from 37 to 153 all ranks in less than a year, restoring its status as a major unit and bringing Meagher promotion to lieutenant-colonel. Perhaps more importantly, Olson let it be known at DND Headquarters in Ottawa that anybody who tried to mess with the Medicine Hat militia unit would be messing with him and the result was that the disconcerting rumours about the impending demise of the Light Horse abruptly ceased. The Regiment was safe for the time being but it had been a very near run thing and every Light Horse officer who served during that time knew who was responsible – as Major Paul Mast put it, "the only thing that saved our butt was the fact that Bud Olson was both our Honorary Colonel and the local Member of Parliament."[30]

"Make It Happen": The stand up of B Squadron, 1978-1980

The early Trudeau years, from 1968 to 1978, were a desperate and depressing time for the Canadian army, now Mobile Command of the Canadian Forces. It laboured to serve a government which seemed to regard it as an embarassment and which itself exhibited considerable confusion over defence matters. On the one hand, budgets and manpower were cut back; on the other the government insisted, to keep up international face, that the army continue to carry out its NATO and UN peacekeeping commitments. It became a question of constantly having "to do more with less." On the subject of armoured vehicles, the government decided to retire the regular forces' Centurion main battle tanks in favour of something they termed a "light, tracked, direct-fire support vehicle" that would be air transportable.[31] In the early 70s, a requirement for an Armoured Vehicle General Purpose (AVGP) therefore was given international distribution and a number of prototypes were tested. At the same time, however, the West German government, noting Canada's recent reduction of its NATO forces, began to exert pressure on Ottawa by threatening to link future trade agreements between the two countries directly to Canadian willingness to deploy capable military forces in Europe. The result was an abrupt reversal on the part of the Trudeau government which approved the purchase of new tanks for Mobile Command with the choice, not surprisingly, being the German Leopard which, with some improvements, began to enter service in 1978.

The Die-Hards, summer camp, 1975   jeep id

Despite all their problems in the 1970s, the Light Horse never gave up and, occasionally during that long decade, they had some high points. One such came in the summer of 1975 when they held their concentration at CFB Shilo in Manitoba where they got to watch the German *Bundeswehr* at work. Here, a group of Light Horsemen pause from work to pose for a photo, wearing the new combat dress of olive green nylon-cotton introduced between 1964 and 1974 to replace battle and bush dress. Standing from left to right are: Bill Heib, John Bray, Robert McKenzie, Alex Van Rooyen, Trooper Vandam, Jim Ogston, Dayle Mytton, Sergeant R. Purdy (instructor from the Strathconas), Ray Gradwell, Barry Gramlich and Alex Symington. Kneeling left to right are Dave Symington, Jim Lutz, Pat Major, Lee Cluff, Richard Gage and Paul Mast. In this group are four future SALH RSMs and one future commanding officer.

SALH ARCHIVES

Honorary Colonel H.B. Olson and Mrs. Olson
The Honourable Horace ("Bud") Olson, a rancher from near Medicine Hat, who was a long-serving Liberal Member of Parliament, agreed to become the Honorary Colonel of the Light Horse in 1970. He served in that appointment for 18 years during which he managed to preserve the unit from extinction as he was a powerful figure in the Liberal government of Pierre Elliot Trudeau, a government that seemed hellbent on the destruction of its own armed forces. In this 1999 photo, Olson, now lieutenant-governor of Alberta, and his wife, Lucille, pose with Captain Alex Van Rooyen, serving as his aide-de-camp. Captain Van Rooyen is wearing the dark green service dress jacket of the Canadian Forces. COURTESY, ALEX VAN ROOYEN

In the meantime, the requirement for a light armoured vehicle had grown into a requirement for a family of wheeled armoured vehicles that would serve as direct fire support vehicles, personnel carriers and recovery vehicles. Products from a number of companies were tested but the clear winner was the Swiss MOWAG firm's Piranha and, in 1977, Ottawa made the decision to acquire this product, to be manufactured in Canada by General Motors, with the direct fire support variant to be the Cougar while the personnel carrier variant would be the Grizzly. The Cougar, a vehicle weighing 11.5 tons and armed with a 76 mm gun and a co-axial machinegun, would be issued to the regular and militia armoured regiments, and thus, for the first time in a quarter century, the two components of the army would have the same fighting platform. The effect of this decision on the militia armoured regiments was electrifying – after a long and depressing decade, they would get modern equipment and, with the infantry possessing a similar vehicle, they would be able to undertake combined arms training. At the time, there was some understandable confusion as to exactly what the Cougar was – a direct fire support vehicle, a tank trainer or an armoured car – and perhaps the best analysis of the vehicle is found in the history of the Royal Canadian Armoured Corps:

At the unit level, the Cougar gave crew commanders and gunners a 76 mm Alvis turret-mounted gun to train on, and there was provision for a laser sighting system. The acquisition of the RADNIS night-sight and the image intensification driving system allowed units to reconstruct their night-fighting skills with relatively up-to-date equipment. In effect, the Cougar acquisition permitted non-tank units to be 60 per cent compatible with tank units, so that if and when a new MBT arrived, conversion time would be reduced. The psychological effect of training on and with a tank-like vehicle should not be underestimated, but there were many limitations. The Cougar was not a tank, it was a tank-trainer.[32]

After much discussion, DND HQ decided to provide one troop of four Cougars to selected militia armoured regiments across the country, with distribution beginning in 1980-1981.

In Alberta both the Light Horse and the King's Own Calgary Regiment were chosen to receive the new vehicle and, thus, to convert from their recce to an armoured role. As both regiments were closely connected with the Strathconas, then stationed at Currie Barracks in Calgary and Sarcee Camp just outside the city, this apparently made good sense as the regulars could provide technical assistance. The problem was that by this time Alberta had been divided into two separate militia districts: Southern District with headquarters at Calgary, and Northern District with headquarters at Edmonton. Each district nominally fielded an armour/infantry battlegroup but, since the SALH and KOCR were in the Southern District, the Northern District was without an armoured component, a fact that did not please Colonel Arnold Mottershead, the district commander. A former 19th Dragoon, Mottershead and a number of other officers, regular and militia, conceived a plan to re-introduce an armoured presence into the provincial capital by transferring a squadron's worth of positions from the Light Horse in Medicine Hat north to Edmonton. In the light of what was to follow, it probably would have made more sense to badge this new entity as the 19th Alberta Dragoons. Ottawa refused to permit this because the Royal Canadian Armoured Corps Association had been pressuring hard for the return of the regiments placed on the Supplementary Order of Battle in 1965 and the fear was that, if the Dragoons were stood up again, it would set a bad precedent that would only increase pressure to bring back the other units on the Supplementary Order. Mottershead was therefore more or less told that the new Edmonton squadron had to be badged as SALH.

Lieutenant-Colonel Charles Meagher of the Light Horse agreed to this plan, which would see A Squadron in Medicine Hat remain recce while the new B Squadron in Edmonton would eventually become a Cougar-equipped armoured unit. As Captain Lindsay Fraser recalled, RHQ regarded this as the correct decision as it

would be a great opportunity to go to the big city and compete with other units with a recruiting tool, that is the Cougar. Who is going to join a jeep unit when they can join a Cougar unit?

Another reason that we gave the Cougars to B Squadron

was that there was a Forces maintenance facility in Edmonton. We knew the problems we were having getting repairs in Medicine Hat even for a jeep, we didn't know what would happen when we got this big cumbersome thing that nobody knew how to work on. There was technical support available in Edmonton, or at we least thought there was.[33]

For the time being, however, until it received Cougars, B Squadron would be a jeep-equipped recce squadron and, to get them started, RHQ transferred five late-model jeeps of the type commonly called "Ugly Girls" (because they had "fat bottoms") and four .30 calibre General Purpose Machine Guns (GPMG) northward.

The new squadron was officially authorized in late 1977 with headquarters at Griesbach Barracks, named after the distinguished Albertan soldier who has made frequent appearances in this story. Griesbach Barracks was a large two-mile square base on the outskirts of Edmonton and the former home of the Canadian Airborne Regiment, which the Liberals transferred to Petawawa in Ontario in the late 1970s. The squadron shared somewhat crowded quarters with the Loyal Edmonton regiment and a number of support and service units. It is one thing, however, to authorize a unit on paper, it is quite another to actually stand it up – that is, to staff, equip and train it. For the first eighteen months of its existence, B Squadron was a small, wayward and nearly lost orphan in the greater Edmonton garrison.

The first seven recruits, known in B Squadron legend as "The Magnificent Seven," joined in the first week of January 1978. The "Seven" actually thought they were enlisting in the Loyal Eddies and it was only after they were sworn in that they learned that they had just signed on with the armoured corps – but, once again, if you can't take a joke, etc., etc. The infant squadron encountered immediate problems when they tried to access their vehicles which were parked in the lines or compound of the service battalion at Griesbach. One of the "Seven", Trooper Sean Thirlwell, now a Light Horse captain, remembered how his comrades overcame this obstacle:

Things were a little different, a little looser in those days, and we would go down and break into the service battalion compound and get the jeeps we needed and use them to train. They were our own squadron's vehicles but because we did not have a secure compound, they were kept in the service battalion lines and we had to go through that unit to get per-

mission to drive our own vehicles and it took too long. So we got them out by our own means but, having said that, there were some members of the squadron who liked to drive other units' vehicles.[34]

Trooper Troy Steele, No. 3 of the "Seven" and also a captain in the Light Horse in 2005, quickly became the little unit's leading specialist in the fine art of vehicle acquisition. As Steele remembered:

The problem was that we had no control over our own equipment, kit or vehicles. We could not get our vehicles on the road, we couldn't get fuel for them, we couldn't get lubricants, we couldn't get the paperwork, work tickets, etc., and the only way we could train was to break the rules as we just couldn't get the authorization to drive them out of the compound. Since it was our own equipment, we made it available by learning how to pick locks and we actually learned how to remove and then replace whole sections of wire fence. We got away with it for a long time until the day I was caught driving the jeep of the RSM of the Loyal Edmonton Regiment. That wasn't a very bright idea and it was one of three such incidents where I was re-allocated temporary housing [i.e. placed in the detention cells].[35]

The squadron also faced hurdles getting proper uniforms, particularly winter gear. They solved that by outfitting themselves at local surplus stores and, being an imaginative bunch, became fond of ex-Rhodesian Army camouflage smocks and somewhat exotic, peaked, camouflage caps of unknown but probably Communist origin. They wore these items proudly in the field until the day they were seen by a senior officer and ordered to remove them in quick time.

Thus fitted out, one way or another, the "Magnificent Seven" mounted up and rode out to train although, initially, this was also difficult because they had no qualified officers and NCOs. As Steele notes, however, this was just another challenge to be met and overcome:

Our highest rank was a corporal so, to train, we took the pam [pamphlet or manual] and drove into farmer's fields around St. Albert or Morinville [north of Edmonton]. It was kind of a "discover, learn, think," and totally unproductive in many ways but we eventually got to know what recce was about.

The culture that we developed in those crazy, early years

The regimental symbol

A pronghorn antelope, the symbol of the Light Horse which features on their cap badge, pauses to stare at an intruder at Suffield. The pronghorn, blessed with phenomenal vision and hearing, is the fastest mammal in North America and the second fastest, after the cheetah, in the world, being able to run at speeds up to 50 mph for brief periods and maintain a steady 30-40 mph for longer periods. Always alert and quick to react, the pronghorn is a very suitable symbol for a light cavalry unit.

COURTESY, ALEX VAN ROOYEN

The "Magnificent Seven" prepare to ride

In late 1977, a decision was made to stand up a squadron of the SALH in Edmonton and the first seven recruits, known in legend as the "Magnificent Seven," joined in January 1978. This new entity was independent of RHQ in Medicine Hat and for the first year or so of its existence was an orphan unit in the Edmonton garrison and had problems getting vehicles, equipment and uniforms. The squadron solved these problems by using their own initiative, becoming experts in the fine art of vehicle acquisition, and uniformed themselves in local surplus stores. Here, B Squadron, whose motto became "Make It Happen!", prepare to ride out. Note the camouflage jackets, which are Rhodesian army in origin, and the peaked caps, which may or may not be Czechoslovakian. Note also that the M38A1 CDN jeep in the foreground has been painted in what appears to be a non-regulation camouflage pattern. COURTESY, TROY STEELE

The coming of the Cat

In the early 1980s, militia armoured units were re-equipped with the Armoured Vehicle General Purpose (AVGP) or Cougar, a wheeled tank trainer armed with a 76 mm main gun and a 7.62 mm co-axial machine-gun. The Cougar provided an immediate boost to their morale, improved training and increased recruiting. Here, five SALH Cougars, followed by soft-skinned vehicles, take part in the festivities surrounding the 100th Anniversary of the founding of Medicine Hat in 1983. SALH ARCHIVES

is still evident in B Squadron today and it is a mindset of "Make It Happen" – it is a kind of a cowboy culture, but a disciplined cowboy culture. It made B Squadron and, eventually the Regiment, very aggressive in achieving any task set for them. Of the original group of seven, three are now in leadership roles in the Sally Horse in 2004 because, although those early days were wild times, they made us always want to serve with the Light Horse.[36]

Steele is not exaggerating. In January 1980, two years after the first recruits joined B Squadron, its AHR (Annual Historical Report) states that, in the previous twelve months,

There was one officer and one senior NCO at this time. Unfortunately the senior NCO was not armoured trained. For the fall [1979] training period three additional officers, all untrained in armoured tactics, reinforced the unit. The addition of a trained sergeant and two MCpls certainly enhanced the level of expertise in the unit.[37]

From the beginning, whatever it lacked in expertise or equipment, B Squadron never lacked spirit. Consider the infamous Exercise WOLF CAKE held in March 1979 which required the squadron to drive from Edmonton to Suffield down Highway 41 through one of the most wide open, windswept, and sparsely populated areas of southern Alberta. As Steele recalled, it was quite the experience:

We had to drive down to Suffield from Edmonton in open jeeps with no tops or side windows, and that's distance of about 350 miles. We left in mid afternoon because we knew it would be a long trip and, at first it was okay but then it began to snow.

None of the windshield wipers worked and so we had guys hanging over the front of the windshield scraping the ice off the glass by hand, in a snowstorm. Soon they wrapped themselves in sleeping bags, covering the tops of their heads and hung over the windshields with just one arm sticking out, scraping the glass. It was so cold that some were bordering on hypothermia but, fortunately, we had an enclosed one-ton truck with us and

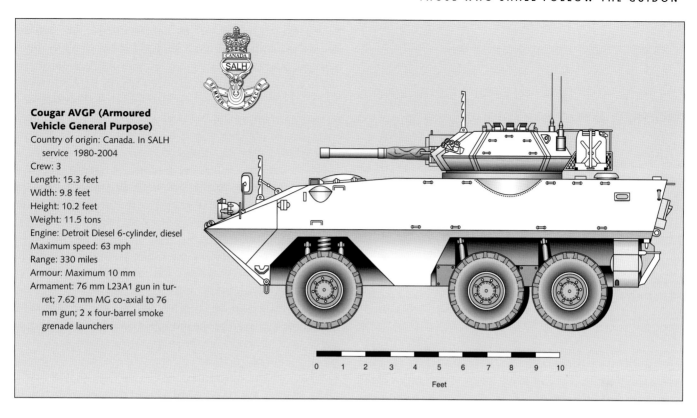

Cougar AVGP (Armoured Vehicle General Purpose)
Country of origin: Canada. In SALH service 1980-2004
Crew: 3
Length: 15.3 feet
Width: 9.8 feet
Height: 10.2 feet
Weight: 11.5 tons
Engine: Detroit Diesel 6-cylinder, diesel
Maximum speed: 63 mph
Range: 330 miles
Armour: Maximum 10 mm
Armament: 76 mm L23A1 gun in turret; 7.62 mm MG co-axial to 76 mm gun; 2 x four-barrel smoke grenade launchers

```
0   1   2   3   4   5   6   7   8   9   10
```
Feet

we placed the frozen ones into the heated cab and drove on. Eventually, we had to drag guys out of the truck and tell them to get back in the jeeps to relieve other frozen ones.

I do not know how we survived that trip, which took twelve hours. It was the Gong Show from Hell, it was Stalingrad, and it was great fun.[38]

Another B Squadron trait, also evident from its earliest days, was its strong interest in the heritage of the western cavalry. In September 1979, no less than ten members, or about a third of the squadron's strength, took to horse and participated in the "Queen's Ride" from Calgary to Edmonton when 85 men from the RCMP, the Strathconas, the KOCR and the Light Horse donned period uniform to recreate the 180-mile march of General "Gunner Jingo" Strange's Alberta Field Force in 1885, described in Chapter One above. It took them seven days in the saddle and the group hauled along one of the original 9-pdr. field guns from Strange's column, although they were fortunate to receive better rations than the original cast.

"Let the eastern bastards freeze in the dark": Alberta and Canada in the 1980s – two steps forward, one step back

As the 1970s ended, there were hopes in the Canadian army, now Mobile Command, that the Liberal government was finally beginning to take a serious interest in defence matters. The acquisition of new tanks and armoured vehicles was a positive sign and they hoped for more such measures because, along with the armed forces of the other NATO nations, the Canadian Forces were becoming increasingly concerned about the Soviet military build-up that occurred during the decade – supposedly a

time of *"détente"* between the two global power bocs. In 1975, the same year that South Vietnam fell to the Communists, the Soviet Union gained nuclear parity with the west and embarked on a programme of upgrading and increasing its land forces. In 1979 the Soviets, apparently learning nothing from the American experience in southeast Asia, invaded Afghanistan and directly threatened the borders of India. Throughout most of the latter years of the decade, the United States was in a state of retrenchment, trying to heal the bitter divisions caused by the Vietnam War and and the lack of national self-confidence that had resulted. Canada's Liberal government, however, displayed less concern about international events than about its domestic situation. Trudeau had been quick to call in the armed forces in 1970 to apprehend what he believed was a nascent revolt in Quebec, but the forces got little thanks and, in any case, the strength of the Quebec separatist movement increased, culminating in the election of the *Parti Québécois* to power in that province in 1976. Defeating the separatist threat became Trudeau's overwelming concern, to the detriment of other national matters, including the increasing alienation of Western Canada.

Throughout the 1970s, the Lougheed government fought battles with Ottawa over the control and pricing of oil, particularly in 1973-1974 when the Liberals froze domestic oil prices after OPEC raised global prices following the 1973 Egyptian-Israeli War. Tempers had calmed by the time of the brief Conservative government of Joe Clark in 1978-1979 and Alberta profited from the global increase in oil prices brought about by the Iran-Iraq war which began in 1980. When Trudeau returned to power after winning a majority government that same year, however, without any attempt at negotiation with the Lougheed

Winter ex

Canada being a northern country, all Canadian soldiers participate in winter training, which can either be great fun or horrible. Here, a group of Light Horse undergo it at either Suffield or Wainwright in the early 1990s. SALH ARCHIVES

government, the Liberals introduced the National Energy Program. This program was an attempt by the federal government to increase its control over the oil and gas industry and its revenues, by means of a complex mix of domestic price controls, production and corporate income taxes directed specifically toward the petroleum industry, a complicated set of financial regulations and creation of a new entity, Petro-Canada, which would buy out those private companies that did not wish to do business in Canada under the new system. The result was outright war between Edmonton and Ottawa in 1980-1981, a war perhaps best summed up for Albertans by three bumper stickers widely seen in the province at this time:

"Let the eastern bastards freeze in the dark!"

"This Car Doesn't Brake for Liberals."

"I'd rather push this thing a mile than buy from Petro-Canada."

After a very tense year, and some protracted negotiations, Ottawa backed off and the two governments resolved their differences by signing an energy pricing agreement in 1981 which returned some control of the oil and gas industry to the province, increased domestic oil prices and gave Alberta greater revenues.

The damage, however, was done and the psychological impact of the NEP, combined with falling world oil prices, rampant inflation and a general global recession sent Alberta into an economic tailspin in 1982. In one year, unemployment increased from 3.8% to 10.2%, and thousands lost their homes because they could not keep up their mortages. This, in turn, led to the collapse of financial and lending institutions that had invested heavily in real estate, notably the Canadian Commercial Bank and the Northlands Bank. Many left the province and,

for the first time in decades, the population was static. Alberta was just climbing out of this recession in 1986 when oil prices took a massive drop as increasing volumes of British North Sea oil came on the international market – by early 1987, the unemployment rate in Edmonton was 12.9% and 68,000 people were on welfare in the province. The economy gradually crept back but it was not until the early 1990s that it recovered to the level that prevailed when the "dismal 80s" began.

Not all was doom and gloom in Alberta during the 1980s. For example, the Edmonton Eskimos, beginning in 1978, won the Grey Cup for five successive years. Late in the decade, the West Edmonton Mall, the world's biggest indoor shopping centre, was completed and drew hundreds of thousands of visitors to that city. In 2004, these visitors pump an estimated 7.6 billion dollars a year into the provincial economy. Not to be outdone by its northern rival, Calgary hosted the 1988 Winter Olympics and gave the world a stirring example of perfect hospitality, Alberta fashion. Edmonton, on the other hand, was proud of its Oilers, arguably one of the best hockey teams to ever take the ice, led by the incredible Wayne Gretzky (a native of Ontario, like the author, it should be noted) which brought the Stanley Cup to that city in 1984, 1985, 1987 and 1988. All Albertans (even Calgarians) and many Canadians went into shock and mourning on 9 August 1988, truly a black day in the history of both the province and the nation because a flint-hearted owner traded Gretzky, "the Great One," to the Los Angeles Kings. A downcast Edmonton became even more dispirited the following year when the Calgary Flames won the Stanley Cup. Edmonton rebounded, however, under the leadership of St. Albert native Mark Messier, to win the Cup in 1990.

To drop back a little in time, it should come as no surprise to the reader that many Canadian soldiers rejoiced when the Liberal Party, no longer led by Trudeau, was defeated in the general election of 1983 and replaced by the Conservatives under Prime Minister Brian Mulroney. One of Mulroney's election planks had been a promise to undertake a sweeping review of defence policy and increase funding to the Canadian Forces, which had been on a starvation diet for more than a decade. This promise was kept, at least partly, and defence spending was increased in the middle 1980s, permitting both the regular and reserve force (as the militia was now re-titled) to obtain much-needed new equipment and to increase the tempo of training activities. One of the most popular decisions by the new government was to give each of the three main components of the Canadian Forces (air, land and sea) different uniforms, a measure which went a long way to restoring the pride of soldiers, sailors and airmen, who had always disliked being lumped together as a common herd.

The review of defence policy, entitled *Challenge and Commitment*, was released as a White Paper to great fanfare in 1987 and incorporated the most recent staff planning concept, called "Corps 86." Under this plan, on full mobilization, the army (and people were beginning to quietly call it that again) would consist of two mechanized infantry divisions and an armoured division, as well as an independent brigade group, an artillery division and an independent cavalry (light armour) brigade. It was an ambitious model that would never be fully realized but it led to the "Total Force" concept "in which composite Militia-Regular units of varying ratios would be employed, depending on the nature of the emergency."[39] What this meant was that, in the future, the militia, for so long the poor stepsister of the army, and formerly intended to be only fully mobilized in time of war, would be more closely integrated with the regular force during peacetime. As the history of the Royal Canadian Armoured Corps points out, the militia was now

to augment the Regular units, contribute to the Defence of Canada and train replacements for overseas operations. Such a concept demanded that the training standards at all levels be equalized and Militia officers also had to understand how to operate at battle group and brigade group levels, not just at the sub-unit level. Militia Training Support Centres were [to be] established and the existing armoured vehicles pooled at them. …… [and] a greater effort [would be] made to integrate Militia personnel, and even sub-units, into Regular units in West Germany.[40]

It took some time to implement this policy but by the early 1990s it was in place and, with some modifications, remains so today.

As usual, however, just as things were looking better for the Canadian army, both regular and militia, Ottawa took two steps back, a retrograde movement caused by financial constraints and a changing international situation. The Mulroney government, re-elected in 1988, experienced difficulties trying to deal with the tremendous deficits that were a hangover from the Trudeau years and therefore began to cut defence spending. At the same time, the United States, having recovered from its Viet Nam troubles, steadily increased its military power throughout the decade by introducing a plethora of high-technology weapons systems. The Soviet Union, with its artificial and weak state-run economy (for more than two decades the Soviets had been unable to feed their own population and had been forced to import food), could not match the American ante and the resultant strain caused Moscow to change its hitherto belligerent international stance and adopt a policy of *glasnost* (openness) to the west, which was shortly followed by *perestroika* (economic and social restructuring) in the Communist Bloc. Once the door was open to reform, however, the shaky Communist house of cards quickly fell apart and the Eastern European nations, no longer held in thrall by Soviet military power, moved swiftly to establish democratic governments while the Soviet Union itself disintegrated into several independent states, the largest of which was Russia. After more than four decades, the Cold War had ended and, for most Canadians, the event that symbolized its end was the dismantling of the Berlin Wall in 1989. This being the case, defence matters moved from the front to the back burner of Ottawa's agenda and since a Canadian government, no matter what party, is always quick to trim its defence budget

at the slightest excuse, military spending was further reduced in the last years of the decade.

During this roller coaster decade, the South Alberta Light Horse soldiered on in Edmonton and Medicine Hat. The stress must be put on the two different cities because, as the commanding officers at RHQ in Medicine Hat quickly learned, they were permitted only limited contact with B Squadron in Edmonton because their Regiment was divided between two militia districts. The respective district commanders, jealous of their own prerogatives, restricted the Light Horse Commanding Officers' authority over their own sub-units. The result was that the SALH existed as two distinct elements, each of which evolved separately, so they must be discussed separately.

"This neat little unit": B Squadron, 1980-1988

By 1980, after its wild, woolly, early days, B Squadron was beginning to settle down. Although it was slated to receive the Cougar and convert from recce to armour, Cougars were in short supply and it was some time before the first arrived in the squadron lines. Trooper Brett Walton, who joined the squadron in 1980, remembered that the squadron had five jeeps, two with .30 calibre machineguns mounted on pintles, and the remainder with the same weapon resting on a sandbag placed on the front passenger's side of the dashboard. "We were basically like Rat Patrollers back them," Walton recalled. "We had a lot of fun in the field but I don't know how much actual planning for our training was done, because it seemed a little haphazard at times."[41] Throughout the first eight years of the decade, the squadron's strength averaged between 45 and 50 but there were continual problems in getting men paid and, like many dedicated militiamen, the members put in many unpaid hours. The squadron could have increased its strength because there was strong interest and support for it in Edmonton, but its numbers were restricted by Ottawa.

Major Bob Caldwell of the Fort Garry Horse, having escaped from a close brush with the Suffield rattlers in 1966, became aware of the presence of a substantial armour community in Edmonton when he was posted to that city in 1982 as a staff officer at North Alberta Militia District. His assigned duties had nothing to do with the armoured corps but Caldwell, a veteran black hat, quickly learned about B Squadron. "When I got there," he remembered,

I found this neat little unit called B Squadron, SALH, so I head straight for it and it is really neat. All I have to do is babysit it. I was never sure whether this thing had ever been authorized by Ottawa but it was certainly all done within Mobile Command. I went out of my way to spend time with them and make sure they were all right.[42]

By the time B Squadron received its first Cougar in late 1981, it had enough personnel qualified in the three Cougar trades – driver, gunner and crew commander – to be able to man the vehicle. It took more than three years, however, before it received three more Cougars to complete its troop of four vehicles and began to form a support troop, or A1 Echelon, to carry out more advanced training at Wainwright. Corporal Dave Bergt never forgot the time when, shortly after the squadron had it full roster of Cougars, some of the younger troopers persuaded him, much against his will, to take the vehicles out into muddy fields behind Griesbach Barracks for "a little proficiency run" after the weekly parade night had ended. Bergt reluctantly led the column of four into the field and promptly got his Cougar bogged. The second vehicle in line, ignoring his frantic hand signals and shouts to stay away, came alongside to help and also bogged as did, in succession, the third and fourth. All attempts to free the Cougars being unavailing, Bergt returned to the armoury to get a 2.5 ton truck to tow them free only for it to get stuck as well. By now, it was approaching midnight and a desperate Bergt, after many entreaties and promises, managed to get a crew from the service battalion to bring a 5-ton wrecker out and free all five Light Horse vehicles. His problems, however, had not yet ended as the Cougars and the truck were coated with thick mud and, as this nocturnal escapade was not authorized, they had to be spotless by the next morning before the RSS (Regular Support Staff) showed up for work. Some of the "boggees" helped him for a little while but, one by one, they slipped away leaving Bergt to finish the job by himself. He kept at it, and when the RSS staff arrived in the morning, they found Bergt sound asleep and five spotless vehicles parked in the squadron lines.

There were no Milcons in 1983 and 1984, funding being diverted to the regulars who, throughout the decade, staged large "Rendezvous" training exercises, nominally involving both regular and militia soldiers. Two of these events, RV 85 and RV 87, were held in Western Canada but the militia discovered that, if their personnel participated, they were often relegated to secondary roles such as the drivers of B Echelon or non-combat vehicles while the regulars took over their F Echelon or fighting vehicles ("thanks very much") and were often slow to return them. Even worse, B Squadron found that if one their vehicles required repair, it had to go to the regular force workshops in Calgary and took a long time to come back. "Due to the breakdown rate of our AVGP (Cougars)," its Annual Historical Report noted in 1986, "the Squadron has not been able to operate to its full capacity."[43] The problem was compounded by the fact that the government, in its infinite wisdom, had not seen fit to purchase a full set of spares for the Cougars and Grizzlies, and thus parts were always in short supply. The regulars got first call on what was available, keeping the militia waiting that much longer to get their vehicles back on the road. By 1989, the annual average VOR (Vehicle Off Road) rate for B Squadron's four Cougars was 42.5% meaning that the vehicles were not available for that percentage of time during that year. Unfortunately the rate would have been about the same, if not worse, for every other militia armoured unit in Canada.

The mechanical condition of the Cougars became of primary concern one evening in November 1988 when two vehicles were returning to Edmonton from a small field exercise they had staged out in the country. Corporal Greg Yanda was driving the lead Cougar and remembered that

It was -20 Fahrenheit and ungodly cold. I was driving the lead vehicle and it ran okay but half the gauges didn't seem to function. We had taken it out anyway because back then so many things were broken on our "Moolisha" vehicles (we would never even get it out of the hangar today). We were almost inside the Edmonton city limits when my warning light came on. I looked to the right at the engine and there was one hell of a lot of white smoke coming out of the cover and so I thought I had an engine fire (my temperature gauge didn't work but I had actually blown my thermostat housing and had no coolant and the engine was heating up very fast). I slowed down and began to pull over.

Corporal Ken Lastiwka was driving the Cougar behind and he followed me but, when he tried his brakes, they didn't work. Ken tried to avoid me by pulling left back onto the road but it was too late and he hit us. Our vehicle was thrown to the right, still going about 20 mph or so and ended up running out of control down into the ditch. My helmet had been ripped off with the impact of the collision and I was flying around inside the hatch and, because of all the bumping along the ditch, I couldn't find the brakes so I finally just stabbed my feet out and managed to hit them.

Overall we had three crew members hurt but not seriously and they went to the hospital. My vehicle was undriveable so everyone went back into town but Ken Anderson and I stayed with my Cougar for five hours in -25 degree weather and we had difficulty keeping warm because without an engine, we had no heat.[44]

The damage amounted to $22,000 and mounds of paperwork followed.

Despite such minor blips, B Squadron continued to evince an interest in its cavalry heritage and in the late 1980s created a mounted Ceremonial Troop which wore the stetson and scarlet tunic with yellow facings of the 15th Light Horse. In this, it was only carrying on the tradition of having ceremonial units available in the provincial capital that the 19th Dragoons had started eight decades before and had continued well into the late 1950s. There was no problem mounting the troop, as almost every Albertan who owns a few hundred square feet of ground outside an urban area (and some inside) seems to keep a few horses grazing on it. It was difficult, however, to keep the troop going as no government money was available, at least not legally, and the squadron paid the troop's expenses out of its own pockets. Unfortunately, the costs became too much for slender purses to bear, and, with regret, the Ceremonial Troop had to be disbanded after a few years.

Although it was, in administrative and operational terms, an independent unit, B Squadron did maintain links with RHQ in Medicine Hat. Both elements of the Light Horse often staged joint exercises at Suffield (notably winter warfare indoctrination)

and sent representatives to each other's ceremonial events while Edmonton officers always made an effort to attend the annual Vimy Dinner held each spring at Patterson Armoury. Light Horse commanding officers at the Hat tried to get up to Edmonton – although the government would rarely fund their travel expenses – as frequently as possible but they were told in no uncertain terms by successive commanders of Northern Militia District, that their authority over a squadron of their own regiment was limited to matters of regimental tradition and ceremony. It was a difficult, if not impossible, situation and the source of continuing frustration for Regimental Headquarters and perhaps it is time to see how the other element of the Light Horse fared during this time.

"It was amazing why these people would put up with all the crap": RHQ and A Squadron, 1980-1988

A militia regiment has an annual cycle. Most units are stood down over the summer but in early September weekly parades commence and the annual training cycle begins, and generally culminates in one or two weekend exercises or gun camps in the autumn. The unit will take a break over the Christmas holidays and then resume its activities in January and the new year, this being the Canadian army after all, usually includes a winter in-doctrination or winter warfare exercise, which can be good or terrible, but usually interesting. Generally, more weekend exercises will be held in the spring and early summer as, typically, a unit has more qualified personnel available in the second half of the annual cycle than in the first and, if nothing more elaborate is on the agenda, the second part will usually include a major gun camp. In June the unit will stand down although its personnel may attend a major exercise, if one is staged by its militia area command. Throughout the year the unit will conduct ceremonial events – participation at a local Remembrance Day Ceremomy is mandatory – and hold its own social events for all personnel.

This was the pattern followed by Regimental Headquarters and A Squadron of the Light Horse throughout the 1980s, a cycle almost as fixed in its course as the stars in theirs. Generally, during this decade, the Regiment's strength was better than it had been in the 1970s – recruits were coming into the SALH who couldn't remember the Vietnam War and social attitudes, as they do, started to change as the public became slightly less anti-military. That is to say that most Canadians, unless they lived in the vicinity of a major military base, more or less forgot their nation even had armed forces. Throughout the 1980s, the strength of RHQ and A Squadron fluctuated between 125 and 150 all ranks, a marked improvement over earlier years. The problem was that not all Light Horse personnel were authorized to receive pay – in 1984 for example, the overall strength was 148 but the payroll only provided for 66 paid positions. No matter. By a little judicious juggling of figures and some creative accounting, the Light Horse managed to get at least some pay for everyone – much less than they were entitled to but still something – although, only too often, resort was made to the traditional militia tactic of parading without pay. Some things never change.

I'm sorry, I'm so sorry...
Trooper Clayton Meilihe regards the doleful result of careless driving as a casualty is removed after being run over by his vehicle at Suffield. Actually, although heavily-bandaged, the man on the stretcher is not hurt at all, this 1987 exercise just featured casualty treatment and evacuation training. Note that Meilihe is wearing the black denim overalls that were still in service in Canadian armoured units. The shape of the Cougar gives an idea why their crews nickname these vehicles "boats." SALH ARCHIVES

The Regiment's 75th Birthday, which came in 1980, was a good year for the Light Horse as it not only celebrated the occasion by means of "a good old fashioned western barbecue with a dance," it also won the Murphy Trophy as the best armoured regiment in Western Canada.[45] In 1982, Lieutenant-Colonel Charles Meagher, who had served as commanding officer for seven years, turned over to Lieutenant-Colonel Brian McKinley, a former officer of the Fort Garry Horse militia regiment in Winnipeg. Bringing in a commanding officer from outside, necessary because of the problems encountered in recruiting officers in the previous decade meant that none of the Light Horse officers presently serving were qualified for command. It did not prove, however, to be a problem as McKinley

knew the Sally Horse because I had had them in the field in a composite squadron in training. It was a nice, tight little organization but it wasn't that hard to run as there was only RHQ and A Squadron. I thought they were a pretty good, little unit, certainly up to par with the Garries, but not a big city unit and that was their problem as they didn't have a big recruiting base. But, shortly after I got to the Hat, the economy in Alberta hit a bad patch and we could get more recruits. The facilities were okay, although we had a shared mess with the warrants and NCOs which was a little different.[46]

In June 1983, with elements of B Squadron participating, the Regiment staged a Roll Past in the Hat to mark the Centennial of the city.

Unfortunately, McKinley's employers transferred him in the autumn of 1984 before his term was completed. As the two officers he was grooming for command, Captains Fraser and CWO Robert McKenzie, were still not fully qualified, he managed to convince Major Brian Moore, a Royal Canadian Dragoon who had served as an RSS officer with the Light Horse from 1981 to 1983 before retiring in Medicine Hat, to again put on uniform and take over the Regiment. Moore recalled the time he first entered Patterson Armoury as a regular officer and his reactions:

My first impression was that these guys must have tremendous dedication to survive under these conditions. They had racked out, crappy old vehicles and everything was done on a shoestring, they got pennies for wages and they were doing any thing they could to keep the darn unit going. I was also very surprised with their persistence because it was amazing to me why these people would put up with all the crap they had to, just to serve. They had a lot of initiative, which isn't that common in the regular force. When I became commanding officer, my object became to keep the Sally Horse alive.[47]

Moore's complaints about "racked out, crappy old vehicles" were entirely warranted. At this time A Squadron's tasking was to provide a 7-car recce troop to the commanding officer of Lord Strathcona's Horse as requested and, over the years, Strathcona commanders had come to like having the Light Horse under command, particularly when they came to Suffield to train as, by this time, the Sally Horse knew that sprawling exercise area like the backs of their hands. There was some resentment that B Squadron, those northern upstarts, were equipped with Cougars but Master Warrant Officer John Bray recalled that, once the members of A Squadron learned about the problems that the Edmonton boys were having in keeping Cougars on the road, "the fellows from the Hat began to think that we had the better of the two vehicles as they spent a lot of their time doing maintenance and we had jeeps and they were simple to maintain and so we had more free time."[48] The problem was that, by this time, the most modern jeep in A Squadron was 12 years old and the vehicles were so worn out that it became difficult for the squadron to keep seven in working order, out of the fifteen or so on strength. Gradually, as the jeeps got more worn, the repairs became more extensive, meaning that they had to be sent to the regular workshops in Calgary where, given the perennial lack of spare parts, they remained unavailable for long periods. As if all this was not bad enough, the regulars hijacked the squadron's jeeps for Rendezvous 85 in that year and, when they finally came back, they were in even worse shape.

For this reason, the SALH rejoiced in 1986 when they received 15 new Iltis vehicles. The Iltis, a Volkswagen design, was a small jeep-like utility vehicle manufactured under licence by Bombardier, a Quebec firm which received the majority of federal government vehicle contracts in the 1970s and 1980s (shades of Sam Hughes and the Ross rifle). The Germans have a reputation for building good vehicles but, this time, something must have got lost in the translation because the Iltis was not nearly as good as the worn-out jeeps it replaced. For one thing, it was too small and Light Horse troopers are often very big so they were cramped. For another, it would not take a pintle mount for a machinegun so crews were forced to fire them from sandbags placed on the dashboard. On top of that, the vehicle was actually intended to be used in Europe where even minor farm lanes are paved and was not suitable for the steppes of Alberta and had a tendency to roll easily. But what really annoyed everyone was that the early models of Iltis came with left and right tires, which had different tread patterns – as Captain Neil Douglas noted, "if you put a left tire on a right wheel, the vehicle became difficult to steer and this meant, on exercise, a recce troop commander had to make sure that there were both left and right spares being carried in the troop, which was yet another thing to worry about."[49] In Mast's phrase, the Light Horse had no choice but to "suck it up" and carry on, which they did – to the extent that at Milcon 86 that summer, they managed to field two 7-car Iltis recce troops and win the RCAC Howard Trophy for the best overall improvement of a militia armoured regiment.

Vehicles were not the only things changing in the mid-1980s, the makeup of the army was undergoing a transformation as women soldiers began to enter the combat arms. Following unification, the number of women in the Canadian Forces markedly increased and they were no longer segregated in the "women's services," which were disbanded, but joined the military mainstream. This trend continued throughout the decade, powered not only by social trends in the civilian world and government policy, but also because the Forces recognized that, with the tendency in the western world toward smaller families, they would shortly be facing competition from the private sector to recruit from a population that would not grow at the same rate it had in the previous three decades. As a result, it would have to offer women a greater role.

The armed forces of most western nations arrived at a similar conclusion and, throughout the 1970s, women personnel in modern armed forces moved from being useful adjuncts to male personnel, to becoming fully-fledged members of their respective services. In the Canadian Forces, more and more trades were opened to women until, by the end of the decade, there were women personnel attached to all branches. Restrictions remained, however, on their employment in combat roles – in the armoured corps, for example, they might train with their units but they were not permitted to go into the field with them, a limitation many women soldiers regarded as being discriminatory. Between 1979 and 1989 the Canadian Forces carried out a series of highly-publicized experiments, the SWINTER (Service Women in Non-Traditional Roles) and CREW (Combat Related Employment of Women). Even before these programmes had been completed, Mobile Command began to post women soldiers into combat roles in both regular and militia units. By the 1990s, the only barrier to women in the combat arms was that they must be able to perform the job and the presence of women soldiers in combat units soon became common and accepted by most of their male comrades.

Over the last two decades much has been written – perhaps too much – on the subject of women in the combat arms and, too often, this extensive literature has focussed on differences rather than similarities. In the South Alberta Light Horse, although the arrival of women soldiers initially caused some difficulties and a number of adjustments, their presence is now completely accepted. As Warrant Officer Brett Walton, a 25-year veteran of the Light Horse, notes, when he joined in 1980,

> the women trained on the same weapons and equipment but felt like they were hard done by because they couldn't go out in the field with the guys. When they were permitted to go into the field, some guys were pretty close minded about it but my feeling was "give them a chance" and the fact is that they have given us refreshing views on a lot of things and we have got some very good troops from this arrangement. Certainly, I don't hear any more complaining from our women soldiers that "we can't come out and play."[50]

Beginning in the 1980s the SALH has adopted a common sense attitude to the employment of women soldiers: when someone wears the pronghorn cap badge, they are a member of the Light Horse and their gender is not important. Light Horse soldiers have tasks to accomplish and they will be judged on how well they accomplish them, and no other criteria – in the words of Major Paul Mast:

> When we started getting women within the troops, we accepted it and got on with it. They were called on to do a job and, if they slacked off on the job, you called them on it and told them that they could not expect special treatment because of their gender.[51]

This straightforward approach has paid dividends, although it would be foolish to deny that there has not been the occasional problem, particularly in the early years. The majority of women soldiers in the Regiment, however, would agree with the sentiments expressed by Master-Corporal Sarah Thompson, a Cougar driver, who is quite clear about the matter:

> I have never had any problems being a woman soldier in an armoured combat trade. We share tents, meals and all facilities with the men. The only real issues I have ever had are with older male soldiers who were in the military before women entered the combat trades because you can tell they are somewhat uncomfortable around women soldiers. They really don't know how to treat us so they end up treating us like we are more fragile than we really are. I can do my job and if I need help doing some of the heavy physical tasks, my crew gives it to me just as I help them when they need it.[52]

That being said, all members of the Light Horse would agree with Master-Corporal's Thompson's conclusion on the matter of women in the military: "If a young woman came to me and asked if she should join the reserves, my response would be: 'Go for it but make sure you join the armoured corps!'"[53]

CHAPTER EIGHTEEN

"There Are Some Things About This Outfit They Didn't Tell Me When I Signed On."

TOWARD A NEW CENTURY, 1988-2004

"A lady had found 'this army gun'":
The Regiment carries on, despite some misadventures

On 19 November 1988, Lieutenant-Colonel Lindsay Fraser assumed command of the South Alberta Light Horse from outgoing Lieutenant-Colonel Brian Moore. A Medicine Hat police officer in civilian life, Fraser had joined the Light Horse as a trooper in 1965 and had been commissioned in the late 1970s. He was the first of a younger generation of officers who had been groomed for command throughout the 1980s by Lieutenant-Colonels Meagher, McKinley and Moore. Fraser's tenure of command, which lasted until 1992, would prove to be an important and interesting period as it witnessed major changes in the organization and training of the militia, the overseas deployment of many Light Horsemen and the beginning of a coming together of the various elements of the Light Horse family.

It was not, however, to be an easy time for Fraser. Shortly after taking over, he ran into trouble when he tried to sort out the confusing command situation with B Squadron in Edmonton by asking the area commander to clarify his relationship with an organization that "wears my cap badge."[2] The result, as Fraser later recalled with some amusement, was that he was paraded before the commander of Southern Alberta Militia District who asked him "what the hell did he think he was doing by going over

> A yellow bird, with a yellow bill,
> Was sitting on my window sill.
> I lured it in, with a piece of bread,
> And then I smashed its effing head.
>
> The prettiest girl you ever saw,
> Was sipping bourbon through a straw.
> I picked her up, I laid her down,
> Her long blonde hair lay all around.
>
> And all I got, is a father-in-law,
> And sixteen kids that call me "paw."
> And all I got, is a mother-in-law,
> And sixteen kids that call me "paw."
>
> The moral of this story is,
> Don't sip your bourbon,
> DRINK YOUR BEER![1]

his [the district commander's] head to the area commander." Fraser's reply – that "he had not bothered to consult Southern District because he already knew what their answer would be" – was not regarded as satisfactory and he received a severe tongue lashing for violating chain of command. Like his predecessors in Medicine Hat, Fraser was frustrated with an inane situation which worked against his regiment's solidarity – he remembered that, for his first three years in command, "there was no authority for me to get travel money at government expense to attend B Squadron functions, I had to pay out of my own pocket."[3] Like his predecessors, he did so but, fortunately, the divide within the Light Horse was not to last much longer.

Fraser also encountered problems with the media. Gone were the golden days of the 1960s when the Light Horse could draft their own press releases and expect to have them printed. By the late 1980s, the Canadian press did not regard their military very favourably – during those rare occasions when they even bothered to notice them – and Fraser learned this bitter truth the hard way in November 1990 when, along with the rest of the militia, the Light Horse began to turn in their FN C1 rifles for the new C-7 weapon, basically a Canadian variant of the American M-16 assault rifle. After Southern District informed the SALH that their issue of C-7s was ready to be picked up at the ordnance stores in Suffield, an RSS NCO attached to the Light Horse sent a trooper, unarmed and without escort, in a ¾ ton truck with a canvas top, to collect them. As he was returning, a box containing a C-7 fell off the vehicle when the trooper encountered the frozen, bumpy surface of an unpaved road leading to Patterson Armoury and landed in the middle of the street. As Fraser remembered the incident:

> I was a police officer in the city of Medicine Hat at the time and when the RSS NCO told me that there was a box with

---

(Facing) **Feeding the cat**

Corporal Brett Walton loads the 76 mm main gun of his Cougar while on exercise in the late 1980s. The interior of a Cougar turret is not only cramped; it contains entirely too many hard, pointed projections that can inflict punishment on the unwary. Walton is wearing the one-piece air force crew suit issued to armoured personnel in the 1980s, which was disliked because it was hot and tight and not fitted with a rear hatch for natural functions. SALH ARCHIVES

MILCON 88
Defence spending, curtailed drastically by the Liberals from 1968 to 1983, was increased in the later 1980s and this permitted more intense levels of training for the militia. Here, B Squadron Cougars participate in Militia Concentration (MILCON) 88 at Wainwright in that year. SALH ARCHIVES

a rifle missing from the truck and he didn't know where it was, I listened on the police radio. When I heard a patrol car being dispatched to a house on a the street just down from the armoury where a lady had found "this army gun" lying in the road, I called the responding officer and gave him a description of the markings on the box and told him if they matched, he should take it over to Patterson Armoury.

He did so and so the weapon was back under our control within a matter of minutes.[4]

So far, so good, but reporters from the *Medicine Hat News* had also been listening to the police radio band and, the following day, contacted Fraser about the incident. It was at this point that he freely admits that he made a fatal error – he allowed the press to take his picture with the C-7 in question lying across his desk in front of him. To Fraser's horror, the syndicates took up the story and, within two days, his photo appeared in most major newspapers across Canada above headlines that varied in their wording, but which were not particularly laudatory to either the Light Horse or the Canadian Forces. It was not the best example of media-military relations, and things did not get any better in the following months.

In 1990 a highly-publicized break-in at an armoury in Quebec occurred, resulting in the theft of military weaponry and equipment. Not unnaturally, considering his own recent experience with weapons control, Fraser decided to hold a nighttime "defence of Patterson Armoury" exercise.[5] He contacted all the relevant municipal authorities, explained what he wished to do, and received permission to go ahead. Exercise FORCE FIELD, carried out on the night of 1-2 December 1990, saw RHQ and A Squadron defend the armoury against a hand-picked "OP FOR" (Opposing Force) dressed completely in black, including black ski masks, and armed with submachineguns. The Sallies really enjoyed themselves on this one, and had great fun chasing each other around the vicinity of the armoury using night vision equipment. Unfortunately, a civilian, unaware of what was going on, attempted to walk his dog through the middle of the melee and was understandably mistaken for a cunningly-camouflaged member of the "OP FOR." Both Rover and his master were quickly surrounded by Light Horsemen armed to the teeth and determined to protect their home turf. Things eventually got sorted out but the irate civilian complained to the mayor, the press, the local radio and TV, and just about anyone else who would listen, that his dog had been "traumatized" by a brutal and uncontrolled soldiery. Things simmered down after the municipal authorities and police came to Fraser's defence by stating that the exercise had received their approval. Regarding these two incidents, the Light Horse Historical Report for

Lunch in the field
Lieutenant Sean Funk uses the hood of an Iltis jeep to eat lunch in the field during MILCON 88. The Iltis, a German-designed but Canadian-manufactured, vehicle replaced the jeep in Canadian service but was not particularly successful in the recce role. Lieutenant Funk is wearing olive green combat dress. SALH ARCHIVES

1990 wryly comments that the "press and local media created a nightmare for [the] CO" but "lessons were learned by the local populace and the Regiment."[6]

To return to more routine matters, both elements of the Light Horse carried out their normal annual cycles, training, field exercise, ceremonial and social events. A cryptic but fascinating reference in the Historical Report for 1989 tells us that Lieutenant-Colonel Fraser and RSM Alex Van Rooyen judged "a drill competition held by Job's Daughters" and were "impressed by the level of competency," but unfortunately adds no further information.[7] RHQ and A Squadron celebrated the 85th Birthday of the Regiment by staging a Roll Past of City Hall in the Hat with Lieutenant Governor Helen Hunley taking the salute. Mrs. Isabel Currie, the widow of Lieutenant-Colonel David Currie, VC, was in attendance and dedicated the newly-named Currie Park beside Patterson Armoury. These celebrations were concluded by a military ball attended by more than 300 persons. In Edmonton, B Squadron founded an annual Cavalry Dinner in 1989, their counterpart to the Vimy Dinner, and officers from Edmonton and Medicine Hat tried their best to attend both functions. The Cavalry Dinner is a popular event and, over the fifteen years it has been run, the guest speakers have included prominent British and Canadian soldiers, journalists and diplomats.

Training suffered somewhat in the late 1980s and early 1990s as the Conservative government, faced with a massive deficit

They also serve who only wait
Corporal John Hare monitors the radio at the firing point during a B Squadron range exercise at Wainwright on a very cold day in March 1992. SALH ARCHIVES

and encouraged by the end of the Cold War in Europe, began to cut defence expenditures. B Squadron kept encountering problems keeping their Cougars on the road – the Cougar VOR rate in 1990 was a terrible 88%, meaning that the squadron only had the vehicles available for just over one of every ten days in the year. A Milcon attended by both A and B Squadron was held in 1989 but the big exercise in these years was ON GUARD 90 in July 1990. This was one of a series of ON GUARD exercises staged across Canada in an attempt by the regular forces to revitalize the militia and were carried out by militia brigades augmented by regular troops. In the western ON GUARD, armoured regiments from Saskatchewan, Alberta and British Columbia formed a two-squadron Cougar regiment. One squadron, commanded by Major Brian Hodgson of the SALH, was composed of personnel from the Light Horse, the KOCR, the BCDs and Saskatchewan Dragoons, the other was largely formed by regular crews from the Strathconas. Lieutenant-Colonel Fraser commanded this composite unit which also included a recce troop in Iltis vehicles and a company of infantry. He remembered it as being a "combined arms" exercise that was "awesome" and the high point of his military career.[8] Unfortunately, it was the first and last of these exercises to be staged. Two months later, Northern and Southern Militia Districts were amalgamated to form a single Alberta Militia District within the newly-established Land Forces Western Area with headquarters at Calgary, thus finally re-uniting the two components of the SALH after twelve years of frustrating separation. This change would take some time to implement and, in the meantime, tragedy struck the Regiment.

Just one of Mother's favourite recipes
From left to right, Lieutenant Ian Douglas, Lieutenant Ray Hogard, Captain Graham Skjenna and MWO Jim Ogston serve a hot meal in the range shack at Range 16 in Wainwright during a gun camp in the early 1990s. Douglas is wearing the combat shirt, Hogard a combat jacket over his combat shirt, while Ogston wears the one-piece cloth armoured crew overall. The rations and the servers look suspect enough but the sign on the wall is enough to put anyone off their feed. On the other hand, if you can't take a joke.... SALH ARCHIVES

"The first casualty the Regiment suffered since the war": The death of Trooper James Leckie, 1991

On the weekend of 20 April 1991, B Squadron of the Light Horse held a Cougar gun camp at Wainwright. This exercise, which took place at Range 16 on Jeep Hill, was successfully completed by late afternoon and Sergeant David Bergt led a work party, comprising Master-Corporal Greg Yanda, Corporal Chuck Howie and Trooper James Leckie, onto Range 16 to "de-target" it – to tear down the targets that had been erected for the exercise. This range had been used for mortar practice by both armoured and infantry units during the previous year and, knowing this, Bergt's party was careful to watch where they stepped and to avoid any fins or pieces of fins on the ground, as it was not unknown for unexploded projectiles to be present. At the range the party divided into two pairs – Howie and Leckie, Bergt and Yanda – and set to work taking down the targets, and tossing the angle irons that supported them into piles located in safe areas clear of fins.

At 5.10 P.M., an explosion occurred near the target where Howie and Leckie were working. Master-Corporal Yanda, who was about 20 feet away, at first thought "that someone had thrown a "Thunderflash" [a noise grenade] and my ears were ringing but I saw this giant column of smoke" obscuring Howie and Leckie.[9] Then, to Yanda's horror,

> Chuck Howie came running out of the smoke and I could see that his hand was badly injured so I removed my combat shirt and T-shirt and wrapped the latter around his hand. It was only then I saw that he had abdominal wounds so I took my combat shirt and wrapped that around his stomach and put pressure on it.[10]

Bergt, meanwhile, went into the smoke to look for Leckie and, when he found him, it was clear that Leckie had caught the full force of the explosion. The unconscious trooper was very badly cut up in his chest, face and throat and Bergt did what he could to staunch the extensive bleeding, cradled the young man in his arms and told him: "Hold on, buddy, hold on."[11]

Fortunately, Sergeant H. Hauschildt from Medicine Hat was close by Bergt's party when the explosion occurred. Guessing what had happened, he drove back to the firing point in record time and, in Yanda's words, "hit the brakes and skidded into a 180 degree turn, jumped out yelling for the medic."[12] Corporal Bill Swift of 15 Medical Company drove immediately to the scene in an Iltis ambulance. Swift tended first to the unconscious Leckie but, tragically, his wounds were too severe and he died within a few minutes. Swift then turned to Howie, who was seriously wounded. As Howie recalled:

> I lost fingers, teeth and had two puncture wounds in my stomach. They determined it was an 81 mm mortar round from the lot number engraved on the driving band they took out of my abdomen. I know exactly what time the incident took place because my watch stopped at precisely 5.10 P.M. that day.[13]

Howie, who had been hit by more than 200 fragments of shrapnel, was to spend considerable time in hospital but eventually made a full recovery. It was only after he was placed in an ambulance that Bergt and Yanda realized just how close they themselves had come – Yanda discovered that he had been hit in the hand by a fragment while Bergt found that his boot had been cut open by another fragment.

A subsequent investigation of the incident concluded that, during a mortar practice held the previous year, an 81 mm round had buried itself on Range 16 without exploding and had not been discovered by the infantry when they cleared the range after their shoot. In the following spring, rain and melting snow had thinned out much of the earth cover above the round and it detonated after being struck or jarred by a piece of target iron. As a result of this investigation, major changes were made to range safety procedures.

Trooper James Lee Leckie was a married 25-year-old medical technician who had only been with the Light Horse a few months when he was killed. Major Brian Hodgson, commanding B Squadron, and SSM John Szram paid the necessary but painful official call on the Leckie family to inform them of the death of their son and it was a duty Major Hodgson never forgot:

> Sergeant-Major Szram and I wore service dress. We spoke little on the drive to the Leckie residence. It was a cool, dull day. After introductions to members of the family, mother, father, his young widow and a brother, I explained the circumstances of Trooper Leckie's death. It was one of the most difficult tasks that I have had to do in my service life. Mere words seemed inadequate and far less than he deserved. There was no anger; only sorrow and this made the grief all the more intense. At the time, I recall thinking what it must have been like for those officers who so often in war, had to carry out much the same sad task. The family were resolute and incredibly stoic despite the tears. I came away feeling a greater loss having gained a fuller appreciation as to the quality and sterling character of this fine young man.
>
> After dropping off SSM Szram, I stopped at my parents' house and unburdened myself to my father who sensibly gave me a large dram of Scotch but his best intentions had slight effect. And this is as it should be for the death of soldier, however caused, warrants more than a transitory thought and a drink. I still think of Trooper Leckie as I do about every soldier that I have known who has been killed whether on operational service, training or by any misfortune.[14]

The Light Horse gave Trooper James Leckie a full military funeral at which, Major Hodgson remembered, "we had nearly every soldier in the squadron there as well as many from RHQ and A Squadron in Medicine Hat and from many other units. It was a very emotional day for us."[15] As the squadron Historical Report for 1991 stated, Trooper James Leckie was "the first casualty the Regiment suffered since the war."[16] This young man is remembered today by a B Squadron trophy and, as it is right that it should be, his name has been included on the Roll of Honour of those soldiers of the Light Horse and its predecessor units who have died in the service of their country.

"We think a lot about our connections": The Regimental family draws together

The death of Trooper Leckie was a sad event in the recent history of the South Alberta Light Horse but there were also positive happenings. The late 1980s and early 1990s witnessed a "coming together" of the various elements of the Regimental family. During Lieutenant-Colonels Moore and Fraser's terms of command, an attempt was made to renew links with the SAR Veteran's Association, which itself was becoming more active as its members reached retirement age and had more time to devote to their old comrades. Much of the responsibility for this new development was due to the efforts of the honorary colonels and lieutenant-colonels. In 1983, Harry Quarton, ex-SAR and 19th Dragoons, became Honorary Lieutenant-Colonel of the Light Horse, with the specific function of looking after the interests of B Squadron. Two years later, when Bud Olson stepped down, Alan Graham, a Calgary businessman, became Honorary Colonel of the Regiment. Harry Quarton and Major Brian Hodgson, commanding B Squadron, were instrumental in creating an organization, "The Friends of the South Alberta Light Horse," to oversee the long-term future of the Regiment, and brought several prominent Albertans –among them Edmonton oil executive Stanley Milner, brother of Sergeant Tom Milner, DCM, of the SAR – into the Light Horse family. Stan Milner succeeded Harry Quarton as Honorary Lieutenant-Colonel in 1988 and, shortly afterward, the South Alberta Light Horse Foundation – whose activities will be discussed below – was created.

A determined effort was also made to affirm the link between the Light Horse and the South Alberta Regiment, its distinguished wartime predecessor, a relationship that had not been as strong as it might have been. It became the custom for Light Horse commanding officers and RSMs to attend, if possible, the annual reunions of the SAR veterans and in 1990, when Lieutenant-Colonel Fraser was present at the SAR reunion in Edmonton, a plan was conceived to hold a joint SAR/SALH battlefield tour in Europe. Honorary Colonel Graham was prominent in the fundraising for this tour which took place in the autumn of 1992. Lieutenant-Colonel Fraser and ten members of the SALH accompanied the SAR veterans on a three-week pilgrimage to those far-off places with names familiar to the younger Light Horse soldiers from the Battle Honours on their Guidon – St. Lambert, Moerbrugge, Bergen-op-Zoom, the Hochwald and all the rest. During this journey, the South Alberta veterans, thus encouraged, conceived three further projects: the publication of their wartime history, the marking of their battlefields with memorial plaques; and the procurement of their Regimental Colour.

The bonds that form between soldiers who have fought together are very close and the comradeship that results does not readily admit strangers into its midst. It would be wrong to claim that relations between the modern Light Horse and the wartime South Albertas have always been easy, but from the 1992 tour onward, there has been a gradual strengthening of ties. To the Light Horse, their relationship with the wartime SAR is an important one as, though they have a number of distinguished predecessors, they take special pride in this particular link. As Captain Sean Thirlwell explains:

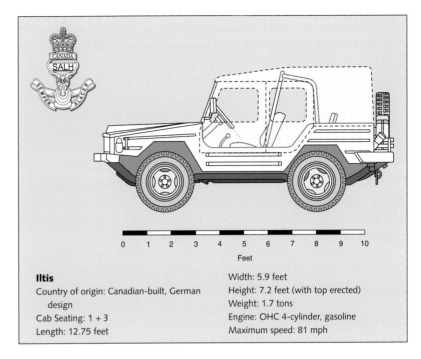

Iltis
Country of origin: Canadian-built, German design
Cab Seating: 1 + 3
Length: 12.75 feet

Width: 5.9 feet
Height: 7.2 feet (with top erected)
Weight: 1.7 tons
Engine: OHC 4-cylinder, gasoline
Maximum speed: 81 mph

We think a lot about our connections with the SAR. In our lines we have the Sergeant Tom Milner, DCM, room with pictures and displays relating to the South Albertas and their deeds in the Second World War and every member of the Sally Horse knows and is very proud of the SAR and their accomplishments. We have a very lengthy heritage but the South Albertas are to us perhaps the most important of our predecessor units as – and this is not to take away from our other predecessors who were also fine soldiers – we are an armoured regiment and the wartime SAR form the armoured part of our heritage and are the ancestor unit we talk most about.[17]

The elimination of the two separate militia districts in Alberta also meant that the Light Horse itself came closer together, particularly after 1992 when the operational tasking of the Regiment was changed. Prior to this time, A Squadron in Medicine Hat had trained to provide two recce troops equipped with Iltis vehicles while B Squadron in Edmonton had the responsibility of providing a Cougar troop, with RHQ in the Hat providing elements of a squadron headquarters. Now the Regiment was tasked with providing three Cougar troops and elements of a squadron headquarters, as well as first line echelon detachments. Overall, this meant that A Squadron would have to retrain on the Cougar and, in future, both squadrons would work closely together in the field under the control of RHQ. It took some time for this change of tasking to be accomplished and at first, there was not a little friction between two squadrons that had existed separately for so long.

This was inevitable because, without putting too fine a point on it, neither squadron entirely liked the other. The Light Horsemen from the Hat were naturally suspicious of the Edmonton squadron because it is established wisdom in southern Alberta that the provincial capital is full of liars, thieves and politicians.

On the other side, the sophisticates from the big city were somewhat scornful of their red-necked, rube cousins from southern cow country. What made it worse was that both squadrons drew on a different heritage – many senior members of A Squadron had joined the Light Horse during its glory days of the 1960s when it was one of the largest and best militia armoured regiments in Canada. B Squadron, on the other hand, drew heavily on the "Make It Happen" culture that evolved during the crazy days of the "Magnificent Seven" in the late 1970s and early 1980s. Both squadrons were proud and, as a result, some people remained a bit stiff with each other for quite some time – as Major Hodgson of B Squadron remarked, "the problem was always between individuals, not between the squadrons."[18]

There is an old Arab saying, "My brother and I against my cousin, my cousin and I against the world," which can aptly be applied to the Light Horse in the early 1990s. Whereas neither A nor B squadron would admit the other was its equal, both were determined that no outsiders from any other unit would be permitted to think that they were, in any way, shape or form, superior to the the South Alberta Light Horse. As the squadrons began to work together on a more frequent basis, they came to know and respect each other – and, ultimately, to like each other. As Captain Troy Steele of B Squadron, a card-carrying member of the "Magnificent Seven," puts it:

When we first came together, it was a bit of a problem because the two squadrons were different; they came from very different cities, from very different parts of the province. But we quickly learned that the Hat people have a tremendous group of skills that we didn't have and they learned that we had similar attributes. We were very different people and, before the elimination of the two militia districts, it was a tough because the unit was kept from coming together and the net effect was that B Squadron had evolved into an independent unit. It took some time for us to mesh well with A Squadron but not that long, and certainly now we are all Sally Horse.[19]

These sentiments are echoed by Lieutenant Greg Yanda:

In the early years there sure was a lot of rivalry. They didn't like us and we didn't like them. Once we started to train together, that lessened but, let's face it, there will always be some rivalry, always, but it actually can be a good thing. The point is that, when we go into the field now, the two squadrons integrate to form the field squadron and we don't think of each of other as being A or B Squadron but just plain Light Horse.[20]

The unification of the Regiment in the early 1990s could not have come at a better time because, in that decade, the world became a much more dangerous place.

"We were pretty scared": The Light Horse overseas, 1992-2004

The collapse of the Soviet Union ended the threat of nuclear holocaust but did not lead, as many expected, to a new era of global peace. Instead, it created an instability that gave rise to an entirely new set of international problems. As one historian succinctly puts it:

The Cold War had had a dampening effect on local, regional, and ethnic conflicts outside of the NATO area since both sides realized that sparks on the periphery could lead to conflagrations in Europe with nuclear consequences. This *status quo* no longer applied, however, and suddenly smouldering hot spots in Africa, the Middle East and the Balkans began to burst forth in waves of mass savagery. New phrases like "ethnic cleansing" entered the vocabulary. The immediacy of satellite-transmitted TV news beamed the viciousness right into the living rooms of the West, which, in turn, prompted cries to "Do something, do anything!"[21]

Canada, along with the rest of the western world, was caught off guard by this unforeseen development. For the army, the result was a period of crisis and turmoil, particularly after the election of Jean Chrétien's Liberal government in 1993, as the Liberals, while cutting its budget, also deployed more soldiers overseas than in three previous decades of peacekeeping operations. The deployments of the 1990s were a far cry from the traditional UN assignments that Canadian troops had been undertaking since 1956 and they would become involved in their first sustained combat since the Korean War. Stretched to the breaking point, the regular force turned to the militia to augment its strength and, as a result, members of the Light Horse began to serve overseas.

Attachments to regular units were nothing new for the Light Horse. The Regiment had occasionally sent members to serve briefly with the NATO brigade in Germany in the 1970s and it was normal for members to serve on "call outs" with regular units in Canada, usually in the summer. As far as can be ascertained, the first Lighthorsemen to be deployed on a UN mission were Corporal Alex Symington and Trooper Ray Gradwell who served with the Royal Canadian Dragoons in Germany before doing a six-month deployment with the Canadian component of the UN Peacekeeping Force in Egypt in 1975-1976. Beginning in 1988 and continuing until Canadian troops withdrew from the island, a number of Light Horsemen served with Operation SNOW GOOSE rotations to the Canadian Peacekeeping Force in Cyprus, one of the largest Canadian UN responsibilities in the 1970s and 1980s. Egypt and Cyprus were fairly stable and the members of the Regiment who served with the UN in these places, reported their tours as being fairly quiet. In 1992, however, Canada became involved in the Balkans, a region that was anything but quiet.

In 1991, the former Communist nation of Yugoslavia disintegrated along ethnic, linguistic and religious lines into a number of small, mutually hostile, nations which engaged in a series of conflicts that, fuelled by six centuries of hatred, were marked by brutality, viciousness and bloodshed. In the spring of 1992, Canadian troops from the NATO brigade at Lahr in Germany, a base that was in the process of being shut down, were included in UNPROFOR (United Nations Protection Force) with the object of protecting four Serbian enclaves in Croatia from being "ethnically cleansed" by the Croats. This was the beginning of a Canadian commitment in the Balkans which continues to this day. It soon became obvious that a deployment in this region was quite unlike previous peacekeeping missions – none of the warring peoples were inclined to listen to reason and, ironically, they were often much better armed than the UN or NATO forces sent to keep peace in the region. From the outset of the UNPROFOR mission, Canadian troops were fired upon and, for self-preservation, forced to return fire as, although the Canadian public was blissfully unaware of it, a war was taking place in the Balkans.

Many Light Horse members have served in Balkans since 1992 – one soldier, for example, has completed three deployments to that area as well as one to Haiti in the past decade – and their experiences have varied. Among the first to go over were Master-Corporal Greg Yanda and Corporal Chuck Howie of the Light Horse, who were members of a battlegroup formed around the 2nd Battalion, PPCLI, that was mobilized for a Balkan deployment in the winter of 1992-1993. This unit, which had given up one of its rifle companies to fill out the deployment of its sister 3rd Battalion in the previous year, was ordered to conduct a test of the "Total Force" concept, or the augmentation of a regular unit with reservists. More than 700 militia volunteers from across Canada travelled to the 2 PPCLI base in Winnipeg to be tested in their military skills. Howie, who had just recovered from the wounds suffered during the fatal range accident the previous year, recalled that he decided to join because "I was looking for something and attracted by the intrigue of going to a continent I had read about and I thought it would be interesting and I could help."[22] Yanda, who had left his civilian job to take part, noted the risks involved for militia personnel: "You give up everything you have, with no guarantee you are going to go. If you give up a good job, you have problems if you don't make it onto the deployment."[23] Three hundred of the militia augmentees were found wanting and sent home as the standards were high. In Howie and Yanda's group of 50 western Canadian militiamen, only four were retained, among them Howie and Yanda, who became, respectively, weapons detachment commanders in Alpha and Delta Companies of 2 PPCLI. Howie remembered that when "we started pre-training there were some problems with the regulars as they didn't know us" but once "we could show that we were up to the job, there were no problems and we were just part of the platoon although I retained my SALH badge and flashes."[24] The good news was, that it being winter in Canada, the battalion carried out its preliminary

Master-Corporal Greg Yanda, Medak Pocket, September 1993
In the summer of 1993, as part of UN-PROFOR, the 2nd Battalion, Princess Patricia's Canadian Light Infantry, deployed in the Medak Pocket in Croatia. The battalion quickly realized that they had entered a very hot area and, over the course of a three month deployment, engaged in some of the heaviest fighting Canadian troops have experienced since the Korean War. Master-Corporal Yanda of the Light Horse was on deployment with the 2nd Battalion, PPCLI, and appears here wearing a flak vest over his combat shirt and pants and an American kevlar helmet painted UN blue. Yanda is armed with a C-7 assault rifle, the Canadian version of the American M-16, which replaced the FN C1 in Canadian service in the late 1980s. COURTESY, GREG YANDA

training at an American base in California and then, in April 1993, crossed the Atlantic.

The first three months of 2 PPCLI's employment were spent in a relatively quiet area of Croatia called Sector West. In late June, however, the battalion deployed to a new area, known to UN Forces as Sector South, but to the troops as the Medak Pocket because it was a sliver of Croatia, centred around the town of Medak and almost surrounded by Bosnian and Serb territory. The Medak Pocket, as Yanda recalled,

was a free-fire zone and the three months I spent there were hot. We were pretty scared and Delta Company was up front all the time and my job was to make sure the heavy weapons were where the company commander wanted them to be. We had to deal with a fair amount of sniping and shelling, both mortars and artillery – I think they just did it for fun. We were building a big, red earth bunker and we had to work at night because they would shell us during the day but we eventually abandoned the thing because it seemed to draw fire. They were using 105 mm guns, sometimes lighter rounds, possibly 76 mm light artillery. Basically we slept beside our vehicles or in our vehicles, in our clothes, because the threat level was always high. The plan was that, if something happened, you got in the tracks [M-113 APCs] and drove away. At nighttime we would sit and watch the tracers going by in the sky. During the day, they would fire random shots at us when we were driving, again probably just trying to have some fun, and we would drive away from it.[25]

On several occasions, 2 PPCLI returned fire in self-defence, particularly against Croatian forces engaged in the "ethnic cleansing" or mass murder of Serbian civilians around their positions. The Princess Pats did what they could but they were nearly powerless, under the restrictions placed on them by the UN authorities, to stop this awful activity. The worst time was September 1993 when, in four particularly heavy days of fighting that month, it has been estimated that 2 PPCLI killed or wounded more than two dozen Croatian soldiers in what was the most sustained combat experienced by Canadian soldiers since the Korean War. Howie of Alpha Company remembered the Medak:

Our primary function was to man a checkpoint or OP called Whisky Charlie 8, the closest point within the ceasefire line where the Serbs and the Croats came together. It was a major crossover point between the two sides so we would handle everything from UN traffic to common traffic, we would provide overwatch in our area for families divided by the war to get together, to have reunions. We were billeted in Pakrac where we lived in the town hospital, which had been bombed out. We had our own platoon mess and kitchen because we were isolated.

The situation was partially tense, but you could always tell if something was going to go down because the locals would keep their kids off the streets because they had been prewarned. We had a lot of sniping and, one night, we had to do a clear sweep of the hospital complex. After that, we put up trip wires with early warning devices so that we had some "heads up" time. One of our sergeants lost his leg on a booby trap in early May 1993 but, overall, our relations with the civilians were good because the average person didn't want anything to do with the war. We bought locally and we did

Job well done
Lieutenant-General Rick Hillier, appointed Chief of the Defence Staff in January 2005, presents Corporal Ryan Ogston with the NATO medal for Bosnian service at a ceremony held at Patterson Armoury in 2001. Ogston is one of many Light Horsemen who have served in overseas deployments in the last two decades. Two British soldiers, wearing that army's camouflage uniform, are also receiving this medal. Corporal Ogston is wearing combat dress which will be replaced, within a few months, by CADPAT camouflage clothing. SALH ARCHIVES

the usual things like giving candies to the kids and that cemented good relations.

My closest call came one night when we spotted a Croatian sniper firing bursts from near our position into Serbian territory. We cornered him in some rose bushes and surrounded him but he pulled a fragmentation grenade out of his pocket at which point I pulled my Browning 9 mm and pointed it at his head. It was a stand-off but in the end it worked out – but I was surely scared at the time.[26]

After getting through their tours, both Light Horsemen experienced the letdown common to Canadian soldiers who served in the Balkans when they returned home to a country which didn't seem to know about, or even be concerned about the terrible things that were taking place in that blighted region. As Yanda recalls:

You know they told us that when we came back to Canada, that "nobody would care" and they were absolutely right, nobody cared. But I was indestructible at that time (or at least I thought I was) although now I know that I am not indestructible.[27]

This was only the beginning. In September 1993, Trooper Jason Watt volunteered as part of a militia augmentation to the Strathconas who were deployed to Bosnia the following spring. Watt served as a Cougar driver since the army, strained to its limits, was forced to employ this thinly-armoured training vehicle in the Balkans. Watt spent six months with the Strathconas in and around the town of Visoko and saw a fair amount of action, taking and returning fire and trying to protect Bosnians from Serbs and Serbs from Bosnians. To their chagrin, as they did not have the weaponry to do it, the Strathconas were forced to watch one day as a Danish Leopard squadron destroyed five Serbian tanks in an engagement near their positions. As Watt remembers his tour:

It was an exciting time because there was a shooting war on at the time and you got to see perhaps why you joined the army. We manned the OP line for two months, a little bit back from the opposing positions. It would get interesting at night – depending on how much alcohol the locals had consumed. You might get rounds through the UN flag flying over your head. During the last four months we rotated between the OP line and camp security. On the other hand, for me, it was a chance to travel and see the world – I went to London for two weeks on leave.[28]

Watt returned to Bosnia with the Strathconas in 1996-1997 and went back yet again with the 1st Battalion of the PPCLI in 2002-2003. Having been commissioned in the meantime, he served on this latter deployment in a CIMIC (Civil-Military Cooperation) detachment which he defines as being sort of a "sales

CIMIC officers in Haiti, spring 2003

In the spring of 2003, the 2nd Battalion, Royal Canadian Regiment, deployed as part of a UN Force to strife-torn Haiti to provide political stabilization. Captain Jason Watt of the Light Horse served in the CIMIC (Civil-Military Co-operation) detachment attached to this unit and is seen discussing local problems with civilian leaders in Port-au-Prince. From left to right: unknown Haitian civilian; Captain J.R. Watt, SALH; Master-Corporal Reginald Obas; Mr. Patrick Souffrance of Haiti; and Captain Shawn Courty. The soldiers are wearing the new CADPAT (Canadian Army Disruptive Pattern) camouflage uniforms, based on the design of the combat dress that preceded them, and field hats, politely called a "bush hat" but rudely called many other things. COURTESY, JASON WATT

rep for the military, you sell the army and you ensure that the activities of the military overlap as much as possible with what the international [UN and relief agencies] community wants."[29] His duties primarily involved being an information officer for his battalion group and communicating messages that the group wanted transmitted to local organizations, community and religious leaders. CIMIC personnel often become involved in helping people in distress and their duties are far from the military norm. As Corporal Sean MacIntyre of the Light Horse, who served with Watt in the CIMIC detachment of 1 PPCLI in Bosnia, notes:

Having served for five years before I went overseas I was a highly trained soldier. Highly trained for war, that is. What I found and all other "peacekeepers" like me found on these tours is that the situations we had trained for, did nothing to prepare us for what we found over there. How would doing section attacks till you can hardly walk, prepare you for helping a blind old widow light her stove to keep her invalid son from freezing through the night? How does perfecting an armoured "advance to contact" prepare you for helping an old one-armed man bury his dead brother? This is the 21st century "Canadian war story." We are too often left to clean up the destruction other nations reduce themselves to.[30]

Captain Watt was only back in Canada for five days after his 2003 Bosnian deployment when he went out on an emergency CIMIC deployment with 2nd Battalion, Royal Canadian Regiment, to strife-torn Haiti in March of that year. His description of this tour illustrates the non-combat roles that Canadian troops carry out overseas:

The situation in Haiti was deplorable. This little country has the highest levels of poverty, early death, AIDs and illiteracy in the western hemisphere. A corrupt government had taken some US $800 million from this backward nation and we went into Haiti to establish a safe and secure environment and to establish the conditions under which humanitarian

assistance could be delivered by the UN and other international relief agencies. Security was restored very quickly but there were a few shooting incidents early in the deployment, mainly on American patrols. In each case, the Americans responded aggressively and decisively and attacks on foreign troops quickly came to an end. There was still some lawlessness in the outlying areas as the multi-national military force was too small to impose order on a mountainous country such as Haiti but we were able to render the large population centres safe and secure in a few months.

I served in Port-au-Prince and our efforts in CIMIC focused on assessing the area and its problems – getting an understanding, for example, of how many children were going to school because armed gangs threatened parents who sent their children to school, in the hopes that they could intimidate them and shut the country down. Once we were on the ground, however, this sort of activity became much less common.

We then looked for ways we could clean up the garbage and sewage situation in a city of two million people where sanitation was completely lacking. Using locally-contracted equipment, we began to remove rotting garbage from the streets where it posed the greatest health risk and, after a few weeks of watching us, the Haitians began to do it themselves. Garbage, I learned on this deployment, produces 17 different and distinct odours depending on its organic content, how long it has been left out, its mixture with water, its mixture with human waste, and its exposure to sun.[31]

By 1996, ten members of the Light Horse had served in the Balkans and this activity has continued up to the present day. There were twelve soldiers on ROTO 12 (Rotation 12) in 2002-2003 and two on ROTO 13 in 2003-2004 and, at the date of writing (November 2004), there are three members of the SALH serving overseas including Lieutenant-Colonel Brian Hodgson (who commanded the SALH in 1996-2000) with the international force in Kabul, Afghanistan. Hodgson contributes the following comments on the situation in that battle-scarred nation:

Kabul is relatively quiet, compared to the rest of Afghanistan despite the fact that we have had a few rocket attacks and a car bomb down the street (which interrupted my dinner). The people here appreciate what the ISAF forces are doing in terms of providing stability, a stability they have not had in 25 years or more. They don't want us to be here forever but they appreciate the fact that they do not have to be concerned with wild events and atrocities being perpetrated.[32]

As Light Horse personnel overseas always retain their regimental identity, the pronghorn cap badge is now seen around the globe. Perhaps more importantly, the Light Horse soldiers who have participated in the overseas deployments of the last thirteen years, are learning new skills which they have brought back to the Regiment. As Warrant Officer Chuck Howie notes, his time in the Medak Pocket

taught me a lot of soldiering skills that I never would have got any other way because I found 2 PPCLI to be very professional. I have brought those skills back to the SALH, skills such as weapons and dismounted training, weapons effects, and how to employ heavy weapons. I learned new weapons systems and how to deploy them and, since the Medak was a learning experience for the army, we were doing new things that have since become standard doctrine.

Looking back on it, I realize it was one of the major turning points in my life. I learned more in that six months in Croatia than in any other six-month period of my life. I grew up really fast.[33]

The knowledge gained on these attachments to the regulars is important for the future because, in the last decade or so, the training and role of the militia – and its relation to the regular army – has undergone a major shift. It is now time to take up again the main story of the Light Horse.

"It makes people jump through the proper hoops": The mid-1990s

In September 1993, Lieutenant-Colonel Lindsay Fraser turned over command to Lieutenant-Colonel Robert B. McKenzie. A teacher in civilian life, McKenzie had enlisted as a trooper in the Light Horse in 1966 and served three terms as RSM before being commissioned. The second of the two future regimental commanders that Meagher, McKinley and Moore had groomed during the 1980s, McKenzie also had a family connection with the Regiment. His father, Lieutenant-Colonel Bruce McKenzie, DSO, ED, who had served in the prewar South Alberta Regiment and the wartime Calgary Highlanders, had been the last commanding officer of the SAR before the amalgamation that created the SALH in 1954. Such pedigrees are not uncommon in the Light Horse – during much of his tenure in command, McKenzie's RSM was John Bray, the great-grandson of John Gresham Bray who had held the same appointment with the Rocky Mountain Rangers in 1885.

McKenzie's command period, which lasted until 1996, witnessed some important changes. In 1992, the Light Horse's operational tasking had been significantly changed to providing three Cougar troops and elements of a squadron headquarters. This meant that A Squadron in Medicine Hat had to be retrained to take over armoured vehicles and, toward this end, four Cougars arrived at Patterson Armoury in 1993 so that the squadron could get to work. Such was the hard effort put in, not just by A Squadron but by the entire regiment, that by 1995, A Squadron was completely retrained and the Light Horse were able to field four troops of Cougars, a squadron headquarters and elements of an A1 and A2 Echelon which permitted the Regiment to re-supply itself in the field, without depending on outside resources. At first, the unit's eight Cougars were located at Griesbach Barracks in Edmonton and Patterson Armoury in the Hat but, when the creation of Land Forces Western Area in 1991 led to Wainwright being established as the Western Area Training Centre (WATC), a Militia Training Support Centre (MTSC) was organized at that base to maintain a general pool of the western armoured units' stock of Cougars, about 40 vehicles. The MTSC was not fully operational until the autumn of 1994 and, at first, units had some problems accessing their vehicles. McKenzie remembered that it seemed that, any time the Light Horse needed the Cougars, "it took tremendous amounts of paper work and effort" but, as the start up problems at the MTSC were gradually worked out, he recalled that, in the last year of his command, the assistance provided by that organization was "exceptional."[34] This was one of the changes prompted by the increasing use of militia personnel to augment the regular force, both in Canada and abroad, as the "Total Force" concept gradually became a reality.

Training methods also changed. Now, when the Light Horse went into the field at Wainwright, they had to pass "Gateway" testing, which checked their basic vehicle and tactical skills and made sure that all personnel were up to the required professional level before they were let out to play. Training exercises became more realistic and the testing became more rigorous as the Light Horse, along with other militia armoured regiments, were gradually brought up to regular force standards. Warrant Officer Chuck Howie summarizes these innovations:

There's operational experience filtering down to the unit both from the regulars and from our people serving overseas. The way the training is formatted now, especially through the MTSC which was created in 1994, is much better. In the past, each unit was left to their own devices and, in a nutshell, it was too often just a bunch of dummies dressing up like soldiers and going out and blowing off some blanks, then coming home and telling war stories. The MTSC is structured that, right from the commanding officer down, they are assessed by the professionals and they have to go through certain "Gateways" in order to carry on to the next phase, so it makes people jump through the proper hoops.[35]

Troy Steele and Shawn Thirlwell, who had served as enlisted personnel in the Light Horse in the 1980s before leaving to pursue their education, were amazed by the changes they found when they returned in the 1990s. As Steele describes it:

When I returned in 1992, things had altered significantly, the leadership, attitudes and requirements of the Militia had changed substantially. We took a more professional standard when training with the regulars as we worked more and more with them, and as we did not want to look like the knobs, their country cousins, so our officers really tightened things up. We were now "in the game," so to speak, and we began to act like it.[36]

Thirlwell agrees:

When I first joined in the 1970s, you got one set of combats, one set of boots and that was it. If you wanted winter clothing, you only got that on a winter indoctrination course. When I came back to the regiment in 1995, it was part of a professional army and we received the needed kit. Before, the Militia only too often acted like an extension of the cadets. Now we have a very professional infrastructure with professional leadership at all levels and the equipment is there.[37]

As usual, however, just as things appeared to be going well for the militia, Ottawa dropped the ball. There had been fiscal restraint in the last years of the Conservative government which ended in 1993, but when the Liberals under Prime Minister Jean Chrétien took office that year, they initiated a major cost-cutting programme that had such an adverse effect on the Canadian Forces that they have not, to this day, fully recovered. The militia suffered the worst and, although the organization and the equipment was there, their personnel and training budgets were cut back. In some years, even the equipment wasn't there as the regulars often plundered the militia's Cougars to carry out overseas deployments. There were no major summer exercises or Milcons held in Western Canada for five years after ON GUARD 90, and such was the effect of the budget crunch that the Light Horse Historical Report complains in 1994 that,

Due to financial restraints, more initiative, resourcefulness and effort has been demanded from the Officers and Senior NCOs. In view of the limitation on AVGP [Cougar] training more emphasis has therefore been placed on basic individual skills.[38]

That is to say, there was a return to basic infantry fieldcraft including route marching using "black Cadillacs" (boots), and small arms training. The same comment, using almost exactly the same words, appeared in the 1995 Report which, although it doesn't say much for the ingenuity of the officer tasked to write it, was doubtless entirely accurate. A perusal of the Historical Reports for the

middle 90s indicates that some of the most effective training done at this time were four weekend exercises, dubbed ARMOUR WARRIER I to IV, carried out at Wainwright between January and April 1995. That summer, a major exercise WESTERN CHALLENGE 95 took place, involving all the western militia armoured units but, "due to constant changes of taskings by higher headquarters," the Light Horse had too many personnel on training courses and it attendance was poor.[39] WESTERN CHALLENGE was repeated in 1996 and although Light Horse attendance "could have been better … those attending had a good week of realistic training."[40] Unfortunately, this was to be the last major militia training exercise to be held in Western Canada for eight years.

There were other problems. The Regiment's strength in the mid-1990s was good, between 150 and 200 all ranks, but it could have been better if it had not been harmed by a decision by Ottawa to centralize the recruiting system, both regular and militia, across the country. Recruiting funds were removed from individual units and administered centrally, paperwork increased, waiting time lengthened and, inevitably, the number of recruits dropped. Limited budgets also meant fewer courses and, too often, the length of these courses and the time of year they were held, precluded militia personnel from taking them, because they could not take the time off from their jobs or studies. There were, however, in these years no shortage of compulsory courses in such non-military subjects as sexual harassment, ethnicity, and racial discrimination, etc., etc. It was also during this time, that the uniformed lawyers in the Judge Advocate General's Department began to raise a fuss about "liability issues" that might arise from militia soldiers being injured while training without pay. This traditional militia procedure – which has more or less kept the force alive in peacetime for much of the 20th century – was prohibited and training was hampered until a method was figured out to get around the prohibition. The interference from lawyers led one anonymous but brilliant Light Horseman interviewed for this book to quip: "Since there is some concern about the thin armour plate on the Cougars, in case we take them into action, what we should do is strap JAG lawyers to the front and sides and we would thus solve two problems at once."[41]

Good things did happen during this time. Lieutenant-Colonels Fraser and McKenzie were able to get a major addition built for Patterson Armoury that included an indoor rifle range and modern classrooms. It was completed in February 1994 and officially opened by Lieutenant-General J.R. Gutknecht, CMM, CD, Colonel-Commandant of the RCAC. McKenzie also created a compact but complete Regimental Museum in Medicine Hat to house a collection put together by Master Warrant Officer Jim Ogston, the Light Horse Historian and Curator. Opened in June 1996, it was named the "Captain Kenneth E. Perrin Museum" after a young South Alberta officer from the Hat who had been killed in the Hochwald in 1945.

One of the most impressive ceremonial events carried out by the Regiment during McKenzie's command was the joint parade the SALH staged with the South Alberta Veterans Association on

(Below) Corporal Sean MacIntyre and friend, February 2003
Corporal MacIntyre from Edmonton served with the CIMIC detachment of 1st Battalion, PPCLI, in Bosnia-Herzegovina in 2003. Here, he poses with his one-armed Bosnian friend (the right arm is a prosthetic), Nebosja, in the town of Titov Dvar. CIMIC personnel, whose job is to assist the civilian population in areas where the Canadian army operates, can get involved in some very different activities. In the case of Nebosja, a routine request to provide transport resulted in MacIntyre helping Nebosja take a coffin to the home of his dead brother, a recluse, and assisting the one-armed Bosnian to place the body in a coffin and transport it to a grave site. It was an experience that MacIntyre will never forget. COURTESY, SEAN MACINTYRE

(Above) SNOW GOOSE 50, Cyprus, 1989
SNOW GOOSE was the codename for rotations to UNFICYP (UN Forces in Cyprus), where Canadian soldiers served in a peacekeeping role for almost two decades. In 1989, six men of B Squadron, SALH, deployed for six months on that island. Top left is Trooper Giessman, top is Trooper Walton, top right is Trooper Van Patten, centre is Sergeant Walton and bottom left is Trooper Kolke and bottom right is Trooper Lund. These men are wearing flak vests over their combat dress and UN blue berets or field caps, and are armed with the C-7 rifle or the C-9 7.62 mm machinegun. SALH ARCHIVES

(Above) Moving to Sector South, Croatia, July 1993

Master-Corporal Greg Yanda poses with his vehicle as his mechanized infantry company of 2nd Battalion, Princess Patricia's Light Infantry prepares to move into Sector South, the Medak Pocket, in Croatia in the early summer of 1993. Note that the vehicles have been painted white for visibility. COURTESY, GREG YANDA

In the lee of the Hindu Kush, 2004

As this book goes to press, Lieutenant-Colonel Brian Hodgson, CD, who commanded the SALH from 1996 to 2000, is serving with NATO forces in Kabul, Afghanistan. He is seen here posing in the lee of the Hindu Kush wearing Arid Environment (i.e. desert) CADPAT uniform. COURTESY, BRIAN HODGSON

(Right) Inspection of the guard
Lieutenant-General J.A.R. Gutknecht, CMM, CD, Colonel-Commandant of the Royal Canadian Armoured Corps, inspects the guard at the official opening of the new addition to Patterson Armoury in April 1994. Behind Gutknecht is the guard commander, Master-Sergeant Darryl C. Risk. The guard is wearing the Canadian Forces service dress jacket called, since 1985, the DEU (Distinctive Environment Uniform) in No. 1 Order with belts and medals. COURTESY, ALEX VAN ROOYEN

(Left) Upgrading – the addition at Patterson Armoury
In February 1994, an addition was completed at Patterson Armoury in Medicine Hat that added an indoor smallarms range and a classroom wing. The old wooden hangar still remains but it has been considerably expanded over the years. SALH ARCHIVES

the grounds of the provincial Legislature Building in Edmonton in September 1995 to mark the veterans' receipt of their Colour which was laid up in the Building beside the Colours of other Alberta regiments that had fought in both world wars. Nearly 250 Light Horse and South Albertas were present that day and the Historical Report for 1995 enthused that

The Regiment was on parade for this very important event for the South Alberta Regiment. This event was long overdue as the SARs were never presented their Colours during or after the Second World War. To our knowledge, no other Regiment "struck off the order of battle" has ever received Colours fifty years after the event. The parade was a most moving event and the SARs and the SALH have become a much more cohesive group because this parade took place. ...... a great day in the unit's history.[42]

If needed, the Light Horse and its predecessors have always assisted the civil authorities in times of emergency. They have fought fires, searched for lost children, provided communications, traffic pickets and security at major public events and dynamited ice floes. In the late spring of 1995, RHQ and A Squadron was called out to aid the civil power after a combination of heavy rain and melting snow caused the South Saskatchewan River to overflow its banks in its worst flood in a century. The crisis came during the night of 8-9 June when the river rose about 15 feet over its normal level and the city of Medicine Hat declared a state of emergency and evacuated 4,000 residents from some 1,500 homes in the lower areas of the city. McKenzie was ready to order the Light Horse out to help but his intentions ran afoul of bureaucracy – the mayor of the Hat had not made an official request for assistance to the Canadian army and, without this formality, LFWA could not approve the military participation. RSM John Bray remembered that,

it was a very strange situation as the city had asked for volunteers to sandbag and most of our troops were down on the dykes. The CO had requested formal permission to help out but there was some bureaucratic screw up but things changed quickly when the television media reported that British troops and helicopters from BATUS were taking part in the rescue work as that shamed the higher ups into action.[43]

As McKenzie himself recalled:

Most of my soldiers were down working as volunteer sandbaggers on the dykes but they couldn't wear uniform as we did not have permission to render assistance as a military unit. Meanwhile, the British forces from Suffield were helping out with their helicopters and engineering equipment. I asked for permission from LFWA to mobilize the Light Horse to assist but was told that this could not be done as there had been no official request for assistance from the civil authorities. However, they came back a few hours later and said "go ahead." I gather that was one of the first times that they had gotten involved in something like this without a formal request for assistance from the civil authorities. A couple of years down the road, they changed the system and allocated funds for emergency duties.

The unit was called out for three days on what we called Exercise SANDBAG ASSIST and helped the police to secure the homes that had been evacuated. We set up OP points and blocked off all routes into that area, turning people away. A few tried to sneak in but we simply notified the police and let them handle it.[44]

In October 1996, when Lieutenant-Colonel McKenzie turned over command of the Regiment to Lieutenant-Colonel Brian Hodgson, he could take pride in having held the Light Horse together during a time of difficult fiscal restraint. It is his belief that

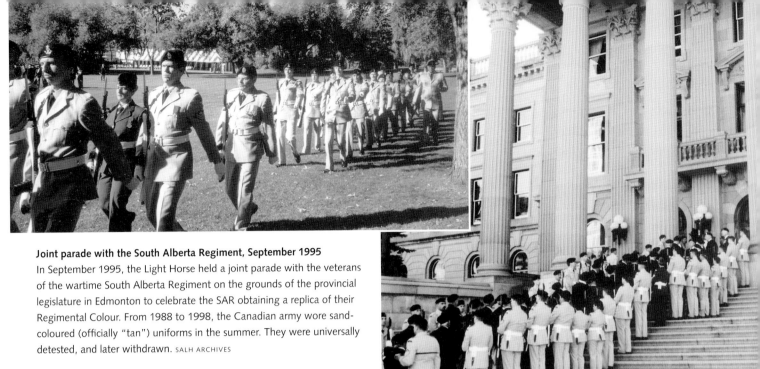

Joint parade with the South Alberta Regiment, September 1995
In September 1995, the Light Horse held a joint parade with the veterans of the wartime South Alberta Regiment on the grounds of the provincial legislature in Edmonton to celebrate the SAR obtaining a replica of their Regimental Colour. From 1988 to 1998, the Canadian army wore sand-coloured (officially "tan") uniforms in the summer. They were universally detested, and later withdrawn. SALH ARCHIVES

(Right) **Honouring the veterans**
The South Alberta Light Horse lines the steps of the Alberta Legislature Building and presents arms as the veterans of their predecessor unit, the wartime South Alberta Regiment, enter the building to lay up their replica Colour in September 1995. During the 1990s, all the components of the Regimental Family drew closer together. SALH ARCHIVES

The most satisfying accomplishment during my tenure was to still maintain a unit despite the continuing uncertainty about our future, continued reduction of resources and budgets, ineffective recruiting and training support above unit level, … and lack of realization and awareness of the real problems and effective solutions available to build the reserves.[45]

"The FAX and phone and Electronic Mail gets used a lot": Headquarters shifts to Edmonton, 1996-2000
Lieutenant-Colonel Hodgson had an interesting background. A native of Edmonton, he had joined in the British army as a private in the early 1970s and served two tours in Northern Ireland before returning to Edmonton and enlisting in the Loyal Edmonton Regiment. In 1980, when he was commissioned, Hodgson transferred to the SALH and rose steadily in rank, taking over B Squadron as a major in 1988. In civilian life the Sergeant-at-Arms of the Alberta Legislative Assembly, Hodgson was the first commanding officer of the Light Horse to come from the

provincial capital and, as a result, RHQ moved north but, as the unit Historical Report stressed: "no problems have risen having our CO and RSM 360 miles from Medicine Hat, the FAX and phone and Electronic Mail gets used a lot and monthly visits to Medicine Hat are working well."[46]

Light Horse Headquarters wasn't the only thing that moved to Edmonton in 1996. By this time Alberta had shaken off the economic doldrums of the previous decade and resumed its economic prosperity, a prosperity fuelled by the estimated 450,000 oil and gas wells located in the province. Peter Lougheed, having won a measure of victory in his battles with Ottawa over energy policy, retired in 1985 to be replaced by Don Getty who proved to be not as adroit in office. This, combined with considerable dissatisfaction over the state of the provincial economy in the late 1980s, had resulted in a resurgence in the fortunes of the provincial Liberal party, led by the popular former mayor of Edmonton, Laurence Decore. Decore, however, was neatly balanced by the even more popular former mayor of Calgary, Ralph Klein, who succeeded Getty as head of the provincial Conserva-

Exercise SANDBAG ASSIST, June 1995
In early June 1995, a combination of heavy rain and melting snow caused the South Saskatchewan to overflow its banks in the worst flood for nearly a century. The Light Horse participated in an aid to the civil power exercise by providing communications and patrols in residential areas that had been evacuated. SALH ARCHIVES

441

tives in 1989 and, at the date of writing (January 2005), has just won his fourth straight election. Premier Klein's party now has 33 years at the helm of the province and will eventually surpass the previous Canadian record set by the Alberta Social Credit Party, which formed the provincial government for 36 years.

In 1996, as part of a major re-structuring of the Canadian army, a decision was made to close CFB Calgary and move the regular 1st Canadian Mechanized Brigade Group, built around the Strathconas and 1 PPCLI, to a new "mega-base" at Edmonton. This move, which affected some 3,500 regular soldiers and their families, has been attributed by some cynics as being Prime Minister Jean Chrétien's reward to Edmonton for returning a number of Liberal MPs in the 1993 federal election which brought him to power. Be that as it may, it has had a very positive impact on the South Alberta Light Horse and the other units of the Edmonton militia garrison who have benefited from the proximity of a large regular combat formation and its supporting infrastructure. From that time until now, the Light Horse have held numerous joint activities with 1 CMBG besides normal training – the Regiment has acted as an "OP FOR" on a number of occasions for the regulars and has been involved in trials of the next generation of Canadian armoured vehicles, the 8-wheeled Coyote and LAV (Light Armoured Vehicle) III. Perhaps most important, having a large regular garrison nearby has provided a standard to be met and a model to be emulated and, just as importantly, many regular soldiers have opted to join the Regiment after their term of regular service has expired.

Unfortunately for the Light Horse, this advantage was offset by financial restraints in the late 1990s, particularly in the 1996-1997 and 1997-1998 training years when, on many occasions, the SALH was reduced to using their unreliable Iltis vehicles to train as Cougars were not available. Matters improved somewhat in the 1998-1999 year with more money available and, in the spring of 1999, the Light Horse were able to carry out four good weekend exercises at Wainwright, dubbed ARMOURED ASSAULT I to IV, which were an excellent refresher in basic armour tactics. This was followed by a similar series of exercises, the BOLD HUSSAR series in the spring of 2000. The problem is that military units are often like revolving doors, with personnel constantly coming and going, and when qualified Cougar personnel left the Regiment, budget restrictions meant that it was often difficult to train replacement personnel. For example, much of the Light Horse's focus in the autumn of 1999 was on getting enough personnel qualified so that it could take the field in the ARMOURED ASSAULT programme. As for gunnery, although gun camps were held at regular intervals to keep crew skills up to date, government parsimony meant that fewer and fewer live firing exercises were permitted and, when they were, the number of rounds was restricted. This was offset, however, by the increasing use of electronic training devices, including Cougar turret gunnery simulators and electronic small arms ranges, as the SALH is always quick to adopt any new technology that will assist them in their tasks.

The Light Horse is also fortunate to be the militia armoured regiment in closest proximity to the Training Centre at Wainwright and probably spends more time on that base than any other militia unit in Western Canada. The regiment has acted as an "OP FOR," not only against regular Canadian units but also the militia and British units who use Wainwright. In the POND JUMP WEST series of exercises held at Wainwright in the summer and autumn of 2000, they were opposing troops to British forces, including the Coldstream Guards. The Sallies, however, were somewhat puzzled by the Coldstreams because, promptly at 7.30 A.M. every morning a platoon of Guardsmen would march past their lines at double time under a sergeant – "marched beautifully" as Major Paul Mast recalled – but were never seen to come back. This went on for some time until a Light Horseman finally asked a Guards sergeant whether this fast-moving platoon was perhaps the Coldstreams' drill and demonstration team. "Not at all," was the reply, "those are just the defaulters," (soldiers charged with minor misdemeanours), "being marched down to have a little chat with the RSM."[47] The reason they never came back was that, after their little chat, these miscreants were dispersed throughout the Coldstream lines doing the worst fatigues their RSM could think up, generally involving laborious and dirty lifting jobs, or painting things white. It was an interesting comment on the traditional methods of discipline still in use in the British army.

Since Lieutenant-Colonel Hodgson had once served in that army and still maintained close links with it, in 1997 the Light Horse B Squadron fielded, in conjunction with members of the Loyal Edmonton Regiment, a team to compete in the Cambrian Patrol. It was coached by Captain David Broomfield, a former member of the 15th/19th King's Royal Hussars, and led by Captain Sean Thirlwell who explains what it was all about:

The Cambrian Patrol is an international military competition for long range patrolling which draws teams from almost every army in NATO and some non-NATO armies. Basically, it is a gruelling 40-hour trek, carrying a stipulated amount of equipment weighting between 65 and 72 lbs for each man, over 40 miles of the Black Mountains near Sennybridge in Wales, the same area where the British SAS do their training. It is partly an endurance test but it is also a test of basic military fieldcraft skills such as observation, first aid, river crossing, etc. and you are tested on these skills at various stands located along the route.[48]

The combined Light Horse/Loyal Eddies team began training on their own time six months before the event was held in October 1997. They knew they were facing stiff competition from regular army teams from the Royal Canadian Regiment and Royal 22e Régiment who had been training seven days a week for more than a year, not to mention teams from the American, British, French and German armies. Up to the time they took part, no reserve team had ever placed high enough in stand-

Weapons training

Members of B Squadron train with the Browning 9 mm automatic, the standard sidearm of the Canadian army, in March 1998. From left to right, Troopers Pitts, Foulkes, Ogilvie, Corporals Elliott and Comie, Troopers Winton and Caudle. In the Light Horse, training is ceaseless. These personnel are wearing the combat dress of olive green nylon-cotton issued in the Canadian army for nearly four decades. SALH ARCHIVES

ing to be awarded a medal but, ignoring the odds, the Alberta militia team decided to participate in the regular contest, not the reserve competition which was less rigorous. To their unending delight they not only beat out the Canadian teams but emerged from this test of soldier skills and knowledge with a bronze medal.

Under Lieutenant-Colonel Hodgson's leadership, a Regimental Ceremonial Troop was raised again in the late 1990s. Consisting of between 6 and 8 soldiers, it sometimes appears mounted but, more often, parades on foot and is dressed in the scarlet tunic and stetson of the 15th Light Horse. Unfortunately, this uniform is so similar to that of the RCMP that the Troop is often mistaken as Mounties by the unenlightened. In order to end the confusion, the Ceremonial Troop occasionally switches to a blue patrol jacket with shoulder chains so that, in Warrant Officer Dave Bergt's words, "we look more like cavalry than police officers."[49] The Ceremonial Troop parades whenever it is required but one function it carries out faithfully every year on Remembrance Day is to mount a Guard of Honour at the War Memorial in the little of town of Chipman, outside Edmonton, in memory of those soldiers of the Regiment or its predecessors who have died in the service of their country.

The Light Horse continued to maintain an active social calendar and, as always, rallied around to support members of the Regimental family which experienced distress. In July 1997 RSM John Szram died very suddenly in Edmonton, at the age of 47. A well liked and well respected warrant officer, his loss was keenly felt by all members of the Regiment but particularly by Lieutenant-Colonel Hodgson as he had served as an NCO with Szram in the Loyal Eddies and had been instrumental in convincing him to transfer to the SALH. The Light Horse gave RSM Szram a full military funeral and was "of great assistance to Mrs. Szram" in her bereavement.[50] RSM John Szram is still remembered in

the SALH today, nearly eight years after his untimely passing.

The Light Horse also stood by to assist the civil power if required and, in this respect, Operation ABACUS deserves to be mentioned. As the minutes ticked away on the evening of 31 December 1999, much of the globe held its breath in fear that, when the clocks struck midnight, a world heavily dependent on computers would be plunged into chaos by the "Y2K" syndrome or the inability of computers to adjust from the 20th to the 21st century. Governments around the world, including the Canadian, prepared emergency programmes should they be required and the Light Horse was tasked to provide a detachment of 33 all ranks in support of Operation ABACUS which, along with a detachment from 18th Air Defence Regiment in Lethbridge, shared responsibility for emergency measures in the southern part of the province. As the SALH Historical Report records, almost wistfully, "nothing happened on 01 Jan 00" and the world exhaled again.[51]

"He's up there, Sir": Into a new century and a new conflict, 2000-2003

In the last year of Lieutenant-Colonel Hodgson's tenure in command, his RSM was Chief Warrant Officer Tom Smith, a veteran of the 15th/19th Hussars. For a brief period, until Hodgson turned over command in September 2000, the Light Horse thus had both a commander and a regimental sergeant-major who had seen service in the British army, a unique occurrence. Lieutenant-Colonel Neil Douglas, who succeeded Hodgson, was a veteran Light Horseman who joined the Regiment in the early 1980s and had an extensive and impressive military background both in and out of the Regiment. He had served on a SNOW GOOSE rotation to Cyprus in 1991 and on the Strathcona deployment to Bosnia in 1994, which he recalled as "being a good tour, with plenty of action and some shelling and mortaring."[52] Douglas had returned to Canada to run advanced training at CFB Dundurn for militia augmentees on the various Balkan deployments, a duty which had honed his basic soldier skills to a high degree. A building contractor in civilian life, Douglas was highly regarded in the Light Horse as a field soldier *par excellence* and, as he was from the south of the province, RHQ now shifted back to Medicine Hat.

Douglas's command style was very down to earth and he would never order a subordinate to carry out a task he was not willing to do himself. Captain Michael Onieu of Lord Strathcona's Horse became aware of this quality when, in 2001, he reported at Patterson Armoury to serve as an RSS officer with the SALH. A graduate of the Royal Military College in Kingston and an armoured officer who had taken a troop of Leopard tanks to Kosovo in the late 1990s, Onieu was used to the more conservative ways of the regular force. When he walked into Patterson Armoury, his first duty was to report to his commanding officer, but when he asked an enlisted soldier where the CO was to be found, the trooper pointed to the roof and replied: "Up there, Sir." Gazing skyward, Onieu was amazed to see Lieutenant-

Colonel Douglas, having grown impatient at the unwillingness of government caretakers to do the job, perched on the top of a very high and rickety ladder, changing the light bulbs in the armoury ceiling. It was a "heads up" for young Captain Onieu that he had just entered a different world and, as he later remarked about his years with the Light Horse, they could best be summed up by the poster in the officers' mess in Medicine Hat which depicts a grizzled old cowpoke complaining: "There are some things about this outfit they didn't tell me when I signed on."[53]

Douglas's time in command was hampered, as he later commented, "by financial cutbacks, distance and the unavailability of Cougars" for training.[54] His regiment had the largest payroll in 41 Brigade Group, the Alberta militia brigade, but, "although I was parading 180 all ranks in Medicine Hat and Edmonton, I was only receiving pay for 90 officers and men."[55] To get pay for his people required administrative sleight of hand but the government cutbacks were so severe in 2000-2001 that, as the Historical Report for that year sorrowfully stated, it "made the maintenance of our core skills increasingly difficult."[56] In that year, the Light Horse only got weekend camps at Wainwright and not all of these involved armoured training and had to be satisfied with small arms work, simulators and cloth model exercises. As his predecessors had also discovered, being the commanding officer of a regiment whose two components are separated by a distance of 360 miles does not make for an easy life and Douglas estimates that he was travelling as much as 3,000 miles a year between the two squadrons. It is somewhat ironic that, as has only recently been learned, while Chrétien's Liberal government was starving its armed forces between 1993 and 2003, it was wasting billions of dollars on poorly-managed programmes.

Winter gun camp, 2001

The Light Horse trains in all seasons, in all weathers. Here the unit holds a winter gun camp at Wainwright in March 2001. The officer in the foreground is Lieutenant Ken Anderson. SALH ARCHIVES

In 2001, the Light Horse squadron in Edmonton finally moved out of the overcrowded and ramshackle Griesbach Barracks into the new and modern Jefferson Armoury in the northern part of the city. Named after Brigadier James Jefferson who commanded 10th Brigade in Northwest Europe in 1944-1945, it resembles a modern high school more than it does a military establishment but offers clean, modern office space, classrooms, garages, drill halls and large and bright messes. For Lieutenant-Colonel Douglas, this move was the high point of a term of command during which he experienced many difficulties not of his own making. But, as all Light Horse commanding officers have done since the Regiment was formed, he brought it through, intact, and in good form.

This was just as well as, in the second week of September 2001, an event occurred that provided an object lesson for the western world about just how dangerous is the new international reality. The deaths of thousands of innocent people on a bright, sunny morning in New York began a new global conflict against a new and terrible enemy who, because they are impelled by religious fanaticism, do not follow the precepts that civilized nations have established over the last century or so to lessen the horrors attendant on war. Despite the general rundown of its armed forces over the past three decades, Canada has joined in the struggle against international terrorism and Canadian soldiers, both regulars and militia, are today serving in the Middle East and a number of other global hotspots. The militia are involved in this struggle as the "Total Force" concept is no longer a concept, it is a reality – there are currently 10,000 reservists serving full time with the Canadian regular army, approximately a third of its strength, and when the men and women of the

South Alberta Light Horse train today, they do so knowing that they may be called upon to use their military skills in the defence of their country against an opponent ready and willing to strike anywhere on the globe, against any target. This was the new reality that Canadian soldiers faced when Lieutenant-Colonel Neil Douglas turned over command to Lieutenant-Colonel Thomas E. Putt in April 2003.

"My soldiers wouldn't have it any other way": Coming up to the mark, 2003-2004

A veteran of 30 years in the militia and regular force, Lieutenant-Colonel Thomas E. Putt served with the 8th Hussars and the Strathconas before assuming command of the Western Area Training Centre at Wainwright in 2001. On Putt's retirement from the regular army in early 2003, Honorary Colonel Stanley Milner of the SALH asked him to assume command of the Regiment, and Putt thus became the first commanding officer of the Light Horse not to come from either Edmonton or Medicine Hat – actually Lieutenant-Colonel Putt hails originally from Calgary and once served in the KOCR. He is no stranger to the militia, having served as an RSS officer with the First Hussars in London, Ontario, and certainly no stranger to the Light Horse, whom he had previously encountered during his service. He recalls that, among the regular personnel of the Training Centre, the Light Horse had a reputation for "doing things on the fly," – not always according to regulations, it should be noted, but, despite that, usually landing on their feet.[57]

The new commanding officer brought with him another former Strathcona to serve as RSM. Chief Warrant Officer Adrian Thomas is a veteran with 23 years of service in the regular army who has seen service on several overseas deployments. Thomas, too, is no stranger to the Light Horse, having previously served at the Western Training Centre in Wainwright. Not a man to be easily fooled, RSM Thomas is impressed by the sheer enthusiasm evident in his new regiment – as he puts it: "the amount of dedication a reserve soldier has to have to meet the requirements of his duties is unbelievable but these people have it, in spades, and there is no equivalent in the regular forces to the dedication the SALH displays."[58] Together, these two officers (who have risen above their humble regular force origins and ascended to the ranks of the anointed) will take the SALH into its second century.

One of Lieutenant-Colonel Putt's first major tasks after he assumed command was to prepare

Honorary but important

Throughout the history of the South Alberta Light Horse, the Regiment's honorary colonels and lieutenant-colonels have proved to be not only benefactors but leaders in shaping the future of the unit. In November 2003, the Light Horse held a dinner to thank former Honorary Colonel Alan Graham. From left to right: Lieutenant-Colonel T.E. Putt, CD, commanding officer of the SALH; former Honorary Lieutenant-Colonel Harry Quarton, CD, ADC; Honorary Colonel Stanley Milner, OC, AOE, CD, LL.D; former Honorary Colonel Alan Graham, SBStJ, CLJ, LCM; and present Honorary Lieutenant-Colonel John Watson, FCA. Harry Quarton served in the wartime SAR and in the postwar 19th Dragoons before ending his military career as commanding officer of the Loyal Edmonton Regiment. COURTESY, HARRY QUARTON

Mr. Thomas, the RSM

Chief Warrant Officer Adrian Thomas, CD, Regimental Sergeant-Major of the South Alberta Light Horse, poses at Wainwright during the training exercises held to prepare for ACTIVE EDGE 04. A former member of Lord Strathcona's Horse, RSM Thomas brings more than two decades of experience to his job of preparing the Light Horse for their second century of service. SALH ARCHIVES

the Regiment to take the field in Exercise ACTIVE EDGE, the largest militia exercise to be held since WESTERN CHALLENGE in 1996. ACTIVE EDGE, to be staged by 41st Brigade Group of Alberta was, in Putt's words, "crafted and created by the reserves for the reserves" and a great deal of time and energy was put into its planning and preparations.[59] It was scheduled to take place in August 2003 but, unfortunately, nature intervened that summer when massive forest fires began to rage out of control in the interior of British Columbia and the provincial government requested military help for its overburdened provincial firefighting service. ACTIVE EDGE was therefore cancelled in favour of Operation PEREGRINE, the deployment of more than 2,600 regular and militia personnel to assist the civil authorities. The Regiment's contribution was a detachment of 22 all ranks.

Among them was Warrant Officer Dave Bergt who was on holiday in the Okanagan Valley in British Columbia when he learned of the SALH's deployment in Operation PEREGRINE. Cutting

Future Light Horse

The South Alberta Light Horse and the South Alberta Light Horse Foundation support six cadet corps in Camrose, Edmonton and Medicine Hat where young boys and girls learn citizenship values and participate in adventure training. Above, 2313 SALH Cadet Corps parade at Patterson Armoury in the Hat. Many of these cadets will join the Regiment when they are of age. Some of the cadets are wearing the old Canadian Forces "work dress" of green pants and a short zippered jacket, called the "bus-driver suit" when it was worn by soldiers. In the photo at left, an adult instructor attempts to sneak up on cadets, whose heads can just be seen in the grass beyond the road. The instructor is about to get a big surprise. In the cadets, the emphasis is on having fun as well as learning useful skills. BOTH COURTESY, PETE DAVISON

short the family vacation he rushed back to Edmonton and was able to get on the bus that took the personnel of the Light Horse/ Loyal Edmonton Regiment to the deployment area. The troops arrived at 6 P.M. on a Friday and were billeted at a cadet camp in Vernon. They expected to go into action immediately but instead spent two days taking courses in fighting fires, most of which seemed reasonably basic. Bergt was not particularly impressed when a nice young lady instructor lined up the military detachment with shovels one morning, preparatory to teaching them how to dig a ditch. Being the senior warrant officer present, he ordered the Loyal Eddies to dig a trench and the flatfeet, eager to show off one of their most crucial skills, went to work with a will, flinging dirt in all directions until the instructor allowed as to how it was clear that soldiers did know how to dig ditches and dropped that subject from the curriculum. Once they got through their instruction, the detachment spent nearly two weeks in the Kelowna area, under the direction of professional "fire bosses," taking two hours on the fire line and two hours off, looking for "hot spots" or hidden areas of combustion under the surface of the ground.[60]

The postponement of ACTIVE EDGE was fortuitous because it allowed Lieutenant-Colonel Putt to take his new unit into the field "to measure where it stood operationally."[61] In October 2003, the Light Horse carried out a 3-day offensive exercise at Wainwright, followed by Exercise TASK FORCE NORTH in November, a "combined arms" exercise with the regulars. In Putt's words, TASK FORCE NORTH,

included armour, artillery infantry and combat engineers, supported by two regular force army units who came with Coyote reconnaissance vehicles and the new, "state of the art," LAV III [Light Armoured Vehicle] Fighting Vehicles while aviation support was provided by 408 Tactical Helicopter Squadron. I organized these elements into a 250-soldier combat team centred on a SALH Cougar Squadron consisting of Squadron HQ (2 Cougars), three Cougar troops (12 Cougars), supported by a complete armour Echelon. The Light Horse Cougar squadron was formed by combining A Squadron from Medicine Hat and B Squadron from Edmonton into what would be a permanent field organization for training throughout the coming year.[62]

Based on what he already knew about the Light Horse, Putt had no doubts that the unit would perform well in this advanced exercise but even he was impressed with the results:

The officers and senior non-commissioned members were superb. They knew their business at the squadron and troop level and were very keen to take on the challenge of working at the higher level as part of an "all arms" combat team in the advance and attack. I noted that the Regiment's leadership represented all walks of life in Alberta, ranging from independent businessmen to police officers. The soldiers were a good mix of students, full time workers and ex-regular army veterans whose background largely mirrored that of the officers and senior NCOs from both Edmonton and Medicine Hat. I was also pleasantly surprised to find that several soldiers from both squadrons actually live in other major urban centres, hours away by car from either Edmonton or Medicine Hat, but see no problem commuting to parade with the Light Horse – this is true *esprit de corps*.

As the exercise culminated with a mounted attack on an

enemy combat outpost, I listened to the radio as Major Wayne Lockhart, Officer Commanding (OC) of the Light Horse field squadron and the "all arms" combat team, gave a crisp set of radio orders putting a Cougar troop into a fire base to suppress the enemy outpost while he manoeuvred his assault force, consisting of more than 20 armoured vehicles, through a breach in an enemy minefield blown by the attached combat engineers. The supporting artillery was well co-ordinated by the FOO and "smoked off" the front of the enemy position as the assault force formed up to attack, just over the breach. As the OC's call sign [vehicle] and his other two Cougar troops (10 Cougars) led the LAV III-mounted infantry onto the objective on time and on target, I was confident that, with proper leadership and preparation, the SALH could do anything.

TASK FORCE NORTH, November 2003

In the autumn of 2003, Lieutenant-Colonel Thomas Putt, the new commanding officer of the Light Horse, carried out two major "combined arms" training exercises to prepare for ACTIVE EDGE. Here, he is conducting an After Action Review with the personnel of the SALH combat team following Exercise TASK FORCE NORTH, which was staged with regular army units at Wainwright Camp. COURTESY, T.E. PUTT

I knew then that I was going to truly enjoy command of this Regiment. I also knew I could and would ride the SALH hard into its 100th year of service. My soldiers wouldn't have it any other way.[63]

Putt continued to work with the Regiment over the winter of 2003 in preparation for Exercise ACTIVE EDGE, now rescheduled for August 2004. Throughout that winter and into the spring, RHQ staff put considerable effort into planning for this event and, in March, a preliminary tactical camp to brush up on basic skills was held at the United States Army base at Yakima in Washington State, using Cougars brought in by rail from Canada. By the time the summer of 2004 arrived, the Regiment was ready.

"This regiment is in fine fettle": The Light Horse approaches its second century

Hard training was not the only thing that occupied the Regiment from the time Lieutenant-Colonel Putt assumed command. The SALH was nearing its 100th Birthday which will occur on 3 July 2005 and, under the overall stewardship of the SALH Foundation, preparations for this important event were begun at an early date. The Foundation has been mentioned before and it is now time to discuss its role and activities at greater length. Lieutenant-Colonel Putt confesses that one thing that amazed him when he assumed command was the "depth of commitment" the Foundation displays toward the Regiment.

This non-profit organization, headed by Honorary Colonel Stan Milner, was created to fulfill a number of important aims. It assists Light Horse soldiers obtain post-secondary education by providing financial scholarships – for example, a serving member of the SALH attending a college or university, who is in good

standing in the Regiment, can receive up to $1,000 per year in tuition assistance. It supports activities that celebrate the heritage of the Western Cavalry in general, and the Light Horse and its predecessors in particular. Toward this end, it has supported the writing and free distribution of historical publications about these subjects – including the very well-received history of the wartime South Alberta Regiment* – and, indeed, this present volume. It has assisted the SAR Veterans to place 15 plaques in Europe to commemorate that unit's campaign from Normandy to the Rhineland, sustains the Light Horse Ceremonial Troop and the Captain Kenneth E. Perrin Regimental Museum in Medicine Hat, and promotes cultural and social events, primarily museum and gallery displays. In times of need, it is always there for the soldiers of the Regiment and their families. It has provided emergency assistance to members, both serving and retired – it has helped a severely-injured cadet to obtain special medical aids; it has succoured Light Horse members who have experienced financial problems caused by accidents or major illness; and it has supported the families of Light Horsemen on overseas deployments who have suffered economic hardship. As Lieutenant-Colonel Brian Hodgson emphasizes:

In my judgement, by any objective measure, there isn't a regiment that looks after its soldiers as well as the SALH does and the credit for that is entirely due to the Foundation – frankly, it is unparalleled. Other regiments may have more mess silver or grander furniture, or spend more on social events but the Foundation looks after our people very well.[65]

---

* *South Albertas: A Canadian Regiment at War*, Robin Brass Studio, Toronto, 1998, revised edition 2004.

Not the least of the Foundation's many worthy activities concern the SALH cadet organizations and mention must be made of these youngest family members, who have hitherto gone unnoticed. Their lineage is almost as old as that of the Regiment itself, as the creation of a national organization to provide training in citizenship for schoolboys was authorized in 1887. The first cadet corps in Alberta was organized in Calgary in 1898 and by 1914 thousands of boys were enrolled in cadet corps across Canada. Although its fortunes have risen and fallen with public interest in military matters, the modern Royal Canadian Army Cadet Corps (RCAC) is a thriving and popular organization that provides adventure training for young people, both boys and girls, from 12 to 18 years of age. All the predecessor units of the Light Horse had attached cadet organizations and, in 2005, no less than six cadet corps are affiliated with the Regiment – in Medicine Hat there are 2313 SALH RCAC (Kiwanis), #15 Royal Canadian Air Cadets, Navy League Cadets Corps #66 and #145 Royal Canadian Sea Cadet Corps while in the northern part of the province are 2051 19th Alberta Dragoons in Edmonton and 3068 SALH RCAC in Camrose. Many Light Horsemen began their service as cadets and it is a tradition that, when their active careers end, they will spend a few years as cadet officers to encourage what will, after all, be the future of the Regiment. It is a simplistic but entirely fitting analogy to state that the cadet corps, the Regiment itself, and its veterans, represent the three generations of a Light Horse family and all three benefit from the work of their guardian angel, the SALH Foundation.

This fact was brought home to the author when the South Alberta Veterans Association recently held a reunion in Edmonton and the Regiment hosted a barbecue buffet for the veterans and cadets at Jefferson Armoury. The Light Horse took the opportunity to show off their modern vehicles, weapons and equipment to the South Albertas. Sadly, the once-young troopers who, in 1944-1945, could jump into their Shermans in two bounds and roar off to wreak havoc on the *Wehrmacht,* are older now and it is getting rather difficult for them to get in and out of the cramped confines of armoured vehicles but they tried gamely, helped by a discreet hand. The South Albertas have always been a plain-talking bunch and the following comments, overheard on the occasion, testify that they were not all that impressed by modern weapons and high-tech widgetry: "These electronic gadgets are nice, to be sure, but it won't stand up in the field, I can tell you that, better to have the old 19 Set, never let you down," or, "So it can go 50 miles an hour, so what, an 88 would go through this armour like a knife through butter." They were, however, intrigued by the modern CADPAT (Canadian Pattern Disruptive) camouflage uniforms of the Light Horse soldiers and also their IMP rations: "You mean you don't have to sew your badges on any more but slap them on velcro and pull them off?" and "Are you telling me you get all this stuff in a single meal ration … well I never." What made this particular occasion even more delightful was the presence of the Light Horse cadets who,

while the older folks tried to come to grips with the changing nature of the service, bounced in and out of, ran behind and around, and crawled under, vehicles like a pack of frisky puppies and occasionally – when they thought they were not being observed – made a raid on the dessert table. The whole affair resembled nothing so much as a big, happy, family picnic for that is very much what it was.

As the South Alberta Light Horse moved toward its second century, it set in motion a number of initiatives and projects to celebrate this landmark. In the autumn of 2003, a decision was made that the Regiment would amalgamate with the 19th Alberta Dragoons, who have been on the Supplementary Order of Battle since 1965. This amalgamation would not only get one of the province's most distinguished cavalry units back in the saddle but it would ensure that the Dragoon's hard-won Battle Honours would not be lost if the "axe man in Ottawa" started casting about for fresh victims. When the process is complete, the Light Horse will acquire the Honours earned by the Canadian Light Horse in the First World War, including "Ypres 1915," Gravenstafel, 1915," "St. Julien, 1915" and "Festubert, 1915." It will also mean that the SALH, the direct successor of the 15th Light Horse, will also trace a lineage back to the 19th Dragoons and the Edmonton Fusiliers. The Regiment will thus be linked with four of the five militia cavalry regiments that existed in Alberta in 1914 and one of the two infantry regiments, making it truly a provincial regiment, if not *the* provincial regiment.

Since the Centennial of Alberta falls within two days of that of the Regiment, July 2005 will be a special time for both enitities. In conjunction with The Provincial Museum of Alberta in Edmonton, an exhibit entitled "Hoof Prints to Tank Tracks," entirely devoted to the history of the South Alberta Light Horse, will be that institution's premier Centennial project and will open in May 2005. It will be followed in October by a second exhibit of Regimental history in the new Medicine Hat Museum and, to honour the occasion, the Light Horse will parade through the Hat to celebrate and re-affirm the Freedom of the City granted to it in May 1967. A third project put in motion is the writing of this present volume, intended to tell the story of "Her Majesty's Cowboys" from their earliest beginnings. Finally, in late 2003 the Regiment launched a fourth project and one very dear to its heart – the complete restoration of "Old Reliable," the SAR's wartime command vehicle, to its original pristine state.

After the Guidon, "Old Reliable" is the Light Horse's most cherished possession. The old veteran became known internationally after its story was told in *South Albertas: A Canadian Regiment at War*, released in 1998. In fact, "Old Reliable" is so famous that in 2004 it was selected by the Corgi Company of Britain to serve as that firm's "60th Anniversary of D-Day" product and the interested reader can purchase a splendidly detailed, metal scale model of this distinguished campaigner. Unfortunately, the decades since 1974, when it was put on static display in Calgary, had not been kind to their hallowed trooper. "Old Reliable" came north when 1st Canadian Mechanized Brigade

Group moved to Edmonton in 1996 but, for seven years, sat rather forlornly on the airstrip at Namao between a Soviet-built T-34 tank and its newer cousin, a T-72. The Light Horse never forgot "Old Reliable," however, and in August 2003 it was moved to Jefferson Armoury to be a static display.

At this point, Sergeant Rob McCue, the senior NCO of the Ceremonial Troop, who had been watching over "Old Reliable" for more than a decade, decided that the vehicle could be restored to running order. He convinced Lieutenant-Colonel Putt that the idea was feasible, the Foundation made the funds available, and in January 2004 the half-track was moved inside Jefferson Armoury where McCue and a volunteer Light Horse restoration team, led by Corporals Ian Christie and Adrian Winton, both apprentice mechanics, commenced the laborious and exacting task of bringing it back to health. They were assisted by Reg Hodgson of St. Albert, a member of the board of the Military Vehicle Preservation Association and editor of that organization's journal, *Army Motors*, who rendered much expert and useful advice on procuring parts and information. Another person who assisted McCue's team was Dr. Ken Armstrong of Edmonton who, as a sergeant in the wartime SAR, was part of "Old Reliable's" original crew. The engine was found to be in good shape but areas of the interior, where water had seeped in over the years, had to be fully replaced, involving great time and effort. Although the configuration of "Old Reliable" was changed when it was first rebuilt in the early 1960s, the team was determined to restore the vehicle to its wartime state and that determination increased when they discovered brass .303 calibre shell casings stamped "1943" embedded in small cavities in the half-track's frame.

Juggling their civilian jobs and their military duties, the team members had, by February 2005, put 8,900 hours of labour into this project. The vehicle and its White Motor Company 6-cylinder engine (386-inch capacity and 147 bhp) were completely disassembled, cleaned and painted, and damaged parts replaced. The team was fascinated to discover that some vehicle and engine parts were still held in manufacturer's stocks

On the road again

Beginning in late 2003, a volunteer SALH team led by Sergeant Rob McCue put in 8,900 hours of hard work over a 14-month period to restore "Old Reliable" to running order. Here, the oldest trooper in the Light Horse poses proudly at Jefferson Armoury in pristine condition and in its wartime paint scheme complete with the "45" tac sign of the 29th Canadian Armoured Reconnaissance Regiment (South Alberta Regiment) and the gold maple leaf/green patch of 4th Canadian Armoured Division. It is believed that "Old Reliable" is one of the few running Second World War vehicles still on the muster rolls of a military unit. COURTESY, ROB MCCUE

but experienced particular difficulties obtaining slot-head oval armour bolts with a fine-pitch screw as made in the 1940s, and the nuts to secure them, as they are no longer manufactured. Finding tracks was another major problem but, fortunately, the Israeli Army, which used a similar vehicle until well into the 1980s, had surplus stocks for sale, as did the French army. The restoration team expects to have the engine running in March 2005 and the vehicle, tracks and all, in perfect running order with its original wartime paint scheme, by the following month. When the Regiment celebrates its 100th birthday in July 2005, the oldest serving member of the unit will be back on parade, complete with two plaques, donated by the SAR Veterans' Association, listing the members of the original wartime crew and the restoration team.[66]

As the Regiment prepares to begin its second century of service, it is time to sum up where it stands today. Consider the words of Lieutenant-Colonel Brian Hodgson, grandson of a 19th Dragoon and commanding officer of the Regiment from 1996 to 2000:

The SALH is a pan-Alberta regiment, it is more an all-Alberta regiment than any other militia unit in the province. If you look at our lineage, look all the units we perpetuate, you quickly realize that the Light Horse are connected with every part of Alberta. We have many advantages. We have an educated work force in this province and, thus, an educated recruiting base; we have two excellent training areas in Suffield and Wainwright; and we are in close proximity to a large regular army base. This Regiment is in fine fettle and our future is bright.[67]

That being said – and said well – the time has come for us to end this long and colourful story and all that remains is to rejoin the battle squadron at Wainwright Camp. When we left them to commence our tale, it was Monday, 23 August 2004, and they were in their "hide" for the night, eating their evening meal and looking out from their shelters at the rain, which was still coming down ……

Cougars after attack: ACTIVE EDGE 2004

A Cougar troop pauses after carrying out an attack exercise. Left to right are: Corporal Byers in turret; Warrant Officer Bergt on Cougar; Lieutenant Greg Yanda; Lieutenant Peeling; and Corporal Stock.

"Her Majesty's Cowboys": Battle squadron, Wainwright, 2004

On the last day of Exercise ACTIVE EDGE 04, the battle squadron poses for their picture. In the back row from left to right are Captain Watt, Lieutenant Yanda, Corporal Byers, Corporal Duffield, Corporal Osborne, Sergeant Rosendal, Master-Corporal Rosadiuk, Corporal Critchley, Corporal Burrows, Trooper Lojkowski, Corporal Hildebrandt, Sergeant Petr, Warrant Officer Moore and Lieutenant Hisdal. In the front from left to right are Corporal Adby, Corporal Gutowski, Lieutenant Peeling, Warrant Officer Bergt, Warrant Officer Walton, Major Lockhart, Corporal O'Callaghan, Corporal Markwell, Corporal Rolls, Corporal Buntain. BOTH COURTESY, BRETT WALTON

"No Matter How Much B.S. ... Today Made It All Worthwhile."

WAINWRIGHT, ALBERTA, AUGUST 2004

It rained throughout the night but it began to tail off on Tuesday morning. The Light Horse were up and about by 5.30 A.M. and after breakfast (blueberry apple cereal, cinnamon-flavoured oatmeal, or crunchie cereal, and lots of coffee) they performed routine maintenance and communications checks before moving out of their "hides" to take up the day's work. The squadron's task that Tuesday was to provide covering fire for the regular sappers of 1st Combat Engineer Regiment and the militia sappers of 8th Field Engineer Regiment while they dealt with an anti-tank ditch and a minefield. Once that job was done, the squadron would make a tactical move through these obstacles.

Everybody was in place, on time, and better still, it had stopped raining by the time the fun began. While the Cougar troops laid down suppressing fire and smoke using rounds from their 76 mm guns, the sappers moved in and blew a path through the minefield with C-4 charges, a very dangerous task in peace or war. Once the minefield was gapped, the engineers brought in their big Badger AEVs (Armoured Engineer Vehicles) equipped with ploughs and buckets, and began constructing an earth bridge over the anti-tank ditch on the far side of the field, their activities being covered by the squadron. When the sappers were finished, the squadron moved through the field and over the ditch, troop by troop, the first troop to cross establishing a fire base to protect the next troop, and so on until everyone was in position on the far side of the obstacle. The whole business went smoothly and one Light Horse troop leader confessed to being "so happy about it that I nearly couldn't breathe."

The remainder of Tuesday was spent preparing targets for the three days of range work that were to follow – the main event in the minds of the Light Horse. Many of these targets, to add a touch of realism, were high-technology "pop up" items activated by the Lockheed-Martin company whose representatives, most former soldiers, were on the ground to control them. The Light Horse worked hard on this preparatory job and that evening they were rewarded by being permitted to go back to the main camp to get hot showers and clean uniforms – a great morale booster after three days of rain – before returning, squeaky clean, to their "hide" to get some sleep.

Unfortunately, things did not go as smoothly on Wednesday, 25 August 2004, a bright but cool day. In the morning the squadron continued working on the targeting of the range with the hope that firing would commence at 1 P.M. but there was some confusion resulting in delays caused by what Clausewitz terms "friction" or unforeseen eventualities but soldiers call "another screw-up by the staff." The Military Police company, who were training in the second block of the "Three Block War" (security operations, if the reader has forgotten after all this time), became so enthusiastic about conducting vehicle searches that they hampered movement to and from the range. Next, a strange vehicle was observed entering the live fire area which, on investigation, turned out to be truck full of Ghurkhas (a not uncommon sight at Wainwright as the British army uses this base to train) who had to be put on the correct path. All this, however, is about normal for any military operation, training or active – and after things got sorted out, range practice commenced at 3 P.M.

The firing continued until 6.30 P.M. after which the squadron wrapped up and went into their "hide" for the night. After a meal, the crews carried out routine maintenance while troop leaders attended the squadron O Group (a nightly occurrence it should be noted). ACTIVE EDGE being the first big exercise in years and one involving many different arms and services, everybody wanted to have their say, and these squadron O Groups tended to stretch out a bit. While the armoured officers listened to the gunners, engineers, flatfeet – and just about everyone else – drone on, the crews, having finished the daily chores, got in a few hands of Euchre while they waited for the troop leaders to return. When they did, the troop leaders held their own O Groups for the crews and, by the time these were finished, it was nearly 11 P.M.

Thursday, Day 5, 26 August 2004, was a good day. The squadron carried out a controlled advance-to-contact exercise ("keep moving until you run into the enemy") using live ammunition, mainly SHPRAC (Squashed Head, Practice Round). Each troop practised firing on the move – actually since the main gun of the Cougar is not stabilized, they moved, stopped, fired, moved – which can be fatiguing given the constant jolting of the vehicle, but was certainly interesting. Before making a move to

Cougars on the range
The Cougars of the battle squadron prepare to carry out range practice on the last day of the exercise. The echelon crews are still loading ammo through the rear hatches of some of the vehicles. COURTESY, BRETT WALTON

Winding down
As ACTIVE EDGE comes to a successful conclusion, headquarters staff begin to relax at the battle group command post vehicle. From left to right are Captain Colin Michaud, CD, operations officer of the SALH; Chief Warrant Officer Adrian Thomas, CD, Regimental Sergeant-Major; Captain Tom Smith, CD, Officer Commanding A Squadron; and Captain Kristian Gustafson, SALH. Gustafson, Michaud and Thomas are former members of the Lord Strathcona's Horse while Smith previously served with the 15th/19th Hussars of the British army. Michaud and Thomas wear the Goretex weather jacket of the combat dress clothing, necessary because, even in August, Wainwright can be cold and wet – in fact Wainwright is generally miserable at any time of year. COURTESY, KRISTIAN GUSTAFSON

that night's "hide," the squadron had to tear down the range and, since the Echelons were short of bodies, the Cougar crews pitched in to help. This took until early evening and was followed by a lengthy move to a new area on the eastern side of Highway 41 but it went well, the squadron found its guides and its 25 vehicles had no problem locating and settling down in a "hide" area that had been selected by the battlegroup staff and well prepared by the squadron sergeant-major. Dinner was late, as were the O Groups and maintenance activities, all of which combined to make bedtime not much before midnight.

It was about this time that Lieutenant-Colonel Thomas Putt,

who was acting as the Exercise Director for ACTIVE EDGE, visited the battle squadron to talk to his soldiers. A number of them commented that they now realized why he had worked them so hard the previous autumn on Exercise TASK FORCE NORTH as they were doing the same scenarios on the same ground – and they knew their job. Putt was pleased, both with his soldiers' performance and with their "intelligence and their grip of the situation."[1] Better still, he had been able to carry out further assessments of his personnel and, "in the best traditions of the Regiment," which likes to grow its own, had "identified a couple of potential officer candidates from within the enlisted ranks."

Thursday had been a good day and the Light Horse were on a high, but they were all looking forward to Friday, 27 August, which they reckoned would be a great day. Once things were organized in the morning, the squadron prepared to move to a new range to carry out a major live fire exercise, to be undertaken not only by armour but also the artillery and infantry. The plan was to pick up ammunition at a location known as "Dillon's Folly," load it up and then move to the range. While one troop went ahead to the firing line, the crews of the other troop helped the Echelon personnel unload two large trucks piled high with wooden crates, each containing four rounds of 76 mm HESH (High Explosive, Squash Head) or Smoke BE (Base Ejection). Undoing the five metal hasps that secured each crate and kicking them open, these work details loaded 40 rounds into each of the troop's Cougars, 10 in the ready-use rack and 30 in the "wine rack," or storage bin. This completed, the ammunitioned troop proceeded to the range followed by the hardworking Echelon personnel who stopped behind each vehicle of the other troop, already in position, and ammunitioned them, assisted by their crews.

By this time the party had started as the 105 mm howitzers of 20th Field Regiment from Edmonton and Red Deer began to lay down a smoke and HE bombardment on the targets. The gunners were followed by the armour squadron which contributed more smoke and HE and, when that was over, the infantry rolled into the assault, supported by a troop of Leopard C-2 tanks, and accompanied by sappers who blew a bunker. Everyone thought it was just glorious and, better still, when it was finished, they got to do it all over again – hurrah! The only problem was that, this being the first large exercise in Western Canada for some time, the place was crawling with brass ("too many bars" commented one Light Horseman, referring to rank insignia as the more bars, the higher the rank) and media – one calculation was that there were two senior officers and two journalists for every armoured vehicle actually firing. But that didn't really matter to the Light Horse or their comrades, they were just happy to send about 60 rounds per Cougar down range during the event, more than they had in many a long day. When it was all over, late in the afternoon, a woman corporal summed up everybody's feelings: "No matter how much b.s. there was the rest of the week, today made it all worthwhile." Amen.

And then it was time to pack up. The usual chores remained to be done and the squadron had yet to stage a "running replen" (running replenishment or field refuelling) before returning to the Militia Training Support Centre to turn in their vehicles and equipment.

We will leave them at this point, for the time has come to bid farewell to the South Alberta Light Horse. We set out on their trail in the 19th century and have followed it all the way into the 21st century. Along the way we have seen them fight as cavalry, infantry, artillery and armour in times of war and struggle to stay alive in times of peace. We have heard them called rangers, mounted rifles, dragoons, gunners, hussars and fusiliers and armoured reconnaissance, to list but a few of their many handles. Whatever they are called, however, the Light Horse will be ready, as they have always been, to serve their nation if needed.

So wave 'em goodbye and wish 'em luck as they move off in their Cougars along the muddy trails of Wainwright.

"All stations, 4-1 this is 4-1. Prepare to move to compound on order, Bravo leads. Route is Black, Green, Red, then White. All acknowledge … over."

"Alpha, acknowledged… over"

"Bravo"

"Charlie"

"All stations 4-1, this is 4-1, move now… out"

THE END

ROLL OF HONOUR, SOUTH ALBERTA LIGHT HORSE AND PREDECESSOR UNITS

Note that these lists include men who died on active service from causes other than enemy action

South Alberta Light Horse

Trooper James L. Leckie[1]

29th Canadian Armoured Reconnaissance Regiment (South Alberta Regiment), Canadian Armoured Corps, 1940-1945

Captain K.E. Perrin
Captain A.C. Scrimger
Lieutenant R.C. Burns
Lieutenant J.M. Guyot
Lieutenant G.M. Johnston
Lieutenant W. Kennedy
Lieutenant K.W. Little
Lieutenant I.J. Reed
Lieutenant J.M. Roberts
Lieutenant R.C. Smith
Lieutenant W.H. Young
Sergeant A. Bell
Sergeant F.W. Clark
Armourer-Sergeant R.R. Coté
Sergeant T. Donald
Sergeant E.W. Fortin
Sergeant J.S. Wagner
Lance-Sergeant G.J. Hussey
Lance-Sergeant H.B. Jacobson
Lance-Sergeant M.J. Nickel
Lance-Sergeant T.E. Palfrenier
Corporal E.E. Ely
Corporal E.E. Gendron
Corporal H.D. McFadden
Corporal J.G. McRae
Corporal F.B. Moan
Corporal G.W. Tourond
Lance-Corporal L.J. Golby
Lance-Corporal R.H. Goodyer
Trooper A.R. Allen
Trooper H.H. Amey
Trooper W.H. Andrew
Trooper J.F. Bartlett
Trooper A.E. Bateman
Trooper F.C. Belsey
Trooper M.E. Bergquist

Trooper C.E. Brewer
Trooper V.L. Carpenter
Trooper W.B. Carr
Trooper J.C. Carragher
Trooper D. Colwell
Trooper M.A. Danielson
Trooper M.M. Devreker, MM
Trooper A. Dutka
Trooper E.V. Easton
Trooper E.G. Edwards
Trooper L.A. Evans
Trooper E.M. Foster
Trooper J.M. Foster
Trooper E.O. Frankson
Trooper A.G. Gee
Trooper G.F. Hamm
Trooper D.E. Harper
Trooper W.L. Hinson
Trooper D. Hoare
Trooper W.N. Homer
Trooper T.O. Lafoy
Trooper L. Laprade
Trooper W. Laughton
Trooper C.W. Lorenson
Trooper D.A. Low
Trooper P.J. Lynch
Trooper J.A. MacInnis
Trooper G. McCaffrey
Trooper G.A. McDonald
Trooper J.A. McDonell
Trooper D.S. McIntyre
Trooper F.R. McKee
Trooper K.F. Merritt
Private S. Milan
Private H. Moreau
Private F.J. Mullan
Trooper G.W. Mungall
Trooper H.W. Neff
Trooper G.W. Noble
Trooper D. Ouelette
Trooper E.M. Owen
Trooper W.F. Pachal
Trooper C.L. Quinnel
Trooper J. Rathwell
Trooper A.J. Robertson
Trooper K. Rowe
Trooper G.S. Scott
Trooper J.V. Seidler
Trooper J.C. Stone
Trooper V.E. Storvik
Trooper H.G. Walker
Trooper H.W. Walton
Trooper K.J. Wickstrom
Trooper L.A. Woods
Trooper W. Zwicker

13th Field Regiment, Royal Canadian Artillery, 1940-1945

Major G.F. Rainnie
Major J.D. Young
Captain W.M. Dirks
Lieutenant R.J. MacDonald
Battery Quartermaster-sergeant R. Brakewell
Sergeant J. Burkosky
Sergeant J. Muir
Lance-Sergeant M.C. Hays
Bombardier C.A. MacDonald
Bombardier H.G. McDougall
Bombardier L.R. Thorburn
Bombardier J.M. Wiley
Corporal N.A. Hauk
Lance-Bombardier A.H. Josephson
Signalman C.E. Allison
Gunner H.F. Bailey
Gunner J.F. Birney
Gunner J.R. Carter
Gunner R.C. Casselman
Gunner K.R. Collyer
Gunner F.B. Curliss
Gunner R.V. Darnell
Gunner R.E. Edwards
Craftsman V.A. Essen
Gunner R.G.F. Filsinger
Gunner L.G. Ford
Gunner V.L. Fredericskon
Gunner W.A. Higgs
Craftsman Humphries*
Gunner J.F. Hunter
Gunner J.K. Jeffrey
Gunner S. Lebel
Gunner A.A. MacLellan
Gunner D. McDonald
Gunner W. Mowbray
Gunner A.J. Perry
Gunner S.E. Renault
Gunner J.F. Robinson
Gunner J.R.A.A. Roy
Gunner J.A.E. St.Louis
Gunner F.H. Siddons
Gunner R.F. Taylor
Gunner R.W. Varcoe
Gunner E.T. Waynert
Gunner J. Whittey

19th Alberta Dragoons Service Squadron/Canadian Corps Cavalry Regiment/Canadian Light Horse, 1914-1918

Lieutenant-Colonel C.T. van Straubenzie
Major C.F. McEwen, DSO
Captain W. de M. King
Captain G. Robinson
Lieutenant R.H. Hocken
Lieutenant A.R. Leggo (attached Royal Flying Corps)
Lieutenant T.H. Murray
Lieutenant R.W.W. Teasdale
Lieutenant E. Wadge
Squadron Quartermaster-sergeant N.F. Trafford
Sergeant C.E. Dickinson
Sergeant E.W.B. Montgomery
Sergeant E. Morris
Lance-Sergeant L.K. Franklin
Lance-Sergeant W.H. Pryce
Lance-Sergeant H.J. Munro
Corporal H. Hastings
Corporal A. Henderson
Corporal A. Inglis, MM
Corporal G.H. Marlow
Corporal P. Stewart
Lance-Corporal A. Forsyth
Lance-Corporal G. Pilkington
Lance-Corporal H.A. Silcox
Private J.R. Alder
Private S. Baldwin
Private A. Banford
Private G.A. Bishop
Private E.S. Blackford
Private J. Blundell
Private J. Bruce
Private W.C. Butler
Private A.F. Clarke
Private S. Crawford
Private R.M. Cornwall
Private F. Delplancke
Private A.D. Dickinson
Private R.J. Dunbar
Private W.H. Eearp
Private H.W. Ellis
Private H. Fisher

Private G.H. Ford
Private S. Gayer
Private R. Gee
Private S.W. Gibson
Private L. Grisdale
Private J.W. Hamilton
Private G.L. Hardwick
Private W.P. Harwood
Private A. Hastie
Private A.O. Imison
Private Z.V. Ingram
Private W. James
Private F.A. Jarvis
Private A.R. Jenkins
Private W.A. Johns
Private T. Johnson
Private A.S. Kilgour
Pirvate G. Lane
Private G. Lewis
Private A.K. MacKinven
Private J.P. McConville
Private L. McKay
Private W.S. McKibbon
Private R.D. Mungall
Private R.H. Nelson
Private W. Parsons
Private H.A. Pruden
Private W.R. Reynolds
Private E. Rogers
Private A.E.G. Sanderson
Private J. Scanlon, MM
Private W.B. Skinner
Private L.B. Smith
Private W.F.B. Smith
Private R. Stanley
Private J.M. Stirton
Private A.R. Walker
Private F.W. Walterson
Private C.E. Watts
Private R.R. Weir
Private, C.D. Westgate
Private T. Wilcock

31st (Alberta) Battalion, Canadian Expeditionary Force, 1914-1918

Officers

Major J.S. Gilker
Major G.D. Powis
Major W.F. Seaton, MC
Major H.M. Splane
Captain V.J.L. Eccles.
Captain W.N. Graham, MC
Captain A.L.B. Johnson
Captain H. Norris, DSO

Lieutenant N. Appleby, MM & bar
Lieutenant J.F. Arbuckle
Lieutenant H.A. Baker
Lieutenant R.H. Barnes
Lieutenant W.R. Barnes, MC
Lieutenant C.A. Bateman
Lieutenant E.A. Boucher
Lieutenant R.W. Buchanan
Lieutenant J.H. Cameron, DSO
Lieutenant D.J.M. Campbell
Lieutenant J.H. Carson, MC
Lieutenant E.S. Conrad
Lieutenant G.A. Cunliffe
Lieutenant R.G.W. Ecland
Lieutenant E.A. Finn
Lieutenant D.B. Forbes
Lieutenant C. Gordan
Lieutenant C.H. Irvine
Lieutenant A.F. Keyes
Lieutenant P. Kingsmith
Lieutenant J.L. Macpherson
Lieutenant A.E. Metcalfe, MC
Lieutenant A. McCormick, MM.
Lieutenant S.M. McNally
Lieutenant J.N. Mee
Lieutenant H.P. Morgan, MM
Lieutenant J.M. Morton
Lieutenant E.F. Pinkham
Lieutenant J.V. Richards
Lieutenant D. Richmond
Lieutenant J.T.L. Sara
Lieutenant C.M. Scadden, MC
Lieutenant G.H. Scott, MC
Lieutenant E.A. Sharples
Lieutenant H.N. Simpson
Lieutenant L.R. Swain
Lieutenant E.C. Thom
Lieutenant P.G. Tofft
Lieutenant E.T. Toole
Lieutenant H.H. Whitehead
Lieutenant W. Whyte, MC

Other Ranks[2]

Abbott, A.F.
Adam, G.E.

Adamson, A.R.	Bird, J.H.	Clark, F.W.	Dodridge, P.C.	Fraser, A.P.	Harvey, J.C.
Adamson, J.G.C.	Birkill, T.M.	Clarke, H.	Doheny, J.	Fraser, B.	Haslam, J.M.
Adsett, J.W.	Bisset, R.	Clarkson, L.	Doherty, J.H.	Fraser, R.St.C.	Hawker, H.
Adsit, W.R.	Bissonette, L.	Cleary, J.	Doleman, W.	Fraser, W.W.	Hawkins, W.H.
Aitken, D.	Black, W.	Clifton, F.	Donald, A.	Frederick, C.	Hazelton, J.D.
Aitken, G.	Blair, J.	Coad, R.G.	Donaldson, D.	French, R.C.A.	Heath, F.C.
Aitken, R.	Blakeley, W.E.	Coates, C.R.	Donegan, G.W.	Frith, F.H.	Heffernan, E.J.
Alcock, A.H.	Blight, H.	Coghill, A.C.	Donnelly, W.H.	Fuller, J.H.	Helem, W.R.
Alcock, J.	Bliss, F.	Coldons, H., MM	Dordige, P.C.	Fulton, E.	Hellawell, T.
Alderson, C.	Blossom, W.E.	Coldwell, W.E	Douglas, C.D.	Furley, G.F.	Henderson, T.
Allan, G.F.	Bodwell, J.F.	Coleman, J.	Dower, J.	Gaetz, R.F.	Hermanson, A.
Allan, J.M.	Boles, D.E.	Collin, W.J.	Downing, G.A.	Galloway, H.E.	Hewitt, A.J.
Allardyce, J.H.	Borthwick, S.A.	Collins, E.C.	Downing, W.J.	Galway, J.L.	Hicks, C.H.
Allison, J.	Botsford, J. McK.	Collins, V.	Doyle, J.H.	Gardiner, O.E.	Hicks, E.K.
Anderson, A.	Boughey, G.E.	Comfort, A.M.	Dravinski, J.P.	Gardner, T.	Hicks, H.P.
Anderson, D.S.	Boulden, P.	Condon, J.F.B.	Duff, J., 160691	Garrison, H., MM	Hildreth, J.G.
Anderson, J.	Bourns, W.P.	Connelly, I.W.	Duff J., 79229	Gay, A.H.	Hoad, W.F.
Anderson, J.C.	Bowerman, J.W.	Conning, J.	Duffy, H.	Geddes, A.C.	Hodge, C.F.
Anderson, L.H.	Bowker, J.H.G.	Connolly, E.B.	Duhaime, N.	Geprage. D.St.C.	Hodge, R.F.
Armstrong, A.W.	Bowman, O.R.	Connolly, T.	Duncan, J.E.	Gillison, D.	Hodgkins, J.W.
Armstong, G.H.	Boyce, S.L.	Cook, W.	Duncan, W.J.	Gilman, C.I.	Hogarth, P.
Ashford, A.	Bramwell, W.F.	Corbett, R.J.	Dunn, A.	Gilory, H.	Holborn, C.S.
Ashton, H.C.	Brazeau, G.	Corby, H.	Dunn, R.E.	Gittens, W.A.	Holder, J.G.
Ashton, R.G.	Brenner, T.	Corfield, A.	Dyer, J.B.	Given, C.	Holm, H.
Atkinson, A.H.	Brewster, C.	Coutts, C.R.	Eagle, F.G.	Glasscock, G.J.	Holmes, A.H, MM & bar
Atkinson, R.E.	Broadhead, K.H.	Cowie, A.	Eccles, A.E.	Glover, F.H.	Hooten, W.
Attard, A.	Bromwell, W.F.	Cox, H.C.	Edgar, D.W.	Goad, A.H.	Hopkins, S.H.
Austin, G.B.	Brown, J., 696901	Cox, J.H.	Edstrom, C.E.	Goggs, F.	Hordman, T.
Austin, T.	Brown, J., 79242	Crain, P.L.	Edwards, F.	Good, J.H.	Hornett, A.E.
Avery, T.	Brown, J.E.	Crane, H.F.	Elliot, W.R.	Gooderham, R.	Horrock, R.
Bagget, M.G.	Brown, J.G.	Crawford, A.B.	Elliott, E.G.	Gordan, R.O.	Howard, J.
Baillie, G.	Brunyee, J.	Cressey, H.S. MM	Elliott, H.	Gower, H.R.	Hughes, J.
Baker, B.G.	Buchan, J.	Crossland, W.A.	Elliott, W.	Graham, F.G.	Hughes, L.
Balkenstein, D.L.	Buckley, J.A.	Crow, F.G.	Elliott, W.W.	Grant, D.K.	Hughson, H.E.
Balwin, W.	Buist, R.H.	Cruise, R.W.	Ellis, M.L.	Grant, F.J.	Huguet, E.R., MM
Bannan, J.C.	Bunyan, N.	Cullen, B.L.	Ellis, T., 160391	Grant, J.	Humphreys, R.C.
Barclay, J.W.	Burchell, T.E.	Cumming, A.E.	Ellis, T., 231617	Grant, J.F.	Hunt, C.J.
Barker, J.S.	Burke, T.	Cumming, G.	Elsey, J.J.,	Grawbarger, G.	Hunt, G.S.
Barley, A.H.	Burney, H.	Cupples, D.	Emslie, J., MM	Gray, J.E.	Hunt, L.T.
Barnes, E., MM	Burwell, W.H.	Currie, A., 80112	Erickson, C.G.	Grayburn, A.	Hunter, J.
Barnes, P.J.	Bury, C.L.	Currie, A., 183565	Erskine, W.R.	Greenough, T.	Husley, F.R.
Barron, J.	Butcher, N.S.	Curtis, C.F.	Essles, A.E.	Gregalait, C.	Hutten, C.P.R.
Barry, O.	Butler, J.V.	Cutler, T.	Evans, C.S.	Grieve, W.	Imrie, W.J.
Baxter, G.I.	Butterfield, P.	Cutmore, E.W., MM	Evans, E.	Gross, H.A.	Inglis, J.
Bayles, J.	Buttress, F.	Dalziel, W., DCM	Evans, E.M.	Groves, A.J.	Ingram, J.J.
Beach, O.	Cagney, J.	Darling, D.	Evans, G.O.	Gruzelier, C.	Inkster, A.F.R.
Beardman, A.T.	Caldeleugh, E.G.	Darragh, J.E.	Evans, W.R.	Gurney, A.E.	Inkster, J.C.
Bearn, R.	Callaghan, L.E.	Davenport, A.	Eyre, W.	Guscott, T.A.	Irven, E.
Beaton, D.	Cameron, H.D.	Davidson, A.W.	Falconer, A.	Gustafson, O.	Ivens, C.I.
Beaton, H.E.	Campbell, F.H.	Davidson, F.R.	Farquhar, W.	Gwilliam, F.	Jacklin, R.
Beatt, S.M.	Campbell, H.B.	Davidson, W.M.	Fenby, H.	Haggerty, A.	Jackson, E.J.
Beattie, F.M.	Campbell, J.	Davies, F.	Ferguson, J.	Hamon, P.J.	Jackson, J.H.
Beattie, W.F.	Campbell, J.A.	Davis, A.E.	Fergusson, A.M.	Hannah, J.D.	Jackson, G.R.E..
Bell, J.	Campbell, N.H.	Dawson, H.J.	Ferris, W.H.	Hanslip, A.G.	Jacobs, A.C.
Bell, J.A.	Campbell, P.J.	De Santos, J.	Field, J.	Hanson, E.E.	James, F.V.
Bell, J.T.	Campbell, S.	Deadman, W.J.	Figuers, H.J.	Hardman, T.	James, J.
Benjamin, W.	Campbell, W.	Deal, A.E.	Fiske, K.R.	Hardy, L.	James, O.
Bennett, F.	Canavan, P.	Dean, G.	Flynn, D.J.	Hargreaves. W.	James, W.
Benoit, J.S.	Cannon, A.	Delamere, S.	Ford, A.J.	Harmon, W.	James, W.H.
Bentley, J.S.	Cantrell, J.	Derouin, J.	Ford, W.	Harris, H.T.	Jamieson, H.F.
Benwell, T.L.	Capucci, N.	Dewar, W.J.	Ford, W.J.	Harris, L.G.	Jenson, F.
Berget, O.	Carr, F.E.	Diffey, H.E.	Forshaw, A.E.	Harris, R.N.	Jobel, E.
Berry, J.	Carson, C.M.	Dixon, G.E.	Fortune, G.C.	Harrison, F.	Jobling, E.S.
Berry, W.	Chadwick, J.F.	Dobias, L.H.	Foster, J.	Harvey, A.E.	Johnson, A.A.
Berube, F.	Chalker, W.H.	Dobson, I.	Franklen, J.	Harvey, A.O.	Johnson, C.E.
Bilkey, F.	Chard, R.A.	Dodds, J.G.W.	Franklin, A.E.	Harvey, J.	Johnson, J.N.

Johnson, P.
Johnson, W.H.
Johnston, S.E.
Johnston, W.A.
Jones, B.
Jones, D.
Jones, E.T.
Jones, F.
Jones, I.
Jones, R.
Jones, R.F. 100421
Jones, W.
Jovetich, P.
Jull, G.F.
Junck, V.H.
Kachina, N.
Kain, J.
Kane, C.
Karpuck, G.
Keith, J.M.
Kelly, F.P.
Kelly, J.T.
Kelly, T.
Kemp, A.J.
Kennedy, H.W.
Kenworthy, J.L.
Kerr, A.D.
Keyes, W.E.G.
Kidd, J.
Kidd, W.
Kimball, J.
King, F.W.
King, H.
King, W.N.
Kinnear, G.W.
Kinsella, W.W.
Kirkman, C.F.
Knott, W.
Kunz, C.
LaBrie, L.G.
LaForet, E.D.
Lafranier, G.A.
Laidlaw, W.J.
Laird, R.J
Lambert, W.E.
Lancaster, C.
Langlands, J.A.
Langridge, H.A.
Laurie, A.
Law, A.J.W.
Leach, J.
LeClaire, F.
Lee, E.R.
Lee, J.F.
Leeder, H.N.
Leeman, T.S.
Leif, W.R.
Leish, H.L.
Lemnoux, J.
Lewis, W.R.
Light, A.N.
Lightle, A.I.
Lind, A.
Lister, T.
Llewellyn, J., MM
Lloyd, C.

Lloyd, J.O.
Lobban, E.A.
Lock, F.C.
Lockyer, J.
Logan, S.B.
Lomax, G.
Lomax, J.
Lomax, W.
Loomis, S.A.
Loucks, S.
Loughborough, E.
Loveland, C.V.
Lovell, L.
Low, C.T.
Luxton, H.M.
MacAldin, T.G.
MacBeth, F.H.
MacDonald, A.
MacDonald, A.R.
MacDonald, C.A.
Macdonald, J.
MacDonald, J.C.G.
MacNeil, F.T.
MacGregor, W.
MacIntosh, J.H.
MacLean, I.
MacPherson, C.J.
MacPherson, G.
MacRae, D., DCM
Madden, E.
Maguire, J.
Maitland, G.R.A.
Major, C.R.
Maley, H.
Mallory, H.
Malone, J.V.
Manley, W.J.
Mann, A.J.
Mann, L.
Manning, C.B.
March, G.
March, W.
Marment, V.W.
Marquis, G.
Marsh, G., 425025
Marsh, G., 446897
Marsh, W.J.
Marshall, A.A.
Martin, F.G.
Martin, G.H.
Mathews, G.B., MM
Matthews, H.J.
Matthews, J.G.
Matthews, W.E.
Matthewson, T.
Mayhew, W.
McAlister, A.J.
McAlister, R.S.
McArthur, J.
McBain, A.
McBain, W.
McCleary, W.
McColl, G.H.
McCombe, A.
McCracken, J.
McCracken, W.

McCreedy, H.
McCullock, T., MM
McDairmaid, D.D.
McDonald, A.
McDonough, E.A.
McDougall, C.F.
McDowall, D.
McDowell, E.
McGonigal, V.
McInnes, F.D.
McIntosh, J.D.
McIsaac, J.
McKay, W.A.
McKie, V.H.
McKie, W.
McKinnon, W.
McKinnon, W.D.
McLeen, W., MM
McLennan, K.
McLeod, N.
McMillan, A.G.
McMullen, C.C.
McMurtry, R.F.
McNabb, M.C.
McNair, A.
McQuade, W., MM
McWalter, J.
McWilliams, J.
Mearns, J.
Meechan, P.
Meers, A.
Melvin, A.
Merkley, M.E.
Metters, L.
Mewton, L.J.M.
Millar, J.
Miller, A.
Miller, A.J.
Miller, E.
Miller, J.R.
Mills, C.R.
Milne, A.W.
Milne, J.W.
Milnes, H.
Mitchell, A.
Mitchell, D.
Mitchell, F.W.
Mitchell, W.
Mole, W.
Montague, J.E.
Mooney, C.A.
Mooney, W.I.
Moore, A.
Moore, A.S.
Moore, C.E.
Moore, H.E.
Moore, J.C.
Moore, P.J.
Morrell, G.
Morris, A.T.
Morris, C.P.S.
Morris, D.
Morris, H.W.
Morris, M.
Morris, W.P.
Morrison, A.D.

Morrison, D.A.
Morrison, H.B.
Mortimer, A.
Morton, J.
Mould, H.J.
Mousley, W.J.
Moyer, L.
Muir, H.
Muncrieff, A.
Mungham, H.W.
Murray, E.F.
Murtha, J.
Musgrave, W.L.
Nail, M.D., MM
Neave, W.
Neilsen, N.S.
Neilson, W.A.
Nelson, T.W.
Newbold, W.K.
Nicholson, A.P.
Norman, T.
Norton, A.
Nunn, C.
Nunn, R.R.
Nuttall, J.L.
O'Hearn, P.P.
O'Keefe, J.
Oakes, J.R.
Oates, A.
Oliver, J.
Oliver, T.E.
Oppliger, P.
Orgar, J.E.
Orr, S.
Osborne, J.
Ostrowiec, E.
Ouimette, E.
Owen, C.A.
Owen, H.W.
Page, T.
Page, W.
Park, C.C
Park, R.
Parker, E.H.
Parker, L.
Patey, S.
Pattison, H.W.
Patton, S.P.
Pavey, H.W.
Peacock, S.
Pearce, R.S.
Pearson, H.
Peck, A.L.
Peck, W.
Pelkey, L.
Pembrooke, J.
Penrose, J.L.
Percy, H.
Peters, R.E.
Phillips, E.
Pickard, J.
Pickering, E.R.
Pinkham, C.W.
Pirie, J.
Pitchford, S.
Porter, S.S.

Portway, P.
Potts, T.
Power, G.
Pownall, E.W.
Poyers, J.E.B.
Pratt, A.
Preston, R.
Price, H.A.
Prince, G.
Profit, J.A., DCM
Proven, J.S.
Proven, W.
Pyecraft, R.W.
Quinney, G.H.
Radzevev, W.
Rae, M.H.
Rayfield, F.W.
Recknell, C.E.
Redshaw, A.R.
Redshaw, J.W.
Reid, W.G.
Reynard, F.
Rice, A.L.
Rich, J.H.
Richardson, J.J.
Richardson, J.M.
Richmond, E.
Ripley, R.J.
Ritchie, J.
Robb, J.
Roberts, H.
Roberts, J.W., MM
Robertson, C.E.
Robertson, R.J.
Robins, H.F.
Robinson, H.M.
Robinson, J.M.
Robson, W.H.
Rogers, G.
Rope, L.G.
Ross, J.
Ross, W.
Ross, W.H., MM
Rowlands, J.
Rowley, F.E.
Rowlinson, A.
Rumberg, O.A.
Runham, T.
Rushworth, J.
Russ, M.W.
Russell, A.
Russell, H.
Russell, R.
Rustad, G.
Rutherford, N.N.
Sager, J.E.
Salter, J.E.
Saunders, J.
Saunders, J.A.
Saunders, W.
Saunders, W.E.
Scammell, W.W.
Schoemperlen, A.F.
Scollen, B.
Setter, P.
Seward, J.B.

Sewell, J.
Sexsmith, C.C.
Shakalevich, K.
Sharon, H.F.
Sharpe, G.S.
Shaw, A.F.
Shaw, A.I.
Shaw, C.T.
Shaw, E.
Shaw, R.E.
Shaw, W.G.
Shaw, W.L.
Sheperd, E.B.
Sheridan, S.
Sherlock, C.J.
Silcox, J.H.B.
Simmons, C.E., DCM
Simpson, J.W.E.
Sims, E.G.
Sims, W.
Skelly, G.
Skinner, F.R.
Smart, H.A., MM
Smith, C.H.
Smith, C.T.
Smith, E.
Smith, G.A.
Smith, G.F.
Smith, H.G.
Smith, H.L.
Smith, J., 151914
Smith, J., 427523
Smith, T.
Smith, O.
Smith, W.J.
Sogge, O.
Soulecho, F.
South, E.
Spence, G.J.
Squires, G.F.
Stanley, H.M.
Steeds, F.H.
Steels, A.E.
Steen, E.R.
Stephan, J.
Stephenson, J.
Stevens, L., 435713
Stevens, L., 654768
Stewart, G.
Stewart, J.
Stewart, R.
Stiles, J.A.
Stitt, J.
Stone, E.A.
Storry, C.W.J.
Strachan, T.E.L.
Strang, W.
Stratton, A.P.
Stromberg, G.A.
Stuart, C.R.
Stump, L.E.
Swannell, F.W.
Symons, W.
Talbot, H.F.
Taylor, A.H.
Taylor, J.W.

Teape, G.F.	Webber, F.W.
Teel, F.D.	Weddell, J.W.
Teel, N.A.	Wedderburn, L.H.
Temple, J.	Weeger, E.A.
Thatcher, W.	Wemp, O.
Theaker, T.	Wesley, A.
Thiebot, J.F.	West, W.M.
Thom, A.W.	Whetham, P.G.
Thomas, D.	Whitaker, E.
Thomas, H.	Whitcutt, F.C.
Thomas, P.	White, W.K.
Thompson, D.	Whitehead, A.
Thurlow, H.V.	Whithead, G.
Tilson, H.	Wiberg, E.F.
Tindall, J.F.	Wik, J.
Todd, P.E.	Williams, H.M.
Tole, F.E.	Williams, O.C.
Toole, E.	Williamson, E.
Torrens, E.	Williamson, J.
Treavor, C.	Wilson, C.
Tull, H.	Wilson, F.
Turner, A.H.	Willox, G.
Turner, W.H.	Wilson, G.
Tyson, J., 696509	Wilson, J., 160270
Tyson, J., 696153	Wilson, J., 883754
Veno, A.	Wilson, J.S.
Vig, J.O.	Wilson, R.
Waddington, S.	Wilson, W.C.
Wade, H.W.	Winkles, S.J.
Wainwright, J.S.	Winskell, E.
Wakeham, J.	Winter, J.A.S.
Walker, E.	Wishart, J.
Walker, J.	Wither, N.A.
Walker, J.H.	Witherby, N.G.
Wall, J.	Wood, A.S.
Ward, A.R.	Wood, G.
Warmington, J.	Woodger, S.G.
Warren, J.D.	Woodland, V.B.
Watlig, S.R.	Woods, C.
Watson, J.	Workman, G.H.S.
Watson, T.	Worster, H.E.
Watson, W.R.	Wright, H.A.
Watters, J.E.	Wyseman, A.
Waugh, V.E.	Yarr, W.J.
Weaver, C.	Young, A.S.L.

Sources

W.W. Barrett, *The History of 13 Canadian Field Regiment, Royal Canadian Artillery, 1940-1945* (n.p., n.d., c. 1946); Donald E. Graves, *South Albertas: A Canadian Regiment at War* (Toronto, 1998); Major (Retd.) M.R. McNorgan, "Notes on the Casualties of Canadian Mounted Units, 1914-1918," compiled for the history of the Royal Canadian Armoured Corps published as J.M. Marteinson and M.R. McNorgan, *The Royal Canadian Armoured Corps: An Illustrated History* (Toronto, 2000); and H.C. Singer with A.A. Peebles, *History of the 31st Canadian Infantry Battalion, C.E.F.* (n.d., c. May 1939).

Notes

1. Killed in a training accident in April 1991.
2. Note that the original source did not provide ranks of enlisted personnel.

APPENDIX B

BATTLE HONOURS
OF THE SOUTH ALBERTA LIGHT HORSE

NORTHWEST REBELLION

North West Canada, 1885

FIRST WORLD WAR

Battle Honours won by the 19th Alberta Dragoons, CEF (Special Service Squadron) and Canadian Light Horse, 31st Battalion, CEF, (The Alberta Regiment) and 66th Battalion, CEF

Ypres, 1915*   Gravenstafel*   St. Julien*   Festubert, 1915*

Mount Sorrel	Somme, 1916	Flers-Courcelette
Thiepval	Ancre Heights	Arras, 1917,1918
Vimy, 1917	Arleux	Scarpe, 1917,1918
Hill 70	Ypres, 1917	Passchendaele
Amiens	Drocourt-Quéant	Hindenburg Line
Canal du Nord	Cambrai, 1918	Pursuit to Mons

France and Flanders, 1915-1918

SECOND WORLD WAR

Battle Honours of the 29th Canadian Armoured Reconnaisance Regiment (The South Alberta Regiment)

Falaise	Falaise Road	The Laison
St. Lambert-sur-Dives	Moerbrugge	The Scheldt
The Lower Maas	Kapelsche Veer	The Rhineland
The Hochwald	Veen	Twente Canal
Bad Zwischenahn	Woensdrecht	

North-West Europe, 1944 - 1945

* Battle Honours held by the 19th Alberta Dragoons which will come to the South Alberta Light Horse on the completion of the amalgamation of the two units.

Sources

Directorate of History and Heritage, Department of National Defence, Ottawa, Files on Battle Honours for units indicated; Donald E. Graves, *South Albertas: A Canadian Regiment at War* (Toronto, 1998); and H.C. Singer with A.A. Peebles, *History of the 31st Canadian Infantry Battalion, C.E.F.* (n.d., c. May 1939).

MAJOR AWARDS AND DECORATIONS WON BY THE PERSONNEL
OF THE PREDECESSOR UNITS OF THE SOUTH ALBERTA LIGHT HORSE, 1914-1945

19th Alberta Dragoons Service Squadron/Canadian Corps Cavalry Regiment/Canadian Light Horse, 1914-1918

Distinguished Service Order

Lieutenant-Colonel E.I. Leonard

Lieutenant-Colonel S.F. Smith

Major C.F. McEwen

Major J.A.G. White

Military Cross

Captain H.M. Dawson

Captain W. de M. King

Captain G. Robinson

Lieutenant L.F. Askwith

Lieutenant J.W. Barnard

Lieutenant H. B. Campbell

Lieutenant C.G. Cockshutt

Lieutenant A.J. Everett

Lieutenant D.N. Ferris

Lieutenant G.L. Greenlay

Military Cross (Bar)

Lieutenant A.J. Everett

Lieutenant E.M. Haliday

Lieutenant F.A. Matheson

Lieutenant A.H.D. Sharp

Lieutenant H.G. Stevens

Lieutenant G. Stirrett

Lieutenant F.A. Taylor

Lieutenant J.A.G. White

Distinguished Conduct Medal

Acting Squadron Sergeant-Major G. Stirrett

Sergeant S. Cook

Sergeant E. Pendrich

Sergeant T. Smith

Sergeant R.R. Tooley

Private R. Frendiger

Private S.J. Thornton

Distinguished Conduct Medal (Bar)

Private G.F. Clarke

Meritorious Service Medal

Regimental Sergeant-Major J.M. Heselton

Squadron Quartermaster-sergeant C.V. Statia

Farrier-Sergeant W. Lewis

Sergeant E.C. Gurnett

Sergeant D.S. Guy

Private H.W. Gore

Military Medal

Squadron Sergeant-Major G. Duncan

Squadron Sergeant-Major W.J. Johnson

Sergeant G.T. Aiken

Sergeant J.E. Bolingbroke

Sergeant J.W. Clarke

Sergeant E. Davis

Sergeant C. Duncan

Sergeant J.K. Greenfield

Sergeant I.N. Lawson

Sergeant C.A. Martin

Sergeant Rolan Munro

Sergeant W.L. Nixon

Sergeant T.A. O'Connor

Sergeant D. Wilson

Corporal H.W. Dafoe

Corporal H. Gilham

Corporal F. Hawkins

Corporal E. Haynes

Corporal R.C. Hill

Corporal A. Inglis

Corporal J. Inkster

Corporal T. John

Corporal J.P. Lucas

Corporal C. O'Connell

Corporal J.V. Sigurdson

Corporal W.E. Sutton

Corporal R.R. Tooley

Corporal H.O. Wilson

Acting Corporal D.S. Charleson

Lance-Corporal E.G. Clements

Lance-Corporal C. Price

Lance-Corporal R.J. Rogers

Lance-Corporal G.H. Spriggs

Private W. Adderly

Private N.L. Ashcroft

Private Arthur Challons

Private J.P. Chamberlain

Private A. Dudgeon

Private G.F. Dudley

Private C. Durham

Private H. Elmer

Private R. Ferguson

Private H. Hodge

Private E.E. Kivell

Private T. Knowles

Private Z.L. Lafrance

Private A.D. Mann

Private W.G. Richards

Private W.H. Richards

Private F.G. Sanderson

Private J. Scanlan

Private J.W. Wells

Private F.J. Spicer

Private L.L. Stevens

Military Medal (Bar)

Sergeant G.P. Lucas

Sergeant C. Price

Croix de Guerre (Belgium)

Sergeant W.D. Munroe

Private E.E. Kivell

Croix de Guerre (France)

Lieutenant C.G. Cockshutt

Médaille Militaire (France)

Squadron Sergeant-Major A.S. Turnbull

Lance-Corporal G.P. Greer

Medal of the Order of St. George, 4th Class (Silver) (Russia)

Sergeant G.T. Aiken

Order of the Rising Sun, 5th Class (Japan)

Lieutenant A.J. Everett

31st Battalion, Canadian Expeditionary Force, 1915-18

Commander of the Order of St. Michael and St. George

Lieutenant-Colonel A.H. Bell

Order of the British Empire

Major W.H. Hewgill

Major J.D.R. Stewart

Captain A.E. Myatt

Distinguished Service Order

Lieutenant-Colonel A.H. Bell

Lieutenant-Colonel E.S. Doughty

Lieutenant-Colonel N. Spencer

Captain H. Kennedy

Captain H. Norris

Lieutenant J.A. Cameron

Military Cross

Major H.C. Chase

Major W. Jewitt

Major W.F. Seaton

Captain W.M. Gilbert

Captain W.N. Graham

Captain W.M. Harris

Captain P. Hunter

Captain J.C. Hutchinson

Captain J.H. L'Amy

Captain R. Pouncey

Captain D.C. Robertson

Captain G.S. Robertson

Captain P.B.R. Tucker

Captain L.B. Yule

Honorary Captain G. Wainwright

Honorary Captain G. Wright

Lieutenant W.T. Bannan

Lieutenant W.R. Barnes

Lieutenant H.C.C. Beaumont

Lieutenant W.N. Bradley

Lieutenant W.S. Brett

Lieutenant J.H. Carson

Lieutenant R.O. Edgar

Lieutenant N. Franks

Lieutenant W.H. French

Lieutenant J.H. Gainor

Lieutenant J.S.P. Guy

Lieutenant W.K. Jull

Lieutenant G. Lawson

Lieutenant F.S. Long

Lieutenant A.F. Metcalfe

Lieutenant J. Millington

Lieutenant H.P. Morgan

Lieutenant W.A. McGregor

Lieutenant F.P.D. Newland

Lieutenant J. O'Hara

Lieutenant N.C. Pearce

Lieutenant H.N. Petty

Lieutenant H.G. Rogers

Lieutenant G.H. Scott

Lieutenant L.G. Shillinglaw

Lieutenant A.J. Toole

Lieutenant W.G. West

Lieutenant W. Whyte

Lieutenant W.H. Williams

Military Cross (Bar)

Major H.C. Chase

Major W. Jewitt

Captain G.S. Robertson

Distinguished Conduct Medal

Avison, D.J.

Bell, G.

Campbell, T.

Muncaster, J.W.M.

Nurse, U.

Profit, J.A.

Rees, S.

Roberts, J.W.

Rodwell, J.F.

Rowden, M.

Rumford, W.

Sheasby, H.G.

Simmons, C.

Stewart, C.

Thompson, H.

Tidswell, I.

Westover, G.E.

Meritorious Service Medal

Calder, R.

Military Medal (Bar)

Lieutenant W. B. Curtis

Bennett, M.J.

Collins, M.E.

Hill, G.F.

Holmes, A.H.

MacPhee, K.H.

Park, C.H.

Sparrow, J.A.

Military Medal

Captain W.M. Gilbert

Captain D. Murray

Lieutenant R.H. Barnes

Lieutenant R. Calvert

Lieutenant J.F. Clement

Lieutenant W.B. Curtis

Lieutenant W. Langtry

Lieutenant A.R. Leek

Lieutenant H.P. Morgan

Lieutenant A. McCormick

Lieutenant D.N. MacKenzie

Lieutenant F.G. Parker

Lieutenant A.J.M. Talbourdet

Lieutenant W.G. West

Adams, A.E.

Anderson, C.L.

Arber, C.W.

Ashton, L.H.

Atherton, S.

Avery, W.

Avison, D.J.

Bainbridge, G.E.

Barnes, B.J.

Barnes, E.

Barrons, W.

Bateman, J.W.

Beaumont, B.

Bell, G.

Bennett, F.C.

Bennett, M.J.

Bicknell, F.J.

Black, H.H.

Boucher, C.T.

Broderick, C.A.

Brown, A.E.

Brown, E.J.

Bruce, G.

Cameron, J.A.

Campbell, D.

Carter, A.

Clegg, A.H.

Cohen, A.

Collins, W.L.

Colson, H.

Connor, A.F.

Cook, J.E.

Corp, W.J.

Creasey, H.S.
Croft, H.
Cross, C.T.A.
Cutmore, E.W.
Day, G.O.
Decastro, G.
Dey, J.
Dixon, J.F.
Dryburgh, W.
Dunbar, F.G.
Durieux, H.
Dyet, D.M.
Ede, P.J.
Emslie, J.
Ferrier, C.J.
Findlay, J.
Flemons, R.G.
Forbes, P.D.
Foster, H.V.
Fraser, J.E.
Fudge, W.F.
Garret, E.
Garrison, H.
Gayton, L.F.
Gillilan, L.
Girling, W.E.
Given, W.G.
Gleghorn, W.
Glynn, A.A.
Grieve, W.J.
Gunning, A.J.
Gush, E.W.
Haigh, J.W.
Harrison, D.
Harrod, J.E.
Harrow, W.F.
Hart, W.D.
Hastings, D.W.
Hawkins, H.
Hawthorne, A.J.G.
Hayes, R.J.
Hicks, E.
Hill, G.F.
Hollyfield, V.
Holmes, A.H.
Huckelsbee, L.
Huguet, E.R.
Hunt, W.J.
Hushagen, A.J.
Jardine, A.M.
Johnston, N.
Keith, O.J.
Kelly, F.
Kerr. A.
Kerr, I.T.
Leadbeater, G.
Leitch, J.
Lent, L.L.
Lewis, A.J.
Llewellyn, J.
Lockhead, C.J.
Lovette, W.S.
Lowe, T.A.
Lowes, R.P.
Lumby, E.
McAlpine, J.M.

McArthur, H.
MacBean, F.A.
McCaskie, A.A.
McCormick, T.
McCreery, A.N.
McCulloch, T.
McDonald, A.P.
McDonald, E.
McGarrachie, A.
McIlveen, A.N.
MacKay, D.
McKay, N.
McLean, M.
McLean, M.A.
McLean, T.
McLean, W.
McLeod, D.A.
McMillan, W.
McMurchie, J.
McNieve, E.
McNintch, S.
MacPhee, K.H.
Macqualter, G.P.
Mann, G.H.
Mapstone, W.
Martin, G.
Martin, R.S.
Mathews, G.B.
Maynard, C.C.
Metcalf, A.
Miller, J.
Milton, E.
Mitchell, D.
Mitchell, J.
Moore, N.A.
Morgan, C.M.
Mott, W.T.
Murray, R.
Nail, M.D.
Nesbitt, E.T.
Neuroh, H.
Newman, P.J.
Newton, J.
O'Neill, A.D.
Ofstedahl, E.
Olsen, E.T.
Orr, J.E.
Otterson, O.H.
Oxley, C.
Park, C.H.
Parker, E.H.
Parker, H.W.
Pendle, W.H.
Price, M.
Proudlove, C.
Ralph, G.
Reid, G.R.
Richardson, W.
Roberts, J.W.
Robertson, J.H.
Robertson, R.
Rodwell, F.J.
Rogers, T.R.
Ross, J.L.
Ross, W.H.
Roy, C.H.

Samson, C.
Sarrasin, W.J.
Simmons, G.
Simpson, W.
Smart, H.A.
Smith, C.E.
Smith, F.
Smith, H.C.
Smith, J.E.
Smith, P.
Solfleet, T.
Sparrow, J.A.
Stark, F.B.
Stewart, W.
Strachan, H.E.R.
Strong, J.A.
Sullivan, G.S.
Swann, L.C.
Symonds, H.A.
Taylor, A.F.
Thompson, C.A.
Tidswell, I.
Tooke, H.A.
Townsend, C.W.
Tregellas, W.
Trelford, A.R.
Upton, H.W.
Velge, R.M.
Ward, J.T.
Watson, A.W.
Wear, C.A.
Weighill, A.J.
Weiler, H.
Westover, G.E.
Willis, P.
Wilson, G.F.
Wilson, J.
Witherly, W.C.
Wolfenden, J.R.
Wright, J.
Wyatt, R.

Croix de Guerre (Belgium)
Lieutenant E.L. Scott
Bell, G.
Bradbury, D.
Bryden, N.
Doull, G.
Jackson, F.W.

Croix de Guerre (France)
Lieutenant-Colonel A.H. Bell

Cross of St. George (Russia)
Jackson, A.H.
Korchuk, J.

Médaille d'Honneur (France)
Turner, H.

29th Canadian Armoured Reconnaissance Regiment (South Alberta Regiment), 1944-1945

Victoria Cross
Major D.V. Currie

Member, Order of the British Empire
Honorary Captain A.P. Silcox
Squadron Quartermaster-sergeant-Major W.J. Doherty

Distinguished Service Order
Lieutenant-Colonel A.F. Coffin
Lieutenant-Colonel G. de S. Wotherspoon
Major T.B. Nash

Military Cross
Captain J.L. Summers
Lieutenant S.F. Bowick
Lieutenant L. Caseley
Lieutenant W.J. McLeod

Distinguished Conduct Medal
Sergeant T.E. Milner
Trooper A.G. Broadbent

Military Medal
Sergeant L.F. Freeman
Sergeant F.E. Freer
Sergeant A.E. Halkyard
Sergeant J.F. Kroesing
Sergeant H. Roulston
Sergeant G.L. Woolf
Corporal A. Haddow
Corporal M. Ottenbreit
Trooper A. Devreker
Trooper J.E. Forbes

Bronze Lion (Netherlands)
Lieutenant-Colonel G. de S. Wotherspoon

Bronze Cross (Netherlands)
Captain D.E. Stewart
Sergeant A.M. Holmes
Sergeant W.G. Penney

Bronze Star (United States)
Captain F.N. Hughes

Croix de Guerre (Belgium)
Major A. Lavoie

Croix de Guerre with Silver Star (France)
Captain G.E. Irving

Croix de Guerre with Bronze Star (France)
Sergeant D.S. Prenevost

Knight of the Order of Leopold II (Belgium)
Major A. Lavoie

13th Field Regiment, Royal Canadian Artillery, 1944-45

Military Cross
Captain R.D. Baugh
Captain W.L. Hogg
Captain W.M. McNabb
Captain H.L. Thomas

Military Medal
Sergeant H.E.R. Roberts
Sergeant C.H. Van Aggellan
Lance-Sergeant R.D. Buswell
Bombadier H.W. Sulis
Lance-Bombardier R.D. Kerr
Lance-Bombardier O. Shaw
Lance-Corporal C.H. McNeill
Gunner H.D. Gingell
Gunner J. Holtzman
Gunner J. McMullan
Gunner W.G. Maynes
Gunner L.K. Smith
Gunner J.R. Stromquist

Chevalier of Leopold III et Croix de Guerre (Belgium)
Lieutenant J.P. Grenier

Croix de Guerre (Belgium)
Corporal W.E.E. Hall

Croix de Guerre with Silver Star (France)
Captain J.R. Milani

Croix de Guerre with Bronze Star (France)
Lance-Bombardier E. Schauer
Gunner E. Barton

Knight Officer of the Order of Orange-Nassau, with Swords (Holland)
Captain A.K. Pousette

Bronze Cross (Holland)
Gunner D.P. Hamilton

Sources
Directorate of History and Heritage, Department of National Defence, Ottawa, Citations File, Northwest Europe, 1944-1945; W.W. Barrett, *The History of 13 Canadian Field Regiment, Royal Canadian Artillery, 1940-1945* (n.p., n.d., c. 1946); Donald E. Graves, *South Albertas; A Canadian Regiment at War* (Toronto, 1998); Hugh Halliday, "Notes on Awards and Decorations of the South Alberta Regiment and 13th Field Regiment, Second World War;" Major (Retd.) M.R. McNorgan, "Notes on the Awards and Decorations of Canadian Mounted Units, 1914-1918," compiled for the history of the Royal Canadian Armoured Corps published as J.M. Marteinson and M.R. McNorgan, *The Royal Canadian Armoured Corps: An Illustrated History* (Toronto, 2000); and H.C. Singer with A.A. Peebles, *History of the 31st Canadian Infantry Battalion, C.E.F.* (n.d., c. May 1939).

COMMANDING OFFICERS AND REGIMENTAL SERGEANTS-MAJOR, THE SOUTH ALBERTA LIGHT HORSE, 1954-2005

Commanding Officers

Lieutenant-Colonel P.W.H. Higgs, CD	1954-1957
Lieutenant-Colonel C.D. Williams, CD	1958-1960
Lieutenant-Colonel N.R. Ray, CD	1960-1964
Lieutenant-Colonel R.W. Ainscough, CD	1964-1968
Lieutenant-Colonel J.D. Heine, CD	1968-1972
Lieutenant-Colonel E.M. Moore, CD	1972-1975
Lieutenant-Colonel C.J. Meagher, CD	1975-1982
Lieutenant-Colonel B.F. McKinley, CD	1982-1984
Lieutenant-Colonel B. Moore, CD	1984-1988
Lieutenant-Colonel H.L. Fraser, CD	1988-1993
Lieutenant-Colonel R.B. McKenzie, MMM, CD*	1993-1996
Lieutenant-Colonel B. Hodgson, CD	1996-2000
Lieutenant-Colonel N. Douglas, CD	2000-2003
Lieutenant-Colonel T.E. Putt, CD	2003-

Regimental Sergeants-Major

WO 1 William Ross, CD	1954-1958
WO 1 M. Clelland, CD	1958-1960
WO 1 T. Buchanan, CD	1960-1964
WO 1 J. Paterson, CD	1964-1968
CWO A. Arelis	1968-1974
WO R.B. McKenzie	1975-1976
MWO W. Hieb	1976-1978
MWO R.B. McKenzie, CD*	1978-1980
CWO R.B. McKenzie, MMM, CD	1980-1984
CWO J. Hamill, CD	1984-1987
CWO A. van Rooyen, CD	1987-1991
CWO J. Bray, CD	1991-1996
CWO J. Szram, CD	1996-1997
CWO S. Ballard, MMM, CD	1997-1998
CWO T. Smith	1999-2002
MWO J. Bray, CD	2002-2003
CWO A. Thomas, CD	2003-

Sources

Directorate of History and Heritage, Department of National Defence, Ottawa, Annual Historical Reports, South Alberta Light Horse, 1954 to 2004; files in SALH Archives, Medicine Hat.

Notes

* Lieutenant-Colonel McKenzie has served both as RSM and Commanding Officer.

NATIONAL AND COMMAND COMPETITIONS WON BY THE SOUTH ALBERTA LIGHT HORSE, 1954-1997

Note: The Royal Canadian Armoured Corps stopped holding national competitions when cutbacks in the defence budget led to the inability of instructional staff to provide gunnery and inspection teams for the testing of militia armoured units. As a result all RCAC competitions were ended in 1997. The actual trophies are currently held at the Armour School in CFB Gagetown.

NATIONAL LEVEL COMPETITIONS

The Worthington Trophy

Presented by the founder of the Royal Canadian Armoured Corps, Major-General F.F. Worthington, to the best Militia regiment in the Corps.

1962	The South Alberta Light Horse
1963	The South Alberta Light Horse tie with The Elgin Regiment (RCAC)
1964	The South Alberta Light Horse tie with the King's Own Calgary Regiment (RCAC) and The Elgin Regiment (RCAC)

The Howard Trophy

Presented by Major-General William Howard and awarded to the armoured unit showing the greatest improvement from the previous year.

1983	The South Alberta Light Horse
1986	The South Alberta Light Horse

REGIONAL COMPETITIONS

The Dunwood Trophy

Presented by Colonel J.M. Dunwoody, this trophy was awarded for the best unit at summer camp in Prairie Command (1953-1964). It was later awarded to the unit attaining the highest overall standard in the Prairie and Pacific Areas (1966-1996).

1972	The South Alberta Light Horse tie with The British Columbia Regiment (DCO) (RCAC)

The Leonard Challenge Trophy

First presented in 1936 by Colonel I.B. Leonard, former commanding officer of the Canadian Light Horse, this trophy was originally awarded (1936-1939) for NCO horsemanship. It was later re-designated as a trophy for the best armoured car regiment (1949-1964). Finally it was awarded to the runner-up unit in the Central Area (1966-1996).

1962	The South Alberta Light Horse
1963	The South Alberta Light Horse

The Murphy Trophy

First presented by Brigadier W.C. Murphy in 1953 for the best unit at summer camp in Western Command (1953-1957), it was also for a period (1960-1967) awarded to the best reconnaissance regiment in Canada. Finally, (1972–1996) it was awarded to the runner-up unit in the Prairie and Pacific Areas.

1961	The South Alberta Light Horse
1980	The South Alberta Light Horse
1994	The South Alberta Light Horse

TRADES COMPETITIONS

The Merritt Challenge Cup

Originally presented by Lieutenant-Colonel W.H. Merritt in 1913 for the highest standard of horsemanship for cavalry officers, it was later (1924-1963) presented to the unit with the hightest percentage of specialists on strength and finally (1981-1987) awarded for the highest standard of skill in the reconnaissance role.

1962	The South Alberta Light Horse

The Nash Memorial Challenge Trophy

Originally presented in honour of Major-General A.E. Nash and presented to the Militia unit having the highest percentage of trained mechanics qualified during the current training year (1939-1963), it was later awarded (1985-1987) to the militia troop displaying the highest standard of skills in the reconnaissance role.

1962	The South Alberta Light Horse

Sources

Directorate of History and Heritage, Department of National Defence, Ottawa, Annual Historical Reports, South Alberta Light Horse, 1954-1997; "Notes on RCAC Competitions and Trophies" compiled by Major (Retd.) M.R. McNorgan for the history of the Royal Canadian Armoured Corps published as J.M. Marteinson and M.R. McNorgan, *The Royal Canadian Armoured Corps: An Illustrated History* (Toronto, 2000).

AN OUTLINE HISTORY OF THE LINEAGE OF THE SOUTH ALBERTA LIGHT HORSE

The lineage of the South Alberta Light Horse is a complex and convoluted subject because the SALH is the oldest militia unit in the Alberta and has, in terms of military lineage, a connection, one way or another, with most of the military units raised in that province during the 20th century. What follows is an attempt to outline the Regiment's lineage in the simplest possible form.

Prior to the First World War

The **Rocky Mountain Rangers** were raised and disbanded in 1885. The SALH perpetuates this unit and holds its Battle Honour, "North West Canada, 1885," through its later connection with the **South Alberta Horse** (see below).

In 1901, three squadrons of **Canadian Mounted Rifles** were authorized at Calgary, Fort Macleod and Medicine Hat. Although the SALH has no official connection with these units, many of the personnel of G Squadron at Calgary ended up in the **15th Light Horse** when it was authorized to be raised in 1905.

The SALH officially originated on 3 July 1905 when General Order 154/05 authorized the raising of its direct predecessor, the **15th Light Horse**, with Regimental Headquarters at Calgary. The date, 3 July 1905, is the Regiment's birthday.

In 1906, an independent squadron, the **Alberta Rangers**, was authorized at Fort Macleod.

In 1908, four militia units were raised in Alberta that would later become linked with the SALH. On 1 February 1908, General Order 11/08 authorized the formation of the **19th Alberta Mounted Rifles** from four independent squadrons of mounted rifles existing in the province. On 1 April 1908, a General Order authorized the formation of the **21st Alberta Hussars** to be based on the independent squadron of mounted rifles in existence at Medicine Hat since 1901. On 1 April 1908, the squadron of **Alberta Rangers** at Fort Macleod was raised to regimental status as the **23rd Alberta Rangers**. Also on 1 April 1908, the **101st Regiment**, an infantry unit, was authorized to be raised in Edmonton by General Order 60/08.

In 1909 the **101st Regiment** became the **101st Regiment, "Edmonton Fusiliers"** and, in 1911, the **19th Alberta Mounted Rifles** became the **19th Alberta Dragoons**.

The First World War, 1914-1918

During the First World War, only the **19th Alberta Dragoons** served overseas under their original title as the Divisional Cavalry Squadron of the 1st Canadian Division. In 1916 this squadron became A Squadron of the newly-formed **Canadian Light Horse**. The other five militia regiments who play a role in the lineage of the SALH contributed personnel to many of the units of the Canadian Expeditionary Force, of which the **31st Battalion, CEF** is most relevant to the lineage of the Light Horse.

All units of the Canadian Expeditionary Force were disbanded by 1919 but were perpetuated by selected postwar militia units who hold their Battle Honours. (See Appendix H for those units perpetuated by the SALH.)

The Interwar Period, 1919-1939

In 1920, all Canadian military units, both permanent and non-permanent, disbanded for organizational purposes before assuming their postwar form. This was done in an attempt to amalgamate prewar and wartime officers, and wartime units, into the new organization. During the next four years, there were considerable changes in the Alberta militia.

The **15th Light Horse** was redesignated the **15th Canadian Light Horse** on 15 March 1920. In May 1921 the **21st Alberta Hussars** became the 1st Regiment of the new **Alberta Mounted Rifles** with Headquarters at Medicine Hat while, in June 1922, the **23rd Alberta Rangers** became the 2nd Regiment of the same unit. The **101st Regiment, "Edmonton Fusiliers"** was redesignated the **Edmonton Regiment** in March 1920 and, in May 1924, was split into two units, the **Edmonton Fusiliers** and the **Edmonton Regiment**.

A direct predecessor of the modern SALH was formed in February 1920 when the **22nd Battery, Canadian Field Artillery**, was authorized at Gleichen. This battery perpetuated the **22nd Battery, Canadian Field Artillery**, CEF, a wartime unit raised in Ontario. It was redesignated the **22nd Field Battery, Canadian Artillery**, in July 1925 and **22nd Field Battery, Royal Canadian Artillery** in June 1935.

Another direct predecessor was created in March 1920 when the **Alberta Regiment** was authorized. It perpetuated and held the Battle Honours of the **31st Battalion, CEF**. In May 1924, this regiment was split into two separate units, the **South Alberta Regiment**, with Headquarters at Medicine Hat, and the **North Alberta Regiment** with Headquarters at Killam and, later, Ponoka.

Also to become a minor part of the SALH lineage was the **13th Machine Gun Brigade** (later Battalion), authorized in 1919, with companies at Calgary, Edmonton and Medicine Hat.

In 1931, the **2nd Regiment, Alberta Mounted Rifles** was redesignated the **South Alberta Horse** and its Headquarters moved from Medicine Hat to Pincher Creek. That same year, the **1st Regiment, Alberta Mounted Rifles** was redesignated the **Alberta Mounted Rifles** with Headquarters at Vegreville.

The year 1936 was a time of important change in the Alberta militia. The **15th Canadian Light Horse** amalgamated with the **South Alberta Horse** to form the **15th Alberta Light Horse**. The **19th Alberta Dragoons** amalgamated with the **Alberta Mounted Rifles** but retained their original title. The **13th Machine Gun Battalion** was disbanded but the **Edmonton Fusiliers** now became the **Edmonton Fusiliers (Machine Gun)**. The **South Alberta Regiment** took over C Company of the **13th Machine Gun Battalion** in Medicine Hat. The **North Alberta Regiment** was disbanded.

The Second World War, 1939-1945

In June 1940, the **15th Alberta Light Horse**, **19th Alberta Dragoons**, **Calgary Regiment (Tank)**, **Edmonton Fusiliers (MG)** and the **South Alberta Regiment** each contributed a company to form a unit of the Canadian Active Service Force, which was originally planned to be titled **"The Alberta Regiment"** but this title was changed to the **South Alberta Regiment (Canadian Active Service Force)**. This unit was redesignated the **29th Canadian Armoured Regiment (South Alberta Regiment)**, Canadian Armoured Corps, in 1942 and the **29th Canadian Armoured Reconnaissance Regiment (South Alberta Regiment)** in 1943. This unit was disbanded in early 1946.

The **22 Battery, RCA**, joined 44 Battery, RCA, and 78 Battery, RCA, to form **13th Field Regiment, RCA**. This wartime unit disbanded in 1946.

The **15th Alberta Light Horse** and **19th Alberta Dragoons** were made dormant in 1942 but contributed, along with the **Calgary Regiment (Tank)**, to form the **31st Alberta Reconnaissance Battalion, Canadian Armoured Corps (Canadian Active Service Force)**. This wartime unit was redesignated the **31st Armoured Reconnaissance Regiment (CASF)** in June 1942 and was disbanded in February 1945.

The **Edmonton Fusiliers (MG)** mobilized **The Edmonton Fusiliers (CASF)** in May 1940. This wartime unit was later redesignated **1st Battalion, The Edmonton Fusiliers (CASF)** and disbanded in late 1945. When the active service battalion was redesignated, the reserve or militia battalion became the **2nd Battalion, The Edmonton Fusiliers**. In 1942, it mobilized the **3rd Battalion, The Edmonton Fusiliers (CASF)** which only served briefly before being disbanded in 1943.

The militia or reserve battalion of the **South Alberta Regiment** was redesignated the **2nd (Reserve) Battalion, South Alberta Regiment** in late 1940 and the **2nd (Reserve) Battalion, South Alberta Regiment (MG)** in 1942.

Another predecessor unit originated in Calgary in April 1942 when the **41st (Reserve) Field Regiment (RCA)** was authorized.

The Battle Honours won by the **29th Canadian Armoured Reconnaissance Regiment (South Alberta Regiment)** in Northwest Europe in 1944-1945 were authorized to be held by the postwar **South Alberta Regiment**. Being an artillery unit, **13th Field Regiment, RCA**, did not receive Battle Honours.

The Modern Period, 1946-2005

In 1946 the dormant **15th (Reserve) Alberta Light Horse** was amalgamated with the **22nd (Reserve) Field Battery, RCA**, to form the **68th Light Anti-Aircraft Regiment, RCA**, with Headquarters at Calgary. This is a direct predecessor of the SALH.

That same year, the **19th Alberta Dragoons** were amalgamated with the **Edmonton Fusiliers** to form the **19th Armoured Car Regiment (Edmonton Fusiliers)**.

The **41st (Reserve) Field Regiment** was redesignated the **41st Anti-Tank Regiment (Self-Propelled), RCA**, in 1946.

The **19th Armoured Car Regiment (Edmonton Fusiliers)** was redesignated the **19th Armoured Car Regiment** in 1949 and the **19th Alberta Dragoons (19th Alberta Armoured Car Regiment)** in 1954.

On 18 September 1954, the **41st Anti-Tank Regiment**, the **68th Light Anti-Aircraft Regiment** and the **South Alberta Regiment** were amalgamated to form the **South Alberta Light Horse** with Headquarters at Calgary.

In 1958 the **19th Alberta Dragoons (19th Alberta Armoured Car Regiment)** was redesignated the **19th Alberta Dragoons**.

In 1959 the Headquarters of the **South Alberta Light Horse** was made dormant and the unit was reduced to an independent armoured squadron at Medicine Hat with the title, **South Alberta Light Horse**.

In 1961, the **South Alberta Light Horse** regained regimental status with Headquarters at Medicine Hat.

In 1965 the **19th Alberta Dragoons** were placed on the Supplementary Order of Battle.

In 2003, the **South Alberta Light Horse** and the Regimental Association of the **19th Alberta Dragoons** requested that the latter unit be removed from the Supplementary Order of Battle and amalgamated with the **SALH**. At the time of writing (January 2005), official approval has not yet been received but it is hoped that it will come before the Regiment's 100th birthday on 3 July 2005. When this amalgamation takes place, the **South Alberta Light Horse** will hold not only the Battle Honours of the **31st Battalion, CEF** and **29th Canadian Armoured Reconnaissance Regiment (South Alberta Regiment)** but also those of the **19th Alberta Dragoons**, **Canadian Light Horse** and **66th Battalion, CEF**.

Source

Directorate of History and Heritage, Department of National Defence, Ottawa: Unit Lineage Files, 19th Alberta Dragoons and South Alberta Light Horse.

APPENDIX G

COMMANDING OFFICERS OF THE PREDECESSOR UNITS OF THE SOUTH ALBERTA LIGHT HORSE

PRIOR TO 1914

Rocky Mountain Rangers (1885)

Major J.O. Stewart	1885

Alberta Squadrons, Canadian Mounted Rifles (authorized 1901)
G Squadron, Calgary

Captain W.M. Inglis	1901
Captain W.B. Barwis	1902

H Squadron, Fort McLeod

Captain D.J. d'Urban Campbell	1901
Captain C. Genge	1903
Captain A.F. O'Grady	1903
Captain D.J. d'Urban Campbell	1908

I Squadron, Medicine Hat

Captain E.F. Fewings	1901
Captain F.O. Sissons	1903

15th Light Horse (authorized 1905)

Lieutenant-Colonel James Walker	1905-1910
Lieutenant-Colonel G. Macdonald	1910-1920

Alberta Squadrons, Canadian Mounted Rifles (authorized, 1901-1907)
A Squadron, Edmonton

Major S.C. Paton	1906

B Squadron, Strathcona

Major F.C. Jamieson	1906

C Squadron, Fort Saskatchewan

Major P. Aylen	1906

D Squadron (former I Squadron), Medicine Hat

Major F.O Sissons	1905

E Squadron, Morinville/St. Albert

	1907

19th Alberta Mounted Rifles (authorized 1908)

Lieutenant-Colonel R. Belcher	1908-1911

19th Alberta Dragoons (redesignated 1911)

Lieutenant-Colonel R. Belcher	1911-1912
Lieutenant-Colonel F.C. Jamieson	1912-1914

21st Alberta Hussars (authorized 1908)

Major F.O. Sissons	1908
Lieutenant-Colonel F.O. Sissons	1908-1913
Lieutenant-Colonel H. Jenkins	1913-1921

23rd Alberta Rangers (authorized 1908)

Major D.J. d'Urban Campbell	1908-1911
Lieutenant-Colonel A.C. Kemmis	1911-1914

FIRST WORLD WAR (1914-1919)

19th Alberta Dragoons, Divisional Cavalry Squadron, 1st Canadian Division (1914-1916)

Major F.C. Jamieson	1914-1915

Canadian Corps Cavalry Regiment/Canadian Light Horse (1916-1919)

Lieutenant-Colonel L. Elmsley	1916
Lieutenant-Colonel C.C. van Straubenzie	1916-1917
Lieutenant-Colonel E.I. Leonard	1917-1918
Lieutenant-Colonel S.F. Smith	1918-1919

31st Battalion, Canadian Expeditionary Force (1914-1919)

Lieutenant-Colonel A.H. Bell	1914-1918
Lieutenant-Colonel E.S. Doughty	1918
Lieutenant-Colonel N. Spencer	1918
Lieutenant-Colonel E.S. Doughty	1918-1919

INTERWAR PERIOD, 1919-1939

15th Canadian Light Horse (1920-1936)

Lieutenant-Colonel A.G. Wolley-Dod	1920-1923
Lieutenant-Colonel H.C.A. Hervey	1923-1926
Lieutenant-Colonel W.E.A. Tidball	1926-1930
Lieutenant-Colonel R.E.A. Lloyd	1930-1934
Lieutenant-Colonel J.F. Scott	1934-1936

15th Alberta Light Horse (1936-1939)

Lieutenant-Colonel E.G. Studd	1936-1937
Lieutenant-Colonel J.F. Scott	1937-1939

19th Alberta Dragoons (1919-1939)

Lieutenant-Colonel C.Y. Weaver, DSO	1920-1923
Lieutenant-Colonel P.E. Bowen	1923-1927
Lieutenant-Colonel H. de N. Watson	1927-1931
Lieutenant-Colonel W.L. Oliver, MC	1931-1936
Lieutenant-Colonel E.A. Pitman	1936-1938
Lieutenant-Colonel M.H. Wright	1938-1940

21st Alberta Hussars (1919-1921)

Lieutenant-Colonel H. Jenkins	1913-1921

1st Regiment, The Alberta Mounted Rifles (1921-1931)

Major T. Snedden	1921-1923
Lieutenant-Colonel H.W.D. Cox, DSO	1923-1928
Major J. McK. Hughes	1929
Lieutenant-Colonel J. McK. Hughes	1930-1931

The Alberta Mounted Rifles (1931-1936)

Lieutenant-Colonel J. McK. Hughes	1931-1934
Lieutenant-Colonel E.A. Pitman	1934-1936

23rd Alberta Rangers (1919-1921)

Major W.A. Lyndon	1919-1921

2nd Regiment, The Alberta Mounted Rifles (1922-1931)

Lieutenant-Colonel W.A. Lyndon	1922-1925
Lieutenant-Colonel J.H. Jackson	1925-1928
Lieutenant-Colonel W.W. Henderson	1928-1931

The South Alberta Horse (1931-1936)

Lieutenant-Colonel W.W. Henderson, VD	1931-1933
Lieutenant-Colonel E.G. Studd	1933-1936

22nd Battery, Canadian Field Artillery (1920-1940)

Major A.G.B. Lewis	1920-1933
Major R. Dodson, MM	1933-1939

The Edmonton Regiment (authorized 1920)
1st Battalion, (Edmonton Fusiliers)

Lieutenant-Colonel R.H. Palmer, DSO	1920-1924

2nd Battalion, (Edmonton Regiment)

Lieutenant-Colonel P. Anderson, DSO	1920-1924

The Edmonton Fusiliers (from 1924)

Lieutenant-Colonel R.H. Palmer, DSO	1924
Lieutenant-Colonel A.C. Gillespie	1924-1929
Lieutenant-Colonel A.W. Bannard, MM	1929-1933
Lieutenant- Colonel E. Brown, MM	1933-1936

Edmonton Fusiliers (MG) (redesignated in 1936)

Lieutenant- Colonel E. Brown, MM	1936-1938
Lieutenant Colonel A.H. Davies	1938-1939

13th Machine Gun Brigade (authorized 1919)

Major J. Basevi, DSO	1919-1923
Lieutenant-Colonel G.W.H. Millican, MC	1923-1926
Lieutenant-Colonel A.E. Ladler	1926-1931
Major A.H. Highton	1931-1936

The Alberta Regiment (authorized 1920)
1st Battalion, Medicine Hat
    Lieutenant-Colonel W.T Bannan, MC
                         1922-1924

2nd Battalion, Killam
    Lieutenant-Colonel A.S. McCulloch   1922-1924

The South Alberta Regiment (authorized 1924)
Lieutenant-Colonel W.T. Bannan, MC   1924-1926
Lieutenant-Colonel M.E. Patterson   1926-1934
Lieutenant-Colonel C.A. Hooker   1934-1936
Lieutenant-Colonel G.A. Hoover   1936-1937
Lieutenant-Colonel G.G. Elder   1937-1939

THE SECOND WORLD WAR, 1939-1945

The South Alberta Regiment (CASF) (1940-1942)
Lieutenant-Colonel J.H. Carvosso, MM, MC
                         1940-1941
Lieutenant-Colonel W. Bristowe   1941-1942

29th Canadian Armoured Regiment (South Alberta Regiment) (CASF) (1942-1943)
Lieutenant-Colonel W. Bristowe   1942-1943

29th Canadian Armoured Reconaissance Regiment (South Alberta Regiment) (CASF) (1943-1946)
Lieutenant-Colonel W. Bristowe   1943
Lieutenant-Colonel G. de S. Wotherspoon,
    DSO   1943-1945
Lieutenant-Colonel T.B. Nash   1945-1946

31st Alberta Reconaissance Battalion, CASF (1942)
Lieutenant-Colonel F.C. Smith   1942

31st Alberta Reconnaisance Regiment, CASF (1942)
Lieutenant-Colonel F.C. Smith   1942-1943
Lieutenant-Colonel H.H. Riley, MM   1943-1945

13th Field Regiment, Royal Canadian Artillery (CASF) (1940-1946)
Lieutenant-Colonel G.S. Howard   1940-1941
Lieutenant-Colonel J.W.G. Thompson,
    MM, ED   1941-1942
Lieutenant-Colonel H.A. Sparling   1942-1943
Lieutenant-Colonel W.S. Zeigler   1943
Lieutenant-Colonel F. le P.T. Clifford 1943-1944
Lieutenant-Colonel F.D. Lace   1944
Lieutenant-Colonel C.R. Ostrander   1944-1945
Lieutenant-Colonel J.D. Baird   1945

POSTWAR PERIOD, 1945-1965

19th Armoured Car Regiment (Edmonton Fusiliers) (authorized 1946)
Lieutenant-Colonel J. Proctor, OBE   1946-1949

19th Alberta Armoured Car Regiment (1949)
Lieutenant-Colonel J. Proctor, OBE   1949-1950
Lieutenant-Colonel F.N. Hughes   1950-1952
Lieutenant-Colonel A.J. Lavoie   1952-1954

19th Alberta Dragoons (19th Armoured Car Regiment) (1954)
Lieutenant-Colonel E.S. Bryant, CD   1954
Lieutenant-Colonel D.F. Cameron, CD 1954-1958

19th Alberta Dragoons (1958)
Lieutenant-Colonel R.A. Cawsey, CD   1958-1961
Lieutenant-Colonel R.H. Summergill, CD 1961-1965

41st Anti-Tank Regiment (SP), RCA
Lieutenant-Colonel D.S. Harkness, GM, ED
                         1946-1948
Lieutenant-Colonel J.V. Rose   1948-1951
Lieutenant-Colonel R.E. Lucy, MBE,
    MC, ED
                         1951-1954

68th Light Anti-Aircraft Regiment, RCA
Lieutenant-Colonel J.H.R. Thomson, MBE, ED
                         1946-1949
Lieutenant-Colonel W.G. Ledingham   1949-1951
Lieutenant-Colonel C.S. McKay   1951-1953
Lieutenant-Colonel P.W.H. Higgs, CD   1954

The South Alberta Regiment
Lieutenant-Colonel J.L. Wyatt   1946-1949
Lieutenant-Colonel W.H. Buchanan   1949-1951
Lieutenant-Colonel W.H. Buchanan, ED 1949-1951
Lieutenant-Colonel B. McKenzie, DSO, ED 1951-1954

See Appendix D for the Commanding Officers of the South Alberta Light Horse from 1954 to date.

Sources
Canada, Department of Militia and Defence, *Militia Lists*, 1903-1948; Directorate of History and Heritage, Department of National Defence, Ottawa; Annual Historical Reports: 19th Alberta Dragoons, 41st Anti-Tank Regiment, 68th Light Anti-Aircraft Regiment, and South Alberta Regiment, 1946-1954.

APPENDIX H

UNITS OF THE CANADIAN EXPEDITIONARY FORCE RAISED WHOLLY OR PARTLY IN ALBERTA, 1914–1918 AND THEIR PERPETUATION

Key to Abbreviations

Bn	Battalion
CE	Canadian Engineers
CEF	Canadian Expeditionary Force
CFA	Canadian Field Artillery
Coy	Company
MD	Military District
Regt	Regiment

UNIT	FATE	PERPETUATION
Mounted Units		
19th Alberta Dragoons, Special Service Squadron	Became A Squadron, Canadian Light Horse in 1916	**South Alberta Light Horse,** after forthcoming amalgamation
3rd Regt, Canadian Mounted Rifles	Converted to infantry	North Saskatchewan Regt
12th Regt, Canadian Mounted Rifles	Broken up for reinforcements	**South Alberta Light Horse**
13th Regt, Canadian Mounted Rifles	Converted to infantry	**South Alberta Light Horse**
Cyclist Units/Establishments		
Cyclist Depot, MD 13	Created in 1916 at Calgary	Not perpetuated
Artillery Units		
20th Field Battery, CFA, CEF	Fought as an artillery unit	18th Air Defence Regt, RCA
39th Field Battery, CFA, CEF	Fought as an artillery unit	39th Air Defence Battery, RCA
61st Field Battery, CFA, CEF	Fought as an artillery unit	61st Heavy AD Battery, RCA
78th Field Battery, CFA, CEF	Broken up for reinforcements	
Engineer Units		
2nd Tunneling Company, CE, CEF	Formed at Calgary, 1915	Not perpetuated
Infantry Units		
Princess Patricia's Canadian Light Infantry	Made a regular unit in 1919	Regiment still exists
5th Bn (Western Cavalry)	Fought as an infantry unit	North Saskatchewan Regiment
6th Bn	Fought as an infantry unit	12th Manitoba Dragoons (SOB)
9th Bn	Became 9th (Reserve Bn)	**South Alberta Light Horse**
10th Bn (Canadians)	Fought as an infantry unit	Royal Winnipeg Rifles & Calgary Highlanders

Unit	Note	Perpetuation
31st (Alberta) Bn	Fought as an infantry unit	**South Alberta Light Horse**
49th Bn (Edmonton Regt)	Fought as an infantry unit	Loyal Edmonton Regt
50th (Calgary) Bn	Fought as an infantry unit	King's Own Calgary Regt
51st (Edmonton) Bn	Utilized for garrison duty and reinforcements	King's Own Calgary Regt
56th (Calgary) Bn	Broken up for reinforcements	Calgary Highlanders
63rd (Edmonton) Overseas Bn	Broken up for reinforcements	Loyal Edmonton Regt
66th Overseas Bn (Edmonton Guards)	Broken up for reinforcements	**South Alberta Light Horse**
82nd Overseas Bn (Calgary Light Infantry)	Broken up for reinforcements	Calgary Highlanders
89th (Alberta) "Overseas" Bn	Broken up for reinforcements	King's Own Calgary Regt
113th "Overseas" Bn (Lethbridge Highlanders)	Broken up for reinforcements	**South Alberta Light Horse**
137th (Calgary) "Overseas" Bn	Broken up as reinforcements	King's Own Calgary Regt
138th (Edmonton) "Overseas" Bn	Broken up as reinforcements	**South Alberta Light Horse**
151st (Central Alberta) "Overseas" Bn	Broken up as reinforcements	Not perpetuated
175th (Medicine Hat) Overseas Bn	Broken up as reinforcements	**South Alberta Light Horse**
187th (Central Alberta) Overseas Bn	Broken up as reinforcements	**South Alberta Light Horse**
191st (Southern Alberta) Overseas Bn	Broken up as reinforcements	Not perpetuated
192nd (Crow's Nest Pass) Overseas Bn	Broken up as reinforcements	Not perpetuated
194th Overseas Bn (Edmonton Highlanders)	Broken up as reinforcements	Not perpetuated
196th Overseas Bn (Western Universities)	Broken up as reinforcements	Not perpetuated
197th Overseas Bn (Vikings of Canada)	Broken up as reinforcements	Not perpetuated
202nd (Sportsman's) Overseas Bn	Broken up as reinforcements	**South Alberta Light Horse**
211th Overseas Bn (American Legion)	Broken up as reinforcements	Not perpetuated
223rd (Overseas) Bn (Canadian-Scandinavians)	Broken up as reinforcements	Not perpetuated
233rd Overseas Bn (*Canadien Français du Nord Ouest*)	Broken up as reinforcemnts	Not perpetuated
260th Bn, Canadian Rifles	Served in Siberia in 1919	Princess Patricia's Canadian Light Infantry

Infantry Drafts Recruited by Militia Cavalry Regiments
15th Light Horse Draft	A reinforcement draft	Not perpetuated
19th Alberta Dragoons Overseas Draft	A reinforcement draft	Not perpetuated
35th Central Alberta Horse Overseas Draft	A reinforcement draft	Not perpetuated

Infantry Drafts Recruited by Militia Infantry Regiments
101st Regt (Edmonton Fusiliers) Draft	A reinforcement draft	Not perpetuated
103rd Regt (Calgary Rifles) Draft	A reinforcement draft	Not perpetuated

Territorial Regiment
Alberta Regiment, comprising

    Regimental Depot

    21st Reserve Bn (provided reinforcements to 10th, 31st, 49th and 50th Bns)

    9th Reserve Bn (absorbed by 21st Reserve Bn in 1917)

Medical Units/Establishments
8th Canadian Field Ambulance	Raised in Calgary in 1915	Not perpetuated
11th Canadian Field Ambulance	Raised in Edmonton in 1915	Not perpetuated

Ogden Military Convalescent Hospital (Calgary)
Strathcona Military Hospital
Wetaskiwin Military Convalescent Hospital
Canadian Military Hospital, Calgary
Wetaskiwin Military Hospital
Edmonton Military Convalescent Hospital
Colonel Belcher Military Hospital (Calgary)
Sarcee Camp Hospital (Venereal Disease)
Military Convalescent Camp, Banff
No. 13 Army Medical Corps Unit, Calgary
No. 13 Canadian Army Dental Corps, Calgary
Mo. 13 Medical Stores Detachment, Calgary

Miscellaneous Units
No. 13 Canadian Army Pay Corps Detachment, Calgary
Alberta University Canadian Officers Training Company, Edmonton.

Sources
Directorate of History and Heritage, DND, Ottawa: CEF Unit files; List of Canadian Artillery Units during the First World War, 1963; and Joseph Harper, "The Canadian Expeditionary Force 1914-1919," unpublished manuscript in the Directorate.

GLOSSARY OF MILITARY TERMS, ABBREVIATIONS AND ACRONYMS

"40 and 8s" A corruption of "*40 hommes, 8 chevaux (longs)*," the sign stencilled on the standard French railway box car in the First World War indicating that it could hold 40 men or 8 horses.

"A & T" staff Administrative and Training Staff. Regular army personnel attached to militia units to ensure that standards were met and maintained. Now known as RSS (Regular Support Staff).

AALMG Anti-Aircraft Light Machine Gun. A Second World War term which usually means a Bren light machinegun.

ADS Advanced Dressing Station, see that term.

Advanced Dressing Station See "Medical Evacuation System."

AEV Armoured Engineer Vehicle, see "Badger."

AFV Armoured Fighting Vehicle.

AHR See "Annual Historical Report."

Air Defence Command One of five commands of the Canadian Forces which replaced the traditional three services after unification in 1968.

Air Transport Command One of five commands of the Canadian Forces which replaced the traditional three services after unification in 1968.

Angriffsdivisionen Literally "assault" or "attack" divisions, formations capable of carrying out offensive operations.

Annual Historical Report Every unit of the Canadian Forces is required to submit an annual report of its activities in a calendar year. The quality of the reporting varies with the interest of the unit in its own history.

ANZAC Australian and New Zealand Army Corps, these Dominions' equivalent to the Canadian Expeditionary Force.

AVGP Armoured Vehicle, General Purpose, see "Cougar."

Badger The Badger is an Armoured Engineer Vehicle based on the chassis of the Leopard tank. It is equipped with a plough and bucket.

bastion A projection from a main line of fortification permitting weapons to be fired along the face of the main line.

battalion See "terminology, military."

battalion group An infantry battalion to which has been added additional combat and logistical elements, including artillery and armour.

battery (arty.) The basic unit in the artillery arm, a battery consists of between 6 and 8 artillery pieces and can operate independently of its parent regiment

battle exhaustion See "combat stress."

Battle Honour In the Commonwealth military tradition, units that perform well in a specific action are granted a "Battle Honour" for that action. A regiment's most famous engagements are emblazoned on its Regimental Colour or Guidon.

BCD British Columbia Dragoons

BEF see "British Expeditionary Force."

bell tent A circular tent with a centre pole used in the Canadian army from about 1900 until the late

1970s. It was uncomfortable for standing, sitting or sleeping.

"Boat" Crew nickname for the Cougar AVGP

Bofors gun The 40 mm Bofors gun was the standard medium anti-aircraft weapon of the Canadian army from 1940 to well into the 1980s

bomb, bomber In the First World War, hand grenades were known as "bombs" and those soldiers who specialized in using them were known as "bombers."

Box lunch A pre-packaged ration issued in the modern Canadian Forces which usually includes sandwiches or their equivalent, a beverage and a piece of fruit.

Boy's anti tank rifle An oversized .50 calibre anti-tank rifle used by Commonwealth military forces from 1939 to 1943. Almost useless, it was replaced by the PIAT.

brigade (arty) A term used prior to 1939 to indicate the basic artillery unit. It was replaced by "regiment."

brigade, (inf., arm.) A formation composed of two or more units. See also "terminology, military."

brigade group A brigade to which has been added additional combat, logistic or administrative elements. A brigade group is usually based on infantry units with armour and artillery elements attached.

Brigadeführer, **rank** A brigadier-general in the Waffen SS.

British Expeditionary Force In the First World War, the Canadian Corps served in the BEF and in the Second World War, the term was used again for British troops sent to France in 1939-1940

bronco See "quarter horse."

BSM Battery Sergeant-Major

bugle Infantry units used bugles for signalling, cavalry and artillery units used trumpets.

Bundeswehr The army of Federal German Republic in the postwar period

"bus driver uniform" Term of derision for garrison dress uniform issued to Canadian soldiers shortly after unification. It was possibly one of the most unattractive and unmilitary styles of dress inflicted on the soldiers of any nation.

CADPAT Acronym for new disruptive camouflage uniforms which came into service about 2000 which led to Canadian soldiers calling themselves "the relish jars from hell."

calibre Most armed forces used the measurement of the internal diameter of a gun barrel as a means of classifying weapons, thus a 20 mm or 76 mm calibre weapon. Prior to about 1960, the Commonwealth armies also used an older system of classifying artillery weapons by the weight of the shell they fired and this classification is used for some weapons discussed in this book. The conversion for the types discussed above are as follows:

2-pdr.	40 mm
6-pdr.	57 mm
9-pdr.	107 mm
13-pdr.	76.2 mm (World War I)
17-pdr.	76.2 mm (World War II)
18-pdr.	83.8 mm
25-pdr.	85 mm

Weapons with calibres less than one inch were often designated by a decimal point, thus a .50 calibre (half inch) and .303 calibre (nearly a third of an inch) weapons.

camp school A militia summer camp for selected officers and NCOs only

Canadian Expeditionary Force The active service Canadian army during the First World War

Canadian Active Service Force The active service Canadian army during the Second World War

Canadian Forces The term for the unified Canadian armed forces after 1968.

Canadian Corps The four-division corps that was the main field force of the Canadian Expeditionary Force during the First World War

Carabiniers Rifles. Term for militia Rifle regiments in Quebec.

carrier Lightly-armoured tracked vehicle used in the Second World War for a number of purposes including carrying mortars and machineguns, towing small artillery pieces and communications work.

CASF Canadian Active Service Force, see that term.

Casualty Clearing Station See "Medical Evacuation System."

Cavalry Generally, the term "cavalry" refers to soldiers who fight on horseback, as opposed to fighting on their own feet. In the British and Commonwealth military tradition, cavalry units have always carried a bewildering variety of titles, most of which are absolutely meaningless to anyone but members of a regiment. This confusing variety of terminology began shortly after the establishment of a permanent regular army in Britain in 1688. This army consisted of two types of units: *Horse* (cavalry) and *Foot* (infantry). This simple, happy and innocent state of affairs only lasted a few years until regiments of *Dragoons* were added to the army. Dragoons were soldiers who rode to battle on horses and, once there, fought on foot. Looked down upon by the *Horse* (or true cavalry) who both rode and fought mounted, the *Dragoons* began to agitate to progress upward, so to speak, in the military social scale and began to both move and fight on horseback.

By the 1780s, they had achieved this goal and had become divided into two types: *Dragoons* (sometimes *Dragoon Guards*) and *Light Dragoons*. *Dragoons* or *Dragoon Guards* were "heavy cavalry," mounted soldiers riding big horses whose primary tactic was the charge with the *arme blanche* (swords) while *Light Dragoons* were "light cavalry" who might mount a charge but whose primary function was reconnaissance, front, flank and rear protection, and the pursuit of a beaten enemy. Heavy cavalry (which also included many of the original regiments of *Horse* which adopted the title of *Dragoon Guards* because it sounded better) generally despised light cavalry as being of minor significance while light cavalry despised their heavy brothers as big, stupid men on big, stupid horses.

During the nearly two decades of warfare with Revolutionary and Imperial France (1793-1815), the British mounted arm encountered French heavy and light cavalry units with impressive uniforms and interesting titles: *Carabiniers* (actually *Dragoon Guards* but wearing metal chest armour or *cuirasses* and armed with a carbine), Cuirassiers (*Carabiniers* without quite the *éclat*), *Lancers* (light cavalry who used lances (spears) as their main weapon), *Hussars* (light cavalry with fantastic and highly impractical uniforms) and *Chevaux Légers* (actually French for "light horse" but it sounds better in a foreign language). After 1815, therefore, many *Light Dragoon* regiments converted to *Hussars* and *Lancers* while one *Dragoon Guard* began to sub-title itself *Carabiniers*. All these changes in titles, which required changes in uniform (making military tailors both happy and wealthy), were meaningless as cavalry units were either light or heavy, depending on their function.

In the middle to late 19th century, as the British Empire began to reach its zenith, a number of factors came into play that created a new wave of confusing cavalry unit terminology. First, the British army found itself campaigning in distant and large foreign lands such as India where the local people did not fight according to European customs of war – which is to say that they did not stand still long enough to be cut down by a cavalry charge. Second, campaigning in such terrain required large numbers of mounted troops and, since the regular British cavalry establishment was always small in size and disliked serving in foreign climates, numbers of local mounted units were raised, which were called, variously, *Scouts*, *Guides*, *Rangers* (a term first used in the British army in the 18th Century), *Light Horse* (*Chevaux Légers* re-translated into English) and, sometimes, when infantry units were hastily and temporarily converted to cavalry, just plain *Mounted Infantry*. The third factor was the introduction of rifled weapons which could effectively counter traditional cavalry tactics which depended on the use of the sword and lance.

By the time of the war in South Africa in 1899-1902, British and Dominion mounted troops served in the field under a bewildering variety of titles (*Dragoons, Light Dragoons, Hussars, Horse Guards, Life Guards, Dragoon Guards, Lancers, Horse, Light Horse, Guides, Rangers* and others, including *Mounted Police*). It was about this time that a new term came into being, *Mounted Rifles*, to designate those cavalrymen whose main weapon was the rifle, not the sword or lance, and who rode to battle but fought on foot. The cynic might opine that *Mounted Rifles* was but a fancier and more socially grand term for *Mounted Infantry* as they performed the same function. As

explained in the text of this book, however, the post-South African War British military establishment carefully delineated the difference between cavalry (rode to battle and fought mounted with edged weapons but might fight dismounted with rifles); mounted rifles (rode to battle and fought dismounted with rifles but also might fight mounted with edged weapons) and mounted infantry (an inferior breed who rode to battle but always fought dismounted with rifles as they were apparently not trusted with edged weapons).

The militia cavalry establishment that existed in Alberta prior to 1939 exhibited this incredible profusion of titles as it included *Mounted Rifles, Light Horse, Rangers, Hussars* and *Dragoons*.

In 1940 all Canadian cavalry regiments became part of the newly-formed Canadian Armoured Corps as did a number of infantry regiments who were converted to armour (notably the South Alberta Regiment). Instead of eliminating the confusing matter of regimental titles, things actually got worse when the 32 units – armour, tank, armoured car, reconnaissance and armoured reconnaissance – in the new corps were assigned corps numbers (1-12 and 14-33) based on seniority and ordered to use them in all official correspondence with their old titles in brackets. This resulted in such unwieldy handles as the *15th (Reserve) Armoured Regiment (6th Duke of Connaught's Royal Canadian Hussars)* being heard across the land. The regiments in the Corps fought a determined battle against these numbers and, by the postwar period, got them reduced to brackets as sub-titles, as in *Lord Strathcona's Horse (Royal Canadians) (2nd Armoured Regiment)* before finally getting them eliminated completely in 1958.

Today, Canadian armoured regiments whose titles do not indicate that they have cavalry origins place "(RCAC)" for Royal Canadian Armoured Corps in brackets after their title – as in *King's Own Calgary Regiment (RCAC)* while those whose titles indicate a cavalry origin – as in *South Alberta Light Horse* or *British Columbia Dragoons* – do not. Among the 19 active regiments in the Corps, the old cavalry terminology is still extant as there are *Dragoons, Hussars, Light Horse* and *Rangers* on the Order of Battle in 2005. There is also a *12e Régiment blindé du Canada* but this definition will end now because there are limits to knowledge beyond which it is unwise to venture.

cayuse See "quarter horse."

CCS Casualty Clearing Station, see "Medical Evacuation System."

CD Canada Defence, a medal for service, commonly called "5 Years of Undetected Crime"

CEF Canadian Expeditionary Force, see that term

Centaur A Cromwell tank mounting a 95 mm close support weapon.

Central Powers See "Triple Alliance."

Centurion Main battle tank of the Canadian army, 1953-1978.

CF Canadian Forces. The unified Canadian armed forces after 1968.

CFB Canadian Forces Base

Chinese attack A false attack or demonstration.

Chinese Hussars Mobile Bath and Laundry Detachment

CIMIC Civil Military Cooperation. A CIMIC de-

tachment accompanies its parent unit on most overseas deployments and carries out civil-military relations.

CLH Canadian Light Horse

Cold War The state of undeclared hostility just short of war that dominated global politics from about 1948 to the demise of the Soviet Union in the late 1980s.

Colonel-Commandant An honorary appointment in the Royal Canadian Armoured Corps, the colonel-commandant (who may hold a higher actual rank) is the final arbiter in all matters of dress and tradition in the Corps and represents its concerns to higher authorities.

Colour See "Regimental standards."

Colt Depending on the period, a reference to one of the many varieties of handguns manufactured by the Colt company. Canadian soldiers have used Colt .38 and .45 calibre revolvers and .45 calibre automatics.

Combat Engineer Regiment The regular engineer units of the modern Canadian Forces, which are capable of carrying out many different tasks beyond simple field engineering, including the construction of air fields.

Combat stress Throughout history, it was known and accepted that soldiers exposed to the stress of combat might suffer immediate or long-term psychological trauma. Disciplinary methods were imposed to ensure such men performed in battle. In the late 19th century, investigators in several nations began to research the motivation of soldiers in battle as a means of improving performance and began to examine more positive methods of coping with combat stress.

The advent of long-range artillery weapons and the lengthened duration of combat during the First World War led to an increase in psychological casualties caused by stress, particularly from prolonged bombardment by artillery. These casualties were first treated as suffering from "shell shock," that is a condition brought on by the physical effects of High Explosive, but it later became apparent that the cause of such casualties was also psychological in origin. The high number of "shell shock" casualties and the attempts by some soldiers to use the condition as a means of avoiding combat led to a decision in the British Expeditionary Force not to use the term "shell shock" when treating such men, instead the term "Not Yet Diagnosed (Nervous)" was applied to all soldiers who exhibited signs of psychological trauma. This caused a marked reduction in the number of such casualties as the term was regarded negatively by soldiers.

During the Second World War an attempt was made to provide medical treatment for casualties caused by "battle exhaustion," the period term for those afflicted by combat stress. In the Canadian army, attempts were made to identify men in the early stages of their military service who were psychologically unfit for combat and to place them in non-combat trades. At the same time both active corps of the Canadian army in the field were provided with psychiatric units for the treatment of the victims of combat stress. The problem was that soldiers who were referred to these specialized medical units, identified as suffering from "battle exhaustion" rarely returned to their units when they recovered as, once tagged an "exhaustion" casualty, they were evacuated through the medical system and often spent long periods under treatment. As it was known in frontline units that "combat exhaustion" was often a transitory affliction, brought on by prolonged artillery bombardment and lack of sleep, most combat units established a system by which real or potential "battle exhaustion" casualties were sent to the rear echelon for a period, to give them a chance to recover. By this method, many soldiers were retained and ultimately returned to combat, who might have been lost if they had been evacuated through the medical system.

The current word for combat stress is post-traumatic stress disorder and it is not a satisfactory term as it includes all types of stress suffered by soldiers and non-soldiers. Since life is basically stressful, all humans will experience some form of post-traumatic stress, to a greater or lesser extent, during the course of their lives. Soldiers in combat, however, experience extreme stress that has both short and long term effects. Since it is highly unlikely that humanity will ever do away with war, this fact must be recognized and some method or methods must be found of preventing or lessening the effect of combat stress.

company (inf.) The basic infantry sub-unit, consisting of, according to period, anywhere between 75 and 175 officers and soldiers.

Cougar A 6-wheeled tank-trainer introduced into the Canadian Forces in the late 1970s, this is a wheeled armoured vehicle equipped with a 76 mm gun.

counter-battery Artillery that fires on the opposing artillery, rather than other targets, is engaged in counter-battery fire.

Coyote An 8-wheeled armoured vehicle currently in Canadian service in a variety of roles.

CP See "Command Post."

DF Defensive Fire. One of the common tasks carried out by artillery units.

Division (RCMP) A police squadron. The term is still used in the modern RCMP for its various administrative districts.

DND HQ Department of National Defence Headquarters, Ottawa, the Canadian "Pentagon." Among the kinder names given this building are "The Headshed," "Fort Fumble" and "Bedlam on the Rideau."

dragoon See "Cavalry."

DSO Distinguished Service Order

dugout A cave dug in the area of a trench system and usually reinforced with wooden props, dugouts were used for sleeping and important functions such as medical posts and command posts.

ED Empire Defence Medal

edged weapons Swords, bayonets and lances.

elevate To align in the vertical plane.

Entente Cordiale The official term for the alliance of Britain, France and Russia during the First World War.

F Echelon See "Fighting Echelon."

FAT See "Field Artillery Tractor."

Fenian Raids A series of raids launched against Canada from American territory by Irish militants during a four-year period, 1866-1870. The Fenian Raids were one of the first tests of the Canadian militia and resulted in many changes.

Field Artillery Tractor A 4-wheel drive truck used to tow field artillery pieces during the Second World War, also called a "Quad."

Field Engineer Regiment The basic militia engineer unit in the Canadian army.

Field Punishment Introduced in the late 19th century to replace the traditional measure of flogging in the British and Imperial armies, Field Punishments which involved heavy labour, being chained to inanimate objects for long periods and other elements were regarded as a more humane method of punishing military offenders.

Fighting echelon That part of a combat unit that actually fights: the batteries in an artillery unit, the tanks in an armoured unit and the rifle companies in an infantry unit.

firing bay That part of a frontline trench from which soldiers fired their weapons.

Freedom of the City A privilege granted by certain municipalities to military units which accords them the honour of marching through the streets with bayonets fixed, drums beating and flags flying. The custom derives from the British army where the movement of soldiers through cities was always strictly regulated.

funk hole A man-size hold dug into the side of a trench for protection from artillery fire.

fusilier In the late 17th century, units of infantry were raised with the specific task of protecting the artillery in battle. For this reason, they were armed with "fusils" or flintlock muskets rather than the standard matchlock muskets which were very dangerous around a gun position because of the presence of black powder. Gradually, fusiliers, as they were termed, evolved in an elite form of infantry. The title today is largely honorific.

GPMG General Purpose Machinegun. The Browning .30 calibre in widespread use in Canadian service from 1958 to 1988.

GPO Gun Position Officer, see that term.

Granatenwerfer Grenade launcher or small mortar.

Guidon See "Regimental Standards."

gun number Each gunner in a gun detachment is numbered according to the task he has to perform while loading and firing the weapon. The detachment commander is usually No. 1.

gun detachment The sub-unit in the artillery which mans and fires one artillery piece, often incorrectly called a "gun crew."

gun camp Range training with live ammunition usually held over a period of days.

Gun Position Officer The officer in command of firing an artillery battery.

Hauptsturmführer A captain in the Waffen SS

HESH High Explosive, Squash Head

HF Harassing Fire, one of the standard tasks carried out by artillery.

hide A temporary overnight bivouac sometimes, but not always camouflaged.

Honorary Lieutenant-Colonel See "Honorary Colonel."

Honorary Colonel In the Commonwealth military tradition, many regiments have Honorary Colonels and Lieutenant-Colonels which are usually prominent citizens, community leaders or former members of the regiment who rendered distinguished service, who work to the benefit of their respective regiments. Honorary colonels have no power of command.

horse Grain-fuelled, four-legged member of the equine species used until the advent of the internal combustion engine as a prime mover and personnel carrier.

Horse See "Cavalry."

Hussar See "Cavalry."

Iltis A small utility vehicle introduced in the Canadian Forces in the 1980s to replace the jeep.

Individual Meal Pack Individual package containing enough food for one soldier for one meal, IMPs come in a great variety of menus and, if things are going well, each soldier gets 3 per day.

IMP Individual Meal Pack, see that term.

Jagdpanther A particularly dangerous German AFV which was an 88 mm gun mounted on a Panther tank chassis with very thick and well-sloped armour.

Judge Advocate General The legal branch of the army. Military lawyers are as well liked and respected as their civilian counterparts.

Kangaroo A Ram tank with its turret removed to create an Armoured Personnel Carrier.

khaki From the Hindu word *khak*, meaning "dust." Khaki is a dull brown colour and, until unification of the Canadian armed forces, Canadian army uniforms were made of cotton twill or wool in this colour.

KOCR King's Own Calgary Regiment

Kriegsmarine The German navy of the Second World War.

lancer See "Cavalry."

Land Forces Western Area Created in 1991, the westernmost geographical command in Canada, encompassing the Prairie provinces, northern Ontario, British Columia and the northern Territories.

Landing Craft, Assault A small landing craft that could carry and land between 30 and 40 infantrymen to make an assault landing. Equipped with a bow ramp.

Landing Craft, Tank A landing craft designed to carry and land tanks or other vehicles. Equipped with a bow ramp.

LAV III Light Armoured Vehicle III, see that term.

LCA Landing Craft, Assault, see that term.

LCT Landing Craft, Tank, see that term.

Leopard German-built Main Battle Tank, used by the Canadian army since the late 1970s.

LFWA Land Forces, Western Area, see that term.

Light Armoured Vehicle III An 8-wheeled armoured vehicle currently coming into service in the Canadian army which will function as an armoured personnel carrier and in other roles.

light horse See "Cavalry."

lines A military term that derives from "tent lines," it is now commonly used to mean a unit's specific area, whether in the field or in garrison.

line, phase line An objective marked by an imaginary line on a map, rather than a terrain feature.

line crew (arty.) Gunners tasked with the job of maintaining land line communcations between Observation Posts and the gun positions. A very dangerous job.

load-carrying equipment The soldier's basic harness to which is attached all the items and implements he needs for combat.

Local Headquarters Training A militia interwar term meaning training carried out only at a unit's local armoury or drill hall.

M-10 A self-propelled 17-pdr. mounted on a Sherman tank chassis and equipped with a turret

"Maggie Ross" One of the kinder terms used by Canadian soldiers during the First World War for their wretched Ross rifles.

Main Battle Tank The standard tank of an army. In the Canadian army, since 1943, this has progressively been the Sherman, the Centurion and the Leopard.

March Past A military ceremony in which a unit marches past a senior officer or dignitary.

Maritime Command The post-unification term for the Canadian navy. Lately, it has taken to using the traditional term more and more.

Materiel and Training Command One of the five commands into which the Canadian armed forces were split after unification in 1968. This basically included everything not in the other four commands.

MBT Main Battle Tank, see that term.

McAdam shovel An infamous piece of equipment foisted on the Canadian army prior to 1914. Invented by Sam Hughes, the minister of militia, and patented in the name of his secretary, Ena McAdam, it was a small, folding shovel with a hole for a rifle muzzle in the blade that could supposedly either function as a digging implement or as a shield. It was entirely useless and soon discarded, officially or unofficially.

ME 109 Messerschmitt 109. One of the two standard German fighter aircraft during the Second World War.

Medical Evacuation System In both world wars, a medical evacuation system was followed by which a wounded man passed through progressive stages during which he was given progressively more advanced treatment. For the seriously wounded, the evacuation system usually ended in a military hospital. Main stages in the system were the RAP (Regimental Aid Post), Advanced Dressing Station (ADS), Casualty Clearing Stations (CCS) and a variety of forward surgical units.

Mike Target A target engaged by all the guns in an artillery regiment, between 16 and 24 weapons.

Milcon Militia concentration. A term that began to be used in the 1970s for what was once called "summer camp." The militia had no weapons, money or personnel so, instead, the government issued them with fancy terminology, a process that is still ongoing.

Military District Administrative districts were created in the late 1890s across Canada to control the regular and militia units in a specific area. Military District 13 was the Province of Alberta from 1907 until the late 1940s.

militia The Canadian equivalent of the American Army Reserve or British Territorial Army.

Militia Group Formation created in the 1950s and 1960s to control militia units in a specific geographical area.

Militia Training Support Centre Created in the early 1990s, these regional support centres provide a variety of back up support for militia units.

mine In the military sense, as used in the First World War, a tunnel under an enemy position in which explosives are placed to destroy the opponent.

Minenwerfer A large mortar.

Mobile Command What was left of the Canadian army after unification in 1968, one of the five functional commands that replace the former

three armed services.

mounted infantry See "Cavalry."

mounted rifles See "Cavalry."

MQMSM Mechanical Quartermaster-sergeant-Major. The warrant officer in an armoured regiment tasked with keeping the unit's vehicles in running order.

Mulberry Artificial port constructed from large pontoons and old ships in Normandy to serve as a temporary logistics point.

Musical Ride A ceremonial display of intricate team horsemanship created in the British army for equestrian training but now carried out only for entertainment.

musketry A traditional British military term for rifle and range training that was used right up until the Second World War.

Nähmaschine Sewing machine. German army slang for the Maxim machinegun of the First World War.

Nebelwerfer German term for a multi-barrelled smoke mortar which evolved into a very useful weapon system feared by Allied troops during the Second World War. The most common type fired six 150 mm rounds every 90 seconds and the distinctive noise these projectiles made coming towards you gave rise to the sobriquets, "Moaning Minnie," or "Sobbing Sister."

"New Armies" Name given to the essentially civilian force raised by Britain in 1914-1916 to replace the heavy loss she suffered in regular soldiers during the opening months of the First World War.

Non-Permanent Active Militia Official term used in Canada prior to 1941 for the militia.

NPAM Non-Permanent Active Militia, see that term.

NST National Survival Training. Between 1959 and 1965, assisting the civil authorities in the event of nuclear war was the official mission of the Canadian militia and it was universally detested.

NWMP North West Mounted Police, see "Royal Canadian Mounted Police."

NYD(N) Not Yet Diagnosed (Nervous). See "combat stress."

O Group Orders group, see that term.

O Pip Observation Point, see that term.

OBE Order of the British Empire.

Obersturmbannführer Lieutenant-colonel in the Waffen SS.

Obersturmführer First lieutenant in the Waffen SS.

Observation Point A location from which the enemy can be seen and fire brought to bear on him.

Oerlikon The 20 mm Oerlikon was the standard light anti-aircraft weapon in the Canadian army until the mid-1950s.

OP FOR Opposing Force, see that term.

OP Observation Point, see that term.

Opposing Force In training exercises, the "enemy."

Order of Battle The official list of the military units of Canada which are listed according to a strict order of precedence. If a unit is struck from the Order of Battle, it is disbanded.

Orders Group A meeting at which orders are given for a forthcoming operation or movement

overalls The one-piece black denim garment which was standard issue in Canadian armoured units from 1940 until well into the late 1980s.

"Pals battalions" Units raised in Britain in 1915-1916 which permitted the enlistment of young men who belonged to the same athletic team, social club or place of employment to train and

serve together.

parados The back wall of a trench.

parapet The front wall of a trench, facing the enemy.

Parham system A system of artillery command and control, introduced into the Commonwealth armies in 1942-1943 which permitted quick response and heavy fire on selected targets.

PIAT Projector, Infantry, Anti-Tank. An anti-tank weapon introduced into Commonwealth service in 1943, the PIAT was a spring-loaded device that fire a projectile with a hollow charge that was capable of penetrating the armour of most German tanks at close range. Although it required a good sense of humour and a steady hand to be used properly, the PIAT was surprisingly effective.

"Porpoise" Codename for a metal sled loaded with extra ammunition dragged behind the vehicles of the four Canadian field artillery regiments which landed in Normandy on D-Day.

PPCLI Princess Patricia's Canadian Light Infantry. One of the three regular infantry regiments in the modern Canadian army.

Priest The name given to the American M-7 self-propelled 105 mm howitzer manned by the four field artillery regiments which supported 3rd Canadian Division in the opening stages of the Normandy campaign.

Provost Marshal The officer or section responsible for maintaining discipline. The military police or provosts are under his command.

Quad Field Artillery Tractor, see that term.

quarter horse A horse originally bred in North America to run quarter-mile races, hence the name. Quarter horses tend to be somewhat small in size, powerful in build, even in temperament and to possess great stamina.

RA Royal Artillery.

Range Safety Officer The officer tasked with ensuring that all safety regulations during a live firing exercise are followed, the word of the RSO is supreme on the range.

Rangers See "Cavalry."

RAP Regimental Aid Post, see that term.

RCA Royal Canadian Artillery.

RCMP Royal Canadian Mounted Police, see that term

Red Ensign Prior to 1965, the Red Ensign was the flag of Canada. It was replaced by the current maple leaf flag.

Regimental standards In the Commonwealth military tradition, infantry regiments carry Colours, armoured regiments carry Guidons and Horse Guards units carry Standards. These emblems are a military unit's proudest possession and the living embodiment of its service and heritage as they are emblazoned with the Battle Honours of its major engagements. Artillery units and rifle regiments do not receive these items.

Regular Support Staff Regular army officers, warrant officers and non-commissioned officers attached to militia units for the purposes of assisting in administration and training.

regiment A term that means different things to different armies, see "terminology, military."

Regimental Aid Post See "Medical Evacuation system."

Relay Point The point at which walking stretcher bearers transfer the wounded to vehicle ambulances.

Remount Depot The central quartering unit for replacement horses.

Rifles In the first decade of the 19th century, units

of infantry armed with rifled, as opposed to smoothbore muskets, were formed. They quickly became elite troops and the tradition is carried on today, although like "Fusiliers," rifle regiments are armed and equipped in an identical fashion to standard infantry regiments.

Roll Past The armoured equivalent of the infantry March Past, a ceremonial function.

ROTO Acronym for Rotation.

Royal Canadian Mounted Police Formed in 1873 as the Northwest Mounted Police, the RCMP is the federal police force of Canada and the provinical police force in 8 of the 10 provinces and the two northern Territories. It carries out a number of diverse functions that are usually handled in other countries by separate forces or agencies.

Royal Artillery The artillery arm of the British army.

RPG Rounds per gun.

RPM Rounds per minute.

RSO Range Safety Officer, see that term.

RSS Regular Support Staff, see that term.

RV Rendezvous.

Scale Level of artillery fire. Scale 1 is one round per gun, Scale 10 is ten rounds per gun.

Scouts See "Cavalry."

self-inflicted wound In desperation to get out of combat, some soldiers would deliberately wound themselves. Authorities frowned on this practice and the punishments were severe.

shell shock See "Combat stress."

Sherman HVSS The last wartime model of Sherman, powered by diesel engines and armed with a high-velocity 76 mm. gun.

"smoker" A military stag night, so called because there was no restriction on smoking, which would not have been the case if it was a more formal occasion.

SMTP Special Militia Training Plan. This was basically an employment programme created by the Canadian government to help alleviate high unemployment in the early 1960s. Men were given weeks of basic military training with an emphasis on non-weapons training and paid at regular army rates. Many of the graduates joined either the regular army or the militia.

"Sobbing sister" See *Nebelwerfer*.

SOS Emergency firing task for artillery.

Special Air Service The elite British special forces unit.

squadron The armoured/cavalry equivalent to the infantry rifle company. Depending on the period, a squadron would consist of up to 225 mounted soldiers or about 20 AFVs.

"Stables" The duty, carried out several times a day, when cavalrymen groomed and fed their mounts.

stand to Manning weapons and positions in readiness to defend against a possible attack.

stand up Army slang word meaning the creation, organization and training of a new unit.

stand down When the "stand to" is finished, soldiers "stand down."

Standard See Regimental standards.

Standartenführer Colonel in the Waffen SS.

Stellungsdivisionen "Static" or "position" divisions. Formations capable of only limited offence but sound defence.

Stosstruppen "Assault" or "attack" troops. Small units of well-trained soldiers who made the initial assault.

Sturmmann Lance-corporal in the Waffen SS.

Stottertante "Stuttering aunt." German soldiers' slang for First World War Maxim machinegun.

sub-unit A component of a unit (see that terms). A company is a sub-unit of an infantry battalion, a squadron of an armoured regiment and a battery of an artillery regiment.

subalterns Officers of captain's rank and below.

Supplementary Order of Battle Units placed on the Supplementary Order of Battle are disbanded in all but name.

Tannoy A primitive loudspeaker and voice communications system used during the Second World War.

tent-pegging A form of cavalry weapons training by which a mounted soldier attempted to use either a lance or a sword to impale a tent peg imbedded in the ground, while at full gallop. Supposedly good training for the *arme blanche*, it was also whacking great fun.

terminology, military Commonwealth armies use terminology for units and formations that differ somewhat from other western armies. In most armies, a "regiment" is a permanently organized military unit with two or more battalions – the Commonwealth equivalent is a "brigade." In the Commonwealth, the term "regiment" is used in the titles of units that are really only of battalion size. Thus Commonwealth infantry, armour and artillery regiments are actually battalions in size. The reader unfamiliar with this usage should simply translate "battalion" for "regiment" every time the latter word appears and "regiment" for "brigade." American equivalents for Commonwealth unit and formation terminology are as follows:

Commonwealth	American
brigade	reinforced regiment
regiment (armour)	tank battalion
regiment (infantry)	infantry battalion
regiment (artillery)	artillery regiment
company (infantry)	company
squadron (armour)	tank company
squadron (engineer)	engineer company
battery (artillery)	artillery battalion
troop (armour)	tank platoon
platoon (infantry)	platoon
section (infantry)	squad

"Three Block War" A term used to describe the different but connected levels of activity that Canadian soldiers face on overseas deployments. In one block, they might be providing humanitarian aid to the distressed; in the second block they might carrying out security operations against armed terrorists; and in the third block they might be engaged in full scale war fighting.

Tiffie Nickname for Typhoon tactical attack aircraft.

Tommy Nickname for British soldier.

TOT Time on Target. An artillery tactic by which a great number of rounds are landed on the target at the same time.

traverse To align in the horizontal plane.

trench torpedo Mortar bomb.

Triple Alliance Germany, Austria-Hungary and Italy (later Turkey).

troop (cav.) The basic cavalry sub-unit which, depending on the period, could consist of between 25 and 75 all ranks.

troop (arm.) The smallest armour sub-unit, consisting of between 3 and 5 AFVs, commanded by an officer.

trumpet Artillery and cavalry units used trumpets for signalling, infantry units used bugles.

U-boat A German submarine in both world wars.

Uncle Target A target fired at by every artillery piece in a division, between 48 and 72 weapons.

unit Basic tactical organization of one arm (artillery, armour or infantry). In the infantry, the normal unit is the battalion (see "terminology, military units and formations"). In the armour and artillery, the normal unit is the regiment.

Unterscharführer Sergeant in the Waffen SS.

Untersturmführer Second lieutenant in the Waffen SS.

Victor Target A target fired at by every artillery piece in a corps.

Voltigeurs Literally "leapers," the French term for Light Infantry.

VOR Vehicle Off Road. The higher the VOR rate of a unit, the fewer vehicles it had running.

War Office The headquarters of the British army in London.

War Diary Prior to the late 1940s, every Canadian unit was required to keep a daily war record of its activities for examination by higher authority. Although War Diaries constitute an important historical source, their quality is uneven, according to the interest of the junior officer who was usually changed with keeping them up to date. Replaced by the Annual Historical Report, see that term.

Wasp A carrier mounting a flamethrower unit.

WATC Western Area Training Centre, located at Wainwright Camp, Alberta.

Western Command One of the five area commands that replaced the traditional military districts after the Second World War. Western Command encompassed Alberta and British Columbia.

Western Area Training Centre The major training base for Land Forces Western Area is located at Wainwright Camp, Aberta

William Target A target fired at by every artillery piece in an army.

Winchester An American weapons manufacturer. In the 19th century, its products were issued to a number of Canadian units, including the Rocky Mountain Rangers.

Woodbine A British soldier, derived from the most common British ration cigarette.

Yeomanry A traditional term for the mounted units of the Territorial Army, the British equivalent to the American Army Reserve or Canadian militia.

Yoke Target A target fired at by every artillery piece within range.

YSTP Young Soldier Training Plan. A recruiting programme that existed in the late 1950s and early 1960s by which young men received basic military training carried out on weekends and in the summer. Although administered by the militia, it was not a militia programme although many of the graduates of the YSTP ended up in either the militia or the regular army.

Zombie Term of approbation for a soldier drafted under the National Resources Mobilization Act of 1940 who was neither an active service man nor a militia man.

Zug German for platoon.

NOTES

Abbreviations Used in Notes

Owing to their great number, abbreviated forms of both published and archival sources have been utilized in the notes. The full citations will be found in the bibliography that follows.

AHR	Annual Historical Report
AI	Author's interview
CEA	City of Edmonton Archives
DHH	Directorate of History and Heritage, DND HQ, Ottawa
GM	Glenbow Museum, Calgary
WD	War Diary
MG	Manuscript Group
PAM	Provincial Archives of Manitoba, Winnipeg
NAC	National Archives and Library, Ottawa
RG	Record Group
SALH Archives	Records of the South Alberta Light Horse, Medicine Hat
SAR Archives	Records of the South Alberta Regiment Veterans Association
vol	volume

Sources: Prologue

Information from the planning documents for Exercise ACTIVE EDGE 04 and author's interviews and communications with D. Bergt, C. Howie, R. McKenzie, C. Michaud, T. Putt, S. Thirlwell, B. Walton, J.Watt and G. Yanda

Sources: Chapter One

Unless otherwise noted, this chapter is based on the following sources.

Sources for the early history of the west and Alberta to 1905 were: William Brandon, *American History Book of the Indian*; Ted Byfield, ed., *The Great West Before 1900*; Hugh Dempsey, ed., *Best from Alberta History* and *Men in Scarlet*; W.B. Fraser, *Calgary*; Gerald Friesen, *Canadian Prairies*; W.A. Griesbach, *I Remember*; Archibald MacRae, *History of the Province of Alberta*; James MacGregor, *History of Alberta*; J.W. Morrow, *Early History of the Medicine Hat Country*; George Stanley, *The Birth of Western Canada*; Samuel Steele, *Forty Years in Canada*.

Also consulted were issues of the *Calgary Herald*, the *Eye-Opener* and the *Fort Macleod Gazette*, 1885-1905.

The major sources used for James Walker, the NWMP, the Northwest Rebellion and the Rocky Mountain Rangers were: Canada. *Annual Report of the Militia Department* and *Sessional Papers*, 1886; *Canadian Pictorial and Illustrated War News*, 1885; Hugh Dempsey, ed., *Men in Scarlet* and "Rocky Mountain Rangers" in *Alberta Historical Review*; Cecil Denny, *The Law Marches West* and *Riders of the Plains*; F.C. Jamieson, *Alberta Field Force*; R.G. Macbeth, *Making of the Canadian West*; Grant MacEwan, *Colonel James Walker*; R.C. Macleod, *The N.W.M.P. and Law Enforcement*; Desmond Morton, *The Last War Drum*; Desmond Morton and Reg Roy, eds., *Telegrams of the North-West Campaign*; George Stanley, *Birth of Western Canada* and *Canada's Soldiers*; Samuel Steele, *Forty Years in Canada*; Thomas B. Strange, *Gunner Jingo's Jubilee*; and Gordon Tolton, *Rocky Mountain Rangers*.

For the Boer War the major sources are: Marquis of Anglesey, *History of British Cavalry*, Vol. IV; Canada. *Sessional Papers, 1900-1903*; Ernest Chambers, *Governor-General's Body Guard*; Richard Cunniffe, *Story of a Regiment*; W.A. Griesbach, *I Remember*; E.W.B. Morrison, *With the Guns*; Brian Reid, *Our Little Army in the Field*, "For God's Sake … Save Your Guns!" in Donald E. Graves, ed., *Fighting for Canada: Seven Battles* and "A Most Dashing Advance" in Donald E. Graves, ed., *More Fighting for Canada: Five Battles*; and Samuel Steele, *Forty Years in Canada*.

For cavalry tactics and early militia matters in the province from 1885 to 1905 the sources are: Marquis of Anglesey, *History of British Cavalry*, Vol. IV; Canada. *Sessional Papers 1886* and *1902*; *Calgary Herald*, various issues, 1903-1905; Canada. *Annual Report of the Militia Department*, 1886 and 1898, and *Militia Lists*, 1902-1905; Richard Cunniffe, "Militia Regiments of Alberta" and *Story of a Regiment*; Brereton Greenhous, *Dragoon*; and G.M. Hogarth, "The Canadian Military Tradition in the West."

Biographical information is from the *Canadian Encyclopedia*; the *Dictionary of Canadian Biography*; Archibald MacRae, *History of the Province of Alberta* as well as relevant town and city directories for the period.

Notes: Chapter One

1. A soldier's song of the 1885 Rebellion, these lyrics were sung to the tune of "Solomon Levi" by Canadian militiamen in Lieutenant-Colonel William D. Otter's column during the Northwest Rebellion of 1885. See Morton, *Last War Drum*, xix-xx.
2. Brandon, *American History Book of the Indian*, 45.
3. Quoted in Friesen, *Canadian Prairies*, 55.
4. Quoted in R.C. Macleod, *The N.W.M.P. and Law Enforcement*, 8.
5. Quoted in R.C. Macleod, *The N.W.M.P. and Law Enforcement*, 8.
6. Mary Inderwick, "A Lady and Her Ranch," in Dempsey, *Best from Alberta History*, 66
7. MacGregor, *History of Alberta*, 131.
8. Steele, *Forty Years in Canada*, 111.
9. Griesbach, *I Remember*, 66.
10. Steele, *Forty Years in Canada*, 112.
11. Macdonald to Middleton, 8 Mar 1885, quoted in Morton and Roy, eds., *Telegrams of the North West Campaign, 1885*, 226.
12. Cottingham to Caron, 5 Apr 1885, quoted in Morton, *Last War Drum*, 111.
13. Steele, *Forty Years in Canada*, 337.
14. Strange, *Gunner Jingo's Jubilee*, 419.
15. Strange, *Gunner Jingo's Jubilee*, 408.
16 R.G. MacBeth, *The Making of the Canadian West*, 158-159.
17. Strange, *Gunner Jingo's Jubilee*, 408.
18. Strange, *Gunner Jingo's Jubilee*, 408.
19. Steele, *Forty Years in Canada*, 212-213
20. Strange, *Gunner Jingo's Jubilee*, 430.
21. Strange, *Gunner Jingo's Jubilee*, 430.
22. Steele, *Forty Years in Canada*, 213.
23. Steele, *Forty Years in Canada*, 214.
24. Strange, *Gunner Jingo's Jubilee*, 445.
25. Griesbach, *I Remember*, 71.
26. MacBeth, *Making of the Canadian West*, 171.
27. MacBeth, *Making of the Canadian West*, 172.
28. Strange, *Gunner's Jingo Jubilee*, 416.
29. Stewart to Caron, 25 Mar 1885, quoted in Tolton, *Rocky Mountain Rangers*, 30-31.
30. Quoted in Tolton, *Rocky Mountain Rangers*, 51.
31. Quoted in Tolton, *Rocky Mountain Rangers*, 51.
32. *Fort Macleod Gazette*, 2 May 1885.
33 *Canadian Pictorial and Illustrated War News*, 20 June 1885.
34. *Fort Macleod Gazette*, 11 Aug 1885.
35. Quoted in Cunniffe, "Militia Regiments of Alberta," 7.
36. Middleton to Hutton, 2 May 1885, in Morton and Roy, eds., *Telegrams of the North-West Campaign 1885*, 230.
37. Canada, *Sessional Papers 1886*, Paper 6, Middleton to Caron, quoted in Cunniffe, *Story of a Regiment*, 22.
38. *Annual Report of the Militia Department*, 1886.
39. Major Andrews quoted in Anglesey, *History of the British Cavalry*, Vol. 4, 389.
40. *Annual Report of the Militia Department*, 1898.
41. *Calgary Herald*, 30 Sept 1899.
42. *Calgary Herald*, 24 Oct 1899.
43. Canada, *Sessional Papers 89*, quoted in Reid, *Our Little Army*, 32.
44. Steele, *Forty Years in Canada*, 339.
45. Steele, *Forty Years in Canada*, 340.
46. Robertson, *Dragoons*, 93, quoted in Brian Reid, "For God's Sakes … Save Your Guns," in Graves, *Fighting for Canada*, 197.
47. Major-General Redvers Buller, quoted in Cunniffe, *Story of a Regiment*, 77.
48. Morrison, *With the Guns*, 216.
49. Griesbach, *I Remember*, 316.
50. Morrison, *With the Guns*, 304.
51. Griesbach, *I Remember*, 315.
52. Moeller, *Two Years at the Front*, 162.
53. Smith-Dorien, *Memories*, 276.
54. Canada, *Sessional Papers, 35A*, 85, Macdonell to Adjutant-General, 31 Aug 1902.
55. Quoted in Reid, *Our Little Army*, 6.
56. Chambers, *Governor-General's Body Guard*, 121.
57. *Calgary Herald*, 12 Mar 1902.
58. Cunniffe, "Militia Regiments of Alberta," 22.
59. Cunniffe, "Militia Regiments of Alberta," 23.

Sources for Chapter Two

Unless otherwise noted, the sources for this chapter are as follows.

Sources for the history of Alberta from 1900 to 1914 were: Ted Byfield, ed., *The Birth of the Province*, and *The Boom and the Bust*; Hugh Dempsey, ed., *Best from Alberta History*; Gerald Friesen, *Canadian Prairies*; W.A. Griesbach, *I Remember*; James MacGregor, *History of Alberta*; Samuel Steele, *Forty Years in Canada*. Also consulted were issues of the *Calgary Herald* and *Calgary Standard*, the *Edmonton Bulletin* and *Edmonton Journal*, the *Lethbridge Herald*, *Medicine Hat News* and *Red Deer News* for the period, 1905-1914.

The following sources were used for the Alberta and Canadian militia in the decade prior to 1914: Canada, *Annual Reports of the Department of Militia* and *Militia Lists*, 1900-1914; John Cashman, *More Edmonton Stories*; Richard Cunniffe, "The Militia Regiments of Alberta," *Story of a Regiment* and *Scarlet and Riflegreen*; D.J. Goodspeed, *The Armed Forces of Canada*; William Griesbach, *I Remember*; Ronald Jack, "The Colonel … Willoughby C. Bryan, 1865-1947;" F.C. Jamieson, notes on the early history of the 19th Alberta Dragoons in various issues of *The 19th*; H.G. Kennedy, *History of the Edmonton Fusiliers*; and Christopher Kilford, *Lethbridge at War*.

On military tactics, training and warfare in the immediate pre-1914 period, the sources were: Marquis of Anglesey, History of British Cavalry, vol. 4; Shelford Bidwell and Dominick Graham, *Fire-Power*; Robert Citino, *Quest for Decisive Victory*; H.K. Johnson, *Breakthrough*; Bill Rawling, *Surviving Trench Warfare*; and S.F. Wise and Richard Preston, *Men at Arms*.

Sources for the 1914 summer camp were: Cunniffe, "Militia Regiments in Alberta"; and articles dated June 1914 in the *Calgary Herald*, *Calgary Standard*, *Edmonton Bulletin*, *Edmonton Journal*, and *Medicine Hat News*.

The sources for the origins and causes of the First World War and the opening events of the conflict were: A.F. Duguid, *History of the Canadian Forces in the Great War*; D.J. Goodspeed, *The Road Past Vimy*; J.L Granatstein and Desmond Morton, *Marching to Armageddon*; Robert Massie, *Dreadnought*; Desmond Morton, *When Your Number's Up*; G.W.G. Nicholson, *The C.E.F.*; Peter Simkins, *The Western Front*; Barbara Tuchman, *The Guns of August* and *The Proud Tower*; and J.M. Winter, *The Experience of World War I*.

Biographical information is taken from the *Canadian Encyclopedia*; the *Dictionary of Canadian Biography*; Archibald MacRae, *History of the Province of Alberta* as well as relevant town and city directories for the period.

Notes: Chapter Two

1. Often thought of as a Boer War song, "Dolly Gray" is actually an American composition dating from the Spanish-American War of 1898. It remained popular with soldiers into the early part of the First World War, a popularity perhaps due to its marching rhythm, patriotic and emotional sentiments – and the fact that the most common version, recorded by Canadian singer Harry MacDonough in 1901, included the bugle call for "Reveille" at the beginning and "Last Post" at the end of the song.
2. *Eye Opener*, 24 June 1905.
3. Quoted in MacGregor, *History of Alberta*, 180.
4. Cunniffe, "Militia Regiments of Alberta," 31.
5. Griesbach, *I Remember*, 337.
6. Griesbach, *I Remember*, 338.
7. Quoted in Cunniffe, "Militia Regiments of Alberta," 35.
8. Samuel Steele, *Forty Years in Canada*, 411.
9. Steele, *Forty Years in Canada*, 411-412.
10. Quoted in Cunniffe, "Militia Regiments of Alberta," 39.
11. Quoted in Cunniffe, "Militia Regiments of Alberta," 39.
12. Byfield, ed., *The Birth of the Province*, 140-141.
13. Cunniffe, "Militia Regiments of Alberta," 47.
14. Quoted in Cunniffe, "Militia Regiments of Alberta," 65.
15. Cunniffe, "Militia Regiments of Alberta," 65.
16. H.G. Kennedy, *History of the Edmonton Fusiliers*, n.p.
17. Quoted in Cunniffe, "Militia Regiments of Alberta," 71.
18. DHH File 11.1001, "Short History of the Alberta Mounted Rifles," c. 1931.
19. Henry Borden, ed., *Robert Laird Borden: His Memoirs*, 463.

20. Griesbach, *I Remember*, 350.
21. Andrew Macphail, *Medical Services*, 201.
22. Duguid, *History of the Canadian Forces in the Great War*, vol. 2, 3.
23. Duguid, *History of the Canadian Forces in the Great War*, vol. 2, 11.
24. G. Tylden, "Mounted Infantry," *JSAHR*, 22 (1943-1944), 177.
25. Anglesey, *History of British Cavalry*, vol. 4, 396-397.
26. Anglesey, *History of British Cavalry*, vol. 4, 391.
27. Anglesey, *History of British Cavalry*, vol. 4, 401.
28. Anglesey, *History of British Cavalry*, vol. 4, 401.
29. *Yeomanry and Mounted Rifle Training*, 1.
30. Griesbach, *I Remember*, 350.
31. Griesbach, *I Remember*, 350.
32. Griesbach, *I Remember*, 338.
33. Griesbach, *I Remember*, 338.
34. Griesbach, *I Remember*, 348.
35. Griesbach, *I Remember*, 338.
36. Griesbach, *I Remember*, 350.
37. Griesbach, *I Remember*, 351.
38. Griesbach, *I Remember*, 350.
39. Griesbach, *I Remember*, 339.
40. Griesbach, *Observations on Cavalry Duties*, 34.
41. Griesbach, *Observations on Cavalry Duties*, 5.
42. Griesbach, *I Remember*, 348.
43. *Edmonton Journal*, 17 June 1914.
44. *Calgary Herald*, 16 June 1914.
45 Morton, *When Your Number's Up*, 11.
46. *Calgary Herald*, 16 June 1914.
47. *Calgary Herald*, 17 June 1914.
48. *Calgary Western Standard*, 20 June 1914
49. Cunniffe, "Militia Regiments of Alberta," 82.
50. Griesbach, *I Remember*, 352.
51. *Edmonton Journal*, 29 Jun 1914.
52. News items from the *Calgary Herald*, Edmonton Journal, and Medicine Hat News, July 1914.
53. Morton, *When Your Number's Up*, 3.
54. *Lethbridge Herald*, 4 Aug 1914.
55. *Edmonton Journal*, 4 Aug 1914.

Sources: Chapter Three
Archival sources used for this chapter were as follows. DHH, Ottawa: Shipping Lists, CEF. NAC, Ottawa: RG 9 III D-3, vol. 4955, WD, 19th Light Dragoons and vol 4936, WD, 31st Battalion; MG 30: E15, Diary of Major W.A. Griesbach, 19th Dragoons; and E16, Diary of Major W. Hewgill, 31st Battalion. PAM, Winnipeg: MG 7, H11, Diary of Trooper George Hambley, Canadian Light Horse.

Newspapers consulted were the *Calgary Herald* and *Calgary Standard*, *Edmonton Bulletin* and *Edmonton Journal*, *Lethbridge Herald*, *Medicine Hat News* and the *Red Deer News*, August 1914-March 1915.

Other published sources used were: Ted Byfield, ed., *The Great War and Its Consquences*; Daniel Dancocks, *Welcome to Flanders Fields*; A.F. Duguid, *History of the Canadian Forces in the Great War*; D.J. Goodspeed, *The Road Past Vimy*; J.L. Granatstein, *Hell's Corner*; J.L Granatstein and Desmond Morton, *Marching to Armageddon*; ; Dianne Graves, *A Crown of Life*; F.C. Jamieson, "The 19th Alberta Dragoons in the First World War;" H.K. Johnson, *Breakthrough*; Lyn Macdonald, *1914*; Andrew Macphail, *The Medical Services*; Robert Massie, *Dreadnought*; Steven Mills, *Task of Gratitude*; Desmond Morton, *When Your Number's Up*; G.W.G. Nicholson, *The C.E.F.*; Bill Rawling, *Surviving Trench Warfare*; Peter Simkins, *The Western Front*; H.C. Singer, *31st Battalion*; Barbara Tuchman, *The Guns of August*; War Office. *Field Service Pocket Book, 1914*; and J.M. Winter, *The Experience of World War I*.

Biographical information is from the *Canadian Encyclopedia*; the *Dictionary of Canadian Biography*; Archibald MacRae, *History of the Province of Alberta* as well as relevant town and city directories for the period.

Notes: Chapter Three
1. A 1914 Canadian variant of "Fred Karno's Army," a British soldiers' song that celebrated Army Service Corps, sung to the tune of the hymn, "The Church's One Foundation." From Steven Mills, *Task of Gratitude*. Fred Karno was a popular music hall entertainer in the immediate postwar period.
2. Report of the Privy Council, 6 Aug 1914, in Duguid, *History of the Canadian Forces in the Great War*, vol 2, 37.
3. Duguid, *History of the Canadian Forces in the Great War*, vol 2, 11.
4. Debates, House of Commons, 20 January 1916, quoted in Duguid, *History of the Canadian Forces in the Great War*, vol. 2, 13.
5. Jamieson, "The 19th Dragoons," 22.
6. Duguid, *History of the Canadian Forces in the Great War*, vol. 1, 86.
7. *Edmonton Journal*, 16 Aug 1914.
8. *Edmonton Journal*, 25 Aug 1914.
9. *Red Deer News*, 27 Aug 1914.
10. Griesbach, Diary, 26 Aug 1914.
11. Granatstein and Morton, *Marching to Armageddon*, 10.
12. Granatstein and Morton, *Marching to Armageddon*, 11.
13. *Edmonton Journal*, 23 Nov 1914.
14. Griesbach Diary, 26 Sep 1914.
15. Macphail, *Medical Services*, 23.
16. Duguid, *The Canadian Forces in the Great War*, vol. 2, 122.
17. *Red Deer News*, 19 Aug 1914.
18. Herbert Russell, quoted in Graves, *A Crown of Life*, 169.
19. Macphail, *Medical Services*, 46.
20. Macphail, *Medical Services*, 23.
21. Dancocks, *Welcome to Flanders Fields*, 65.
22. *Field Service Pocket Book. 1914*, 223.
23. "Stables" call from Hambley, Diary 6.
24. WD, 19th Alberta Dragoons, Dec 1914-Jan 1915.
25. Simkins, *The Western Front*, 40.
26. *Edmonton Journal*, 25 Nov 1914.
27. Hewgill, Diary, 10 Mar 1915.
28. DHH, Shipping List, 31st Battalion, CEF.
29. Singer, *31st Battalion*, 15.
30. *Calgary Herald*, 26 Apr 1915 and *Red Deer News*, 28 Apr 1915.
31. Jamieson, ""19th Alberta Dragoons," 24.
32. Jamieson, "19th Alberta Dragoons," 24.
33. Jamieson, "19th Alberta Dragoons," 24.
34. Dancocks, *Welcome to Flanders Fields*, 125.
35. Dancocks, *Welcome to Flanders Fields*, 127.
36. Dancocks, *Welcome to Flander's Fields*, 176.
37. Jamieson, "19th Alberta Dragoons," 26.
38. Dancocks, *Welcome to Flander's Fields*, 240.
39. Morton, *When Your Number's Up*, 45-46.
40. *Calgary Western Standard*, 8 May 1915.
41. Singer, *31st Battalion*, 19.
42. Hewgill, Diary, 31 Aug 1915.
43. Quoted in Simkins, *Western Front*, 71.
44. Duguid, *The Canadian Forces in the Great War*, vol. 2, 87.
45. Macphail, *Medical Services*, 46.

Sources: Chapter Four
Unless otherwise noted, the archival sources used for this chapter were as follows. DHH, Ottawa, DHH 74/633, Stirrett, "A Soldier's Story." NAC, Ottawa: RG 9 III D-3, vols. 4954 and 4955, WD, 19th Light Dragoons and Canadian Light Horse; vols 4936 and 4938, War Diaries, 31st Battalion; MG 30: E16, Diary of Major W. Hewgill, 31st Battalion; and E241, Diary of Lieutenant-Colonel D.E. McIntyre, 28th Battalion. PAM, Winnipeg: MG 7, H11, Diary of Trooper George Hambley, Canadian Light Horse. GM, Calgary: M 742/1, Diary of Captain H.W. McGill, 31st Battalion.

Newspapers consulted were the *Calgary Herald* and *Calgary Standard*, *Edmonton Bulletin* and *Edmonton Journal*, *Lethbridge Herald*, *Medicine Hat News* and the *Red Deer News*, 1915-1916.

Published sources used were: David Beatty, *Memories of the Forgotten War*; Will R. Bird, *Ghosts Have Warm Hands*; A.F. Duguid, *History of the Canadian Forces in the Great War*; Arthur Empey, *Over the Top*; Bill Gammage, *The Broken Years*; D.J. Goodspeed, *The Road Past Vimy*; J.L. Granatstein, *Hell's Corner*; J.L Granatstein and Desmond Morton, *Marching to Armageddon*; F.C. Jamieson, "The 19th Alberta Dragoons in the First World War;" H.K. Johnson, *Breakthrough*; Joyce Kennedy, *Distant Thunder*; William Kerr, *Shrieks and Crashes*; Frederic Manning, *The Middle Parts of Fortune*; Lyn Macdonald, *The Roses of No Man's Land*; Andrew Macphail, *The Medical Services*; William Mathieson, *My Grandfather's War*; Desmond Morton, *When Your Number's Up*; G.W.G. Nicholson, *The C.E.F.*; Bill Rawling, *Surviving Trench Warfare*; Reg Roy, ed., *The Journal of Private Fraser*; Siegfried Sassoon, *Memoirs of an Infantry Officer*; Peter Simkins, *The Western Front*; H.C. Singer, *The 31st Battalion*; and J.M. Winter, *The Experience of World War I*.

Biographical information is from the *Canadian Encyclopedia*; the *Dictionary of Canadian Biography*; Archibald MacRae, *History of the Province of Alberta* as well as relevant town and city directories for the period.

Notes: Chapter Four
1. "When Very Lights are Shining" was a soldier's song from the mid-war period sung to the tune of "When Irish Eyes are Smiling." Very lights were a type of flare, Maxims were the standard German machinegun and "five nines" referred to the German 5.9 inch field gun, a much-feared high velocity weapon.
2. Roy, *Journal of Fraser*, 25.
3. Singer, *31st Battalion*, 41.
4. Singer, *31st Battalion*, 41.
5. Singer, *31st Battalion*, 42-43.
6. Roy, *Journal of Private Fraser*, 36.
7. Kerr, *Shrieks and Crashes*, 127.
8. Kerr, *Shrieks and Crashes*, 128.
9. Roy, *Journal of Private Fraser*, 81.
10. Kerr, *Shrieks and Crashes*, 131.
11. Singer, *31st Battalion*, 48.
12. Roy, *Journal of Private Fraser*, 33.
13. Roy, *Journal of Private Fraser*, 26.
14. Kerr, *Shrieks and Crashes*, 133.
15. Hewgill, Diary, 27 and 28 Oct 1915.
16. Singer, *31st Battalion*, 56.
17. Roy, *Journal of Private Fraser*, 47.
18. Singer, *31st Battalion*, 63.
19. Singer, *31st Battalion*, 59.
20. Hewgill, Diary, 23 Feb 1916.
21. Kerr, *Shrieks and Crashes*, 83.
22. Roy, *Journal of Private Fraser*, 36.
23. Roy, *Journal of Private Fraser*, 37.
24. Singer, *31st Battalion*, 52.
25. Roy, *Journal of Private Fraser*, 113.
26. Singer, *31st Battalion*, 78.
27. Roy, *Journal of Private Fraser*, 113-114.
28. McGill, Diary, 5-6 Apr 1916.
29. Roy, *Journal of Private Fraser*, 120.
30. Singer, *31st Battalion*, 84.
31. Hambley, Diary 6.
32. Roy, *Journal of Private Fraser*, 151.
33. Roy, *Journal of Private Fraser*, 150.
34. Roy, *Journal of Private Fraser*, 152.
35. Singer, *31st Battalion*, 128.
36. Singer, *31st Battalion*, 128-129.
37. Gammage, *Broken Years*, 162.
38. Macdonald, *The Roses of No Man's Land*, 166-167.
39. Roy, *Journal of Private Fraser*, 193.
40. Hewgill, Diary, 12 Sept 1916.
41. Hewgill, Diary, 12 and 13 Sept 1916.
42. Roy, *Journal of Private Fraser*, 201. All of the following quotations concerning the attack on Courcelette in Sep 1916 are from this source, 201-215.
43. Hewgill, Diary, 15 Sept 1916; McIntyre, Diary, 15 Sept 1916.
44. Hewgill, Diary, 16 Sept 1916.
45. McIntyre, Diary, 15 Sept 1916.
46. McIntyre, Diary, 15 Sept 1916.
47. Singer, *31st Battalion*, 162.
48. Singer, *31st Battalion*, 163.
49. Roy, *Journal of Private Fraser*, 224.
50. Singer, *31st Battalion*, 164.
51. McGill, Diary, 26-27 Sept 1916.
52. Hewgill, Diary, 29 Sept 1916.
53. Stirrett, "Soldier's Story." The phrase, "War is Hell," has been attributed to General William Tecumseh Sherman of the Union Army.
54. Simkins, *Western Front*, 122.
55. Hewgill, Diary, 8 Oct 1916.

Sources: Chapter Five
Unless otherwise noted, the sources for this chapter were as follows.

The sources for the wartime history of the province of Alberta, 1914-1919, were: Ted Byfield, ed., *The Great War and Its Consequences*; Richard Cunniffe, *Scarlet and Riflegreen*; Grant McEwen, *James Walker*; James MacGregor, *History of Alberta*. Also consulted were issues of the *Calgary Herald* and *Calgary Herald*, the *Edmonton Bulletin* and *Edmonton Journal*, the *Medicine Hat News* and the *Red Deer News*, 1914-1918.

On military units and recruiting in Alberta, DHH files on CEF unit recruiting and Shipping Lists were utilized.

On the Calgary "Riot," see P.W. Lackenbauer, "The Military and Mob Rule in Calgary.".

The sources for the wartime history of Canada in general were: Henry Borden, ed., *Robert Laird Borden*; A.F. Duguid, *History of the Canadian Forces in the Great War*; D.J. Goodspeed, *The Road Past Vimy*; J.L. Granatstein, *Hell's Corner*; J.L Granatstein and Desmond Morton, *Marching to Armageddon*; William Kerr, *Shrieks and Crashes*; Andrew Macphail, *The Medical Services*; Desmond Morton, *When Your Number's Up*; and G.W.G. Nicholson, *The C.E.F.*

Biographical information is from the *Canadian Encyclopedia*; the *Dictionary of Canadian Biography*; Archibald MacRae, *History of the Province of Alberta* as well as relevant town and city directories for the period.

Notes: Chapter Five
1. Wartime verse added to the "God Save the King" quoted in W.D. Lightall, "War Experiences of Canadian Cities," *National Municipal Review*, 8, No. 1 (June 1918).
2. Nicholson, *The CEF*, 214.
3. Quoted in Morton, *When Your Number's Up*, 63.
4. MacEwan, *James Walker*, 4.
5. *Calgary Standard*, 26 Nov 1916.
6. *Red Deer News*, 7 July 1915.
7. *Edmonton Journal*, 16 Feb 1916.
8. *Medicine Hat News*, 21 Oct 1915.
9. *Field Service Pocket Book. 1914*, 223.
10. Byfield, ed., *The Great War and Its Consequences*, 319.
11. Manning, *The Middle Parts of Fortune*, 51.
12. Kerr, *Shrieks and Crashes*, 145.
13. Byfield, *The Great War and Its Consequences*, 299.
14. Quoted in Granatstein and Morton, *Marching to Armageddon*, 170.

Sources: Chapter Six
The following sources were used for this chapter, unless otherwise noted:

The archival sources consulted for this chapter were as follows. DHH, Ottawa: DHH 74/633, Stirrett, "A Soldier's Story." NAC, Ottawa: RG 9 III D-3, vols. 4954 and 4955, WD, Canadian Light Horse, and vols. 4937, WD, 31st Battalion; MG 30: E16, Diary of Major W. Hewgill, 31st Battalion; and E241, Diary of Lieutenant-Colonel D.E. McIntyre, 28th Battalion, CEF; and E351, Diary of Signaller Craig, 28th Battalion, CEF. PAM, Winnipeg: MG 7, H11, Diary of Trooper George Hambley, Canadian Light Horse. GM, Calgary: M 742/1, War Diary of Captain H.W. McGill, 31st Battalion.

Newspapers consulted included the *Calgary Herald* and *Calgary Standard*, *Edmonton Bulletin* and *Edmonton Journal*, *Lethbridge Herald*, *Medicine Hat News* and the *Red Deer News*, 1916-1917.

Published sources used were: Daniel Dancocks, *Welcome to Passchendaele*; A.F. Duguid, *History of the Canadian Forces in the Great War*; Bill Gammage, *The Broken Years*; D.J. Goodspeed, *The Road Past Vimy*; J.L. Granatstein, *Hell's Corner*; J.L. Granatstein and Desmond Morton, *Marching to Armageddon*; Dianne Graves, *A Crown of Life*; Brereton Greenhous and Steve Harris, *The Battle of Vimy Ridge*; A.M.J. Hyatt, *General Sir Arthur Currie*; F.C. Jamieson, "The 19th Alberta Dragoons in the First World War;" H.K. Johnston, *Breakthrough*; William Kerr, *Shrieks and Crashes*; Lyn Macdonald, *The Roses of No Man's Land*; Andrew Macphail, *The Medical Services*; Desmond Morton, *When Your Number's Up*; G.W.G. Nicholson, *The C.E.F.*; Bill Rawling, *Surviving Trench Warfare*; Reg Roy, ed., *The Journal of Private Fraser*; Peter Simkins, *The Western Front*; H.C. Singer, *The 31st Battalion*; and J.M. Winter, *The Experience of World War I.*

Biographical information is from the *Canadian Encyclopedia*; the *Dictionary of Canadian Biography*; Archibald MacRae, *History of the Province of Alberta* as well as relevant town and city directories for the period.

Notes: Chapter Six

1. "Hanging on the Old Barbed Wire" was a popular soldiers' song sung in the late war period with verses that castigated everyone from politicians down to corporals – with good reason in every case.
2. Singer, *31st Battalion*, 177.
3. Hewgill, Diary, 30 Dec 1916.
4. Singer, *31st Battalion*, 181.
5. Hambley, Diary 3.
6. Singer, *31st Battalion*, 181.
7. Nicholson, *The CEF*, 244.
8. Singer, *31st Battalion*, 185.
9. Craig, Diary, 31 March 1916.
10. Craig, Diary, 1 April 1916.
11. Singer, *31st Battalion*, 190-191.
12. Craig, Diary, 8 April 1916.
13. Singer, *31st Battalion*, 200.
14. Roy, *Journal of Private Fraser*, 270.
15. Hambley, Diary 3.
16. Craig, Diary, 9 April 1917.
17. Roy, *Journal of Private Fraser*, 263.
18 WD, Canadian Light Horse, April 1917, Annex, Report of Sergeant Smith.
19. Graves, *A Crown of Life*, 237.
20. Graves, *A Crown of Life*, 238.
21. Singer, *31st Battalion*, 217.
22. Roy, *Journal of Private Fraser*, 280.
23. Roy, *Journal of Private Fraser*, 287-288.
24. Singer, *31st Battalion*, 220.
25. Roy, *Journal of Private Fraser*, 218.
26. Singer, *31st Battalion*, 221.
27. Roy, *Journal of Private Fraser*, 283.
28. Roy, *Journal of Private Fraser*, 287.
29. MacPhail, *Medical Services*, 130.
30. Macphail, *Medical Services*, 274.
31. Macphail, *Medical Services*, 136.
32. Macphail, *Medical Services*, 136.
33. Macphail, *Medical Services*, 133.
34. Macphail, *Medical Services*, 305.
35. Macphail, *Medical Services*, 275.
36. Roy, *Journal of Private Fraser*, 268.
37. Macphail, *Medical Services*, 279.
38. Singer, *31st Battalion*, 223.
39. Singer, *31st Battalion*, 226.
40. Roy, *Journal of Private Fraser*, 189.
41. Kerr, *Shrieks and Crashes*, 247.
42. Kerr, *Shrieks and Crashes*, 247.
43. Singer, *31st Battalion*, 228.
44. Quoted in Dancocks, *Passchendaele*, 123.
45. Hyatt, *General Sir Arthur Currie*, 79.
46. Kerr, *Shrieks and Crashes*, 173.
47. McIntyre, Diary, 1 Nov 1917.
48. Macphail, *Medical Services*, 101.
49. Macphail, *Medical Services*, 101.
50. Hyatt, *General Sir Arthur Currie*, 145.
51. Singer, *31st Battalion*, 262.
52. Dancocks, *Passchendaele*, 127.
53. Singer, *31st Battalion*, 267.
54. Singer, *31st Battalion*, 269.
55. Craig, Diary, 6 Nov 1917.
56. Singer, *31st Battalion*, 275.
57. Singer, *31st Battalion*, 276.
58. Singer, *31st Battalion*, 275
59. WD, 31st Battalion, 11 Nov 1917.

Sources: Chapter Seven

The following sources were used for this chapter, unless otherwise noted:

The archival sources consulted for this chapter were as follows. DHH, Ottawa: DHH 74/633, Stirrett, "A Soldier's Story." NAC, Ottawa: RG 9 III D-3, vols. 4954 and 4955, WD, Canadian Light Horse, and vols. 4937, WD, 31st Battalion; MG 30: E16, Diary of Major W. Hewgill, 31st Battalion; and E241, Diary of Lieutenant-Colonel D.E. McIntyre, 28th Battalion, CEF; and E351, Diary of Signaller Craig, 28th Battalion, CEF. PAM, Winnipeg: MG 7, H11, Diary of Trooper George Hambley, Canadian Light Horse.

Other sources used were: Will R. Bird, *Ghosts Have Warm Hands*; John Brophy and Eric Partridge, eds., *Songs and Slang of the British Soldiers, 1914-1918* and *The Long Trail*; A.F. Duguid, *History of the Canadian Forces in the Great War*; Bill Gammage, *The Broken Years*; D.J. Goodspeed, *The Road Past Vimy*; J.L. Granatstein, *Hell's Corner*; J.L Granatstein and Desmond Morton, *Marching to Armageddon*; Basil Hargreaves, *Origins and Meanings of Popular Phrases and Names*; Harold Harvey, *A Soldier's Sketches under Fire*; A.M.J. Hyatt, *General Sir Arthur Currie*; F.C. Jamieson, "The 19th Alberta Dragoons in the First World War;" H.K. Johnston, *Breakthrough*; William Kerr, *"Shrieks and Crashes"*; Lyn Macdonald, *The Roses of No Man's Land*; Andrew Macphail, *The Medical Services*; Michael McNorgan, "My God, Look at them houses moving," in Donald E. Graves, *More Fighting for Canada*; Desmond Morton, *When Your Number's Up*; G.W.G. Nicholson, *The C.E.F.*; Bill Rawling, *Surviving Trench Warfare*; Reg Roy, ed., *The Journal of Private Fraser*; Shane B. Schreiber, *Shock Army of the British Empire*; Peter Simkins, *The Western Front*; H.C. Singer, *The 31st Battalion*; D.S. Tamblyn, *The Horse in War*; and J.M. Winter, *The Experience of World War I.*

Biographical information is from the *Canadian Encyclopedia*; the *Dictionary of Canadian Biography*; Archibald MacRae, *History of the Province of Alberta* as well as relevant town and city directories for the period.

Notes: Chapter Seven

1. "I want to go home" was a popular soldier's song of the late war period. "Alleyman" was a corruption of the French *allemand* or German. From Harvey, *A Soldier's Sketches*, 36.
2. Hambley, Diary 8.
3. Singer, *31st Battalion*, 278-279
4. Hambley, Diary 8
5. Roy, *Journal of Private Fraser*, 48.
6. Singer, *31st Battalion*, 283.
7. Singer, *31st Battalion*, 65.
8. Hambley, Diary 8.
9. Hambley, Diary 8
10 Hambley, Diary 8
11. Hambley, Diary 9.
12. Quoted in Singer, *31st Battalion*, 304-305.
13. Singer, *31st Battalion*, 337.
14. Singer, *31st Battalion*, 340.
15. Hambley, Diary 10.
16. Singer, *31st Battalion*, 341.
17. Singer, *31st Battalion*, 349.
18. Singer, *31st Battalion*, 357-358.
19. Nicholson, *The CEF*, 407.
20. Singer, *31st Battalion*, 368.
21. Singer, *31st Battalion*, 389.
22. Singer, *31st Battalion*, 389.
23. McNorgan, "My God, look at them houses moving," in Graves, ed., *More Fighting for Canada*, 212-213.
24. Hambley, Diary 9.
25. Hambley, Diary 9.
26. Hambley, Diary 9.
27. Hambley, Diary 10.
28. Hambley, Diary 9.
29. Hambley, Diary 11.
30. Singer, *31st Battalion*, 411.
31. Stirrett, "A Soldier's Story."
32. Hambley, Diary 11.
33. Singer, *31st Battalion*, 417.
34. Kerr, *Shrieks and Crashes*, 134-135.
35. Stirrett, "A Soldier's Story."
36. Singer, *31st Battalion*, 430.
37. Singer, *31st Battalion*, 435.
38. Singer, *31st Battalion*, 437.
39. Singer, *31st Battalion*, 439.
40. Singer, *31st Battalion*, 440.
41. Singer, *31st Battalion*, 441.
42. Hambley, Diary 14.
43. Hambley, Diary 17.
44. *Calgary Herald*, 1 June 1919.
45. Singer, *31st Battalion*, 445.
46. Dave Husdal, "War Pony Found New Home in Banff," *Banff Craig and Canyon*, 9 Nov 2004.

Sources: Chapter Eight

The sources for the history of Alberta from 1919 to 1939 were: Ted Byfield, ed., *Brownlee and the Triumph of Populism, Fury and Futility: The Onset of the Great Depression*; *Aberhart and the Alberta Insurrection*; Gerald Friesen, *Canadian Prairies*; and James MacGregor, *History of Alberta.* Also consulted were issues of the *Calgary Herald, Edmonton Journal* and *Medicine Hat News.*

Archival sources consulted were as follows. GM, Calgary: J.F. Scott, "As I Saw It"; NAC, Ottawa: RG 24, vol. 4591: Historical Record of the South Alberta Regiment, 1931; Regimental History of the Edmonton Fusiliers, 1935; Regimental History of the 19th Dragoons; Notes for Regimental History of the Alberta Mounted Rifles; A Short History of the South Alberta Horse. SALH Archives: Ms. History of the 15th Light Horse; History of the SAR, 1931-1941. SAR Archives: Whiffen, History of the SAR, 1921-1931.

The following sources were also consulted: David Bercuson, *Battalion of Heroes*; Shelford Bidwell, *Gunners at War*; Shelford Bidwell and Dominick Graham, *Fire-Power*; Canada. *Militia Lists*, 1920-1939; Canada. *Annual Reports of the Department of Militia and Defence* (title varies), 1919-1939; Robert Citino, *Quest for Decisive Victory*; James Corum, *Roots of Blitzkrieg*; Richard Cunniffe, "The Militia Regiments of Alberta;" *Scarlet and Riflegreen*; and *Story of a Regiment*; Alec Douglas, *Creation of a National Air Force*; Alec Douglas and Brereton Greenhous, *Out of the Shadows*; James Eayrs, *Defence of Canada*, vol 1; Tony Foster, *Meeting of Generals*; J.L. Granatstein, *Canada's Army*; Donald E. Graves, *South Albertas*; James Gray, *Ten Lost Years*; Brereton Greenhous, *Dragoon*; Michael Horn, ed., *The Dirty Thirties*; R.G. Maltby, *The Calgary Regiment*; John Marteinson and M.R. McNorgan, *The Royal Canadian Armoured Corps*; Grant McEwen, *James Walker*; M.R. McNorgan, "Notes on Armoured and Cavalry Trophies;" G.W.L. Nicholson, *Gunners of Canada*, vol. 2; Harry Quarton, "19 Alberta Dragoons"; C.P. Stacey, *Arms, Men and Governments* and *Six Years of War*; "Sword Thrusts" (newsletter of the 19th Dragoons); and John Wallace, *Dragons of Steel.*

Biographical information is from the *Canadian Encyclopedia*; the *Dictionary of Canadian Biography*; Archibald MacRae, *History of the Province of Alberta* as well as relevant town and city directories for the period.

Notes: Chapter Eight

1. Officers' mess song of the 19th Alberta Dragoons in the 1920s sung to the tune of "Yes, we have no bananas!." It was attributed to Captain R.E. Washburn, the Dragoons' Medical Officer, but Washburn vigorously denied that he had anything to do with its creation, which is understandable. See "Sword Thrusts," Volume I, 1924.
2. *Militia Lists*, 1919-1924; Cunniffe, "Milita Regiments of Alberta," 102-117.
3 *Edmonton Journal*, 23 May 1925.
4. SALH Archives, Whiffen, "History of the SAR," n.p.
5. DHH, File 11.1.001, "Short History of the Alberta Mounted Rifles," n.p.
6. Letter from unidentified woman in Benton, Alberta, to Bennett, 19 Feb 1935, in Horn, ed., *Dirty Thirties*, 236-237.
7. General Staff Review of Militia, 1931, quoted in Eayrs, *Defence of Canada*, vol. 1, 309.
8. DHH, File 11.1.001, "Short History of the Alberta Mounted Rifles," n.p.
9. SALH Archives, "History of the 15th Light Horse," n.p.
10. SALH Archives, "History of the 15th Light Horse," n.p.
11. Cunniffe, "Militia Regiments of Alberta," 129-132.
12. Quoted in Eayrs, *Defence of Canada*, vol. 1, 312.
13. NAC, Regimental History, Edmonton Fusiliers, 1935.
14. For examples, see *Annual Reports* for 1930, 1932, 1934, 1936 and 1938.
15. Cunniffe, "Militia Regiments of Alberta," 120.
16. *Strathconian*, 1934, quoted in Cunniffe, "Militia Regiments of Alberta," 139.
17. SALH Archives, "Sword Thrusts," vol. 4, Sept 1924.
18. SALH Archives, Whiffen, "History of the SAR, 1921-1931," n.p.
19. NAC, History of the Calgary Highlanders, n.p.
20. SALH Archives, "History of the 15th Alberta Light Horse," n.p. The menu for this occasion has survived.
21. SALH Archives, "History of the 15th Alberta Light Horse," n.p.
22. "Sword Thrusts," vol. 2 (c. 1923).
23 "Sword Thrusts," vol. 4, Sept 1924.
24. "Sword Thrusts," vol. 2, (c. 1922).
25. SALH Archives, "History of the 15th Alberta Light Horse," n.p.
26. SALH Archives, "History of the 15th Alberta Light Horse," n.p.
27. *Medicine Hat News*, 12 Nov 1936.
28. Quoted in Horn, ed., *Dirty Thirties*, 647.
29. Stacey, *Arms, Men and Governments*, 1.
30. McNaughton to Minister of Defence, 5 April 1934, quoted in Eayrs, *In Defence of Canada*, vol 1, 314-315.
31. Cunniffe, "Militia Regiments of Alberta," 143.
32. SALH Archives, "History of the 15th Light Horse," n.p.
33. GM, J.F. Scott, "As I saw it."
34. Tony Foster, *Meeting of Generals*, 61-62.
35. Douglas and Greenhous, *Out of the Shadows*, 19.
36. *Edmonton Journal*, 3 June 1939.
37. Stacey, *Six Years of War*, 41.
38. GM, J.F. Scott, "As I Saw It."

Sources: Chapter Nine

Unless otherwise stated, the sources for this chapter were as follows.

Author's interviews (AI) with A. Brennand, P. Clay, D. Cotterill, H. Cunningham, T. Greenlees, G. Lynch-Staunton, W. McCrie, J. Moffat, and R. Porter.

Archival sources are: CEA, Edmonton: Inspection Reports of W.A. Griesbach. NAC, Ottawa: WDs, SAR; WD, 41 Brigade Group; WD, 31st Alberta Recce Regiment; and WD, 13th Field Regiment.;, 13 Fd Regt, 31 Arr.

Newpapers consulted were the *Canadian Press News*, 1942-1944, *Edmonton Journal*, 1939-1944 and *Medicine Hat News*, 1939-1944.

Other sources used were: W.W. Barrett, *History of the 13 Canadian Field Regiment*; T.J. Bell, *Into Action with the 12th Field*; Shelford Bidwell, *Gunners at War*; Shelford Bidwell and Dominick Graham, *Fire-Power*; A. Brennand, "13 Field Regiment"; Ted Byfield, ed., *The War that United the Province*; Canada. *Department of National Defence. Artillery in Battle. Vol.11. Gun Drill, 105 mm Howitzer*; Canada. *History of the Brigadier Royal Artillery Branch*; Alec Douglas, *Creation of a National Air Force*; Alec Douglas and Brereton Greenhous, *Out of the Shadows*; Barbara Dundas, *Women in the Canadian Military*; D.W. Falconer, *Battery Flashes of WW II*; Tony Foster, *Meeting of Generals*; John Galipeau, *Peewees on Parade*; Donald E. Graves, *South Albertas*, and *In Peril on the Sea*; Brereton Greenhous, *Dragoon*; Brereton Greenhous and Steven Harris, *Crucible of War*; J.M. Hitsman and J.L. Granatstein, *Broken Promises*; Ian Hogg, *Artillery in Colour*, *Barrage: The Guns in Action* and *The Guns, 1939-45*; Christopher Kilford, *Lethbridge at War*; R. Maltby, *The Calgary Regiment*; John Marteinson and M.R. McNorgan, *The Royal Canadian Armoured Corps*; G.W.L. Nicholson, *Gunners of Canada*, vol. 2; R.A. Paterson, *Tenth Infantry Brigade*; Harry Quarton "19 Alberta Dragoons"; G.E.M. Ruffee, *The History of the 14th Field Regiment*; C.P. Stacey, *Arms, Men and Governments*, *Six Years of War* and *The Victory Campaign*; and John Wallace, *Dragons of Steel.*

Notes: Chapter Nine

1. "Marching Song of the Fighting S.A.R.," sung to the tune of "I've been Working on the Railroad," *Medicine Hat News*, 31 Aug 1940.
2. Stacey, *Six Years of War*, 53.
3. Stacey, *Six Years of War*, 63.
4. AI with George Lynch-Staunton, 22 May 04.
5. *Edmonton Journal*, 3 June 1940.
6. Galipeau, *Peewees*, 8.
7. Barrett, *13 Canadian Field Regiment*, 13.
8. AI with T.C. Greenlees, 27 April 2004.
9. AI with J. Moffat, 29 April 2004.
10. AI with J. Moffat, 29 April 2004.
11. AI with D. Cotterill, 14 April 2004.
12. AI with R.J. Porter, 15 April 2004.
13. AI with J. Moffat, 29 April 2004.
14. AI with A. Wagner, 12 Aug 1996.
15. CEA, W.A. Griesbach, Report on South Alberta Regiment, C.A. (A), 23 April 1941.
16. CEA. W.A. Griesbach, Report on South Alberta Regiment, C.A. (A), 23 April 1941.
17. Galipeau, *Peewees*, 102-103.
18. WD, SAR, 31 July 1942.
19. Stacey, *Arms, Men and Governments*, 400.
20. Hitsman and Granatstein, *Broken Promises*, 177.
21. CEA, W.A. Griesbach, Inspection Report of 3rd Battalion, Edmonton Fusiliers, 7 Mar 1941.
22. CEA, W.A. Griesbach, Inspection Reports of 15th Alberta Light Horse, 13 March 1941, and 19th Alberta Dragoons, 2 April 1941.
23. Foster, *Meeting of Generals*, 265.
24. Author's conversation with Brigadier-General J.L. Summers (Retd.), MC, CD, c. 1977. Summers was a troop leader in the SAR in 1944-1945.
25. WD, 31 Recce, 26 June 1944.
26. Douglas and Greenhous, *Out of the Shadows*, 110.
27. Macdougall, *Short History of the SAR*, 37.
28. Wiley interview with Wotherspoon, 1986.
29. SAR, WD, June 1943, Appendix, Training Instruction No. 2. The Carrier Troop.
30. AI with R.H. Porter, 15 April 2004.
31. Bidwell and Graham, *Fire-Power*, 200.
32. Barrett, *13 Canadian Field Regiment*, 21.
33. Barrett, *13 Canadian Field Regiment*, 23.
34. Nicholson, *Gunners*, vol. 2, 268.
35. Barrett, *13 Canadian Field Regiment*, 24.
36. WD, 13 Field Regiment, 22 May 1944.
37. Paterson, *Tenth Brigade*, 15.
38. Wiley interview with Wotherspoon, 1986.
39. AI with R.H. Porter, 15 April 2004.
40. AI with J.O. Moffat, 29 April 2004.
41. Brennand, "13 Field Regiment."
42. Barrett, *13 Canadian Field Regiment*, 24.
43. Barrett, *13 Canadian Field Regiment*, 24.
44. AI with R.H. Moffat, 29 April 2004.
45. AI with W. McCrie, 8 April 2004.
46. Brennand, "13 Field Regiment."
47. Brennand, "13 Field Regiment."
48. AI with R.H. Moffat, 29 April 2004.
49. AI with N. Hunter, 17 April 2004.
50. AI with W. McCrie, 8 April 2004.
51. Barrett, *13 Canadian Field Regiment*, 29.

Sources: Chapter Ten

Unless otherwise stated, the sources for this chapter are as follows.

Author's interviews with A. Brennand, P. Clay, D. Cotterill, H. Cunningham, J. Galipeau, N. Hall, G. Henning, N. Hunter, G. Irving, G. Lynch-Staunton, W. McCrie, J. Moffat, J. Porter and G. Pugh.

Archival sources used were as follows. NAC, Ottawa: MG 24: WD, South Alberta Regiment; WD, 13th Field Regiment; WDs, 22 Battery and 78 Battery; Operations Log, 10th Infantry Brigade; First Canadian Army Daily Intelligence Summary, June-August 1944.

Other sources were: W.W. Barrett, *History of 13 Canadian Field Regiment*; T.J. Bell, *Into Action with the 12th Field*; Shelford Bidwell, *Gunners at War*; Shelford Bidwell and Dominick Graham, *Fire-Power*; Alex Brennand, "13 Canadian Field Regiment"; Canada. Department of National Defence. *Artillery in Battle. Vol. 11. Gun Drill, 105 mm Howitzer*; Canada. *History of the Brigadier Royal Artillery Branch*; Terry Copp and W.J. McAndrew, *Battle Exhaustion*; Carlo D'Este, *Decision in Normandy*; Jack English, *Canadian Army and the Normandy Campaign*; Tony Foster, *Meeting of Generals*; John Galipeau, *Peewees on Parade*; Donald E. Graves, *South Albertas*; Donald E. Graves, W.J. McAndrew and Michael Whitby, *Normandy 1944*; Brereton Greenhous and Steven Harris, *Crucible of War*, Ian Hogg, *Artillery in Colour* and *Barrage*; John Marteinson and M.R. McNorgan, *The Royal Canadian Armoured Corps*; Glen McDougall, *Short History of the SAR*; Stanislaw Maczek, *Mes Blindés*; Hubert Meyer, *12th Waffen SS Panzer Division*; W. McCrie, "Memoir;" G.W.L. Nicholson, *Gunners of Canada*, vol 2; R.A. Paterson, *Tenth Infantry Brigade*; Brian Reid, *No Holding Back*; R.L Rogers, *Lincoln and Welland*; G.E.M. Ruffee, *History of the 14th Field Regiment*; and C.P. Stacey, *Victory Campaign*.

Notes: Chapter Ten

1. "Battle Song of the 44 Canadian Field Battery, RCA," written by Major T. O'Shea and sung to the tune of "John Brown's Body," from Barrett, *13 Canadian Field Regiment*, 188.
2. AI with W. McCrie, 8 April 2004.
3. AI with R. Porter, 15 April 2004.
4. AI with G. Lynch-Staunton, 22 May 2004.
5. AI with R. Porter, 15 April 2004.
6. AI with W. McCrie, 8 April 2004.
7. AI with N. Hunter, 17 April 2004.
8. AI with G. Lynch-Staunton, 22 May 2004.
9. AI with G. Lynch-Staunton, 22 May 2004.
10. Stacey, *Victory Campaign*, 130.
11. WD, 13th Field Regiment, 7 June 1944.
12. AI with J. Moffat, 22 April 2004.
13. Meyer, *12th SS Division*, 55.
14 Meyer, *12th SS Division*, 55.
15. Graves et al., *Normandy 1944*, 56.
16. Meyer, *12th SS Division*, 56.
17. AI, W. McCrie, 8 April 2004.
18. Meyer, *12th SS Division*, 56.
19. Quoted in Stacey, *Victory Campaign*, 137.
20. Quoted in Stacey, *Victory Campaign*, 152.
21. Quoted in Stacey, *Victory Campaign*, 137.
22. AI, R. Porter, 15 April 2004.
23. Meyer, *12th SS Division*, 123.
24. AI with R.J. Moffat, 29 April 2004.
25. AI with J. Moffat, 29 April 2004.
26. AI, with G. Pugh, 17 April 2004.
27. WD, 78 Battery, entries for days indicated.
28. AI, with J. Moffat, 29 April 2004.
29. WD, 78 Battery, 30 June 1944.
30. WD, 22 Battery, 24 June 2004.
31. AI, G. Hall, 12 April 2004.
32. WD, 13th Field Regiment, 25 June 1944.
33. WD, 13th Field Regiment, 26 June 1944.
34. Paterson, *Tenth Brigade*, 21.
35. Bidwell, *Gunners at War*, 148-149.
36. AI with H. Cunningham, 13 April 2004.
37. AI with J. Moffat, 29 April 2004.
38. WD, 22 Battery, 7 July 1944.
39. AI, with G. Hall, 12 April 2004.
40. Stacey, *Victory Campaign*, 139.
41. Report by 2nd Panzer Divsion, 8 Aug 1944 in 1st Canadian Army Daily Intelligence Summary, No. 40.
42. 1st Canadian Army Daily Intelligence Summary, No. 38.
43. 1st Canadian Army Daily Intelligence Summary, No. 294, Interrogation of *Oberst* Semmler.
44. 1st Canadian Army Daily Intelligence Summary, No. 35.
45. 1st Canadian Army Daily Intelligence Summary, No. 35.
46. Meyer, *12th SS Division*, 104.
47. Graves et al, *Normandy 1944*, 115.
48. Graves et al., *Normandy 1944*, 115.
49. WD, 78 Battery, 11 July 1944.
50. AI with J. Moffat 29 April 2004.
51. WD, 78 Battery, on dates indicated.
52. WD, 78 Battery, 31 July 1944.
53. Paterson, *Tenth Brigade*, 16.
54. AI with G. Irving, 23 Sept 1995.
55. AI, J. Redden, 3 Jan 1996.
56. AI with J. Galipeau, 24 Sept 1995.
57. AI with H. Cunningham, 13 April 2004.
58. AI with H. Cunningham, 13 April 2004.
59. AI with J. Porter, 15 April 2004.
60. Directive by Montgomery, 11 Aug 1944, quoted in Stacey, *Victory Campaign*, 234.
61. Interview by W. Wiley with G.D. Wotherspoon, 1986.
62. Macdougall, *Short History*, 39.
63. Graves et al., *Normandy 1944*, 146.
64. Paterson, *Tenth Brigade*, 25.
65. Graves et al., *Normandy 1944*, 148.
66. Rogers, *Lincoln and Welland*, 153.
67. AI with W. McCrie, 8 April 2004.
68. AI with J. Moffat, 29 April 2004.
69. AI with J. Porter, 15 April 2004.
70. AI with H. Cunningham, 13 April 2004.

Sources: Chapter Eleven

Unless otherwise stated, the sources for this chapter were as follows.

Author's interviews with T. Aspleset, A. Brennand, P. Clay, D. Cotterill, H. Cunningham, J. Galipeau, N. Hall, G. Henning, N. Hunter, G. Irving, G. Lynch-Staunton, W. McCrie, J. Moffat, J. Porter and G. Pugh.

Archival sources used were as follows. NAC, Ottawa; MG 24: WD, South Alberta Regiment; WD, 6th Anti-Tank Regiment; WD, 13th Field Regiment; WDs, 22 Battery and 78 Battery; Operations Logs, 9th Infantry Brigade and 10th Infantry Brigade; First Canadian Army Daily Intelligence Summary, June-August 1944.

Other sources used were: W.W. Barrett, *History of 13 Canadian Field Regiment*; T.J. Bell, *Into Action with the 12th Field*; Shelford Bidwell, *Gunners at War*; Shelford Bidwell and Dominick Graham, *Fire-Power*; Alex Brennand, "13 Canadian Field Regiment"; Canada. Department of National Defence. *Artillery in Battle. Vol. 11. Gun Drill, 105 mm Howitzer*; Canada. *History of the Brigadier Royal Artillery Branch*; G.L. Cassidy, *Warpath*; Terry Copp and W.J. McAndrew, *Battle Exhaustion*; David Currie, "St. Lambert;" Carlo D'Este, *Decision in Normandy*; Jack English, *Canadian Army and the Normandy Campaign*; Tony Foster, *Meeting of Generals*; John Galipeau, *Peewees on Parade*; Donald E. Graves, *South Albertas*; Donald E. Graves, W.J. McAndrew and Michael Whitby, *Normandy 1944*; Brereton Greenhous and Steven Harris, *Crucible of War*; *History of the 5th Canadian Anti-Tank Regiment*; Ian Hogg, *Artillery in Colour* and *Barrage*; John Marteinson and M.R. McNorgan, *The Royal Canadian Armoured Corps*; Glen McDougall, *Short History of the SAR*; Stanislaw Maczek, *Avec Mes Blindés*; Hubert Meyer, *12th Waffen SS Panzer Division*; W. McCrie, "Memoir;" G.W.L. Nicholson, *Gunners of Canada*, vol 2; R.A. Paterson, *Tenth Infantry Brigade*; Brian Reid, *No Holding Back*; R.L Rogers, *Lincoln and Welland*; G.E.M. Ruffee, *History of the 14th Field Regiment*; Morton Schulman, *Defeat in the West*; R. Spenser, *Fifteenth Field*; and C.P. Stacey, *Victory Campaign*.

Notes: Chapter Eleven

1. The SAR "War Dance," a ritual chant performed late at night in the mess by happily-intoxicated South Albertans, the words of which are a disgrace in these politically correct times.
2. AI with T. Aspleset, 26 Aug 96.
3. SAR Archives, MBE Citation, Honorary Captain A.P. Silcox.
4. AI with C. Daley, 12 Aug 1996.
5. Currie, "St. Lambert".
6. Currie, "St. Lambert."
7. Currie, "St. Lambert."
8. AI with G. Adams, 22 Nov 1995.
9. Paterson, *Tenth Brigade*, 26-27.
10. AI with J. Redden, 5 Jan 1996.
11. WD, SAR, 19 Aug 1944.
12. AI, R. Rasmussen, 21 Sept 1995.
13. AI, with D. Grant, 10 Dec 1995.
14. AI, with R. Fairhurst, 19 Aug 1996.
15. Currie, "St. Lambert.".
16. W. Wiley interview with G. Wotherspoon, 1986.
17. Currie, "St. Lambert"; W. Wiley interview with G. Wotherspoon, 1986.
18. Ops Log, 10th Brigade, 19 Aug 1944.
19. Currie, "St. Lambert."
20. AI with E. Davies, 21 Aug 1996.
21. Ops Log, 10th Brigade, 20 Aug 1944.
22. Ops Log, 10th Brigade, 20 Aug 1944.
23. Currie, "St. Lambert."
24. Ops Log, 10th Brigade, 20 Aug 1944.
25. WD, SAR, 20 Aug 1944.
26. Galipeau, *Peewees*, 170.
27. Galipeau, *Peewees*, 171.
28. Ops Log, 10th Brigade, 20 Aug 1944.
29. Barrett, *13 Canadian Field Regiment*, 60.
30. Robert Spenser, *Fifteenth Canadian Field Regiment*, 119.
31. Nicholson, *Gunners of Canada*, vol 2, 327.
32. Quoted in Schulman, *Defeat in the West*, 281.
33. Paterson, *Tenth Brigade*, 29-30.
34. W. Wiley interview with G. Wotherspoon, 1986.
35. Von Lüttwitz quoted in Schulman, *Defeat in the West*, 182.
36. Currie, "St. Lambert."
37. AI with E. Davies, 21 Aug 1995.
38. Currie, VC Citation, Statement of Captain R.F. Dickie.
39. Currie, VC Citation, Statement of Sergeant John Gunderson, c. Sept 1944.
40. AI with J. Lardner, 19 Sept 1995, and J. Eastman, 30 Aug 1996.
41. SAR Archives, BBC interview with Dave Currie, c. 4 Dec 1944.
42. WD, 6th Anti-Tank Regiment, 20 Aug 1944.
43. Ops Log, 10th Brigade, 20 Aug 1944.
44. Ops Log, 10th Brigade, 20 Aug 1944.
45. Ops Log, 10th Brigade, 20 Aug 1944.
46. Maczek, *Mes Blindés*, 218.
47. WD, 10th Brigade, 20 Aug 1944.
48. Ops Log, 10th Brigade, 20 Aug 1944.
49. Currie, "St. Lambert."
50. W. Wiley interview with G. Wotherspoon, 1986.
51. AI with J. Gove, 15 Aug 1996.
52. Nicholson, "1940-1945."
53. *History of the First Hussars*, 97.
54. AI with G. Stoner, 11 Jan 1996.
55. Currie, "St. Lambert."
56. SAR Archives, Currie VC Citation, Statement of Sergeant J. Gunderson.
57. AI with J. Galipeau, 21 Sept 1995.
58. AI with E. Hyatt, 26 Aug 1996.
59. AI with W. Boothroyd, 18 Nov 1995.
60. AI with T. Clausen, 28 Aug 1996.
61. AI with R. Porter, 15 April 2004.
62. Currie, "St. Lambert."
63. Author's conversation with J.L. Summers, 1994.
64. Clipperton, "Memories."
65. SAR Archives, BBC interview with D. Currie, c. 4 Dec 1944.
66. Currie, "St. Lambert."

Sources: Chapter Twelve

Unless otherwise stated, the sources for this chapter are as follows.

Author's interviews with T. Aspleset, A. Brennand, P. Clay, D. Cotterill, H. Cunningham, J. Galipeau, N. Hall, G. Henning, N. Hunter, G. Irving, G. Lynch-Staunton, W. McCrie, J. Moffat, J. Porter and G. Pugh.

Archival sources used were: NAC, Ottawa, MG 24: WD, South Alberta Regiment; WD, 13th Field Regiment; WDs, 22 Battery and 78 Battery; Operations Log, 10th Infantry Brigade; First Canadian Army Daily Intelligence Summaries, August-November 1944.

Other sources consulted were: W.W. Barrett, *History of 13 Canadian Field Regiment*; T.J. Bell, *Into Action with the 12th Field*; David Bercuson, *Battalion of Heroes*; Shelford Bidwell, *Gunners at War*; Shelford Bidwell and Dominick Graham, *Fire-Power*; Alex Brennand, "13 Canadian Field Regiment"; Canada. *History of the Brigadier Royal Artillery Branch*; G.L. Cassidy, *Warpath*; Tony Foster, *Meeting of Generals*; John Galipeau, *Peewees on Parade*; Donald E. Graves, *South Albertas*; *History of the 5th Canadian Anti-Tank*, Ian Hogg, *Artillery in Colour* and *Barrage*; John Lakes, "Tomorrow's Rainbow"; David Marshall, "Me and George"; John Marteinson and M.R. McNorgan, *The Royal Canadian Armoured Corps*; Glen McDougall, *Short History of the SAR*; W. McCrie, "Memoir;" G.W.L. Nicholson, *Gunners of Canada*, vol 2; Jim Nicholson, "1940-1945"; R.A. Paterson, *Tenth Infantry Brigade*; John

Raycroft, *A Signal War*; R.L Rogers, *Lincoln and Welland*; G.E.M. Ruffee, *History of the 14th Field Regiment*; R. Spenser, *Fifteenth Field*; C.P. Stacey, *Victory Campaign*; War Office. *Gun Drill for Q.F. 25-Pr., Mark II Gun*; and Denis and Sheila Whittaker, *Tug of War*.

Notes: Chapter Twelve

1. "The Fitters' Lament," from T.J. Bell, *Into Action with the 12th Field* (Holland, c. 1945), 99. This song, sung by the fitters or mechanics of 12th Field commemorates the fact that, following the mistaken bombing of 14 August 1944, all three field regiments in 3rd Division received replacement vehicles including "Quads," the four-wheel drive artillery tractor/truck. Unfortunately the replacements were British vehicles built by MG (Morris Garage), not Canadian-built vehicles, and they were a nightmare to maintain, as the song indicates.
2. Barrett, *13 Canadian Field Regiment*, 62
3. Barrett, *13 Canadian Field Regiment*, 64
4. Lakes, "Tomorrow's Rainbow."
5. Galipeau, *Peewees*, 176.
6. Lakes, "Tomorrow's Rainbow."
7. AI with J. Moffat, 29 April 2004.
8. SAR Archives, Bob Clipperton to Andy Clipperton, 23 Aug 1944.
9. Foster, *Meeting of Generals*, 388.
10. Galipeau, *Peewees*, 174.
11. SAR Archives, John Neff, Diary, 2 Sept 1944.
12. Barrett, *13 Canadian Field Regiment*, 67.
13. Paterson, *Tenth Brigade*, 34.
14. Galipeau, *Peewees*, 178.
15. Marshall, "George and Me," 37.
16. Marshall, "George and Me," 38.
17. Foster, *Meeting of Generals*, 403.
18. Fraser, *Black Yesterdays, info to come.*
19. SAR Archives, John Neff, Diary, 9 Sept 1944.
20. Paterson, *Tenth Brigade*, 35.
21. Quoted in Fraser, *Black Yesterdays*, 276.
22. Paterson, *Tenth Brigade*, 35.
23. SAR Archives, John Neff Diary, 10 Sept 1944.
24. WD, South Alberta Regiment, 12 Sept 1944.
25. Stacey, *Victory Campaign*, 361.
26. AI, Danny Mcleod, 24 Aug 1996.
27. AI, J. Moffat, 29 April 2004.
28. Brennand, "13 Field Regiment."
29. AI, H. Cunningham, 13 April 2004.
30. AI, J. Moffat, 29 April 2004.
31. AI, H. Cunningham, 13 April 2004.
32. Barrett, *13 Canadian Field Regiment*, 78.
33. AI with J. Moffat, 29 April 2004.
34. WD, 22 Battery, 12 Oct 1944.
35. Barrett, *13 Canadian Field Regiment*, 79.
36. AI, J. Shemrock, 28 April 2004.
37. DHH, 1st Canadian Army Intelligence Summary No 92.
38. WD, 22 Battery, 13 Oct 1944.
39. Barrett, *13 Canadian Field Regiment*, 86.
40. Quoted in Whitaker, *Tug of War*, 311.
41. Barrett, *13 Canadian Field Regiment*, 161.
42. SAR Archives, John Neff, Diary, 26 Oct 1944.
43.
44. *Globe and Mail*, n.d., (c. early Nov 1944).
45. The "Bergen op Zoom" song, written by Lieutenant-Colonel Bill Cromb of the Lincoln and Welland Regiment and sung to the tune of the "Blue Danube," had its first performance at a 10th Brigade officers' dinner held at the Hotel de Draak in Bergen on Halloween Night, October 1944. The words vary according to the audience.
46. Raycroft, *Signal War*, 58.
47. Raycroft, *Signal War*, 58.
48. AI with W. McCrie, 8 April 2004.
49. AI, D. Cotterill, 14 April 2004.
50. Brennand, "13th Canadian Field Regiment."
51. Raycroft, *Signal War*, 61.

Sources: Chapter Thirteen

The sources for the history of Alberta from 1939 to 1945 were: Ted Byfield, ed., *The War that United the Province*; Gerald Friesen, *Canadian Prairies*; Ken Tingley, ed., *For King and Country*; and James MacGregor, *History of Alberta*.

Newspapers consulted were the *Calgary Herald*, *Edmonton Journal* and *Medicine Hat News*, 1939-1945 and the *Canadian Press News*, 1942-1945

Archival sources used were as follows. NAC, Ottawa: WDs of SAR and 31st Alberta Recce Regiment. SAR Archives: Clipperton correspondence, 1943-1945

Other sources used were: Alec Douglas, *The Creation of a National Airforce*; Alec Douglas and Brereton Greenhous, *Out of the Shadows*; Alec Douglas et al, *No Higher Purpose*; Donald E. Graves, *In Peril on the Sea*; Barry Broadfoot, *Six War Years*; Brereton Greenhous et al., *Crucible of War*; J.M. Hitsman and J.L. Granatstein, *Broken Promises*; Christopher Kilford, *Lethbridge at War*; John Raycroft, *A Signal War*; C.P. Stacey, *Arms, Men and Government* and *Six Years of War*; and Norman Tucker, *The Naval Service of Canada*.

Notes: Chapter Thirteen

1. *Canadian Press News, 13 June 1944.* "Salute to a Zombie," sung to the tune of "Oh, My Darling Clementine," was composed by three returned soldiers and a member of the CWAC at Military District 11 in the summer of 1944. At this time, tensions between active service and NRMA personnel were running high and there were a series of riots between the two types of Canadian soldiers at military bases across Canada. The song quickly entered the civilian world and became very popular in the last year of the war.
2. Tingley, ed., *For King and Country*, 208-209.
3. *Canadian Press News*, 10 June 1944.
4. *Canadian Press News*, 26 Aug 1944.
5. SAR Archives, correspondence of Andy and Bob Clipperton on dates indicated.
6. SAR Archives, Andy Clipperton to Bob Clipperton, 23 Nov 1943.
7. *Canadian Press News*, 23 Sept 1944
8. Stacey, *Arms, Men and Government*, 443.
9. Stacey, *Arms, Men and Government*, 464.
10. Stacey, *Arms, Men and Government*, 597.
11. Stacey, *Arms, Men and Government*, 595.
12. Stacey, *Arms, Men and Government*, 470.
13. Stacey, *Arms, Men and Government*, 471-472.
14. WD, 31 Recce Regt, 28 Nov 1944.
15. WD, 31 Recce Regt, 1 Dec 1944.

Sources: Chapter Fourteen

Unless otherwise stated, the sources for this chapter are were follows.

Author's interviews with T. Aspleset, A. Brennand, P. Clay, D. Cotterill, H. Cunningham, J. Galipeau, N. Hall, G. Henning, N. Hunter, G. Irving, G. Lynch-Staunton, W. McCrie, J. Moffat, J. Porter and G. Pugh.

Archival sources used were NAC, Ottawa: MG 24: WD, South Alberta Regiment; WD, Argyll and Sutherland Highlanders; WD, 13th Field Regiment; WDs, 22 Battery and 78 Battery; WD and Operations Log, 10th Infantry Brigade; First Canadian Army Daily Intelligence Summary, December 1944-March 1945. SAR Archives: Clipperton and Dryer correspondence.

Other sources consulted were: W.W. Barrett, *History of 13 Canadian Field Regiment*; T.J. Bell, *Into Action with the 12th Field*; Shelford Bidwell, *Gunners at War*; Shelford Bidwell and Dominick Graham, *Fire-Power*; Alex Brennand, "13 Canadian Field Regiment"; Canada. *History of the Brigadier Royal Artillery Branch*; G.L. Cassidy, *Warpath*; Tony Foster, *Meeting of Generals*; Robert Fraser, *Black Yesterdays*; John Galipeau, *Peewees on Parade*; Donald E. Graves, *South Albertas*; *History of the 5th Canadian Anti-Tank*; Geoffrey Hayes, *The Lincs*; Ian Hogg, *Artillery in Colour* and *Barrage*; John Lakes, "Tomorrow's Rainbow"; Bill Luton, "Seven Days"; David Marshall, "Me and George"; John Marteinson and M.R. McNorgan, *The Royal Canadian Armoured Corps*; Glen McDougall, *Short History of the SAR*; W. McCrie, "Memoir;" G.W.L. Nicholson, *Gunners of Canada*, vol 2; Jim Nicholson, "1940-1945"; R.A. Paterson, *Tenth Infantry Brigade*; John Raycroft, *A Signal War*; R.L Rogers, *Lincoln and Welland*; M.O. Rollefson, *Green Route Up*; G.E.M. Ruffee, *History of the 14th Field Regiment*; R. Spenser, *Fifteenth Field*; C.P. Stacey, *Victory Campaign*; Joe Strathearn, "Escape from Civvies"; Denis and Sheila Whittaker, *Rhineland*; and H.F. Wood, "Operation Elephant."

Notes: Chapter Fourteen

1. LOB means "Left out of Battle." A certain number of officers and enlisted personnel were always LOB to form a cadre in case a unit took such heavy casualties that it had to rebuild itself. Not unnaturally, LOB personnel rejoiced and this song, sung to the tune of "Lili Marlene," was very popular in the last year of the war.
2. Barrett, *13 Canadian Field Regiment*, 95.
3. WD, 78 Battery, 4 Dec 1944.
4. WD, 78 Battery, 13 Dec 1944.
5. Nicholson, "1940-1945."
6. Galipeau, "Pee Wees," 172.
7. AI with J. Moffat, 29 April 2004.
8. AI with W. McCrie, 8 April 2004.
9. WD, 22 Battery, 16 Dec 1944.
10. SAR Archives, A. Dryer to fiancee, 4 Jan 1945.
11. WD, 78 Battery, 14 Jan 1945.
12. AI with W. McCrie, 8 April 2004.
13. WD, 22 Battery, 1 Jan 1945.
14. Paterson, *Tenth Brigade*, 52.
15. Cassidy, *Warpath*, 244.
16. Wood, "Operation Elephant," 9.
17. Graves, "If only we had the wisdom," 231.
18. A. Earp to author, n.d. (c. Oct 1995).
19. Rollefson, *Green Route Up*, 67.
20. Paterson, *Tenth Brigade*, 56.
21. WD, SAR, Feb 1945, Annexed Report of Lieutenant Ken Wigg.
22. AI with J. Wiebe, 24 Sept 1995.
23. SAR Archives, R. Clipperton to wife, 30 Jan 1945.
24. AI with G. Irving, 15 Sept 1995.
25. J. Strathearn, "Escape from Civvies."
26. Quoted in Fraser, *Black Yesterdays*, 352.
27. Paterson, *Tenth Brigade*, 56.
28. Foster, *Meeting of Generals*, 429.
29. Hogg, *Barrage*, 145.
30. WD, 13th Field Regiment, 5 Mar 1945.
31. Barrett, *13 Canadian Field Regiment*, 103.
32. Raycroft, *Signal War*, 103.
33. Bell, *Into Action with the 12th Field*, 117.
34. WD, 22 Battery, 8 Feb 1945.
35. Quoted in McAndrew et al., *Liberation*, 132.
36. WD, 22 Battery, 9 Feb 1945.
37. AI with G. Pugh, 17 April 2004.
38. Brennand, "13 Canadian Field Regiment."
39. Raycroft, *Signal War*, 116.
40. T.J. Bell, *Into Action with the 12th Field*, 119.
41. Marshall, "George and Me."
42. Luton, "Seven Days."
43. Cassidy, *Warpath*, 254.
44. WD, ASH, 28 Feb 1945.
45. Paterson, *Tenth Brigade*, 61.
46. Barrett, *13 Canadian Field Regiment*, 110.
47. Raycroft, *Signal War*, 150.
48. WD, SAR, 6 Mar 1945.
49. SAR Archives, R. Clipperton to wife, 12 March 1945.
50. SAR Archives, John Neff, Diary, 6 and 7 Mar 1945.
51. Luton "Seven Days."
52. SAR Archives, John Neff diary, 18 March 1945.
53. AI with E.V. Nieman, 26 Aug 1995.
54. Marshall, "George and Me."
55. SAR Archives, John Neff, Diary, 19 March 1945.
56. Luton, "The Rhine."
57. Raycroft, *Signal War*, 168-170.
58. Barrett, *13 Canadian Field Regiment*, 117-118.

Sources: Chapter Fifteen

Unless otherwise stated, the sources for this chapter are as follows.

Author's interviews with T. Aspleset, A. Brennand, P. Clay, D. Cotterill, H. Cunningham, J. Galipeau, N. Hall, G. Henning, N. Hunter, G. Irving, G. Lynch-Staunton, W. McCrie, J. Moffat, J. Porter, G. Pugh.

Archival sources used were as follows: NAC, Ottawa: MG 24: War Diaries, South Alberta Regiment; 13th Field Regiment War Diary, 22 Battery and 78 Battery; War Diary and Operations Log, 10th Infantry Brigade; First Canadian Army Daily Intelligence Summary, June-August 1944.

Other sources consulted were: W.W. Barrett, *History of 13 Canadian Field Regiment*; T.J. Bell, *Into Action with the 12th Field*; Shelford Bidwell, *Gunners at War*; Shelford Bidwell and Dominick Graham, *Fire-Power*; Alex Brennand, "13 Canadian Field Regiment"; Canada. *History of the Brigadier Royal Artillery Branch*; G.L. Cassidy, *Warpath*; Tony Foster, *Meeting of Generals*; Robert Fraser, *Black Yesterdays*; John Galipeau, *Peewees on Parade*; Donald E. Graves, *South Albertas*; *History of the 5th Canadian Anti-Tank*; Geoffrey Hayes, *The Lincs*; Ian Hogg, *Artillery in Colour* and *Barrage*; John Lakes, "Tomorrow's Rainbow"; Bill Luton, "The Rhine" and "Armoured Reconaissance"; David Marshall, "Me and George"; John Marteinson and M.R. McNorgan, *The Royal Canadian Armoured Corps*; Glen McDougall, *Short History of the SAR*; W. McCrie, "Memoir;" G.W.L. Nicholson, *Gunners of Canada*, vol 2; Jim Nicholson, "Personal Recollection"; R.A. Paterson, *Tenth Infantry Brigade*; John Raycroft, *A Signal War*; R.L Rogers, *Lincoln and Welland*; M.O. Rollefson, *Green Route Up*; G.E.M. Ruffee, *History of the 14th Field Regiment*; R. Spenser, *Fifteenth Field*; C.P. Stacey, *Victory Campaign* and *Six Years of War*; Joe Strathearn, "Escape from Civvies"; War Office. *Gun Drill for Q.F. 25-Pr., Mark II Gun*; and Denis and Sheila Whittaker, *Rhineland*.

Notes: Chapter Fifteen

1. "Ode to a Sten Gun," poem by Gunner S.N. Tweed in *The Maple Leaf Scrapbook*, 10.
2. WD, 22 Battery, 30 Apr 1945.
3. Luton, "The Rhine."
4. Raycroft, *Signal War*, 187.
5. AI with W. McCrie, 8 April 2004.
6. AI, G. Lynch-Staunton, 22 May 2004.
7. Luton, "The Rhine."
8. Luton, "The Rhine."
9. Luton, "The Rhine."
10. Luton, "The Rhine."
11. Luton, "The Rhine."
12. Luton, "The Rhine."
13. Barrett, *13 Canadian Field Regiment*, 120.
14. Barrett, *13 Canadian Field Regiment*, 120.
15. Barrett, *13 Canadian Field Regiment*, 128.
16. Raycroft, *Signal War*, 215.
17. Barrett, *13 Canadian Field Regiment*, 128.
18. McDougall, *Short History*, 78.
19. Marshall, "George and Me."
20. Marshall, "George and Me."
21. AI with W.J. McLeod, 24 Aug 1996.
22. AI with C. Daley, 12 Aug 1995.
23. AI, T. Milner, 26 Nov 1995.
24. AI with R. Fairhurst, 19 Aug 1996.
25. WD, SAR, 16 April 1945.
26. AI with P. Konvitsko, 6 Dec 1995.
27. Galipeau, *Peewees*, 226.
28. Galipeau, *Peewees*, 227.
29. Galipeau, *Peewees*, 228.
30. Galipeau, *Peewees*, 229.
31. SAR Archives, John Neff, Diary, 20-23 April 1945.
32. Marshall, "George and Me."
33. WD, SAR, 25 April 1945.
34. Paterson, *Tenth Brigade*, 69.
35. Barrett, *13 Canadian Field Regiment*, 131.
36. Raycroft, *Signal War*, 247-248.
37. Raycroft, *Signal War*, 248.
38. Raycroft, *Signal War*, 263-264.
39. AI with J. Shemrock, 28 April 2004.
40. Raycroft, *Signal War*, 268.
41. Paterson, *Tenth Brigade*, 70.
42. WD, SAR, Nov 1945, Appendix containing Padre Silcox's notes on fatal casualties.
43. Barrett, *13 Canadian Field Regiment*, 141.
44. Barrett, *13 Canadian Field Regiment*, 142.
45. Barrett, *13 Canadian Field Regiment*, 142.
46. Barrett, *13 Canadian Field Regiment*, 146.
47. Galipeau, *Peewees*, 234.
48. SAR Archives, R. Clipperton to wife, 24 June 1945.
49. SAR Archives, R. Clipperton to wife, 24 June 1945.

50. Marshall, "George and Me."
51. SAR Archives, R. Clipperton to wife, 6 July 1945.
52. SAR Archives, R. Clipperton to wife, 6 July 1945.
53. SAR Archives, M. Clipperton to R. Clipperton, 29 Nov 1945.
54. SAR Archives, telegram, R. Clipperton, 9 December 1945.
55. Galipeau, *Peewees*, 235.
56. Galipeau, *Peewees*, 236.
57. H. Quarton to author, 23 Aug 2004.

Sources: Chapter Sixteen
Unless otherwise noted, the following sources were used for this chapter.
Author's interviews with A. Arelis, L. Fraser, P. Fuog, H. Quarton, G. Lynch-Staunton, P. Mast; L. MacDonald, R. McKenzie and G. McQueen.
Archival sources were as follows. DHH, Ottawa: AHRs of the 19th Alberta Armoured Car Regiment and 19th Alberta Dragoons, 1946-1964; 41st Anti-Tank Regiment, 1946-1954; 68th Light Anti-Aircraft Regiment, 1946-1954; South Alberta Regiment, 1946-1954; and South Alberta Light Horse, 1955-1964. DHH 112.352.003 (D10), Amalgamation of the SAR and Other Units, 1954. SALH Archives, records and correspondence, 1945-1964 in Edmonton and Medicine Hat including copies of *Sabre and Spur* (unit newsletter) and correspondence for the period, 1955-1964.
Newspapers were consulted were the *Calgary Herald*, 1952-1958; *Edmonton Journal*, 1950-1955 and the *Medicine Hat News*, 1950-1964.
Other sources were Ted Byfield, ed., *Leduc, Manning and the Age of Prosperity*; Tony Foster, *Meeting of Generals*; J.L. Granatstein, *Canada's Army*; John Marteinson and M.R. McNorgan, *The Royal Canadian Armoured Corps*; *The 19th*, [newletter], 1954-1962; Harry Quarton, "The 19th Alberta Dragoons; and *Sabre and Spur*, various issues, 1958-1966.

Notes: Chapter Sixteen
1. "Going Home," an adaptation of an old soldier's poem by the personnel of the SALH, Sarcee Camp, July 1961, *Greggsville Herald* (camp newspaper), 3 July 1961.
2. Nicholson, *Gunners of Canada, II,* 544.
3. AI with H. Quarton, 27 Aug 2004.
4. AI, with G. Lynch-Staunton, 22 May 2004.
5. AI with H. Quarton, 27 Aug 2004.
6. Foster, *Meeting of Generals*, 507.
7. AI with G. Lynch-Staunton, 22 May 2004.
8. DHH 112.352.003 (D10), Adjutant-General's Instructions, Amendment No. 2, 25 Aug 1954.
9. SALH Archives, Higgs to Vokes, 9 July 1954.
10. *Calgary Herald*, 15 July 1954.
11. DHH, 470.009(D2), Murdoch to VCGS, 9 Aug 1954.
12. DHH, 470.009(D2), Simonds to Defence Secretary, 13 Aug 1954.
13. DHH, 470.009(D2), Brief by DSD, 13 Sept 1954.
14. DHH, 470.009(D2), Memo, DSD, 7 Sept 1954.
15. AI with G. McQueen, 9 Aug 2004.
16 AI with A. Arelis, 10 Aug 2004.
17. SALH Archives, Higgs to RCAC, 20 Dec 1955.
18. SALH Archives, Higgs to RCAC, 20 Dec 1955.
19. SALH Archives, Higgs to RCAC, 6 Sept 1956.
20. SALH Archives, Higgs to RCAC, 20 Dec 1955.
21. *The 19th*, June 1956.
22. *The 19th*, March 1956.
23. SALH Archives, Memo on Ex BOOMERANG by Ray, Feb 1961.
24. SALH Archives, Address by Ray, 9 Nov 1964.

25. AI with L. MacDonald, 11 Aug 2004.
26. *Medicine Hat News*, 15 April 1961.
27. AI with P. Mast, 12 Aug 2004.
28. AI with A. Arelis, 10 Aug 2004.
29. AI with A. Arelis, 10 Aug 2004, and *Medicine Hat News*, 1 April 1961.
30. AI with A. Arelis, 10 Aug 2004.
31. AI with A. Arelis, 10 Aug 2004.
32. AI with R. McKenzie, 8 Aug 2004.
33. Recruiting Poster, "The SALH Wants You," in *Medicine Hat News*, 14 May 1961.
34. *Medicine Hat News*, 15 July 1961.
35. *Medicine Hat News*, 16 Oct 1961.
36. *Medicine Hat News*, 16 Oct 1961.
37 AI with Arelis, 10 Aug 2004.
38. AI with G. McQueen, 8 Aug 2004.
39. AI with A. Arelis, 10 Aug 2004.
40. AI with P. Mast, 12 Aug 2004.
41. SALH Archives, Ray to 22 Militia Group, 21 Nov 1961.
42. SALH Archives, Ray to 22 Militia Group, 21 Nov 1961.
43. SALH Archives, Ray to 22 Militia Group, 21 Nov 1961.
44. SALH Archives, Ray to 22 Militia Group, 21 Nov 1961.
45. SALH Archives, Ray to 22 Militia Group, 21 Nov 1961.
46. SALH Archives, Memo on regimental history by Ray, March 1962.
47. SALH Archives, Memo on regimental history by Ray, March 1962.
48. AI with A. Arelis, 10 Aug 2004.
49. SALH Website, Ray to West, 29 Dec 1978.
50. AI with G. McQueen, 8 Aug 2004.
51. AI with G. MacDonald, 11 Aug 2004.
52. AI with A. Arelis, 10 Aug 2004.
53. AI with R. McKenzie, 8 Aug 2004.
54. SALH Archives, Memo on regimental history by Ray, June to Oct 1962.
55. AI with A. Arelis, 10 Aug 2004.
56. SALH Archives, address by Ray, 9 Nov 1964.

Sources: Chapter Seventeen
Unless otherwise noted, the following sources were used for this chapter.
Author's interviews with A. Arelis, D. Bergt, J. Bray, R. Caldwell, N. Douglas, L. Fraser, D. Heine, H. Quarton, G. Lynch-Staunton, P. Mast; L. MacDonald, R. McKenzie, B. McKinley, G. McQueen, B. Moore, E. Moore. A. Mottershead, T. Steele, R. Summersgill, S. Thirlwell, S. Thompson, B. Walton, and G. Yanda.
Archival sources were as follows. DHH, Ottawa: AHRs for the 19th Alberta Dragoons, 1964-1965; and the South Alberta Light Horse, 1964-1988; and B Squadron, SALH, 1978-1988. SALH Archives, Medicine Hat, correspondence and records for the period, 1964-1988.
Newspapers consulted were the *Calgary Herald* and *Medicine Hat News*, 1964-1988.
Other sources were Paul Bunner, ed., *The Sixties Revolution and the Fall of Social Credit* and *Lougheed and the War with Ottawa*; J.L. Granatstein, *Canada's Army*; John Marteinson and M.R. McNorgan, *The Royal Canadian Armoured Corps*; *Presentation of the Colours and Guidon*; Harry Quarton, "The 19th Alberta Dragoons;" and *Saber and Spur* [newsletter], 1964-1968; and *Standing Orders and Regulations for the Army in Ireland*.

Notes: Chapter Seventeen
1. Regimental song of the 19th Alberta Dragoons in the post-1945 period, sung to the tune of "Lili Marlene." From Harry Quarton, "19 Alberta Dragoons."
2. AI with H. Quarton, 27 Aug 2004.
3. SALH Archives, Mulford to Inglis, 25 Feb 1965.
4. SALH Archives, Mulford to Inglis, 24 Feb 1965.

5. AI with R. Caldwell, 15 Aug 2004.
6. AI with A. Arelis, 10 Aug 2004.
7. AI with P. Mast, 12 Aug 2004.
8. AI with L. MacDonald, 11 Aug 2004.
9. AI with E. Moore, 9 Aug 2004.
10. SALH Archives, *Sabre and Spur*, Dec 1966.
11. AI with R. Caldwell, 15 Aug 2004.
12. AI with R. Caldwell, 15 Aug 2004.
13. AI with R. Caldwell, 15 Aug 2004.
14. SALH Archives, *Presentation of Guidon* booklet.
15. AI with A. Arelis, 10 Aug 2004.
16. AI with R. McKenzie, 8 Aug 2004.
17. AI with P. Mast, 12 Aug 2004.
18. . AI with L. Fraser, 24 Aug 2004.
19. SALH Archives, *Presentation of Guidon* booklet.
20. AI with P. Mast, 12 Aug 2004.
21. AI with P. Mast, 12 Aug 2004.
22. AI with D. Heine, 9 Aug 2004.
23. AI with E. Moore, 9 Aug 2004.
24. AI with P. Mast, 12 Aug 2004.
25. AI with L. Fraser, 24 Aug 2004.
26. AI with J. Bray, 11 Aug 2004.
27. AI with R. McKenzie, 8 Aug 2004.
28. AI with J. Bray, 11 Aug 2004.
29. AI with P. Mast, 12 Aug 2004.
30. AI with P. Mast, 12 Aug 2004.
31. Marteinson and McNorgan, *Royal Canadian Armoured Corps*, 381.
32. Marteinson and McNorgan, *Royal Canadian Armoured Corps*, 391.
33. AI with L. Fraser, 24 Aug 2004.
34. AI with S. Thirlwell, 13 Aug 2004.
35. AI with T. Steele, 12 Aug 2004.
36. AI with T. Steele, 12 Aug 2004.
37. DHH, AHR, B Squadron, SALH, 1979.
38. AI with T. Steele, 12 Aug 2004.
39. Marteinson and McNorgan, *Royal Canadian Armoured Corps*, 396.
40. Marteinson and McNorgan, *History of the RCAC*, 396.
41. AI with B. Walton, 14 Aug 2004.
42. AI with R. Caldwell, 15 Aug 2004.
43. AI with D. Bergt, 9 Aug 2004.
44. Yanda to Graves, 8 Oct 04.
45. DHH, AHR, SALH, 1980.
46. AI with B. McKinley, 9 Aug 2004.
47. AI with B. Moore, 8 Aug 2004.
48. AI with J. Bray, 11 Aug 2004.
49. AI with N. Douglas, 7 Sept 2004.
50. AI with B. Walton, 14 Aug 2004.
51. AI with P. Mast, 12 Aug 2004.
52. AI with S. Thompson, 17 Aug 2004.
53. AI with S. Thompson, 17 Aug 2004.

Sources: Chapter Eighteen
Unless otherwise noted, the following sources were used for this chapter.
Author's interviews with D. Bergt, J. Bray, R. Caldwell, N. Douglas, L. Fraser, C. Howie, H. Quarton, G. Lynch-Staunton, P. Mast, R. McKenzie, M. Onieu, T. Putt, T. Steele, R. Summersgill, S. Thirlwell, A. Thomas, S. Thompson, B. Walton, J. Watt, A. Van Rooyen and G. Yanda.
Archival sources were as follows. DHH, Ottawa: AHRs of the SALH, 1988-2003. SALH Archives, records and correspondnece for 1988-2004.
Newspapers were consulted were the *Edmonton Journal* and *Medicine Hat News*, 1988-2004.
Other sources were Paul Bunner, ed., *Alberta Takes the Lead*; J.L. Granatstein, *Canada's Army*; and John Marteinson and M.R. McNorgan, *The Royal Canadian Armoured Corps*.

Notes: Chapter Eighteen
1. "The Yellow Bird Song," an American boy scout campfire song, was adapted by the U.S. Army which passed it on to the SALH who

sang it (with suitably modified words) in the 1990s.
2. AI with L. Fraser, 24 Aug 2004.
3. AI with L. Fraser, 24 Aug 2004.
4. AI with L. Fraser, 24 Aug 2004.
5. AI with L. Fraser, 24 Aug 2004.
6. DHH, AHR, SALH, 1990.
7. DHH, AHR, SALH, 1989.
8. AI with L. Fraser, 24 Aug 2004.
9. AI with G. Yanda, 12 Aug 2004.
10. AI with G. Yanda, 12 Aug 2004.
11. AI with D. Bergt, 9 Sept 2004.
12. AI with G. Yanda, 12 Aug 2004.
13. AI with C. Howie, 14 Aug 2004.
14. Communication from LCol Hodgson, 15 Oct 04.
15. AI with B. Hodgson, 11 Oct 2004.
16. DHH, SALH AHR 1991.
17. AI with S. Thirlwell, 13 Aug 2004.
18. AI with B. Hodgson, 11 Oct 2004.
19. AI with T. Steele, 12 Aug 2004.
20. AI with G. Yanda, 12 Aug 2004.
21. Marteinson and McNorgan, *Royal Canadian Armoured Corps*, 397.
22. AI with C. Howie, 14 Aug 2004.
23. AI with C. Howie, 12 Aug 2004.
24. AI with C. Howie, 14 Aug 2004.
25. AI with G. Yanda, 12 Aug 2004.
26. AI with C. Howie, 14 Aug 2004.
27. AI with G. Yanda, 12 Aug 2004.
28. AI with J. Watt, 14 Aug 2004.
29. AI with J. Watt, 14 Aug 2004.
30. MacIntyre to author, 18 Oct 2004.
31. AI with J. Watt, 14 Aug 2004.
32. AI with B. Hodgson, 9 Oct 2004.
33. AI with C. Howie, 14 Aug 2004.
34. R. McKenzie, Report to historian of RCAC, c. 1996.
35. AI with C. Howie, 14 Aug 2004.
36. AI with T. Steele, 12 Aug 2004.
37. AI with S. Thirlwell, 13 Aug 2004.
38. DHH, SALH, AHR, 1994.
39. DHH, SALH AHR, 1995.
40. DHH, SALH, AHR, 1996.
41. Name withheld by request.
42. DHH, SALH, AHR, 1995.
43. AI with J. Bray, 11 Aug 2004.
44. AI with R. McKenzie, 9 Aug 2004.
45. R. McKenzie, report to RCAC, c. 1996.
46. DHH, SALH, AHR, 1996.
47. AI with P. Mast, 12 Aug 2004.
48. AI with S. Thirlwell, 13 Aug 2004.
49. AI with D. Bergt, 9 Sept 2004.
50. AI with B. Hodgson, 9 Sept 2004.
51. DHH, SALH, AHR, 2000.
52. AI with N. Douglas, 7 Sept 2004.
53. AI with M. Onieu, 11 Aug 2004.
54. AI with N. Douglas, 7 Sept 2004.
55. AI with N. Douglas, 7 Sept 2004.
56. DHH, SALH, AHR, 2000.
57. AI with T. Putt, 11 Sept 2004.
58. AI with A. Thomas, 11 Sept 2004.
59. AI with T. Putt, 11 Sept 2004.
60. AI with D. Bergt, 9 Sept 2004.
61. LCol Putt to author, 17 Nov 2004.
62. LCol Putt to author, 17 Nov 2004.
63. LCol Putt to author, 17 Nov 2004.
64. AI with T. Putt, 11 Sept 2004.
65. AI with B. Hodgson, 9 Sept 2004.
66. R. McCue to author, 28 Oct 2004.
67. AI with B. Hodgson, 9 Sept 2004.

Sources: Epilogue
Based on information from planning documents for Exercise ACTIVE EDGE 04 and author's interviews and communications with D. Bergt, C. Howie, R. McKenzie, C. Michaud, T. Putt, S. Thirlwell, B. Walton, J.Watt and G. Yanda.

Notes: Epilogue
1. T. Putt to author, 17 Nov 2004.

BIBLIOGRAPHY

UNPUBLISHED SOURCES

ARCHIVAL SOURCES

CITY OF EDMONTON ARCHIVES
Inspection Reports, 1941-1942, by Major-General W.A. Griesbach of the 15th Alberta Light Horse, 19th Alberta Dragoons, South Alberta Regiment and Edmonton Fusiliers

DIRECTORATE OF HISTORY AND HERITAGE, DND, OTTAWA
Annual Historical Reports
19th Alberta Dragoons, 1946-1965
South Alberta Light Horse, 1954-2003
41st Anti-Tank Regiment, RCA, 1946-1954
68th Light Anti-Aircraft Regiment, RCA, 1946-1954
South Alberta Regiment, 1946-1954
Battle Honours files
South Alberta Regiment (CASF), 1940-1945
13th Field Regiment, RCA
31st Battalion, CEF
Citations File, Northwest Europe, 1944-1945
DHH 74/633, George Stirrett, "A Soldier's Story"
Lineage Files
Canadian Expeditionary Force: Units of the CEF and their Perpetuations
Joseph Harper, "The Canadian Expeditionary Force, 1914-1918," manuscript on file.
Notes on the Composition of the 31st Canadian Battalion
Shipping Lists, Canadian Expeditionary Force
19th Alberta Dragoon Squadron, 1914
31st Battalion, 1915
First Canadian Army Daily Intelligence Summaries, 1944-1945

GLENBOW MUSEUM, CALGARY
Manuscript 742/1: Diary of Captain H.W. McGill, 31st Battalion, 1915-1917
J. Fred Scott, "As I Saw It"

NATIONAL LIBRARY AND ARCHIVES OF CANADA, OTTAWA
Manuscript Group 30
E 15, Diary of Major W.A. Griesbach, 19th Dragoons, 1914
E 16, Diary of Major W.A. Hewgill, 31st Battalion, 1914-1918
E 241, Diary of Lieutenant-Colonel D.E. McIntyre, 28th Battalion, CEF
E 351, Diary of Signaller Craig, 28th Battalion
Record Group 9 III, D-3
vol. 4936, 4937 and 4938, War Diary, 31st Battalion, CEF, 1915-
vol. 4954 and 4955, War Diaries, 19th Alberta Dragoons, 1914-1916 and Canadian Light Horse, 1916-1919
Record Group 24, C3, War Diaries and Operations Logs
War Diary, 3rd Canadian Infantry Division, 1944
Operations Log, 7th Canadian Infantry Brigade, 1944
Operations Log, 9th Infantry Brigade, 1944
War Diary and Operations Log, 10th Infantry Brigade, 1944-1945,
War Diary, 41st (Reserve) Brigade Group, 1942-1944
War Diary, South Alberta Regiment (CASF), 1940-1945
War Diary, 31st Alberta Reconnaissance Regiment, 1942-1945
War Diary, 13th Field Regiment, RCA, 1940-1945
War Diary, 6th Anti-Tank Regiment, RCA
Record Group 24
vol 4591: Historical Record of the South Alberta Regiment, 1931; Regimental History of the Edmonton Fusiliers, 1935; Regimental History of the 19th Alberta Dragoons; Notes for Regimental History of the Alberta Mounted Rifles; A Short History of the South Alberta Horse.

PROVINCIAL ARCHIVES OF MANITOBA, WINNIPEG
Manuscript Group 7
H 11, Diaries of Trooper G.W. Hambley, Canadian Light Horse, 1916-1919

SOUTH ALBERTA REGIMENT and SOUTH ALBERTA LIGHT HORSE HISTORICAL COLLECTIONS AND ARCHIVES

RECORDS

Files Relating to the History of the South Alberta Regiment, 1922-1940, the 15th Alberta Light Horse, 1922-1935 and the South Alberta Light Horse, 1954-2004, held in the SALH Museum and Archives, Medicine Hat.

DOCUMENTS

Manuscript History of the 15th Canadian Light Horse, c. 1924-1935
Manuscript History of the South Alberta Regiment, c. 1921-1940
Reports on Regimental History by Lieutenant-Colonel N.R. Ray, c. 1959-1964

CORRESPONDENCE, WARTIME

Robert and Myrtle (Andy) Clipperton, 1943-1945
Arnold Dryer to his fiancee, 1943-1945
Honorary Captain A.P. Silcox

CORRESPONDENCE, POSTWAR

Author's correspondence relating to the writing of the history of the South Alberta Regiment, 1994-1998.
Author's correspondence relating to the writing of the history of the South Alberta Light Horse, 2003- 2004.

DIARIES

George Gallimore, January-May 1945
John Neff, 1 August 1944-May 1945
Joe Strathearn, January-May 1945

INTERVIEWS BY D.E. GRAVES

South Alberta Regiment (CASF), 1940-1946
G. Adams, 22 Nov 95; T. Aspleset, 26 Aug 96; W. Boothroyd, 18 Nov 1995; T. Clausen, 28 Aug 96; A. Coffin, 14 Aug 06; C. Daley, 12 Aug 96; E. Davies, 21 Aug 96; J. Eastman, 30 Aug 96; R. Fairhurst, 19 Aug 96; J. Galipeau, 24 Sep 95; J. Gove, 15 Aug 96; D. Grant, 10 Dec 95; G. Henning, 14 Aug 96; E. Hyatt, 26 Aug 96; G. Irving, 23 Sep 96; P. Konsvitsko, 26 Dec 95; J. Lardner, 10 Sep 95; W.J. McLeod, 24 Aug 96; T. Milner, 26 Nov 95; E.V. Nieman, 26 Aug 95; R. Rasmussen, 21 Sep 95; J. Redden, 3 Jan 96; G. Stoner, 11 Jan 96; A. Wagner, 12 Aug 96; and J. Wiebe, 24 Sep 95.
13th Field Regiment, RCA, 1940-1945
A. Brennand, 12 Apr 04; P. Clay, 12 Apr 04; D. Cotterill, 14 Apr 04; H. Cunningham, 13 Apr 04; T.C. Greenlees, 27 Apr 04; G. Hall, 12 Apr 04; N. Hunter, 17 Apr 04; G. Lynch-Staunton, 22 May 04; W. McCrie, 8 Apr 04; J. Moffat, 29 Apr 04; R. Porter, 15 Apr 04; G. Pugh, 17 Apr 04; and J. Shemrock, 28 Apr 04.
19th Alberta Dragoons and South Alberta Light Horse, 1954-2004
A. Arelis, 10 Aug 04; D. Bergt, 9 Sep 04; J. Bray, 11 Aug 04; R. Caldwell, 15 Aug 04; N. Douglas, 7 Sep 04; L. Fraser, 24 Aug 04; P. Fuog, 12 Aug 04; D. Heine, 9 Aug 04; B. Hodgson, 11 Aug 04; C. Howie, 14 Aug 04; G. Lynch-Staunton, 22 May 04; P. Mast, 12 Aug 04; L. MacDonald, 11 Aug 04; R. McKenzie, 8 Aug 04; B. McKinley, 9 Aug 04; G. McQueen, 8 Aug 04; C. Michaud, 11 Sep 04; B. Moore, 8 Aug 04; E.M. Moore, 9 Aug 04; A. Mottershead, 12 Aug 04; M. Onieu, 11 Aug 04; T.E. Putt, 11 Sep 04; H. Quarton, 27 Aug 04; T. Steele, 12 Aug 04; R. Summersgill, 14 Aug 04; S. Thirlwell, 13 Aug 04; A. Thomas, 11 Sep 04; S. Thompson, 17 Aug 04; A. Van Rooyen, 14 Sep 04; B. Walton, 14 Aug 04; J. Watt, 14 Aug 04; and G. Yanda, 12 Aug 04.

INTERVIEWS BY OTHERS
G.D. Wotherspoon by Bill Wiley, 1986

MEMOIRS, POSTWAR
Alec Brennand, "13 Field Regiment, RCA".
Robert Clipperton, "My Personal Memories of the South Alberta Regiment from 1940 to 1946"
David Currie, "St. Lambert-sur-Dives," c. 1963
John Galipeau, manuscript copy of "Pee Wees on Parade"
John Lakes, "Tomorrow's Rainbow: Memoirs of John Rutherford Lakes."
W.C. Luton, "The Seven Days. A Troop Leader's Memories of the Battle for the Hochwald Gap;" "The Rhine and the Twente;" and "Armoured Reconnaissance, the Last Days."
David Marshalll, "Me and George," c. 1993.
William McCrie, "My Wartime Memories"
Tom Milner, "Action at Varrelbusch," and "DCM Action," 1995.
Jim Nicholson, "1940-1945 with the South Alberta Regiment. A Personal Recollection by J.L. Nicholson."

REGIMENTAL NEWSLETTERS
"The 19th," newsletter of the 19th Dragoons, various issues, 1952-1962
"Sabre and Spur," newsletter of the South Alberta Light Horse, various issues, 1958-1967
South Alberta Regiment Christmas Magazine 1941.
"Sword Thrusts," newsletter of the officers' mess of the 19th Alberta Dragoons, various issues, 1922- 1930.

UNPUBLISHED MANUSCRIPTS, THESES AND STUDIES

Brigadier, Royal Artillery Branch. "The History of Brigadier Royal Artillery Branch of Headquarters, First Canadian Army. Second Great War." Brigadier Royal Artillery Branch, Holland, November 1945.
Cunniffe, Richard. "Militia Regiments of Alberta." Typescript, c. 1972.
English, Jack. "A Perspective on Infantry." MA Thesis, Royal Military College of Canada, Kingston, 1980.
Graves, Donald E. "Lost Opportunity: The Royal Canadian Navy and Combined Operations, 1939-1945." Background narrative for the official history of the Royal Canadian Navy in the Second World War.
———. "Fists of Mail, Walls of Steel, Armoured Warfare, 1914-1945."
———. "Five Questions and Answers Concerning the History of the South Alberta Regiment, 1939-1954." SAR Association, 1995.
Halliday, Hugh. "Notes on Awards and Decoration of the South Alberta Regiment and 13th Field Regiment, Second World War."
Hogarth, G.M. "The Canadian Military Tradition in the West, 1870-1900." Unpublished MA Thesis, Royal Military College, 1973.
MacDonald, J.A. "Summary History of the South Alberta Light Horse," n.p. 1976.
McNorgan, M.R. "Notes on Casualties of Canadian Mounted Units, 1914-1918."
———. "Notes on the Decorations and Awards of Canadian Mounted and Armoured Units."
———. "Notes on Royal Canadian Armoured Corps Competitions and Awards."
Quarton, Harry. "19 Dragoons." Author's publication, n.d. [c. 1995].
Rutherdale, Robert A. "The Home Front: Convergence and Conflict in Lethbridge, Guelph and Trois Rivières during the Great War." PhD. Thesis, York University, Toronto, 1993.
van Rooyen, Alex. "Notes on Matters Relating to the History of the SALH."

AUDIO-VISUAL SOURCES

BRITISH BROADCASTING CORPORATION
Interview with Major David Currie, VC, n.d., c. December 1944

BRITISH PATHE CORPORATION
"British Troops Liberating France" [sic], film of SAR shot in March 1945

CANADIAN FORCES FILM UNIT, OTTAWA
Film shot by Sergeant Jack Stollery at St. Lambert-sur-Dives, 19 August 1944

NATIONAL FILM UNIT, OTTAWA
Film Footage of the D-Day Landing, 6 June 1944

NATIONAL LIBRARY AND ARCHIVES OF CANADA, OTTAWA
Canadian Army Newsreel No. 49, February 1945
Canadian Army Newsreel No. 64, March 1945

SOUTH ALBERTA REGIMENT HISTORICAL COLLECTION
South Alberta Regiment Pictorial Record, 1941-1944

PUBLISHED SOURCES

NEWSPAPERS AND PERIODICALS

Banff Craig and Canyon, November 2004
Calgary Herald, 1899-1958
Calgary Standard, 1905-1918
Canadian Pictorial and Illustrated War News, 1914-1915
Canadian Press News, 1942-1945
Edmonton Bulletin, 1914-1918
Edmonton Journal, 1908 to 1945
Edmonton Sun, August 2004
Eye-Opener, 1905-1907
Fort Macleod Gazette, 1885-1905
Globe and Mail, August 1914

Lethbridge Herald, 1914-1918
Medicine Hat News, 1908-2004
Red Deer News, 1914-1918

MILITARY MANUALS AND TECHNICAL LITERATURE

[Chatwin, J.V.P.] *Armoured Car Squadron Precis. 19th Alberta Dragoons.* Edmonton: B Squadron, 19th Alberta Dragoons, n.d. [c. 1958].
Department of Militia, Canada. *Cavalry Training, Canada. 1904.* Ottawa: Department of Militia, 1904.
Department of National Defence, Canada. *Artillery in Battle Field Artillery. Volume 11. Gun Drill, 105mm Howitzer, C1.* Ottawa; Department of National Defence, 1974.
Griesbach, W.A. *Observations on Cavalry Duties. Some Hints for Western Cavalry Men.* Edmonton: Author's publication, 1914.
War Office. *List of Changes in British War Material in Relation to Edged Weapons, Firearms and Assorted Ammunition and Accoutrements. Vol II: 1886-100; Vol II: 1900-1910; Vol IV: 1910-1918.* London: War Office, 1886-1918, reprinted Arms and Militaria Press, 2000-2002.
———. *Cavalry Training. 1904.* London: War Office, 1904.
———. *Cavalry Training. 1910.* London: War Office, 1910.
———. *Yeomanry and Mounted Rifle Training. Parts I and II. 1912.* London: War Office, 1912
———. *Field Service Pocket Book. 1914. Reprinted, with Amendments, 1916.* London: His Majesty's Stationery Office, 1916.
———. *Cavalry Training. Vol. I. Training.* London: War Office, 1924
———. *Gun Drill for Q.F. 25-Pr., Mark II Gun on Carriage 25-Pr., Mark I.* London: War Office, 1944.

BOOKS

Anglesey, Marquess of, [G.C.H.V. Paget]. *A History of British Cavalry, Volume IV: 1899 to 1913.* London: Pen and Sword, 1986.
Barrett, W.W. *The History of 13 Canadian Field Regiment, Royal Canadian Artillery, 1940-1945.* N.p., n.d. [c. 1945].
Beatty, David Pierce. *Memories of the Forgotten War. The World War I Diary of Pte. V.E. Goodwin.* Port Elgin: Baie Verte Editions, 1986.
Bell, T.J. *Into Action with the 12th Field.* N.p., n.d. [c. 1945].
Bercuson, David. *Battalion of Heroes: The Calgary Highlanders in World War II.* Calgary: Calgary Highlanders Regimental Funds Foundation, 1994.
Bidwell, Shelford. *Gunners at War.* London: Arrow Books, 1972.
———. and Dominick Graham. *Fire-Power. British Army Weapons and Theories of War 1904-1945.* Boston: Allen and Unwin, 1985.
Bird, Will R. *Ghosts Have Warm Hands.* Toronto: Clarke, Irwin, 1968.
Blue, John. *Alberta Past and Present, Historical and Biographical.* Chicago: Pioneer Historical Publichsing Company, 1924.
Borden, Henry, ed. *Robert Laird Borden: His Memoirs.* Toronto: Macmillan, 1938.
Brandon, William. *American Heritage Book of the Indians.* New York: American Heritage, 1961.
Broadfoot, Barry. *Six War Years, 1939-1945: Memories of Canadians at Home and Abroad.* Toronto: Doubleday, 1974.
Brophy, John and Eric Partridge, eds. *Songs and Slang of the British Soldier, 1914-1918.* London: Scholarctic Press, 1930.
———. *The Long Trail: What the British Soldier Sang and Said in the Great War of 1914-1918.* London: A. Deutsch, 1965.
Brown, Gordon and Terry Copp. *Look to Your Front – Regina Rifles, A Regiment at War, 1944-1945.* Waterloo: Laurier Centre for Military, Strategic, Disarmament Studies, 2001.
Byfield, Ted and Paul Brunner, eds., *The Journalistic History of Alberta.* Edmonton: 12 volumes, United Western Communications and History Book Publications, 1991-2003. Vol. 1: *The Great West before 1900;* Vol. 2: *The Birth of the Province;* Vol. 3: *The Boom and the Bust;* Vol. 4: *The Great War and Its Consequences;* Vol. 5: *Brownlee and the Triumph of Populism;* Vol. 6: *Fury and Futility: The Onset of the Great Depression;* Vol. 7: *Aberhart and the Alberta Insurrection;* Vol. 8: *The War that United the Province;* Vol. 9: *Leduc, Manning and the Age of Prosperity;* Vol. 10: *The Sixties Revolution and the Fall of Social Credit;* Vol. 11: *Lougheed and the War with Ottawa;* Vol. 12: *Alberta Takes the Lead.*
Canada. *Sessional Papers*, 1885-1886, 1898-1903.
———. *Annual Reports of the Department of Militia and Department of National Defence* [titles vary], 1896-1914, 1920-1939
———. *Militia Lists*, 1898-1914, 1919-1939, 1948
Canadian Encyclopedia. Edmonton: Hurtig Publishers, 1985.
Cashman, Tony. *More Edmonton Stories: The Life and Times of Edmonton.* Edmonton: Institute of Applied Arts, 1958.
Cassidy, G.L. *Warpath. The Story of the Algonquin Regiment, 1939-1945.* Toronto: Ryerson, 1948.
Chambers, Ernest. *The Governor-General's Body Guard.* Toronto: E.L. Ruddy, 1992.
Citino, Robert. *Quest for Decisive Victory: From Stalemate to Blitzkrieg in Europe, 1899-1940.* Lawrence: University of Kansas Press, 2002.
Copp, Terry and Bill McAndrew. *Battle Exhaustion: Soldiers and Psychiatrists in the Canadian Army, 1939-1945.* Montreal: McGill-Queen's Press, 1990.
Corum, James S. *The Roots of Blitzkrieg: Hans Seeckt and German Military Reform.* Lawrence: University of Kansas Press, 1992.
Cunniffe, Richard. *Scarlet, Rifle Green and Khaki: The Military in Calgary.* Calgary: Calgary Century Publishing Company, 1975.
Dancocks, Daniel. *Welcome to Flanders Fields. The First Canadian battle of the Great War; Ypres, 1915.* Toronto: McClelland and Stewart, 1988.
———. *The Story of a Regiment. Lord Strathcona's Horse (Royal Canadians).* Calgary: Lord Strathcona's Horse Regimental Society, 1995.
———. *Legacy of Valour: The Canadians at Passchendaele.* Edmonton: Hurtig Press, 1980.
———. *Spearhead to Victory: Canada in the Great War.* Edmonton: Hurtig, 1987.
Dempsey, Hugh, ed. *Men in Scarlet.* Calgary: Historical Society of Alberta and McClelland and Stewart, 1974.
———, ed. *The Best from Alberta History.* Saskatoon: Western Producer Prairie Books, 1981.
Dennison, George T. *A History of Cavalry from the Earliest Times.* London: Macmillan, 1913.
Denny, Cecil. *Riders of the Plains: A Reminiscence of the Early and Exciting Days in the North-West.* Calgary: Herald Company, 1905.
———. *The Law Marches West.* Toronto: Dent, 1939.
D'Este, Carlo. *Decision in Normandy. The Unwritten Story of Montgomery and the Allied Campaign.* London: Collins, 1983.
Dictionary of Canadian Biography. Toronto: University of Toronto Press, 1979 to date.
Douglas, W.A.B. *The Creation of a National Air Force.* Ottawa: Department of National Defence, 1988.
——— and Brereton Greenhous. *Out of the Shadows. Canada in the Second World War. Revised Edition.* Toronto: Dundurn, 1995.
Duguid, A.F. *Official History of the Canadian Forces in the Great War 1914-1919. Volume I. From the Outbreak of War to the Formation of the Canadian Corps August 1914-September 1915.* Ottawa: Department of National Defence, 1938.
Dunbar, Francis J., and Joseph Harper. *Old Colours Never Die: A Record of Colours and Military Flags in Canada.* Ottawa: Department of National Defence, 1992.
Dundas, Barbara. *A History of Women in the Canadian Military.* Montreal: Art Global, 2000.
Eayrs, James. *In Defence of Canada. From the Great War to the Great Depression.* Toronto: University of Toronto Press, 1964.
Empey, Arthur G. *Over the Top. By an American Soldier Who Went … together with Tommy's Dictionary of the Trenches.* Toronto: W. Briggs, 1917.
English, Jack. *The Canadian Army and the Normandy Campaign. A Study of Failure in High Command.* New York: Praeger, 1991.
Falconer, D.W. *Battery Flashes of W.W. II.* Author's publication, 1985.
Foster, Tony. *Meeting of Generals.* Toronto: Methuen, 1986.
Fraser, Robert. *Black Yesterdays: The Argylls' War.* Hamilton: The Regiment, 1996.
Fraser, W.B. *Calgary.* Toronto: Holt, Rinehart and Winston, 1967.
Friesen, Gerald. *The Canadian Prairies: A History.* Lincoln: University of Nebraska Press, 1984.
Galipeau, John and Pattie Whitehouse. *Peewees on Parade. Wartime Memories of a Young (and small) Soldier.* Toronto: Robin Brass Studio, 2000.
Gammage, Bill. *The Broken Years: Australian Soldiers in the Great War.* London: Penguin, 1975.
Goodspeed, D.J. *The Armed Forces of Canada: A Century of Achievement.* Ottawa: Department of National Defence, 1967.
———. *The Road Past Vimy: The Canadian Corps 1914-1918.* Toronto: Macmillan, 1969.
Gould, Ed. *All Hell for a Basement.* Medicine Hat: City of Medicine Hat, 1981.
Granatstein, J.L. *Canada's Army. Waging War and Keeping the Peace.* Toronto: University of Toronto Press, 2002.
———. *Hell's Corner: An Illustrated History of Canada's Great War, 1914-1918.* Vancouver: Douglas and MacIntyre, 2004.
——— and J.M. Hitsman. *Broken Promises: A History of Conscription in Canada.* Toronto: Oxford University Press, 1977.
——— and Desmond Morton. *Marching to Armageddon: Canada and the Great War, 1914-1919.* Toronto: Lester, Orpen and Denys, 1989.
Graves, Dianne L. *A Crown of Life: The World of John McCrae.* St. Catharines: Vanwell, 1997.
Graves, Donald E. *South Albertas: A Canadian Regiment at War.* Toronto: Robin Brass Studio, 1998.
———. *In Peril on the Sea: The Royal Canadian Navy and the Battle of the Atlantic.* Toronto: Robin Brass Studio, 2003.
———, Bill McAndrew and Michael Whitby. *Normandy 1944: The Canadian Summer.* Montreal: Art Global, 1994.
———, ed. *Fighting for Canada: Seven Battles, 1758-1945.* Toronto; Robin Brass Studio, 2000.
———, ed. *More Fighting for Canada: Five Battles, 1760-1944.* Toronto: Robin Brass Studio, 2004.
Greenhous, Brereton. *Dragoon. The Centennial History of The Royal Canadian Dragoons, 1883-1993.* Ottawa: The Regiment, 1983.
——— and Stephen Harris. *Canada and the Battle of Vimy Ridge.* Montreal: Art Global, 1992.
——— and Stephen J. Harris, William C. Johnston and William G.P. Rawling. *The Crucible of War 1939-1945.* Ottawa: Department of National Defence, 1994.
Griesbach, William A. *I Remember.* Toronto: Ryerson, 1946.
Hargreaves, Basil. *Origins and Meanings of Popular Phrases and Names, Including Those Which Came into Use during the Great War.* London: T.W. Laurie, 1925.
Harvey, Harold. *A Soldier's Sketches Under Fire.* Toronto: Thomas Allen, c. 1916.
Hayes, Geoffrey. *The Lincs: A History of the Lincoln and Welland Regiment at War.* Alma: Maple Leaf Route, 1986.
Hickey, Raymond. *The Scarlet Dawn.* Campbelltown: Tribune Publishing, 1949.
Higginbotham, John D. *When the West was Young: Historical Reminiscences of the Early Canadian West.* Lethbridge: 2nd edition, Lethbridge Herald, 1980.
Hillsman, John. *Eleven Men and a Scalpel.* Winnipeg: Columbia Press, 1948.
A History of the First Hussars Regiment. London: The Regiment, 1951.
Hogg, Ian. *The Guns 1939-1945.* New York: Ballantine Publishing, 1970.
———. *Barrage: The Guns in Action.* New York: Ballantine Publishing, 1970.
———, Ian, Peter Sarson and Tony Bryan. *Artillery in Colour, 1920-1935.* New York, Arco Publishing, 1980.
——— and John S. Weeks. *Military Small Arms of the 20th Century.* Iola: Krause Publications, 2000.
Holt, Tonie and Valmai. *In Search of a Better 'Ole: The Life, Works and the Collectables of Bruce Bairnsfather.* Woodnesborough: Milestone Press, 1985.
Horn, Michiel, ed. *The Dirty Thirties. Canadians in the Great Depression.* Toronto: Copp, Clark, 1972.
House, Jonathan. *Towards Combined Arms Warfare: A Survey of 20th-Century Tactics, Doctrine and Organization.* Leavenworth: Combat Studies Institute, 1984.
Hyatt, A.M.J. *General Sir Arthur Currie: A Military Biography.* Toronto: Macmillan, 1987.
Jackson, H.M., ed. *The Argyll and Sutherland Highlanders of Canada (Princess Louise's), 1928-1953.* Hamilton: The Regiment, 1953.
Jamieson, F.C. *The Alberta Field Force of 1885.* Battleford: Canadian North-West Historical Society, 1931.
Johnson, H.K. *Breakthrough: Tactics, Technology, and the Search for Victory on the Western Front in World War I.* Novato: Presidio Press, 1994.
Kennedy, H.G., ed. *History of the 101st Edmonton Fusiliers.* Edmonton: The Regiment, 1912.
Kennedy, Joyce M. *Distant Thunder: Canada's Citizen Soldiers on the Western Front.* Manhattan: Sunflower University Press, 2000.
Kerr, William B. *"Shrieks and Crashes": Being Memories of Canada's Corps in 1917.* Toronto: Hunter, Rose, 1929.
Kilford, Christopher R. *Lethbridge at War. The Military History of Lethbridge from 1900 to 1996.* Lethbridge: Battery Books and Publishing, 1996.
Kitching, George. *Mud and Green Fields.* Vancouver: Battleline Books, 1986.
Macbeth, R.G. *Making of the Canadian West: Being the Reminiscences of an Eye-Witness.* Toronto: W. Briggs, 1898.
Macdonald, J.A. *Keen-Eyed Prairie Men: A Summary History of the SALH and of Medicine Hat and District Military Units.* N.p., c. 1976.
Macdonald, Lyn. *1914.* London: Penguin, 1987.
———. *The Roses of No Man's Land.* London: Penguin, 1993.
MacEwan, J.W. Grant. *A Short History of Western Canada.* Toronto: McGraw-Hill-Ryerson, 1968.
———. *James Walker, Man of the Western Frontier.* Edmonton: Brindle and Glass, 2000.
MacGregor, James C. *A History of Alberta.* Edmonton: Hurtig Publishers, 1977.
Macleod, R.C. *The N.W.M.P. and Law Enforcement, 1873-1905.* Toronto: University of Toronto, 1976.
Macphail, Andrew. *Official History of the Canadian Forces in the Great War 1914-191. The Medical Services.* Ottawa: Department of National Defence, 1925.
MacRae, Archibald O. *History of the Province of Alberta.* Calgary: Western Canada History Company, 1912.
Maczek, Stanislaw. *Avec mes Blindés.* Paris: Presses de la Cité, 1967.
Maltby, R.G. *The Calgary Regiment (Tank).* Hilversum: The Regiment, 1945.
Manning, Frederick. *The Middle Parts of Fortune. Somme and Ancre 1916.* London: Buchan and Endwright, 1986.
Maple Leaf Scrapbook. Holland: Maple Leaf, 1945.
Marteinson, John and Michael R. McNorgan. *The Royal Canadian Armoured Corps: An Illustrated History.* Toronto: Royal Canadian Armoured Corps Association and the Canadian War Museum, 2000.
Massie, Robert. *Dreadnought. Britain, Germany, and the Coming of the Great War.* New York: Random House, 1991.
Mathieson, William. *My Grandfather's War:*

Canadians Remember the First World War. Toronto: Macmillan of Canada, 1981.

McAndrew, W.J, W. Rawling and M. Whitby. *Liberation: The Canadians In Europe.* Montreal; Art Global, 1995.

McDougall, Glenholm L. *A Short History of the 29 Cdn Armd Recce Regt (South Alberta Regiment).* Amsterdam: Spin's Publishing Co., 1945.r

McNorgan, Michael R. *The Gallant Hussars: A History of the 1st Hussars, 1856-2004.* London: 1st Hussars Cavalry Fund, 2004.

Meek, John. *Over the Top: The Canadian Infantry in the First World War.* Orangeville: author's publication, c. 1971.

Meyer, Hubert. *The History of the 12. SS-Panzerdivision Hitlerjugend.* Winnipeg: J.J. Fedorowicz Publishing, 1994.

Miller, Carmen. *Painting the Map Red. Canada and the South African War, 1899-1902.* Montreal: McGill-Queen's Press, 1993.

Mills, Stephen. *Task of Gratitude: Canadian Battlefields of the Great War.* Calgary: Vimy Ventures, 1997.

Moeller, Bertie. *Two Years at the Front with the Mounted Infantry.* London: Grant, Richards, 1903.

Morrison, E.W.B. *With the Guns in South Africa.* Hamilton: Spectator Printing, 1901.

Morrow, J.W. *Early History of the Medicine Hat Country.* Medicine Hat: Medicine Hat and District Historical Society, 1963, revised 1998.

Morton, Desmond. *The Last War Drum: The North West Campaign of 1885.* Toronto: Hakkert, 1972.

———. *When Your Number's Up: The Canadian Soldier in the First World War.* Toronto: Random House, 1993.

———. and Reginald Roy, eds., *Telegrams of the North-West Campaign of 1885.* Toronto: Champlain Society, 1972.

Moulton, J.L. *Battle for Antwerp. The Liberation of the City and the Opening of the Scheldt 1944.* New York: Hippocrene, 1978.

Nicholson, G.W.G. *Canadian Expeditionary Force, 1914-1919. Official History of the Canadian Army in the First World War.* Ottawa: Queen's Printer, 1964.

———. *The Gunners of Canada. The History of the Royal Regiment of Canadian Artillery. Volume I, 1534-1919.* Toronto: McClelland and Stewart, 1967.

———. *The Gunners of Canada. The History of the Royal Regiment of Canadian Artillery. Volume II 1919-1967.* Toronto: McClelland and Stewart, 1972.

Palmer, Howard. *Alberta: A New History.* Edmonton: Heritage Publishers, 1990.

Paterson, R.A. *The Tenth Canadian Infantry Brigade. A Short History.* Holland: The brigade, 1945.

Rawling, Bill. *Surviving Trench Warfare: Technology and the Canadian Corps.* Toronto: University of Toronto Press, 1992.

Raycroft, John. *A Signal War: A Canadian Soldier's Memoir of the Liberation of the Netherlands.* Prescott: Babblefish Press, 2002.

Reid, Brian. *Our Little Army in the Field: The Canadians In South Africa 1899-1902.* St. Catharines: Vanwell Publishing, 1996.

———. *No Holding Back. Operation Totalize, Normandy, August 1944.* Toronto: Robin Brass Studio, 2005.

Reid, Gordon. *Pure Bloody Murder: Personal Memoirs of the First World War.* Oakville: Mosaic Press, 1980.

Rogers, H.L. *The History of the Lincoln and Welland Regiment.* St. Catharines: The Regiment, 1954.

Roy, Reginald. *1944: The Canadians in Normandy.* Toronto: Macmillan, 1984.

———, ed., *The Journal of Private Fraser, 1914-1918, Canadian Expeditionary Force.* Nepean: CEF Books, 1998.

Ruffee, G.E.M. and J.B. Dickie. *The History of the 14th Field Regiment, Royal Canadian Artillery.* Amsterdam: Wereldbibliotheek, 1945.

Sassoon, Siegfried. *Memoirs of an Infantry Officer.* London: Faber and Faber, 1974.

Savage, J.M. *History of the 5th Canadian Anti-Tank Regiment, 10 September 1941-10 June 1945.* Lochern: The Regiment, 1945.

Schreiber, Shane B. *Shock Army of the British Empire: The Canadian Army in the Last 100 Days of the Great War.* Westport: Praeger, 1997.

Schulman, Morton. *Defeat in the West.* London: Coronet Books, 1968.

Scott, Frederick G. *The Great War as I Saw It.* Toronto: D.F. Goodchild, 1922.

Simkins, Peter. *World War I. The Western Front.* New York: Random House, 1991.

Singer, H.C. *History of the 31st Infantry Battalion C.E.F. Compiled from Its Diaries and Other Papers.* Medicine Hat: The Battalion, [1939].

Smith-Dorrien, Horace. *Memoirs of Forty-Eight Years Service.* London: John Murray, 1925.

Snowie, J.A. *Bloody Buron.* Erin: Boston Mills Press, 1984.

South Alberta Light Horse; Calgary Highlanders; the Ceremony of the Presentation of Guidon and New Colours by Her Royal Highness Princess Alexandra, Currie Barracks, Calgary, Alberta, Thursday, May 25th, 1967. Calgary: Burnand Print Co., c. 1967.

South Alberta Light Horse Regimental Parades. Regimental Inspection and March Past. Freedom of the City Ceremony. Drumhead Service. May 27 and May 28, 1967.

Spenser, Robert A. *A History of the Fifteenth Canadian Field Regiment.* Amsterdam: Elsevier, 1945.

Stacey, C.P. *Six War Years. The Army in Canada, Britain and the Pacific.* Ottawa: Department of National Defence, 1955.

———. *The Victory Campaign. The Operations in North-West Europe, 1944-1945.* Ottawa: Department of National Defence, 1960.

———. *Arms Men and Government. The War Policies of Canada 1939-1945.* Ottawa: Department of National Defence, 1970.

Stanley, George. *The Birth of Western Canada: A History of the Riel Rebellions.* Toronto: University of Toronto, 1961.

———. *Canada's Soldiers, 1604-1954. The Military History of an Unmilitary People.* Toronto; Macmillan, 1974.

Steele, Samuel B. *Forty Years in Canada: Reminiscences of the Great North-West with Some Account of His Service in South Africa.* Winnipeg: R. Lang, 1915.

Steven, Walter. *In This Sign.* Toronto: Ryerson, 1948.

Strange, Thomas B. *Gunner Jingo's Jubilee.* Edmonton: University of Alberta Press, 1988.

Tamblyn, David S. *"The Horse in War": and Famous Canadian War Horses.* Kingston: Jackson Press, 1930.

Tingley, K.W., ed. *For King and Country: Alberta in the Second World War.* Edmonton: Reidmore Books, 1995.

Tolton, Gordon. *Rocky Mountain Rangers: Southern Alberta's Cowboy Cavalry in the Northwest Rebellion, 1885.* Lethbridge: Lethbridge Historical Society, 1996.

Travers, Timothy. *The Killing Ground: The British Army, the Western Front, and the Emergence of Modern Warfare.* London: Allen and Unwin, 1987.

Tuchman, Barbara. *The Guns of August.* New York: Macmillan, 1962.

———. *The Proud Tower. A Portrait of the World Before the War, 1890-1914.* New York: Macmillan, 1966.

Tucker, Glenn. *The Naval Service of Canada. Its Official History.* Ottawa: 2 vols, Department of National Defence, 1952.

Wallace, John F. *Dragons of Steel: Canadian Armour in Two World Wars.* Burnstown: General Store Publishing, 1995.

Whitaker, Denis and Shelagh. *Tug of War: The Canadian Victory that Opened Antwerp.* Toronto: Stoddart, 1984.

———. *Rhineland: The Battle to End the War.* Toronto: Stoddart, 1989.

Winter, J.M. *The Experience of World War I.* London: Guild, 1988.

Wise, S.F. and Richard Preston, *Men in Arms. A History of Warfare and Its Interrelationships with Western Society.* New York: 4th Edition, Holt, Rinehart and Winston, 1979.

ARTICLES

Dempsey, Hugh. "Rocky Mountain Rangers," *Alberta Historical Review,* vol 5 (Spring, 1952), No. 2, 3-8.

Herman, Len. "Field Force Rides Again," *Sentinel,* 1980, no. 1, 28-32.

Jack, Ronald. "The Colonel: An Inquiry into the Life of Willoughby Charles Bryan, 1865-1947. Part One: Red Serge Days." *Canadian Military Biography,* vol 1, no 2, Autumn 1989, 21-37.

Jamieson, F.C. "The 19th Alberta Dragoons in the First World War," *Alberta Historical Review* (Autumn 1959), 22-28.

Lackenbauer, P.W. "The Military and 'Mob Rule:' The CEF Riots in Calgary, February 1916," *Canadian Military History,* vol 10, no 1 (Winter 2001), pp. 31-43.

Lightall, W.D. "War Experiences of Canadian Cities," *National Municipal Review,* 8, No. 1 (June 1918).

Tylden, G., "Mounted Infantry," *Journal of the Society for Army Historical Research,* 22 (1943-1944), 177.

Wood, Hubert F. "Operation ELEPHANT. The Battle for the Kapelsche Veer," *Canadian Army Journal* (September 1949), 8-12.

INDEX

INDEX TO ILLUSTRATIONS

The South Alberta Regiment, November 1944
This diagram shows the more than 200 tanks and other vehicles as they would have appeared with the unit at full strength in November 1944. Unfortunately, the South Alberta Regiment was rarely at full strength.

Regimental Headquarters (RHQ) contained the command element of and controlled the Reconnaissance Troop of eleven Stuart VI tanks and the Anti-Aircraft Troop of seven Crusader AA tanks. The Inter-Communication Troop was usually dispersed throughout the unit.

The fighting element consisted of the three "sabre" squadrons (A, B and C) each with its command element and four troops, each with one Sherman Firefly tank and three Sherman V tanks.

Headquarters Squadron (a separate entity from Regimental Headquarters) controlled all the various administrative elements of the unit including the A2 Administrative (Supply Echelon), which resupplied the A1 Administrative (Supply) Echelons of the squadrons, which resupplied the squadrons.

Attached were sub-units of the Royal Canadian Corps of Signals which handled communications and a Light Aid Detachment of the Royal Canadian Electrical and Mechanical Engineers which provided first line mechanical repairs.

Drawing by Chris Johnson

The South Alberta Regiment, November 1944

Regimental Headquarters

Command Vehicles

Humber Scout Car
Commanding Officer

Truck, 15-cwt, Armoured,
White Half-track,
Armoured Command Vehicle

RHQ Troop

Tank, Control
Sherman V
2 x No.19 Wireless

Tank, Rear Link
Sherman V
2 x No. 19 Wireless

Sherman V

Sherman V

Headquarters Squadron

Truck, 15-cwt, Armoured,
M14 Half-track,
Medical Officer

Truck, 15-cwt, Armoured,
M14 Half-track,
Signals Officer

Reconnaissance Troop

Stuart VI   Stuart VI   Stuart VI   Stuart VI   Stuart VI   Stuart VI   Stuart VI   Stuart VI   Stuart VI   Stuart VI   Stuart VI

A A Troop

Crusader III   Crusader III   Crusader III   Crusader III   Crusader III   Crusader III   Crusader III
AA Mk. II   AA Mk. II   AA Mk. II   AA Mk. II   AA Mk. II   AA Mk. II   AA Mk. II

Note: Seventh Crusader
Acquired Informally.

Intercommunication Troop

Humber Scout Car   Humber Scout Car   Humber Scout Car   Humber Scout Car

Note: Nine in total dispersed
through the regiment

"A" Squadron

Squadron Headquarters Troop

Humber Scout Car

Sherman V   Sherman V   Sherman V

Truck, 15-cwt, Armoured
M14 Half-track,
Collection Of Casualties

Tank, Recovery
Sherman V

Truck, 15-cwt, Armoured
M14 Half-track, Fitters

No. 1 Troop

Sherman V   Sherman V   Sherman V   Sherman VC or IC Hybrid

No. 3 Troop

Sherman V   Sherman V   Sherman V   Sherman VC or IC Hybrid

No. 2 Troop

Sherman V   Sherman V   Sherman V   Sherman VC or IC Hybrid

No. 4 Troop

Sherman V   Sherman V   Sherman V   Sherman VC or IC Hybrid

"B" Squadron

Squadron Headquarters Troop

Humber Scout Car

Sherman V   Sherman V   Sherman V

Truck, 15-cwt, Armoured
M14 Half-track,
Collection Of Casualties

Tank, Recovery
Sherman V

Truck, 15-cwt, Armoured
M14 Half-track, Fitters

No. 1 Troop

Sherman V   Sherman V   Sherman V   Sherman VC or IC Hybrid

No. 3 Troop

Sherman V   Sherman V   Sherman V   Sherman VC or IC Hybrid

No. 2 Troop

Sherman V   Sherman V   Sherman V   Sherman VC or IC Hybrid

No. 4 Troop

Sherman V   Sherman V   Sherman V   Sherman VC or IC Hybrid

"C" Squadron

Squadron Headquarters Troop

Humber Scout Car

Sherman V   Sherman V   Sherman V

Truck, 15-cwt, Armoured
M14 Half-track,
Collection Of Casualties

Tank, Recovery
Sherman V

Truck, 15-cwt, Armoured
M14 Half-track, Fitters

No. 1 Troop

Sherman V   Sherman V   Sherman V   Sherman VC or IC Hybrid

No. 3 Troop

Sherman V   Sherman V   Sherman V   Sherman VC or IC Hybrid

No. 2 Troop

Sherman V   Sherman V   Sherman V   Sherman VC or IC Hybrid

No. 4 Troop

Sherman V   Sherman V   Sherman V   Sherman VC or IC Hybrid